Restaurant Guide 2011

AA Lifestyle Guides

This 18th edition published 2010

Please contact
Advertisement Sales: advertisingsales@theaa.com
Editorial Department: lifestyleguides@theaa.com

AA Media Limited would like to thank the following photographers, companies and picture libraries for their assistance in the preparation of this book.
Abbreviations for the picture credits are as follows: (t) top; (b) bottom; (l) left; (r) right; (c) centre; (AA) AA World Travel Library.
Front cover: (t & br) Andrew Fairlie at Gleneagles, Auchterarder, Scotland; (bl) Von Essen Hotels
Back cover: (l) Babylon Restaurant (c) Von Essen Hotels; (r) Gilpin Hotel and Lake House.
Every effort has been made to trace the copyright holders, and we apologise in advance for any accidental errors. We would be happy to apply any corrections in the following edition of this publication.

Typeset/Repro: Keenes, London
Printed by Trento Srl, Italy.
This directory is compiled by AA Lifestyle Guides; managed in the Librios Information Management System and generated by the AA establishment database system.

AA Restaurant Guide edited by Andrew Turvil, assisted by Fiona Griffiths

Restaurant descriptions have been contributed by the following team of writers: Miles Chapman, Fiona Griffiths, David Hancock, Mike Pedley, Carina Simon, Allen Stidwill, Mark Taylor, Stuart Taylor, Andrew Turvil, Joel Wright

Published by AA Publishing, a trading name of AA Media Limited, whose registered office is Fanum House, Basing View, Basingstoke, Hampshire RG21 4EA.
Registered number 06112600.
A CIP catalogue for this book is available from the British Library.
ISBN: 978-0-7495-6682-1
A04312

Contents

Welcome to the Guide

Welcome to the 18th edition of the AA Restaurant Guide. This book is the result of hundreds of meals undertaken over the course of the year by the experienced AA inspection team, with thousands of facts gathered and checked, and countless descriptive words used to bring the restaurants to life on the page. Whether you are looking to celebrate a big occasion, or it is simply Wednesday night and you can't be bothered to cook, there is somewhere in the Guide that fits the bill.

This is the 18th edition of the AA Restaurant Guide and we're spoiled for choice when it comes to where to go out and celebrate. Just a couple of decades ago a celebration meal meant dressing up and heading out to the posh place, the one where you might spend a little more than you're comfortable with, but feel bad griping about it because, well, it's a special day. Things have changed. The British have a more relaxed attitude towards going out to eat these days. That's partly because there's more choice and, I'm delighted to say, more good quality places out there. You can still dress up and head off to an expensive place and tuck into haute cuisine of the old school if you wish, but you can also keep your jeans on and head to a local foodie pub that keeps things relatively simple but still delivers a memorable meal. And, of course, you could always push the boat out and seek out one of those fancy experimental places that blow away your culinary expectations and serve up something that may well live in your memory forever. Or go for a top-notch curry – old or new school. The strength of the UK dining scene is its diversity.

That is not to say all is hunky dory. When researching this guidebook we look for restaurants serving good, fresh ingredients, cooked from scratch on the premises. Sounds simple enough, but if you turn up in any town in the UK you'll find more places relying on pre-packaged foods and taking shortcuts than you will cooking up fresh stuff from scratch. If you take pot luck when choosing a restaurant in the UK, disappointment is a distinct possibility. There are nearly 2,000 restaurants listed within these pages and they should be congratulated for flying the flag for good food in this country, for constantly raising the bar. Without their hard work, dedication and commitment, the AA Restaurant Guide would not exist.

On the Menu

An AA inspector eats a lot of meals in a given year and casts their eyes over stacks of menus. What can we glean from these menus? They reveal trends in food, certainly, but can they tell us something about the broader food culture? Pollock is big on menus this year and that's good news for the environment and sustainable fish stocks; according to the Marine Conservation Society, Pollock is a fish we can eat with a clear conscience, one that helps ensure the long-term sustainability of fish stocks in the UK. Sounds like a good reason to put it on the menu, and it's pleasing to see so many pollock dishes mentioned in the Guide this year. For a comprehensive and clear list of what seafood is at risk and what's sustainable, check out the society's website: www.mcsuk.org. Perhaps the increasing presence of pollock reflects the restaurant industry's awareness of the crises in the fishing industry.

What does the rather regular appearance of pease pudding have to say? In the midst of a recession, perhaps it reflects a nostalgia for the comfort foods of yesteryear, or more simply a desire to bring a touch of trendy retro-chic to the menu. The same goes for piccalilli. They both cropped up a lot in 2010.

Salted caramel is a fabulous blend of sweet and salty, the sea salt combining brilliantly with the sweet, rich caramel. It's addictive stuff and a small amount goes a long way. It turns up in desserts such as Marcus Wareing's Granny Smith apple crème construction and even at food-focused pubs, such as with spiced banana cake at the Punchbowl Inn at Crosthwaite in the Lake District. This shows, perhaps, how ideas filter down from the top restaurants, where trends and innovations in the top fine-dining restaurants make their way into the broader food culture.

Three, it turns out, is the magic number. Trios are big on restaurant menus. That is to say explorations of one ingredient in three different ways in the same dish. Thus a trio of lamb might bring forth loin, shoulder and sweetbread, or rhubarb, perhaps poached, as a sorbet and in a shot glass perked up with some ginger. The trio of meats, particularly, shows a refreshing willingness to embrace the different cuts of meat from the same animal – nose-to-tail eating, as it were, making full use of the beast and not just serving up the prime cuts.

The provenance of ingredients is listed on more and more menus each year as restaurants realise that the customer does care where the food comes from. It has become a selling point for the restaurant – local, home-grown, hand-dived, this farm, that ocean. Some places choose to list suppliers in one go on the back of the menu, or even on a blackboard, freeing up the menus so that they are not too cluttered by farmers' names. Whichever way the restaurateur chooses to let the customer know that the food is sourced with care and not just bought from the nearest cash-and-carry, the point is they now realise that this information is worth sharing with their customers. Is it a question of trust? Perhaps these days we're a little more cynical than we used to be and like to be reassured that they've gone to some effort to serve us some decent ingredients.

Menus continue to evolve, fads and fashions come and go, and if we look back at this Guide in 20 years time, we'll doubtless smile nostalgically at some of the food we used to eat back in the good/bad old days (delete where appropriate).

A Good Read

We've some more interesting articles for you again this year. There's a piece about the growing number of all-day restaurants (talking of trends), which are seemingly meeting the demand for flexibility in what we eat and when; cheese guru Juliet Harbutt writes about the amazing range of British cheeses available and wonders why we don't see more of them on restaurant menus; and we also look at what goes on behind the scenes, as Fiona Griffiths investigates what makes a service brigade tick.

I hope you enjoy some great meals at the restaurants listed within these pages.

Good Eating

Andrew Turvil
Editor

How to Use the Guide

1 MAP REFERENCE

The atlas section is at the back of the Guide. The map page number is followed by the National Grid Reference. To find a location, read the first figure horizontally and the second figure vertically within the lettered square. For Central London and Greater London, there is a 13-page map section starting on page 218.

2 PLACE NAME

Restaurants are listed in country and county order, then by town and then alphabetically within the town. There is an index by restaurant at the back of the book and a similar one for the Central & Greater London sections on pages 214-217.

3 RESTAURANT NAME

4 THE AA ROSETTE AWARD

Entries have been awarded one or more Rosettes, up to a maximum of five.
See page 9.

5 FOOD STYLE

Food style of the restaurant is followed by a short summary statement.

6 PHOTOGRAPHS

Restaurants are invited to enhance their entry with up to two photographs.

7 CHEF(S) AND OWNER(S)

The names of the chef(s) and owner(s) are as up-to-date as possible at the time of going to press, but changes in personnel often occur, and may affect both the style and quality of the restaurant.

8 PRICES

Prices are for fixed lunch (2 courses) and dinner (3 courses) and à la carte dishes. Service charge information (see also opposite). Note: Prices quoted are a guide only, and are subject to change.

HAMPSHIRE

2 **EVERSLEY** Map 5 SU76 1

3 **The New Mill Riverside Restaurant**

4 Modern European NOTABLE WINE LIST 19

5

6

Modern European cooking in an idyllic riverside setting

☎ 0118 973 2277
New Mill Rd RG27 0RA
e-mail: info@thenewmill.co.uk
web: www.thenewmill.co.uk 17
10 **dir:** Off A327 2m S of Arborfield Cross. N of village follow brown signs. Approach from New Mill Rd

The historic building became a restaurant in 1973, having served as a corn mill for many a century prior to that. It retains a working waterwheel, and the setting on the banks of the Blackwater, amid carefully tended gardens, is enhanced by interior beams and the warmly hospitable approach of staff. Modern European menus deal in complex, satisfying dishes such as a pressed terrine of rabbit, chorizo and black pudding, dressed with apple and caraway relish and pesto, followed perhaps by seared sea bass with braised butter beans, wild mushrooms and kale in a shrimp butter sauce. Dishes are generally well-balanced, and impress for their subtle ranges of flavours. Desserts might include cherry clafoutis, or pecan treacle tart with mascarpone cream. 16

7 **Chef** Colin Robson-Wright **Owner** Cindy & John Duffield
15 **Times** 12-2/7-10 Closed 1-2 Jan, Mon **Prices** Fixed L 2 course £15, Fixed D 3 course £25, Service optional, Groups min 8 service 10% **Wines** 150 bottles over £20, 10 bottles under £20, 10 by glass **Notes** Tasting menu available, Sunday L, Vegetarian available, Dress restrictions, Smart casual, Civ Wed 150 **Seats** 80, Pr/dining room 32 **Children** Portions **Parking** 60 8 14 9 13

12 11

---

9 NOTES

Additional information e.g. availability of vegetarian dishes, civil weddings, air conditioning etc.

10 DIRECTIONS

Directions are given if supplied.

11 PARKING DETAILS

On-site parking is listed if applicable, then nearby parking.

12 CHILDREN

Menu, portions, age restrictions etc.

13 NUMBER OF SEATS

Number of seats in the restaurant, followed by private dining room (Pr/dining room).

14 NUMBER OF WINES

Number of wines under and over £20, and available by the glass.

15 DAILY OPENING AND CLOSING TIMES

Daily opening and closing times, the days of the week it is closed and seasonal closures. Note that opening times are liable to change without notice. It is wise to telephone in advance.

16 DESCRIPTION

Description of the restaurant and the food.

17 E-MAIL ADDRESS AND WEBSITE

18 VEGETARIAN MENU

V Indicates a vegetarian menu. Restaurants with some vegetarian dishes available are indicated under Notes.

19 NOTABLE WINE LIST

NOTABLE WINE LIST Indicates notable wine list (See p18-19).

20 LOCAL AND REGIONAL PRODUCE

Indicates the use of local and regional produce. More than 50% of the restaurant food ingredients are produced within a 50-mile radius. Suppliers are mentioned by name on the menu.

All establishments take major credit cards, except where we have specified otherwise.

All information is correct at the time of printing but may change without notice. Details of opening times and prices may be omitted from an entry when the establishment has not supplied us with up-to-date information. This is indicated where the establishment name is shown in *italics*.

Service Charge

We ask restaurants the following questions about service charge (their responses appear under Prices in each entry):

- Is service included in the meal price, with no further charge added or expected?
- Is service optional – charge not automatically added to bill?
- Is service charge compulsory, and what percentage?
- Is there a service charge for larger groups, minimum number in group, and what percentage?

Many establishments automatically add service charge to the bill but tell the customer it is optional.

Smoking Regulations

From July 2007 smoking was banned in all enclosed public places in the United Kingdom and Ireland. A hotel or guest accommodation proprietor can designate one or more bedrooms with ventilation systems where the occupants can smoke, but communal areas must be smoke-free. Communal areas include the interior bars and restaurants in pubs and inns.

Facilities for Disabled Guests

The Disability Discrimination Act (access to Goods and Services) means that service providers may have to consider making adjustments to their premises. For further information see disability.gov.uk/dda.

The establishments in this Guide should all be aware of their responsibilities under the Act. Always phone in advance to ensure that the establishment you have chosen has appropriate facilities. See also holidaycare.org.uk.

Website Addresses

Where website addresses are included they have been supplied and specified by the respective establishment. Such websites are not under the control of AA Media Limited and as such AA Media Limited has no control over them and will not accept any responsibility or liability in respect of any and all matters whatsoever relating to such websites including access, content, material and functionality. By including the addresses of third-party websites the AA does not intend to solicit business or offer any security to any person in any country, directly or indirectly.

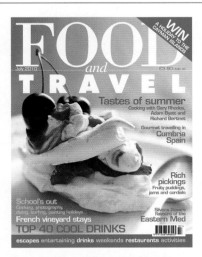

AA Restaurants of the Year

Potential Restaurants of the Year are nominated by our team of full-time Inspectors based on their routine visits. In selecting a Restaurant of the Year, we look for somewhere that is exceptional in its chosen area of the market. Whilst the Rosette awards are based on the quality of the food alone, Restaurant of the Year takes into account all aspects of the experience.

ENGLAND

THE HARROW INN ◎◎◎

LITTLE BEDWYN, WILTSHIRE

Page 431

What sounds like a village pub in a little hamlet near the Kennet and Avon Canal is actually a top-flight country restaurant, owned and lovingly run for 12 years by Roger and Sue Jones. Sue leads a super front-of-house team in the sharp-looking dining room, while Roger directs the kitchen's output. Passion about the freshness, sourcing and quality of raw materials is the cornerstone here; fish and seafood come from Brixham, Lyme Bay and the Scilly Isles; meat and game is from specialist farmers and butchers. Put together in subtle combinations with top-level technical skill, the results are memorable. A ceviche of langoustine, turbot and sea bass is set on nori seaweed, its flavours framed with a salpicon of cucumber, carrot and red pepper. Next up, the game season kicks off with roast grouse, celeriac crisps and purée, and a Wiltshire truffle jus served in a shot glass. The wine list is world-class.

LONDON

GALVIN LA CHAPELLE ◎◎◎

LONDON

Page 231

First came Galvin Bistrot de Luxe, then Galvin at Windows, and now it's the turn of Galvin La Chapelle to wow London restaurant-goers and critics alike. The latest venture from chef brothers Chris and Jeff Galvin is housed in a former Victorian school hall in Spitalfields. It's a glamorous brasserie-style affair, complete with marble-clad pillars soaring up to the vaulted ceiling, a mezzanine area for private dining, and tables dressed to thrill. The service is impeccable, the atmosphere incredible, and the cooking trademark Galvin – French, technically brilliant, and founded on absolutely tip-top ingredients. Lasagne of Dorset crab with a velouté of chanterelles shows great technical dexterity and an eye for richly appealing flavour combinations, while tagine of Bresse pigeon, aubergine purée and harissa sauce is a wonderful marriage of tastes and textures, beautifully presented in a tagine pot. The superb wine list offers several vintages of Hermitage La Chapelle – the restaurant's namesake.

SCOTLAND

THE PEAT INN ⚙⚙⚙

PEAT INN, FIFE

Page 502

Geoffrey and Katherine Smeddle have been running the Peat Inn since 2006, taking the baton from the celebrated David Wilson. An inn since the 1700s, today's incarnation is elegantly kitted out, with roaring fires, old beams and smartly laid, linen-clad tables in the three intimate dining rooms. Geoffrey mans the stoves, cooking up a storm with the carefully-sourced produce, much of it from the region, delivering well-judged dishes where flavour is paramount and contemporary sensibilities combine with classical technique. Pumpkin and parmesan soup comes with a poached quail's egg, ricotta gnocchi and pumpkin seed oil in a first course, while John Dory might turn up in a main course with a gratin of razor clams, creamed Swiss chard, glazed salsify and a shellfish velouté. The food is as pretty as a picture, including desserts such as lemon tart with poached rhubarb and pistachio ice cream.

WALES

THE HARDWICK ⚙⚙

ABERGAVENNY, MONMOUTHSHIRE

Page 555

The setting, in an old country pub on a main road close to Abergavenny, is pleasant enough, but what lies within is a bit special, definitely worthy of a detour. This is down to chef-proprietor Stephen Terry – a man with over 20 years cooking experience under his belt and a CV that reads like a dream. There's nothing flashy about the interior – bare wooden tables and chairs confirm its country pub status. The daily-changing menu of rustic modern British grub shows some Italian influences and offers a remarkable choice given the high quality. To start, how about a generous portion of house-cured salt duck breast with Italian stem and globe artichokes, fontina and rocket? Main course might bring forth a hot raised venison pie with mashed potato, organic carrots and cavolo nero, or a superb piece of pan-fried organic Shetland salmon, served with a Black Mountain smoked salmon and fennel risotto cake.

AA Wine Awards

The AA Wine Award

The annual AA wine award, sponsored again by T&W Wines, attracted a huge response from our AA recognised restaurants with over 1,000 wine lists submitted for judging. Three national winners were chosen – Hambleton Halll, Rutland, England, The Kitchin, Edinburgh, Scotland and Fairyhill, Reynoldston, Swansea, Wales. Hambleton Hall, Rutland was selected as the Overall Winner, and a member of their wine team wins an all-expenses-paid trip to Willi Opitz's vineyards at Illmitz in Austria's Burgenland.

All 2,000 or so Rosetted restaurants in last year's guide were invited to submit their wine lists. From these the panel selected a shortlist of 182 establishments who are highlighted in the guide with the Notable Wine List symbol NOTABLE WINE LIST.

The shortlisted establishments were asked to choose wines from their list (within a budget of £70 per bottle) to accompany a menu designed by John Hoskins, last year's winner, and proprietor of The Old Bridge, Huntington.

The final judging panel included Simon Numphud, AA Hotel Services Manager, John Hoskins, Master of Wine, last year's winner from The Old Bridge Hotel at Huntingdon, Trevor Hughes, Managing Director of T&W Wines (our sponsor) and Fiona Sims, an independent wine journalist. The judges' comments are shown under the award winners on page 19.

Other wine lists that stood out in the final judging included La Trompette and Bibendum, London, Northcote in Lancashire, Le Manoir in Oxfordshire, The Witchery, The Peat Inn and 21212 in Scotland and The Crown in Wales.

Notable Wine Lists

What makes a wine list notable?

We are looking for high-quality wines, with diversity across grapes and/ or countries and style, the best individual growers and vintages. The list should be well presented, ideally with some helpful notes and, to reflect the demand from diners, a good choice of wines by the glass.

What disappoints the judges are spelling errors, wines under incorrect regions or styles, split vintages (which are still far too common), lazy purchasing (all wines from a country from just one grower or negociant) and confusing layouts. Sadly, many restaurants still do not pay much attention to wine, resulting in ill considered lists.

To reach the final shortlist, we look for a real passion for wine, which should come across to the customer, a fair pricing policy (depending on the style of the restaurant) an interesting coverage (not necessarily a large list), which might include areas of specialism, perhaps a particular wine area, sherries or larger formats such as magnums.

The AA Wine Awards are sponsored by
T&W Wines Ltd, 5 Station Way, Brandon, Suffolk, IP27 0BH
Tel: 01842 814414 email: contact@tw-wines.com
web: www.tw-wines.com

Hambleton Hall - Winning Wine Selection

Menu	Wine selection
Canapés – Gougères	Non Vintage Pol Roger White Foil
Appetiser – Gazpacho	2008 Viña Farnadas Treixadura, Ribeiro
Starter – Tuna tempura with nori seaweed, pickled pink ginger, coriander, wasabi and Asian dipping sauce	2007 Grosset Polish Hill Riesling, Clare Valley
Main course – Haunch of Denham Estate venison with rösti potato, ruby chard, caramelised apple and blackberry sauce	1999 St Joseph Domaine du Cornilhlac
Cheese – Colston Bassett Stilton with quince chutney and oatcakes	1985 Offley Boa Vista Port
Dessert – Poached pear in mulled wine with cinnamon ice cream	2002 Tokaji Aszu 5 Puttonyos, Crown Estates
Coffee and chocolates	1966 Armagnac Magud

WINNER FOR ENGLAND AND OVERALL WINNER

HAMBLETON HALL ®®

OAKHAM, RUTLAND Page 360

Overlooking Rutland Water, and set amid glorious gardens, Hambleton Hall is a supremely graceful pile. The interiors are pastorally pretty, with much use of gentle light green in the lounge, and shimmering deep red in the dining room. Here, service is as slick as can be, while table settings, with their fine stemware, wine cradles and crisp linen, are the last word in refinement. Aaron Patterson's cooking style is not one of technological wizardry; dishes are not about foams and dusts so much as the coaxing of magisterial depth from ingredients whose integrity is respected. The wine list is extremely comprehensive, covering all corners of the Old and New Worlds.
Judges' comments: A sensibly sized list, beautifully presented and clearly laid out. Easy to read and navigate, showing wines of great maturity, quality and value. A truly personal list.

WINNER FOR SCOTLAND

THE KITCHIN ®®®

EDINBURGH, CITY OF EDINBURGH Page 493

Chef Tom Kitchin's name lends itself to his restaurant as naturally as the regenerated spaces of the Leith Dockyards lend themselves to funky drinking and dining venues. Kitchin is obsessive about seasonal Scottish ingredients, while razor-sharp French technique underpins his modern European style of cooking. The wine list features an extensive range of premium French classic wines, plus a sophisticated selection from the rest of the world, many of which are available by the glass.
Judges' comments: The list fits very well with the style of the restaurant, nicely chosen wines with very good quality selections throughout. The informed presentation includes seasonal recommendations in keeping with the restaurant's overall focus and philosophy.

WINNER FOR WALES

FAIRYHILL ®®

REYNOLDSTON, SWANSEA Page 565

Style, low-key luxury and top-notch food are the attractions of this Gower favourite. The elegant interior is kitted out in a stylish modern country-house idiom, with well-spaced tables in the two dining rooms, which are looked after by a clued-up and efficient front-of-house team. The kitchen is keen on keeping food miles to a minimum, so most of the ingredients – Welsh Black beef, salt marsh lamb, Penclawdd cockles and fresh fish, for example – come from Gower and the surrounding area, and form the backbone of modern Welsh dishes. The extensive wine list, cellared in the old vaults of the house, includes wines from Wales.
Judges' comments: The exciting wine selections show exceptional value for some rare bins. There's a useful section of white and reds below £25, plus a quality half bottle selection.

OPEN *all*

HOURS

Want breakfast in the middle of the afternoon or lunch at 4pm? No problem. More and more restaurants are ripping up the rulebook and serving food all day, as Fiona Griffiths discovers...

A couple of years ago Trevor Tobin was the head chef at one of London's top restaurants.

He'd taken Chapter Two in Blackheath Village to three AA Rosettes, and was working towards achieving a fourth.

But now the AA plate on the wall shows two Rosettes, not four, and instead of dishes such as mosaic of confit canard with shiitake mushrooms, baby leeks, grilled sourdough and truffle mayonnaise, Tobin is turning out the likes of steak, fish and chips, eggs Benedict and American-style waffles.

So what went wrong?

Well, actually, it's more of a case of what went right.

Restaurant director and executive chef Andrew McLeish spotted a gap in the market in Blackheath for a venue serving high quality food all-day – from breakfast through to morning pastries, brunch, lunch, afternoon tea and dinner.

Chapter Two was 10-years-old and due a refurbishment anyway, so after a makeover to give it a more modern, casual feel, Chapters All Day Dining was born.

It was a brave move, especially at the beginning of a recession, but there's been no looking back.

Left: Chapters All Day Dining in Blackheath has been a hit with the locals

Top left: Andrew McLeish and and Trevor Tobin at Chapters All Day Dining.

Above: Galvin Café a Vin

"Before, because we were fine dining, people had the impression that we were too expensive, so they'd come in once a month," says Tobin.

"Now we get mums coming in for breakfast after dropping their kids off at school, and people having business meetings over breakfast or afternoon tea. Some of our customers come in three or four times a week.

"People love it because they know they can sit and relax and have whatever they want – not feel pressured to have three courses."

You might imagine that Tobin and his team would miss the fine-dining style of cooking of Chapter Two, and possibly even resent having to turn out breakfasts and bake cakes, but far from it.

Tobin says his chefs enjoy the variety an all-day menu provides, while for him, it's a relief not to be cooking for accolades anymore.

"I'm happier now than I've ever been because I don't have to worry about all the fancy stuff and be constantly looking over my shoulder thinking, 'are we going to get four Rosettes?'

"The pressure has gone and we're just doing simple things the best we can and at the best available price.

"We may not get the accolades but it's about us as a team serving our customers and knowing that they're happy and that they feel welcome - that's what we're here for."

That attitude is certainly shared by chef brothers Chris and Jeff Galvin.

When they launched their latest London restaurant, the three AA Rosette Galvin La Chapelle, at the end of 2009, they also opened a cafe next door offering all-day dining, more as a service to the local community in Spitalfields than anything else.

"We wanted to be good neighbours – to fit in with Spitalfields rather than the other way around. I wouldn't necessarily say it's highly profitable but we're offering a service," says Chris.

Galvin Café a Vin opens at 8am to serve porridge, croque-monsieur, sausage sandwiches and the like, and carries on right through until late with an all-day menu ranging from pizza of smoked and confit duck with figs and red onions, to wood roast sea bream with fennel and ratte potatoes.

"The locals love the cafe because it's always open and they don't have to book, they can just turn up whenever they want.

"To my mind there's nothing worse than arriving somewhere to eat and finding that you're just five minutes too late," says Chris.

"We're brilliant in our industry at saying 'no' to people. On the Continent, if you haven't got to a restaurant by 2pm you're stuck.

"We've decided we need to move with the times and give people what they want, which is flexibility." A flexible approach has proven a surefire winner for Sam Harrison, who owns London restaurants Sam's Brasserie and Bar in Chiswick, and Harrison's in Balham.

Both offer casual, all-day dining and were inspired by Harrison's time spent in Sydney and New York.

"People eat at different times of the day in those cities – not just traditional lunch and dinner times – and I think we're moving towards that in London," says Harrison.

"More and more people are working from home and not working a traditional Monday to Friday, so they might want a brunch or a lazy late afternoon lunch on a Tuesday because to them that's Saturday or Sunday.

"I think there are quite a few people in Chiswick who have given up their offices as a way of saving money during the recession, so they use Sam's almost as an office."

Harrison believes eating out is becoming less of an occasion now, too, and that's fueling the growth in informal restaurants serving food all day.

He explains: "Traditionally, in London people would go out for lunch or dinner and that would be the main event. That's still the case in many restaurants, but for a lot of people now eating out is just part of their plans for the day, and it might be at the traditional lunch or dinner time or it might be at 4pm before going out to meet friends."Similarly to Harrison, it was "the cafe culture" of Australia and New Zealand that provided inspiration for Anna Hansen's The Modern Pantry in Clerkenwell, London.

Above: Breakfast at Sam's Brasserie and Bar

"People eat at different times of the day in (Sydney and New York) – not just traditional lunch and dinner times – and I think we're moving towards that in London

"I'm from New Zealand and back home places open first thing in the morning and just stay open," says Hansen.

"I really like that approach to eating – to be able to drop into places as and when suits and know you can actually have something decent and substantial to eat."

At The Modern Pantry the formula works well, with office workers dropping into the restaurant throughout the day for meetings, residents popping in for everything from breakfast to afternoon tea, and people travelling from all over London for Hansen's weekend brunches.

"Weekends are enormous. The great thing about brunch is people are quite happy to travel a fair distance for it because it's still early in the day and they can then head off and do some exploring," says Hansen.

"There aren't many restaurants doing it either, so once you get a reputation, people do keep coming back."

Hansen has been so encouraged by the response to her slice of New Zealand-style living, that she plans to do it all over again.

"We will do something similar in the future. There are more and more places opening doing the same thing already – changing the approach to eating."

She adds: "Hopefully this will spread outside of London, too, because it's a bit depressing when you're away somewhere and you're starving in the middle of the afternoon and can't find anywhere to eat.

"That does tend to be the case outside London, where the restaurants operate to pretty limited hours. To change that, operators just have to take the

Right: Anna Hansen's Modern Pantry was inspired by the café culture of New Zealand

In a location where there's trade all day it makes sense to do it

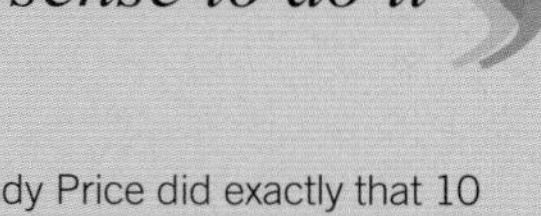

plunge." Andy Price did exactly that 10 years ago when he opened West Beach on Bournemouth's seafront, and again when he launched sister restaurant The Print Room in the town centre in 2007.

"At West Beach we made it all-day dining because there was footfall down on the beach all day, and because I didn't want anybody walking all the way down the prom, getting to the restaurant and finding it had stopped serving," explains Price.

Left: Eggs Benedict for breakfast (or lunch, or dinner) at The Print Room, Bournemouth

"With the Print Room we've got business people coming in during the day, particularly for meetings over afternoon tea. We've also got the pre-theatre market and people who are in the town on conferences and want to eat whenever.

"In a location where there's trade all day it makes sense to do it."

When Catherine Hardy and Jacqueline Fennessy opened The Left Bank in Glasgow in 2006, there was no question that it would offer all-day dining.

"It's quite a high flow area with the university right next door and a lot of small businesses, so we thought there was a gap in the market for somewhere serving breakfast and food in the afternoon," explains Hardy.

"You need staff in at 9am anyway to do prep for lunch and dinner, and to take deliveries, so the opportunity to have customers in at the same time so you can be generating some money as well as spending it makes good economic sense."

After three successful years Hardy and Fennessy opened a second all-day dining restaurant in Glasgow, The Two Figs, which has also taken off.

"It's a bit quieter because it's not on the main road up to the university, but it's definitely still been worthwhile," says Hardy.

"I think in the modern day and age people don't like to be constricted to eating between 12-2pm and 7-9pm, so in populated urban areas I think we're going to see a lot more restaurants like ours."

Left: Afternoon tea is good for business at The Print Room

Above: The Left Bank in Glasgow

British Cheese
on the menu

By Juliet Harbutt

Cheese is a combination of man's ingenuity and one of nature's finest miracles – the conversion of lush grass, wild herbs and meadow flowers into sweet, white, milk; this amazing natural bounty turned by man into cheese. Over the last 25 years, the revitalisation of UK cheese producers has seen more than 700 unique English, Welsh and Scottish cheeses come to market. Made in a myriad of different shapes, tastes and sizes, these cheeses, like great wines, are the fruit of the soil or terroir – never uniform, never predictable.

Why is it, then, that most UK-based chefs seem almost perversely determined to ignore this extraordinary diversity and quality? Many still insist on serving up the usual suspects of European cheeses, or to dish up the same old Stilton and Cheddar – the equivalent of prawn cocktail and steak Diane. For many, the cheese board is a footnote on the dessert menu.

Since 1994, the British Cheese Awards have attracted entries from over 70% of British cheesemakers and in 2009, 189 British and Irish cheese makers entered 884 washed, brushed, pressed or polished cheeses made with Ayrshire, Jersey, Old Gloucester, goat, ewe and (even) water buffalo milk. In the blue category alone, excluding Stilton, there were 50 entries and another eight in the 'new blue' class. There is no excuse for chefs not to make use of these fabulous cheeses.

There are, luckily, an increasing number of chefs who are totally dedicated to local producers. This band of enthusiasts have sought out good, local producers who ripen their own cheeses, and are proud to sell them, describing them in the same loving or even salacious terms as a wine list. And serving them with excellent home-made bread and biscuits.

So, how should a restaurateur approach the cheese board? What should they look for to guarantee a perfect combination of cheeses, of tastes and textures, and bring a true local flavour to their menu? The following cheeses are examples of what the UK has to offer and show there is no excuse for not putting great British cheeses on the menu.

THE 7 DIFFERENT TYPES OF CHEESE

The perfect blend lies not in the variety of animal but in the rind of a cheese for, unlike the cover of a book, a cheese displays its heart on its sleeve. Using the rind method, a system I created to help me understand cheese, with just a glance and a gentle squeeze you can categorise 99% of any cheese you meet whether in a French market, a New York cheese shop or British restaurant. There is the odd exception but most are very obvious.

Fresh Cheeses No rind

Classic Examples: Cream Cheese, Ricotta, Feta, Mozzarella

These cheeses are high in moisture so do not have time to develop a rind and need to be eaten at around 1-15 days old. As they are very young they have a subtle 'lactic' or milky, fermenting fruit flavour and a lemony freshness. Some, like Feta, are preserved in brine or oil, others like Mozzarella are made by stretching the curd in hot water, creating a marvellously elastic texture.

Rosary Ash Log [goat]
Rosary Goats
Wiltshire
5 time winner of Best Fresh cheese

Chris and Claire Moody make a range of superb fresh goats' cheeses and this is particularly attractive with its dusting of ash which provides a stark contrast against the pure white interior. Delicate, almost mousse-like, with the subtle aromatic character of the goat coming through.

Aged Fresh Cheese Pale blue-grey to grey-black moulds and wrinkly rind

Classic Examples: Crottin de Chavignol, Selles sur Cher, Banon, Cerney Ash

Some fresh cheeses are encouraged to age and gradually dry out when they develop a delicate bluish grey mould, a wrinkled rind and the flavour intensifies with age. The texture develops from chalky to dry when it feels thick, almost gluggy in the mouth, then becoming flaky, almost brittle. Most are found in France and are usually made with goats' milk.

Tymsboro [goat]
Sleight Farm
Somerset
1997 & 1998 Best Aged Fresh

Created by Mary Holbrooke using milk from her own small herd that graze the Mendip Hills, home to Britain's best-known cows' milk cheese, Cheddar. An elegant truncated pyramid dusted with ash, over which grows the white and grey moulds which help break down the curd so it becomes soft, nutty, aromatic and quite pungent when it is almost runny just under the rind.

Soft White White fuzzy rind

Classic Examples: Camembert, Brie, Capricorn Goat, Little Wallop, Tunworth, Vignotte

These cheeses are characterised by their soft, white, fuzzy rind of Penicillium Candidum while inside the texture gradually changes from chalky to soft and almost liquid. Raw milk varieties often develop a reddish-brown ferment on the rind, while adding cream to the milk gives some a more luxurious taste and texture. At first the flavour is mild, like mushrooms in melted butter with a salty tang. With age the mushroomy aroma becomes more distinct and there is a hint of sherry on the finish.

Flower Marie [ewe]
Golden Cross Cheese
Sussex
1999 Best Soft White

Produced by Kevin and Alison Blunt

Page 26: Cheese board with an impressive spread of English cheeses

Page 27: Stilton with cranberry

Above: Goats' cheese

Below: Keen's Farmhouse Cheddar

Left: Denhay cheese store, near Bridport, Dorset

Above: Shropshire Blue

at Greenacres Farm, Flower Marie has a gentle fragrance, like that of fresh mushrooms, and a soft rind that envelops the firm yet moist interior. It melts like ice cream in the mouth to reveal a lemony freshness under the characteristic sweetness of the sheep's milk.

Semi-Soft Dry, grey-brown to sticky, orange-brown rind

Classic Examples: Edam, Reblochon, Pont l'Evêque, Ardrahan, Wyfe of Bath

Supple to rubbery texture because they have been lightly pressed to eliminate some of their moisture. Gradually various moulds develop which are removed by dipping the cheese into baths of brine (salty water). Some are encouraged to grow moulds, which are regularly brushed or washed off gradually building up a dry, leathery rind. Those 'washed' frequently in brine develop a soft orange-pink to brown-orange rind with a strong, farmyardy flavour and aroma.

Stinking Bishop [cow]
Charles Martell & Son
Gloucestershire

A wash-rind cheese dating back to the Cistercian monks who once settled in Dymock where this cheese is made. Washed in fermented pear juice or Perry, the rind develops a smelly, pungent, orange sticky rind while the texture is smooth and voluptuous. Named after an old variety of local pear – Stinking Bishop.

Hard Thick, dense, leathery rind often waxed or oiled

Classic Examples: Cheddar, Lancashire, Parmigiano Reggiano, Emmental, Gouda

Thick, crusty or leathery and often waxed rinds, they are typically large cheeses that have been pressed for hours or even days to remove their whey

Above: A selection of modern English cheeses, including Cornish Yarg, with the distinctive nettle leaf pattern on the rind. For more information visit www.britishcheese.com

Above right: Local cheeses on the menu at Terre à Terre in Brighton

There is no excuse for chefs not to make use of these fabulous cheeses

or moisture. They are then ripened for weeks, months or even years when they develop a more complex, full bodied character than softer cheeses.

Redesdale [ewe]
Northumberland Cheese Co
Northumberland

One of several excellent cheeses made by Northumberland. Beneath the thin leathery rind dusted with white and grey moulds, the sweet, local ewes' milk has a subtle sweetness that hints of nuts and caramelised onions, while the texture is firm yet pliable.

Blue Gritty, rough, dry or sticky rind

Classic Examples: Stilton, Shropshire Blue, Cornish Blue, Oxford blue, Buffalo Blue

These range from mild and very creamy like Blue Brie to pungent, almost vicious with a strong kick on the finish. The blue mould, added to the milk before it is curdled, is from the penicillin family but will not turn blue until the young cheese is pierced with rods (normally steel but could be wood or plastic), the blue then grows along the tunnel, cracks and trails between the roughly packed curd.

Blue Monday [cow]
Highland Fine Cheese
Scotland

A small, square blue, softer and creamier than most British blues, its flavour is steely blue, with some sweet notes only revealing its spicy, sea-breeze character as it melts on the palate. An example of how the very essence of the grazing can be evoked in the hands of a good cheesemaker.

Flavour Added varied

Classic Examples: Gouda with cumin, Yarg with Nettles, Wensleydale with Cranberries

These are hard cheeses to which a variety of different ingredients are added to the curd or rubbed into the rind such as nuts, fruit, spices, herbs, hops and nettles, and also include smoked cheeses. Blended cheeses also belong in this category and are made by breaking up young cheeses, combining them with various sweet or savory ingredients, then re-forming them into cheese.

Cornish Yarg [cow]
Lynher Dairies Cheese Co
Cornwall
Best Flavour Added 2001

Made from a traditional 17th century recipe it is one of the most distinctive and attractive cheeses on the market. It is wrapped in interwoven nettle leaves which contrast with the pale ivory interior and impart a hint of spring, while the finish is fresh and lemony.

These examples are just a taster of the fabulous cheeses that are available across the country. If your favourite restaurant doesn't feature exciting local cheeses, ask for them, encourage them to think local and bring wonderful cheeses to the table.

GREAT BRITISH CHEESE FESTIVAL

The festival was created by Juliet Harbutt in 2000 to educate and inspire foodies from across Britain. Having moved around the Cotswolds it has found its permanent home at Cardiff Castle where it continues to attract 1,000's of cheese lovers every year, lured by the prospect of seeing, tasting and buying over 500 British and Irish cheeses. Plus visitors can visit Cardiff Castle, sample over 35 artisan beers and ciders, listen to great live music and, of course, watch cheese tossing. For more information check out www.thecheeseweb.com

SERVICE *with a*

It seems every time you switch on the TV these days there's a programme about a top chef, but what about the professionals who serve the food (and wine) at your table? Fiona Griffiths meets some of the country's best front-of-house talents...

It's 11.45am on a Thursday at the Waterside Inn in Bray, and general manager Diego Masciaga is addressing the troops.

Reservations book in hand, he reads out the names of each and every guest expected for lunch.

Some of the names are familiar to the staff – despite its high prices, The Waterside has plenty of regulars – while others are probably first-time guests whose names aren't recognised, but everyone still needs to know who's coming, where they'll be sitting, whether they have any dietary requirements, and whether they're celebrating a special occasion.

I recognise one of the names myself; Lord Alan Sugar will be dining today in a party of five. Masciaga designates one of his waiters to look after the business tycoon over lunch, which produces a big smile from the chosen young man.

If he can keep that cheerful look on his face throughout service, he'll have a happy boss.

Left: The Waterside Inn's front-of house team line up for inspection before lunch service

 *When the door is open the show is open, because at the end of the day this is a theatre. Every day the actors have to perform and they have to be 100 per cent* 

"Remember, priority one is to smile," Masciaga tells his assembled team – the comment is directed more towards the newer recruits than the old hands, but it's a lesson that can never be learnt too many times.

"If a guest asks for something and you don't understand, it's not a problem. Just say 'I'm sorry, I'm just starting, and I'm going to ask someone who understands'. As long as you keep smiling, that's what matters."

There's just enough time for a brief inspection of the staff's uniforms – a quick check to make sure their shoes are polished, their clothes clean and pressed, their ties straight and their hair neat – and then that's it, the curtain is up, and at midday the show begins.

"When the door is open the show is open, because at the end of the day this is a theatre," says Masciaga.

"Every day the actors have to perform and they have to be 100 per cent – clean shaven, with their shoes and clothing clean."

An early start

Masciaga has been preparing for this moment – the curtain up moment – since 8.30 this morning, when he arrived for work and went for his daily walk around the premises. He checked in with the gardener and the housekeeping staff, and made sure everything was looking spotless.

At 9.10am he had his usual meeting with his department heads – to talk about how things went yesterday and who is expected to dine today and stay the night – and then spent 30 minutes in his office dealing with bookings for private dining, before another check on the progress of the cleaning operation.

This morning he also fitted in a staff training session in the restaurant. The subject? How to carve a duck and make a sauce from the carcass, how to carve a chicken, and how to remove a lobster from its shell and serve it – all at the table.

He makes it look so easy, but it takes quite some strength to cut through the bone of the chicken to remove the legs and wings.

"The guest mustn't see that it's hard – you still have to smile and talk to the guest as you work," Masciaga says, switching effortlessly from one language to another for the benefit of his multinational team.

Later, he tells me: "There are restaurants and there are restaurants.

"There are restaurants where guests will only go for one reason – which is the food – and then there are restaurants like The Waterside where, because of our setting by the river, the valet who parks your car, the waiters who still work a lot at the table, it's more of a show and you go for the complete experience."

At some point before the "show" starts, Masciaga always finds time to have a quick read through the newspapers. It's not so much a chance to put his feet up, as an essential part of his role as host.

"It's not enough to be able to talk about the food or the wine – I read the newspapers every day because I have to know what's happening in the world, otherwise I'll appear ignorant in front of the guests," he explains.

From starting at 8.30am to finishing after evening service at 1.30am (having prepared the books for the next day and checked the news headlines on Teletext), Masciaga only has an hour's break (it's a good job he only lives a short distance down the road), but if he's tired and longing for some time off, he never lets it show.

He never forgets his own lesson – to keep smiling – and he's constantly on the ball, eyes scanning the room for a guest who wants to order something, or needs a top up of wine. He's constantly observing his staff too, looking to make sure everyone's keeping up the pace and, most importantly, making the guests feel relaxed and welcome.

"I always say that if you go to a restaurant of this level and your food is perfect but you don't feel comfortable with the place, if there's no warmth, yes, it's nice, but you're not going to go back because it doesn't give you anything," says Masciaga.

"On the other hand, if you go to a place where maybe the food is okay, the

Left: Diego Masciaga at The Waterside Inn demonstrates Canard à la presse (pressed duck) to his team

Below: The Waterside Inn sits on the banks of the Thames

Wine and product knowledge can be learnt, but I think to work front-of-house, communication skills and a good personality are the biggest things you need

steak is a bit overcooked but when you tell the head waiter he listens and does something about it straight away, and you feel comfortable with the people around you, then you'll go back, because we're all human."

Dining room theatre

Fellow Italian Donato Colasanto, at The Capital in London's Knightsbridge, shares Masciaga's passion for the profession of service.

Within three weeks of joining The Capital as restaurant manager at the beginning of 2010, he had reintroduced gueridon service (where a dish is partially prepared in the kitchen and finished at the table) in a move to bring some theatre back to the dining room.

"What I'm trying to do here is revive some of the values of front-of-house, not only because I believe there's demand for gueridon service, but to give the front-of-house respect as a profession," says Colasanto.

"In fine-dining, front-of-house is not a job, it's a profession and an art."

The carving trolley – used to serve roast meats and salmon – has certainly gone down well with the customers, and perhaps even more so with the staff, who are enjoying the chance to pick up new skills from an old hand like Colasanto.

"With the carvery the two most important things to get right are presentation and speed. I've been giving my staff training and they love doing it – I haven't seen such enthusiasm in young people for years," says Colasanto.

"Front-of-house has always been the front of the theatre, and the carving trolley is one of the tools that we use when we go on stage."

Seamless service

There are no carving trolleys at Vito Scaduto's Italian restaurant Red or White in Trowbridge, Wiltshire (a new entry to this year's guide), but what there is is Scaduto's relaxed but "slick" style of service.

Scaduto, who managed the restaurant at The Bath Priory for 12 years before launching Red or White in late 2008, says: "In the last 10 years I think service in this country has become a little bit more relaxed because that's what the customer wants. If you go to a restaurant you don't want to feel embarrassed about the way you hold the fork or the glass, you want to feel comfortable."

He adds: "Good service is where you're sitting there and things happen but you don't notice the waiter – it's almost as though he's invisible."

Of course, fundamental to a polished performance – be it in a restaurant or on the stage – is a strong and harmonious relationship between front-of-house and back-of-house.

One won't work without the other,

Right: Bradley Gent of Opus in Birmingham carves a chicken during the final heat of the Master of Culinary Arts Awards

Below: Peter Avis of Babylon at the Roof Gardens with his Restaurant Manager of the Year Award

as Peter Avis, restaurant manager at Babylon at the Roof Gardens in Kensington, explains: "Restaurant managers have a huge responsibility to build a relationship between front and back-of-house. It's a clear balance between the two – a really good dish presented by the chef and a really good delivery by front-of-house is what constitutes a good dining experience."

And Avis should know – he was the winner in 2009 of the Academy of Food and Wine Service's inaugural Restaurant Manager of the Year Award.

"The award was set up to shine a light on what we do in front-of-house and to show how important our role actually is," says Avis.

"We've had a long time focusing on getting chefs to a certain level in the UK, and now the shift is going to front-of-house. A lot of people are discovering now that they can have a very successful career in front-of-house, just as they can as a chef."

You don't need to tell that to Bradley Gent. He's been restaurant manager at Opus in Birmingham since he was 26 and is one of the youngest people ever to be awarded the Master of Culinary Arts (MCA) by the Academy of Culinary Arts.

Like Masciaga, Colasanto and Scaduto – all previous winners of the MCA – Gent has learnt the art of good service, plus he has the all-important personality to go with it.

"Wine and product knowledge can be learnt, but I think to work front-of-house, communication skills and a good personality are the biggest things you need," says Gent.

"What it's really all about is a passion for food and drink, a passion for people, and having the ability to spot what the customer wants before they tell you."

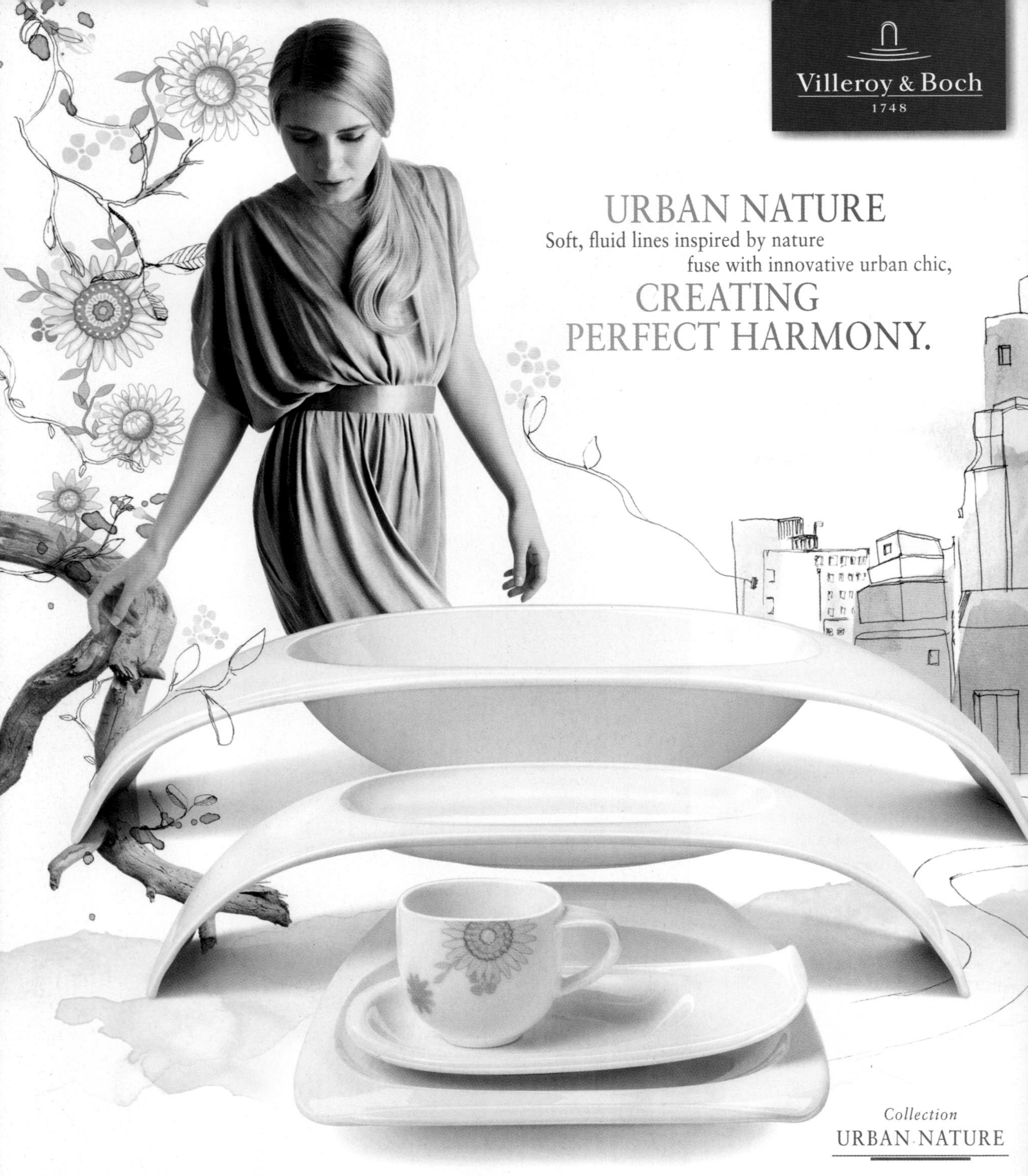

Villeroy & Boch
1748
URBAN NATURE
Soft, fluid lines inspired by nature
fuse with innovative urban chic,
CREATING
PERFECT HARMONY.
Collection
URBAN NATURE

The Top Ten Per Cent

Each year all the restaurants in the AA Restaurant Guide are awarded a specially commissioned plate that marks their achievement in gaining one or more AA Rosettes.The plates represent a partnership between the AA and Villeroy & Boch two quality brands working together to recognise high standards in restaurant cooking.

Restaurants awarded three, four or five AA Rosettes represent the Top Ten Per Cent of the restaurants in this Guide. The pages that follow list those establishments that have attained this special status

The Top Ten Per Cent

5 ROSETTES

LONDON

Marcus Wareing at The Berkeley
The Berkeley, Wilton Place, Knightsbridge, SW1
020 7235 1200

Tom Aikens
43 Elystan Street, SW3
020 7584 2003

Sketch (Lecture Room & Library)
9 Conduit Street, W1
0870 777 4488

ENGLAND

BERKSHIRE
The Fat Duck
High Street, BRAY, SL6 2AQ
01628 580333

CUMBRIA
L'Enclume
Cavendish Street, CARTMEL, LA11 6PZ
01539 536362

NOTTINGHAMSHIRE
Restaurant Sat Bains with Rooms
Lenton Lane, NOTTINGHAM, NG7 2SA
0115 986 6566

OXFORDSHIRE
Le Manoir aux Quat' Saisons
GREAT MILTON, OX44 7PD
01844 278881

4 ROSETTES

LONDON

Restaurant Gordon Ramsay
68 Royal Hospital Road, SW3
020 7352 4441

The Greenhouse
27a Hay's Mews, W1
020 7499 3331

Hélène Darroze at The Connaught
Carlos Place, W1
020 3147 7200

Hibiscus
29 Maddox Street, W1
020 7629 2999

Pied à Terre
34 Charlotte Street, W1
020 7636 1178

The Square
6-10 Bruton Street, W1
020 7495 7100

LONDON, GREATER

Chapter One
Farnborough Common, Locksbottom, BROMLEY, BR6 8NF
01689 854848

ENGLAND

BERKSHIRE
Waterside Inn
Ferry Road, BRAY, SL6 2AT
01628 620691

BUCKINGHAMSHIRE
Adam Simmonds at Danesfield House
Henley Road, MARLOW, SL7 2EY
01628 891010

CAMBRIDGESHIRE
Midsummer House
Midsummer Common, CAMBRIDGE, CB4 1HA
01223 369299

CHESHIRE
Simon Radley at The Chester Grosvenor
Chester Grosvenor & Spa, Eastgate, CHESTER, CH1 1LT
01244 324024

DERBYSHIRE
Fischer's Baslow Hall
Calver Road, BASLOW, DE45 1RR
01246 583259

DEVON
Gidleigh Park
CHAGFORD, TQ13 8HH
01647 432367

GLOUCESTERSHIRE
Le Champignon Sauvage
24 Suffolk Road, CHELTENHAM, GL50 2AQ
01242 573449

LANCASHIRE
Northcote
Northcote Road, LANGHO, BB6 8BE
01254 240555

RUTLAND
Hambleton Hall
Hambleton, OAKHAM, LE15 8TH
01572 756991

SURREY
The Latymer
Pennyhill Park Hotel & Spa
London Road, BAGSHOT, GU19 5EU
01276 471774

WILTSHIRE
Whatley Manor
Easton Grey, MALMESBURY, SN16 0RB
01666 822888

YORKSHIRE, NORTH
The Burlington Restaurant, The Devonshire Arms Country House Hotel & Spa
BOLTON ABBEY, BD23 6AJ
01756 718111

JERSEY

Bohemia Restaurant
The Club Hotel & Spa, Green Street, ST HELIER, JE2 4UH
01534 880588

SCOTLAND

CITY OF EDINBURGH
The Kitchin
78 Commercial Quay, Leith, EDINBURGH, EH6 6LX
0131 555 1755

Restaurant Martin Wishart
54 The Shore, Leith, EDINBURGH, EH6 6RA
0131 553 3557

HIGHLAND
The Boath House
Auldearn, NAIRN, IV12 5TE
01667 454896

PERTH & KINROSS
Andrew Fairlie @ Gleneagles
AUCHTERARDER, PH3 1NF
01764 694267

NORTHERN IRELAND

CO BELFAST
Deanes Restaurant
36-40 Howard Street,
BELFAST, BT1 6PF
028 9033 1144

REPUBLIC OF IRELAND

DUBLIN
Restaurant Patrick Guilbaud
Merrion Hotel, 21 Upper
Merrion Street, DUBLIN
01 676 4192

3 ROSETTES

LONDON

E1
Galvin La Chapelle
35 Spital Square
020 7299 0400

EC1
Club Gascon
57 West Smithfield
020 7796 0600

EC2
1901 Restaurant
ANdAZ London
40 Liverpool Street
020 7618 7000

Rhodes Twenty Four
Tower 42, Old Broad Street
020 7877 7703

N7
Morgan M
489 Liverpool Road,
ISLINGTON
020 7609 3560

NW1
Odette's
130 Regent's Park Road
020 7586 8569

York & Albany
127-129 Parkway
020 7388 3344

SW1
Apsleys at
The Lanesborough
Hyde Park Corner
020 7259 5599

Nahm
The Halkin Hotel,
Halkin Street
020 7333 1234

One–O–One
Sheraton Park Tower,
101 Knightsbridge
020 7290 7101

Pétrus
1 Kinnerton Street,
Knightsbridge
020 7592 1609

Seven Park Place by
William Drabble
St James's Hotel & Club
7-8 Park Place
020 7316 1600

Zafferano
15 Lowndes Street
020 7235 5800

SW3
Rasoi Restaurant
10 Lincoln Street
020 7225 1881

SW4
Trinity Restaurant
4 The Polygon,
Clapham Old Town
020 7622 1199

SW10
Aubergine
11 Park Walk, Chelsea
020 7352 3449

SW17
Chez Bruce
2 Bellevue Road,
Wandsworth Common
020 8672 0114

W1
Alain Ducasse
The Dorchester,
53 Park Lane
020 7629 8866

The Albemarle
Brown's Hotel,
Albemarle Street
020 7518 4004

Arbutus Restaurant
63-64 Frith Street
020 7734 4545

L'Autre Pied
5-7 Blandford Street
020 7486 9696

Corrigan's Mayfair
28 Upper Grosvenor Street
020 7499 9943

Galvin at Windows
London Hilton on Park Lane,
Park Lane
020 7208 4021

Le Gavroche Restaurant
43 Upper Brook Street
020 7408 0881

Gordon Ramsay at
Claridge's
Brook Street
020 7499 0099

Locanda Locatelli
8 Seymour Street
020 7935 9088

Murano
20 Queen Street
020 7592 1222

3 ROSETTES

W1 CONTINUED

Rhodes W1 Restaurant
Great Cumberland Place
020 7616 5930

Roka
37 Charlotte Street
020 7580 6464

Sketch (The Gallery)
9 Conduit Street
0870 777 4488

Texture Restaurant
34 Portman Street
020 7224 0028

Umu
14-16 Bruton Place
020 7499 8881

Wild Honey
12 Saint George Street
020 7758 9160

W4

La Trompette
5-7 Devonshire Road,
CHISWICK
020 8747 1836

W6

The River Café
Thames Wharf,
Rainville Road
020 7386 4200

W8

Kitchen W8
11-13 Abingdon Road,
Kensington
020 7937 0120

Launceston Place Restaurant
1a Launceston Place
020 7937 6912

Min Jiang
Royal Garden Hotel
2-24 Kensington High Street
020 7361 1988

W11

The Ledbury
127 Ledbury Road,
NOTTING HILL
020 7792 9090

Notting Hill Brasserie
92 Kensington Park Road
020 7229 4481

WC1

Pearl Restaurant & Bar
Renaissance
Chancery Court,
252 High Holborn
020 7829 7000

WC2

L'Atelier de Joël Robuchon
13-15 West Street
020 7010 8600

Clos Maggiore
33 King Street,
COVENT GARDEN
020 7379 9696

LONDON, GREATER

The Glasshouse
14 Station Road,
KEW, TW9 3PZ
020 8940 6777

Bingham
61-63 Petersham Road,
RICHMOND-UPON-THAMES,
TW10 6UT
020 8940 0902

ENGLAND

BEDFORDSHIRE

Paris House Restaurant
Woburn Park, WOBURN,
MK17 9QP
01525 290692

BERKSHIRE

The Vineyard at Stockcross
Stockcross, NEWBURY,
RG20 8JU
01635 528770

L'ortolan
Church Lane, SHINFIELD,
RG2 9BY
01189 888 500

BRISTOL

Casamia Restaurant
38 High Street,
WESTBURY-ON-TRYM
BS9 3D2
0117 959 28840

BUCKINGHAMSHIRE

Hartwell House Hotel, Restaurant & Spa
Oxford Road,
AYLESBURY, HP17 8NR
01296 747444

Aubergine at
The Compleat Angler
Macdonald Compleat Angler,
Marlow Bridge, MARLOW,
SL7 1RG
01628 484444

The Hand & Flowers
126 West Street,
MARLOW, SL7 2BP
01628 482277

CAMBRIDGESHIRE

Restaurant Alimentum
152-154 Hills Road,
CAMBRIDGE, CB2 8PB
01223 413000

CHESHIRE

The Alderley Restaurant, Alderley Edge Hotel
Macclesfield Road,
ALDERLEY EDGE, SK9 7BJ
01625 583033

The Church Green
Higher Lane, LYMM,
WA13 0AP
01925 752068

CORNWALL & ISLES OF SCILLY

Hell Bay
BRYTHER, Isles of Scilly
TR23 0PR
01720 422947

Well House Hotel
St Keyne, LISKEARD,
PL14 4RN
01579 342001

The Seafood Restaurant
Riverside, PADSTOW,
PL28 8BY
01841 532700

Driftwood
Rosevine, PORTSCATHO,
TR2 5EW
01872 580644

Restaurant Nathan Outlaw
The St Enodoc Hotel
ROCK, PL27 6LA
01208 863394

Hotel Tresanton
Lower Castle Road,
ST MAWES, TR2 5DR
01326 270055

CUMBRIA

Rampsbeck Country House Hotel
WATERMILLOCK, CA11 0LP
017684 86442

Gilpin Lodge Country House Hotel & Restaurant
Crook Road,
WINDERMERE, LA23 3NE
015394 88818

Holbeck Ghyll Country House Hotel
Holbeck Lane,
WINDERMERE, LA23 1LU
015394 32375

The Samling
Ambleside Road,
WINDERMERE, LA23 1LR
015394 31922

DEVON

The Horn of Plenty
GULWORTHY, PL19 8JD
01822 832528

Lewtrenchard Manor
LEWDOWN, EX20 4PN
01566 783222

Corbyn Head Hotel & Orchid Restaurant
Sea Front, TORQUAY,
TQ2 6RH
01803 213611

The Elephant Restaurant & Brasserie
3/4 Beacon Terrace,
TORQUAY, TQ1 2BH
01803 200044

DORSET

Sienna Restaurant
36 High West Street,
DORCHESTER, DT1 1UP
01305 250022

Summer Lodge Country House Hotel, Restaurant & Spa
EVERSHOT, DT2 0JR
01935 482000

GLOUCESTERSHIRE

Lords of the Manor
UPPER SLAUGHTER,
Cheltenham, GL54 2JD
01451 820243

5 North Street
5 North Street,
WINCHCOMBE, GL54 5LH
01242 604566

HAMPSHIRE

36 on the Quay
47 South Street,
EMSWORTH, PO10 7EG
01243 375592

Chewton Glen Hotel & Spa
Christchurch Road,
NEW MILTON, BH25 6QS
01425 275341

JSW
20 Dragon Street,
PETERSFIELD, GU31 4JJ
01730 262030

Avenue Restaurant
Lainston House Hotel,
Sparsholt, WINCHESTER,
SO21 2LT
01962 863588

HERTFORDSHIRE

Collette's at The Grove
Chandler's Cross,
RICKMANSWORTH,
WD3 4TG
01923 807807

Auberge du Lac
Brocket Hall Estate,
WELWYN, AL8 7XG
01707 368888

KENT

The West House
28 High Street,
BIDDENDEN, TN27 8AH
01580 291341

Apicius
23 Stone Street,
CRANBROOK, TN17 3HF
01580 714666

Read's Restaurant
Macknade Manor,
FAVERSHAM, ME13 8XE
01795 535344

Thackeray's
TUNBRIDGE WELLS,
TN1 1EA
01892 511921

LANCASHIRE

The Longridge Restaurant
104-106 Higher Road,
LONGRIDGE, PR3 3SY
01772 784969

LINCOLNSHIRE

Harry's Place
17 High Street,
Great Gonerby,
GRANTHAM, NG31 8JS
01476 561780

MERSEYSIDE

Fraiche
11 Rose Mount,
Oxton Village,
BIRKENHEAD, CH43 5SG
0151 652 2914

NORFOLK

Morston Hall
Morston, Holt,
BLAKENEY, NR25 7AA
01263 741041

The Neptune Restaurant with Rooms
85 Old Hunstanton Road,
HUNSTANTON, PE36 6HZ
01485 532122

NORTHAMPTONSHIRE

Equilibrium
Fawsley Hall, Fawsley,
DAVENTRY, NN11 3BA
01327 892000

SHROPSHIRE

Old Vicarage Hotel and Restaurant
BRIDGNORTH, WV15 5JZ
01746 716497

La Bécasse
17 Corve Street,
LUDLOW, SY8 1DA
01584 872325

SOMERSET

Bath Priory Hotel, Restaurant & Spa
Weston Road, BATH,
BA1 2XT
01225 331922

The Olive Tree at The Queensberry Hotel
4-7 Russell Street,
BATH, BA1 2QF
01225 447928

3 ROSETTES

CONTINUED

SOMERSET continued

Homewood Park Hotel
Abbey Lane,
HINTON CHARTERHOUSE,
BA2 7TB
01225 723731

Little Barwick House
Barwick Village,
YEOVIL, BA22 9TD
01935 423902

SUFFOLK

The Bildeston Crown
104 High Street,
BILDESTON, IP7 7EB
01449 740510

SURREY

The Oak Room at Great Fosters
Stroude Road, EGHAM,
TW20 9UR
01784 433822

Drake's Restaurant
The Clock House,
High Street, RIPLEY,
GU23 6AQ
01483 224777

SUSSEX, WEST

Amberley Castle Hotel
AMBERLEY, BN18 9LT
01798 831992

West Stoke House
Downs Road, West Stoke,
CHICHESTER, PO18 9BN
01243 575226

Ockenden Manor
Ockenden Lane,
CUCKFIELD, RH17 5LD
01444 416111

The Pass
South Lodge Hotel
LOWER BEEDING,
RH13 6PS
01403 891711

TYNE & WEAR

Jesmond Dene House
Jesmond Dene Road,
NEWCASTLE UPON TYNE,
NE2 2EY
0191 212 3000

WARWICKSHIRE

Mallory Court Hotel
Harbury Lane,
Bishop's Tachbrook,
ROYAL LEAMINGTON SPA,
CV33 9QB
01926 330214

WEST MIDLANDS

Loves Restaurant
The Glasshouse,
Canal Square
Browning Street
BIRMINGHAM, B16 8FL
0121 454 5151

Purnell's
55 Cornwall Street,
BIRMINGHAM, B3 2DH
0121 212 9799

Simpsons
20 Highfield Road,
Edgbaston,
BIRMINGHAM, B15 3DU
0121 454 3434

WIGHT, ISLE OF

Robert Thompson
The Hambrough
Hambrough Road,
VENTNOR, PO38 1SQ
01983 856333

WILTSHIRE

The Bybrook at the Manor
CASTLE COMBE, SN14 7HR
01249 782206

The Park Restaurant
Lucknam Park
COLERNE, SN14 8AZ
01225 742777

The Harrow at Little Bedwyn
LITTLE BEDWYN, SN8 3JP
01672 870871

YORKSHIRE, NORTH

Samuel's at Swinton Park
MASHAM, Ripon, HG4 4JH
01765 680900

Judges Country House Hotel
Kirklevington, YARM,
TS15 9LW
01642 789000

YORKSHIRE, WEST

Box Tree
35-37 Church Street,
ILKLEY, LS29 9DR
01943 608484

Anthony's Restaurant
19 Boar Lane,
LEEDS, LS1 6EA
0113 245 5922

JERSEY

Ocean Restaurant at the Atlantic Hotel
Le Mont de la Pulente,
ST BRELADE, JE3 8HE
01534 744101

Grand, Jersey
The Esplanade,
ST HELIER, JE4 8WD
01534 722301

Longueville Manor Hotel
ST SAVIOUR, JE2 7WF
01534 725501

SCOTLAND

ABERDEENSHIRE

Darroch Learg Hotel
Braemar Road,
BALLATER, AB35 5UX
013397 55443

The Green Inn
9 Victoria Road,
BALLATER, AB35 5QQ
013397 55701

ARGYLL & BUTE

Isle of Eriska
ERISKA, PA37 1SD
01631 720371

The Ardanaiseig Hotel
KILCHRENAN,
Taynuilt, PA35 1HE
01866 833333

Airds Hotel and Restaurant
PORT APPIN, PA38 4DF
01631 730236

DUMFRIES & GALLOWAY

Knockinaam Lodge
PORTPATRICK, DG9 9AD
01776 810471

EDINBURGH

Norton House Hotel
Ingliston, EDINBURGH,
EH28 8LX
0131 333 1275

Number One, The Balmoral Hotel
Princes Street, EDINBURGH, EH2 2EQ
0131 557 6727

Plumed Horse
50-54 Henderson Street, Leith, EDINBURGH, EH6 6DE
0131 554 5556

21212
3 Royal Terrace, EDINBURGH, EH7 5AB
0131 523 1030

FIFE

The Cellar
24 East Green, ANSTRUTHER, KY10 3AA
01333 310378

The Peat Inn
PEAT INN, KY15 5LH
01334 840 206

The Road Hole Restaurant
Old Course Hotel Golf Resort & Spa, ST ANDREWS, KY16 9SP
01334 474371

The Seafood Restaurant
The Scores, ST ANDREWS, KY16 9AS
01334 479475

GLASGOW

Hotel du Vin Bistro at One Devonshire Gardens
1 Devonshire Gardens, GLASGOW, G12 0UX
0141 339 2001

HIGHLAND

Inverlochy Castle Hotel
Torlundy, FORT WILLIAM, PH33 6SN
01397 702177

Abstract Restaurant
Glenmoriston Town House Hotel, Ness Bank, INVERNESS, IV2 4SF
01463 223777

The Cross at Kingussie
Tweed Mill Brae, Ardbroilach Road, KINGUSSIE, PH21 ILB
01540 661166

SCOTTISH BORDERS

The Horseshoe Inn
EDDLESTON, Peebles, EH45 8QP
01721 730225

SOUTH AYRSHIRE

Glenapp Castle
BALLANTRAE, KA26 0NZ
01465 831212

Lochgreen House Hotel
Monktonhill Road, Southwood TROON, KA10 7EN
01292 313343

STIRLING

Roman Camp Country House Hotel
CALLANDER, FK17 8BG
01877 330003

WEST DUNBARTONSHIRE

Martin Wishart at Loch Lomond
Cameron House on Loch Lomond, BALLOCH, G83 8QZ
01389 722504

SCOTTISH ISLANDS

Kinloch Lodge
Sleat, ISLE ORNSAY, IV43 8QY
01471 833214

The Three Chimneys
COLBOST, Isle of Skye IV55 8ZT
01470 511258

Ullinish Country Lodge
STRUAN, Isle of Skye, IV56 8FD
01470 572214

WALES

CARDIFF

Le Gallois-y-Cymro
6-10 Romilly Crescent, CARDIFF CF11 9NR
029 2034 1264

CEREDIGION

Ynyshir Hall
EGLWYSFACH, Machynlleth, SY20 8TA
01654 781209

CONWY

Tan-y-Foel Country House
Capel Garmon, BETWS-Y-COED, LL26 0RE
01690 710507

Bodysgallen Hall and Spa
LLANDUDNO, LL30 1RS
01492 584466

MONMOUTHSHIRE

Walnut Tree Inn
Llandewi Skirrid, ABERGAVENNY, NP7 8AW
01873 852797

NEWPORT

The Crown at the Celtic Manor Resort
Coldra Woods, NEWPORT, NP18 1HQ
01633 410262

POWYS

Carlton Riverside
Irfon Crescent, LLANWRTYD WELLS, LD5 4SP
01591 610248

REPUBLIC OF IRELAND

CO CLARE

Gregans Castle
BALLYVAUGHAN
065 7077005

CO KILDARE

The Byerley Turk
The K Club, STRAFFAN
01 601 7200

CO MONAGHAN

Restaurant at Nuremore
CARRICKMACROSS
042 966 1438

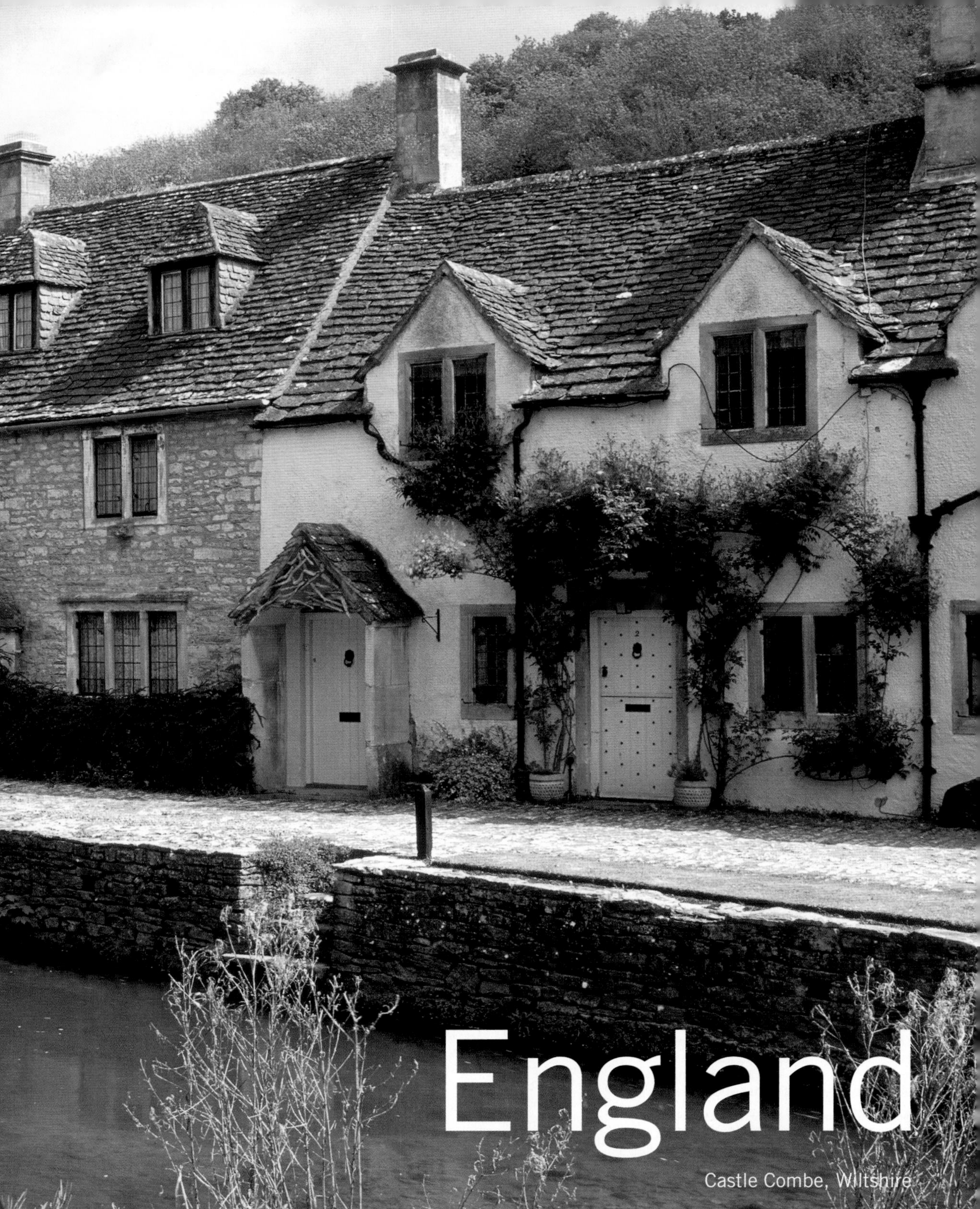

England

Castle Combe, Wiltshire

BEDFORDSHIRE

BEDFORD Map 12 TL04

The Bedford Swan

Modern British NEW V

Modern food in refurbished Georgian hotel

☎ 01234 346565
The Embankment MK40 1RW
e-mail: info@bedfordswanhotel.co.uk
dir: M1 junct 13, take A421 following signs to city centre (one way system)

After a lavish refurbishment, Bedford's most historic hotel is looking sharp. The 18th-century building's elegant bow windows overlook the River Ouse, while the made-over interior décor showcases its period charm - bare stone walls, oak panelling and fancy plaster ceilings mingling with contemporary colours and textures. In the River Room restaurant, exposed stone walls and burnished wooden tables make an attractive setting for uncomplicated, modern comfort-food cooking. Roast scallops with cauliflower cream, caper and raisin dressing and pea shoots might set the ball rolling, followed by rack of local pork teamed with cider apples, sage mash, green beans and red wine sauce.

Chef James Parsons **Owner** BDL **Times** 12-3/6-10 **Prices** Fixed L 2 course £13.95-£16.95, Starter £4.95-£9.95, Main £10.95-£25, Dessert £4.95 **Wines** 23 bottles over £20, 15 bottles under £20, 6 by glass **Notes** Vegetarian menu, Dress restrictions, Smart casual, Civ Wed 250 **Seats** 90, Pr/dining room 20 **Children** Portions, Menu **Parking** 90

BOLNHURST Map 12 TL05

The Plough at Bolnhurst

Modern British

Extensive modern European menu in Tudor pub

☎ 01234 376274
Kimbolton Rd MK44 2EX
e-mail: theplough@bolnhurst.com
dir: A14/A421 onto B660 for approx 5m to Bolnhurst village

The low-beamed whitewashed country inn in north Bedfordshire harks back to the Tudor era, as you might infer from its tiny windows. It's a well-run fine-dining destination for the region, with a chalkboard menu at lunchtimes, and a more extensive roll call of modern European dishes in the evenings. Sautéed foie gras with quince, potato galette and sherry vinegar sauce is the hot-button starter, and could be followed by braised brill in Noilly Prat, with tomato and coriander chowder. Anglo-Irish cheeses come from Neal's Yard, and there are eye-catching desserts such as honey and Grand Marnier nougat glacé with orange compôte and sugared almonds.

Chef Martin Lee **Owner** Martin Lee, Jayne Lee, Michael Moscrop **Times** 12-2/6.30-9.30 Closed 27 Dec-14 Jan, Mon, D Sun **Prices** Fixed L 2 course fr £14, Starter £5.75-£10.95, Main £11.95-£24.95, Dessert £5-£6.95, Service optional **Wines** 80 bottles over £20, 42 bottles under £20, 12 by glass **Notes** Sunday L, Vegetarian available **Seats** 80, Pr/dining room 40 **Children** Portions **Parking** 30

FLITWICK Map 11 TL03

Menzies Flitwick Manor

Modern British

Georgian manor house with confident kitchen

☎ 0871 472 4016
Church Rd MK45 1AE
e-mail: flitwick@menzies-hotels.co.uk
dir: M1 junct 12, follow Flitwick after 1m turn left into Church Rd. Manor 200 yds on left

With a full complement of antiques, oil paintings, and oriental rugs on oak parquet floors, Flitwick Manor is a handsome Georgian country house done out in a classic vein. An impressive acreage of wooded parkland and peaceful gardens with a croquet lawn gives guests plenty of breathing space, while the restaurant fits the bill with its traditional look and lovely views over the grounds. Classic dishes are given a modern spin on a well-thought-out repertoire, opening with seared breast of pigeon with creamed leeks and hazelnuts, ahead of fillet of pork which appears wrapped in Parma ham and served with Savoy cabbage, Chantenay carrots and sage gnocchi.

Times 12-2.30/7-9.30

LUTON Map 6 TL02

Adam's Brasserie

Modern British NEW

Vibrant brasserie cooking in smartly restyled stables

☎ 01582 734437 & 698888
Luton Hoo Hotel, Golf & Spa, The Mansion House LU1 3TQ
e-mail: enquiries@lutonhoo.co.uk
dir: M1 junct 10A, 3rd exit to A1081 towards Harpenden/St Albans. Hotel less then a mile on left

This airy brasserie is named for the renowned 18th-century architect Robert Adam, who designed the stables building on the Luton Hoo estate in which it is housed. Huge A-frame rafters hung with stylish chandeliers soar above an expansive space, kitted out with smart green leather booths and burnished wooden tables left modishly unclothed. Luton Hoo is a bit of a film star, so you can amuse yourself by identifying pictures of the various movies that have been shot here while mulling over the menu of modern British brasserie favourites. Potted shrimps are well-partnered with shellfish mayonnaise and lime crème fraîche, ahead of a vibrantly fresh main course of seared mackerel fillets with citrus crushed potatoes, sautéed spring greens and white wine and caviar sauce. To finish, textbook wobbly pannacotta is teamed exotically with passionfruit cream, caramelised mango and coconut sorbet.

Chef Kevin Clark **Owner** Elite Hotels **Times** 12-3/6-10 Closed Mon, L Tue **Prices** Fixed L 2 course fr £19.50, Fixed D 3 course fr £29.50, Service optional **Notes** Sunday L

Wernher Restaurant

Modern European

Modern cooking in a resplendent stately home setting

☎ 01582 734437 & 698888
Luton Hoo Hotel, Golf and Spa, The Mansion House LU1 3TQ
e-mail: reservations@lutonhoo.com
dir: M1 junct 10A, 3rd exit to A1081 towards Harpenden/St Albans. Hotel less than a mile on left

This magnificent Grade I listed mansion at Luton Hoo in 1,000 acres of 'Capability' Brown-designed parkland and gardens is the stuff of film-set grandeur. Indeed, the walls of Adam's Brasserie in the former stables are lined with stills and memorabilia of the many films and TV productions in which the grand old pile has played a starring role. Priceless tapestries, oil paintings and sculptures, chandeliers and sweeping staircases ensure the opulence factor is high throughout. The majestic Wernher Restaurant was the original state dining room and it looks every inch the part. This is where the kitchen pulls out all the stops with the confidence to come up with some adventurous modern British ideas that show real culinary flair. The menu is full of interest - perhaps a lobster and lemongrass ravioli in a shellfish, tomato and coriander broth to start, followed by roast breast of guinea fowl with sweet potato gnocchi, snail and mushroom fricassée and wild garlic purée. Formality runs to the very core of the service, but not at the expense of friendliness.

Chef Kevin Clark **Owner** Elite Hotels **Times** 12.30-2/7-10 Closed L Sat **Prices** Fixed L 2 course fr £25, Fixed D 3 course fr £42, Service optional **Wines** 338 bottles over £20, 18 by glass **Notes** Sunday L, Vegetarian available, Dress restrictions, Jacket or tie, Civ Wed 380 **Seats** 80, Pr/dining room 280 **Children** Portions, Menu **Parking** 316

WOBURN Map 11 SP93

The Inn at Woburn

Modern British

Seamless blend of old and modern in lovely market town

☎ 01525 290441
George St MK17 9PX
e-mail: enquiries@theinnatwoburn.co.uk
dir: 5 mins from M1 junct 13. Follow signs to Woburn. Inn in town centre at x-rds, parking to rear via Park St

The handsome Georgian inn at the heart of Woburn is a fine example of that classic British institution - the upmarket country hostelry. If you're as hungry as a lion after a visit to the historic abbey or the safari park, afternoon tea in the beamed Tavistock bar and lounge should fill the gap until it's time to return for an aperitif before dinner in Olivier's restaurant. Named after chef Olivier Bertho, it sports a classic country-house look, involving button-backed chocolate leather seats, fragrant lilies in blue-and-white Chinese vases, burnished wooden floors and tables, and neutral tones of mushroom and cream. An inviting contemporary menu of British and Mediterranean themes might open with ceviche of scallops partnered by tomato vierge, black olive tapenade, and anchovy oil, then progress to monkfish with crab ravioli, and white bean cassoulet in tomato coulis. To finish, an assiette of three desserts brings forth chocolate tart with Chantilly cream, orange pannacotta, and golden syrup sponge.

The Inn at Woburn

Times 12-2.30/6-10.15

Paris House Restaurant

– see below

WYBOSTON Map 12 TL15

Wyboston Lake Hotel

Modern NEW

Honest brasserie grub with a lakeside view

☎ 01480 212625
Wyboston Lakes, Great North Rd MK44 BA
e-mail: reservations@wyboston.co.uk
web: www.wybostonlakes.co.uk
dir: Off A1/A428, follow brown Cambridge signs. Wyboston Lakes & hotel on right, marked by flags

Popular with golfers and the business crowd, the modern Wyboston Lake Hotel is just off the A1 between Cambridge

continued

Paris House Restaurant

WOBURN Map 11 SP93

French V

Creative French cooking in parkland setting

☎ 01525 290692 **Woburn Park MK17 9QP**
e-mail: gail@parishouse.co.uk
web: www.parishouse.co.uk
dir: M1 junct 13. From Woburn take A4012 Hockliffe, 1m out of Woburn village on left

Following the sad death of long-time owner Peter Chandler, a new chapter has begun at this beautiful Tudoresque black-and-white timber framed building in Woburn Park - Paris House is now part of the small group of fine-dining restaurants run by Alan Murchison (see entries for L'ortolan, Shinfield, and La Bécasse in Ludlow). Built in 1878 for the Paris Exhibition, the house was shipped over lock, stock and chimneys to this beautiful spot by the 9th Duke of Bedford. It meets current expectations on the inside - chic and understated with vibrant modern artworks - and there's the obligatory chef's table with views of all the action in the kitchen. Chef-patron Phil Fanning describes the food as French retro classic, which seems a reasonable description of a main-course 'pork and apple sauce' (confit belly with sage and smoked apple purée). Things start as they mean to go on with superb bread (apricot and caraway, perhaps) and some clever little amuse-bouche such as a Scotch egg filled with a nicely soft quail's egg. The kitchen sources with due diligence, local ingredients get a fair showing and technical skills are sharp. First-course roasted scallops come with black pudding and celeriac and apple dressing, while main-course kedgeree is a reinvention with halibut and a well-judged curry risotto, topped with a quail's egg and curry foam. For dessert, carrot and ginger cake with a carrot sorbet and ginger cream looks a picture on the plate.

Chef Phil Fanning **Owner** Alan Murchison **Times** 12-2/6.30-10 Closed D 26 Dec-8 Jan, Mon, L Tue, D Sun **Prices** Fixed L 2 course £24-£49, Fixed D 3 course £38-£59, Starter £9-£15, Main £17.50-£32, Dessert £9-£12, Service added 10% **Wines** 80 bottles over £20, 8 by glass **Notes** ALC 3 course £59, Gastronomic menu 7 course £65, Sunday L, Vegetarian menu, Dress restrictions, Smart casual **Seats** 48, Pr/dining room 16 **Children** Portions, Menu **Parking** 24

WYBOSTON *continued*

and Bedford in 350 acres of countryside. The Waterfront Brasserie turns out uncomplicated, crowd-pleasing dishes. It overlooks the south lake and leads out onto decking, so alfresco dining is a good bet in warm weather. The simple brasserie fare served by friendly staff might include a well-timed smoked haddock and spinach risotto with a poached egg, followed by pork two ways - pan-roasted fillet and braised belly - served with mashed potato, roasted parsnips, cabbage and a cider jus. An all-day menu is available in the lounge.

Chef Leigh Morris **Times** 11.30-3/6.30-9.30 **Prices** Food prices not confirmed for 2011. Please telephone for details

BERKSHIRE

ASCOT — Map 6 SU96

Bluebells Restaurant & Garden Bar

Ⓡ Modern, International **NEW**

Contemporary European cookery in relaxed surroundings

☎ 01344 622722
Shrubbs Hill, London Rd SL5 0LE
e-mail: info@bluebells-restaurant.co.uk
dir: From M25 junct 13, A30 towards Bagshot. Between Wentworth & Sunningdale

A 300-year-old building lies at the heart of this clean-cut modern restaurant - not that you'd know it since a stylish facelift has kitted out the interior with a calm, understated contemporary look. Gauzy voile screens split the open-plan space into bar, main restaurant and conservatory areas, while textures of exposed brick, darkwood floors, olive carpets and white leather seats provide a contemporary finish. The kitchen team has an impressive classically-trained pedigree, deployed in a winning formula that subjects prime British produce to vibrant modern international influences. Pressed ham hock with boudin noir, cider-glazed apples and celeriac spaghetti is a typical starter, while main courses might be pan-fried sea bass with truffle linguini, pickled girolles and a ginger and lemongrass emulsion.

Chef Adam Turley **Owner** John Rampello
Times 12-3/6.30-9.45 Closed Mon, D Sun **Prices** Fixed L 2 course fr £13, Starter £7.95-£12.95, Main £16.50-£26, Dessert £7.50-£8.95, Service added but optional 10% **Wines** 76 bottles over £20, 13 bottles under £20, 12 by glass **Notes** Sunday L, Vegetarian available, Dress restrictions, Smart casual **Seats** 90, Pr/dining room 14 **Children** Portions, Menu **Parking** 100

Hyperion at Macdonald Berystede Hotel & Spa

Ⓡ Modern European

Elegant dining room offering contemporary cuisine

☎ 01344 623311 & 0844 8799 104
Bagshot Rd, Sunninghill SL5 9JH
e-mail: general.berystede@macdonald-hotels.co.uk
dir: M3 junct 3/A30, A322 then left onto B3020 to Ascot or M25 junct 13, follow signs for Bagshot. At Sunningdale turn right onto A330

The historic Berystede Hotel is an amazing piece of Victorian Gothic whimsy with witches' hat turrets, faux-Tudor timbers and fish-scale shingle tiles. Inside, the hotel's long horseracing heritage is celebrated for fans of the sport of kings - Ascot racecourse is, after all, just a short length away - but if you're not tempted to lose your shirt on the gee gees, there's a full complement of 21st-century leisure facilities to keep you busy. Named after a legendary Derby-winning racehorse, the Hyperion Restaurant deals in modern European ideas, presented simply: smoked haddock terrine opens in the company of a crème fraîche and caper dressing, then a well-executed main course teams rump of lamb with saffron creamed potatoes, roasted vegetables and rosemary jus.

Times 12.30-2/7-9.45 Closed L Sat

BRACKNELL — Map 5 SU86

Rowans at Coppid Beech

Ⓡ European, Pacific Rim

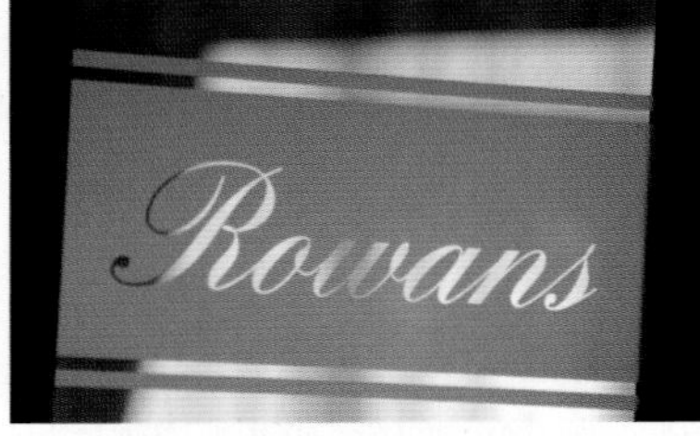

Alpine atmosphere and modern food by the Thames

☎ 01344 303333
The Coppid Beech Hotel, John Nike Way RG12 8TF
e-mail: sales@coppidbeech.com
web: www.coppidbeech.com
dir: From M4 junct 10 follow A329(M) (Bracknell/Wokingham) to 1st exit. At rdbt take 1st exit to Binfield (B3408); hotel 200yds on right

This one-off hotel has the look of an alpine resort transposed to the Thames Valley - as well as its amazing Swiss chalet design, there's even a dry-ski slope, an ice rink and toboggan run in the complex. There's no cheese fondue and glühwein on the menu in the fine dining Rowans restaurant, though: beneath a soaring timbered ceiling hung with crystal chandeliers, the style is traditional with heavy drapes, linen-clothed tables and formal service from uniformed staff. The menu ranges widely through a broad repertoire of modern European dishes, taking in slow-cooked pork belly with date purée, roasted parsnips, smoked mash and a passionfruit reduction, or a more orthodox combination of corn-fed chicken breast with shiitake mushroom and smoked bacon risotto, cauliflower purée and thyme gravy.

Chef Paul Zolik **Owner** Nike Group Hotels Ltd
Times 12-2/7-9.45 Closed L Sat **Prices** Fixed L 2 course £15-£20, Fixed D 3 course £25-£31, Starter £6.50-£8.50, Main £14.50-£18.25, Dessert £5.25-£8.50, Service optional **Wines** 61 bottles over £20, 7 bottles under £20, 11 by glass **Notes** Sunday L, Vegetarian available, Dress restrictions, Smart casual, Civ Wed 300 **Seats** 120, Pr/dining room 20 **Children** Portions, Menu **Parking** 350

BRAY — Map 6 SU97

The Fat Duck

ⓇⓇⓇⓇⓇ – *see opposite page*

Hinds Head

ⓇⓇ Traditional British

The best of British pub food Blumenthal style

☎ 01628 626151
High St SL6 2AB
e-mail: info@hindsheadhotel.co.uk
dir: M4 junct 8/9, at rdbt take exit to Maidenhead Central, next rdbt take exit Bray & Windsor, after 0.5m take B3028 to Bray

The 15th-century former hunting lodge is a fascinating place, not only for its celebrated past but for its current incarnation as the boozy younger sibling to the Fat Duck (see entry), located a few doors away along the High Street. This is a different kettle of fish, of course, with chef-owner Heston Blumenthal probing the delights of British tavern food. Classic pub dishes, served without fuss or unnecessary garnish and clear, defined flavours, echo the pub's Tudor roots and fit perfectly into the traditional pub setting of oak panelling and beams, crackling log fires, leather chairs, and a warm, inviting and informal atmosphere. Start with potted shrimps with watercress salad or raw Scotch beef with caper and shallot dressing, before moving on to time-honoured dishes like chicken, ham and leek pie with mustard sauce, blade of beef with spring cabbage and Irish black and white pudding, or roast black bream with fennel salad. Interesting side dishes include broccoli with anchovies and almonds, and Heston's renowned triple-cooked chips. Old-fashioned puddings include Sussex pond pudding and banana Eton mess. The Crown, another Bray pub, just across the road from the Fat Duck, has also joined the Heston family.

Chef Clive Dixon **Owner** Hinds Head Ltd
Times 11-2.30/6.30-9.30 Closed 25-26 Dec, D 1 Jan **Prices** Starter £6.35-£9.50, Main £11.95-£29.50, Dessert £6.50-£8.95, Service added but optional 12.5% **Wines** 69 bottles over £20, 10 bottles under £20 **Notes** Tasting menu available 7 course, Sunday L, Vegetarian available **Seats** 100, Pr/dining room 22 **Children** Portions, Menu **Parking** 40

The Fat Duck

BRAY Map 6 SU97

Modern British V NOTABLE WINE LIST

The home of Heston - a culinary Wonderland

☎ 01628 580333
High St SL6 2AQ
dir: M4 junct 8/9 (Maidenhead) take A308 towards Windsor, turn left into Bray. Restaurant in centre of village on right

We can safely say Heston goes by just the single name these days, alongside Marco, Jamie and a few others. So 2010 turned out to be somewhat of a watershed year for Heston. The telly work continues at a pace with ever more thrilling and visceral experiences for one bunch of lucky celebs or another in the *Feast* series, but the notable, tangibly exciting prospect is a London opening, due to happen as the guide is published; make hot-foot for The Mandarin Oriental Hyde Park. London is bound to deliver a different experience than the Fat Duck, and indeed it is not the intention to replicate Bray in a metropolitan five-star hotel. The Berkshire village setting of the FD is part of its charm, the unpretentious nature of the room making it pretty much unique among the top flight of UK restaurants - it is smart, certainly, with wooden floors and bold contemporary artworks, but it is by no means a shrine. Eating chez Heston is a fun experience and doubtless he wouldn't have it any other way. The service is utterly confident inasmuch as staff engage with diners in a charming manner whilst demonstrating supreme professionalism. The tasting menu is £150 these days. Sounds like a lot, but you get a lot. Not in terms of volume - although you won't leave hungry that is for sure - rather in multi-sensory experiences based on years of research, relentless endeavour, obsessive perfectionism, heart and soul. That's got to be worth 150 quid of anyone's money. The menu evolves, old favourites remain - as expected as *Let it Be* at a Paul McCartney gig - while new dishes arrive, some of them as seen lovingly developed on TV. 'Lime Grove', the nitro-poached green tea and lime mousse, typifies the thrill of it all, with the liquid nitrogen producing an ultra-light meringue-like texture that dissolves on the tongue delivering tantalisingly invigorating flavours, and is accompanied by a spray of lime grove (lime blossom, zest and leaf) that is deftly delivered by the waiter. 'Mock turtle Soup' was developed for the Mad Hatter's tea party (it's not often you get the chance to say that) and is a thing of complex beauty that is magical to look at and divine to consume. 'Sound of the Sea' comes with an iPod to deliver aural stimulation alongside the beautifully fresh fish and three types of seaweed, and 'Powdered Anjou Pigeon' comes with a superb blood pudding and confit umbles (offal in today's parlance). 'Tafferty Tart' is a dessert dating from the 17th century that is in Heston's hands an alluring combination of the flavours and textures of caramelised apple, fennel, rose and candied lemon. The experience hopes to trigger the memory - perhaps the 'BFG' (Black Forest gâteau) will do it for you - and there is evident passion for rediscovering and reinventing the culinary heritage of this country.

Chef Heston Blumenthal **Owner** Fat Duck Ltd **Times** 12-1.45/7-9.45 Closed 2 wks at Xmas, Mon, D Sun **Prices** Tasting menu £150, Service added but optional 12.5% **Wines** 500 bottles over £20, 13 by glass **Notes** Vegetarian menu **Seats** 40 **Children** Portions **Parking** Two village car parks

BRAY *continued*

The Riverside Brasserie

◎◎ Modern European

Relaxed riverside dining in Bray marina

☎ 01628 780553
Bray Marina, Monkey Island Ln SL6 2EB
e-mail: info@riversidebrasserie.co.uk
dir: Off A308, signed Bray Marina

Tucked away down the wonderfully named Monkey Island Lane, this modest, café-like building set along the bank of the River Thames at Bray marina is a hidden gem. As well as being a pit stop for boats on the Thames, this riverside eatery draws the summer crowds for leisurely lunches on the waterside decked terrace. Expect a relaxed atmosphere, and unpretentious yet accomplished brasserie fare from the open kitchen. Using well-sourced ingredients, simple, well-presented dishes mix classics such as a starter of venison and pork terrine with piccalilli, followed by skate wing, brown butter, lemon and capers or pollock with Savoy cabbage and applewood-smoked bacon, with Mediterranean-inspired ideas such as fettuccine, artichoke and peas. Classic puddings include apple crumble and custard or sticky toffee pudding.

Chef Phil Boardman **Owner** Alfie Hitchcock **Times** 12-2.30/7-9.30 Closed Mon-Thu (Oct-Mar), L Fri (Oct-Mar) **Prices** Food prices not confirmed for 2011. Please telephone for details **Wines** 20 bottles over £20, 3 bottles under £20, 6 by glass **Notes** Vegetarian available **Seats** 36 **Children** Portions, Menu **Parking** 30

Waterside Inn

◎◎◎◎ *– see opposite*

CHIEVELEY **Map 5 SU47**

The Crab at Chieveley

◎◎ Modern British

Dedicated seafood paradise in a Berkshire country pub

☎ 01635 247550
Wantage Rd RG20 8UE
e-mail: info@crabatchieveley.com
dir: M4 junct 13, towards Chieveley. Left into School Rd, right at T-junct, 0.5m on right

Landlocked Berkshire may not be your first port of call for a dedicated seafood restaurant of great flair, nor may you expect to find it in a downland country pub, but there it is. The Crab happily confounds expectations in every way. The seafood makes its way here from Devon and is served in three dining rooms hung about with fishing-nets and with pictures crowding the walls. Prepare for grilled red mullet in pistachio crumb, scallops with watercress purée, or crab consommé with lobster cannelloni to start, perhaps followed by one of the signature main-course platters of fruits de mer, served cold with wasabi mayonnaise, or hot with garlic butter. Meat-eaters can opt for the likes of braised oxtail with foie gras if they don't want to join the party. Desserts pique the interest at meal's end with strawberry torte, served with a granola biscuit and daiquiri granité.

Chef Dave Horridge, Jamie Hodson **Owner** Andrew Hughes **Times** 12-2.30/6-9.30 Closed D 25 Dec **Prices** Fixed L 2 course £15.95, Fixed D 3 course £19.95, Starter £8.50-£12.50, Main £18.50-£44, Dessert £6-£14, Service added but optional 10% **Wines** 150 bottles over £20, 15 by glass **Notes** Sunday L, Vegetarian available, Civ Wed 50 **Seats** 120, Pr/dining room 30 **Children** Portions **Parking** 80

COOKHAM **Map 6 SU88**

Malik's

◎◎ Indian

Precision Indian cooking in rural Berkshire

☎ 01628 532914 & 520085
High St SL6 9SF
dir: M4 junct 7, take A4 towards Maidenhead, 2m

When you have big guns such as Mr Blumenthal and the Waterside Inn in your neck of the woods, the culinary bar is raised rather high. Accordingly, Malik's steps up to the plate with classic tandoori cooking that is a cut above the average high street Indian. The building itself, in a primped stockbroker-belt village near the Thames, also refuses to conform to sub-continental stereotypes: we're dealing with a classic old English ivy-clad coaching inn here, decked out with arty monochrome shots of Indian spices on the walls, and candlelit tables swathed in crunchy white linen. Clued-up staff talk you through the finer points of the kitchen's output, as the menu is a compendium of accurately-cooked, taste-led Indian classics, some familiar, others less so. King prawn tandoori relies on top-class plump prawns and subtle spicing for its effect, ahead of a lamb halim dish, which pulls out all the flavour stops in a rich tomato and lentil sauce with fried ginger, garlic and chilli. Finish with firni - a Bengali take on rice pudding, infused with saffron, cardamom and fresh coconut.

Chef Malik Ahmed, Shapon Miah **Owner** Malik Ahmed **Times** 12-2.30/6-11 Closed 25-26 Dec, L Eid festival **Prices** Fixed L 2 course £12-£18, Fixed D 3 course fr £40, Starter £4-£8, Main £7.50-£16, Dessert £3.50-£6, Service added but optional 10% **Wines** 40 bottles over £20, 10 bottles under £20, 7 by glass **Notes** Sunday L, Vegetarian available, Dress restrictions, Smart dress **Seats** 70, Pr/dining room 30 **Children** Portions **Parking** 26

Waterside Inn

BRAY Map 6 SU97

French

Gastronomic Thames-side legend delivering classic French cuisine and impeccable service

☎ 01628 620691
Ferry Rd SL6 2AT
e-mail: reservations@waterside-inn.co.uk
dir: M4 junct 8/9, A308 (Windsor) then B3028 to Bray. Restaurant clearly signed

The Roux brothers pitched up in this spot beside the Thames in 1972, placing the sleepy village of Bray firmly on the culinary map. At the time, Michel Roux's son Alain was in short trousers, but over the years he learned his father's craft and in 2001 took the helm. Indeed, the Waterside has seen many changes in the last 39 years, not least the addition of 13 luxurious bedrooms and suites, and, in 2009, the installation of a £2 million state-of-the-art kitchen. Having said that, plenty of things have stayed steadfastly the same since 1972 and that's part of the appeal to the many loyal fans. Now there's no hiding from the fact it is pricey - very - but it will be an experience you won't forget. Service plays its part in making it memorable, from the moment you pull up outside and the immaculately turned-out valet appears, as if from nowhere, to park your car, you just know you're going to be in very safe hands. In fact, service is so intuitive, so seamless, it's practically invisible. Drinks and canapés out on the terrace, or in one of the little heated summerhouses overlooking the river, is a great way to enjoy the setting while making your choice from one of two set menus, or à la carte. Whichever you choose, this is classic French haute cuisine at its best, with a few contemporary flourishes and everything prepared from superb seasonal ingredients. The impeccably trained staff seem to have the pace just so, thus when the time is right you'll be shown to your table in the bright and airy dining room, with its floor-to-ceiling windows looking out across the Thames. There's certainly plenty to watch, from people messing about on boats to the waiters carving meat at your table - a tradition which has never gone out of fashion here. First course pan-fried scallops - cooked with absolute precision - come wrapped in a light veil of breadcrumbs with sesame seeds to give great contrast of texture, complemented by a classic curry scented cauliflower mousseline and some crisp baby artichokes. In a wonderfully simple but inspired main course, fillet of salmon is cooked, to perfection, en papillote with pine needles, giving it a beautifully smoky flavour. Fillet of Angus beef - pan-fried, studded with black olives and served with soft potato and tapenade croquettes and a basil scented Graves sauce - is so tender you could cut it with a fork. From the incredible cellar comes a choice of no less than 2,000 wines, including some which would easily add a good few noughts to your total bill.

Chef Michel Roux, Alain Roux
Owner Michel Roux & Alain Roux
Times 12-2/7-10 Closed Mon, L Tue, D Tue (ex Jun-Aug) **Prices** Fixed L 2 course fr £41.50, Fixed D 4 course fr £112.50, Starter £33.50-£58, Main £49-£69.50, Dessert £28-£39, Service included
Wines 650 bottles over £20, 14 by glass
Notes Sunday L, Vegetarian available, Dress restrictions, Smart casual, Civ Wed 70 **Seats** 75, Pr/dining room 8
Children Menu **Parking** 20

FRILSHAM Map 5 SU57

The Pot Kiln

Traditional British, European

Hearty country cooking in rural Berkshire pub

☎ 01635 201366
RG18 0XX
e-mail: info@potkiln.org
dir: From Yattendon follow Pot Kiln signs, cross over motorway. Continue for 0.25m pub on right

Persevere down narrow lanes to find TV chef and presenter Mike Robinson's wonderfully rustic and rural country pub. Come for the views across rolling fields to woodland, pints of Good Old Boy in the charmingly unpretentious bar, and plates of hearty country food served by the blazing fire at unclothed scrubbed tables in the relaxing dining room. The modern European menu changes with the seasons and bristles with local meat and game dishes, with much of the venison shot by Mike. Cooking may be straightforward and presentation simple, but expect quality ingredients and modern, gutsy flavours, as seen in a stunningly delicious pavé of Linkenholt fallow deer with pommes purée and peppercorn sauce. Alternatively, tuck into a warm wood pigeon salad with smoked bacon and black pudding, followed by wild rabbit in cider, apple and mustard, and sticky toffee pudding.

Chef Mike Robinson **Owner** Mike & Katie Robinson **Times** 12-2.30/7-9.30 Closed 25 Dec, Tue, D Sun **Prices** Fixed L 2 course fr £14.50, Starter £5.95-£7.50, Main £12.95-£16.50, Dessert £5.95, Service added but optional 10% **Wines** 51 bottles over £20, 8 bottles under £20, 6 by glass **Notes** Sunday L, Vegetarian available **Seats** 48, Pr/dining room 16 **Children** Portions **Parking** 70

HUNGERFORD Map 5 SU36

The Bear Hotel

Modern British

Modernised historic coaching inn showcasing British cuisine

☎ 01488 682512
41 Charnham St RG17 0EL
e-mail: info@thebearhotelhungerford.co.uk
dir: M4 junct 14, follow A338/Hungerford signs. 3m to T-junct turn right onto A4 over 2 rdbts. Hotel 500yds on left

The Bear has impressive historical connections, including ownership by Henry VIII and operating as a headquarters for Charles I during the English Civil War. Both monarchs might marvel at how the old girl is getting on these days. Whitewashed brick walls and imposing black beams contrast with the restaurant's original artwork and tables are laid with crisp white linen and silver cutlery. The accomplished modern British cooking sees pressed terrine of tea-smoked pheasant and foie gras perfectly partnered with a scrumpy apple and thyme purée, while griddled rib-eye of beef comes with a braised oxtail and pepper sauce. Save room for apple and blackberry bread-and butter-pudding with rhubarb ice cream and toffee custard. The carte is supplemented by weekly specials and lighter options are available in the bar.

Chef Philip Wild **Owner** The Bear Hungerford Ltd **Times** 12-3/7-9.30 Closed D Sun **Prices** Food prices not confirmed for 2011. Please telephone for details **Wines** 24 bottles over £20, 26 bottles under £20, 8 by glass **Notes** Sunday L, Vegetarian available, Civ Wed 80 **Seats** 50, Pr/dining room 18 **Children** Portions **Parking** 68

HURLEY Map 5 SU88

Black Boys Inn

Traditional French

French home cooking in the Chilterns

☎ 01628 824212
Henley Rd SL6 5NQ
e-mail: info@blackboysinn.co.uk
dir: M40 junct 4, A404 towards Henley, then A4130. Restaurant 3m from Henley-on-Thames & Maidenhead

Dating back to the 16th century and given its current name as early as the 17th in tribute to the future Charles II, who popped in following defeat at the Battle of Worcester in 1651, the current incarnation of the building is a smart restaurant with rooms, where owner Adrian Bannister shows his passion for bourgeois French cooking. It's got a lovely rural aspect, just outside Henley-on-Thames, in a pretty part of the Chilterns. Inside there's plenty of rustic charm in the form of unclothed wooden tables, traditional beams and well-worn leather armchairs, but the overall effect is lightened with smart modern touches. In the kitchen local produce is king, combined with ingredients sourced from small suppliers in France to create beautifully presented dishes. Smoked duck and dandelion salad, perhaps, with hazelnut dressing and warm poached duck egg in filo may precede confit goose with red wine, juniper and caramelised pear. On the 100-strong wine list, around 40 are available by the glass.

Chef Marc Paley, Adrian Bannister **Owner** Adrian & Helen Bannister **Times** 12-2/7-9 Closed D Sun **Prices** Starter £5.95-£9.95, Main £13.50-£22.50, Dessert £5.95-£9.95, Service optional **Wines** 105 bottles over £20, 6 bottles under £20, 32 by glass **Notes** Carte du jour & drink £9.95, Sunday L, Vegetarian available **Seats** 45, Pr/dining room 12 **Parking** 45

LAMBOURN Map 5 SU37

The Hare Restaurant and Bar

British, French

Daring modern British cooking in horse racing country

☎ 01488 71386
Ermin St RG17 7SD
e-mail: cuisine@theharerestaurant.co.uk
dir: M4 junct 14, A338 towards Wantage, left onto B4000 towards Lambourn, restaurant 3m on left

The former village inn in Berkshire racing country has recently seen an enlargement of its eating options, which now extend over four separate areas, including a garden room that can be transformed into a private space. Stripped wood tables are stylishly set, and there are prints of the sport of kings adorning the walls. A well-wrought version of modern British cooking is on offer, with dishes that are both daring and informed by sound culinary logic. A shellfish starter partners a seared scallop, a tempura-battered prawn and an oyster with shallot vinaigrette, the whole unified by a rich lobster sauce. Mains might furnish more seafood with the likes of lemon sole stuffed with salmon and crab in beurre noisette, or roast pork belly rolled around black pudding and apricot, alongside parsnip purée, caramelised apple and a cider jus. Fruity desserts will prove a strong lure at the finishing stage, perhaps lemon tart with pomegranate and satsuma salad and crème fraîche.

Chef Paul Reed **Owner** John Kirby **Times** 12-2.30/7-9.30 Closed 2 wks Jan, 2 wks summer, Mon, D Sun **Prices** Fixed L 2 course £20, Fixed D 3 course £28-£38, Starter £6.50-£8.50, Main £15-£21, Dessert £6.50-£8.50, Service optional, Groups min 10 service 10% **Wines** 70 bottles over £20, 6 bottles under £20, 6 by glass **Notes** Sunday L, Vegetarian available, Dress restrictions, Smart casual **Seats** 75, Pr/dining room 25 **Children** Portions **Parking** 30

MAIDENHEAD Map 6 SU88

Fredrick's Hotel Restaurant Spa

Modern British, French

Contemporary British cooking in grand hotel and spa

☎ 01628 581000
Shoppenhangers Rd SL6 2PZ
e-mail: reservations@fredricks-hotel.co.uk
dir: From M4 junct 8/9 take A404(M), then turning (junct 9A) for Cox Green/White Waltham. Left on to Shoppenhangers Rd, restaurant 400 mtrs on right

Owned by the same family for the past 33 years, this grand hotel close to Windsor Castle and Wentworth and Sunningdale golf courses is also a short hop from the M4 and only 30 minutes from London. Spa therapies and beauty treatments are on offer amid the comfortable luxury. The grand dining room has a traditional and formal air, with polished silver accoutrements, gleaming glassware and crisp white napery all adding to the elevated tone. A la carte or fixed-price menus deliver modern British cooking; fresh crab with tuna carpaccio and pea shoot salad might open proceedings, while main courses might feature the likes of supreme of halibut with scallops and fricassée of woodland mushrooms. Finish with white chocolate parfait with caramelised pear.

Chef Brian Cutler **Owner** R Takhar **Times** 12-2.30/7-10 Closed 23-27 Dec, L Sat **Prices** Fixed L 2 course fr £18.95, Fixed D 3 course fr £38.95, Service optional **Wines** All bottles over £20, 6 by glass **Notes** Sunday L, Vegetarian available, Dress restrictions, Smart casual, Civ Wed 120 **Seats** 60, Pr/dining room 140 **Children** Portions **Parking** 90

The Royal Oak at Paley Street

British

Historic inn with ambitious, exciting cooking

01628 620541
Paley St, Littlefield Green SL6 3JN
e-mail: royaloakmail@aol.com
dir: M4 junct 8/9. Take A308 towards Maidenhead Central, then A330 to Ascot. After 2m, turn right onto B3024 to Twyford. Second pub on left

The whitewashed pub looks exactly as classic inside as you hope, with black beams, exposed brick supports and slate-tiled floors. A portrait shot of David Beckham with the late George Best ensures there is a little corner of Berkshire that will be forever Man United. It makes a fitting environment for some seriously ambitious, classy cooking, which is built around ingredients of demonstrable quality. Dish after dish scores highly: a bowl of deep-fried sand eels with mayonnaise; fabulous foie gras and chicken liver parfait with salt flakes, fig chutney and a doorstop wodge of brioche; peppered haunch of resonantly flavoured venison on creamed spinach with sauce poivrade. Fish is treated with due sensitivity, as when lemon sole fillets turn up with brown shrimps, tomatoes and basil, while pannacotta in a pot, layered with strawberries and melt-in-the-mouth shortbread, is a fine note to end on. There's a pedigree wine list, too.

Chef Dominic Chapman **Owner** Nick Parkinson **Times** 12-3/6-12 Closed 1-4 Jan, D Sun **Prices** Fixed L 2 course fr £17.50, Starter £6-£12.50, Main £12.50-£28, Dessert £6.50-£9, Service added but optional 12.5% **Wines** 300 bottles over £20, 30 bottles under £20, 20 by glass **Notes** Sunday L, Vegetarian available **Seats** 50 **Children** Portions **Parking** 70

NEWBURY **Map 5 SU46**

Donnington Valley Hotel & Spa

Modern British

Elegant, wine-themed restaurant in stylish spa and golfing hotel

01635 551199
Old Oxford Rd, Donnington RG14 3AG
e-mail: general@donningtonvalley.co.uk
dir: M4 junct 13, A34 towards Newbury. Take immediate left signed Donnington Hotel. At rdbt take right, at 3rd rdbt take left, follow road for 2m, hotel on right

Surrounded by rolling Berkshire countryside and with its own 18-hole golf course, this very modern hotel conceals a surprisingly stylish interior behind its rather plain red-brick façade. The smart, contemporary feel extends to the impressive conference facilities and a state-of-the-art spa. The Wine Press restaurant is an airy, split-level space, with a wine theme, and a skilful kitchen team delivering simple, modern British dishes. Expect imaginative renditions of classic favourites prepared from fresh, locally-sourced produce. Start with juicy, perfectly cooked scallops with shallot purée and crispy aubergine, then perhaps lamb shank with roasted garlic mash and ratatouille, and finish with a hazelnut terrine with chocolate ice cream. The mighty wine list is well balanced and includes a comprehensive choice by the glass.

Chef Kelvin Johnson **Owner** Sir Peter Michael **Times** 12-2/7-10 **Prices** Fixed L 2 course fr £19.45, Fixed D 3 course fr £27.60, Starter £6.15-£12.30, Main £17.40-£25, Service optional **Wines** 190 bottles over £20, 34 bottles under £20, 30 by glass **Notes** Sunday L, Vegetarian available, Dress restrictions, Smart casual, Civ Wed 85 **Seats** 120, Pr/dining room 130 **Children** Portions, Menu **Parking** 150

Regency Park Hotel

Modern

Appealing seasonally-changing modern menu

01635 871555
Bowling Green Rd, Thatcham RG18 3RP
e-mail: info.newbury@pedersenhotels.com
dir: M4 junct 13, follow A339 to Newbury for 2m, then take the A4 (Reading), the hotel is signed

The Watermark restaurant overlooks a well designed landscaped garden, with a fabulous giant water feature the other side of the floor-to-ceiling windows. It's a modern hotel, red-brick and glass, with an open-plan interior and comfortably contemporary fixtures and fittings. There's a relaxed and friendly feel to proceedings. The seasonal menu is a mix of French and European flavours; confit breast of lamb for example, served with a tart of chanterelle mushrooms, roast garden beetroot and yellow carrots; braised belly of pork with baby squid; and for dessert perhaps a hot passionfruit soufflé with passionfruit cream and a pink grapefruit sorbet.

Regency Park Hotel

Chef Laurent Guyon **Owner** Pedersen Caterers **Times** 12.30-2/7-9.30 Closed L Sat **Prices** Food prices not confirmed for 2011. Please telephone for details **Wines** 25 bottles over £20, 26 bottles under £20, 11 by glass **Notes** Sunday L, Vegetarian available, Civ Wed 100 **Seats** 100, Pr/dining room 140 **Children** Portions, Menu **Parking** 200

River Bar Restaurant

Modern European

Delightful riverside restaurant serving good food

01635 528838
Newbury Manor Hotel, London Rd RG14 2BY
e-mail: enquiries@newbury-manor-hotel.co.uk
web: www.riverbarrestaurant.co.uk
dir: M4 junct 13, A34 Newbury, A4 Thatcham, 0.5m on right opposite Swan Pub

Newbury Manor is an elegant Grade II listed Georgian house, set in nine idyllic acres of lush woodland and water meadows that are a haven for wildlife. The short walk through fragrant herb gardens and over wooden bridges is a delight, as is the setting: the conservatory-style River Bar Restaurant occupies part of an old watermill, with floor-to-ceiling windows looking across an alfresco decking terrace to the confluence of the Rivers Kennet and Lambourn. You may catch the electric blue flash of a kingfisher as you put the kitchen's repertoire of unfussy

continued

NEWBURY *continued*

Anglo-French dishes through their paces: foie gras comes with brioche and a fried duck egg, all perfectly timed and pretty as a picture. Next, a subtly gamey roasted partridge arrives with dauphinoise potato, Savoy cabbage with cream, chestnuts and bacon, and bread sauce.

Chef David Horridge, John Harrison **Owner** Heritage Properties & Hotels **Times** 12-2.30/6-10 **Prices** Food prices not confirmed for 2011. Please telephone for details **Wines** 29 bottles over £20, 15 bottles under £20, 12 by glass **Notes** Sunday L, Vegetarian available, Civ Wed 100 **Seats** 48, Pr/dining room 40 **Parking** 80

The Vineyard at Stockcross

@@@ – *see below*

PANGBOURNE Map 5 SU67

The Elephant at Pangbourne

@ Modern British

Modern British classics in an Indian-colonial setting

☎ 0118 984 2244 & 07770 268359
Church Rd RG8 7AR
e-mail: reception@elephanthotel.co.uk
dir: A4 Theale/Newbury, right at 2nd rdbt signed Pangbourne. Hotel on left

A fond nod to the days of the Raj seems to infuse this singular hotel, which is adorned with Indian furniture and rugs, and, of course, elephants. Choose from an enclosed garden, the BaBar bistro, or the smart dining room, which has views over the garden and the local church. A little Indian seasoning may crop up in the bowl of mussels that starts a meal in the bistro, but essentially this is modern British cooking, with many recognised contemporary dishes on the slate. Seared scallops with black pudding and cauliflower purée, monkfish wrapped in Parma ham, and succulent local rib-eye with skinny chips and béarnaise tick all the boxes, as might a finisher of zesty lemon tart with a dollop of clotted cream.

Times 12-2.30/7-9

READING Map 5 SU77

Acqua Restaurant & Bar

@@ Modern British

Modern cooking on the banks of the Thames

☎ 0118 925 9988
Crowne Plaza Reading, Caversham Bridge, Richfield Av RG1 8BD
e-mail: info@cp-reading.co.uk
dir: M4 junct 11, take the Inner Distribution Rd to Caversham

Within the town's Crowne Plaza Hotel, the light and spacious Acqua Restaurant mixes contemporary elegance with stunning views across the River Thames, which flows by right outside. The kitchen caters for a wide range of tastes but the cornerstone is local, seasonal produce and high quality ingredients. Start, perhaps, with white bean and roast garlic soup with charred artichoke and chorizo oil, or a classic Caesar salad, before moving on to chargrilled Exmoor rib-eye steak with goose fat chips, roquette salad and béarnaise sauce. Dessert could be banana soufflé with maple and walnut ice cream and banana sandwich.

Times 12-2.30/6.30

Cerise Restaurant at The Forbury Hotel

@ Modern European

Smart brasserie dining at stylish townhouse hotel

☎ 0800 078 9789 & 0118 952 7770
The Forbury Hotel, 26 The Forbury RG1 3EJ
e-mail: reservations@theforburyhotel.co.uk
dir: M4 junct 11/A33 towards town centre, then right onto A329. Follow station signs & continue forward over flyover. At traffic lights bear left into Watlington St & continue to Forbury Rd. Take left turns into Blagrove St, Valpy St and at War Memorial. Hotel on the left

The Forbury is a smart boutique hotel full of striking design features - how about the chandelier with 86,000 Italian glass beads which runs the height of the building in the old lift shaft? There's an opulent cocktail lounge

The Vineyard at Stockcross

NEWBURY Map 5 SU46

Modern French V Notable Wine List

Alluringly confident modern French cuisine

☎ 01635 528770
Stockcross RG20 8JU
e-mail: general@the-vineyard.co.uk
dir: M4 junct 13/A34 Newbury bypass southbound, take 3rd exit signed Hungerford/Bath road interchange. Take 2nd exit at 1st and 2nd rdbts signed Stockcross, 0.6 mile on right

There's been a changing of the guard at the Vineyard. John Campbell has gone to new terroirs in the form of the Dorchester's country-house hotel, Coworth Park, and Daniel Galmiche has arrived with his style of contemporary French cuisine, rooted in the classics and showing a light touch and a sure hand. The luxurious modern hotel's sweeping gravel driveway leading past the 'Fire and Water' sculpture makes a good first impression. The Vineyard is certainly big on luxury and delivers first-class service; the spa and conference facilities are five-star, and the restaurant remains a destination in its own right. As well as a handsome split-level mellow toned dining room - linked by a sweeping staircase with a balustrade fashioned as if it were a grapevine snaking between the spaces, and tables smartly set with crisp white linen - Daniel Galmiche has inherited a wine list of some repute; the Californian list is as diverting as any you'll find in the UK, and the 'rest of the world' section can hold its own in most company. Daniel's menus are based on impeccable produce, change with pleasing regularity and showcase his confident, intelligent style. Things get off to a flying start with an amuse-bouche such as a luscious pumpkin velouté with goats' cheese and a beetroot crisp. Then on to the first course, perhaps a beautiful looking dish of pressed duck leg and foie gras terrine, the richness cut perfectly by the partnering pear compôte. Main-course pan-fried red mullet - perfectly fresh, perfectly cooked - comes à la Niçoise, and for dessert, perhaps a top-notch tarte Tatin with Tahitian vanilla ice cream and caramel sauce.

Chef Daniel Galmiche **Owner** Sir Peter Michael **Times** 12-2.30/7-9.30 **Prices** Fixed L 2 course £20, Fixed D 3 course £70, Tasting menu £46-£99, Service optional **Wines** 3000 bottles over £20, 60 bottles under £20, 50 by glass **Notes** ALC 2 course £60, 3 course £70, Tasting menu available L & D, Sunday L, Vegetarian menu, Civ Wed 120 **Seats** 86, Pr/dining room 120 **Children** Portions, Menu **Parking** 100

with a superb list, and the restaurant is done out in a stylishly modern way with splashes of cerise and bare wooden tables. In fine weather you can dine in the garden under the shade of a pomegranate tree. The menu is broadly modern European, so a meal might begin with carpaccio of beef with pesto, basil oil, roquette and parmesan, and follow on with oven baked sea bream with prawn colcannon and parsley velouté, or Highland rib-eye steak or free-range, corn-fed chicken from the grill.

Chef Michael Parke **Owner** von Essen Hotels **Times** 12-3/7-10.30 **Prices** Fixed L 2 course £10-£25, Fixed D 3 course £35-£55, Starter £6.50-£12, Main £15-£21, Dessert £6.50-£8, Service optional **Wines** 200 bottles over £20, 8 by glass **Notes** Vegetarian available **Seats** 72, Pr/dining room 35 **Children** Portions, Menu **Parking** 18

Forbury's Restaurant

French, European NOTABLE WINE LIST

Refined, confident cooking in smartly contemporary venue

☎ 0118 957 4044
1 Forbury Square RG1 3BB
e-mail: forburys@btconnect.com
dir: In town centre, opposite Forbury Gardens

Forbury's is a stylish contemporary restaurant on the ground-floor of an office block designed by the same architect who created Canary Wharf. It is very smartly dressed in the contemporary manner, with large canvases of modern art, high-backed leather chairs, rich colours and well-spaced linen-clad tables. Floor-to-ceiling windows overlook Forbury Square and you can sit outside, too, under heated parasols. There's a popular wine bar area where you can choose something from the excellent wine list, and go for something off the menu as well. The cooking is based on classic French thinking with plenty of contemporary ideas, with excellent British ingredients to the fore. The menu changes regularly according to what is in season, presentation is a strength, and the dishes show a good degree of refinement. Start with warm salad of quail with Muscat grapes, beetroot and balsamic dressing, move on to roasted Cornish John Dory with braised oxtail, herb potato and a red wine sauce, and finish with a tarte Tatin made with Braeburn apples and served with salted butter caramel and vanilla ice cream.

Chef Gavin Young **Owner** Xavier Le-Bellego **Times** 12-2.15/6-10 Closed 26-28 Dec, 1-2 Jan, Sun **Prices** Fixed L 2 course £11.95, Fixed D 3 course £21, Starter £7.50-£12.50, Main £16.95-£22.95, Dessert £8-£9.50, Service optional, Groups min 4 service 12.5% **Wines** 145 bottles over £20, 9 bottles under £20, 22 by glass **Notes** Tasting menu available, Vegetarian available **Seats** 80, Pr/dining room 16 **Children** Portions **Parking** 40

Malmaison Reading

Modern European

Contemporary brasserie dining in rejuvenated former Great Western Rail hotel

☎ 0118 956 2300 & 956 2302
Great Western House, 18-20 Station Rd RG1 1JX
e-mail: reading@malmaison.com
dir: Next to Reading station

Reading's Great Western Railway Hotel dates from the golden age of steam in the mid 19th-century, but its lustre was rather tarnished until Malmaison revamped it with their trademark contemporary boutique chic. Railway memorabilia give a nod to its heritage in the brasserie-style restaurant, where bare brick walls are teamed with exposed industrial ducting, black floor tiles and theatrical lighting. The kitchen does a nice line in good honest modern brasserie cooking led by great quality produce, so cream of haricot blanc soup comes with tasty chunks of confit duck, followed by pot-roast chicken with sage dumplings and leek and bacon broth. Don't skip pudding as the head chef is a whizz with pastry and has a thing for chocolate - try slow-cooked chocolate fondant with passionfruit sorbet and honeycomb.

Chef Andrew Holmes **Owner** MWB Malmaison Holdings Ltd **Times** 12-2.30/6-10.30 Closed L Sat **Prices** Fixed L 2 course £17.50-£28.50, Fixed D 3 course £25-£35, Starter £5.25-£8.50, Main £12.50-£19.50, Dessert £5.95-£8.50, Service added but optional 10% **Wines** 142 bottles over £20, 10 bottles under £20, 18 by glass **Notes** Sunday L, Vegetarian available, Civ Wed 35 **Seats** 64, Pr/dining room 40 **Children** Portions, Menu **Parking** NCP across road

Millennium Madejski Hotel Reading

British, International V

Contemporary cuisine in striking, modern stadium complex

☎ 0118 925 3500
Madejski Stadium RG2 0FL
e-mail: sales.reading@millenniumhotels.co.uk
dir: 1m N from M4 junct 11. 2m S from Reading town centre

The stylish Cilantro restaurant in the glitzy hotel part of the Madejski Stadium complex of Reading FC has a trendy buzz, with moody lighting falling on black, white and red walls. Hidden behind a style-statement wall of wine bottles, the kitchen sends out contemporary reworkings of French-accented classics that are totally in tune with the surroundings. Foie gras terrine might be paired with camomile jelly, while a halo of garlic foam adds oomph to cream of artichoke soup. Main courses range from pan-fried John Dory with scallops, fennel and sauce vierge to medallions of lamb with asparagus, minted hollandaise and potato gratin.

Chef Denzil Newton **Owner** Madejski Hotel Co **Times** 7-10 Closed 25 Dec, 1 Jan, BHs, Sun-Mon, L all week **Prices** Food prices not confirmed for 2011. Please telephone for details **Wines** 64 bottles over £20, 36 bottles under £20, 12 by glass **Notes** Vegetarian menu, Dress restrictions, Smart casual **Seats** 55, Pr/dining room 12 **Children** Portions **Parking** 100

The Mill House Hotel

Modern European NEW

Classic cooking in tranquil hotel

☎ 0118 988 3124
Old Basingstoke Rd, Swallowfield RG7 1PY
e-mail: info@themillhousehotel.co.uk
dir: M4 junct 11, S on A33, left at 1st rdbt onto B3349. Approx 1m after sign for Three Mile Cross & Spencer's Wood, hotel on right

Set in ten acres of well-tended lawns with weeping willows and a millpond complete with rustic bridges, this smart Georgian house occupies a peaceful spot next to the River Loddon. Light meals are served in the bar, whilst the conservatory restaurant is the place to head to for fine dining with well-defined, classic flavours: Scotch quail's egg salad with spicy red onion jam might be followed by beef fillet medallion with baby spinach and wild mushroom and Madeira jus. Round things off with bread-and-butter pudding scented with orange and served with custard.

Chef Robert John **Owner** Mark & Kim Pubus **Times** 12-2.30/7-9.30 Closed 26 Dec-4 Jan, L Mon, D Sun **Prices** Fixed L 2 course £19.50-£29.50, Fixed D 2 course £19.50-£29.50, Starter £5, Main £19.50, Dessert £5, Service added but optional 10% **Wines** 24 bottles over £20, 20 bottles under £20, 6 by glass **Notes** Sunday L, Vegetarian available, Civ Wed 120 **Seats** 45, Pr/dining room 30 **Children** Portions **Parking** 60

SHINFIELD **Map 5 SU76**

L'ortolan

– see page 58

SONNING Map 5 SU77

The French Horn

British, French

Classical dining on the Thames

0118 969 2204
RG4 6TN
e-mail: info@thefrenchhorn.co.uk
dir: From Reading take A4 E to Sonning. Follow B478 through village over bridge, hotel on right, car park on left

The French Horn blows its trumpet for the joys of timeless Gallic gastronomy in a quintessentially-English *Wind in the Willows* setting beside a lazy stretch of the Thames. The elegant dining room revels in old-school opulence; a glass frontage opens onto an idyllic terrace overlooking the willow-fringed river - the sort of spot where a glass of chilled bubbly is de rigueur before skilful waiters present your meal with a flourish. To whet your appetite, there's a spit-roast duck turning above the fire, or should that be canard rôti à l'Anglaise, as it is the signature dish on a menu heavily accented with French classics. Kick off with a terrine of duck foie gras served with marinated fig and port relish and warm brioche. Keeping things French, follow with a sole bonne femme - Dover sole with mushrooms and creamy white wine and chive sauce.

Times 12-2.15/7-9.45 Closed 26-30 Dec

STREATLEY Map 5 SU58

Cygnetures

British, International

Fine-dining hotel restaurant with a gorgeous Thames-side vista

01491 878800
The Swan at Streatley, High St RG8 9HR
e-mail: sales@swan-at-streatley.co.uk
web: www.swanatstreatley.co.uk
dir: Follow A329 from Pangbourne, on entering Streatley turn right at lights. Hotel on left before bridge

Tradition has it that Jerome K Jerome checked into the 17th-century Swan at Streatley to pen his bestseller *Three Men in a Boat*. The Swan, and the whole Thames-side tourism industry, owe him a great debt as it contributed significantly to the river becoming a tourist attraction. The hotel has not let the grass grow beneath its feet and now offers the full pampering and spa experience as well as contemporary dining in its Cygnetures restaurant, complete with the unspoilt bucolic backdrop of weeping willows dipping into the Thames. A clean-cut, minimal look favours sailing images on white walls and a single flower at each table to inject a note of colour, while the cooking takes in modern British staples with European influences, built on top-quality materials. Dinner might begin with suprême of wood pigeon with walnut gnocchi and cranberry jus, and go on to pan-fried bream with risotto nero, red pepper piperade, pea shoots and samphire.

Cygnetures

Chef Andrew West-Letford **Owner** Nike Group Hotels **Times** 12.30-2/7-10 **Prices** Food prices not confirmed for 2011. Please telephone for details **Wines** 89 bottles over £20, 31 bottles under £20, 18 by glass **Notes** Sunday L, Vegetarian available, Dress restrictions, Smart casual, Civ Wed 150 **Seats** 70, Pr/dining room 130 **Children** Portions, Menu **Parking** 130

L'ortolan

SHINFIELD Map 5 SU76

French V Notable Wine List

Confident cooking in elegant former vicarage

0118 988 8500
Church Ln RG2 9BY
e-mail: info@lortolan.com
web: www.lortolan.com
dir: From M4 junct 11 take A33 towards Basingstoke. At 1st rdbt turn left, after garage turn left, 1m turn right at Six Bells pub. Restaurant 1st left (follow tourist signs)

Dating back to the 17th century, this charming red-brick former vicarage amid pretty, tranquil grounds is a stand-out gastronomic destination these days, thanks to Alan Murchison's impressive French cooking. Pastel greens and chocolate colours prevail in the modern, elegant dining room, and the chefs can be spotted working their magic through a fish tank 'window'. The classy cuisine is rooted in the French classics with no lack of contemporary ideas and creative touches, and top-notch seasonal ingredients are treated with due diligence and a great degree of technical skill. Everything from the excellent breads and amuse-bouche through to the pre-dessert and petits fours show this to be a kitchen firing on all cylinders. From the menu du jour comes a starter of confit of organic salmon, given a Far-Eastern flavour by pickled mooli and wasabi mayonnaise, while from the carte a main-course pan-fried tranche of halibut is paired with crab risotto and a tempura of soft-shell crab. Finish with a warm bitter chocolate tart and peanut butter ice cream, or a perfectly risen soufflé.

Chef Alan Murchison **Owner** Newfee Ltd **Times** 12-2/7-9 Closed 2 wks Xmas/New Year, Sun-Mon **Prices** Food prices not confirmed for 2011. Please telephone for details **Wines** 400 bottles over £20, 1 bottle under £20, 11 by glass **Notes** Vegetarian menu, Dress restrictions, Smart casual, Civ Wed 62 **Seats** 62, Pr/dining room 22 **Children** Portions **Parking** 45

WINDSOR Map 6 SU97

The Dining Room

Modern British, French

Riverside dining in a Gothic country-house hotel

☎ 01753 609988 & 609900
Oakley Court Hotel, Windsor Rd, Water Oakley SL4 5UR
e-mail: reservations@oakleycourt.com
dir: M4 junct 6 to Windsor. At rdbt right onto A308. Hotel 2.5m on right

If this Victorian Gothic country-house hotel close to Windsor looks familiar then chances are you've seen one of those 1960s Hammer Horror films or *The Rocky Horror Picture Show*, which were made here. You won't get a shiver down your spine these days, though. It's a relaxing place to stay, set in 35 acres of landscaped gardens which wend their way down to the Thames. The restaurant has been rebranded since the hotel was bought by the Principal Hayley hotel group. The elegant Dining Room turns out some classy modern European cuisine made with good quality local produce. Start with a trio of foie gras appetisers with their own garnishes and truffle dressing or a main of red mullet fillet, warm spiced couscous salad, tempura broccoli and sauce vierge.

Chef Darran Kimber **Owner** Principal Hayley Hotels & Conference Venues **Times** 12-2/7-9.30 Closed L Sat **Prices** Fixed L 2 course fr £16.95, Fixed D 3 course fr £29.95, Starter £10-£16, Main £20-£32, Dessert £8.50-£10.50, Service optional **Wines** 40 bottles over £20, 4 bottles under £20, 7 by glass **Notes** Sunday L, Vegetarian available, Dress restrictions, Smart casual, Civ Wed 200 **Seats** 110, Pr/dining room 25 **Children** Portions, Menu **Parking** 180

Mercure Castle Hotel

Modern European

Contemporary dining in the heart of Windsor

☎ 0870 4008300 & 01753 851577
18 High St SL4 1LJ
e-mail: h6618@accor.com
dir: M25 junct 13 take A308 towards town centre then onto B470 to High St. M4 junct 6 towards A332, at rdbt first exit into Clarence Rd, left at lights to High St

For grandstand views of the castle and the Changing of the Guard, this 16th-century coaching inn in the heart of Windsor can't be beaten. Tailor-made for the Home Counties affluence of this Royal town, the classy, contemporary Eighteen restaurant sports plush aubergine high-backed chairs at modishly bare darkwood tables against a soft-focus backdrop of beige and white. The kitchen reworks classic themes with an intelligent contemporary approach, and is not afraid to use some quite daring flavour combinations on a menu that dips happily into global influences. There are plenty of appealing ideas on show here: green asparagus soup might appear with goats' cheese tortellini and piquillo pepper coulis, ahead of breast and confit of Gressingham duck teamed with Parma ham roulade, braised red cabbage purée and semolina gnocchi. Finish with dark chocolate fondant and marshmallow ice cream.

Chef Gregory Watts **Times** 12-2.30/6.30-9.45 **Prices** Food prices not confirmed for 2011. Please telephone for details **Wines** 67 bottles over £20, 22 bottles under £20, 14 by glass **Notes** Sunday L, Dress restrictions, Smart casual, Civ Wed 80 **Seats** 60, Pr/dining room 300 **Children** Portions, Menu **Parking** 112

Strok's at Sir Christopher Wren's House Hotel & Spa

Modern British

Elegant restaurant with riverside views

☎ 01753 861354
Thames St SL4 1PX
e-mail: reservations@windsor.wrensgroup.com
dir: M4 junct 6, 1st exit from relief road, follow signs to Windsor, 1st major exit on left, turn left at lights

As its name rather suggests, this was once the family home of Sir Christopher Wren, architect of St Paul's Cathedral. Living in the shadow of Windsor Castle may well have given the great man the inspiration for his own masterful building projects - the Georgian hotel certainly has a lovely setting on the Thames at Eton Bridge. The terrace of Strok's restaurant can't be beaten when it comes to aperitif time, sipping bubbly as the sun dips behind the tree-lined riverbank, while the interior goes for an elegant contemporary look that suits the unfussy modern cooking. Menus move with the seasons, starting, perhaps, with a ballottine of duck teamed with pan-fried foie gras, red onion jam and brioche, followed by confit cheeks and leg of pork with pommes Maxim and white cabbage.

Chef Stephen Boucher **Owner** The Wrens Hotel Group **Times** 12.30-2.30/6.30-10 Closed L 31 Dec & 1 Jan **Prices** Fixed L 2 course £22.50, Starter £7-£15, Main £15.50-£26, Dessert £7.50-£10, Service optional **Wines** 74 bottles over £20, 2 bottles under £20, 10 by glass **Notes** Pre-theatre D available, Sunday L, Vegetarian available, Dress restrictions, Smart casual preferred, Civ Wed 100 **Seats** 65, Pr/dining room 100 **Children** Portions **Parking** 14, Riverside train station

BRISTOL

BRISTOL Map 4 ST57

The Avon Gorge

Modern British NEW

Stylish modern cafe with views over iconic bridge

☎ 0117 973 8955
Sion Hill, Clifton BS8 4LD
dir: From S: M5 junct 19, A369 to Clifton Toll, over suspension bridge, 1st right into Sion Hill. From N: M5 junct 18A, A4 to Bristol, under suspension bridge, follow signs to bridge, exit Sion Hill

The grand semicircular terrace of the Victorian Avon Gorge hotel conjures images of Bristol's high society sipping tea after taking the cure in the Hot Wells springs. Nowadays, the hotel's stylish Bridge Café is the place to head for the best view in town of Brunel's masterpiece suspension bridge. It's a friendly and welcoming place that serves up an eclectic menu of contemporary, Mediterranean-inspired dishes with enticing flavour combinations, as in a crab cake starter served with spiced couscous and mango and chilli salsa. Mains run to chicken supreme with gorgonzola and smoked bacon gnocchi, or a pavé of lamb with tempura sweetbreads, Jersey Royals and mint vinaigrette.

Chef Damien Awford-Nash **Owner** Swire Hotels **Times** 12-2.30/6-10 **Prices** Fixed L 2 course £9.95, Starter £5-£7.50, Main £9.95-£18.50, Dessert £5-£6.50, Service added but optional **Wines** 34 bottles over £20, 15 bottles under £20, 11 by glass **Notes** Sunday L, Vegetarian available, Civ Wed 100 **Seats** 50, Pr/dining room 20 **Children** Portions, Menu **Parking** 25

Bells Diner

Modern European

Ambitious food in revamped grocery shop

☎ 0117 924 0357
1-3 York Rd, Montpellier BS6 5QB
e-mail: info@bellsdiner.com
web: www.bellsdiner.com

Behind its shop-style frontage in a bohemian part of Bristol, Bells Diner serves up food of genuine creativity and invention - this is contemporary European food as imagined by Christopher Wicks, the chef-patron. It's a comfortable, restrained space, the front dining room showcasing some of the original grocery shop fittings. The menu changes in tune with the seasons while the latest kitchen gadgetry allows the kitchen to continually develop. There's a tasting menu if you fancy going with the flow, or a carte full of clever combinations and well-judged ideas. To start, foie gras is partnered perfectly with pineapple, ginger bread and a tea fluid gel, before a main course of macaroni cheese with wild mushrooms, spinach and black truffle, or rabbit with lemon risotto, pancetta and parmesan. Desserts are no less inventive: melon salad with an olive oil biscuit, cucumber sorbet and balsamic.

Chef Christopher Wicks **Owner** Christopher Wicks **Times** 12-2/7-10 Closed 24-30 Dec, Sun, L Mon & Sat **Prices** Tasting menu fr £45, Starter £6.50-£10.50, Main £14.50-£19.50, Dessert £7.50-£8.50, Service added but optional 10% **Wines** 181 bottles over £20, 3 bottles under £20, 15 by glass **Notes** Tasting menu 8 course, wine flight 6 glasses £34.50, Vegetarian available, Dress restrictions **Seats** 60 **Children** Portions **Parking** On street

BRISTOL *continued*

Bordeaux Quay

European

Local and ethical cooking in magnificent dockside location

0117 906 5550
V-Shed, Canons Way BS1 5UH
e-mail: info@bordeaux-quay.co.uk
dir: Canons Rd off the A4

Former dockland warehouses tend to lend themselves to re-development and this one on the Bristol Docks is a real gem. Named for the fact that French wines were once off-loaded here, today's incarnation is no longer the middleman, but the destination. The restaurant is up on the first floor - and by the way, there's also a brasserie, deli, bakery and cookery school on site - with elegant table settings and fine wood alongside industrial pipe work. The ethos puts West Country produce at the top of the agenda, along with sustainability and ecological principles. The daily-changing menu of astute European cooking brings forth a bright salad of gorgonzola, pear, chicory and walnuts, or perhaps a venison, juniper and orange terrine, partnered with a cranberry and rosemary jelly. As a main course, meltingly tender braised beef shin and oxtail sits perfectly with its accompanying polenta mash, spinach and a flavoursome red wine jus. Caramelised Amalfi lemon tart with Campari and blood orange sorbet is a taste of the Italian sunshine.

Chef Liz Payne **Owner** Alex & Luke Murray
Times 12.30-3/6-10 Closed Mon, L Sat, D Sun
Prices Fixed L 2 course fr £21.50, Fixed D 3 course fr £28.50, Starter £5.50-£9.50, Main £13.50-£23, Dessert £6.50-£8.50, Service added but optional 10% **Wines** 140 bottles over £20, 20 bottles under £20, 30 by glass
Notes Express menu availble L & pre-theatre, Sunday L, Vegetarian available **Children** Portions

The Bristol Marriott Royal

Modern

Imaginative British cooking in spectacular dining room

0117 925 5100
College Green BS1 5TA
e-mail: bristol.royal@marriotthotels.co.uk
dir: Next to cathedral by College Green

The Palm Court restaurant is the jewel in the crown of this landmark Victorian city-centre hotel next to the cathedral and historic harbour front. Only a hard heart could fail to be impressed by the Empire-era pomp of its balconied sandstone walls, statuary and spectacular stained glass panels. The kitchen is a proud advocate of all things West Country in its creative contemporary repertoire - expect the likes of warm black pudding salad with Somerset apples and balsamic to start the ball rolling, followed by fennel and dill-crusted monkfish with barley 'risotto' and beurre blanc, or roasted Somerset gammon with cider and honey glaze. End with a retro knickerbocker glory, or bread-and-butter pudding with Devon cream and whisky syrup.

Times Closed Sun

Casamia Restaurant

– *see below*

City Café

Modern European

Seasonal cooking in chic city centre hotel

0117 910 2700
City Inn Bristol, Temple Way BS1 6BF
e-mail: bristol.citycafe@cityinn.com
dir: M4 junct 19, M32 to Bristol, follow signs to Temple Meads Station. Hotel on right after underpass

A stone's throw from Temple Meads railway station, this contemporary, chic hotel is an ideal base for exploring Bristol's throbbing city centre. When the sun is shining, a seat on the terrace overlooking the avenues of mature trees and church ruins in Temple Gardens is hard to beat. Inside awaits a spacious and airy dining room, with polished wooden floors and crisp white linen clothed tables. The kitchen has a serious approach to seasonality, and the well-presented modern European dishes make good use of local produce. Roast wild pigeon breast with onion tart, crispy shallots and raisin purée might be followed by a more classic coq au vin or

Casamia Restaurant

BRISTOL **Map 4 ST57**

Modern

Highly inventive modern cooking in Bristol suburbs

0117 959 2884
38 High St, Westbury Village, Westbury-on-Trym BS9 3DZ
e-mail: 0117 959 2884
dir: Close to Westbury College Gatehouse

Paco and Susan Sanchez-Iglesias ran a well-loved neighbourhood Italian trattoria on Westbury Village High Street in Bristol's northern fringes for many years. There was nothing wrong with it at all, but they ignored the 'if it ain't broke don't fix it' mantra, and stepped aside to let their sons' youthful ambition and creativity fulfil its potential. With Jonray and Peter at the stoves and mum and dad taking over front-of-house, the operation has morphed into a hotbed of contemporary cooking at the more cutting-edge end of the culinary spectrum. The restaurant goes for a simple Mediterranean look of whitewashed walls hung with Italian scenes, but that's where simplicity stops. The Italian roots are still there, reworked in an adventurous way with hints of France and Spain thrown into the mix, but these chefs are clearly excited by the whizz-bang world of froths, foams and powders, off-the-wall flavour combinations and scene-stealing presentations. Menus are 8- or 10-course tasting events - maybe chicken liver parfait with mushroom jelly, parsley and crostini as an opening gambit. Beetroot risotto with iced yoghurt, pickled fennel and pistachios, might follow, then raw wild roe deer teamed with chestnut honey, young onions and ubriaco rosso - an Italian cheese soaked in wine and matured in a grape skin coating. Equally thrilling desserts might include velouté of kettle corn with Amalfi lemon sorbet, or Italy's finest Amedei chocolate with assorted textures and essences of plum, lime and hazelnut.

Chef Peter & Jonray Sanchez-Iglesias **Owner** Paco & Susan Sanchez-Iglesias **Times** 12.30-2.30/7-10 Closed Sun-Mon, L Tue-Fri **Prices** Food prices not confirmed for 2011. Please telephone for details **Wines** 30 bottles over £20, 8 bottles under £20, 20 by glass
Notes Tasting menu 6/10 course, Vegetarian available, Dress restrictions, Smart casual **Seats** 40 **Parking** On street

smoked haddock and salmon fishcakes with creamed leeks and grain mustard. Finish with Manuka honey and Amaretto parfait.

Chef Matthew Lord **Owner** City Inn Ltd
Times 12-2.30/6-10.30 **Prices** Fixed L 2 course £9.95-£27.90, Fixed D 3 course fr £21.95, Starter £4.95-£7.95, Main £10.50-£19.95, Dessert £3.50-£5.95, Service optional **Wines** 36 bottles over £20, 12 bottles under £20, 29 by glass **Notes** Sunday L, Vegetarian available, Dress restrictions, Smart casual, Civ Wed 50 **Seats** 72, Pr/dining room 28 **Children** Portions, Menu **Parking** 45

Culinaria

Traditional British, Mediterranean

Excellent bistro cooking amid cheerful informality

☎ 0117 973 7999
1 Chandos Rd, Redland BS6 6PG

Culinaria is the sort of neighbourhood foodie heaven that we'd all like on our block: Stephen and Judy Markwick's great idea is to offer a three-pronged approach to their love of food. A deli sells the finest local produce, which forms the basis of Stephen's honest, confidently-cooked food, available in an easygoing bistro, or to take away fresh or frozen. The Markwicks have been stalwarts of the Bristol dining scene for over 30 years, so Stephen's experience in the kitchen gives him the confidence to keep things simple, underpinned by sound technique and a natural feel for flavour combinations. The dining room is refreshingly simple - stripped pine floors, bare blond-wood tables - and the vibe is easygoing. A classic Provençal fish soup with aïoli and sauce rouille is a signature starter, ahead of mains such as braised ox cheek with horseradish mash and root vegetables. End with an old favourite - perhaps walnut and treacle tart with clotted cream.

Chef Stephen Markwick **Owner** Stephen & Judy Markwick **Times** 12-2.30/6.30-10 Closed Xmas, New Year, BHs, 4 wks during year, Sun-Wed **Prices** Fixed L 2 course fr £15, Starter £6.95-£8.50, Main £13-£17.50, Dessert £6-£6.50, Service optional **Wines** 13 bottles over £20, 20 bottles under £20, 6 by glass **Notes** Vegetarian available **Seats** 30 **Children** Portions **Parking** On street

Ellipse Bar & Restaurant

Modern British

Stylish riverside setting for modish food

☎ 0117 933 8200 & 929 1030
Mercure Brigstow Bristol, 5-7 Welsh Back BS1 4SP
e-mail: h6548@accor.com
dir: M32, follow signs for Bristol Temple Meads train station. At rdbt turn into Victoria St. Continue over Bristol bridge turn left and immediately left and then left again onto Welsh Back, hotel on left

In an impressive and fashionable waterside location close to the city centre, the modern, purpose-built Mercure Brigstow Hotel stands proud. The Ellipse Bar and lounge runs from brunch to evening cocktails, while the contemporary restaurant, with its mezzanine level, delivers a short menu of modern British dishes that suit the fashionable mood. Tuck into king prawn and spring onion samosa before main-course smoked garlic and thyme warm choux bun filled with vegetable ratatouille topped with gruyère, with spiced mango and lime mousse for dessert.

Times 11-5/6-9.45 Closed 25 Dec

Glass Boat Restaurant

Modern Mediterranean

Unfussy, well-sourced food on the water

☎ 0117 929 0704
Welsh Back BS1 4SB
e-mail: bookings@glassboat.co.uk
dir: Moored below Bristol Bridge in the old centre of Bristol

Moored close to Bristol Bridge, this stylish, modern brasserie housed on a splendid 1920s barge has a special charm. Located in the heart of Bristol city centre, its glass walls offer an impressive backdrop for lunch and make for a uniquely romantic setting for candlelit dinner à deux. The kitchen deals in uncomplicated European cooking, with strong Italian leanings, and uses a lot of local produce, some of which is grown in the restaurant's own kitchen garden on the outskirts of the city. The daily-changing menus offer good value and recommendations include Cornish mussels with fennel, saffron and cream, followed by pan-fried bream with Umbrian lentils, home-cured pancetta and anchovy. Finish, perhaps, with orange and polenta cake and blood orange curd.

Chef Dan Wilson **Owner** Arne Ringer
Times 12-2.30/5.30-10.30 Closed 24-26 Dec, 1-10 Jan, L Mon, D Sun **Prices** Fixed L 2 course fr £10, Fixed D 3 course £17.50-£27.50, Starter £5-£10, Main £9-£20, Dessert £5-£8, Service optional, Groups min 8 service 10% **Wines** 40 bottles over £20, 10 bottles under £20, 12 by glass **Notes** Pre-theatre menu 2 or 3 course £12.50-£17.50, Sunday L, Vegetarian available, Civ Wed 120 **Seats** 120, Pr/dining room 40 **Children** Portions, Menu **Parking** NCP Queen Charlotte St

Goldbrick House

Classic British

Multi-purpose city eatery with traditional British food

☎ 0117 945 1950
69 Park St BS1 5PB
e-mail: info@goldbrickhouse.co.uk
dir: M32, follow signs for city centre. Left side of Park St, going up the hill towards museum

Located in a bustling quarter of the city, Goldbrick House is an amalgam of two Georgian townhouses and a Victorian bread factory, and comprises an expansive restaurant with private dining rooms, a champagne and cocktail bar, and a speedy bistro-café. You can buzz in and out for a plate of smoked mackerel and pancetta and a wild mushroom risotto, or linger longer for a starter serving of rare roast beef with mini-Yorkshire pudding, horseradish cream and parsnip crisps, followed by a mash-topped fish pie combining smoked haddock and salmon with leeks and spinach. The accent in most dishes is unashamedly trad Brit, with sticky toffee pudding and butterscotch sauce to finish. Service is professional, efficient and unobtrusive.

Chef Matthew Peryer **Owner** Dougal Templeton, Alex Reilley, Mike Bennett **Times** noon-10.30 Closed 25-26 Dec, 1 Jan, Sun **Prices** Fixed L 2 course £10-£20, Fixed D 3 course £20-£32, Starter £4.50-£7.50, Main £10.50-£18.50, Dessert £5-£7, Service added but optional 10% **Wines** 36 bottles over £20, 20 bottles under £20, 12 by glass **Notes** Early evening D menu 6-7pm, Vegetarian available, Civ Wed 100 **Seats** 180, Pr/dining room 20 **Children** Portions, Menu **Parking** On street, NCP

Hotel du Vin Bristol

Modern European NOTABLE WINE LIST

Brasserie food and great wine in a sugar warehouse

☎ 0117 925 5577
The Sugar House, Narrow Lewins Mead BS1 2NU
e-mail: info.bristol@hotelduvin.com
dir: From M4 junct 19, M32 into Bristol. At rdbt take 1st exit & follow main road to next rdbt. Turn onto other side of carriageway, hotel 200yds on right

The Bristol outpost of Hotel du Vin occupies an 18th-century sugar warehouse not far from the waterfront. As at other branches, the dining room is an expansive, civilised place with brisk service and an agreeably informal atmosphere, in which you will eat modern brasserie food that does what it says on the tin. A chunk of ham hock and oyster mushroom terrine comes with cornichons and brioche, and might be followed by rump of Welsh lamb on buttery crushed new potatoes and highly seasoned pea purée, or crab-crusted lemon sole in cockle velouté. Finish with an evenly caramelised, properly creamy crème brûlée, perhaps spiked with passionfruit. The monster wine list is, of course, half the fun.

Chef Marcus Lang **Owner** Hotel du Vin Ltd
Times 12-2/6-10 **Prices** Fixed L 2 course £10-£28, Fixed D 3 course £35, Starter £4.50-£8.95, Main £9.95-£19.95, Dessert £4.50-£5.50, Service added but optional 10% **Wines** 400 bottles over £20, 15 bottles under £20, 10 by glass **Notes** Sunday L, Vegetarian available, Civ Wed 70 **Seats** 85, Pr/dining room 72 **Children** Portions, Menu **Parking** NCP Rupert St

BRISTOL *continued*

The Kensington Arms

Traditional British NEW

Easygoing urban gastro-pub with hearty cooking

0117 944 6444
35-37 Stanley Rd, Redland BS6 6NP
e-mail: info@thekensingtonarms.co.uk

After a recent makeover, this down-at-heel watering hole for students and sundry boozers in the residential Redland area has morphed into a smart dining pub. The place is still first and foremost a pub, in the 21st-century style: that's to say, relaxed, inclusive and in tune with the local community - you could just drop in and read the paper with a coffee or prop up the bar with a pint. Downstairs is a casual vibe, uncluttered, bare wooden floors and tables; move upstairs for a more formal restaurant ambience. Wherever you eat, the food is gutsy stuff, prepared with care and skill from local, often organic produce. You could keep things simple along the lines of burgers, mussels, or faggots with cauliflower cheese and Guinness gravy, or put the kitchen through its paces with something more ambitious - maybe salt-baked sea bass with lemon thyme-braised chicory, or pot-roast beef brisket with rosemary dumplings. To finish, perhaps, baked egg custard tart with home-made nutmeg ice cream.

Chef Dan Snelling **Times** 12-3/6-10 Closed 25-26 Dec, D Sun **Prices** Starter £5.50-£8.50, Main £10.50-£13.50, Dessert £3.50-£7.50, Service optional **Wines** 14 bottles over £20, 10 bottles under £20, 12 by glass **Notes** Sunday L, Vegetarian available **Seats** 60, Pr/dining room 60 **Children** Portions **Parking** On street

No. 4 Restaurant & Bar

Modern European

Bright modern hotel dining in smart Clifton

0117 973 5422
Rodney Hotel, 4 Rodney Place, Clifton BS8 4HY
e-mail: info@numberfourrestaurant.co.uk
dir: M5 junct 19, follow signs across Clifton Bridge. At mini rdbt turn onto Clifton Down Rd. Hotel 150yds on right

The Rodney Hotel is a stylish Georgian townhouse in a handsome terrace in fashionable Clifton village. Its No. 4 Restaurant has a clean-cut contemporary look and easygoing ambience, plus the promise of alfresco dining in a secluded garden on fine days. The kitchen sources its ingredients from Bristol and Somerset, and goes in for a refreshingly simple take on modern classics, often basking in a Mediterranean glow. Chicken liver parfait with red onion marmalade and home-made focaccia bread is a cracking way to start, followed by the likes of cod with green beans, crushed potatoes and a white wine, parsley and bacon sauce. Finish with a Sailor Jerry rum and vanilla pannacotta with fruit coulis.

Chef David Jones **Owner** Hilary Lawson **Times** 6-10 Closed Xmas, Sun, L all week **Prices** Starter £4.50-£5.95, Main £10.50-£14.95, Dessert £4.95-£5.95, Service added 10% **Wines** 7 bottles over £20, 15 bottles under £20, 5 by glass **Notes** Vegetarian available **Seats** 35, Pr/dining room 35 **Children** Portions **Parking** 10

The Restaurant @ Cadbury House

Modern British

Modern cooking in relaxed, stylish contemporary hotel

01934 834343
Cadbury House Hotel, Frost Hill, Congresbury BS49 5AD
e-mail: info@cadburyhouse.com
dir: M5 junct 20, left at rdbt, turn onto B133 at next rdbt towards Congresbury. Continue through village of Yatton for 4m, hotel is on left after village

This sleek newly-built hotel has quickly built a reputation on the Bristol foodie scene for stylish dining. Chef Mark Veale paid his dues with Ramsay Inc and his ethos is that of tracking down the best local seasonal materials and treating them without undue fuss. Herbs, fruit and wild garlic come from just outside the kitchen door, other ingredients come from within a 30-mile radius, and the day's catch comes fresh from the West Country - as in a starter of grilled Cornish mackerel with celeriac remoulade, confit cherry tomatoes and caper dressing. Next up, suckling pig is teamed with fondant potato, wild mushrooms and smoked bacon sauce; desserts mix comfort with a touch of class - how about dark chocolate fondant with lavender ice cream?

Chef Mark Veale **Owner** Nick Taplin **Times** 6.30-9.30 Closed L Mon-Sat **Prices** Food prices not confirmed for 2011. Please telephone for details **Wines** 24 bottles over £20, 12 bottles under £20, 10 by glass **Notes** Tasting menu 7 course, Vegetarian tasting menu available, Sunday L, Vegetarian available, Dress restrictions, Smart casual, Civ Wed 140 **Seats** 80, Pr/dining room 80 **Children** Portions, Menu **Parking** 350

riverstation

Modern European

Brasserie food in designer waterfront venue

0117 914 4434 & 9463
The Grove BS1 4RB
e-mail: relax@riverstation.co.uk
dir: On the dock side in central Bristol

The two-storey restaurant (upstairs is where the main menu is offered) is a handsomely designed contemporary venue right on the river, with one glassed end wall and outdoor terrace ensuring it makes the most of its location. Modern brasserie cooking is the name of the game, and dishes are presented with evident panache. Herb-crusted crottin with candied beets and pecan salsa makes an interesting appetiser. Mains run from smoked haddock choucroute with Morteau sausage and wheat beer sauce to well-wrought shoulder of lamb with parsnip gratin, red cabbage and mint jus. Crunchy-topped apple and quince crumble comes with Calvados ice cream.

Chef Peter Taylor **Owner** J Payne & P Taylor **Times** 12-2.30/6-10.30 Closed 24-26 Dec, L Sat (open by arrangement), D Sun (except BH) **Prices** Fixed L 2 course fr £12, Fixed D 3 course fr £18.50, Starter £5-£11, Main £13.50-£19.50, Dessert £4.50-£5.50, Service optional, Groups min 8 service 10% **Wines** 56 bottles over £20, 12 bottles under £20, 10 by glass **Notes** Sunday L, Vegetarian available **Seats** 120, Pr/dining room 26 **Children** Portions, Menu **Parking** Pay & display, meter parking opposite

The Rockfish Grill & Seafood Market

British, Mediterranean NEW

Vibrant fish bistro and seafood market

0117 973 7384
128 Whiteladies Rd, Clifton BS8 2RS
e-mail: enquiries@rockfishgrill.co.uk
dir: From city centre follow signs for Clifton, restaurant half way along Whiteladies Rd

This lively bistro in fashionable Clifton is a shrine to seriously fresh fish and seafood, the brainchild of Mitch Tonks, fishmonger, chef, and champion of all things fishy. Inside, it's an immediately likeable place with an easygoing vibe, pictures of fish on the walls, shelves stacked with wine, and the buzz of an open kitchen working to an eminently sound formula: get hold of the best piscine produce and don't fiddle about with it too much. Sound supply lines to the fishing ports of South Devon mean that each day's catch brings new ideas to the table. Crisp-fried Brixham squid comes with aïoli - what else do you need? Main course is red gurnard tasting deliciously of a charcoal grill, and dusted with freshly-chopped herbs, a simple half of lemon and a dash of olive oil. Other options are fritto misto, roast ray with anchovy and capers, or pollock fried in beer batter. Check out the seafood market next door.

Chef Jake Platt **Owner** Mitch Tonks **Times** 12-2.30/6-10.30 Closed 25 Dec, Sun-Mon **Prices** Fixed L 2 course £15, Starter £5-£10, Main £11-£28, Dessert £5-£7, Service optional **Wines** 40 bottles over £20, 8 bottles under £20 **Notes** Fixed L menu available before 7pm, Vegetarian available, Air con **Seats** 52 **Children** Portions **Parking** On street

Second Floor Restaurant

◎◎ Modern European NEW

Cuisine of the moment in a glamorous venue

☎ 0117 961 8898
Harvey Nichols, Philadelphia St, Quakers Friars BS1 3BZ
e-mail: Reception.Bristol@harveynichols.com

Harvey Nicks has sashayed onto the Bristol dining scene, bringing a hit of the brand's trademark sleek metropolitan glamour to the top floor of its boutique store in the town centre Cabot's Circus development. French architect and designer Christian Biecher is responsible for the bling factor in a décor of shimmering gold walls and ceilings, lustrous leather banquettes and caramel chairs - a look that certainly appeals to Bristol's ladies who lunch and shop - while head chef Louise McCrimmon is cooking up a storm with her assured modern repertoire. Menus bristle with engaging ideas taken from Europe and further afield - a deep understanding of how flavours work together is evident in a starter uniting Ragstone goats' cheese with black olive crumb, red wine poached pears and a spiced wine dressing. Next, a saffron aïoli is an indulgent foil to roast chicken breast with Puy lentils, carrots and swede. A dessert of Valrhona chocolate mousse with peanut butter cookies makes a great finish.

Chef Louise McCrimmon **Owner** Harvey Nichols Restaurants Ltd **Times** 12-3/6-10 Closed 25 Dec, Etr Sun, D Sun-Mon **Prices** Fixed L 2 course fr £12, Fixed D 3 course fr £18, Starter £5.50-£8, Main £11.50-£22, Dessert £5-£6.50, Service added but optional 10% **Wines** 230 bottles over £20, 4 bottles under £20, 14 by glass **Notes** Afternoon tea 3-5.30pm, Vegetarian available **Seats** 60, Pr/dining room 10 **Children** Portions, Menu **Parking** NCP/Cabot Circus multi

The Square Kitchen

◎◎ European NEW

Classy hotel with sure hand in the kitchen

☎ 0117 925 4000
Berkeley Square Hotel, 15 Berkeley Square, Clifton BS8 1HB
e-mail: berkeley@cliftonhotels.com
web: www.cliftonhotels.com/chg.html
dir: M32 follow Clifton signs. 1st left at lights by Nills Memorial Tower (University) into Berkeley Sq

A modern, stylish venue in the elegant Berkeley Square Hotel, the flagship of Bristol-based Clifton Hotels, The Square Kitchen overlooks a tranquil, tree-lined square close to the university and Clifton village. Small, intimate and furnished in contemporary style, with well-spaced tables and those views, it offers a relaxed ambience, efficient service and changing seasonal menus. The small kitchen team show passion for quality local produce and endeavour to cook with accuracy and simplicity, allowing the flavour combinations to shine through. A memorable twice-baked blue cheese soufflé comes well matched with a spicy tomato jam, as does a tender, melt-in-the-mouth blade of beef, served with watercress risotto and green beans wrapped in pancetta. Cappuccino crème brûlée, with a crisp topping and strong coffee flavours, finishes proceedings off nicely.

Times 12-3/6-10.30 Closed L Sun-Mon

BUCKINGHAMSHIRE

AMERSHAM Map 6 SU99

The Artichoke

◎◎ Modern European

Smart high-street restaurant with refined cooking

☎ 01494 726611
9 Market Square, Old Amersham HP7 0DF
e-mail: info@artichokerestaurant.co.uk
dir: M40 junct 2. 1m from Amersham New Town

This intimate restaurant weaves a clever blend of 16th-century old-world charm and knife-sharp 21st-century cooking. Classily refurbished after a fire in 2008 closed it down for over a year, the décor looks the part, bringing together ancient gnarly beams with whitewashed brick walls, tasty walnut tables and modern art. When closed, its loyal fan base didn't desert it: the place is back on its feet and winning new devotees with modern French cooking built on a conscientious, quality-first approach to sourcing top-grade Chilterns produce. A Jerusalem artichoke soup with Isle of Skye scallops starts with subtle contrasts in flavours and textures, then saddle of local wild venison comes with glazed pears, pontack sauce (made with elderberries, vinegar and spices), elderflower capers, Savoy cabbage, roasted onion and pumpkin gnocchi. The overtly French style concludes with a hot prune and Armagnac soufflé with vanilla ice cream.

Chef Laurie Gear **Owner** Laurie & Jacqueline Gear **Times** 12-3/6.30-11 Closed 1 wk Xmas, 1 wk Apr, Sun, Mon **Prices** Fixed L 2 course £18.50, Fixed D 3 course £39.50, Starter £8.50-£13.50, Main £16.50-£23, Dessert £6-£8.50, Service added but optional 12.5% **Wines** 76 bottles over £20, 5 bottles under £20, 8 by glass **Notes** Tasting menu 7 course, Vegetarian available **Seats** 25 **Children** Portions **Parking** On street, nearby car park

AYLESBURY Map 11 SP81

Hartwell House Hotel, Restaurant & Spa

◎◎◎ – *see page 64*

BLETCHLEY Map 11 SP83

The Crooked Billet

◎ Modern British

Carefully-cooked food and well-chosen wines in 17th-century pub

☎ 01908 373936
2 Westbrook End, Newton Longville MK17 0DF
e-mail: john@thebillet.co.uk
dir: M1 junct 14 follow A421 towards Buckingham. Turn left at Bottledump rdbt to Newton Longville. Restaurant on right as you enter the village

A red-brick old inn with a thatched roof, The Crooked Billet is run by chef Emma Gilchrist and husband John, a former Sommelier of the Year. Needless to say food and drink are taken seriously. A pub for some 300 years, the 17th-century interior of oak beams and inglenook fireplace has plenty of charm, and there's a country garden, too. Ingredients are locally-sourced with due diligence (vegetables are likely to come from the pub's own veg patch) and all of the 300 wines are available by the glass. Off the evening carte might come warm onion tart with Mrs Kirkham's Lancashire cheese and walnuts, followed by duck 'cassoulet' (pan-fried breast, duck sausage, crispy leg and pan-fried foie gras), and, to finish, vanilla and forced rhubarb cheesecake with honey and crème fraîche ice cream.

Chef Emma Gilchrist **Owner** John & Emma Gilchrist **Times** 12-2.30/7-10 Closed 27-28 Dec, L Mon, D Sun **Prices** Fixed L 2 course fr £16.75, Fixed D 3 course fr £23, Starter £4.75-£10.50, Main £12-£28, Dessert £5-£9, Service optional, Groups min 6 service 12% **Wines** 200 bottles over £20, 20 bottles under £20, 170 by glass **Notes** Tasting menu 8 course, Sunday L, Vegetarian available **Seats** 70, Pr/dining room 16 **Children** Portions **Parking** 30

BUCKINGHAM Map 11 SP63

Villiers Hotel Restaurant & Bar

Modern British

Modern British cooking in characterful coaching inn

01280 822444
3 Castle St MK18 1BS
e-mail: reservations@villiershotels.com
web: www.villiers-hotel.co.uk
dir: Town centre - Castle Street is to the right of Town Hall near main square

There's been an inn and hostelry on this spot since the mid-16th century, and something of the feel of days gone by is preserved in the Villiers bar with its fireplace, oak panelling and flagstone floor. The low-ceilinged, white-walled restaurant offers a more contemporary look in furnishings and wall decorations, and the cooking is bang up to date too. Based on the gentle combinations of the modern British mode, it deals in the likes of lemon sole and crab rillettes with gingered leeks and crème fraîche, pasta variations in starter or main-course servings, and well-conceived mains such as slow-roast pork belly with caramelised apple, braised leeks and chestnuts in cider cream sauce. Finish with rhubarb and ginger mousse and champagne jelly.

Villiers Hotel Restaurant & Bar

Chef Paul Stopps **Owner** Oxfordshire Hotels Ltd **Times** 12-2.30/6-9.30 **Prices** Fixed L 2 course £10.95-£15.90, Fixed D 3 course £19.95-£25.95, Starter £4.35-£7.20, Main £9.20-£19.95, Service optional, Groups min 6 service 10% **Notes** Sunday L, Vegetarian available, Civ Wed 150 **Seats** 70, Pr/dining room 150 **Children** Portions **Parking** 52

BURNHAM Map 6 SU98

Grays Restaurant

British, European

Classic cooking in historic setting

0844 736 8603 & 01628 600150
Burnham Beeches Hotel, Burnham Beeches, Grove Rd SL1 8DP
e-mail: burnhambeeches@corushotels.com
web: www.corushotels.com
dir: off A355, via Farnham Royal rdbt

Burnham Beeches is a Georgian mansion and former hunting lodge set in 10 acres of gardens and is believed to have been the inspiration for Thomas Gray's *Elegy to a Country Churchyard*. The appropriately titled restaurant has a relaxed air with oak-panelled walls, floral curtains and lovely views of the grounds. The food leans towards

Hartwell House Hotel, Restaurant & Spa

AYLESBURY Map 11 SP81

British, European NOTABLE WINE LIST

Classy, modern cooking in sumptuous stately home

01296 747444
Oxford Rd HP17 8NR
e-mail: info@hartwell-house.com
dir: 2m SW of Aylesbury on A418 (Oxford road)

The one time home in exile of Louis XVIII of France (he wasn't exactly welcome back in his own country at the time), is now in the safe hands of the National Trust and operates as a luxury hotel in 90 acres of unspoilt parkland. Grade I listed, the stately home has both Jacobean and Georgian features and is bedecked with outstanding decorative ceilings and panelling, fine paintings and antiques in its elegant rooms. But that's not to say that dining here is stuffy or stuck in the past: service is friendly and well briefed, while the high-ceilinged, neo-classical restaurant is bright and elegant. The modern English cooking is underpinned by classic French techniques and there is a clear understanding of ingredients - some as local as Hartwell's own gardens and orchards. Breast of wood pigeon and sausage cassoulet with parsley purée and red wine sauce is a typical starter, followed by pan-fried John Dory fillets with rösti potato, confit shallots, creamed leeks and champagne cream sauce. Blood orange soufflé with blood orange compôte is an uplifting finale.

Chef Daniel Richardson **Owner** Historic House Hotels/National Trust **Times** 12.30-1.45/7.30-9.45 **Prices** Fixed L 2 course £22.95, Fixed D 3 course £29.95, Starter £8.50-£12, Main £22-£28, Dessert £7.75-£10.75, Service included **Wines** 300 bottles over £20, 11 bottles under £20, 15 by glass **Notes** Tasting menu available, Sunday L, Vegetarian available, Dress restrictions, Smart casual, No jeans, tracksuits/trainers, Civ Wed 60 **Seats** 56, Pr/dining room 30 **Children** Portions **Parking** 50

the classics; start, perhaps, with chicken and duck liver parfait with roasted fig and onion chutney and toasted brioche, progress to herb topped fillet of salmon with truffled pommes purée and seasonal vegetables and end with a pear and almond frangipane tart with toffee and almond ice cream.

Chef John Dickson **Owner** Corus Hotels
Times 12-2/7-9.30 **Prices** Food prices not confirmed for 2011. Please telephone for details **Wines** 19 bottles over £20, 5 bottles under £20, 6 by glass **Notes** Sunday L, Vegetarian available, Dress restrictions, Smart casual, Civ Wed 120 **Seats** 70, Pr/dining room 120
Children Portions, Menu **Parking** 150

The Grovefield House Hotel

◎◎ Traditional Mediterranean

Refurbished country-house hotel with ambitious cooking

☎ 01628 603131
Taplow Common Rd SL1 8LP
e-mail: gm.grovefield@classiclodges.co.uk
dir: From M4 left on A4 towards Maidenhead. Next rdbt turn right under railway bridge. Straight over mini rdbt, garage on right. Continue for 1.5m, hotel on right

After a £2 million facelift, this Edwardian country house has been brought fully up to speed with the 21st century, with Hamilton's Restaurant at the heart of its culinary endeavours. The place was once the rural bolthole of John Fuller of the brewing family, who gave the world the treasure that is Fuller's London Pride. What he would have made of a menu that serves crab and langoustine tortellini with spaghetti of carrot and cucumber and langoustine bisque is anybody's guess. There is also plenty of traditionalism, though, on an up-to-date menu that reads well - roast saddle of lamb with Sarladaise potato, glazed vegetables and rosemary jus, for example, or Angus beef sirloin served with fondant potatoes, honey-roast vegetables and port wine sauce. Pistachio soufflé with rosewater ice cream makes an exotic finale.

Times 12-2.30/7-9.30 Closed L Sat

CHENIES — Map 6 TQ09

The Bedford Arms Hotel

◎ Modern International

Pastoral charm in the Chilterns

☎ 01923 283301
WD3 6EQ
e-mail: contact@bedfordarms.co.uk
dir: M25 junct 18/A404 towards Amersham, after 2m follow signs on right for hotel

Chenies is a pretty village in the Chilterns, with a picturesque green, ancient parish church and a manor house that once belonged to the Dukes of Bedford - yet the M25 is just two miles away. The red-brick Victorian Bedford Arms slots perfectly into the bucolic surroundings, a proper, homely pub with an unpretentious bar serving straight-up pub food - Bedford pie, pork and leek sausage with onion gravy and mash, say - and a smart oak-panelled restaurant. The easygoing menu offers an eclectic choice of modern dishes, topped up with daily fish specials. Confit pork terrine with pickled apples and sage cream is a good way to start, ahead of rack of lamb with potato fondue, cavalo nero, girolles and lamb jus.

Chef Christopher Cloonan **Owner** Arthur & Celia Rickett
Times 12-2.30/7-9.30 Closed 26 Dec-5 Jan, D Sun
Prices Fixed D 3 course £26.50-£32.75, Service optional
Wines 21 bottles over £20, 20 bottles under £20, 10 by glass **Notes** Sunday L, Vegetarian available, Dress restrictions, Smart casual, Civ Wed 55 **Seats** 55, Pr/dining room 24 **Children** Portions **Parking** 55

GREAT MISSENDEN — Map 6 SP80

Nags Head Inn

◎ British, French

Charming pub offering well-cooked Anglo-French food

☎ 01494 862200 & 862945
London Rd HP16 0DG
e-mail: goodfood@nagsheadbucks.com
web: www.nagsheadbucks.com
dir: N from Amersham on A413 signed Great Missenden, left at Chiltern Hospital onto London Rd (1m S of Great Missenden)

After a lavish refurbishment this 15th-century inn in the rolling Chiltern Hills has been transformed into a stylish foodie pub serving inventive Anglo-French fusion cooking. The place has had its fair share of famous visitors in the past: various Prime Ministers called in for a pint on their way to Chequers, and it was author Roald Dahl's local - his prints hang on the walls, and the Nags Head appears in the film of his children's book *Fantastic Mr Fox*. Top-class organic produce is at the heart of the cooking, and the kitchen keeps it simple - nothing overworked, no outlandish combinations - to let the flavours shine. Foie gras mi-cuit served with fig chutney and focaccia sets the tone, before wild rabbit slow-cooked in red wine and game stock with barley and vegetable strudel.

Chef Alan Bell, Howard Gale & Claude Paillet
Owner Alvin, Adam & Sally Michaels
Times 12-2.30/6-9.30 Closed 25 Dec **Prices** Food prices not confirmed for 2011. Please telephone for details
Wines 80 bottles over £20, 28 bottles under £20, 12 by glass **Notes** Sunday L, Vegetarian available, Dress restrictions, Smart casual **Seats** 60 **Children** Portions
Parking 35

IVINGHOE — Map 11 SP91

The King's Head

◎ Modern British, French V

Classic village inn with Anglo-French cooking and excellent service

☎ 01296 668388
Station Rd LU7 9EB
e-mail: info@kingsheadivinghoe.co.uk
web: www.kingsheadivinghoe.co.uk
dir: From M25 junct 20 take A41 past Tring. Turn right onto B488 (Ivinghoe), hotel at junct with B489

A 17th-century village inn on the Bucks-Beds county border, the King's Head looks every inch the part. Roaring fires, exposed beams, crisp linen and candlelight are only the half of it. Impeccable traditional service also makes a strong impression. Lengthy menus aim to offer plenty of choice, and the style is nicely poised between old school and modern thinking. Cappuccino leek soup with flaked smoked haddock and truffle oil could be the curtain-raiser for roast breast of guinea fowl wrapped in pancetta, with rissole potatoes and Madeira jus. The carving of Aylesbury duckling, or flambéing of crêpes suzette, offer tableside theatre, or you might finish less ostentatiously with a crème brûlée and white chocolate ice cream.

Chef Jonathan O'Keeffe **Owner** G.A.P.J. Ltd
Times 12-2.45/7-9.45 Closed 27-30 Dec, D Sun
Prices Fixed L 3 course £19.95-£20.25, Fixed D 4 course £36.50-£50, Service added but optional 12.5% **Wines** 80 bottles over £20, 8 bottles under £20, 4 by glass
Notes Sunday L, Vegetarian menu, Dress restrictions, Smart casual **Seats** 55, Pr/dining room 40
Children Portions **Parking** 20, On street

Adam Simmonds at Danesfield House

MARLOW Map 5 SU88

Modern European NOTABLE WINE LIST

Grand Chiltern pile with outstanding cooking

☎ 01628 891010
Henley Rd SL7 2EY
e-mail: reservations@danesfieldhouse.co.uk
web: www.danesfieldhouse.co.uk
dir: M4 junct 4/A404 to Marlow. Follow signs to Medmenham and Henley. Hotel is 3m outside Marlow

Victorian Gothic usually comes in stern red brick, but Danesfield House sports a more playful Dracula-does-Disneyland look, with its sweeping whitewashed façade, crenellated roofline and fantasy turrets. This is a country pile on a grand scale, sitting in 65 acres of impeccably trimmed and topiaried Thames-side gardens between Marlow and Henley-on-Thames. The grandiose interior has all the oak panelling, fancy plasterwork and baronial marble fireplaces you'd expect, but the fine-dining restaurant goes for a light café crème look with bleached white panelling, courtesy of Anouska Hempel. It also began 2010 with a new name: as a tribute to Adam Simmonds, the chef whose edgy, innovative wizardry has earned it a place in the gastronomic Premier League, the former Oak Room now bears his name. The highly experienced kitchen brigade all come from high-profile backgrounds and set about their task with serious culinary intentions. Simmonds' creativity is unmistakable from the arrival of a gin and tonic jelly and lime foam that nails the essential flavours and fizz of a G&T - the first of several stunning amuse-bouche and intensely-flavoured pre-desserts. Expect moments of sheer revelation, when daring juxtapositions of taste and texture force you to revise your culinary preconceptions. As well as pulling off head-spinning depth and clarity of flavours, the kitchen plays with the full contemporary arsenal of sorbets and purées, foams and jellies to keep the entertainment factor on the boil. Roasted breast of quail is super-tender, pink and perfectly judged, and comes matched with the moistness of Cornish crab salad, and the textural contrasts of sweetcorn purée and popcorn. A main course of hyper-fresh fillets of red mullet, enhanced by scallop ceviche, fennel salad, tomato and olive oil sorbet is, overall, a light, joyously-refined dish taken to a higher level by the textural contrast of crisp tuiles. Flavours and textures are again subtly balanced in complex desserts: take 'strawberry' - centre stage is a silky fromage frais mousse with a dizzying depth of flavour, encircled by pillows of strawberry ravioli; add in the crunch of green almonds, the pungency of basil sorbet, a light chilled strawberry soup and alpine and wild strawberries for a truly inspirational finish. The entire team here pulls together to ensure that the whole package is presented with polished customer service skills from start to finish.

Chef Adam Simmonds
Times 12-2/7-9.30 Closed 15-31 Aug, 19 Dec-3 Jan, BHs, Sun-Mon, L Tue-Thu
Prices Fixed D 3 course £55, Tasting menu fr £68.50, Service added but optional 12.5% **Wines** 400 bottles over £20, 14 by glass **Notes** ALC 3 course £55, Vegetarian available, Dress restrictions, Smart casual, Civ Wed 100
Seats 30, Pr/dining room 14
Children Portions **Parking** 100

LONG CRENDON Map 5 SP60

The Angel Restaurant

Mediterranean, Pacific Rim NOTABLE WINE LIST

Confident cooking in 16th-century coaching inn

☎ 01844 208268
47 Bicester Rd HP18 9EE
e-mail: angelrestaurant@aol.com
dir: M40 junct 7, beside B4011, 2m NW of Thame

A 16th-century coaching inn situated in a picturesque village on the Buckinghamshire and Oxfordshire borders, this popular place is more restaurant than pub these days. There is a small bar and plenty of original features including wattle-and-daub wall, exposed timbers, slate floors and inglenook fire; the overall impression, though, is rather chic. But food is the thing: eat in one of the various dining areas or opt for the spacious conservatory, or go for the heated sun terrace. The menu takes in British classics with evident Mediterranean leanings and a few ideas from farther afield. A starter of breast of woodland pigeon arrives with a vegetable rösti and wild mushroom and thyme ragoût, while mains might see a breast of Gressingham duck glazed with honey and served on apple and potato rösti with steamed baby pak choi and blueberry sauce. Round things off with Calvados rice pudding with caramelised apple.

Chef Trevor Bosch **Owner** Trevor & Annie Bosch
Times 12-3/7-10 Closed D Sun **Prices** Fixed L 2 course fr £14.95, Starter £4.95-£8.25, Main £13.50-£27.50, Dessert £6.50, Service optional, Groups min 8 service 10% **Wines** 58 bottles over £20, 29 bottles under £20, 12 by glass **Notes** Tasting menu 5 course Mon-Fri, Sunday L, Vegetarian available, Dress restrictions, Smart casual **Seats** 75, Pr/dining room 14 **Children** Portions **Parking** 30

MARLOW Map 5 SU88

Adam Simmonds at Danesfield House

– *see opposite page*

Aubergine at the Compleat Angler

– *see below*

Bowaters

Modern British

Modern British food served in a charming Thames-side setting

☎ 0844 879 9128 & 01628 484444
The Compleat Angler Hotel, Marlow Bridge SL7 1RG
e-mail: compleatangler@macdonald-hotels.co.uk
dir: M4 junct 8/9 or M40 junct 4. A404 to rdbt, take Bisham exit, 1m to Marlow Bridge, hotel on right

It is hard to dream up a more quintessentially English tableau than dinner at the elegant Georgian Compleat Angler Hotel, seated out on the Thames-side lawn, candlelight glinting off the water as it glides towards the thundering weir at Marlow. Of course, the English climate doesn't always oblige, in which case the historic Bowaters restaurant puts on a fashionable face in a slick pastel-hued blend of classic and contemporary style - and river views come as standard whatever the season. The kitchen cooks with great precision and intelligence, delivering eye-catching modern British dishes with razor-sharp flavours and combinations that work on the plate. A vibrant cream of parsley soup with truffle oil opens an autumn dinner with plenty of wow factor, ahead of confit belly and pan-fried fillet of pork with braised cabbage and Bramley apple sauce. Aubergine (see entry below) is the hotel's other restaurant option.

Chef David Smith **Owner** Macdonald Hotels
Times 12.30-2/7-10 **Prices** Fixed L 2 course £19.95, Starter £7.50-£11.95, Main £17.50-£23.50, Dessert £6.95-£9.95, Service added but optional 12.5% **Wines** 138 bottles over £20, 2 bottles under £20, 13 by glass **Notes** Sunday L, Vegetarian available, Civ Wed 100 **Seats** 90, Pr/dining room 120 **Children** Portions, Menu **Parking** 100

Aubergine at the Compleat Angler

MARLOW Map 5 SU88

Modern European

Daring cookery transplanted from Chelsea to the Home Counties

☎ 0844 879 9128 & 01628 484444
Macdonald Compleat Angler, Marlow Bridge SL7 1RG
e-mail: aubergineca@londonfinedininggroup.com
web: www.auberginemarlow.com
dir: M4 junct 8/9 or M40 junct 4. A404 to rdbt, take Bisham exit, 1m to Marlow Bridge, hotel on right

The peaceful setting of a riverside hotel, overlooking a Home Counties stretch of the Thames and its weeping willows, is home to the sister operation of the renowned Chelsea operation (see entry). The design theme has survived the journey (how could it not?), with depictions of the zeppelin-shaped vegetable on chargers and cutlery, and both hues - the purple skin and beige interior - represented in the décor. It all fits in seamlessly with the tranquil location, and even the daring food, which may once have come as something of a jolt in the environs, has garnered a base of local support. Combinations may raise the odd eyebrow, but they are properly thought through, as when crispy pig's head and crayfish join forces in the context of a potato salad. There is even the confidence to offer dishes that might be thought modern European classics by now, such as monkfish wrapped in Parma ham on a casserole of peas, as well as stalwarts of fine dining - beef fillet in red wine and shallots with horseradish cream - made exponentially finer by quality materials and nerveless timing. Desserts ring the changes with bright fruit flavours, encompassing iced lemon chiboust with rhubarb jelly and passionfruit sauce, or apricot soufflé with dark chocolate sauce.

Chef Miles Nixon **Owner** London Fine Dining Group
Times 12-2.30/7-11 Closed Mon-Tue **Prices** Fixed L 2 course £18.50, Starter £11-£18, Main £22-£27, Dessert fr £8, Service added but optional 12.5% **Wines** 50+ bottles over £20, 4 bottles under £20, 6 by glass
Notes Gourmand menu 5 course from £55 (with cheese £65), Sunday L, Vegetarian available, Dress restrictions, Smart casual **Seats** 49, Pr/dining room 120
Children Portions **Parking** 100

The Hand & Flowers

MARLOW **Map 5 SU88**

British, European

Superbe cooking in relaxed, stylish pub

☎ 01628 482277
126 West St SL7 2BP
e-mail: theoffice@thehandandflowers.co.uk
web: www.thehandandflowers.co.uk
dir: M40 junct 4/M4 junct 8/9 follow A404 to Marlow

Marlow is a pretty town on the River Thames with a nice line in Georgian architecture which has of late become something of a mecca for foodies. Amongst its many gems is The Hand & Flowers, a pub which matches a serious attitude to food with a refreshingly unpretentious and relaxed approach that satisfies 21st-century sensibilities. It still has the look of a pub, from the white-painted exterior hung with hanging baskets to the rustic interior, where old beams, wooden and flagged floors, chunky wooden tables and chairs and exposed brick walls meet neutral colours, leather banquettes and cloth-less, smartly-set tables. Chef-patron Tom Kerridge is able to walk adroitly the high wire between simplicity and sophistication, his food is not overworked but nor does it lack impact (presentation is always eye-catching). First-rate produce is at the heart of everything, with attention to detail running though the place from top to bottom. The menu, which offers up six or so choices per course, is broadly modern British, though there is much evidence of respect for French classical ways. Start with glazed omelette of smoked haddock and parmesan or maybe moules marinière with warm stout and brown bread. High technical skills and an eye for contemporary combinations can be found in a main-course fillet of bass served with pork belly, pickled apple, cockles and honey gravy. There are side dishes where required (chips, pommes boulangère and buttered spring greens among them) and to finish there could be warm pistachio sponge cake with melon sorbet and marzipan.

Chef Tom Kerridge **Owner** Tom & Beth Kerridge **Times** 12-2.30/6.30-9.30 Closed 24-26 Dec, D Sun, 1 Jan **Prices** Food prices not confirmed for 2011. Please telephone for details **Wines** 63 bottles over £20, 2 bottles under £20, 11 by glass **Notes** Sunday L, Vegetarian available **Seats** 50 **Children** Portions **Parking** 20

MARLOW *continued*

The Hand & Flowers

@@@ – *see opposite page*

The Vanilla Pod

@@ Modern British, French V

Historic house offering imaginative modern cuisine

☎ 01628 898101
31 West St SL7 2LS
e-mail: contact@thevanillapod.co.uk
dir: From M4 junct 8/9 or M40 junct 4 take A404, A4155 to Marlow. From Henley take A4155

Literary heavyweight TS Eliot once lived in this handsome townhouse on Marlow high street, but a thorough refurbishment has ushered in a chic contemporary feel, matched by a sociable atmosphere and politely correct, clued-up service. Chef-patron Michael Macdonald worked with Nico Ladenis, Pierre Koffman and Eric Chavot and brings red-hot skills to his deftly-realised brand of modern British cooking, which gives French-influenced classics a bold makeover. Not surprisingly, given the restaurant's name, vanilla is something of a leitmotif, as in a spot-on starter of roasted scallops teamed with a swipe of Bourbon vanilla pear purée. Meat-lovers might be taken with main-course pot-roasted pheasant with a cassoulet-style sauce of white beans and bacon, and silky parsnip purée. An exemplary bitter chocolate fondant with coffee parfait and milk chocolate mousse is as pretty as a picture for pudding. The three-course lunch menu is an absolute steal for this level of cooking.

Chef Michael Macdonald **Owner** Michael & Stephanie Macdonald **Times** 12-2/7-10 Closed 24 Dec-3 Jan, Sun-Mon **Prices** Fixed L 2 course £15.50, Fixed D 3 course £40, Tasting menu £50, Service optional **Wines** 102 bottles over £20, 3 bottles under £20, 10 by glass **Notes** Tasting menu 8 course, Vegetarian menu, Dress restrictions, Smart casual **Seats** 28, Pr/dining room 8 **Parking** On West Street

STOKE POGES Map 6 SU98

The Dining Room

@@ British, European NEW

Modern British cooking in magnificent country club

☎ 01753 717171 & 717176
Stoke Park, Park Rd SL2 4PG
e-mail: info@stokepark.com
dir: M4 junct 6 or M40 junct 2, take A355 towards Slough, then B416. Stoke Park in 1.25m on right

A country club since the Edwardian epoch, Stoke Park is a classical manor house designed as a private residence by James Wyatt, architect to George III. Its sparkling-white monumental look has fitted it over the years to be a much-used film location, as James Bond fans will doubtless recognise. Surrounded by 350 acres of parkland and gardens, the place lacks nothing in magnificence, and the dining room plays its part with its rich wall coverings, high windows and imposing mantelpiece mirrors. Well-drilled, highly skilled staff are knowledgeable and chatty, while the cooking, under Chris Wheeler, offers a refined version of modern British thinking. Lightly caramelised scallops are accompanied by baby fennel and beetroots with a gentle lemongrass sauce, while loin of lamb is voguishly teamed with a mini-shepherd's pie, rosemary-scented roasted roots and redcurrant jus. A languidly risen, subtle banana soufflé with a spoonful of fine rum and raisin ice cream is a lighter alternative to something like sticky toffee pudding with butterscotch sauce.

Chef Chris Wheeler **Owner** Roger King
Times 12-2.30/7-10 Closed 24-26 Dec, 1st wk Jan **Prices** Fixed D 3 course £39.50, Starter £6.50-£16.50, Main £13.50-£28.50, Dessert £6.50-£9.50, Service added 12.5% **Wines** 67 bottles over £20, 3 bottles under £20, 8 by glass **Notes** Sunday L, Vegetarian available, Dress restrictions, Smart casual, no trainers or T-shirts, Civ Wed 120, Air con **Seats** 50, Pr/dining room 120 **Parking** 400

Waldo's Restaurant, Cliveden

Rosettes not confirmed at time of going to press

TAPLOW Map 6 SU98

Modern European V NOTABLE WINE LIST

Fine-dining restaurant in historic stately home

☎ 01628 668561
Cliveden Estate SL6 0JF
e-mail: info@clivedenhouse.co.uk
dir: M4 junct 7, A4 towards Maidenhead for 1.5m, onto B476 towards Taplow, 2.5m, hotel on left

Perhaps the jewel in the National Trust's crown, Cliveden is an Italianate stately home with a past that has seen it placed firmly at the centre of the British establishment for several hundred years. It's as grand as they come, and the 21st-century incarnation as a luxury hotel is entirely in keeping with its stature. The hotel's flagship restaurant is Waldo's, named after the sculptor of the famous *Fountain of Love* in the sweeping driveway. As we go to press, there is a change in the kitchen once again, following the departure of Chris Horridge. The setting remains the same: a traditionally elegant room with oak-panels, tables dressed in the formal manner, with impeccable service from the formally dressed team. Start with a salad of red tuna sashimi before a main course such as medallions of veal with braised lettuce, sautéed girolles, celeriac purée and truffle jus, and finish with a deconstructed apple and blackberry crumble with custard. The wine list is a fine piece of work.

Chef Sebastien Audou **Owner** von Essen Hotels **Times** 7-9.30 Closed Xmas, New Year, 2 wks Aug, Sun-Mon, L all week **Prices** Tasting menu £79, Starter £12-£17, Main £22-£34, Dessert £10.50-£15, Service optional **Wines** All bottles over £20, 10 by glass **Notes** Vegetarian menu, Dress restrictions, Jacket & tie, Civ Wed 120 **Seats** 28, Pr/dining room 12 **Parking** 60

TAPLOW Map 6 SU98

Berry's at Taplow House Hotel

Modern British

Architectural, horticultural and culinary interest combined

01628 670056
Berry Hill SL6 0DA
e-mail: reception@taplowhouse.com
dir: M4 junct 7 towards Maidenhead, at lights follow signs to Berry Hill

Taplow House certainly stands out from the herd of country piles sprinkled liberally around these sceptred isles. The singular-looking Georgian confection has a symmetrical façade of red brick and cream stucco with decorative battlements, and splendid gardens with a centuries-old Cedar of Lebanon and Europe's tallest tulip trees. Berry's Restaurant makes a suitably elegant setting: with its tall windows, plush swagged curtains, and crystal chandelier, it's all very traditional, but the food has evolved into the contemporary British realm of country-house cooking, enlivened by clear European accents. Confit leg and seared breast of wood pigeon is served with plum salad, beetroot and red chard to start; mains might take in stuffed pork tenderloin with sage and apple, spring onion mash and Calvados sauce. Awaiting you at the end could be something like lemon and ginger cheesecake with orange sauce and candied lemon zest.

Chef Robert Lacey **Owner** Taplow House Hotel Ltd **Times** 12-2/7-9.30 Closed L Sat **Prices** Fixed L 2 course fr £15, Fixed D 3 course fr £25, Starter fr £6.50, Main fr £17.50, Dessert fr £5, Service added but optional 12.5% **Wines** 36 bottles over £20, 8 bottles under £20, 10 by glass **Notes** Gastronomic menu 7 course £45, Sunday L, Vegetarian available, Dress restrictions, Smart casual, Civ Wed 90 **Seats** 40, Pr/dining room 90 **Children** Portions, Menu **Parking** 100

The Terrace Dining Room, Cliveden

Traditional European

Fine dining in famous country house

01628 668561
Cliveden Estate SL6 0JF
e-mail: info@clivedenhouse.co.uk
dir: M4 junct 7, A4 towards Maidenhead for 1.5m, onto B476 towards Taplow, 2.5m, hotel on left

Set in 350-acres of parkland and gardens overlooking the Thames, this remarkable and majestic hotel occupies one of England's finest country houses, now owned by the National Trust. The sumptuous, sun-washed Terrace Dining Room looks through six French windows over a classical parterre garden to the distant Thames, while Waterford chandeliers, wood panelling and oil paintings combine in an elegant setting. The kitchen delivers what you'd expect of a top-ranking country house: imaginative interpretations of classic French cuisine, with correctly formal service to match. Starters might include seared scallops with cauliflower purée and curry oil, or wild mushroom risotto with cep sauce. Next up, loin of venison with salsify, chicory and Cassis sauce, followed by cherry soufflé with pistachio ice cream and Kirsch sauce. The hotel is also home to Waldo's (see entry).

Times 12-2.30/7-9.30

Waldo's Restaurant, Cliveden

– see page 69

WAVENDON Map 11 SP93

The Plough Wavendon

Modern French NOTABLE WINE LIST

Excellent food served in elegant surroundings

01908 587576
72 Walton Rd MK17 8LW
e-mail: info@theploughwavendon.com
web: www.theploughwavendon.com
dir: M1 junct 13, 7m from central Milton Keynes

The name may sound like a pub, but the Plough is a stylish contemporary bar and restaurant resurrected on the site of a 16th-century coaching inn and bake house. Inside, a pared-back modern look combines linen-jacketed high-backed chairs with bare darkwood tables on walnut-hued floors, pastel lemon walls, or you could move outdoors to the expansive terrace for alfresco dining. There's clearly some talent and a lively creative mind at the stoves, coupled with well-sourced raw materials. Pan-seared scallops served with truffled black pudding, Granny Smith apple and celeriac purée set the standard. Next up, pork belly is teamed with poached lobster in a visually stunning picture involving purées of vanilla potato and smoked apple, and a cinnamon crumble topping. To reinforce the fine dining feel-good factor, the meal comes interspersed with amuse-bouche, intermediate nibbles and pre-desserts.

Chef Chris Smith **Owner** Jon Todd **Times** 12-2.30/5.30-10.30 Closed 1 Jan, Mon, L 26 Dec, D 25 Dec **Prices** Fixed L 2 course £20, Fixed D 3 course £25, Service optional, Groups min 6 service 10% **Wines** 290 bottles over £20, 14 by glass **Notes** Tasting menu 7-9 course. ALC menu 2/3 course £45-£55, Sunday L, Vegetarian available, Dress restrictions, Smart casual **Seats** 48 **Children** Portions **Parking** 30

see advert on opposite page

WOOBURN COMMON Map 6 SU98

Chequers Inn

British, French

Chilterns coaching inn with impressive modern British food

☎ 01628 529575
Kiln Ln HP10 0JQ
e-mail: info@chequers-inn.com
dir: M40 junct 2, A40 through Beaconsfield Old Town towards High Wycombe. 2m from town left into Broad Ln. Inn 2.5m on left

The red-brick inn with its oak beams and flagstone floors sits comfortably in a Chilterns village, a soothing enough retreat that is not all that distant from London. Crisp white linen and interesting prints set a refined tone in the restaurant, where the modern British cooking hits some impressive high notes. A fishcake dressed with pistou and salad leaves is a good way to begin, and might be succeeded by corn-fed lemon chicken with black pudding fritters, or monkfish in Provençal sauce with rice. Finish with sticky toffee pudding and vanilla ice cream, or bitter-sweet lemon tart.

Owner PJ Roehrig **Times** 12-2.30/7-9.30 Closed D 25 Dec, 1 Jan **Prices** Fixed L 2 course £13.95-£21.95, Fixed D 3 course £23.95-£27.95, Starter £5.75-£9.75, Main £10.95-£18.95, Dessert £5.95-£6.95, Service optional **Wines** 36 bottles over £20, 25 bottles under £20, 11 by glass **Notes** Sunday L, Vegetarian available **Seats** 60, Pr/dining room 60 **Children** Portions **Parking** 50

CAMBRIDGESHIRE

CAMBRIDGE Map 12 TL45

Best Western Cambridge Quy Mill Hotel

Modern European

Converted watermill with focus on local produce

☎ 01223 293383
Newmarket Rd, Stow Cum Quy CB25 9AF
e-mail: info@quymillhotel.co.uk
dir: exit A14 at junct 35, E of Cambridge, onto B1102 for 50yds. Entrance opposite church

At Quy Mill, a Grade II listed complex of 19th-century watermill, miller's house and timber-framed barns in 11 acres of riverside meadows, has been converted into a smart hotel on the fringes of Cambridge. The old miller's dining room, parlour and study are now home to the intimate restaurant, or you could go more casual and eat in the bar, or out on the terrace in good weather. The menu proudly lists regional suppliers whose materials form the backbone of the kitchen's repertoire of traditional and globally-accented modern dishes. Kick off with devils on horseback with prunes and Armagnac, and follow with braised lamb shank, black colcannon, shallot and Madeira sauce. Hard-to-resist puddings might include caramelised black figs with mascarpone mousse and caramel syrup.

Chef Josh Fox **Owner** David Munro **Times** 12-2.30/6.30-9.45 Closed 24-31 Dec **Prices** Fixed L 2 course £12, Starter £4.95-£9.95, Main £10.95-£26.50, Dessert £4.95-£7.95, Service optional, Groups min 8 service 10% **Wines** 55 bottles over £20, 13 bottles under £20, 27 by glass **Notes** Sunday L, Vegetarian available, Dress restrictions, Smart dress/smart casual - no shorts (men), Civ Wed 80 **Seats** 48, Pr/dining room 80 **Children** Portions, Menu **Parking** 90

Graffiti at Hotel Felix

Modern British

Vibrant modern brasserie dining in a boutique Victorian mansion

☎ 01223 277977
Whitehouse Ln CB3 0LX
e-mail: help@hotelfelix.co.uk
dir: M11 junct 13. From A1 N take A14 turn onto A1307. At City of Cambridge sign turn left into Whitehouse Ln

Don't be fooled, this grand-looking Victorian mansion set in three acres of landscaped grounds hides a sleek 21st-century hotel inside, where period charm and elegance fuses effortlessly with pastel tones, dark hardwood flooring, clean lines and a swish contemporary décor. The chic, bistro-style Graffiti restaurant overlooks the garden and is a stunning dining space, with walls bedecked in modern art, and it has a fabulous terrace for alfresco aperitifs and fine weather dining. Like the décor, food is vibrant and modern British in style with more than a nod to the Mediterranean for inspiration. Take rillette of confit guinea fowl with pancetta, roasted quince and chorizo oil for a starter, and main dishes like chargrilled rump and braised cheek of beef with balsamic onion mash, sautéed morels and Perigueux sauce. Puddings may include warm pear and almond Charlotte with iced pear cream.

Chef Tom Stewart **Owner** Jeremy Cassel **Times** 12-2/6.30-10 **Prices** Fixed L 2 course £12.95, Starter £4.75-£6.75, Main £12.95-£21, Dessert £5.50-£7.95, Service added but optional 10%, Groups min 10 service 10% **Wines** 37 bottles over £20, 14 bottles under £20, 14 by glass **Notes** Sunday L, Vegetarian available, Civ Wed 60 **Seats** 45, Pr/dining room 60 **Children** Portions **Parking** 90

Midsummer House

CAMBRIDGE Map 12 TL45

Modern British NOTABLE WINE LIST

Creative cooking of the highest order

☎ 01223 369299
Midsummer Common CB4 1HA
e-mail: reservations@midsummerhouse.co.uk
web: www.midsummerhouse.co.uk
dir: Park in Pretoria Rd, then walk across footbridge. Restaurant on left

In a city filled with students seeking enlightenment and tourists rapt by the antiquity of the great colleges, there is a man, down by the River Cam, who has put Cambridge on the gastronomic map. Daniel Clifford's inexorable quest for perfection and innovation has resulted, after much hard work, in a restaurant of considerable class and calibre. The Victorian villa has the river flowing past on one side and the common on the other, and views over the water can be best enjoyed from the upstairs bar and terrace. The conservatory extension dining room looks out over the fragrant walled herb garden, while within, pristine white walls, slate floors and generously-sized, well-spaced tables give an air of imperturbable refinement. The cooking of Clifford and his team (not a large brigade by today's standards) is bold, exciting and technically innovative, taking meticulously sourced ingredients and creating an array of memorable dishes, fizzing with thrilling flavour combinations and inventive presentations. There's a tasting menu and a carte, and whichever you go for you are guaranteed there will be no holds barred from the off: an amuse-bouche, for example, of pink grapefruit and champagne foam, theatrically served at the table, invigorates the palate like no other. A first course of maple caramelised sweetbreads is a truly inspired combination, served with ox tongue, turnip and maple jelly, laying bare the confidence of the kitchen. Portions can be generous, as with main-course venison, slow-roasted and presented with parsnip purée and sautéed chestnuts, and powerfully flavoured with blue cheese and chocolate. Desserts show no less invention, as in a triumphant orange cheesecake, with flavours of fresh coriander and caramelised oats, and finished with a Hoegaarden sorbet. The young service team are delightful and the wine list deserves a moment of your time.

Chef Daniel Clifford **Owner** Midsummer House Ltd **Times** 12-1.45/7-9.30 Closed 2 wks late Aug, 2 wks from 25 Dec, 1 wk Etr, Sun-Mon, L Tue **Prices** Fixed L 2 course £29.50, Fixed D 3 course £65, Tasting menu £85, Service added but optional 12.5% **Wines** 900 bottles over £20, 12 by glass **Notes** Vegetarian available **Seats** 45, Pr/dining room 16 **Children** Portions **Parking** On street

CAMBRIDGE ***continued***

Hotel du Vin Cambridge

Modern British V

Bistro cooking in a medieval building

01223 227330
15-19 Trumpington St CB2 1QA
e-mail: info.cambridge@hotelduvin.com
dir: M11 junct 11 Cambridge S, pass Trumpington Park & Ride on left. Hotel 2m on right after double rdbt

The beautiful building on Trumpington Street, close to the historic heart of Cambridge, has been sensitively transformed into a unique boutique hotel in typical Hotel du Vin style, enhancing its many quirky features. Bare wooden floors and rough-cast walls set a pleasingly rustic tone in the bistro dining room, and the menus tack to the successful, refreshingly straightforward Anglo-French culinary style that is the chain's hallmark. Start with seared scallops with cauliflower purée and black pudding, follow with duck on potato rösti with orange confit, or a classic dish of beef and ox cheek casserole, and finish with hot chocolate tart with raspberry sorbet.

Chef Jonathan Dean **Owner** MWB **Times** 12-2/6-10 Closed L 31 Dec **Prices** Fixed L 2 course £13.50-£15.50, Starter £4.95-£10.50, Main £14.50-£19.95, Dessert £6.95-£9.50, Service added but optional 10% **Wines** 400 bottles over £20, 30 bottles under £20, 15 by glass **Notes** Sunday L, Vegetarian menu **Seats** 76, Pr/dining room 24 **Children** Portions **Parking** On street, Lyons Yard NCP

Midsummer House

– see opposite page

Restaurant 22

Modern European

Accomplished cooking in intimate setting

01223 351880
22 Chesterton Rd CB4 3AX
e-mail: aandstommaso@restaurant22.co.uk

Once a Victorian residence, the candlelit dining room at 22 still retains the intimate atmosphere of a private home. The tables are close together, adding to the homely feel, and the atmosphere is suitably mellow. The monthly-changing fixed-price menu takes on a modern British style with a definite French influence. Pheasant breast stuffed with date and apple mousse served with fondant potato and Brussels sprouts is a typical main course from the fixed price menu, which always offers a fish option. For dessert, go for a comforting orange steamed pudding with ginger crème anglaise.

Chef Mr Kipping **Owner** Mr A & Mrs S Tommaso **Times** 7-9.45 Closed 25 Dec & New Year, Sun-Mon, L all week **Prices** Fixed D 4 course £27.95, Service optional **Wines** 40 bottles over £20, 30 bottles under £20, 4 by glass **Notes** Vegetarian available **Seats** 26, Pr/dining room 14 **Children** Portions **Parking** On street

Restaurant Alimentum

– see below

DUXFORD **Map 12 TL44**

Duxford Lodge Hotel

British, European

Ambitious cooking in historic country house

01223 836444
Ickleton Rd CB22 4RT
e-mail: admin@duxfordlodgehotel.co.uk
web: www.duxfordlodgehotel.co.uk
dir: M11 junct 10, onto A505 to Duxford. 1st right at rdbt, hotel 0.75m on left

continued

Restaurant Alimentum

CAMBRIDGE **Map 12 TL45**

Modern European

Strong ethical principles and classy, contemporary cooking

01223 413000
152-154 Hills Rd CB2 8PB
e-mail: info@restaurantalimentum.co.uk
dir: Opposite Cambridge Leisure Park

Cambridge's new leisure park is not the first landmark that springs to mind when you think of this great city of learning, but head out that way to a smart building opposite and you're in for a culinary treat. Alimentum, a restaurant named after the Latin word for food, stands out from the crowd for a number of reasons. First off, there's its strikingly modern décor, with smoked glass, black-lacquered surfaces and bold red seating; secondly, a decidedly chilled out attitude to service; thirdly, a progressive and sensitive approach to environmental sustainability and animal welfare; and, finally, an innovative and creative kitchen team led by Mark Poynton. That desire to source produce with ethical concern seems to pay dividends on the plate, with some first-rate ingredients turning up in dishes. This is contemporary cooking based on sound classical principles and bringing some modern techniques into play. Hand-dived Scottish scallops appear in a first-course delivering superb flavours and textural contrasts, while main-course fillet and belly of pork is partnered with a pineapple purée, powerful garlic confit and sage jus. A touch of showmanship turns up at dessert - the lid is lifted on a kilner jar at the table and out pours hickory smoke, and within is an inventive dish of smoked milk jam mousse with caramel, honeycomb and banana.

Chef Mark Poynton **Owner** Mark Poynton **Times** 12-3/6-10 Closed 24-31 Dec, BHs, D Sun **Prices** Fixed L 2 course £13.50, Fixed D 3 course £18.50, Starter £7.50-£9.50, Main £17.50-£21, Dessert £7.95-£9.50, Service added but optional 12.5% **Wines** 83 bottles over £20, 8 bottles under £20, 40 by glass **Notes** Pre-theatre D Mon-Fri 6-7pm, Sunday L, Vegetarian available, Dress restrictions, Smart casual **Seats** 62, Pr/dining room 34 **Children** Portions, Menu **Parking** NCP Cambridge Leisure Centre (3 min walk)

DUXFORD ***continued***

The attractive red-brick building, built in the early part of the last century, and located in the heart of a delightful village, these days earns its crust as a country-house hotel. It's steeped in history, serving as an officers' mess and, in the 1940s, was a magnet for a range of visiting dignitaries and stars, from Sir Winston Churchill to Bing Crosby. The pastel-coloured restaurant offers ambitious modern dining on fixed-price and à la carte menus. Expect confit chicken and foie gras terrine with Provençal dressing to begin, followed by poached salmon and sautéed king prawns with spinach, wild mushrooms, new potatoes and sauce vierge.

Chef Jason Burridge **Owner** Mr Hemant Amin **Times** 12-2/7-9.30 Closed 24 Dec-2 Jan, L Mon, Fri, Sat **Prices** Starter £5.50-£8.25, Main £12.50-£16.50, Dessert £4.25-£10.25, Service optional **Wines** 12 bottles over £20, 10 bottles under £20, 6 by glass **Notes** Sunday L, Vegetarian available, Dress restrictions, Smart dress/smart casual, Civ Wed 46 **Seats** 45, Pr/dining room 24 **Children** Portions **Parking** 30

ELTISLEY — Map 12 TL25

The Eltisley

Modern British NEW

Well-tuned modern food in smart dining pub

☎ 01480 880308
2 The Green PE19 6TG
e-mail: theeltisley@btconnect.com
dir: Between St Neots & Cambridge, 500 yds from A428

This ambitious modern dining pub sits on the green of a lovely village close to St Neots. The former Leeds Arms has a smart new look to go with its new name. A welcoming bar appeals with its down-to-earth bare wooden floors and tables, thirst-inducing array of real ales, and chalkboard menus - a pie of the day, or organic sausages with mustard mash and apple and cider sauce might catch the eye - while the restaurant goes for a striking modern look beneath a high-beamed ceiling. Top-class local ingredients are the bedrock of the kitchen's imaginative modern British cooking; twice-cooked local pork belly is teamed with white wine-poached apples and black pudding purée, ahead of mains such as corn-fed chicken breast with potato and tarragon croquette, confit shallots and shallot purée.

Chef Simon Turner **Owner** John Steans **Times** 12-2/6-9 Closed Mon (except BHs), D Sun **Prices** Starter £4.50-£7.95, Main £9.95-£23.95, Dessert £5.95, Service optional **Notes** Sunday L, Vegetarian available **Seats** 70, Pr/dining room 35 **Children** Portions

ELTON — Map 12 TL09

The Crown Inn

Modern British NEW

Dreamy country inn with appealing modern menu

☎ 01832 280232
8 Duck St PE8 6RQ
e-mail: inncrown@googlemail.com
dir: A1 take A605 towards Oundle for 3m. Exit right for Oundle. Restaurant next to village green

The Crown is the very image of an English country inn - built in the 16th century of honey-hued stone, topped with thatch and festooned with bright flower baskets, it sits next to an ancient horse chestnut tree on the green of an idyllic village. It's still a proper local too, with a nice line in modern Anglo-French cooking. Food is served in a trio of eating venues - the classic beamed bar, with a real fire sizzling in a stone inglenook, the cosy Snug, or the smart modern Orangery restaurant. Local materials are garnered by the kitchen and sent out with a cross-channel spin, as in a no-nonsense starter of ham hock, mushroom, leek and parmesan tart, followed by a breaded chicken breast stuffed with ham and cheese and served with proper home-made chips. Fish lovers might go for a seafood broth with crab ravioli, spring onion and coriander, and round things off with sticky toffee pudding and tiramisù ice cream.

Chef Pierre Kolabukoff **Owner** Marcus Lamb **Times** 12-2/6.30-9 Closed 1st wk Jan, L Mon, D Sun **Prices** Fixed L 2 course fr £12, Starter £4.95-£8.50, Main £10.50-£18.95, Dessert £4.95-£6.95, Service optional **Wines** 27 bottles over £20, 9 bottles under £20, 6 by glass **Notes** Sunday L, Vegetarian available, Dress restrictions, Smart casual **Seats** 40 **Children** Portions **Parking** 15

ELY — Map 12 TL58

The Anchor Inn

Modern British

Creative cooking in rural East Anglian inn

☎ 01353 778537
Bury Ln, Sutton Gault, Sutton CB6 2BD
e-mail: anchorinn@popmail.bta.com
dir: Signed off B1381 in Sutton village, 7m W of Ely via A142

Built in 1650 to provide shelter for workers digging the New Bedford River to help drain the Fens, this old inn retains plenty of character. Uneven tiled floors, antique pine furniture and roaring fires in winter all make for a warm welcome. The menu isn't tied to one genre, skipping from traditional English to elsewhere in the world, with plenty of European leanings. East Anglian ingredients get a good showing, too. Bottisham-smoked pigeon breast with bacon and pine nut salad and Earl Grey syrup shows the confident, modish style of the cooking. Follow on with pan-fried tenderloin of pork with spring onion croquet potato, curly kale and a ginger and apricot glaze, and finish with orange and cinnamon pannacotta.

Chef Adam Pickup **Owner** Adam Pickup & Carlene Bunten **Times** 12-3.30/7-11 **Prices** Fixed L 2 course £11.95, Starter £4.95-£8.25, Main £10-£21, Dessert £4.50-£7, Service optional, Groups min 10 service 10% **Wines** 21 bottles over £20, 32 bottles under £20, 12 by glass **Notes** Sunday L, Vegetarian available **Seats** 70 **Children** Portions, Menu **Parking** 16

HINXTON — Map 12 TL44

The Red Lion Inn

Modern British

Modern British food in a pink pub

☎ 01799 530601
32 High St CB10 1QY
e-mail: info@redlionhinxton.co.uk
dir: M11 junct 10, at rdbt take A505 continue to A1301 signed Saffron Walden/Hinxton for 0.75m & follow signs for Red Lion

The Lion is not so much red as blush-pink, and lurks peaceably in a pretty conservation village near the Cambridgeshire-Essex border. An informal dining room with beamed ceiling and unclothed tables is the setting for wide-ranging modern British cooking of some flair. Asian influences surface in a stir-fry to accompany saffron-scented red mullet, or in the sea bass with Thai noodle salad and coconut foam, but there are classic pub dishes too on the bar menu, so seekers after steak and ale pie with shortcrust pastry and gravy need not feel neglected. Finish with a poached pear in a brandy snap basket, served with strawberry jelly and lemongrass granité.

Chef Peter Friskey **Owner** Alex Clarke **Times** 12-2/6.45-9 **Prices** Starter £4-£9, Main £9-£20, Dessert £5-£8, Service optional, Groups min 8 service 10% **Notes** Sunday L, Vegetarian available **Seats** 60 **Parking** 43

HUNTINGDON Map 12 TL27

The Old Bridge Hotel

Modern British

Charming hotel with versatile dining options and great wines

01480 424300
1 High St PE29 3TQ
e-mail: oldbridge@huntsbridge.co.uk
dir: From A14 or A1 follow Huntingdon signs. Hotel visible from inner ring road

Owner and Master of Wine, John Hoskins, has set up an in-house wine shop here, where a couple of dozen bottles are up for tasting each day. If that isn't inducement enough for a trip to this 18th-century ivy-clad townhouse hotel, there's the location by the ancient stone bridge over the River Ouse and a glorious riverside terrace, or the classic bar, which pulls a fine pint of Adnams. Then there's the Terrace Restaurant, a buzzy and relaxed place with its bold murals, bleached wood panelling and brass buddha in the fireplace. On the menu is a blend of traditional crowd-pleasers and modern bistro dishes that speak with a strong French or Italian accent. Seared diver-caught scallops are nicely caramelised and partnered with celeriac purée and the invigorating tang of a caper, apple and sherry vinegar dressing, followed by roast breast of free range chicken with potato, leek and artichoke hash, pancetta and a light sherry cream sauce. The wine list is, of course, a thing of joy.

Chef Simon Cadge **Owner** J Hoskins **Times** 12-2/6.30-10 **Prices** Fixed L 2 course £16, Starter £6.95-£9.95, Main £12.95-£25, Dessert £5.95-£9.95, Service optional **Wines** 350 bottles over £20, 50 bottles under £20, 35 by glass **Notes** Sunday L, Vegetarian available, Civ Wed 80 **Seats** 100, Pr/dining room 60 **Children** Portions, Menu **Parking** 60

KEYSTON Map 11 TL07

Pheasant Inn

British Mediterranean

Unfussy seasonal cooking in comfortable country inn

01832 710241
Loop Rd PE28 0RE
e-mail: info@thepheasant-keyston.co.uk
dir: 0.5m off A14, clearly signed, 10m W of Huntingdon, 14m E of Kettering

At the heart of picture-postcard Keyston, beneath a huge sycamore tree, sits the Pheasant, formed from classic 16th-century thatched cottages. Within, it is quintessentially 'olde England'; old farming implements, hunting and shooting prints, a mass of blackened beams, brick inglenooks, flagstone floor and stripped boards. The atmosphere is relaxed and informal and cooking is simple, traditional British and French and based on quality local produce, with vegetables from the kitchen garden, and beef, lamb and pork sourced from farms within a 10-mile radius. Follow carrot and coriander soup with roast partridge, game chips, rosehip jelly and curly kale, or grilled mackerel with gremolata, and finish with treacle suet sponge pudding with custard.

Chef Jay Scrimshaw, Liam Goodwill **Owner** Jay & Taffeta Scrimshaw **Times** 12-2.30/6.30-9.30 **Prices** Fixed L 2 course fr £14.50, Fixed D 3 course fr £19.50, Starter £5.50-£9, Main £12.50-£25, Dessert £5.50-£8, Service optional, Groups min 10 service 10% **Wines** 60 bottles over £20, 20 bottles under £20, 12 by glass **Notes** Sunday L, Vegetarian available **Seats** 80, Pr/dining room 30 **Children** Portions, Menu **Parking** 40

LITTLE WILBRAHAM Map 12 TL55

Hole in the Wall

Modern British

Fine old country pub with modern approach in the kitchen

01223 812282
2 High St CB21 5JY
e-mail: jenniferleeton@btconnect.com
dir: A14 junct 35. A11 exit at The Wilbrahams

Chris and Jenny Leeton's heavily-beamed 15th-century pub may be rather more of a dining destination than it was in the days when farm labourers picked up their barrels of beer through a hole in the wall of the bar, but it is still at heart a real pub without any pretensions. The unvarnished interior says it all: logs piled beside a roaring fire, hop bines garlanding the rafters and a battery of real ales on tap. The food takes a similar unfussy line - hearty, full-flavoured contemporary ideas built on fresh local produce. Go for haggis fritters in beer batter with pickled cabbage and sour cream, followed by free-range pork tenderloin with black pudding mash, apple purée and cider sauce. To finish, the kitchen might put together winter-spiced Cambridgeshire burnt cream with mulled pear and mulled wine.

Chef Christopher Leeton **Owner** Christopher & Jennifer Leeton, Stephen Bull **Times** 12-2/7-9 Closed 2 wks Jan & 2 wks Oct, Mon (except L BH), D Sun, 26 Dec, 1 Jan **Prices** Fixed L 2 course £17.50-£24, Starter £4.25-£8.50, Main £11-£16, Dessert £5.75, Service optional **Wines** 15 bottles over £20, 26 bottles under £20, 12 by glass **Notes** Sunday L, Vegetarian available **Seats** 65 **Children** Portions **Parking** 30

PETERBOROUGH Map 12 TL19

Best Western Orton Hall Hotel

British

Impressive historic building serving modern cuisine

01733 391111
The Village, Orton Longueville PE2 7DN
e-mail: reception@ortonhall.co.uk
dir: off A605 E, opposite Orton Mere

The former home of the Marquis of Huntly is a rambling, tastefully restored 17th-century country manor, set in 20 acres of parkland in a quiet village close to Peterborough. Expect a traditional country-house feel throughout and a wealth of period features in the elegant restaurant, including notably exquisite stained glass and some fine oak panelling. A competent kitchen delivers a seasonal menu of modern British dishes that show good use of quality local produce. Take partridge and pheasant terrine with prune and whiskey chutney, roast cod with a mussel minestrone broth, and warm banana cake with condensed milk ice cream. The on-site pub, the Ramblewood Inn, offers an alternative, informal dining venue.

Best Western Orton Hall Hotel

Chef Kevin Wood **Owner** Abacus Hotels **Times** 12.30-2/7-9.30 Closed 25 Dec, L Mon-Sat **Prices** Fixed D 3 course fr £81, Starter £5-£10, Main £12-£20, Dessert £5-£10, Service optional **Wines** 23 bottles over £20, 42 bottles under £20, 6 by glass **Notes** Sunday L, Civ Wed 150 **Seats** 34, Pr/dining room 40 **Parking** 200

ST NEOTS Map 12 TL16

The George Hotel & Brasserie

Modern British

Modern British in laid-back brasserie

01480 812300
High St, Buckden PE19 5XA
e-mail: mail@thegeorgebuckden.com
dir: Off A1, S of junct with A14

The ground-floor brasserie in the chic George Hotel in the pretty village of Buckden has the cool confidence of many a metropolitan venue. The old Georgian inn got a contemporary makeover back in 2004, including the twelve bedrooms, which are named after different Georges (Orwell and Harrison to name but two). The brasserie sports polished darkwood tables and a splendid metal bar. Modern British cooking is the order of the day, with influences drawn from across Europe; foie gras and smoked eel terrine, for example, with artichoke salad, then maybe fillet of sea bass with clams, agretti (a marsh grass), brunoise potatoes and chive velouté. The informal lounge bar also serves food by the open fire.

Chef Chris Cheah **Owner** Richard & Anne Furbank **Times** 12-2.30/7-9.30 **Prices** Starter £5.50-£9.50, Main £12.50-£25.50, Dessert £5.50-£7.50, Service optional **Wines** 35 bottles over £20, 35 bottles under £20, 16 by glass **Notes** Sunday L, Vegetarian available, Dress restrictions, Smart dress, Civ Wed 40 **Seats** 60, Pr/dining room 30 **Children** Portions **Parking** 25

STILTON — Map 12 TL18

Bell Inn Hotel

British, French V

Modern British cuisine in delightful 16th-century surroundings

☎ 01733 241066
Great North Rd PE7 3RA
e-mail: reception@thebellstilton.co.uk
dir: A1(M) junct 16, follow Stilton signs. Hotel in village centre

The Bell has history in spades. It's said that Stilton cheese was first served here in the 18th century and Dick Turpin dropped by to quaff ale regularly. Nothing much has changed since those days - cockerels and livestock aren't allowed inside, and smart modern rooms have been built around the courtyard - such details apart, much of the timeless character is intact. The kitchen deals in a happy fusion of hearty British and French crowd-pleasers, served in the ancient bar and bistro, or up in the beamed gallery restaurant. Chicken liver parfait with fennel seed toast and gooseberry chutney is a typical starter, followed by main-course chargrilled cannon of lamb with pea and mint purée, root vegetables and redcurrant jus.

Chef Robin Devonshire **Owner** Mr Liam McGivern **Times** 12-2/7-9.30 Closed 25 Dec, 31 Dec, L Mon-Sat, D Sun **Prices** Food prices not confirmed for 2011. Please telephone for details **Wines** 30 bottles over £20, 30 bottles under £20, 8 by glass **Notes** Sunday L, Vegetarian menu, Dress restrictions, Smart casual, Civ Wed 90 **Seats** 60, Pr/dining room 20 **Children** Portions, Menu **Parking** 30

WISBECH — Map 12 TF40

The Moorings

Modern, Traditional

Rural setting for crowd-pleasing food

☎ 01945 773391
Crown Lodge Hotel, Downham Rd, Outwell PE14 8SE
e-mail: office@thecrownlodgehotel.co.uk
dir: 5m SE of Wisbech on A1122, 1m from junct with A1101, towards Downham Market

With its contemporary interior and peaceful location, the Crown Lodge Hotel, on the banks of Welle Creek, has a lot to offer. Not least, the smart brasserie-style restaurant, with its leather chairs, darkwood tables and modern crockery and cutlery. It's an open plan space, incorporating a bar and lounge area. On the broad menu expect straightforward crowd-pleasers, including a grill section. Eat where you like, including on the terrace, and expect prawn tian followed by chargrilled chicken breast served with a flat field mushroom, roasted plum tomato and hand-cut chips, and for pud, pecan nut and banoffee pie.

Times 12-2.30/6-10 Closed 25-26 & 31 Dec, 1 Jan

CHESHIRE

ALDERLEY EDGE — Map 16 SJ87

The Alderley Restaurant

– see opposite page

BROXTON — Map 15 SJ45

Redmonds Restaurant

Modern British **NEW**

Luxury modern hotel with cuisine to match

☎ 01829 731615 & 01829 731616
De Vere Carden Park Hotel, Golf Resort & Spa CH3 9DQ
e-mail: hamish.ferguson@devere-hotels.com
dir: A41 signed Whitchurch to Chester, at Broxton rdbt turn on to A534 towards Wrexham. After 2m turn into Carden Park Estate

Carden Park estate has occupied 1,000 acres of green and pleasant Cheshire countryside since the 17th century. The original mansion burned down long ago, but megabucks investment over the last decade has seen a luxury development rise in the grand spirit of the location. Two championship golf courses, plus state of the art spa and fitness facilities are a big draw for many, while the split-level Redmonds Restaurant - a glossy, contemporary space with candle-lit dark mahogany tables - is where the serious cooking takes place. Cracking local produce is used to great effect in a repertoire of modern British dishes, such as seared scallops and black pudding fritters with caramelised apple purée to start, followed by Llandudno Smokery chicken breast with buttered baby leeks, and sweetcorn done as a relish, purée and tempura.

Times 12-2/6.30-9.30

CHESTER — Map 15 SJ46

La Brasserie at The Chester Grosvenor & Spa

Modern International

French brasserie cooking in a grand Chester hotel

☎ 01244 324024
Eastgate CH1 1LT
e-mail: hotel@chestergrosvenor.co.uk
dir: A56 follow signs for city centre hotels. Opposite Town Hall on Northgate St

Playing a strong second fiddle to Simon Radley's restaurant at the Chester Grosvenor (see separate entry), La Brasserie is for more informal fare in an ambience that aims for as much Parisian chic as a Cheshire hotel can provide. Burnished granite tabletops and black leather seating, together with a hand-painted skylight, establish the tone, and the menu does the rest. Despite the presence of French onion soup, and a main-course feuilleté of veal kidneys and sweetbreads with ceps and Madeira, there are references to other culinary traditions too, as in roast Gressingham duck with bacon gnocchi in sweet-and-sour redcurrant sauce. Go French again at dessert with floating island in blood orange soup with Grand Marnier bavarois.

Times 12-10.30 Closed 25-26 Dec

Langdale Restaurant

Traditional British

Magnificent Georgian country-house hotel with fine dining

☎ 01244 335262
Rowton Hall Hotel & Spa, Whitchurch Rd, Rowton CH3 6AD
e-mail: reception@rowtonhallhotelandspa.co.uk
dir: M56 junct 12, A56 to Chester. At rdbt left onto A41 towards Whitchurch. Approx 1m, follow hotel signs

This regal Georgian manor house sits in eight acres of manicured gardens just a couple of miles outside the walls of Chester. A glitzy health and beauty spa takes care of body and soul with a spot of pampering, or if you want to raise your heart rate rather than de-stress, you could have a flutter down at Chester races. Oak panelling and Robert Adam fireplaces play their part in a classy interior that pulls together period elegance with flourishes of understated contemporary style, as typified in the Langdale restaurant. The kitchen takes a straightforward modern approach to good quality produce, focusing on what works best with what, in starters along the lines of confit chicken pressing with coarse grain mustard. Mains again reflect a sensible choice of produce, teaming pan-fried sea bream with ratatouille and potato rösti, or the crowd-pleasing combination of roast rump of lamb with creamed mushrooms and fondant potato.

Chef Matthew Hulmes **Owner** Mr & Mrs Wigginton **Times** 12-2/7-9.30 **Prices** Fixed L 3 course £13-£18, Fixed D 3 course £19.95-£26.50, Starter £5.25-£12.50, Main £8.95-£19.95, Dessert £4.25-£7.50, Service optional **Notes** Sunday L, Vegetarian available, Dress restrictions, Smart casual, Civ Wed 170 **Seats** 70, Pr/dining room 30 **Children** Portions, Menu **Parking** 200

Simon Radley at The Chester Grosvenor

– see page 78

The Alderley Restaurant

ALDERLEY EDGE Map 16 SJ87

British V

Dynamic modern British cooking amid the Cheshire smart set

☎ 01625 583033
Alderley Edge Hotel, Macclesfield Rd SK9 7BJ
e-mail: sales@alderleyedgehotel.com
dir: A538 to Alderley Edge, then B5087 Macclesfield Rd

Built in the 1850s for a member of the Manchester business elite, the Elizabethan-Gothic house stands on a wooded rise overlooking Cheshire's smartest community, where many of the present day elite of professional footballers are domiciled. Views over the surrounding countryside from the conservatory dining room are as breathtaking as David Beckham's free kicks once were, and chef Chris Holland works with the grain of the modern British culinary movement, while adding in some dynamic ideas of his own. The menu makes dishes sound fun, especially when you might start with a hot lobster sausage, served with organic salmon cooked sous-vide, along with limoncello purée, compressed melon and langoustine jelly. Holland has the modern chef's feeling for texture as well as flavour combination, seen again in a main course of fillet of sea bass with spiced cauliflower, roasted scallops and smoked raisins, or loin of Conwy Valley lamb with hotpot, candied beetroot and creamed leeks. Desserts aim to amaze too, with the likes of Granny Smith beignets, dry butterscotch powder, toffee, and spiced ice cream. Pedigree British cheeses are served with fruit bread and chutneys.

Chef Chris Holland **Owner** J W Lees (Brewers) Ltd **Times** 12-2/7-10 Closed 1 Jan, L 31 Dec, D 25-26 Dec **Prices** Fixed L 2 course £17.95, Fixed D 3 course £29.95, Tasting menu £54.50-£79, Starter £10.75-£11.50, Main £21.95-£23.85, Dessert £8.25, Service optional **Wines** 450+ bottles over £20, 30 bottles under £20, 7 by glass **Notes** Tasting menu available 6 course (with wine £79), Sunday L, Vegetarian menu, Dress restrictions, Smart casual, Civ Wed 150 **Seats** 80, Pr/dining room 150 **Children** Portions, Menu **Parking** 82

Simon Radley at The Chester Grosvenor

CHESTER Map 15 SJ46

Modern French V NOTABLE WINE LIST

Cutting-edge cooking in a grand city hotel

☎ 01244 324024
Chester Grosvenor & Spa, Eastgate CH1 1LT
e-mail: hotel@chestergrosvenor.co.uk
dir: City centre (Eastgate St) adjacent to Eastgate Clock & Roman walls

Right next to Chester's landmark Eastgate Clock, within the city's Roman walls (also next to a multi-storey car park, but enough of that), the Grosvenor is something of a local landmark in itself. Owned by the Duke of Westminster, its reputation throughout the northwest has been carefully maintained over the years, not only as a supremely refined five-star hotel, but as a premier dining magnet. Simon Radley, after whom the main restaurant is now fittingly named, has achieved a stunning efflorescence here, taking the place from somewhere that simply did opulent high-end dining to the kind of venue that can justly consider itself to be at the epicentre of current developments in British cooking. The pillared room is less ostentatious than you may be expecting, with comfortable high-backed chairs and minimal wall adornment, but it's what goes on on the table that excites the closest attention. Dishes are often given titles that may sound like indie album tracks: 'Pond Life' turns out to involve crayfish tails, garlic snails and a frog leg bonbon, along with a substance described as watercress whip, while 'Cheek to Cheek' puts together the said parts of Gloucestershire Old Spot pig and halibut, with caramelised cauliflower and raisins. Foreign culinary modes are accorded in-depth study, rather than being casually employed, as witness the Chinese references that abound in a dual serving of sea bass with lacquered oysters and a fresh oyster sauce. And there are remixes of classic dishes too, as when a combination of yellowfin tuna and Limousin veal fillet, each in the other's sauce, along with cannellini beans and basil, is entitled 'Vitello Tonnato'. Even desserts explore and recast textbook gastronomic ideas, perhaps in the form of pear and Roquefort, where the accompaniments of walnut ice and milk chocolate jelly turn what was once a bistro salad into an unforgettable conclusion. The Tasting Menu is a tour de force. Oh, and there are 60 pages of wines to consider.

Chef Simon Radley, Ray Booker **Owner** Grosvenor - Duke of Westminster **Times** 7-9.30 Closed 25-26 Dec, 1 wk Jan, Sun-Mon, L all week (except Dec) **Prices** Fixed D 3 course £69, Tasting menu £80, Service added but optional 12.5% **Wines** 620 bottles over £20, 5 bottles under £20, 15 by glass **Notes** Tasting menu 8 course, Vegetarian menu, Dress restrictions, Smart dress, no jeans, shorts or sportswear, Civ Wed 120 **Seats** 45, Pr/dining room 240 **Parking** NCP attached to hotel

CREWE Map 15 SJ75

The Brasserie

Modern European

Contemporary brasserie in new wing of old stately home

☎ 01270 253333 & 259319
Crewe Hall, Weston Rd CW1 6UZ
e-mail: crewehall@qhotels.co.uk
dir: M6 junct 16 follow A500 to crewe. Last exit at rdbt onto A5020. 1st exit next rdbt to Crewe. Crewe Hall 150yds on right

The grand old Crewe Hall with its old-world charms and stunning period features also has a modern wing, linked via a glass walkway which acts like a time tunnel in transporting you from one age to another. A world of luxurious facilities awaits such as a state-of-the-art spa and the vibrant brasserie with its modish open kitchen. A drink in the revolving bar is a suitable place to whet the appetite for the confident modern European cooking. Start with smoked trout with dill scones and horseradish cream before moving on to maize-fed chicken with herb gnocchi or a rib-eye steak from the grill.

Chef Andrew Fletcher **Owner** Q Hotels **Times** all day **Prices** Fixed L 2 course £12, Starter £4.50-£7.50, Main £12-£25, Dessert £5-£6.50, Service optional **Wines** 34 bottles over £20, 9 bottles under £20, 15 by glass **Notes** Vegetarian available, Civ Wed 280 **Seats** 140 **Children** Portions, Menu **Parking** 500

Hunters Lodge Hotel

Traditional British

Traditional cooking in attractively situated hotel

☎ 01270 539100
Sydney Rd, Sydney CW1 5LU
e-mail: info@hunterslodge.co.uk
dir: 1m from Crewe station, off A534

With 16 acres of impressive grounds, this 18th-century former farmhouse now earns its crust as a family-run hotel. Extended and modernised, it is geared up for weddings and conferences, and has a spacious, beamed restaurant delivering a classically-inspired menu amid smart formality. Start, perhaps, with the globally-inspired tempura of prawns served with sweet chilli dip and a salad of rocket leaves, before main-course fillet of salmon with a leek and prawn risotto cake and roasted tomatoes. End with a comforting Bramley apple crumble with custard or well-made crème brûlée with compôte of seasonal berries. There's a bar offering good value, straightforward dishes.

Chef David Wall **Owner** Mr A Panayi **Times** 12-2/7-9.30 Closed BHs, D Sun **Prices** Fixed D 3 course £19.95, Starter £3.95-£5.95, Main £8.95-£15.95, Dessert £4.95, Service optional **Wines** 26 bottles over £20, 27 bottles under £20, 7 by glass **Notes** Sunday L, Vegetarian available, Civ Wed 130 **Seats** 60, Pr/dining room 30 **Children** Portions, Menu **Parking** 200

The Ranulph

Modern European

Fine dining in Victorian splendour

☎ 01270 253333
Crewe Hall, Weston Rd CW1 6UZ
e-mail: crewehall@qhotels.co.uk
web: www.qhotels.co.uk
dir: M6 junct 16 follow A500 to Crewe. Last exit at rdbt onto A5020. 1st exit next rdbt to Crewe. Crewe Hall 150yds on right

Restraint was not in the vocabulary of Victorian architect Edward Barry when he set about rebuilding stately Crewe Hall after a fire sent most of the original 17th-century pile up in smoke. Expect all the pomp of marble fireplaces, oak panelling, fancy plasterwork and stained glass from the man who designed London's Charing Cross Station. But it is not preserved in aspic: this is a 21st-century hotel doing a roaring trade in weddings and conferences, so the slick contemporary brasserie wouldn't look out of place in any big city centre, while the Ranulph restaurant sticks to timeless opulence. The kitchen takes a modern European approach, bringing together potato gnocchi with Blacksticks Blue cheese, quail's egg and truffled emulsion, before an Asian take on sea bass, which comes pan-fried with wilted pak choi, crab, lemongrass and chilli mousse, and ginger soy vinaigrette.

Chef Andrew Hollinshead **Owner** Q Hotels **Times** 12-3/7-10 Closed Mon-Wed, L Thu-Sat, D Sun **Prices** Food prices not confirmed for 2011. Please telephone for details, Service optional **Wines** 40 bottles over £20, 10 bottles under £20, 21 by glass **Notes** Fixed D 5 course incl tea & coffee £45, Sunday L, Vegetarian available, Dress restrictions, Smart casual, Civ Wed 280 **Seats** 40, Pr/dining room 280 **Children** Portions, Menu **Parking** 500

KNUTSFORD Map 15 SJ77

Cottons Hotel & Spa

Modern British NEW

Appealing modern food in contemporary setting

☎ 01565 650333
Manchester Rd WA16 0SU
e-mail: cottons@shireinns.co.uk
dir: On A50, 1m from M6 junct 19

There's a friendly buzz within the cream walls of the Cottons Hotel's Magnolia Restaurant, which scores with a pleasingly clean-cut contemporary décor and an unfussy line in modern cooking to match. The menu plays it sensibly safe with an appealing range of tried-and-tested combinations cooked in a broadly modern British vein, kicking off with anything from seared king scallops with Bury black pudding and minted pea purée, to Moroccan harissa-spiced fresh sardines on toasted bruschetta. Main courses might embrace rump of roast new season lamb perked up with the flavours of garlic and rosemary, and served with wilted spinach and gratin dauphinoise. At dessert, a vanilla pannacotta with poached rhubarb is a great marriage of simple flavours.

Times 12.15-2/7-9.30 Closed L Sat-Sun & BHs

Mere Court Hotel & Conference Centre

Mediterranean

Modern British cooking with lake views

☎ 01565 831000
Warrington Rd, Mere WA16 0RW
e-mail: sales@merecourt.co.uk
web: www.merecourt.co.uk
dir: A50, 1m W of junct with A556, on right

In seven acres of gardens and grounds with a private lake, Mere Court was built in 1903 as a private residence before being reborn as a country-house hotel. Part of the original Arts and Crafts-style house, the fine dining Arboretum Restaurant is resplendent with oak panelling and views across the ornamental lake. Mediterranean influences are apparent in the modern British cookery with the likes of carpaccio of Derbyshire beef with baby capers, shaved parmesan and pickled leaves, and pan-fried trout served with beetroot pasta, asparagus velouté and melange of green vegetables. Rhubarb tarte Tatin and strawberry ice cream brings things to a satisfactory conclusion.

Owner Mr. Chawla **Times** 12-2/7-9.30 **Prices** Fixed L 2 course fr £15.95, Fixed D 3 course fr £19.95, Starter £5.95-£8.95, Main £11.95-£22, Dessert £6.50, Service optional **Notes** Sunday L, Vegetarian available, Dress restrictions, Smart casual, Civ Wed 120 **Seats** 40, Pr/dining room 150 **Children** Portions, Menu **Parking** 150

LYMM Map 15 SJ68

The Church Green

@@@ – *see below*

NANTWICH Map 15 SJ65

Rookery Hall

@@ Modern British

Classic country-house cooking in a handsome Cheshire hall

☎ 01270 610016
Main Rd, Worleston CW5 6DQ
e-mail: rookeryhall@handpicked.co.uk
dir: B5074 off 4th rdbt, on Nantwich by-pass. Hotel 1.5m on right

A sweeping drive leads up to the front of the stone-built Rookery Hall, with its porticoed façade and sumptuous, dark-panelled interiors. Built in the late Georgian era, it's a handsome pile all round, and its modestly sized dining room makes a pleasingly intimate backdrop for the classic country-house cooking on offer. Baked Crottin goats' cheese in filo, served with a tomato and basil salad, is a lighter way to start, but old favourites like scallops and black pudding, or ham hock terrine, are present too. At main course, local beef fillet might come with dauphinoise, roast beetroot, shallots and wild mushroom cream, and the curtain is brought down with something like iced strawberry mousse, served with strawberry doughnuts and whole strawberries poached in champagne.

Times 12-2/7-9.30 Closed L Sat

PECKFORTON Map 15 SJ55

1851 Restaurant at Peckforton Castle

@@ Modern British

Gothic castle serving up imaginative combinations

☎ 01829 260930
Stonehouse Ln CW6 9TN
e-mail: info@peckfortoncastle.co.uk
dir: 15m from Chester, situated near Tarporley

Built in the mid-19th century in the style of a medieval castle, it will come as no surprise to hear that the castle has starred in several films. Converted to a hotel in 1988 and in the Naylor family for five years, it's certainly a memorable location. The gothic splendour takes in a chapel, gatehouse and keep while outside you might encounter a peacock or three. Unsurprisingly Peckforton does a good line in medieval banquets and is a popular wedding venue, but fine dining restaurant 1851 is also a major draw. With a low ceiling, dark heavy curtains and large stone arches, you could be forgiven for expecting the headless lady to pass through between courses. The food is by no means an afterthought here though. Classically trained Stephen Ramsden impresses with balanced flavours and artistic presentation using modern British style as a starting point. Pigeon breast with celeriac and apple pickle, butternut squash purée, candied bacon and corn fritter is well thought out, as is a fresh, sustainable thick-cut cod loin topped with morel crust, sautéed wild mushrooms, Swiss chard, chervil juices and roasted garlic caramel. Cheshire Guernsey Gold yoghurt pannacotta, forced rhubarb soup, Granny Smith granité and frozen cinnamon provide a vibrant finish.

Chef Stephen Ramsden **Owner** Naylor Family **Times** 12-6/6-9 **Prices** Food prices not confirmed for 2011. Please telephone for details **Wines** 21 bottles over £20, 12 bottles under £20, 9 by glass **Notes** Sunday L, Vegetarian available, Civ Wed 180 **Seats** 60, Pr/dining room 165 **Children** Portions, Menu **Parking** 100

PRESTBURY Map 16 SJ87

White House Restaurant

@ Modern British

Bistro cooking with a loyal local following

☎ 01625 829336
SK10 4DG
e-mail: enquiries@thewhitehouseinprestbury.com
dir: Village centre on A538 N of Macclesfield

A long-established and smartly decorated modern restaurant housed in a converted 18th-century farmhouse in the village centre. It has retained a loyal, enthusiastic

The Church Green

LYMM Map 15 SJ68

Modern British

A class act in a refurbished village pub

☎ 01925 752068
WA13 0AP
dir: M6 junct 20 follow signs for Lymm along B5158 after 1.5m turn right at T-junct onto A56 towards Altrincham pub on right after 0.5m

Aiden Byrne is the very model of a modern British chef. He learned his trade under some of the UK's top chefs (Tom Aikens and David Adlard to name but two), he's got a book on the shelves (*Made in Great Britain* shows where his heart lies) and he's done a fair share of telly. And with his wife, Sarah, runs The Church Green, a refreshingly relaxed place, where serious food is not encumbered by a repressive atmosphere. It's all very charming, with the old pub spruced up in neutral tones with plenty of natural wood and open brickwork on display, plus a large conservatory to one side. There's a lounge area with its own menu, served all day, which runs to sandwiches and cooked dishes such as fish and chips and braised ox cheek with caramelised onions and mash. The main restaurant brings forth a range of menus from the Menu of the Day, via full carte to the Surprise Menu, and there's also a children's menu which is as lovingly put together as you'll find anywhere. Byrne's cooking is based on classical principles and top-quality produce (a good deal of it local), and his class shines through in dishes such as beetroot poached salmon with slow-baked beetroot, caviar and orange from the Tasting Menu. Chestnut and apple soup is a beguiling first course from the Menu of the Day; next up, pan-fried silver bream with green olive and celery purée and mussels. A traditional British dessert might be English apple and cinnamon egg custard tart, and there are local artisan cheeses with home-made chutney to boot.

Chef Aiden Byrne **Owner** Aiden Byrne **Times** 12-3/6-9.30 Closed 25 Dec **Prices** Fixed L 2 course £18.50, Tasting menu £68-£98, Starter £10-£14, Main £22-£28, Dessert £5-£6, Service optional **Wines** 42 bottles over £20, 14 bottles under £20, 13 by glass **Notes** Tasting menu 7 or 12 course, Sunday L, Vegetarian available, Dress restrictions, Smart casual preferred **Seats** 50 **Children** Portions, Menu **Parking** available

following, the draw being the modern bistro cooking and the extensive menu choice. 'To commence,' as the menu has it, there might be pressed ham hock terrine with sauce gribiche, or asparagus risotto with poached egg and mustard vinaigrette. Continue with roast rack of lamb with dauphinoise, wilted spinach and a basil lamb jus, or roast cod with olive mash and a pancetta and red wine sauce, and finish with iced raspberry parfait with forest fruit compôte.

Times 12-2/6-9 Closed 25 Dec, 1 Jan, Mon, D Sun

PUDDINGTON **Map 15 SJ37**

Macdonald Craxton Wood

Modern British

Relaxed hotel dining in a leafy setting

☎ 0151 347 4000 & 0844 879 9038
Parkgate Rd, Ledsham CH66 9PB
e-mail: info@craxton.macdonald-hotels.co.uk
dir: from M6 take M56 towards N Wales, then A5117/A540 to Hoylake. Hotel on left 200yds past lights

Standing in 27 acres of mature woodland and well-tended gardens, and approached via a tree-lined drive, the Macdonald Craxton Wood Hotel is a quiet oasis just a short drive away from the centre of historic Chester. The Garden Room restaurant makes the most of the setting, with large windows and an adjoining conservatory looking out over the gardens. The kitchen makes good use of local and organic suppliers and offers a broad range of dishes - a classic Caesar salad with free-range, organic chicken could be followed by 21-day aged Scottish rib-eye steak with all the traditional accoutrements. Finish with dark chocolate tart with honeycomb and vanilla ice cream.

Times 12.30-2/7-9.30 Closed L Sat

SANDIWAY **Map 15 SJ67**

Nunsmere Hall Country House Hotel

British, European

Sumptuous dining room with lake views and modern British food

☎ 01606 889100
Tarporley Rd, Oakmere CW8 2ES
e-mail: reservations@nunsmere.co.uk
dir: M6 junct 18, A54 to Chester, at x-rds with A49 turn left towards Tarporley, hotel 2m on left

Having done a rather splendid job with the design of his house, which dates from the turn of the last century, Sir Aubrey Brocklebank turned his attention to designing the first Queen Mary ocean liner. Bounded on three sides by a 60-acre lake, Nunsmere is a luxurious retreat, where the elegant dining room enjoys views of a sunken Italian garden and the lake, and the tables are set with full-drop cloths. A range of Cheshire and Lancashire suppliers furnishes the kitchen with tip-top produce, which is transformed into a refreshingly straightforward version of modern British cooking. Well-presented dishes might include roast Goosnargh chicken terrine with sautéed foie gras and pickled girolles, and loin of majestic Tarporley venison with cabbage, smoked bacon and pine nuts, sauced with a strong reduction of port and juniper. At dessert, parsnip ice cream outshouts its accompanying crisp apple tart, but incidentals such as canapés and 'home-made dainties' with coffee are up to snuff.

Chef Craig Malone **Owner** Prima Hotels **Times** 12-2/7-10 **Prices** Food prices not confirmed for 2011. Please telephone for details **Wines** 140 bottles over £20, 12 bottles under £20, 8 by glass **Notes** Sunday L, Vegetarian available, Dress restrictions, No jeans, trainers or shorts, Civ Wed 100 **Seats** 60, Pr/dining room 45 **Children** Portions **Parking** 80

TARPORLEY **Map 15 SJ56**

Macdonald Portal Hotel

Modern British

Sophisticated country-club setting for contemporary cuisine

☎ 0844 879 9082
Cobbiers Cross Ln CW6 0DJ
e-mail: general.portal@macdonald-hotels.co.uk
dir: Off A49 in village of Tarporley

With three golf courses on-site, it's no surprise that the game is high on the agenda for many guests at this luxurious modern hotel in rolling Cheshire countryside. There's a full complement of health, fitness and beauty facilities, too. The modish Ranulf Restaurant looks slick in butch tones of tobacco with darkwood tables, romantically candlelit in the evening for the kitchen's straightforward modern cooking. Flavour combinations tend towards the classic, as in a seared breast of wood pigeon with celeriac remoulade and walnut dressing, or a main-course roast saddle of venison teamed with braised red cabbage, fondant potato, parsnip purée and thyme jus.

Owner Macdonald Hotels **Times** 6-9.30 Closed L all week **Prices** Fixed D 3 course £16-£25, Starter £6.25-£8.50, Main £10-£19.95, Dessert £5-£7.50, Service optional **Wines** 25 bottles over £20, 5 bottles under £20, 12 by glass **Notes** Early bird available before 7pm, Vegetarian available, Dress restrictions, Smart casual **Seats** 100 **Children** Portions, Menu

WILMSLOW **Map 16 SJ88**

Stanneylands Hotel

Modern European

Modern cooking in country-house hotel

☎ 01625 525225
Stanneylands Rd SK9 4EY
e-mail: enquiries@stanneylandshotel.co.uk
dir: from M56 at airport turn off, follow signs to Wilmslow. Left into Station Rd, onto Stanneylands Rd. Hotel on right

Set in four acres of attractive grounds, this traditional country-house hotel is handy for Manchester airport and the city centre. The spruce dining room has elegant panelled walls and is a suitably refined setting for the ambitious modern European cooking. There is a choice of contemporarily done out lounges for a pre-dinner drink. Start with duck marinated in ras el hanout and served up with chargrilled courgette and feta salad with a mint yoghurt dressing or a salad of red mullet and orange with a citrus emulsion. Main-courses range from pan-fried brill with a lentil ragoût, Parmentier potatoes and a lime vinaigrette to a vegetarian option such as Thai chick pea curry with coconut rice. For dessert, Baileys rice pudding with poached pear, mulled wine syrup and black pepper tuile catches the eye.

Chef Carl North **Owner** Mr L Walshe **Times** 12.30-2.30/7-9.45 **Prices** Fixed L 2 course £9.95-£12.95, Fixed D 3 course £19.95-£31.50, Starter £7-£12, Main £16-£23, Dessert £6.95-£7.95, Service optional **Wines** 108 bottles over £20, 31 bottles under £20, 18 by glass **Notes** Sunday L, Vegetarian available, Dress restrictions, Smart casual, Civ Wed 100 **Seats** 60, Pr/dining room 120 **Children** Portions, Menu **Parking** 110

CORNWALL & ISLES OF SCILLY

BODMIN **Map 2 SX06**

Trehellas House Hotel & Restaurant

Modern European

Local produce in a former Cornish courthouse

☎ 01208 72700
Washaway PL30 3AD
e-mail: enquiries@trehellashouse.co.uk
dir: Take A389 from Bodmin towards Wadebridge. Hotel on right 0.5m beyond road to Camelford

Just off the A389 between Bodmin and Wadebridge, Trehellas is a stone-built former courthouse dating from the early 18th century. Within the low-ceilinged, timbered dining room with its smartly dressed tables, some gently adventurous European cooking is offered. Consider fried scallops with Parma ham in hazelnut and coriander butter, before duck breast and red cabbage with couscous in a honey and balsamic reduction. Cornish cheeses and local ice creams and sorbets await, or you might opt for something along the more elaborate lines of banana and honey bread-and-butter pudding with bourbon crème anglaise.

Chef Tim Parsons **Owner** Alistair & Debra Hunter **Times** 12-2/6.30-9 **Prices** Fixed L 2 course £21-£40, Starter £5-£14, Main £12-£25, Dessert £6-£9, Service included **Wines** 7 bottles over £20, 24 bottles under £20, 6 by glass **Notes** Sunday L, Vegetarian available **Seats** 40 **Children** Portions, Menu **Parking** 25

BOSCASTLE Map 2 SX09

The Wellington Hotel

Modern British

Imaginative cooking in popular Cornish fishing village

☎ 01840 250202
The Harbour PL35 0AQ
e-mail: info@boscastle-wellington.com
dir: A30/A395 at Davidstowe follow Boscastle signs. B3266 to village. Right into Old Rd

The 'Welly' has had its share of time under the media spotlights over the last decade: the Boscastle floods in 2004 were a low point, but coverage in BBC's *Changing Rooms* makeover series gave the old place a contemporary design spin with a heritage colour scheme. Boscastle is back to its old self nowadays, while this venerable 16th-century turreted coaching inn goes about the business it knows best - making sure visitors are well-fed and watered. Chef Scott Roberts goes about his work with flair and dexterity, whether he's serving roast scallops with buttered haggis, crispy ham and balsamic, or braised pork belly with apple fritters, courgettes and cream. The food takes its cue from French and British, old and new themes, while the ingredients are as local as possible. Mains might feature seared fillet steak together with a veal shin burger, caraway dauphinoise, onion confit, beetroot purée and marrow.

Chef Scott Roberts **Owner** Paul Roberts **Times** 6.30-9.30 Closed Thu **Prices** Starter £5.50-£10, Main £11-£22, Dessert £6-£8.50, Service optional **Wines** 20 bottles over £20, 48 bottles under £20, 8 by glass **Notes** Tasting menu available with advance notice **Seats** 35, Pr/dining room 28 **Children** Portions, Menu **Parking** 15

BUDE Map 2 SS20

The Castle Restaurant

Modern European

Ambitious cooking in bistro with sea views

☎ 01288 350543
The Wharf EX23 8LG
e-mail: enquiries@thecastlerestaurantbude.co.uk
dir: From A39 into Bude onto mini-rdbt straight ahead along 'The Crescent'. Then 1st right towards The Castle Heritage Centre. Restaurant within centre.

This unpretentious and relaxed bistro with superb sea views shares its castellated home with a museum and art gallery. The simple style of unclothed wooden tables, local artwork on the walls and an open kitchen is matched by the unfussy cooking and friendly, attentive service. Dishes on the weekly changing menu let well-sourced ingredients speak for themselves and there is a lightness of touch in the kitchen. A meal starting with scallops with Jerusalem artichokes, followed by roast pollock with braised oxtail, could finish with a classic crème brûlée. A seven-course tasting menu is also available.

The Castle Restaurant

Chef Kit Davis **Owner** Kit Davis **Times** 12-2.30/6-9.30 Closed D Sun **Prices** Fixed L 2 course £10.50-£12.50, Fixed D 2 course £19.50, Starter £5-£8, Main £12-£25, Dessert £5-£6, Service optional **Wines** 4 bottles over £20, 15 bottles under £20, 7 by glass **Notes** Tasting menu available, Sunday L, Vegetarian available, Civ Wed 120 **Seats** 40, Pr/dining room 25 **Children** Portions, Menu **Parking** Parking nearby

CALLINGTON Map 3 SX36

Langmans Restaurant

Modern British

Stylish restaurant serving contemporary food in a multitude of courses

☎ 01579 384933
3 Church St PL17 7RE
e-mail: dine@langmansrestaurant.co.uk
dir: From the direction of Plymouth into town centre, left at lights and second right into Church St

This Grade II listed former bakery is the place to head to for a relaxed fine-dining experience delivered via a multi-course tasting menu. It's all very charming on the inside with mellow yellow tones on the walls and tables laid with crisp white linen and quality glassware. The husband-and-wife-team lead from the front and have created a pleasingly unpretentious environment for the ambitious, confident cooking. The seven-course tasting menu follows the seasons, changing every four weeks, and there is plenty of local produce on show. Things might begin with tea-smoked duck breast with Jerusalem artichoke, Puy lentils and crackling, before a fish course such as wild sea bass and shellfish risotto. Fillet of Cornish beef comes with a port and shallot sauce, plus ceps purée, dauphinoise potatoes and purple sprouting broccoli, and for dessert (where there's a choice), perhaps an apple tart with vanilla ice cream.

Chef Anton Buttery **Owner** Anton & Gail Buttery **Times** 7.30 Closed Sun-Wed, L all week **Prices** Tasting menu £35, Service optional **Wines** 50 bottles over £20, 34 bottles under £20, 11 by glass **Notes** Tasting menu 6 course, Vegetarian available, Dress restrictions, Smart casual preferred **Seats** 24 **Parking** Town centre car park

FALMOUTH Map 2 SW83

Best Western Penmere Manor Hotel

Modern French, European V

Modern seasonal cooking in charming Georgian hotel

☎ 01326 211411
Mongleath Rd TR11 4PN
e-mail: reservations@penmere.co.uk
dir: Turn right off A39 at Hillhead rdbt, over double mini rdbt. After 0.75m left into Mongleath Rd

Penmere Manor offers country-house dining, with a comfortable lounge where a nightly pianist adds to the experience. Dating back to Georgian times, the house sits in five acres of well-groomed grounds. The restaurant is laid out formally with linen-clad tables but service is extremely friendly at the hands of a well-established team. The kitchen makes good use of local seasonal produce to create simple dishes skilfully prepared. Try Cornish scallops with crisp prosciutto and orange salad to start followed by Cornish game stew and herb mash. The bar is the place to head to for ham, egg and chips or a ploughman's.

Chef Joe Lado Devesa **Owner** Nick Moore **Times** 7-9.30 Closed 21-26 Dec, L all week **Prices** Food prices not confirmed for 2011. Please telephone for details **Wines** 20 bottles over £20, 16 bottles under £20, 9 by glass **Notes** Vegetarian menu, Civ Wed 70 **Seats** 80, Pr/dining room 40 **Children** Portions, Menu **Parking** 60

Falmouth Hotel

Modern British V

Victorian coastal hotel with aspirational cooking

☎ 01326 312671
Castle Beach TR11 4NZ
e-mail: reservations@falmouthhotel.com
dir: A30 to Truro then A390 to Falmouth. Follow signs for beaches, hotel on seafront near Pendennis Castle

Occupying pole position on the Falmouth coast, this Victorian hotel overlooks Pendennis Castle, the sandy beaches and the sea. In the Trelawney dining room, model ships and maritime pictures remind you where you are, and the approach is fairly formal. Skilled, aspirational cooking draws on the plentiful produce of Cornwall and the southwest for dishes such as seared pigeon breast with celeriac remoulade and beetroot jus, roast neck and braised belly of local lamb with spectacularly intense artichoke purée, and fish dishes like grilled brill fillet with garlic-sautéed potatoes in olive and dill velouté. Local cheeses or banoffee crème brûlée end things well.

Chef Paul Brennan **Owner** Richardson Hotels of Distinction **Times** 12-2/6.45-8.45 Closed L Sat **Prices** Food prices not confirmed for 2011. Please telephone for details **Wines** 21 bottles over £20, 29 bottles under £20, 7 by glass **Notes** Sunday L, Vegetarian menu, Dress restrictions, Smart casual, no sportswear, Civ Wed 250 **Seats** 150, Pr/dining room 40 **Children** Portions, Menu

Harbourside Restaurant

Modern British

Regionally-based cooking with sweeping harbour views

01326 312440
The Greenbank, Harbourside TR11 2SR
e-mail: sales@greenbank-hotel.co.uk
web: www.greenbank-hotel.co.uk
dir: Approaching Falmouth from Penryn, take left along North Parade. Follow sign to Falmouth Marina and Greenbank Hotel

Spacious and comfortable with a laid-back ambience, the light-drenched Greenbank Hotel bathes in sweeping views across Falmouth harbour. In keeping with the watery location, the kitchen majors in fish and seafood, served in a clean-cut contemporary restaurant with vast picture windows giving wide-angle views across the bay. An extensive menu delivers well-tuned modern food, kicking off with crisp-fried Cornish crab risotto balls with pickled beetroot and tomato relish; main course delivers a whole grilled lemon sole served simply with sautéed potatoes and seasonal salad, while a chargrilled rib-eye of West Country beef with dripping-fried chips and Madeira sauce should catch a meat eater's eye.

Chef Prosenjit Bhattacharya **Owner** Greenbank Hotel (Falmouth) Ltd **Times** 12-2/7-9.15 **Prices** Food prices not confirmed for 2011. Please telephone for details **Wines** 20 bottles over £20, 42 bottles under £20, 10 by glass **Notes** Fixed L 3 course, Sunday L, Dress restrictions, Smart casual, Civ Wed 90 **Seats** 60, Pr/dining room 16 **Children** Portions **Parking** 60

The Terrace Restaurant

Modern International

Flexible approach in a grand seaside hotel

01326 313042
The Royal Duchy Hotel, Cliff Rd TR11 4NX
e-mail: info@royalduchy.co.uk
dir: on Cliff Rd, along Falmouth seafront

The pale grey hotel with its balustraded terraces occupies a prime position on the Falmouth seafront, overlooking the bay. Pendennis Castle lurks in the middle distance. As in the most alluring seaside hotels, there is a deeply agreeable air of times gone by, of grandeur worn lightly, and of proper relaxation not often found in big-city hotels. In the Terrace Restaurant, which opens up at the front in the summer months, the mood is complete, with friendly, attentive staff and a range of dishes that can be taken in starter or main-course sizes. Sea bass Niçoise salad, local mussels in cider with celery, apple and focaccia, or smoked chicken Caesar, with quail eggs, anchovies and croûtons, are the kinds of things to expect. Then treat yourself to warm chocolate tart with sour cherry ice cream.

Times 12.30-2/6.30-9 Closed L Mon-Sat

FOWEY **Map 2 SX15**

The Fowey Hotel

Modern European V

Modern European food with calming harbour views

01726 832551
The Esplanade PL23 1HX
e-mail: info@thefoweyhotel.co.uk
dir: A30 to Okehampton, continue to Bodmin. Then B3269 to Fowey for 1m, on right bend left junct then right into Dagands Rd. Hotel 200mtrs on left

Fowey is a great little town for a saunter, its crooked houses and shops tumbling towards the water in a beautifully unspoiled setting. This expansive Victorian hotel looks like lord of all it surveys, and indeed the dining room makes the most of those calming harbour views. An uncontroversial modern European style of cooking based on locally-sourced materials brings on main dishes such as seared bream with fennel confit, basil and balsamic, or guinea fowl with Savoy cabbage and pancetta in a red wine sauce, bookended perhaps by gravad lax and buttermilk pannacotta in orange syrup.

Chef Mark Griffiths **Owner** Keith Richardson **Times** 12-3/6.30-9 **Prices** Fixed D 3 course £35, Starter £8.95, Main £18.95, Dessert £7.95, Service optional **Wines** 14 bottles over £20, 29 bottles under £20, 7 by glass **Notes** Sunday L, Vegetarian menu, Dress restrictions, Smart casual, no torn denim, trainers, shorts, Civ Wed 120 **Seats** 60 **Children** Portions, Menu **Parking** 20

Hansons

British, French

Accomplished cuisine in plush family-friendly surroundings

01726 833866
Fowey Hall Hotel, Hanson Dr PL23 1ET
e-mail: info@foweyhall.com
dir: Into town centre, pass school on right, 400yds turn right onto Hanson Drive

A strong family focus sets the tone at Fowey Hall, a grandiose Victorian château-style country house perched above Fowey harbour, with sweeping views over the estuary to the rugged coast and sea beyond. Allegedly the inspiration for Toad Hall in the children's classic *Wind in the Willows*, it is apt that the place is run with a family-friendly ethos. It is, however, a very grown-up hotel, fully-loaded with all the ingredients for a thorough blowout: antiques, chandeliers and oodles of style. There's a spa too, and after the kids are sorted out with nannies and baby-listening services, the classy adults-only Hansons restaurant is the place for romantic dining amid gilt-framed mirrors, oak panels and flooring. The kitchen is firing on all cylinders, sourcing the best Cornish materials, which are handled with a serious level of skill and brought together in intelligent combinations in its creative contemporary take on the country-house idiom. Pigeon breast with cep risotto might open proceedings, before equally forthright mains - whole roast partridge with wild mushrooms and blackberry jus, say - with comforting desserts such as vanilla and gingerbread cheesecake with blueberry ice cream.

Times 12-2.15/7-10

The Old Quay House Hotel

British, French

Fresh local produce overlooking the Fowey estuary

01726 833302
28 Fore St PL23 1AQ
e-mail: info@theoldquayhouse.com
web: www.theoldquayhouse.com
dir: From A390 through Lostwithiel, take left onto B3269 to Fowey town centre, on right next to Lloyds TSB bank

The white-fronted Victorian building was once a customs-house, and faces the river at Fowey, where it has become a fine dining destination for this part of

continued

FOWEY *continued*

Cornwall. Boutique styling within makes for a contemporary feel, with mosaic tiles on the dining room walls a striking feature. A strong approach to fresh local food is maintained, and menus are well aligned to modern European style. Honeyed coppa with potato and shallot salad, and an egg that has been poached and then quickly deep-fried, is a thought-provoking starter. Mains might take in bistro-style Angus sirloin with frites and Café de Paris butter, but there is a strong emphasis on seafood too, perhaps in red mullet with saffron potatoes and bouillabaisse sauce. Finish with rhubarb trifle served in a glass, along with a rhubarb sorbet.

Chef Ben Bass **Owner** Jane & Roy Carson
Times 12.30-2.30/7-9 Closed 1 month in winter, L Mon-Fri (Oct-May) **Prices** Food prices not confirmed for 2011. Please telephone for details **Wines** 15 bottles over £20, 15 bottles under £20, 5 by glass **Notes** Sunday L, Vegetarian available, Civ Wed 40 **Seats** 38

GOLANT Map 2 SX15

Cormorant Hotel and Restaurant

Modern British

Fine modern British food with sumptuous river views

☎ 01726 833426
PL23 1LL
e-mail: relax@cormoranthotel.co.uk
dir: A390 onto B3269 signed Fowey. In 3m left to Golant, through village to end of road, hotel on right

The setting is fabulous - perched on a hill with stunning views across the River Fowey. You get the expansive views from formal clothed tables in the restaurant, or can get even closer with a table on the terrace on sunny days. Well-drilled service and a light, airy feel add gloss to proceedings, and so does the adventurous cooking. Flair and consistency distinguish dishes such as a beautifully presented terrine of chicken confit with baby leek and mushrooms served with onion marmalade, or a tender, moist and full-flavoured roast loin and confit leg of wild rabbit. To finish, try an intense coconut flavoured pannacotta served with seared mango and basil salad.

Chef Martin Adams **Owner** Mrs Mary Tozer
Times 12.30-2.30/6.30-9.30 Closed Jan, L Mon-Tue (summer) **Prices** Tasting menu £55, Starter £8-£12, Main £18-£23, Dessert £9, Service optional, Groups min 7 service 12% **Wines** 41 bottles over £20, 30 bottles under £20, 8 by glass **Notes** Tasting menu 6 course, Vegetarian available, Dress restrictions, Smart casual, no shorts **Seats** 30 **Children** Portions **Parking** 18

HELSTON Map 2 SW62

New Yard Restaurant

Modern British

Serious commitment to local food in an 18th-century stable yard

☎ 01326 221595
Trelowarren Estate, Mawgan TR12 6AF
e-mail: kirsty.newyardrestaurant@trelowarren.com
dir: 5m from Helston

Sir Ferrers Vyvyan inherited his family's 1,000-acre Trelowarren estate at the heart of the Lizard Peninsula in 1995, and embraced the 21st century with an eco-friendly, self-sufficient, carbon-neutral ethos. The estate's restaurant occupies a converted carriage house in the stable yard, a bright, buzzy space with tables made of local ash. Sir Ferrers learned how to keep guests happy when he waited on tables here: a cursory glance at the

The Well House Hotel

LISKEARD Map 2 SX26

Modern European V

Culinary hideaway in a tranquil valley

☎ 01579 342001
St Keyne PL14 4RN
e-mail: enquiries@wellhouse.co.uk
dir: From Liskeard on A38 take B3254 to St Keyne (3m). At church fork left, hotel 0.5m down hill on left

The Victorian tea planter who built his country house among the secluded pleats of the Looe Valley had a keen eye for a plum location. Little did he know that a century later the hoi polloi would be queuing not far away in their overheated horseless carriages to gain entrance to the Eden Project's futuristic dome. Modern guests remain mercifully oblivious too, as nothing disturbs the peaceful tinkle of afternoon teacups ringing out on the terrace, guarded by a green and pleasant English idyll of buxom hills and meadows all around. It's hard to think of a more completely tranquil hidey-hole, in an unstuffy smallscale country-house ministered to by attentive and friendly staff. The neutral tones of the smart contemporary restaurant make a fitting backdrop for displays of sculpture and fine art. Tom Hunter is the inventive young spirit at the stoves, with a personal passion for sourcing superb ingredients as the building blocks of his precise and polished modern European cooking. The tersely-worded menu descriptions don't give away much, but what arrives on the plate is always intelligently conceived and realised with panache - perhaps a winning combination of seared scallops with spring pea risotto and mint oil, followed by turbot in the company of samphire, brown shrimps and saffron, while local meat aficionados might go for roast loin and shoulder of Cornish lamb with seasonal vegetables and roasted garlic.

Chef Tom Hunter **Owner** R A & D A Farrow
Times 12-3.30/6.30-10.30 **Prices** Fixed L 2 course £18.50, Fixed D 3 course £37.50, Tasting menu £42.50, Service optional **Wines** 79 bottles over £20, 39 bottles under £20, 6 by glass **Notes** Tasting menu 6 course, Sunday L, Vegetarian menu, Civ Wed 70 **Seats** 26 **Children** Menu **Parking** 30

menu shows minimal food miles - 90% of what's on your plate is sourced from within a 10-mile radius - and the kitchen keeps things simple, fresh and vibrant. Pan-fried pigeon breasts with orange salad and pomegranate molasses might start things off, while Cornish venison loin with buttered kale and chocolate oil, or roasted monkfish with Jerusalem artichoke and oxtail ravioli showcase the area's top-class fish and meat.

Chef Olly Jackson **Owner** Sir Ferrers Vyvyan **Times** 12-2/7-9 Closed Mon (mid Sep-Whitsun), D Sun **Prices** Fixed L 2 course fr £15.95, Fixed D 3 course fr £23.50, Starter £5.95-£8.95, Main £12.95-£18.95, Dessert £5.50-£6.75, Service optional **Wines** 29 bottles over £20, 28 bottles under £20, 6 by glass **Notes** Sunday L, Vegetarian available, Dress restrictions, Smart casual **Seats** 50 **Children** Portions **Parking** 20

LISKEARD — Map 2 SX26

The Well House Hotel

◎◎◎ – *see opposite page*

LOOE — Map 2 SX25

Barclay House

◎◎ Modern British

Relaxed dining with river views

☎ 01503 262929
St Martin's Rd PL13 1LP
e-mail: info@barclayhouse.co.uk
dir: 1st house on left on entering Looe from A38

Surrounded by six acres of grounds, this whitewashed Victorian House stands above this Cornish town overlooking the harbour and across the estuary and the East Looe River. The hotel's bright and contemporary restaurant has a plum spot at the front of the house, and when the doors open out onto the terrace for pre-dinner aperitifs, there's no better place to be. Candlelight brings a charming atmosphere in the evening, with wooden tables and vibrant local art on the walls. The daily-changing menu delivers what's best and in season locally from sea and land. Take seared Looe scallops with celeriac and apple purée, pea shoots, curry oil and black pudding, or from the land, perhaps Treweers Farm fillet steak with duck fat chips and béarnaise sauce.

Chef Benjamin Palmer **Owner** Malcolm, Graham & Gill Brooks **Times** 12-3.30/7-9 Closed 24-26 Dec, Sun in winter, L winter by arrangement only **Prices** Fixed D 4 course £25, Starter £6.95-£9.95, Main £14.95-£23.95, Dessert £5.95-£9.95, Service added but optional 10% **Wines** 41 bottles over £20, 12 bottles under £20, 18 by glass **Notes** Sunday L, Vegetarian available, Dress restrictions, Smart casual, Civ Wed 120 **Seats** 50 **Children** Portions, Menu **Parking** 25

Trelaske Hotel & Restaurant

◎ Modern, Traditional British

Locally-sourced produce in verdant Cornwall

☎ 01503 262159
Polperro Rd PL13 2JS
e-mail: info@trelaske.co.uk
dir: Over Looe bridge signed Polperro. After 1.9m signed on right

In the rolling Cornish hinterland between Looe and Polperro, this whitewashed modern hotel sits in four acres of verdant grounds where fruit, vegetables and herbs for the restaurant are grown year-round in poly-tunnels. Run by hands-on owners, it's the personal and attentive service that raises Trelaske above the herd - that and the kitchen's accomplished modern British cooking. An old favourite turns up to start - richly-flavoured potted beef, with horseradish cream, apple and cress, followed by loin of Trewithen Estate venison, braised red cabbage and parsnip purée and crisps. Fish fans might be treated to brill, fresh off the Looe day boats that very morning, and served with wild mushroom fricassée and mint pesto.

Chef Ross Lewin **Owner** Ross Lewin & Hazel Billington **Times** 12-2/7-9 **Prices** Food prices not confirmed for 2011. Please telephone for details **Wines** 11 bottles over £20, 23 bottles under £20, 32 by glass **Notes** Sunday L, Vegetarian available, Dress restrictions, Smart casual **Seats** 70 **Children** Portions **Parking** 60

MARAZION — Map 2 SW53

Mount Haven Hotel & Restaurant

◎◎ Modern British

Ambitious modern cookery on the Cornish coast

☎ 01736 710249
Turnpike Rd TR17 0DQ
e-mail: reception@mounthaven.co.uk
dir: From centre of Marazion, up hill E, hotel 400yds on right

Just along the coast from Penzance, this smart converted coach-house hotel overlooks the bay with the majestic hulk of St Michael's Mount rising from it. The decorative touches inside are full of originality, an Asian theme predominating in the various figurines, ornamental caskets and tapestries on display, while the dining room is a predominantly white, airy space with a wood floor. A fair indication of the ambitious modern cooking might be had from a meal that takes in fillets of John Dory with herb gnocchi, a quail's egg and samphire, followed by loin of Gloucestershire Old Spot pork with braised leeks, capers and gherkins in Madeira sauce, and closing with banana tarte Tatin with hazelnut ice cream.

Times 12-2.30/6.30-10.30 Closed mid Dec-mid Feb

MAWGAN PORTH — Map 2 SW86

Bedruthan Steps Hotel

◎ Modern British

Vibrant cooking with panoramic ocean views

☎ 01637 860555 & 860860
TR8 4BU
e-mail: stay@bedruthan.com
dir: From A39/A30 follow signs to Newquay Airport. Turn right at T-junct to Mawgan Porth. Hotel at top of hill on left

Bedruthan Steps overlooks a stupendous North Cornish beach at Mawgan Porth, a location tailor-made for de-stressing with soothing sea-gazing views all day long, from breakfast through to sundowner aperitifs before dinner in the contemporary-style restaurant. It's a family-friendly place where the kids can surf in the waves, and a hammam spa takes care of adult pampering. Food-wise, the kitchen takes a suitably modern British tack with an output that is built on mostly West Country produce. Tuck into cider-soused gurnard, sardines and clams with locally-picked sea purslane, then hay-baked rump of lamb with haricot bean cassoulet, white wine and rosemary jus, and finish with banana sticky toffee pudding and Cornish crème fraîche.

Times 12-2/7.30-9.30 Closed Xmas

The Scarlet Hotel

◎◎ Modern European NEW

Eco-friendly hotel with highly-skilled contemporary cooking

☎ 01637 861800
Tredragon Rd TR8 4DQ
e-mail: stay@scarlethotel.co.uk
dir: Follow signs for Newquay Airport on A3059. Just after garage turn right signed St Mawgan & Airport. After airport, right at T-junct signed Padstow (B3276). At Mawgan Porth turn left half way up hill at red Scarlet sign. Hotel 250yds on left

The ethos of this award-winning newly-built hotel is that luxury and eco-friendly sustainability are not mutually exclusive. The stealth design camouflages the structure against the cliff at Mawgan Porth; once inside, the world is full of sea and sky. Light bathes everything through floor-to-ceiling windows with the sleek minimal look of an art gallery - not surprising given the splashes of colourful art that relieve the neutral décor; curvy furniture adds a retro Scandinavian feel. The in-crowd won't be disturbed by children: the hotel is an adults-only bolthole. Chef Ben Tunnicliffe's cooking is grown-up stuff too, served in a luminous dining room done out in gâteau colours of chocolate, cherry and cream. His food is about flavour foremost, simplicity second and aesthetics last. A well-constructed starter of paupiette of sole is teamed with a warm salad of mussels, clams and potatoes; the same sense of balance runs through a breast and braised wing of chicken with foie gras, purple sprouting broccoli and

continued

MAWGAN PORTH ***continued***

Madeira sauce. Dessert brings superb textures, in a perfect peanut parfait with bread-and-butter pudding, crème anglaise and crunchy candied peanuts.

Chef Ben Tunnicliffe **Owner** Red Hotels Ltd
Times 12-2/7-9.30 Closed 4 Jan-12 Feb **Prices** Fixed L 3 course £19.75, Starter £7-£11, Main £12.75-£23, Dessert £7-£8, Service included **Wines** 57 bottles over £20, 3 bottles under £20, 32 by glass **Notes** Sunday L, Vegetarian available, Civ Wed 74 **Seats** 70, Pr/dining room 16 **Parking** 37

MAWNAN SMITH Map 2 SW72

Budock Vean - The Hotel on the River

British V

Opulent Cornish setting for modern British cooking

01326 252100 & 250288
TR11 5LG
e-mail: relax@budockvean.co.uk
dir: from A39 follow tourist signs to Trebah Gardens. 0.5m to hotel

Set in 65 acres of organic, sub-tropical garden (this is Cornwall after all), Budock Vean is a traditional country-house hotel with expansive dining room, a sun terrace and conservatory as dining choices. A good local following pours in for the locally based, modern British cooking, seen in menu options such as a salad of duck egg with sautéed potatoes, bacon and white pudding, and roast veal fillet with robust dauphinoise and a wild mushroom cream sauce. A choice of soup or sorbet intervenes, and meals end with the likes of strawberry and kiwi vacherin.

Chef Darren Kelly **Owner** Barlow Family
Times 12-2.30/7.30-9 Closed 3 wks Jan, L Mon-Sat **Prices** Fixed D 4 course £39, Starter £8.15-£18.75, Main £15.50-£35, Dessert £6, Service optional **Wines** 55 bottles over £20, 39 bottles under £20, 7 by glass **Notes** Sunday L, Vegetarian menu, Dress restrictions, Jacket & tie, Civ Wed 60 **Seats** 100, Pr/dining room 40 **Children** Portions, Menu **Parking** 100

MOUSEHOLE Map 2 SW42

The Cornish Range Restaurant with Rooms

Modern British

The best local seafood in charming village restaurant

01736 731488
6 Chapel St TR19 6SB
e-mail: info@cornishrange.co.uk
web: www.cornishrange.co.uk
dir: From Penzance 3m S to Mousehole, via Newlyn. Follow road to far side of harbour

Mousehole is a pretty coastal village that packs in the tourists in the summer. Down one of its quaintly narrow roads (best to park at the top of the village or by the harbour), you'll find this charming restaurant, once a factory for salting and packing the local catch of pilchards, and these days still earning its crust from the fruits of the sea, albeit in a more refined manner. It looks more like a quaint cottage than a former industrial building and inside it is smartly done out in neutral, contemporary tones with a decidedly seafaring theme in the local artworks. It's open for brunch from 10am (pop in for a locally-smoked kipper, maybe) and then the restaurant menu kicks in, bringing forth a modern British repertoire that runs from crispy monkfish and sesame king prawns with sweet chilli jam, to fillets of gurnard served with seared scallops and potatoes braised with bacon, onion and Cornish cheddar. There's meat and vegetarian options, too.

The Cornish Range Restaurant with Rooms

Chef Keith Terry **Owner** Chad James & Keith Terry
Times 10-2.15/6-9.30 **Prices** Food prices not confirmed for 2011. Please telephone for details **Wines** 13 bottles over £20, 19 bottles under £20, 6 by glass
Notes Vegetarian available **Seats** 42 **Children** Portions, Menu **Parking** Harbour car park

NEWQUAY Map 2 SW86

Sand Brasserie

Modern British

Locally-sourced cooking with majestic sea views

01637 872211
Headland Hotel, Fistral Beach TR7 1EW
e-mail: management@headlandhotel.co.uk
dir: A30 onto A392 towards Newquay, follow signs to Fistral Beach, hotel is adjacent

A grand old building perched on a clifftop overlooking Fistral beach, the Headland surveys the foaming brine with an air of unruffled majesty. A pair of sculpted mussels dominates the Sand Brasserie, where locally-sourced fish and seafood, as well as pedigree meats, form the backbone of the Mediterranean-influenced menus. An intricate terrine of duck breast, liver and leg confit is sweetly offset with orange and honey dressings, while mains might offer lamb ragout with chorizo, tomato and garlic, or a chunky seafood mixed grill with pea purée and double-fried chips. Good dessert ideas include coconut rice pudding with star anise ice cream and pineapple compôte.

Chef Nick Hodges **Owner** John & Carolyn Armstrong
Times 12.30-2.30/6.30-9.45 Closed 25-26 Dec, L Mon-Sat **Prices** Fixed D 3 course £26.95, Service optional **Wines** 79 bottles over £20, 51 bottles under £20, 13 by glass **Notes** Sunday L, Vegetarian available, Civ Wed 200 **Seats** 250, Pr/dining room 40 **Children** Portions, Menu **Parking** 200

PADSTOW Map 2 SW97

Custard

British NEW

Funky Cornish diner with a heart-warming menu

01841 532565
1a The Strand PL28 8AJ
e-mail: info@custardpadstow.com

As its name might suggest, there's a sense of light-hearted funky fun in this retro-styled eatery in the heart of Padstow. An eclectic décor evokes rose-tinted English nostalgia with a casual vintage look - touches of Cath Kidston, a juke box, an old Philips radio, a toy cabinet and a sideboard with jars of sweeties - all in a high-ceilinged loft-style venue with broad oak floorboards and button-backed caramel leather banquettes. A certain Mr Stein has set the culinary bar high in Padstow, so you have to come up with the goods to cut it here. Luckily, the chef is ex-Seafood Restaurant (see entry) so knows a thing or two about freshness, clear flavours and where to get his hands on the best local produce. A punchy duo of olive tapenade and devilled tomatoes make deeply-satisfying partners for fresh grilled sardines, ahead of a straight-up grilled rump steak with roasted tomatoes and chips. Sticky sherry poured over ice cream with honeycomb biscuits makes a great finale.

Chef Dan Gedge **Owner** Vanessa Pinto
Times 12-2.30/7-10 Closed 25-26 Dec, 1 May, Mon (winter only), D Sun **Prices** Starter £5.95-£7.95, Main £11.95-£18.95, Dessert £5-£8.50, Service optional **Wines** 24 bottles over £20, 6 bottles under £20, 6 by glass **Notes** Sunday L, Vegetarian available, Air con **Seats** 65 **Children** Portions, Menu

Margot's

British

Friendly family-run bistro with a genuine local flavour

01841 533441
11 Duke St PL28 8AB
e-mail: enquiries@margots.co.uk

A characterful shop front down one of Padstow's busy side streets is the setting for this intimate French-style bistro. It is family run, informal and, with only nine tables, it's wise to book. Local paintings hang on the walls and local produce fills the menu; expect plenty of fresh seafood and vegetables and salads from nearby growers. A typical meal may take in local crab soup with cream and chives, a meaty main course of confit duck leg with spring onion mash and sage cream sauce, or a simply grilled lemon sole, and pannacotta with baked plums for pudding. Service is genuinely friendly and the chef-proprietor likes to pop out of his kitchen from time to time, and might even bring your food to the table.

Times 12-2/7-9 Closed Nov, Jan, Sun-Mon

The Metropole

Modern British

Modern British cooking with commanding views of Padstow

01841 532486
Station Rd PL28 8DB
e-mail: info@the-metropole.co.uk
web: www.richardsonhotels.co.uk
dir: M5/A30 past Launceston, follow signs for Wadebridge and N Cornwall. Then take A39 and follow signs for Padstow

The hotel commands panoramic views over everybody's favourite north Cornish fishing town, as well as the Camel estuary. Indeed, it looks like just about the grandest building in Padstow. Within the Victorian splendour of the dining room, with its crisp white linen and well-drilled service, a version of complex modern British cooking scores some hits. Seafood is strong, as in a sea bream starter that comes with stewed chorizo and chick peas, while mains might include two cuts of pork, pan-roasted tenderloin and braised belly, with a savoury apple tart, creamed cabbage and bacon, and Calvados jus. Spotted Dick and custard gets an outing at dessert stage.

Chef Adam Warne **Owner** Richardson Hotels Ltd
Times 6.30-9.00 Closed L Mon-Sat **Prices** Fixed L 2 course £23-£23.50, Fixed D 2 course £36.45, Service included **Wines** 21 bottles over £20, 26 bottles under £20, 8 by glass **Notes** Sunday L, Vegetarian available, Dress restrictions, No jeans, shorts, swimwear, trainers **Seats** 70 **Children** Portions, Menu **Parking** 40

Paul Ainsworth at No. 6

Modern British

Confident cooking in smart townhouse

01841 532093
6 Middle St PL28 8AP
e-mail: enquiries@number6inpadstow.co.uk
dir: A30 follow signs for Wadebridge then sign to Padstow

A Victorian townhouse with a shady past as a smugglers' den, No. 6 these days cuts a dash and satisfies contemporary sensibilities with its classy demeanour and cooking that takes the classics as a solid foundation and adds a bit of modern fizz. There's been a change in approach since the previous edition of the guide, a shift away from the fine dining end of the spectrum to a more mellow, relaxed approach across the board, and it works a treat. The attractively contemporary dining room fits this mood and there's chilled out music too. The food looks good on the plate and the main ingredient is given room to shine, and there's certainly no stinting when it comes to sourcing first-class produce. Dave Thommason scallops come with Charles Macleod black pudding and carrot in a starter that wears its provenance with pride; next up, perhaps local day-boat cod with cockles, chorizo and chick peas, or ox cheek and tongue with Lyonnaise potatoes, 'carrot 'n' swede' and beef juices. The set lunch is a sensational deal. There's a great selection of British cheeses with raisin and treacle bread, and for pudding, perhaps an espresso brûlée with fairground doughnuts.

Chef Paul Ainsworth **Owner** Paul Ainsworth
Times 12-2/6.30-10 Closed 23-26 Dec, 3-26 Jan, Mon, L Sun (out of season), D Sun **Prices** Fixed L 2 course £10, Starter £5-£10, Main £11-£18, Dessert £6, Service optional **Wines** 42 bottles over £20, 13 bottles under £20, 11 by glass **Notes** Tasting menu available, Sunday L, Vegetarian available **Seats** 40, Pr/dining room 28 **Children** Portions **Parking** Harbour car park and on street

Rosel & Co

Modern British NEW

Confident cooking and a relaxed vibe near Padstow

01841 521289
The Dog House, St Merryn PL28 8NF
dir: Off B3276, at the centre of St Merryn

Not everything happening on the Cornish restaurant scene is going on in Padstow, and in this appealing little village a couple of miles away, is to be found another exciting contender. It's an intimate place in the heart of the village, stylishly understated with scrubbed wooden tables and bench seating strewn with scatter cushions, run by attentive, knowledgeable and approachable staff. Zane Rosel keeps the menus short, and cooks confidently in the modern British style, without unnecessary flounce but achieving bold, positive results. A bowl of deep green, velvet-textured spinach soup is enriched with parmesan, and comes with a poached egg sitting jauntily on a croûton in the middle of it. A piece of superbly fresh cod gains from its underlay of finely diced bacon, celeriac and leek in a parsley jus, while the finale may be a well-made hot chocolate sponge pudding with fondant-style liquid centre, accompanied by a gentle coconut ice cream. Fine breads contribute to the overall quality. One to watch.

Times 7-9 Closed Sun-Mon, L all week

St Petroc's Hotel and Bistro

French, Mediterranean

Informal bistro cooking from the Stein camp

01841 532700
4 New St PL28 8EA
e-mail: reservations@rickstein.com
dir: Follow one-way around harbour, 1st left, establishment 100yds on right

The bistro at St Petroc's Hotel represents another way of getting your knife and fork on some Rick Stein cooking if the Seafood Restaurant (see entry) is chock-a-block, or you want somewhere a little lighter on the wallet. The laminate floors and unclothed tables set an informal tone, and some lively modern artworks adorn the dining room. Seafood isn't quite the predominant theme that it is down the road, but there are still reliable offerings such as grilled prawns with ouzo, tomatoes, chilli and feta, or whole lemon sole with béarnaise. Otherwise, look to the grill, from which 28-day-aged beef emerges in various cuts and guises, including half-pound sirloin with peppercorn and chive butter. Finish with baked lemon cheesecake and berry compôte.

Chef Paul Harwood, David Sharland **Owner** R & J Stein
Times 12-2/7-10 Closed 25-26 Dec, 1 May, D 24 Dec
Prices Fixed L 3 course fr £17.50, Starter £6.80-£7.65, Main £12.75-£20.40, Dessert £5-£6.05, Service optional
Wines 23 bottles over £20, 1 bottle under £20, 12 by glass **Notes** Fixed L menu only available in winter, Sunday L, Vegetarian available **Seats** 54 **Children** Portions, Menu **Parking** Car park

The Seafood Restaurant

– see page 88

Treglos Hotel

Modern British V

Locally-based cooking with glorious bay views

01841 520727
PL28 8JH
e-mail: stay@tregloshotel.com
dir: At St Merryn x-rds take B3276 towards Newquay. In 500mtrs right to Constantine Bay, follow brown signs

Overlooking Constantine Bay and a glorious sweep of Cornish beach, the white-walled, late Victorian house was converted into a seaside hotel with art-deco features in the 1930s. Seasonal, locally-inspired cooking is on

continued

PADSTOW ***continued***

offer in the trimly decorated dining room. Expect to start, perhaps, with a velvety bisque of local fish and shellfish, served with rouille and parmesan, or mussels in vermouth, garlic and cream. Rack of lamb comes with Puy lentils, rosemary potatoes and a mead jus for main course, and meals end with either regional cheeses and walnut bread, or something like poached plums with brandy syllabub.

Chef Paul Becker **Owner** Mr & Mrs J Barlow
Times 7.15-9.15 Closed Jan-Feb & Dec, L Mon-Sat (except by arrangement) **Prices** Fixed D 4 course £29, Service optional **Wines** 44 bottles over £20, 25 bottles under £20, 3 by glass **Notes** Sunday L, Vegetarian menu, Dress restrictions, Jacket or tie **Seats** 90 **Children** Menu **Parking** 40

PENZANCE **Map 2 SW43**

The Bay Restaurant

Modern British

Locally-sourced, contemporary cooking in hotel with great sea views

☎ 01736 366890 & 363117
Hotel Penzance, Britons Hill TR18 3AE
e-mail: table@bay-penzance.co.uk
dir: from A30 pass heliport on right, left at next rdbt for town centre. 3rd right onto Britons Hill. Restaurant on right

With its fabulous views across Mount's Bay, the light and airy restaurant of this elegantly redesigned Edwardian building doubles as a gallery displaying work by local artists. The contemporary dining room has a stylish look with stripped floors and doors leading out to a decked area for alfresco dining and the best of those views. The kitchen has a modern approach to cooking fresh Cornish produce, whether it's from the sea or the land. Dishes might include pan-fried breast of wood pigeon served with pea purée, black pudding with rosemary and juniper oil, followed by roast fillet of skate wing with aubergine, garlic and herb purée and saffron-braised leeks. There's a plate of local cheeses such as Vintage Menallack and Keltic Gold, while desserts run to red wine poached pear with vanilla macaroons and hazelnut cream.

Chef Ben Reeve, Katie Semmens, Roger Hosken **Owner** Yvonne & Stephen Hill **Times** 11-2/6.15-11 Closed L Sat **Prices** Fixed L 2 course fr £12.50, Fixed D 3 course fr £29.95, Service optional, Groups min 8 service 10% **Wines** 15 bottles over £20, 16 bottles under £20, 10 by glass **Notes** Tasting menu available 7 course, Sunday L, Vegetarian available, Dress restrictions, Smart casual, no shorts **Seats** 60, Pr/dining room 12 **Children** Portions, Menu **Parking** 12, On street

Harris's Restaurant

Modern European

Simple, freshly cooked food in a charming restaurant

☎ 01736 364408
46 New St TR18 2LZ
e-mail: contact@harrissrestaurant.co.uk
dir: Located down narrow cobbled street opposite Lloyds TSB & the Humphry Davy statue

Harris's Restaurant is tucked away down a skinny cobbled side street in the heart of Penzance, but it shouldn't be too hard to find - the owners have been in business for pushing 40 years and any local can point you in the right direction. Chef-proprietor Roger Harris is on to a winner with his brand of unpretentious cooking that lets top-grade local ingredients - fish from Newlyn and game from nearby estates, for example - take centre stage. Falmouth estuary mussels might star in a classic moules marinière, ahead of grilled Dover sole with chive butter; meat aficionados might prefer noisettes of local lamb with spinach and pommes purées. Finish with a straight-up crème brûlée or apple strudel with clotted cream.

Chef Roger Harris **Owner** Roger & Anne Harris
Times 12-2/7-9.30 Closed 3 wks winter, 25-26 Dec, 1 Jan, Sun-Mon (winter), L Mon **Prices** Food prices not confirmed for 2011. Please telephone for details **Wines** 27 bottles over £20, 17 bottles under £20, 6 by glass **Notes** Vegetarian available, Dress restrictions, Smart casual **Seats** 40, Pr/dining room 20 **Parking** On street, local car park

The Seafood Restaurant

PADSTOW **Map 2 SW97**

International Seafood V

HQ of the Rick Stein empire

☎ 01841 532700
Riverside PL28 8BY
e-mail: reservations@rickstein.com
dir: Follow signs for town centre. Restaurant on left of riverside

The large, buzzy restaurant on the Padstow waterfront is one of the reference addresses of the recent British restaurant scene. It's where what has become Rick Stein's empire began, humbly enough, and is still dedicated to serving the freshest fish and seafood in ways that can be as simple or as inventive as you desire. Centred on a great seafood counter, where you can watch it all coming together, it's an infectiously relaxed place, run with positive cheer by staff who clearly love what they do. Japanese notes are rung in an opening dish of sashimi, comprised of scallop, salmon, sea bass and kingfish, served with wasabi, pickled ginger and soy, or you might opt for shangurro, a Basque dish of stuffed crab baked in the shell under a parsley and breadcrumb topping. At main course, the most straightforward offerings are often the most favoured ones, such as chargrilled whole Dover sole seasoned with sea salt and lime, and served with a light butter sauce, or steamed lobster with mayonnaise and salads. There is meat for those who want it - perhaps duck breast with red wine sauce and sautéed potatoes - and desserts include a mandarin soufflé worth waiting for, served with lemon and yoghurt sorbet.

Chef Stephane Delourme, David Sharland **Owner** R & J Stein **Times** 12-2/7-10 Closed 25-26 Dec, 1 May, D 24 Dec **Prices** Fixed L 3 course fr £28.50, Tasting menu £65.60, Starter £10.50-£26.50, Main £17.50-£49, Dessert £8.70, Service optional **Wines** 156 bottles over £20, 4 bottles under £20, 21 by glass **Notes** Fixed L menu only available in winter, Tasting menu 6 course, Vegetarian menu **Seats** 120 **Children** Portions, Menu **Parking** Pay & display opposite

The Navy Inn

Modern British

Penzance local with an ambitious kitchen

☎ 01736 333232
Lower Queen St TR18 4DE
e-mail: keir@navyinn.co.uk
dir: In town centre, follow Chapel St for 50yds, right into Queen St to end

Just off the prom in Penzance, the Navy Inn is an easygoing pubby restaurant with an invitingly casual shabby chic look. As the name might imply, the interior smacks of things nautical - ship's rigging block-and-tackle festoons the beams above exposed stone walls and scrubbed-up wooden tables on flagstone floors. Bag a table by a window, and you get great views across Mount's Bay to go with a menu that majors in superb Cornish produce, treated simply and without undue fuss. Classic pubby fodder such as pies and casseroles change daily, or you could test the kitchen's mettle with more contemporary concepts - perhaps seared local scallops with crispy bacon, cauliflower purée and fig and almond dressing, or rump of organic lamb slow-cooked in lemon and parsley sauce and teamed with a lamb patty and pearl barley.

Times 12-10 Closed D 25 Dec

PERRANUTHNOE Map 2 SW52

The Victoria Inn

Modern British

Well-judged menu of local produce in friendly coastal pub

☎ 01736 710309
TR20 9NP
e-mail: enquiries@victoriainn-penzance.co.uk
dir: A30 to Penzance, A394 to Helston. After 2m turn right into Perranuthnoe, pub is on right on entering the village

The unspoilt coastal village overlooking Mount's Bay is a good base for exploring Penwith and the Lizard. The inn with its wood-burning fire, cosy nooks and roaring log fires, has a deservedly strong local following who have cottoned on to the fact they've got a bit of a gem in their midst. The owner-chef, Stew (a good name for a chef), is passionate about sourcing local produce and his menus serve up excellent seafood and seasonal ingredients, the dishes packed with flavour. A starter of Cornish crab and potato salad gets a lift from some curry spicing, and comes with a mango and lime chutney, while main-course garlic and herb-roasted West Country chicken breast is accompanied by bubble-and-squeak, Savoy cabbage and bacon. To finish, try the West Country artisan cheeses or vanilla and lemon crème brûlée with poached plums and mulled wine syrup (or go for both).

Chef Stewart Eddy **Owner** Stewart & Anna Eddy **Times** 12-2/6.30-9 Closed 25-26 Dec, 1 Jan, 1st wk Jan, Mon (off season), D Sun **Prices** Starter £4.95-£7.50, Main £9.95-£17.95, Dessert £5.25-£8.25, Service optional, Groups min 8 service 10% **Wines** 10 bottles over £20, 20 bottles under £20, 8 by glass **Notes** Sunday L, Vegetarian available **Seats** 60 **Children** Portions, Menu **Parking** 10, On street

PORTHLEVEN Map 2 SW62

Kota Restaurant with Rooms

British, Pacific Rim

Asian-influenced modern British cooking by the sea

☎ 01326 562407
Harbour Head TR13 9JA
e-mail: kota@btconnect.com
dir: B3304 from Helston into Porthleven, Kota on harbour head opposite slipway

Kota is Maori for shellfish, and this easygoing bistro in a cosy, beamed 18th-century corn mill in the horseshoe harbour of Porthleven is in pole position for sourcing the raw ingredients that give Kota its name and culinary focus. The menu here is full of good ideas executed with skill and exuberant creativity. If the modern cooking style has a clear Asian leaning, that's because chef-proprietor Jude Kereama is half-Maori, quarter Chinese and quarter

continued

Driftwood

PORTSCATHO Map 2 SW83

Modern

Accomplished cooking in a stunning coastal location

☎ 01872 580644
Rosevine TR2 5EW
e-mail: info@driftwoodhotel.co.uk
dir: 5m from St Mawes off the A3078, signposted Rosevine

Thanks to its glorious location perched on a Cornish cliff top, crashing waves are the soundtrack to cocktails on the decking terrace of this contemporary boutique bolt-hole. There's a certain well-heeled Cape Cod surfer chic about the stripped-out modern décor, as well as views to die for across Gerrans Bay. Huge picture windows make the most of this panorama in the relaxed dining room, where bleached out neutral colours and a pale wood floor are counterpointed with seaside splashes of blue and yellow. Light, contemporary cooking fits the mood perfectly, with spanking fresh fish and seafood straight off local boats showcased on seasonal menus. A skilful kitchen team serves hand-dived scallops with pork belly, cauliflower, toasted grains and sherry, or might match Somerset snails with wild garlic, pearl barley, celeriac, Madeira and thyme. Prime West Country produce also turns up in main courses such as Woolley Park guinea fowl teamed with onion fondue, gnocchi, morels and roasting juices. There are artisan Cornish cheeses served with home-made digestive biscuits, membrillo, and fig and hazelnut bread, and desserts run to caramelised banana with gingerbread and salted peanut ice cream.

Chef Christopher Eden **Owner** Paul & Fiona Robinson **Times** 7-9.30 Closed mid Dec-mid Feb, L all week **Prices** Fixed D 3 course £42, Service optional **Wines** 50 bottles over £20, 7 bottles under £20, 6 by glass **Notes** Vegetarian available **Seats** 34 **Parking** 20

PORTHLEVEN *continued*

Malaysian; thus Cornish mussels are given a Thai-style spin with lemongrass, lime leaves, coconut milk and coriander, ahead of pan-fried turbot with fennel and blood orange salad, salmon cakes and miso saké dressing. And it's not all about fish and seafood: Cornish beef comes with an oxtail raviolo.

Chef Jude Kereama **Owner** Jude & Jane Kereama **Times** 12-2/5.30-9 Closed 25 Dec, Jan, Sun (off season), L Sun-Thu **Prices** Fixed L 2 course £14, Fixed D 3 course £18.50-£19.50, Starter £4.50-£8.95, Main £11.50-£18.95, Dessert £5.50-£6.50, Service optional, Groups min 6 service 10% **Wines** 30 bottles over £20, 23 bottles under £20, 13 by glass **Notes** Early bird 2 course £14, Tasting menu available (pre-order), Vegetarian available **Seats** 40 **Children** Portions, Menu **Parking** On street

PORTLOE Map 2 SW93

The Lugger Hotel

Modern British

Top seafood in harbour hotel with stunning views

☎ 01872 501322
TR2 5RD
e-mail: office@luggerhotel.com
dir: A390 to Truro, B3287 to Tregony, A3078 (St Mawes Rd), left for Veryan, left for Portloe

At first sighting, the Lugger looks like the 16th-century inn that it once was, shoehorned into a postcard-perfect cove with a pocket-sized harbour. Once inside, it's clear that the place has traded up and is now a bijou luxury hotel, complete with a modern harbourside restaurant. It's hard to imagine anywhere better placed to flip fish straight from the boat to the grill, and the sunny terrace is the best imaginable place to eat it - although when the waves are crashing in, the contemporary dining room is a slick act too. Fresh-from-the-boats seafood is, naturally, high on the agenda: uncomplicated pairings - crab with crème fraîche and herb oil, or grilled John Dory with fennel, chargrilled vegetables, and dill butter cream sauce - set the tone. Main course could be a bouillabaisse of Cornish fish, while unreconstructed carnivores might prefer roast breast of guinea fowl filled with tarragon mousse.

Chef Didier Bienaime **Owner** Oxford Hotels **Times** 12-2.30/7-9.30 **Prices** Food prices not confirmed for 2011. Please telephone for details **Wines** 31 bottles over £20, 8 bottles under £20, 8 by glass **Notes** Sunday L, Vegetarian available, Civ Wed 60 **Seats** 54 **Parking** 24

PORTSCATHO Map 2 SW83

Driftwood

– see page 89

PORTWRINKLE Map 3 SX35

Whitsand Bay Hotel & Golf Club

Modern British

Fine local produce on a Cornish clifftop

☎ 01503 230276
PL11 3BU
e-mail: whitsandbayhotel@btconnect.com
dir: A38 from Exeter over River Tamar, left at Trerulefoot rdbt onto A374 to Crafthole/Portwrinkle. Follow hotel signs

Standing high on a Cornish clifftop, the imposing Victorian limestone hotel was designed in the Tudor-Gothic style, and these days boasts a golf course with sea views. An elegant dining room with light panelling and smartly attired tables offers Cornish seasonal produce in a style that pleases locals as well as guests from afar. Crab tian with mango salsa and citrus dressing, followed by roast venison loin with Calvados sauce and dauphinoise, might be a good way to experience the repertoire, with Treleavans ice creams and sorbets, or a bowl of seasonal strawberries and clotted cream, to finish.

Times 12-2/7-9

Restaurant Nathan Outlaw

ROCK Map 2 SW97

British V NEW

The Outlaw returns to Rock

☎ 01208 863394
The St Enodoc Hotel PL27 6LA
e-mail: mail@nathan-outlaw.co.uk
dir: M5/A30/A39 to Wadebridge. B3314 to Rock

Rock's period of mourning is over. Nathan Outlaw has returned to the village where he first stepped into the limelight. It is now the turn of Fowey to lament the absence of this prodigious talent. The Seafood & Grill paved the way when Nathan opened up a vibrant bit of fishy paradise in the St Enodoc Hotel, and now he has moved his fine-dining operation, lock, stock and sous-chef, into the hotel as well. It is a reserved and mellow space, halfway between minimalism and metropolitan chic, with neutral colours throughout, well-spaced tables and a refreshing lack of overwrought designer flourishes. This is Cornwall after all. There is some nice art on the walls and the overall effect is smart and confident - perfect for what follows. And what follows is some supremely confident, creative modern cooking. First-rate Cornish produce shines on the menus as brightly as the summer sun shines over the Camel Estuary outside, and everything that arrives at the table is beautifully crafted and intelligently rendered. Scallops are perfectly timed in a first course that shows perfect poise, with a deeply flavoured hog's pudding and contrasting Jerusalem artichoke and apple purées. Next up, a superb piece of brill is as fresh and flavoursome as it gets, served up with angels on horseback, seaweed and squash. Desserts are no less thrilling and well judged; Amaretto mousse with coffee sponge and chocolate sorbet is a delectable piece of sculpture. The Seafood & Grill is open all day, has great views over the water and a fab terrace on which to enjoy them, and serves up more straightforward - but still high quality - stuff; grilled sardines with thyme bread, for example. Visit Cornwall, eat Outlaw.

Chef Nathan Outlaw **Owner** Nathan Outlaw **Times** 7-9 Closed Xmas, Jan, Sun-Mon, L all week **Prices** Tasting menu £65-£125 **Wines** 200+ bottles over £20, 6 bottles under £20, 20 by glass **Notes** Tasting menu 6 course (with wine £125), Veg tasting menu, Vegetarian menu, Dress restrictions, Smart casual **Seats** 24, Pr/dining room 20 **Parking** 30

ROCK Map 2 SW97

Restaurant Nathan Outlaw

– see opposite page

RUAN HIGH LANES Map 2 SW93

Fish in the Fountain

British, Mediterranean

Georgian hotel with unpretentious homely cooking

01872 501336
The Hundred House Hotel TR2 5JR
e-mail: enquiries@hundredhousehotel.co.uk
dir: On A3078 towards St Mawes, hotel 4m after Tregony on right, just before Ruan High Lanes

The mid-Georgian house was once the home of an Admiralty surgeon, and retains a feeling of gracious living today, sitting as it does in the heart of the Roseland peninsula near Truro. Its airy, pastel-hued dining room is easy on the eye, and is a restful place to enjoy some unpretentious homely cooking, served in the form of a daily-changing dinner menu. Pesto-topped goats' cheese wrapped in puff pastry could be the opener to a main course of braised lamb leg steak in red wine, rosemary and shallots, with blackberry fool, or sultana-filled baked apple and clotted cream, to finish.

Chef Richard Maior-Barron **Owner** Richard Maior-Barron **Times** 6.45-8 Closed Jan-Feb, L all week **Prices** Food prices not confirmed for 2011. Please telephone for details **Wines** 7 bottles over £20, 33 bottles under £20, 4 by glass **Notes** Vegetarian available, Dress restrictions, Smart casual **Seats** 24 **Children** Portions **Parking** 15

ST AGNES Map 2 SW75

Valley Restaurant

Traditional British

Accomplished cooking in a tranquil setting

01872 562202
Rose-in-Vale Hotel, Mithian TR5 0QD
e-mail: reception@rose-in-vale-hotel.co.uk
dir: Take A30 S towards Redruth. At Chiverton Cross rdbt take B3277 signed St Agnes. In 500mtrs turn at tourist info sign for Rose-in-Vale. Into Mithian, right at Miners Arms, down hill

The Rose-in-Vale Hotel is a real getaway - a gorgeous Georgian manor house in the tranquil village of Mithian on the North Cornish coast. The Valley Restaurant is a bright, traditional space, elegantly turned-out with smart table settings and formal-yet-friendly service, and there are views of the beautifully kept garden to further enhance the soothing surroundings. The kitchen makes great use of local produce in seasonal, traditional British dishes; start perhaps with pan-fried Falmouth Bay scallops on a pea purée, served with Parma ham crisps, followed by 'Celebration of Cornish beef', the local meat coming as an oven-roasted fillet, braised ox tongue and a beef pudding, served with fondant potato and sautéed mushrooms. For desserts there could be Bramley apple crumble with the obligatory (and welcome) Cornish clotted cream on the side.

Chef Colin Hankins, Shane Hodges, Aaron Rawlings **Owner** James & Sara Evans **Times** 12-2/7-9 Closed 2 wks Jan, L Mon-Wed (winter) **Prices** Food prices not confirmed for 2011. Please telephone for details **Wines** 14 bottles over £20, 25 bottles under £20, 7 by glass **Notes** Sunday L, Vegetarian available, Dress restrictions, Smart dress, Civ Wed 100 **Seats** 80, Pr/dining room 12 **Children** Portions **Parking** 50

ST AUSTELL Map 2 SX05

Austell's

Modern British

Contemporary dining in Carlyon Bay

01726 813888
10 Beach Rd PL25 3PH
e-mail: brett@austells.net
dir: From A390 towards Par, 0.5m after Charlestown rdbt at 2nd lights turn right. Left at rdbt. Restaurant 600yds on right

Located on Beach Road a stone's throw from the glorious strand at Carlyon Bay, and with a half-dozen golf courses and the Eden Project a short drive away, Austell's casts a wide net. The dining area - a modish space of darkwood floors and polished mahogany-hued tables - is raised so that diners get a good view of the brigade doing their thing in the open kitchen. Chef Brett Camborne-Paynter has paid his dues at The Ivy, The Waldorf and The Four Seasons, a classical pedigree that underpins his straightforward modern British food. Slow-cooked pork belly with apple purée and black pudding shows how to wring deep flavours from local seasonal materials; main course might be poached monkfish with white wine sauce, broccoli and potato purée; dessert finishes with an assiette of chocolate: a spot-on fondant, an unctuous white chocolate cheesecake and smooth-as-silk ice cream.

Chef Brett Camborne-Paynter **Owner** J & S Camborne-Paynter **Times** 11.30-3/7-10.30 Closed 25-26 Dec, 1-15 Jan, Mon, L Sun-Thu **Prices** Fixed D 3 course £29.95, Service optional **Wines** 37 bottles over £20, 7 bottles under £20, 9 by glass **Notes** Vegetarian available **Seats** 48 **Children** Portions **Parking** 30

Carlyon Bay Hotel

Modern, Traditional

West Country produce and fantastic sea views

01726 812304
Sea Rd, Carlyon Bay PL25 3RD
e-mail: info@carlyonbay.co.uk
dir: From St Austell, follow signs for Charlestown. Carlyon Bay signed on left, hotel at end of Sea Rd

The sprawling, creeper-curtained Carlyon Bay Hotel surveys the rugged Cornish coast from its cliff-top perch above St Austell. With a full complement of spa and leisure facilities and a championship golf course in 250 acres of grounds, there's no excuse for not bringing a good appetite to dinner in the aptly-named Bay View restaurant. 'Clean-cut and contemporary' is a good way to describe both the décor and the kitchen's modern style of cooking. Seasonal West Country produce - particularly fish and seafood - is backed up by good technical skills to result in starters that might take in crab soup with tempura mussels, followed by pan-fried bass with lobster fumet, or for carnivores, perhaps pot-braised chicken in tarragon cream with chanterelle fricassée.

Times 12-2/7-9.30

The Cornwall Hotel, Spa & Estate

British **NEW**

Ambitious modern cooking in resurrected Victorian country house

01726 874050
Pentewan Rd, Tregorrick PL26 7AB
e-mail: enquiries@thecornwall.com
dir: A391 to St Austell then B3273 towards Mevagissey. Hotel approx 0.5m on right

After a lavish £30 million restoration, this abandoned Cornish country house now stands resplendent in 43 acres of parkland. The white-painted Victorian mansion - appropriately known as the White House - opened for business at the start of 2010, with classy contemporary rooms split between the old manor and a stylish modern annexe. There are original works by Plymouth-based artist Robert Lenkiewicz to admire before settling into the Arboretum Restaurant overlooking the terrace, croquet lawn and estate. Head chef Tom Bradbury returned to his Cornish roots after a spell in top London kitchens, and comes to his new task fully loaded with ambition, an arsenal of contemporary twists, turns and techniques, plus a sound local knowledge of where to get his hands on the best Cornish produce. The tight-lipped menu descriptions don't give much away: take, for example, 'scallops, celeriac, truffle' - which delivers the scallops on a swipe of celeriac purée, with diced sour apples, rice balls and a hint of truffle. Next up is John Dory with cheese-filled macaroni, speck, grilled leeks and parmesan, and to finish, banana soufflé with pecan praline and chocolate ice cream.

Prices Food prices not confirmed for 2011. Please telephone for details

ST IVES — Map 2 SW54

Alba Restaurant

Modern European

Fish-focussed menu in the former lifeboat house

☎ 01736 797222
Old Lifeboat House, Wharf Rd TR26 1LF
e-mail: albarestaurant@aol.co.uk
dir: 1st building on St Ives harbour front, opposite new lifeboat house

The old lifeboat house at St Ives has been creatively transformed into a clean-lined modern restaurant with a light, sandy colour scheme and fine harbour views from the upstairs window. Fish is the theme, as well it might be, with diamond-fresh produce going into dishes like black bream with olive oil mash and provençal vegetables, or hake with crab in sweetcorn chowder. Well-made fish soup with rouille and garlic croûtons is an apposite way to cast the net, there is properly aged fillet steak in red wine for the meat-eaters, and you might opt to finish with Neal's Yard cheeses, or a dessert such as custard tart with poached rhubarb.

Chef Grant Nethercott **Owner** Harbour Kitchen Co Ltd **Times** 12-2/6-9.45 Closed 25-26 Dec **Prices** Fixed L 2 course fr £13.95, Fixed D 3 course fr £16.95, Starter £4.95-£8.50, Main £10.95-£18.95, Dessert £1.50-£5.95, Service optional, Groups min 6 service 10% **Wines** 23 bottles over £20, 39 bottles under £20, 25 by glass **Notes** Fixed price menus before 7pm in season or 7.30pm rest of year, Sunday L, Vegetarian available **Seats** 60 **Children** Portions, Menu

Garrack Hotel & Restaurant

Modern British

Modern British cooking with commanding Atlantic views

☎ 01736 796199 & 792910
Burthallan Ln, Higher Ayr TR26 3AA
e-mail: aarest@garrack.com
dir: Exit A30 for St Ives, then from B3311 follow brown signs for Tate Gallery, then brown Garrack signs

Sitting proud above Porthmeor beach and commanding Atlantic views, the Garrack is a family-run hotel that aims to offer a retreat from the normal tourist bustle. It's a homely place with a cosy bar (where you might partake of one of the extensive collection of gins) and a smart dining room that capitalises on that coastal view. The modern British cooking does some neat interpretations of dishes such as Cullen skink and Waldorf salad, as well as ideas like baked local goats' cheese with sweetcorn and courgette blinis and tomato and onion salsa. Duck breast is served with cocotte potatoes, kale and spinach, and the chocolate cheesecake lacks nothing in intensity.

Chef Neil O'Brien **Owner** Kilby family **Times** 12.30-2/6-9 Closed 5 days Xmas, L Mon-Sat **Prices** Fixed D 3 course fr £27.50, Starter £5.25-£10.50, Main £16-£20, Dessert £4.95-£7.95, Service optional **Wines** 16 bottles over £20, 47 bottles under £20, 8 by glass **Notes** Early D 6-7pm 2 course £12.95, Sunday L, Vegetarian available, Dress restrictions, Smart casual **Seats** 40 **Children** Portions, Menu **Parking** 36

Porthminster Beach Restaurant

Modern International V

Thrilling location and divertingly confident global cooking

☎ 01736 795352
TR26 2EB
e-mail: pminster@btconnect.com
dir: On Porthminster Beach, beneath the St Ives Railway Station

A deckchair store and a tea room in its former life, this whitewashed art deco building slap bang on Porthminster Beach has views out to sea and across the coast that are second to none. Eating on the terrace is a treat in all but the most horrendous weather, but, anyway, inside has windows large enough to frame the view in all seasons. It's a relaxed, unpretentious space, with bare-wood tables and the whitewashed walls hung with vibrant works of art. The food fits the place to a tee, with the excellent local larder (they grow some of their own, too) combining with the Australian chef's evident passion for Asian and Mediterranean flavours. Thus you might start with crispy fried squid with citrus miso, black spices and coriander and chilli salad, or Cornish fish soup with garlic croûton, wild garlic, crab and lemon. Fish is perhaps not unsurprisingly a high point: Cornish hake, perhaps, with wild garlic, salt-cod croquettes, smoked tomato and langoustine velouté, and desserts are no less appealing (honey and pine nut tart with lavender and cream cheese ice cream). The lunch menu is a little more straightforward and there is a take-away on the beach if you fancy first-rate fish and chips in the open air.

Chef M Smith, Isaac Anderson **Owner** Jim Woolcock, David Fox, Roger & Tim Symons, M Smith **Times** 12-3.30/6 Closed 25 Dec, Mon (Winter) **Prices** Starter £5-£10, Main £10-£20, Dessert £5-£6, Service optional **Wines** 13 bottles over £20, 15 bottles under £20, 9 by glass **Notes** Sunday L, Vegetarian menu **Seats** 60 **Children** Portions **Parking** 300yds (railway station)

Sands Restaurant

Traditional Mediterranean

Tranquil beachside hotel with traditional dining

☎ 01736 795311
Carbis Bay Hotel, Carbis Bay TR26 2NP
e-mail: carbisbayhotel@btconnect.com
dir: A3074, through Lelant. 1m, at Carbis Bay 30yds before lights turn right into Porthrepta Rd to sea & hotel

Built in 1894 by Cornish architect Sylvanus Trevail, the family-run Carbis Bay Hotel sits above its own sandy beach and offers stunning views across the bay. Expect a traditional style of European cooking in the light and airy refurbished restaurant. Seasonality and local produce are the cornerstones of the menu, which could include line-caught mackerel with pancetta salad and citrus crème fraîche or roast guinea fowl with lemon and thyme sauce. Finish with almond tart with clotted cream or a plate of Cornish cheeses.

Chef Paul John Massey **Owner** Mr M W Baker **Times** 12-3/6-9 Closed 3 wks Jan **Prices** Food prices not confirmed for 2011. Please telephone for details **Wines** 15 bottles over £20, 20 bottles under £20, 8 by glass **Notes** Sunday L, Vegetarian available, Dress restrictions, Smart casual, Civ Wed 150 **Seats** 150, Pr/dining room 40 **Children** Portions, Menu **Parking** 100

The Wave Restaurant

Modern Mediterranean

Modern Mediterranean cooking close to St Ives harbour

☎ 01736 796661
17 St Andrews St TR26 1AH
e-mail: lcowling2000@yahoo.com
web: www.wave-restaurant.co.uk
dir: Just outside town centre, 100yds from parish church

The dinky bright blue frontage of this smart contemporary restaurant opens Tardis-like into a rather slick cosmopolitan split-level space with unclothed blond wood tables and chairs and vibrant blue abstracts on white walls. It's a relaxed and cheery place in a quiet street just back from the harbour - an ideal spot to make the most of locally-landed fish. The kitchen deals in sunny modern Mediterranean cooking with the odd foray into Asian territory here and there, as in a starter of Thai-spiced crab and prawn cakes with Asian coleslaw and spicy cucumber relish. Mains could take in cod fillet roasted with sun-dried tomato pesto and served with saffron mash and buttered spinach. Local meat is not ignored - pistachio and honey-crusted Cornish lamb rump might get an outing in the company of oven-dried plum and apricot tabouleh and harissa dressing.

Chef S M Pellow **Owner** Mr & Mrs Cowling, Mr & Mrs Pellow **Times** 6-9.30 Closed end Nov-beg Mar, Sun, L all week **Prices** Food prices not confirmed for 2011. Please telephone for details **Wines** 4 bottles over £20, 20 bottles under £20, 8 by glass **Notes** Vegetarian available, Dress restrictions, Smart casual, no swimwear or bare chests **Seats** 50 **Children** Portions, Menu **Parking** Station car park

ST MAWES Map 2 SW83

Hotel Tresanton

– *see below*

Idle Rocks Hotel

Modern European

Modern cuisine in picturesque fishing port

01326 270771
Harbour Side TR2 5AN
e-mail: reception@idlerocks.co.uk
dir: From St Austell A390 towards Truro, left onto B3287 signed Tregony, through Tregony, left at T-junct onto A3078, hotel on left on waterfront

Perched on the harbour wall in fashionable St Mawes, you can't get any closer to the waves than the Idle Rocks Hotel. The aptly-named Water's Edge restaurant is suitably decked-out in pale wood and modern seaside shades of blue and gold; a split-level layout means everyone gets a sea view through sweeping picture windows. Better still, the terrace gets you right down to the water in summer - any closer and you'll need a towel. Head chef Stephen Marsh is passionate about local Cornish produce and so in touch with suppliers that he can point out the crab and lobster man's pots from the window, while a local forager turns up edible seaweed and wild herbs. Dishes follow a modern European line and show a lively imagination without needing to resort to showy tricks. Seared Cornish scallops turn up in a starter with bok choy, kaffir lime leaf and chilli ice cream, and mango crisps; local seafood stars again in a main-course fillet of pan-seared brill with garlic chive risotto, and smoked mussel and clam ragout.

Chef Stephen Marsh **Owner** E K Richardson
Times 12-2.30/6.30-9 Closed Xmas **Prices** Fixed L 2 course £25-£39.50, Service optional **Wines** 42 bottles over £20, 8 bottles under £20, 11 by glass **Notes** Sunday L, Vegetarian available, Dress restrictions, Smart casual **Seats** 70 **Children** Portions **Parking** 5

SALTASH Map 3 SX45

The Farmhouse

Modern British

Quality cooking in a converted farmhouse

01752 854664 & 854661
China Fleet Country Club PL12 6LJ
e-mail: sales@china-fleet.co.uk
dir: A38 towards Plymouth/Saltash. Cross Tamar Bridge, take slip road before tunnel. Right at lights, 1st right follow signs, 0.5m

The China Fleet Country Club offers a range of facilities for the sporting type, including a championship golf course, along with the light, airy Farmhouse restaurant, which is set apart from the main hotel. Quality table settings and a careful, seasonally-based culinary approach indicate a classy operation, confirmed in dishes such as pigeon breast with crispy ham in grape and walnut jus, an intense and cleverly conceived first course. Mains might bring on a well-timed piece of cod, offset with braised lentils and sautéed kale, while Salcombe apple tarte Tatin with smooth vanilla ice cream ends proceedings on a high.

Chef Marc Slater **Times** 12-2/7-9.30 Closed 24 Dec-10 Jan, Mon, L Tue-Sat, D Sun **Prices** Fixed D 3 course £18, Starter £4.50-£8.95, Main £9.95-£24.95, Dessert £4.50-£7.95, Service optional **Wines** 6 bottles over £20, 23 bottles under £20, 11 by glass **Notes** Sunday L, Vegetarian available, Civ Wed 200 **Seats** 45, Pr/dining room 200 **Children** Portions, Menu **Parking** 400

Hotel Tresanton

ST MAWES Map 2 SW83

Modern British, Mediterranean

Reassuringly straightforward cooking in a stylish seafront hotel

01326 270055
Lower Castle Rd TR2 5DR
e-mail: info@tresanton.com
dir: On the waterfront in town centre

A lane heading out of town along the water's edge leads to this jewel of a hotel. The entrance off the lane is somewhat discreet, the main body of the building, including the restaurant, a few steps up the hillside, where the sea view is even more stunning. Fashioned from a straggle of old houses set at different levels, it was once the yachting club, until Olga Polizzi turned it into a boutique hotel, a template now much imitated across the country. There's more than a whiff of the Mediterranean in the décor of the restaurant, where fashionable off-white-painted tongue-and-groove woodwork and a mosaic-tiled floor paint a neutral picture, the large windows opening onto the splendid views over the water to Falmouth being all that is needed by way of a diversion. The food tacks a modern European course on daily-changing menus, with local produce figuring prominently, and there's a pleasingly uncomplicated approach to the construction of dishes. John Dory with squid, steamed clams, grilled potatoes and baby leeks is a fresh and appealing combination in a first course, while main-course Calenick Farm best end of lamb is ably supported by fondant potato, Savoy cabbage, carrots and honey-roast parsnips. Finish with West Country cheeses or on a sweet note with Tunisian orange cake with yoghurt sorbet and a poppy seed tuile.

Chef Paul Wadham **Owner** Olga Polizzi
Times 12-2.30/7-9.30 Closed 2 wks Jan (essential maintenance) **Prices** Fixed L 2 course fr £26.50, Fixed D 3 course fr £42, Service optional **Wines** 114 bottles over £20, 8 by glass **Notes** Sunday L, Vegetarian available, Civ Wed 50 **Seats** 50, Pr/dining room 45 **Children** Menu **Parking** 30

TALLAND BAY Map 2 SX25

Terrace Restaurant at Talland Bay Hotel

Modern British

Good-looking modern food on the Cornish coastline

01503 272667
PL13 2JB
e-mail: reception@tallandbayhotel.co.uk
dir: Signed from x-rds on A387 between Looe and Polperro

The sparkling-white hotel looks out to sea from the Cornish coast near Looe. A strikingly contemporary interior look includes zebra-striped sofas, colourful modern artworks and sky-blue walls, with tub seats upholstered in rich claret fabric in the bar. The oak-panelled dining room is light and airy, with huge windows that open on to a summer terrace, and the approach is slick and unobtrusive. Carefully prepared, good-looking dishes based on local sourcing are Steve Buick's stock-in-trade, whether it be the simplicity of chicken liver parfait with pistachio brioche and tomato chutney, or a high-stakes main course such as roast halibut with a confit duck croquette and Jerusalem artichoke purée in lentil jus. A rendition of wild mushroom risotto with parmesan and pine nuts achieves resonant flavour, while lemon tart displays the perfect balance of sharp and creamy, the former emphasised with an accompaniment of rhubarb terrine, the latter with vanilla ice cream.

Times 12.30-2/7-9 Closed L Mon-Sat (Oct-mid Apr)

TRURO Map 2 SW84

Alverton Manor

Traditional British

Contemporary cooking in a former convent

01872 276633
Tregolls Rd TR1 1ZQ
e-mail: reception@alvertonmanor.co.uk
dir: From Truro bypass take A39 to St Austell. Just past church on left

Within walking distance of the city centre, but artfully concealed on its hillside, the former convent does a roaring trade in local weddings. Many of the vegetables, fruits and herbs the kitchen uses are grown in the extensive grounds, and the interiors are decorated with a host of artefacts, such as model trains and toy soldiers for guests to pore over. Keith Brooksbank is a skilled chef and brings a degree of contemporary style to Alverton, in the form of lightly seared mackerel with pear and celeriac remoulade and anchovy dressing, duck breast with a risotto of curly kale and gésiers in a red wine reduction, and well-rendered vanilla pannacotta with sharp blackberry compôte.

Owner Mr M Sagin **Times** 11.45-1.45/7-9.15 Closed L Mon-Sat **Prices** Food prices not confirmed for 2011. Please telephone for details **Wines** 80 bottles over £20, 40 bottles under £20, 15 by glass **Notes** Sunday L, Vegetarian available, Dress restrictions, Smart casual, Civ Wed 80 **Seats** 30, Pr/dining room 80 **Children** Portions, Menu **Parking** 80

Bustophers Bar Bistro

Modern British

Buzzy, contemporary setting for well-crafted cooking

01872 279029
62 Lemon St TR1 2PN
e-mail: info@bustophersbarbistro.com
dir: Located on right, past Plaza Cinema up the hill

Snug in the historic heart of Truro, Bustophers is a lively contemporary wine bar-bistro among the architectural grandeur of Lemon Street. Head straight for the long zinc-topped bar for a sip of something interesting from the vast range of wines by the glass, then move into the clean-cut glassed-over atrium-style restaurant, where the chefs at work in the open kitchen add to the upbeat buzz. The kitchen nails its sourcing policy to the mast, listing a roll-call of local suppliers on the menu; simplicity is the key here - unpretentious modern crowd-pleasers to go with the vivacious vibe. Start, perhaps, with a Cornish take on moules marinières - River Fowey mussels steamed in Cornish Orchard cider with Baker Tom's bread - followed by local venison with root vegetable dauphinoise and blackberry jus.

Chef Rob Duncan **Owner** Simon & Sue Hancock **Times** 12-2.30/5.30-9.30 Closed 25-26 Dec, 1 Jan **Prices** Fixed L 3 course £14, Fixed D 3 course £14, Starter £5-£8, Main £9-£22, Dessert £4-£7, Service optional, Groups min 8 service 10% **Wines** 68 bottles over £20, 17 bottles under £20, 19 by glass **Notes** Pre-theatre menu available £14, Sunday L, Vegetarian available **Seats** 110, Pr/dining room 30 **Children** Portions, Menu **Parking** Moorfield NCP at rear of property

Probus Lamplighter Restaurant

Modern British

Locals' favourite lets ingredients shine through

01726 882453
Fore St, Probus TR2 4JL
e-mail: maireadvogel@aol.com
dir: 5m from Truro on A390 towards St Austell

Housed in a 300-year-old former farmhouse, Probus is a cosy, candlelit restaurant with a roaring open fire (seasonally, of course), wooden beams and smartly dressed tables. It enjoys a good local following having been part of the high street's landscape for over 50 years. Now run by a husband-and-wife team, the atmosphere is convivial and service friendly and relaxed. Chef-patron Robert Vogel produces modern British dishes, using local and seasonal produce, in which he allows the high quality of the ingredients to speak for themselves. Pig's cheek, ear and trotter salad with crisp barley is a typical way to begin. Follow that with loin of Cornish veal wrapped in prosciutto with port wine morel sauce and spinach pasta, ending with an unusual take on a classic dessert - maple crème brûlée with cinnamon doughnut.

Chef Robert Vogel **Owner** Robert & Mairead Vogel **Times** 7-10 Closed Sun-Mon, L all week **Prices** Fixed D 3 course £29.90 **Wines** 16 bottles over £20, 17 bottles under £20, 7 by glass **Notes** Vegetarian available, Dress restrictions, Smart casual **Seats** 32, Pr/dining room 8 **Children** Portions **Parking** On street & car park

Tabb's

Modern British

Contemporary dining championing local produce

01872 262110
85 Kenwyn St TR1 3BZ
e-mail: n.tabb@virgin.net
dir: Down hill past train station, right at mini rdbt, 200yds on left

Tabb's has enjoyed a strong local fan base since opening on a trendy town centre street in 2005. The chic modern restaurant is done out with calming lilac walls, black slate floors and high-backed leather chairs in cream and lilac, but it is the food that makes the real impact. In the kitchen, Nigel Tabb takes no short cuts: everything is made in-house, such as splendid breads to go with inventive soups - say smoked haddock with chilli and Devon Blue relish. Another starter might be seared duck fillets with smoked paprika pasta, soft-boiled duck egg and wild mushroom jus. Main courses also make admirable use of local produce: braised leg of wild rabbit is teamed with its seared fillet, celeriac and snow peas with star anise jus. Locally-caught fish appears too, as in grilled red gurnard with crisp polenta, shredded leeks, cockles and chive butter sauce. Don't skip dessert - Nigel is an expert chocolatier.

Chef Nigel Tabb **Owner** Nigel Tabb **Times** 6.30-9.30 Closed 25 Dec, 1 Jan, 1 wk Jan, Sun-Mon, L all week **Prices** Starter £6.95-£9.75, Main £14.75-£22.50, Dessert £6.50, Service optional **Wines** 26 bottles over £20, 11 bottles under £20, 6 by glass **Notes** Vegetarian available **Seats** 30 **Children** Portions **Parking** 200yds

VERYAN Map 2 SW93

Nare Hotel

Traditional British

Elegant country-house hotel by the sea

01872 501279
Carne Beach TR2 5PF
e-mail: office@narehotel.co.uk
dir: from Tregony follow A3078 for approx 1.5m. Left at Veryan sign, through village towards sea & hotel

The delightful Nare Hotel offers a relaxed country-house atmosphere in a spectacular coastal setting with stunning views across Gerran's Bay. Although stylish and contemporary in many respects, it retains a genteel feel and you can expect old-fashioned service from the friendly staff. There are two dining options, and you get those magnificent sea views from both rooms. The nautically-themed Quarterdeck restaurant injects a contemporary note, with a more modern brasserie-style menu - see entry below. If you go for the five-course table d'hôte in the formal dining room, expect silver service and straightforward, classic cooking, starting with, perhaps, seared Cornish scallops with cauliflower purée and pancetta crisps followed by a fish course of red gurnard with watercress and pink grapefruit salad.

Chef Richard James **Owner** T G H Ashworth **Times** 12.30-2.30/7.30-10 Closed L Mon-Sat **Prices** Food prices not confirmed for 2011. Please telephone for details, Service optional **Wines** 300 bottles over £20, 200 bottles under £20, 18 by glass **Notes** Fixed D 5 course £48, Sunday L, Vegetarian available, Dress restrictions, Jacket and tie **Seats** 75 **Children** Portions, Menu **Parking** 70

The Quarterdeck at the Nare

Modern British **NEW**

Great local produce accompanied by fab sea views

☎ 01872 501111
Carne Beach TR2 5PF
e-mail: stay@narehotel.co.uk
dir: From Tregony follow A3078 for approx 1.5m. Left at Veryan sign, through village towards sea & hotel

Part of the Nare Hotel (see entry) but with its own separate entrance, The Quarterdeck has a different vibe from the rest of the hotel, the theme being 'J-class' yachts - this means lots of beautiful polished teak, square rails and yachting prints on the walls. The position overlooking the bay is breathtaking and it is easy to imagine yourself at sea as you sit on the terrace or gaze through the large floor-to-ceiling windows. Local produce is the focus in the kitchen, with seafood at the forefront as you might hope. The setting is ideal for the light lunches and afternoon tea on offer, but in the evening the boat is pushed out to deliver hand-dived scallops with lemon vierge, or breast of wood pigeon with ceps and parsnip purée, followed by fillet of John Dory with lobster and truffle oil potato purée. Finish with baked chocolate cake with vanilla ice cream.

Chef Richard James **Owner** Toby Ashworth **Times** 12.30-2.30/7-9.30 Closed 25 Dec, D 31 Dec **Prices** Starter £5.85-£7.50, Main £19.50-£23, Dessert £6.50-£8.50 **Notes** Vegetarian available, Dress restrictions, Smart casual **Children** Menu **Parking** 70

WATERGATE BAY — Map 2 SW86

Fifteen Cornwall

Modern British, Italian

Freshest fish and seafood with views of the rolling surf

☎ 01637 861000
On The Beach TR8 4AA
e-mail: restaurant@fifteencornwall.co.uk
dir: M5 to Exeter & join A30 westbound. Exit Highgate Hill junct, following signs to airport and at T-junct after airport, turn left & follow road to Watergate Bay

In case you're not up to speed on the concept, Jamie Oliver's Fifteen Foundation was set up to help youngsters who have had a rough deal in life get onto the first rung of a career in the restaurant industry. And this is a very cool place to start out from, looking through a glass wall over the sand as surfers bob in the waves. The hip interior sports a designer beach bum look with darkwood floors, teardrop light shades and pink 1960s flowers painted on columns and walls. The kitchen delivers all-day food, kicking off at breakfast, while lunch brings a medley of Jamie O's pukka rustic Italian dishes - pan-fried brill with aubergine caponata, purple sprouting broccoli and wild garlic, for example. Amazing fresh seafood stars again in the evening tasting menu, perhaps pan-fried John Dory with Charlotte potatoes, mussels and rainbow chard in a crab broth with bottarga fish roe.

Chef Andy Appleton **Owner** Cornwall Foundation of Promise **Times** 12-3/6.15-9.45 **Prices** Fixed L 3 course £26, Tasting menu £55, Starter £7.25-£10.50, Main £16.50-£22, Dessert £6.40-£7.15, Service optional **Wines** 90 bottles over £20, 3 bottles under £20, 10 by glass **Notes** Tasting menu 5 course D only, Vegetarian available **Seats** 100, Pr/dining room 12 **Children** Portions, Menu **Parking** In front of restaurant

ZENNOR — Map 2 SW43

The Gurnard's Head

Modern British NOTABLE WINE LIST

Roadside inn with appealing modern menu

☎ 01736 796928
Treen TR26 3DE
e-mail: enquiries@gurnardshead.co.uk
dir: 6m W of St Ives by B3306

On the rugged north-west edge of Cornwall, with the sea on one side and the moors on the other, stands this sturdy, traditional-looking Cornish pub. It combines a country atmosphere - log fires, solid wood floors and tables - with modern cooking in both bar and dining areas. Good local produce meets modern British and European sensibilities on the carte, so oyster rissoles with asparagus are alongside confit pork belly with cauliflower purée and spiced jus as starters. Main-course sole is given a European flavour with white beans, pearl onions and spinach sauce, as is spring lamb with boulangère potatoes and a mint and caper jus, and desserts such as chocolate terrine with coffee ice cream come with dessert wine suggestions. The bar serves a good pint of local beer, and service gets the tone of friendly efficiency just right.

Times 12-2.30/6.30-9.30 Closed 24-25 Dec

SCILLY, ISLES OF

BRYHER — Map 2 SV81

Hell Bay

– *see page 96*

ST MARY'S — Map 2 SV91

St Mary's Hall Hotel

International **NEW**

Environmentally conscious food in a smart townhouse hotel

☎ 01720 422316
Church St, Hugh Town TR21 0JR
e-mail: recp@stmaryshallhotel.co.uk

A couple of minutes' from the sandy beaches of St Mary's, this smart townhouse hotel maintains a keen environmental policy, with much local sourcing, as well as growing its own produce. A breezy Mediterranean style runs through the menu, bringing on such dishes as roasted tomato and olive oil soup served with toasted ciabatta, and majestic paella incorporating lobster tail and crab, River Exe mussels, Newlyn scallops and chorizo. There's also the more obviously British steak and ale pie, its chunky filling bound with the hotel's own Spirit Level ale under a buttery puff-pastry lid. Lemon and almond polenta cake for dessert is served warm with vanilla crème fraîche.

Times 12-2/6-8 Closed Xmas, Sun (exc residents)

TRESCO — Map 2 SV81

New Inn

Traditional British

Great local seafood and more close to the beach

☎ 01720 422844 & 423006
TR24 0QQ
e-mail: newinn@tresco.co.uk
dir: Ferry or helicopter from Penzance; 250yds from harbour (private island, contact hotel for details)

Very much the convivial hub of the beautiful, tranquil island of Tresco with its exotic gardens and sandy beaches and turquoise sea, The New Inn is practically on the beach. The pub combines old-world character with a beachcomber-chic and much of the Driftwood Bar has been created from reclaimed wood from shipwrecks over the years. The light and airy bistro-style Pavilion restaurant has a New England-style décor and the menus and daily specials are the same as in the bar. A sea-facing garden is the place to dine when the weather allows (which is quite often in these parts). Quality local ingredients - fish and seafood in particular - are the backbone of a crowd-pleasing menu full of old favourites. Grilled mackerel fillets with potato and watercress salad might start you off, followed by crayfish, crab, chilli and bok choi linguini with coriander.

Chef Peter Marshall **Owner** Mr Robert Dorrien-Smith **Times** 12-2/6.30-9 **Prices** Starter £4.95-£8, Main £9-£16, Dessert £5.50, Service optional **Wines** 14 bottles over £20, 13 bottles under £20, 12 by glass **Notes** Sunday L, Vegetarian available **Seats** 30 **Children** Portions, Menu

Hell Bay

BRYHER **Map 2 SV81**

Modern British

Formidably talented chef in a dramatic island hotel

☎ 01720 422947
TR23 0PR
e-mail: contactus@hellbay.co.uk
dir: Helicopter from Penzance to Tresco, St Mary's. Plane from Southampton, Bristol, Exeter, Newquay or Land's End

The address may sound a little like something out of Rider Haggard, while the journey here is refreshingly not the usual matter of looking for the right motorway junction. This dramatically sited island hotel is unquestionably worth the journey. Lavishly adorned with artworks by local artist Richard Peace, as well as the odd Barbara Hepworth piece, it is a singular environment for a visit or a stay. The full-length windows and high vaulted wood ceiling of the dining room fit the ambience perfectly, and Glenn Gatland is a formidably talented chef who brings a finely attentive sensibility to menus that balance innovation with modern classics. First course might be a late spin on breakfast, a roasted local tomato appearing with grilled black pudding and a poached egg, or else a fresh rendition of that well-worked combination of seared scallops, cauliflower purée and pancetta. Clear-headed thinking is in evidence in a stunning main course trio of beef, comprised of braised oxtail, seared fillet and a little steak-and-kidney pudding, accompanied by fine ancillaries in the forms of soft, smooth mash, local spinach and crunchy green beans. Dessert assiettes are as tempting as ever - a strawberry one brings on cheesecake, mousse and parfait. Cornish cheeses, brilliant canapés and petits fours that might extend to a blob of elderflower sorbet in lemonade, complete a richly impressive picture.

Chef Glenn Gatland **Owner** Tresco Estate **Times** 12-2/7-9.30 Closed Nov-Feb **Prices** Fixed L 2 course £15-£30, Fixed D 3 course fr £35, Service optional **Wines** 32 bottles over £20, 17 bottles under £20, 16 by glass **Notes** Sunday L, Vegetarian available, Dress restrictions, No jeans, T-shirts in eve **Seats** 75, Pr/dining room 20 **Children** Portions, Menu **Parking**

CUMBRIA

ALSTON **Map 18 NY74**

Lovelady Shield Country House Hotel

Modern British

Family-run country-house hotel with innovative cuisine

☎ 01434 381203
CA9 3LF
e-mail: enquiries@lovelady.co.uk
web: www.lovelady.co.uk
dir: 2m E of Alston, signed off A689 at junct with B6294

How many times have you said you want to get away from it all? Well, this charming Georgian country house lost among the wilds of the North Pennines with the River Nent trundling through three acres of secluded gardens should fit the bill. The delightfully-named Lovelady Shield seduces visitors with its intimate ambience - it is run with charm by hands-on owners who like to foster the feel of a house party rather than a formal hotel. The neatly decorated dining room is a suitably refined setting for ambitious, well-presented modern cooking which majors on seasonality and local suppliers. Creative combinations and top-class materials are present from the off, in home-cured wild boar bacon with pan-fried thyme porridge, quail's egg and tomato salsa, say, and mains that might see a trio of beef - rare roasted rump, slow-braised feather and cottage pie - on the same plate as horseradish mousse and red cabbage purée. Equally inventive desserts might include a white chocolate and passionfruit marquise with milk chocolate fritter and passionfruit coulis.

Times 12-2/7-8.30 Closed L Mon-Sat

AMBLESIDE **Map 18 NY30**

Drunken Duck Inn

British

Superb local produce in a glorious Lakeland setting

☎ 015394 36347
Barngates LA22 0NG
e-mail: info@drunkenduckinn.co.uk
web: www.drunkenduckinn.co.uk
dir: Take A592 from Kendal, follow signs for Hawkshead (from Ambleside), in 2.5m sign for inn on right, 1m up hill

The 400-year-old Drunken Duck has been run by the same family for 35 years and has built a reputation that extends far beyond the knot of winding lanes where it sits above Ambleside. It's a nice idea to drop by for a lunchtime pint of the pub's own Barngate Brewery ales at the black slate bar: admire the classy leather chairs, wide oak floorboards, hopbines festooning the roof and tuck into hearty pub grub from the lunch menu; perhaps a slab of local pork, chicken and stuffing pie with air-dried ham and piccalilli, or potted duck with a boiled duck egg, pickled onions and gherkins. But you'll need to come back in the evening to see what the kitchen can really do. Things take a fancier turn at dinner when rich and hearty modern brasserie-style cuisine is the deal: take a classic fillet beef tartare to start, followed by braised belly pork and home-made black pudding, boulangère potatoes, wilted baby gem lettuce, and Calvados apples and jus. Puddings keep up the momentum - carrot cake with cream cheese frosting is served with candied walnuts and cinnamon ice cream.

Drunken Duck Inn

Chef Luke Shaw, Jim Metcalfe **Owner** Stephanie Barton **Times** 12-4/6.30-9 Closed 25 Dec **Prices** Food prices not confirmed for 2011. Please telephone for details **Wines** 200 bottles over £20, 26 bottles under £20, 26 by glass **Notes** Sunday L, Vegetarian available **Seats** 52 **Children** Portions **Parking** 40

The Log House

Modern Mediterranean

Unique Norwegian log-house restaurant with rooms

☎ 015394 31077
Lake Rd LA22 0DN
e-mail: info@loghouse.co.uk
dir: M6 junct 36. Situated on A591 on left, just beyond garden centre

This charming and historic Norwegian building is located midway between Ambleside's town centre and the shore of Lake Windermere. The Log House was imported in the late 19th century by the artist Alfred Heaton Cooper. Nowadays, Cooper's studio and family home serves as a restaurant with rooms, with the interior of the split-level restaurant and bar remodelled to suit modern tastes - smart lightwood floors and terracotta-washed walls, for example. The kitchen follows the seasons and uses classic techniques to produce modern European food such as a first-course confit of slow-cooked Gressingham duck leg with wild mushroom tartlet and hazelnut dressing. Next up, perhaps Gloucestershire Old Spot pork belly with roasted parsnips, Savoy cabbage, chilli jam and pork demi-glaze, and sticky toffee pudding for dessert.

Chef Heath Calman **Owner** Nicola & Heath Calman **Times** 5-9.30 Closed 7 Jan-7 Feb, Mon, L all week **Prices** Fixed D 3 course £18.95-£19.95, Starter £5.50-£7.95, Main £12.95-£22.95, Dessert £5.50-£7.25, Service optional **Wines** 32 bottles over £20, 31 bottles under £20, 5 by glass **Notes** Chef's choice menu available 5-6.30pm, Vegetarian available **Seats** 40 **Children** Portions, Menu **Parking** 3, Pay & display opposite

Rothay Manor

Traditional British V

Lakeland country dining in family-run hotel

☎ 015394 33605
Rothay Bridge LA22 0EH
e-mail: hotel@rothaymanor.co.uk
web: www.rothaymanor.co.uk
dir: In Ambleside follow signs for Coniston (A593). Manor 0.25m SW of Ambleside opposite rugby pitch

The Regency-style mansion is handy for Ambleside, but well insulated from its touristy bustle by over an acre of gorgeous secluded grounds. The same family have been at the helm of Rothay for 43 years, giving the place the deeply traditional feel of a comfy well-established country house. Lounges have squashy sofas to sink into, while the dining room has a relaxed, informal ambience; soft candlelight glows from burnished mahogany tables at dinner, which runs to five courses, with a soup or sorbet after the starter, and English cheeses after dessert. Classic country-house cuisine might open with sautéed scallops on butternut squash purée with lime and chilli dressing, and move on via cream of carrot and coriander soup to loin of Cumbrian lamb on a bed of ratatouille with Anna potatoes and rosemary jus.

Chef Jane Binns **Owner** Nigel Nixon **Times** 12.30-1.45/7.15-9 Closed 3-28 Jan, L 1 Jan, D 25 Dec **Prices** Fixed L 2 course £14-£20, Fixed D 3 course £42, Starter £5-£7, Main £9-£13, Dessert £5-£6, Service optional **Wines** 95 bottles over £20, 28 bottles under £20, 12 by glass **Notes** ALC L only, Sunday L, Vegetarian menu, Dress restrictions, Smart casual **Seats** 65, Pr/dining room 34 **Children** Portions, Menu **Parking** 35

Waterhead Hotel

Modern British **NEW**

Classy modern cooking on the water's edge

☎ 015394 32566
Lake Rd LA22 0ER
e-mail: waterhead@elhmail.co.uk
dir: A591 into Ambleside, hotel opposite Waterhead Pier

Right on the shore of Lake Windermere, the Waterhead hotel got a contemporary makeover a few years back and has scrubbed up very nicely indeed to meet the needs of the modern traveller. It is not possible to improve the location, but everything else has been subject to a keen eye for contemporary design. The Bay Restaurant and Bar has views over the water and a smart but unpretentious interior, with unclothed darkwood tables, retro lampshades and innovative evening lighting. It's a civilised and comfortable space for some accomplished modern British cooking. There's plenty of local produce on the menu in a happy blend of traditional and modern dishes. Start perhaps with an oriental squid salad with the kick of chilli and ginger, and for main course perhaps a fillet of cod with leeks and a mussel cream sauce. To finish there might be rhubarb cheesecake with rhubarb syrup.

Chef Michael Wilson **Owner** English Lakes Hotels **Times** 12.30-2.30/7-9.30 Closed Xmas, New Year (only open to residents), L Mon-Sat **Prices** Fixed D 3 course £23.65-£35.40, Starter £4.75-£7.95, Main £12.95-£19.95, Dessert £5.95-£7.50, Service optional **Wines** 38 bottles over £20, 29 bottles under £20, 12 by glass **Notes** Sunday L, Vegetarian available **Seats** 70 **Children** Portions, Menu **Parking** 50, Nearby pay & display

APPLEBY-IN-WESTMORLAND **Map 18 NY62**

Appleby Manor Country House Hotel

Modern British V

Hearty classic cooking in relaxed country-house hotel

☎ 017683 51571
Roman Rd CA16 6JB
e-mail: reception@applebymanor.co.uk
dir: M6 junct 40/A66 towards Brough. Take Appleby turn, then immediately right. Continue for 0.5m

Whether you pull up a seat in the traditional oak-panelled dining room or the summery conservatory, the award-winning gardens of this delightful family-run country house look a treat while you eat. And the food is accomplished stuff too, produced by a kitchen that favours hearty traditional dishes, but is far from stuck in the mud; interesting flavours and combinations put a new spin on time-honoured classics. An ambitious starter plays variations on a William pear theme, bringing together boozy pear jelly, black pepper-roasted pear, and Yorkshire blue cheese with pear salad and pear cider syrup. Main-course calves' liver is flash-fried and served with savoury roly poly, white onion cream, Bury black pudding and thyme jus.

Chef Chris Thompson **Owner** Dunbobin Family **Times** 12-2/7-9 Closed 24-26 Dec **Prices** Starter £5.95-£9.95, Main £14.95-£20, Dessert £6.95, Service optional **Wines** 31 bottles over £20, 50 bottles under £20, 6 by glass **Notes** Sunday L, Vegetarian menu, Dress restrictions, Smart casual **Seats** 96, Pr/dining room 20 **Children** Portions, Menu **Parking** 62

BARROW-IN-FURNESS Map 18 SD26

Clarence House Country Hotel & Restaurant

@@ British, International **NEW**

Enjoyable dining in comfortable conservatory surroundings

☎ 01229 462508
Skelgate LA15 8BQ
e-mail: info@clarencehouse-hotel.co.uk

Sandwiched between the beautiful beaches of the Cumbrian coast and the Lake District, Clarence House is a welcoming country-house hotel that does everything right. Solicitous staff ensure polished service and a relaxed mood - it's the sort of place where afternoon tea is hard to resist, but go easy on the cakes and sandwiches as there's a real sense of occasion in the ritzy Victorian-styled restaurant at dinner too. High-backed pyjama-striped chairs at linen-clad tables look through full-length windows over St Thomas' Valley, and on balmy evenings you can dine alfresco on the terrace. The menu ranges widely around modern European themes with a peppering of global flourishes. Cumbrian meats could star in a starter plate of pressed ham hock, Waberthwaite ham, and Carmel smoked duckling with pickled red cabbage and beetroot relish, while mains could deliver an exotic tempura of monkfish and tiger prawns with coconut, lemongrass and chilli risotto.

Times 12-4/7-9

BASSENTHWAITE Map 18 NY23

The Pheasant

@ Modern British

Quality Cumbrian ingredients in a revamped dining room

☎ 017687 76234
CA13 9YE
e-mail: info@the-pheasant.co.uk
dir: M6 junct 40, take A66 (Keswick and North Lakes). Continue past Keswick and head for Cockermouth. Signed from A66

One of the last remaining traditional Cumbrian hostelries, this 500-plus year old former coaching inn enjoys a peaceful location close to Bassenthwaite Lake. The new dining room is a formal affair (think sparkling cutlery and crystal glasses) overlooking the gardens, fells and forests behind the hotel. Modern British dishes might include ham hock and rabbit terrine with apple and mustard jelly and boozy raisins, and a main course of pan-fried pavé of cod with clams, courgettes, almonds, spiced merguez sausage and minted potatoes. A new bistro opened in summer 2010.

Times 12-1.30/7-9 Closed 25 Dec

BORROWDALE Map 18 NY21

Hazel Bank Country House

@ British, European

Sound cooking in Victorian house with stunning Lakeland views

☎ 017687 77248
Rosthwaite CA12 5XB
e-mail: enquiries@hazelbankhotel.co.uk
dir: A66 Keswick, follow B5289 signed Borrowdale, turn left before Rosthwaite over humpback bridge

The Victorian gentleman who built this house chose a heavenly corner of the Borrowdale Valley. Hazel Bank sits in four acres of gardens and woodlands with lovely streams running through, and with inspirational views of the Lakeland peaks - enjoy them at leisure over aperitifs by the fireside in the lounge. The smartly traditional dining room makes an intimate setting with a convivial ambience, while the kitchen takes a traditional line with its four-course dinners, making maximum use of Cumbria's fine produce in dishes that have a continental accent. Things might get underway with home-smoked duck breast with ceps and truffle oil, followed by seared Lakeland lamb steak with redcurrants and capers. Finish with gooseberry farmhouse pie and vanilla sauce.

Times 7 Closed 25-26 Dec, L all week

Leathes Head Hotel

@ Modern British

Honest cooking in the beautiful Borrowdale Valley

☎ 017687 77247
CA12 5UY
e-mail: enq@leatheshead.co.uk
dir: 3.75m S of Keswick on B5289, set back on the left

This Edwardian country-house hotel built of local slate is set in two and a half acres of grounds, elevated and set back from the road in the magnificent Borrowdale Valley. It's a family business, with chef David Jackson manning the stoves for the last 20 years. Comfort is the name of the game, in the elegant bedrooms and spacious conservatory lounge, cosy well-stocked bar and the traditional restaurant. Typical options on the daily-changing menu of hearty British dishes might include Cumbrian brie with traditional Waldorf salad and salami, then pan-seared medallions of beef fillet with pearl barley risotto and rich port red wine sauce, and chilled lemon syllabub with Cumberland flapjack to finish.

Times 7.30-8.15 Closed mid Nov-mid Feb

BRAITHWAITE Map 18 NY22

The Cottage in the Wood

@@ Modern British V NOTABLE WINE LIST

Excellent food and service in dramatic Lake District setting

☎ 017687 78409
Whinlatter Forest CA12 5TW
e-mail: relax@thecottageinthewood.co.uk
dir: M6 junct 40, A66 signed Keswick. 1m after Keswick take B5292 signed Braithwaite, hotel in 2m

This former 17th-century coaching inn sits in the embrace of Whinlatter Forest near Keswick, with glorious views dropping away down the valley to Lakeland mountains much beloved of the famous walker A W Wainwright. After a recent makeover the restaurant with rooms looks spruce, and dinner is served in a classy, contemporary light-flooded conservatory setting to a dreamy backdrop of the Skiddaw peaks. Chef-proprietor Liam Berney draws his influences from Europe as well as the native larder, so English asparagus might be teamed in a first course with grilled haloumi and lemon dressing. Flavour combinations are full of good ideas, but nothing is fussy or forced - main courses might run to pan-roasted wild halibut with oxtail croquette and wild garlic, or roast Goosnargh duck with vanilla mash and shiitaki mushrooms. Interesting dessert combinations could take in lemon cheesecake with apple and ginger jelly, and lemon and bayleaf custard.

Chef Liam Berney **Owner** Liam & Kath Berney
Times 12-2.30/6.30-9 Closed Jan, Mon, D Sun
Prices Fixed D 3 course £28.50-£32.50, Service included, Groups min 8 service 10% **Wines** 20 bottles over £20, 20 bottles under £20, 6 by glass **Notes** Degustation menu 6 course £55, Sunday L, Vegetarian menu **Seats** 36
Children Portions **Parking** 16

BRAMPTON Map 21 NY56

Farlam Hall Hotel

@ Modern British V

Traditional cooking with relaxing pastoral views

☎ 016977 46234
Hallbankgate CA8 2NG
e-mail: farlam@relaischateaux.com
web: www.farlamhall.co.uk
dir: On A689, 2.5m SE of Brampton (not in Farlam village)

Not far from Carlisle, the hotel is a Victorian re-creation of a medieval manor house. It looks a picture, with its half-cladding of creepers and the rise of immaculate grounds that swell up towards it. Those peaceful views are still to be enjoyed from the formally attired dining room, where the cooking maintains the gentle tone. A daily-changing menu offers the likes of crayfish and avocado timbale to start, perhaps followed by pork fillet of exemplary flavour, served with pasta in a gingery cream sauce. Well-kept English cheeses precede the sweet stuff, perhaps a light orange mousse with robustly rich Grand Marnier ice cream.

Chef Barry Quinion **Owner** Quinion Family **Times** 8-8.30 Closed 24-30 Dec, 4-15 Jan, L all week **Prices** Fixed D 4 course £43-£45, Service optional **Wines** 37 bottles over £20, 7 bottles under £20, 12 by glass **Notes** Vegetarian menu, Dress restrictions, Smart dress, no shorts **Seats** 40, Pr/dining room 20 **Children** Portions **Parking** 25

BRIGSTEER **Map 18 SD48**

The Wheatsheaf

Modern, Traditional British **NEW**

Rural pub making good use of local ingredients

☎ 015395 68254
LA8 8AN
e-mail: wheatsheaf@brigsteer.gb.com
dir: Off A591 signed Brigsteer, Wheatsheaf at bottom of hill

The spruced-up Wheatsheaf has stood at the crossroads in sleepy Brigsteer, close to the Lakes and Kendal, since 1762 and today wows the locals with hearty gastro-pub cooking. The attractive bar and dining room has a rustic feel, with warm colours and real fires adding to the comfort factor. The kitchen makes good use of local and regional produce to deliver robust modern British dishes with plenty of flair. Take potted Morecambe Bay shrimps and Millom crab with lemon and caper jelly for starters and a main course of roast chump of Helsington lamb with roast garlic mash, crushed broad beans and mint pickle. Puddings may include rhubarb and custard crème brûlée with home-made ginger biscuits.

Times 12-2/5.45-9

CARTMEL **Map 18 SD37**

Aynsome Manor Hotel

British

Long-standing Lakeland hotel with comfortingly traditional approach

☎ 015395 36653
LA11 6HH
e-mail: aynsomemanor@btconnect.com
dir: M6 junct 36, A590 signed Barrow-in-Furness towards Cartmel. Left at end of road, hotel before village

The original Georgian manor was extended by those compulsive makeover pioneers, the Victorians, and has been handed down through various incumbents, including wealthy clergy, to the welcoming stewardship of the Varley family for the last couple of generations. Lakeland country-house tradition in its oak-panelled interior is the order of the day; it is all looking spick and span, too, after a thorough facelift at the start of 2010. The kitchen's comforting country-house cooking fits the bill, on a well-balanced menu studded with local materials. Pan-seared scallops with Higginson's black pudding and celeriac purée drizzled with white truffle oil is one way to start, and if you fancy something meaty, roast venison comes with spiced red cabbage, potato rösti and a gin and berry jus.

Chef Gordon Topp **Owner** P A Varley **Times** 1-7 Closed 25-26 Dec, 2-28 Jan, L Mon-Sat, D Sun (ex residents) **Prices** Fixed L 3 course £15.95, Fixed D 3 course £26-£27, Service optional **Wines** 25 bottles over £20, 60 bottles under £20, 6 by glass **Notes** Sunday L, Vegetarian available, Dress restrictions, Smart dress **Seats** 28 **Children** Portions, Menu **Parking** 20

L'Enclume

– see page 100

Rogan & Company Bar & Restaurant

European

Classic dining at L'Enclume's younger sister

☎ 015395 35917 & 07813 347475
Devonshire Square LA11 6QD
e-mail: reservations@roganandcompany.co.uk
dir: From M6 junct 36 follow signs for A590. Turn off at sign for Cartmel village

While Simon Rogan is making great culinary waves down the road at L'Enclume (see entry), more straightforward cooking is the name of the game at little sister Rogan & Company, which sits beside the river in the heart of Cartmel. The 16th-century building, formerly an antiques shop, is part lively bar, part casual restaurant, with wooden flooring, beamed ceilings, wooden tables and modern artwork on the walls. You can have a drink in the bar at the back, or on one of the comfy leather sofas at the front, before dining upstairs or down. The cooking is mostly classic British, with a few modern European influences, and much of the seasonal produce comes from Rogan's own farm nearby. Nibble on some crispy devilled whitebait before moving on to a first-class gazpacho with a crunchy wafer and tartar of salmon. Grilled plaice fillet with tarragon mash and Muncaster crab velouté is a typically simple but effective main course.

Chef Simon Rogan, Adam Wesley **Owner** Simon Rogan & Penny Tapsell **Times** 12-2.30/6.30-9 Closed Mon (winter only) **Prices** Food prices not confirmed for 2011. Please telephone for details **Notes** Sunday L, Vegetarian available **Seats** 100, Pr/dining room 24 **Children** Portions **Parking** On street

CROSTHWAITE **Map 18 SD49**

The Punchbowl Inn at Crosthwaite

Modern British NOTABLE WINE LIST

Historic, elegantly refurbished inn with refined cooking

☎ 015395 68237
Lyth Valley LA8 8HR
e-mail: info@the-punchbowl.co.uk
dir: A590 then A5074 signed Bowness/Crosthwaite. Inn within 3m on right

The Lyth Valley is an area of genuine tranquility, with the unspoilt, gently rolling Lakeland countryside possessing a timeless quality. Next to the village church in the small community of Crosthwaite is the Punchbowl - a country inn and restaurant of sheer class. There's plenty of country character if that's what you're after - open fireplaces, slate floors (and bar), and enough oak boards and beams to satisfy purists - but classy leather chairs and chic styling give it a contemporary sheen. Eat in the bar or restaurant and expect excellent food with classical sensibilities, based on top-notch regional produce, and cooked with flair. Home-smoked saddle of venison, for example, with beetroot and salad leaves, followed by roasted halibut, served up with brown shrimps and cockles, Lincolnshire potatoes, and finished with a lemon and chervil butter.

Chef Christopher Meredith **Owner** Paul Spencer, Richard Rose **Times** 12-6/6-9.30 **Prices** Food prices not confirmed for 2011. Please telephone for details **Wines** 58 bottles over £20, 15 bottles under £20, 14 by glass **Notes** Vegetarian available, Civ Wed 50 **Seats** 50, Pr/dining room 16 **Children** Portions **Parking** 40

L'Enclume

CARTMEL Map 18 SD37

Modern NOTABLE WINE LIST

Exhilarating, innovative cuisine to stir a quiet Lakeland village

☎ 015395 36362
Cavendish St LA11 6PZ
e-mail: info@lenclume.co.uk
web: www.lenclume.co.uk
dir: Follow signs for A590 W, turn left for Cartmel before Newby Bridge

To set up shop intending to voyage to the edge of culinary possibilities in the heart of Lakeland country-house chintz territory takes some audacity. Then there's the setting: a 700-year-old smithy (the name is French for 'anvil') in a snoozy village that induces contemplation. Not the most obvious foundations for a restaurant that aims to stay in the vanguard of 21st-century gastronomy, then. But it all works beautifully, and has done since day one, back in 2002. Within the dining room, gnarled beams, flagstones and rough whitewashed walls are a nod to antiquity, while contemporary sensibilities are stroked by bare darkwood tables with corduroy place mats, slate floors and abstract artworks. While stopping short of monastic, the stark look makes no attempt to vie with the food for diners' attention. Service is intelligent, attentive and knowledgeable - necessarily so, as the menus require explanation: the names given to dishes intrigue rather than enlighten. There are three multi-course workouts, the most ambitious running to 15 or so courses, but whichever way you jump, superb produce underpins everything - vegetables and herbs come from their own farm, which also breeds pigs and sheep. And so to the food. Simon Rogan is a chef working at a level of innovation and technical skill shared by maybe a handful of people in the UK, an edgy explorer striving for an elusive perfection - out with the bombastic meat stocks and reliance on dairy produce, and in with forgotten flowers and subtle herbs. He is a tireless researcher, using an experimental kitchen as a test bed for new ideas, constantly striving to pop preconceptions by pushing the boundaries of what tastes and textures work; if this all sounds a bit too serious, there is a sense of humour at work too. 'Humphrey's Pool' is a light seafood broth flavoured with sea lettuce - a clean ocean-flavoured dish of whelks, clams, cockles and winkles; next up, 'sea scallop meat and pearls' delivers a big fat scallop centre stage, atop tapioca infused with scallop essence, with a stunning red pepper emulsion; pan-seared skate gets esoteric company next to an ambrosial pine nut purée, Douglas fir foam, and stems of wild celery and Alexander; desserts bring more mind-spinning textures and flavours with caramelised quince, Ribston Pippin sorbet, cobnut crisp for added crunch, and a soft rosehip jelly. (See Rogan & Company for the Rogan take on modern brasserie cooking.)

Chef Simon Rogan **Owner** Simon Rogan, Penny Tapsell **Times** 12-1.30/6.30-9.30 Closed L Mon-Tue **Prices** Fixed L 3 course £25, Service optional, Groups min 8 service 10% **Wines** 356 bottles over £20, 4 bottles under £20, 10 by glass **Notes** Fixed D 8 course £60, 13 course £80, Sunday L, Vegetarian available **Seats** 50, Pr/dining room 8 **Parking** 7, On street

ELTERWATER Map 18 NY30

Purdeys

Modern, Traditional British

Culinary fireworks in a former gunpowder factory

015394 37302 & 38080
Langdale Hotel & Country Club LA22 9JD
e-mail: purdeys@langdale.co.uk
web: www.langdale.co.uk
dir: M6 junct 36, A591 or M6 junct 40, A66, B5322, A591

Sited in what was once a gunpowder factory (the cannon that was once used to test it now lies dormant in the restaurant), Purdey's is otherwise a blamelessly tranquil place, built of local stone and with a working waterwheel in the walled garden. Pardoning ourselves the pun, we might expect the cooking to be suitably explosive, and there are certainly fireworks going on in dishes such as a starter study in salmon, which brings together rillettes, a slice of ballottine and smoked salmon alongside an earthy beetroot sorbet. Follow on with Gressingham duck in the classic pairing of breast and confit leg, garnished with seared foie gras, a fig tart and celeriac cream. It's highly worked cooking, but the efforts pay off, even if dishes often feel as though they have one too many elements. Banana parfait and caramel ice cream are the accompaniments to a well-rendered dark chocolate fondant.

Chef Graham Harrower **Owner** Langdale Leisure **Times** 6.30-9.30 Closed L Group L booking essential **Prices** Starter £7.50-£11.50, Main £14.50-£26, Dessert £6-£7.50, Service optional **Wines** 22 bottles over £20, 40 bottles under £20, 9 by glass **Notes** Vegetarian available, Dress restrictions, Smart casual, Civ Wed 60 **Seats** 80, Pr/dining room 40 **Children** Portions, Menu **Parking** 50

GLENRIDDING Map 18 NY31

The Inn on the Lake

Modern European V

Varied menu and sumptuous views across Ullswater

017684 82444
CA11 0PE
e-mail: info@innonthelakeullswater.co.uk
dir: M6 junct 40, A66 Keswick, A592 Windermere

A sumptuously sited Victorian Lakeland hotel, the Inn offers photogenic views of the fells and Ullswater. Pleasure boats and steamers ply the lake, and the whole scene can be taken in from the windows of the plushly decorated dining room. Where other Lake District hotels go in for set menus, the choice here is wide and varied, with starters embracing braised pig's cheek with chorizo and button onions in port, and mains running a range from seared monkfish tail with curly kale and grain mustard, to roast Gressingham duck in truffled jus with swede confit. Finish with the regional speciality, sticky toffee pudding with butterscotch sauce and toffee ice cream.

Chef Fraser Soutar **Owner** Charles & Kit Graves **Times** 12.30-2/7-9 Closed L Sat **Prices** Fixed D 4 course fr £35.95, Service optional **Wines** 38 bottles over £20, 12 bottles under £20, 8 by glass **Notes** Sunday L, Vegetarian menu, Dress restrictions, Smart casual, Civ Wed 110 **Seats** 100, Pr/dining room 40 **Children** Portions, Menu **Parking** 100

GRANGE-OVER-SANDS Map 18 SD47

Clare House

Modern British

Confident cooking in elegant Victorian mansion with views

015395 33026 & 34253
Park Rd LA11 7HQ
e-mail: info@clarehousehotel.co.uk
dir: From M6 take A590, then B5277 to Grange-over-Sands. Park Road follows the shore line. Hotel on left next to swimming pool

Built in the late 1800s as some lucky gentleman's private residence, Clare House has been run by the same family for the past 40 years. These days a relaxing country-house hotel between the Lakes and the sea, this splendid Victorian mansion retains a wealth of period features including stained-glass windows, deep cornices and open fireplaces. Once across the threshold, it feels a bit like stepping back in time to a more unhurried, elegant era. With gorgeous gardens and spectacular views over Morecambe Bay, it makes an ideal setting for traditional country-house fare (with plenty of contemporary ideas alongside). Confit of duck leg with cider reduction and apple and vanilla chutney is a well-judged first course; next up, perhaps a roast loin and slow-cooked belly of Gloucestershire Old Spot pork with herb jus. Finish with apple and blackberry crumble with toasted nuts, oats and cinnamon.

Chef Andrew Read, Mark Johnston **Owner** Mr & Mrs D S Read **Times** 6.45-7.15 Closed Dec-Apr, L all week **Prices** Food prices not confirmed for 2011. Please telephone for details **Wines** 7 bottles over £20, 30 bottles under £20, 2 by glass **Notes** Vegetarian available **Seats** 32 **Children** Portions, Menu **Parking** 16

GRASMERE Map 18 NY30

Grasmere Hotel

Traditional European

Traditional country-house hotel with good food

015394 35277
Broadgate LA22 9TA
e-mail: enquiries@grasmerehotel.co.uk
dir: Off A591 close to village centre

The River Rothay runs through the lovely gardens of this traditional Victorian hotel in the heart of the Lake District. A thorough refurbishment in recent years has given the place a dapper look without impacting on the period charm of its wood panelling and grand staircase. Food-wise, tradition is the watchword, both in the style of the dining room, where an eye-catching acanthus chandelier hangs from the vaulted ceiling, and in the old-school approach to the daily four-course menu. The kitchen takes no short cuts, so you can be sure that everything it sends out is prepared from scratch using the best local produce. Peppered mackerel and horseradish pâté is a typical starter, then soup - carrot and dill, perhaps, or mango sorbet - intervenes before oven-baked breast of Barbary duck with a Demerara glaze and honey, orange and Cointreau jus.

Times 7pm Closed Jan-early Feb, L all week

Oak Bank Hotel

Modern British **NEW**

Accomplished modern cooking in friendly Lakeland hotel

015394 35217
Broadgate LA22 9TA
e-mail: info@lakedistricthotel.co.uk
dir: N'bound: M6 junct 36 onto A591 to Windermere, Ambleside, then Grasmere. S'bound: M6 junct 40 onto A66 to Keswick, A591 to Grasmere

The River Rothay runs along the foot of the gardens of the Oak Bank Hotel, a substantial Victorian house in the

continued

GRASMERE *continued*

Lakeland village of Grasmere, with a delightful, light-flooded conservatory restaurant. The kitchen places a strong emphasis on local produce, proudly naming suppliers on the menu. Dinners are set-price affairs, where you can go for two, three, or four courses of creative modern British dishes, cooked with skill, and presented in a way that is always easy on the eye. A starter salad of Eyemouth crab is served with a full-flavoured jellied crab essence and watercress vichysoisse, ahead of a ham hock ballottine, that comes with breaded pork cheek, apple purée and dried apple ring, crackling and a port and raisin reduction to emphasise different textures. Main course teams John Dory with parmesan gnocchi, mussel beignets, scallops, baby onions, wilted spinach and a shellfish emulsion.

Chef John Cook, Dexton Gooden **Owner** Glynis & Simon Wood **Times** 6.30-8.30 Closed Jan, L all week **Prices** Fixed D 3 course £30, Service optional, Groups min 6 service 10% **Wines** 8 bottles over £20, 28 bottles under £20, 6 by glass **Notes** Vegetarian available **Seats** 32 **Children** Portions **Parking** 14

Rothay Garden Hotel & Restaurant

Modern British

Superb fell views and ambitious cooking

☎ 015394 35334
Broadgate LA22 9RJ
e-mail: stay@rothaygarden.com
dir: From N M6 junct 40, A66 to Keswick, then S on A591 to Grasmere. From S M6 junct 36 take A591 through Windermere/Ambleside to Grasmere. At N end of village adjacent to park

Surrounded by typically magnificent views of the fells, this attractive Lakeland-stone hotel and restaurant is tucked away in tranquil riverside gardens on the edge of bustling Grasmere village. Admire the stunning scenery whilst eating in the traditional conservatory restaurant, which is candlelit at night and looks onto the floodlit gardens. Expect modern British cooking on daily menus; seared tuna, perhaps, with warm Niçoise salad, pesto dressing and a balsamic glaze to start, followed by garlic roast aubergine and spinach charlotte with ginger and chilli roast vegetables, and crème brûlée with strawberry compôte and shortbread to finish.

Rothay Garden Hotel & Restaurant

Times 12-1.45/7-9.30 Closed 25-26 Dec, 1 Jan

Signature Restaurant @ Wordsworth Hotel

Modern British

Lovely Lakeland hotel delivering modern British flavours

☎ 015394 35592
LA22 9SW
e-mail: enquiry@thewordsworthhotel.co.uk
dir: From Ambleside follow A591 N to Grasmere. Hotel in town centre next to church

In two acres of beautiful landscaped gardens at the heart of one of the Lake District's loveliest villages, the Wordsworth offers a traditional country-house experience on the doorstep of the area's world-renowned literary attractions. Peaceful lounges furnished with fine antiques overlook the well-kept lawns and beyond to the spectacular mountains. In the light and airy conservatory the new fine-dining Signature restaurant has been decked out in shades of brown, beige and burgundy giving it a more contemporary look than the former Prelude restaurant. Locally-sourced ingredients take pride of place on the modern British menu - so expect the likes of rich local game terrine with cranberry chutney to start - followed by pot-roasted guinea fowl with broad beans and pancetta, thyme dauphinoise, sautéed spinach and battered cauliflower. Save room for an inventive dish of 'Northern Treats' featuring parkin ice cream, dandelion and burdock sorbet and frozen yoghurt desserts. The 'bodega' for storing wine is a major feature of the new restaurant with an impressive wine list of over 130 bins. For something simpler, settle down by the roaring fire in the Wordsworth Bistro.

Chef David Farrar **Owner** Iain & Jackie Garside **Times** 12.30-2/7-9.30 **Prices** Fixed L 2 course £12.50-£20, Fixed D 3 course £25-£39.95, Starter £3.95-£9.95, Main £12.95-£27, Dessert £4.95-£9.50 **Wines** 50 bottles over £20, 51 bottles under £20, 10 by glass **Notes** Sunday L, Vegetarian available, Dress restrictions, Smart casual, Civ Wed 100 **Seats** 65, Pr/dining room 18 **Children** Portions, Menu **Parking** 50

HAWKSHEAD **Map 18 SD39**

Queens Head Hotel

British, International

Charming old-world inn serving contemporary food

☎ 015394 36271 & 0800 137263
Main St LA22 0NS
e-mail: enquiries@queensheadhotel.co.uk
dir: Village centre

This venerable Lakeland inn has been at the heart of Hawkshead life since the 16th century. It has seen William Wordsworth go by on his way to school, and visits from Beatrix Potter, whose solicitor husband's former offices now house her illustrations. Behind the black-and-white timbered façade you'll find head-skimming oak beams, panelled walls and bare tables on a well-worn slate floor. Well-kept real ales make a perfect foil to timeless pub classics, but there's also an up-to-date, hearty repertoire with plenty of local colour. Start with venison and wild mushroom terrine served with home-baked brioche toast and pear and date chutney, and move on to local pheasant with caramelised Bramley apples, prunes and baby onions.

Queens Head Hotel

Chef Vincent Mulama **Owner** Anthony Merrick **Times** 12-2.30/6.15-9.30 **Prices** Fixed L 2 course £7, Starter £4.50-£7.25, Main £10.95-£18.50, Dessert £5.75, Service optional **Wines** 18 bottles over £20, 41 bottles under £20, 17 by glass **Notes** ALC menu available 3 course, Sunday L, Vegetarian available, Dress restrictions, Smart casual **Seats** 38, Pr/dining room 20 **Children** Menu **Parking** NCP permits issued

See advert on opposite page

HOWTOWN **Map 18 NY41**

Sharrow Bay Country House Hotel

British, International

Country-house cooking of great continuity on the shores of Ullswater

☎ 017684 86301
Sharrow Bay CA10 2LZ
e-mail: info@sharrowbay.co.uk
dir: M6 junct 40. From Pooley Bridge right fork by church towards Howtown. Right at x-rds, follow lakeside road for 2m

The continuity at Sharrow Bay (the present kitchen team are protegés of the hotel's founders) is one of its great strengths. Its position on the edge of Ullswater, in one of Lakeland's loveliest spots, is doubtless another, and the tone of gracious high living, bolstered by seasonally informed careful cookery, exercises as strong a lure now as ever it did. Contemporary fashion is gently acknowledged in a dish of sautéed scallops with truffled creamed leeks, asparagus and a rich shellfish velouté, while a main course of perfectly timed venison noisettes, served with a mighty portion of braised red cabbage, apple and raisins, sauced with cider, recalls the Sharrow Bay of old. A flurry of spun sugar announces the arrival of a dessert such as banana Tatin with liquorice ice cream.

Times 1-8pm

IREBY **Map 18 NY23**

Overwater Hall

Modern British

Fine country house with creative cooking

☎ 017687 76566
CA7 1HH
e-mail: welcome@overwaterhall.co.uk
dir: A591 at Castle Inn take road towards Ireby. After 2m turn right at sign

Bookended by turrets and with battlements along the roof, Overwater Hall stands in a lovely spot: guests regularly spot deer and red squirrels in its 18 acres of grounds guarded by the peak of Skiddaw and surrounding fells. Just eleven bedrooms make for a civilised, intimate ambience. Sip an aperitif and nibble canapés in the mahogany-panelled bar, then install yourself amid the sunny yellow and blue Georgian elegance of the dining room. Classical music plays, staff are correctly formal, and the kitchen approaches country-house classics with modern British creativity. Dinner takes a four-course format, kicking off with the well-balanced flavours of pan-fried quail scented with orange and thyme, continuing via a fish course to the main event: Cumbrian game three ways delivers loin of venison pan-fried with juniper on braised red cabbage, supreme of partridge on root vegetable rösti, and a rabbit pie with bramble jus.

Chef Adrian Hyde **Owner** Adrian & Angela Hyde, Stephen Bore **Times** 12.30-3/7-8.30 Closed 1st 2 wks Jan, L Mon **Prices** Fixed D 4 course £40, Service optional **Wines** 46 bottles over £20, 18 bottles under £20, 9 by glass **Notes** Light lunch available Tue-Sun 12.30-3, Vegetarian available, Dress restrictions, Smart casual, Civ Wed 30 **Seats** 30 **Children** Portions **Parking** 15

KENDAL **Map 18 SD59**

Best Western Castle Green Hotel in Kendal

Modern British, European

Ambitious cooking in modern Lakeland hotel

☎ 01539 734000
Castle Green Ln LA9 6RG
e-mail: reception@castlegreen.co.uk
web: www.castlegreen.co.uk
dir: M6 junct 37, A684 towards Kendal. Hotel on right in 5m

A tranquil Lakeland location with views of Kendal castle is the backdrop for this smart hotel. The Greenhouse restaurant looks sharply contemporary in neutral tones - an uncluttered space that doesn't vie for attention with the dramatic views outside the full-length picture windows. Ambitious modern cooking suits the surroundings, deploying superb local ingredients with dexterity and a feel for current trends. A starter of seared scallops with Gloucestershire Old Spot pork belly, garden peas and pea purée with mint delivers good depth of flavour, ahead of a modish marriage of fish and meat - fillet of brill with beef cheeks, shallots, garlic and carrots. A keenly-priced five-course tasting menu is available.

Chef Justin Woods **Owner** James & Catherine Alexander **Times** 12-2/6-10 **Prices** Fixed D 3 course £25, Tasting menu £25-£30, Starter £4.95-£8, Main £11.50-£22.50, Dessert £5-£7.95, Service included **Wines** 23 bottles over £20, 27 bottles under £20, 7 by glass **Notes** Tasting menu 3 or 5 course, Vegetarian available, Dress restrictions, Smart casual, Civ Wed 100 **Seats** 80, Pr/dining room 200 **Children** Portions, Menu **Parking** 200

KESWICK **Map 18 NY22**

Dale Head Hall Lakeside Hotel

Modern British V

Country-house dining in stunning spot

☎ 017687 72478
Lake Thirlmere CA12 4TN
e-mail: onthelakeside@daleheadhall.co.uk
dir: 5m from Keswick on A591

Dale Head Hall sits in wooded seclusion in one of the finest spots in the Lake District, with the waters of Lake Thirlmere at the foot of the garden, and the peak of Helvellyn towering in the background. The hotel, parts of which date from the 16th century, is run with a comfortingly traditional ambience, which extends to the beamed restaurant, where daily-changing dinner menus take a straightforward approach to the country-house idiom. Tried-and-tested combinations could kick off with a chicken and wild mushroom terrine with plum and sultana compôte, then proceed to pork loin wrapped in pancetta and teamed with Calvados sauce and basil-infused potato purée. Dessert could bring treacle and pecan tart with nutmeg cream.

Chef Jose Lopez, Gary Cooper **Owner** Mr & Mrs P Hill **Times** 7-8.30 Closed Jan, L all week **Prices** Fixed L 3 course £19.95, Fixed D 4 course £42.50, Service included **Wines** 55 bottles over £20, 17 bottles under £20, 8 by glass **Notes** Sunday L, Vegetarian menu, Dress restrictions, No jeans or casual wear, Civ Wed 50 **Seats** 28, Pr/dining room 12 **Children** Portions **Parking** 30

KESWICK *continued*

Highfield Hotel & Restaurant

@@ Modern European

Modern cooking in comfortable Lakeland hotel with stellar views

☎ 017687 72508
The Heads CA12 5ER
e-mail: info@highfieldkeswick.co.uk
dir: M6 junct 40, A66, 2nd exit at rdbt. Left to T-junct, left again. Right at mini-rdbt. Take 4th right

Just a short stroll from the centre of Keswick, and offering stunning views of Skiddaw, Catbells and Derwentwater, this elegant slate-built Lakeland country-house hotel typifies the Victorian style. The recently refurbished dining room with its bay windows and views down the Borrowdale Valley boasts traditional features - cornicing and chandeliers - but has a light and fresh feel. The hotel may offer traditional comforts, but the kitchen creates a more modern British approach with its innovative, dinner-only menus. Top-notch local ingredients are treated with respect in dishes such as twice-baked blue Stilton soufflé served on a ratatouille of Mediterranean vegetables or breast of Gressingham duck marinated in port on a cassoulet of haricot beans with cinnamon red cabbage.

Chef Gus Cleghorn **Owner** Howard & Caroline Speck **Times** 6.30-8.30 Closed Jan-early Feb, L all week **Prices** Fixed D 2 course £29.50-£34, Fixed D 4 course £42.50-£47, Service optional **Wines** 22 bottles over £20, 41 bottles under £20, 7 by glass **Notes** Vegetarian available, Dress restrictions, Smart casual **Seats** 40 **Children** Portions **Parking** 20

Lyzzick Hall Country House Hotel

@ European

Country-house cooking in the shadow of Skiddaw

☎ 017687 72277
Under Skiddaw CA12 4PY
e-mail: info@lyzzickhall.co.uk
dir: M6 junct 40 onto A66 to Keswick. Do not enter town, keep on Keswick by-pass. At rdbt 3rd exit onto A591 to Carlisle. Hotel 1.5m on right

The Hall is a greystone country house on the lower slopes of Skiddaw in the heart of Lakeland walking country. Owned by a wealthy Lancashire textile merchant in the first tourist rush that followed Wordsworth's death, it has been a hotel since the 1970s. Traditional country-house cooking is the order of the day in the blue-toned dining room with its majestic views. Expect air-dried Cumberland ham with feta and mango dressing, and then pheasant with sweet potato, cherries and port, with the option of a fish course or sorbet in between. Pear and almond tart with raspberry coulis is among the dessert options.

Times 12-2/7-9 Closed Jan

Swinside Lodge Country House Hotel

@@ Modern British V

Enticing no-choice menu near Derwentwater's edge

☎ 017687 72948
Grange Rd, Newlands CA12 5UE
e-mail: info@swinsidelodge-hotel.co.uk
web: www.swinsidelodge-hotel.co.uk
dir: M6 junct 40, A66, left at Portinscale. Follow to Grange for 2m ignoring signs to Swinside & Newlands Valley

The whitewashed Lodge is a trim Georgian house lying at the foot of Catbells, not five minutes' stroll from the shore of Derwentwater. Take a volume of Wordsworth with you for a walk among the hills, but be sure to be back in time for dinner. The format is traditional Lakeland: a fixed-start service and table-d'hôte menu of four courses with a choice at the final stage. A winter menu might take in red mullet with lobster, celeriac and orange remoulade, curried parsnip soup, and maple- and thyme-roasted corn-fed chicken with stuffed courgettes and sherry jus, before the final decision must be made. Will it be dark chocolate brownie with Kirsch cherries and vanilla ice cream, or liquorice and rum pannacotta with pineapple and passionfruit salad?

Chef Clive Imber **Owner** Mike & Kath Bilton **Times** 7-10.30 Closed 20-26 Dec, L all week **Prices** Fixed D 4 course £40, Service optional **Wines** 111 bottles over £20, 12 bottles under £20, 12 by glass **Notes** Vegetarian menu, Dress restrictions, Smart casual **Seats** 14 **Children** Portions **Parking** 12

KIRKBY LONSDALE **Map 18 SD67**

Hipping Hall

@@ Modern British, French

Modern British food in a medieval hall

☎ 015242 71187
Cowan Bridge LA6 2JJ
e-mail: info@hippinghall.com
dir: 8.5m E of M6 junct 36 on A65

Not far from the appealing market town of Kirkby Lonsdale, and surrounded by some of northern England's lushest scenery, the wisteria-clad Hipping Hall is a 17th-century house of great elegance. Two hundred years older, however, is the hall that now houses the restaurant, with its minstrels' gallery and tapestries. Detailing is impressive, from the sandstone salt-shakers to the Lakeland slate slab on which the petits fours arrive, and the cooking is an imaginative rendition of the modern British country-house idiom. Loin of rabbit and trotter of pig comprise one faintly Macbethian first course, served with a simple purée of chervil roots, while main course might deliver a roast fillet of brill with gnocchi, pied de mouton mushrooms, Swiss chard and a mushroom foam. Finish with the show-stopping whole orange pudding, accompanied by star anise parfait and honeycomb.

Times 12-2/7-9.30 Closed 3-8 Jan, L Mon-Thu

The Sun Inn

@ Modern British

Appealing modern British food in a historic market town

☎ 015242 71965
6 Market St LA6 2AU
e-mail: email@sun-inn.info
dir: From A65 follow signs to town centre. Inn on main street

Visitors to the historic market town of Kirkby Lonsdale, perched on the borders of the Lake District and the Yorkshire Dales, can revel in the famous 'Ruskin's View' across the Lune Valley. It's definitely worth taking in the white-painted 17th-century Sun Inn too, though, with its confident mix of traditional and modern décor and serious commitment to simple dishes using the best local ingredients. It's a proper pub with oak beams, log fires and cask ales in the elegantly traditional bar, and a contemporary feel in the dining room. The self-assured modern British menu might offer up ham hock terrine with pineapple chutney, then loin of local lamb, the shoulder served up as a confit, with cauliflower purée, baby root vegetables and dauphinoise potatoes. Lunchtime offers up 'Light Bites' or the likes of steak and kidney pudding.

Chef Sam Carter **Owner** Lucy & Mark Fuller **Times** 12-2.30/7-9 Closed L Mon **Prices** Starter £3.95-£6.95, Main £13.95-£19.95, Dessert £4.25-£6.95, Service optional **Wines** 8 bottles over £20, 23 bottles under £20, 7 by glass **Notes** Sunday L, Vegetarian available **Seats** 36 **Children** Portions, Menu **Parking** On street & nearby car park

NEAR SAWREY **Map 18 SD39**

Ees Wyke Country House

British, French

Splendid Lakeland views and tip-top country-house cooking

☎ 015394 36393
LA22 0JZ
e-mail: mail@eeswyke.co.uk
web: www.eeswyke.co.uk
dir: On B5285 on W side of village

Deep in the heart of Beatrix Potter country, this Georgian country house basks in quintessential Lakeland views over sheep-speckled fells to Esthwaite Water. The welcoming owners take good care of their guests, serving aperitifs outside in the summer months, or making sure there's a warming log fire in the lounge when things get nippy. After a day's hiking up Coniston Old Man or the Langdale Pikes, what's needed is dinner in true Lakeland style: five courses served in a plushly-upholstered dining room. Dinner might begin with apple and almond black pudding with red onion marmalade and wild boar sausage, ahead of grilled salmon and garlic pea mash with lemon butter sauce. Main courses bring on the likes of roast breast of duckling with thyme, ginger and honey sauce, then comes dessert - perhaps chocolate truffle with raspberry coulis - ahead of local Cumbrian cheeses.

Chef Richard Lee **Owner** Richard & Margaret Lee **Times** 7.30pm **Prices** Food prices not confirmed for 2011. Please telephone for details **Wines** 32 bottles over £20, 26 bottles under £20, 5 by glass **Notes** Vegetarian available **Seats** 16 **Parking** 12

NEWBY BRIDGE **Map 18 SD38**

Lakeside Hotel

Modern British V

Lakeside dining with a choice of restaurants

☎ 015395 30001
Lakeside LA12 8AT
e-mail: sales@lakesidehotel.co.uk
dir: M6 junct 36 follow A590 to Newby Bridge, straight over rdbt, right over bridge. Hotel within 1m

On the shores of Lake Windermere, this former 17th-century coaching inn retains many original period features and offers a warm welcome in its choice of two restaurants. As well as the lake, the hotel has views over a typical Lakeland landscape of forests, fells and streams. Within, snug lounges and traditional bars beckon. The Lakeview restaurant, with its oak panelling, is the more formal place to take dinner. Local produce features heavily on the modern British menu. You might find foie gras with burnt orange, rhubarb and nougatine to start, followed by veal tortellini, carrot purée, morels, glazed onion and salsify with pineapple, and strawberry jelly, lavender ice cream and meringue for dessert.

Lakeside Hotel

Chef Richard Booth **Owner** Mr N Talbot **Times** 12.30-2.30/6.45-9.30 Closed 23 Dec-15 Jan **Prices** Fixed D 3 course £33-£38, Starter £5-£9, Main £9-£22, Dessert £5-£9, Service included **Wines** 190 bottles over £20, 15 bottles under £20, 12 by glass **Notes** Fixed 6 course from £45, Vegetarian menu, Dress restrictions, Smart casual, no jeans, Civ Wed 80 **Seats** 70, Pr/dining room 30 **Children** Portions, Menu **Parking** 200

PENRITH **Map 18 NY53**

The Martindale Restaurant

Traditional British

Brasserie dishes in a Cumbrian spa hotel

☎ 01768 868111
North Lakes Hotel & Spa, Ullswater Rd CA11 8QT
e-mail: nlakes@shirehotels.com
dir: M6 just off junct 40

Not far from the northern stretches of the M6, the North Lakes Hotel is home to the Martindale restaurant, a pleasantly spacious room with white walls and ceiling beams, where the cooking uses good Lakeland produce in some appealing modern brasserie dishes. Roast rump of flavourful local lamb might come with roasted cherry tomatoes, rocket and parmesan, or there could be a serving of sea bass with risotto containing Whitby crab and spring onion. Well-made crème brûlée with hazelnut shortbread makes a satisfying conclusion, or you might choose to finish with a scoop of espresso ice cream.

Chef Mr Doug Hargeaves **Owner** Shire Hotels Ltd **Times** 12.15-1.45/7-9.15 Closed L Sat-Sun **Prices** Food prices not confirmed for 2011. Please telephone for details **Wines** 41 bottles over £20, 17 bottles under £20, 14 by glass **Notes** Sunday L, Vegetarian available, Dress restrictions, Smart casual, Civ Wed 200 **Seats** 112 **Children** Portions, Menu **Parking** 120

SEASCALE **Map 18 NY00**

Cumbrian Lodge

British, International

Modern global cooking in Victorian lodge

☎ 019467 27309
58 Gosforth Rd CA20 1JG
e-mail: cumbrianlodge@btconnect.com
dir: From A595 onto B5344, hotel on left after 2m

Dating back to 1874, this sky-blue Victorian house was converted to a small hotel back in 1999 and inside it still looks spruce and contemporary. The restaurant is an unfussy rather smart room done out in shades of caramel and white, with modern art on the walls and deep blue glassware on crisp linen-clothed tables. The bistro-style menu majors in traditional British dishes, but takes its influences from around the globe, ranging from home-made chicken and noodle soup to salmon and leek fishcake, and main courses such as Cajun chicken and pan-fried duck breast with blackcurrant sauce. There are pretty little thatched outbuildings in the grounds used for sheltered alfresco dining throughout the year.

Chef R Hickson, C Brown **Owner** David J Morgan **Times** 6.30-9.30 Closed Xmas, New Year, BHs, Sun, L Mon & Sat **Prices** Starter £5.95-£6.95, Main £16.95-£17.95, Dessert £4.95-£5.95, Service optional **Wines** 17 bottles over £20, 19 bottles under £20, 15 by glass **Notes** Vegetarian available **Seats** 32 **Parking** 17

TEBAY **Map 18 NY60**

Westmorland Hotel

Modern British

Friendly modern hotel dining overlooking rugged moorland

☎ 015396 24351
Orton CA10 3SB
e-mail: reservations@westmorlandhotel.com
dir: Signed from Westmorland Services between M6 junct 38 & 39

Although this modern independent hotel sits just a mile away from the M6, it has dramatic views of the Howgill fells. Its natural materials lend it something of a Tyrolean feel, and the lounge-bar and restaurant come on split-levels with floor-to-ceiling windows. The kitchen stocks its larders with produce from the local farming community, while Herdwick lamb and Galloway beef come from the hotel's own farm just up the road. Appealing and ambitious modern dishes come well presented; perhaps a 21-day aged rump steak (from their own herd, of course) served with mash potato, roast parsnip, fresh asparagus, foie gras and a red wine and thyme jus, or seared mackerel fillet with celeriac purée and a smoked milk and anchovy dressing.

Chef Bryan Parsons **Owner** Westmorland Ltd **Times** 6.30-9 **Prices** Starter £4.95-£7.50, Main £12.95-£19.50, Dessert £5.50-£6.95, Service optional **Wines** 9 bottles over £20, 36 bottles under £20, 7 by glass **Notes** Set menus can be provided for pre-booked groups, Vegetarian available, Dress restrictions, Smart casual, Civ Wed 120 **Seats** 100, Pr/dining room 40 **Children** Portions, Menu **Parking** 60

Rampsbeck Country House Hotel

WATERMILLOCK Map 18 NY42

Modern British, French

Confident cooking in serene setting

☎ 017684 86442
CA11 0LP
e-mail: enquiries@rampsbeck.co.uk
web: www.rampsbeck.co.uk
dir: M6 junct 40, A592 to Ullswater, T-junct turn right at lake's edge. Hotel 1.25m

The inspirational view over Ullswater is reason enough to retreat to Rampsbeck, but the 18th-century hotel is also blessed with 18 acres of glorious grounds to wander in. Add to that a traditionally plush country-house interior brimming with period character, ornate marble fireplaces, antiques and a cossetting feel of well-being, and you have a package that is every inch the serene Lakeland hideaway. A recent makeover has given the dining room a snazzy look using cherry-red floral silk wall panels set against a café crème carpet, while staff deliver confident service in a polished, formal style. Chef Andrew McGeorge has headed the kitchen for long enough to have well-established supply lines to the best local materials, which underpin his exciting modern British and French cooking. Braised pig's cheek with parsnip purée, apple jelly and star anise jus is a typically appealing idea to start, followed by a classic steamed fillet of Dover sole with puréed potatoes and mussel and saffron sauce. Meat dishes might include a perfect marriage of roast fillet of beef with veal sweetbreads wrapped in Cumbrian air-dried ham alongside seared foie gras, shallot confit and Madeira sauce. Desserts keep up their end: hot kumquat soufflé is teamed with bitter chocolate sorbet, while a classic vanilla crème brûlée is pointed up by rhubarb compôte and sorbet.

Chef Andrew McGeorge
Owner Blackshaw Hotels Ltd
Times 12-1.45/7-9 Closed 4-27 Jan, L booking only **Prices** Fixed L 2 course £24-£26, Fixed D 3 course £47-£49.50, Service optional **Wines** 84 bottles over £20, 47 bottles under £20, 9 by glass **Notes** Sunday L, Vegetarian available, Dress restrictions, Smart casual, no shorts, Civ Wed 60 **Seats** 40, Pr/dining room 15 **Children** Portions **Parking** 30

TEMPLE SOWERBY   Map 18 NY62

Temple Sowerby House Hotel & Restaurant

@@ Modern British

Peaceful bolt-hole offering creative modern food

☎ 017683 61578
CA10 1RZ
e-mail: stay@templesowerby.com
dir: 7m from M6 junct 40, midway between Penrith & Appleby, in village centre

This intimate 18th-century country-house hotel close to Ullswater is an ideal base for exploring the northern Lake District. Overlooking the Pennine fells and quiet village green, expect traditionally elegant décor and personable staff. Head chef Ashley Whittaker takes full advantage of the fabulous local larder to deliver dishes that draw on contemporary British ideas supported by French classical technique. There are expansive views over the garden from the restaurant. Begin with a sophisticated starter such as home-smoked venison with a lasagne of wild mushrooms, red cabbage and cranberry marmalade and a gingerbread crisp. Follow on with pan-fried Goosnargh duck with jasmine rice, a spring roll flavoured with five spice, pickled plums and a five spice sauce. Vanilla 'arctic roll' with poached plums and mulled berry consommé keeps the creative sparks flying to the very end.

Chef Ashley Whittaker **Owner** Paul & Julie Evans **Times** 7-9 Closed 8 days Xmas, L all week **Prices** Fixed D 3 course £35.50, Service optional **Wines** 30 bottles over £20, 10 bottles under £20, 7 by glass **Notes** Vegetarian available, Dress restrictions, Smart casual preferred, Civ Wed 40 **Seats** 24, Pr/dining room 24 **Parking** 20

WATERMILLOCK   Map 18 NY42

Macdonald Leeming House

@ Modern British

Luxurious country-house cooking by Ullswater

☎ 0870 4008131
CA11 0JJ
e-mail: leeminghouse@macdonald-hotels.co.uk
dir: M6 junct 40, continue on A66 signed Keswick. At rdbt follow A592 towards Ullswater, at T-junct turn right, hotel 3m on left

The house itself may not be the grandest in the Lake District, but it does boast over 20 acres of magnificent gardens, direct access to Ullswater, and its own fishing licence. A sweeping prospect of the gardens and lake can be enjoyed from the windows of the Regency Restaurant, where swagged curtains and a busily patterned carpet set the tone. The cooking is country-house luxurious, with starters such as foie gras and duck terrine with quince purée and golden raisins, succeeded by mains like sea bass with lobster tortellini and baby fennel in shellfish foam, or Scottish venison loin with violet potatoes, spiced red cabbage and salsify, sauced with port.

Times 12-2/6.30-9

Rampsbeck Country House Hotel

@@@ – *see opposite page*

WINDERMERE   Map 18 SD49

Burn How Garden House Hotel

@ Modern British V

Traditional dining a short walk from Lake Windermere

☎ 015394 46226
Back Belsfield Rd, Bowness LA23 3HH
e-mail: info@burnhow.co.uk
dir: Exit A591 at Windermere, following signs to Bowness. Pass Lake Piers on right, take 1st left to hotel entrance

Work up an appetite hiking around the shores of Lake Windermere, which lie just a couple of minutes' stroll from this deliciously tranquil Victorian hotel. Large windows make for a luminous restaurant with gorgeous views of lush, leafy gardens, while the kitchen deals in hearty British fare spiked with influences from the Mediterranean, as well as more exotic shores. Starters such as Morecambe Bay potted shrimps or Thai fishcakes with ginger dipping sauce show the variety, while mains might be rack of Lune Valley lamb with pea purée and basil, and minted fondant potato. Cumbrian cheeses such as Keldthwaite Gold and Roegill Red make a tempting alternative to pudding.

Chef Jane Kimani **Owner** Michael Robinson **Times** 6.30-8.30 Closed Xmas, L all week **Prices** Fixed D 3 course £25-£29.50, Starter £4-£8, Main £12-£22, Dessert £5, Service optional **Notes** Vegetarian menu **Seats** 40 **Children** Portions, Menu **Parking** 28

Cedar Manor Hotel & Restaurant

@ Modern British

Romantic dining at a peaceful country retreat

☎ 015394 43192
Ambleside Rd LA23 1AX
e-mail: info@cedarmanor.co.uk
dir: From A591 follow signs to Windermere. Hotel on left just beyond St Mary's Church at bottom of hill

Formerly a gentleman's residence (clearly a gentleman of some taste), the hotel takes its name from the 200-plus-year-old cedar tree that dominates the garden. On the outskirts of Windermere with a peaceful walled garden, it has a dinner-only restaurant decked out in crisp white linen with high-backed leather chairs and a menu that is as unstuffy as the house. Produce is judiciously sourced and brings a local flavour to the broadly modern British dishes. Tovey tart is made with the eponymous local goats' cheese (named in honour of a Lake District food hero), and comes with red onion marmalade, mixed leaves and a verjus walnut oil dressing. Follow on with a casserole of Lake District venison and finish with black cherry frangipane tart (with clotted cream and chocolate syrup).

Chef Roger Pergl-Wilson **Owner** Caroline & Jonathan Kaye **Times** 6.30-8.30 Closed Xmas & 6-25 Jan, L all week **Prices** Fixed D 3 course £26.95-£34.95, Service optional **Wines** 14 bottles over £20, 16 bottles under £20, 7 by glass **Notes** Vegetarian available, Dress restrictions, Smart casual, no mountain wear **Seats** 22 **Children** Portions **Parking** 12

Fayrer Garden Hotel

@ Modern British, Traditional

Traditional country-house dining with lake views

☎ 015394 88195
Lyth Valley Rd, Bowness on Windermere LA23 3JP
e-mail: lakescene@fayrergarden.com
dir: M6 junct 36, A591. Past Kendal, at rdbt left onto B5284 signed Crook Bowness & Ferry, 8m, left onto A5074 for 400yds

This former Edwardian gentleman's Lake District hideout perches above Lake Windermere in five acres of delightful gardens. Contemporary chic combines with luscious textures and understated style to ensure that the hotel has a high feelgood factor. The kitchen jazzes up its repertoire of traditional British dishes with a few modern twists, served in the Terrace Restaurant to a beautiful backdrop of garden and lake views. Five-course, daily-changing dinner menus might begin with breast of wood pigeon with glazed parsnips and game jus, then move on via soup or sorbet to pan-fried supreme of chicken with green beans, potato gratin, sage and onion quiche and cep and Madeira sauce.

Times 7-8.30 Closed 1st 2wks Jan, L all week

Gilpin Hotel & Lake House

@@@ – *see page 108*

Gilpin Hotel & Lake House

WINDERMERE Map 18 SD49

Modern British V

Elegant family-run hotel with first-class food

☎ 015394 88818
Crook Rd LA23 3NE
e-mail: hotel@gilpinlodge.co.uk
web: www.gilpinlodge.co.uk
dir: M6 junct 36 & A590, then B5284 for 5m

In 1917 Joseph Cunliffe needed to escape the smog of Manchester after suffering lung damage during WWI, so he bought an Edwardian house in 22 acres of peaceful gardens, moors and woodland near Windermere. Gilpin Lodge remained in the family until the 1960s when it became a bed and breakfast. These days - well, since 1988 in fact - it's back in the hands of the Cunliffe family, run as a luxurious country-house hotel. Whether you're staying the night, or just staying for dinner, the Cunliffes' love of the old house, which dates from 1901, and their passion for what they do is evident for all to see, and that's something they've passed on to their staff, too. The style of cooking is modern British, with an emphasis on the finest, mainly locally-sourced, ingredients, and attractive, unfussy presentation. There are four dining rooms to choose from, each distinctly different in feel and design, but all beautifully furnished, elegant and atmospheric. Relax in the cosy lounge, the stylish champagne bar or on the pretty terrace with a drink and some canapés while taking your pick from the menu, which is split into 'signature dishes' and 'classic dishes'. The latter offers more straightforward options such as smoked salmon with a classic garnish, and coq au vin, while the former shows Plowman's more creative side. The good news is you can mix and match between the two. An evenly-risen twice-baked Stichelton cheese soufflé with a deconstructed Waldorf salad and red wine reduction makes a fine opener. A main-course of Shetland organic salmon poached in olive oil comes beautifully cooked and complemented by a chive butter sauce and well-made champ. Dessert might take in a light and delightfully smooth chocolate mousse with a contrastingly sharp blackcurrant sorbet. The 200-strong wine list offers an excellent range representing 13 countries.

Chef Russell Plowman **Owner** The Cunliffe Family **Times** 12-2/6.30-9.15 **Prices** Fixed L 3 course £27, Starter £6-£10, Main £11-£22, Dessert £6.50-£8, Service optional **Wines** 235 bottles over £20, 1 bottle under £20, 15 by glass **Notes** Fixed menu D 5 course £52.50, Tasting menu with wine, Sunday L, Vegetarian menu, Dress restrictions, Smart Casual **Seats** 60, Pr/dining room 20 **Parking** 40

WINDERMERE *continued*

The Hideaway at Windermere

Modern British

Intimate and relaxed dining in Lakeland restaurant with rooms

015394 43070
Phoenix Way LA23 1DB
e-mail: eatandstay@thehideawayatwindermere.co.uk
web: www.thehideawayatwindermere.co.uk
dir: M6 junct 36/A5391. Pass sign to Windermere Village, then take 2nd left into Phoenix Way. Restaurant on right

Completely refurbished in January 2010, the restaurant of this handsome Lakeland Victorian house now sports a neat mix of contemporary style, 19th-century elegance and Sam Toft artwork for a bit of fun. It is a very personal operation led by owners Richard and Lisa Gornall to ensure first-class service and consistent, appealing food. The kitchen produces simple modern British cooking spiked here and there with creative global influences, and underpinned by super local ingredients - say griddled Lancashire black pudding with sautéed apple and onion and Dijon mustard cream, followed by Cumbrian lamb shank with rosemary and garlic and grain mustard mash.

Chef Craig Sherrington **Owner** Richard & Lisa Gornall **Times** 12-2.30/6.30-11 Closed Mon-Tue, L Wed-Sat **Prices** Fixed L 2 course £12.50, Fixed D 3 course £19.50-£24.50, Starter £4.25-£7.95, Main £10.95-£19.95, Dessert £5.50-£6.50, Service optional, Groups min 10 service 10% **Wines** 6 bottles over £20, 28 bottles under £20, 4 by glass **Notes** Sunday L, Vegetarian available, Dress restrictions, Smart casual, no sportswear or trainers **Seats** 30, Pr/dining room 12 **Parking** 15

Holbeck Ghyll Country House Hotel

 *– see below*

Jerichos At The Waverley

Modern British

Modern British cooking in a well-converted Victorian hotel

015394 42522 & 07885 544503
College Rd LA23 1BX
e-mail: info@jerichos.co.uk
dir: M6 junct 36. A591 to Windermere. 2nd left towards Windermere then 1st right onto College Rd. Restaurant 300mtrs on right

The restaurant with rooms on a quiet road in the centre of Windermere was built in Victorian times as a temperance hotel, and retains many of its original features, such as stained-glass windows, pitch-pine doors, tiled floors and a Carrara marble fireplace. Simple, light décor in the dining room, where plain white walls are hung with jazz-themed pictures, sets the tone for the smartly presented, inventive modern British cooking. Expect chorizo, spinach and Gorgonzola risotto, followed by parsley-crusted turbot on stir-fried new potatoes with a seared scallop in tomato coulis, or more traditional prime Scottish steak with chips in Cabernet wine sauce. Dessert might be a slice of apricot and pecan frangipane tart with lemon ice cream and crème anglaise.

Chef Chris Blaydes, Tim Dalzell **Owner** Chris & Jo Blaydes **Times** 7-9.30 Closed 1st 2 wks Nov, 24-26 Dec, 1 Jan, last 3 wks Jan, D Thu **Prices** Starter £4.25-£9.50, Main £15.25-£25, Dessert £6.25-£9.50, Service optional, Groups min 6 service 10% **Wines** 32 bottles over £20, 32 bottles under £20, 8 by glass **Notes** Vegetarian available **Seats** 28 **Children** Portions **Parking** 13

Holbeck Ghyll Country House Hotel

WINDERMERE **Map 18 SD49**

Modern British V

Breathtaking views and classy cooking

015394 32375
Holbeck Ln LA23 1LU
e-mail: stay@holbeckghyll.com
dir: 3m N of Windermere on A591, right into Holbeck Lane (signed Troutbeck), hotel 0.5m on left

Traditional country-house elegance is the order of the day at this 19th-century mansion with breathtaking views over Lake Windermere. The house was once owned as a hunting lodge by Lord Lonsdale, the first president of the Automobile Association whose name adorns the belts around the rippling midriffs of boxing champions. A man who moved with the times, he gave the place the modish Arts and Crafts makeover you see in its lovely stained glass windows and the carved wooden panels that feature in the elegant dining rooms. This is every inch the serene Lakeland retreat - a fact that sinks in as you step onto the terrace outside the more contemporary of the two dining rooms for aperitifs with a view that inspired Romantic poets. Although it has a long and unbroken line of gastronomic awards, the kitchen here does not live off its past reputation: chef David McLaughlin is always as much on the lookout for new ideas as he is for the region's finest produce. A modish marriage of meat and fish brings together honey-glazed Gloucestershire Old Spot pork belly with spiced carrot, sautéed langoustines and pea foam. Next up, best end of lamb arrives on a bed of Puy lentils with crisp haggis beignets, all pointed up by the sweetness of roast garlic and swede purée. The momentum is maintained at dessert - a riff on cherries delivers different varieties as cherry clafoutis with almond ice cream, cherry sorbet, cherry sauce and confit cherries. The lovingly-described cheeses are hard to resist, while the wine list is clearly a labour of love, with a good selection by the glass.

Chef David McLaughlin **Owner** Stephen & Lisa Leahy **Times** 12-2/7-9.30 **Prices** Fixed L 3 course £29.95, Fixed D 4 course £56.50, Service optional **Wines** 264 bottles over £20, 19 bottles under £20, 14 by glass **Notes** Gourmet menu £74, Sunday L, Vegetarian menu, Dress restrictions, Smart casual, Civ Wed 65 **Seats** 50, Pr/dining room 20 **Children** Portions, Menu **Parking** 34

WINDERMERE *continued*

Lindeth Fell Country House Hotel

Modern British

Traditional British cooking in elegant Lakeland hotel

☎ 015394 43286 & 44287
Lyth Valley Rd, Bowness-on-Windermere LA23 3JP
e-mail: kennedy@lindethfell.co.uk
dir: 1m S of Bowness-on-Windermere on A5074

Enjoying breathtaking Lakeland views, this smart, elegant Edwardian residence stands at the top of a tree-lined drive in seven acres of glorious, landscaped gardens stretching away to Lake Windermere below and the mountains in the distance. Equally impressive are the panoramic views from the dining room extended along the lake side of the house. Home-made soup, perhaps tomato and tarragon, might kick things off, then comes a sorbet before straightforward main courses such as roast rack of Lakeland lamb with apricot and rosemary compôte. Finish with hazelnut meringues with chocolate sauce.

Times 12.30-1.45/7.30-9 Closed 3 wks in Jan

Lindeth Howe Country House Hotel

Modern British

Modern British cooking in Beatrix Potter's former Windermere home

☎ 015394 45759
Lindeth Dr, Longtail Hill LA23 3JF
e-mail: hotel@lindeth-howe.co.uk
dir: 1m S of Bowness onto B5284, signed Kendal and Lancaster. Hotel 2nd driveway on right

There may not be any shortage of delightful Lakeland hotels, nor of any overlooking Lake Windermere, but this is the only one that can lay claim to having once been home to Beatrix Potter. Don't be surprised to be greeted by the outsize figure of one of her characters, or to see deer roaming the grounds. A dress code is in force in the dining room, where, amid an atmosphere of comfortable civility, French chef Marc Guibert has taken to the modern British idiom like a duck to water. Ham hock and sweet pepper terrine wrapped in Cumbrian ham in mango and vanilla dressing might be the curtain raiser for main courses such as rarebit-crusted cod with ratatouille in beurre blanc, or haunch of venison with courgette rösti in whisky sauce. Finish with a dessert trio, or with top-notch English farmhouse cheeses.

Chef Marc Guibert **Owner** Lakeinvest Ltd
Times 12-2.30/6.30-9 **Prices** Fixed L 2 course £10.95-£12.95, Starter £5.95-£10.50, Main £19.50-£28, Dessert £6.50-£7.95, Service optional **Wines** 29 bottles over £20, 37 bottles under £20, 8 by glass **Notes** Fixed D 5 course £39.95, Trilogy menu available, Sunday L, Vegetarian available, Dress restrictions, Smart casual, no jeans or sleeveless T-shirts **Seats** 70, Pr/dining room 20 **Children** Portions, Menu **Parking** 50

Linthwaite House Hotel

Modern British V

Elegant hotel dining with modern, classy food

☎ 015394 88600
Crook Rd LA23 3JA
e-mail: stay@linthwaite.com
dir: M6 junct 36. A591 towards The Lakes for 8m to large rdbt, take 1st exit (B5284), 6m, hotel on left. 1m past Windermere Golf Club

The views at this erstwhile Edwardian gentlemen's residence, with over 14 acres of wooded gardens on a hillside looking over Lake Windermere, are rather magical at sunset. Linthwaite is a top-drawer country house that trades on its sincere warmth and hospitality; style-wise, it has chucked out the chintz and moved up a gear with modish furnishings. The restaurant was restyled by the designer behind Malmaison's chic look - in fact, the place is so switched on these days that you can even follow the hotel's latest news on Twitter and Facebook. The kitchen also stays in touch with current trends, while placing a strong emphasis on sourcing the pick of local materials. Pan-roasted scallops with sticky chicken wing, parsnip salsa and cumin foam is a typical opener, and might be

The Samling

WINDERMERE **Map 18 SD49**

Modern British V

Impressive dining in Lakeland hillside retreat

☎ 015394 31922
Ambleside Rd LA23 1LR
e-mail: info@thesamlinghotel.co.uk
dir: On A591 towards Ambleside. 1st on right after Low Wood Hotel. 2m from Windermere

A stay at the Samling is rather like being given the keys to an impossibly wealthy friend's country hideaway; the white-painted 18th-century house, set high on a wooded hillside above Lake Windermere in a 67-acre estate, awaits your pleasure. Inside, the standards of country-house luxury reach new heights, driven by a service ethos that really does impress. Of course, food is a key element of the lavish set-up, so two intimate dining areas are done out in the same opulent blend of old and contemporary style as a backdrop to the kitchen's inventive modern output. The bedrock is fresh seasonal produce, much of it local, put together with a serious level of skill and a lightness of touch. Well-defined flavours are the hallmark in a starter of pan-fried red mullet served with a pannacotta-like parmesan custard, with a tuile and foam of the same cheese and courgette pearls. Next up, sea trout is married with a tian of crunchy samphire, fresh crab and crab jelly, Shetland Black potatoes and white asparagus velouté. Pink grapefruit - carpaccio, jelly and ice cream - is pointed up with honey and ginger and given crunch with granola biscotti in a playful finale. All breads, canapés and intermediate amusements hit the same heights, and there's a menu gourmand with wine suggestions for a serious blowout.

Chef Nigel Mendham **Owner** von Essen Hotels
Times 12.30-2/7-9.30 **Prices** Fixed L 3 course £25-£38, Fixed D 4 course £55-£67, Service optional **Wines** 97 bottles over £20, 15 by glass **Notes** Gourmand tasting menu, Sunday L, Vegetarian menu, Civ Wed 20 **Seats** 22 **Children** Portions, Menu **Parking** 15

followed by poached fillet of brill, fennel cannelloni, herb spätzle noodles and a soup of mussels and clams. Finish with a caramelised apple parfait with blackcurrant gel and cinnamon beignets.

Chef Richard Kearsley **Owner** Mike Bevans
Times 12.30-2/6.45-9.30 Closed Xmas & New Year (ex residents) **Prices** Fixed L 2 course £14.95, Fixed D 4 course £49, Service optional **Wines** 100 bottles over £20, 10 bottles under £20, 13 by glass **Notes** Sunday L, Vegetarian menu, Dress restrictions, Smart casual, Civ Wed 64 **Seats** 64, Pr/dining room 16 **Children** Portions, Menu **Parking** 40

Miller Howe Hotel & Restaurant

Modern British V

Classy modern cooking in a much-loved Lakeland hotel

☎ 015394 42536
Rayrigg Rd LA23 1EY
e-mail: info@millerhowe.com
dir: M6 junct 36. Follow the A591 bypass for Kendal. Enter Windermere, continue to mini rdbt, take left onto A592. Miller Howe is 0.25m on right

A Lakeland classic, Miller Howe has outstanding views over Windermere and the Langdale Pikes, a vista that can be enjoyed from the restaurant within the Arts and Crafts hotel. The five-acre plot heading down to the water is as tranquil a spot as you'll find, and lunch on the terrace is a warm weather treat. Large arched windows frame the view in the restaurant, where understated contemporary design and formally laid tables make an ideal setting for the modern British cooking. Technical dexterity and first-rate produce combine to deliver seared squab pigeon with cauliflower purée and a smoked pancetta jus, and main-course Cumbrian pork three ways - roast fillet, confit belly, braised cheek - with pease pudding and a cider jus. It is worth taking your eyes off the view to peruse the excellent wine list.

Miller Howe Hotel & Restaurant

Chef Andrew Beaton **Owner** Martin & Helen Ainscough **Times** 12.30-1.45/6.45-8.45 **Prices** Fixed L 2 course £18.50, Fixed D 3 course £35-£40, Starter £9-£14, Main £14-£24, Dessert £7-£10, Service optional **Wines** 100 bottles over £20, 10 bottles under £20, 8 by glass **Notes** Gourmet D 5 courses £40, Sunday L, Vegetarian menu, Dress restrictions, Smart casual, Civ Wed 64 **Seats** 80, Pr/dining room 30 **Children** Portions **Parking** 40

The Samling

– see opposite page

Storrs Hall Hotel

Modern British V

Accomplished, imaginative cuisine in luxurious country surroundings

☎ 015394 47111
Storrs Park LA23 3LG
e-mail: storrshall@elhmail.co.uk
web: www.elh.co.uk/hotels/storrshall
dir: on A592 2m S of Bowness, on Newby Bridge road

Not to be confused with John Storrs Hall, who is eminent in the field of molecular nanotechnology, this handsome Georgian mansion on the shores of Lake Windermere is the epitome of timeless Lakeland beauty. Landscaped gardens look over the lake to wild fells all around - there's even a National Trust-owned temple folly to explore. Inside are the requisite antiques, oil paintings and opulent furnishings of the classic country-house hotel. The ornate solid oak and intricate glass bar is architectural salvage of the highest order: it was recycled from Blackpool Tower. There's plenty of

continued

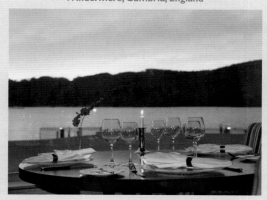

WINDERMERE *continued*

thought, imagination, and considerable ambition in the kitchen's contemporary British cooking; local materials make a good showing and are presented using eye-catching props such as slates and mini Kilner jars. A pressing of cured foie gras, Puy lentils, braised ox tongue and Jerez jelly opens with plenty of visual impact, followed by a globe-trotting main course of roasted spiced monkfish with harissa and spring onion couscous, Asian cock crab spring roll, and whipped parsley root.

Storrs Hall Hotel

Chef Will Jones **Owner** English Lakes Hotels **Times** 12.30-2/7-9 **Prices** Fixed L 3 course £19.75-£22.75, Fixed D 3 course fr £42.50, Service included **Wines** 154 bottles over £20, 14 bottles under £20, 6 by glass **Notes** Tasting menu and themed evenings available, Sunday L, Vegetarian menu, Dress restrictions, Smart casual, no jeans or trainers, Civ Wed 90 **Seats** 64, Pr/dining room 40 **Children** Portions **Parking** 50

Vinand Restaurant at the Old England Hotel & Spa

Classic British, International

Stylish modern dining and stunning lake views

☎ 0844 879 9144
Macdonald Old England Hotel, Church St, Bowness LA23 3DF
e-mail: sales.oldengland@macdonald-hotels.co.uk
web: www.macdonaldhotels.co.uk
dir: Through Windermere to Bowness, straight across at mini-rdbt. Hotel behind church on right

Occupying arguably one of the best positions on Lake Windermere, this elegant Victorian mansion has stunning views across the lake and surrounding woodland, which are best enjoyed from the beautifully furnished Vinand Restaurant. The cooking makes great use of quality local produce such as fell-bred lamb or Gressingham duck to produce innovative and refined dishes. Start, perhaps, with oxtail roulade with fondant potato, shallot purée and roast jus, moving on to wild sea bass with smoked haddock rösti and vanilla hollandaise, and finish with dark chocolate fondant with pistachio ice cream.

Times 6.30-9 Closed L all week

See advert on page 111

DERBYSHIRE

ASHBOURNE — Map 10 SK14

Callow Hall

Traditional British (Notable Wine List)

Classic British cuisine in Peak District country-house hotel

☎ 01335 300900
Mappleton Rd DE6 2AA
e-mail: info@callowhall.co.uk
dir: A515 through Ashbourne towards Buxton, left at Bowling Green pub, then 1st right

A small-scale Victorian country-house hotel on the edge of the Peak District National Park, Callow Hall is a mere five-minute drive from busy Ashbourne, yet feels remote, secluded in 44 acres of gardens and woodlands overlooking Bentley Brook and the River Dove valley. Inside the ivy-clad house, you're greeted with exemplary service and a time-warp ambience of plaster cornicing, oak galore and opulent fabrics. The dining room is a refined setting for sure-footed, unaffected country-house cooking. There's a real feel of dedication to the job in the kitchen - sausages are home-made, meats and fish are smoked and cured in-house, and all breads, cakes and pastries are freshly baked. A creamy lobster bisque is raised to a higher level by adding a skewer of tiger prawns and scallops, with crème fraîche and chives, while main course brings on a fine, fresh cod fillet with potato purée, mussels, and saffron and leek sauce. To finish, there's warm raspberry and blueberry frangipane tart with vanilla ice cream.

Chef Anthony Spencer **Owner** von Essen Hotels **Times** 12-1.45/7.15-9 **Prices** Food prices not confirmed for 2011. Please telephone for details **Wines** 71 bottles over £20, 8 bottles under £20, 11 by glass **Notes** Sunday L, Vegetarian available, Dress restrictions, Smart casual, Civ Wed 40 **Seats** 70, Pr/dining room 40 **Children** Portions **Parking** 30

The Dining Room

Modern European

A virtuoso culinary one-man band

☎ 01335 300666
33 St John St DE6 1GP
dir: On A52 (Derby to Leek road)

Dating back to the early years of the reign of James I, the building comes brimming with character; think low-beamed ceilings, original cast-iron range and a wood-burning stove. Peter Dale cooks here single-handedly for a mere half-dozen tables, producing modern British food driven by seasonal local produce in a complex, highly technical and unique style. His no-choice daily-changing seven-courser comes with plenty of between-course action, while the main event might take in wild Snelston wood pigeon paired with 12-hour pork belly, Herefordshire snails, 'Richard's' bunch carrots and turnips, leeks, pea purée, rapeseed oil and piccalilli. Desserts stay with the multi-component action; witness a carrot muffin with cox apple sous-vide, confit ginger carrots, damson cheese foam, pecans and clementine carrot purée.

Chef Peter Dale **Owner** Peter & Laura Dale **Times** 7.30 Closed 2 wks 26 Dec, 1 wk Sep, 1 wk Mar, Sun-Mon, L all week **Prices** Food prices not confirmed for 2011. Please telephone for details **Wines** 43 bottles over £20, 3 by glass **Notes** Tasting menu 7 course wk days D, Dress restrictions, Smart casual **Seats** 16 **Children** Portions **Parking** Opposite restaurant (evening)

ASHFORD-IN-THE-WATER — Map 16 SK16

Riverside House Hotel

Modern French

Fine dining in elegant country-house hotel

☎ 01629 814275
Fennel St DE45 1QF
e-mail: riversidehouse@enta.net
dir: off A6 (Bakewell/Buxton road) 2m from Bakewell, hotel at end of main street

Set in an acre of peaceful grounds on the banks of the River Wye in one of Derbyshire's most picturesque villages, this handsome ivy-clad Georgian country house is close to the Chatsworth Estate. The Riverside Room restaurant makes a grandly elegant setting for a meal - it's easy to imagine you're in a BBC period drama - with an inglenook that was part of the original kitchen and antique polished tables and chairs. The kitchen deals in first-class ingredients and treats them with imagination and intelligence. The beautifully-presented dishes range from a starter of guinea fowl terrine with apple and thyme salad, to a precisely-timed main course of roasted fillet of local beef with vegetables and creamed potatoes. To finish, try a refreshing passionfruit delice with home-made raspberry ripple ice cream.

Chef John Whelan **Owner** Penelope Thornton **Times** 12-2.30/7-9.30 **Prices** Food prices not confirmed for 2011. Please telephone for details **Wines** 200 bottles over £20, 26 bottles under £20, 32 by glass **Notes** Sunday L, Vegetarian available, Dress restrictions, Smart casual, jacket & tie preferred, Civ Wed 32 **Seats** 40, Pr/dining room 30 **Parking** 25

BAKEWELL Map 16 SK26

Monsal Head Hotel

® Modern British

Crowd pleasing food and spectacular views

☎ 01629 640250
Monsal Head DE45 1NL

Three miles from Bakewell in a unique location overlooking the Monsal Dale in the heart of the Peak District National Park, this hotel and restaurant has a friendly atmosphere and delivers hearty platefuls of food. The view also takes in the famous railway viaduct dating back to 1867 and the River Wye. The Longstone Restaurant serves substantial portions of down-to-earth dishes. Start perhaps with chicken liver pâté, cured with brandy and Madeira, served with red onion marmalade and toast, moving onto a main of Lamb President - lamb with pea purée baked in puff pastry with rich red wine and tomato jus. Meanwhile, real ales sourced from local micro breweries can be found in the Stables Bar.

Chef Rob Cochran, Adrian Billings **Owner** Penelope Thornton Hotels **Times** 12-9.30 **Prices** Food prices not confirmed for 2011. Please telephone for details **Notes** Sunday L, Vegetarian available **Seats** 50 **Children** Portions, Menu **Parking** 20

Piedaniel's

® French, European

Impeccably served traditional French-European cuisine

☎ 01629 812687
Bath St DE45 1BX
dir: From Bakewell rdbt in town centre take A6 Buxton exit. 1st right into Bath St (one-way)

Tones of white and beige punctuated by vivid lime greens bring a contemporary spin to Piedaniel's intimate dining room and lounge-bar. Though tucked-away down a side street in the centre of town, there are pleasing views over its pretty cottage garden, while natural light, whitewashed exposed brick and beams add character and white linen and modern high-backed chairs deliver comfort. There's a friendly hands-on approach, with chef-patron Eric Piedaniel's French heritage shining through on the plate in well-constructed dishes: witness a starter of rabbit rillette served with home-made warm brioche and sweet tomato chutney, and to follow, perhaps pan-fried calves' liver with potato galette and a port and raisin sauce.

Chef E Piedaniel **Owner** E & C Piedaniel **Times** 12-2/7-10 Closed Xmas & New Year, 2 wks Jan, 2 wks Aug, Mon, D Sun **Prices** Fixed L 2 course £12, Starter £5, Main £14-£18.50, Dessert £5, Service included **Wines** 6 bottles over £20, 23 bottles under £20, 10 by glass **Notes** Sunday L, Vegetarian available **Seats** 50, Pr/dining room 16 **Children** Portions **Parking** Town centre

The Square

® Modern British

Creative cooking in the home of Bakewell pudding

☎ 01629 812812
The Rutland Arms Hotel, The Square DE45 1BT
e-mail: enquiries@rutlandarmsbakewell.co.uk
dir: On A6 in Bakewell centre opposite war memorial. Parking opposite side entrance

The Rutland Arms sits in superb walking country on the fringes of the Chatsworth Estate, bookended by the spa towns of Buxton and Matlock. The period interior of this classic Georgian coaching inn lends a comforting air of prosperity, while an army of antique clocks beats time in the background, celebrating every half-hour with a massed outbreak of chimes. The Square restaurant might share the same period look, but the young, adventurous kitchen team have no intention of leaving the food stuck in the past. Creative contemporary dishes are the deal - perhaps scallops with black and white foam, laverbread and crisp pancetta to start, while peerless Peak District produce is the foundation of mains such as cannon of Derbyshire lamb teamed with crushed petits pois, baby carrots, dauphinoise potato, minted jelly and pan jus.

Chef Greg Wallace **Owner** David Donegan **Times** 12-2.30/7-9.30 **Prices** Food prices not confirmed for 2011. Please telephone for details **Notes** Sunday L, Vegetarian available, Dress restrictions, Smart casual **Seats** 50, Pr/dining room 30 **Children** Menu **Parking** 25

BASLOW Map 16 SK27

Cavendish Hotel

®® Modern British

Confident cooking in historic coaching inn

☎ 01246 582311
Church Ln DE45 1SP
e-mail: info@cavendish-hotel.net
web: www.cavendish-hotel.net
dir: M1 junct 29 follow signs for Chesterfield. From Chesterfield take A619 to Bakewell, Chatsworth & Baslow

Dating back to the 18th century, this historic building is delightfully situated on the outskirts of the Chatsworth Estate. The antiques and original artworks are a reminder that owners the Duke and Duchess of Devonshire had a hand in the design. Eat in the more informal conservatory Garden Room or in the elegant Gallery Restaurant with its silver tableware and professional yet friendly service. There is a modern approach to classic British dishes and an emphasis on vibrant flavours, unfussy presentation and some hearty local flavours. Start with braised oxtail soup with horseradish and Bakewell beer dumplings, then move on to six-hour cooked saddle of lamb with Vichy carrots, mini shepherd's pie and mint gravy, and end creatively with a fennel pannacotta served with Pontefract cake ice cream. There's a good choice of British cheeses, too.

Chef Wayne Rogers **Owner** Eric Marsh **Times** 12.30-2.30/6.30-10 Closed D 25 Dec **Prices** Fixed L 2 course £30.25, Fixed D 3 course £39.45, Service added 5% **Wines** 44 bottles over £20, 12 bottles under £20, 11 by glass **Notes** Sunday L, Vegetarian available, Dress restrictions, No trainers, T-shirts **Seats** 50, Pr/dining room 18 **Children** Portions **Parking** 40

Fischer's Baslow Hall

®®®® *– see page 114*

Rowley's Restaurant & Bar

®® Modern British

Informal pub offshoot of Fischer's Baslow Hall

☎ 01246 583880
Church Ln DE45 1RY
e-mail: info@rowleysrestaurant.co.uk
dir: A619/A623 signed Chatsworth, Baslow edge of Chatsworth estate

In the pretty village of Baslow, on the edge of the Chatsworth Estate, the former Prince of Wales pub has been revitalised by the team behind Fischer's Baslow Hall. With its all-day bar and stylish brasserie dining rooms done out in deep purple and blond wood, this is a world apart from the country house gentility of its big brother, but the same commitment to local produce is still evident. The kitchen sources its materials astutely for a crowd-pleasing modern British repertoire. A 'light bites' option might tempt with a posh take on the burger (a venison version, perhaps, with smoked paprika on cumin bread), or give the kitchen a chance to show what it can do with mains such as braised ox cheek with pan-fried lamb's sweetbread, celeriac rösti, roasted swede and ox jus. Finish with coconut and lemongrass rice pudding with caramelised pineapple.

Chef Rupert Rowley **Owner** Susan & Max Fischer, Rupert Rowley **Times** 12-2/6-8.45 Closed 1 Jan, D Sun **Prices** Fixed L 2 course £19.50, Starter £5-£7, Main £13-£19, Dessert £4-£5.50, Service optional **Wines** 21 bottles over £20, 14 bottles under £20, 10 by glass **Notes** Sunday L, Vegetarian available **Seats** 64, Pr/dining room 18 **Children** Portions, Menu **Parking** 17, On street

Fischer's Baslow Hall

BASLOW Map 16 SK27

Modern European V 

Elegant manor house with confident kitchen

☎ 01246 583259
Calver Rd DE45 1RR
e-mail: reservations@fischers-baslowhall.co.uk
dir: From Baslow on A623 towards Calver. Hotel on right

You can't beat a sweeping chestnut-lined driveway by way of an introduction, and Baslow Hall is an enterprise that more than exceeds expectations after such an august approach. On the edge of the Chatsworth Estate, the house is an Edwardian pastiche of a 17th-century manor, and it exudes refinement with its gabled façade, mullioned windows and balustraded entrance. The grounds are worth a wander whatever the time of year, and the kitchen garden is an important link in the supply chain for head chef Rupert Rowley and his team. The house is furnished with some beautiful pieces, carefully chosen by Max and Susan Fischer, creating a sophisticated and formally elegant setting which extends to the restaurant with its smartly laid tables. The modern European cooking is underpinned by classical French techniques, and a meal includes all the de rigueur extras from amuse-bouche (smoked haddock and whisky soup, perhaps) to a Black Forest trifle pre-dessert served in a shot glass. First-course pan-fried scallops are partnered with confit duck and vibrant butternut squash purée and herb salad, and main-course roast squab pigeon comes with braised Puy lentils, pan-fried foie gras and a delicious Madeira sauce. Finish with a lemon chiboust served up with a limoncello jelly, bayleaf ice cream and pain d'épice.

Chef Max Fischer, Rupert Rowley
Owner Mr & Mrs M Fischer
Times 12-1.30/7-8.30 Closed 24-26 Dec, 31 Dec, L Mon, D Sun (ex residents)
Prices Fixed L 2 course £28, Fixed D 3 course £48, Tasting menu £68, Service optional **Wines** 119 bottles over £20, 1 bottle under £20, 5 by glass
Notes Tasting menu Mon-Sat, Gourmet menu £72, Sunday L, Vegetarian menu, Dress restrictions, Smart casual, no jeans, sweatshirts, trainers, Civ Wed 38
Seats 38, Pr/dining room 20
Children Portions **Parking** 38

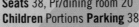

BEELEY Map 16 SK26

Devonshire Arms-Beeley

Modern British

Highly accomplished cooking in an up-to-date, English country inn

01629 733259
Devonshire Square DE4 2NR
e-mail: enquiries@devonshirebeeley.co.uk
dir: 6m N of Matlock & 5m E of Bakewell, located off B6012

From the outside this charming building looks like the classic English country inn, set in the sweet little village of Beeley. Initially inside is much as you'd expect - exposed beams, stone-brick walls and a great selection of real ales - but a surprise awaits as you move into the dining area: a colourful, modern brasserie, contemporary in style, but no less appealing for that. The cooking is refined but with a stout heart, with traditional British dishes rubbing shoulders with some French classics. A typical dinner might comprise cauliflower and curd cheese mousse with ham hock roulade, apple jelly, aniseed cress and grape vinaigrette followed by a main of Porkingtons pork fillet with spicy confit fennel, belly pork, braised pork cheek and a prune and Armagnac sauce. For dessert try the staple; Mrs Hill's Lemon Tart (the chef's mum's recipe.)

Chef Alan Hill **Owner** Duke of Devonshire **Times** 12-9.30 **Prices** Food prices not confirmed for 2011. Please telephone for details **Wines** 120 bottles over £20, 30 bottles under £20, 20 by glass **Notes** Sunday L, Vegetarian available **Seats** 60 **Children** Portions

BRADWELL Map 16 SK18

The Samuel Fox Country Inn

Modern British NEW

Modern cooking in a stylishly converted pub

01433 621562
Stretfield Rd S33 9JT
e-mail: thesamuelfox@hotmail.co.uk
dir: M1 junct 29, A617 towards Chesterfield, onto A619 towards A623 Chapel-en-le-Frith. B6049 for Bradwell, restaurant located on left

Renamed after Bradwell's most famous son, the industrial magnate Samuel Fox, this former village local was revamped in 2008 and is now a modern and stylish inn. In a glorious location and retaining its rustic charm, with glowing log fires, candles and fresh flowers on wooden tables, and stunning Hope Valley views from large windows, it draws discerning locals for its informal atmosphere and enjoyable modern British cooking. Seasonal menus make sound use of fresh locally-sourced produce and the emphasis is on simple, uncomplicated dishes with vibrant flavours. Typically, tuck into plump scallops with crispy pancetta and spiced sweet potato purée, and slow-braised lamb shoulder with creamy mash, Savoy cabbage and jus, leaving room for chocolate and amaretti torte. Service is highly attentive - nothing is too much trouble.

Chef Charlie Curran **Owner** Bakewell Developments **Times** 12-2.30/6-9.30 **Prices** Fixed L 2 course £12, Starter £3.90-£6.50, Main £8.95-£15.95, Dessert £3.95-£6.50, Service optional **Wines** 19 bottles over £20, 30 bottles under £20, 15 by glass **Notes** Sunday L, Vegetarian available **Seats** 50 **Children** Portions, Menu **Parking** 15

BREADSALL Map 11 SK33

Priory Restaurant

Modern British

Good contemporary cooking in historic setting

01332 832235
Marriott Breadsall Priory, Hotel & Country Club, Moor Rd DE7 6DL
e-mail: allayne.broom@marriotthotels.com
dir: M1 junct 25, A52 to Derby, then follow Chesterfield signs. Right at 1st rdbt, left at next. A608 to Heanor Rd. In 3m left then left again

Dating all the way back to the 13th century, Breadsall Priory is the oldest hotel in the Marriott chain. A luxuriously extended mansion house, it is set in 400 acres of parkland and well-tended gardens complete with an ornamental lake and golf course. The exposed beams and archways of the medieval priory's wine cellar make a fittingly atmospheric venue for the modern British cooking, where the emphasis is firmly on seasonal, local produce. Grilled sardines are perked up with a pink grapefruit, orange and chervil salsa, and served with spinach and rocket salad, as an appealing first course, followed, perhaps, by guinea fowl breast with basil mousse, butternut purée and white wine sauce.

Chef Karl J Kenny **Owner** Royal Bank of Scotland **Times** 1-2/7-10 Closed L Mon-Sat (private functions only) **Prices** Food prices not confirmed for 2011. Please telephone for details **Wines** 40 bottles over £20, 20 bottles under £20, 10 by glass **Notes** Sunday L, Vegetarian available, Dress restrictions, Shirt with collar, long trousers required, Civ Wed 100 **Seats** 104 **Children** Portions, Menu **Parking** 300

BUXTON Map 16 SK07

Best Western Lee Wood Hotel

British, International

Conservatory restaurant serving modern British menu

01298 23002
The Park SK17 6TQ
e-mail: leewoodhotel@btinternet.com
dir: M1 junct 24, A50 towards Ashbourne, A515 to Buxton. From Buxton town centre follow A5004 Long Hill to Whaley Bridge. Hotel approx 200mtrs beyond University of Derby campus

Fashioned into a hotel when the railway came to Buxton, Lee Wood was once three houses, built at the end of the Georgian era. It's set in impressive mature gardens and boasts a spacious bar-lounge area, where a nip of something appetising can be enjoyed before you progress through to the attractive conservatory restaurant, Elements. Here, you may expect to feast on ballottine of salmon with clams in dill cream, followed by Lancashire spring lamb medallions with stuffed tomatoes and wild mushrooms, finishing fruitily with pineapple carpaccio and pomegranate with mango sauce and coconut mist.

Times 12-2.15/7.15-9.30

CLOWNE Map 16 SK47

Hotel Van Dyk

British NEW

Modern British cooking in an atmospheric hotel with a boutique finish

01246 810219
Worksop Rd S42 4TD
dir: M1 junct 30, 2nd right towards Worksop, 2nd rdbt 1st exit, 3rd rdbt straight over. Through lights, hotel 100yds on right

Hotel Van Dyk is a grand Grade II listed building on the edge of the Dukeries Estate, which has been fully restored and transformed into an elegant and contemporary boutique hotel. There are two eating options, with the Bowden Restaurant being the hotel's fine-dining venue, housed in a converted chapel. With its oak-panelled walls, chandeliers, tables dressed in crisp white linen, and a self-playing baby grand in the corner, it's an elegant, atmospheric setting for some modern British cooking. Dinner begins with canapés and amuse-bouche, while a typical starter might be bonbon of quail, pigeon and goose liver on a mosaic of beetroot and celery. Chatsworth lamb with peppered sweetbreads, black pudding sausage, smoked garlic fondant and shallot jus could be one way to proceed, rounding off with roasted pears with honey ice cream and a pineapple tuile.

Times 7-10 Closed L Mon-Sat

DARLEY ABBEY Map 11 SK33

Darleys Restaurant

Modern British V

Modern British cooking by the water's edge

01332 364987
Hashams Ln DE22 1DZ
e-mail: info@darleys.com
dir: A6 N from Derby (Duffield road). Right in 1m into Mileash Ln, to Old Lane, right, over bridge. Restaurant on right

A converted cotton mill complete with its own toll bridge down at the water's edge of the River Derwent sounds like a trip back to olde worlde England, but Darley's is clean-cut and contemporary inside. The designer interior sports easy-on-the-eye shades of warm pink and earthy brown - it's a world apart from the days when the place was a canteen for cotton-mill workers. There's nothing archaic going on in the kitchen either: the team takes an unpretentious line with its modern British cooking, getting off to a modish start with home-cured venison

continued

DARLEY ABBEY *continued*

with chocolate jelly and pickled red cabbage, while fillet of pork with carrot purée, black pudding bonbon and slow-braised cheek continues with serious intent. A decking terrace overlooking the Derwent weir is the place to head to for alfresco dining when the sun shines.

Darleys Restaurant

Chef Jonathan Hobson, Mark Hadfield **Owner** Jonathan & Kathryn Hobson **Times** 12-2/7-10 Closed BHs, 1st 2 wks Jan, D Sun **Prices** Fixed L 2 course fr £15.95, Starter £6.95-£8.50, Main £17.90-£21.50, Dessert £6.95-£7.50, Service optional **Wines** 42 bottles over £20, 41 bottles under £20, 15 by glass **Notes** Sunday L, Vegetarian menu **Seats** 70 **Children** Portions **Parking** 12

DERBY — Map 11 SK33

Cathedral Quarter Hotel

Modern British

Exciting modern repertoire in a luxurious Victorian hotel

☎ 01332 546080
16 St Mary's Gate DE1 3JR
e-mail: opulence@cathedralquarterhotel.com
dir: Follow brown signs to Cathedral Quarter. Hotel on one-way road

Derby's Victorian council offices have been put to good use as a stylishly-converted hotel. How well those old-school civil servants once lived: the mosaic floors of the grand foyer are splendidly restored, and a regal Scagliola marble staircase sweeps up to the Opulence restaurant, where oak-panelled walls and period plasterwork cornices are offset by retro flock wallpaper and Italian glass chandeliers. The kitchen works in a modern idiom, keeping an eye open for fashionable ingredients, flavour combinations and textures. Braised belly of local pork partnered with carrots, pickled shemiji and sweetbread ravioli is a good way to start, then main-course lamb appears as slow-poached fillet and braised shoulder with potato purée, almonds and lentil vinaigrette.

Times 12-2.30/7-9.30 Closed L Sat, D Sun

Masa Restaurant

Modern British V

Immaculate cuisine in converted chapel

☎ 01332 203345
The Old Chapel, Brook St DE1 3PF
e-mail: enquiries@masarestaurantwinebar.com
dir: 8m from M1 junct 25. Brook St off inner ring road near BBC Radio Derby

This stylish restaurant and wine bar in the centre of Derby pulls in a faithful congregation with its good-looking contemporary interior and food to match. The converted Wesleyan chapel has tables perched up on the chapel's soaring galleries above the buzzy wine bar - good for people-watching. The room is done out in slick style with chestnut-hued floors and slabs of white and deep purple. The kitchen subjects sound British ingredients to modern European treatment, and keeps to straightforward flavour combinations. Sharp flavours are to the fore in a well-balanced starter of slow-cooked pork belly with caramelised white asparagus, creamed Savoy cabbage and Calvados jus. Main courses continue in the same vein, as in seared fillet of beef with wilted spinach, Roquefort Pithiviers and bordelaise sauce.

Chef José Vega **Owner** Didar & Paula Dalkic **Times** 12-2.30/6-9.30 Closed 26 Dec-1 Jan, Mon-Tue **Prices** Fixed L 3 course £18, Fixed D 3 course £22, Starter £4.50-£8.50, Main £13.50-£21, Dessert £5.95-£7.45, Service added but optional 10% **Wines** 20 bottles over £20, 24 bottles under £20, 20 by glass **Notes** Tasting menu 5 course, Sunday L, Vegetarian menu, Dress restrictions, Smart casual, black tie when specified, Civ Wed 220 **Seats** 120 **Children** Portions **Parking** On street (pay & display), Car park Brook St

FROGGATT — Map 16 SK27

The Chequers Inn

British

Homely country inn in the Peak District

☎ 01433 630231
S32 3ZJ
e-mail: info@chequers-froggatt.com
dir: On A625 between Sheffield & Bakewell, 0.75m from Calver

The Chequers is a whitewashed roadside inn in the rugged Peak District, not far from Chatsworth. A homely, no-nonsense air pervades the dining area, with its plainly set tables and welcoming staff, and the menu is supplemented by blackboard specials. A range of culinary influences is in evidence, from grilled sardines on toast with caper oil, to mains such as saffron-scented seafood risotto, or guinea fowl with champ potatoes in tomato and Madeira sauce. Desserts tend to the lighter end of the spectrum, with attractive offerings such as blackcurrant and elderflower mousse, garnished with a tuile.

Chef Karim Maoui **Owner** Jonathan & Joanne Tindall **Times** 12-2/6-9.30 Closed 25 Dec **Prices** Starter £4.75-£7, Main £10.50-£16, Dessert £5.50-£6.50, Service optional **Wines** 11 bottles over £20, 29 bottles under £20, 9 by glass **Notes** Sunday L, Vegetarian available **Seats** 90 **Children** Portions, Menu **Parking** 50

GRINDLEFORD — Map 16 SK27

The Maynard

Modern British

Stylishly renovated hotel with imaginative food

☎ 01433 630321
Main Rd S32 2HE
e-mail: info@themaynard.co.uk
dir: M1/A619 into Chesterfield, onto Baslow, A623 to Calver right into Grindleford

Amid immaculate landscaped gardens on a hillside just outside the village, this handsome Victorian building enjoys glorious views across the Peak District National Park. Stylishly reworked with a hip boutique hotel décor, it has a voguish dining room packed with funky modern art on the walls and ceiling. The cooking, too, takes a contemporary line, juggling classics with imagination and a hint of the Orient here and there in its simple flavour combinations; materials are local and organic as far as possible. Among starters might be grilled sardines with chilli couscous and a tomato, ginger and orange sauce; follow with braised pork belly with baked apple and black pudding beignet, and finish with lemongrass, ginger and lime leaf chocolate tart.

Times 12-2/7-9 Closed L Sat

HATHERSAGE — Map 16 SK28

George Hotel

Modern British

Accomplished modern cooking in traditional coaching inn

☎ 01433 650436
Main Rd S32 1BB
e-mail: info@george-hotel.net
dir: In village centre on junction of A625/B6001

This 500-year-old coaching inn has a firm connection to the literary Brontë sisters, as Charlotte frequently dropped by for a snifter while visiting friends at the vicarage, and used Hathersage and its local characters in her novel *Jane Eyre*. The George was once an inn, but nowadays it's more of a stylish contemporary hotel after a makeover that blends funky colours, clever lighting and wooden floors with its original stone walls in the restaurant. The kitchen's output matches the surroundings, with a long-standing commitment to making everything in-house using top local produce in an unfussy yet inventive way. Punchy flavours are to the fore in a starter of beetroot tarte Tatin with herb-crusted goats' cheese, walnut dressing and aged balsamic, while mains might offer roasted lamb cutlets with 8-hour braised shoulder of lamb Wellington with fondant potato, beetroot purée and thyme jus.

Chef Helen Heywood **Owner** Eric Marsh **Times** 12-2.30/7-10 Closed D 25 Dec **Prices** Fixed L 2 course £28.65, Fixed D 3 course £35.75, Service included **Wines** 31 bottles over £20, 18 bottles under £20, 10 by glass **Notes** Early bird menu Mon-Fri 6.30-7.30pm, Sunday L, Vegetarian available, Dress restrictions, Smart casual, no T-shirts, Civ Wed 45 **Seats** 45, Pr/dining room 80 **Children** Portions **Parking** 45

The Plough Inn

Modern British

Good honest food in a traditional inn

01433 650319
Leadmill Bridge S32 1BA
e-mail: sales@theploughinn-hathersage.co.uk
web: www.theploughinn-hathersage.co.uk
dir: 1m SE of Hathersage on B6001. Over bridge, 150yds beyond at Leadmill

The Plough is a great place for a pitstop in the Peak District. The interior is cosy and welcoming, the beer is well kept, and it sits on the banks of the Derwent in beautiful Derbyshire countryside. There's clearly some talent at the stoves too, turning out an appealing line in classic and modern British cooking, peppered with European accents. Whether you eat in the convivial bar or the more intimate dining room, the crowd-pleasing menu is built on diligently-sourced local materials. Black pudding Scotch egg with a foie gras yolk and apple purée sets the standard, ahead of roast wood pigeon with a cassoulet of haricots blancs, kale, bacon and mushrooms. Finish with something like red wine-poached figs with praline ice cream.

Chef Robert Navarro **Owner** Robert & Cynthia Emery **Times** 11.30-2.30/6.30-9.30 Closed 25 Dec **Prices** Fixed L 2 course £15.75-£19, Starter £4.50-£9, Main £11-£19, Dessert £4.75-£7, Service optional **Wines** 27 bottles over £20, 22 bottles under £20, 14 by glass **Notes** Sunday L, Vegetarian available, Dress restrictions, Smart Casual **Seats** 40, Pr/dining room 24 **Children** Portions **Parking** 40

HIGHAM Map 16 SK35

Santo's Higham Farm Hotel

Traditional Italian

Simple food big on flavour in the lush Amber Valley

01773 833812
Main Rd DE55 6EH
e-mail: reception@santoshighamfarm.co.uk
dir: M1 junct 28, A38 towards Derby, then A61 to Higham, left onto B6013

With fine views over the lush Amber Valley in the heart of rugged Derbyshire, the farm hotel is licensed for weddings, as well as offering a base for some serious walking. It's run with friendly, approachable cheer, and the comfortable, candlelit dining room incorporates a seafood station and lobster tanks. Food comes in gargantuan portions and is all about big flavours. Tuna carpaccio dressed in lemon and black pepper with saffron mascarpone and endive, classic tournedos Rossini with foie gras, and spiced ginger pudding with butterscotch sauce and custard are the kinds of things to expect.

Chef Raymond Moody **Owner** Santo Cusimano **Times** 12-2/7-9.30 Closed L Mon-Sat, D Sun **Prices** Food prices not confirmed for 2011. Please telephone for details **Wines** 26 bottles over £20, 23 bottles under £20, 3 by glass **Notes** Sunday L, Vegetarian available, Dress restrictions, Smart casual, Civ Wed 70 **Seats** 50, Pr/dining room 34 **Children** Portions **Parking** 100

See advert below

HOPE Map 16 SK18

Losehill House Hotel & Spa

Modern British

Imaginative cooking in an idyllic Peak District location

01433 621219
Lose Hill Ln, Edale Rd S33 6AF
e-mail: info@losehillhouse.co.uk
dir: On entering Hope follow signs to Edale opposite church. Turn right at brown tourist sign after 1.5m. Located on left

It takes a bit of effort to track down Losehill House, but the investment is well-rewarded. The stylishly-refurbished country house and spa is tucked down a tranquil single-track lane in the heart of the Peak District National Park - a hideaway made for hiking all day over the dales, before recharging with a snifter on the terrace with wide-open, sheep-grazed hills all around. That view is the backdrop at dinner in the Orangery restaurant, a feminine, soft-focus sort of place with fancy wrought-iron seats, blond wood floors and honey-hued walls. As for the food, astute sourcing ensures supplies from meat and dairy farmers on the doorstep, which appear in no-nonsense modern British dishes. Daily-changing menus might kick off with lamb's kidneys sautéed with mustard and wild mushrooms served on brioche, ahead of fillet of White Peak beef with potato galette, wild mushrooms and béarnaise sauce.

Chef Darren Goodwin **Owner** Paul & Kathryn Roden **Times** 12-2.30/7-9 **Prices** Fixed L 2 course £14-£17.50, Fixed D 3 course £32.50-£35, Service optional **Wines** 6 by glass **Notes** Sunday L, Vegetarian available, Civ Wed 80 **Seats** 50, Pr/dining room 12 **Parking** 20

MATLOCK — Map 16 SK35

The Red House Country Hotel

Traditional British

Simple country cooking in a fine Victorian house

☎ 01629 734854
Old Rd, Darley Dale DE4 2ER
e-mail: enquiries@theredhousecountryhotel.co.uk
dir: off A6 onto Old Rd signed Carriage Museum, 2.5m N of Matlock

Built in the 1890s for a Manchester architect, the house is an appealing mix of comfortable domestic interiors and large public rooms, where stained-glass windows look out over the neatly maintained gardens. The dining room looks properly elegant and the staff know their stuff, making for a relaxing experience all round. The cooking avoids over-elaboration in favour of a simpler country-house approach, taking in smoked trout pâté with toast, pork escalope with mushrooms in Madeira, and salmon on pea purée, topped with diced pancetta and drizzled in mint oil. Desserts are of the 'wickedly delicious' variety, according to the menu, so expect the likes of sticky toffee pudding and cream.

Chef Alan Perkins **Owner** David & Kate Gardiner **Times** 7-8.30 Closed 25-29 Dec, 1st 2 wks Jan, L all week **Prices** Fixed D 4 course £27-£30.50, Service optional **Wines** 17 bottles over £20, 11 bottles under £20, 6 by glass **Notes** Vegetarian available, Dress restrictions, Smart casual **Seats** 24 **Parking** 15

Stones Restaurant

Modern British V

Basement venue with modern British classics

☎ 01629 56061
1c Dale Rd DE4 3LT
e-mail: info@stones-restaurant.co.uk

Stones is in a basement and yet misses nothing of the daylight with its sun terrace that overlooks the River Derwent. A brasserie-style layout done in warm caramel tones with exposed brick feels up-to-date, and the cooking is a Mediterranean-based rollcall of modern British ideas. Seared scallops with black pudding purée, poached apple and rosemary foam might be the prelude to mains such as ballottine of guinea fowl with a leg meat sausage, celeriac purée and mustard sauce, or sea bass with baby fennel in a vanilla-scented shellfish sauce. Crowd-pleasing desserts include the likes of chocolate pudding with peanut butter mousse and caramelised banana. A compact list of internationally mixed wines comes at manageable prices.

Chef Kevin Stone **Owner** Kevin Stone, Jade Himsworth, Katie Temple **Times** 12-2/6-9 Closed 26 Dec, 1 Jan, Mon, L Tue-Wed, D Sun **Prices** Fixed L 2 course £14.95, Fixed D 3 course £16.95-£21, Starter £7.20-£8.50, Main £15-£18.50, Dessert £5.95, Service optional **Wines** 12 bottles over £20, 17 bottles under £20, 7 by glass **Notes** Fixed D 2/3 course available 6-7pm, Sunday L, Vegetarian menu **Seats** 30 **Children** Portions, Menu **Parking** Matlock train station

MELBOURNE — Map 11 SK32

The Bay Tree

Modern British

Eclectic modern cooking in the heart of the village

☎ 01332 863358
4 Potter St DE73 8HW
e-mail: enquiries@baytreerestaurant.co.uk
dir: Please telephone for directions

First opening its doors 23 years ago, this unpretentious eatery occupies a fine 17th-century building in the village centre and continues to draw a loyal local clientele for robust brasserie-style cooking. The smart, airy dining room has timber floors and contemporary artwork on the walls. The modern menu has an international flavour with local produce used to create dishes such as mustard and coriander-crusted beef carpaccio with chilli and lime dressing, followed by seared sea bass with tomato risotto and basil cream sauce. Puddings include sticky toffee pudding with vanilla ice cream.

Times 10.30-3/6.30-10.30

MORLEY — Map 11 SK34

The Morley Hayes Hotel - Dovecote Restaurant

Modern British

Upbeat modern cooking in golfing destination

☎ 01332 780480
Main Rd DE7 6DG
e-mail: enquiries@morleyhayes.com
dir: 4m N of Derby on A608

Set in rolling countryside, this contemporary hotel and golfing destination started out life as an 18th-century farmstead. Its first-floor Dovecote Restaurant (the top-drawer dining option) comes brimful of character, with a vaulted roof, massive exposed beams, bare brickwork walls and clothed tables. Sip cocktails in the small piano bar while you ponder the modern brasserie-style menu driven by quality local produce. House classics immediately catch the attention, like matured Derbyshire rib-eye with frites, roasted tomatoes, Portabello mushrooms and béarnaise, or perhaps an apple tarte Tatin finish (with marzipan ice cream). Otherwise check out options like roasted fillet of cod served with curly kale, creamed potatoes and a brown shrimp and chive butter cream sauce.

Chef Nigel Stuart **Owner** Robert & Andrew Allsop/Morley Hayes Leisure Ltd **Times** 12-2/7-9.30 Closed 1 Jan, L Sat, Mon **Prices** Fixed L 2 course fr £13.95, Fixed D 3 course fr £19.95, Starter £5.95-£9.95, Main £13.95-£18.95, Dessert £5.95-£7.25, Service optional **Wines** 25 bottles over £20, 15 bottles under £20, 12 by glass **Notes** Fixed L 1 course £9.95, Sunday L, Vegetarian available, Dress restrictions, Smart casual, Civ Wed 80 **Seats** 100, Pr/dining room 24 **Children** Portions, Menu **Parking** 250

RISLEY — Map 11 SK43

Risley Hall

European

Traditional hotel dining in ancient manor house

☎ 0115 939 9000
Derby Rd DE72 3SS
e-mail: enquiries@risleyhallhotel.co.uk
dir: M1 junct 25, Sandiacre exit into Bostock Ln. Left at lights, hotel on left in 0.25m

Risley Hall is a handsome Saxon country house dating back to the 11th century, with a splendid Baronial Hall inside which is, in fact, a legacy from the 16th century. In recent years the house has been tastefully restored and refurbished, and nowadays it's a happy blend of the old and the new, sitting in 10 acres of beautiful landscaped grounds. The Abbey restaurant is the scene for some straightforward cooking based around seasonal ingredients. Chicken liver parfait with caramelised onion chutney and melba toast is a typical starter, followed by rack of lamb with a mustard and herb crust, fondant potato and redcurrant sauce. Finish with pear and almond tart with vanilla ice cream.

Times 12-6.30/7-10.30

ROWSLEY Map 16 SK26

East Lodge Country House Hotel

Modern British

Modern British cooking in the Peak District

☎ 01629 734474
DE4 2EF
e-mail: info@eastlodge.com
dir: On A6, 5m from Matlock & 3m from Bakewell, at junct with B6012

In the heart of the Peak District, not far from Chatsworth, East Lodge makes its own creditable stab at grandeur with 10 acres of lush grounds, a conservatory bar and its own extensive kitchen garden. That last detail means that menus can't help but be impeccably seasonal, and the modern British food is full of bright ideas. Derbyshire black pudding is used in a little pie that is accompanied by celery and apple, crispy pig's ear and grated crackling. A tranche of halibut is dressed with a profusion of Morecambe Bay shrimps, capers, lemon and chives, while locally-farmed lamb appears as the now-fashionable trio (braised shoulder, roast best end and sweetbreads) with broccoli couscous spiced with ras el hanout. Finish with the Great British hot pudding of the day.

Times 12-2/7-9.30

The Peacock at Rowsley

Modern British V

Inventive, modern dining in luxury Derbyshire hotel

☎ 01629 733518
Bakewell Rd DE4 2EB
e-mail: reception@thepeacockatrowsley.com
dir: A6, 3m before Bakewell, 6m from Matlock towards Bakewell

Set in the heart of the Peak District, the former dower house dates from the 1640s and is now a small luxury hotel, marrying period features with modern design to great effect. Designed by Paris-based India Mahdavi, contemporary chandeliers and other well-chosen fixtures and fittings rub along nicely with the bare-wood tables in the restaurant; there's a diverting view over the garden, too. Head chef Dan Smith's time with Tom Aikens shows in his technical dexterity and the creativity of his menu, the dishes based on excellent local seasonal produce. Start, perhaps, with duck liver paired with fig, hazelnuts and a frangelico reduction; next up, a beautifully balanced main-course has sea bass served with a crab lasagne, leeks, chervil vierge and shellfish foam. Desserts are no less creative: chocolate parfait comes with an espresso reduction, Amaretto jelly and milk sorbet. Slick service comes from a young team. For a pint, or some more straightforward food, pull up a seat at an antique table in front of the roaring fire in the bar.

Chef Daniel Smith **Owner** Rutland Hotels **Times** 12-2/7-9 Closed D 24-26 Dec **Prices** Fixed L 2 course fr £19, Starter £5.95-£13.25, Main £26.25-£31.50, Dessert £7.50-£8.75, Service optional **Wines** 45 bottles over £20, 8 bottles under £20, 15 by glass **Notes** Sunday L, Vegetarian menu, Civ Wed 20 **Seats** 40, Pr/dining room 20 **Children** Portions, Menu **Parking** 25

THORPE Map 16 SK15

Izaak Walton Hotel

Modern European

New-fangled cooking in a hotel named after author of *The Compleat Angler*

☎ 01335 350555
Dovedale DE6 2AY
e-mail: reception@izaakwaltonhotel.com
dir: A515 onto B5054, to Thorpe, continue straight over cattle grid & 2 small bridges, 1st right & sharp left

The creeper-covered house enjoys fabulous views over the Dovedale valley, an especially delectable part of the Peak District National Park. In the smart dining room, with its gathered curtains and elegant table-settings, some modern doings are afoot. New-fangled ways with fish that might have come as a surprise to Walton include steamed cod with a carrot and coriander salad in a passionfruit reduction with coconut foam. Bookend that with seared pigeon on creamed leeks with celeriac chips and hazelnuts, and honey and lavender pannacotta with strawberry compôte and lemon meringue.

Times 12.30-2.30/7-9

DEVON

ASHBURTON Map 3 SX77

Agaric

Modern British

Skilful cooking in charming restaurant with rooms

☎ 01364 654478
30 North St TQ13 7QD
e-mail: eat@agaricrestaurant.co.uk
dir: Opposite town hall. Ashburton off A38 between Exeter & Plymouth

A friendly and welcoming restaurant with rooms housed in a listed 300-year-old building, Agaric was formerly a double-fronted shop. It's small and intimate and the low ceilings, wooden floors, wood-burning stove, and simple wooden tables create a relaxing, unpretentious atmosphere. Nick Coiley once cooked alongside the legendary Joyce Molyneux at the Carved Angel, and there is a refreshing honesty about his style. His daily menus showcase technically accomplished dishes prepared from home-grown and local produce and wild ingredients. Fish soup comes with all the accoutrements, while main-course pan-fried brill is served with stir-fried squid, mustard leaves and sweet chilli sauce, and for dessert, perhaps a local rhubarb and strawberry clafoutis. There's a beautiful courtyard garden with wood-fired bread oven.

Chef Nick Coiley **Owner** Mr N Coiley & Mrs S Coiley **Times** 12-2/7-9.30 Closed 2 wks Aug, Xmas, 1 wk Jan, Sun-Tue, L Sat **Prices** Fixed L 2 course fr £14.95, Starter £4.95-£9.50, Main £14.95-£18.95, Dessert £5.95-£6.95, Service optional **Wines** 16 bottles over £20, 9 bottles under £20, 4 by glass **Notes** Vegetarian available **Seats** 30 **Children** Portions **Parking** Car park opposite

ASHWATER Map 3 SX39

Blagdon Manor Restaurant with Rooms

Traditional British

Confident cooking in charming country-house hotel

☎ 01409 211224
EX21 5DF
e-mail: stay@blagdon.com
dir: From A388 towards Holsworthy, 2m N of Chapman's Well take 2nd right towards Ashwater. Next right by Blagdon Lodge. Hotel 2nd on right

continued

ASHWATER ***continued***

A Devon longhouse dating back to the 16th century, Blagdon makes the best of its location close to the border with Cornwall to dish up some fine West Country produce. A dog-friendly country-house hotel set in rolling countryside, the traditionally elegant décor mixes well with the original features in its comfortable lounges, snug bars, and through to the restaurant, part of which is in a handsome conservatory extension. That fine regional produce is used to great effect in creative dishes that reflect the ambition and flair in the kitchen. White onion pannacotta is a complex first course, the clearly flavoured cream supported by chargrilled new potatoes, ham hock salad, mustard seeds and some deep-fried parsley. A tasting of West Country pork is a generous serving of tip-top meat, served as roast loin, confit belly and the deeply-flavoured liver sautéed, while a dessert might be a summer berry pudding with clotted cream.

Chef Stephen Morey **Owner** Stephen & Liz Morey **Times** 12-2/7-9 Closed 1-31 Jan, Mon-Tue, L Wed-Thu **Prices** Fixed L 2 course fr £17, Fixed D 3 course fr £38, Service optional **Wines** 22 bottles over £20, 8 bottles under £20, 7 by glass **Notes** Sunday L, Vegetarian available, Dress restrictions, Smart casual **Seats** 24, Pr/dining room 16 **Parking** 12

AXMINSTER — Map 4 SY29

Fairwater Head Country House Hotel

Modern, Traditional

Lovely views and elegant cooking

☎ 01297 678349
Hawkchurch EX13 5TX
e-mail: info@fairwaterheadhotel.co.uk
dir: A358 into Broom Lane at Tytherleigh, follow signs to Hawkchurch & hotel

This countryside hideaway built in Edwardian times exudes a sense of calm with its two acres of gardens, a feeling helped along by the experienced and amiable owners. The Greenfields restaurant is bright and airy with stripped wooden floorboards, simple white and cream fittings, chunky wooden tables dressed in linen and tan high-back leather chairs. Large windows allow for stunning views across Axminster Valley and the rolling Devon countryside. Elegant cooking using classic British and modern French influences, with the occasional foray further afield, plunders the local larder to great effect. Salad of tempura plaice with mixed leaves and gribiche dressing, perhaps, before sautéed breast of Barbary duck with fondant potatoes, braised red cabbage, cinnamon and port reduction and a pud of white chocolate pannacotta, satsuma marmalade and honeycomb crumble. There are good local cheeses and Devon wines, too.

Chef Mike Reid **Owner** Adam & Carrie Southwell **Times** 12-2/7-8.30 Closed Jan, L Mon & Tue **Prices** Fixed L 2 course £10.50-£14.75, Fixed D 3 course fr £31, Starter £5-£7, Main £14.50-£19.50, Dessert £5-£7, Service optional **Wines** 33 bottles over £20, 27 bottles under £20, 12 by glass **Notes** Sunday L, Vegetarian available, Dress restrictions, Smart casual, Civ Wed 50 **Seats** 60, Pr/dining room 18 **Children** Portions, Menu **Parking** 40

BEESANDS — Map 3 SX84

The Cricket Inn

Modern British

Quaint seaside inn serving tip-top seafood and more

☎ 01548 580215
TQ7 2EN
e-mail: enquiries@thecricketinn.com
dir: From Kingsbridge follow A379 towards Dartmouth, at Stokenham mini-rdbt turn right for Beesands

There are fabulous views from the Cricket Inn, built back in 1867 (the vista hasn't really changed since then, since it is only the shingle beach and the open water of Start Bay out front). Sympathetically restored, the inn retains a quaint feel, courtesy of fishing memorabilia and historical black-and-white photos of the old fishing village on the walls. Friendly, informal service mirrors the simple set-up. Blackboard menus are changed regularly to include the local fishermen's latest catch and dishes don't mess around too much with the quality ingredients. Tuck into Beesands crab soup or diver-caught Beesands scallops before trying the signature seafood pancake, or traditional fish and chips. Devonshire sirloin or calves' liver provide good carnivorous choices. An extension is underway as we go to print.

Chef Scott Simon **Owner** Nigel & Rachel Heath **Times** 12-3/6-9 **Prices** Starter £5-£9, Main £9-£20, Dessert £4.50-£7, Service optional **Wines** 8 bottles over £20, 19 bottles under £20, 9 by glass **Notes** Sunday L, Vegetarian available **Seats** 65, Pr/dining room 40 **Children** Portions, Menu **Parking** 30

BIDEFORD — Map 3 SS42

Yeoldon Country House Hotel

British

Traditional cooking with lovely river views

☎ 01237 474400
Durrant Ln, Northam EX39 2RL
e-mail: yeoldonhouse@aol.com
dir: A39 from Barnstaple over River Torridge Bridge. At rdbt right onto A386 towards Northam, then 3rd right into Durrant Lane

Run by husband-and-wife-team Brian and Jennifer, Yeolden offers unpretentious food using local produce in peaceful, traditional surroundings. The handsome house dates back to Victorian times and is in a very pretty location, with views over the garden across to the River Torridge. There are no airs and graces in the dining room, just warm hospitality and well-spaced tables. The simple, traditional British menu might include duck liver and orange pâté served with an apricot and ginger chutney and melba toast, followed by chump of West Country lamb served with parsnip and horseradish mash with a redcurrant and rosemary gravy. Devonshire farmhouse ice creams hit the spot for afters; try whisky and ginger or raspberry Pavlova.

Chef Brian Steele **Owner** Brian & Jennifer Steele **Times** 7-8 Closed Xmas, Sun, L all week **Prices** Fixed D 3 course £32.50, Service included **Wines** 7 bottles over £20, 32 bottles under £20, 4 by glass **Notes** Vegetarian available, Dress restrictions, Smart casual, Civ Wed 60 **Seats** 30 **Children** Portions **Parking** 30

BRANSCOMBE — Map 4 SY18

The Masons Arms

Traditional British

Characterful village inn near one of Devon's loveliest beaches

☎ 01297 680300
EX12 3DJ
e-mail: reception@masonsarms.co.uk
dir: Village off A3052 between Sidmouth and Seaton

The setting is a postcard-perfect 14th-century pub in the heart of beautiful Branscombe above its famous beach. And inside, the Masons Arms is a gem too: you can still order a ploughman's and a pint in the original cider house bar built from ship's timbers, slate floors and stone walls, but the place has evolved to focus on a busy restaurant where crowds spill out into the outdoor seating in summer. Keeping things local is high on the agenda: lobster and crab are landed down on the beach, and most ingredients come from within a 10-mile radius of the village. Simple dishes kick off along the lines of seared scallops with roasted butternut squash purée, then progress to main courses that point up the locality: pan-fried West Country pork tenderloin with cider beurre blanc and apple fritter, or roast rack of local lamb with aubergine caviar and a light jus.

Chef S Garland, A Deam **Owner** Mr & Mrs C Slaney **Times** 12-2/7-9 Closed L Mon-Sat **Prices** Fixed D 3 course £29.95, Starter £4.50-£7.50, Main £10.95-£16.25, Dessert £5.25, Service optional **Wines** 27 bottles over £20, 17 bottles under £20, 14 by glass **Notes** Sunday L, Vegetarian available, Dress restrictions, No shorts or jeans **Seats** 70, Pr/dining room 20 **Parking** 45

BRIXHAM — Map 3 SX95

Quayside Hotel

Modern British **NEW**

Skilful cooking in popular quayside hotel

☎ 01803 855751
41-49 King St TQ5 9TJ
e-mail: reservations@quayside.co.uk
dir: From Exeter take A380 towards Torquay, then A3022 to Brixham

Formerly six cottages, the engaging, long-established Quayside Hotel is positioned to exploit the panoramic views over the bustling harbour and bay. Sound technical skills and creativity are very much in evidence from the committed kitchen team, with care taken in the sourcing of ingredients and the presentation on the plate. With Brixham Fish Market just along the quay, excellent fish is cooked with simplicity; crispy gurnard served with scallops, herb couscous and lemon sabayon, for example. Alternatives may include Thai-style mussels, black bream with saffron velouté, and meaty options like beef fillet with wild mushroom ragoût and Madeira jus. The cosy restaurant has low ceilings, clothed tables, flickering candlelight, and those soothing harbour views.

Chef Andy Sewell **Owner** Mr & Mrs C F Bowring **Times** 6.30-9.30 Closed L all week **Prices** Food prices not confirmed for 2011. Please telephone for details **Wines** 5 bottles over £20, 27 bottles under £20, 10 by glass **Notes** Vegetarian available, Dress restrictions, Smart casual preferred **Seats** 40, Pr/dining room 18 **Children** Portions, Menu **Parking** 30

BURRINGTON **Map 3 SS61**

Northcote Manor

Modern British V NOTABLE WINE LIST

Modern British cooking in a former monastery

☎ 01769 560501
EX37 9LZ
e-mail: rest@northcotemanor.co.uk
dir: M5 junct 27 towards Barnstaple. Left at rdbt to South Molton. Do not enter Burrington village. Follow A377, right at T-junct to Barnstaple. Entrance after 3m, opp Portsmouth Arms railway station and pub

High on a hill, and reached via a drive through lovely woodland, Northcote is all about tranquility. It was originally a monastery, until Henry VIII put paid to that, but has managed to retain an aura of unruffled calm nonetheless. You dine in candlelit intimacy, with crisp white linen and skilled service maintaining a rarefied tone. The food is squarely in the modern British mould, with regional ingredients proudly showcased throughout. A starter sausage fashioned from free-range chicken is served with wilted spinach and watercress sauce, to achieve a nice balance of textures. Move on to North Devon beef tournedos of excellent pedigree, ably supported by wild mushroom casserole and a sweet rendition of sauce Diane, not forgetting a bowl of delicious chips, and finish with dark chocolate and caramel mousse and honeycomb ice cream.

Chef Richie Herkes **Owner** J Pierre Mifsud **Times** 12-2/7-9 **Prices** Fixed L 2 course fr £15, Fixed D 3 course fr £42, Service optional **Wines** 87 bottles over £20, 9 bottles under £20, 10 by glass **Notes** Sunday L, Vegetarian menu, Dress restrictions, Smart casual preferred, Civ Wed 80 **Seats** 34, Pr/dining room 30 **Children** Portions, Menu **Parking** 30

CHAGFORD **Map 3 SX78**

Gidleigh Park

– see page 122

Mill End

Modern British

Confident cooking in charming riverside setting

☎ 01647 432282
TQ13 8JN
e-mail: info@millendhotel.com
dir: From A30 turn on to A382. Establishment on right before Chagford turning

In a secluded Dartmoor valley, part of the appeal of this country-house hotel by the River Teign is the charming service led by its owner. It feels like a home-from-home (albeit one with six miles of on-site angling). The 18th-century building is still a working water mill and restaurant diners get a view of the restored wheel. The interior is a calming sage green, the tables crisply laid with white linen and fine crockery and cutlery. An exciting modern menu utilises local produce to great effect in the likes of smooth chicken liver parfait with poached plums, loin of pork with black pudding mousse and a cider and apple sauce and dark chocolate marquise with mint chocolate chip ice cream.

Chef Wayne Pearson **Owner** Keith Green **Times** 12-2/7-9 Closed 1st 3 wks Jan, L Mon-Sat (except by appointment) **Prices** Fixed D 3 course £42, Service optional, Groups min 8 service 10% **Wines** 41 bottles over £20, 16 bottles under £20, 7 by glass **Notes** Sunday L, Vegetarian available, Dress restrictions, No jeans, trainers **Seats** 42 **Parking** 30

22 Mill Street Restaurant & Rooms

Modern European V

Inspiring cooking in Dartmoor village

☎ 01647 432244
22 Mill St TQ13 8AW
e-mail: info@22millst.com
web: www.22millst.com
dir: A382/B3206 enter village into main square, Mill St is on the right

David and Chantel Jenkins took over the helm at 22 Mill Street at the start of 2010, bringing new vitality and enthusiasm. This small but stylish restaurant in a spirited little moorland town has clean-cut contemporary décor with wooden louvred blinds, local art on the walls, toffee-hued leather chairs and white-clothed tables making for a stylish ensemble to match the food. David Jenkins cooks impressively in a modern British vein with tight, punchy flavour combos that show a clear sense of purpose in each dish. Langoustine soufflé with langoustine and Cognac bisque opens with reassuring depth of flavour, followed by a superb-looking main course of crisp Gloucestershire Old Spot pork belly with carrot purée, River Exe mussels and fondant potato - a superbly coherent piece of cooking. Save room for moreish desserts such as pineapple tarte Tatin with burnt honey ice cream.

Chef John Hooker, David Jenkins **Times** 12-4/6.30-10 Closed 2 wks Jan, Mon, D Sun **Prices** Fixed L 2 course £14.95-£24.95, Fixed D 3 course fr £42, Tasting menu £59, Service optional **Wines** 50 bottles over £20, 10 bottles under £20, 8 by glass **Notes** Tasting menu 7 course, Sunday L, Vegetarian menu **Seats** 28, Pr/dining room 14 **Children** Portions **Parking** On street

DARTMOUTH **Map 3 SX85**

Jan and Freddies Brasserie

Modern British

Lively brasserie in the centre of Dartmouth

☎ 01803 832491
10 Fairfax Place TQ6 9AD
e-mail: info@janandfreddiesbrasserie.co.uk
dir: Fairfax Place runs parallel to S Embankment. Restaurant faces Hawley Rd

Right in the heart of Dartmouth, this stylish bar and brasserie has a thoroughly modern look with funky lighting, an abundance of mirrors and undressed wooden tables. The relaxed and friendly service fits the bill, as does the unfussy modern British food prepared with an emphasis on good local ingredients. Begin with River Teign mussels steamed in a shallot and white wine broth, or maybe a twice-baked Devon cheese soufflé with pear and celery salsa. Follow on with diver-caught scallops with squid and crisp pork belly on a pea and saffron risotto, and don't miss out on desserts, such as a superb strawberry cheesecake with gingerbread crumb, foamed lemon jelly and basil coulis, a dish displaying echoes of molecular gastronomy.

Chef Richard Hilson **Owner** Jan & Freddie Clarke **Times** 12.30-2/6.30-9 Closed Xmas, Sun, L Mon **Prices** Fixed D 3 course fr £19.95, Starter £5.95-£7.95, Main £13.95-£19.95, Dessert £4.95-£8.95, Service optional **Wines** 16 bottles over £20, 22 bottles under £20, 10 by glass **Notes** Vegetarian available **Seats** 40 **Children** Portions **Parking** On street

Gidleigh Park

CHAGFORD Map 3 SX78

Modern European V NOTABLE WINE LIST

First-class country-house fine dining in beautiful Dartmoor hotel

☎ 01647 432367
TQ13 8HH
e-mail: gidleighpark@gidleigh.co.uk
dir: From Chagford Sq turn right at Lloyds TSB into Mill St, after 150yds right fork, across x-rds into Holy St. Restaurant 1.5m

Gidleigh Park is a masterpiece of understatement. The handsome half-timbered mansion built in the 1920s in the Arts and Crafts style stands on the fringes of Dartmoor in a 54-acre haven of immaculate gardens and woodland with an impressive water feature, otherwise known as the River Teign, running past the foot of the sweeping lawn. It's all undeniably lovely - but what, you may wonder, makes Gidleigh stand out from the multitude of eye-wateringly expensive country-house hotels all over Britain? A perfectionist ethos pervades this silky smooth operation, which is perhaps best illustrated by its tasteful restraint: in 2006 Gidleigh underwent a major refurbishment and tacked on an extension to add 10 bedrooms, taking the total to 24 - many hotels would have built a money-spinning glamorous spa too, but Gidleigh resisted the temptation that would have introduced the feeling of a more commercial operation of a different nature. Instead, the top-level rooms got their own private steam and sauna facilities. And that's what keeps the Gidleigh experience magical: small-scale, intimate, no detail overlooked. Three dining rooms, each with its own stylishly understated character, form the arena for the kitchen's intelligent take on contemporary French cuisine. Ambition and complexity can be bad news in the wrong hands, but Michael Caines MBE is one of a handful of chefs currently working in the UK at a level of technical ability that can pull off elaborate cooking of this order. Highly-intricate dishes of intense, luxury-laden flavours are immaculately presented, and delivered to table by staff who know their business and go about it without any airs and graces. The opening gambit of an eight-course tasting menu is a tartare of marinated tuna, scallops and lime with Oscietra caviar, soused turnip and beetroot, wasabi cream, honey and soy vinaigrette, ahead of a classic terrine of foie gras with Madeira jelly and truffled green bean salad. Ingredients are firmly rooted in the West Country - Cornish duckling with honey and spices marries perfectly with an apple galette, while Dartmoor lamb is partnered by fondant potato, vegetable Niçoise and tapenade jus. Perfectly-kept Devonshire cheeses appear before desserts culminate in a rhubarb jelly with rhubarb and lemongrass foam, and a textbook orange and Grand Marnier soufflé with an intense confit orange sorbet. Prices are, of course, high, but you can worry about the bill later - just enjoy and you'll probably agree that, whatever the cost, benchmark food like this is worth the money.

Times 12-2/7-9.45

DARTMOUTH *continued*

The New Angel Restaurant & Rooms

See below

River Restaurant

◎◎ Modern British

Balanced modern cooking in riverside hotel restaurant

☎ 01803 832580
The Dart Marina Hotel, Sandquay Rd TQ6 9PH
e-mail: info@dartmarinahotel.com
dir: A3122 from Totnes to Dartmouth. Follow road which becomes College Way, before Higher Ferry. Hotel sharp left in Sandquay Rd

A riverside hotel restaurant in photogenic Dartmouth, this stunning venue benefits from full-length windows, smartly laid tables with fresh flowers, and slick, professional staff. What's on offer is modern, inspirational cooking from a seasoned kitchen team, using much of Devon's quality produce in a style that is all about balancing tastes and textures among an array of elements. Salmon to start materialises in the various shapes of a terrine, a tartare and a ballottine of smoked salmon, garnished with pea shoots, with appreciable tang coming from a citrus dressing. Main course might spin variations on pork, with servings of glazed belly, tenderloin, trotter, and wonderfully intense black pudding, the dish unified with light purées of apple and celeriac. Finish with nougat glacé, served with blackcurrant sorbet and a cashew tuile.

Times 12-2/6-9

The Seahorse

◎◎ Seafood

Top-notch fish and seafood on the River Dart

☎ 01803 835147
5 South Embankment TQ6 9BH
e-mail: enquiries@seahorserestaurant.co.uk

Mitch Tonks, founder of the popular FishWorks chain of seafood restaurants and fishmongers is an ambassador of all things fishy. His Seahorse restaurant overlooks the boats see-sawing on the River Dart estuary, and if it's true that competition drives up quality, the rivalry between the Seahorse and near neighbour the New Angel (see entry) can only be a good thing. Inside it has a timeless French bistro look, combining button-backed mustard leather banquettes with darkwood tables and a large window opening up the kitchen to diners' view. A lovely picture of a John Dory underlines the business in hand: the quality and freshness of the fish and seafood is as good as it gets here, cherry-picked from what was landed in Brixham that morning. A charcoal-fired oven is the focus of the action in the kitchen - and what better way is there to cook sea-fresh fish with the minimum of complication? Scallops from Lyme Bay are roasted in the shell with garlic and white port, while Italian-inspired dishes run to brill cooked 'al cartoccio' in fennel, onion and leeks, or cuttlefish braised in Chianti and served with grilled polenta. A rib of Devon beef roasted over the fire shows the kitchen can treat local meat with the same precision. The wine list is big on Italy, and features a changing cast of wines sold by the glass.

Chef Mat Prowse & Mitch Tonks **Owner** Mat Prowse & Mitch Tonks **Times** 12-3/6-10 Closed Sun-Mon, L Tue **Prices** Food prices not confirmed for 2011. Please telephone for details **Wines** 109 bottles over £20, 14 bottles under £20, 6 by glass **Notes** Vegetarian available **Seats** 40 **Children** Portions **Parking** On street

The New Angel Restaurant & Rooms

Rosettes not confirmed at time of going to press

DARTMOUTH **Map 3 SX85**

French

Fresh seafood and quality meats at the river's edge

☎ 01803 839425
2 South Embankment TQ6 9BH
e-mail: info@thenewangel.co.uk
dir: Town centre, on water's edge

The New Angel has started a new chapter in its illustrious culinary journey - the post John Burton-Race years. The celeb chef has moved onto pastures new and James Barber is manning the stoves. The location just across the road from the water is a prime spot in the town, the gun-metal frontage, ornate tiling and large picture windows hooking in passers-by. If you prefer a quiet time, go for the more sedate setting of the upstairs dining room, as the brightly-lit ground floor arena is where all the action takes place: the chef and his team do their thing in a bustling open kitchen. Local sourcing is still at the heart of this operation, so they are off to a flying start with fish and seafood delivered to the door from the day boats moored a few feet away. Start with ravioli of Dartmouth crab with a bisque enriched with Cognac and cream, moving onto steamed fillet of turbot with a scallop mousseline, or something meaty - veal kidneys, perhaps, in a green peppercorn sauce.

Chef James Barber **Owner** Clive Jacobs **Times** 12-2.30/6.30-10 Closed Jan, Sun-Mon **Prices** Fixed L 2 course fr £19.50, Tasting menu £65, Service added but optional 12.5% **Wines** 150 bottles over £20, 32 bottles under £20, 8 by glass **Notes** Vegetarian available, Dress restrictions, Smart casual **Seats** 80 **Children** Portions, Menu **Parking** Dartmouth central car park

EGGESFORD Map 3 SS61

Fox & Hounds Country Hotel

Traditional British

Extensive menu in friendly West Country inn

01769 580345
EX18 7JZ
e-mail: relax@foxandhoundshotel.co.uk
dir: M5 junct 27, A361 towards Tiverton. B3137 signed Witheridge. After Nomansland follow signs to Eggesford Station, hotel in 50m

'Kick off your wellies and relax,' the brochure invites visitors, who may well have been tramping nearby Eggesford Forest to work up an appetite. Set amid the teeming wildlife of north Devon, the Fox & Hounds is a former coaching-inn run sympathetically and with aplomb. The ambitious menus served in both dining room and bar offer a breadth of choice, from caramelised scallops on chorizo cassoulet to start, to rabbit in puff pastry and white wine jus for main. Crème brûlées arrive in threes - perhaps lemon and blueberry versions with the traditional vanilla - or there are pedigree West Country cheeses to consider.

Chef Alex Pallatt **Owner** Nick & Tara Culverhouse **Times** 12-2.30/6.30-9 **Prices** Fixed D 3 course £25-£30, Starter £5.25-£8.25, Main £10.50-£17.95, Dessert £5.50-£7.95 **Wines** 23 bottles under £20, 8 by glass **Notes** Sunday L, Vegetarian available, Civ Wed 120 **Seats** 60, Pr/dining room 120 **Children** Portions, Menu **Parking** 100

EXETER Map 3 SX99

Barton Cross Hotel & Restaurant

British, French V

Sound cooking in 17th-century thatched hotel

01392 841245
Huxham, Stoke Canon EX5 4EJ
e-mail: bartonxhuxham@aol.com
dir: 0.5m off A396 at Stoke Canon, 3m N of Exeter

At Barton Cross, a 17th-century thatched longhouse blends seamlessly with modern style in a delightful rural spot near to Exeter. Low beams and cob walls abound, and while the galleried restaurant looks like it could do service as a medieval banqueting hall, the kitchen is rather more likely to send out roast scallops with pea purée and crispy pancetta, or Thai crab fishcakes with soy ginger and lime dipping sauce than, say, roast swan. At main course, monkfish fillet might turn up with herb risotto and local River Exe mussels, and to finish, fine West Country cheeses offer a savoury alternative to desserts such as caramelised rice pudding with apricots and Amaretto ice cream.

Chef Nicholas Beattie **Owner** Brian Hamilton **Times** 6.30-11.30 Closed Sun, L all week **Prices** Fixed D 3 course fr £29.50, Starter £6.50-£8.50, Main £14.50-£18.50, Dessert £6.50-£8.50, Service optional **Wines** 49 bottles over £20, 52 bottles under £20, 10 by glass **Notes** Vegetarian menu, Dress restrictions, Smart casual **Seats** 50, Pr/dining room 26 **Children** Portions, Menu **Parking** 50

The Olive Tree Restaurant

Modern British

Elegant city hotel with confident modern cuisine

01392 272709
Queens Court Hotel, 6-8 Bystock Ter EX4 4HY
e-mail: enquiries@queenscourt-hotel.co.uk
dir: Exit dual carriageway at junct 30 onto B5132 Topsham Rd towards city centre. Hotel 200yds from station

A short walk from the city centre, this elegant townhouse hotel occupies three terraced buildings on a quiet leafy Exeter square that was once the home of wealthy merchants (perhaps it still is today). The charming Olive Tree restaurant is Mediterranean through and through, with Venetian masks, olive oil bottles and flickering candles, and dishes that arrive at the table with a flourish. The unfussy, well-presented food is modern British-meets-Med, so expect plenty of European preparations and great British produce. A starter of garlic- and thyme-infused rabbit ravioli is served with leek linguine and wholegrain mustard and cider sauce, followed perhaps by seared locally-farmed chicken breast served with a chicken and mushroom pie, sweet potato purée, Savoy cabbage and roast chicken foam. The West Country cheeses are a boon, and there's sweet things like creamy ginger and mascarpone cheesecake served with rhubarb.

Chef Darren Knockton **Owner** C F & B H Bowring **Times** 12-2/7-9.30 Closed Xmas, L Sun **Prices** Starter £5.95-£6.95, Main £16-£21, Dessert £5.95-£6.95, Service optional **Wines** 12 bottles over £20, 15 bottles under £20, 7 by glass **Notes** Vegetarian available, Civ Wed 60 **Seats** 24, Pr/dining room 16 **Children** Portions **Parking** Public car park in front of hotel

EXMOUTH Map 3 SY08

Les Saveurs at The Seafood Restaurant

Modern European NEW

Fresh fish cooked with superb care in family-run restaurant

01395 269459
9 Tower St EX8 1NT
e-mail: lessaveurs@yahoo.co.uk
dir: A376 to Exmouth, left at rdbt. At traffic lights, right onto one way system Rolle Street. Tower Street on right

Tucked away in a quiet pedestrianised lane behind a lovely church, this delightful family-run fish specialist hits you with a wave of what's in store as soon as you open the door and the stock pot wafts across. The vibe is rustic-meets-romantic, an intimate space with exposed brick walls, distressed white chairs and pristine tablecloths. The man you see working the stoves behind the glass-panelled doors is French and brings an unmistakable pedigree to the kitchen. He exploits the very best of the local catch with a simple, sensitive approach: pan-fried Brixham scallops are teamed with a velvety pea purée and minted mussel jus; next up, a stunning fillet of turbot is served with champagne sauce and silky smooth mash. A classic Madagascar crème brûlée makes a spot-on finish.

Chef Olivier Guyard-Mulkerrin **Owner** Olivier & Sheila Guyard-Mulkerrin **Times** 7-9.30 Closed Variable (bkg advised), Sun-Mon (except special arrangement), L all week **Prices** Starter £6.50-£7.90, Main £15.95-£19.95, Dessert £5.50-£6.50, Service optional, Groups min 6 service 10% **Wines** 15 bottles over £20, 11 bottles under £20, 4 by glass **Notes** Vegetarian available, Dress restrictions, Smart casual **Seats** 30, Pr/dining room 36 **Parking** On street/council offices

GULWORTHY Map 3 SX47

The Horn of Plenty

– *see opposite page*

HAYTOR VALE Map 3 SX77

Rock Inn

Traditional British

Wild Dartmoor scenery at a classic country inn serving accomplished British food

01364 661305 & 661556
TQ13 9XP
e-mail: reservations@rockinn.co.uk
dir: From A38 at Drum Bridges, onto A382 to Bovey Tracey. In 2m take B3387 towards Haytor for 3.5m, follow brown signs

A coaching inn from around 1750, the civilised Rock Inn stands in a tiny Dartmoor village below Haytor, the best known of the Dartmoor tors. After a day on the moor, retreat into the rambling traditional bar and dining rooms, filled with antique furnishings and warmed by roaring log fires, for some hearty classic British food, cooked with flair and imagination from top-notch local produce. Typically, tuck into River Teign mussels cooked in white wine, garlic and cream, rump of Devon lamb with dauphinoise potatoes and red wine sauce, or pan-fried halibut on truffle oil mash with sautéed wild mushrooms, leaving room for treacle and lemon tart with clotted cream.

Chef Sue Beaumont Graves & Mark Tribble **Owner** Mr C Graves **Times** 12-2.15/6.30-9 Closed 25-26 Dec **Prices** Food prices not confirmed for 2011. Please telephone for details **Wines** 44 bottles over £20, 26 bottles under £20, 11 by glass **Notes** Sunday L, Vegetarian available, Dress restrictions, No jeans **Seats** 75 **Children** Portions, Menu **Parking** 25

The Horn of Plenty

GULWORTHY Map 3 SX47

Modern International

Fabulous flavour combinations and beguiling English countryside views

☎ 01822 832528
PL19 8JD
e-mail:
enquiries@thehornofplenty.co.uk
dir: From Tavistock take A390 W for 3m. Right at Gulworthy Cross. In 400yds turn left, hotel in 400yds on right

Built in the 19th century for the Duke of Bedford's mine captain, The Horn of Plenty has a setting of beguiling bucolic appeal. There's the stunning views across the Tamar Valley (an Area of Outstanding Natural Beauty, no less), plus five acres of wild orchards and gardens to get stuck into. Despite the undoubted charm of the bedrooms, or the elegance of the public spaces, they say it themselves: 'the heart of The Horn of Plenty is the kitchen.' The restaurant's layout makes the very best of the panoramic views through large windows, and the tables are dressed in their best whites; smartly turned out staff add to the sense of occasion. Peter Gorton is as dedicated a chef as you'll find anywhere, and is rigorous in ensuring the quality of the seasonal ingredients (much of them local) that turn up on the plate. His 30-year career has taken him all over the world and the menu reflects this, as does the good spread of international wines on offer. A first-course pan-fried risotto cake with Vulscombe goats' cheese and a lightly spiced carrot emulsion shows wonderful technique and well-judged flavours. Fillet of cod with crushed new potatoes and a saffron and white wine velouté, or whole roasted partridge with rösti potato and creamed sprouts, are typical main courses, and a clever warm espresso and chocolate tart with milk ice cream is a finely judged finish.

Chef Peter Gorton & Stuart Downie **Owner** Mr & Mrs P Roston, Peter Gorton **Times** 12-4/7-12 **Prices** Fixed L 3 course £26.50, Fixed D 3 course £47, Tasting menu £55, Service optional, Groups min 10 service 10% **Wines** 115 bottles over £20, 20 bottles under £20, 11 by glass **Notes** Tasting menu available most Fri & Sat, Sunday L, Vegetarian available, Dress restrictions, Smart casual, Civ Wed 150 **Seats** 60, Pr/dining room 12 **Children** Portions, Menu **Parking** 20

HONITON Map 4 ST10

Combe House - Devon

Modern British V

Classic cooking in handsome Elizabethan manor

01404 540400
Gittisham EX14 3AD
e-mail: stay@combehousedevon.com
web: www.combehousedevon.com
dir: M5, junct 29 to Airport, exit Patterson Cross or off A30 1m S of Honiton, follow Gittisham Heathpark signs

Surrounded by 3,500 acres of lush Devon estate, Combe House is one of the finest country-house hotels in the country. A Grade I listed gabled Elizabethan mansion with oak panelling, walk-in fireplaces, ancestral oils and fine antiques, it lies hidden at the end of a mile-long winding drive surrounded by roaming pheasants and Arabian horses. The kitchen makes good use of the local larder, including herbs, fruits and vegetables from their own walled garden, and all meat and fish is local. The three dining areas match the elegant formality of the house. Modern British ideas are complemented by a classic skills set to combine refined and well-flavoured dishes such as blinis with Portland crab, smoked salmon and caviar, finished with a sweet citrus dressing. Follow on with slow-roast loin of venison with balsamic Puy lentils, braised red cabbage and potato fondant. Finish with an exemplary carpaccio of pineapple with a parfait of the same fruit and a coconut and Malibu sorbet.

Chef Hadleigh Barrett, Stuart Brown **Owner** Ken & Ruth Hunt **Times** 12-2/7-9.30 Closed 3-18 Jan **Prices** Fixed L 2 course £27, Fixed D 3 course £48, Service optional **Wines** 88 bottles over £20, 1 bottle under £20, 10 by glass **Notes** Sunday L, Vegetarian menu, Dress restrictions, Smart casual, Civ Wed 100 **Seats** 75, Pr/dining room 48 **Children** Portions, Menu **Parking** 35

The Holt Bar & Restaurant

Modern British

Buzzy pub-restaurant with a local flavour

01404 47707
178 High St EX14 1LA
e-mail: enquiries@theholt-honiton.com

On the High Street in the market town of Honiton, this buzzy, rustic-style pub is owned by the Otter Brewery. It's the place to come for a cracking pint and some confident, hearty cooking using great local produce, including home-smoked fish and meats. At simple wooden tables tuck into excellent tapas dishes or something from the daily-changing menu. Start with a flavoursome smoked goose terrine with a deconstructed piccalilli to cut through the richness, follow on with grilled fillet of bream with spiced courgette fritter, glazed potatoes and saffron sauce, and finish with a passionfruit shortcake, served with Greek yoghurt sorbet.

Chef Josh McDonald Johnson **Owner** Joe & Angus McCaig **Times** 12-2/7-10 Closed 25-26 Dec, Sun-Mon **Prices** Food prices not confirmed for 2011. Please telephone for details **Wines** 9 bottles over £20, 18 bottles under £20, 9 by glass **Notes** Vegetarian available **Seats** 50 **Children** Portions **Parking** On street, car park 1 min walk

Monkton Court

Modern British **NEW**

Smartly refurbished hotel majoring on local produce

01404 42309
Monkton EX14 9QH
e-mail: enquiries@monktoncourthotel.co.uk
dir: 2m E A30

This former vicarage turned small hotel and restaurant on the edge of the Blackdown Hills, beside the A30, blends traditional country style with a more contemporary spin in the restaurant. The kitchen makes good use of the local larder in well-judged dishes; perhaps seafood from the Dorset coast (seared Lyme Bay scallops with parsnip purée and gravad lax vinaigrette as an opener), or a main-course trio of Blackdown Hills lamb (roasted rack, spring roll of roasted shoulder and sweetbread - served with gratin potatoes, ratatouille, creamed cabbage and a shallot and port jus). There are daily specials, too, with lighter, simpler options also available.

HORNS CROSS Map 3 SS32

The Hoops Inn & Country Hotel

British, French NOTABLE WINE LIST

Gastro-pub fare at an ancient inn

01237 451222
EX39 5DL
e-mail: sales@hoopsinn.co.uk
dir: A39 from Bideford towards Clovelly/Bude, through Fairy Cross & Horns Cross, restaurant on right

If you're striding along the North Devon coast, you won't regret a short detour to the Hoops, a postcard-pretty, thatched 13th-century roadside hostelry in heavenly natural gardens. Beers brewed locally for the pub are tapped from the wood in a bar where gnarled beams are festooned with tankards, and there's a rabbit warren of cosy nooks and crannies for eating and drinking, as well as a more formal restaurant. It is a common refrain nowadays, but the kitchen here really does have a sincere commitment to sourcing locally, and goes about its work in an unpretentious way, delivering ingredients that taste honestly and forthrightly of themselves. To start, Devon game terrine with plum, cinnamon and port chutney vies with fresh crab, served with brioche and mayonnaise, while mains might include grilled lemon sole with pesto butter and new potatoes.

The Hoops Inn & Country Hotel

Times 12-2/6-11

ILFRACOMBE Map 3 SS54

The Quay

Modern British

Unpretentious food with Damien Hirst's Brit art for company

01271 868090 & 868091
11 The Quay EX34 9EQ
e-mail: info@11thequay.com
dir: Follow signs for harbour and pier car park. Restaurant on left before car park

The Damien Hirst tag is enough to get The Quay noticed, particularly as the artist's works provide visual entertainment on its walls. The handsome red-brick and stone building sits smack on the harbour in Ilfracombe. Entering the cool ground-floor bar, you are struck by the proportions of the light-drenched space - all high ceilings, soaring pillars and alcoves. After a sharpener here, choose from two dining venues: the Atlantic room has an arching ceiling like an upturned boat, and features Hirst's seashell artworks, or there's the Harbourside room, where you get his 'Modern Medicine' artworks as a talking point. Considering the artist's reputation for shock effects, it's all very relaxed, sober and sedately modern, and the kitchen takes a down-to-earth approach in tune with the setting; expect unfussy contemporary food such as ham roulade with celeriac mustard and parsley to start, then salmon fillet with French bean and artichoke salad.

Times 10-3/6-9 Closed 25-26 Dec, 2-25 Jan, Mon & Tue

ILSINGTON Map 3 SX77

Ilsington Country House Hotel

◎◎ Modern European

Great Dartmoor views and confident cooking

☎ 01364 661452
Ilsington Village TQ13 9RR
e-mail: hotel@ilsington.co.uk
dir: A38 to Plymouth, exit at Bovey Tracey. 3rd exit from rdbt to Ilsington, then 1st right, hotel on right, past village shop

The family-run Ilsington has a lot going for it. It's up on the sweeping hills of Dartmoor, for a start, with views across to the Haytor Rocks, and then there's the 10 acres of grounds to explore, good conference and spa facilities, and a delightful restaurant with large picture windows framing that dramatic view. The regularly changing seasonal menu points its compass firmly at Europe and much of the sourcing of ingredients is local. A classical foundation is embellished with some modish ideas, thus confit duck leg comes with the familiar celeriac remoulade and the more outré cucumber and kumquat salad and balsamic dressing. For main course, perhaps, seared loin of lamb with a chick pea, green bean and chorizo cassoulet, served with black pudding and Madeira sauce, and to finish, treacle tart gets treated to an orange and cardamom anglaise alongside vanilla ice cream.

Chef Mike O'Donnell **Owner** Hassell Family
Times 12-2/6.30-9 **Prices** Fixed D 3 course £33.95-£36, Starter £6.50-£9.50, Main £16.50-£22.50, Dessert £6-£7.50, Service included **Wines** 31 bottles over £20, 40 bottles under £20, 9 by glass **Notes** Sunday L, Vegetarian available, Dress restrictions, Shirt with a collar (smart casual) no shorts, Civ Wed 120 **Seats** 75, Pr/dining room 70 **Children** Portions **Parking** 60

INSTOW Map 3 SS43

Decks Restaurant

◎ Modern British

Hearty modern cooking with superb sea views

☎ 01271 860671
Hatton Croft House, Marine Pde EX39 4JJ
e-mail: decks@instow.net
dir: From Barnstaple follow A38 to Bideford. Follow signs for Instow, restaurant at far end of seafront

With a prime location on the beachfront at Instow, this shipshape restaurant is an ambassador for all things piscine. Decks is an airy, light-flooded venue, with a ship's mast spearing through the ceiling into the first-floor dining area, where the views open up through a sweep of picture windows to the Torridge estuary, pretty Appledore and the elephantine dunes of Braunton Burrows. The menu is packed with great fishy ideas, cooked with restraint and intelligence - nothing flashy, just great West Country produce left to speak for itself. Start with a Thai-accented fish broth involving sea bass, skate and cod poached in a lightly-spiced coconut and coriander broth, and proceed to steamed halibut on spinach and rocket tagliatelle with grain mustard dressing, or for fans of local meat there could be rolled rib-eye of Exmoor beef with chips and salad.

Times 12-2.30/7-9.30 Closed 25-26 Dec, 1 Jan, Sun-Mon, L ex by appointment

KNOWSTONE Map 3 SS82

The Masons Arms

◎◎ Modern British

Assured cooking in pretty Devon village inn

☎ 01398 341231
EX36 4RY
e-mail: dodsonmasonsarms@aol.com
dir: Signed from A361, turn right once in Knowstone

A delightful country inn deep in the Devon countryside, The Mason's Arms is situated midway between the market towns of South Molton and Tiverton in a village with a population of a little over 200. It's an idyllically rustic setting for sure and as pretty as a postcard - the thatched pub retains its village inn atmosphere despite being a gastronomic destination in its own right. The restaurant at the rear offers fabulous views of the rolling hills of Exmoor. Chef-patron Mark Dodson used to be head chef at the Waterside Inn at Bray (see entry) and his cooking displays confidence and a high level of skill. His modern British cooking is firmly rooted in the French classics and he's a dab hand at getting hold of top-notch produce. Start with scallops with pear and a vanilla and vermouth sauce or a risotto of parmesan, flaked smoked haddock and a poached egg. Main-courses might bring forth Devon beef fillet, served with calves' sweetbreads, shallot purée and sauce diable.

Chef Mark Dodson **Owner** Mark & Sarah Dodson
Times 12-2/7-9 Closed 1st wk Jan, Mon, D Sun
Prices Starter £8.50-£12.50, Main £17.50-£22, Dessert £7.50-£8.75, Service optional **Wines** 30 bottles over £20, 12 bottles under £20, 9 by glass **Notes** Sunday L, Vegetarian available **Seats** 28 **Children** Portions **Parking** 10

LEWDOWN Map 3 SX48

Lewtrenchard Manor

◎◎◎ *– see page 128*

LIFTON Map 3 SX38

Arundell Arms

◎◎ Modern British V

Old coaching inn with local flavours on the menu

☎ 01566 784666
Fore St PL16 0AA
e-mail: reservations@arundellarms.com
web: www.arundellarms.com
dir: Just off A30 in Lifton, 3m E of Launceston

A short hop to the uplands of Dartmoor, this upmarket, creeper-clad old Devon inn is a favoured haunt among those who enjoy the country pursuits of shooting, riding and in particular fishing - the inn boasts 20 miles of fishing rights on the River Tamar. A civilised air pervades throughout the smart interior, from the elegant lounge with deep comfortable sofas, antique furnishings, blazing log fires and classic country chintz to the airy, classically-styled restaurant with its yellow and cream décor, crisp linen and sparkling glassware. Accomplished modern British cooking from a chef with passion and flair, who champions top-notch West Country produce, reveals chicken, artichoke and rosemary soup with nutmeg cream, wild garlic-crusted duck fillet with Savoy cabbage and oyster mushrooms, and crème brûlée with mango sorbet and berry syrup.

Chef Steven Pidgeon **Owner** Anne Voss-Bark
Times 12.30-2.30/7.30-10 **Prices** Food prices not confirmed for 2011. Please telephone for details **Wines** 37 bottles over £20, 3 bottles under £20, 7 by glass
Notes Sunday L, Vegetarian menu, Dress restrictions, Smart casual, Civ Wed 80 **Seats** 70, Pr/dining room 24
Children Portions, Menu **Parking** 70

LIFTON *continued*

Tinhay Mill Guest House and Restaurant

British, French

Former 15th-century mill cottages with locally-inspired cooking

☎ 01566 784201
Tinhay PL16 0AJ
e-mail: tinhay.mill@talk21.com
dir: From M5 take A30 towards Okehampton/Launceston. Lifton off A30 on left. Follow brown tourist signs. Restaurant at bottom of village near river

Dating back to the 15th century, these former mill cottages have been transformed into a smart restaurant with rooms. Open fireplaces and beamed ceilings lend a certain charm to the interior making it a great place to unwind after a day exploring the north Cornish coast or west Devon. Margaret Wilson (co-owner with husband Paul) is in the kitchen and prides herself on using the best local produce and making everything in-house, from the bread at the beginning to the truffles at the end. Simple signature dishes include chicken liver crêpe with a brandy and cream sauce followed by Cornish pork tenderloin and a pudding of ginger crème brûlée.

Times 7-9.30 Closed 2 wks Xmas & New Year, 3 wks Feb & Mar, Sun & Mon (ex residents), L all week

LYDFORD **Map 3 SX58**

Dartmoor Inn

Modern British

Stylish and original country inn with first-class food

☎ 01822 820221
EX20 4AY
e-mail: info@dartmoorinn.co.uk
dir: On A386 (Tavistock to Okehampton road)

On the edge of Dartmoor's spectacular moorland landscape and just a short drive from Lydford Gorge stands Philip and Karen Burgess's 16th-century roadside coaching inn. Lovingly restored and refurbished, it's a charming inn and represents the passions and hard work of its proprietors, who have fashioned an idyllic Dartmoor retreat. There's a small bar (a fire blazes in the cool months) where real ales and high class pub classics are on offer, and a restaurant made up of a series of rooms where original features and contemporary styles are interwoven, and the tables are laid with crisp white linen. The menu is based on seasonal ingredients, sourced locally, and turned into intelligently uncomplicated dishes. Kick off with ham hock terrine with apricot chutney, followed by halibut with fish mousseline and saffron butter sauce, and round off with hot chocolate fondant or a plate of West Country cheeses.

Times 12-2.15/6.30-9.30 Closed Mon, D Sun

LYNMOUTH **Map 3 SS74**

Rising Sun Hotel

British, French **NEW**

Harbourside dining in characterful thatched inn

☎ 01598 753223
Harbourside EX35 6EG
e-mail: risingsunlynmouth@easynet.co.uk
dir: M5 junct 23 (Minehead). Take A39 to Lynmouth. Opposite the harbour

The 14th-century Rising Sun has no problem pulling in the punters; on a sunny day, the drinkers spill out from the postcard-perfect thatched inn smack on Lynmouth harbourfront. The wonky ceiling beams, stone walls and creaky floorboards have many a tale to tell - of smugglers, of the poet Shelley's honeymoon, and of R D Blackmore writing chunks of *Lorna Doone* here. The candlelit oak-panelled dining room is the setting for

Lewtrenchard Manor

LEWDOWN **Map 3 SX48**

Modern British

Majestic old manor with exemplary modern food

☎ 01566 783222
EX20 4PN
e-mail: info@lewtrenchard.co.uk
dir: Take A30 signed Okehampton from M5 junct 31. 25m, exit at Sourton Cross. Follow signs to Lewdown, then Lewtrenchard

On the edge of timelessly rugged Dartmoor, Lewtrenchard is a Jacobean manor (built in 1626 no less) of inspiring antiquity surrounded by equally diverting gardens. Any house this old must have an historical connection or two and this one includes being home to Reverend Sabine Baring-Gould of *Onward Christian Soldiers* fame; his desk is still in the hallway. Inside, the grand old house is crammed with period detail from oak panelling, beautifully ornate ceilings, stained-glass windows, large fireplaces, period furnishings and family portraits, but there is nothing stuffy about the place: everything is comfortingly luxurious and the service formal but never oppressive. The candlelit, panelled dining room overlooks the pretty colonnaded courtyard - a real boon in fair weather - and the Purple Carrot private dining room (a take on the chef's table concept) reflects the ambition of chef-patron Jason Hornbuckle and his team. The kitchen garden ensures seasonality is a given, bolstered by local suppliers, and the well-crafted menus overflow with great British flavours and plenty of modern ideas. A superb piece of sea bream is pan-fried in a first course with creamed white beans and a chervil and celeriac purée, and flavours are well judged in a main-course roasted leg of Cornish lamb with sweetly caramelised onions, liquorice marmalade and suet dumplings. Hot chocolate tart with toasted marshmallows and Cornish milk ice cream is a fitting finale.

Chef Jason Hornbuckle, Carl Maxfield **Owner** von Essen Hotels **Times** 12-1.30/7-9 **Prices** Fixed L 2 course £15, Fixed D 3 course £50.50, Service optional **Wines** 234 bottles over £20, 5 bottles under £20, 13 by glass **Notes** The Chef's Table - Purple Carrot - 8 course, Sunday L, Vegetarian available, Dress restrictions, L smart casual, D no jeans or T-shirts, Civ Wed 100 **Seats** 45, Pr/dining room 22 **Children** Portions, Menu **Parking** 40

confident, unfussy cooking - but we're not talking pub grub classics - this is inventive modern food, starting with squid piri piri with rocket and lemon, while main course brings confit duck leg with red cabbage, sweet potato mash and sumac dressing. To finish, there's a textbook wobbly pannacotta with poached rhubarb and home-made shortbread.

Times 7-9 Closed L all week

Tors Hotel

Modern British

Versatile hotel menu on a wooded Devon hillside

☎ 01598 753236
EX35 6NA
e-mail: torshotel@torslynmouth.co.uk
dir: M5 junct 23 (Bridgwater). Continue 40m on A39 through Minehead. Hotel at base of Countisbury Hill on left

The broad-fronted white hotel cosies into its surrounding wooded hillside on the Exmoor coast. Lynmouth is barely more than a straggle of buildings by the harbour, making for a glorious tranquil setting. The Tors dining room aims for understated, candlelit intimacy against the backdrop of those breathtaking sea views. A fixed-price menu, changing daily, shows great versatility in moving from a tian of white crabmeat with pink grapefruit, chive mayonnaise and powdered fennel, to spiced lamb meatballs with couscous, pepper tagine, minted yoghurt and preserved lemon. West Country cheeses complement the dessert selection.

Chef Andy Collier **Owner** Mrs Glover, Mrs Dalgarno **Times** 7-9 Closed 3 Jan-4 Feb (wknds only in Feb), L all week **Prices** Fixed D 3 course £30, Service included **Wines** 11 bottles over £20, 39 bottles under £20, 3 by glass **Notes** Vegetarian available, Civ Wed 80 **Seats** 50 **Children** Portions, Menu **Parking** 40

LYNTON Map 3 SS74

Lynton Cottage Hotel

Modern British V

Stunning clifftop views and skilfully cooked food

☎ 01598 752342
North Walk EX35 6ED
e-mail: enquiries@lynton-cottage.co.uk
dir: M5 junct 27, follow A361 towards Barnstaple. Follow signs to Lynton A39. In Lynton turn right at church. Hotel on right

The jagged North Devon coastline unfurls a stunning backdrop for dining in an elegant setting at this historic country house perched on the clifftop above the Valley of the Rocks. Shelley, Wordsworth and Coleridge all found inspiration in the elemental romance of this area, and you too might begin to wax lyrical when chef Matthew Bailey's cooking appears at the table. His experience conjures beautifully-balanced dishes with subtle seasoning and exciting contrasts in flavour and textures - nothing leaves the kitchen unless it is correct in every way. Top-notch Exmoor produce is given modern British treatment, but its roots remain firmly in the classics. And presentation is always eye-catching - it has to be to draw diners' attention away from those views. Pan-fried scallops with cauliflower and a raisin and verjus dressing is a typical starter; main-course pork loin and braised belly are paired with swede, black pudding and spiced honey, while yoghurt pannacotta with rhubarb sorbet, pistachios and vanilla syrup ends on a refined note.

Chef Matthew Bailey **Owner** David Mowlem, Heather Biancardi **Times** 7-9 Closed Dec & Jan **Prices** Food prices not confirmed for 2011. Please telephone for details **Wines** 15 bottles over £20, 18 bottles under £20, 4 by glass **Notes** Vegetarian menu **Seats** 30 **Children** Portions **Parking** 18

MORETONHAMPSTEAD Map 3 SX78

Best Western The White Hart Hotel

British, International

Devon coaching inn with smart brasserie dining

☎ 01647 441340
The Square TQ13 8NQ
e-mail: enquiries@whitehartdartmoor.co.uk
dir: A30 towards Okehampton. At Whiddon Down take A382 for Moretonhampstead

The White Hart has been at the heart of life in this bustling Dartmoor village since 1639. The 21st-century incumbents have brought it smartly up to date: its contemporary brasserie dining room looks good in duck egg blue, with bare oak tables, wooden floors and stag's antler chandelier. The kitchen deals in modern British cooking that doesn't faff about with hearty local ingredients - black pudding with poached egg, pancetta lardons and wholegrain mustard hollandaise being a typical starter. Main-course Gressingham duck comes with fondant potato, celeriac purée and braised white cabbage, while dessert-lovers will find joy in a russet and Bramley apple crumble with butterscotch sauce and ice cream.

Chef Simeon Baber **Owner** Hart Inns Limited **Times** 12-2.30/6-9 **Prices** Starter £4.95-£6.50, Main £6.50-£16.95, Dessert £5.95-£7.50, Service optional **Wines** 15 bottles over £20, 15 bottles under £20, 15 by glass **Notes** Sunday L, Vegetarian available, Civ Wed 100 **Seats** 62 **Children** Portions, Menu **Parking** Public car park 100mtrs

Edwardian Grill

Modern European **NEW**

Elegant dining in opulent surroundings

☎ 01647 445000
Bovey Castle TQ13 8RE
e-mail: enquiries@boveycastle.com
dir: A30/A382 to Moretonhampstead, onto B3212 signed Postbridge. Hotel 2m outside Moretonhampstead on left

Don't expect turrets and battlements at this grandiose country pile - it's not that sort of castle. In fact it's not really a castle at all, but the former seat of the WH Smith family. Run with the sort of immaculate service that its Edwardian masters would have been familiar with, Bovey Castle has all the five-star bells and whistles you'd expect in a top-flight country-house hotel. A liveried doorman meets and greets guests, public rooms are an exercise in unrestrained opulence, and the Edwardian Grill restaurant is the very image of romance; candlelight plays on hand-painted Chinese silk wallpaper, and a pianist tinkles away in the background, while service is well-drilled yet friendly. Head chef Darron Bunn has a fine pedigree, including stints with Nico and Marco, and lives up to his refined surroundings with ease, delivering intelligent modern dishes of intense flavours. Goats' cheese tortellini is served with a punchy mushroom ragoût and Jerusalem artichokes in an intriguing starter; main course delivers a single rib-eye of beef with a ballottine of braised beef wrapped in bacon, pearl barley and watercress, and dessert ends in fine style - a lush fig tarte Tatin with walnut mascarpone ice cream.

Times 7-10 Closed Sun, L all week

NEWTON ABBOT Map 3 SX87

Sampsons Farm & Restaurant

British

Fresh local produce in charming family-run restaurant

☎ 01626 354913
Preston TQ12 3PP
e-mail: nigel@sampsonsfarm.com
dir: M5/A380/B3195 signed Kingsteington. Pass Ten Tors Inn on left & take 2nd rd signed B3193 to Chudleigh. At rdbt 3rd exit, left after 1m

This charming Tudor thatched farmhouse in the Devon countryside offers a snug getaway with its crackling log fires, old black oak beams and panelling and rare breed hens pecking away under the apple trees. Artist and illustrator of the Archers' cookbook Sarah Bell's original watercolours hang on the walls. Husband and owner Nigel grew up on the farm, which has been in his family for four generations. The local larder is put to good use in dishes that show British sensibilities; Brixham scallops, for example, on a butternut squash purée with a smoked bacon salad and sherry dressing, followed by South Devon sirloin steak with dauphinoise potato and mustard sauce. Finish with an English strawberry Eton mess with strawberry jam and raspberry sorbet.

continued

NEWTON ABBOT *continued*

Chef Andrew Shortman **Owner** Nigel Bell **Times** 12-2/7-9 Closed 25-26 Dec, Sun **Prices** Fixed L 2 course £10-£19, Starter £5-£9, Main £12-£21, Dessert £5-£7.50 **Wines** 6 by glass **Notes** Vegetarian available **Seats** 36, Pr/dining room 20 **Children** Portions, Menu **Parking** 20

NEWTON POPPLEFORD Map 3 SY08

Moore's Restaurant & Rooms

Modern British

Enjoyable food in friendly family-run restaurant

☎ 01395 568100
6 Greenbank, High St EX10 0EB
e-mail: info.moores@btconnect.com
dir: On A3052 in village centre

In the village of Newton Poppleford, with Sidmouth just a few miles down the road, this family-run restaurant with rooms serves up a bit of genuinely warm hospitality. Formerly two cottages, one of which doubled as a grocer's store, the intimate country-style restaurant overlooks the village street, and there's a small conservatory dining area which is used at busier times, plus the option of eating in the pretty garden. Modern British dishes make use of good quality, locally-sourced ingredients and the attractively presented food delivers well defined flavours. A starter of crab and smoked salmon timbale comes with the exoticism of a mango and chilli dressing, whilst main-course haunch of local wild venison is served with a mustard and chive mash and finished with a blackberry jus. Round off with lavender and honey crème brûlée.

Chef Jonathan Moore **Owner** Jonathan & Kate Moore **Times** 12-1.30/7-9.30 Closed 1st 2 wks in Jan, Mon, D Sun **Prices** Fixed L 2 course £12.95-£14.95, Fixed D 3 course £17.90-£27.50, Service optional **Wines** 19 bottles over £20, 12 bottles under £20, 6 by glass **Notes** Sunday L, Vegetarian available **Seats** 32, Pr/dining room 12 **Children** Portions **Parking** 2, On street & free car park behind church

PLYMOUTH Map 3 SX45

Artillery Tower Restaurant

British

Confident cooking in historic maritime building

☎ 01752 257610
Firestone Bay, Durnford St PL1 3QR
dir: 1m from city centre & rail station

A 16th-century stone tower on Plymouth's seafront built to keep out the Spanish Armada and other historic foes is the setting for Peter and Debbie Constable's characterful restaurant. At high tide waves lap at the foot of the tower, adding to the atmosphere inside the thick stone walls of the round dining room, which is kitted out with simple bare wooden tables and moody lighting. The food is based on supplies from within 30 miles of the tower, cooked with skill and brought together in intelligent combinations. Belly pork is partnered by scallops and apple, while rump of lamb appears with rosemary, garlic, and gratin dauphinoise. End with dark chocolate fondant and Amaretto ice cream.

Chef Peter Constable **Owner** Peter Constable **Times** 12-2.15/7-9.30 Closed Xmas & New Year, Sun-Mon, L Sat **Prices** Fixed D 3 course fr £36, Service optional, Groups min 8 service 6% **Wines** 60 bottles over £20, 30 bottles under £20, 6 by glass **Seats** 40, Pr/dining room 16 **Children** Portions **Parking** 20, (Evening only)

Barbican Kitchen

Modern British

A modern city brasserie in antique surroundings

☎ 01752 604448
Plymouth Gin Distillery, 60 Southside St PL1 2LQ
e-mail: info@barbicankitchen.com
dir: On Barbican, 5 mins walk from Bretonside bus station

The Tanner brothers' restaurant is to be found in Plymouth's oldest domestic house, a 15th-century building behind St Andrew's Church. Enter through the Plymouth Gin distillery, and try not to get distracted on the way. The roughcast walls and open-plan kitchen create a nice blend of ancient and modern, and the food is unpretentious and big on flavour. Pressed pork terrine is chunky, wrapped in bacon and served with a fruity chutney, and might be followed by beef medallions with buttery champ mash and wild mushroom sauce. Finish with a classic vanilla pannacotta served with enlivening tropical fruit sorbet. Good home-made bread comes with olive oil.

Chef Mark Turton, C & J Tanner **Owner** Christopher & James Tanner **Times** 12-3/5-10 Closed 25-26 & 31 Dec **Prices** Fixed L 2 course £9.95, Starter £3.95-£7.95, Main £7.95-£18.50, Dessert £5.50-£6.95, Service included **Wines** 16 bottles over £20, 22 bottles under £20, 13 by glass **Notes** Fixed 2/3 course L menu also available pre-theatre, Sunday L, Vegetarian available, Civ Wed 60 **Seats** 80 **Children** Portions, Menu **Parking** Drakes Circus, Guildhall

Best Western Duke of Cornwall Hotel

British, European V

Classic Victorian hotel with appealingly unfussy food

☎ 01752 275850 & 275855
Millbay Rd PL1 3LG
e-mail: enquiries@thedukeofcornwall.co.uk
dir: City centre, follow signs 'Pavilions', hotel road is opposite

When Brittania ruled the waves and the sun never set on the empire, they built hotels like the Duke of Cornwall. It is a glorious old pile, lording it over Plymouth's cityscape with its tower and turret. Once through the revolving doors of the grand entrance, all the period oak panelling and elaborate plasterwork is present and correct; in the dining room, chandeliers hang from high ceilings above gilt-framed paintings and generously-spaced tables. The kitchen delivers crowd-pleasing British and European dishes on a menu spanning from wild boar and apple sausage with spring onion mash, streaky bacon and redcurrant jus, to grilled sea bass with braised leeks, cockles and mussels.

Chef Darren Kester **Owner** W Combstock, J Morcom **Times** 7-10 Closed 26-31 Dec, L all week **Prices** Starter £5.75-£6.95, Main £13.50-£18.50, Dessert £5.50-£6.75 **Wines** 50% bottles over £20, 50% bottles under £20, 8 by glass **Notes** Vegetarian menu, Dress restrictions, Smart casual, Civ Wed 300 **Seats** 80, Pr/dining room 30 **Children** Portions, Menu **Parking** 40, also on streeet

Langdon Court Hotel & Restaurant

British

Tudor property serving the best of local produce

☎ 01752 862358
Down Thomas PL9 0DY
e-mail: enquiries@langdoncourt.com
dir: From A379 at Elburton, follow brown tourist signs

This magnificent Grade II listed manor house set in 10 acres of mature gardens and woodlands is brimming with history. Henry VIII and his last wife, Catherine Parr (she survived him so don't worry, it's not a haunted house) lived here and there's a mention of a manor house here in the Domesday Book. In the elegant restaurant, polished tables are dressed with crisp linen and fine glassware. Long-standing head chef Carl Smith cooks traditional British food with flair and imagination using local fish and meat and vegetables and herbs from the hotel's garden. Start perhaps with smooth duck parfait, toasted brioche and red onion marmalade, then try South Hams fillet of venison with apricot and spinach, root vegetable gratin and a rich venison jus. Finish with an apple tarte Tatin.

Times 12-2.30/6.30-9.30

Tanners Restaurant

Modern British V Notable Wine List

Unique medieval setting for contemporary British cooking

01752 252001
Prysten House, Finewell St PL1 2AE
e-mail: enquiries@tannersrestaurant.com
dir: Town centre. Behind St Andrews Church on Royal Parade

This stunning medieval building is one of the oldest in Plymouth, dating from 1490, but the restaurant it now accommodates is as modern as a parmesan biscuit (served with hand-picked Looe crab and sweet apple, by the way). Much character remains in the premises, though, from flagged floors, exposed stone walls and large oil canvases. It is the food on the plate that reflects 21st-century sensibilities; broadly modern British, the focus firmly on the local larder, with those carefully-sourced ingredients given room to breathe. Kick off with a slow-cooked Devon duck egg with peas and ham, then perhaps seared day boat John Dory with fresh egg linguini, chorizo and smoked shrimp sauce, winding up with a rhubarb semi-fredo. The Tanner brothers have written numerous cookery books and you may have seen James on the telly; the pair also run a popular brasserie in the city - The Barbican Kitchen (see entry).

Chef Christopher & James Tanner **Owner** Christopher & James Tanner **Times** 12-2.30/7-9.30 Closed 25, 31 Dec, 1st wk Jan, Sun-Mon **Prices** Fixed L 2 course £17.50, Fixed D 3 course fr £39, Service optional, Groups min 8 service 10% **Wines** 40 bottles over £20, 20 bottles under £20, 8 by glass **Notes** Tasting menu 6 course, Vegetarian menu, Dress restrictions, Smart casual preferred, no trainers **Seats** 45, Pr/dining room 26 **Children** Portions **Parking** On street, church car park next to restaurant

ROCKBEARE Map 3 SY09

The Jack In The Green

Modern British V

Comfortable Devon pub with innovative food

01404 822240
EX5 2EE
e-mail: info@jackinthegreen.uk.com
dir: 3m E of M5 junct 29 on old A30

The long-established Devon hostelry is a supremely comfortable place, where you can sink into a sofa near a crackling log fire, and where there is always a convivial local crowd. Smiling, fully engaged service lifts the restaurant operation into the ranks of the most professional, while the owner candidly states that the intention of the cooking is to give 'pub grub classics a delicious kick up the backside'. Sunday lunchers may indeed be favoured with top-drawer roast sirloin and Yorkshire pudding, or lamb shank with redcurrant and rosemary, but there is plenty else going on. Seared sesame tuna with avocado and lime purée is not exactly pub grub, and the care and attention lavished on roast duck breast in its own juices, with potato fondant and rhubarb chutney, transforms it into something special. Finish with white chocolate and macadamia cheesecake, or a deconstructive homage to the unassuming Jaffa Cake.

Chef Matthew Mason, Craig Sampson **Owner** Paul Parnell **Times** 12-2/6-9.30 Closed 25 Dec-5 Jan **Prices** Fixed L 2 course £19.50-£25, Fixed D 3 course £25, Tasting menu £39.50, Starter £4.95-£7.95, Main £9.50-£23.50, Dessert £5.95-£7.95, Service optional **Wines** 40 bottles over £20, 60 bottles under £20, 12 by glass **Notes** Sunday L, Vegetarian menu, Dress restrictions, Smart casual **Seats** 80, Pr/dining room 60 **Children** Portions, Menu **Parking** 120

SALCOMBE Map 3 SX73

Soar Mill Cove Hotel

Modern British

Classical cooking in a coastal Devon hotel

01548 561566
Soar Mill Cove, Marlborough TQ7 3DS
e-mail: info@soarmillcove.co.uk
dir: A381 to Salcombe, through village follow signs to sea

The jewel in the crown of a stretch of National Trust Devon coastal country, the hotel boasts a dazzling, spacious dining room enhanced by floor-to-ceiling windows. There is nothing quite like a sea view to stimulate the appetite, the more so when fish and seafood from Salcombe and Brixham are on the menu. An appetite-whetting cup of lobster and crab bisque sets the ball rolling, and might lead on to a voguish pairing of scallops and chorizo in tomato dressing. The dishes are classically informed, despite the odd modern flourish, so expect a main course like grilled West Country beef fillet, served with celeriac purée in a sauce of roasted shallots and Madeira. Dessert proper may well be anticipated by a taster portion of rose-scented crème brûlée.

Chef I Macdonald **Owner** Mr & Mrs K Makepeace & family **Times** 7.15-9 Closed Jan, L all week **Prices** Fixed D 3 course £29, Service optional **Wines** 40 bottles over £20, 11 bottles under £20, 4 by glass **Notes** Vegetarian available, Civ Wed 150 **Seats** 60 **Children** Portions, Menu **Parking** 25

Tides Reach Hotel

Modern British

Stunning seaside setting for good British food

01548 843466
South Sands TQ8 8LJ
e-mail: enquire@tidesreach.com
dir: Take cliff road towards sea and Bolt Head

Tides Reach is a delightfully relaxed family-run hotel in a gorgeous location overlooking Salcombe's South Sands. The Garden Room restaurant is airy and light with stunning views of Salcombe Estuary through the large picture windows. The area is blessed in terms of local produce and the kitchen uses this well in the simple, effective cooking on display. Enjoy seared Falmouth Bay scallops with braised cabbage to start, honey-glazed lamb shank with redcurrant and rosemary jus, confit of vegetables, spring onion and mashed potatoes for main and chocolate marquise to finish.

Chef Finn Ibsen **Owner** Edwards Family **Times** 7-9 Closed Dec-Jan, L all week **Prices** Fixed D 4 course £33.50, Service included **Wines** 90 bottles over £20, 14 bottles under £20, 6 by glass **Notes** Vegetarian available, Dress restrictions, Smart casual, no jeans or T-shirts **Seats** 80 **Parking** 80

SHALDON Map 3 SX97

ODE

◎◎ Modern British

Top-quality local and organic produce in coastal village

☎ 01626 873977
21 Fore St TQ14 ODE
e-mail: info@odetruefood.co.uk
dir: Cross bridge from Teignmouth then 1st left into Fore St

Discreetly set in a three-storey Georgian townhouse in this picturesque coastal village, ODE's owners, Tim and Clare Bouget, believe in true food values and are passionate about sourcing quality seasonal and local ingredients. The same ethos applies to the intimate interior, which has been refurbished with environmentally-friendly materials. Impeccable 'green' credentials aside, ultimately it's the quality of the cooking that impresses, the innovative modern British style underpinned by French technique and dotted with occasional global influences, though with subtlety and intelligence. Take pan-seared line-caught sea bass with a black lentil dhal and coconut and turmeric cream, or perhaps slow-cooked rump of Pitts Farm spring lamb accompanied by a potato terrine and black olive toffee. (ODE is certified 'organic' by the Soil Association, and wines follow the theme.)

Times 12-1.30/7-9.30 Closed 25 Dec, BHs, Mon-Tue, L Wed, D Sun

SIDMOUTH Map 3 SY18

Riviera Hotel

◎ Modern British

Traditional cooking in stylish hotel with sea views

☎ 01395 515201
The Esplanade EX10 8AY
e-mail: enquiries@hotelriviera.co.uk
web: www.hotelriviera.co.uk
dir: From M5 junct 30 take A3052 to Sidmouth. Situated in centre of Esplanade

Overlooking the sea and close to the town centre, the bay-fronted Riviera Hotel is a fine example of Regency architecture and still the jewel in the crown of Sidmouth's historic Esplanade. Inside, traditional comfort and elegance sets the tone in the restaurant, where a daily-changing menu balances traditional fare with forays into modern innovative dishes. Expect starters such as ham hock and flageolet bean terrine with pineapple crisps, pineapple and chilli compôte, followed by steamed paupiette of lemon sole filled with salmon mousse and baby spinach served with couscous, asparagus, tomato compôte and saffron foam. Leave room for pudding - perhaps a strawberry delice or chocolate mousse. In summer, dine on the sunny terrace with lovely views over Lyme Bay.

Chef Matthew Weaver **Owner** Peter Wharton **Times** 12.30-2/7-9 **Prices** Starter £8.50-£12, Main £22.50-£33.50, Dessert £6-£7.50, Service optional **Wines** 70 bottles over £20, 7 bottles under £20, 6 by glass **Notes** Fixed L 5 course £28, Fixed D 6 course £39.50, Sunday L, Vegetarian available **Seats** 85, Pr/dining room 65 **Children** Portions, Menu **Parking** 26

The Salty Monk

◎◎ Modern British

Charming restaurant with rooms with creative kitchen

☎ 01395 513174
Church St, Sidford EX10 9QP
e-mail: saltymonk@btconnect.com
dir: From M5 junct 30 take A3052 to Sidmouth, or from Honiton take A375 to Sidmouth, left at lights in Sidford, 200yds on right

Salt is in the air around these parts. The house that this charming restaurant with rooms now occupies is the last house in the parish of Salcombe Regis ('salty vale'), and it once housed the salting operation of local monks who sold the stuff out of Exeter Cathedral. These days, the Witheridges run a welcoming, nicely unreconstructed country-house operation, with candelight and garden views, although the locally-based cooking is open to cosmopolitan influences. Try herbed ravioli filled with ham and broad bean mousse in minted pea cream to begin, followed perhaps by fillets of red mullet on rösti in red wine sauce. Local fruit and hedgerow wines supplement a list supplied by Devon specialist Christopher Piper.

Chef Annette & Andy Witheridge **Owner** Annette & Andy Witheridge **Times** 12-1.30/6.30-9.30 Closed 3 wks Jan, 2 wks Nov, L Mon-Wed **Prices** Fixed D 3 course fr £42, Service optional, Groups min 10 service 10% **Wines** 24 bottles over £20, 56 bottles under £20, 10 by glass **Notes** Tasting menu 8 course, Sunday L, Vegetarian available, Dress restrictions, Smart casual **Seats** 55, Pr/dining room 14 **Children** Portions **Parking** 18

Victoria Hotel

◎ Traditional

Turn-of-the-century splendour and appealing menu at seafront hotel

☎ 01395 512651
The Esplanade EX10 8RY
e-mail: info@victoriahotel.co.uk
dir: At western end of The Esplanade

The imposing Victoria was built in the early years of the 20th century, and stands in five acres of landscaped grounds at the end of Sidmouth's lovely Georgian esplanade. Tradition reigns inside, from the dignified period style involving high ceilings and fancy plasterwork cornices, right down to the dress code that requires gentlemen to turn up in jacket and tie for dinner; a piano plays in the background and well-drilled staff swish professionally between tables. In tune with the ambience, the kitchen takes a traditional approach, partnering trout mousse and rillettes with horseradish cream, ahead of guinea fowl breast with bacon and peas, and fondant potato. Dessert concludes with a more modern trio of passionfruit, served as jelly, sorbet and cheesecake.

Times 1-2/7-9

SOUTH BRENT Map 3 SX66

Glazebrook House Hotel & Restaurant

◎ British

Stylish country house in tranquil garden setting

☎ 01364 73322
TQ10 9JE
e-mail: enquiries@glazebrookhouse.com
dir: From A38, between Ivybridge & Buckfastleigh exit at South Brent, follow hotel signs

With a tranquil location next to the Dartmoor National Park, this former home of an 18th-century gentleman is set within four acres of pretty gardens. These days, it's a comfortable country-house hotel but the classic style has been maintained and the intimate restaurant is elegantly done out in natural tones with white linen-clad tables. The menu focuses on local produce and follows a broadly British path. A starter of Devon crab cakes with Thai spices is served with a sweet chilli sauce and mixed leaves, and might be followed by noisettes of South Devon lamb with celeriac dauphinoise and port wine sauce.

Chef David Merriman **Owner** Dave & Caroline Cashmore **Times** 7-9 Closed 2 wks Jan, 1 wk Aug, Sun, L all week **Prices** Fixed D 3 course £19.50, Starter £4.50-£6.50, Main £16.50-£20.50, Dessert £4.50-£5.95, Service optional **Wines** 13 bottles over £20, 19 bottles under £20, 8 by glass **Notes** Vegetarian available, Civ Wed 80 **Seats** 60, Pr/dining room 12 **Children** Portions **Parking** 40

STRETE Map 3 SX84

The Kings Arms

◎ Modern British

Local seafood in charming, family-run old pub

☎ 01803 770377
Dartmouth Rd TQ6 0RW
e-mail: kingsarms_devon_fish@hotmail.com
dir: A379 coastal road from Dartmouth to Kingsbridge, 5m from Dartmouth

An elegant Victorian building with a fine ornate cast-iron balcony, The Kings Arms is a pub and restaurant with a happy mix of traditional bar and more modern dining room. It is relaxed, unpretentious and confident throughout, with modern art adding splashes of bright colour to the neutral tones on the walls. There are great views of Start Bay from the back, too. Fresh fish is king here (although there is always an interesting meaty alternative available), the daily catch from local boats, including crabs and lobsters directly from the bay, form the bedrock of the daily-changing menu. The kitchen knows that the best fish and seafood dishes are the simple ones and starters might include smoked sprats with lemon wedges and Brixham mussels steamed in white wine, garlic, cream and herbs. For main course, perhaps roast cod 'Spanish style' on chorizo, pepper and potato stew.

Times 12-2/6.30-9

The Laughing Monk

Modern British **NEW**

Top-notch local produce cooked with care and attention

☎ 01803 770639
Totnes Rd TQ6 0RN
e-mail: thelaughingmonk@btconnect.com
dir: A38 & follow signs toward Dartmouth, 700yds past Dartmouth Golf Club take right turn to Strete

Sandwiched by the glorious South Hams beaches of Blackpool Sands and Slapton, this former school house dating from 1839 is a good bet for unfussy modern British food at any time of year. New owners took over in 2008 and have de-cluttered the place, giving it a fresh modern look to go with the original oak floors and doors and a welcoming open fire. Chefs are blessed with cracking produce in this part of the world, and this kitchen's sourcing is exceptional; raw materials travel but a few miles from local Devon farmers and fishermen. Start Bay crabs, scallops, lobsters and fish are treated simply to let freshness speak for itself, as in a main course of pan-seared scallops with local black pudding mash, crispy pancetta and red wine sauce. Carnivores are well catered for too with the likes of slow-roasted crispy belly pork with a Luscombe organic cider gravy.

Chef Ben Handley **Owner** Ben & Jackie Handley **Times** 6.30-10.30 Closed Jan, Sun, L all week **Prices** Food prices not confirmed for 2011. Please telephone for details **Wines** 5 bottles over £20, 16 bottles under £20, 5 by glass **Notes** Vegetarian available **Seats** 50 **Parking** 4, On street

TAVISTOCK — Map 3 SX47

Bedford Hotel

Modern British

Historic building with appealing menu

☎ 01822 613221
1 Plymouth Rd PL19 8BB
e-mail: enquiries@bedford-hotel.co.uk
dir: M5 junct 31, A30 (Launceston/Okehampton). Then A386 to Tavistock, follow town centre signs. Hotel opposite church

Built on the site of a former Benedictine Abbey in a prominent position at the edge of Tavistock, this eye-catching old building with a stone, castellated frontage was formerly home to the Dukes of Bedford. Inside, there's a comfortable lounge and bar and smart restaurant serving up a good amount of local ingredients in a mixture of classic and modern dishes. Start, perhaps, with grilled sardine bruschetta with buttered red chard, spinach with a garlic, parsley and caper butter, and poached egg. Move on to West Country beef fillet topped with a wild mushroom gratin served with fondant potato and a port and rosemary jus.

Times 12-2.30/7-9.30 Closed L Mon-Sat

THURLESTONE — Map 3 SX64

Thurlestone Hotel

Modern British

Classy modern British food on the south Devon coast

☎ 01548 560382
TQ7 3NN
e-mail: enquiries@thurlestone.co.uk
dir: A38 take A384 into Totnes, A381 towards Kingsbridge, onto A379 towards Churchstow, onto B3197 turn into lane signed to Thurlestone

The prime coastal location in south Devon, not far from Salcombe, is a joy in itself, and this classy hotel has appetising views of the shoreline. Gentlemen, don your jackets for the elegant, spacious dining room, where an unmistakable style of modern British cooking is offered in the form of a fixed-price menu. Organic gravad lax with blinis, caviar and lime crème fraîche is an appealing way to open proceedings, slow-cooked belly pork confit with prosciutto, Bramley apple purée, mustard mash and cider jus a satisfying follow-up. Finish with glazed lemon tart and melba sauce with fresh raspberries.

Chef H Miller **Owner** Grose Family **Times** 12.30-2.30/7.30-9 Closed 4-20 Jan, L Mon-Sat **Prices** Fixed L 3 course fr £19.50, Fixed D 4 course £35, Service optional **Wines** 113 bottles over £20, 40 bottles under £20, 8 by glass **Notes** Fish tasting menu, Sunday L, Vegetarian available, Dress restrictions, Jacket, Civ Wed 150 **Seats** 150, Pr/dining room 150 **Children** Portions, Menu **Parking** 120

TORQUAY — Map 3 SX96

Corbyn Head Hotel & Orchid Restaurant

– see page 134

The Elephant Restaurant and Brasserie

– see page 135

Grand Hotel

Modern

Fine local ingredients cooked with aplomb in characterful sea view hotel

☎ 01803 296677
Torbay Rd TQ2 6NT
e-mail: reservations@grandtorquay.co.uk
dir: M5 junct 31, follow signs for Torquay. At the Penn Inn rdbt follow signs for seafront

With stunning views over Torbay, this lordly Edwardian hotel dominates Torquay's seafront and retains more than a whiff of that elegant era in grand lounges and public rooms. Agatha Christie, no less, once had her own suite in the hotel. The Gainsborough restaurant is its fine dining venue, a spacious buzzy place with a soothing décor and efficient staff keeping things purring along smoothly. The kitchen team thinks local with its sourcing of produce, and deals in straightforward modern dishes, cooked with care and presented without affectation. Typical choices may include Ruby Devon beef fillet with béarnaise, and grey mullet with cauliflower and vanilla purée, samphire, surf clams, confit tomato and bisque.

Times 12.30-2.30/7-9.30 Closed L Mon-Sat

No 7 Fish Bistro

Mediterranean, European

Unpretentious, friendly seafood bistro above the harbour

☎ 01803 295055
7 Beacon Ter TQ1 2BH
e-mail: paul@no7-fish.com
dir: Close to Royal Torbay Yacht Club & Imperial Hotel

It's appropriate that this unpretentious, family-run harbourside fish specialist on the English Riviera should have a whiff of the Mediterranean about it. As you open the door of No 7 Fish Bistro a lovely waft of garlic and grilled fish sharpens the appetite; then take in the nautical blue and white interior decked out with wooden floors and chairs, wipe-clean tablecloths and fishy-themed prints and objets. The menu relies on the day's catch from local boats - displayed on a platter for diners to view - treated simply, as seen in a rustic starter of squid fried with olive oil and lemon and served in the pan. Main courses might serve up baked monkfish with black pepper and sea salt.

Chef Graham, Jill, Oliver & Paul Stacey **Owner** Graham & Jill Stacey **Times** 12.15-1.45/6-9.30 Closed 2 wks Xmas & New Year, Sun, Mon (Nov-May), L Mon-Tue **Prices** Starter £5.25-£9.75, Main £12.75-£21.50, Dessert £4-£6.50, Service optional, Groups min 6 service 10% **Wines** 20 bottles over £20, 16 bottles under £20, 12 by glass **Notes** Vegetarian available **Seats** 38 **Children** Portions, Menu **Parking** Car park opposite

Corbyn Head Hotel & Orchid Restaurant

TORQUAY Map 3 SX96

Modern British V

First-class cooking and fabulous sea views

☎ 01803 296366
Sea Front TQ2 6RH
e-mail: dine@orchidrestaurant.net
dir: Follow signs to Torquay seafront, turn right on seafront. Hotel on right with green canopies

The English Riviera is never more deserving of its name than when seen through the half-moon windows of the Orchid Restaurant, up on the first floor of the Corbyn Head Hotel. If the weather isn't exactly on a par with St Tropez, no matter, the climate control will keep up the illusion. The views from the restaurant are a draw day or night, but no more so than the food, which is as confident and beguiling as you'll get in these parts. The room is easy on the eye, done out in creamy toffee hues with plush velvet seats and well-distanced linen-clothed tables; a formal, comfortable setting for the refined modern cooking. There's a good use of local and regional produce in dishes that show sound judgement when it comes to letting the flavours shine out. Creativity and culinary good sense are evident in a starter of goats' cheese spring roll, which comes with beetroot in a salad and as a sorbet. Texture is given due consideration, too, as with a main course slow-cooked Ruby Red beef (nicely pink), served with parsnip three ways and sauce d'épice. For dessert, vanilla cheesecake is partnered with rhubarb, or go for a crème brûlée, flavoured with lemongrass and served up with a coconut sorbet. The amuse-bouche, breads and petits fours are produced with the same care and attention and the wine list lays out an impressive spread with plenty of choice by the glass.

Chef Daniel Kay, Marc Evans
Owner Rew Hotels Ltd
Times 12.30-2.30/7-9.30 Closed 2 wks Jan, 2 wks Nov, 1 wk Apr, Sun-Mon, L Tue **Prices** Food prices not confirmed for 2011. Please telephone for details
Wines 47 bottles over £20, 65 bottles under £20, 11 by glass **Notes** Vegetarian available, Vegetarian menu, Dress restrictions, Smart casual, Civ Wed 80
Seats 26 **Children** Portions, Menu
Parking 50

TORQUAY *continued*

Orestone Manor Hotel & Restaurant

Modern British

Slick cooking in a colonial-style restaurant

☎ 01803 328098
Rockhouse Ln, Maidencombe TQ1 4SX
e-mail: info@orestonemanor.com
dir: From Teignmouth take A379, through Shaldon towards Torquay. 3m take sharp left into Rockhouse Lane. Hotel signed

This luxurious manor house set in landscaped gardens and rolling countryside is a secluded place to relax with the added bonus of a beautifully furnished colonial-style restaurant. Wonderful, distant, elevated sea views and confident, sophisticated service make this a memorable place to eat. The menu reads simply, in places like a list of ingredients, but don't be fooled: this is ambitious cooking based on excellent seasonal and local produce, incorporating herbs and vegetables from the hotel's garden. Head chef Chris May has sound technique and turns out some well-crafted dishes; Brixham crab, for example, with mango, curry risotto and caviar, then pavé of sirloin and summer vegetable tea. Vanilla custard, crème caramel ice cream and praline rounds things off.

Times 12-2/7-9 Closed 2-26 Jan

TWO BRIDGES **Map 3 SX67**

Two Bridges Hotel

Modern British

Scenic moorland spot with fine-dining approach

☎ 01822 890581
PL20 6SW
e-mail: enquiries@twobridges.co.uk
dir: 8m from Tavistock on B3357, hotel at junct with B3312

Beside the West River Dart in the heart of the Dartmoor National Park, this fine hotel is next to the two bridges that give the village its name. Full of charm and character, it provides a choice of lounges and a traditional-style restaurant with oak panelling, linen tablecloths, great views and attentive service that is formal but very friendly all the same. The seasonally-changing menu offers skilfully cooked British dishes, using quality local produce, with an emphasis on game. Start with rabbit terrine with wild mushrooms and parsnip purée, move on to black bream with saffron gnocchi, braised fennel and spinach, or local beef fillet with mushroom ravioli and oxtail jus, and finish with dark chocolate tart with raspberry sorbet.

Times 12-2/6.30-9.30

WOODBURY **Map 3 SY08**

The Atrium Restaurant

British

Golf and motor-racing themes in a West Country retreat

☎ 01395 233382 & 234735
Woodbury Park Hotel, & Golf Club, Woodbury Castle EX5 1JJ
e-mail: enquiries@woodburypark.co.uk
dir: M5 junct 30, take A376/A3052 towards Sidmouth, turn right opposite Halfway Inn onto B3180 towards Budleigh Salterton to Woodbury Common, hotel signed on right

When he wasn't screaming around in a Formula One car, Nigel Mansell could often be found on a golf course. The former champion once owned this country hotel in 550 acres of rolling Devon countryside with its own PGA championship golf course, and his racing car and trophy collection is still here. Light floods into the glass-roofed Atrium restaurant, where the kitchen delivers fuss-free modern English cooking - the team is Devon born-and-bred and keen to showcase the county's peerless produce. Terrine of local ham hock is paired with Otter ale and spiced raisin chutney in a hearty starter, ahead of roast rump of Devon lamb with roast Provençal vegetables, Parisienne potatoes and black olive tapenade.

continued

The Elephant Restaurant and Brasserie

TORQUAY **Map 3 SX96**

Modern British

Classy, confident cooking in contemporary harbourside restaurant

☎ 01803 200044
3-4 Beacon Ter TQ1 2BH
e-mail: info@elephantrestaurant.co.uk
dir: Follow signs for Living Coast, restaurant opposite

Two dignified and rather elegant Georgian houses overlooking the marina and the bay are the setting for some of the best cooking on the English Riviera. If the façade is old-school, what lies within is anything but, with the wealth of period details supported by a personally-chosen eclectic range of fixtures and fittings, from old barrels to bold pieces of art on the walls. This elephant has two faces: on the ground floor is a brasserie serving up appealing things like pickled beetroot samosas with creamed Vulscombe goats' cheese with apple and grain mustard salad, followed by lemon sole with shellfish ragoût and Noilly Prat cream, while upstairs is the main restaurant, where Simon Hulstone opens up the throttle to full speed. The views are best admired from the restaurant, with its smart blue leather seats at well-spaced, well-dressed tables. West Country produce has a starring role, sourced with pride and due diligence. Start with hand-dived Torbay scallops on a lemon and cabbage risotto, before a rump of new season lamb (from Cornwall) with summer vegetables and thyme gnocchi. Technical skill and a confident hand are evident right through to the finale, perhaps in the form of a Netherton Farm raspberry millefeuille with vanilla ice cream.

Chef Simon Hulstone **Owner** Peter Morgan, Simon Hulstone **Times** 7-9.30 Closed 1st 2wks Jan, Sun-Mon, L all week **Prices** Food prices not confirmed for 2011. Please telephone for details **Wines** 34 bottles over £20, 10 bottles under £20, 8 by glass **Notes** Tasting menu available, Vegetarian available **Seats** 24 **Parking** Opposite restaurant

WOODBURY *continued*

Chef Matthew Pickett **Owner** Sue & Robin Hawkins **Times** 12.30-2.30/6.30-9.30 Closed L Mon-Sat, D 31 Dec **Prices** Fixed L 2 course £12.95, Starter £5.50-£8.50, Main £14.50-£22.50, Dessert £5.50-£8.95, Service optional **Wines** 21 bottles over £20, 31 bottles under £20, 10 by glass **Notes** Sunday L, Vegetarian available, Dress restrictions, Smart casual, Civ Wed 150 **Seats** 120, Pr/dining room 180 **Children** Portions **Parking** 350

WOOLACOMBE **Map 3 SS44**

Watersmeet Hotel

European

Rugged coastline setting for fine local cuisine

☎ 01271 870333
Mortehoe EX34 7EB
e-mail: info@watersmeethotel.co.uk
dir: M5 junct 27. Follow A361 to Woolacombe, right at beach car park, 300yds on right

Spectacular views over Woolacombe Bay to Hartland Point and Lundy Island mark out this former Edwardian gentleman's residence, now a smartly appointed country-house hotel with direct access to the beach. Every table in the Pavilion Restaurant has a magnificent sea view, so expect candlelit dinners with spectacular sunsets (hopefully). Good-quality local produce, particularly fresh fish, is used to create well-balanced dishes such as lobster, crab and saffron risotto to start, followed by Exmoor venison with Puy lentils, smoked bacon and a whisky cream sauce. Save room for a rhubarb and vanilla pudding with crème anglaise.

Times 12-2/7-8.30

DORSET

BEAMINSTER **Map 4 ST40**

BridgeHouse

Modern British

Classy mix of traditional and modern in a medieval house

☎ 01308 862200
3 Prout Bridge DT8 3AY
e-mail: enquiries@bridge-house.co.uk
web: www.bridge-house.co.uk
dir: From A303 take A356 towards Dorchester. Turn right onto A3066, 200mtrs down hill from town centre

A stone-built priest's house dating from the 13th century, BridgeHouse certainly has no lack of old-world charm, but a classy injection of contemporary style has brought things into the 21st century. The kitchen is very much at the heart of the enterprise: for over 20 years the hotel's reputation as a foodie venue has flourished, and you have a trio of dining areas to choose from - an intimate and chic Georgian beamed dining room perfect for a candlelit dinner, a modern conservatory brasserie, and an alfresco terrace shielded beneath a vast canvas canopy. The cooking is founded on Dorset produce and takes its cues primarily from France, although a sprinkling of influences from wider afield adds spice. Seared Lyme Bay scallops with squash and truffle purée, and hazelnut and sage butter shows the style, while mains run from Goan fish curry with sticky chai rice and crispy noodles, to roast rack of local lamb with dauphinoise potatoes, roasted vegetables and nettle and mint jus.

Chef Mr Stephen Pielesz **Owner** Mark and Joanna Donovan **Times** 12-2.30/6.30-9.30 **Prices** Food prices not confirmed for 2011. Please telephone for details **Wines** 52 bottles over £20, 22 bottles under £20, 17 by glass **Notes** Sunday L, Vegetarian available, Civ Wed 50 **Seats** 36, Pr/dining room 30 **Children** Portions, Menu **Parking** 20

The Wild Garlic

Modern British **NEW V**

Careful sourcing and considered cooking from Masterchef winner

☎ 01380 861446
4 The Square DT8 3AS
e-mail: mail@thewildgarlic.co.uk
dir: From A303, exit A3066 Crewkerne and follow signs to Bridport. Restaurant located in town square

Mat Follas, the 2009 *Masterchef* winner, is settling into this engaging and popular restaurant overlooking the square in bustling Beaminster. Décor is simple and rustic, with wooden floors, pale green painted beams, and solid mismatched tables, and the atmosphere is very chilled out. In keeping, Mat's cooking is refreshingly straightforward, allowing the flavours of the main ingredient to shine through, and his sensibly short daily-changing chalkboard menu champions top-notch produce from local artisan producers and foragers. Served with minimum fuss, dishes may include gutsy, accurately-cooked pigeon breasts with beetroot and berry compôte, beautifully fresh whole brill with caper and lemon butter, and lemon tart with pink rhubarb sorbet.

Chef Mat Follas **Owner** Mat Follas **Times** 12-2/7-11 Closed Sun, D Mon-Tue **Prices** Starter £6-£9, Main £12-£20, Dessert £6-£8, Service optional **Notes** Vegetarian menu **Seats** 40 **Children** Portions **Parking** Car park at front

BOURNEMOUTH **Map 5 SZ09**

Blakes @ Best Western The Connaught Hotel

Modern British

Friendly, relaxed hotel restaurant serving unfussy cuisine

☎ 01202 298020
30 West Hill Rd, West Cliff BH2 5PH
e-mail: dining@theconnaught.co.uk
web: www.theconnaught.co.uk
dir: Follow Town Centre West & BIC signs

The Victorian gentleman who built his seaside residence here on Bournemouth's West Cliff chose his spot well, right by the renowned Blue Flag beach and a five minute walk from the town centre action. Blakes restaurant has been reworked in recent years in a comfy traditional style, and there's also a lovely garden terrace for alfresco dining. Well-prepared, unfussy dishes show a loyalty to fresh local produce, and might start, typically, with chicken and mushroom terrine with home-made piccalilli, followed, perhaps, by honey and mustard pork tenderloin served with garlic mashed potatoes and buttered green beans. Finish with the comfort of strawberry Eton mess.

Chef Danny Green **Owner** Franklyn Hotels Ltd **Times** 6.30-9 Closed L all week **Prices** Food prices not confirmed for 2011. Please telephone for details **Wines** 6 bottles over £20, 24 bottles under £20, 9 by glass **Notes** Vegetarian available, Dress restrictions, Smart casual, no jeans, T-shirts or mobiles, Civ Wed 150 **Seats** 80, Pr/dining room 16 **Children** Menu **Parking** 66

Chine Hotel

Modern British, European

Seaside hotel with sumptuous gardens

☎ 01202 396234
Boscombe Spa Rd BH5 1AX
e-mail: reservations@chinehotel.co.uk
dir: From M27, A31, A338 follow signs to Boscombe Pier. Boscombe Spa Rd is off Christchurch Rd near Boscombe Gardens

This majestic Victorian hotel is surrounded by three acres of mature gardens from which a path leads down to the promenade. Expect stained-glass windows and burnished wood panelling within and huge picture windows in the dining room, which look out over Poole Bay and with tables so arranged that no-one misses out. Shortish menus keep things simple, but the cooking shows care and thought, from trout roulade with leek and beetroot chutney and a lemon dressing, to breast of duck with fondant potato, green beans and orange sauce, and cardamom and vanilla rice pudding with home-made jam to finish.

Chef Carl Munroe **Owner** Brownsea Haven Properties Ltd **Times** 12.30-2/7-9 Closed L Sat **Prices** Food prices not confirmed for 2011. Please telephone for details **Wines** 21 bottles over £20, 8 bottles under £20, 10 by glass **Notes** Sunday L, Vegetarian available, Dress restrictions, No jeans, T-shirts or trainers at D, Civ Wed 120 **Seats** 150, Pr/dining room 120 **Children** Portions, Menu **Parking** 55

Hermitage Hotel

Modern British

Unpretentious cooking in seafront hotel

☎ 01202 557363
Exeter Rd BH2 5AH
e-mail: info@hermitage-hotel.co.uk
dir: Follow A338 (Ringwood-Bournemouth) & signs to pier, beach & BIC. Hotel directly opposite

The Hermitage sits in pole position facing the pier and seafront promenade smack in the centre of Bournemouth, handy for all the events at the Bournemouth International Centre and Pavilion Theatre. It is a smartly-refurbished grand hotel with a suitably impressive dining room as a setting for the kitchen's crowd-pleasing repertoire of unfussy modern dishes. You might start with steamed local mussels with pesto sauce and garlic bread, then move onto something along the lines of braised shoulder of lamb with bubble-and-squeak, buttered kale and redcurrant and rosemary jus, or confit duck leg teamed with new potatoes sautéed with rosemary and garlic, green beans wrapped in pancetta, and raspberry sauce.

Chef Paul Groves **Owner** Mr P D Oram **Times** 12.30-2/6.15-9 Closed L Mon-Sat **Prices** Food prices not confirmed for 2011. Please telephone for details **Wines** 12 bottles over £20, 40 bottles under £20, 8 by glass **Notes** Vegetarian available, Dress restrictions, No T-shirts or shorts **Children** Portions, Menu **Parking** 69

Highcliff Grill

Modern British

Contemporary dining with great views in a traditional hotel

☎ 01202 557702
Highcliff Marriott Hotel, St Michael's Rd, West Cliff BH2 5DU
e-mail: reservations.bournemouth@marriotthotels.co.uk
dir: Take A338 dual carriageway through Bournemouth, then follow signs for International Centre to West Cliff Rd, then 2nd right

Bournemouth has gone to great lengths to shed its blue-rinse image in recent years, so the Marriott chain's £4.5 million facelift of this grand old Victorian seaside hotel is right in tune with the chuck-out-the-chintz ethos. The Highcliff Grill is now looking rather rakish with its modish banquettes and seats in jazzy shades of cerise and lime green, and bare darkwood tables - get the right ones and you have sweeping views over Bournemouth's golden beaches to boot. The cooking toes the line: contemporary but not trying to get too clever with its blend of classic and modern dishes driven by well-sourced ingredients. Fish soup with croûtons, rouille and gruyère is a time-honoured way to start, ahead of straight-up grilled meats or a more refined roast spiced monkfish with bok choy and saffron mussel broth.

Chef Clyde Hollett **Owner** Marriott Hotels **Times** 1-3/6-9.30 Closed L Mon-Sat **Prices** Fixed L 3 course £19.95, Starter £6.50-£7.50, Main £14-£23, Dessert £5.95-£8, Service included **Wines** 43 bottles over £20, 13 bottles under £20, 13 by glass **Notes** Sunday L, Vegetarian available, Civ Wed 250 **Seats** 80, Pr/dining room 14 **Children** Portions, Menu **Parking** 100

Langtry Restaurant

Modern

Edwardian setting for some contemporary cooking

☎ 0844 3725 432 & 01202 553887
Langtry Manor, 26 Derby Rd, East Cliff BH1 3QB
e-mail: lillie@langtrymanor.com
dir: On East Cliff, at corner of Derby & Knyveton Roads

Romantics take note that this handsome manor was built as a love nest by Edward VII in 1877 for his mistress Lillie Langtry. Although the hotel has recently had a stylish modern makeover, Victorian character is still present in spades - nowhere more so than in the spectacular restaurant, where a minstrels' gallery, Tudor tapestries, stained glass windows and a grand fireplace are tailor-made for gourmet Edwardian banquets. The kitchen also squares the demands of traditionalists and modernists with sound cooking underpinned by great ingredients. Start with a corn-fed chicken and confit pheasant terrine with spiced red wine jelly, and proceed to cannon of lamb with potato and spiced carrot cake, sautéed sweetbreads and spring greens. Awaiting you at the end will be something like a Bramley apple soufflé with rose cookies and Calvados cream.

Chef Chris Corbett **Owner** Mrs P Hamilton-Howard **Times** 7-9 Closed L all week **Prices** Fixed D 3 course £34, Service optional **Wines** 25 bottles over £20, 30 bottles under £20, 5 by glass **Notes** ALC 3 course £34-£44, Vegetarian available, Dress restrictions, Smart casual, Civ Wed 100 **Seats** 60, Pr/dining room 16 **Children** Portions, Menu **Parking** 20

BOURNEMOUTH *continued*

The Print Room & Ink Bar & Brasserie

Classic Brasserie

Buzzy art-deco brasserie with appealing menu

01202 789669
Richmond Hill BH2 6HH
e-mail: info@theprintroom-bournemouth.co.uk
dir: Town centre - located in landmark art deco listed Daily Echo newspaper building

Housed in the Daily Echo's former press hall, this buzzy brasserie-style grand café has been described as the South Coast's answer to London's Wolseley (see entry). It certainly looks the part with its art-deco styling, double-height windows, hanging lanterns lit with church candles and chequerboard-tiled floor; there's an authentic charcuterie bar, patisserie counter and partially open kitchen to add to the vibe. The extensive menu offers breakfast and afternoon tea, with the main menu kicking off at noon and running until late. Expect classics like pressed ham hock terrine with shallot marmalade, followed by a modern construction of pan-fried Scottish scallops with honey-glazed pork belly, langoustine and potato purée. Finish with rosemary crème brûlée with pink grapefruit sorbet or apple and cherry crumble tart with clotted cream.

Chef Michael Lecouteur **Owner** Andy Price **Times** 8am-10pm Closed D 25-26 Dec, 1 Jan **Prices** Fixed L 2 course £12.50, Fixed D 3 course £20-£30, Starter £4.95-£9.50, Main £6.75-£25.95, Dessert £6.50-£6.95, Service added but optional 10%, Groups min 8 service 10% **Wines** 85 bottles over £20, 12 bottles under £20, 9 by glass **Notes** Sunday L, Vegetarian available **Seats** 145, Pr/dining room 18 **Children** Portions, Menu **Parking** NCP - 100yds

West Beach

Modern Seafood

Great local seafood right by the beach

01202 587785
Pier Approach BH2 5AA
e-mail: enquiry@west-beach.co.uk
dir: 100yds W of the pier

Metres from the shore by Bournemouth Pier, West Beach enjoys panoramic views across Poole Bay from its stunning beachside location. You can almost touch the sea when you dine out on the wooden deck terrace of this easy-going seafood-oriented modern restaurant. Inside, the stripped-out beachcomber-chic pastel shades and bleached wood almost fool you into thinking you could be Down Under not Dorset. Chefs are at work in the open kitchen, taking daily deliveries of fresh fish caught by local fishermen right in front of the restaurant. The simple, clean flavoured dishes incorporate old favourites and modern interpretations of classics. Start with the prawn cocktail, then go for roast John Dory fillets with New Forest mushroom gnocchi and parmesan or classic moules marinière. There are meat and vege options, plus desserts such as Jasmine white tea pannacotta with lemon confit.

Chef Ese Kousin **Owner** Andrew Price **Times** 9.30am-10pm Closed D 26 Dec, 1 Jan **Prices** Fixed L 3 course £20-£50, Fixed D 3 course £20-£50, Starter £5.50-£10.90, Main £7.50-£19.90, Dessert £4.50-£6, Service optional, Groups min 10 service 10% **Wines** 47 bottles over £20, 14 bottles under £20, 11 by glass **Notes** Tasting menu available, Sunday L, Vegetarian available, Dress restrictions, No bare feet or bikinis **Seats** 90 **Children** Portions, Menu **Parking** NCP 2 mins

BRIDPORT **Map 4 SY49**

Riverside Restaurant

Seafood, International

The pick of local seafood in a waterside setting

01308 422011
West Bay DT6 4EZ
e-mail: artwatfish@hotmail.com
dir: A35 Bridport ring road, turn to West Bay at Crown rdbt

Anthony Newley was topping the charts back in March 1960 when the Watson family took over this waterfront restaurant in West Bay on the Jurassic Coast. These days it's a jaunty nautical-feeling place, done out with a beach-shack look in lavender blue and pine, that deals in immaculately-fresh fish and seafood treated with a light touch and served without any palaver. What's on the menu depends on what's been landed, of course, but expect to kick off with classics such as Lyme Bay dressed crab with home-made mayonnaise, or local Portland oysters - some things need no messing with. Brill with crispy spinach and sorrel sauce, fresh fish in a bourride sauce, or bounteous seafood platters are next in line. If you're an unreconstructed carnivore, braised Dorset beef with shallots, pancetta, rosemary and red wine might be up for grabs, while pear tarte Tatin with home-made rum and raisin ice cream wraps things up.

Chef N Larcombe, G Marsh, A Shaw **Owner** Mr & Mrs A Watson **Times** 12-2.30/6.30-9 Closed 30 Nov-14 Feb, Mon (ex BHs), D Sun **Prices** Fixed L 2 course £16.50-£17.50, Starter £6-£12.50, Main £12.95-£25.75, Dessert £4.50-£6.50, Service optional, Groups min 7 service 10% **Wines** 23 bottles over £20, 35 bottles under £20, 10 by glass **Notes** Sunday L, Vegetarian available **Seats** 70, Pr/dining room 30 **Children** Portions, Menu **Parking** Public car park 40 mtrs

CHRISTCHURCH Map 5 SZ19

Captain's Club Hotel

Modern European

Contemporary riverside restaurant focusing on locally-sourced ingredients

☎ 01202 475111
Wick Ferry, Wick Ln BH23 1HU
e-mail: enquiries@captainsclubhotel.com
web: www.captainsclubhotel.com
dir: Hotel just off Christchurch High St, towards Christchurch Quay

This markedly contemporary hotel has acres of glass to make the most of the views over the yachts on the River Stour and Christchurch Quay, and the building (it isn't five years old yet) is designed to meet the needs of the 21st-century customer. It's all very sleek and stylish, with an open-plan ground floor providing everything from live music in the popular bar, to a fine terrace on which to watch the sunset, a chic lounge, and Tides Restaurant, where the modern European food is a real hit. It has the air of eating on a grand ocean liner, but is by no means stuffy, and the service is on the ball. The seasons and locale are reflected on the carte and fixed-price menus, which might see ham hock, potato and parsley terrine partnered with pease pudding and sherry vinaigrette, and main-course slow-cooked ox cheek served with confit garlic creamed potatoes, an oxtail and liver faggot and baked salsify.

Chef Andrew Gault **Owner** Platinum One Hotels Ltd **Times** 12-2.30/7-10 **Prices** Fixed L 2 course fr £12.50, Fixed D 3 course fr £25, Starter £6-£10, Main £12-£17, Dessert £5-£7, Service optional **Wines** 90 bottles over £20, 35 bottles under £20, 14 by glass **Notes** Sunday L, Vegetarian available, Civ Wed 100 **Seats** 72, Pr/dining room 44 **Children** Portions, Menu **Parking** 41

Christchurch Harbour Restaurant

Modern European

Complex modern European cooking with gorgeous coastal views

☎ 01202 483434
95 Mudeford BH23 3NT
e-mail: christchurch@harbourhotels.co.uk
dir: A35/A337 to Highcliffe. Right at rdbt, hotel & restaurant 1.5m on left

The discreet, three-storey building dates from the onset of the Victorian era, and was recently treated to a lavish makeover, complete with state-of-the-art spa facilities, and a light-filled dining room done in stone shades, complete with coastal views. Polished service adds class to the operation, as does the modern European cooking. Complex but effective productions are typified by a starter comprised of a cake of local crabmeat with citrus polenta and avocado in orange and vanilla syrup, or main courses like fillet and sweetbreads of veal with caramelised shallots, sweet potato purée and a pink peppercorn sauce. All elements pull together, and the result is a satisfying whole. An impressive dessert is the spiced poached pear, which arrives in a red wine and rosemary reduction, along with buttermilk panncaotta.

Chef John Parham **Owner** Harbour Hotels Group **Times** 12-2.30/6.30-9.30 **Prices** Starter £4.95-£6.95, Main £14.95-£19.95, Dessert £4.95-£5.95, Service optional, Groups min 10 service 10% **Wines** 22 bottles over £20, 14 bottles under £20, 9 by glass **Notes** Sunday L, Vegetarian available, Civ Wed 120 **Seats** 80, Pr/dining room 100 **Children** Portions, Menu **Parking** 70

Crooked Beam Restaurant

Modern British

Genuinely friendly welcome and plenty of old-world charm

☎ 01202 499362
Jumpers Corner, 2 The Grove BH23 2HA
e-mail: info@crookedbeam.co.uk
web: www.crookedbeam.co.uk
dir: Situated on corner of Barrack Road A35 and The Grove

Once inside, it is clear where this cosy little neighbourhood restaurant gets its name. At 300 years old, the venerable Crooked Beam is a true Dorset veteran - but olde-worlde charm only goes so far, and what makes this restaurant so outstanding is the hands-on owners Simon and Vicki Hallam, a sincerely welcoming couple who put heart and soul into their work. Everything is made in-house by Simon, who uses top-class local materials in his well-executed dishes. A tart plum chutney cuts through the richness of a duck and pistachio pâté served with port and cream, and buttery toasted brioche. Next, a main course of perfectly-judged pan-fried sea bass comes with delicate lemon risotto and vermouth cream sauce. Dessert finishes with a vibrant, citrus hit of lemon cheesecake. Make sure to visit the Hallam's deli down the road, which sells home-made cakes, bread and biscuits as well as dishes from the restaurant.

Times 12-2/7-11 Closed Mon, L Sat, D Sun

The Kings Hotel & Restaurant

Modern British

Tapas-style or full dishes in a chic seaside setting

☎ 01202 588933
18 Castle St BH23 1DT
e-mail: restaurant@thekings-christchurch.co.uk
dir: Turn off A35 onto Christchurch High St, turn left at rdbt, hotel 20mtrs on left

The former Kings Arms pub has been rescued from dereliction and turned into this smart boutique hotel, complete with a stylish brasserie and bar. It's a delicious exercise in understated modish décor, all dark hardwood floors, muted colours, classy fabrics, and well-spaced linen-swathed tables laid with designer cutlery. The cooking stays simple and honest in true brasserie style, with flavour-packed dishes prepared from local seasonal produce, including fish landed just down the road at Mudeford Quay. Seared pigeon with chicory salad and red wine dressing is an impressive starter, followed by perfectly-cooked lamb rump with a well-balanced onion mash and a spot-on thyme jus. Finish with Bakewell tart with vanilla ice cream.

Times 12-2.30/6-9.30 **Prices** Fixed L 2 course fr £10, Starter £4.50-£8, Main £8.50-£22.50, Dessert £4.50-£7.95 **Notes** Sunday L

The Lord Bute & Restaurant

British, European

Ambitious cooking in elegant dining room

☎ 01425 278884
179-185 Lymington Rd, Highcliffe-on-Sea BH23 4JS
e-mail: mail@lordbute.co.uk
dir: Follow A337 to Lymington, opposite St Mark's churchyard in Highcliffe

The elegant Lord Bute stands directly behind the original entrance lodges of Highcliffe Castle, close to the beach at Christchurch. Named after an erstwhile resident and 18th-century Prime Minister, portraits of the many distinguished visitors to the castle welcome you in the entrance hall. The elegant, black marble floored dining room is a traditional, classy space which sets the stage for the ambitious modern British food. Top-notch Dorset ingredients are used to create dishes such as a starter of seared scallops with fennel purée, ginger cream sauce and micro cress salad, and main-course grilled Cornish beef fillet with wild mushroom confit, oxtail pudding, fat chips and tarragon jus.

Times 12-2/7-9.30 Closed Mon, L Sat, D Sun

CHRISTCHURCH *continued*

Rhodes South

Modern British

Eco-friendly harbourside restaurant from the Gary Rhodes stable

☎ 01202 483434
95 Mudeford BH23 3NT
e-mail: reservationenquiries@rhodes-south.co.uk
dir: A35/A337 to Highcliffe. Right at rdbt, hotel & restaurant 1.5m on left

The single-storey, timber-framed building within the grounds of the Christchurch Harbour Hotel houses the Dorset outpost of the Gary Rhodes empire. Its sumptuous full-drop windows offer uplifting views of the quay, and ecological concerns have informed the design of the place, as well as much of its menu, with local produce predominating. Dishes from the Rhodes repertoire are brought off with great aplomb, as in red mullet with pissaladière and rosemary cream, or mains such as treacled duck breast with parsnip and date purée, or steamed Jerusalem artichoke mousse glazed with Barkham Blue, served with chestnuts and celery leaf. Cheesecakes, jellies and lemon meringue are the kinds of desserts to expect.

Chef Mike Jennings **Owner** Harbour Hotels Ltd
Times 12-2.30/6.30-10 Closed Xmas, Sun, Mon
Prices Fixed L 2 course £15.95, Starter £5.95-£11.50, Main £16.95-£25, Dessert £7, Service optional **Wines** 55 bottles over £20, 2 bottles under £20, 13 by glass
Notes Vegetarian available **Seats** 60 **Children** Portions
Parking 40

Splinters Restaurant

Modern International

Modern European cooking by the Priory

☎ 01202 483454
12 Church St BH23 1BW
e-mail: eating@splinters.uk.com
dir: Directly in front of Priory gates

In a row of ancient buildings on a cobbled street, close by the gates of Christchurch Priory, is this green-fronted, family-run restaurant that has become a firm favourite in the town over nearly 50 years of operation. A variety of different eating areas awaits, from the elegant Blue Room with its framed pictures to more informal wooden booths, with classy efficient service throughout. Paul Putt cooks a modern European menu using fine local materials and daily fish, with breads, ice creams and much else made in-house. Seared scallops wrapped in Parma ham, served with asparagus in lemongrass foam, is a starter that ticks a fair few contemporary boxes, and may be followed by herb-crusted Dorset lamb with a liver and bacon pie and pomme purée. To finish, you could surrender to the lure of a grande assiette of sweet things.

Splinters Restaurant

Chef Paul Putt **Owner** Paul & Agnes Putt
Times 11-2/7-10 Closed 26 Dec, 1-10 Jan, Sun-Mon
Prices Fixed L 2 course fr £11.95, Fixed D 3 course fr £24.95, Service optional, Groups min 8 service 10%
Wines 105 bottles over £20, 37 bottles under £20, 5 by glass **Notes** ALC 2 course £31.95, 3 course £38.95, Vegetarian available, Dress restrictions, Smart casual
Seats 42, Pr/dining room 30 **Children** Portions
Parking Priory car park

Sienna

DORCHESTER **Map 4 SY69**

Modern British

Small is beautiful on Dorchester's high street

☎ 01305 250022
36 High West St DT1 1UP
e-mail: browns@siennarestaurant.co.uk
dir: Near top of town rdbt in Dorchester

Proving that size isn't everything, Sienna on Dorchester's high street wows with fantastic food and service for each of its 15 covers. Run for the past seven years by a husband-and-wife-team - Russell Brown in the kitchen and Elena leading service - the intimate and contemporary room, painted sienna and cream with comfortable seating and white clothed tables, is a regional high-flyer. The relaxed, unhurried ambience is aided by Elena's pleasant and helpful service. Russell's cooking is refreshingly unfussy but, make no mistake, his deft touch means every dish is bang on the money. In his careful hands, the freshest seasonal local produce packs a flavoursome punch from the canapés through to the coffee and everything in-between. The good value lunch is popular, while dinner and a tasting menu offer more complex combinations. A perfectly balanced spaghetti with crab might give way to roast breast of wood pigeon with pan-fried potato gnocchi, beetroot and horseradish foam. The Tahitian vanilla cheesecake is a fine example of its type, served with blackcurrant jelly, poached apple and green apple sorbet. The wine list is also a thing of beauty and includes plenty by the glass and carafe.

Chef Russell Brown **Owner** Russell & Elena Brown
Times 12-2/7-9 Closed 2 wks Feb/Mar, 2 wks Sep/Oct, Sun-Mon **Prices** Fixed L 2 course £23.50, Fixed D 3 course £41, Tasting menu £50, Service optional **Wines** 28 bottles over £20, 11 bottles under £20, 7 by glass **Notes** Tasting menu 6 course, Vegetarian available **Seats** 15
Parking Top of town car park, on street

CORFE CASTLE **Map 4 SY98**

Mortons House Hotel

Traditional British

Tudor elegance and old style hospitality

01929 480988
East St BH20 5EE
e-mail: stay@mortonshouse.co.uk
dir: In village centre on A351

Dating back to Tudor times, the manor house is now a luxurious small hotel housing a charming restaurant split into two elegant dining rooms. Both of these, plus a drawing room complete with log fire, are traditionally decorated and table settings are also old school with crisp linen and high quality glassware. The cooking is classic country-house fare with a grounding in classical French cooking brought into the present with some modern ideas. Try not to over indulge in the delicious home-made breads and leave room to enjoy white onion velouté, breakfast garnish and poached free-range egg, and a main course of roasted chicken breast, lentil purée, Savoy cabbage and smoked bacon, red wine and grape jus. The large wine list features some excellent new and old world choices.

Chef Ed Firth **Owner** Mrs Hageman, Mr & Mrs Clayton **Times** 12-1.45/7-9 **Prices** Fixed L 2 course £25-£30, Fixed D 3 course £30-£35, Service optional, Groups min 20 service 10% **Wines** 40 bottles over £20, 5 bottles under £20, 4 by glass **Notes** Sunday L, Vegetarian available, Dress restrictions, Smart casual preferred, Civ Wed 60 **Seats** 60, Pr/dining room 22 **Children** Portions, Menu **Parking** 40

CORFE MULLEN **Map 4 SY99**

The Coventry Arms

Modern British

Classic pub with quality ales and great food

01258 857284
Mill St BH21 3RH
e-mail: info@coventryarms.co.uk
dir: A31, 2m from Wimborne

Describing itself as a 'Chop and Ale House', the Coventry Arms lives up to the billing with an excellent range of real ales (a pint of Cocker Hoop, anyone?) and a menu of a mostly British flavour that goes from kipper pâté with toast and lemon to crumble of the season with vanilla custard, via 12oz veal chop with hand-cut chips and béarnaise sauce, or cottage pie of local venison with Chantenay carrots. All this in a converted 15th-century watermill bursting with character and charm right by the river (the terrace is a treat). Local produce is central to the menu, the atmosphere unpretentious, and a proper espresso the icing on the cake.

Times 12-2.30/6-9.30

DORCHESTER **Map 4 SY69**

Sienna

– see opposite page

Summer Lodge Country House Hotel, Restaurant & Spa

EVERSHOT **Map 4 ST50**

Modern British NOTABLE WINE LIST

Creative country-house cooking in a pastoral setting

01935 482000
Fore St DT2 0JR
e-mail: summer@relais.com
web: www.summerlodgehotel.com
dir: 1.5m off A37 between Yeovil and Dorchester

A country-house spa hotel in the heart of tranquil Dorset, Summer Lodge feels a little like one of those well-kept secrets. Once a dower house, and partly designed by Wessex author Thomas Hardy, it has been decorated with an English pastoral air, with the green and reddish-pink hues of a garden in summer predominating in the main dining room. A conservatory extension affords views of the real thing. The welcome level of informality in the service reassures us that we're all on the same side, and the cooking, while firmly in the country-house idiom, nonetheless encompasses some appealing creative touches. A quartet of seared scallops on a swipe of parsley sauce is accompanied by a new take on choucroute, lightly pickled white cabbage and caraway seeds, adding contrast. Sweetly tender Creedy Carver duck makes a majestic main course, served alongside a vol-au-vent of spring vegetables in a glossy jus studded with golden raisins. Dessert might be an intense banana parfait crunchy with hazelnuts, topped with sharp lemon sorbet, sauced with swirls of caramel. Extras such as the foie gras 'crème brûlée' appetiser and fine breads add value to the whole package.

Chef Steven Titman **Owner** Red Carnation Hotels **Times** 12-2.30/7-9.30 **Prices** Fixed L 3 course £28, Tasting menu £75, Starter £14.50-£17.95, Main £21.95-£34.95, Dessert £11-£12.95, Service included, Groups min 12 service 12.5% **Wines** 1500 bottles over £20, 15 bottles under £20, 15 by glass **Notes** Tasting menu 8 course, Sunday L, Vegetarian available, Dress restrictions, No shorts, T-shirts or sandals, Jackets pref, Civ Wed 30 **Seats** 60, Pr/dining room 20 **Children** Portions, Menu **Parking** 60

EVERSHOT Map 4 ST50

The Acorn Inn

Modern British

Romantic old inn in Hardy country

☎ 01935 83228
28 Fore St DT2 0JW
e-mail: stay@acorn-inn.co.uk
dir: 2m off A37, between Dorchester and Yeovil. In village centre

This charming 16th-century village inn located in picturesque Evershot has oodles of character in its bar and dining room with low beams, flagged floors and roaring log fires. It has a genuinely relaxed atmosphere, helped along by the staff. If you're on a Thomas Hardy pilgrimage, you may be interested to know that the inn was said to have inspired *Tess of the D'Urbervilles* Sow and Acorn inn. The seasonally-changing menu, plus daily specials board of modern British fare, might feature scallops with parsnip cream and crispy pancetta and a main course of braised and rolled shoulder of lamb, pan haggerty and seasonal vegetables.

Chef Justin Mackenzie **Owner** Red Carnation Hotels **Times** 12-2/7-9 **Prices** Food prices not confirmed for 2011. Please telephone for details **Wines** 29 bottles over £20, 7 bottles under £20, 8 by glass **Notes** Sunday L, Vegetarian available **Seats** 45, Pr/dining room 35 **Children** Portions **Parking** 40

Summer Lodge Country House Hotel, Restaurant & Spa

– *see page 141*

FARNHAM Map 4 ST91

The Museum Inn

Modern British

Gastro-pub with accomplished cooking and contemporary vibe

☎ 01725 516261
DT11 8DE
e-mail: enquiries@museuminn.co.uk
dir: 12m S of Salisbury, 7m N of Blandford Forum on A354

The museum in question once housed the collection of artefacts gathered by eminent Victorian ethnologist and archaeologist General Augustus Lane Fox Pitt Rivers. The exhibition is no more, but the brick and thatch inn built to put up its visitors is still going strong, showing the enduring attraction of good food and drink and convivial company. A contemporary facelift has sharpened up the interior, but not to the detriment of its original flagstone floors and cosy nooks filled with the background thrum of contented diners and chirpy drinkers. Eat in the buzzy bar, or if you prefer a posher setting, there's the Shed, a light-flooded barn-like dining room. The menu is the same in both venues, a polished modern British affair that produces full-on flavours from superb Dorset ingredients: an earthy starter of pig's head is served with chorizo, capers, apple and a crispy pig's ear, followed by cannon, shoulder and sweetbreads of Dorset spring lamb teamed with dauphinoise potatoes, smoked peppers and roasting juices.

Chef Owen Sullivan **Owner** David Sax **Times** 12-2/7-9.30 Closed 25 Dec **Prices** Starter £6.95-£11.95, Main £16.50-£22.50, Dessert £6.95-£8.50, Service optional **Wines** 120 bottles over £20, 28 bottles under £20, 12 by glass **Notes** Tasting menu available, Sunday L, Vegetarian available **Seats** 80, Pr/dining room 30 **Children** Portions, Menu **Parking** 20, On street

MAIDEN NEWTON Map 4 SY59

Le Petit Canard

Modern British, French

Honest, accomplished cooking in pretty village restaurant

☎ 01300 320536
Dorchester Rd DT2 0BE
e-mail: craigs@le-petit-canard.co.uk
web: www.le-petit-canard.co.uk
dir: In centre of Maiden Newton, 8m W of Dorchester

In its 350-year-life the cottagey building has been a coaching inn amongst other things, and for the last 10 years it has been in the capable hands of Gerry and Cathy Craig. It is indeed as diminutive as the name suggests, with beams and exposed stone combining well with the traditional furnishings and palette of pastel colours. Harmony reigns between front-of-house and kitchen as the husband-and-wife-team run the place with charm and efficiency. Gerry's cooking is imbued with influences from these shores and across the Channel, plus a few ideas from the Far East. Honest and well-executed dishes might include seared scallops with bacon and cream, slow-roast belly pork with cider gravy and crackling, and to finish, perhaps sticky toffee pudding with caramel sauce and cream.

Chef Gerry Craig **Owner** Mr & Mrs G Craig **Times** 12-2/7-9 Closed Mon, L all week (ex 1st & 3rd Sun in month), D Sun **Prices** Fixed D 3 course £32-£35, Service optional **Wines** 18 bottles over £20, 13 bottles under £20, 6 by glass **Notes** Sunday L, Vegetarian available, Dress restrictions, Smart casual preferred **Seats** 28 **Parking** On street/village car park

POOLE Map 4 SZ09

Harbour Heights Hotel

Modern British, French

Modern bistro with unbeatable harbour views

☎ 01202 707272
Haven Rd, Sandbanks BH13 7LW
e-mail: enquiries@harbourheights.net
dir: From A338 follow signs to Sandbanks, restaurant on left past Canford Cliffs

After a 21st-century boutique makeover, this 1920s hotel on top of a hill has a classy new look. Harbour Heights is just a short walk from the sea, and has sweeping views over Poole Harbour, Brownsea Island and the Purbecks, best appreciated from the sprawling alfresco terrace for a real Riviera touch, or when the weather does its worst, through vast floor-to-ceiling picture windows in the contemporary, open-plan brasserie. Top- quality local produce forms the backbone of the kitchen's creative modern repertoire. Poole Bay oysters are a great way to start, or go for grilled salmon medallions with citrus quinoa salad, and tomato and basil coulis. Moving on, pan-fried cod may be teamed with clams and mussels, bouillabaisse broth and new potatoes, while chargrilled pork loin is served with marjoram potato rösti, onion purée, Savoy cabbage and wholegrain mustard jus.

Times 12-2.30/7-9.30

Haven Hotel

◎◎ Modern British V

Delightful Poole Bay views and confident modern cooking

☎ 01202 707333
161 Banks Rd, Sandbanks BH13 7QL
e-mail: reservations@havenhotel.co.uk
dir: Follow signs to Sandbanks Peninsula; hotel next to Swanage ferry departure point

Radio pioneer Guglielmo Marconi deservedly made a few quid with his invention of the radio telegraph, the first step in the global communications network, and chose to live in this house on this spot. He had a keen eye as well as a keen brain. With its enticing art-deco entrance, the hotel is geared up for the 21st-century visitor, with spas, bars and the appealing La Roche restaurant. The views across the water are quite something and when the sun is shining, a table on the terrace is as evocative as many a Mediterranean vista. The sharp, French-influenced menu makes the most of local ingredients from sustainable sources. Start, perhaps, with some spanking fresh Poole Harbour rock oysters with the customary shallot dressing, then move onto roast fillet of pork with a lasagne made with the belly meat and caramelised onions, plus Bramley apple, salsify and smoked bacon, and finished with the roasting juices.

Chef Claudio Norbotello **Owner** Mr J Butterworth
Times 12-2.30/7-9.30 **Prices** Fixed L 2 course fr £20, Fixed D 3 course fr £26, Starter £6-£14, Main £15-£56, Dessert £6.50-£14, Service optional **Wines** 82 bottles over £20, 8 bottles under £20, 12 by glass **Notes** Sunday L, Vegetarian menu, Dress restrictions, No shorts or beach wear, Civ Wed 99 **Seats** 80, Pr/dining room 156 **Children** Portions, Menu **Parking** 90

Hotel du Vin Poole

◎ Modern British, French

European bistro classics in a Georgian townhouse

☎ 01202 685666
Thames St BH15 1JN
dir: A350 into town centre follow signs to Channel Ferry/ Poole Quay, left at bridge, 1st left is Thames St

The former Mansion House hotel, an elegant Georgian building just off Poole's bustling harbourfront, was revamped by Hotel du Vin in their trademark boutique style in 2008. The swish facelift swept in a more Gallic tone, a buzzier vibe and a more open, lighter feel in the bistro, with wood floors, leather banquette seating and quality glassware on bare polished wood tables. Wine buffs can savour the expertly-chosen, French dominated list, while youthful, helpful staff serve modern bistro dishes; start, perhaps, with twice-baked Dorset cheddar soufflé with herb cream, and follow on with smoked haddock cake with watercress purée, poached egg and horseradish butter, or rib-eye steak with green peppercorn sauce.

Times 12.30-2/7-10

The Rising Sun

◎◎ British NEW

Skilful cooking in popular gastro-pub

☎ 01202 771246 & 01202 471858
3 Dear Hay Ln BH15 1NZ
dir: From A349, take A350 signed Poole

For many years a pub serving Thai food, The Rising Sun has been transformed - in looks and cooking style - into the very model of a modern gastro-pub. Inside it's all very stylish, with black leather banquettes, bare wooden tables, neutral coloured walls, white pillars and lamps dotted about. There are lots of intimate little nooks and crannies, a couple of open fires for colder nights, a terrace for dining alfresco, and a relaxing lounge-bar with tub chairs and sofas. Head chef Greg Etheridge and brother Phil employ a lightness of touch on top-quality local ingredients, producing a menu of pub classics and brasserie-style dishes. Start with a textbook pea, mint and feta risotto, following on with plump salmon fishcakes and a well-made dark chocolate fondant to finish.

Chef Greg Etheridge **Owner** Dick Goemaas
Times 12-2.30/6-9.30 Closed D Sun **Prices** Starter £4.75-£9.95, Main £8.95-£19.95, Dessert £5.95-£6.50, Service optional, Groups min 12 service 10% **Wines** 15 bottles over £20, 16 bottles under £20, 14 by glass **Notes** Sunday L, Vegetarian available, Dress restrictions, Smart casual **Seats** 65, Pr/dining room 16 **Children** Portions **Parking** Car park opposite

Sandbanks Hotel

◎ Mediterranean, European V

Vibrant beachside brasserie

☎ 01202 707377 & 709884
15 Banks Rd, Sandbanks BH13 7PS
e-mail: reservations@sandbankshotel.co.uk
dir: From Poole or Bournemouth, follow signs to Sandbanks Peninsula. Hotel on left along peninsula

Stratospheric property prices in the Sandbanks area of Poole have become so legendary in recent years that people forget the real reason the place is worth a visit, namely a fantastic seven-mile Blue Flag beach. The waterside hotel sits in pole position, its terrace and garden with their toes in the sand, looking across Poole Bay. The Sandbanks Brasserie will never want for customers, thanks to its glorious beachside setting and an octagonal layout that gives just about everyone a sea view - but it doesn't sit on its laurels: the food is up to the mark too, on a menu majoring in appealing, straightforward modern brasserie dishes. Expect the likes of seared scallops with celeriac purée, chorizo and baby clams, followed by turbot teamed with baby spinach, white onion purée and seared squid.

Chef Paul Harper **Owner** Mr J Butterworth
Times 12-3/6-10 Closed Mon-Tue, D Sun **Prices** Fixed L 2 course £10-£18, Fixed D 3 course £25, Starter £6.50-£9.50, Main £13.50-£19, Dessert £5-£6, Service optional **Wines** 73 bottles over £20, 10 bottles under £20, 17 by glass **Notes** Sunday L, Vegetarian menu, Dress restrictions, Smart casual, Civ Wed 80 **Seats** 65, Pr/dining room 25 **Children** Portions, Menu **Parking** 112

PORTLAND Map 4 SY67

The Bluefish Restaurant

Modern European

Flavourful cooking a stone's throw from Chesil Beach

☎ 01305 822991
15-17a Chiswell DT5 1AN
e-mail: thebluefish@tesco.net
web: www.thebluefishcafe.co.uk
dir: Take A354 by Chesil Bank, off Victoria Square in Portland, over rdbt towards Chesil Beach, next to 72hr free car park

This simple, unpretentious and much-loved neighbourhood eatery is located on the ground floor of a 400-year-old Portland stone building wedged between Portland Harbour and Chesil Beach. Dine in one of the two interconnecting dining rooms under twinkling lights from ceiling spots and tea-lights dotted around, or go alfresco in the summer. The atmosphere is relaxed and welcoming and the food is gutsy, flavour packed and refreshingly simple, with effective and intelligent ingredient combinations. With the sea just a stone's throw away, the modern European menu offers plenty of fish and seafood, but there are good meat choices, too. Expect Galician-style braised octopus with capers, parsley and paprika, followed by sea bream with squid ink risotto and artichoke pesto.

Times 12-3/6.45-9 Closed Mon & Tue, L Wed-Fri, D Sun (in Winter)

SHAFTESBURY Map 4 ST82

The Byzant

Modern British

Appealing menu in picture-postcard Dorset

☎ 01747 853355
Best Western Royal Chase Hotel, Royal Chase Roundabout SP7 8DB
e-mail: royalchasehotel@btinternet.com
dir: On rdbt at A350 & A30 junction (avoid town centre)

Named after an ancient rite that allowed the townsfolk of Shaftesbury to draw water from a local well, the restaurant of this welcoming Georgian hotel in rolling Dorset countryside is run with a friendly attitude. Add in an unbuttoned ambience, and good-value food that aims for all-round satisfaction, and you're on to a winner. Expect starters along the lines of black pudding and apple terrine with caramelised grape chutney and toasted brioche, ahead of grilled salmon served with saffron potatoes, buttered asparagus and lemon butter sauce, or local meat fans might go for a Dorset sirloin steak with horseradish mash and red onion gravy.

Times 12-2/7-10

Le Chanterelle

French, British

Ambitious Anglo-French cooking with a twist

☎ 01747 852821
Sherborne Causeway SP7 9PX
e-mail: le_chanterelle@yahoo.co.uk
dir: On A30 from Shaftsbury to Yeovil

A former cottage with roaring log fire and many original features intact, the family-run Chanterelle has a modern, bright décor which suits the old building nicely. In the kitchen, there's a good deal of confidence and ambition in the modern Anglo-French cooking, the complex and immaculately presented dishes showing considerable class. Start with a twice-baked Denhay cheddar soufflé or the contemporary pairing of slow-braised daube of pork with roasted langoustines and a light ginger jus. Follow on with pan-fried fillet of venison with a venison faggot, served with creamy Savoy cabbage, a red wine poached pear and walnuts. And to finish, indulge in a hot chocolate fondant with chestnut ice cream and caramelised banana.

Chef Ryan Lamb **Owner** Susan Lamb **Times** 12-3/7-9.30 Closed Mon-Tue **Prices** Food prices not confirmed for 2011. Please telephone for details **Wines** 35 bottles over £20, 15 bottles under £20, 9 by glass **Notes** Sunday L, Vegetarian available, Dress restrictions, Smart casual **Seats** 32 **Children** Portions

La Fleur de Lys Restaurant with Rooms

British, French

Traditional cooking in charming town-centre hotel

☎ 01747 853717
Bleke St SP7 8AW
e-mail: info@lafleurdelys.co.uk
dir: Junct A350/A30

A girls' boarding school in a previous life, since the early 1990s this restaurant with rooms has earned a good reputation for its French-inflected cooking. The L-shaped dining room is traditionally dressed with fine linen and china, candles flicker in the evening, and there's a homely lounge in which to nurse a pre-dinner drink. The small kitchen team sources good quality ingredients and puts them to good use in a range of Anglo-French dishes, with some broader European preparations as well. Thus, hot lobster ravioli is dressed with a Dijon mustard sauce, while main-course honey-roasted breast of guinea fowl comes with wild mushrooms in a creamy tarragon and brandy sauce. An inventive honey, halva and fig crème brûlée served with sesame brandy snaps is an enticing finish.

Chef D Shepherd & M Preston **Owner** D Shepherd, M Preston & M Griffin **Times** 12-2.30/7-10.30 Closed 3 wks Jan, L Mon-Tue, D Sun **Prices** Fixed L 2 course £23-£24, Fixed D 3 course £30, Starter £6-£10, Main £18-£26, Dessert £6-£8, Service optional **Wines** 180 bottles over £20, 20 bottles under £20, 8 by glass **Notes** Sunday L, Vegetarian available, Dress restrictions, Smart casual, No T-shirts **Seats** 45, Pr/dining room 12 **Children** Portions **Parking** 10

SHERBORNE Map 4 ST61

Eastbury Hotel

Modern British

Contemporary cooking in an attractive Dorset townhouse

☎ 01935 813131
Long St DT9 3BY
e-mail: enquiries@theeastburyhotel.com
dir: 5m E of Yeovil, follow brown signs for The Eastbury Hotel

The boutique townhouse hotel, with its handsome stone-built façade and one-acre walled garden, is just a short stroll from the centre of Sherborne. It's the kind of place where time ticks along at its own reassuringly sedate pace, although staff lack nothing in ready efficiency. The dining room is a split-level affair, the higher level within the main building, the rest within a conservatory-style extension. A contemporary sensibility informs the cooking, as witnessed in a starter pairing of seared scallops and braised chicken wings, accompanied by langoustine jelly, or a main-course autumn serving of locally shot partridge, with thyme gnocchi, and an array of supporting vegetables. Desserts might include slow-cooked seasonal rhubarb, served with mascarpone and crushed ginger nuts.

Chef Brett Sutton **Owner** Mr & Mrs P King **Times** 12-2/7-9.30 Closed L Sun **Prices** Fixed L 2 course £19-£22, Fixed D 3 course £36-£38, Tasting menu £45, Service optional, Groups min 6 service 10% **Wines** 61 bottles over £20, 30 bottles under £20, 6 by glass **Notes** Tasting menu 7 course, Vegetarian available, Civ Wed 80 **Seats** 40, Pr/dining room 12 **Children** Portions, Menu **Parking** 20

The Grange at Oborne

Modern British

Confident cooking in country-house hotel with pretty gardens

01935 813463
Oborne DT9 4LA
e-mail: reception@thegrange.co.uk
dir: From A30 turn left at sign & follow road through village to hotel

Set in beautiful gardens in a tiny hamlet just one mile from Sherborne itself, this 200-year-old country-house hotel built of Purbeck stone is handsome enough to make a grand wedding venue. The candlelit restaurant is also part of the appeal. It's a smart and comfortable room with well-spaced, linen-clad tables and views of the floodlit garden and fountain through lofty Georgian windows. In the kitchen, locally-sourced produce is king and is put to good use on the seasonal menu. Start with spiced Lyme Regis crab pointed up by pink grapefruit and served with green bean and artichoke heart salad and a honey and lime dressing. Next up, perhaps a roasted loin of Dorset venison with mushrooms, baby figs, buttered spinach, apple and ginger galette and rum jus. Finish with rhubarb and apple Charlotte served with rhubarb and ginger sorbet.

Chef Nick Holt **Owner** Mr & Mrs K E Mathews **Times** 12-1.30/7-9 Closed D Sun **Prices** Fixed L 2 course £18.95-£20, Fixed D 3 course £31-£34, Service optional **Wines** 18 bottles over £20, 24 bottles under £20, 5 by glass **Notes** Sunday L, Vegetarian available, Dress restrictions, Smart casual, Civ Wed 120 **Seats** 30, Pr/dining room 120 **Children** Portions **Parking** 50

The Green

Modern British

Modern British cooking near Sherborne Abbey

01935 813821
3 The Green DT9 3HY
e-mail: green.restaurant@tiscali.co.uk
dir: A30 towards Milborne Port, at top of Greenhill turn right at mini rdbt. Restaurant located on the left

Your sat nav may tell you otherwise, but The Green is a little way from its advertised postcode. However, when the smart green painted woodwork hoves into view, you know you've made it. The team have made the most of this Grade II listed building, keeping the heart and soul of the old place, whilst dressing it up nicely. Service is pleasingly unfussy and genial and considerable effort has been made to keep local produce at the heart of the action. Beetroot-cured gravad lax with pickled cucumber and dill mustard is a simple, sincere first course, before the likes of Dorset rose veal, flavoured with rosemary and lemon, and served up with almondine potatoes, carrots and hispi cabbage. The intelligent, well-judged modern British style continues at dessert stage, with puds such as pannacotta flavoured with passionfruit and mangoes, and served with candied Macadamia nuts.

Chef Michael Rust **Owner** Michael & Judith Rust **Times** 12-2/7-9 Closed 2 wks Jan,1 wk Jun,1 wk Sep, BHs, Xmas, Sun-Mon **Prices** Starter £6-£8, Main £9.50-£18, Dessert £6.95, Service optional, Groups min 8 service 10% **Wines** 19 bottles over £20, 31 bottles under £20, 12 by glass **Notes** Vegetarian available **Seats** 40, Pr/dining room 25 **Parking** On street, car park

SYDLING ST NICHOLAS Map 4 SY69

The Greyhound Inn

International NEW

Popular village inn with good, unfussy cooking

01300 341303
26 High St DT2 9PD
e-mail: info@thegreyhound.net

You couldn't ask for a more welcoming foodie pub than this quintessential Dorset local wrapped in lush Hardy countryside. The Greyhound is a gorgeous 17th-century inn with a walled garden in a picturesque village - step into the flagstoned bar and you are greeted with convivial banter, good local ales and food cooked with care and intelligence. The kitchen knows its business and keeps things simple, allowing the flavours of top-notch local materials to speak for themselves. A simple but effective starter teams pigeon breast with oxtail faggot, port wine and shallot marmalade. Next up, an excellent piece of pan-fried brill is served with wilted red chard, local mussels and a light broth pepped up with saffron. Almond tart with vanilla ice cream wraps things up in the comfort zone.

Chef Dan Clarke & Dervke Tee **Owner** John Ford, Karen Trimby, Ron Hobson & Cherry Ball **Times** 12-2/6.30-9 Closed 25-26 Dec, D Sun **Prices** Starter £4.50-£7.50, Main £11-£19, Dessert £4.95-£5.95, Service optional **Wines** 11 bottles over £20, 23 bottles under £20 **Notes** Sunday L, Vegetarian available **Seats** 60, Pr/dining room 30 **Children** Portions, Menu **Parking** 20

WAREHAM Map 4 SY98

Kemps Country House

International

Country-house dining in Thomas Hardy country

0845 8620315 & 01929 462563
East Stoke BH20 6AL
e-mail: info@kempscountryhouse.co.uk
web: www.kempshotel.com
dir: A352 between Wareham & Wool

Close to the Dorset coastline and with views across the Frome Valley and Purbeck Hills, this sensitively refurbished Victorian former rectory is home to a charming country-house restaurant. It's all very traditional and soothingly calm within. The menu follows a broad path which goes from international classics such as Caesar salad and Peking-style duck to more inventive dishes such as a main-course lightly-spiced Moroccan monkfish served with rustic chick pea, cumin and coriander purée and chermoula infused oil. There's a bespoke steak menu, too, and save room for comforting desserts such as warm Dorset pear cake with clotted cream and nutmeg.

Chef Matt Allen **Owner** John Smyth **Times** 12-3/6.30-9.30 **Prices** Fixed L 2 course £12.95, Fixed D 2 course £12.95, Starter £4.95-£7.25, Main £9.95-£21.95, Dessert £5-£6.95 **Wines** 6 bottles over £20, 17 bottles under £20 **Notes** Fixed D ALC, Sunday L, Vegetarian available, Dress restrictions, Smart casual **Seats** 60, Pr/dining room 20 **Children** Portions, Menu **Parking** 50

WEYMOUTH Map 4 SY67

Moonfleet Manor

Modern British

Med-influenced cooking on the Dorset coast

01305 786948
Fleet DT3 4ED
e-mail: info@moonfleetmanor.com
dir: A354 from Dorchester, right into Weymouth at Manor Rdbt, right at next rdbt, left at next rdbt, up hill (B3157) then left, 2m towards sea

The trim Georgian manor house overlooks Chesil Beach and the Fleet Lagoon near Weymouth, in a photogenic stretch of Dorset coastline. The dining room makes the most of those marine views, and on summer days, lunch or dinner can be taken on the decked patio, with the whispering of the tide not far off. A fresh, breezy style of Mediterranean-influenced modern British food is offered, taking in monkfish carpaccio with marinated crayfish, cucumber and avocado, roast breast of guinea fowl with an open raviolo of wild mushrooms and asparagus, served with pea purée and thyme foam, and chocolate and mascarpone crème brûlée with Amaretto ice cream. The hotel makes a virtue of its child-friendliness: children will be sure to relish the option of their own high tea, served buffet-style, with not an item of processed food in sight.

Times 12.30-2/7-9.30

WEYMOUTH *continued*

Perry's Restaurant

British, French

Waterside location for good honest food

01305 785799
4 Trinity Rd, The Old Harbour DT4 8TJ
e-mail: perrysrestaurant@hotmail.co.uk
dir: On western side of old harbour - follow signs for Brewers Quay

This long-established Weymouth eatery continues to deliver the goods with a menu reflecting its location and the seasons. The waterside position offers a superb opportunity to watch the waterborne comings and goings so window seats are popular at this intimate restaurant. The lovely old building set over two floors dates back to Georgian times and is the setting for some technically ambitious cooking. Dishes are well-executed yet still retain an honesty about them; expect ham hock and wood pigeon terrine with baby herb salad, pear and saffron, followed by main-course rosemary and prosciutto wrapped cod fillet with lemon and herb crushed potatoes, confit peppers and baby caper and anchovy dressing. The excellent wine list is a real boon.

Times 12-2/7-9.30 Closed 25-27 Dec, 1 Jan, Mon (winter), L Mon (summer), D Sun (winter)

WIMBORNE MINSTER — Map 5 SZ09

Les Bouviers Restaurant with Rooms

French

Restaurant with rooms offering a taste of France

01202 889555
Arrowsmith Rd, Canford Magna BH21 3BD
e-mail: info@lesbouviers.co.uk
web: www.lesbouviers.co.uk
dir: 1.5m S of Wimborne on A349, turn left onto A341. In 1m turn right into Arrowsmith Rd. 300yds, 2nd property on right

Chef-proprietor James Coward has clocked up almost two decades at the helm of Les Bouviers and is still going great guns after relocating three years ago to this smart modern restaurant with rooms in five acres of landscaped grounds with a lake and a stream. It's a great spot on several fronts: Bournemouth and Wimborne are a short drive away, yet the place feels secluded and remote, and the best produce from Dorset farms plus fish and seafood landed in Poole harbour is readily to hand. Inside, a country-house ambience prevails - expect opulent shades of claret and gold and modern artworks on the walls, and elaborate cooking rooted in the classics. Accents of France and the Mediterranean run through various fixed-price menus offering a wide choice, starting, perhaps, with roasted quail with home-smoked duck breast, mushy peas and a wine and oregano reduction. Moving on, local sea bass is teamed with star anise, braised fennel, grilled courgettes and Pastis and dill butter sauce, or local meat fans might go for roasted best end of lamb in herb crumbs with fondant potato, carrot tarte Tatin, buttered spinach and mustard sauce.

Chef James Coward **Owner** James & Kate Coward **Times** 12-2.15/7-9.30 Closed D Sun **Prices** Fixed L 2 course £16.95-£18.95, Fixed D 3 course £29.95, Starter £15-£20, Main £25-£35, Dessert £8-£10, Service optional, Groups min 7 service 10% **Wines** 100+ bottles over £20, 100+ bottles under £20, 24 by glass **Notes** ALC 2 course £39, Tasting menu 7 course (incl wine), Sunday L, Vegetarian available, Dress restrictions, No ripped jeans or shorts, Civ Wed 100 **Seats** 50, Pr/dining room 120 **Children** Portions, Menu **Parking** 50

CO DURHAM

BEAMISH — Map 19 NZ25

Beamish Park Hotel

Modern International

Inventive food against a thoroughly modern backdrop

01207 230666
Beamish Burn Rd NE16 5EG
e-mail: reception@beamish-park-hotel.co.uk
web: www.beamish-park-hotel.co.uk
dir: A1 junct 63 onto A693 Stanley. Exit rdbt onto A6076, hotel 2m on right

Newcastle's buzzing city centre is a mere 10-minute drive from this stylish modern hillside hotel by Beamish's renowned North of England Open Air Museum - although, many guests get no further than the PGA golf academy next door. The conservatory bistro is a funky place, with a modern brasserie feel, and an appealing modern menu to match. Choice pickings from the hotel's garden find their way into the larder, along with bountiful supplies from local producers. The kitchen's approach to revisiting classic dishes with imagination might produce a starter of home-made black pudding with a poached egg and devilled gravy, followed by pot-roast beef brisket teamed with chestnut suet pudding, bashed carrot and swede with rich gravy. Puddings keep the good ideas coming - perhaps a burnt lemon curd cream with poached Yorkshire rhubarb and shortbread.

Chef Christopher Walker **Owner** William Walker **Times** 12-2.30/7-10.30 **Prices** Starter £4.95-£10.50, Main £10.95-£18, Service optional **Wines** 16 bottles over £20, 19 bottles under £20, 9 by glass **Notes** Sunday L, Vegetarian available, Dress restrictions, Smart casual preferred, Civ Wed 100 **Seats** 70, Pr/dining room 150 **Children** Portions **Parking** 100

BILLINGHAM — Map 19 NZ42

Wynyard Hall Hotel

Modern British NEW

Modern British cooking in a grand mansion

01740 644811
Wynyard Village TS22 5NF
dir: A19 onto A1027 towards Stockton. At rdbt 3rd exit B1274 (Junction Rd). At next rdbt 3rd exit onto A177 (Durham Rd). Right onto Wynyard Rd signed Wolviston. Left into estate at gatehouse

A long winding drive leads to this magnificent 19th-century mansion set in vast grounds overlooking a lake. Be wowed in the stately dining room, a grand space with high ceilings, twinkling chandeliers, huge military portraits and fabulous red wallpaper; it's an impressive setting for some sound modern British cooking using seasonal ingredients, including home-grown fruit and vegetables. A typical meal may take in mackerel escabèche with vodka gazpacho and salt-and-pepper squid, followed by roast garlic pork belly with red wine sauce, and a selection of delicious mini crème brûlées (green tea, citrus, chocolate and ginger, almond biscotti).

DARLINGTON — Map 19 NZ21

Hansard's

British

Contemporary cooking in 12th-century castle hotel

01325 485470
Best Western, Walworth Castle Hotel, Walworth DL2 2LY
e-mail: enquiries@walworthcastle.co.uk
dir: A1 junct 58, follow A68 Corbridge for 1m. At rdbt keep left for 1m

It's not often you get to dine in a proper English castle, which is exactly what makes Hansard's rather special. Although the restaurant dates back *merely* to the 16th century, it's within 12th-century Walworth Castle, which has been run as a hotel since the 1980s. Under its current ownership the castle, in 18 acres of grounds, has been extensively refurbished, with Hansard's gaining a smart new look whilst retaining its period charms. Here, locally sourced, seasonal ingredients are put to good effect in modern British dishes such as Doreen's grilled black pudding triangle served with plum and apple chutney, and main-course roast organic chicken breast stuffed with spinach and asparagus, served with garlic and roast carrots. Save room for the apple and golden raisin crumble with cider sorbet.

Times 12-2/7-9.30 Closed L Mon-Sat

Headlam Hall

British, French

High quality produce in a Jacobean mansion

☎ 01325 730238
Headlam DL2 3HA
e-mail: admin@headlamhall.co.uk
dir: 8m W of Darlington off A67

Dating back to the 18th century, this impressive manor house stands in beautiful walled gardens surrounded by rolling countryside and retains many original features. The feeling of spaciousness extends to the restaurant, which is housed in a conservatory, and two further rooms, one with deep green walls, gilt mirrors and elegant pictures and the other a stately panelled space. British and French cooking techniques make good use of top quality ingredients. Think maple syrup glazed pork belly with cockles cooked in thyme and cider with a scrumpy reduction, a veggie main of caramelised onion and chicory marmalade open tartlet, blue cheese fritters, walnut and pear salad and a walnut dressing. Excellent spa facilities (there's also a spa brasserie) and a nine-hole golf course add to the appeal.

Chef David Hunter **Owner** J H Robinson
Times 12-2.30/7-9.30 Closed 25-26 Dec **Prices** Fixed L 2 course £13, Starter £7-£8.50, Main £15-£23, Dessert £7-£8.50, Service optional **Wines** 25 bottles over £20, 30 bottles under £20, 10 by glass **Notes** Sunday L, Vegetarian available, Dress restrictions, Smart casual, no shorts or T-shirts, Civ Wed 150 **Seats** 70, Pr/dining room 30 **Children** Portions, Menu **Parking** 80

DURHAM Map 19 NZ24

Bistro 21

Modern British, French V

Anglo-French bistro food in a converted farmhouse

☎ 0191 384 4354
Aykley Heads House, Aykley Heads DH1 5TS
e-mail: admin@bistrotwentyone.co.uk
dir: Off B6532 from Durham centre, pass County Hall on right & Dryburn Hospital on left. Turn right at double rdbt into Aykley Heads

Owned by north-east restaurant supremo Terry Laybourne, this converted farmhouse on the edge of Durham makes an imaginative setting for an Anglo-French bistro. The cooking gently updates the bistro idiom, so expect scallops with cucumber, kimchi, watercress and smoked apple juice, in among the chicken and foie gras parfait, mackerel with potato salad, fillet steak with wild mushrooms in red wine, and halibut with tartare sauce, mushy peas and chips. There's a separate vegetarian menu and desserts push all the right buttons with crème brûlée, fig tart, and treacle sponge and custard.

Chef Robbie Bell **Owner** Terence Laybourne
Times 12-2/6-10.30 Closed 25 Dec, 1 Jan, BHs, Sun **Prices** Fixed L 2 course fr £15, Fixed D 3 course fr £18, Starter £5.50-£10, Main £14.50-£25.50, Dessert £5-£7.50, Service added but optional 10% **Wines** 48 bottles over £20, 5 bottles under £20, 7 by glass **Notes** Early D menu available, Vegetarian menu **Seats** 55, Pr/dining room 20 **Children** Portions **Parking** 11

ROMALDKIRK Map 19 NY92

Rose & Crown Hotel

Traditional British

Cosy upmarket country inn in a quintessentially English setting

☎ 01833 650213
DL12 9EB
e-mail: hotel@rose-and-crown.co.uk
dir: 6m NW of Barnard Castle on B6277

You know you're on to a good thing as soon as you arrive in Romaldkirk: not one, but three village greens complete with Saxon church, village pump and stocks, bracket the Rose & Crown. After 20 years in the engine room, Chris and Alison Davy have their country inn running like a well-oiled machine on all levels; it is steeped in tradition, yet bang up-to-date where it matters. The creaky bar is the sort of place you dream of finding for a pint of Black Sheep on a winter's night by a sizzling log fire - you're welcome to eat here, but at dinner, many guests go for the romantic candlelit vibe of the elegant oak-panelled dining room. The kitchen buys locally and looks to French classics for its inspiration. Seared king scallops with leek and bacon risotto, pancetta and herb pesto kicks off a four-course dinner with full-on flavours; next, comes courgette and sweet pear soup before chargrilled calves' liver and bacon, confit onions, roasted rosemary potatoes and green peppercorn sauce.

Chef Chris Davy, Andrew Lee **Owner** Mr & Mrs C Davy
Times 12-1.30/7.30-9 Closed Xmas, L Mon-Sat
Prices Fixed L 3 course £17.95-£21, Fixed D 4 course £32.50-£38.50, Service optional **Wines** 46 bottles over £20, 20 bottles under £20, 14 by glass **Notes** Sunday L, Vegetarian available **Seats** 24 **Children** Portions **Parking** 24

SEAHAM Map 19 NZ44

The Ozone Restaurant

Asian Fusion Notable Wine List

East Asian spices in a state-of-the-art spa

☎ 0191 516 1400
Seaham Hall Hotel, Lord Byron's Walk SR7 7AG
e-mail: info@seaham-hall.co.uk
dir: Leave A1018 onto A19, at rdbt take 2nd exit onto B1285/Stockton Rd. Turn left at Lord Byron's Walk, in 0.3m turn right

A state-of-the-art spa hotel with luxurious treatment rooms, Seaham Hall also offers a number of stimulating eating options, not least this vibrantly flame-coloured restaurant, which deals predominantly in East Asian dishes. You could start with grilled goats' cheese, Parma ham and beetroot, but that would be to miss the more enlivening flavours and spices on offer in chick pea and Asian vegetables in yellow curry sauce. These are further elaborated in main courses that go from classic Thai green curry to duck breast roasted in five spice, served with pak choi in a soy and sesame dressing. To finish, there's a whole greengrocer's store of ice cream and sorbet fruit flavours.

Chef Andrew Laurie **Owner** von Essen Hotels
Times 11-5/6-9 Closed 25 Dec, D Sun **Prices** Starter £4.50-£7, Main £9.95-£16, Dessert £4.50, Service optional **Wines** 10 bottles over £20, 3 bottles under £20, 5 by glass **Notes** Vegetarian available, Dress restrictions, Smart casual, no robes after 6pm, Civ Wed 100 **Seats** 60 **Children** Portions **Parking** 200

Seaham Hall - The White Room Restaurant

Modern European V

Ambitious contemporary cooking in luxury spa hotel

☎ 0191 516 1400
Lord Byron's Walk SR7 7AG
e-mail: info@seaham-hall.co.uk
dir: A19 at 1st exit signed B1404 Seaham and follow signs to Seaham Hall

Seaham Hall is a luxurious hotel and spa with a flagship restaurant - The White Room - delivering classy modern European food which follows the seasons and puts fine north-eastern produce at the top of the agenda. The elegant Georgian façade displays the heritage of the building, a past which saw Lord Byron's wedding back in 1815, but today's hotel meets the demand for high-end comforts and 21st-century facilities. There's a certain

continued

SEAHAM ***continued***

timelessness to The White Room's restrained minimalism, with its neutral and natural tones and large floor-to-ceiling windows, while the views over the coast and countryside, and charming, professional service, put one at ease. Amuse-bouche such as foie gras parfait and celeriac mousse show a steady hand and a classical eye in the kitchen, but there is plenty of ambition and creativity, too, such as a first-course Atlantic halibut, in a busy dish with Whitby crab, gem lettuce, mussels and razor clams. Organic pork comes in a strikingly contemporary main course as honey-glazed belly, roast tenderloin and a brawn beignet, served with langoustines, pease pudding, butternut squash and leeks.

Chef Max Wilson **Owner** von Essen Hotels **Times** 12-2/7-10 Closed L Mon-Sat **Prices** Fixed L 3 course £30, Fixed D 3 course £50, Tasting menu £65-£80, Service optional **Wines** 350 bottles over £20, 6 bottles under £20, 25 by glass **Notes** Tasting menu 6 & 9 course, Sunday L, Vegetarian menu, Dress restrictions, Smart casual, Civ Wed 100 **Seats** 42, Pr/dining room 30 **Children** Portions **Parking** 145

SEDGEFIELD Map 19 NZ32

Best Western Hardwick Hall Hotel

Modern British

Basement restaurant in a venerable Durham location

☎ 01740 620253
TS21 2EH
e-mail: info@hardwickhallhotel.co.uk
dir: Off A1(M) junct 60 towards Sedgefield, left at 1st rdbt, hotel 400mtrs on left

The hall's foundations lie in the early 15th century, when it started out as a manor house. Much has changed since those days: it still lies in 120 acres of English parkland, but after a few million quid's worth of updating it provides 21st-century levels of comfort and service. The Ha Ha restaurant in the basement deserves attention: contemporary wooden floors, leather chairs and bistro tables make a thoroughly modish setting for an inventive menu of modern British dishes. A typical dinner might kick off with rare breed pork belly with prune and apple pudding and cider jus, ahead of North Sea monkfish combined unusually, but effectively, with confit duck spring roll, pak choi and red wine sauce.

Times 7-9.30

ESSEX

BRENTWOOD Map 6 TQ59

Marygreen Manor

Modern European V

International cuisine in Tudor hall

☎ 01277 225252
London Rd CM14 4NR
e-mail: info@marygreenmanor.co.uk
dir: M25 junct 28, onto A1023 over 2 sets of lights, hotel on right

Any meal in the high-beamed baronial hall of 16th-century Marygreen Manor is guaranteed to fizz with a certain sense of occasion. The vaulted ceiling, barley-twist columns, blackened timbers and coats of arms of Tudors Restaurant might seem the perfect setting for a medieval-themed banquet, but there's nothing archaic about the cooking. The kitchen dealeth not in roast ox, larks and lampreys, but rather in classic modern European dishes, skilfully cooked and built on well-sourced seasonal materials. Tiger prawns are served with confit pork belly, bok choy, mango, tomato and salmon caviar in a typical starter, while mains might include venison fillet with parsnip purée, baby beetroot, ceps and game jus. End with chocolate mousse with pain d'épice ice cream and Cassis jelly.

Chef Mr Majid Bourote **Owner** Mr S Bhattessa **Times** 12.30-2.30/7.15-10.15 Closed D Sun & BHs **Prices** Fixed L 2 course £13.50, Fixed D 3 course £22.50-£39.50, Starter £9.50, Main £25.50, Dessert £8.50, Service added but optional 12% **Wines** 80 bottles over £20, 21 bottles under £20, 7 by glass **Notes** Tasting menu 6 course, Sunday L, Vegetarian menu, Dress restrictions, No jeans or trainers, Civ Wed 60 **Seats** 80, Pr/dining room 85 **Children** Portions **Parking** 100

CHELMSFORD Map 6 TL70

County Hotel

Modern British

Town-centre hotel serving seasonal British cuisine

☎ 01245 455700
29 Rainsford Rd CM1 2PZ
e-mail: kioftus@countyhotelgroup.co.uk
dir: Off Chelmsford ring road close to town centre and A12 junct 18

Just a short stroll from the town centre and railway station, this family-run hotel is done out in a cheerful contemporary style. Leather seats in summery pastel shades of tangerine, ochre and jade add splashes of colour to the neutral uncluttered décor of the dining room, while a sunny terrace is just the job for alfresco dining when the weather allows. The kitchen makes good use of seasonal, locally-sourced produce in its repertoire of straightforward modern British cooking, starting with the likes of duck and ham hock terrine with celeriac remoulade and walnut bread; mains might offer lemon flattened chicken with creamed potatoes and Savoy cabbage, or slow-roasted pork belly with sage mash, apples and cider jus.

Chef Wayne Browning **Owner** Richard & Ginny Austin **Times** 12-2.30/6-10 **Prices** Fixed L 2 course £14.50-£30, Starter £4.50-£7.95, Main £11.25-£19.95, Dessert £4.50-£5.50 **Wines** 55 bottles over £20, 15 bottles under £20, 6 by glass **Notes** Sunday L, Vegetarian available **Seats** 64, Pr/dining room 50 **Children** Portions, Menu **Parking** 70

COGGESHALL Map 7 TL82

Baumann's Brasserie

British, French

Gutsy cooking in buzzy brasserie

☎ 01376 561453
4-6 Stoneham St CO6 1TT
e-mail: food@baumannsbrasserie.co.uk
dir: A12 from Chelmsford, exit at Kelvedon into Coggeshall. Restaurant in centre opposite clock tower

Located in a 16th-century half-timbered hall house in the heart of town, Baumann's is a buzzy and informal restaurant popular with regulars and visitors for over 20 years. The building was converted by ebullient restaurateur Peter Langan, of Langan's Brasserie fame, alongside his then young head chef Mark Baumann (these days chef-patron and star of TV). Antique chairs, stripped floors and whitewashed walls hung with colourful artwork provide an eclectic backdrop for the kitchen's innovative take on French and British dishes. Expect the likes of flaked hot-smoked salmon crumpet with lavender honey crème fraîche to start, followed by sautéed slivers of calves' liver with wild rocket and ricotta ravioli and merlot juices. And to finish, there's the house speciality: Mars Bar cheesecake with crushed Melba sauce and vanilla whipped cream.

Chef Mark Baumann, Chris Prichard **Owner** Baumann's Brasserie Ltd **Times** 12-2/7-9.30 Closed 2 wks Jan, Mon-Tue **Prices** Fixed L 2 course £10, Fixed D 3 course £23, Starter £5-£9, Main £15-£20, Dessert £6, Service optional **Wines** 20 bottles over £20, 24 bottles under £20, 11 by glass **Notes** Sunday L, Vegetarian available **Seats** 80 **Children** Portions **Parking** Opposite

White Hart Hotel

British, European

Modern classics in splendid medieval inn

01378 561654
Market End CO6 1NH
e-mail: 6529@greeneking.co.uk
dir: From A12 through Kelvedon & onto B1024 to Coggeshall

A delightful 15th-century inn in the centre of the market town of Coggeshall, the White Hart serves up European cuisine in a traditional pub setting. Public areas retain the medieval feel with lots of oak beams and roaring fires, while the two-level restaurant has formally dressed tables with flickering candles. The menu incorporates locally-sourced, seasonal produce in the likes of wild mushroom vol-au-vent, fillet of beef with vegetable fricassée and fig compôte and brandy and apple tart with crème anglaise. There's a bar and terrace menu, too.

Chef Richard Allan **Owner** Greene King
Times 12-2.30/7-9 **Prices** Starter £6-£9, Main £12.50-£24.95, Dessert £5-£9, Service optional **Wines** 29 bottles over £20, 20 bottles under £20, 8 by glass **Notes** Sunday L, Vegetarian available **Seats** 80, Pr/dining room 40 **Parking** 20

COLCHESTER **Map 13 TL92**

The North Hill Hotel

Modern British

Well-prepared food in a smartly-refurbished Colchester bistro

01206 574001
51 North Hill CO1 1PY
e-mail: info@northhillhotel.com
web: www.northhillhotel.com
dir: Follow signs for town centre. Up North Hill, hotel on right

You can't mess with the external appearance of a Grade II listed Georgian building in the heart of historic Colchester, but the inside of the North Hill Hotel comes as quite a surprise, looking rather chic and contemporary after a stylish facelift. Bright and swirly modern art adds a funky touch in the modish Green Room bistro, a style that suits the modern British cooking to a T. The kitchen works to the seasons with earthy bistro classics and a liking for local produce. Wood pigeon breast with braised Puy lentils and parsnip shavings, followed by confit Blythburgh pork belly, spiced Marsala sauce, roasted sweet potato and carrot mash and buttered curly kale show the style. Finish with a pear and frangipane tart with clotted cream.

Chef John Riddleston **Owner** Rob Brown
Times 12-2.30/6-9.30 **Prices** Food prices not confirmed for 2011. Please telephone for details **Wines** 13 bottles over £20, 21 bottles under £20, 13 by glass **Notes** Sunday L, Vegetarian available **Seats** 45 **Children** Portions **Parking** NCP opposite

DEDHAM **Map 13 TM03**

milsoms

International

Eclectic cooking in hip riverside brasserie

01206 322795
Stratford Rd CO7 6HN
e-mail: milsoms@milsomhotels.com
web: www.milsomhotels.com
dir: 7m N of Colchester, just off A12

Right by the river in a village near Colchester is to be found one of the more diverting branches of the Milsom Group. The split-level restaurant couldn't shun the country-house idiom more forcefully, with its no-bookings policy and little notepads on the tables on which you write down your own orders. People love it, as they also do the outdoor dining option on a heated terrace. The brasserie menu trades in notable dishes such as deep-fried squid with chilli and cucumber dipping sauce, North African-style roast lamb rump with toasted almond couscous, baba ghanoush and harissa, and peanut cookies with chocolate ice cream and chocolate sauce.

Chef Sarah Norman, Ben Rush **Owner** The Milsom Family
Times 12-9.30 **Prices** Starter £5.25-£13.95, Main £9.75-£24.95, Dessert £5.75-£6.75, Service optional **Wines** 34 bottles over £20, 16 bottles under £20, 11 by glass **Notes** Sunday L, Vegetarian available **Seats** 80, Pr/dining room 24 **Children** Portions, Menu **Parking** 60

The Sun Inn

Modern Italian **NEW**

Village pub with an Italian soul

01206 323351
High St CO7 6DF
e-mail: office@thesuninndedham.com
dir: In village centre opposite church

Lovingly restored and transformed from run-down village boozer to a classy dining destination, Piers Baker's timbered old coaching inn overflows with 16th-century charm and character. Both bar and dining areas boast blazing log fires, thick oak beams, rustic wooden floors and unclothed tables, alongside a contemporary décor, providing a relaxed and informal atmosphere in which to enjoy some good Italian cooking. Sound traditional techniques combine with fresh locally-sourced produce and quality Italian ingredients, such as cured meats, cheeses and oils, in uncomplicated, well-executed dishes. Perhaps an earthy, full-flavoured pasta starter with spicy Calabrian salami, radicchio and garlic, followed by a moist and succulent Gloucestershire Old Spot pork chop with beetroots, turnips and salsa verde. Leave room for strawberry ravioli with vanilla and cinnamon cream.

Times 12-2.30/6.30-9.30

Le Talbooth

Modern British NOTABLE WINE LIST

Ambitious modern cooking in beautiful Tudor house by the river

01206 323150
Gun Hill CO7 6HN
e-mail: talbooth@milsomhotels.com
web: www.milsomhotels.com
dir: 6m from Colchester follow signs from A12 to Stratford St Mary, restaurant on the left before village

The setting on the banks of the River Stour is rather special, as quintessentially English as you can imagine. Needless to say alfresco eating is a real treat here. In the same family for more than 50 years, the former toll house, dating from the Tudor period, oozes character and

continued

DEDHAM *continued*

charm and you can see why John Constable immortalised it in paint. Inside leaves no less of an impression, with original low beams, whitewashed walls and tables dressed to impress in their best whites. Expect cooking in the modern British vein: sea bass with cockle popcorn, herb pasta and broad bean and shrimp velouté, for example, might precede a dessert such as steamed treacle pudding with orange Chantiily cream and custard.

Le Talbooth

Chef Ian Rhodes, Tom Bushell **Owner** The Milsom Family **Times** 12-2/6.30-9 Closed D Sun (Oct-Apr) **Prices** Fixed L 2 course £22.50, Service included **Wines** 560 bottles over £20, 38 bottles under £20, 10 by glass **Notes** Sunday L, Vegetarian available, Dress restrictions, Smart casual, No jeans, Civ Wed 50 **Seats** 80, Pr/dining room 34 **Children** Portions, Menu **Parking** 50

FELSTED — Map 6 TL62

Reeves Restaurant

Modern British

Character building serving up top-notch East Anglian produce

☎ 01371 820996
Rumbles Cottage, Braintree Rd CM6 3DJ
e-mail: reevesrestaurant@tiscali.co.uk
dir: A120 E from Braintree, B1417 to Felsted

Housed in a 14th-century cottage which used to be the village shop, Reeves offers fine dining in the historic village of Felsted. The heavily timbered interior combined with low sloping ceilings lends a certain charm, as do the cheerful staff. Fresh flowers and candles set off the crisply laid tables. East Anglian ingredients crop up on the globally-influenced menu. You might find a petit leaf salad of tiger prawns, smoked salmon and baby mozzarella, with a light creamy blue cheese dressing, and a main-course pan-seared sea bass and red mullet on a spring onion and potato rösti with a garden herb beurre blanc. Lavender drizzle cake is a signature pudding. The top floor houses a lovely sitting room and small private dining room.

Times 12-2/7 Closed Mon-Wed

GREAT CHESTERFORD — Map 12 TL54

The Crown House

Modern British

Traditional cooking in a peaceful village setting

☎ 01799 530515
London Rd CB10 1NY
e-mail: stay@thecrownhouseonetel.net

History abounds at The Crown House. The smartly-restored coaching inn presents a Georgian façade, but inside, the plot thickens: parts of it pre-date Tudor times, and it is actually built on the ruins of the old Roman wall of Great Chesterford. Needless to say, the old place has heaps of character throughout, and an atmospheric oak-panelled restaurant kitted out with modern blond wood tables and blue high-backed chairs. In good weather, a terrace between the main house and the walled garden is a great spot for alfresco dining. Good, honest straightforward cooking built on great local materials is the order of the day - expect starters along the lines of chicken liver parfait with red onion marmalade, followed by pan-seared sea bass with crayfish risotto and hollandaise sauce, or pan-roasted loin of Gloucestershire Old Spot pork with white pudding, caramelised apple, scallop potatoes, and sage and cider jus.

Times 12-2/7-9

GREAT YELDHAM — Map 13 TL73

The White Hart

British, European NEW

Characterful old inn with contemporary cooking

☎ 01787 237250
Poole St CO9 4HJ
e-mail: mjwmason@yahoo.co.uk
dir: On A1017, between Halstead & Haverhill

It is a peach of a building, 500 years old and still going strong, and it's probably fair to say it has never been in such fine fettle. On the outside the black-and-white timber frontage would melt the heart of the most ardent modernist and inside a plethora of beams is a constant reminder that you're amid British architectural history. The restaurant has a modern European bent, name-checking local produce in a first course of breast of Yeldham Hall wood pigeon with wild mushrooms wrapped up in a cabbage parcel and finished with a deeply-flavoured port jus. Poached breast of chicken comes with chorizo, Puy lentils and a tian of Mediterranean vegetables, and maple and walnut crème brûlée comes with a home-made biscotti.

Chef Dominic Ash **Owner** Matthew Mason **Times** noon-mdnt Closed 25 Dec D **Prices** Starter £4.95-£11.95, Main £14.95-£24.95, Dessert £4.95-£9.95, Service optional, Groups min 7 service 10% **Wines** 39 bottles over £20, 23 bottles under £20, 7 by glass **Notes** Sunday L, Vegetarian available, Dress restrictions, Smart casual, Civ Wed 200 **Seats** 60, Pr/dining room 200 **Children** Portions, Menu **Parking** 50

HARWICH — Map 13 TM23

The Pier at Harwich

British, Seafood

Stellar seafood in stylish harbourside hotel

☎ 01255 241212
The Quay CO12 3HH
e-mail: pier@milsomhotels.com
web: www.milsomhotels.com
dir: A12 to Colchester then A120 to Harwich Quay

As locations for seafood restaurants go, they don't get much better than this. Up on the first floor of the Pier Hotel, a pleasingly four-square hotel given a classy modern makeover, the view from the Harbourside Restaurant takes in Harwich Quay together with the Stour and Orwell estuaries. It's a stylish space with a pewter bar, natural colours, leather banquettes and those views. The menu is focused on all the delights of the sea, much of it with local provenance assured. Perhaps a platter of smoked fish with a mild horseradish relish or Thai-flavoured salmon fishcakes to start, then a simple cold-poached lobster with lemon mayonnaise, or Dedham Vale sirloin steak if you must. Finish with a classic dark chocolate fondant with honeycomb ice cream. The Ha'penny bistro on the ground floor offers an informal alternative along with less of a fishy focus.

Chef Chris Oakley **Owner** The Milsom Family **Times** 12-2/6-9 Closed D 25 Dec **Prices** Fixed L 2 course £19.50, Starter £6.95-£15, Main £13.95-£35, Dessert £5.85-£6.80, Service added 10% **Wines** 82 bottles over £20, 25 bottles under £20, 6 by glass **Notes** Sunday L, Vegetarian available, Dress restrictions, Smart casual, Civ Wed 50 **Seats** 80, Pr/dining room 16 **Children** Portions, Menu **Parking** 20, On street, pay & display

MANNINGTREE Map 13 TM13

The Mistley Thorn

International

America meets Italy in Essex

01206 392821
High St, Mistley CO11 1HE
e-mail: info@mistleythorn.co.uk
web: www.mistleythorn.co.uk
dir: From A12 take A137 for Manningtree & Mistley

This charming restaurant with rooms in a former Georgian inn has a peach of a setting in the centre of the village right beside the River Stour. The bistro-style restaurant feels like it could be in New England, which is no surprise given the American heritage of chef-patron Sherri Singleton. There are terracotta tiles on the walls, exposed beams, tongue-and-groove walls and plenty of things to remind one of the waterside location, which goes for the menu, too, which is full of fresh local seafood. There are both American and Italian influences on display in dishes that show confidence in their simplicity. Start with smoked haddock chowder or steamed Cornish mussels, before moving onto Cioppino - a Cal-Ital seafood stew brimming with local fish, shellfish, tomato and herbs. There are meat (and vegetarian) options as well, such as the Mistley Thorn burger. Who could resist Chez Panisse chocolate cake with home-made coffee ice cream and chocolate sauce to finish? If the food leaves you feeling inspired, cookery classes are also available.

Chef Sherri Singleton, Rino Scalco **Owner** Sherri Singleton, David McKay **Times** 12-2.30/6.30-9.30 **Prices** Fixed L 2 course £11.95, Starter £4.95-£8.95, Main £10.25-£14.95, Dessert £5.50-£6.95, Service optional, Groups min 8 service 10% **Wines** 22 bottles over £20, 19 bottles under £20, 17 by glass **Notes** Sunday L, Vegetarian available **Seats** 75, Pr/dining room 28 **Children** Portions, Menu **Parking** 7

TENDRING Map 7 TM12

The Fat Goose

Modern British NEW

Fresh, local food in refurbished pub

01255 870060
Heath Rd CO16 0BX
e-mail: eat@fat-goose.co.uk
dir: A120 to Horsley Cross, follow B1035 to Tendring/ Thorpe-le-Soken. 1.5 m on right

A goose rather than a phoenix has risen from the ashes (or a state of disrepair at least) to become a smart roadside pub with a focus on food, and fresh, local food at that. It looks unassuming from the outside, but within a sensitive makeover has kept a country feel while bringing it up-to-date with some clean lines and comfortable touches such as Chesterfield armchairs in the bar area. The restaurant has been extended in a conservatory style and there is a large garden. Suffolk ham and gruyère soufflé is finished with a cheese and chive glaze among first courses, following on with steak and mushroom suet pudding or, from the daily-changing fish menu, baked salmon with creamed leeks, bacon and champ.

Chef Philip Hambrook-Moore **Owner** Philip Hambrook-Moore **Times** 12-2.30/6.30-9.30 **Prices** Fixed L 2 course fr £10, Starter £5-£7, Main £12-£19, Dessert £5-£7.50, Service optional, Groups min 8 service 10% **Wines** 37 bottles over £20, 15 bottles under £20, 15 by glass **Notes** Tasting menu available for groups 6-8, Sunday L, Vegetarian available **Seats** 100, Pr/dining room 50 **Children** Portions **Parking** 50

TOLLESHUNT KNIGHTS Map 7 TL91

The Camelot Restaurant at Five Lakes

Modern British

Modern British cooking in a multi-resourced hotel

01621 868888
Five Lakes Hotel, Golf, Country Club & Spa, Colchester Rd CM9 8HX
e-mail: enquiries@fivelakes.co.uk
dir: M25 junct 28, then on A12. At Kelvedon take B1024 then B1023 to Tolleshunt Knights, clearly marked by brown tourist signs

The Five Lakes hotel encompasses a country club, spa resort and golfing, so guests won't be short of something to do, while the range of eating options is almost as varied. The trump card is the Camelot Restaurant, where a sober decorative tone of burgundy and darkwood lends class to the expansive, split-level space. Contemporary British cuisine with one or two nods to French fashion is the order of the day, in a repertoire that might offer confit sea bass with pancetta, broad beans and ratte potatoes in tomato and basil dressing, beef fillet with braised ox cheek, pommes purée, leeks and mushrooms in a port jus, and apricot bread-and-butter pudding with Baileys custard and vanilla ice cream.

Times 7-10 Closed 26, 31 Dec, 1 Jan, Sun-Mon

GLOUCESTERSHIRE

ALMONDSBURY Map 4 ST68

Quarterjacks Restaurant

Modern British

Eclectic modern menu in vibrant room

01454 201090
Aztec Hotel & Spa, Aztec West BS32 4TS
e-mail: quarterjacks@shirehotels.com
dir: M5 junct 16/A38 towards city centre, hotel 200mtrs on right

Named after a famous Bristol clock, this modern British restaurant in the modern Aztec Hotel & Spa is in a great looking room, with a high vaulted ceiling (the cross-beams are Jacobean, no less) and a large open fire. Having said that, it is very much a contemporary-feeling space, which suits the Nordic style of the hotel; light-wood floors, bright and bold modern art on the walls, and a relaxed attitude from the staff. There's a pleasing emphasis on produce from the South West in dishes in a broad modern British vein which suit the relaxed vibe: tiger prawn tempura with chilli sauce and lime, followed by slow-cooked shank of salt marsh lamb with mint dumpling and vegetable broth. There's a self-service hors d'oeuvres table, plus an all-day menu.

Chef Mike Riordan **Owner** Shire Hotels **Times** 12.30-2/7-9.30 Closed L Sat, D 25-26 Dec **Prices** Fixed L 2 course £12.95, Starter £5.75-£8.95, Main £12.50-£22.50, Dessert £6.75, Service optional **Wines** 25 bottles over £20, 10 bottles under £20, 12 by glass **Notes** Sunday L, Vegetarian available, Civ Wed 160 **Seats** 80, Pr/dining room 40 **Children** Portions, Menu **Parking** 200

ALVESTON Map 4 ST68

Carriages at Alveston House Hotel

Modern European

Seasonal produce in a refurbished period house hotel

01454 415050
Davids Ln BS35 2LA
e-mail: info@alvestonhousehotel.co.uk
dir: On A38, 3.5m N of M4/M5 interchange. M5 junct 16 N'bound or junct 14 S'bound

A whitewashed Georgian country house on the outside, but smartly made-over in a clean-cut contemporary style within, Alveston House is handily placed for exploring Bristol; when the day's business is done, there's a secluded walled garden for afternoon tea or pre-dinner drinks. Its Carriages restaurant is kitted out in elegant hues of cream and gold with a romantic candlelit evening ambience and friendly, welcoming vibe. The kitchen takes an unpretentious tack with dishes built on soundly-sourced ingredients and tried-and-true flavour pairings. Slow-cooked lamb shank in red wine, garlic and herbs with parsnip mash, or pan-fried sea bass with smoked bacon, leeks and peas show the style.

continued

ALVESTON ***continued***

Chef Ben Halliday **Owner** Julie Camm
Times 12-1.45/7-9.30 **Prices** Starter £5.25-£6.75, Main £13.75-£19.50, Dessert £5-£5.75, Service optional **Wines** 11 bottles over £20, 28 bottles under £20, 5 by glass **Notes** Vegetarian available, Civ Wed 75 **Seats** 75, Pr/dining room 40 **Children** Portions, Menu **Parking** 60

ARLINGHAM Map 4 SO71

The Old Passage Inn

@@ Seafood

Riverside restaurant with tip-top seafood

☎ 01452 740547
Passage Rd GL2 7JR
e-mail: oldpassage@ukonline.co.uk
web: www.theoldpassage.com
dir: M5 junct 13/A38 towards Bristol, 2nd right to Frampton-on-Severn, over canal, bear left, follow to river

It's hard to beat a riverside setting and the Old Passage has the River Severn flowing past with all its majestic beauty; there used to be a ford here, hence the name. Now it is a relaxing seafood restaurant with rooms that combines high quality food with a definite air of tranquility. There's also the splendid backdrop of the wooded hills of the Forest of Dean and a garden terrace, which cannot be ignored when the weather is mild. The menu deals almost exclusively in fish and seafood, brought in fresh from Pembrokeshire or Cornwall, while the restaurant's seawater tanks guarantee impeccably fresh lobsters. Dishes are kept simple and presented attractively, as in whole lemon sole with nut brown butter, parsley, lemon juice and new potatoes or the fish pie packed with pollock, smoked haddock and North Atlantic prawns. Fruits de mer or the shellfish tasting menu might prove too hard to resist.

Chef Mark Redwood **Owner** Sally Pearce
Times 12-2/7-9.30 Closed 25-26 Dec, Mon, D Sun
Prices Fixed L 2 course £15, Fixed D 3 course £20, Starter £8-£12, Main £16.50-£25, Dessert £7.50-£9, Service optional **Wines** 53 bottles over £20, 36 bottles under £20, 15 by glass **Notes** Shellfish tasting menu, Sunday L, Vegetarian available **Seats** 60, Pr/dining room 12
Children Portions **Parking** 40

BARNSLEY Map 5 SP00

The Village Pub

@@ Modern British

Cotswold inn with deserved reputation for good food

☎ 01285 740421
GL7 5EF
e-mail: info@thevillagepub.co.uk
dir: 4m from Cirencester, on B4425 to Bibury

'Green and pleasant' could have been coined specifically to describe the rolling fields of Gloucestershire all around this contemporary country inn. As with most stylishly reworked pubs, food is high on the agenda; and the food here is good, with five country-chic dining rooms at hand to accommodate the faithful. There are flagstone and oak floors, exposed timbers and open fireplaces, mixed with antiques, oil paintings, cosy settles and polished candlelit tables in a country chic décor. The operation likes to promote local produce, which means serving locally-produced real ales and soft drinks, while the area's best ingredients - some of which come no further than the vegetable garden at Barnsley House (the pub's posh sibling up the road) - form the backbone of an unfussy modern repertoire. To start, locally-smoked sea trout might be teamed with green beans, crème fraîche and citrus dressing, while mains could bring slow-roasted belly pork with root vegetable gratin.

Times 12-2.30/7-9.30

BIBURY Map 5 SP10

Bibury Court

@@ British

Confident modern cooking in stunning country-house hotel

☎ 01285 740337
GL7 5NT
e-mail: info@biburycourt.com
web: www.biburycourt.com
dir: On B4425 between Cirencester & Burford; hotel behind church

An imposing 17th-century manor house hidden away in six acres of grounds beside the River Coln, on the edge of a picture-postcard Cotswold village. Within, it oozes historic charm and character, with roaring log fires, flagstone floors and wood panelling maintaining the traditional country-house feel, while period features blend with a smart, contemporary décor in the newly refurbished restaurant. The food is modern British with a classic edge, yet there are plenty of Mediterranean influences, as seen in risotto of black truffles and scallops, and roast bream with spiced aubergine, tomato and cumin, sautéed squid and salsa verde. Menus change with the seasons and make good use of local produce, perhaps roast Bibury trout with Coln Valley smoked salmon, horseradish and chive-crushed potatoes, and Aldsworth venison with smoked mash and red cabbage. Eat in the more informal conservatory at lunch and the formal restaurant at dinner.

Chef Antony Ely **Owner** John Lister **Times** 12-2/7-9
Prices Fixed L 2 course £13.50-£14.50, Starter £7.50-£12.95, Main £15.50-£24, Dessert £6.50-£10, Service added but optional 10% **Wines** 117 bottles over £20, 24 bottles under £20, 8 by glass **Notes** Sunday L, Vegetarian available, Civ Wed 32 **Seats** 65, Pr/dining room 30
Children Portions, Menu **Parking** 100

Swan Hotel

@ International

Assured modern cooking in charming Cotswold village

☎ 01285 740695
GL7 5NW
e-mail: info@swanhotel.co.uk
web: www.cotswold-inns-hotels.co.uk/swan
dir: 9m S of Burford A40 onto B4425. 6m N of Cirencester A4179 onto B4425. In town centre by bridge

The riverside setting by an old stone bridge in an endearing Cotswold village looks almost edible in itself, and this charming hotel, part of the Cotswold Inns group, doesn't disappoint. A comfortable modern dining room with well-spaced tables, and courtyard seating for fine days, is the setting for some assured contemporary cooking based on good country produce. A generous slab of duck and orange terrine with a sharp, fruity chutney is a good start, and is ably succeeded by crisp-skinned sea bass fillets in a light saffron cream sauce. A meat main course might be pork belly with apple mash, pak choi and Calvados jus, with a fitting finale such as raisin crème brûlée with rhubarb compôte.

Chef Chris Hutchings **Owner** Cotswold Inns & Hotels
Times 12-2.30/7-9 **Prices** Fixed D 3 course fr £32.50, Service optional **Wines** 40 bottles over £20, 20 bottles under £20, 2 by glass **Notes** Sunday L, Vegetarian available, Dress restrictions, Smart casual, no jeans or trainers, Civ Wed 90 **Seats** 60, Pr/dining room 30
Children Portions **Parking** 20, On street

BOURTON-ON-THE-WATER Map 10 SP12

The Dial House Hotel & Restaurant

@@ Modern British

Bags of character and top local ingredients

☎ 01451 822244
The Chestnuts, High St GL54 2AN
e-mail: info@dialhousehotel.com
dir: Just off A429

Built from the famous Cotswold mellow stone, the Dial House dates back to 1698 making it the oldest building still standing in chocolate box Bourton-on-the-Water. Until 30 years ago it was a private house and after a careful refurbishment, today the hotel is rich with period details such as inglenook fireplaces, low stone arches, beamed ceilings and poor boxes. The dining rooms are formal, yet not overbearing, while slick service from a well-trained team adds to the sense of occasion. The best of local Cotswold produce, skilfully prepared, dominates the menu. Tuck into a multi-dimensional starter of grilled Cornish mackerel, curried lentils, beetroot, apple and sorrel salad, before moving onto a tender pot-roast squab pigeon with caramelised shallot and Alsace bacon.

Times 12-2/6.30-9.30

BUCKLAND Map 10 SP03

Buckland Manor

@@ Traditional British NOTABLE WINE LIST

Ancient manor-house setting overlooking the Vale of Evesham

☎ 01386 852626
WR12 7LY
e-mail: info@bucklandmanor.com
dir: 2m SW of Broadway. Take B4632 signed Cheltenham, then take turn for Buckland. Hotel through village on right

Ten acres of superb grounds with grand views over the Vale of Evesham make a marvellous setting for this tranquil Cotswold-stone manor, whose history dates back as far as the 13th century. Inside, antiques, fine paintings, crackling log fires and panelled walls create a true country-house atmosphere and the air of refinement extends to jacket-and-tie order for male diners. The light, airy and spacious dining room, with views over the rolling hills, combines elegance with comfort and is the perfect place to enjoy modern country-house cooking based around top quality seasonal ingredients. Follow an impressive starter of rabbit terrine with confit leg, celeriac remoulade and thyme reduction, with tender, full-flavoured fillet of Cotswold venison served with a port and redcurrant jus, then round off with a delicious pear poached in Cassis with cinnamon ice cream. The impressive wine list includes an extensive Bordeaux collection.

Chef Matt Hodgkins **Owner** Buckland Manor Country House Hotel Ltd **Times** 12.30-1.45/7.30-9 **Prices** Fixed L 2 course £15, Starter £7.95-£12.50, Main £25.50-£29.50, Dessert £9, Service optional **Wines** 532 bottles over £20, 6 bottles under £20, 10 by glass **Notes** Pre-theatre D available, Sunday L, Vegetarian available, Dress restrictions, Jacket & tie **Seats** 40 **Children** Portions **Parking** 30

CHARINGWORTH Map 10 SP13

The John Greville Restaurant

@ Modern International

☎ 01386 593555
Charingworth Manor GL55 6NS
e-mail: charingworthmanor@classiclodges.co.uk
dir: M40 exit at signs for A429/Stow. Follow signs for Moreton-in-Marsh. From Chipping Camden follow signs for Charingworth Manor

Rooted into the Cotswolds scenery for 700 years, Charingworth Manor is a full-dress country-house hotel decked out in a fetching blend of old and new - stylish modern fabrics, colour schemes and designer touches set against ancient flagstone and wood floors, exposed stone walls, huge fireplaces and beams showing medieval decoration. Beamed ceilings and rag-rolled walls make the John Greville Restaurant an intimate venue for the kitchen's straightforward contemporary food; start, perhaps, with ballottine of chicken with pistachio mousse, sherry and mustard dressing, then continue with roast rump and slow-braised shoulder of lamb with confit potato, spring greens, squash purée and lamb jus.

Times 12-2/7-9.30

See advert below

Le Champignon Sauvage

CHELTENHAM **Map 10 SO92**

Modern

Cheltenham's shining star

☎ 01242 573449
24-28 Suffolk Rd GL50 2AQ
e-mail: mail@lechampignonsauvage.co.uk
dir: S of town centre, on A40, near Cheltenham College

There are many good reasons for a visit to the still-beautiful spa town of Cheltenham, and the Champignon has to be one of them. David and Helen Everitt-Matthias have been running the place since the late 1980s, and time hasn't in the least dimmed their enthusiasm. In the case of David's cooking, it has rather refined it to a pitch of sublime accomplishment. This is a place every keen eater-out should get to sooner or later. There is nothing startling in the decorative ambience, just the feeling of stepping straight off the street into a gracious private home, albeit one owned by a collector of eye-catching modern artworks. The culinary style is still appreciably founded on classical technique, but has absorbed the more experimental modes of today with great subtlety. Some dishes incorporate lesser-known wild ingredients, for which our chef has foraged locally, and although much energy is spent on presentation, so that dishes can look surprisingly busy, their components are nonetheless accorded their due status. A luxuriant ruffle of cep-flavoured foam crowns a dish of guinea-fowl raviolo, the pasta delicately sheer, the chunks of meat offset with golden raisins, pine nuts and chard. Cornish sea bass arrives with a welter of accompaniments in the forms of caramelised cauliflower, smoked almonds, wild mushrooms and a resonant red wine and liquorice sauce, or there might be red-legged partridge in the game season, served with turnip 'choucroute' and a turnip and verjus purée, a daring foray into the bitter and sour end of the flavour spectrum. Desserts go for it, with strong flavour notes such as bergamot, chicory root, coconut and basil, hardly more so than in a profoundly concentrated chocolate and olive tart with fennel ice cream. An impeccable French-led wine list adds the final gloss to a quality enterprise.

Chef David Everitt-Matthias
Owner Mr & Mrs D Everitt-Matthias
Times 12.30-1.30/7.30-8.30 Closed 10 days Xmas, 3 wks Jun, Sun-Mon
Prices Fixed L 2 course £25-£30, Fixed D 3 course £35-£55, Service optional
Wines 100+ bottles over £20, 45 bottles under £20, 6 by glass **Seats** 40
Parking Public car park (Bath Rd)

CHELTENHAM Map 10 SO92

Le Champignon Sauvage

@@@@ – *see opposite page*

The Cheltenham Regency Hotel

@ Traditional

Traditional cooking in quiet Cotswold setting

☎ 01452 713226 & 0845 1949867
Staverton Rd GL51 0ST
e-mail: gm@cheltenhamregency.co.uk
dir: M5 junct 11 onto A40 to Cheltenham. Left at rdbt, hotel 1m on left

Recently refurbished, this friendly hotel is just outside the famous spa town, and has a large function room which appeals to the wedding and business markets. In the dining room, the well-spaced tables and comfortable chairs make for a calming traditional setting. The crowd-pleasing menu caters for most tastes with its good selection of simple dishes created from good quality produce. Think grilled mackerel fillet with new potato and chive salad followed by chicken and mushroom pie with buttered carrots. Desserts include sticky toffee pudding and butterscotch sauce.

Times 12-2/7-9.30

The Daffodil

@ Modern European

Brasserie cooking in a former art-deco cinema

☎ 01242 700055
18-20 Suffolk Pde, Montpellier GL50 2AE
e-mail: eat@thedaffodil.com
dir: S of town centre, just off Suffolk Rd, near Cheltenham Boys' College

Originally a cinema built in grand art-deco style, this unique and glamorous dining venue has been refurbished under the guidance of TV design guru Laurence Llewelyn-Bowen. The sweeping entrance staircase with original mosaic tiles, period film posters, old vending machines and even an antique projector are all still on view, and where once you might have been gazing in wonder at the silver screen, there is now an open-to-view bustling kitchen. A menu of modern European brasserie dishes features some adept and appetising cooking; seared scallops with pork belly confit and pea purée before halibut with buttered samphire and sorrel sauce. Glazed lemon tart with raspberry compôte and crème fraîche makes for a happy ending.

Chef Mark Davidson **Owner** Mark Stephens & James McAlpine **Times** 12-3/6-10.30 Closed 25 Dec & 1 Jan, Sun **Prices** Fixed L 2 course £13.50-£14.50, Fixed D 3 course £15.50-£16.50, Starter £3.95-£9.95, Main £10.95-£22.50, Dessert £4.50-£6.50, Service added but optional 10% **Wines** 46 bottles over £20, 14 bottles under £20, 20 by glass **Notes** Fixed price menu Mon-Fri until 7.30pm, daily lunch special (main course and glass of wine) £10, Vegetarian available **Seats** 140 **Children** Portions, Menu **Parking** On street

The Greenway Hotel

@@ British, European V

Ambitious cooking amid the elegance of a historic house

☎ 01242 862352
Shurdington GL51 4UG
e-mail: info@thegreenway.co.uk
dir: 3m S of Cheltenham on A46 (Stroud) & through Shurdington

On the fringes of Cheltenham, this creeper-swathed Elizabethan manor sits in eight acres of immaculate grounds with a sunken garden and lily pond to wander, cocktail in hand, as you take in the view of the Cotswold Hills at sunset. The same view is the backdrop to dining in the classy restaurant amid an opulent décor blending traditional elegance with modern design. The cooking suits the surroundings with its polished modern British repertoire of ambitious ideas, presented with eye-catching pizzazz. Starters announce the style - risotto of South Coast crab is served with celeriac ice cream, while roast saddle of rabbit comes with rabbit bolognese and squash purée. Main course might bring Cotswold venison cutlet with juniper and blackcurrant sorbet and mixed berry jus, or a modish fish and meat pairing such as monkfish and citrus-cured pork belly with potato purée and lie-de-vin sauce.

Chef Paul Mottram **Owner** von Essen Hotels **Times** 12-2.30/7-9.30 **Prices** Fixed L 2 course £18, Fixed D 3 course £48.50, Tasting menu £65, Service optional **Wines** 150 bottles over £20, 6 bottles under £20, 10 by glass **Notes** Tasting menu 6 course, Sunday L, Vegetarian menu, Dress restrictions, Smart casual, No jeans, T-shirts or trainers, Civ Wed 45 **Seats** 56, Pr/dining room 22 **Children** Portions **Parking** 50

Hotel du Vin Cheltenham

@ British, European

Bistro menu in boutique hotel

☎ 01242 588450
Parabola Rd GL50 3AQ
e-mail: info.cheltenham@hotelduvin.com
dir: M5 junct 11, follow signs for city centre. At rdbt opposite Morgan Estate Agents take 2nd left, 200mtrs to Parabola Rd

The boutique HdV group's Cheltenham hotel is close to the famed Ladies' College in the fashionable Montpellier district. A wine glass chandelier dominates the contemporary interior and shelves and windowsills are filled with the trademark bottles. Olive and brown leather furnishings and a pewter topped bar make way for a more classic style in the basement restaurant where French dishes mostly rule. Try pan-fried scallops glazed with hollandaise sauce and cheese followed by chargrilled Donald Russell beef burger with bacon, cheese, home-made ketchup and pommes frites. Take advantage of the sommelier service to guide you through the lengthy wine list.

Chef Jon Parsons **Owner** MWB **Times** 12-2/6.30-10.30 **Prices** Fixed L 2 course £10, Fixed D 2 course £10, Starter £4.50-£9.95, Main £12.50-£25, Dessert £6.95, Service added but optional 10% **Wines** 450 bottles over £20, 20 bottles under £20, 20 by glass **Notes** 2 course with wine £15, Sunday L, Vegetarian available **Seats** 92, Pr/dining room 32 **Children** Portions, Menu **Parking** 23

Monty's Brasserie

@@ Modern International

Brasserie cooking in Grade II listed building

☎ 01242 227678
George Hotel, 41 St Georges Rd GL50 3DZ
e-mail: info@montysbraz.co.uk
dir: M5 junct 11, follow signs to town centre. At lights (TGI Fridays) turn left onto Gloucester Rd. Straight on, at lights turn right, Monty's 0.75m on left

Sitting adjacent to the main entrance of the elegant George Hotel, an imposing Regency-style building dating from the 1840s, Monty's Brasserie is a cleanly designed, up-to-date space with simple table settings, a wood floor, and a colour scheme in the brown-to-yellow range. The comprehensive brasserie menu is punctuated with an M-symbol denoting the house signature dishes (Thai crispy duck with chilli and sesame dipping sauce and pancakes, beef Wellington in red wine sauce), but there is also a healthy emphasis on seafood. Seared Cornish mackerel Niçoise with a split bean and shallot salad, followed by stone bass with squid, artichokes and basil cream, might be typical of that route, while desserts celebrate the renaissance of baked Alaska, this one filled with strawberries and clotted cream.

Chef Rob Owen **Owner** Jeremy Shaw **Times** 12-2/6-10 Closed 25-26 Dec **Prices** Fixed L 2 course £12.50, Starter £6-£9, Main £12-£22, Dessert £4-£7, Service added but optional 10% **Wines** 32 bottles over £20, 11 bottles under £20, 7 by glass **Notes** Sunday L, Vegetarian available **Seats** 40, Pr/dining room 32 **Children** Portions, Menu **Parking** 30

The Royal Well Tavern

@ Modern British

Remodelled town-centre pub with well-conceived bistro menu

☎ 01242 221212
5 Well Place GL50 3DN
e-mail: info@theroyalwelltavern.com
dir: In town centre close to the Royal Crescent & Promenade, W of A46

The Royal Well Tavern had a reputation as a bit of a rough joint before a complete makeover brought together the best elements of a classic town-centre pub with a French bistro. The interior now has a dark masculine look involving leather banquettes, bare darkwood tables and gilt-framed sketches on the walls, and a buzzy vibe. To go with the Anglo-French look, the kitchen's style is a fusion of modern British and classic French bistro cooking, with

continued

CHELTENHAM *continued*

the accent on great local ingredients. The daily-changing menu's lack of florid waffle echoes the unembellished approach to its food - perhaps ox cheek and lentil soup or rabbit terrine with fig chutney and toast, followed by leg of lamb with fennel, garlic, spring greens and chestnuts.

Chef Andy Martin **Owner** Sam Pearman **Times** 10-3/5-11 Closed 25 Dec **Prices** Fixed L 2 course £10, Starter £4-£12, Main £12-£50, Dessert £4-£7, Service added but optional **Wines** 9 bottles over £20, 6 bottles under £20, 3 by glass **Notes** Tasting menu availlable, Prix fixe theatre menu 5-7pm, Sunday L, Vegetarian available **Seats** 50 **Children** Portions **Parking** NCP 5 min walk

CHIPPING CAMPDEN **Map 10 SP13**

The Kings

Modern British

Cotswold inn with contemporary style

☎ 01386 840256 & 841056
The Square GL55 6AW
e-mail: info@kingscampden.co.uk
web: www.kingscampden.co.uk
dir: In centre of town square

The Kings is a classic Georgian Cotswold stone inn at the heart of the pretty town's historic centre, brought up-to-date with dollops of contemporary style. While the bar retains a pubby vibe, the operation clearly has its heart in the gastro side of life. There's a relaxed contemporary brasserie, or, overlooking the square, the buzzy restaurant with chocolate and cream leather seats at antique tables, and vibrant art blending with wonky beams. Here, exceptional raw ingredients are the cornerstone of the kitchen's output, put together in intelligent combinations to form a menu with wide-ranging appeal. Honey-roasted duck confit with Toulouse sausage and haricot bean cassoulet makes for a rib-sticking starter, followed by braised shank of Lighthorne lamb with sweet potato mash, minted peas and lettuce and lamb gravy. Don't skip dessert when there's the prospect of warm rhubarb cake with baked vanilla custard and rhubarb ice cream.

Chef Gareth Rufus **Owner** Sir Peter Rigby **Times** 12-2.30/6.30-9.30 **Prices** Food prices not confirmed for 2011. Please telephone for details **Wines** 47 bottles over £20, 13 bottles under £20, 10 by glass **Notes** Sunday L, Vegetarian available, Civ Wed 60 **Seats** Pr/dining room 20 **Children** Portions, Menu **Parking** 8

Three Ways House

British

Welcoming home of the famous Pudding Club

☎ 01386 438429
Chapel Ln, Mickleton GL55 6SB
e-mail: reception@puddingclub.com
dir: On B4632, in village centre

You can take it for granted that the Cotswolds home of the famous Pudding Club won't be serving up any foams, froths or drizzles. As its name might hint, the club is famous for championing Great British Puddings, but there's a lot more to appreciate here before we get as far as dessert. The Victorian hotel has oodles of period character, although the restaurant bucks the trend with a more up-to-date look. The food is weighted towards traditional British and classical themes, but put together with a contemporary lightness of touch. Local, seasonal ingredients get top billing, as in a ham hock and Tewkesbury mustard terrine with Bramley apple compôte for starters, followed by roast chump of Cotswold lamb with a mustard and herb crust. Although other desserts are available, there's only one real choice: it's back to school for a selection of steamed puddings served with lashings of custard.

Chef Mark Rowlandson **Owner** Simon Coombe & Peter Henderson **Times** 12-2.30/7-9.30 Closed L Mon-Sat **Prices** Fixed L 2 course £21, Fixed D 3 course fr £36, Service optional **Wines** 36 bottles over £20, 22 bottles under £20, 15 by glass **Notes** Sunday L, Vegetarian available, Civ Wed 80 **Seats** 80, Pr/dining room 70 **Children** Portions, Menu **Parking** 37, On street parking

CIRENCESTER **Map 5 SP00**

Hare & Hounds

International **NEW**

Diverting country-pub food by a Roman road

☎ 01285 720288
Fosse-Cross GL54 4NN
e-mail: stay@thehareandhoundsinn.com
dir: On A429 (Stow road), 6m from Cirencester

Standing by the old Fosse Way Roman road, not far from Cirencester, the Hare & Hounds is a Cotswold-stone country inn, complete with original fireplaces with bread ovens built into them, and a clutch of guest rooms around an inner courtyard. Restored flagstones and undressed tables create a welcoming modern-rustic feel in the dining room, where Gerry Ragosa offers a menu of diverting country-pub food. Start with a filo basket of chicken livers cooked in port and topped with foie gras, before setting about a main course of baked monkfish Catalan-style, with something homely like raspberry and ginger steamed sponge pudding and custard to round it all off.

Times 12-3/6-10 Closed Xmas, New Year, BHs

CLEARWELL **Map 4 SO50**

Tudor Farmhouse Hotel & Restaurant

Modern British

Confident modern cooking in atmospheric old farmhouse

☎ 01594 833046
High St GL16 8JS
e-mail: info@tudorfarmhousehotel.co.uk
dir: Off A4136 onto B4228, through Coleford, turn right into Clearwell, hotel on right just before War Memorial Cross

A 13th-century converted farmhouse deep in the Forest of Dean, as the name suggests, much of its original character has been preserved. Exposed stonework, wall panelling, inglenook fireplaces and an abundance of beams prevail. The food on the other hand, takes a more contemporary point of view: the confident modern British menu changes with the seasons and utilises high quality local ingredients. The cooking is not overly complex or overwrought, delivering clear flavours and taking inspiration from a broadly European template. Rillette of ham knuckle with pineapple relish and a lightly curried hen's egg is the sort of thing you might find in some classy metropolitan brasserie; next up, perhaps loin of Lydney Park venison with bubble-and-squeak, red cabbage and beetroot jus. A well made fine apple and frangipane tart with caramel ice cream shows the confidence runs right through to the finish.

Chef Blaine Reed **Owner** Colin & Hari Fell **Times** 12-2/7-9 Closed 24-27 Dec **Prices** Fixed L 2 course fr £16.50, Fixed D 3 course fr £32.50, Service optional **Wines** 22 bottles over £20, 24 bottles under £20, 8 by glass **Notes** Sunday L, Vegetarian available **Seats** 36, Pr/dining room 22 **Children** Portions, Menu **Parking** 30

COLN ST ALDWYNS Map 5 SP10

The New Inn at Coln

Modern British

Modern British cooking in a charming village inn

01285 750651
GL7 5AN
dir: 8m E of Cirencester, between Bibury & Fairford

The Inn is the cherry on the cake of an almost edible-looking Cotswold village. Choose from the bar or restaurant for eating, but don't overlook the terrace seating in summer weather. Red-washed walls and simple table settings in the restaurant retain the country ethos, and a modern British menu is founded on sound culinary principles. Richly flavoured mushroom and thyme broth with croûtons reminds us what a pleasure a good bowl of soup can be, or there may be crab, chargrilled pepper and lime tian with sweet chilli dressing to start, if you're in the mood for something racier. Mains run from steamed hake with smoked salmon, beetroot risotto and leek and horseradish cream to tender, positively flavoured slow-roast honey-glazed pork belly with black pudding and a rich red wine jus. Gooseberry and elderflower parfait with a honeycomb meringue and mint ice cream is a delightful summer dessert.

Chef Oli Addis **Owner** Hillbrooke Hotels
Times 12.30-2.30/7-9 **Prices** Food prices not confirmed for 2011. Please telephone for details **Wines** 30 bottles over £20, 6 bottles under £20, 8 by glass
Notes Vegetarian available **Seats** 40 **Children** Portions, Menu **Parking** 25

CORSE LAWN Map 10 SO83

Corse Lawn House Hotel

British, French V NOTABLE WINE LIST

Genteel Queen Anne house with a skilled team in the kitchen

01452 780771
GL19 4LZ
e-mail: enquiries@corselawn.com
dir: 5m SW of Tewkesbury on B4211, in village centre

Since 1978, the Hine family (of Cognac fame) have called this handsome red-brick Queen Anne house their home. Set back from the village green behind an ornamental pond that was originally a coach wash in the days of horse-drawn transport, it's an operation based on traditional values of courteous yet friendly service from a smartly-uniformed team. Baba Hine may have handed over the culinary helm to Andrew Poole, but remains very hands-on in a front-of-house role. The kitchen takes no short cuts: its sourcing of local seasonal produce is meticulous, and everything from bread to petits fours is made in-house. The result is seriously good food; classically minded and displaying spot-on technical skills. An exemplary Mediterranean fish soup with garlic rouille makes a fine start, followed by super-fresh roast fillet of pollock with saffron crushed potatoes and mussel sauce.

Chef Andrew Poole & Martin Kinahan **Owner** Hine Family **Times** 12-2/7-9.30 Closed 24-26 Dec **Prices** Fixed L 2 course £22.50, Fixed D 3 course fr £32.50, Starter £4.95-£10.95, Main £14.95-£19.95, Dessert £5.95-£6.95, Service optional **Wines** 400 bottles over £20, 39 bottles under £20, 10 by glass **Notes** Sunday L, Vegetarian menu, Civ Wed 70 **Seats** 50, Pr/dining room 28
Children Portions, Menu **Parking** 60

DAYLESFORD Map 10 SP22

Daylesford Farm Café

British NEW

Organic cooking at its best

01608 731700
GL56 0YG
e-mail: enquiries@daylesfordorganic.com

Quite the most luxurious farm shop you're ever likely to come across. Originally set up as an organic deli by Lady Bamford in a beautifully converted barn on her Cotswold estate, it has evolved into a trendy, lifestyle shopping experience, with the emphasis firmly on organic food and products. Browse the fascinating deli, complete with on-site creamery, butchery, fishmonger and bakery, explore the garden nursery, country clothes and local crafts shop, and be pampered in the beauty therapy barn before rounding off with a meal in the restaurant or on the impressive alfresco terrace. The ethos of the cooking is simple, seasonal and organic, so begin with a great carpaccio of estate-reared beef with spiced mayonnaise, follow with moist and tender pork chop with a rich, full-flavoured café au lait sauce, and finish with a perfect chocolate fondant.

Times 9am-5pm

EBRINGTON Map 10 SP14

The Ebrington Arms

Modern British

Village inn with great British food

01386 593223
GL55 6NH
e-mail: claire.alexander@mac.com
dir: Take B4035 from Chipping Campden towards Shipston on Stour. After 0.5m turn left signed Ebrington

In green-and-pleasant Cotswolds countryside near Chipping Campden, this gorgeous stone inn is firing on all cylinders. First of all, it's a real pub at the heart of Ebrington village life, that takes its real ales and real fires seriously; the vibe inside is fun and totally unpretentious, from the characterful flagstoned bar to the beamed rustic-chic dining room. The kitchen draws on the best local materials for its switched-on contemporary pub cuisine. Daily-changing menus might offer a salad of wood pigeon breast, with parsnip crisps, raspberry and Puy lentil vinaigrette, ahead of a casserole of local Todenham Manor Farm steak, ale and mustard with horseradish dumplings, or a classic beer-battered pollock with tartare sauce, minted pea purée and home-cut chips. For pudding, you're onto a winner with pineapple tarte Tatin and honeycomb ice cream.

Chef James Nixon, Andrew Lipp **Owner** Claire & Jim Alexander **Times** 12-2.30/6.30-9.30 Closed 25 Dec, D Sun **Prices** Food prices not confirmed for 2011. Please telephone for details **Wines** 11 bottles over £20, 9 bottles under £20, 6 by glass **Notes** Vegetarian available
Seats 50, Pr/dining room 30 **Children** Portions
Parking 13

LOWER SLAUGHTER Map 10 SP12

Lower Slaughter Manor

See page 158

Washbourne Court Hotel

Modern British, French

Quintessential Cotswold hotel with innovative cooking

01451 822143
GL54 2HS
e-mail: info@washbournecourt.co.uk
dir: Off A429, village centre by river

Standing by the river Eye in a lush pastoral setting, Washbourne Court was once a crammer for boys on their way to Eton. If that evokes suggestions of Latin prep and gowned headmasters, rest assured it's a lot more convivial these days. The place has a neat contrast of modern interior design in 17th-century surroundings, and the cooking is absolutely of its time, right down to the conscientious extras such as piping-hot mini-loaves with unsalted butter. Some classic contemporary notes are sounded in dishes like smoked trout served warm with chunky black pudding, puréed celeriac and apple syrup to start. Afterwards might come fine lamb saddle, pink and tender, with rösti, wilted greens and rosemary jus, a main course that displays solid technical skills. Desserts might encompass the pace-setting hot mango Tatin with Thai green curry ice cream, or a straightforward, if loose-textured crème brûlée.

Times 12.30-2.30/7-9.30

Lower Slaughter Manor

Rosettes not confirmed at time of going to press

LOWER SLAUGHTER Map 10 SP12

Modern British V

Chic manor house with modern British cooking

☎ 01451 820456
GL54 2HP
e-mail: info@lowerslaughter.co.uk
dir: Off A429, signed 'The Slaughters'. 0.5m into village on right

Lower Slaughter Manor is as English as cricket on a village green with a jug of Pimm's. The elegant 17th-century mansion is the jewel in the crown of the honeypot Cotswold village, secluded in expansive grounds with mature trees, immaculate lawns and a lovely secretive walled garden. Inside, the décor has been brought into the modern world; an upmarket country-house chic blends plush fabrics and tasteful colour schemes with stately architecture and period elegance. It all adds up to premium comfort and quality at premium prices. A change of chef has resulted in Rosette suspension for this edition of the guide. The ambience in the intimate Sixteen58 dining room is as suave and refined as its chocolate-brown silk walls and Murano crystal tableware. Expect modern British cooking along the lines of home-smoked quail with Stornoway black pudding, soft-poached quail's egg, crisp pancetta and plum purée, followed by fillet of Gloucestershire Old Spot pork with Asian spices with crackling, warm belly pork jelly, honey-glazed parsnips and lentils.

Owner von Essen Collection **Times** 12.15-2/6.30-10 **Prices** Fixed L 2 course £19.50, Starter £9.50-£13, Main £19.50-£37.50, Dessert £8.50-£10.50, Service optional **Wines** All bottles over £20, 14 by glass **Notes** Sunday L, Vegetarian menu, Dress restrictions, Smart, no jeans or trainers, Civ Wed 70 **Seats** 55, Pr/dining room 20 **Children** Portions, Menu **Parking** 30

MORETON-IN-MARSH Map 10 SP23

Mulberry Restaurant

◎◎ Modern British V

Classy, modern cooking in a 16th-century gem

☎ 01608 650501
Manor House Hotel, High St GL56 0LJ
e-mail: info@manorhousehotel.info
web: www.cotswold-inns-hotels.co.uk/manor
dir: Off A429 at south end of town

A happy blend of old and new, the 16th-century origins of the former coaching inn are laid bare in the honeyed-Cotswold-stone walls, while the gently contemporary fixtures and fittings bring it up-to-date without ever looking out of place. The cooking served up in the elegant Mulberry Restaurant treads a similar path, with some classy modern dishes based on both classic and inventive interpretations. Thus home-smoked salmon is paired with a pea shoot salad, vanilla pannacotta and spinach purée, and loin of Cotswold venison comes with a suet pudding, dauphinoise, parsnip purée and a roast plum. To finish, perhaps try the assiette of citrus, including lemon posset and orange Madeleine. There's a tasting menu with the option of accompanying wines selected by the sommelier.

Chef Nick Orr **Owner** Michael & Pamela Horton **Times** 12-2.30/7-9.30 **Prices** Fixed L 3 course £19.95, Fixed D 3 course £37.50, Service added but optional 10% **Wines** 53 bottles over £20, 26 bottles under £20, 8 by glass **Notes** Tasting menu 7 course, Sunday L, Vegetarian menu, Dress restrictions, Smart casual, no jeans, shorts or trainers, Civ Wed 120 **Seats** 55, Pr/dining room 120 **Children** Portions **Parking** 32

Redesdale Arms

◎ British

Relaxed dining in historic Cotswold inn

☎ 01608 650308
High St GL56 0AW
e-mail: info@redesdalearms.co.uk
dir: On A429, 0.5m from rail station

Like so many buildings in this quintessential Cotswolds town, the venerable Redesdale Arms is built of honey-hued stone and exudes an air of well-established comfort. It is a relaxed place that pulls together a classy fusion of old and new: age is there in its wood panelling and oak floorboards, while contemporary sensibilities are catered for with modern art, subtly understated colour schemes and touchy-feely textures. Depending on your mood - and the weather - you can eat in the bar, the conservatory restaurant, the courtyard garden or the stylish dining room. The lengthy menu is a crowd-pleasing affair built on local, seasonal produce, delivering the likes of local wood pigeon terrine with macerated grapes to start, followed by lamb shank with smoked garlic, potato purée, ratatouille and balsamic jus.

Times 12-2.30

NAILSWORTH Map 4 ST89

The Wild Garlic Restaurant

◎◎ Modern British

Relaxing atmosphere and top-quality ingredients

☎ 01453 832615
Heavens Above, 3 Cossack Square GL6 0DB
e-mail: info@wild-garlic.co.uk
dir: M4 junct 18. A46 towards Stroud. Enter Nailsworth, turn left at rdbt and then an immediate left. Restaurant opposite Britannia Pub

Chef-proprietor Matthew Beardshall jumped ship from heading up the kitchen of nearby Calcot Manor (see entry) back in 2007 and continues to run his own restaurant with rooms with an energetic hands-on approach. The former blacksmith's quarters has been given a stylish contemporary look - tables, chairs, and lovely stained glass panels are all hand-made by local craftsmen. Local artisans also provide the lion's share of the kitchen's materials, combined in modern dishes that have a sound classical basis, tweaked with a nice streak of creativity. You might find wild garlic and mushroom soup with sautéed field mushrooms and wild garlic pesto among unfussy starters, then proceed to honey-roast Gloucestershire Old Spot pork belly teamed with soft polenta, pickled carrots and celeriac. Desserts - perhaps rhubarb consommé with light ginger pannacotta and basil ice cream - are all made to the same high standard. Sincerely welcoming and clued-up staff are the icing on the cake.

Times 12-2/7-9 Closed 1st 2 wks Jan, Mon-Tue, D Sun

NEWENT **Map 10 SO72**

Three Choirs Vineyards

◎◎ Modern British

Mediterranean-style vineyard restaurant with views

☎ 01531 890223
GL18 1LS
e-mail: ts@threechoirs.com
dir: 2m N of Newent on B4215, follow brown tourist signs

As you sit on the terrace and look out across the sloping vines of this award-winning vineyard, sipping a glass of wine, you could be forgiven for thinking you are in Burgundy or Tuscany rather than Gloucestershire. Whether it's the vine-covered terrace of this converted farmhouse or the elegant, airy dining room overlooking the estate, the Mediterranean-inspired food makes good use of local ingredients in simply prepared and well-executed dishes. Pork belly, cheek and hock terrine, for example, wrapped in Parma ham is served with lightly spiced beetroot and pear compôte, followed by fillet tail of Cotswold beef with roasted shallots and rich red wine and thyme jus. Finish with iced English rhubarb parfait with shortbread, honeycomb crumble and crème anglaise.

Chef Darren Leonard **Owner** Three Choirs Vineyards Ltd **Times** 12-2/7-9 Closed Xmas, New Year **Prices** Fixed L 2 course £19.50, Fixed D 3 course fr £35, Starter £4.50-£8.75, Main £12.95-£19.95, Dessert £5.50-£6.95, Service optional, Groups min 10 service 10% **Wines** 20 bottles over £20, 34 bottles under £20, 12 by glass **Notes** Sunday L, Vegetarian available **Seats** 50, Pr/dining room 20 **Children** Portions, Menu **Parking** 50

NORTHLEACH **Map 10 SP11**

The Puesdown Inn

◎◎ Modern British

Refurbished coaching inn with confident kitchen team

☎ 01451 860262
Compton Abdale GL54 4DN
e-mail: inn4food@btopenworld.com
dir: On A40 (Cheltenham-Oxford), 7m from Cheltenham, 3m W of Northleach

Standing proudly at 800ft above sea level, the unique name for this charming pub derives from an ancient English phrase meaning 'windy ridge.' The interior has had a mellow and inviting contemporary makeover with the addition of comfortable sofas alongside the fire in the lounge, warm colours and exposed stone on the walls, and, best of all, a serious approach to good food. There's a bar menu, plus a range of pizzas (available to takeaway), but the main culinary action takes place in the dining room. The kitchen turns out some high quality stuff, based on good produce, much of it local. Start with warm salad of confit duck with apple and pistachios, moving on to rump of lamb with dauphinoise potatoes, aubergine caviar and green beans. Bread-and-butter pudding with vanilla ice cream or a thin apple tart with honey ice cream are two satisfying ways to end a meal.

Chef John Armstrong **Owner** John & Maggie Armstrong **Times** 10-3/6-11 Closed D Sun-Mon **Prices** Fixed L 2 course £12.50-£17.50, Fixed D 3 course £19.50-£23.50, Starter £4.75-£8.50, Main £12.50-£17, Dessert £5.50-£6.25, Service optional, Groups min 8 service 10% **Wines** 11 bottles over £20, 15 bottles under £20, 11 by glass **Notes** Sunday L, Vegetarian available **Seats** 48, Pr/dining room 24 **Children** Portions **Parking** 80

PAINSWICK **Map 4 SO80**

Cotswolds88 Hotel

◎◎ British, French **NEW**

Hip boutique hotel with creative modern cooking

☎ 01452 813688 & 810062
Kemps Ln GL6 6YB
e-mail: reservations@cotswolds88hotel.com

Arriving in the Cotswolds idyll of Painswick, there's little to indicate that anything out of the ordinary lies behind the grand greystone façade of the palladian mansion that is Cotswolds88. The interior - rather like a hip London hangout displaced to the countryside - goes for the chic boutique look, blending off-the-wall vintage pieces and splashes of colour with a touch of psychedelia. The restaurant is an eye-catching exercise in monochrome pyjama stripes, like a set from Tim Burton's *Alice in Wonderland*, with an eclectic soundtrack of chill-out music. Luckily the kitchen reins in any temptation to rival the designer's flamboyance, and takes a French-inflected, modern British approach to its output of well-balanced, creative dishes. An 'all-day breakfast' teams smoked breast of quail with black pudding, crispy pancetta, a boiled quail's egg and date and caper purée; next up, roasted cod with nicely crispy skin comes with pommes Anna layered with shredded duck, braised gem lettuce, celeriac and truffle purée, and cep velouté. Desserts keep things in the modern and funky zone, with a lemon and pine nut parfait, crème fraîche and black pepper ice cream, lemon curd and blueberries.

Chef Lee Scott **Owner** Mr & Mr Harris
Times 12-2.30/6.30-10 **Prices** Fixed L 2 course £10-£21, Fixed D 2 course £32.50-£35, Fixed D 4 course £45, Tasting menu £45, Starter £5.50-£14, Main £12.50-£26, Dessert £5.50-£7.50, Service added but optional 12.5% **Wines** 24 bottles over £20, 2 bottles under £20, 6 by glass **Notes** Tasting menu 6 course, Sunday L, Vegetarian available, Civ Wed 120 **Seats** 42, Pr/dining room 14

St Michaels

◎ Modern British **NEW**

Imaginative modern cooking in pretty Painswick

☎ 01452 814555
Victoria St GL6 6QA
e-mail: info@stmickshouse.co.uk

St Michael's House is a gorgeous 17th-century listed building overlooking the church in pretty Painswick village - the 'Queen of the Cotswolds'. The restaurant/B&B is a classy mix of exposed stone and mullioned windows and clean-cut contemporary style - chocolate leather chairs, oak parquet floors, cream walls and linen-clad tables. The kitchen takes a modern British approach, built around sensible combinations of well-sourced local produce. A white bean soup with ceps is served with a fragrant truffle foam, then local Gloucestershire Old Spot pork gets a workout, in the shape of a crispy trotter croquette, a tender and sweet chargrilled loin, and a full-flavoured seared kidney. Puddings might be as delicate as a compôte of marinated seasonal fruit with organic iced yoghurt, or as lush as apple and cinnamon beignets with boozy apple custard.

Times 12-3/7-10 Closed Mon & Tue

PAXFORD **Map 10 SP13**

Churchill Arms

◎◎ Modern, Traditional British

Confident cooking in a charming Cotswold pub

☎ 01386 594000
GL55 6XH
e-mail: info@thechurchillarms.com
dir: A429 from The Fosse, then A44 to Bourton-on-the-Hill. Turn right at end of village to Paxford via Blockley

A quick glance over the menu shows that the kitchen of the Churchill Arms sets its sights a notch or so higher than your average foodie pub. The building itself has all the elements you might expect in a honey-stone Cotswold pub - inglenook fireplace, beams overhead, oak and flagstones underfoot - plus an easygoing informality in its chalkboards for both food and wine, and relaxed pub vibe that includes ordering at the bar. Local lamb, venison and beef, and fish brought in from Brixham, all appear in good-looking, accurately-cooked modern dishes, that might include braised lamb's tongue with carrot and cumin purée, followed by parsley-crusted turbot with mussels and chestnut mushrooms. Finish with a roasted hazelnut parfait with banana curd and poached fig.

Chef William Guthrie **Times** 12-2/7-9 Closed 25 Dec **Prices** Fixed L 2 course £15.50-£27.90, Starter £4.50-£8.95, Main £8.95-£18.95, Dessert £4.50-£6.95, Groups min 10 service 10% **Wines** 12 bottles over £20, 13 bottles under £20, 8 by glass **Notes** Fixed L menu - main course & glass of wine £10, Sunday L, Vegetarian available **Seats** 55 **Children** Portions, Menu **Parking** On street

SOUTH CERNEY Map 5 SU09

The Old Boathouse

British NEW

Lakeside gastro-pub with classic British cooking

☎ 01285 864000
Cotswold Water Park Four Pillars Hotel, Lake 6, Spine Road East GL7 5FP

There are binoculars and a wildlife information board at hand to help you make the best of the stunning lakeside position of this thriving gastro-pub within the grounds of the Cotswold Water Park Four Pillars Hotel. Not surprisingly the terrace is a big hit. At bare wooden tables in the relaxing, nautically-themed bar and dining areas you can tuck into simple, traditional British dishes, the extensive seasonal menus taking in sandwiches, deli-boards to share, salads and risottos at lunchtime. At dinner, follow smoked haddock fishcakes with rocket and lemon mayonnaise, with roast duck with Madeira jus, or lemon sole with lemon and parsley, and apple and blackberry crumble.

SOUTHROP Map 5 SP10

The Swan at Southrop

British, European V

A touch of the Mediterranean in the Cotswolds

☎ 01367 850205
GL7 3NU
e-mail: info@theswanatsouthrop.co.uk
web: www.theswanatsouthrop.co.uk
dir: Off A361 between Lechlade & Burford

Country inns don't come more thickly swathed in climbing foliage than the Swan, and yet if you were expecting it to be correspondingly dark inside, you're in for a pleasant surprise. Whitewashed walls and white seating make for a light, summery feel, and there are modern paintings to divert the eye. A definite Italian influence is detectable in the earlier dishes on the menus, with pasta, prosciutto and risottos to the fore, as well as side dishes of artichokes. Crab linguini can be sized up to main-course proportions, and comes with upstanding notes of chilli and garlic. Otherwise, rack of local lamb might be accoutred with a soufflé of sundried tomato and goats' cheese for a labour-intensive dish. Ice creams such as Baileys and Horlicks are one way to round things off, or there might be a traditional English pudding such as sticky toffee with caramel sauce and clotted cream.

Chef Sebastian Snow **Owner** Sebastian & Lana Snow **Times** 12-3/6-10 Closed 25 Dec, D Sun **Prices** Fixed L 2 course fr £13, Fixed D 3 course fr £16, Starter £6-£9.50, Main £11.25-£18, Dessert £6-£6.50, Service optional, Groups min 8 service 12.5% **Wines** 80 bottles over £20, 22 bottles under £20, 16 by glass **Notes** Sunday L, Vegetarian menu **Seats** 70, Pr/dining room 24 **Children** Portions, Menu

STONEHOUSE Map 4 SO80

Stonehouse Court

Modern British

Modern British style in Elizabethan manor, plus ghost

☎ 0871 8713240
Bristol Rd GL10 3RA
e-mail: info@stonehousecourt.co.uk
dir: M5 junct 13, off A419. Follow signs for Stonehouse, hotel on right 0.25m after 2nd rdbt

There's nothing like the prospect of a ghostly visitation to add a frisson to staying in a country house - and this Elizabethan manor in six acres of lovely gardens overlooking the Stroud Canal comes with the shade of a spurned butler-turned-arsonist. He is said to have started the fire in 1908 that left only the stone walls and some sections of Tudor panelling intact. In Henry's Restaurant, clean-cut modern style sits happily with dark oak panelling as a backdrop to Mediterranean-accented modern cooking made from fine local materials. You might start with seared scallops with celeriac, Granny Smith apples and truffle vinaigrette as a build up to loin and 16-hour-cooked belly of Cotswold pork accompanied by apple and black pudding purée and Stowford Press cider sauce. Desserts put a modern spin on classics - perhaps lemongrass crème brûlée with strawberry jus and sorbet.

Times 7-10

STOW-ON-THE-WOLD Map 11 SP12

Fosse Manor

Modern British

Accomplished cooking in elegant country-house hotel

☎ 01451 830354
GL54 1JX
e-mail: enquiries@fossemanor.co.uk
dir: From Stow-on-the-Wold take A429 S for 1m

Set in five acres of peaceful grounds, Fosse Manor sits in the heart of the Cotswolds on the fringes of the tourist honeypot of Stow-on-the-Wold. The honey-hued, creeper-swathed stone façade of the former rectory looks like it might open onto an interior of country chintz, but the interior has been brought smartly up-to-date with a seamless blend of contemporary and traditional themes. The kitchen, too, has moved with the times, evolving an appealing repertoire of modern British cuisine built on classic flavour combinations. A typical starter pairs Cotswold chicken and morel mushroom ravioli with parsley broth, followed by roast suprême of cod with onion purée, potato rösti, salsify and Shiraz butter sauce. Meat fans might prefer the comfort of honey-roast pork belly with bubble-and-squeak, crackling and apple sauce.

Times 12-2/7-9

The Kings Head Inn

Traditional British

Charming village-green inn serving accomplished traditional food

☎ 01608 658365
The Green, Bledington OX7 6XQ
e-mail: kingshead@orr-ewing.com
dir: On B4450, 4m from Stow-on-the-Wold

Picture this: a mellow stone Cotswolds pub looking onto a village green with ducks playing in a meandering brook; inside are wobbly floors - wobblier still after a few jars of Hook Norton - heart-warming log fires, head-cracking beams and an unbuttoned dining room kitted out with solid oak tables on a flagstone floor. A popular place, it is run by genuinely welcoming people and the inventive cooking is a cut or two above your average pub. Exceptional raw ingredients - largely free-range, organic and local - lead the cooking, starting with a pigeon breast, chicken liver and black pudding salad, then Aberdeen Angus beef from the family's Fifield farm is the star in a steak and ale pie with puff pastry and fries.

Chef Charlie Loader **Owner** Archie & Nicola Orr-Ewing **Times** 12-2/7-9.30 Closed 25-26 Dec **Prices** Starter £5-£7.50, Main £9.50-£22, Dessert £5.50-£6.50, Service optional, Groups min 8 service 10% **Wines** 17 bottles over £20, 28 bottles under £20, 8 by glass **Notes** Sunday L, Vegetarian available **Seats** 32 **Children** Portions **Parking** 20

The Old Butcher's

European

Appealing modern cooking in informal surroundings

☎ 01451 831700
Park St GL54 1AQ
e-mail: info@theoldbutchers.com

Peter Robinson's contemporary brasserie-style eaterie, squeezed into an old butcher's shop, certainly stands out in civilised Stow, which oozes traditional Cotswold charm. Beyond the decked terrace and modern glass frontage, expect to find polished wood tables, banquette seating, tasteful artwork on white walls, a stylish bar area, and a relaxing, buzzy vibe. Equally bang up-to-date are the refreshingly uncomplicated and well-presented dishes listed on simply described daily menus. Flavours shine through due to careful handling of quality local ingredients. Well-judged dishes may include marinated squid with dill, red onion and rocket, followed by slow-cooked lamb shank with paprika and peas, grilled rabbit with salsa verde, or calves' brains with capers and lemon. Leave room for pannacotta with almond caramel and grappa. There's an excellent value set lunch menu, too.

Chef Peter Robinson **Owner** Louise & Peter Robinson **Times** 12-2.30/6-9.30 Closed 1 wk in May & Oct **Prices** Fixed L 2 course £12, Starter £5.50-£8, Main £12.50-£17.50, Dessert £5.50-£7, Service optional **Wines** 55 bottles over £20, 19 bottles under £20, 14 by glass **Notes** Sunday L, Vegetarian available **Seats** 45 **Children** Portions **Parking** On street

STROUD Map 4 SO80

Burleigh Court Hotel

British, European

Grand old house, confident cooking

☎ 01453 883804
Burleigh, Minchinhampton GL5 2PF
e-mail: info@burleighcourthotel.co.uk
dir: 2.5m SE of Stroud, off A419

The superb views from Burleigh over the Golden Valley can be admired from the terraced gardens designed in the 1930s by Clough Williams-Ellis. The house is no slouch either, built on a grand scale at the beginning of the 19th century out of local Cotswold stone, with a delightful oak-panelled bar, traditionally decorated bedrooms and a formal dining room. The menu is fittingly refined and not overly complicated, based around high quality produce, and making good use of local ingredients. Simple ideas are well executed, such as a starter of glazed goats' cheese in a salad with walnuts, pears and flat-leaf parsley pesto, or rack of Cornish lamb (perfectly cooked, covered in a brioche crust) with fondant potato, spinach and a purple mustard jus. A summer dessert might be strawberry and basil parfait, supported by strawberries as both compôte and consommé. Service hits the right notes.

Chef Adrian Jarrad **Owner** Louise Noble **Times** 12-2/7-9 Closed 24-26 Dec **Prices** Food prices not confirmed for 2011. Please telephone for details **Wines** 50 bottles over £20, 15 bottles under £20, 7 by glass **Notes** Sunday L, Vegetarian available, Civ Wed 50 **Seats** 34, Pr/dining room 18 **Children** Portions, Menu **Parking** 28

TETBURY Map 4 ST89

The Conservatory at Calcot Manor

Modern British NOTABLE WINE LIST

Charming 14th-century Cotswold retreat with vibrant modern cuisine

☎ 01666 890391
Calcot GL8 8YJ
e-mail: reception@calcotmanor.co.uk
dir: M4 junct 18, A46 towards Stroud. At x-roads junct with A4135 turn right, then 1st left

The days when Calcot Manor was a lowly farmhouse are long gone: it is now resurrected as a design-led boutique-style country-house hotel for 21st-century sybarites with pampering on the agenda. A fabulous health spa takes care of the body, while the contemporary rustic chic of the luminous Conservatory Restaurant panders to the palate. The kitchen takes a strong stance on sourcing locally for its repertoire of modern British dishes; flavours have real punch - spot the stylish wood-burning oven that adds an authentically rustic Mediterranean edge. Seared scallops are teamed with a vibrant coriander sauce and lentils, ahead of a garlic and parsley-crusted roast rack of lamb served with confit shoulder, sweetbreads and boulangère potatoes. Dessert puts a new spin on a classic - baked Alaska with rum-roasted pineapple. A second eating option - the casual pub-style Gumstool Inn - offers unfussy comfort-food dining.

Chef Michael Croft **Owner** Richard Ball (MD) **Times** 12-2/7-9.30 **Prices** Fixed L 2 course £19.50, Starter £7.50-£13.95, Main £17-£24, Dessert £8.75, Service optional **Wines** 6 bottles under £20, 12 by glass **Notes** Sunday L, Vegetarian available, Civ Wed 100 **Seats** 100, Pr/dining room 16 **Children** Portions, Menu **Parking** 150

THORNBURY Map 4 ST69

Ronnie's

Modern European NOTABLE WINE LIST NEW

Confident seasonal cooking at a fair price

☎ 01454 411137
11 St Mary St BS35 2AB
e-mail: info@ronnies-restaurant.co.uk

Tucked away in the town's small shopping arcade, Ronnies is something of a lifestyle choice, with an all-day café lounge bolstering the restaurant's output. It's a stylish modern affair, sympathetically crafted from a one-time 17th-century schoolhouse; minimalist yet smart, with exposed natural stone walls, solid-oak floors and leather chairs all fitting the relaxed but upbeat brief. Ronnie Faulkner's cooking takes an equally modern approach while ticking all the right boxes - quality, local and seasonal ingredients put to good use in carefully-prepared, accomplished dishes that meld classic thinking with contemporary verve. Wild mushroom risotto with black chanterelles, champagne and truffle oil, for example, or local Badminton Estate venison Wellington served with celeriac purée, baby carrots and a port and juniper jus. There's good value here too, with fixed-price lunch and early-evening proving something of a steal.

Chef Ron Faulkner & George Kostka **Owner** Ron Faulkner **Times** 12-3/6.30-10.30 Closed 25-26 Dec, 1 Jan, Mon, D Sun **Prices** Fixed L 2 course fr £9.75, Fixed D 3 course fr £19, Starter £4.50-£9.50, Main £13.50-£19.75, Dessert £4.95-£6.95, Service optional, Groups min 7 service 10% **Wines** 55 bottles over £20, 12 bottles under £20, 13 by glass **Notes** Sunday L, Vegetarian available **Seats** 68 **Children** Portions **Parking** Car park

Thornbury Castle

Modern British

Up-to-date cooking in a majestic Tudor castle

☎ 01454 281182
Castle St BS35 1HH
e-mail: info@thornburycastle.co.uk
dir: M5 junct 16, N on A38. 4m to lights, turn left. Follow brown Historic Castle signs. Restaurant behind St Mary's church

Technically, Thornbury isn't a castle, not in the fortress sense, as its minimal defences were never meant for any serious scrapping - but that's just splitting hairs. Henry VIII once courted Anne Boleyn in this majestic Tudor manor house before it all ended in tears. Dining in the hexagonal restaurant is a treat: its cross-shaped arrow slit windows and tobacco-brown panelled walls evoke images of Tudor banquets, but you won't find any medieval hog roasts here - the kitchen takes a rather more modern country-house route, using well-sourced ingredients in classic combinations. Wine lovers take note: Thornbury Castle still has its own bijou vineyard where wine has been made for 500 years. Tian of foie

continued

THORNBURY *continued*

gras and confit duck leg with Sauternes jelly and pear and fig chutney is a typical opener; next might come fried halibut with cocotte potatoes and a saffron and mussel consommé, or cannon of local lamb with braised shoulder, black olive mash, confit fennel and a goats' cheese beignet.

Chef Lee Heptinstall **Owner** von Essen **Times** 11.45-2/7-9 **Prices** Food prices not confirmed for 2011. Please telephone for details **Wines** 278 bottles over £20, 2 bottles under £20, 7 by glass **Notes** Sunday L, Vegetarian available, Dress restrictions, Smart casual, No jeans, trainers, T-shirts, Civ Wed 50 **Seats** 72, Pr/dining room 22 **Children** Portions, Menu **Parking** 50

UPPER SLAUGHTER **Map 10 SP12**

Lords of the Manor

– see below

WICK **Map 4 ST77**

Oakwood

Modern British

Well-judged cooking in a classy stone manor house

☎ 0117 937 1800
The Park, Bath Rd BS30 5RN
e-mail: info@tpresort.com
dir: Just off A420

The Cotswold manor house stands in a 240-acre estate mentioned in the Domesday Book. Today, it is an opulent golfing hotel, with an intimate feature restaurant, where chefs are on parade behind a counter, in a kitchen centred on a wood-burning oven. Stone walls and subdued lighting form the backdrop to a culinary operation of great class, with high quality produce predominating and a finely judged approach to flavour combinations. Choose from main dishes such as salt-cured duck leg on a mixed bean casserole, in tomato, thyme and white wine sauce, or brill with Cornish mussels and saffron. A winter menu delivers an inventive dessert in the shape of white chocolate and vodka parfait with new season's rhubarb.

Chef Phil Clench **Owner** TP Resort Ltd **Times** 12-2.30/7-9.30 Closed L Mon-Sat **Prices** Starter £4.95-£6.95, Main £10.75-£14.90, Dessert £4.75-£5.95, Service added but optional 12.5% **Wines** 48 bottles over £20, 15 bottles under £20, 9 by glass **Notes** Sunday L, Vegetarian available, Civ Wed 130 **Seats** 36, Pr/dining room 130 **Children** Portions, Menu **Parking** 250

WINCHCOMBE **Map 10 SP02**

5 North Street

– see opposite page

Lords of the Manor

UPPER SLAUGHTER **Map 10 SP12**

Modern British 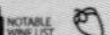

Gutsy modern European cooking in a stylishly-refurbished country house

☎ 01451 820243
GL54 2JD
e-mail: enquiries@lordsofthemanor.com
dir: Follow signs towards The Slaughters 2m W of A429. Hotel on right in centre of Upper Slaughter

The honey stone 17th-century former rectory presents an unchanged exterior of that chocolate-box Cotswoldy Englishness so beloved of well-heeled international guests. But inside, it's another story altogether: a major facelift in 2008 has delivered 1.8 million quid's worth of vibrant splashes of colour, funky fabrics, and contemporary furnishings, all rubbing along seamlessly with antiques, mullioned windows and grand fireplaces. It's a décor that works particularly well in the dining room, where vast modern artworks explode against ivory walls. A passion for French classical cooking informs chef Matt Weedon's endeavours - expect elaborately-crafted modern dishes with big, bold, clearly-defined flavours founded on top-drawer local, seasonal produce. A restlessly inventive streak is evident right from the off: perhaps mi-cuit Adlestrop Estate wood pigeon, served with pastilla of leg meat, tartare, beetroot sorbet, pickled mushrooms and fig purée. Main course might serve Middlewhite pork three ways - as fillet, braised belly, and steamed suet pudding of shoulder, with red cabbage, apple pork jus and crackling, while desserts demonstrate the same mastery of technical skills - perhaps prune and Armagnac soufflé with Earl Grey tea mousse, and prune and Armagnac ice cream. An outstanding wine list majors in Italian vintages, with some gilt-edge Tuscans as well as plenty of more affordable bottles.

Chef Matt Weedon **Owner** Empire Ventures **Times** 12-2.30/7-9.30 Closed L Mon-Sat **Prices** Food prices not confirmed for 2011. Please telephone for details **Wines** 700+ bottles over £20, 10 bottles under £20, 15 by glass **Notes** Sunday L, Vegetarian available, Dress restrictions, Smart casual, no trainers or jeans, Civ Wed 50 **Seats** 50, Pr/dining room 30 **Children** Portions, Menu **Parking** 40

5 North Street

WINCHCOMBE Map 10 SP02

Modern European V

Cotswold star serving emphatically-flavoured, first-class food

☎ 01242 604566
5 North St GL54 5LH
e-mail: marcusashenford@yahoo.co.uk
dir: 7m from Cheltenham

Squeezed into an ancient bow-fronted building of sagging timbers just off the high street, this pocket-sized restaurant shows that good things really do come in small packages: the Ashenfords' restaurant is a serious contender in the constantly evolving Cotswolds dining scene. The two rustic dining rooms may have a subtly understated cottagey familiarity - albeit with high-backed chocolate leather chairs and terracotta walls to inject a note of contemporary style - but the kitchen is certainly working on a higher plane. Marcus Ashenford cooks in an unpretentious but highly confident style that brings together some of the gutsy aspects of British cooking with pedigree ingredients and the finesse of French classical technique. Combinations are intelligent and result in head-spinning depth of flavour. Dinner offers three fixed-price options to suit most pockets, plus a seven-course Gourmet menu. There's some bold thinking in a starter of scallops with foie gras, creamed cauliflower, sweet braised onion and beetroot syrup; next up, chump of local lamb is teamed with sweetbreads, Savoy cabbage, crisp artichokes, carrot and star anise purée, lamb and thyme jus. Dessert might bring the fine-tuned flavours of bayleaf and vanilla pannacotta, lemon meringue, lime curd, caramelised banana and plum sauce. Under Kate Ashenford's guidance, service fits the bill too - unstuffy and friendly, but always on-the-ball and informed.

Chef Marcus Ashenford **Owner** Marcus & Kate Ashenford **Times** 12.30-1.30/7-9 Closed 1st 2 wks Jan, 1 wk Aug, Mon, L Tue, D Sun **Prices** Fixed L 2 course fr £22, Fixed D 3 course £36-£46, Tasting menu £57-£67, Service optional **Wines** 60 bottles over £20, 12 bottles under £20, 6 by glass **Notes** Gourmet menu 7/10 course, Sunday L, Vegetarian menu **Seats** 26 **Children** Portions **Parking** On street, pay & display

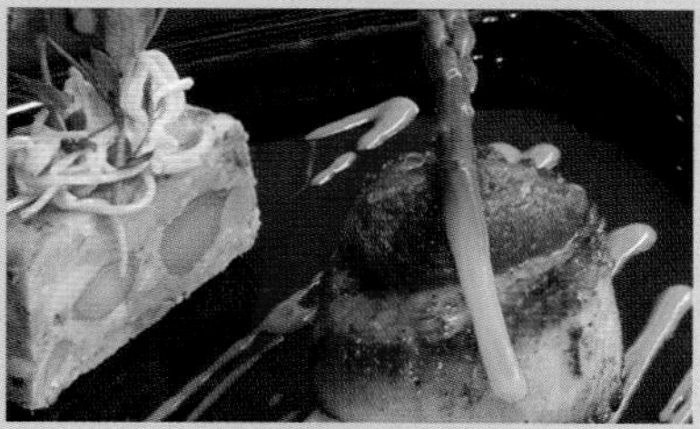

WINCHCOMBE ***continued***

Wesley House

Modern British

Sound cooking in historic Cotswold building

01242 602366
High St GL54 5LJ
e-mail: enquiries@wesleyhouse.co.uk
web: www.wesleyhouse.co.uk
dir: In centre of Winchcombe

A half-timbered property in the heart of this bustling Cotswold town, Wesley House was named after the Methodist preacher who once stayed here in the 18th century. Full of traditional character, with beamed ceilings, exposed stone, and open fireplaces, the restaurant also incorporates a stylish glass atrium with unique modern lighting and stunning floral displays from a renowned local florist. The kitchen concentrates on seasonal produce and well-defined flavour combinations. Start with fillet of beef, oxtail raviolo, mashed potato and Madeira sauce and follow with roasted guinea fowl with gratin potatoes, Savoy cabbage and tarragon sauce. Dark chocolate tart with orange compôte and chocolate crisp makes for a well-judged finale. Look out for special offers at lunchtime.

Chef Martin Dunn **Owner** Matthew Brown **Times** 12-2/7-9 Closed D Sun **Prices** Fixed L 2 course fr £12.50, Fixed D 3 course fr £24.50, Starter £5.50-£7.50, Main £13.50-£24.50, Dessert fr £6.95, Service optional **Wines** 65 bottles over £20, 20 bottles under £20, 15 by glass **Notes** Sunday L, Vegetarian available, Civ Wed 60 **Seats** 70, Pr/dining room 24 **Children** Portions **Parking** In the square

Wesley House Bar & Grill

European **NEW**

Wesley House's funky sibling

01242 602366
High St GL54 5LJ
e-mail: enquiries@wesleyhouse.co.uk
dir: In the centre of Winchcombe

Wesley House (see entry) has another string to its bow in the form of this relaxed bar and grill next door. It mixes old-world character and contemporary verve with some style - it looks rather cool with its brightly coloured furniture, funky bar and an appropriately relaxed approach to service. Whereas next door is the place to go for a more formal gastronomic experience, the bar and grill is about lighter dishes, express lunches and a lively atmosphere, but rest assured the same high quality produce and attention to detail are in evidence. A starter of Fowey mussels with lemongrass, ginger, coriander and coconut shows the style, following on, perhaps, with main-course escalope of chicken with crushed new potatoes, mushrooms and Madeira sauce, or fishcakes with fennel salad and tartare sauce.

Chef Martin Dunn **Owner** Matthew Brown **Times** 12-2/6-10 Closed Sun-Mon **Prices** Food prices not confirmed for 2011. Please telephone for details **Notes** Vegetarian available **Seats** 50 **Children** Portions

WOTTON-UNDER-EDGE **Map 4 ST79**

Orangery Restaurant

Modern British

A local flavour in an inspiring conservatory setting

01454 263000
Tortworth Court Four Pillars, Tortworth GL12 8HH
e-mail: tortworth@four-pillars.co.uk
web: www.four-pillars.co.uk
dir: M5 junct 14. Follow B4509 towards Wotton. Turn right at top of hill onto Tortworth Rd, hotel 0.5m on right

A grandiose Victorian Gothic manor in 30 acres of grounds with an arboretum and expansive swathes of lawn makes a strong enough impression, but the Orangery Restaurant beats it by a length. An elegantly curvaceous free-standing glass conservatory built in 1899 has been restored to its full grandeur and fitted out as a one-off dining venue. Top-grade local produce from nearby farms is sold in the Tortworth Estate shop, which supplies a goodly share of what appears on your plate. Classic dishes are done simply and with skill: take lobster, langoustine and salmon ravioli with olive tapenade and lobster bisque for starters, then follow with Saxon Farm pork belly and pistachio roulade with parsnip purée, braised pork cheeks, and pickled walnut and apple chutney.

Chef Nigel Jones **Owner** Four Pillars
Times 12-2.30/6.30-10 Closed Sun-Mon, L Sat
Prices Fixed L 2 course fr £15.95, Starter £6-£9, Main £16-£22, Dessert £6.50-£8, Service included **Wines** 24 bottles over £20, 28 bottles under £20, 13 by glass **Notes** Vegetarian available, Dress restrictions, Smart casual, Civ Wed 120 **Seats** 90, Pr/dining room 12 **Children** Portions **Parking** 150

GREATER MANCHESTER

DELPH **Map 16 SD90**

The Saddleworth Hotel

Modern European **NEW**

Confidently modern food in the lush Castleshaw valley

01457 871888
Huddersfield Rd OL3 5LX
e-mail: enquiries@thesaddleworthhotel.co.uk
dir: A62, located between A6052 & A670

Barely half-an-hour from Manchester, in the heart of the Castleshaw valley, the Saddleworth stands amid nine acres of woodland and gardens, not far from the site of a Roman fortress. If you like, they'll collect you in a chauffeur-driven Roller from the railway station, setting the tone for the formal, but appreciably warm approach. Black table linen and crystal glassware make a dramatic visual impact in the dining room. Anthony Byrom cooks a fashionably understated modern menu, with thoroughbred meats - Millstone Farm aged beef fillet, for example - among the headline ingredients. Start with a big fresh langoustine, accompanied by riotously rich truffled tortellini, before a pairing of halibut and scallops in butter sauce with pickled vegetables. An avant-garde dessert might be chocolate (fondant) with parsnip (ice cream) and bee pollen. This is a kitchen that may well achieve even greater things.

Chef Anthony Byrom **Owner** A J Baker **Times** 12-2/7-10 **Prices** Fixed L 2 course £20-£30, Fixed D 4 course fr £50, Tasting menu £75, Starter £6-£12, Main £11-£22, Dessert £6-£10, Service optional **Wines** 4 bottles over £20, 3 bottles under £20 **Notes** Sunday L, Vegetarian available, Dress restrictions, Smart casual, Civ Wed 400 **Seats** 30, Pr/dining room 6 **Children** Portions **Parking** 200

MANCHESTER Map 16 SJ89

City Café

Modern European

Contemporary European cooking in the bustling heart of Manchester

☎ 0161 242 1020 & 242 1000
City Inn Manchester, One Piccadilly Place, 1 Auburn St M1 3DG
e-mail: manchesteradmin@cityinn.com
dir: M56 onto A5103 to end of Princess Parkway, at rdbt take 3rd exit onto Mancunian Way, take 1st exit at traffic lights, turn left and follow road round to the right

In a prime location at the heart of the action, this stylish modern restaurant at the City Inn Hotel ticks all the right in-place boxes. If you're into people gazing, watch the world go by on Piccadilly Place from the outdoor terrace, otherwise, head indoors to the smart, softly stylish restaurant to tuck into the appealing and assured modern European cooking. Take pressed ham hock and parsley terrine served with white peach chutney and a pan-fried quail's egg, while to follow, perhaps rack of lamb Niçoise with creamed white onion and basil lamb jus. Finish on a smile with classic glazed lemon tart or a chocolate fondant.

Times 12-2.30/5.30-10

The Dining Rooms @ Worsley Park

British

Country club with appealingly modish food

☎ 0161 975 2000
Walkden Rd, Worsley M28 2QT
e-mail: anna.collier@marriotthotels.com
dir: M60 junct 13, over 1st rdbt take A575. Hotel 400yds on left

Near to Manchester centre, and with the motorways close to hand, this country club hotel has a great location, complete with its own golf course in 200 acres of parkland that was once the Duke of Bridgwater's estate. The Dining Rooms - three of them, to be precise - are done out in a luminous contemporary style that attracts a strong local following for uncomplicated modern British food, prepared by a kitchen that makes sourcing prime North West of England ingredients a priority. Seared king scallops come with Bury black pudding - the best there is, according to its fans - and mustard sauce, followed by roast loin and confit belly of local pork with young leeks and red wine jus. Puddings take a similar no-nonsense approach - perhaps Manchester tart with Gornall's dairy cream.

Chef Sean Kelly **Owner** Marriott Hotels **Times** 1-3/5-10 Closed L Mon-Sat **Prices** Fixed L 3 course fr £17, Fixed D 3 course fr £29, Tasting menu £40, Starter £6.50-£10.50, Main £14.50-£22.50, Dessert £5-£7.50, Service optional **Wines** 40 bottles over £20, 27 bottles under £20, 20 by glass **Notes** Signature taster menu 3 course & coffee, Sunday L, Vegetarian available, Dress restrictions, Smart casual, Civ Wed 200 **Seats** 140, Pr/dining room 14 **Children** Portions, Menu **Parking** 250

The French

British, French

Lovingly preserved Edwardian hotel in the city centre

☎ 0161 236 3333
The Midland Hotel, Peter St M60 2DS
e-mail: midlandsales@qhotels.co.uk
dir: M602 junct 3, follow Manchester Central Convention Complex signs, hotel opposite

The Midland Hotel opened in 1903 in the Belle Epoque era of railways and waxed moustaches, and remains a time-warp bubble of Edwardian opulence to savour in a world of functional minimalism. The French Restaurant comes with a whiff of pre-war Paris - fleur-de-lys wallpaper, high ceilings and chandeliers, and just out of sight, a pianist floating his music unobtrusively into the dining room. The ambience says silver cloche service, dishes flambéed at the table by waiters named Serge, but the cooking, although rooted in the classics, takes a rather more modern route. You might start with a bang up-to-date match of scallops with caramelised cauliflower and pig's cheek, then follow with a cutlet and belly of Lakeland pork with black pudding, dates and celeriac; fish might appear in the form of brill teamed with parsley, risotto, cockles and chicken wings. The French's soufflés are renowned as a high point on which to finish - perhaps a treacle tart version with praline ice cream.

Chef Paul Beckley **Owner** QHotels **Times** 7-11 Closed BHs, Sun-Mon, L all week **Prices** Fixed D 3 course fr £35, Starter £7.95-£14.95, Main £22.95-£75, Dessert £7.95, Service optional **Wines** 69 bottles over £20, 13 by glass **Notes** Dress restrictions, Smart casual, No sportswear, Civ Wed 50 **Seats** 55 **Children** Portions **Parking** NCP behind hotel

Greens

Modern Vegetarian V

Well-established vegetarian restaurant

☎ 0161 434 4259
43 Lapwing Ln, West Didsbury M20 2NT
e-mail: simoncgreens@aol.com
dir: Between Burton Rd & Palatine Rd

A stalwart of the Mancunian veggie scene for almost two decades, Greens has gone from strength to strength in its trendy Didsbury base. Simon Rimmer's high profile as a TV celeb chef has certainly helped to boost an interest in meatless eating, as the vibrant bistro-style operation has doubled in size after expanding into the neighbouring premises. His approach kicks any notion of stodgy lentil bakes into touch: dishes are conceived with verve and creativity, dipping freely into the world's larder to come up with eclectic and kaleidoscopic combinations of flavours to keep the taste buds tickled. You could start with a classic Greek salad with red onion shortbread, or a more inventive lemongrass and chilli-spiced beetroot mousse with poppy seed straws, ahead of a hearty Lancashire hotpot with barley, root vegetables and cabbage.

Chef Simon Rimmer **Owner** Simon Connolly & Simon Rimmer **Times** 12-2/5.30-10.30 Closed BHs, L Mon **Prices** Fixed D 3 course £15.95, Starter £3.50-£6.50, Main £9.95-£12.95, Dessert £5.50-£6.50, Service optional, Groups min 6 service 10% **Wines** 6 bottles over £20, 16 bottles under £20, 6 by glass **Notes** Sunday L, Vegetarian menu **Seats** 84 **Children** Portions, Menu **Parking** On street

Harvey Nichols Second Floor Restaurant

Modern European

Trendy dining overlooking Exchange Square

☎ 0161 828 8898
21 New Cathedral St M1 1AD
e-mail: secondfloor.reservations@harveynichols.com
dir: Just off Deansgate, town centre. 5 min walk from Victoria Station, on Exchange Sq

The snazzy bar and brasserie on the second floor of this trendy department store has vast full-length glass walls giving sweeping views over the Manchester skyline. It's the place to meet and eat for fashionable foodie shoppers who know about the kitchen's confident modern European cooking. Expect well-proven combinations on a menu that is never at a loss for good ideas - take, for example, a starter of superbly caramelised sweetbreads with Cheshire bacon, mushroom bhaji and onion purée, then follow with an inventive main-course Morecambe brill with pea tortellini, clam chowder and bacon foam. Finish with a fragrant Earl Grey parfait with citrus fruits.

Chef Stuart Thomson **Owner** Harvey Nichols **Times** 12-3/6-10.30 Closed 25-26 Dec, 1 Jan, Etr Sun, D Sun-Mon **Prices** Tasting menu £50, Starter £8-£11, Main £15-£22, Dessert £8-£10, Service added but optional 10% **Wines** 100+ bottles over £20, 30 bottles under £20, 20 by glass **Notes** Tasting menu 5 course, Pre-theatre menu Tue-Fri 6-7pm £25, Sunday L, Vegetarian available **Seats** 50 **Children** Portions, Menu **Parking** Under store, across road

Lowry Hotel, The River Restaurant

Modern British

Unfussy British classics in stylish modern hotel

☎ 0161 827 4000 & 827 4041
50 Dearmans Place, Chapel Wharf, Salford M3 5LH
e-mail: hostess@roccofortehotels.com
dir: M6 junct 19, A556/M56/A5103 for 4.5m. At rdbt take A57(M) to lights, right onto Water St. Left to New Quay St/ Trinity Way. At 1st lights right onto Chapel St for hotel

A fashionable address on the Manchester dining scene, and part of the über-cool Lowry Hotel, The River Restaurant looks across the River Irwell from the glass-fronted luxury of its five-star home. It's on the Salford side of the river, but only a short walk to Manchester's heart. The clean-cut designer décor ticks all the right boxes, with leather banquettes, crisp, white linen-clad

continued

MANCHESTER ***continued***

tables, wooden flooring, and bright artwork to jazz up the neutral tones; friendly, well-informed staff ensure everything ticks along nicely. The unfussy British brasserie fare is taken seriously, carefully prepared and based on well-sourced ingredients, the farmers and producers duly name checked. To start, fried Burford Brown egg with Bury black pudding and baby squid seems a wholly appropriate beginning, following on with Cheshire Belgium Blue rib steak (on the bone) with hollandaise sauce and chips. Black cherry cheesecake hits the spot for dessert.

Chef Oliver Thomas **Owner** Sir Rocco Forte & family **Times** 12-2.30/6-10.30 **Prices** Fixed L 3 course £15-£19.50, Fixed D 3 course £15, Starter £7-£11.50, Main £12.50-£32.50, Dessert £7-£10.50, Service added but optional 10% **Wines** 100 bottles over £20, 10 bottles under £20, 8 by glass **Notes** Sunday L, Vegetarian available, Civ Wed 108 **Seats** 108, Pr/dining room 20 **Children** Portions, Menu **Parking** 100, NCP

Malmaison Manchester

® British, French

Brasserie menu in a city-centre boutique hotel

☎ 0161 278 1000
1-3 Piccadilly M1 1LZ
e-mail: manchester@malmaison.com
dir: From M56 follow signs to Manchester, then to Piccadilly

The former warehouse with its handsome brick facings in the city centre makes a particularly head-turning boutique hotel. Chic interior styling in red and black is very much in the Malmaison house style, and the wood-floored, candlelit restaurant maintains the spirit with a menu of informal brasserie eating. Leek vinaigrette with Fourme d'Ambert and caramelised pecans, or a plate of Iberico Bellota ham, might set the ball rolling, and lead on to rump of new season's lamb with crushed new potatoes and Niçoise jus. Superior burgers with bacon and gruyère will prove hard to resist for many.

Times 12-2.30/6-11

Moss Nook

® British, French V

Traditional haute cuisine not far from the airport

☎ 0161 437 4778
Ringway Rd, Moss Nook M22 5NA
e-mail: enquiries@mossnookrest.co.uk
dir: 1m from airport at junction of Ringway Road with B5166

In a village just a mile from Manchester airport, Moss Nook is a rustic traditional restaurant at ease with its soft-edged comfort. No stripped-out modern minimalism here, thank you - just the old-school look of spotless white linen laid with silverware, crystal and fresh flowers, and there's an alfresco pergola terrace for warm day dining. Confident Anglo-French cooking from a chef who has manned the stoves for over 25 years is what keeps the customers happy here. Start with pan-seared Scottish scallops accompanied by asparagus, and lime and dill butter sauce, before moving on to loin of Cheshire venison with chive and mustard mash and Madeira sauce. To finish, go for a crème brûlée with blueberry sorbet.

Chef Kevin Lofthouse **Owner** P & D Harrison **Times** 12-1.30/7-9.30 Closed 1 wk Jan, Sun-Mon, L Sat **Prices** Fixed L 2 course fr £15, Starter £8.75-£12, Main £20-£23, Dessert £6.75-£7 **Wines** 100 bottles over £20, 10 bottles under £20, 8 by glass **Notes** Fixed L 5 course £21, Fixed D 6 course £38.50, Vegetarian menu, Dress restrictions, No jeans, trainers **Seats** 72 **Parking** 30

Signatures

® Modern British

Mezzanine restaurant with city skyline views

☎ 0844 879 9088
Macdonald Manchester Hotel, London Rd M1 2PG
e-mail: sales.manchester@macdonald-hotels.co.uk
web: sales.manchester@macdonald-hotels.co.uk
dir: Opposite Piccadilly Station

Bright by day, intimate by night, the relaxed and spacious Signatures Restaurant commands stunning views across Manchester's skyline from its lofty location within this smart modern hotel. The menus offer an ever-growing range of organic foods, grass-fed beef and fish; salmon, kippers and haddock are supplied by the Loch Fyne Oysters company. Classic dishes are prepared with flair and imagination in the open kitchen, and might include duck and quail terrine with sweet wine jelly and toasted brioche to start, with main courses such as pan-fried monkfish with white onion tart, caramelised chicory and red wine sauce.

Times 6-10

MANCHESTER AIRPORT Map 15 SJ88

Etrop Grange Hotel

® Modern Mediterranean NEW

Georgian splendour beside the airport

☎ 0161 499 0500
Thorley Ln M90 4EG
e-mail: etropgrange@foliohotels.com
dir: Off M56 junct 5. Follow signs to Terminal 2, take 1st left (Thorley Ln), 200yds on right

If you can filter out the sound of planes taking off and landing at Manchester Airport next-door, and focus on the Georgian elegance of this Grade II listed mansion, you can imagine yourself right out in the countryside. Recently refurbished to the tune of £1.8 million, Etrop Grange has retained all the charm and character you'd expect to find in a house built in 1780. The Coach House Restaurant hasn't missed out on the refurb, and it's now a light and airy space decorated in a contemporary but sympathetic style. Apple and Bury black pudding salad with a softly poached egg is a typical starter, which might be followed by seared sea bass fillet with brown shrimps, spinach and new potatoes, and cappuccino chocolate fondant with vanilla bean ice cream.

Times 12-2/6.30-10 Closed L Sat

OLDHAM Map 16 SD90

White Hart Inn

®® Modern, Traditional British

Modern British with heritage puddings in a Lancashire inn

☎ 01457 872566
51 Stockport Rd, Lydgate OL4 4JJ
e-mail: bookings@thewhitehart.co.uk
dir: M62 junct 20, A627, continue to end of bypass, then A669 to Saddleworth. Enter Lydgate turn right onto Stockport Rd. White Hart Inn 50yds on left

Standing opposite an old church on an A-road leading out of Oldham, the White Hart is a traditional Lancashire inn full of period charm. The beamed interiors and low windows evoke times past, although there is a restrained contemporary feel to the design approach in the main restaurant, which is open for business in the latter half of the week, but serves the same menu as the less formal Brasserie. Interesting dishes may include curried cauliflower risotto cakes with lemon and coriander mayonnaise, wild sea bass and king scallop in chorizo butter sauce with new potato and watercress salad, and some good vegetarian options, but puddings revert to the heritage recipe-book for jam roly-poly and custard, or lemon posset and shortbread.

Times 12-2.30/6-9.30 Closed 26 Dec, 1 Jan, L Mon-Sat, D Tue & Sun

ROCHDALE Map 16 SD81

Nutters

Modern British V NOTABLE WINE LIST

Technically skilful cooking using the best of Lancashire

☎ 01706 650167
Edenfield Rd, Norden OL12 7TT
e-mail: enquiries@nuttersrestaurant.com
dir: From Rochdale take A680 signed Blackburn. Edenfield Rd on right on leaving Norden

The name is not a gimmick - it belongs to Andrew Nutter, who cooks in the grand environs of Wolstenholme Manor in six acres of manicured parkland overlooking Ashworth Moor. Andrew is no stranger to the world of celebrity chef TV, but there's no grandstanding here - the place may be lavish with its theatrical Gothic arches and soaring ceilings, but it's a welcoming family-run concern whose friendliness has won a loyal following. There's a serious level of technical skills at work in the kitchen that showcases the pick of local produce and paints attractive pictures on the plate - ginger beer-battered brill with coriander, lime and chilli dressing, for example. Ambition and creativity continue in a main-course fillet of St Asaph lamb 'Wellington' with basil mousseline, broad beans and a port reduction, while desserts could be white chocolate and whisky bread-and-butter pudding or warm treacle tart with vanilla mascarpone.

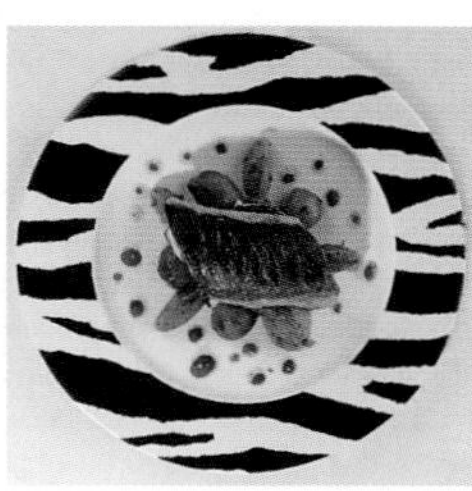

Chef Andrew Nutter **Owner** Mr A Nutter, Mr R Nutter, Mrs K J Nutter **Times** 12-2/6.30-9.30 Closed 1-2 days after Xmas and New Year, Mon **Prices** Fixed L 2 course £13.95, Tasting menu £38, Starter £4.80-£9.50, Main £16.95-£21, Dessert £3.95-£7.80, Service optional, Groups min 8 service 10% **Wines** 159 bottles over £20, 24 bottles under £20, 9 by glass **Notes** Gourmet menu 6 course £38, afternoon tea Tue-Sat £14.50-£22, Vegetarian menu, Dress restrictions, Smart casual, Civ Wed 120 **Seats** 143, Pr/dining room 100 **Children** Portions, Menu **Parking** 100

The Peacock Room

Modern British

Art-deco design and modern British food

☎ 01706 368591
The Crimble, Crimble Ln, Bamford OL11 4AD
e-mail: crimble@thedeckersgroup.com
dir: M62 junct 20 follow signs for Blackburn, left onto B6222 (Bury road) contine for 1m Crimble Lane on left

Peacocks strut their stuff in the grounds and even in the car park, at The Crimble, which dates back to the 17th century when it was a farm. The main restaurant - the Peacock Room - was inspired by ocean liners and retains a decadent art-deco theme with its mirrored ceilings and luxurious fabrics. A small, ornate bar with mullioned glass windows embraces the same look. The modern British menu deals in quality seasonal and regional ingredients to turn out hand-dived seared scallops, for instance, served with crispy pork belly and spiced lentil dressing, followed by chargrilled monkfish, with baby fennel, a warm tomato and chervil vinaigrette. Blackberry macaroon, blackberry sauce and crème anglaise makes a fine end.

Chef Rob Walker **Owner** The Deckers Group **Times** 12-2/6.30-10 Closed Mon-Tue **Prices** Fixed L 2 course £13.50, Fixed D 3 course £18.50, Starter £4.90-£9.50, Main £14.95-£23.95, Dessert £5.95-£6.95, Service optional **Wines** 64 bottles over £20, 10 bottles under £20, 6 by glass **Notes** Tasting menu available 12-2 & 6.30-7.30 Wed-Fri, Sunday L, Vegetarian available, Dress restrictions, Smart casual, no sportswear or trainers, Civ Wed 80 **Seats** 80 **Children** Portions **Parking** 130

WIGAN Map 15 SD50

Bennetts Restaurant

Modern International **NEW**

Contemporary surroundings for confident modern British cooking

☎ 01257 425803
Wrightington Hotel, Moss Ln, Wrightington WN6 9PB
e-mail: info@wrightington.co.uk
dir: M6 junct 27, 0.25m W, hotel on right after church

Handy for the M6, the Wrightington Hotel stands in tranquil landscaped grounds on the edge of the town. A contemporary hotel with a light-filled modern design, it has two bars and Bennetts Restaurant, a stylish, minimalist space with bold artwork, polished tables and pretty views. Expect modern British dishes with plenty of originality and flavour and good use of quality produce. Take terrine of salmon and lobster with tartare sauce, well-cooked roast pork fillet wrapped in Parma ham with pancetta, shallot and grain mustard cream, and cherry pie with home-made ginger ice cream.

Times 6.30-9.30 Closed Sun, L all week

Laureate Restaurant

Modern British

Confident cooking in conservatory restaurant with views

☎ 01257 472100
Macdonald Kilhey Court Hotel, Chorley Rd, Standish WN1 2XN
e-mail: general.kilheycourt@macdonald-hotels.co.uk
dir: M6 junct 27, through village of Standish. Take B5239, left onto A5106, hotel on right

Set in ten acres of private grounds, this impressive Victorian-style country-house hotel is convenient for Liverpool and Manchester. The hotel has fabulous views of Worthington Lake, and a split-level restaurant in a large and airy conservatory provides impressive views of the garden. The seasonal menu features some contemporary ideas and innovative flavour combinations. Oven-roast Gressingham duck breast, for example, comes with pickled sauerkraut and jasmine sauce, and might be preceded by fresh egg linguini with garlic, flat parsley and John Ross-cured oak smoked salmon. Finish with fine apple tart with prune and Armagnac ice cream.

Chef Steve Peel **Owner** Macdonald Hotels **Times** 12.30-2.30/6.30-9.30 Closed L Sat **Prices** Fixed L 2 course £12-£18, Starter £4.95-£7.95, Main £9.95-£19.95, Dessert £4.95-£6.95, Service optional **Wines** 24 bottles over £20, 16 bottles under £20, 13 by glass **Notes** Vegetarian available, Civ Wed 350 **Seats** 80, Pr/dining room 22 **Children** Portions, Menu **Parking** 300

HAMPSHIRE

ALTON Map 5 SU73

Alton Grange Hotel

@@ Modern European

Modern European cooking in the heart of Jane Austen country

☎ 01420 86565
London Rd GU34 4EG
e-mail: info@altongrange.co.uk
dir: 300yds from A31 on A339

Just off the A31, between Farnham and Winchester, Alton Grange is a family-owned hotel in an attractive market town. It also happens to be in the heart of Jane Austen country (her house at Chawton is not far away), so literary tourists will find it a most commodious recourse, as indeed one of Austen's titled ladies might have done. The Tiffany lamps add kaleidoscopic colour to the scene, and the bright style of modern European cooking in Truffles restaurant enhances the appeal. Chorizo, pea and sage risotto, or a crab fritter with pickled red peppers and potato salad, are possible ways to open proceedings, with a follow-up of slow-cooked local lamb in shallots and Madeira heading in a more traditional direction. Inviting combinations of flavours inform desserts such as warm lemon cake with blueberry compôte and ginger ice cream.

Chef David Heath **Owner** Andrea & David Levene **Times** 12-2/7-9.30 Closed 24 Dec-3 Jan (ex 31 Dec) **Prices** Starter £5.50-£7.50, Main £10.95-£15.95, Dessert £5.50, Service added but optional 10% **Wines** 40 bottles over £20, 18 bottles under £20, 12 by glass **Notes** Sunday L, Vegetarian available, Dress restrictions, No shorts or jeans, Civ Wed 100 **Seats** 45, Pr/dining room 18 **Children** Portions **Parking** 40

The Anchor Inn

@@ Traditional British

Great British inn with classy British cooking

☎ 01420 23261
Lower Froyle GU34 4NA
e-mail: info@anchorinnatlowerfroyle.co.uk
dir: Leave A31 at exit for Bentley, follow signs for Lower Froyle. Inn on left

The Anchor Inn is part of a small group and, more importantly, it is part of a vision. A vision to create classic, quintessentially British pubs, such as its sister establishment, The Peat Spade Inn (see entry). Everything from the classy bedrooms, the bar stocked with local ales, the fixtures and fittings and the copious original features reflect the owners' philosophy, and it is all as wonderful as you might hope it to be. That goes for the food, too, which embraces a nose-to-tail ethos, draws on the splendid local larder and turns out some first-rate British dishes. Smoked mackerel pâté on toast with pickled cucumber is a perfectly simple starter done with attention to detail: great home-made soda bread, flavour-packed pâté and the sharpness from the pickle to bring it all together. Lamb three ways includes the beautifully glazed sweetbreads, and sticky toffee pudding is a dessert packed with comforting richness.

Chef Kevin Chandler **Owner** The Millers Collection **Times** 12-2.30/6.30-9.30 Closed 25 Dec, D 26 Dec & 1 Jan **Prices** Starter £5-£10, Main £10-£22, Dessert £6-£8, Service optional **Wines** 58 bottles over £20, 8 bottles under £20, 9 by glass **Notes** Sunday L, Vegetarian available, Civ Wed 30 **Seats** 70, Pr/dining room 20 **Children** Portions **Parking** 36

ANDOVER Map 5 SU34

Esseborne Manor

@ Modern British V

Timeless country-house setting

☎ 01264 736444
Hurstbourne Tarrant SP11 0ER
e-mail: info@esseborne-manor.co.uk
web: www.esseborne-manor.co.uk
dir: Halfway between Andover & Newbury on A343, just 1m N of Hurstbourne Tarrant

Pleasingly intimate and reassuringly traditional, Esseborne is a country-house hotel with plenty of charm and its feet on the ground. It sits high above the beautiful Bourne Valley, surrounded by rolling countryside, with three acres to explore, including a herb garden. The Victorian house retains the feel of a private house, albeit a rather grand one, and inside it is handsomely furnished and decorated in warm, traditional colours. The dining room is suitably formal, with large sash windows, smartly laid tables and comfortably upholstered high-back chairs. The cooking does not ignore the local bounty and delves into traditional British and classical European cooking with some contemporary touches, starting, perhaps, with a tian of local crab with 'elements of gazpacho', following on with a middle course (home-made gravad lax with asparagus vichyssoise) and main-courses such as local pork three ways, served with spiced Bramley apple and butter fondant.

Chef Charles Murray **Owner** Ian Hamilton **Times** 12-2/7-9.30 **Prices** Fixed L 2 course fr £14, Fixed D 3 course £20-£28, Service optional **Wines** 97 bottles over £20, 34 bottles under £20, 13 by glass **Notes** Fixed menu with wine available 2, 3 or 4 course £27-£37, Sunday L, Vegetarian menu, Dress restrictions, Smart dress, Civ Wed 100 **Seats** 35, Pr/dining room 80 **Children** Portions **Parking** 40

BARTON-ON-SEA Map 5 SZ29

Pebble Beach

@ French, Mediterranean

Stunning views and simply prepared, quality local ingredients

☎ 01425 627777
Marine Dr BH25 7DZ
e-mail: mail@pebblebeach.uk.com
dir: Follow A35 from Southampton onto A337 to New Milton, turn left onto Barton Court Av to clifftop

Situated atop a cliff, this restaurant and bar with rooms looks out over the south coast towards the Needles. The restaurant is geared up to make the most of its location with panoramic views across two tiers and an outside terrace. Tables are simply set with polished bare wood and a single gerbera to add a splash of colour, while an open-plan kitchen and oyster counter add to the bustling atmosphere. Service is relaxed and knowledgeable. It's not all about the seafood here, but it's a good starting point - perhaps a Lymington crab, shrimps and prawn terrine. A meat main course might be braised pork cheek with confit belly and black pudding, or it is back to the sea for skate wing with baby capers and lemon.

Chef Pierre Chevillard **Owner** Michael Caddy **Times** 11-2.30/6-11 Closed D 25 Dec, 1 Jan **Prices** Starter £5.25-£9.95, Main £12.95-£21.90, Dessert £6.60, Service optional, Groups min 10 service 10% **Wines** 74 bottles over £20, 14 bottles under £20, 10 by glass **Notes** Sunday L, Vegetarian available, Dress restrictions, Smart casual, no beach wear **Seats** 90, Pr/dining room 8 **Children** Portions **Parking** 20

BASINGSTOKE Map 5 SU65

Audleys Wood

@@ European

Modern cooking in relaxing Hampshire countryside

☎ 01256 817555
Alton Rd RG25 2JT
e-mail: info@audleyswood.com
dir: M3 junct 6. From Basingstoke take A339 towards Alton, hotel on right

Just a short drive from Basingstoke, this extended Victorian country-house hotel is set in seven acres of wooded gardens. The impressive, high-vaulted Gallery Restaurant makes a stylish backdrop for some accomplished and often adventurous cooking. Expect wooden tables dressed with candles and hyacinths and skilful service. The eye-catching menu sees some modern classics alongside a few more interesting combinations: pea and mint soup with ham hock roulade and white truffle dressing, for example. For main course try, perhaps, pigeon with pineapple tart, beetroot purée, garlic dauphinoise and pancetta-flavoured jus, and dessert might take in ice prune parfait with candied prunes and chocolate tartlet.

Times 12.30-2/7-9.45 Closed L Sat, BHs (booking only)

The Hampshire Court Hotel

Modern British

Smart, modern hotel restaurant with appealing menu

☎ 01256 319700
Centre Dr, Great Binfields Rd, Chineham RG24 8FY
e-mail: hampshirecourt@qhotels.co.uk
dir: M3 junct 6, A33 towards Reading. Right at Chineham centre rdbt onto Great Binfields Rd. Hotel 400mtrs on left

The clue is in the name: the 'court' in question here is the tennis variety - a refreshing change, some might say, from all those shrines to golf. At the heart of this eye-catching modern hotel are eight tennis courts and a smart contemporary restaurant overlooking the centre court. The kitchen offers good honest classic cooking on a menu that ranges widely from pasta dishes to grilled meats and more modern British dishes along the lines of pan-fried red mullet with prawn tian and fennel and chilli salsa, or slow-cooked lamb shank served with double cream mash, ratatouille, and rosemary and mint jus. Desserts include the likes of Tia Maria bread-and-butter pudding with home-made custard.

Chef Ali Bensarda **Owner** QHotels **Times** 12-2/7-9.30 Closed L Sat **Prices** Starter £4.50-£5.95, Main £12.50-£18.50, Dessert £4.50-£6.95, Service optional **Wines** 23 bottles over £20, 10 bottles under £20, 13 by glass **Notes** Vegetarian available, Dress restrictions, Smart casual, no shorts or swimwear, Civ Wed 200 **Seats** 200, Pr/dining room 170 **Children** Portions, Menu **Parking** 200

Oakley Hall Hotel

Modern European **NEW**

Country-house hotel with classy modern cooking

☎ 01256 783350
Rectory Rd, Oakley RG23 7EL
e-mail: enquiries@oakleyhall-park.com
dir: M3 junct 7, follow Basingstoke signs. Turn left at lights on A30 towards Oakley, then immediately right onto unclass road towards Oakley. After 3m turn left at T-junct, into Rectory Rd & then left again onto B3400. Hotel signed 1st on left

Built in 1795 and formerly owned by the Bramston family, close friends of Jane Austen, this beautifully restored mansion stands at the end of an impressive drive and enjoys stunning country views. Transformed into a country-house hotel following huge investment, it offers luxury rooms and a swish contemporary restaurant sporting stylish mirrors, leather seats, well-dressed tables and a striking striped carpet. The kitchen delivers an ambitious broadly modern European repertoire, focusing on flavour. Take smoked salmon ravioli with rocket and lemongrass cream, followed by rump and rack of lamb with cauliflower mousse and candied courgette, and a tip-top lemon tart served with raspberry coulis.

Chef Graham Weston **Owner** Jon Huxford
Times 12-2/7-9.30 **Prices** Food prices not confirmed for 2011. Please telephone for details **Wines** 20 bottles over £20, 4 bottles under £20, 8 by glass **Notes** Sunday L, Vegetarian available, Dress restrictions, Smart, no jeans or T-shirts, Civ Wed 100, Air con **Seats** 40, Pr/dining room 200 **Children** Portions, Menu **Parking** 100

Vespers

International

Smart and stylish modern hotel dining

☎ 01256 796700
Apollo Hotel, Aldermaston Roundabout RG24 9NU
e-mail: admin@apollo-hotels.co.uk
dir: From M3 junct 6 follow ring road N & signs for Aldermaston/Newbury. Then follow A340 (Aldermaston) signs, at rdbt take 5th exit onto Popley Way. Hotel entrance 1st left

The smart modern Apollo Hotel sits just a short distance from the M3 on the edge of Basingstoke, with the Vespers restaurant as its fine-dining venue. It's a clean-cut contemporary space done out in neutral tones with banquettes or leather tub chairs at tables swathed in linen, and splashes of colour provided by modern artworks. The dinner-only menu offers a balanced repertoire of modern European dishes - first course might be seared scallops with fennel purée and parmesan cannelloni; to follow, monkfish could be wrapped in pancetta and paired with chorizo risotto, while Hampshire meat is showcased as lamb medallions with dauphinoise potatoes and celeriac mash.

Chef Jo Booth **Owner** Huggler Hotel **Times** 12-2/7-10 Closed Xmas, New Year, Sun, L Sat **Prices** Starter £5-£8, Main £15-£21, Dessert £6, Service included **Wines** 13 bottles over £20, 20 bottles under £20, 14 by glass **Notes** Fixed D carvery, Dress restrictions, Smart casual, Civ Wed 200 **Seats** 28, Pr/dining room 200 **Children** Portions **Parking** 120

BAUGHURST **Map 5 SU56**

The Wellington Arms

Modern British

Honest cooking with lots of home-grown and local produce

☎ 0118 982 0110
Baughurst Rd RG26 5LP
e-mail: hello@thewellingtonarms.com
dir: M4 junct 12 follow Newbury signs on A4. At rdbt left signed Aldermaston. Through Aldermaston. Up hill, at next rdbt 2nd exit, left at T-junct, pub 1m on left

Amid Hampshire countryside, this charming Grade II listed pub-restaurant gets its name from its former incarnation as the Duke of Wellington's hunting lodge. The intimate room has just eight large oak tables, simple antique chairs, open fire, original art and beeswax candles - it looks and feels like a 'proper' pub, but food is the thing here. The daily-changing blackboard menu is a treat to read and delivers on the promise. Eggs come from the pub's 200 free-range, rare-breed and rescue hens, honey from their bees and vegetables and herbs from the garden. Other ingredients are diligently sourced as locally as possible. Dishes are simple and honestly presented. Start with gazpacho of home-grown tomatoes, cucumbers and red peppers with extra virgin olive oil, move onto 'a rather large piece of Cornish skate' with capers, flat leaf parsley, brown butter and sautéed greens and finish with a comforting pud of steamed sponge topped with damson jam and proper custard. The same attention to detail shines through in the friendly service.

Chef Jason King **Owner** Simon Page & Jason King **Times** 12-2.30/6.30-9.30 Closed D Sun **Prices** Fixed L 2 course fr £15, Starter £5.50-£9.50, Main £10.50-£19, Dessert £2.50-£6, Service added but optional 10% **Wines** 51 bottles over £20, 8 bottles under £20, 9 by glass **Notes** Sunday L, Vegetarian available **Seats** 22 **Children** Portions **Parking** 25

BEAULIEU **Map 5 SU30**

Beaulieu Hotel

Modern British

Modern British cooking in the New Forest

☎ 023 8029 3344
Beaulieu Rd SO42 7YQ
e-mail: beaulieu@newforesthotels.co.uk
dir: On B3056 between Lyndhurst & Beaulieu. Near Beaulieu Rd railway station

Built on open heathland in the New Forest conservation area, amid cantering ponies and panoramic views, the hotel is ideal for what convention demands we style a 'romantic break'. Whether you're loved-up or not, though, the glossy-magazine elegance of the interiors makes a classy impression, and the cream-coloured dining room is serviced by knowledgeable and attentive staff. A well-constructed menu of seasonal local produce, informed by modern British combinations, delivers the likes of Wye Valley smoked salmon with toasted brioche and a poached egg, thoroughly tasty roast belly pork with roasted apple, sage mash and pan juices, and crème brûlée garnished with a little ramekin of gorgeous forest fruits jam.

Chef Michael Mckell **Owner** New Forest Hotels plc **Times** 7-9 Closed L all week **Prices** Starter £3.50-£6, Main £14.50-£19.50, Dessert £3.50-£6.50, Service optional **Wines** 19 bottles over £20, 19 bottles under £20, 8 by glass **Notes** Sunday L, Vegetarian available, Civ Wed 300 **Seats** 60, Pr/dining room 80 **Children** Portions, Menu

BEAULIEU *continued*

The Master Builders at Bucklers Hard

Modern British **NEW**

Contemporary dining in historic maritime setting

☎ 01590 616253
Bucklers Hard SO42 7XB
e-mail: res@themasterbuilders.co.uk
dir: From M27 junct 2 follow signs to Beaulieu. Turn left onto B3056, then 1st left, hotel in 2m

The grassy areas in front of this recently spruced-up 18th-century hotel run right down to the banks of the River Beaulieu, where ships were once built for Nelson's fleet. Back on song ever since Hillbrooke Hotels took over the former home of master shipbuilder Henry Adams in May 2009, its attractions include the Yachtsman's Bar and informal, brasserie-style dining room next door. Expect sound modern British cooking based on top-notch local ingredients. With tranquil views across the river, tuck into oysters three ways (shallot vinaigrette, bloody Mary shot, grilled with garlic and parmesan), followed by roast fillet and belly of pork with black pudding, Savoy cabbage and cider. Round off with chestnut pannacotta, hazelnut meringue and dark chocolate sorbet. In summer, dine outside on the terrace under the stars. Smart bedrooms and good summer barbecue menus complete the pleasing picture.

Times 12-3/7-10

The Montagu Arms Hotel

British, European V

Luxurious country house serving accomplished cuisine

☎ 01590 612324
Palace Ln SO42 7ZL
e-mail: reservations@montaguarmshotel.co.uk
dir: From M27 junct 2 take A326 & B3054 for Beaulieu

The Montagu Arms Hotel is a charming rural retreat with an enviable location in the heart of the New Forest. Built in 1742, the traditional English country house is still very much in evidence; there's stunning oak panelling, an old brick fireplace, roaring open fires and squashy sofas to provide that extra comfort factor. With delightful views of the well-tended gardens, the Terrace restaurant is worth dressing up for - jeans and trainers are a no-no. Head chef and previous Roux Scholarship winner, Matthew Tomkinson, sets great store by local, free-range and organic produce and presents his food beautifully. Spiced diver-caught scallops with cauliflower purée, apple, coriander and cumin velouté comes highly recommended. Then, go for an assiette of New Forest Pannage pork with braised cheek, stuffed cabbage, confit belly and roast fillet, followed by a well-conceived banana soufflé with banana ice cream, butterscotch sauce and honeycomb. Monty's offers home-cooked dishes and real ales.

The Montagu Arms Hotel

Chef Matthew Tomkinson **Owner** Greenclose Ltd, Mr Leach **Times** 12-2.30/7-9.30 Closed Mon **Prices** Fixed L 2 course fr £17, Tasting menu fr £70, Starter £10-£16, Main £28-£35, Dessert £10-£12, Service optional **Wines** 200+ bottles over £20, 9 bottles under £20, 12 by glass **Notes** Tasting menu available, Sunday L, Vegetarian menu, Dress restrictions, Smart casual, Civ Wed 60 **Seats** 60, Pr/dining room 32 **Children** Portions **Parking** 45

BOTLEY Map 5 SU51

Macdonald Botley Park, Golf & Country Club

British, European

Simple, honest cooking in relaxed hotel

☎ 01489 780888 & 0870 194 2132
Winchester Rd, Boorley Green SO32 2UA
e-mail: botleypark@macdonald-hotels.co.uk
dir: M27 junct 7, A334 towards Botley. At 1st rdbt left, past M&S store, over the next 5 mini rdbts. At 6th mini rdbt turn right. In 0.5m hotel on left

Set in 176-acres of landscaped gardens with an 18-hole championship golf course, this large country hotel is only 15 minutes from Southampton Airport and within easy reach of the M3. There is a traditional feel to the restaurant. The light-and-airy dining room is contemporary in style with wood panelling and decorated mirrors. It all creates a comfortable setting for the unpretentious cooking. A starter of rich and creamy gorgonzola gnocchi with sage butter could be followed by rump of lamb with roasted root vegetables, and a classic crème brûlée. For a more casual dining experience, relax in the Swing and Divot Sports Bar overlooking the 18th green.

Times 12.30-2.30/7-9.45 Closed L Sat

BRANSGORE Map 5 SZ19

The Three Tuns

British, European

A pretty village inn serving classic pub grub and more

☎ 01425 672232 & 07850 713406
Ringwood Rd BH23 8JH
e-mail: threetunsinn@btconnect.com
web: www.threetunsinn.com
dir: On A35 at junct for Walkford/Highcliffe follow Bransgore signs, 1.5m, restaurant on left

A picture-postcard 17th-century thatched gem deep in the New Forest National Park. A delight in summer, festooned with flowers, and cosy in winter, with blazing log fires warming the low beamed bar and dining areas, the Three Tuns draws foodies and Forest visitors for its charm and character, its buzzy atmosphere, the glorious sun-drenched garden, and an eclectic menu that lists pub classics alongside more adventurous dishes. Using game from surroundings estates, locally-shot venison, farm meats and fish delivered to door, the seasonal menu may list plump scallops with a compôte of Chinese cabbage marinated in soy sauce, perfectly cooked pigeon breasts with prunes, polenta and wilted chard, and tonka bean crème brûlée. Alternatively, tuck into a ploughman's lunch, cod and chips, or rib-eye steak with all the trimmings.

Chef Colin Nash **Owner** Nigel Glenister
Times 12-2.15/6.30-9.15 Closed 25 Dec, D 31 Dec
Prices Food prices not confirmed for 2011. Please telephone for details **Wines** 2 bottles over £20, 21 bottles under £20, 11 by glass **Notes** Sunday L, Vegetarian available, Dress restrictions, Smart casual **Seats** 60, Pr/dining room 50 **Children** Portions **Parking** 50

BROCKENHURST **Map 5 SU30**

Balmer Lawn Hotel

Modern British

Fine dining at grand New Forest hotel

01590 623116 & 625725
Lyndhurst Rd SO42 7ZB
e-mail: info@balmerlawnhotel.com
dir: Take A337 towards Brockenhurst, hotel on left after 'Welcome to Brockenhurst' sign

This imposing pavilion-style Victorian hunting lodge stands in a gorgeous New Forest setting just outside Brockenhurst. With a fascinating history - it has hosted prime ministers and presidents - it's now a friendly family-owned hotel refurbished in a classy style blending modern interior aesthetics with period character. The Beresfords restaurant shares the same understated contemporary chic, with its high-backed leather seats at bare darkwood tables and restful mustard colour scheme. The kitchen deals in modern British cuisine with an impressive showing of local produce. Chicken liver and foie gras parfait with greengage relish is a typical starter, with main courses such as pan-fried salmon with braised gem and fennel purée.

Times 12.30-2.30/7-9.30

Carey's Manor Hotel

Modern British

Carefully-sourced produce in the heart of the New Forest

01590 623551
SO42 7RH
e-mail: stay@careysmanor.com
dir: M27 junct 2, follow Fawley/A326 signs. Continue over 3 rdbts, at 4th rdbt right lane signed Lyndhurst/A35. Follow A337 (Lymington/Brockenhurst)

A smart modern spa hotel tucked away in the depths of the New Forest, Carey's Manor pampers its guests with a globetrotting array of sybaritic treatments, and an equally multinational choice of dining. French cuisine is the deal in the Blaireau bistro, while the Zen Garden Restaurant's thing is Thai cooking. But when only fine dining will do, go for the Manor Restaurant, where the kitchen scours the local area for the best materials - often free-range and organic - for its creative modern British dishes with clear influences from France and Europe. Terrine of lightly-smoked Hampshire garlic sausage is teamed to good effect with a chervil crust, Dijon mustard and compressed figs. Mains also display inventiveness and sound flavour combinations, with a spot-on piece of pan-roasted Lymington cod served with chorizo bubble-and-squeak, wilted spinach, parsnip purée, rocket pesto and chorizo oil.

Times 12-2/7-10 Closed L Mon-Sat

New Park Manor Hotel & Spa

Modern

Royal connections and sound modern cooking

01590 623467
Lyndhurst Rd SO42 7QH
e-mail: info@newparkmanorhotel.co.uk
dir: On A337, 8m S of M27 junct 1

Whatever you think of King Charles II, he clearly had a good eye for a nice location: New Park Manor was a favoured hunting lodge. These days the handsome red-brick house in an idyllic New Forest setting is a smart hotel with its own equestrian centre, croquet lawn and spa. His Majesty would surely approve. The restaurant is split into two rooms, with high ceilings and original features - some of which date back to the 15th century - but it's refreshingly informal and large windows provide diverting views of the paddock. The kitchen tacks a predominantly modern British course via a sound classical grounding. Start with Brixham crab beignets with crisp Parma ham and garden pea purée, followed by pan-fried locally-caught gilt head bream served with lemon and chive crushed new potatoes, sauce vierge and spinach tortellini.

Times 12-2/7-9

Rhinefield House

Modern British

Vibrant flavours in the New Forest

01590 622922 & 0845 0727516
Rhinefield Rd SO42 7QB
e-mail: info@rhinefieldhousehotel.co.uk
web: www.rhinefieldhousehotel.co.uk
dir: M27 junct, A337 to Lyndhurst, then A35 W towards Christchurch. 3.5m, left at sign for Rhinefield House. Hotel 1.5m on right

At the heart of the New Forest, set in 40 acres of grounds complete with ornamental gardens and Italian ponds, lies this stunning 19th-century mock-Elizabethan mansion. The fine-dining Armada restaurant proudly showcases a magnificent carving of the Spanish Armada over the fireplace. Fabulous fresh, local and seasonal produce are the order of the day while service is formal and standards exacting. Typical starters include smoked New Forest venison loin with cauliflower beignet, purée, fresh parmesan and mizuna, followed perhaps by roast Hampshire beef with roast bone marrow, parsley salad, Jerusalem artichoke purée and free-range egg ravioli. Butterscotch pannacotta served with a Granny Smith sorbet and cinnamon doughnuts is an exciting twist on a classic dessert.

Chef Mathew Budden **Owner** Hand Picked Hotels Ltd **Times** 12.30-2/7-9.30 **Prices** Food prices not confirmed for 2011. Please telephone for details **Wines** 100+ bottles over £20, 2 bottles under £20, 15 by glass **Notes** Sunday L, Vegetarian available, Dress restrictions, Smart casual preferred, Civ Wed 130 **Seats** 58, Pr/dining room 12 **Children** Portions, Menu **Parking** 150

Simply at Whitley

Modern British, French

Well-defined flavours in peaceful setting

01590 622354
Whitley Ridge Hotel, Beaulieu Rd SO42 7QL
e-mail: info@whitleyridge.co.uk
web: www.whitleyridge.co.uk
dir: From Brockenhurst, 1m along Beaulieu Rd

In secluded grounds in the beautiful New Forest, Whitley Ridge is a smart country-house hotel in a picture-perfect 18th-century country manor. The brasserie - Simply at Whitley - is an elegant and suitably relaxed venue decked out with lime green leather chairs and soft grey wall coverings. Head chef James Golding uses locally-sourced and home-grown (often organic) produce in dishes where the flavours are allowed to shine. The menu is laid out under Larder and Garden, Solent, Forest and Simply Simple. Try new season asparagus soup and crumbled Sway goats' cheese, then perhaps local wild rabbit pie with seared loin, roast cauliflower and watercress purée. Lemon posset with lovage and preserved blackberry sauce makes for an appealingly British finish. An excellent wine list offers plenty by the glass.

Chef James Golding **Times** 12-2/6.30-9.30 **Prices** Fixed L 2 courses fr £15, 3 courses fr £19.50 Main fr £13.50 **Notes** Sunday L

BROOK Map 5 SU21

Briscoe's at The Bell Inn

Modern English

New Forest haven with an ambitious team in the kitchen

☎ 023 8081 2214
SO43 7HE
e-mail: bell@bramshaw.co.uk
dir: M27 junct 1 onto B3079, hotel 1.5m on right

Situated in the heart of the New Forest and part of the Bramshaw Golf Club, the 18th-century Bell Inn is the perfect '19th' hole for post round refreshment, and an ideal base for exploring the National Park. Period features have been retained in the cosy bar and in Briscoe's restaurant, where old-fashioned charm and character blend well with chic modern colours. Expect a sound modern approach to cooking traditional dishes from an ambitious brigade. Dishes are well executed and make good use of locally-sourced ingredients, as in twice-baked crab soufflé, followed by roast venison haunch with braised red cabbage and grain mustard mash, and warm chocolate tart with mint ice cream.

Chef Scott Foy **Owner** Crosthwaite Eyre Family **Times** 7-9.30 Closed L all week **Prices** Food prices not confirmed for 2011. Please telephone for details **Wines** 56 bottles over £20, 18 bottles under £20, 12 by glass **Notes** Vegetarian available, Dress restrictions, No jeans, T-shirts, trainers or shorts **Seats** 50, Pr/dining room 40 **Children** Portions, Menu **Parking** 40

BURLEY Map 5 SU20

Moorhill House

Modern British

Modern British cooking in Edwardian country house

☎ 01425 403285
BH24 4AG
e-mail: moorhill@newforesthotels.co.uk
dir: Exit A31 signed Burley Drive, through village, turn right opposite cricket pitch

An Edwardian country house just outside the village of Burley, Moorhill sports extensive, well-husbanded grounds, and a dining room that opens out on to a raised patio where views of them may be enjoyed. The kitchen tacks to a recognisable modern British style of country-house cooking, with gentle combinations and much skill in execution. Notable dishes may include a terrine of smoked haddock, spinach and potato, with horseradish cream and beetroot salad, seared duck breast with creamy dauphinoise and Savoy cabbage in red wine juices, and desserts such as lemon tart with ginger ice cream, or passionfruit delice with raspberry coulis. Regional cheeses are usually a good selection.

Chef Ben Cartwright **Owner** New Forest Hotels **Times** 12-2/7-9 Closed L Mon-Sat **Prices** Starter £3.50-£6, Main £14.50-£19.50, Dessert £3.50-£5, Service optional **Wines** 19 bottles over £20, 19 bottles under £20, 8 by glass **Notes** Sunday L, Dress restrictions, Smart casual **Seats** 60, Pr/dining room 40

CADNAM Map 5 SZ21

Bartley Lodge

Traditional British

Carefully worked modern British dishes in an ornate dining room

☎ 023 8081 2248
Lyndhurst Rd SO40 2NR
e-mail: bartley@newforesthotels.co.uk
dir: M27 junct 1, A337, follow signs for Lyndhurst. Hotel on left

A member of the New Forest Hotels family, Bartley Lodge is another enviably sited retreat amid the sylvan reaches of Hampshire, with landscaped gardens surrounding a former hunting lodge. The Crystal Restaurant boasts an ornate chandelier of that nature in a dining room done in restful shades of pale blue and gold. Service combines warmth and respect in the proper country-house idiom, while the cooking brings together a repertoire of carefully worked dishes. Start perhaps with an airily light soufflé of smoked haddock and spring onion, served with salad leaves in a mustardy dressing, before moving on to haunch of deeply flavoured venison, served with red cabbage and creamy dauphinoise, and sharpened up with crab-apple and redcurrant jelly.

Chef John Lightfoot **Owner** New Forest Hotels plc **Times** 12-2/7-9 Closed L Mon-Sat **Prices** Starter £3-£7.50, Main £14.50-£19.50, Dessert £3.50-£6.50, Service optional **Wines** 19 bottles over £20, 19 bottles under £20, 8 by glass **Notes** Sunday L, Vegetarian available, Civ Wed 80 **Seats** 60 **Children** Portions, Menu **Parking** 90

DENMEAD Map 5 SU61

Barnard's Restaurant

Modern British

Friendly neighbourhood restaurant

☎ 023 9225 7788
Hambledon Rd PO7 6NU
e-mail: mail@barnardsrestaurant.co.uk
dir: A3M junct 3, B2150 into Denmead. Opposite church

A row of shops opposite the parish church in a sleepy Hampshire village provides the setting for David and Sandie Barnard's homely and long established country restaurant. Expect a warm yellow décor, exposed brick walls lined with bright prints, unclothed darkwood tables and an informal and upbeat atmosphere. Cooking is simple, consistent and modern British in style, relying on top-notch locally-sourced ingredients. Dishes are well presented and clear flavours are evident, as in smoked salmon fishcake on mixed leaves with ginger dressing, lamb rump with onion jus, and a very sticky toffee pudding with a rich toffee sauce and vanilla seed ice cream. Service is friendly and knowledgeable and it is all great value for money.

Chef David & Sandie Barnard **Owner** Mr & Mrs D Barnard **Times** 12-1.30/7-9.30 Closed 25-26 Dec, New Year, Sun-Mon, L Sat **Prices** Fixed L 2 course fr £12.75, Fixed D 3 course fr £15.75, Starter £5.30-£8.50, Main £12.95-£24, Dessert £5.30-£7.95, Service optional **Wines** 8 bottles over £20, 20 bottles under £20, 8 by glass **Notes** Vegetarian available **Seats** 40, Pr/dining room 34 **Children** Portions **Parking** 3, Car park opposite

DOGMERSFIELD Map 5 SU75

Seasons

French, European V

Experimental cooking in a grand Georgian manor

01252 853000
Four Seasons Hotel Hampshire, Dogmersfield Park, Chalky Ln RG27 8TD
e-mail: reservations.ham@fourseasons.com
dir: M3 junct 5 onto A287 Farnham. After 1.5m take left to Dogmersfield, hotel 0.6m on left

The hotel is an imposing red-brick Georgian manor full of sweeping staircases, elaborate mouldings and chandeliers, hearteningly awash with natural daylight in summer, and enjoying glorious views of the Dogmersfield estate. Seasonal menus capitalise on local produce, some of it from the hotel's own gardens. The style is nothing if not experimental: salsify meunière served with parmesan and black pepper cheesecake and port gastrique to start, and then seared gurnard with wild mushrooms, bok choy and saffron fumet. A commendable cheese menu explores the best of British, and you might conclude with a slice of lemon tart, served with hibiscus sorbet and tonka nougatine.

Chef Cyrille Pannier **Owner** Four Seasons Hotels & Resorts **Times** 6-10.30 Closed Mon, L Tue-Sat, D Sun **Prices** Food prices not confirmed for 2011. Please telephone for details **Wines** 167 bottles over £20, 17 by glass **Notes** Sunday L, Vegetarian menu, Dress restrictions, Smart casual, Civ Wed 250 **Seats** 100, Pr/dining room 24 **Children** Portions, Menu **Parking** 100

DROXFORD Map 5 SU61

Bakers Arms

British

Unpretentious country pub serving - local food

01489 877533
High St SO32 3PA
e-mail: adam@thebakersarmsdroxford.com
dir: Off A32

The pretty Meon Valley is a gorgeous corner of rural Hampshire that is always worth exploring, particularly when there's a cracking foodie pub such as the Bakers Arms for refuelling. The place has traded up indoors after a makeover that has injected a modern vibe, but this is still an unpretentious pub in the true sense of the word, with a welcoming buzz and Droxford's Bowman ales on tap. The kitchen tackles robust modern British dishes with skill and intelligence and likes to keep things local seasonal, unfussy and fresh - much of the veg comes from their allotment, and bread is baked freshly twice a day. Fried lamb's kidneys with mustard and onions on toast is a typical starter, followed by slow-roast pork belly with garlic-roasted potatoes, and cider, mustard and cream sauce.

Chef Richard Harrison & Adam Cordery **Owner** Adam & Anna Cordery **Times** 11.45-3/6-11 Closed Mon, D Sun **Prices** Fixed L 2 course £13, Fixed D 2 course £13, Starter £4.75-£6, Main £10.95-£16.95, Dessert £5.50, Service optional, Groups min 8 service 10% **Notes** Sunday L, Vegetarian available **Seats** 35 **Children** Portions **Parking** 30

EAST TYTHERLEY Map 5 SU22

The Star Inn Tytherley

Modern British

Traditional inn with serious attitude to food

01794 340225
SO51 0LW
e-mail: info@starinn.co.uk
dir: Romsey A3057 N, left onto B3084, then left to Awbridge, Kents Oak, through Lockerley on right

Exposed beams, blazing winter log fires, leather Chesterfields and warm colours create a cosy, traditional atmosphere at this 16th-century former coaching inn tucked away in the Test Valley. The dining room follows the relaxed country restaurant theme, with its lightwood tables and pine-clad walls adorned with country prints. You can also eat alfresco in summer in the pretty courtyard garden, which overlooks the village cricket green. The kitchen's approach is to bring a modish twist to traditional dishes, based on local seasonal ingredients. Everything from the flavoured breads to the delicious biscuits or petits fours at the end of the meal is made in the kitchen. Expect dishes such as Winchester cheese soufflé to start and baked cod with braised fennel and a light curry sauce for main course. Finish with glazed lemon and mascarpone tart with raspberry coulis.

Times 11-2.30/6-11 Closed Mon, D Sun

36 on the Quay

EMSWORTH Map 5 SU70

Modern French

Thought provoking modern cooking overlooking the bay

01243 375592 & 372257
47 South St PO10 7EG
e-mail: info@36onthequay.com
dir: Last building on right in South St, which runs from square in centre of Emsworth

The large house stands close to the waterfront, enjoying views over Chichester harbour. It was once a fishermen's pub and, under the careful stewardship of Ramon and Karen Farthing, has long since been a gastronomic landmark in the area. The bar and dining room are both fairly compact, but tables are well-dressed, and the restaurant walls are given over to a display of quality local art. Ramon Farthing leads a small brigade dedicated to demonstrable culinary excellence. Menus are fixed-price, and symmetrically constructed, with four choices at each stage for dinner, two at lunch. Dishes are built around thought provoking combinations in the contemporary way, and are realised by means of wonderful technique and precision. A first course brings together a slow-cooked duck egg with ground Serrano ham on creamed leeks, accompanied by a wild mushroom tortellino in sherry vinegar sauce - a stunning composition. It may be echoed in the conception of a main course that teams garlicky veal loin with dauphinoise, a wild mushroom and spinach tartlet, and another mini-pasta offering in the shape of a lasagne of veal liver, kohlrabi and braised onion, the whole sauced with a light shallot cream. Even the ingredient-themed dessert variation is full of originality, as when an apple selection brings on a tart of Cox's apples, Bramley brûlée and smooth Granny Smith sorbet, all gently enriched with the addition of a delightful cinnamon yoghurt.

Times 12-2/7-10 Closed 1 wk end Oct, 25-26 Dec, 1st 3 wks Jan, 1 wk end May, Sun, Mon

EMSWORTH Map 5 SU70

Fat Olives

British, Mediterranean

Family-run brasserie by the sea with good, honest cooking

01243 377914
30 South St PO10 7EH
e-mail: info@fatolives.co.uk
dir: In town centre, 1st right after Emsworth Square, 100yds towards the Quay. Restaurant on left with public car park opposite

Lawrence and Julia Murphy's smart brasserie in a 17th-century fishermen's cottage by pretty Emsworth harbour ticks all the right boxes for the faithful foodies who have kept it buzzing for over a decade. The stripped-out interior of cream walls, bare wooden floors and unclothed tables is as unvarnished and honest as the food. Lawrence lets the excellent raw materials do the talking, helped by a judicious hand to ensure spot-on accuracy, some eclectic twists and a gentle whiff of the Mediterranean. Starters might offer smoked haddock, cockle and parsley risotto and roasted fennel, followed by lemon sole, gurnard, crevettes and mussels in a saffron nage - all nicely timed to retain natural flavours and textures. To end, blueberry semolina and honey tart comes with blueberry milkshake.

Chef Lawrence Murphy **Owner** Lawrence & Julia Murphy **Times** 12-2/7-9 Closed 2 wks Xmas, 2 wks Jun, Sun-Mon & Tue after a BH **Prices** Fixed L 2 course £16.95, Starter £4.95-£8.50, Main £14.95-£25, Dessert £5.95-£6.50, Service optional, Groups min 10 service 10% **Wines** 36 bottles over £20, 10 bottles under £20, 7 by glass **Notes** Vegetarian available **Seats** 28 **Parking** Opposite restaurant

36 on the Quay

– see page 173

EVERSLEY Map 5 SU76

The New Mill Riverside Restaurant

Modern European

Modern European cooking in an idyllic riverside setting

0118 973 2277
New Mill Rd RG27 0RA
e-mail: info@thenewmill.co.uk
web: www.thenewmill.co.uk
dir: Off A327 2m S of Arborfield Cross. N of village follow brown signs. Approach from New Mill Rd

The historic building became a restaurant in 1973, having served as a corn mill for many a century prior to that. It retains a working waterwheel, and the setting on the banks of the Blackwater, amid carefully tended gardens, is enhanced by interior beams and the warmly hospitable approach of staff. Modern European menus deal in complex, satisfying dishes such as a pressed terrine of rabbit, chorizo and black pudding, dressed with apple and caraway relish and pesto, followed perhaps by seared sea bass with braised butter beans, wild mushrooms and kale in a shrimp butter sauce. Dishes are generally well-balanced, and impress for their subtle ranges of flavours. Desserts might include cherry clafoutis, or pecan treacle tart with mascarpone cream.

Chef Colin Robson-Wright **Owner** Cindy & John Duffield **Times** 12-2/7-10 Closed 1-2 Jan, Mon **Prices** Fixed L 2 course £15, Fixed D 3 course £25, Service optional, Groups min 8 service 10% **Wines** 150 bottles over £20, 10 bottles under £20, 10 by glass **Notes** Tasting menu available, Sunday L, Vegetarian available, Dress restrictions, Smart casual, Civ Wed 150 **Seats** 80, Pr/dining room 32 **Children** Portions **Parking** 60

HAMBLE-LE-RICE Map 5 SU40

The Bugle

Modern British NEW

Contemporary food in lovingly-restored riverside inn

023 8045 3000
High St SO31 4HA
e-mail: manager@buglehamble.co.uk

When developers threatened to demolish this historic waterside pub, a campaign by villagers pulled off a successful rescue. After a loving refurbishment in collaboration with English Heritage, The Bugle is a trumpeting success. Its interior presents an authentic rustic scene of bare brickwork and timbers, flagstone floors, a great slab of oak for a bar, and the comfort of a wood-burning stove; outside is a lovely heated terrace overlooking the River Hamble. On the food front, the place delivers on all counts: a claret-coloured chalkboard spells out the day's specials, the bar menu deals in pub classics done right, while the restaurant menu has an honest populist appeal, starting with ham hock terrine and doorstep toast given the peppery lift of a rocket salad. Haddock and chips with minted peas and chunky home-made tartare is a masterful version of a Great British Classic, or you could give local meat a workout with slow-roasted pork belly, teamed with champ potato cake, grain mustard sabayon and cider gravy.

Chef Jamie Major, Jim Hayward **Owner** Ideal Leisure Ltd **Times** 12-2.30/6-9.30 Closed 25 Dec **Prices** Starter £5-£10, Main £10-£15.50, Dessert £5-£7 **Wines** 10 bottles over £20, 10 bottles under £20, 9 by glass **Notes** Sunday L, Vegetarian available **Seats** 28, Pr/dining room 12 **Children** Portions **Parking** Foreshore car park 50 yds

HAYLING ISLAND Map 5 SU70

Langstone Hotel

British NEW

Well-judged dining in modern conference hotel

023 9246 5011
Northney Rd PO11 0NQ
e-mail: info@langstonehotel.co.uk
dir: From A27 signed Havant/Hayling Island follow A3023 across roadbridge onto Hayling Island & take sharp left on leaving bridge

Not far off the main road through Hayling Island, with views over the salt marsh flats of the north shores, Langstone is a modern hotel, newly refurbished, with leisure and business facilities aplenty. The Brasserie restaurant occupies a large curved room with views through floor-to-ceiling windows over the marina and bay beyond. It's light and bright with some banquette seating, light-wood tables and a digital faux log fire taking centre stage. Confident, honest cooking and good use of excellent ingredients combines with unfussy presentation. A starter of twice-baked Stilton and chive soufflé with poached pears and walnut salad might be followed by belly of pork, sage rösti, crushed peas, apple jelly and Madeira jus. Chocolate tart with espresso ice cream and orange jelly is one of the indulgent desserts.

Times 11-10

HIGHCLERE Map 5 SU45

Marco Pierre White's Yew Tree Inn

Traditional British

Stylish dining pub close to Highclere Castle

☎ 01635 253360
Hollington Cross, Andover Rd RG20 9SE
e-mail: info@theyewtree.net
dir: M4 junct 13, A34 S, 4th junct on left signed Highclere/Wash Common, turn right towards Andover A343, Yew Tree Inn on right

When a chef is identifiable with only one name, any enterprise that bears that name is bound to raise expectations: luckily, Marco's take on the country inn satisfies on every level. The whitewashed 17th-century inn is a classic of the low-beamed-ceiling and crackling-log-fire school, but it's a pretty posh gaff that no-one goes to for a pint, despite an array of beers on tap that would pass muster in any real ale shoot-out. It's all about food, of course, whether you're in the bar or the formal dining room where food-inspired art and memorabilia of Marco's career provide reminders of his legacy to the UK culinary scene. The Marco style is interpreted here on a deceptively simple sounding menu of brasserie-style dishes put together with clinical precision in an uncompromising quest for full-on, deep flavours. Morecambe potted shrimps open with a buttery punch of seaside freshness, then honey-roast belly pork 'Marco Polo' with apple sauce and roasting juices delivers as much succulent sweet pigginess as anyone can reasonably expect.

Chef Neil Thornley **Owner** The Yew Tree (Highclere) Ltd **Times** 12-2.30/6-9.30 Closed D 25-26 Dec **Prices** Fixed L 2 course fr £15.50, Starter £7.50-£14.50, Main £14.50-£22.50, Dessert £7.50-£9.50, Service included **Wines** 58 bottles over £20, 12 bottles under £20, 14 by glass **Notes** Sunday L, Vegetarian available **Seats** 90 **Children** Portions **Parking** 40

LYMINGTON Map 5 SZ39

Stanwell House

Modern European

Contemporary style and choice of venues

☎ 01590 677123
14-15 High St SO41 9AA
e-mail: enquiries@stanwellhouse.com
dir: M27 junct 1, follow signs to Lyndhurst into Lymington centre & High Street

Close to the marina in the Regency town of Lymington, this Georgian coaching inn turned stylish boutique hotel offers two dining options - an informal, Mediterranean-style bistro and a more intimate seafood restaurant. The seafood restaurant serves up tapas-style fishy treats such as smoked salmon and cucumber tortilla and baby octopus with peas and spiced oil, alongside a more traditionally conceived à la carte menu; chargrilled tuna steak, for example, with Mediterranean vegetables, crushed new potatoes and Caesar cream, or the seafood platter for two. Meanwhile, in the bistro, plump for something from the grill. Coconut 'Bounty' for pudding is a winner (coconut sponge with a rich chocolate topping).

Times 12-3/6-10

LYNDHURST Map 5 SU30

The Glasshouse

Modern British

Confident cooking in chic setting

☎ 023 8028 6129 & 8028 3677
Best Western Forest Lodge, Pikes Hill, Romsey Rd SO43 7AS
e-mail: enquiries@theglasshousedining.co.uk
web: www.theglasshousedining.co.uk
dir: M27 junct 1, signed Lyndhurst A337, after 3m right into Pikes Hill

The Forest Lodge is an attractive Georgian building on the outskirts of the busy village of Lyndhurst in the New Forest. The Glasshouse is its gem of a restaurant, a chic space with dramatic black tablecloths, gold crushed velvet curtains and striking artwork on the walls. Service is on the ball which helps the room exude a calm and collected atmosphere. This is technically accomplished cooking which makes great use of top-notch, often local, produce. Things might start with a Cornish crab tian with alfalfa roll and crab bisque, then move on to 'old

continued

LYNDHURST *continued*

Hampshire pork' cooked three ways - loin, belly and cheek - and served with caramelised apple, molasses and sautéed spinach. Finish with chilled rhubarb and custard served with a honey biscuit and clotted cream, and there is an excellent selection of West Country cheeses, too.

Chef Richard Turner **Owner** New Forest Hotels **Times** 12-2/7-9.30 Closed Mon, D Sun **Prices** Fixed D 3 course fr £30, Service optional **Wines** 41 bottles over £20, 30 bottles under £20, 8 by glass **Notes** Sunday L, Vegetarian available, Dress restrictions, Smart dress, Civ Wed 90 **Seats** 40, Pr/dining room 10 **Parking** 60, On street

MILFORD ON SEA **Map 5 SZ29**

One Park Lane

Modern British V

Fine dining in magnificent Victorian mansion with stunning sea views

☎ 01590 643044
Westover Hall Hotel, Park Ln SO41 0PT
e-mail: info@westoverhallhotel.com
dir: From M27 junct 1 take A337 then B3058. Hotel just outside centre of Milford, towards clifftop

Victorian industrial magnate Alexander Siemens quite literally electrified England, and made a bob or two in the process, with which he built his New Forest seaside mansion overlooking the Needles and the Isle of Wight. The place offers as much luxury as anyone can reasonably ask for: gorgeous stained-glass, dark oak panelling, intricate ceiling friezes, and Pre-Raphaelite-designed tiled fireplaces. To cap it all, the classy country house-style restaurant comes with sea views as a backdrop to some pretty snazzy cooking. Dishes are announced with the currently fashionable one-word descriptions, and you can expect complex food that looks as fancy as the surroundings: rabbit trifle, or lobster and pearl barley broth to start, ahead of the classic richness of tournedos Rossini with seared foie gras, black truffle and Madeira sauce; a somewhat lighter option might be seared fillet of sea bass with spring onion risotto and candied carrots. Labour-intensive puddings such as 'coffee' deliver coffee ice cream with chocolate cookies, coffee jellies, ricotta and pecan to finish.

Chef Terry Smith **Owner** David & Christine Smith **Times** 12-2/7-9 Closed D Mon-Wed (winter) **Prices** Fixed L 2 course £15-£20, Fixed D 2 course £20-£24, Starter £4.50-£8.50, Main £19.50-£22, Dessert £8-£10, Service optional **Wines** 60 bottles over £20, 11 bottles under £20, 11 by glass **Notes** Gourmet menu available, Sunday L, Vegetarian menu, Civ Wed 50 **Seats** 40, Pr/dining room 10 **Children** Portions **Parking** 60

NEW MILTON **Map 5 SZ29**

Chewton Glen Hotel & Spa

– see page 177

NORTHINGTON **Map 5 SU53**

The Woolpack Inn

Traditional British **NEW**

Home-cooked British pub grub

☎ 01962 734184 & 0845 2938066
Totford SO24 9TJ
e-mail: info@thewoolpackinn.co.uk
dir: On B3046

Housed in a former skittle alley, this restaurant with rooms has recently reopened under new ownership following an extensive refurbishment. Neutrally painted walls, exposed brickwork and leather high-backed chairs paired with stripy banquettes give a contemporary feel to the dining room. Traditional British pub food is the order of the day in both restaurant, bar and the heated outside area. Start with potted confit duck served with warm crumpets and fruit chutney, followed by salmon and smoked haddock fishcake with roasted fennel and tomato vinaigrette. Treacle tart and toasted pecans to finish. Traditional Sunday roasts with all the trimmings are popular.

Chef Brian Ahearn **Owner** Jarina & Brian Ahearn **Times** 12-3/6.30-9.30 Closed D 25 Dec **Prices** Starter £4.75-£7.25, Main £8.95-£16.95, Dessert £5.50, Service added but optional 10% **Wines** 18 bottles over £20, 8 bottles under £20, 10 by glass **Notes** Sunday L, Vegetarian available **Seats** 60, Pr/dining room 16 **Children** Portions, Menu **Parking**

ODIHAM **Map 5 SU75**

St John Restaurant

Modern

French-influenced modern cooking in a stylish setting

☎ 01256 702697
83 High St RG29 1LB
e-mail: info@stjohn-restaurant.co.uk
dir: M3 junct 5, follow signs to Odiham

St John has hit on a winning formula of unpretentious atmosphere and modern cooking, founded on French classics, which keeps loyal locals coming back time and again. It's an unassuming red-brick building where you look out from a smart contemporary interior through vast windows onto the heart of Odiham. A confident hand in the kitchen takes well-sourced local ingredients as the foundation of an interesting array of menus ranging from a keenly-priced lunchtime 'market' menu, through to a full-on 'menu découverte'. You might start with open ravioli of oyster mushrooms with white onion purée and a truffle and cep foam, and follow with roasted rack and braised shoulder of lamb with sweetbreads, Puy lentils and spiced pumpkin purée.

Chef Steven James **Owner** Mr R Evans **Times** 12-3.30/6-11 Closed Sun **Prices** Fixed L 2 course £16.50, Fixed D 3 course £22.50, Starter £9-£12, Main £17-£27.50, Dessert £6-£6.50, Service added but optional 10% **Wines** 52 bottles over £20, 12 bottles under £20 **Notes** Early bird menu Mon-Fri until 8pm 2 course, Vegetarian available, Dress restrictions, Smart casual **Seats** 55, Pr/dining room 12 **Parking** On street

OLD BURGHCLERE **Map 5 SU45**

The Dew Pond Restaurant

Modern British, French

Country restaurant with fine views and modern cooking

☎ 01635 278408
RG20 9LH

Eating outside on a summer's day, a more glorious bucolic scene is hard to imagine: the raised decking terrace of this 16th-century country-house restaurant looks across the eponymous dew pond to Watership Down among the verdant pleats of rural Hampshire. If nasty weather sends you indoors, two cosy dining rooms feature venerable oak beams, calming pastels and vibrant artwork. The kitchen takes a modern British tack, cooking with intelligence and a feeling for well-sourced local materials. A salad of seared scallops with pea purée and black pudding is a sound opener; main courses might turn up Hampshire lamb - roasted rump and slow-cooked crispy shoulder, with ratatouille, gratin dauphinoise, French beans and a basil and tomato stock reduction.

Times 7-9.30 Closed 2 wks Xmas & New Year, 2 wks Aug, Sun-Mon, L served by appointment only

PETERSFIELD **Map 5 SU72**

Annie Jones Restaurant

Modern European

Confident cooking in market town setting

☎ 01730 262728
10A Lavant St GU32 3EW
e-mail: info@anniejones.co.uk
dir: From A3 into town centre, following Winchester direction. Restaurant is in Lavant St (the road leading to rail station)

Full of character, this cosy restaurant is just a few hundred yards from Petersfield's market place and main shopping area. Once a private cottage, Annie Jones is still chock-full of original features and nooks and crannies, and alongside rich red walls, wooden floors, high-backed leather chairs and simply dressed tables, the picture is confidently traditional but free of chintz. There is a great terrace for when the weather allows. The hands-on owners ensure attention to detail throughout and the

continued on page 178

Chewton Glen Hotel & Spa

NEW MILTON Map 5 SZ29

Traditional British V NOTABLE WINE LIST

Immaculate cooking in internationally renowned country-house hotel

☎ 01425 275341
Christchurch Rd BH25 6QS
e-mail: reservations@chewtonglen.com
web: www.chewtonglen.com
dir: Off A35 (Lyndhurst) turn right through Walkford, 4th left into Chewton Farm Rd

Chewton Glen is in the Premier League of the UK's country hotels. It owes its success to a winning formula of sharp modern boutique style grafted onto an impeccably well-mannered 18th-century English house, backed by polished service - with staff outnumbering guests in a two-to-one ratio, you're pampered like visiting royalty. Add in a myriad of more mod-cons, plus a 9-hole golf course, a state-of-the-art spa with a vast hydrotherapy pool, an indoor pool with lovely views over immaculate gardens, and you can see why this top-drawer New Forest hidey-hole is so seductive. And then there's the food: the classy burgundy-walled restaurant opens through French windows onto a vine-shaded terrace, or there's a luminous conservatory with a softly-tented ceiling, that feels like you're almost sitting out in the garden. The kitchen has its roots firmly in classic techniques and goes about its work with flair and dexterity, producing big flavours and great-looking dishes. Three- and five-course menus place the emphasis firmly on seasonal Hampshire produce - game and wild mushrooms from the New Forest, for example. Among starters might be a tian of Portland crab with Madras crab cakes, roasted mango purée, coconut and coriander, while main courses bring on the likes of fillet and braised cheek of local organic pork teamed with white onion and sage fondue, artichokes and girolles. Desserts end with a creative flourish - braised pineapple with white chocolate and lavender mousse and passionfruit jelly. A remarkable 500-bin wine list is an impressive piece of work.

Chef Luke Matthews **Owner** Chewton Glen Hotels Ltd
Times 12.30-1.45/7.30-9.30
Prices Fixed L 2 course £19.50, Fixed D 3 course £65, Service included
Wines 600 bottles over £20, 20 bottles under £20, 11 by glass **Notes** Gourmand D menu incl wine & private dining £145, Sunday L, Vegetarian menu, Dress restrictions, Jackets preferred, no denim, Civ Wed 120 **Seats** 120, Pr/dining room 120 **Children** Portions, Menu **Parking** 150

PETERSFIELD ***continued***

vibrant atmosphere matches the bold and confident cooking. Roasted scallops with cauliflower purée, smoked haddock tortellini, shellfish velouté and curry oil shows the style. Follow that with roasted and poached fillet of turbot with bacon, lettuce and peas and sauce gribiche, or braised short-rib of beef with creamed potatoes roasted roots and crispy pancetta.

Chef Steven Ranson **Owner** Steven Ranson, Jon Blake **Times** 12-2/6-late Closed 4 wks per year, Mon, L Tue, D Sun **Prices** Fixed L 2 course £14.95, Fixed D 3 course £32, Service added 12.5% **Wines** 12 bottles over £20, 14 bottles under £20, 6 by glass **Notes** Tasting menu 7 course, early bird Tue-Thu 6-7.30pm, Sunday L, Vegetarian available **Seats** 32 **Children** Portions **Parking** On street or Swan Street car park

Frederick's Restaurant, Langrish House

Modern British

Historic setting for accomplished cooking

☎ 01730 266941
Langrish GU32 1RN
e-mail: frontdesk@langrishhouse.co.uk
dir: From Petersfield A272 towards Winchester, turn left into Langrish & follow brown hotel signs

The restaurant at Langrish House was named after an eccentric ancestor of the Talbot-Ponsonby family who was wont to play tennis in a Victorian skirt. This lovely 17th-century pile has been their home for seven generations, and who can blame them for staying put in this enviable location near Petersfield in the buxom embrace of glorious South Downs countryside. Eat in the comfortingly traditional dining room, or to boost the romance factor, go for the softly-lit intimacy of the room in the old vaults. The kitchen takes its cue from the seasons and sources locally for its menu of uncomplicated modern British dishes. Wood pigeon with Hampshire black pudding, bacon lardons and walnut oil dressing makes a robust starter, while mains run from rump of lamb with leek fondue, pancetta crisp and eggplant spring roll, to seared brill with Puy lentils, roasted salsify and beurre rouge. Dessert could offer Granny Smith apple and blackcurrant parfait with cider sorbet.

Chef Peter Buckman **Owner** Mr & Mrs Talbot-Ponsonby **Times** 12-2/7-9.30 **Prices** Fixed L 2 course fr £16.95, Fixed D 3 course fr £35.95, Service added but optional 12.5% **Wines** 15 bottles over £20, 13 bottles under £20, 2 by glass **Notes** Sunday L, Vegetarian available, Dress restrictions, Smart casual, Civ Wed 60 **Seats** 24, Pr/dining room 20 **Children** Portions **Parking** 100

JSW

– see below

The Thomas Lord

British **NEW**

A true local for all seasons

☎ 01730 829244
High St, West Meon GU32 1LN
e-mail: enjoy@thethomaslord.co.uk

Not just another identikit gastro-pub, this unpretentious country inn stays faithful to its pubby roots and an unswerving mission to use 100% local produce, while Hampshire real ales feature at the bar and a duo of local vineyards find a place on the wine list. Fresh, quality, seasonal ingredients - from small-scale producers and farms - are bolstered by eggs from the pub's own hens and quails and produce from its kitchen garden. The cooking shows a light, modern touch with well-presented dishes on daily-changing menus; start with warm bacon-rolled pig's head with apple purée and move onto venison fillet with roasted beetroot and quince and onion gravy, or perhaps pan-fried king scallops and sea bass fillets teamed with celeriac and garlic butter. The pared back no-nonsense interior fits the bill, while candlelight adds its glow in the evening.

JSW

PETERSFIELD **Map 5 SU72**

Modern British V NOTABLE WINE LIST

Confident cooking in understated restaurant with rooms

☎ 01730 262030
20 Dragon St GU31 4JJ
e-mail: jsw.restaurant@btconnect.com
dir: A3 to town centre, follow one-way system to College St which becomes Dragon St, restaurant on left

Every element of Jake Watkins' restaurant in a stylishly restored 17th-century coaching inn makes a virtue of simplicity and understatement: whitewashed outside and done out in natural muted tones within, oak beams span a dining room that caters for just 22 diners at well-spaced linen-clad tables. There's no rush to eat up and make way for the second sitting, since the philosophy has nothing to do with turning tables quickly. This is a chef who cooks with a passion for his craft, starting with the best materials he can lay his hands on: fish from day boats on the Solent - or even caught by the chef himself (he's a keen fisherman) - and the rest from the best suppliers in the UK and France. The food has a confident modern Anglo-French inflection, underpinned by virtuoso technique and an innate feel for what works together on the plate to deliver maximum pleasure to the customer. Fish and seafood are a strong suit - perhaps seared scallops with lightly-spiced mussels and razor clams to start, or a main course of local dover sole with caramelised cauliflower purée, samphire and sea kale. Meat offerings might team pheasant boudin with ham hock, white beans and truffle oil, ahead of 18-hour-cooked ox cheek with curly kale and mash. Desserts also burst with vibrant flavour, say savarin with apple millefeuille and caramelised apple purée. Lurking beneath the restaurant are cellars stocked with over 700 wines, and there's clued-up guidance at hand from professional staff.

Chef Jake Watkins **Owner** Jake Watkins **Times** 12-1.30/7-9.30 Closed 2 wks Jan & summer, Sun-Mon **Prices** Fixed L 2 course fr £19.50, Fixed D 3 course fr £29.50, Tasting menu £40-£50, Service optional, Groups min 10 service 10% **Wines** 556 bottles over £20, 14 bottles under £20, 10 by glass **Notes** ALC 2 course £38.50, 3 course £47, Tasting menu L/D 5 course, Vegetarian menu **Seats** 58, Pr/dining room 18 **Parking** 19

ROTHERWICK **Map 5 SU75**

Oak Room Restaurant

Modern British

Smart formal dining in opulent country-house surroundings

☎ 01256 764881
Tylney Hall Hotel RG27 9AZ
e-mail: sales@tylneyhall.com
dir: M3 junct 5 take A287 (Newnham). From M4 junct 11 take B3349 (Hook), at sharp bend left (Rotherwick), left again & left in village (Newnham) 1m on right

People flock to Tylney Hall - a grand red-brick Victorian country house - for a fine-dining fix and dose of stately wow-factor. It's set in 66 acres of beautiful parkland, which include Gertrude Jekyll-designed gardens, waterfalls, ornamental lakes and woodland walks, while the interior is no less impressive, with its oak panelling and fancy plasterwork - the ceiling in the Italian lounge came from the Grimaldi Palace in Florence. Culinary endeavours focus on the glass-domed and aptly named Oak Room Restaurant, where the cooking takes a modish route, though eschewing culinary fireworks to focus on top-notch British produce, including a sprinkling of luxury (a foie gras pannacotta to start and Chateaubriand to follow). Otherwise, expect the likes of butter poached halibut fillet served with lobster salpiçon and baby leeks.

Chef Stephen Hine **Owner** Elite Hotels
Times 12.30-2/7-10 **Prices** Fixed L 2 course fr £18.50, Fixed D 3 course fr £37.50, Service optional **Wines** 350 bottles over £20, 2 bottles under £20, 10 by glass **Notes** Bill of Fayre menu 3 course £46, Sunday L, Vegetarian available, Dress restrictions, Jacket & tie at D, no jeans Fri-Sat, Civ Wed 100 **Seats** 80, Pr/dining room 100 **Children** Portions, Menu **Parking** 150

SOUTHAMPTON **Map 5 SU41**

Legacy Botleigh Grange Hotel

Modern European

Formal dining in idyllically positioned hotel

☎ 0870 832 9950
Grange Rd, Hedge End SO30 2GA
e-mail: res-botleighgrange@legacy-hotels.co.uk
dir: On A334, 1m from M27 junct 7

Botleigh Grange is a cream-painted Victorian fantasy with turrets, battlements and an Italianate clock tower, set in extensive grounds grazed by Highland cattle. All very idyllic, then, and with the added bonus of being handy for the M27 motorway. Beneath its ornamental glass-domed ceiling, the restaurant has an airy elegance and lovely views over the immaculately-kept gardens. The kitchen makes good use of local Hampshire produce in its creative modern European dishes. A leek, potato and goats' cheese tart is served with a warm balsamic fig and herb salad and rocket oil dressing to start, followed by Gressingham duck 'three ways' - confit leg, roast breast and liver cassoulet, with roast potatoes and apricot and Calvados jus.

Times 12.30-2.30/7-9.45

Vatika

British, Indian V

Vibrant Indian spicing in English country vineyard

☎ 01329 830405
Wickham Vineyard, Botley Rd, Shedfield SO32 2HL
e-mail: info@vatikarestaurant.co.uk
dir: M27 junct 7 through Botley towards Wickham. M27 junct 10, A32 through Wickham towards Bishops Waltham. Turn left into Wickham Rd towards Vineyard

Vatika - meaning 'Vineyard' in Sanskrit and Hindi - is the latest venture from Atul Kochhar of Benares fame (see entry). The English translation certainly sums up its beautiful location as this classy modern Indian restaurant sits in the heart of stunning Wickham Vineyard in deepest Hampshire. Kochhar's cuisine here, overseen by protégé Jitin Joshi who heads up the kitchen, might best be described as 'Indlish' - creative modern British food with a clear Indian influence. The team clearly has a strong understanding of the Indian arsenal of spices and herbs, sharp technical skills and lively imagination to pull off a classy act. Innovative dishes look the part and are named after their two main ingredients, as in a starter of 'crab-parsnip', which delivers crisp soft-shell crab with pickled parsnip and smoked gel, and a main course of 'lamb-spinach' delivers 24-hour cooked lamb shoulder with spinach gnocchi and mint yoghurt. To end, 'chocolate-banana' reveals chocolate cube, banana nuggets and cardamom brûlée.

Chef Jitin Joshi & Atul Kochhar **Owner** Atul Kochhar
Times 12-2.30/6.30-9.30 Closed Xmas, Mon-Tue, L Wed-Thu, D Sun **Prices** Fixed L 2 course £35, Fixed D 3 course £40, Service optional **Wines** 60 bottles over £20, 10 bottles under £20, 14 by glass **Notes** Tasting menu available 6/10 course, Sunday L, Vegetarian menu, Dress restrictions, Smart casual **Seats** 52 **Children** Portions **Parking** 20

White Star Tavern, Dining and Rooms

Modern British

Modern British dining with local flavour

☎ 023 8082 1990
28 Oxford St SO14 3DJ
e-mail: reservations@whitestartavern.co.uk
dir: M3 junct 14 onto A33, towards Ocean Village

Business continues to go from strength to strength at Southampton's first gastro-pub, located just minutes from Ocean Village and West Quay. Housed in a former shipping hotel once owned by the White Star Line, it has been transformed into a smart boutique-style inn and is a favoured dining destination in the city's thriving restaurant quarter. The swish bar area draws a lively drinking crowd, while discerning diners head for the comfortable banquette seating in the spacious, wood-floored and panelled dining areas beyond. Cooking is modern brasserie-style and the changing repertoire of modern British dishes makes sound use of local seasonal ingredients, including day boat fish, organic farm produce and New Forest shoots. Typically, begin with seared scallops with celeriac purée and Spanish black pudding, move on to pan-fried bream with mussels, chorizo mash and fish gravy, and finish with hot dark chocolate and beetroot fondant.

Chef Jim Hayward **Owner** Matthew Boyle
Times 12-2.30/6-9.30 Closed 25-26 Dec **Prices** Starter £4-£8, Main £11-£18, Dessert £5-£8, Service optional, Groups min 6 service 10% **Wines** 22 bottles over £20, 10 bottles under £20, 9 by glass **Notes** Sunday L, Vegetarian available **Seats** 40, Pr/dining room 10 **Children** Portions **Parking** On street or 2 car parks nearby

STOCKBRIDGE **Map 5 SU33**

The Greyhound

Modern British

Popular gastro-pub beside the River Test

☎ 01264 810833
31 High St SO20 6EY
e-mail: enquiries@thegreyhound.info
dir: 9m NW of Winchester, 8m S of Andover. Off A303

Keen anglers flock to the quaint market town of Stockbridge to fish on the River Test, while antique and art enthusiasts come for the shops and galleries. Whatever floats your boat, head to The Greyhound, a stylish gastro-pub in Stockbridge's main street, for some seriously good food. The place has retained much of its original 15th century charm - think inglenook fireplaces, old beams and timbers and bare floorboards - but turns out some distinctly modern fare. Simplicity is the key to the kitchen's approach, but that's not to say the cooking doesn't have a certain degree of finesse. The Greyhound fishcake with poached egg and chive beurre blanc is one way to start, followed by cannon of Welsh lamb with buttered ratte potatoes, crushed peas and rosemary jus. Dessert could be white peach tarte Tatin with honey and toasted almond ice cream.

Times 12-2/7-9 Closed 25-26 Dec, 31 Dec & 1 Jan, D Sun

STOCKBRIDGE *continued*

Peat Spade Inn

British

Good food in Test Valley village pub

01264 810612
Longstock SO20 6DR
e-mail: info@peatspadeinn.co.uk
dir: 1.5m N of Stockbridge on A3057

The River Test, one of Hampshire's finest chalk rivers and famous for fly fishing, is just a short stroll away from this thriving gabled Victorian pub set in a tranquil thatched village. Re-styled as a dining pub with rooms, it sports a small bar area serving Ringwood ales, and two cosy dining areas with candlelit wooden tables, and walls covered with old school pictures and fishing rods. The seasonal menu delivers classic English dishes, using excellent local ingredients and straightforwardly presented. Start with rabbit terrine with pickled carrots and girolles, and follow on with roast halibut with squid ink risotto and sweet fennel. Finish with poached pear with almond parfait and white chocolate ice cream.

Times 12-2/6.30-9.30 Closed 3 wks Feb/Mar & 25-26 Dec, D Sun

WICKHAM Map 5 SU51

Old House Hotel & Restaurant

Modern British

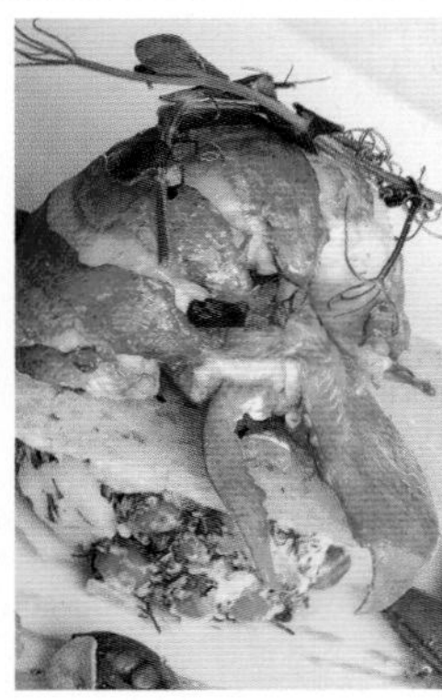

Modern cooking in chic Georgian hotel

01329 833049
The Square PO17 5JG
e-mail: enquiries@oldhousehotel.co.uk
dir: In centre of Wickham, 2m N of Fareham at junct of A32 & B2177

The creeper-covered Old House Hotel has no shortage of Georgian charm and has stood on the pretty village square for a little over 300 years. These days the restaurant, public rooms and bedrooms have both original character and a chic, contemporary gloss. Affable service suits the mood in the various eating areas, including the conservatory and garden room, where classical Victorian prints and works by renowned local artists adorn the walls. The cooking follows a contemporary path with a good deal of Hampshire produce highlighted on the appealing à la carte menu and due diligence paid to the seasons. Crayfish risotto with spring onion and lemon is a typical first course, while local Southdown lamb comes with confit potatoes, glazed carrots and lamb's sweetbreads in a satisfying main. A good way to finish might be caramelised banana bavarois with a warm chocolate brownie, caramel ice cream and toffee popcorn.

Chef David Humphreys **Owner** Mr J R Guess **Times** 12-2.30/7-9.30 Closed D Sun **Prices** Fixed L 2 course £12.95, Starter £6.10-£9.50, Main £14.95-£25, Dessert £6.25-£8, Service optional, Groups min 8 service 10% **Wines** 79 bottles over £20, 14 bottles under £20, 16 by glass **Notes** Tasting menu available, Sunday L, Vegetarian available, Dress restrictions, Smart casual, Civ Wed 60 **Seats** 85, Pr/dining room 14 **Children** Portions **Parking** 12, Street parking

Avenue Restaurant at Lainston House Hotel

WINCHESTER Map 5 SU42

Modern British V

Imaginative modern cooking in a historic house

01962 776088
Woodman Ln, Sparsholt SO21 2LT
e-mail: enquiries@lainstonhouse.com
dir: B3049 Stockbridge road

A gorgeous red-brick 17th-century mansion, Lainston House has certainly had its fair share of high-profile visitors: Charles II dropped by with one of his mistresses, then it was owned by a long roll call of courtiers and members of parliament; since becoming a hotel in 1981 a long list of celebs from the music and film worlds have pitched up. Fittingly, this is the heart of Jane Austen country and the house could easily do service as a film set for a bodice-and-breeches period drama with its romantically-ruined medieval chapel in the grounds and overall air of an archetypal English country manor. Make sure to start in the Cedar Bar, which does a nice line in Bellinis and Martinis to go with the ornate panelling, carved by the master craftsman Grinling Gibbons from a single tree that fell in a storm in 1930. The Avenue Restaurant - named for the graceful mile-long avenue of lime trees that forms an ever-present backdrop - is the venue for chef Andrew MacKenzie's assured, imaginative and highly-skilled cooking. Lainston's kitchen is amply supplied by the exemplary produce of local suppliers championed on the menu, as well as a kitchen garden providing dozens of types of fruit, veg and herbs. Seared scallops with streaky bacon make a grand entrance, served with a purée and fresh leaves of Hampshire watercress and vine tomatoes, while main-course poussin breast, and leg ballottine, is accompanied by lemon thyme potato cake and carrot purée - also present are streaky bacon, spring onions, and a delicious cep foam. The 'exclusive chocolate medley' is too good an option to pass on; it presents a superbly rendered essay in textural contrasts, in the forms of chocolate and caramel mousse, white chocolate and tonka bean tart and a chocolate mint sorbet.

Chef Andrew MacKenzie, Phil Yeomans **Owner** Exclusive Hotels **Times** 12-2/7-10 **Prices** Fixed L 2 course £21.50, Fixed D 3 course £44.50, Tasting menu £65-£110, Starter £10.50-£16.90, Main £18.50-£32, Dessert £10.50, Service added but optional 10% **Wines** 200 bottles over £20, 200 by glass **Notes** Tasting menu with/without wine, Sunday L, Vegetarian menu, Dress restrictions, Smart casual, Civ Wed 200 **Seats** 60, Pr/dining room 120 **Children** Portions, Menu **Parking** 200

WINCHESTER Map 5 SU42

Avenue Restaurant at Lainston House Hotel

◎◎◎ – *see opposite page*

The Black Rat

◎ Modern British

Relaxed, unbuttoned dining in character-packed surroundings

☎ 01962 844465
88 Chesil St SO23 0HX
e-mail: reservations@theblackrat.co.uk
dir: M3 junct 9/A31 towards Winchester & Bar End until T-junct. Turn right at traffic lights, restaurant 600yds on left

The rather unprepossessing exterior of this former 18th-century pub, just a short stroll from the cathedral and city centre, belies the relaxed charm and character to be found within the cosy dining rooms and upstairs bar. Original beams, rug-strewn wooden floors, exposed brickwork, old paintings, log fires crackling in inglenook fireplaces, and chunky bare wood tables set the informal scene for some pleasing modern British cooking with a Mediterranean twist. Monthly menus and chalkboard specials are built around seasonal local produce. Well-presented dishes may take Longhorn bresaola with pecorino, pear and rocket to start, followed by confit pork belly and Toulouse sausage cassoulet, with vanilla bean pannacotta and Yorkshire rhubarb for pudding.

Chef Chris Bailey **Owner** David Nicholson
Times 12-2.15/7-9.30 Closed 2 wks Etr, 2 wks Xmas & New Year, 2 wks Oct /Nov, L Mon-Fri **Prices** Fixed L 2 course £19.50, Starter £6.50-£7.25, Main £16.95-£24, Dessert £6.25-£7.50, Service optional, Groups min 10 service 10% **Wines** 40 bottles over £20, 18 bottles under £20, 6 by glass **Notes** Sunday L, Vegetarian available **Seats** 40, Pr/dining room 14 **Parking** Car park opposite

The Chesil Rectory

◎◎ Modern British

Great British cooking in historic building

☎ 01962 851555
1 Chesil St SO23 0HU
e-mail: enquiries@chesilrectory.co.uk
dir: S from King Alfred's statue at bottom of The Broadway, cross small bridge, turn right, restaurant on left, just off mini rdbt

The name of Winchester's oldest house means 'riverbank' or shingle beach, showing that it once stood beside the river. And as the topography of the town has shifted, so did the focus in the kitchen when a new team took over in October 2008: out went the modern French tag, to be replaced by British classics in a modern vein. The interior changed too: it was built in 1450, so the wonky ceiling, blackened beams and inglenook fireplaces are all sacrosanct, but in came a more funky modern country-house chic featuring vintage chandeliers, bare wood tables and green leather banquettes. Chef Damian Brown's feet are clearly planted firmly in Britain, so expect superb local materials to form the backbone of the cooking - risotto of Portland crab and cockles to start, then slow-cooked belly of local pork with parsnip and potato purée, beetroot and crackling. Rounding off are desserts such as apple and marmalade sponge with custard.

Chef Damian Brown **Owner** Mark Dodd, Damian Brown, Iain Longhorn **Times** 12-2.30/6-9.30 Closed 1 wk Xmas, 1 wk Aug, D Sun **Prices** Fixed L 2 course £14.95, Fixed D 3 course £19.95, Starter £4.50-£8.95, Main £11.95-£18.95, Dessert £6, Service optional, Groups min 10 service 10% **Wines** 50+ bottles over £20, 4 bottles under £20, 9 by glass **Notes** Set menu L Mon-Sat 12-2.30, D Mon-Sat only available 6-7pm, Sunday L, Vegetarian available, Civ Wed 30 **Seats** 75, Pr/dining room 14 **Children** Portions **Parking** NCP Chesil Street 600 spaces

Hotel du Vin Winchester

◎◎ Traditional, International NOTABLE WINE LIST

Bustling bistro and great wines in Georgian townhouse hotel

☎ 01962 841414
14 Southgate St SO23 9EF
e-mail: info@winchester.hotelduvin.co.uk
dir: M3 junct 11, follow signs to Winchester town centre, located on left

Winchester was the original branch of the oenophile hotel chain, and remains architecturally one of the most impressive. Housed in a townhouse dating from the very outset of the Georgian era, 1715, it's a relatively small building less than half a mile from the Cathedral. The house style of modern brasserie dishes, capably rendered and delivering bold, assertive tastes, is in evidence on menus that might take in crayfish and dill on a croûton with basil dressing, roast cod with bok choy in prawn bisque, or pheasant with confit cabbage in wild mushroom jus. As at other Hotels du Vin, a slate of Simple Classics - perhaps traditional fish pie, is offered alongside, while desserts include properly sticky tarte Tatin. The reputation of the wine list goes before it.

Times 12-1.45/7-10

Hutton's Brasserie & Bar

◎ Modern European

British brasserie dishes in a candlelit room

☎ 01962 709988
The Winchester Hotel, Worthy Ln SO23 7AB
e-mail: info.winchester@pedersenhotels.com
dir: M3 junct 9, at rdbt take 3rd exit (A34/Newbury). 0.5m, right & follow A33/Basingstoke signs. 1st left onto B3047 to Winchester. Hotel 2m on right

Plumb in the heart of Winchester, this modern hotel brasserie is all polished wood floors, tabletop candles and hip background music. An atmosphere of stylish intimacy is created around the contemporary culinary repertoire, which deals in fashionable pasta and risotto options amid starters such as goats' cheese, courgette and red pepper pannacotta with sauce vierge, and mains like calves' liver with grain mustard mash, pancetta and Rioja jus. A slate of 'Classics' provides sausages, burgers and fish and chips, while afters such as key lime pie with raspberry sorbet and dark chocolate sauce will send you happily on your way.

Chef Paul Bentley **Owner** Pedersen Hotels
Times 12.30-2/7-9.30 **Prices** Food prices not confirmed for 2011. Please telephone for details **Wines** 15 bottles over £20, 25 bottles under £20, 9 by glass **Notes** Sunday L, Vegetarian available, Dress restrictions, Smart casual, Civ Wed 180 **Seats** 80, Pr/dining room 40
Children Portions, Menu **Parking** 70

The Running Horse

◎ Modern British

Innovation-conscious cooking in a sleek country pub

☎ 01962 880218
88 Main Rd, Littleton SO22 6QS
e-mail: runninghorseinn@btconnect.com
dir: 3m from city centre, 2m off A34

Three miles out of Winchester, the white-fronted country inn has been given a sleek decorative makeover inside, with interesting pictures, a light, minimal tone and blackboard menus. The cooking aims for innovation, by means of up-to-date kitchen equipment and a modern British sensibility. Nicely timed seared scallops are teamed with crisp pancetta, puréed peas, parmesan foam and a wine sauce for a modern classic starter, while main course might be rump and shoulder of Salisbury lamb with ratatouille terrine, basil mash and a reduction of red wine. Finish with silky apple and vanilla crème brûlée in a syrupy apple 'soup' with matching sorbet.

Times 11-3/5.30-11

WINCHESTER *continued*

The Winchester Royal

Modern British

Modern menu in the heart of historic Winchester

01962 840840
St Peter St SO23 8BS
e-mail: winchester.royal@forestdale.com
dir: Take one-way system through Winchester, turn right off St George's Street into St Peter Street. Hotel on right

This ancient hotel pulls off the neat trick of being simultaneously right in the centre of Winchester, yet delightfully tranquil and secluded within its walled garden. Parts of the building date from the 14th century and it has done service as a bishop's house and a Benedictine convent; nowadays, however, there's no need for self denial in the smart Conservatory Restaurant, where the cooking takes in modern British staples with European influences, using quality materials in an unaffected style. Salmon and dill fishcakes with crème fraîche are a good way to start, then follow with roasted halibut on spring onion rösti with butter and sorrel sauce, and finish with pannacotta with roasted rhubarb.

Chef Michael LePoidevin **Owner** Forestdale Hotels **Times** 12-2/7-9.30 **Prices** Starter £5.50-£6.50, Main £16-£20, Dessert £5.50-£7, Service optional **Wines** 11 bottles over £20, 24 bottles under £20, 7 by glass **Notes** Sunday L, Vegetarian available, Civ Wed 120 **Seats** 95, Pr/dining room 30 **Children** Portions, Menu **Parking** 50

HEREFORDSHIRE

HEREFORD **Map 10 SO53**

Castle House

Modern British

Luxury boutique hotel with creative cooking

01432 356321
Castle St HR1 2NW
e-mail: info@castlehse.co.uk
web: www.castlehse.co.uk
dir: City centre, follow signs to Castle House Hotel

Discreetly tucked away close to the cathedral but away from the hubbub of the city centre, this grand Georgian townhouse has lovingly landscaped gardens. Inside, the classical style and gentle pastel colours make for a soothing setting, the plush restaurant suiting the mood with its topiary-themed artworks on mustard walls and lovely views of the garden and river running past the castle moat. The ambitious kitchen turns out inventive combinations based on classical foundations and much of the produce is sourced from the hotel owner's farm. Salad of pigeon with black pudding and quail's egg salad with damson purée might be followed by fillet of Herefordshire beef with beetroot rösti, mushroom duxelle and horseradish cream. Finish with Rhubarb and custard - pannacotta, cream sorbet and rhubarb lollipop.

Times 12-2/7-10

Holme Lacy House Hotel

British **NEW**

Creative cooking in grand country setting

01432 870870
Holme Lacy HR2 6LP
dir: B4399 at Holme Lacy, take lane opposite college. Hotel 500mtrs on right

A Grade I listed 17th century Restoration manor-house hotel not far from Hereford, Holme Lacy is surrounded by 20 acres of Wye Valley parkland. The inspiring grounds are matched by the outstanding architectural features inside. The Orchard Restaurant plays its part with its elegant oak panels and period features, as well as putting the hotel on the regional culinary map. The imaginative menu is accurately cooked by a kitchen that sources much of its produce locally. A well-judged lemon sole with crab risotto and chive hollandaise gets dinner off to a good start, before main-course roast rump of lamb, accurately cooked, is served with celeriac fondant, peas, ceps purée and prosciutto wafer. A rhubarb pannacotta with poached rhubarb and custard ice shows sound technical skills run through from start to finish.

Times Closed L all week

KINGTON **Map 9 SO25**

The Stagg Inn and Restaurant

Modern British V

Welcoming gastro-pub in rural Herefordshire

01544 230221
Titley HR5 3RL
e-mail: reservations@thestagg.co.uk
dir: Between Kington & Presteigne on B4335

Note that this whitewashed Herefordshire hostelry is both inn and restaurant. It is proud of its dual role as both local pub and upscale eatery. Indeed, the whole place is a hive of activity, with vegetables, fruits and herbs grown in the garden, and rare-breed pigs producing sausages, salamis, faggots and more, which are sold off the premises and adorn the menus. Steve Reynolds is a gifted cook, transforming this bounty into dishes of great impact. The in-house chorizo is paired with squid for an appetising starter, while main-course cod with samphire is sauced with smoked lemon beurre blanc. Simpler dishes work convincingly too, as demonstrated by a lunch of crab cake with cucumber relish, followed by local chicken breast wrapped in courgette with olive oil mash. Dessert might be a trio of crèmes brûlées, the familiar vanilla accompanied by its new best friends of coffee and lavender.

Chef S Reynolds, M Handley **Owner** Steve & Nicola Reynolds **Times** 12-3/6.30-9.30 Closed 1st 2wks Nov, 2 wks Jan-Feb, Mon, D Sun **Prices** Starter £4.50-£8.90, Main £14.90-£19.90, Dessert £6.50, Service optional **Wines** 41 bottles over £20, 33 bottles under £20, 8 by glass **Notes** Vegetarian menu **Seats** 70, Pr/dining room 30 **Children** Portions **Parking** 22

LEDBURY **Map 10 SO73**

Feathers Hotel

Modern British

Elizabethan hotel with confident international cooking

01531 635266
High St HR8 1DS
e-mail: mary@feathers-ledbury.co.uk
dir: M50 junct 2. Ledbury on A449/A438/A417. Hotel on main street

Once known as the Plume of Feathers, the heavily timbered building dates back to around the time of Shakespeare's birth. Inside is a plush, well-run hotel with a choice of dining in the smart weekend dining room, Quills, or the more informal Fuggles Brasserie, its name taken from a variety of hops. The menu casts its net wide for global inspiration, turning from crisp-skinned sea bass with Goan-spiced rice and pak choi to oxtail and beef shin pie and mashed potato without a blink. Finish up with blackcurrant posset, garnished with shortbread and apples steeped in Cassis.

Chef Susan Isaacs **Owner** David Elliston **Times** 12-2/7-9.30 **Prices** Starter £5.25-£7.25, Main £11.95-£21.95, Dessert £5.95, Service added but optional 10% **Wines** 97 bottles over £20, 48 bottles under £20, 11 by glass **Notes** Sunday L, Vegetarian available, Civ Wed 100 **Seats** 55, Pr/dining room 60 **Children** Portions **Parking** 30

Verzon House Bar, Brasserie & Hotel

Modern British, European

Quality local produce in modern, stylish surroundings

01531 670381
Hereford Rd, Trumpet HR8 2PZ
e-mail: info@theverzon.com
dir: M5 junct 8, M50 junct 2 (signed Ledbury/A417). Follow signs for Hereford (A438). Hotel on right

An elegant Georgian country-house hotel, Verzon comes set in extensive grounds with far-reaching views of the Malvern Hills. Its relaxed brasserie-style restaurant is an easy-on-the-eye modish place, with stylish furnishings and contemporary natural tones, while service is formal yet friendly. The accomplished modern-British cooking fits the surroundings, driven by high-quality locally-sourced seasonal produce and accurate timing; take seared sea trout teamed with a crayfish risotto, green beans and sauce vièrge, while lamb three ways takes in marinated rack, grilled kidney and slow-cooked shoulder, served with spring vegetable couscous and lemongrass sauce. Finish with the likes of an ethereal millefeuille of local rhubarb, crème anglaise and rhubarb sorbet or caramel sponge pudding served up with rosemary ice cream.

Times 12-2/7-9.30

ROSS-ON-WYE **Map 10 SO52**

The Bridge at Wilton

Modern British, French

Seasonal cooking on the banks of the Wye

☎ 01989 562655
Wilton HR9 6AA
e-mail: info@bridge-house-hotel.com
dir: Off junct A40 & A49 into Ross-on-Wye, 300yds on left

A Georgian house with a walled garden running down to the River Wye, this intimate restaurant with rooms has a rustic chic reminiscent of a French country auberge. The creaky dark oak floorboards underfoot and modern paintings by a local artist on cool cream walls add to the ambience. The kitchen keeps things simple, producing clear flavours and some of the produce is as local as the hotel's own garden. A starter of seared scallops with braised woodland pork might be followed by a trio of lamb with white truffle mash, Savoy cabbage and lamb jus. Glazed lemon tart with berry compôte makes for a refreshing finale.

Chef Nick Seward **Owner** Mike & Jane Pritchard **Times** 12-2/7-9 **Prices** Fixed L 2 course £12.50, Starter £7-£12, Main £18-£23, Dessert £7-£10, Service optional **Wines** 27 bottles over £20, 27 bottles under £20, 4 by glass **Notes** Dress restrictions, Smart casual **Seats** 40, Pr/dining room 26 **Parking** 40

Glewstone Court Country House Hotel & Restaurant

Modern British, French

Fine local produce in Regency house with views

☎ 01989 770367
Glewstone HR9 6AW
e-mail: glewstone@aol.com
web: www.glewstonecourt.com
dir: From Ross Market Place take A40/A49 (Monmouth/Hereford) over Wilton Bridge. At rdbt left onto A40 (Monmouth/S Wales), after 1m turn right for Glewstone. Hotel 0.5m on left

A charming family-run hotel, set in well-tended gardens, enjoying an elevated position with views over Ross-on-Wye, Glewstone is surrounded by orchards within an Area of Outstanding Natural Beauty. Many Georgian features remain in the elegant house, while the restaurant is done out in a gentle contemporary style, the work of local artists adding splashes of colour to the walls. The modern British cooking has a French influence and makes the very best of the abundant local larder, including rack of Usk Valley spring lamb, served up with celeriac and rosemary purée and claret gravy, or pan-fried fillet of Marches venison with pears, parsnip crisps and sloe gin sauce.

Chef Christine Reeve-Tucker, Richard Jefferey, Tom Piper **Owner** C & W Reeve-Tucker **Times** 12-2/7-10 Closed 25-27 Dec **Prices** Fixed L 2 course £11, Starter £6-£9, Main £13-£20, Dessert £6, Service optional **Wines** 23 bottles over £20, 19 bottles under £20, 8 by glass **Notes** Sunday L, Vegetarian available, Dress restrictions, No baseball caps, Civ Wed 72 **Seats** 36, Pr/dining room 40 **Children** Portions, Menu **Parking** 28

Harry's

Modern European

Modern European cooking in Georgian country-house hotel

☎ 01989 763161
Chase Hotel, Gloucester Rd HR9 5LH
e-mail: res@chasehotel.co.uk
dir: M50 junct 4 A449, A440 towards Ross-on-Wye

Set within the Chase Hotel with its landscaped gardens in the picturesque countryside surrounding Ross-on-Wye, Harry's is the place to go for ambitious cooking in elegant surroundings. The original Georgian high ceilings and ornate plaster covings contrast with a modern makeover of plush black- and caramel-toned chairs and pale silk drapes. Seasonal modern European cooking might feature country-style pork and apricot terrine with crackling and cider dressing leading onto Barbary duck breast with sautéed wild mushrooms, spinach and maple syrup dressing. Finish with citrus chiffon mousse with sablé biscuit and orange sorbet.

Times 12-2/7-10 Closed 24-27 Dec

Mulberry Restaurant

British, European

Skilful modern cooking in a riverside setting

☎ 01989 562569
Wilton Court Restaurant with Rooms, Wilton Ln HR9 6AQ
e-mail: info@wiltoncourthotel.com
dir: M50 junct 4 onto A40 towards Monmouth at 3rd rdbt turn left signed Ross-on-Wye then take 1st right, hotel on right

A spacious restaurant with conservatory extension in a house dating back partly to Elizabethan times is the main focus of this Wye Valley riverside hotel. Glass-topped tables, quality tableware and uplifting floral adornments

continued

ROSS-ON-WYE *continued*

are all part of the deal, and the place is run with relaxing professionalism by a knowledgeable team. It's a full-dress dining approach, with canapés, breads and petits fours all suffused with class, and the modern culinary style achieves great depth and balance. A raviolo of wild mushrooms and chestnuts in tomato butter is a fine essay in contrasting sweetness and sharpness, while the Raglan lamb loin is pinkly and accurately cooked to emphasise its tenderness, and cleverly partnered with smoked garlic purée, saffron-hued fondant potato, ratatouille and aubergine caviar. An early spring dessert catches the end of the rhubarb season, with a frangipane tart topped with strips of it, accompanied by creamy vanilla ice.

Chef Michael Fowler **Owner** Roger and Helen Wynn **Times** 12-2.15/7-9 **Prices** Fixed L 2 course £13.95, Tasting menu £49.50, Starter £5.75-£9.50, Main £13.25-£19.95, Dessert £5.95-£8.50, Service optional **Wines** 17 bottles over £20, 16 bottles under £20, 7 by glass **Notes** Tasting menu 7 course, Sunday L, Vegetarian available, Dress restrictions, Smart casual preferred, Civ Wed 50 **Seats** 40, Pr/dining room 12 **Children** Portions, Menu **Parking** 25

Orles Barn

Modern British **NEW**

Confident modern cooking in smart restaurant with rooms

☎ 01989 562155
Wilton HR9 6AE
e-mail: reservations@orles-barn.co.uk
dir: A49/A40 rdbt outside Ross-on-Wye, take slip road between petrol station & A40 to Monmouth. 100yds on left

An old red-brick property with plenty of charm and origins going all the way back to the 14th and 17th centuries, this restaurant with rooms offers a bit of restrained boutique style in pretty Wilton near Ross-on-Wye. The bar with its log fire and comfortable sofas is the place to have a pre-dinner drink and peruse the menus, before moving into the genteel restaurant, where tables are suitably well-spaced, and the décor delivers a pleasing degree of refinement. Expansive windows overlook the lawned gardens. The modern British cooking majors on locally-sourced produce, the suppliers given due credit, and is built on sound classical thinking while showing a confident hand. A duo of local rabbit - roasted loin and the leg meat lasagna - is a classy first course, preceding the likes of roast rack of Buckholt lamb, with crispy braised shoulder and seared liver, served with celeriac gratin, spinach and tomato. Round things off with prune and Armagnac trifle with coffee Chantilly.

Times 12.30-2.30/6.30-9 Closed L Mon, D Sun

ULLINGSWICK — Map 10 SO54

Three Crowns Inn

British, French

Welcoming rural inn offering gutsy modern British fare

☎ 01432 820279
HR1 3JQ
e-mail: info@threecrownsinn.com

The Three Crowns has a long track record of keeping locals well fed and watered since its origins as a cider house in the 16th century. Nowadays, the lovely half-timbered and red-brick country inn trades as a gastro-pub with a laid-back vibe and rustic chic décor of cream washed walls, wooden tables, and church pews. The man behind the stoves is Brent Castle, who sends out creative, bang up-to-date pub food built on the rock-solid foundations of first-class ingredients and sound technical skills. The menu is sensibly concise, and full of great ideas - perhaps roast woodcock with a risotto of its liver and winter vegetables to start, then crisp belly of local pork with home-made black pudding, red cabbage and mustard mash, or line-caught bass with samphire and mussels marinières.

Times 12-3/7-10 Closed 25 Dec, 1 Jan, Mon

WOOLHOPE — Map 10 SO63

Butchers Arms

Modern European **NEW**

Delicious country pub with seriously good food

☎ 01432 860281
HR1 4RF
e-mail: food@butchersarmswoolhope.com
dir: 0.5m out of village, on Ledbury road

The Butchers Arms is every inch the archetypal half-timbered country pub you hope to stumble upon whilst tootling around Herefordshire. Heavily-beamed inside, it has its priorities right: the bar sits centre-stage, serving well-kept local ales, cider and perry, and the place has a down-to-earth, proper pubby feel. The Butchers has always been at the foodie heart of the village - it was indeed a butcher's shop before it started brewing beer and baking bread in an ancient oven that's still on the premises. Nowadays, chef-proprietor Stephen Bull leads a kitchen team down the path of flavour-packed modern European cooking, as witnessed in a powerful pecorino soufflé, cleverly paired with the earthiness of a roasted hazelnut sauce. A classic chargrilled lamb's liver and bacon with crispy onion rings and mash is taken to a higher level by the quality of the materials, and dessert ends with another simple dish done with aplomb - a textbook vanilla pannacotta with poached apricots.

Chef Andreé à Wessel Van Jaarsveld **Owner** Stephen & Annie Bull **Times** 12-2.30/6.30-9.30 Closed Mon (except mid Jul-mid Sep), D Sun **Prices** Starter £3.95-£7.25, Main £9.50-£16, Dessert fr £5.25, Service optional **Notes** Sunday L, Vegetarian available **Seats** 60, Pr/dining room 24 **Children** Portions **Parking** 40

HERTFORDSHIRE

BERKHAMSTED — Map 6 SP90

The Gatsby

Modern European

Modern dining in art-deco picture house

☎ 01442 870403
97 High St HP4 2DG
e-mail: nickpembroke@hotmail.co.uk
web: www.thegatsby.net
dir: M25 junct 20/A41 to Aylesbury in 3m take left turn to Berkhamsted following town signs. Restaurant on left on entering High St

When a restaurant is set in a glorious art deco cinema, you can expect something out of the ordinary. The old 1930s Rex picture house is now a stylish and upbeat 21st-century venue with plenty of nods to the golden age of cinema in its original wooden pillars, huge chandeliers, hand-moulded cornices and nostalgic black-and-white photos; a white baby grand piano adds another touch of pre-war glamour to proceedings. What's on the menu is a crowd-pleasing repertoire of eclectic modern European dishes: start with a gratin of king scallops with caramelised leeks and parmesan crisps, ahead of roast loin of peppered venison teamed with parsnip purée, buttered Savoy cabbage and bitter chocolate sauce.

Chef Matthew Salt **Owner** Nick Pembroke **Times** 12-2.30/5.30-10.30 Closed 25-26 Dec **Prices** Fixed L 2 course £13.95-£18.90, Fixed D 2 course £13.95-£18.90, Starter £6.95-£9.95, Main £14.95-£24.95, Dessert £6.95-£7.25, Groups min 6 service 12.5% **Wines** 25 bottles over £20, 15 bottles under £20, 20 by glass **Notes** Pre cinema menu Mon-Sat 12-2.30 & 5.30-7, Sunday L, Vegetarian available, Dress restrictions, Smart casual **Seats** 65 **Children** Portions **Parking** 10

BISHOP'S STORTFORD **Map 6 TL42**

Ibbetson's Restaurant

Modern British

Modern British menu with a political history

☎ 01279 732100
Down Hall Country House Hotel, Matching Rd, Hatfield Heath CM22 7AS
e-mail: info@downhall.co.uk
web: www.downhall.co.uk
dir: Take A414 towards Harlow. At 4th rdbt follow B183 towards Hatfield Heath, keep left, follow hotel sign

The elegant Down Hall Italianate mansion dates back to 1322, but was rebuilt in the 1870s to become the setting for balls, musical soirées, grand receptions and political entertaining. Grand interiors with ornate ceilings characterise the property while outside there's 110 acres of woodland and landscaped gardens. Ibbetson's is named after former Conservative MP Sir Henry Selwin Ibbetson who lived at the hall. Modern British food with European touches uses produce grown in-house combined with plenty that's locally sourced. Start with salad of duck livers with plum, caramelised red onion, brioche and aged fig balsamic, then move on to pan-fried scallops wrapped in pancetta with a risotto of tiger prawn, asparagus and saffron. Poppyseed parfait with kiwi sauce, fresh cherries and grapefruit tuile provides a fruity finish.

Ibbetson's Restaurant

Chef Mark Jones **Owner** Veladail Collection **Times** 7-9.45 Closed Xmas, New Year, Sun-Mon, L all week **Prices** Food prices not confirmed for 2011. Please telephone for details **Wines** 55 bottles over £20, 12 by glass **Notes** Vegetarian available, Dress restrictions, Smart casual **Seats** 30 **Parking** 100

DATCHWORTH **Map 6 TL21**

The Tilbury

Modern British V

Revitalised village pub serving the best of British

☎ 01483 815550
1 Watton Rd SG3 6TB
e-mail: info@thetilbury.co.uk

Paul Bloxham is a man with endless esprit, as revealed in his countless TV appearances, books, and the kind of restaurants he likes to run. In its previous incarnation the Tilbury was a tired old boozer, but nowadays this pretty village, where cricket is played on the green, is home to a revitalised and invigorated dining pub with a passion for British food of the 'excellent produce, simply cooked' variety. Lucky Datchworth. Bare brick walls, wooden floors, some interesting art and classy table settings suit the mood, too. The modern British menu, which includes daily specials chalked up on the blackboard, runs with the seasons and is peppered with locally-sourced produce. Start with local vegetable minestrone with rocket pesto and home-made focaccia, then perhaps guinea fowl 'In A Jar', served with sauerkraut and chargrilled country bread, or go for the pie of the day from the 'Pub Classics' menu.

Chef Paul Bloxham, Ben Crick **Owner** Paul Bloxham & Paul Andrews **Times** 12-3/6-late Closed 1 Jan, some BHs, D Sun **Prices** Fixed L 2 course fr £13.95, Fixed D 3 course fr £22.50, Starter £4-£11, Main £9.50-£22.95, Dessert £4.50-£8.50, Service optional, Groups min 6 service 10% **Wines** 16 bottles over £20, 16 bottles under £20, 12 by glass **Notes** Sunday L, Vegetarian menu **Seats** 70, Pr/dining room 14 **Children** Portions, Menu **Parking** 40

See advert below

HARPENDEN **Map 6 TL11**

The White Horse

Modern, Traditional

Country gastro-pub with innovative cooking

☎ 01582 469290
Hatching Green AL5 2JP
e-mail: info@thewhitehorseharpenden.com

Under new ownership since celebrity chef Jean-Christophe Novelli went on his way back in 2009, this smart country pub is still very much a destination dining venue. The front bar has retained its pubby atmosphere and is the

continued

HARPENDEN ***continued***

place to go for a pint of real ale, but foodies are drawn to the smart dining room for the likes of smoked Scottish salmon with pickled baby beetroot and red chard. Follow that with a chargrilled pork chop, served with vanilla mash, apple and bacon salsa and cider cream. Smoked chocolate mousse with brioche ice cream and hazelnut dressing is one of the innovative desserts.

Chef Richard Cramer **Owner** Urban 2nd Country Leisure **Times** 12-3.30/6-9.30 Closed 25 Dec,1 Jan **Prices** Fixed L 2 course £10.50-£16.50, Starter £5-£9, Main £15-£26, Dessert £6-£8, Service optional, Groups min 6 service 10% **Wines** 17 bottles over £20, 16 bottles under £20, 20 by glass **Notes** Tasting menu available Mon £17.50, Sunday L, Vegetarian available **Seats** 55, Pr/dining room 12 **Children** Portions, Menu **Parking** 65

HATFIELD — Map 6 TL20

Outsidein at Beales Hotel

Modern British

Contemporary architecture and vibrant contemporary cooking

☎ 01707 288500
Beales Hotel, Comet Way AL10 9NG
e-mail: outsidein@bealeshotels.co.uk
dir: On A1001 opposite Galleria Shopping Mall - follow signs for Galleria

This modern hotel successfully combines natural Cedar wood and huge man-made glass panels to create a striking and unusual building. It was largely rebuilt in 2004 and today houses over 130 original modern pieces of art from the nearby University of Hertfordshire. Outsidein Restaurant doesn't let the side down, being a triumph of contemporary style with its eye-catching lights above every table, modern candles, funky seats and more wood at every turn. Don't think the food is an afterthought here - the creative modern British dishes contain carefully-sourced local ingredients and are cooked with a good degree of skill. Try breast of wood pigeon with spiced Puy lentils and roasted root vegetables before a main-course free-range chicken and Stilton ballottine with fondant potato, and a dessert such as caramel parfait with pear carpaccio and chocolate syrup.

Chef Diego Granada **Owner** Beales Ltd
Times 12-2.30/6.30-10 **Prices** Fixed L 2 course £14.95, Starter £6-£6.50, Main £10-£15, Dessert £6, Service optional, Groups min 8 service 12.5% **Wines** 48 bottles over £20, 15 bottles under £20, 11 by glass **Notes** Sunday L, Vegetarian available, Civ Wed 300 **Seats** 60, Pr/dining room 300 **Children** Portions, Menu **Parking** 126

HEMEL HEMPSTEAD — Map 6 TL00

The Bobsleigh Hotel

British

British classics in a conservatory restaurant

☎ 0844 879 9033
Hempstead Rd, Bovingdon HP3 0DS
e-mail: bobsleigh@macdonald-hotels.co.uk
dir: M1 junct 8, A414 signed Hemel Hempstead. At Plough Rdbt follow railway station signs. Pass rail station on left, straight on at rdbt, under 2 bridges. Left onto B4505 (Box Lane) signed Chesham. Hotel 1.5m on left

Part of the Macdonalds Hotels group, the Bobsleigh is handy for the M1 and M25 and Heathrow and Luton airports, making it useful for the business brigade. It's not without other charms though, namely four-poster beds, spa baths and attractive gardens onto which the aptly named bright and breezy conservatory Garden Room restaurant looks out. A patio proves popular in alfresco weather. The appealing British menu offers lots of classic dishes and traditional flavour combinations such as pea and ham soup followed by roast corn-fed free range chicken, sage and onion gravy and bubble-and-squeak.

Times 12-2.30/7-9.30 Closed L Sat, D Sun

Colette's at The Grove

RICKMANSWORTH — Map 6 TQ09

Modern European NOTABLE WINE LIST

Fine dining in contemporary country estate within the M25

☎ 01923 807807
Chandler's Cross WD3 4TG
e-mail: info@thegrove.co.uk
dir: M25 junct 19, follow signs to Watford. At 1st large rdbt take 3rd exit. 5m, entrance on right

The Grove describes itself as 'London's cosmopolitan country estate', and it lives up to the billing. It is within the M25 for a start, so an easy hop to central London, and a refurbishment in 2004 led to a serious contemporary makeover. As for the country estate bit, well, it stands in 300 acres of beautiful grounds, including a championship golf course. The 18th-century house fits the bill, too, being grand enough to carry the ambitions of the management. The former stables has been converted into a relaxed brasserie-style restaurant, while the fine dining action takes place in Colette's, with its comfortably modern furnishings and funky wooden art on the walls. Head chef Russell Bateman produces classy modern European food with a high level of technique and an eye for appealing presentations. Snail lasagne with celeriac cream makes for a refined starter, while main-course partridge comes with sweetcorn purée, shallots, sprouts and a sticky bacon jus. The flair for balancing flavours continues at dessert stage with a luscious chocolate and chestnut fondant ably supported by coffee ice cream. Service is appropriately professional but there is nothing stuffy about Colette's.

Chef Russell Bateman **Owner** Ralph Trustees Ltd **Times** 7-10 Closed Sun & Mon except BHs, L all week **Prices** Food prices not confirmed for 2011. Please telephone for details **Wines** 250 bottles over £20, 10 by glass **Notes** Vegetarian available, Civ Wed 450 **Seats** 45 **Children** Portions **Parking** 500

HITCHIN Map 12 TL12

Redcoats Farmhouse Hotel

Traditional European

Hearty country food in a medieval farmhouse

☎ 01438 729500
Redcoats Green SG4 7JR
e-mail: sales@redcoats.co.uk
dir: A602 to Wymondley. Turn left to Redcoats Green. At top of hill straight over at junct

Dating from the mid-15th century, this farmhouse in the country between Hitchin and Stevenage has been in the same family ownership for over a hundred years. A warm, homely atmosphere prevails appropriately throughout, and meals are served in the airy, smartly appointed conservatory. Big portions of unpretentiously presented food are high on flavour. Ham hock and parsley terrine is a good opener, and might be followed by parsley-crusted, herb-buttered sea bream on pak choi, or honey-glazed breast and confit leg of Gressingham duck in plum sauce. Finish with pistachio crème brûlée and home-made shortbread. Overnight guests are regaled with a great breakfast menu.

Times 12-6.30 Closed 1 wk after Xmas, BH Mons, L Sat, D Sun

POTTERS BAR Map 6 TL20

Ponsbourne Park Hotel

Modern International

Fine dining in peaceful country setting

☎ 01707 876191 & 879277
SG13 8QT
e-mail: reservations@ponsbournepark.co.uk
web: www.ponsbournepark.com
dir: M25 junct 24/25

Set in 200 acres of the Ponsbourne Park estate, this handsome manor house was rebuilt in fine Regency style after the previous versions were pulled down. Inside, it has been made over with cheerful contemporary hues and modish textures to perk up the period features of the house. The fine-dining Seymours restaurant takes its name from Sir Thomas Seymour, who once lived here with his wife Catherine Parr, the widow of Henry VIII; it's a clean-cut contemporary venue split between two airy high-ceilinged rooms with huge over-mantel mirrors and a grand piano. The kitchen deals in modern European dishes built on a solid foundation of classical technique. Flavours tend to stick to tried-and-tested territory - perhaps smoked haddock served in pannacotta and mousse form, pointed up with tomato vinaigrette, while main-course roast loin and cutlet of lamb could be teamed with champ potato and mint and rosemary cream. Proceedings conclude with something like apple crème brûlée with cinnamon shortbread.

Chef Miles Cobbett **Times** 12-2.30/7-10.30 Closed 1 Jan, D Sun-Wed **Prices** Fixed L 3 course £23.95-£25.95, Fixed D 3 course £27.50, Service optional **Wines** 9 bottles over £20, 14 bottles under £20, 10 by glass **Notes** Sunday L, Vegetarian available, Dress restrictions, Smart casual, Civ Wed 86 **Seats** 60, Pr/dining room 90 **Children** Portions, Menu **Parking** 80

RICKMANSWORTH Map 6 TQ09

Colette's at The Grove

– see opposite page

ST ALBANS Map 6 TL10

Chez Mumtaj

French, Asian

French-Asian fusion in opulent surroundings

☎ 01727 800033
Centurian House, 136-142 London Rd AL1 1PQ
e-mail: info@chezmumtaj.com
web: www.chezmumtaj.com

Don't go thinking there is anything ordinary about Chez Mumtaj. Modern French-Asian cuisine is the thing here and the ambience is modelled on a gentlemen's club; the restaurant and Saffron Lounge are done out with rich mahogany panelled walls, antique mirrors and smart leather banquettes. This swanky appearance is matched by the ambitions of the menu, which takes in South-East Asia and Europe in dishes such as a first-course seared foie gras glazed with kumquats, with a vanilla honey compôte and Szechuan pepper crush, while their take on black cod marries it with kaffir lime curry emulsion. Desserts are similarly on theme - a trio of ice creams featuring pandan leaves and green tea, mango and chilli and cocoa coated coconut.

Chef Chad Rahman **Owner** Chad Rahman **Times** 12-2.30/6-11 Closed 25 Dec, Mon **Prices** Fixed L 2 course £14.95, Fixed D 3 course £17.95, Starter £4.50-£12, Main £14.95-£19.95, Dessert £4.95-£6.95, Service added but optional 10% **Wines** 27 bottles over £20, 18 bottles under £20, 14 by glass **Notes** Early bird dinner menu, Sunday L, Vegetarian available, Dress restrictions, Smart casual **Seats** 100, Pr/dining room 16 **Parking** On street & car park nearby

St Michael's Manor

Modern British

Modern British cooking in tranquil English setting

☎ 01727 864444
Fishpool St AL3 4RY
e-mail: reservations@stmichaelsmanor.com
web: www.stmichaelsmanor.com
dir: At Tudor Tavern in High St into George St. After abbey & school on left, road continues onto Fishpool St. Hotel 1m on left

St Albans is a place of unquestionable historical interest and St Michael's Manor can hold its own amid the antiquity. Set in five acres of tranquil gardens - it is surprisingly close to the centre and the historic cathedral - it dates back to 1585, although it has seen centuries of elegant development and prosperity, and is these days a luxurious country-house hotel. The grand, traditionally-decorated dining room extends into a conservatory and has wonderful views over the gardens and lake. The menu treads a broadly modern British path, with European influences to the fore, thus seared scallops come with pea purée, black pudding and a vierge dressing, and confit pork belly with chorizo, wild mushrooms and butterbean fricassée. Finish with dark chocolate fondant with coffee ice cream and blood orange compôte.

Chef Erick Moboti **Owner** David & Sheila Newling-Ward **Times** 12-2/7-9.30 Closed L 31 Dec, D 25 Dec **Prices** Fixed L 2 course £16.50, Fixed D 3 course £20.50, Starter £5.95-£8.95, Main £14.95-£24.95, Dessert £5.95-£8.50, Service added but optional 12.5% **Wines** 42 bottles over £20, 10 bottles under £20, 11 by glass **Notes** Sunday L, Vegetarian available, Dress restrictions, Smart casual, Civ Wed 90 **Seats** 95, Pr/dining room 24 **Children** Portions, Menu **Parking** 60

TRING Map 6 SP91

Pendley Manor

Modern

Fine dining in an imposing manor house

☎ 01442 891891
Cow Ln HP23 5QY
e-mail: sales@pendley-manor.co.uk
dir: M25 junct 20, A41 (Tring exit). At rdbt follow Berkhamsted/London signs. 1st left signed Tring Station & Pendley Manor

This imposing Tudor-style former manor house was built by the Victorians in 1872, and stands on the site of a much earlier house which was destroyed by fire in 1835. Peacocks roam its 35 acres of wooded parkland, and the public rooms offer period grandeur in spades. The imposing Oak Room restaurant stays true to style, with oak panelling, high ceilings, vast bay windows and heavy drapes. The kitchen's roll call of dishes is based around the modern English canon: first up, baked Golden Cross goats' cheese comes with olive tapenade, rocket, tomato and garlic relish and sherry vinegar treacle, followed by confit pork belly, braised pigs' cheeks, fondant potato, cauliflower purée, pancetta and Granny Smiths.

Times 12.30-2.30/7-9.30

WARE Map 6 TL31

Marriott Hanbury Manor Hotel

French, European

Creative cooking in a Jacobean manor house

☎ 01920 487722
SG12 0SD
e-mail: wendy.traynor@marriotthotels.com
dir: From M25 junct 25, take A10 towards Cambridge, for 12m. Leave A10 Wadesmill/Thundridge/Ware. Right at rdbt, hotel on left

This stately Jacobean county house with its fragrant walled gardens and 200 acres of Hertfordshire countryside boasts an elegant fine-dining restaurant by the name of Zodiac. Dress for dinner in shirts and slacks and take in the view of the championship golf course, plus the chandeliers and oil portraits on the walls. Waiting staff are extremely helpful and knowledgeable as they deliver creative modern dishes with some daring ingredient combinations along the way. Begin with almond-crusted croquette of foie gras with tomato confit, rhubarb tart and cracked black pepper caramel, then move on to roast noisette of lamb with basil purée and asparagus, and finish with a caramel pannacotta, ginger ice cream and gingerbread foam.

Times 12-2/7.30-9.30 Closed Mon, L Sat, D Sun

WELWYN Map 6 TL21

Auberge du Lac

– see below

The Restaurant at Tewin Bury Farm

Modern British V

Confident cooking in converted barn setting

☎ 01438 717793
AL6 0JB
e-mail: maria.finch@tewinbury.co.uk
web: www.tewinbury.co.uk
dir: A1M junct 6 (signposted Welwyn Garden City), 1st exit A1000. 0.25m to B1000 Hertford Rd. Hotel on left

Although still a working farm, the Williams family diversified more than 20 years ago and opened a guest house and restaurant in the 17th-century riverside barn

Auberge du Lac

WELWYN Map 6 TL21

French, European NOTABLE WINE LIST

Innovative cooking in a lakeside hunting lodge

☎ 01707 368888
Brocket Hall Estate AL8 7XG
e-mail: auberge@brocket-hall.co.uk
web: www.brocket-hall.co.uk
dir: A1(M) junct 4, B653 to Wheathampstead. In Brocket Ln take 2nd gate entry to Brocket Hall

Housed in a former hunting lodge dating back to the time of the accession of George III, the Auberge is one of the more singular restaurant operations in the Home Counties. Sitting at one end of the lake on the Brocket Hall Estate, it enjoys enchanting views, and the tone within aims for the kind of timeless elegance that only the combination of a French approach in an English rural setting can deliver. Phil Thompson arrived in 2005 via several stylish London billets, and has conferred a real sense of thrill to the culinary repertoire. Dishes combine influences in dazzling array, seen in a starter of smoked salmon and spiced crab paupiette with yuzu cream and pickled cockles, or a terrine of foie gras, smoked eel and walnut in a reduction of Banyuls with radish and ginger. At main-course stage, the ante is raised still further, perhaps with slow-roasted Devon Vale beef rump, accompanied by Madeira-braised snails and parsnip, with a reduced sauce of Guinness and blue cheese. The technique is sufficiently assured to bring off these daring productions with convincing flair, and if citations of Roquefort, olive oil and salt prove too unnerving among the dessert options, turn to the trolley of British and French cheeses instead.

Chef Phil Thompson **Owner** CCA International
Times 12-2.30/7-10 Closed 27 Dec-14 Jan, Sun & Mon
Prices Food prices not confirmed for 2011. Please telephone for details **Wines** 750 bottles over £20, 14 by glass **Notes** Vegetarian available, Dress restrictions, No jeans or trainers, Civ Wed 60 **Seats** 70, Pr/dining room 32
Children Portions, Menu **Parking** 50

and former chicken shed. Scrubbed wood floors, exposed oak beams and solid oak furniture set the scene for Mediterranean-tinged modern British dishes made from great local ingredients. You could start with an assiette of scallops comprising scallop parfait, seared scallops with peas and bacon and a scallop velouté. Roasted saddle of venison with shallot jam, sour cherry sauce and butternut squash purée is a well-judged main course.

The Restaurant at Tewin Bury Farm

Chef Jon Green **Owner** Vaughan Williams
Times 12-2.30/6.30-9.30 **Prices** Starter £4.95-£6.95, Main £12.95-£17.50, Dessert £5.50-£7, Service optional **Wines** 18 bottles over £20, 12 bottles under £20, 10 by glass **Notes** Tasting menu available, Sunday L, Vegetarian menu, Civ Wed 150 **Seats** 60, Pr/dining room 30 **Children** Portions, Menu **Parking** 400

WILLIAN Map 12 TL23

The Fox

Modern British

Modern British cooking in a Hertfordshire country pub

☎ 01462 480233
SG6 2AE
e-mail: info@foxatwillian.co.uk
dir: A1(M) junct 9 towards Letchworth, 1st left to Willian, The Fox 0.5m on left

Opposite the village pond, next door to the parish church, the Fox is a heart-warming country pub built in the mid-18th century. An atrium ceiling lets in extra daylight and there are terrace tables for when the summer really gets going. Original artworks by a local practitioner add to the sense of vibrancy, as does the thoughtful contemporary cooking. Local ingredients appear in such dishes as smoked salmon and haddock brandade with mustard sauce and shallots, or slow-cooked pork belly glazed in orange and chilli, served with wasabi mash, crispy noodles and plum compôte. Inventive desserts include a lychee and apricot millefeuille with apple galette.

Chef Harry Kodagoda **Owner** Clifford Nye
Times 12-2/6.45-9.15 Closed D Sun **Prices** Starter £4.90-£9.50, Main £8.95-£18.50, Dessert £5.25-£5.50, Service added but optional 10% **Wines** 36 bottles over £20, 16 bottles under £20, 14 by glass **Notes** Sunday L, Vegetarian available **Seats** 70 **Children** Portions **Parking** 40

KENT

ASHFORD Map 7 TR04

Eastwell Manor

British, French

Creative, classical cooking in a grand manor-house setting

☎ 01233 213000
Eastwell Park, Boughton Lees TN25 4HR
e-mail: enquiries@eastwellmanor.co.uk
dir: From M20 junct 9 take 1st left (Trinity Rd). Through 4 rdbts to lights. Left onto A251 signed Faversham. 0.5m to sign for Boughton Aluph, 200yds to hotel

Country houses don't come much more stately or blue-blooded than Eastwood Manor: it has been rooted into the Kentish landscape since the Normans turned up and sits in 62 acres of immaculate landscaped grounds with fragrant rose gardens. Inside, it is every inch the top-drawer country-house hotel, complete with carved oak panelling, baronial fireplaces, and antiques galore as well as a very 21st-century health and beauty spa. The restaurant lives up to the grandeur of the rest of the house, with high coffered ceilings, a huge fireplace, and leaded mullioned windows looking over the gardens. Given all this, the kitchen's repertoire is surprisingly modern, dealing in inventive, contemporary dishes bristling with luxury ingredients. Starters might see hot-smoked salmon teamed with beetroot and vanilla purée, and horseradish cream, followed by turbot fillet with chicken and sage mousse, garlic pommes purées and chicken jus.

Chef Paul Owen **Owner** Turrloo Parrett
Times 12-2.30/7-10 **Prices** Fixed L 2 course fr £12, Fixed D 3 course fr £25, Service optional **Wines** 231 bottles over £20, 25 bottles under £20, 21 by glass **Notes** Tasting menu available, Gourmet evenings, Sunday L, Vegetarian available, Dress restrictions, Jacket preferred at D, no jeans or sportswear, Civ Wed 250 **Seats** 80, Pr/dining room 80 **Children** Portions, Menu **Parking** 120

The Wife of Bath Restaurant with Rooms

Modern NEW

Intimate, stylish village restaurant with accomplished cooking

☎ 01233 812232
4 Upper Bridge St, Wye TN25 5AF
e-mail: relax@thewifeofbath.com
dir: 4m NE of Ashford. M20 junct 9, A28 for Canterbury, 3m right to Wye

'Wye go anywhere else' is something of a mantra at this modern, stylish village restaurant, and, as it ticks all the right boxes, who can argue. It's a fresh, uncluttered, relaxed place with clothed tables, patterned wallpaper, modern art and a small lounge-bar. The appealing menu's modern British approach fits the surroundings, delivering high-quality local and seasonal produce in well-crafted, innovative dishes of interesting combinations and flavours. Home-made breads heighten expectation, while mains don't miss a beat; perhaps roasted fillet of sea bass with nettle, brown shrimp and clam risotto, or a rack of Romney Marsh lamb partnered with artichoke hearts and a mint and pea salsa, while a honey and pine nut tart (with rosemary ice cream) might head-up desserts.

Chef Robert Hymers **Owner** Rupert & Victoria Reeves
Times 12-2.30/6.30-9.30 Closed 25 Dec, Mon, L Tue, D Sun **Prices** Fixed L 2 course £15, Fixed D 3 course £21-£37, Starter £5-£8.50, Main £10-£22, Dessert £6.50, Service optional **Wines** 50 bottles over £20, 19 bottles under £20, 11 by glass **Notes** Sunday L, Vegetarian available **Seats** 45 **Children** Portions, Menu **Parking** 12

AYLESFORD Map 6 TQ75

Hengist Restaurant

British, French V

Modern cooking in classy, contemporary setting

☎ 01622 719273
7-9 High St ME20 7AX
e-mail: restaurant@hengistrestaurant.co.uk
dir: M20 junct 5 & 6, follow signs to Aylesford

Said to be the oldest village in England, Aylesford is the place where Hengist and his brother Horsa led invaders across the Medway in 449 AD and became the first kings of Kent - now that is history. This sleek and contemporary

continued

AYLESFORD *continued*

restaurant may be housed in a 16th-century timbered building, but the interior is as contemporary as they come with decadent chocolate suede walls, smoked glass screens and sparkling chandeliers set against original oak beams and stonework. Part of a Kentish group, along with Thackeray's and Richard Phillips at Chapel Down (see entries), the kitchen here deals in modern European flavours with plenty of classical technique on show and lots of contemporary ideas. Impeccable ingredients are a feature and the dishes make a visual impact on the plate. Ballottine of foie gras with amaretti crumble, roasted quince purée and toasted brioche shows the style - this is refined, intelligent cooking. Follow on with pan-roasted fillet of Atlantic brill with creamed parsley pommes purée, fricassée of sweet shallots and Canterbury snails.

Chef Richard Phillips, Daniel Hatton **Owner** Richard Phillips, Paul Smith & Kevin James **Times** 12-3/6.30-11 Closed 26 Dec & 1 Jan, Mon, D Sun **Prices** Fixed L 2 course fr £12.95, Fixed D 3 course fr £25.50, Starter £7.25-£10.95, Main £16.95-£19.75, Dessert £7.50, Service added but optional 11% **Wines** 71 bottles over £20, 5 bottles under £20, 16 by glass **Notes** Fixed L Tue-Sun, Fixed D Tue-Thu, Sunday L, Vegetarian menu, Dress restrictions, Smart casual **Seats** 70, Pr/dining room 18 **Children** Portions **Parking** Free car park nearby

BEARSTED **Map 7 TQ85**

Soufflé Restaurant

Modern European

Charming village setting for modish cooking

☎ 01622 737065
31 The Green ME14 4DN
dir: M20 junct 7 follow Maidstone signs, bear left towards Bearsted, straight over at rdbt, towards Bearsted Green at next mini-rdbt. Continue for approx 1.5m to the green. Restaurant on left, turn left just before Soufflé sign & park at rear of restaurant

Right on the village green, this charming, 16th-century timbered cottage oozes period character and charm and is an atmospheric place in which to sample some classic cooking with plenty of contemporary influences along the way. The front terrace is great for summer dining, while the interior is full of exposed brickwork, low beams, timbers and an inglenook fireplace. The seasonal carte might deliver a starter of deep-fried crab spring rolls with wild rocket and mango salsa, followed by main-course Chart Farm venison with braised red cabbage and spicy jus. Round things off with hot pistachio soufflé with vanilla ice cream.

Soufflé Restaurant

Chef Nick Evenden **Owner** Nick & Karen Evenden **Times** 12-2.30/7-10 Closed Mon, L Sat, D Sun **Prices** Fixed L 2 course fr £14, Fixed D 3 course fr £25, Starter £6.50-£8.50, Main £16.50-£22, Dessert £7.50-£8.50, Service optional **Wines** 38 bottles over £20, 25 bottles under £20, 7 by glass **Notes** Sunday L, Vegetarian available **Seats** 40, Pr/dining room 25 **Children** Portions **Parking** 15

The West House

BIDDENDEN **Map 7 TQ83**

Modern European

Self-assured cooking in a delightful setting

☎ 01580 291341
28 High St TN27 8AH
e-mail: thewesthouse@btconnect.com
dir: Junct of A262 & A274. 14m S of Maidstone

The 16th-century Flemish weavers' cottages at the heart of a Kentish Weald village are home to West House, where a distinctly 21st-century approach is taken to cuisine. Inside are massive oak beams presiding over a restrained contemporary décor of unclothed darkwood tables and cream leather seats on wide floorboards, and funky food-oriented art on white walls. Chef-patron Graham Garrett earned his stripes in the kitchens of Richard Corrigan and Nico Ladenis, and cooks in a soundly contemporary vein; his intelligent dishes are big on punchy, razor-sharp flavours and endlessly entertaining textures, while a passion for local supplies ensures seasonality. The menu doesn't waste words, and belies the technical skills that have gone into each idea: cured duck foie gras arrives with caramel pineapple, sweet wine jelly and sesame crunch, ahead of a gloriously gutsy celebration of pork - fried pig's head and roast belly teamed with a twice-cooked duck egg, and anchovy and caper vinaigrette. Line-caught cod is simply steamed and served with mussel and parsley broth. The same level of inventiveness and high-art technique extends to desserts: 'all the fun of the fair' involves toffee apple pannacotta, candy floss and a popcorn shot, or a more conventional finale could be Valrhona chocolate and praline pudding with buttermilk sorbet.

Chef Graham Garrett **Owner** Jackie Hewitt & Graham Garrett **Times** 12-2/7-9.30 Closed 25 Dec-1 Jan, Mon, L Sat, D Sun **Prices** Food prices not confirmed for 2011. Please telephone for details **Wines** 46 bottles over £20, 20 bottles under £20, 6 by glass **Seats** 32 **Children** Portions **Parking** 7

BIDDENDEN Map 7 TQ83

The West House

@@@ – see opposite page

BOUGHTON MONCHELSEA Map 7 TQ75

The Mulberry Tree

@@ Modern British

Serious cooking in Kent countryside setting

☎ 01622 749082 & 741058
Hermitage Ln ME17 4DA
e-mail: info@themulberrytreekent.co.uk
dir: B2163 turn into Wierton road straight over at crossroads, first left East Hall Hill

The well-heeled Kentish village of Boughton Monchelsea is the timeless English setting for this erstwhile pub made over into a posh contemporary country restaurant and bar. A fashionable mishmash of contemporary style and traditional furniture rubs along nicely indoors - expect leather sofas to flop into in the bar, wooden floors, and comforting colours on the walls. Accomplished modern British food with influences from Europe and wider afield, married in inventive flavour combinations, forms the backbone of the ambitious, up-to-date menus. Among starters could be paella of Kentish seafood and cured bacon; further evidence of the kitchen's focus on local materials is shown in a main-course line-caught Broadstairs sea bass, served with roasted artichokes, braised salsify, young leeks and lightly-curried velouté. Meals finish strongly with an upside-down blackcurrant and hibiscus cheesecake.

Chef Alan Irwin **Owner** Karen Williams & Mark Jones **Times** 12-2/6.30-9.30 Closed 26 Dec, 1 Jan, Mon, D Sun **Prices** Fixed L 2 course £12.95, Fixed D 3 course £15.95, Starter £5.25-£7.95, Main £13.50-£20.95, Dessert £5.25-£6.95, Service optional, Groups min 10 service 10% **Wines** 16 bottles over £20, 22 bottles under £20, 18 by glass **Notes** Sunday L, Vegetarian available **Seats** 70, Pr/dining room 12 **Children** Portions **Parking** 60

BRANDS HATCH Map 6 TQ56

Brandshatch Place Hotel & Spa

@@ Modern British

Grand location for modern British food

☎ 01474 875000 & 0845 072 7395
Brands Hatch Rd, Fawkham DA3 8NQ
e-mail: brandshatchplace@handpicked.co.uk
dir: M25 junct 3/A20 West Kingsdown. Left at paddock entrance/Fawkham Green sign. 3rd left signed Fawkham Rd. Hotel 500mtrs on right

This former Georgian manor house turned luxury country-house hotel, close to the famous Brands Hatch racing circuit, has impressive grounds and is a good place for a relaxing break whether or not you've been burning rubber all day. Tennis and squash courts, spa treatments and a swimming pool provide plenty to do, while the Dining Room restaurant is a draw in its own right. It has an understated elegance, with views of the garden and smartly dressed tables bedecked with flickering candles and flowers. Modern British dishes are based on good local ingredients, with the seasons duly respected. Try ravioli of rabbit served with a baby leek consommé, moving onto Kent wild mushroom pudding with truffle mash, purple broccoli, or loin of venison with braised red cabbage, fondant potato and celeriac purée. Finish with treacle pudding and lemon meringue ice cream. The Drawing Room, with its doors opening out onto the terrace, is the place to go for elevenses, afternoon tea and cocktails.

Chef Stephen Redpath **Owner** Hand Picked Hotels **Times** 12-2/7-9.30 **Prices** Fixed L 3 course £33-£42, Fixed D 3 course £33, Service optional **Wines** 103 bottles over £20, 2 bottles under £20, 18 by glass **Notes** Sunday L, Vegetarian available, Civ Wed 110 **Seats** 60, Pr/dining room 110 **Children** Portions, Menu **Parking** 100

CANTERBURY Map 7 TR15

The Dove Inn

@ British, French

Anglo-French cooking in deepest Kent

☎ 01227 751360
Plum Pudding Ln, Dargate ME13 9HB
e-mail: pipmacgrew@hotmail.com
dir: 5m NW of Canterbury. A299 Thanet Way, turn off at Lychgate service station

It's always good to see an old village pub serving great food without feeling the need to go for the full gastro-pub-style makeover. Young chef-patron Phillip MacGregor's place has a nice, proper pub vibe, unbuttoned and simple with stripped wooden floors and scrubbed tables, while his cooking pulls together French and British influences in a well-balanced menu built on well-sourced local produce. Dishes 'do what it says on the tin': scallops with black pudding and parsnip purée delivers full-on flavours to start, followed by roasted saddle of Romney Marsh lamb with Savoy cabbage and pumpkin purée. No-nonsense desserts might feature silky-smooth crème brûlée with a sharp blackcurrant sorbet and home-made shortbread.

Chef Phillip MacGregor **Owner** Phillip MacGregor **Times** 12-2.30/7-9 Closed Mon, D Sun **Prices** Starter £4.95-£9.25, Main £13.95-£21.95, Dessert £4-£8, Service added but optional, Groups min 6 service 10% **Wines** 6 bottles over £20, 15 bottles under £20, 12 by glass **Notes** Sunday L, Vegetarian available **Seats** 26 **Children** Portions **Parking** 15

The Goods Shed

@ British

Hearty country cooking overlooking a railway-shed market

☎ 01227 459153
Station Road West CT2 8AN

Next to Canterbury West station, the converted railway shed houses a daily farmers' market, with an eatery serving the pick of the day's produce on a raised level. Blackboard menus and rough wood tables are the order of the day and, if it's a chilly day, wrap yourself in one of the blankets provided before setting about your food. Good things include ham hock and bacon terrine with caramelised pears, served in gigantic portions, goose with turnips and prunes, turbot with leeks in white sauce, and succulent roast pork loin with mashed potato, greens, and redcurrant sauce. The fashion for inveigling savoury ingredients into chocolate desserts is celebrated here with a chocolate and wild mushroom fondant, accompanied (but of course) by tarragon ice cream.

Times 12-2.30/6-mdnt Closed 25 Dec, Mon, D Sun

The Granville

@ British NEW

Relaxed pub with quality food

☎ 01227 700402
Street End, Lower Hardres CT4 7AL
dir: On B2068 in the village of Lower Hardres, about 3m from Canterbury city centre

On a B road outside of Canterbury in a quiet village, this unassuming place is a Shepherd Neame pub, run with conviction by Gabrielle Harris. The bar is still very much a place to sip pints of real ale with the locals, but food, listed on blackboards, is taken seriously. The main restaurant area is light and airy with whitewashed walls dotted with local art and an open circular central fire. Well-sourced local produce is used in well-executed dishes such as wild mushroom risotto, braised fillet of brill with grain mustard sauce and poached spiced pear with ginger ice cream and chocolate sauce.

Times 12-2/6.45-9 Closed Mon **Prices** Food prices not confirmed for 2011. Please telephone for details

Apicius

CRANBROOK Map 7 TQ73

Modern European

Stellar cooking in a Kentish village - book ahead!

01580 714666
23 Stone St TN17 3HF
dir: In town centre, opposite Barclays Bank, 50yds from church

Tim Johnson's mesmerisingly popular restaurant in a little Kentish village remains an object lesson in how many more such apparently modest enterprises could be run. Small, renovated premises on the high street, brightened up with a liberal sploshing of white paint, a few tables that are booked weeks ahead for weekend dining, prices that are surprisingly reasonable - and stellar cooking, honed under various masters of the art. Johnson's food is deeply rooted in local supply lines, firmly seasonal, and capable of delivering quite a punch. A clear understanding of flavours and textures, allied to a vivid imaginative streak, is the hallmark of most dishes. Ingredients multiply, but remain on speaking terms, rather than accumulating into a pile-up, perhaps in a salad of smoked venison, chestnuts, beetroot, cranberry jelly, melon and pickled mushrooms. Then again, the relative simplicity of a main course of roast John Dory with crushed new potatoes, Niçoise garnish and thyme oil, is just as capable of making a splash. Braised beef chuck, an unfashionable cut, is given its moment in the sun, with fine dauphinoise, turnips, carrots and celeriac for company, and desserts mobilise a bouquet of fruit flavours from lime pannacotta, to caramelised banana with praline ice cream, to apple and Calvados mousse with cinnamon cream.

Chef Timothy Johnson **Owner** Timothy Johnson, Faith Hawkins **Times** 12-2/7-9 Closed 2 wks Xmas/New Year, Etr, 2 wks summer, Mon-Tue, L Sat, D Sun **Prices** Fixed L 2 course fr £22.50, Fixed D 3 course fr £32, Service added but optional 12.5% **Wines** 26 bottles over £20, 5 bottles under £20, 10 by glass **Notes** Sunday L, Vegetarian available, Air con **Seats** 24 **Parking** Public car park at rear

Rowhill Grange - Truffles

Rosettes not confirmed at time of going to press

DARTFORD Map 6 TQ57

Modern European

Classy country setting for creative cooking

01322 615136
Rowhill Grange Hotel & Spa DA2 7QH
e-mail: admin@rowhillgrange.com
dir: M25 junct 3, take B2173 towards Swanley, then B258 towards Hextable. Straight on at 3 rdbts. Hotel 1.5m on left

Victorian Rowhill Grange sits in nine acres of delightful grounds comprising mature woodlands, a lake and a walled garden. The Truffles restaurant has the best spot to enjoy those garden views - a luminous conservatory with an alfresco terrace for fine weather dining. It's a classy setting, done out in understated neutral tones, with modern art to inject subtle colour, while staff strike a correct balance between formality and putting guests at ease. The kitchen, under a new chef, deals in vibrant modern European cooking; start perhaps with confit of Loch Duart salmon with pea mousse and horseradish foam, move on to rack of Kent fallow venison with spring greens, celeriac purée and chocolate oil, finishing with a glazed lemon tart with raspberry and elderflower sorbet.

Chef Luke Davis **Owner** Utopia Leisure
Times 12-2.30/7-9.30 Closed L Mon-Sat, D Mon,Tue
Prices Fixed D 3 course £42-£50, Service added but optional 12.5% **Wines** 38 bottles over £20, 11 bottles under £20, 12 by glass **Notes** Sunday L, Vegetarian available, Dress restrictions, No shorts, T-shirts, trainers, Civ Wed 150 **Seats** 90, Pr/dining room 150 **Children** Menu **Parking** 200

CHARING Map 7 TQ94

The Oak

British, European NEW

Hearty British cooking in a smartly renovated village pub

01233 712612
5 High St TN27 0HU
e-mail: www.theoakcharing.co.uk
dir: M20 junct 8 onto A20. At Charing turn left onto High St, 50yds on left

The historic village of Charing sits in glorious Kent countryside at the foot of the North Downs where the ancient Pilgrim's Way runs through to Canterbury. Until recently, the Oak was a run-down high-street boozer, but after a thorough revamp it is once more a welcoming inn in the modern vein: expect stripped wooden floors, bare tables lit by tea lights, leather sofas by a wood-burning stove, and a cosy bar warmed by a log fire. The intimate restaurant is a fresh place with exposed brick and white-painted walls, and low beams, or there's a lovely garden terrace for alfresco eating on good days. The kitchen takes local sourcing seriously and prides itself on its home-baked breads and meats cured in-house. Kick off with a modern British classic such as pan-fried scallops with chorizo and pea purée, and follow with roast belly of pork with mustard mash, black pudding and apple sauce.

Chef Simon Desmond **Times** 12-2.30/7-9.15 Closed 25 Dec **Prices** Starter £5-£8, Main £10-£16, Dessert £4, Service optional, Groups min 8 service 10% **Wines** 25 bottles over £20, 22 bottles under £20, 6 by glass **Notes** Sunday L, Vegetarian available **Seats** 40, Pr/dining room 50 **Children** Portions, Menu **Parking** 20, On street

CRANBROOK Map 7 TQ73

Apicius

– *see opposite page*

DARTFORD Map 6 TQ57

Rowhill Grange - Truffles

See opposite page

DEAL Map 7 TR35

Dunkerleys Hotel & Restaurant

Modern British

Fresh seafood on the seafront

01304 375016
19 Beach St CT14 7AH
e-mail: ddunkerley@btconnect.com
web: www.dunkerleys.co.uk
dir: Turn off A2 onto A258 to Deal - situated 100yds before Deal Pier

At Dunkerley's, a well-established family-run hotel just across the road from the sea, locally-caught fish is quite rightly king of the kitchen's repertoire. It is an unpretentious homely place, where a bar kitted out with old leather armchairs makes a convivial spot for aperitifs before proceeding to dinner in the bistro-style restaurant. Fuss-free dishes bring the area's freshest materials together in well-balanced combinations, as in a starter of mackerel from Deal's pier, pan-fried and served with gin-soaked apple brunoise. Next up, main-course sea bass is teamed with butter-roasted asparagus, creamed potatoes and saffron velouté, while local meat might be represented by rump of Kentish lamb with truffle-scented forest mushrooms and fondant potatoes. At dessert stage, spiced poached pear with pannacotta and Calvados syrup gets the thumbs-up.

Chef Ian Dunkerley **Owner** Ian Dunkerley & Linda Dunkerley **Times** 12-2.30/7-9.30 Closed Mon, D Sun **Prices** Fixed L 2 course £11.95-£31.50, Fixed D 3 course £27.50-£37.50, Service optional **Wines** 29 bottles over £20, 47 bottles under £20, 11 by glass **Notes** Sunday L, Vegetarian available, Dress restrictions, Smart casual preferred **Seats** 50 **Children** Portions **Parking** Public car park adjacent

DOVER Map 7 TR34

The Bay Restaurant at The White Cliffs Hotel

Modern British

Rustic, seasonal cooking in stylish hotel

01304 852229 & 852400
High St, St Margaret's-at-Cliffe CT15 6AT
e-mail: mail@thewhitecliffs.com
dir: From M2/M20 follow signs for Deal onto A258. 1st right for St Margaret's-at-Cliffe & after 2m take right at T-junct. Hotel in centre of village opposite church

Close to those famous white cliffs, this traditional weather-boarded old inn dates back to Elizabethan times. It has been spruced up inside and cuts a contemporary dash with its mix of original features and well chosen fixtures and fittings. The menu is equally unpretentious and makes much of the local larder, espousing environmental and sustainable values, including growing their own veg on an allotment. On the menu, Sussex Cross goats' cheese might turn up in a fritter with fig jampote, and Kentish pheasant with choucroute, smoked sausage, pancetta and roast potatoes. The modern British sensibility continues at desserts, with perhaps a rose blancmange with hot berry compôte.

Chef Gavin Oakley **Owner** Gavin Oakley **Times** 12-2/7-9 **Prices** Fixed L 2 course £10-£15, Fixed D 3 course £25-£35, Starter £4.50-£8, Main £14-£19.50, Dessert £4.50-£7.50, Service optional, Groups min 6 service 10% **Wines** 14 bottles over £20, 16 bottles under £20, 6 by glass **Notes** Sunday L, Vegetarian available **Seats** 50 **Children** Portions, Menu **Parking** 20

The Marquis at Alkham

Modern British

Boutique chic and creative cooking in attractive Kent village

01304 873410
Alkham Valley Rd, Alkham CT15 7DF
e-mail: info@themarquisatalkham.co.uk
dir: M20 continue to A2. Take A260 exit & turn on to the Alkham Valley Rd

This particular Marquis cuts a contemporary dash amid the beautiful Kent Downs. The graceful old building's makeover into a restaurant with rooms has created a chic destination, just a short stroll from the village green, where sumptuous accommodation and a strikingly fashionable bar are part of the lure. The restaurant and Charles Lakin's cooking could be considered the main attraction, with his menus brimming with fine Kentish produce, less commonly seen cuts of meat, and packed with flavour. Crisp pig's trotter, for example, is dished up with ham hock, cauliflower piccalilli and a fried quail's egg in a well-judged first course. Follow that with saddle of Godmersham rabbit stuffed with black pudding and finished with a vintage cider and lovage sauce, and end with British cheeses or banana soufflé with toffee sauce and tonka bean ice cream.

Chef Charles Lakin **Owner** Tony Marsden & Hugh Oxborrow **Times** 12-2.30/6.30-9.30 Closed L Mon, D Sun **Prices** Fixed L 2 course fr £15.50, Fixed D 3 course fr £24.95, Tasting menu fr £50, Starter £8.50-£12.50, Main £22-£27, Dessert £7.50-£10.50, Service optional **Wines** 70 bottles over £20, 35 bottles under £20, 18 by glass **Notes** Tasting menu with wine £57.50, Sunday L, Vegetarian available, Civ Wed 45 **Seats** 70, Pr/dining room 20 **Children** Portions **Parking** 17

DOVER ***continued***

Wallett's Court

Modern, Traditional British

Creative cooking in historic manor

01304 852424
Wallett's Court CHH, St Margarets-at-Cliffe CT15 6EW
e-mail: dine@wallettscourt.com
dir: M2/A2 or M20/A20, follow signs for Deal (A258), 1st right for St Margaret's-at-Cliffe. Restaurant 1m on right

This family-run country-house hotel sits in lovely gardens just inland from the white cliffs of Dover. The 17th-century Jacobean manor house is part of an estate that was recorded in the Domesday Book, and while there's a romantically historic ambience in the restaurant's oak beams, inglenook fireplaces and candlelit tables, there's nothing dated about what's going on in the kitchen. While the modern British menu has a judicious sprinkling of creative touches, there's nothing so radical as to intrude on an intimate dinner à deux. A well-balanced opener brings together parsnip risotto with parmesan crisp, vanilla and mascarpone, while main-course guinea fowl takes a more classic tack, teaming roast breast with ballottine of leg, baby carrots, crushed new potatoes, sage oil and lemon jus.

Chef Ryan Tasker **Owner** Gavin Oakley **Times** 12-2/7-9 Closed 25-26 Dec **Prices** Fixed L 2 course fr £19.50, Fixed D 3 course £40-£50, Service optional **Wines** 60 bottles over £20, 20 bottles under £20, 17 by glass **Notes** Sunday L, Vegetarian available, Civ Wed 50 **Seats** 60, Pr/dining room 40 **Children** Portions, Menu **Parking** 50

EDENBRIDGE **Map 6 TQ44**

Haxted Mill & Riverside Brasserie

Modern British

Unfussy cooking using local produce in rustic, riverside setting

01732 862914
Haxted Rd TN8 6PU
e-mail: david@haxtedmill.co.uk
dir: M25 junct 6, A22 towards East Grinstead. Through Blindley Heath, after Texaco garage left at lights, in 1m 1st left after Red Barn PH. 2m to Haxted Mill

First impressions last, and the idyllic scene of a working watermill is what will stick in your mind long after visiting this cosy restaurant in 500-year-old converted stables next to the mill. Take an aperitif in the dinky downstairs bar, or there's a sun-kissed terrace overlooking the millpond with the millstream racing by. Upstairs, a homely beamed dining room decorated with framed photographs is the setting for unfussy, modern brasserie-style cooking that clearly has its roots in classic French cuisine. Produce from local farmland and the garden of Kent is deployed in simple combinations - pan-fried foie gras with black pudding and sautéed apple is a great way to open, followed by pan-roasted skate wing with black butter and capers.

Chef David Peek **Owner** David & Linda Peek **Times** 12-2/7-9 Closed 23 Dec-6 Jan, Mon, D Sun **Prices** Fixed L 2 course fr £16.95, Fixed D 3 course fr £21.95, Service added but optional 10% **Wines** 30 bottles over £20, 7 bottles under £20, 16 by glass **Notes** Sunday L, Vegetarian available, Dress restrictions, Smart casual **Seats** 52 **Parking** 100

FAVERSHAM **Map 7 TR06**

Read's Restaurant

– *see below*

Read's Restaurant

FAVERSHAM **Map 7 TR06**

Modern British NOTABLE WINE LIST

Classy cooking in an elegant Georgian manor

01795 535344
Macknade Manor, Canterbury Rd ME13 8XE
e-mail: enquiries@reads.com
dir: From M2 junct 6 follow A251 towards Faversham. At T-junct with A2 (Canterbury road) turn right. Hotel 0.5m on right

The five acres of mature gardens that surrounds this elegant Georgian house includes a kitchen garden that provides its bounty for chef-patron David Pitchford. What David and wife Rona can't grow in the grounds is sourced with due diligence from a network of local suppliers. Read's is that kind of place: dedicated, hands-on and in tune with its setting and the rhythms of the seasons. It's a splendidly good-looking manor, not too overbearing, and perfectly proportioned to become the restaurant-with-rooms it is today. It's traditionally done out on the inside - refined, calm and unencumbered by fleeting contemporary tastes. David oversees the kitchen team with confidence, delivering refined modern British dishes, and a sense of fun is revealed in the food-related quotations that adorn the menu. Start with a terrine of ham hock and chicken served with home-made piccalilli and toasted country bread, or organic smoked salmon served up in four different ways. Main-course might bring forth roast breast of local Gressingham duckling with an onion 'tarte Tatin', marmalade purée and almond potatoes. To finish, perhaps a hot golden pineapple soufflé with home-made ice cream, or a selection of British cheeses served traditionally with grapes, biscuits and bread.

Chef David Pitchford, Simon McNamara **Owner** David & Rona Pitchford **Times** 12-2.30/7-10 Closed BHs, Sun-Mon **Prices** Fixed L 3 course £24, Fixed D 3 course £55, Main £55, Service optional **Wines** 250 bottles over £20, 12 bottles under £20, 18 by glass **Notes** Fixed price ALC menu, Tasting menu 7 course, Vegetarian available, Dress restrictions, Smart casual, Civ Wed 60 **Seats** 40, Pr/dining room 30 **Children** Portions **Parking** 30

LENHAM Map 7 TQ85

Chilston Park Hotel

Modern British

Splendid Georgian mansion with elegant restaurant

01622 859803
Sandway ME17 2BE
e-mail: chilstonpark@handpicked.co.uk
dir: M20 junct 8

Chilston Park has been home to a steady procession of nobility and prominent Kentish families through the centuries. Nowadays, the Georgian mansion does business as an upscale country-house hotel tucked away down leafy lanes in the Garden of England. Secluded in 22 acres of sublime landscaped gardens and parkland, its interior brims with enough period authenticity, antiques and oil paintings that you might be inspired to dress as Mr Darcy or Elizabeth for dinner in the unique, sunken Venetian-style Culpeper's restaurant. Intricate plasterwork ceilings, a grand fireplace and fancy crystal chandeliers certainly build a sense of occasion for the French-influenced modern British cuisine. The kitchen has the confidence to come up with some inventive combinations - perhaps beer-battered Whitstable oysters with sautéed scallops, apple purée and Cullen skink, followed by an assiette of Sussex lamb, served as grilled cutlet, braised shoulder and mini shepherd's pie. There's a fine choice by the glass on the noteworthy wine list.

Chef Gareth Brown **Owner** Hand Picked Hotels **Times** 12-2/7-9.30 Closed L Sat **Prices** Fixed L 2 course £11.95, Fixed D 3 course £28.95, Starter £8.75-£9.50, Main £27.50-£35, Dessert £8.50-£9.25, Service added but optional **Wines** 90 bottles over £20, 1 bottle under £20, 18 by glass **Notes** Sunday L, Vegetarian available, Dress restrictions, Smart casual, Civ Wed 90 **Seats** 54, Pr/dining room 8 **Children** Portions, Menu **Parking** 100

MAIDSTONE Map 7 TQ75

Fish on the Green

Seafood **NEW**

Top-class fish and seafood on an English village green

01622 738300 & 01233 820982
Church Ln, Bearsted Green ME14 4EJ
dir: N of A20 on village green

The title says it all: the pretty village green setting is English to the core, while the restaurant occupying a converted stable block near the original coaching house, the Oak on the Green, deals in the finest piscine produce. In the couple of years it has been in operation, the Fish on the Green has netted a strong local fan base - and what's not to like about its fresh, unpretentious interior of whitewashed brick hung with light-hearted paintings on a fishy theme, the smartly-turned-out and clued-up staff, and, of course, the excellent fish and seafood on the menu. Super-fresh materials are partnered with flavours that don't fight on the plate. A blackened fillet of line-caught Scottish mackerel with beetroot, celeriac and horseradish cream brings together vibrant flavours, ahead of seared halibut with béarnaise sauce, wilted spinach and sautéed potatoes.

Chef Peter Baldwin, Sophie Elcomb **Owner** Alexander Bensley **Times** 12-2.30/6.30-10 Closed Xmas, Mon, D Sun (some) **Prices** Fixed L 2 course £14, Starter £6.25-£9.95, Main £14.95-£25.45, Dessert £5.65, Service optional **Notes** Sunday L, Vegetarian available, Air con **Seats** 50 **Children** Portions **Parking** 50

RAMSGATE Map 7 TR36

Harvey's Fish Market & Oyster Bar

British, Seafood **NEW**

Serious about seafood on Ramsgate's harbour front

01843 599707
50 Harbour Pde CT11 8LJ
e-mail: reservations@harveysoframsgate.com

The premises was a fish market in a previous life and today, after an impressive makeover in 2009, it is still dealing in the fruits of the sea, albeit now as a restaurant. Right on the harbour with views over the boats, Harvey's is set over two floors, with exposed beams and wooden tables giving it an authentic rustic feel, alongside comfortable cream leather chairs and well-informed, professional service. Fish and shellfish come straight from local boats, ensuring freshness and a local flavour, and the kitchen team turns this excellent produce into some delightfully creative, yet essentially straightforward dishes. Perfectly cooked scallops are given a textural contrast with an almond topping, finished with a basil and butter sauce, while main-course sea bass comes with local samphire. Kent cherries, cooked until deliciously soft, partner perfectly vanilla pannacotta.

Times 11.45-3/6-10

ROCHESTER Map 6 TQ76

Topes Restaurant

Modern British

An atmospheric gem in historic Rochester

01634 845270
60 High St ME1 1JY
e-mail: julie.small@btconnect.com
dir: M2 junct 1, through Strood High St over Medway Bridge, turn right at Northgate onto High St

Admirers of Dickens will be keen to know that this small but charming house, built in the 15th century, is mentioned in his last novel, *The Mystery of Edwin Drood*. Rooms within have been sensitively updated with much of the character still intact in wooden beams and a narrow staircase to the second dining room. Contemporary high-backed chairs and starched white linen tablecloths provide a pleasing contrast. Owner Julie Small heads up the service with husband Chris in the kitchen. On the varied British menu the emphasis is firmly on local Kentish produce and suppliers are listed; start with smoked haddock and brown shrimp fishball with wilted spinach and cumin-scented cauliflower soup, followed by venison pie with confit mushrooms, butternut squash purée, Brussels sprouts and bacon. To end on a sweet note try walnut, hazelnut and pine nut syrup tart.

Chef Chris Small **Owner** Chris and Julie Small **Times** 12-2.30/6.30-9 Closed Mon-Tue, D Sun **Prices** Fixed L 2 course £16.50, Fixed D 3 course £20.50, Starter £6.50, Main £15.50, Dessert £6, Service optional **Wines** 15 bottles over £20, 25 bottles under £20, 6 by glass **Notes** Bi-annual tasting menu 8 course, Sunday L, Vegetarian available **Seats** 55, Pr/dining room 16 **Children** Portions, Menu **Parking** Public car park

SANDWICH Map 7 TR35

The Bell

Modern British **NEW**

Skilful cooking in a Kentish riverside hotel

01304 626992
The Quay CT13 9EF
e-mail: reservations@olddiningroom.co.uk
dir: Located in the centre of Sandwich next to the Quay

There's no missing the big sign on the side of this building on the bank of the River Stour. Largely Victorian, the hotel has been stylishly renovated, with gentle beige and pastels prevailing throughout, and a dining room that is restfully easy on the eye. An arched mirror is the focal point of the room, and the smart table settings give notice of the seriousness of intent. Fresh fish from Rye and Whitstable, Romney Marsh lamb and salads from local farms are the backbone of a menu that renders classic combinations with great skill and vivacity. Scallops from Rye Bay are gently seared and served with caramelised chicory and a chorizo dressing to give a neat counterbalance of sweet and salty notes. That lamb might appear as the pinkly roasted rump, alongside confit shallots and parsnip mash in a well-worked main dish.

Chef Steve Paddock **Owner** Matthew Collins, Matthew Wolfman **Times** 12-2.30/7-9.30 **Prices** Fixed L 2 course £11.95-£14.95, Starter £4.95-£8.95, Main £10.95-£22, Dessert £5.95-£6.95, Service added but optional 10% **Wines** 28 bottles over £20, 12 bottles under £20, 7 by glass **Notes** Sunday L, Vegetarian available, Civ Wed 70 **Seats** 70, Pr/dining room 120 **Children** Portions **Parking** 7, Pay & display

SEVENOAKS Map 6 TQ55

Gavin Gregg Restaurant

Modern British, European

Popular high street restaurant with hands-on owners

01732 456373
28-30 High St TN13 1HX
dir: 1m from Sevenoaks train station. 500yds from top of town centre towards Tonbridge on left

Gavin and Lucinda Gregg celebrated a decade in business serving the foodies of Sevenoaks in 2010. Ancient head-skimming beams are juxtaposed with the contemporary look of high-backed leather chairs and white-clothed tables within a bay-fronted 400-year-old building. Two different dining experiences are to be had, both singing in tune with the 21st century. On the ground floor, a brasserie serves modern crowd-pleasers, with a set lunch menu offering phenomenal value; upstairs the fine-dining Oak Room opens for dinner only, with imaginative dishes that keep in touch with today's trends. You might start with citrus-cured Loch Duart salmon with prawn toast and chilli dressing, and follow with roast rump of Kentish lamb with celeriac and potato gratin, Savoy cabbage and red wine jus. End with a chocolate délice and Snickers ice cream.

Chef Gavin Gregg **Owner** Gavin & Lucinda Gregg **Times** 12-2/6.30-9.30 Closed Mon, D Sun **Prices** Fixed L 2 course £12-£14.50, Fixed D 3 course £20-£25, Starter £5-£7, Main £12.50-£21, Dessert £6-£7, Service added 10% **Wines** 34 bottles over £20, 16 bottles under £20, 9 by glass **Notes** Sunday L, Vegetarian available **Seats** 80, Pr/dining room 32 **Children** Portions **Parking** Town centre

SISSINGHURST Map 7 TQ73

Rankins

Modern British

Appealing bistro-style cooking in rustic surroundings

01580 713964
The Street TN17 2JH
e-mail: rankins@btconnect.com
dir: Village centre, on A262

A charming, white clapboard cottage on the high street, just a mile from the world-famous Sissinghurst Castle Gardens, is the setting for uncomplicated, soundly-cooked British bistro-style food. Run by a husband-and-wife-team for over 20 years, it has a classic cottagey interior that is subtly-lit, cosy, but with well-spaced tables. They know where to source the Garden of England's finest produce, snapping up fish from Rye and lamb from Romney Marsh, to form a concise menu of unpretentious, eclectic dishes. Take a spicy stew of salmon, cockles and smoked mussels to start, followed by lamb steaks with tomato, haricot bean and rosemary cassoulet, and coffee fudge pudding with espresso ice cream for pudding.

Chef Hugh Rankin **Owner** Hugh & Leonora Rankin **Times** 12.30-2/7.30-9 Closed BHs, Mon, Tue, L Wed-Sat, D Sun **Prices** Fixed L 2 course fr £24.50, Fixed D 3 course fr £33.50, Service optional, Groups min 20 service 10% **Wines** 11 bottles over £20, 9 bottles under £20, 2 by glass **Notes** Sunday L, Vegetarian available, Dress restrictions, Smart casual **Seats** 25 **Children** Portions **Parking** On street

SITTINGBOURNE Map 7 TQ96

Lakes Restaurant

British, European

Refined cooking in a smart conservatory restaurant

01795 428020
Hempstead House Country Hotel, London Rd, Bapchild ME9 9PP
e-mail: lakes@hempsteadhouse.co.uk
dir: On A2 1.5m E of Sittingbourne

The restaurant at Hempstead House gets its name from the Lake family whose forbears built the original Victorian country house in 1850. In the last years of the 20th century, the current owners added a sizeable extension, including the conservatory-style restaurant, a plush, candlelit space that stays true to the character of the old house, with heavy swagged drapes, plasterwork mouldings and a grand centrepiece crystal chandelier. The family-run ambience makes it a welcoming place, while the kitchen treads a line between classic English and French dishes. Starters might include a duck and pigeon salad with cherry and fennel chutney, ahead of mains such as roasted monkfish wrapped in Parma ham teamed with ratatouille and saffron potatoes, or roasted rack of lamb in a rosemary crust with sweet potato rösti, creamed cannellini beans and a port reduction.

Chef John Cosgrove, Aaron Goldfinch **Owner** Mr & Mrs A J Holdstock **Times** 12-2.30/7-10 Closed D Sun (non residents) **Prices** Fixed L 2 course £10-£12.50, Fixed D 3 course £24.50, Starter £5.50-£8.50, Main £14.50-£21.50, Dessert £6.50, Service optional **Wines** 30 bottles over £20, 25 bottles under £20, 4 by glass **Notes** Sunday L, Vegetarian available, Dress restrictions, Smart casual, Civ Wed 150 **Seats** 70, Pr/dining room 30 **Children** Portions, Menu **Parking** 100

TENTERDEN

Richard Phillips at Chapel Down

Modern British NEW V

Modern British cooking amongst the vines

01580 761616
Tenterden Vineyard, Small Hythe TN30 7NG
e-mail: reservations@chapeldownrestaurant.co.uk
dir: A28 towards Rolvenden, left B2082 Smallhythe Rd near the William Caxton Pub. Entrance to vineyard on right in 1m

Richard Phillips' restaurant is on the first-floor of a fabulous wooden building that houses the wine shop at the renowned Chapel Down vineyard. It's a lovely open, bright and contemporary space, with classily set wooden tables and some pretty cool fixtures and fittings, not least the silver bonbon tree that keeps the petits fours tantalisingly on display until they're let loose at the end of the meal. Kentish produce jumps off the menu, the suppliers duly heralded, and wine is not surprisingly a big deal here, although the list is not so partisan as to ignore the rest of the world. The modern British cooking is well-judged, not unambitious but neither overcomplicated. Crab and fennel risotto has just the right consistency and excellent flavour, served with diver-caught scallops. For main-course there might be baked fillet of brill with a wild mushroom and herb crust and a Chapel Down Brut and chive sabayon. Sharp technical skills are on display in a dessert of Willie's Venezuelan Black chocolate tart with local pear compôte and vanilla ice cream.

Chef Richard Phillips, Jose Azevedo **Owner** Kentish Dining Rooms **Times** 12-3/6.30-10.30 Closed Mon, D Tue-Wed, Sun **Prices** Fixed L 2 course fr £12.95, Tasting menu £38-£65, Starter £5.95-£9.95, Main £13.95-£19.75, Service optional, Groups min 9 service 10% **Wines** 34 bottles over £20, 3 bottles under £20, 22 by glass **Notes** Fixed D 3 course Jazz night Thu £25.50, Sunday L, Vegetarian menu, Civ Wed 180 **Seats** 58, Pr/dining room 24 **Parking** 100

TUNBRIDGE WELLS (ROYAL) Map 6 TQ53

Hotel du Vin Tunbridge Wells

British, French NOTABLE WINE LIST

Delightful bistro in elegant townhouse

01892 526455
Crescent Rd TN1 2LY
e-mail: reception.tunbridgewells@hotelduvin.com
dir: Follow town centre to main junct of Mount Pleasant Road & Crescent Road/Church Road. Hotel 150yds on right just past Phillips House

A summer house once used by Queen Victoria is the Kentish outpost of this chain of design-led hotels. Fans of the brand will be au fait with the company's hallmarks: chic 21st-century boutique rooms with classic bistro dining. The bistro of this 18th-century sandstone mansion is a truly regal panelled dining room with gleaming wooden floors and bare antique tables. The kitchen deals in contemporary Anglo-French dishes built on well-sourced local produce, kicking off with warm smoked eel, black pudding, pear purée and chive oil, then moving on to roast and confit leg of guinea fowl with Savoy cabbage and bacon. Wine is taken seriously at all HdVs, so expect a fine and eclectic choice.

Chef Jens Folkel **Owner** Hotel du Vin Ltd
Times 12-2/7-10.30 **Prices** Starter £4.50-£12, Main £10.50-£25, Dessert £5.50-£8.95, Service added but optional 10% **Wines** 700 bottles over £20, 50 bottles under £20, 16 by glass **Notes** Pre-theatre meal offer on selected nights, Sunday L, Vegetarian available, Civ Wed 84 **Seats** 80, Pr/dining room 84 **Children** Portions, Menu **Parking** 30, NCP

Montrose Restaurant

Modern European **NEW V**

Confident modern cooking and passion for wine

☎ 01892 513161
15a Church Rd, Southborough Common TN4 0RX
e-mail: bookings@montroserestaurant.co.uk
dir: M25 junct 5 to A21. Exit A21 Tunbridge Wells/ Tonbridge, to Southborough. Restaurant located on the right after the cricket green

Wine anoraks might spot the reference to Château Montrose - one of the top vineyards of St Estèphe - in the name of this stylishly-refurbished restaurant. Indeed, wine is a large element in the raison d'être here, as the owners keep an exceptional and dynamic cellar. The interior makes a bold design statement, blending Victorian character with peach and apricot pyjama-striped walls, modishly patterned fabrics and black tablecloths. The kitchen cooks in a broadly modern European vein, taking the eminently sound route of sourcing well and keeping dishes simple. A well-balanced starter brings together a terrine of baby leeks with hollandaise sauce, poached egg and aubergine caviar, while a main-course serves roast fillet of herb-crusted cod with garden pea and parmesan risotto. Well-matched flavours arrive in a trio of crème brûlées - cappuccino, vanilla and orange.

Chef Richard Hards **Owner** Richard Hards
Times 12-2.30/6.30-Late Closed D Sun **Prices** Fixed L 2 course £15.95, Fixed D 3 course £35, Starter £6-£8.25, Main £15.25-£20, Dessert £7.95, Service optional, Groups min 8 service 10% **Wines** 60 bottles over £20, 3 bottles under £20, 24 by glass **Notes** L 1 course £9.95, Sunday L, Vegetarian menu, Dress restrictions, Smart casual **Seats** 40, Pr/dining room 18 **Parking** On street

One Restaurant

Modern British

Contemporary cuisine in a sleek boutique hotel

☎ 01892 520587
Brew House Hotel, 1 Warwick Park TN2 5TA
e-mail: reception@brewhousehotel.com
web: www.thebrewhousehotel.net
dir: A267, 1st left onto Warwick Park, hotel immediately on left

Every detail in the über-chic 21st-century interior of this elegant Georgian building near the Pantiles is sure to please those with an eye for style. A cool pair of sunglasses might come in handy - and certainly won't look out of place - as you take in the space-age white and fuchsia-pink décor, complete with wave-patterned walls and curvy fluorescent chandeliers. Expect a well-thought-through menu of modern British dishes that keeps the food miles minimal by sourcing local and seasonal produce. A tian of crab and lobster comes with crème fraîche, caper berries and smoked caviar, while a main course of wild halibut is well-served by flageolet beans with chorizo, clams and fresh herbs in tomato sauce.

Chef Andrew Giles **Owner** Kevin Spencer **Times** 12-10.30 **Prices** Food prices not confirmed for 2011. Please telephone for details **Wines** 28 bottles over £20, 8 bottles under £20, 18 by glass **Notes** Sunday L, Vegetarian available **Seats** 60, Pr/dining room 120 **Children** Portions, Menu **Parking** On street

The Spa Hotel

Modern, Traditional British

Country-house dining beneath crystal chandeliers

☎ 01892 520331
Mount Ephraim TN4 8XJ
e-mail: info@spahotel.co.uk
dir: On A264 leaving Tunbridge Wells towards East Grinstead

Built in 1766 as a country mansion, this imposing building became a hotel in 1880 and stands in beautifully tended parkland and gardens. Recent refurbishment has seen the addition of the new Orangery to complement the traditional lounge. The large Regency-style Chandelier Restaurant lives up to its name, with grand fixtures hanging from ornate high ceilings, plus upholstered chairs and crisp white napery. Service is formal and attentive but never stuffy. Food is classically based, with an emphasis on quality locally-sourced ingredients and simple, clean presentation. Expect roasted scallops with pea purée, black pudding and orange hollandaise, perfectly-cooked wild sea bass with olive and goats' cheese gnocchi, and a trio of chocolate (tart, mousse and sponge) with white chocolate ice cream for pudding.

Times 12.30-2/7-9.30 Closed L Sat

Thackeray's

– see page 198

WEST MALLING **Map 6 TQ65**

The Swan

British, European

Mix of modern and traditional cooking in a contemporary Kentish inn

☎ 01732 521910
35 Swan St ME19 6JU
e-mail: info@theswanwestmalling.co.uk
dir: M20 junct 4 follow signs for West Malling

The Swan may look like a 500-year-old coaching inn, but a radical makeover has transformed the interior into a 21st-century brasserie with a brace of stylish bars. Granite, stainless steel and wood all have their place alongside original oak beams, with an added touch of colour and glamour from contemporary artworks and mirrors. Friendly staff create an easygoing vibe, and the kitchen champions the freshest of local produce on a menu that takes in British and modern European classics. To start, Brixham crab comes with harissa and apple jelly, or oxtail ravioli might be partnered with onions and port. Follow that with belly and cheek of Sussex pork with black pudding and artichoke, and wrap things up with rhubarb mousse and mascarpone sorbet.

Chef S Goss **Owner** Fishbone Ltd **Times** 12-2.45/6-10.45 Closed 26 Dec, 1 Jan, L 27 Dec, 2 Jan **Prices** Food prices not confirmed for 2011. Please telephone for details **Wines** 57 bottles over £20, 10 bottles under £20, 12 by glass **Notes** Sunday L, Vegetarian available, Dress restrictions, Smart casual, Civ Wed 100 **Seats** 90, Pr/dining room 20 **Children** Portions, Menu **Parking** Long-stay car park

WHITSTABLE Map 7 TR16

Crab & Winkle Seafood Restaurant

British Seafood

Local seafood right on the harbour

01227 779377
South Quay, The Harbour CT5 1AB
e-mail: info@seafood-restaurant-uk.com
web: www.seafood-restaurant-uk.com
dir: M2, exit at Whitstable, through town to harbour

The name alludes to the 'Crab and Winkle Line' that from 1830 brought happy tourists down from Canterbury; if you want to follow the old line today it has to be either on foot or bicycle. The nickname stemmed from the seafood delights the town is famous for and today's visitors are no less lucky. Situated above the fish market (and under the same ownership) is the Seafood Restaurant, right on the harbour with views over fishing boats and the open water beyond; grab a seat on the terrace for the best view. The wooden building is light and bright inside with the work of local artists providing even more local flavour. Start with crab bisque or push the boat out with the Whitstable Fish Market platter, before pan-fried cod with lentils, smoked bacon and chorizo or beer-battered fish of the day with chips.

Chef Beverley Ash, Brendon Ellis **Owner** Peter Bennett **Times** 11.30-9.30 Closed 25 Dec, Mon (Nov-Apr), D Sun (Nov-Apr), 26 Dec, 1 Jan **Prices** Starter £5.50-£9.95, Main £9.50-£29.50, Dessert £4.95-£5.50, Service optional **Wines** 12 bottles over £20, 25 bottles under £20, 10 by glass **Notes** Vegetarian available **Seats** 72 **Children** Portions **Parking** Gorrel Tank Car Park

The Sportsman

Modern British

Impeccable local sourcing on the Kent coast

01227 273370
Faversham Rd, Seasalter CT5 4BP
e-mail: contact@thesportsmanseasalter.co.uk
dir: On coast road between Whitstable & Faversham, 3.5m W of Whitstable

There's a pleasing sense of remoteness to this white-fronted former pub on the seafront down a rural road out of Whitstable. Before it is the windswept beach, behind it salt-marsh farmland, from which come fine Kentish lamb, Aberdeen Angus beef and a protean mix of fruit and vegetables. Salt-gleaning and butter-churning are but two of the tireless activities that the Sportsman's kitchen goes in for, and the food, offered via a tasting-menu tour of the repertoire or a daily-changing list of chalkboard specials, aims for a level of metropolitan polish. Blackened mackerel with lettuce cream, properly crackled pork belly with apple sauce, buttered greens and creamy, well-seasoned mash, and full-flavoured roast local chicken with bread sauce, chestnuts and bacon, are dishes to impress. Chocolate mousse served warm alongside salted caramel and milk chocolate ice cream enhances the sensual pleasure we look for in chocolate creations. Excellent home-made breads up the ante still further.

Chef Stephen Harris, Dan Flavell **Owner** Stephen & Philip Harris **Times** 12-2/7-9 Closed 25-26 Dec, 1 Jan, Mon, D Sun **Prices** Starter £4.95-£9.95, Main £14.95-£21.95, Dessert £6.95, Service optional, Groups min 6 service 10% **Wines** 21 bottles over £20, 30 bottles under £20, 8 by glass **Notes** Pre-order tasting menu available Mon-Fri, 48 hrs notice req, Sunday L, Vegetarian available **Seats** 50 **Children** Portions **Parking** 20

Thackeray's

TUNBRIDGE WELLS (ROYAL) Map 6 TQ53

Modern French V

Confident Anglo-European cooking at William Thackeray's place

01892 511921
85 London Rd TN1 1EA
e-mail: reservations@thackeraysrestaurant.co.uk
dir: A21/A26, towards Tunbridge Wells. On left 500yds after the Kent & Sussex Hospital

As the plaque on this listed Georgian house records, Victorian novelist William Makepeace Thackeray once lived here. Without any detriment to its architectural pedigree, the updated interior is a model of elegant modernity: ancient dark oak floors blend with subtle, boutique-style hues of honey and cream in two elegant, surprisingly spacious dining rooms, while a calming Japanese terrace works its magic for alfresco meals. Chef-proprietor Richard Phillips started out with the Roux brothers at Le Gavroche, a grounding in French classicism that still informs his intelligent modern cooking. The coast and hills of Kent and Sussex can be relied on to provide top-class materials for highly-polished results, as in pan-fried Rye Bay scallops with Jerusalem artichoke purée, crispy chicken wing, hazelnut emulsion and jus. Aficionados of local meat will be cheered by the presence of new-season Kentish lamb, its saddle and herb-crusted breast served with stuffed baby artichoke, Niçoise garnish and basil pesto. Fish from the south coast might turn up as a baked tranche of turbot Viennoise in a wild mushroom crust, together with a fricassée of mussels and red peppers, and basil and saffron velouté. Desserts are no less inventive - try a pavé of Valrhona chocolate with milk chocolate mousse, clementine compôte and white chocolate ice cream.

Chef Richard Phillips, Christopher Bower **Owner** Richard Phillips **Times** 12-2.30/6.30-10.30 Closed Mon, D Sun **Prices** Fixed L 2 course £16.50, Tasting menu fr £65, Starter £7.50-£13.50, Main £19.95-£28.50, Dessert £9.95, Service added but optional 12.5% **Wines** 160 bottles over £20, 8 bottles under £20, 21 by glass **Notes** Tasting menu 6 course, Sunday L, Vegetarian menu **Seats** 54, Pr/dining room 16 **Children** Portions **Parking** NCP, on street in evening

LANCASHIRE

ACCRINGTON Map 18 SD72

Mercure Dunkenhalgh Hotel & Spa

British V

Traditional hotel dining in splendid surroundings

01254 303400
Blackburn Rd, Clayton-le-Moors BB5 5JP
e-mail: H6617@accor.com
dir: M65 junct 7, left at rdbt, left at lights, hotel 100yds on left

This popular hotel occupies an imposing 700-year-old manor house with castellated turrets, porticoes and wood-panelled rooms. It's only a few minutes from Blackburn and the M65, but take a stroll in the beautifully maintained grounds, and you could be miles from anywhere. The attractively furnished Cameo Restaurant is the place to head to for some traditional British dishes such as Scottish smoked salmon with horseradish crème fraîche, lemon and buttered wholemeal bread; braised shank of lamb in a rich tomato, rosemary and red wine jus with mashed potato and roasted root vegetables; and apple and blackberry crumble with Cornish clotted cream.

Chef Chris Nicholson **Owner** MREF Ltd **Times** 12-2/7-9.30 **Prices** Fixed L 3 course £12.95-£23.50, Fixed D 3 course £23.50, Starter £4.50-£7, Main £9.50-£23.50, Dessert £5.50-£7 **Wines** 15 bottles over £20, 7 bottles under £20, 10 by glass **Notes** Sunday L, Vegetarian menu, Dress restrictions, Smart dress, Civ Wed 150 **Seats** 80, Pr/dining room 40 **Parking** 300

BLACKBURN Map 18 SD62

The Clog & Billycock

Modern British NEW

Smart gastro-pub showcasing local produce

01254 201163
Billinge End Road, Pleasington BB2 6QB
e-mail: enquiries@theclogandbillycock.com

Co-owned by restaurateur Nigel Haworth, this smart gastro-pub opened in 2008 following a £1.3m refurbishment. Like sister pub the Three Fishes at Mitton (see entry), this is very much a place to celebrate Lancashire's rich larder and black-and-white photos of local food heroes adorn the walls and even appear on the place mats. The cooking philosophy here is keep it local and keep it simple; the seasonal menu might include North Sea smoked cod fishcake with poached free-range egg and watercress sauce followed by Goosnargh duck breast with creamed potato and pickled rhubarb.

Times 12-5.30/6-9

The Millstone at Mellor

Modern British

Traditional setting for modern cooking with regional flavour

01254 813333
Church Ln, Mellor BB2 7JR
e-mail: info@millstonehotel.co.uk
dir: 4m from M6 junct 31 follow signs for Blackburn. Mellor is on right 1m after 1st set of lights

Although it is now a hotel, this stone-built former coaching inn in the Ribble Valley has retained its traditional bar and remains a busy local village pub. If you are looking for a more gastronomic experience, the smart beamed and wood-panelled restaurant is an elegant setting to sample unfussy classic dishes prepared with plenty of locally-sourced seasonal Lancashire produce. Start, perhaps, with potted Curwin Hill ham hock with potato and quail's egg salad, and move on to a honey-roast Goosnargh duck breast with duck leg cottage pie, braised red cabbage and port jus. Finish with Bakewell tart served up with crème anglaise and vanilla ice cream, and there's an excellent board of local Lancashire cheeses to get stuck into.

Chef Anson Bolton **Owner** Shire Hotels Ltd **Times** 12-2.15/6.30-9.30 **Prices** Fixed D 3 course £31.95, Starter £3.75-£7.95, Main £11.95-£19.95, Dessert £5.25-£6.95 **Wines** 55 bottles over £20, 30 bottles under £20, 8 by glass **Notes** Sunday L, Vegetarian available, Dress restrictions, Smart casual, Civ Wed 68 **Seats** 62, Pr/dining room 20 **Children** Portions, Menu **Parking** 45, Also on street

BLACKPOOL Map 18 SD33

Jali Fine Indian Dining

Indian NEW

Inspired Indian cooking in traditional seafront hotel

01253 622223 & 628966
Best Western Carlton Hotel, 286 North Promenade FY1 2EZ
e-mail: blackpool@jalirestaurants.co.uk
dir: M6 junct 32/M55 follow signs for North Shore. Between Blackpool Tower & Gynn Sq

Located on Blackpool's famous North Promenade and making the most of its prime seafront location, this refurbished hotel offers a choice of dining options. Head for the fine dining Jali Restaurant to experience some good Indian cooking. Choose from the intimate, softly-lit dining room or the modern and airy conservatory with sea and promenade views, and sample some interesting, skilfully prepared dishes. Start with Achari fish tikka (cod) or hara bhara kebab (spinach and vegetable cakes), and for main course choose between a classic (and beautifully moist) chicken tandoori or the more unusual meen moilee (hake in a sauce flavoured with coconut milk and curry leaves).

Chef Kasi Shanmugastin, Khagaraj Kandel, Kuldeep & Sanjeev Nanda **Owner** Ablecrest Ltd **Times** 6-10 Closed BH Mon, Sun (except BH wknds), 19-26 Dec, L all week **Prices** Starter £4.25-£6.75, Main £7.95-£11.95, Dessert £3.95-£4.95, Service added but optional 10% **Wines** 6 bottles over £20, 16 bottles under £20, 4 by glass **Notes** Happy Hour menu 3 course £12.95, Vegetarian available, Dress restrictions, No shorts, Civ Wed 90 **Seats** 100, Pr/dining room 18 **Children** Portions, Menu

BURROW Map 18 SD67

The Highwayman

Traditional British NEW

Traditional inn championing regional produce

01524 273338
LA6 2RJ
e-mail: enquiries@highwaymaninn.co.uk
dir: Off A683

Part of Nigel Haworth's thriving mini-empire of swish dining pubs (Ribble Valley Inns), this revamped 18th-century former coaching inn is a real crowd pleaser. Expect handsome wooden furniture on stone floors, blazing winter log fires, acres of alfresco dining terraces, and walls lined with pictures of 'food heroes' (the local farmers and artisan producers who supply the cracking ingredients used in the kitchen). The food ethos focuses on contemporary interpretations of traditional specialities using produce from Cumbria, Lancashire and Yorkshire. A typical meal from the extensive menu may take in North Sea smoked cod fishcake with watercress sauce, a generous, big-flavoured, braised ox cheek pudding served with creamy mash, and burnt English custard with stewed Yorkshire rhubarb.

Chef Michael Ward **Owner** Nigel Haworth & Craig Bancroft **Times** 12-2/6-9 Closed 25 Dec **Prices** Fixed L 2 course £15, Starter £5.50-£7.50, Main £8.50-£19, Dessert £3.50-£5.50, Service optional **Notes** Fixed L 2/3 course available Sun. Open all day Sun & BHs, Sunday L, Vegetarian available **Children** Menu

LANCASTER Map 18 SD46

Lancaster House Hotel

Traditional British

Modern country-house hotel flying the flag for Lancashire produce

01524 844822
Green Ln, Ellel LA1 4GJ
e-mail: lancaster@elhmail.co.uk
dir: 3m from Lancaster city centre. From S M6 junct 33, head towards Lancaster. Continue through Galgate village, and turn left up Green Ln just before Lancaster University

In a rural setting south of the city and close to the university, this modern country-house hotel has a great dining concept in its Foodworks restaurant: to showcase the best of Lancashire's brimming larder and down-to-

continued on page 201

LANCASTER *continued*

earth hospitality. Wooden floors, glass walls with fork and spoon etchings, muted tones, and cups and saucers for light fittings, combine with murals and old sepia prints of a bygone era in a quirky, well-thought out décor. The simple menu is all about the quality of the produce, with the local roots proudly on display all the way from a starter of air-dried ham and poached fig salad, through to pork loin with bubble-and-squeak and red wine sauce, and sticky toffee pudding with butterscotch sauce.

Chef Mr Colin Gannon **Owner** English Lakes Hotels **Times** 12.30-3/7-9.30 Closed L Sat **Prices** Fixed L 2 course £11, Starter £4.50-£11.95, Main £14.50-£24.95, Dessert £1.75-£6.50, Service included **Wines** 33 bottles over £20, 21 bottles under £20, 10 by glass **Notes** Sunday L, Vegetarian available, Dress restrictions, Smart casual, no sportswear, Civ Wed 100 **Seats** 95, Pr/dining room 190 **Children** Portions, Menu **Parking** 140

LANGHO Map 18 SD73

Northcote

◎◎◎◎ – *see page 202*

LONGRIDGE Map 18 SD63

The Longridge Restaurant

◎◎◎ – *see page 203*

LYTHAM ST ANNES Map 18 SD32

Greens Bistro

◎ Modern British

Modish food in pristine, delightful surroundings

☎ 01253 789990
3-9 St Andrews Road South, St Annes-on-Sea FY8 1SX
e-mail: info@greensbistro.co.uk
dir: Just off St Annes Sq

Eight years after opening its doors, the Websters' soothing and delightful cellar bistro is still serving considered plates of food to happy bands of locals and tourists. The décor is charmingly homely and unpretentious, with the linen-clad tables well spaced or tucked away in nooks and crannies. Dapper, uniformed staff ensure a seamless ebb and flow of the modern British food from the kitchen. The menu is keen to promote provenance and seasonality with dishes such as twice baked Lancashire cheese soufflé served with pears and a walnut vinaigrette, followed by the likes of confit of Goosnargh duck with apple purée and duck gravy. Among the half dozen or so desserts might be Baileys crème brûlée with homespun biscuits, and there's a cracking cheese plate, rooted firmly in the county.

Chef Paul Webster **Owner** Paul & Anna Webster **Times** 6-10 Closed 25 Dec, BHs, 2 wks Jan, 1 wk summer, Sun-Mon, L all week **Prices** Fixed D 3 course £16.95, Service optional, Groups min 8 service 10% **Wines** 7 bottles over £20, 15 bottles under £20, 7 by glass **Notes** Vegetarian available **Seats** 38 **Children** Portions **Parking** On street

The West Beach Restaurant

◎ Modern British

Traditional English cooking on the Lytham seafront

☎ 01253 739898
Clifton Arms Hotel, West Beach FY8 5QJ
e-mail: welcome@cliftonarms-lytham.com
dir: M55 junct 4, left onto A583 (Preston), take right hand lane. At lights right onto Peel Rd. Turn right at t-junct into Ballam Rd. Continue onto Lytham town centre. Turn right and then left into Queen St

The 300-year-old red-brick hotel sits on Lytham's seafront, overlooking the West Beach, after which its dining room is named. A narrow room with light peach walls and well-appointed table settings, it deals in traditionally based English cooking, with Lancashire produce to the fore. That modern classic pairing of seared scallops with black pudding takes on special resonance when the two main components are both sourced from hereabouts, while mains run the gamut from grilled leg steak of local lamb with a mini-shepherd's pie and forest mushrooms, richly sauced with red wine, to baked salmon with wilted spinach in white wine cream sauce. Desserts are served from the trolley.

Chef James Rodgers **Owner** David Webb **Times** 12-2.30/6.30-9 **Prices** Food prices not confirmed for 2011. Please telephone for details **Wines** 55 bottles over £20, 19 bottles under £20, 10 by glass **Notes** Sunday L, Vegetarian available, Civ Wed 100 **Seats** 60, Pr/dining room 140 **Children** Portions **Parking** 50

PRESTON Map 18 SD52

Pines Hotel

◎ Traditional British

Straightforward cooking in comfortable surroundings

☎ 01772 338551
570 Preston Rd, Clayton-Le-Woods PR6 7ED
e-mail: mail@thepineshotel.co.uk
web: www.thepineshotel.co.uk
dir: M6 junct 28/29 off A6 & S of B5256

Owner and manager Betty Duffin has been at the helm of the Pines Hotel since 1963 - no wonder, then, that what makes the Pines Hotel stand out is its sincerely friendly, homely touch. Originally built as the home of a Victorian cotton mill owner in four acres of lovely landscaped gardens and woodlands, the house has been extended to take on a booming trade in weddings and conferences, plus a function suite for its busy programme of cabaret nights. The Rosette Restaurant sources well for its extensive menu of European-accented English dishes. Seared scallops are served with cauliflower purée, pan-fried wild mushrooms and truffle dressing in a typical starter, while a good bet for mains is rack of salt marsh lamb with dauphinoise potatoes, broad beans, roasted courgettes, sun-blushed tomatoes and basil jus.

Chef Ryan Greene, Sarah Lowe **Owner** Betty Duffin **Times** 12-2.30/6-9.30 **Prices** Fixed L 2 course fr £12.50, Fixed D 3 course fr £15.50, Starter £4.75-£8.50, Main £9.95-£25, Dessert £5.25-£7, Service optional **Wines** 16 bottles over £20, 28 bottles under £20, 8 by glass **Notes** Fixed menu weekends £28.50 or ALC available, Sunday L, Vegetarian available, Dress restrictions, No jeans, T-shirts/trainers at certain times, Civ Wed 200 **Seats** 95, Pr/dining room 46 **Children** Portions **Parking** 150

See advert on page 199

THORNTON Map 18 SD34

Twelve Restaurant and Lounge Bar

◎◎ Modern British

Lively modern menu in a uniquely fashionable spot

☎ 01253 821212
Marsh Mill Village, Marsh Mill-in-Wyre, Fleetwood Road North FY5 4JZ
e-mail: info@twelve-restaurant.co.uk
web: www.twelve-restaurant.co.uk
dir: A585 follow signs for Marsh Mill Complex. Turn right into Victoria Rd East, entrance 0.5m on left

A converted dance studio beneath a beautifully restored 18th-century windmill is the unique setting for this contemporary-styled restaurant and lounge bar. Expect a touch of urban-chic and modern minimalism - the funky lounge bar and restaurant feature exposed brickwork, steel girders and aluminium, which give this vibrant dining space a minimalist, industrial feel. Take pre-dinner drinks in the lounge bar, where the glazed roof and wall allow stunning views of the 60-foot windmill towering above it. Seasonal menus offer traditional British cuisine with a modern twist, as you might expect, using as much locally-sourced food as possible. Try salt fishcake with seared squid and parsley dressing to start, followed by pigeon with roasted beetroot, watercress dressing and pickled morels. Finish with rhubarb pannacotta with rhubarb sorbet.

continued on page 204

Northcote

LANGHO Map 18 SD73

Modern British V NOTABLE WINE LIST

A powerhouse of regional British gastronomy

☎ 01254 240555
Northcote Rd BB6 8BE
e-mail: reception@northcote.com
dir: M6 junct 31 take A59, follow signs for Clitheroe. Left at 1st traffic light, onto Skipton/Clitheroe Rd for 9m. Left into Northcote Rd, hotel on right

Fans of BBC2's *Great British Menu* could well spot a familiar face - or two - while dining at Northcote. Chef-patron Nigel Haworth is a series regular, and lately his head chef and protégé, Lisa Allen, has taken her turn at impressing the judges with dishes prepared from North West produce. Haworth has been a champion of local and seasonal ingredients since long before it became fashionable and expected. In fact, he's been doing it ever since he and business partner Craig Bancroft took over Northcote as a small hotel back in 1984. From the start the intention was always to turn the former home of a Victorian textile mill owner into a destination for fine food - sourced mostly from the British Isles - and fine wine (Bancroft's area of expertise), and that's still very much the case today. Dinner in the spacious, modern dining room, with views through the large bay windows over the organic kitchen gardens and beyond to the Ribble Valley hills, is certainly the highlight of any stay. Of course, you don't have to be staying the night to dine here - even at breakfast the restaurant is open to non-residents (and it is well worth getting up and driving out for, too). There are several menus to choose from, including an extremely good value seasonal lunch menu, plus the tasting menu and gourmet menu which both display Bancroft's legendary skills at food and wine matching. From the gourmet menu, Whitby cod with langoustine mash and crispy skin is a fine example of Haworth's uncomplicated but refined style; beautifully balanced in terms of flavours and textures, and with a superb piece of fish at its heart. A spring main course of Herdwick lamb baked in butter puff pastry with butter beans, celeriac and pak choi is elegant and stylish, the meat appropriately pink and the flavours all singing in harmony. A perfectly formed dark Valrhona chocolate cylinder with smoked nuts and salted organic sheep's milk ice cream is a truly memorable finish. Breads, canapés and petits fours - particularly the mini Eccles cakes - are as good as it gets, and the wine list is, as you'd imagine, a real stonker.

Chef Nigel Haworth, Lisa Allen
Owner Nigel Haworth, Craig Bancroft
Times 12-1.30/7-9.30 Closed 25 Dec
Prices Fixed L 3 course £25, Tasting menu £80, Starter £9-£18.50, Main £25.50-£35, Dessert £7-£11, Service optional **Wines** 300 bottles over £20, 9 bottles under £20, 6 by glass
Notes Fixed D 5 course £55, Sunday L, Vegetarian menu, Dress restrictions, No jeans, Civ Wed 40 **Seats** 80, Pr/dining room 40 **Children** Portions, Menu
Parking 60

The Longridge Restaurant

LONGRIDGE Map 18 SD63

Modern British V

Chic setting for first-rate British cuisine

01772 784969 & 806545
104-106 Higher Rd PR3 3SY
e-mail: longridge@heathcotes.co.uk
dir: Follow signs for Golf Club & Jeffrey Hill. Higher Rd is beside White Bull Pub in Longridge

Husband-and-wife Chris and Kath Bell are the team behind the success of Paul Heathcote's Longridge Restaurant these days, with Chris at the stoves and Kath as general manager. The Heathcote style of locally-inspired modern British cooking continues in fine fettle. It's a smart looking restaurant in three converted 19th-century cottages, its lounge and three interconnecting dining areas done out with a degree of panache in neutral contemporary tones, plus some exposed brick and lots of original panelling. Kath runs front-of-house with charm and efficiency. Expect all the little extras - canapés (mushroom and truffle oil velouté to name but one), pre-dessert and petits fours, plus an array of breads - and cooking that is neither overly complex nor unrefined. Seared Scottish scallops come in a powerfully-flavoured partnership with pickled shallots and anchovy butter as a first course, while main-course pan-roasted wild sea bass is partnered with olive oil mash, sautéed razor clams and a chilli and oregano butter. There are flashes of exoticism among the British and European flavours, thus coconut cream, roasted pineapple, mango sorbet, sesame, lime and ginger is a successfully striking dessert; there're British cheeses, too, if you want to end on a patriotic note. A meal at Paul Heathcote's flagship restaurant may well inspire you to sign up for a course at the on-site cookery school.

Chef Chris Bell **Owner** Paul Heathcote **Times** 12-2.30/6-10 Closed 1 Jan, Mon-Tue **Prices** Fixed L 2 course £14.50, Fixed D 3 course £50, Tasting menu £60, Starter £7.50-£10, Main £18-£27, Dessert £7-£10, Service optional, Groups min 8 service 10% **Wines** 109 bottles over £20, 25 bottles under £20, 12 by glass **Notes** Gourmet menu available 5/7 course, Sun D last table 7.30, Sunday L, Vegetarian menu **Seats** 60, Pr/dining room 12 **Children** Portions **Parking** 10, On street

THORNTON ***continued***

Chef Paul Moss **Owner** Paul Moss & Caroline Upton **Times** 12-3/6.30-12 Closed 1st 2 wks Jan, Mon, L Tue-Sat **Prices** Fixed L 3 course £15.95, Fixed D 3 course £17.95-£26, Starter £5.95-£10.50, Main £14.95-£24, Dessert £5.50-£7.95, Service optional **Wines** 46 bottles over £20, 29 bottles under £20, 12 by glass **Notes** Sunday L, Vegetarian available **Seats** 90 **Children** Portions **Parking** 150

WHALLEY Map 18 SD73

The Three Fishes

Traditional British

Lancashire produce in a heartwarming village pub

01254 826888
Mitton Rd, Mitton BB7 9PQ
e-mail: enquiries@thethreefishes.com
dir: M6 junct 31, A59 to Clitheroe. Follow signs for Whalley, take B6246 and continue for 2m

The 400-year-old pub sits on a limestone rise above the Ribble, and is the kind of place to refresh the weary soul, with its log fires, roughcast stone walls and cask ales. 'Food with roots' is how the menu is styled, and the roots are firmly and deeply in surrounding Lancashire. Among the fine local produce are corn-fed Goosnargh chicken in devilled sauce, Ribble Valley minced steak in a muffin with dripping-fried chips, and Kirkham's Lancashire cheese, either shredded on to a mash-topped fish pie, or served in splendour alongside other farmhouse cheeses. Home-made ices such as milk chocolate and Bourbon biscuit are a soothing way to finish.

Chef Callum McDonald **Owner** Craig Bancroft & Nigel Haworth **Times** 12-2/6-9 Closed 25 Dec **Prices** Starter £3.50-£5.75, Main £8.50-£19.80, Dessert £3.50-£5.50, Service optional **Wines** 24 bottles over £20, 18 bottles under £20, 10 by glass **Notes** Sunday L, Vegetarian available **Seats** 140 **Children** Portions, Menu **Parking** 70

WHITEWELL Map 18 SD64

The Inn at Whitewell

Modern British

Confident cooking in historic inn with countryside views

01200 448222
Forest of Bowland, Clitheroe BB7 3AT
e-mail: reception@innatwhitewell.com
dir: From S M6 junct 31 Longridge follow Whitewell signs. From N M6 junct 33 follow Trough of Bowland & Whitewell signs

Charles Bowman is the third generation of Bowmans to take the helm of this immensely charming stone inn by the River Hodder among the rolling fells of the Forest of Bowland. There is something for all-comers here: a quirky vibe full of genuine warmth and good humour, in a real, rambling lived-in country inn interior with rustic furniture, antiques, books and eclectic paintings. And everyone is welcome - dogs, kids, the lot. The cooking takes a simple modern British approach using first-rate local produce, with a nod to the Mediterranean here and there. You might start with pork, leek and mustard sausage, with parsnip purée, apple wafers and cider apple jus, ahead of roast loin of lamb with smoked bacon and cabbage polenta cake, ratatouille and aubergine purée. The in-house wine shop guarantees a fine choice.

Chef Jamie Cadman **Owner** Charles Bowman **Times** 12-2/7.30-9.30 **Prices** Starter £4.60-£8.95, Main £15.35-£25.50, Dessert £5.10, Service optional **Wines** 120 bottles over £20, 60 bottles under £20, 20 by glass **Notes** Sunday L, Vegetarian available, Civ Wed 80 **Seats** 60, Pr/dining room 20 **Children** Portions **Parking** 70

WRIGHTINGTON Map 15 SD51

The Mulberry Tree

Modern British

Creative cuisine in a Lancashire gastro-pub

01257 451400
Wrightington Bar WN6 9SE
dir: 4m from Wigan. From M6 junct 27 towards Parbold, right after motorway exit, by BP garage into Mossy Lea Rd. On right after 2m

In the peaceful Lancashire village of Wrightington, just two miles off the M6, the Mulberry Tree is a thriving gastro-pub. There are different seating areas to suit your mood; eat in the lively bar or opt for the more formal restaurant area with its white linen dressed tables. The imaginative seasonal menu of British dishes has foundations in classical French thinking with a few broader influences here and there. Start with Szechuan-spiced sautéed chicken livers with spring onions, coriander and lemon, and move on to main-course home-cured bacon chop with buttered sweetheart cabbage, fondant potatoes and creamy mustard sauce, and finish with a cinder toffee meringue with butterscotch sauce and vanilla ice cream.

Times 12-2.30/6-9.30 Closed 26 Dec, 1 Jan

LEICESTERSHIRE

BELTON Map 11 SK42

The Queen's Head

British

Good, seasonal cooking in a chic, modern gastro-pub

01530 222359
2 Long St LE12 9TP
e-mail: enquiries@thequeenshead.org
web: www.thequeenshead.org
dir: Located just off B5324 between Loughborough and Ashby-de-la-Zouch

A contemporary boutique-style pub with rooms in the picturesque village of Belton, The Queen's Head has plush leather sofas, chunky wooden tables and chairs and modern art on the walls. On the plate you'll find great quality local ingredients skilfully cooked and presented with some style, the classics given an imaginative twist or two along the way. Start with a rather neat mini Queen's Head fish and chips or ham hock terrine with pickled vegetables and home-made brioche, then move on to corn-fed chicken with black pudding, pearl barley risotto and Chantenay carrots. A classic Bakewell tart with mixed berry compôte and vanilla ice cream is a satisfying finale.

Chef David Ferguson **Owner** Henry & Ali Weldon **Times** 12-2.30/6-9.30 Closed 25-26 Dec, L Sun **Prices** Food prices not confirmed for 2011. Please telephone for details **Wines** 49 bottles over £20, 25 bottles under £20, 13 by glass **Notes** Sunday L, Vegetarian available, Civ Wed 60 **Seats** 70, Pr/dining room 40 **Children** Portions, Menu **Parking** 20

CASTLE DONINGTON

For restaurant details see East Midlands Airport

EAST MIDLANDS AIRPORT Map 11 SK42

Donington Manor Hotel

Modern British

Georgian coaching inn with appealing menu

☎ 01332 810253
High St, Castle Donington DE74 2PP
e-mail: enquiries@doningtonmanorhotel.co.uk
dir: 1m into village on B5430, left at lights

Handy for the East Midlands airport, this 18th-century former coaching inn has been thoroughly modernised, emerging as a luxurious hotel and restaurant which does a good wedding trade. The Bistro has retained the best historical details so expect impressive fireplaces and intricate plasterwork set against plush fabrics and well dressed tables. Service is good and friendly and the food covers all the bases. Take a route from smooth chicken liver pâté with onion chutney and herb melba toast to grilled fillet of hake on softened pak choi, served with crushed potatoes and Chardonnay.

Times 12-2.30/7-9.30 Closed Xmas & New Year, L Sat ex by appointment

Orchard Restaurant

Modern European

Creative cooking in relaxed surroundings

☎ 01509 672518
Best Western, Premier Yew Lodge Hotel, Packington Hill, Kegworth DE74 2DF
e-mail: info@yewlodgehotel.co.uk
dir: M1 junct 24, follow signs for Loughborough & Kegworth on A6. At bottom of hill take 1st right onto Packington Hill. Hotel 400yds on right

Despite its handiness for East Midlands Airport and the busy motorway network, this smart, family-run hotel is a surprisingly tranquil bolt-hole. Its Orchard restaurant - a split-level bistro-style venue - is very much on the map for local foodies, who come for accomplished modern cooking that reworks the classics with innovative and bold flavour combinations, as witnessed in a starter of perfectly-seared scallops served with lemongrass cappuccino, rhubarb and ginger purée. Next up, top-quality calves' liver is seared and teamed with caramelised onion, sweet potato mash and a thyme and balsamic jus; finally, a walnut sponge with white chocolate and carrot ice cream closes on a similarly high note. Attentive staff provide the icing on the cake with friendly and well-paced service.

Times 12-2/1.30-9.30 Closed L Sat

The Priest House on the River

Modern British V

Fine dining in historic house

☎ 01332 810649
Kings Mills, Castle Donington DE74 2RR
e-mail: thepriesthouse@handpicked.co.uk
dir: M1 junct 24, onto A50, take 1st slip road signed Castle Donington. Right at lights, hotel in 2m

Better known for the high-octane entertainment of car racing and rock concerts in nearby Donington Park, more sedate pleasures are to be found in Castle Donington in this historic house on the banks of the River Trent. Although it was mentioned in the Domesday Book, the Priest House has been brought smartly up-to-date as a comfy modern country-house hotel with a relaxed contemporary brasserie and more formal fine-dining restaurant. The latter blends exposed stone walls and black beams with classy leather banquettes and an understated neutral décor to suit the modern cooking style. Influences come from Europe as well as the domestic larder on compact menus focused on the seasons. Tried-and-true combinations are the kitchen's draw - perhaps pan-fried scallops with crispy pork belly and apple, ahead of pan-fried fillet of turbot with potato rösti, fennel, and mussels with saffron sauce.

Chef Richard Burchell **Owner** Hand Picked Hotels **Times** 12-3/7-10 Closed L Sat, D Sun **Prices** Food prices not confirmed for 2011. Please telephone for details **Wines** 75 bottles over £20, 2 bottles under £20, 8 by glass **Notes** Sunday L, Vegetarian menu, Civ Wed 90 **Seats** 38, Pr/dining room 100 **Children** Portions, Menu **Parking** 200

HINCKLEY Map 11 SP49

Sketchley Grange Hotel

British, European

Sound modern British cooking in a spa retreat

☎ 01455 251133
Sketchley Ln, Burbage LE10 3HU
e-mail: reservations@sketchleygrange.co.uk
web: www.sketchleygrange.co.uk
dir: From M69 junct 1 take B4109 (Hinckley). Straight on 1st rdbt, left at 2nd rdbt & immediately right into Sketchley Lane. Hotel at end of lane

On the border of Leicestershire and Warwickshire, not far from the motorway network, in an unexpectedly tranquil location, is this half-timbered country-house hotel. Extensive recent refurbishment has resulted in some high-spec guest rooms being added, there are up-to-date spa facilities and, in the Willow Restaurant, with its garden views and grand piano, an elegant place to eat. The menus keep to an appreciable sense of culinary logic, producing goats' cheese en croûte with beetroot carpaccio, diced pear and walnut dressing, pink-cooked Ayrshire beef with buttered spinach and a well-made béarnaise sauce, and sustaining lemon sponge pudding with lemon sauce and vanilla ice cream. Pedigree English cheeses come with dried fruit chutney and sage oatcakes.

Times 7-9.30 Closed Mon, L Tue-Sat, D Sun

KEGWORTH

For restaurant details see East Midlands Airport

KNIPTON Map 11 SK83

The Manners Arms

Modern British

Foursquare country pub with aristocratic connections

☎ 01476 879222
Croxton Rd NG32 1RH
e-mail: info@mannersarms.com
dir: From Grantham take A607 (Melton road), after approx 4m turn right at Croxton Kerrial

Your hosts are the Duke and Duchess of Rutland, as is evidenced by the proximity of their ancestral seat, Belvoir Castle. The Manners Arms, for all that it was built as a Victorian hunting lodge, is now unmistakably a country pub, with its solid wooden tables and bare floorboards. Impeccable raw materials from the Belvoir estate, and from local farmers and growers, inform the menus, which deal in good, substantial rustic cooking. Textbook chicken liver parfait with toasted brioche and pea shoots, mussels cooked in garlic cream, and 30-day rump steak with flawless chips, are satisfying, hearty dishes. Sticky toffee pudding with butterscotch sauce will fill any remaining gaps.

Times 12.30-3/7-9 Closed D Sun (after 8pm), 25 Dec

LEICESTER Map 11 SK50

Hotel Maiyango

Modern European

Innovative cooking in heart of Leicester city centre

0116 251 8898
13-21 St Nicholas Place LE1 4LD
e-mail: reservations@maiyango.com
dir: M1 junct 21, A5460 for 3.5m. Turn right onto A47 round St Nicholas Circle onto St Nicholas Place

The Maiyango brings a touch of boutique glamour to the centre of Leicester. It is right in the centre of town and has a spectacular third-floor rooftop terrace bar where you can look out over the city whilst sipping a classy cocktail. There's lots of natural wood and plenty of contemporary style touches in the vaguely Eastern-themed restaurant, while the menu deals in confident European flavours as well as raiding the global larder here and there. The kitchen is driven by the seasons, and locally-sourced ingredients, some of which are grown exclusively for the hotel on a local farm, are a feature. The food is innovative and interesting: terrine of Gressingham duck with ham hock and mango with rocket and parmesan salad might be followed by soy-scented guinea fowl breast, sweet-and-sour plum jus, sauté sweet potato and spinach.

Chef Phillip Sharpe **Owner** Aatin Anadkat
Times 12-3/6.30-9.45 Closed 25 Dec, 1 Jan, L Sun
Prices Fixed L 2 course fr £15.50, Fixed D 3 course fr £28, Service optional, Groups min 6 service 10% **Wines** 46 bottles over £20, 16 bottles under £20, 12 by glass **Notes** Tasting menu & pre-theatre menu available, Vegetarian available **Seats** 55, Pr/dining room 80 **Children** Portions **Parking** NCP

MEDBOURNE Map 11 SP89

The Horse & Trumpet

Modern British

Stylish former pub with confident, modern cooking

01858 565000
12 Old Green LE16 8DX
e-mail: info@horseandtrumpet.com
dir: Between Market Harborough and Uppingham on B664

Ten years on from when this handsome thatched restaurant with rooms first opened its doors, a slight change in direction is in the air. Intelligent, well-judged dishes are still the order of the day - following the seasons and based on good, local produce - but Gary Magnani's intention, as we go to print, is to make a gear-shift away from fine dining towards a more brasserie-style of cooking. Once inside the old beams knit in well with the warm neutral tones and comfortable furniture. From the lively carte comes a starter of rose-pink breast of local pigeon in pastry with pancetta and duck parfait, before main-course fillet of free-range pork, served up with a delicious Clonakilty black pudding, potato salad and caramelised Granny Smith. Finish with a Valhrona chocolate mousse, judiciously supported by a blood orange sorbet and Cointreau.

Chef G Magnani **Owner** Horse & Trumpet Ltd
Times 12-1.45/7-9.30 Closed 1st week Jan, Mon, D Sun
Prices Fixed L 2 course £15, Starter £4.75-£6.25, Main £11.25-£18.95, Dessert £4.50-£5.75, Service optional, Groups min 16 service 10% **Wines** 40 bottles over £20, 6 bottles under £20, 8 by glass **Notes** Grazing menu 6 course L & D £35, Sunday L, Vegetarian available
Seats 50, Pr/dining room 32 **Parking** On street

MELTON MOWBRAY Map 11 SK71

Stapleford Park Country House Hotel

Modern French

Fine dining amid the splendour of Capability Brown parkland

01572 787000 & 787019
Stapleford LE14 2EF
e-mail: reservations@stapleford.co.uk
dir: A1 to Colsterworth rdbt onto B676, signed Melton Mowbray. In approx 9m turn left to Stapleford

This truly stately home presents a canter through English architecture from the 14th-century to the dying days of the Victorian era, when a wealthy, social-climbing brewer radically changed the old house by grafting on a huge new wing. Nowadays, there's plenty to keep guests occupied - pampering in the spa, and golf in its 500 acres of parkland laid out by Capability Brown, to name just two diversions. The opulent Grinling Gibbons dining room takes its name from the Victorian sculptor and master woodcarver who did the splendid mantelpiece, and is the venue for cuisine of serious intent. The kitchen reworks English and European classics with a modern spin, using heaps of luxury ingredients together with top-quality local materials. A tasting of foie gras delivers the unctuous liver in the form of terrine, parfait and seared with Sauternes jelly and white onion purée. Main-course poussin is served as breast and tortellini of confit leg with leek purée and boulangère potatoes, while dessert is a rich chocolate cup filled with runny toffee rather like a giant Rolo.

Times 12-2/7-9.30 Closed L Sat

NORTH KILWORTH Map 11 SP68

Kilworth House Hotel

Modern British V

Timeless elegance and good cooking techniques

01858 880058
Lutterworth Rd LE17 6JE
e-mail: info@kilworthhouse.co.uk
dir: Located on A4304, 4m E of M1 junct 20 towards Market Harborough

After a painstaking restoration under the watchful eye of English Heritage, this Italianate country house in 38 acres of landscaped parkland now enjoys a new lease of life as a fine upmarket hotel. Period authenticity runs through the whole building, with the deliciously airy Victorian Orangery providing an unbuttoned ambience for eating at any time of day. But when only fine dining will do, the Wordsworth Restaurant offers a particularly delightful confection of crystal chandeliers hanging from a domed ceiling, and oak doors inlaid with colourful stained glass - the sort of place where people feel they should dress for dinner. The kitchen has its roots in country-house classics, given a modern spin, as seen in a large raviolo of smoked chicken and mushroom that delivers punchy flavours pointed up with truffle oil and tomato liquor. Next comes baked hake, accurately cooked and served on crushed new potatoes with sweet crab and basil vinaigrette.

Chef Carl Dovey **Owner** Mr & Mrs Mackay
Times 12-3/7-9.30 **Prices** Fixed D 3 course £40, Service optional **Wines** 49 bottles over £20, 12 bottles under £20, 10 by glass **Notes** Theatre menu in season 3 course £25, Sunday L, Vegetarian menu, Dress restrictions, No jeans or trainers, Civ Wed 130 **Seats** 70, Pr/dining room 130 **Children** Portions, Menu **Parking** 140

STATHERN Map 11 SK73

Red Lion Inn

Traditional British V

Reliable village inn in the Vale of Belvoir

01949 860868
2 Red Lion St LE14 4HS
e-mail: info@theredlioninn.co.uk
dir: From A1 take A52 towards Nottingham signed Belvoir Castle, take turn to Stathern on left

Informality, real ales, fine wines and good quality innovative and traditional food using home-grown and locally-sourced produce sum up the passion and philosophy behind this cracking 16th-century village pub in the beautiful Vale of Belvoir. Expect a warm and rustic atmosphere throughout, from the stone-floored bar and relaxing lounge, kitted out with chunky tables and deep sofas, to the converted skittle alley dining room, replete with low beams and a wood-burning stove. The menu (with map of suppliers) champions local ingredients, the daily choice perhaps delivering ham hock terrine with green bean salad, Old Dalby duck with duck and mushroom pithivier, spring greens and carrot purée, and Rearsby treacle tart with clotted cream.

Chef Sean Hope **Owner** Ben Jones, Sean Hope
Times 12-2/7-9.30 Closed D Sun **Prices** Food prices not confirmed for 2011. Please telephone for details **Wines** 9 bottles over £20, 21 bottles under £20, 8 by glass
Notes Sunday L, Vegetarian menu **Seats** 50
Children Portions, Menu **Parking** 20

WOODHOUSE EAVES — Map 11 SK51

The Woodhouse

Modern British

Modish neighbourhood restaurant with sense of style

01509 890318
43 Maplewell Rd, Woodhouse Eaves LE12 8RG
e-mail: info@thewoodhouse.co.uk
web: www.thewoodhouse.co.uk
dir: M1 junct 23 towards Loughborough, right into Nanpantan Rd, left into Beacon Rd, right in Main St & again into Maplewell Rd

An unassuming whitewashed cottage, tucked away in a small village close to Leicester, conceals a surprisingly vibrant contemporary restaurant. Take time to enjoy cocktails and canapés in the vampishly scarlet bar, before stepping down into the chic dining area, where dark blue high-backed chairs and crisply-set tables contrast with the vibrantly-hued walls. Service, too, hits the spot with a neat balance of confident relaxation and efficiency. The kitchen performs well, with a repertoire of contemporary flavours driven by prime local ingredients, sympathetically balanced and cleverly presented. So, begin with goose liver pâté with caramelised bananas, follow with wild sea bass with samphire and wild sorrel risotto, chorizo, mussels and clams, and round off with pistachio soufflé with blood orange and vodka sorbet.

The Woodhouse

Chef Paul Leary **Owner** Paul Leary **Times** 12-3/6.30-12 Closed BHs, Mon, L Sat, D Sun **Prices** Fixed L 2 course fr £13.95, Fixed D 3 course fr £17.95, Service optional **Wines** 100 bottles over £20, 20 bottles under £20, 8 by glass **Notes** Fixed ALC 3 course £33.50, Tasting menu available, Sunday L **Seats** 50, Pr/dining room 40 **Children** Portions **Parking** 15

LINCOLNSHIRE

GRANTHAM — Map 11 SK93

Harry's Place

– *see below*

HORNCASTLE — Map 17 TF26

Magpies Restaurant

British, European

Creative cooking in small market town

01507 527004
73 East St LN9 6AA
dir: 0.5m from town centre on A158 towards Skegness

A row of 200-year-old terraced cottages in a sedate Lincolnshire Wolds town is the setting for this small family-run restaurant. Inside, the whole place has a charming feel with its russet and honey colour schemes, wood-burning stove and gleaming candlesticks, and there's a tiny outdoor courtyard for fine weather dining. Chef Andrew Gilbert uses local materials in tune with the seasons in his clear-flavoured, creative dishes: a Thai crab cake starter with lemongrass and ginger, artichoke and tomato relish and tempura sea bass injects a note of fusion, although main-course pheasant breast stuffed with cranberry and forcemeat and wrapped in prosciutto,

continued

Harry's Place

GRANTHAM — Map 11 SK93

Modern French

Small restaurant, big heart

01476 561780
17 High St, Great Gonerby NG31 8JS
dir: 1.5m NW of Grantham on B1174

From the outside it just looks like a private house - a very nice Georgian house at that, smartly painted in a sort of duck-egg blue, with some tall trees in the front garden and a neat little gate. Indeed, it's so inconspicuous, so unassuming, you could easily drive or walk past and not even notice it. But while Harry's Place is a private house, it's Harry and Caroline Hallam's house - one of this country's finest (and smallest) restaurants. Harry cooks single-handedly out back, while Caroline single-handedly looks after the diners - 10 at the most, seated at three well-spaced tables. The dining room is elegant and charming - not pretentious or formal in the slightest - with neatly appointed tables dressed in sage green, antique furnishings, fresh flowers, and family pictures and ornaments adding to the homely feel. Caroline is genuinely friendly and yet extremely professional in her role as hostess, while Harry offers a choice of two dishes at each course from his regularly-changing handwritten menu, which is driven by the availability of top-notch, seasonal produce from trusted local suppliers. French technique underpins Harry's cooking, along with a true appreciation of flavour balance and a desire to let the ingredients do the talking. Filey lobster comes with mango, avocado and green leaves, a relish of mango, lime, ginger and basil, a lobster stock reduction and truffle oil in a fresh and vibrant first course. Next up, filleted loin of young roe deer with blueberries, a fresh herb and onion farce and a sauce of red wine, Madeira, sage, thyme and tarragon is a typically well-balanced dish, the meat perfectly cooked and tender. For dessert, something simple and light could be just the ticket after all that has gone before (including a superb amuse-bouche and freshly baked granary bread), so how about cherry brandy jelly served with natural yoghurt and a sprinkling of black pepper?

Chef Harry Hallam **Owner** Harry & Caroline Hallam **Times** 12.30-2.30/7-9 Closed 2 wks from 25 Dec, Sun-Mon **Prices** Starter £9.50-£18.50, Main £35-£39.50, Dessert £8, Service optional **Wines** All bottles over £20, 4 by glass **Seats** 10 **Children** Portions **Parking** 4

HORNCASTLE *continued*

with bubble-and-squeak and a mini game pie has its roots in Lincolnshire.

Chef Andrew Gilbert **Owner** Caroline Gilbert
Times 12-2/7-9.30 Closed 27-30 Dec, Mon-Tue, L Sat
Prices Fixed D 4 course fr £38, Tasting menu £42, Starter £6.50-£7.95, Main £14.95, Dessert £6.50-£7.95, Service optional **Wines** 62 bottles over £20, 50 bottles under £20, 4 by glass **Notes** ALC L only, Tasting menu last Thu each month, Sunday L, Vegetarian available, Dress restrictions, Smart casual **Seats** 34 **Children** Portions **Parking** On street

HOUGH-ON-THE-HILL Map 11 SK94

The Brownlow Arms

British

Popular village inn with locally-focused menu

☎ 01400 250234
High Rd NG32 2AZ
e-mail: paulandlorraine@thebrownlowarms.com
dir: Take A607 (Grantham to Sleaford road). Hough-on-the-Hill signed from Barkston

Looking more like an elegant country house, this magnificent 17th-century inn stands in the heart of a picturesque stone village. In keeping, expect oak beams, open fires, and tapestry-backed chairs in cosy panelled dining rooms. At polished wooden tables, topped with gleaming Riedel glassware, you can tuck into simply presented modern British dishes prepared from local ingredients, including game from surrounding estates. From braised ox tongue with celeriac remoulade, move on to whole lemon sole with parsley and lemon butter, and then round off with caramelised lemon tart with blackcurrant sorbet. The landscaped terrace overlooks fields and is perfect for eating outdoors.

Times 12-3/6.30-9.30 Closed 25-26 Dec, 1-23 Jan, 1 wk Sep, Mon, L Tue-Sat, D Sun

LINCOLN Map 17 SK97

Dining Room Restaurant

Modern British

Straightforward country-house cooking in a Georgian rectory

☎ 01522 790340
Washingborough Hall Hotel, Church Hill, Washingborough LN4 1BE
e-mail: enquiries@washingboroughhall.com
dir: From A46 south to A1434 to city centre, turn right at rdbt onto B1138 towards Branston. Turn left at lights to Washingborough. Turn right at mini rdbt onto Church Hill

The former Georgian rectory is a country-house hotel on a human scale, with smart, comfortable interiors, and a relaxingly friendly front-of-house approach. The dining room with its view of the garden combines pastel hues and quiet civility, and is a good setting for the straightforward modern British food. Expect to start with something like a tian of white crabmeat, prawns and watercress with mango salsa, and continue either with fillet steak and pommes Anna with béarnaise, or a delightfully retro lemon sole and smoked trout roulade with caper mash. Desserts include a refreshing lemon tart with raspberry sorbet.

Chef Dan Wallis **Owner** Mr E & Mrs L Herring
Times 12-2/6.30-9 **Prices** Food prices not confirmed for 2011. Please telephone for details **Wines** 11 bottles over £20, 19 bottles under £20, 5 by glass **Notes** Vegetarian available, Dress restrictions, Smart casual, Civ Wed 50 **Seats** 40, Pr/dining room 36 **Children** Portions **Parking** 40

Lakeside Restaurant

Modern International V

Contemporary food in Victorian country-house splendour

01522 793305
Branston Hall Hotel, Branston Park, Branston LN4 1PD
e-mail: info@branstonhall.com
web: www.branstonhall.com
dir: On B1188, 3m S of Lincoln. In village, hotel drive opposite village hall

Dating from 1885, this imposing country-house hotel is set in 88 acres of wooded parkland and lakes. The elegant Lakeside Restaurant comes with plenty of period feel thanks to its chandeliers, oil paintings, Italian-style chairs and many original features. The kitchen takes a modern approach, treating top-grade regional produce with imagination and a good level of culinary skill to produce a menu whose influences range widely around the globe. Expect starters such as brawn of rabbit and pork knuckle with apple and hazelnut salad, followed by rump of lamb with chick pea purée, cumin-spiced carrot and ras el hanout. Desserts might include toffee mousse with Amaretto mascarpone and chocolate bonbon.

Chef Miles Collins **Owner** Southsprings Ltd **Times** 12-2/7-9.30 **Prices** Food prices not confirmed for 2011. Please telephone for details **Wines** 17 bottles over £20, 36 bottles under £20, 14 by glass **Notes** Sunday L, Vegetarian menu, Dress restrictions, Smart casual, no jeans or T-shirts, Civ Wed 120 **Seats** 75, Pr/dining room 28 **Children** Portions **Parking** 75

see advert on opposite page

The Lincoln Hotel

Modern British **NEW** V

Ambitious cooking close to the cathedral

01522 520348
Eastgate LN2 1PN
e-mail: vgreen@thelincolnhotel.com

The modern Lincoln Hotel has excellent views of the glorious medieval cathedral at the heart of the city. The Green Room, its fine dining venue, has a separate entrance, and with its green walls and dark wooden tables, feels rather discreet and romantic. The kitchen plays up to the setting with a repertoire of modern dishes of some sophistication and complexity. Starters bring on a fashionable fish and meat combo - caramel-flavoured scallops paired with roasted local pork belly, spiced with ras el hanout. Main-course venison is pointed up with juniper and served with potato cake, and fine green beans with pine nuts and parmesan. Desserts wrap up proceedings with a straight vanilla crème brûlée presented prettily with flowers and pistachio croquant.

Chef Sam Owen **Owner** Christopher Nevile, Lady Arnold **Times** 6-9.30 Closed Sun-Mon, L all week **Prices** Fixed L 2 course £10-£15, Starter £3.95-£8.95, Main £6.95-£20.95, Dessert £3.95-£8.95, Service optional **Notes** Sunday L, Vegetarian menu, Air con **Seats** 30, Pr/dining room 12 **Children** Portions, Menu

The Old Bakery

Modern British

Locally-minded cooking in charming former bakery

01522 576057
26-28 Burton Rd LN1 3LB
e-mail: enquiries@theold-bakery.co.uk
web: www.theold-bakery.co.uk
dir: From A46 follow directions for Lincoln North then follow brown signs for The Historic Centre

The Old Bakery is a quaint looking Victorian building in Lincoln's historic cathedral quarter which served the community for over 100 years until the ovens went out in 1954. Brought back to life, these days it serves the community as a delightful restaurant with rooms run by an Italian chef-patron who is passionate about food, from the earth to the fork. The original ovens and quarry tiles remain intact in the charming, pleasingly rustic interior, which includes a bright conservatory-style space. Local produce is sourced with zeal and turned into dishes full of the taste of the Mediterranean; choose between a tasting menu, light lunch option or the full carte. Things might start with free-range chicken liver parfait, served with a Gewürztraminer jelly, fig chutney and pain d'épice croûtons, then proceed to butter-poached free-range guinea fowl with a pink peppercorn sauce. Farmers and producers are duly name-checked on the menu.

Chef Ivano de Serio **Owner** Alan & Lynn Ritson, Tracey & Ivano de Serio **Times** 12-2.30/7-9.30 Closed 26 Dec, 1 Jan, Mon **Prices** Starter £4.75-£10.50, Main £14.50-£20.95, Dessert £5.50-£7.25, Service optional **Wines** 37 bottles over £20, 38 bottles under £20, 9 by glass **Notes** Tasting menu 5 course, Sunday L, Vegetarian available, Dress restrictions, Smart casual **Seats** 85, Pr/dining room 15 **Children** Portions **Parking** On street, public car park 20mtrs

LOUTH Map 17 TF38

Brackenborough Hotel

Modern European

Modern cooking in lively upmarket bistro setting

01507 609169
Cordeaux Corner, Brackenborough LN11 0SZ
e-mail: reception@brackenborough.co.uk
web: www.oakridgehotels.co.uk
dir: Hotel located on main A16 Louth to Grimsby Rd

Just outside Louth, this modern hotel's star attraction is its relaxed bistro bar, where an interesting contemporary menu is built on the best of the region's produce; there's Lincolnshire lamb, pork and poultry, fish comes from a family merchant that has been on Grimsby docks for 70 years, while Cote Hill Farm cheese comes from nearby Market Rasen. The bistro is filled with natural light, and done out in a clean-cut modern style with smart furniture and exposed brickwork. The kitchen keeps on the ball with simple up-to-date ideas and flavour combinations: a plate of pork unites pork belly with white and black pudding, pork sirloin and Lincolnshire sausage with root vegetable purée, mash and red cabbage; pan-seared halibut fillet is served with confit potatoes, fresh tomato concasse and clam beurrre blanc.

Times 11.30-9.45

SCUNTHORPE — Map 17 SE81

Forest Pines Golf and Country Club Hotel

Modern, Traditional

Local seafood in a fine-dining hotel restaurant

☎ 01652 650770
Ermine St, Broughton DN20 0AQ
e-mail: forestpines@qhotels.co.uk
dir: From M180 junct 4, travel towards Scunthorpe on A18. Continue straight over rdbt, hotel is situated on left

Set in 190 acres of grounds, this hotel houses fine-dining Eighteen57 restaurant, named in tribute to the year when nearby Grimsby's No.1 fish dock opened. The restaurant interior follows an aquatic theme; enter through the glass door to find glass walls, blue tiling and a stylish glass wine rack. The kitchen has a light touch, turning fresh local fish into simple, tasty dishes. Sustainability is key so expect the likes of pollock rather than cod. Start perhaps with escabèche of North Sea mackerel with pickled red cabbage and rocket, followed by line-caught Brixham sea bass with mussel, crab and scampi risotto, and finish with a decadent hot fudge soufflé.

Chef Paul Montgomery **Owner** Q Hotels **Times** 6.30-10 Closed Sun-Mon, L all week **Prices** Fixed D 4 course £35, Starter £4.95-£11.75, Main £14.95-£28.25, Dessert £6.25-£8.75 **Wines** 59 bottles over £20, 7 by glass **Notes** Vegetarian available, Dress restrictions, Smart casual, no ripped jeans **Seats** 70 **Parking** 200

SLEAFORD — Map 12 TF04

The Bustard Inn & Restaurant

Modern British, International

Sensitively refurbished old inn in peaceful village

☎ 01529 488250
44 Main St, South Rauceby NG34 8QG
e-mail: info@thebustardinn.co.uk
dir: A17 from Newark, turn right after B6403 to Ancaster. A153 from Grantham, after Wilsford, turn left for S Rauceby

Built by Rauceby Hall Estate in 1860, this striking and sympathetically renovated stone inn retains many original features, including stone-flagged floors, old stone fireplaces, an ornate oriel window, and the original timbers used to build the old brew house and stable that comprise part of the dining area. Solid ash tables, tapestry chairs and exposed stone walls add to the overall charm and provide a relaxing setting for modern cooking that makes good use of locally-sourced produce. Daily menus may take in pork and black pudding terrine, followed by sea bream with pesto mash, chorizo and saffron shallots, and crème brûlée with raspberry sorbet.

Chef Phil Lowe **Owner** Alan & Liz Hewitt **Times** 12-2.30/6-9.30 Closed 1 Jan, Mon, D Sun **Prices** Fixed L 2 course £17.70, Starter £5.60-£12.95, Main £12.95-£25.95, Dessert £5.60-£8.70, Service optional **Wines** 34 bottles over £20, 16 bottles under £20, 9 by glass **Notes** Sunday L, Vegetarian available **Seats** 66, Pr/dining room 12 **Children** Portions **Parking** 18

STAMFORD — Map 11 TF00

The George of Stamford

Traditional British NOTABLE WINE LIST

Coaching inn popular for its old-fashioned charm and food

☎ 01780 750750
71 St Martins PE9 2LB
e-mail: reservations@georgehotelofstamford.com
dir: From A1(N of Peterborough) turn onto B1081 signed Stamford and Burghley House. Follow road to 1st set of lights, hotel on left

A medieval crypt shows that this venerable old Lincolnshire coaching inn has been a fixture on the Great North road for centuries and is knee-deep in history: spot the signs for London and York above the former waiting rooms used by passengers in the days when real horsepower was the only way to get around. The oak-panelled dining room matches the traditional approach to food founded on local ingredients treated with care and skill. Sticklers for old-school ways will love to see fish boned and roast sirloin of beef carved on trolleys, but modernity is present too: pan-fried scallops with pork belly, apple and juniper purée, for example, then sea bass with a parmesan crust, chargrilled vegetable gâteau and basil pesto.

Chef Chris Pitman, Paul Reseigh **Owner** Lawrence Hoskins **Times** 12.30-2.30/7.30-10.30 **Prices** Fixed L 2 course £20.75, Starter £6.20-£20.65, Main £14.25-£38, Dessert £6.99, Service optional **Wines** 149 bottles over £20, 4 bottles under £20, 18 by glass **Notes** Walk in L menu, Sunday L, Vegetarian available, Dress restrictions, Jacket or tie, No jeans or sportswear, Civ Wed 50 **Seats** 90, Pr/dining room 40 **Children** Portions **Parking** 110

Jim's Yard

European, French

Relaxed approach to classic French style

☎ 01780 756080
3 Ironmonger St PE9 1PL
e-mail: jim@jimsyard.biz

Actually two small stone cottages knocked into one in a hidden courtyard in Stamford, Jim's Yard is a relaxed family-run restaurant serving appealing traditionally-inspired French food with a bit of modern style. While the eponymous downstairs space has a conservatory feel, the upstairs dining room has a loft-house vibe with its brick walls, black-and-white pictures of old Stamford, oak beams and simply laid tables contrasted against the modern lighting and metal stairs. The small team produces consistently good flavour combinations for the daily-changing menu along the lines of sautéed king prawns in thermidor sauce, pan-fried calves' liver with mash, braised red cabbage and smoked bacon sauce.

Chef James Ramsay **Owner** James & Sharon Trevor **Times** 12-2.30/6.30-9.30 Closed 24 Dec 2 wks, last wk Jul-1st wk Aug, Sun-Mon **Prices** Fixed L 2 course £13.50, Starter £4.50-£7.95, Main £12-£16.95, Dessert £5-£6.50, Service optional **Wines** 56 bottles over £20, 28 bottles under £20, 13 by glass **Notes** Vegetarian available **Seats** 55, Pr/dining room 14 **Children** Portions **Parking** Broad St

WINTERINGHAM — Map 17 SE92

Winteringham Fields

Modern British, European NOTABLE WINE LIST

Confident, ambitious cooking in luxurious restaurant with rooms

☎ 01724 733096
1 Silver St DN15 9PF
e-mail: wintfields@aol.com
web: www.winteringhamfields.com
dir: Village centre, off A1077, 4m S of Humber Bridge

Parts of this old manor house may well date back to the 1300s, and much of the rest of it from the 16th century, but today's incarnation has been spruced up beyond the wildest dreams of those distant previous incumbents. The Humber Bridge, visible from the grounds, is a reminder of the region's later heritage. Every inch the luxurious contemporary restaurant with rooms, chef-patron Colin McGurran runs a tight ship here, with attention to detail across the board. The richly coloured restaurant is an opulent space dominated by a stained-glass dome in the ceiling, soft furnishings, and smartly laid tables. There is an emphasis on high quality local produce, much of it grown in the garden, and the modern European cooking is well executed and attractively presented. A starter of ham hock and foie gras terrine comes with a parsley cream and marinated mushrooms, before, perhaps, fillet of sea bass with shellfish ravioli, bouillabaisse and confit orange. Round things off with apple tarte Tatin, salted caramel and tonka bean ice cream.

Chef Colin McGurran **Owner** Colin McGurran **Times** 12-1.30/7-9.30 Closed 2 wks Xmas, last 2 wks Aug, Sun-Mon **Prices** Fixed L 2 course £34.50, Fixed D 3 course fr £75, Service optional **Wines** 200 bottles over £20, 20 by glass **Notes** Menu surprise 7 course £79, Vegetarian available, Dress restrictions, Smart dress preferred **Seats** 60, Pr/dining room 12 **Children** Portions **Parking** 20

WOOLSTHORPE **Map 11 SK83**

The Chequers Inn

Modern British

Gastro-pub dining in the shadow of Belvoir Castle

☎ 01476 870701
Main St NG32 1LU
e-mail: justinnabar@yahoo.co.uk
dir: From A1 exit A607 towards Melton Mowbray follow heritage signs for Belvoir Castle

In its early days, back in the 1700s, The Chequers was a farmhouse supplying bread to the village. The original bread oven survives today in the Bakehouse Restaurant, which is the oldest part of the building. The whole place has been stylishly but sympathetically refurbished, and is full of cosy corners with blazing log fires in winter, while the lovely garden has fantastic views across to Belvoir Castle. Cooking is very much in the gastro-pub style and makes good use of local, seasonal ingredients. Start with pear and Colston Bassett stilton salad, then find someone willing to share the rib of beef with hand-cut chips and pepper sauce, and round things off nicely with chocolate and hazelnut truffle cake.

Chef Mark Nesbit **Owner** Justin & Joanne Chad **Times** 12-3/5.30-11 Closed D 25-26 Dec, 1 Jan **Prices** Fixed L 2 course fr £11.50, Fixed D 3 course fr £16.50, Starter £4.95-£8.50, Main £10-£17.50, Dessert £5.50-£6.50, Service optional **Wines** 33 bottles over £20, 34 bottles under £20, 31 by glass **Notes** Early dining offer all week 6-7pm £7, Sunday L, Vegetarian available, Civ Wed 85 **Seats** 70, Pr/dining room 14 **Children** Portions, Menu **Parking** 35

London

City Bankside

Index of London Restaurants

This index shows rosetted restaurants in London in alphabetical order, followed by their postcodes and map references. Page numbers precede each entry.

London Plan 1
0 1 2 miles
0 1 2 3 kilometres
Central London Congestion Charging Zone (The Western Extension Zone is due to be removed late 2010)
Restaurant
AA Restaurant of the Year
Grim's Dyke Hotel
Friends Restaurant
Hawtrey's Restaurant at the Barn Hotel
Incanto Restaurant
Fringe Restaurant (Hendon Hall Hotel)
Crowne Plaza London - Ealing
Momo
E & O
Lonsdale
The Ledbu
Notting Hill Brasserie
Edera
Belved
Cibo
Timo
Anglesea Arms
Ravenscroft Park
High Road Brasserie
Agni
Le Vacherin
La Trompette
Sagar
Sam's Brasserie & Bar
The Devonshire
The Gate
The River Café
Blue Elephant
Sonny's Restaurant
The Harwood Arms
Saran Ro
Wyndham Gra London Chels Harbo
Enoteca Turi
Talad Thai
The Glasshouse
The Depot
Waterfront Brasserie
Bacco Restaurant Italiano
La Buvette
Bingham
A Cena
Richmond Hill Hotel
Gates on the Park (Richmond Gate Hotel)
The Restaurant at The Petersham
Petersham Nurseries
Sheraton Skyline Hotel
Cannizaro House
The Light House Restaurant
Frère Jacques
The French Table
Harrow Weald
Stanmore
Edgware
HARROW
Harrow on the Hill
Wealdstone
Pinner
Eastcote
Kingsbury
Hendon
Golders Green
North Wembley
WEMBLEY
Neasden
Cricklewood
Willesden
Kilburn
Northolt
Ickenham
Greenford
Perivale
Alperton
Harlesden
EALING
Hanwell
Southall
Hayes
Acton
HAMMERSMITH
FULHAM
Brentford
KEW GARDENS
Barnes
Putney
Roehampton
HOUNSLOW
Isleworth
RICHMOND
Twickenham
RICHMOND PARK
WIMBLEDON COMMON
WIMBLEDON
HEATHROW AIRPORT
Feltham
Teddington
Hampton
BUSHY PARK
KINGSTON UPON THAMES
New Malden
Morden
Ashford
Shepperton
A B C D
1 2 3 4 5 6

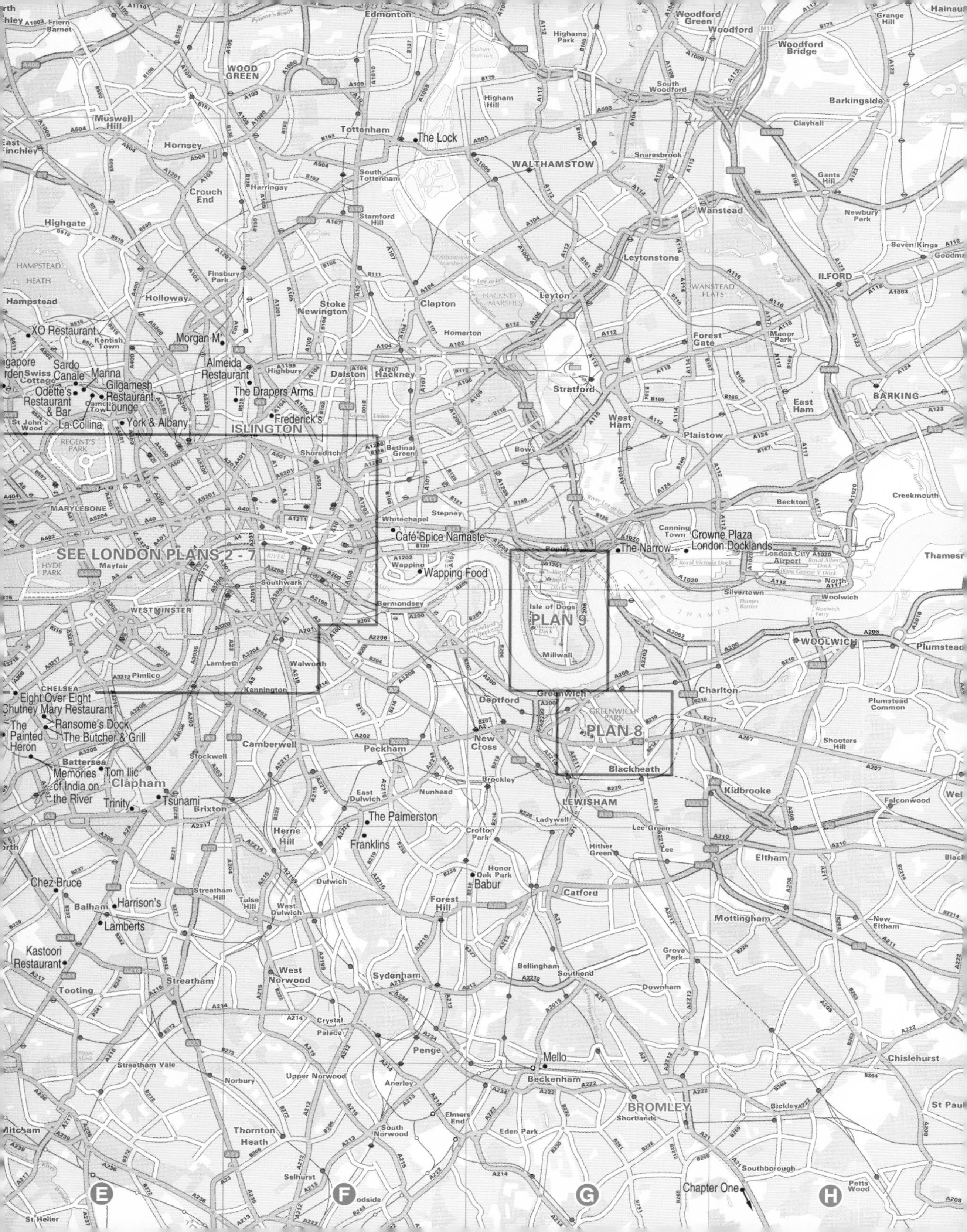

Edmonton
Friern Barnet
Woodford Green
Woodford
Woodford Bridge
Grange Hill
Hainault
Highams Park
WOOD GREEN
Higham Hill
South Woodford
Barkingside
Clayhall
Muswell Hill
Tottenham
The Lock
East Finchley
Hornsey
WALTHAMSTOW
Snaresbrook
Gants Hill
Harringay
South Tottenham
Crouch End
Stamford Hill
Wanstead
Newbury Park
Highgate
HAMPSTEAD HEATH
Leytonstone
Seven Kings
Goodmayes
ILFORD
Finsbury Park
Hampstead
Holloway
Stoke Newington
Clapton
HACKNEY MARSHES
Leyton
WANSTEAD FLATS
XO Restaurant
Kentish Town
Morgan M
Homerton
Forest Gate
Manor Park
Sardo Canale
Swiss Cottage
Manna
Almeida Restaurant
Highbury
Dalston
Hackney
Stratford
Odette's Restaurant & Bar
Gilgamesh Restaurant Lounge
The Drapers Arms
East Ham
BARKING
St John's Wood
La Collina
York & Albany
Frederick's
ISLINGTON
West Ham
Plaistow
REGENT'S PARK
Shoreditch
Bethnal Green
Bow
MARYLEBONE
Stepney
Beckton
Creekmouth
Whitechapel
Café Spice Namasté
Canning Town
Crowne Plaza London Docklands
SEE LONDON PLANS 2 - 7
Poplar
The Narrow
HYDE PARK
Mayfair
Wapping
Wapping Food
London City Airport
Royal Victoria Dock
Royal Albert Dock
King George V Dock
North Woolwich
Thamesmead
Southwark
Silvertown
Thames Barrier
Woolwich
Woolwich Ferry
WESTMINSTER
Bermondsey
Isle of Dogs
PLAN 9
RIVER THAMES
WOOLWICH
Plumstead
Lambeth
Walworth
Millwall
Pimlico
CHELSEA
Kennington
Greenwich
Charlton
Eight Over Eight
Chutney Mary Restaurant
Deptford
GREENWICH PARK
Plumstead Common
The Painted Heron
Ransome's Dock
The Butcher & Grill
Camberwell
Peckham
New Cross
PLAN 8
Shooters Hill
Battersea
Memories of India on the River
Tom Ilic
Clapham
Stockwell
Blackheath
Brockley
Kidbrooke
Trinity
Tsunami
Brixton
East Dulwich
Nunhead
LEWISHAM
Falconwood
The Palmerston
Ladywell
Crofton Park
Herne Hill
Franklins
Lee Green
Lee
Hither Green
Eltham
Chez Bruce
Honor Oak Park
Babur
Dulwich
Balham
Harrison's
Streatham Hill
Tulse Hill
West Dulwich
Forest Hill
Catford
Mottingham
New Eltham
Lamberts
Kastoori Restaurant
Grove Park
West Norwood
Sydenham
Bellingham
Southend
Streatham
Tooting
Downham
Crystal Palace
Penge
Mello
Chislehurst
Streatham Vale
Upper Norwood
Norbury
Beckenham
Anerley
BROMLEY
Shortlands
Bickley
St Paul's
Mitcham
Elmers End
Eden Park
Thornton Heath
South Norwood
Southborough
Selhurst
Chapter One
Petts Wood
St Helier
E
F
G
H

London Plan 2
0
220
440 yards
0
100
200
300
400 metres
Maida Vale
Paddington Recreation Ground
Osteria Stecca
Kilburn Park Station
Maida Vale Station
Middlesex CCC (Lord's Cricket Ground)
Lord's Tour & MCC Museum
The Warrington
BBC Studios
Westbourne Green
Warwick Avenue Station
Little Venice
Westbourne Park Station
Western Extension zone due to be removed late 2010
Royal Oak Station
PADDINGTON
Paddington Basin
Paddington Station
St Marys Hospital
Urban Turban
Le Café Anglais
Assaggi
Bayswater
Bayswater Stn
Queensway Station
Notting Hill Gate Stn
Angelus
Island Restaurant & Bar
Nipa
Lancaster Gate Station
Kensington Place
Kensington Gardens
MAIDA VALE
HARROW ROAD
WESTWAY
BAYSWATER ROAD
NOTTING HL GATE
WESTBOURNE GROVE
QUEENSWAY
EDGWARE ROAD
ST JOHN'S WOOD ROAD
KILBURN PARK ROAD
SHIRLAND ROAD
BISHOP'S BRIDGE ROAD
EASTBOURNE TERRACE
PRAED
PEMBRIDGE VILLAS
CHEPSTOW ROAD
LADBROKE GROVE
KENSINGTON PARK ROAD
A
B
C
D
1
2
3
4
5
6

Congestion Charging Zone boundary
(The Western Extension zone is due to be removed late 2010)
Restaurant
AA Restaurant of the Year
Regent's Park
MARYLEBONE
Lisson Grove
Mayfair
Hyde Park
Queen Mary's Garden
Boating Lake
London Central Mosque
London Business School
Royal Academy of Music
Madame Tussaud's & The London Auditorium
Marylebone Station
Baker Street Stn
Regent's Park Stn
Great Portland St Stn
Warren Street Stn
Oxford Circus Station
Bond Street Stn
Marble Arch Station
Speakers Corner
MARYLEBONE ROAD
EDGWARE ROAD
OXFORD ST
BAKER ST
GLOUCESTER PLACE
PORTLAND PL
REGENT STREET
PICCADILLY
PARK LA
WIGMORE STREET
HAMPSTEAD ROAD
EUSTON RD
TOTTENHAM CT RD
Winter Garden (The Landmark)
Dinings
Park Plaza Sherlock Holmes
Orrery
The Landau
Iberica Food & Culture
Archipelago
Vanilla
Villandry
The Providores and Tapa Room
Galvin Bistrot de Luxe
Canteen Baker Street
Trishna
L'Autre Pied
Yumi Restaurant
deVille (Mandeville Hotel)
Levant
Locanda Locatelli
Texture Restaurant at Best Western Mostyn Hotel
Rhodes W1
Rhodes W1 Brasserie and Bar
Taman Gang
Bar Trattoria Semplice
Ristorante Semplice
Maze Grill
Maze
La Petite Maison
Gordon Ramsay at Claridge's
Mews of Mayfair
Umu
Bellamy's
C London
Avista (Millennium Hotel Mayfair)
Le Gavroche Restaurant
Corrigan's Mayfair
Scott's
Hélène Darroze at The Connaught
Benares
Kai Mayfair
The Only Running Footman
Butler's
The Greenhouse
Alain Ducasse, China Tang & The Grill (Dorchester Hotel)
Tamarind
Murano
Ozer
Eastcastle
Vasco & Piero's Pavilion Restaurant
Aqua Kyoto
Sketch (Lecture Room & Library)
The Gallery
Goodman
Hibiscus
Patterson's
Wild Honey
Via Condotti
La Trouvaille
Dehesa
Andrew Edmunds
Polpo
Artisan (The Westbury Hotel)
Nicole's
Embassy London
Sartoria
The Square
Sumosan
Time & Space
Cecconi's
Veeraswamy Restaurant
The Albemarle (Brown's Hotel)
Alloro
Dolada
Bentley's Oyster Bar & Grill
Nobu Berkeley Street
Brasserie St Jacques
The Wolseley
The Ritz London Restaurant
Le Caprice
Aslan
Al Duca
Petrichor at The Cavendish
Quaglino's
Sake No Hana
Just St James
Fino
Roka
Rasa Samudra
Latium
Salt Yard
Yauatcha
Hix
So Restaurant
Cococo
Ampthill Estate
Euston Centre
University Coll Hosp
Royal Academy of Arts
Emb of USA

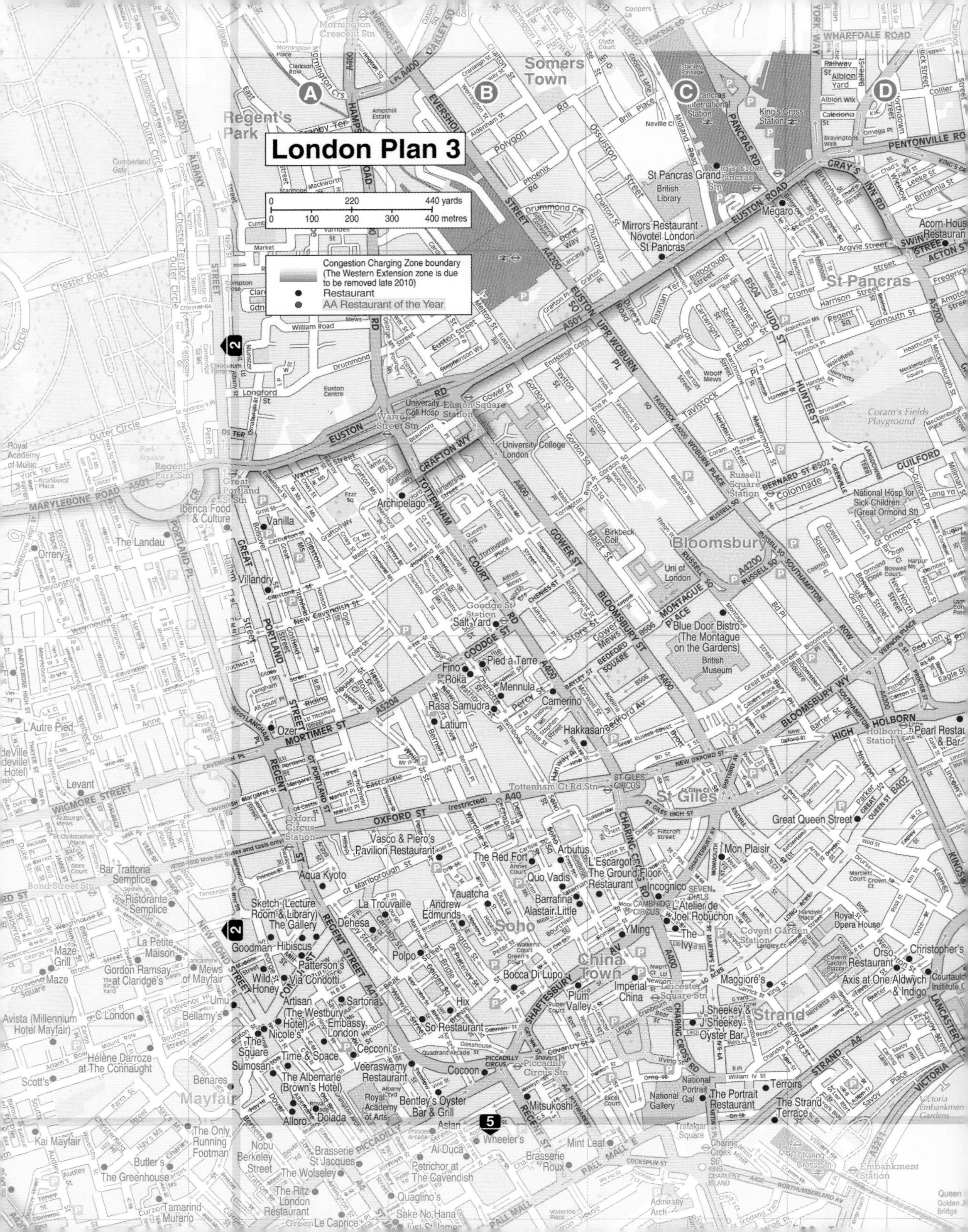
London Plan 3
0 220 440 yards
0 100 200 300 400 metres
Congestion Charging Zone boundary (The Western Extension zone is due to be removed late 2010)
Restaurant
AA Restaurant of the Year
Somers Town
Regent's Park
St Pancras
Bloomsbury
St Giles
Soho
China Town
Strand
Mayfair
St Pancras Grand
Megaro
Mirrors Restaurant - Novotel London St Pancras
Acorn House Restaurant
Archipelago
Iberica Food & Culture
Vanilla
The Landau
Orrery
Villandry
Salt Yard
Fino
Roka
Pied à Terre
Mennula
Camerino
Rasa Samudra
Latium
Blue Door Bistro (The Montague on the Gardens)
Hakkasan
L'Autre Pied
Ozer
Levant
Pearl Restaurant & Bar
Great Queen Street
Vasco & Piero's Pavilion Restaurant
The Red Fort
Arbutus
L'Escargot The Ground Floor Restaurant
Mon Plaisir
Quo Vadis
Incognico
Bar Trattoria Semplice
Aqua Kyoto
Yauatcha
Barrafina
Alastair Little
L'Atelier de Joel Robuchon
Ristorante Semplice
Sketch (Lecture Room & Library)
The Gallery
La Trouvaille
Dehesa
Andrew Edmunds
Yming
The Ivy
Royal Opera House
Goodman
Hibiscus
Maze Grill
La Petite Maison
Polpo
Christopher's
Orso Restaurant
Maze
Gordon Ramsay at Claridge's
Mews of Mayfair
Patterson's
Wild Honey
Via Condotti
Bocca Di Lupo
Plum Valley
Imperial China
Maggiore's
Axis at One Aldwych
& Indigo
Umu
Artisan (The Westbury Hotel)
Sartoria
Avista (Millennium Hotel Mayfair)
C London
Bellamy's
Embassy London
Hix
So Restaurant
J Sheekey
J Sheekey Oyster Bar
The Square
Nicole's
Cecconi's
Hélène Darroze at The Connaught
Sumosan
Time & Space
Veeraswamy Restaurant
Cocoon
Scott's
Benares
The Albemarle (Brown's Hotel)
Bentley's Oyster Bar & Grill
Mitsukoshi
The Portrait Restaurant
Terroirs
The Strand Terrace
Alloro
Dolada
Aslan
Wheeler's
Mint Leaf
Kai Mayfair
The Only Running Footman
Nobu Berkeley Street
Brasserie St Jacques
Al Duca
Petrichor at The Cavendish
Brasserie Roux
Butler's
The Greenhouse
The Wolseley
The Ritz London Restaurant
Quaglino's
Tamarind
Murano
Le Caprice
Sake No Hana
Just St James
British Library
British Museum
National Gallery
National Portrait Gal
Royal Academy of Arts
Uni of London
University College London
Birkbeck Coll
Coram's Fields Playground
National Hosp for Sick Children (Great Ormond St)
Trafalgar Square
St Pancras International Station
King's Cross Station
Euston Square Station
Warren Street Stn
Great Portland St Stn
Regent's Park Stn
Goodge St Station
Russell Square Station
Tottenham Ct Rd Stn
Holborn Station
Oxford Circus Station
Bond Street Stn
Covent Garden Station
Leicester Square Stn
Piccadilly Circus Stn
Charing Cross Stn
Embankment Station
EUSTON ROAD
MARYLEBONE ROAD
OXFORD ST
REGENT STREET
TOTTENHAM COURT RD
SHAFTESBURY AV
CHARING CROSS RD
PICCADILLY
STRAND
HIGH HOLBORN
NEW BOND STREET
BLOOMSBURY WY
GOWER ST
PORTLAND PL

Pentonville
Angel Station
PENTONVILLE ROAD
CITY ROAD
FINSBURY
Clerkenwell
SHOREDITCH
Hoxton
St Luke's
Fifteen London - The Dining Room
Moorfields Eye Hospital
Old Street Station
Great Eastern Dining Room
Eyre Brothers
Moro
The Ambassador
Mount Pleasant (Postal Sorting Office)
The Modern Pantry
Bistrot Bruno Loubet
The Clerkenwell
Malmaison Charterhouse Square
Le Café du Marche
Eastside Inn
Smiths of Smithfield Top Floor
St John
Hix Oyster & Chop House
The Bleeding Heart
Comptoir Gascon
Club Gascon
Farringdon Station
Barbican Station
The Barbican
Chancery Lane Stn
Gray's Inn
Lincoln's Inn
The Chancery
White Swan Pub & Dining Room
City Thameslink Station
Central Criminal Court
St Bartholomews Hospital
Stock Exchange
St Paul's Station
St Paul's Cathedral
Guildhall
Bank of England (& Mus)
Royal Exchange
Moorgate Stn
Liverpool St Stn
Mehek
1901 Restaurant, Catch, Miyako (ANdAZ London)
Tower 42
Rhodes Twentyfour
Bonds
Prism Brasserie & Bar
Restaurant Sauterelle
Lloyd's
Chamberlains Restaurant
Novelli in the City
Royal Courts of Justice
Lutyens Restaurant
Inns of Court and Chancery
Inner Temple
Temple
12 Temple Place Restaurant (Swissotel Howard, London)
Refettorio and Chinese Cricket Club
Blackfriars Stn (closed until late 2011)
CITY OF LONDON
River Thames
Millennium Bridge
Blackfriars Bridge
Southwark Bridge
London Bridge
Cannon Street Stn
Monument Stn
The Oxo Tower Restaurant
Oxo Tower Wharf
Shakespeare's Globe Exhibition & Theatre
Tate Modern
The London Television Centre
Royal National Theatre
National Film Theatre
RSJ, The Restaurant on the South Bank
Cantina Vinopolis
Roast
Southwark Cath
London Bridge Hospital
Hays Galleria
Custom House
VICTORIA EMB
UPPER THAMES ST
HOLBORN VIAD
NEWGATE ST
LONDON WALL
FARRINGDON RD
CLERKENWELL ROAD
FLEET ST
STRAND
ALDERSGATE ST
MOORGATE
BISHOPSGATE
GRACECHURCH ST
KG WILLIAM ST
SOUTHWARK BRIDGE ROAD

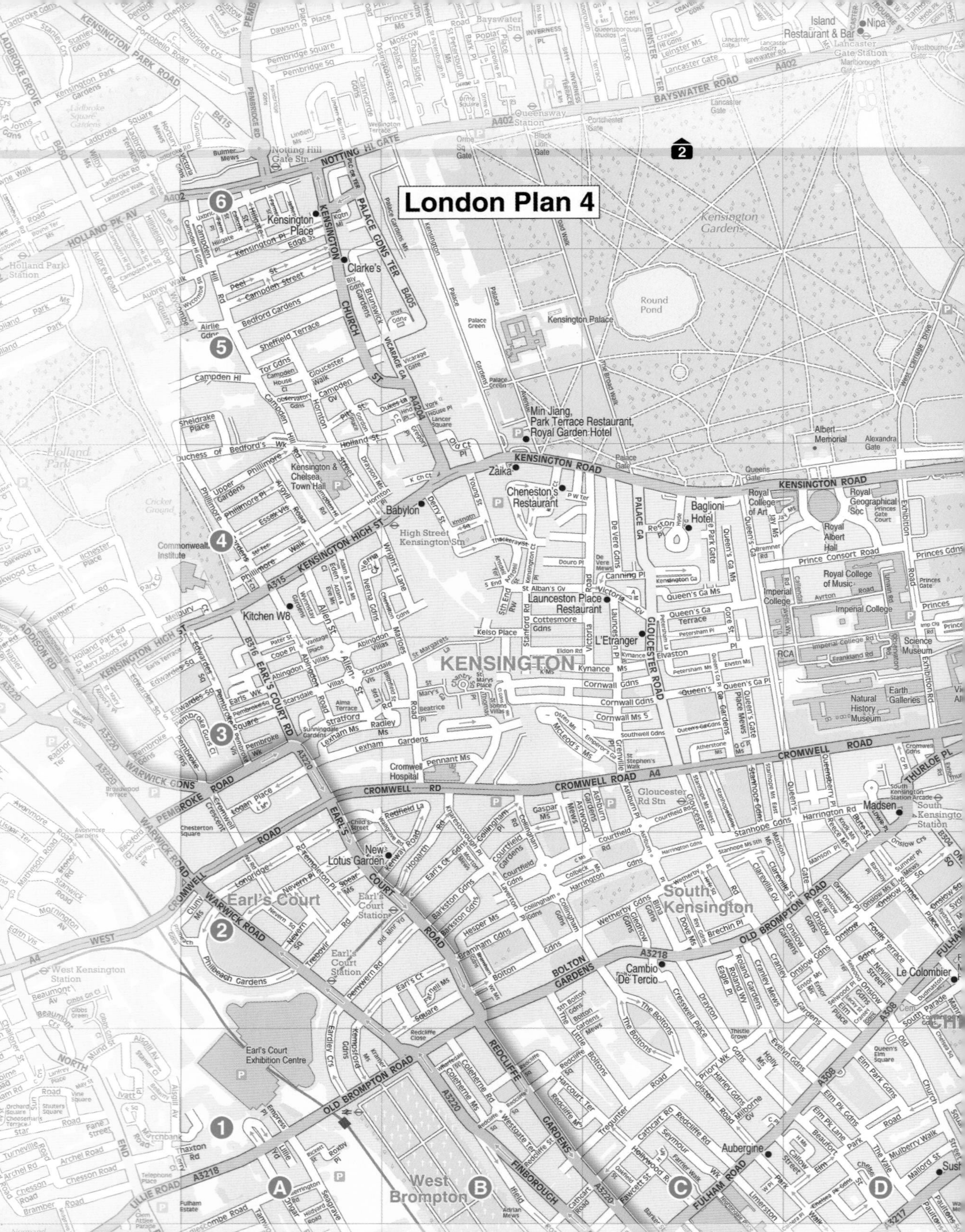
London Plan 4
2
Kensington Gardens
Round Pond
Kensington Palace
Palace Green
The Broad Walk
Albert Memorial
Alexandra Gate
Queens Gate
Palace Gate
Island Restaurant & Bar
Nipa
Lancaster Gate Station
Queensway Station
Bayswater Stn
Notting Hill Gate Stn
Holland Park Station
High Street Kensington Stn
Gloucester Rd Stn
South Kensington Station
Earl's Court Station
West Kensington Station
West Brompton
Kensington Place
Clarke's
Min Jiang, Park Terrace Restaurant, Royal Garden Hotel
Zaika
Cheneston's Restaurant
Babylon
Baglioni Hotel
Kitchen W8
Launceston Place Restaurant
L'Etranger
New Lotus Garden
Madsen
Cambio De Tercio
Le Colombier
Aubergine
KENSINGTON
Earl's Court
South Kensington
Holland Park
Kensington & Chelsea Town Hall
Commonwealth Institute
Royal College of Art
Royal Albert Hall
Royal Geographical Soc
Royal College of Music
Imperial College
Science Museum
Natural History Museum
Earth Galleries
Cromwell Hospital
Earl's Court Exhibition Centre
NOTTING HL GATE
BAYSWATER ROAD
KENSINGTON ROAD
KENSINGTON HIGH ST
KENSINGTON CHURCH ST
CROMWELL ROAD
EARL'S COURT RD
WARWICK ROAD
OLD BROMPTON ROAD
FULHAM ROAD
REDCLIFFE GARDENS
FINBOROUGH
LILLIE ROAD
HOLLAND PK AV
PEMBROKE ROAD
BOLTON GARDENS
1
2
3
4
5
6
A
B
C
D

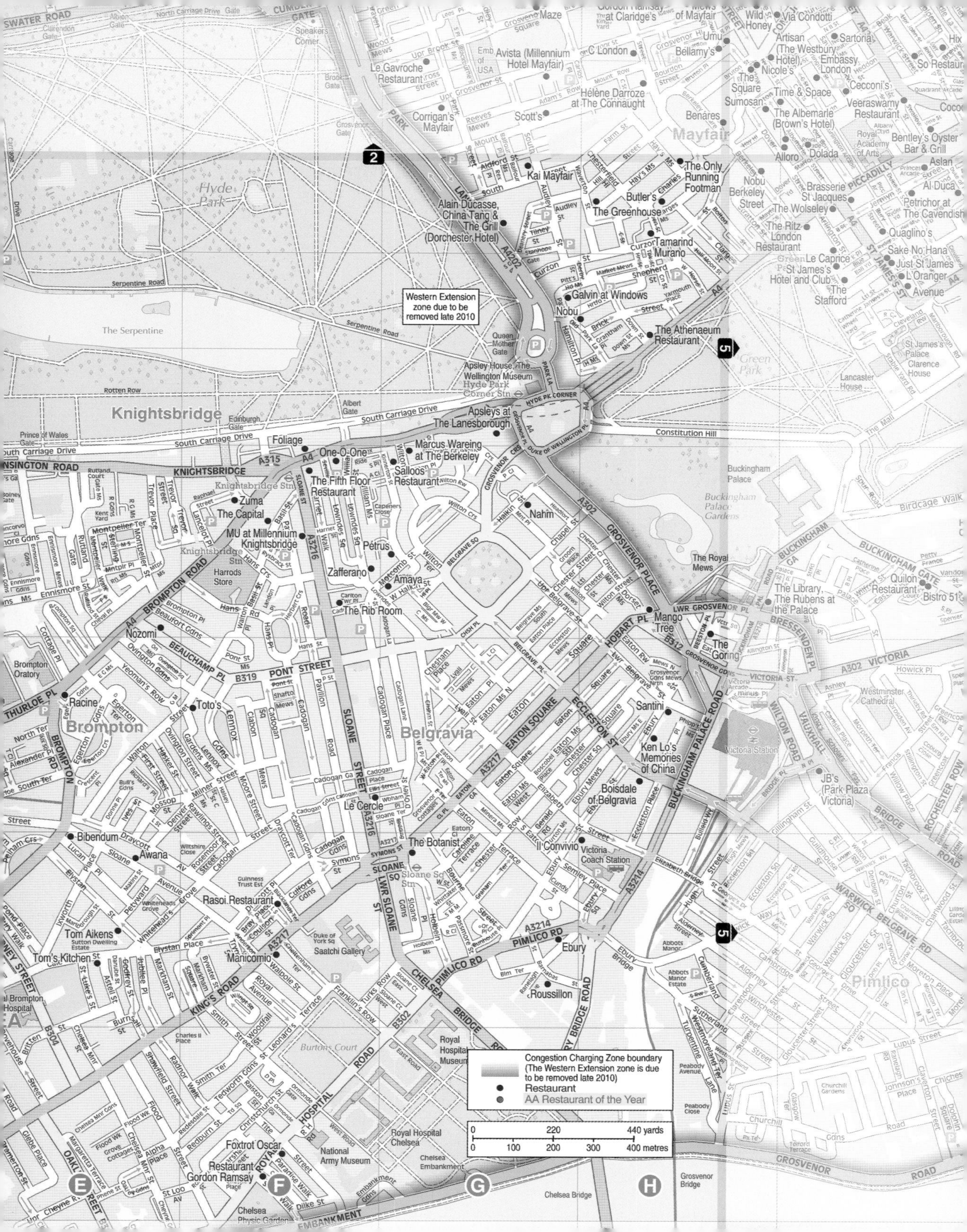

Hyde Park
The Serpentine
Knightsbridge
Mayfair
Belgravia
Brompton
Pimlico
Green Park
Buckingham Palace
Buckingham Palace Gardens
Western Extension zone due to be removed late 2010
Maze
Wild Honey
Via Condotti
Sartoria
Umu
Bellamy's
Artisan (The Westbury Hotel)
Nicole's
Embassy London
The Square
Time & Space
Cecconi's
Sumosan
The Albemarle (Brown's Hotel)
Veeraswamy Restaurant
Benares
Alloro
Dolada
Bentley's Oyster Bar & Grill
Le Gavroche Restaurant
Avista (Millennium Hotel Mayfair)
C London
Hélène Darroze at The Connaught
Corrigan's Mayfair
Scott's
Kai Mayfair
The Only Running Footman
Nobu Berkeley Street
Brasserie St Jacques
Aslan
Al Duca
Petrichor at The Cavendish
The Wolseley
The Ritz London Restaurant
Quaglino's
Sake No Hana
Just St James
L'Oranger
Avenue
Le Caprice
St James's Hotel and Club
The Stafford
Alain Ducasse, China Tang & The Grill (Dorchester Hotel)
Butler's
The Greenhouse
Tamarind
Murano
Galvin at Windows
Nobu
The Athenaeum Restaurant
Apsley House, The Wellington Museum
Hyde Park Corner Stn
Apsleys at The Lanesborough
Foliage
One-O-One
Marcus Wareing at The Berkeley
The Fifth Floor Restaurant
Salloos Restaurant
Zuma
The Capital
MU at Millennium Knightsbridge
Nahm
Pétrus
Zafferano
Amaya
The Rib Room
Harrods Store
Nozomi
Mango Tree
The Goring
The Library, The Rubens at the Palace
Quilon Restaurant
Bistro 51
Racine
Toto's
Santini
Ken Lo's Memories of China
Boisdale of Belgravia
JB's (Park Plaza Victoria)
Victoria Station
Westminster Cathedral
Le Cercle
The Botanist
Il Convivio
Victoria Coach Station
Bibendum
Awana
Rasoi Restaurant
Tom Aikens
Tom's Kitchen
Manicomio
Saatchi Gallery
Ebury
Roussillon
Burtons Court
Royal Hospital Museum
Royal Hospital Chelsea
National Army Museum
Foxtrot Oscar
Restaurant Gordon Ramsay
Chelsea Physic Garden
Chelsea Embankment
Chelsea Bridge
Grosvenor Bridge
KNIGHTSBRIDGE
BROMPTON ROAD
SLOANE STREET
KING'S ROAD
GROSVENOR PLACE
BUCKINGHAM PALACE ROAD
EATON SQUARE
PICCADILLY
PARK LANE
Constitution Hill
The Mall
Birdcage Walk
2
5
5
E
F
G
H
Congestion Charging Zone boundary (The Western Extension zone is due to be removed late 2010)
Restaurant
AA Restaurant of the Year
0 220 440 yards
0 100 200 300 400 metres

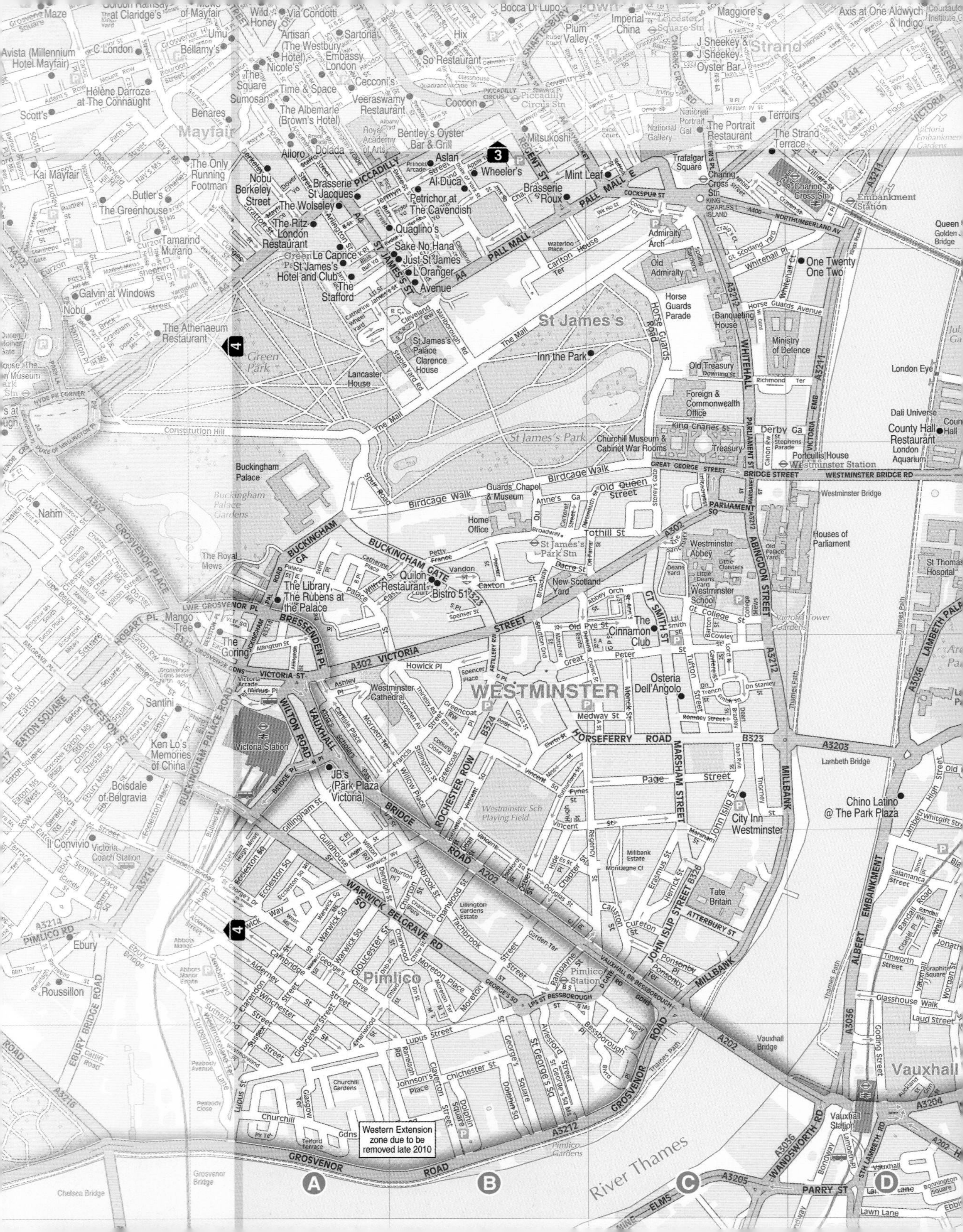
Mayfair
Avista (Millennium Hotel Mayfair)
C London
Hélène Darroze at The Connaught
Scott's
Kai Mayfair
Butler's
The Greenhouse
Tamarind
Murano
Galvin at Windows
Nobu
The Athenaeum Restaurant
Bellamy's
Umu
Benares
The Only Running Footman
Nobu Berkeley Street
The Ritz London Restaurant
The Wolseley
Brasserie St Jacques
Le Caprice
St James's Hotel and Club
The Stafford
Alloro
Dolada
Sumosan
The Square
Nicole's
Artisan (The Westbury Hotel)
Sartoria
Embassy London
Time & Space
Cecconi's
The Albemarle (Brown's Hotel)
Veeraswamy Restaurant
Wild Honey
Via Condotti
Hix
So Restaurant
Cocoon
Bentley's Oyster Bar & Grill
Aslan
Al Duca
Wheeler's
Petrichor at The Cavendish
Quaglino's
Sake No Hana
Just St James
L'Oranger
Avenue
Bocca Di Lupo
Plum Valley
Imperial China
Mitsukoshi
Mint Leaf
Brasserie Roux
Maggiore's
J Sheekey & J Sheekey Oyster Bar
Axis at One Aldwych & Indigo
Terroirs
The Portrait Restaurant
National Portrait Gal
National Gallery
The Strand Terrace
Strand
Trafalgar Square
Charing Cross Stn
Embankment Station
One Twenty One Two
Admiralty Arch
Old Admiralty
Horse Guards Parade
Banqueting House
Ministry of Defence
St James's
Inn the Park
Old Treasury
Foreign & Commonwealth Office
London Eye
Dali Universe
County Hall Restaurant
London Aquarium
Churchill Museum & Cabinet War Rooms
Treasury
Portcullis House
Westminster Station
Westminster Bridge
Houses of Parliament
St James's Palace
Clarence House
Lancaster House
Green Park
St James's Park
Buckingham Palace
Buckingham Palace Gardens
The Royal Mews
Home Office
Guards' Chapel & Museum
St James's Park Stn
New Scotland Yard
Westminster Abbey
Westminster School
Quilon Restaurant
Bistro 51
The Library, The Rubens at the Palace
Mango Tree
The Goring
Nahm
The Cinnamon Club
Osteria Dell'Angolo
WESTMINSTER
Westminster Cathedral
Victoria Station
Victoria Coach Station
Santini
Ken Lo's Memories of China
Boisdale of Belgravia
Il Convivio
JB's (Park Plaza Victoria)
City Inn Westminster
Tate Britain
Chino Latino @ The Park Plaza
Lambeth Bridge
Westminster Sch Playing Field
Pimlico
Pimlico Station
Ebury
Roussillon
Vauxhall Bridge
Vauxhall
Vauxhall Station
River Thames
Pimlico Gardens
Chelsea Bridge
Grosvenor Bridge
Western Extension zone due to be removed late 2010
PICCADILLY
PALL MALL
WHITEHALL
VICTORIA STREET
HORSEFERRY ROAD
MILLBANK
GROSVENOR ROAD
VAUXHALL BRIDGE ROAD
BUCKINGHAM PALACE ROAD
ALBERT EMBANKMENT
3
4
A
B
C
D

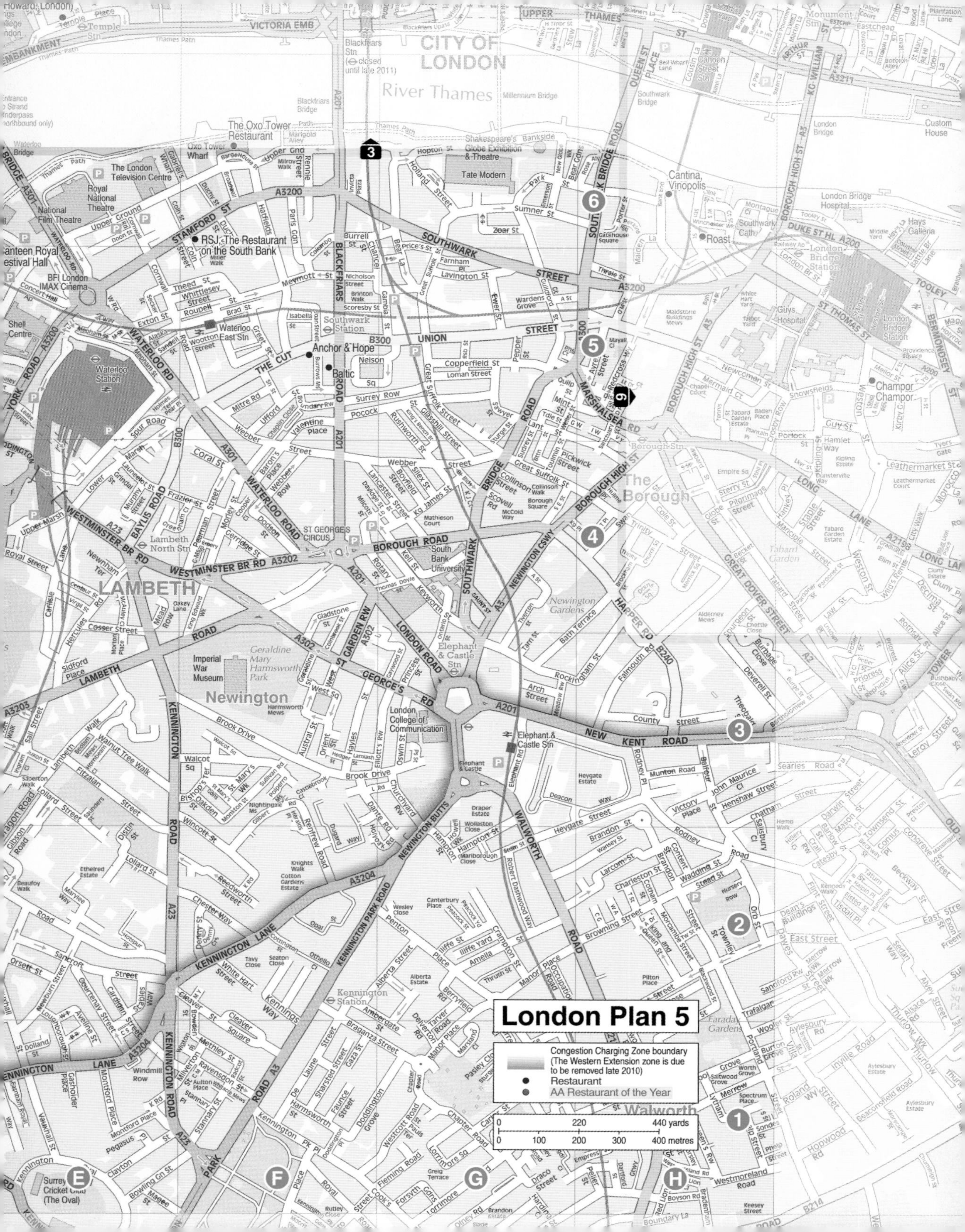

London Plan 5
Congestion Charging Zone boundary (The Western Extension zone is due to be removed late 2010)
Restaurant
AA Restaurant of the Year
0
220
440 yards
0
100
200
300
400 metres
CITY OF LONDON
River Thames
LAMBETH
Newington
The Borough
Walworth
Blackfriars Stn (closed until late 2011)
Blackfriars Bridge
Millennium Bridge
Southwark Bridge
London Bridge
Waterloo Bridge
Waterloo Station
Waterloo East Stn
Southwark Station
Borough Stn
London Bridge Station
Elephant & Castle Stn
Lambeth North Stn
Kennington Station
Cannon Street Stn
Monument Stn
The Oxo Tower Restaurant
Oxo Tower Wharf
The London Television Centre
Royal National Theatre
National Film Theatre
Royal Festival Hall
BFI London IMAX Cinema
Shell Centre
Tate Modern
Shakespeare's Globe Exhibition & Theatre
Cantina Vinopolis
Roast
Southwark Cath
Guys Hospital
London Bridge Hospital
Hays Galleria
Custom House
RSJ, The Restaurant on the South Bank
Anchor & Hope
Baltic
Champor Champor
South Bank University
London College of Communication
Imperial War Museum
Geraldine Mary Harmsworth Park
Newington Gardens
Tabard Garden
Faraday Gardens
Surrey Cricket Club (The Oval)
ST GEORGE'S CIRCUS
VICTORIA EMB
UPPER THAMES ST
STAMFORD ST
SOUTHWARK STREET
UNION STREET
THE CUT
BLACKFRIARS ROAD
WATERLOO ROAD
BOROUGH ROAD
BOROUGH HIGH ST
MARSHALSEA RD
SOUTHWARK BRIDGE ROAD
WESTMINSTER BR RD
NEWINGTON CSWY
LONDON ROAD
ST GEORGE'S RD
NEW KENT ROAD
GREAT DOVER STREET
LONG LANE
TOOLEY ST
WALWORTH ROAD
KENNINGTON ROAD
KENNINGTON LANE
KENNINGTON PARK ROAD
NEWINGTON BUTTS
LAMBETH ROAD
BAYLIS ROAD
YORK ROAD
TOWER BRIDGE ROAD

London Plan 6
St Luke's
SPITALFIELDS
CITY OF LONDON
River Thames
The Borough
Eyre Brothers
Les Trois Garçons
The Modern Pantry
Bistrot Bruno Loubet
The Clerkenwell
Malmaison Charterhouse Square
Le Café du Marche
Eastside Inn
Smiths of Smithfield Top Floor
St John
Hix Oyster & Chop House
Comptoir Gascon
Club Gascon
L'Anima
Galvin La Chapelle
The Luxe
St John Bread & Wine
Marco Pierre White Steak & Alehouse
Boisdale of Bishopsgate
1901 Restaurant, Catch, Miyako (ANdAZ London)
Cinnamon Kitchen
Mehek
Whitechapel Gallery Dining Room
Rhodes Twentyfour
Tower 42
Bonds
Prism Brasserie & Bar
Royal Exchange
Restaurant Sauterelle
Chamberlains Restaurant
Novelli in the City
Addendum
Cantina Vinopolis
Roast
Magdalen
Champor Champor
Le Pont de la Tour
Cantina del Ponte
Anchor & Hope
Baltic
The Barbican
Guildhall
Bank of England (& Mus)
St Paul's Cathedral
Liverpool Street Station
Tower of London
Tate Modern
Shakespeare's Globe Exhibition & Theatre
London Bridge Station
Guys Hospital
London Bridge Hospital
HMS Belfast
Hays Galleria
Greater London Authority Headquarters (City Hall)
Custom House
Tower Bridge
St Katharine Docks
Blackfriars Stn (closed until late 2011)
Millennium Bridge
Southwark Bridge
London Bridge
Tabard Garden
Newington Gardens
London Wall
Moorgate
Bishopsgate
Gracechurch St
Fenchurch Street
Leadenhall Street
Cornhill
Cannon Street
Upper Thames St
Lwr Thames St
Tower Hill
Borough High St
Southwark Bridge Road
Southwark Street
Tooley Street
Long Lane
Great Dover Street
Commercial Street
Aldersgate St
Newgate St
Holborn Viad
Farringdon Rd
New Bridge Street
Blackfriars Road
Borough Road
Congestion Charging Zone boundary (The Western Extension zone is due to be removed late 2010)
Restaurant
AA Restaurant of the Year
0
220
440 yards
0
100
200
300
400 metres

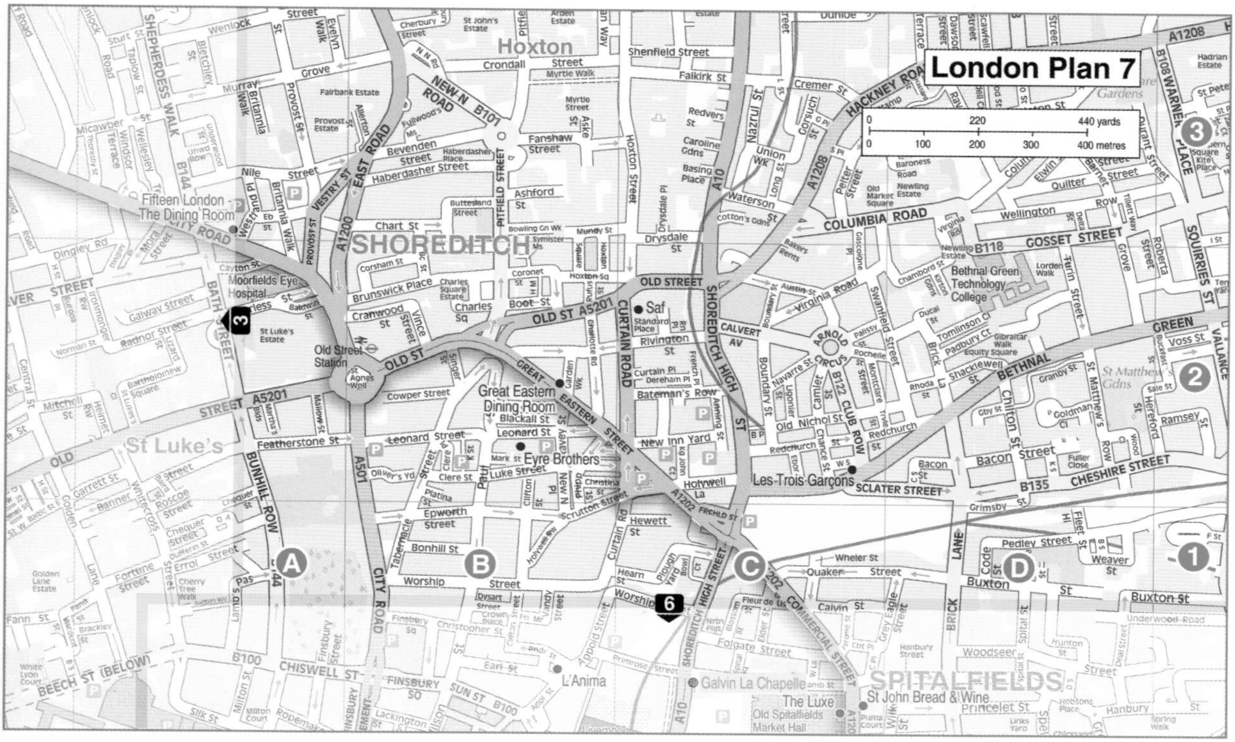
London Plan 7
0 220 440 yards
0 100 200 300 400 metres
Hoxton
SHOREDITCH
St Luke's
SPITALFIELDS
Fifteen London - The Dining Room
Moorfields Eye Hospital
Old Street Station
Great Eastern Dining Room
Eyre Brothers
Saf
Les Trois Garçons
L'Anima
Galvin La Chapelle
The Luxe
St John Bread & Wine
Old Spitalfields Market Hall
Bethnal Green Technology College
OLD ST A5201
CITY ROAD
EAST ROAD
NEW N ROAD B101
GREAT EASTERN STREET
CURTAIN ROAD
SHOREDITCH HIGH ST
HACKNEY ROAD A1208
COLUMBIA ROAD
GOSSET STREET
BETHNAL GREEN
CHESHIRE STREET
SCLATER STREET
COMMERCIAL STREET
BUNHILL ROW
CHISWELL ST
BEECH ST (BELOW)
BRICK LANE
OLD ST
SHEPHERDESS WALK
ARNOLD CIRCUS
A B C D
1 2 3
3 6

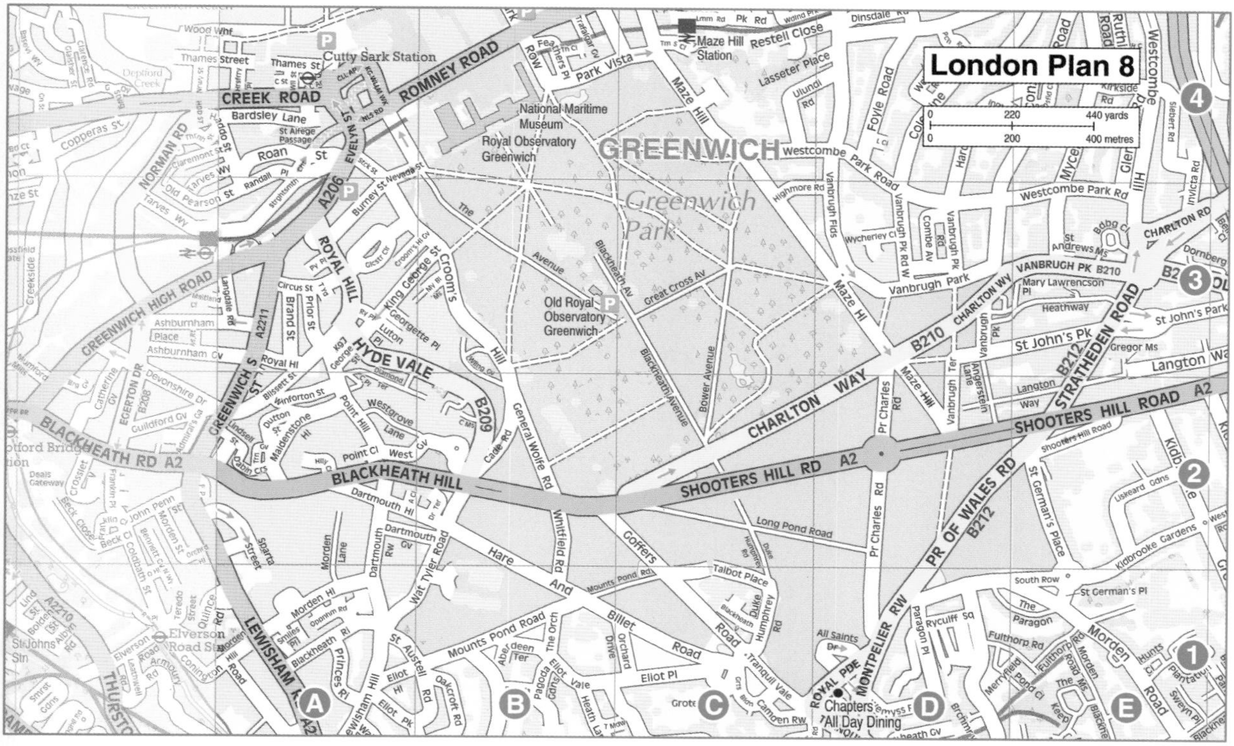
London Plan 8
0 220 440 yards
0 200 400 metres
GREENWICH
Greenwich Park
Cutty Sark Station
Maze Hill Station
National Maritime Museum
Royal Observatory Greenwich
Old Royal Observatory Greenwich
Chapters All Day Dining
Elverson Road Stn
CREEK ROAD
ROMNEY ROAD
GREENWICH HIGH ROAD
ROYAL HILL
HYDE VALE
BLACKHEATH HILL
BLACKHEATH RD A2
SHOOTERS HILL RD A2
SHOOTERS HILL ROAD A2
CHARLTON WAY
PR OF WALES RD B212
STRATHEDEN ROAD
LEWISHAM
Maze Hill
Westcombe Park Road
Vanbrugh Park
Hare And Billet Road
Montpelier Rw
Royal Pde
A B C D E
1 2 3 4

London Plan 9
POPLAR
Canary Wharf
Millwall
Cubitt Town
ISLE OF DOGS
River Thames
DEPTFORD
West India Docks
Millwall Docks
Mudchute Park
Millwall Park
Island Gardens
Greenwich Reach
Limehouse Reach
Surrey Docks
Poplar Dock
Blackwall Basin
Museum in Docklands
Four Seasons Hotel Canary Wharf
Royal China
Plateau
The Gun
HSBC Tower
Citygroup Tower
Billingsgate Fish Market
Guardian Newspapers
London Arena
Daily Telegraph
Mudchute City Farm
Community Centre (Island History Trust)
Millennium Harbour
West India Quay Station
Canary Wharf Station
Heron Quays Station
South Quay Station
Crossharbour Station
Mudchute Station
Island Gardens Station
Poplar Station
Blackwall Station
Westferry Stn
WESTFERRY ROAD
MANCHESTER ROAD
PRESTON'S ROAD
ASPEN WAY
A1261
A1206
Marsh Wall
East Ferry Road
Limeharbour
Greenwich Foot Tunnel
EVELYN STREET
GROVE STREET
SALTER ROAD
0 220 440 yards
0 100 200 300 400 metres
1
2
3
4
5
6
A
B
C
D

LONDON

Greater London Plans 1-9, pages 218-230. (Small scale maps 6 & 7 at back of Guide.) Restaurants are listed below in postal district order, commencing East, then North, South and West, with a brief indication of the area covered. Detailed plans 2-9 show the locations of restaurants with AA Rosette Awards within the Central London postal districts. If you do not know the postal district of the restaurant you want, please refer to the index preceding the street plans for the entry and map pages. The plan reference for each restaurant also appears within its directory entry.

LONDON E1

Café Spice Namasté — PLAN 1 F4

Indian

Pan-Asian food in East London

☎ 020 7488 9242
16 Prescot St E1 8AZ
e-mail: binay@cafespice.co.uk
dir: Nearest station: Tower Gateway (DLR), Aldgate, Tower Hill. Walking distance from Tower Hill

Housed in a former magistrates' court, Parsee murals, hot colours and swags of fabric bring a vivid vibrancy to the place. Mumbai-born Cyrus Todiwala's restaurant deals in regional Indian food (with the occasional influence from elsewhere in Asia) and a good dose of Hindi charm (namasté means gracious hello). As well as an extensive à la carte, there's also a new tasting menu and weekly specialities mean there's plenty of choice. Dishes feature less commonly seen meats and name check great British produce. Start with game samosa followed by ostrich bhuna or guinea fowl til tinka (rolled in sesame seeds and roasted), or roasted collar of Gloucestershire Old Spot vindaloo. Next door, the Ginger Garden offers beer and nibbles.

Chef Cyrus Todiwala, Angelo Collaco **Owner** Cyrus & Pervin Todiwala **Times** 12-3/6.15-10.30 Closed Xmas, BHs, Sun, L Sat **Prices** Fixed L 2 course £22-£30, Fixed D 3 course £25-£35, Starter £5.25-£7.75, Main £13.75-£18.25, Dessert £3.50-£6.75, Service added but optional 12.5% **Wines** 20 bottles over £20, 20 bottles under £20, 10 by glass **Notes** Tasting menu available, Vegetarian available, Dress restrictions, Smart casual **Seats** 120 **Children** Portions **Parking** On street; NCP

Galvin La Chapelle — PLAN 6 C6

– *see below*

The Luxe — PLAN 6 D6

Modern British NEW

All-day dining in contemporary surroundings

☎ 020 7101 1751
109 Commercial St E1 6BG
dir: Nearest station: Liverpool Street

Part of the Spitalfields Market regeneration project, The Luxe is a series of different venues within a refurbished building leading directly onto the market. It retains many of its striking design features - wooden floors, steel girders, exposed brick and large windows. From an open kitchen quality ingredients are skilfully prepared and delivered to bare, well-spaced tables in the informal first-floor dining room. Expect seasonally-changing modern British dishes, perhaps a creamy, well-made green pea and fresh mint risotto, followed by a full-flavoured neck of lamb stew with pearl barley, red cabbage and green sauce, with apple and cinnamon crumble for pudding. There's an excellent café, flower shop, an upstairs private dining room, and evening live music in the basement.

Times 12-3/6-11

Galvin La Chapelle

LONDON RESTAURANT OF THE YEAR

LONDON E1 — PLAN 6 C6

French NEW

Another gem from the brothers Galvin

☎ 020 7299 0400 & 7299 0404
35 Spital Square E1 6DY
e-mail: info@galvinrestaurants.com
dir: Nearest station: Liverpool Street. Close to Old Spitalfields Market

There's a chap wearing a bowler hat to usher you through the door at La Chapelle. This is another hit from the Galvin brothers that is moving them ever closer to the top of the charts - the chart of leading British restaurateurs that is. As a sister to Galvin at Windows and Galvin Bistrot de Luxe (see entries), the Spitalfields restaurant has made an immediate splash and is a must-visit venue on the London dining scene. The former Victorian school hall has scrubbed up extremely nicely and might well take your breath away for a moment or two: there are marble-clad pillars soaring up to the vaulted ceiling, a mezzanine area called The Gallery, swagged curtains, and tables dressed to thrill. It's all very glamorous. The cooking is in the Galvin mould, that is to say it has a decidedly French inflection, but if you're feeling patriotic you can take shelter under the modern British umbrella. Lasagne of Dorset crab with a velouté of chanterelles shows great technical dexterity and an eye for richly appealing flavour combinations. Next up, suprême of Landaise chicken has fantastic flavour, or go for saddle of Denham Estate venison with braised red cabbage, chestnut purée and blackcurrant sauce. The produce is second to none, the cooking on the money, and for dessert, tarte Tatin with crème fraîche or a millefeuille of Yorkshire rhubarb served with a rhubarb sorbet will wind things up nicely until the next time.

Chef Chris & Jeff Galvin **Owner** Chris Galvin, Jeff Galvin, Ken Sanker **Times** 12-2.30/6-11 Closed Xmas, New Year, 25-26 Dec, 1 Jan **Prices** Fixed L 3 course £24.50, Starter £7.50-£14.50, Main £15.50-£28.50, Dessert £8-£10.50, Service added but optional 12.5% **Wines** 10 bottles under £20, 45 by glass **Notes** Sunday L, Vegetarian available **Seats** 110, Pr/dining room 12 **Children** Portions **Parking** On street, NCP

LONDON E1 *continued*

Marco Pierre White Steak & Alehouse PLAN 6 C5

Modern European

Quality City steakhouse in light, modern surroundings

020 7247 5050
East India House, 109-117 Middlesex St E1 7JF
e-mail: info@mpwsteakhouseandgrill.com
dir: Nearest station: Liverpool Street

This collaboration between the eponymous celebrity chef and James Robertson, who started up the venue in its previous life as Lanes Restaurant & Bar, aims squarely at red-blooded carnivorous city slickers. Shielded from the frenzy of Bishopsgate and Liverpool Station in a cool-looking cavernous basement, diners are greeted by a well-lit, stylish modern space done out with classy, cream leather seats, crisp white linen, art deco style mirrors and clocks displaying times across the world's time zones. Top-grade Aberdeen Angus steaks are the stars of the show here: fillet, sirloin, rib-eye or a stonking 16-ounce T-bone, cooked on the grill and served simply with béarnaise sauce and crispy onion rings. If you're not tempted by the hot steak action, true-Brit comfort food along the lines of haddock and chips with mushy peas or a double Barnsley lamb chop should appeal.

Times 12-3/5.30-10 Closed BHs, 25 Dec, 1 Jan, Sun, L Sat

St John Bread & Wine PLAN 6 D6

British

Unpretentious all-day restaurant, bakery and wine shop in Spitalfields

020 7251 0848
94-96 Commercial St E1 6LZ
e-mail: reservations@stjohnbreadandwine.com
dir: Nearest station: Liverpool Street/Aldgate East.

Where else can you get duck hearts, watercress and pickled walnuts these days? Or squirrel and turnips for that matter. Tucked away behind old Spitalfields Market, it perhaps comes as no surprise to learn that it owes the inspiration for such visceral dishes to its elder sibling, St John (see entry), the champion of 'nose-to-tail' eating. It's a simple, canteen-like place, serving trademark British peasant food driven by flavour and simplicity; dishes are timed to appear fresh from the kitchen at certain times of day, so there's no need to follow three-course convention. Take lunch: at 12pm, you might go for hare and kale, blood cake and duck egg; at 1pm the choices might include pigeon and black cabbage. The clue is in the name, but wine and the superb breads - baked in house, of course - are available to take out.

Chef James Lowe **Owner** Trevor Gulliver & Fergus Henderson **Times** 9am-11pm Closed 25 Dec-1 Jan, BHs **Prices** Starter £5.30-£8, Main £9.80-£20, Dessert £5.60-£7, Service optional, Groups min 6 service 12.5% **Wines** 31 bottles over £20, 15 bottles under £20, 25 by glass **Notes** Sunday L, Vegetarian available **Seats** 60 **Parking** on street

Les Trois Garçons PLAN 7 C2

French

Eye-catching, lively French restaurant

020 7613 1924
1 Club Row E1 6JX
e-mail: info@lestroisgarcons.com
dir: Nearest station: Liverpool Street. From station, head along Bishop's Gate towards Shoreditch High St. Turn right after bridge onto Bethnal Green Rd. Restaurant on left

Les Trois Garçons might look like an old-school French bistro, at least until you've crossed the threshold. Those are indeed vintage handbags hanging from the ceiling along with a full-sized stuffed tiger replete with tiara, and a hippo's head on the wall. It may look like a veritable wonderland of the curious and the Baroque, but at its heart is a fine French restaurant. Staff look like fashion models, but they know their stuff. A cocktail seems like a fine place to start in such a place, and they're very good, before tucking into the authentic cooking. From the bilingual menu, there might be fricassée of snails bursting with the flavours of garlic and chilli, followed by seared Gressingham duck breast alongside its slow-cooked leg, served with pickled cucumber, pied bleu mushrooms and a redcurrant orange jus.

Chef Michael Chan, Nathaniel Hancock **Owner** Stefan Karlson, Hussan Abdullah, Michel Lasserre **Times** 7-12 Closed Xmas & New Year, BH Mon, Sun, L all week **Prices** Tasting menu fr £62, Service added but optional 12.5% **Wines** 140 bottles over £20, 13 by glass **Notes** Fixed ALC £39.50-£45.50, tasting menu avail, Vegetarian available, Dress restrictions, Smart casual, no shorts **Seats** 70, Pr/dining room 10 **Children** Portions **Parking** On street

Wapping Food PLAN 1 F4

Modern International

Robust rustic cooking in unique urban setting

020 7680 2080
Wapping Hydraulic, Power Station, Wapping Wall E1W 3SG
dir: Nearest station: Shadwell DLR. Between Wapping Wall & King Edward VII Memorial Park, parallel to the river

A former hydraulic pumping station in London's East End must rank among the most unusual settings in which to eat. In fact, the restaurant and art gallery, which is part of the Wapping Project, is a chic (though most certainly urban) dining space, where you are surrounded by old machinery, tiles and girders, perfectly complemented by dangling chandeliers, designer furniture and flickering candles. The food lives up to the unique setting with a menu of seasonal European dishes conjured from high-quality ingredients. Starters such as ham hock and foie gras terrine with piccalilli precede robust main courses like calves' liver with baked polenta, spring greens and onion jam.

Chef Cameron Emirali **Owner** Womens Playhouse Trust **Times** 12-3/6.30-11 Closed 24 Dec-3 Jan, BHs, D Sun **Prices** Fixed L 3 course £35-£49.50, Fixed D 3 course £35-£49.50, Starter £6.50-£12.50, Main £13.50-£20, Dessert £6-£9.25, Service added but optional 12.5% **Wines** 100 bottles over £20, 6 bottles under £20, 24 by glass **Notes** Brunch at wknds, Sunday L, Vegetarian available **Seats** 150 **Children** Portions **Parking** 20

Whitechapel Gallery Dining Room PLAN 6 D5

Modern British **NEW**

Confident ethically-sound cooking at respected art gallery

020 7522 7896 & 3318
77-82 Whitechapel High St E1 7QX
e-mail: dining@whitechapelgallery.org
dir: Nearest station: Aldgate East

Part of the renowned gallery's recent £13.5 million expansion programme, the small, contemporary, street-facing restaurant is an accomplished act. Chef Michael Paul champions seasonal and sustainable British produce. His creative, deceptively simple dishes show a refreshingly light touch, with clean presentation and a good balance of flavours. Seared scallops come with cauliflower soup and sautéed sea kale in a classic pairing with a twist, while for main course chargrilled rump of Romney Marsh lamb is partnered with a wild garlic potato terrine and a roasted red pepper and saffron dressing. Desserts continue the theme - perhaps rhubarb and almond tart with rosewater crème fraîche. The décor suits the cuisine - it's equally light, fresh and modern with its combination of blond wood and mirrored wall panels.

Chef Michael Paul **Owner** Whitechapel Gallery **Times** 12-2.30/6-11 Closed 24 Dec-2 Jan, Mon, D Sun **Prices** Fixed L 2 course £18, Starter £6.75-£8.50, Main £14.50-£19.50, Dessert £5.75-£7.75, Service added but optional 12.5% **Wines** 14 bottles over £20, 8 bottles under £20, 10 by glass **Notes** Sunday L, Vegetarian available **Seats** 36, Pr/dining room 12 **Children** Portions **Parking** On street

LONDON E14

Four Seasons Hotel Canary Wharf

PLAN 9 A6

Modern Italian

Sophisticated Italian cooking in a smart Docklands hotel

☎ 020 7510 1999
46 Westferry Circus, Canary Wharf E14 8RS
dir: Nearest station: Canary Wharf. Just off Westbury Circus rdbt

Canary Wharf office workers and international travellers (the Docklands airport is close by) are among the clientele at this smart hotel restaurant, which enjoys fantastic views across a secluded garden to the Thames beyond. A strong Italian accent infuses the menu, testing your culinary lingo with risotto mantecato, beccafico swordfish and mixed fish guazzetto. Even the monoglot diner will appreciate what turns up on the plate though, even when the Italian focus is blurred in main courses such as confit duck with raisin polenta and pak choi. Pasta dishes are full of novelty, and meals might conclude with the likes of roasted pineapple with rum and raisin ice cream and a coulis of exotic fruits. Good strong espresso will see you on your way.

Chef Marco Bax **Owner** Four Seasons Hotels **Times** 12-3/6-10.30 **Prices** Food prices not confirmed for 2011. Please telephone for details **Wines** 90 bottles over £20, 29 by glass **Notes** Sun brunch buffet, Vegetarian available, Civ Wed 200 **Seats** 90 **Children** Portions, Menu **Parking** 26

The Gun

PLAN 9 D5

British

Modern brasserie food in a riverside gastro-pub

☎ 020 7515 5222
27 Coldharbour, Docklands E14 9NS
e-mail: info@thegundocklands.com
dir: Nearest station: South Quay DLR, Canary Wharf. From South Quay DLR, E down Marsh Wall to mini rdbt, turn left, over bridge then take 1st right

The Docklands gastro-pub was once a bolt-hole for smugglers, in an area that was previously all iron foundries, producing - among other things - guns. Images of seafaring days gone by adorn the dining room, and there is a splendid outdoor area of decking and brick paving, enjoying commanding views over the Thames towards the O2 Arena. The cooking is impeccably modern brasserie fare from gun to tape, taking in ham hock ravioli with Morteau sausage, smoked bacon and choucroute, fillet of red bream on crushed new potatoes in beurre blanc, and poached peach with matching sorbet and candied hazelnuts.

Times 12-3/6-10.30 Closed 25-26 Dec

The Narrow

PLAN 1 G4

Modern British

Ramsay gets the beers in by the river

☎ 020 7592 7950
44 Narrow St E14 8DP
e-mail: reservations@gordonramsay.com
dir: Nearest station: Limehouse

This Grade II listed former dock master's house stands beside the Thames and commands wonderful views of the river from its decked rear terrace. Sympathetically restored by Gordon Ramsay, the first of his forays into the gastro-pub market, it boasts half-wall panelling, fireplaces and black-and-white vintage artwork. Ramsay it might be but fine dining it ain't: informal, relaxed, casual - in short, a proper pub. The menu boasts classic British dishes with just the right degree of hearty appeal; devilled lambs' kidneys, perhaps, followed by braised neck of lamb with pearl barley and smoked bacon risotto and gremolata, finishing off with cherry tart and hazelnut ice cream. Alternatively, nurse a pint of real ale in the bar and snack on a sausage roll and HP sauce or fill up with a traditional ploughman's.

Times 11.30-3/6-11

Plateau

PLAN 9 B6

Modern French V

Sophisticated, contemporary fine dining in futuristic landscape

☎ 020 7715 7100
4th Floor, Canada Place, Canada Square, Canary Wharf E14 5ER
e-mail: plateaureservations@danddlondon.com
web: www.plateaurestaurant.co.uk
dir: Nearest station: Canary Wharf DLR/Tube. Facing Canary Wharf Tower and Canada Square Park

A lift by Waitrose inside the Canada Place shopping mall beams you up to the fourth floor to emerge in a futuristic realm of steel and glass. The skyscrapers of Canary Wharf surround the rooftop conservatory-style restaurant, a long, sleek complex with vertiginous views over Canada Square. It's all very Manhattan-esque with an open kitchen dividing the buzzy Bar & Grill (offering a simpler menu) from the slightly calmer restaurant, though sensitive souls will find both venues pretty strident. The Conran design is 'the future' as imagined in '60s film classics such as *Barbarella* - neutral colours and white plastic 'tulip' swivel chairs, grey and white Italian marble, and huge arching sci-fi floor lamps. The ambitious modern European cooking is pretty stylish too, and far from lacking in substance: this is a high-energy, committed kitchen team at work, delivering skilled dishes along the lines of braised beef cheeks with mash or simple Dover sole with lemon and extra virgin olive oil, and desserts follow a similar flavour-led path with the likes of mandarin crème brûlée with kumquat confit.

Chef Tim Tolley **Owner** D & D London **Times** 12-3/6-10.30 Closed 25-26 Dec, 1 Jan, BHs, Sun, L Sat **Prices** Fixed L 2 course £28, Fixed D 3 course £31, Tasting menu £54, Starter £7-£15, Main £21-£32, Dessert £6, Service added but optional 12.5%, Groups min 8 service 12.5% **Wines** All bottles over £20, 16 by glass **Notes** Tasting menu 5 course, Fixed menu du jour bar/grill £16-£18, Sunday L, Vegetarian menu, Dress restrictions, Smart casual, Civ Wed 180 **Seats** 124, Pr/dining room 24 **Children** Portions, Menu **Parking** 200

Royal China

PLAN 9 A6

Traditional Chinese V

Accomplished Chinese food with wonderful views of the river

☎ 020 7719 0888
Canary Wharf Riverside, 30 Westferry Circus E14 8RR
e-mail: info@royalchinagroup.co.uk
dir: Nearest station: Canary Wharf. Located near the Four Seasons Hotel & Canary Wharf Pier

The Royal China group now comprises a gang of four, spread around the capital from Fulham to Baker Street to Queensway and Canary Wharf. All come with a signature décor of flying golden geese on black lacquered walls, and stylised silver wave motifs. First-rate dim sum have always pulled in the crowds to the riverside Canary Wharf outpost - lunchtime queues snake out from its imposing glass frontage, hoping to bag a seat on the splendid outdoor terrace. Apart from the legendary dim sum, the extensive menus - with separate sections for abalone, seafood, poultry, beef and pork etc. - wave the flag for Cantonese cuisine, taking in smoked shredded chicken with garlic and chilli, deep-fried eel with spicy salt, steamed Icelandic cod with dried yellow bean, and for high rollers there's braised sliced abalone with sea cucumber.

Chef Man Chau **Owner** Mr Peter Law **Times** Noon-11 Closed 23-25 Dec **Prices** Food prices not confirmed for 2011. Please telephone for details **Wines** 85 bottles over £20, 7 bottles under £20, 2 by glass **Notes** Sunday L, Vegetarian menu **Seats** 155, Pr/dining room 40 **Parking** 2 mins away

LONDON E16

Crowne Plaza London - Docklands
PLAN 1 G4

British, French NEW

Bistro-style dining in contemporary, business-savvy hotel

☎ 020 7055 2000
Royal Victoria Dock, Western Gateway E16 1AL
e-mail: sales@crowneplazadocklands.co.uk
dir: Nearest station: Royal Victoria. A1020 towards ExCeL West, hotel on left 400mtrs before ExCeL

The contemporary Docklands hotel - at the heart of the action close to the ExCel, Canary Wharf and City Airport - overlooks the Royal Victoria Dock. It's geared to the high-octane Docklands business life, with a lively, of-the-moment bar (think high stools and leather banquette seating) and a similarly styled restaurant, both with full-length windows offering views across the dock - there are also fair-weather alfresco opportunities. Modern, easy eating is the style using well-sourced produce, the bistro output available in both bar and restaurant. Go from tuna Niçoise to beef, port and Stilton pie, or perhaps lemon sole with Jersey Royals. Puddings are suitably comforting - rhubarb crumble or vanilla crème brûlée.

Chef Olivier Ruiz **Times** 12.30-2/5.30-10.30 **Prices** Starter £4.50-£7.95, Main £9.95-£18.95, Dessert £5.50, Service added but optional 12.5% **Wines** 17 bottles over £20, 3 bottles under £20, 11 by glass **Notes** Vegetarian available **Seats** Pr/dining room 48 **Children** Menu **Parking** 70

LONDON EC1

The Ambassador
PLAN 3 F5

Modern European

Well-supported all-day venue in Exmouth Market

☎ 020 7837 0009
55 Exmouth Market EC1R 4QL
e-mail: clive@theambassadorcafe.co.uk
dir: Nearest station: Farringdon. Take 1st right off Roseberry Av, heading N from Farringdon Rd junct. Turn right into Exmouth Market

In the heart of Exmouth Market, the Ambassador is a relaxing all-day venue that caters for an enthusiastic local crowd from early-bird breakfasts to the final digestifs of evening. The simple interior design, with its plain furniture and globe light fittings, is in tune with the times, staff are briskly efficient, and the menus undertake an inviting tour of classic European culinary thinking. Expect salt-cod croquettes with aïoli to start, followed perhaps by mussels in cider with chips, spaghetti with butternut squash and sage, dressed in Capezzana olive oil, or grilled rib-eye with bone marrow and peppercorn sauce. Great intensity is coaxed out of these relatively simple dishes, and it all ends with treats such as chocolate and orange mousse with honeycomb.

Chef Chris Dyer **Owner** Clive & Stella Greenhalgh **Times** 12-2.30/6-10.15 Closed 1 wk Xmas, D Sun **Prices** Fixed L 2 course £10, Fixed D 3 course fr £20, Starter £4.50-£9.50, Main £9.50-£18, Dessert £5-£6, Service optional, Groups min 9 service 12.5% **Wines** 49 bottles over £20, 29 bottles under £20, 14 by glass **Notes** Brunch served 11-4 Sat-Sun, Vegetarian available **Seats** 75 **Children** Portions, Menu

Bistrot Bruno Loubet
PLAN 3 F4

French NEW

Authentic French cooking in trendy Clerkenwell

☎ 020 7324 4444
The Zetter Hotel, St John's Square, 86-89 Clerkenwell Rd EC1M 5RJ
e-mail: info@thezetter.com
dir: Nearest station: Farringdon. From west A401, Clerkenwell Rd A5201. Hotel 200mtrs on left

There has been a buzz on the London foodie scene since Bruno Loubet left behind the sun-drenched shores of Oz and returned to London. Great things were expected of this stellar chef who shone brightly during the nineties, and his return has not disappointed the capital's gastronomes. Loubet's collaboration with the hyper-trendy Zetter Hotel sees him set up in a bright and airy ultra-modern space looking out onto the comings and goings of Clerkenwell. A special talent at work in the modish open kitchen is clear from the off, in dishes that display the heart and soul of truly hearty French bistro cooking. Mauricette snails and meatballs arrive in a circular pattern around an airy royale de champignon, pointed up with a light tomato sauce and parsley and tarragon pesto; next up is quail, stuffed with pork, bacon and pistachio, teamed with beans and celeriac purée and a spinach and egg yolk raviolo, all flavours standing to attention and working together. Deeply sinful pleasures continue to the end in a Valrhona chocolate tartlet with caramel and salted butter ice cream.

Times 12-2.30/6-10.30

The Bleeding Heart
PLAN 3 F4

Modern French NOTABLE WINE LIST

Discreet and romantic Hatton Garden favourite

☎ 020 7242 2056
Bleeding Heart Yard, off Greville St EC1N 8SJ
e-mail: bookings@bleedingheart.co.uk
dir: Nearest station: Farringdon. Turn right out of Farringdon Station onto Cowcross St, continue along Greville St for 50mtrs. Turn left into Bleeding Heart Yard

The cobbled courtyard fronting the Bleeding Heart's trio of bar, bistro and romantic cellar was the scene of a gory story of a crime passionnel, when society beauty Lady Elizabeth Hatton was found messily murdered by her lover in the 17th century. Wooden floors, low-beamed ceilings and walls lined with wine-themed prints set a suitably intimate tone in the cellar restaurant, backed by slick service. Expect robust modern French cooking with big, confident flavours using top-notch ingredients: take seared wood pigeon on a shallot tarte Tatin with spiced lentil and smoked bacon vinaigrette to start, followed by an assiette of suckling pig. Finish with the vast selection of perfectly ripened cheeses; wine lovers should take note of the impressive 450-bottle list, including those from the restaurant's own Hawkes Bay estate.

Chef Peter Reffell **Owner** Robert & Robyn Wilson **Times** 12-3/6-10.30 Closed Xmas & New Year (10 days), Sat-Sun **Prices** Starter £5.95-£10.95, Main £12.95-£24.50, Dessert £6.45-£7.25, Service added but optional 12.5% **Wines** 270 bottles over £20, 8 bottles under £20, 20 by glass **Notes** Vegetarian available, Dress restrictions, Smart casual **Seats** 110, Pr/dining room 40 **Parking** 20 evening only, NCP nearby

Le Café du Marché
PLAN 3 G4

French

Provincial, rustic France in converted warehouse

☎ 020 7608 1609
Charterhouse Mews, Charterhouse Square EC1M 6AH
dir: Nearest station: Barbican

Bare-brick walls, floorboards, exposed rafters, French posters and closely-set tables characterise the charmingly rustic interior of this French café-restaurant hidden down a quiet cobbled mews, just a stone's throw from Smithfield Market. Two dining rooms, Le Café on the ground floor and Le Grenier in the bright loft, share the same décor and set-price menu of provincial French bistro-style fare delivered from open kitchens. The careful cooking keeps things simple and fresh, driven on by quality ingredients; take Mediterranean fish soup, pork saltimbocca with Marsala sauce, and marmalade pudding with Drambuie crème anglaise. Attentive service from Gallic staff adds to the colourful joie de vivre.

Chef Simon Cottard **Owner** Anna Graham-Wood **Times** 12-2.30/6-10 Closed Xmas, New Year, Etr, BHs, Sun, L Sat **Prices** Fixed L 2 course £27.50, Fixed D 3 course £33.85, Service added but optional 15% **Notes** Vegetarian available **Seats** 120, Pr/dining room 65 **Children** Portions **Parking** Next door (small charge)

The Clerkenwell
PLAN 3 G4

Modern European

Relaxed fine dining in trendy Clerkenwell

☎ 020 7253 9000
69-73 St. John St EC1M 4AN
e-mail: restaurant@theclerkenwell.com
dir: Nearest station: Farringdon, Barbican. From Farringdon station, continue 60mtrs up Farringdon Rd, left into Cowcross St, left into Peters Ln, left into St John St

The Clerkenwell's dusky façade has the look of an upmarket gastro-pub, opening into a stripped-out contemporary interior with the butch textures of dark herringbone parquet flooring, tobacco-brown leather banquettes and polished darkwood tables. The kitchen's eclectic modern approach favours the Mediterranean in offerings such as sea bass and salt cod with calamari and tomato and red pepper dressing, but is equally at home with a more exotic combination of roast rump of lamb with crisp basmati rice cake with a date and apricot glaze, or in the classic territory of côte de boeuf for two, with hand-cut chips and sage and peppercorn hollandaise. End with a luscious chocolate fondant with prune purée and Baileys cream. The trendy, globetrotting wine list offers plenty of choices by the glass and in 375ml carafes. (Also check out the entry for the Clerkenwell's sibling, the Chancery.)

Times 12-3/6-11 Closed Xmas, BHs, Sun, L Sat

Club Gascon PLAN 3 G3

@@@ – *see below*

Le Comptoir Gascon PLAN 3 F4

@ Traditional French

Gutsy southwestern French dishes opposite Smithfield market

☎ 020 7608 0851
61-63 Charterhouse St EC1M 6HJ
e-mail: info@comptoirgascon.com
web: www.comptoirgascon.com
dir: Nearest station: Farringdon, Barbican, St Paul's, Chancery Ln

The informal French eatery opposite Smithfield, part of the Club Gascon network, incorporates a food hall selling everything from mixed hampers to cheeses, pastries and caviar, as well as a bistro specialising in the gutsy, substantial food of southwest France. 'Piggy Treats', the name of one of the starter selections, just about says it all, while mains are divided into Végétal (such as devilled root vegetable tarte fine), Mer (organic confit salmon and mushy peas), and Terre (beef onglet with sauce bordelaise). Duck is also a major feature. Desserts include a refreshingly simple vanilla cheesecake.

Le Comptoir Gascon

Times 12-2/7-11 Closed 25 Dec -1 Jan, Sun & Mon

Eastside Inn PLAN 3 G4

@@ French, Mediterranean **NEW**

Skilful cooking in a stylish Farringdon venue

☎ 020 7490 9230
40 St John St EC1M 4AY
e-mail: reservations@esilondon.com
dir: Nearest station: Farringdon, Barbican

Divided into two parts, a small, upscale restaurant and a more informal, hang-loose bistro area, the Eastside Inn is Björn van der Horst's version of a contemporary London neighbourhood restaurant. The kitchen is open to view, a big mirror dominates the space, and table settings are exquisite, with beige linen offset by colourful plates, while the leather-upholstered chairs are the last word in comfort. Van der Horst once cooked at the Greenhouse in Mayfair (see entry), and his pedigree speaks for itself. The cooking here may look as though it's aiming for a more obviously domestic vibe, but talent will out. A seafood starter is comprised of sliced scallop sashimi with prawn and crab tempura, topped with little curls of tempura-battered kale, the squeaky-clean freshness of it all fired up by home-made wasabi. Meat mains take in Middlewhite pork, its daily-changing preparation scribbled up on the mirror, or a pair of fabulous beef cuts, aged sirloin and braised feather-blade, served with fondant potato and hollandaise. Theatrical, eye-popping desserts include carpaccio-sliced, passionfruit-dotted pineapple topped with a vacherin meringue ball filled

continued

Club Gascon

@@@

LONDON EC1 PLAN 3 G3

Modern French V NOTABLE WINE LIST

Classy cooking inspired by South West France

☎ 020 7796 0600
57 West Smithfield EC1A 9DS
e-mail: info@clubgascon.com
dir: Nearest station: Barbican, Farringdon

Smithfield is steeped in British history, from the slaying of Wat Tyler, leader of the 1381 Peasants' Revolt, to the execution of the Scottish patriot William Wallace. 57 West Smithfield has enjoyed a more peaceful existence, once as the Lyons Teahouse and these days as Club Gascon, a bastion of refined French cooking, inspired by the cuisine of the South West in particular. Bold displays of fresh flowers bring a glow to the room, where veined marble walls, old oak floors and royal-blue banquettes help create a timelessly opulent ambience. Black-tied waiting staff deliver polished, unhurried service. The restaurant is renowned for its tasting plates - small-scale dishes of impeccably sourced seasonal produce - but this has evolved into slightly larger servings and a variety of menu options. Dishes are intriguingly inventive, ingredients are painstakingly sourced (much from Gascony), and the stunning presentation can result in a sharp intake of breath. Thinly sliced scallops are marinated in red sake and served with piquillos coulis and icy watermelon, looking like a painted flower on the plate, and delivering a masterclass in the juxtaposition of flavours and textures. Smoked beef onglet comes with an equally well-balanced sauce, this time of mandarin and mustard, and technical dexterity is on display in a dessert of pink rhubarb boule, with mixed herbs and hibiscus. The wine list explores the lesser-known wine regions of South West France, as well as serving up plenty of classics.

Chef Pascal Aussignac **Owner** P Aussignac & V Labeyrie **Times** 12-2/7-10 Closed Xmas, New Year, BHs, Sun, L Sat **Prices** Fixed D 3 course fr £29, Service added but optional 12.5% **Wines** 140 bottles over £20, 15 by glass **Notes** Fixed D 5 course £55, Vegetarian menu, Dress restrictions, Smart casual **Seats** 40 **Children** Portions **Parking** NCP opposite restaurant

LONDON EC1 ***continued***

with tropical fruit sorbet. Communal eating is encouraged in the form of Sharing Dishes (four of you could sign up for the braised veal shank in lemon and thyme), and the plats du jour evoke archetypal French bistro eating. Something for everyone, then.

Chef Björn van der Horst **Owner** Justine & Björn van der Horst **Times** 12-3/6-11 Closed 24-30 Dec, D Sun **Prices** Starter £4.50-£9.95, Main £12.95-£30, Dessert £6.95-£7.95, Service added but optional 12.5% **Wines** 275 bottles over £20, 5 bottles under £20, 13 by glass **Notes** Sunday L, Vegetarian available, Air con **Seats** 60, Pr/dining room 14 **Children** Portions **Parking** On street

Hix Oyster & Chop House PLAN 3 G4

Traditional British

First-class seasonal produce cooked without fuss

☎ 020 7017 1930
36-37 Greenhill Rents, Cowcross St EC1M 6BN
e-mail: chophouse@restaurantetcltd.co.uk
dir: Nearest station: Farringdon. Turn left out of underground station (approx 1min walk)

The Clerkenwell outpost of the Mark Hix brand of British comfort food is squirreled away close to Smithfield meat market. The concept is rooted in the past, where seasonal produce takes centre stage and simplicity and a refreshing lack of adornment are hallmarks. As well as an array of oysters (Maldon rocks, perhaps) there are top-notch meats, from a Somerset Barnsley lamb chop to 28-day aged South Devon Ruby Red beef (aka, hanger steak with baked bone marrow). Fish also features, maybe whole lemon sole, while desserts like steamed ginger pudding have a nursery ring. Darkwood panelling, wall tiles, bare floorboards and a marble-topped oyster bar, blend with bistro-style seating, white tablecloths and high decibels in a pared-back interior. There are Hix venues in Soho and Selfridges in London, plus Lyme Regis in Dorset.

Chef Tom Hill **Owner** Mark Hix & Ratnesh Bagdai **Times** 12-3/5.30-11 Closed 25-26 Dec, 1 Jan, BHs, L Sat **Prices** Fixed D 3 course £19.50, Starter £6-£12, Main £12.95-£34, Dessert £2.95-£7.50, Service added but optional 12.5% **Wines** 55 bottles over £20, 5 bottles under £20, 11 by glass **Notes** Pre-theatre menu available, Sunday L, Vegetarian available **Seats** 66 **Children** Portions **Parking** On street (meters)

Malmaison Charterhouse Square PLAN 3 G4

Modern British, French

Boutique hotel with a chic brasserie

☎ 020 7012 3700
18-21 Charterhouse Square, Clerkenwell EC1M 6AH
e-mail: athwaites@malmaison.com
dir: Nearest station: Barbican

The Malmaison chain's London operation has a great location in a cobbled courtyard off Charterhouse Square, and its basement brasserie certainly looks the part, plushly decorated in a rather theatrical Moulin Rouge style, with shades of purple and claret and sexy textures of silk and velvet, wood and brick. It's an intimate place, low-lit and with tables for two tucked into secluded corners. To go with all this is a menu of deeply-French brasserie dishes, built on produce from small producers in the south east. Keeping things 'homegrown and local', you could start with a half-dozen oysters from the River Blackwater, then move on to devilled kidneys or pan-fried sea bass with scallop and liquorice, fennel purée and baby artichoke, finishing with cherry Bakewell tart with pear sorbet.

Chef John Woodward **Owner** Malmaison Hotels **Times** 12-2.30/6-10.30 Closed 23-28 Dec, L Sat **Prices** Food prices not confirmed for 2011. Please telephone for details **Wines** 200 bottles over £20, 6 bottles under £20, 21 by glass **Notes** Vegetarian available **Seats** 70, Pr/dining room 12 **Children** Portions, Menu **Parking** Smithfield Market 200m

The Modern Pantry PLAN 3 F4

Global

Pyrotechnic fusion cooking in trendy Clerkenwell

☎ 020 7553 9210
47-48 St John's Square, Clerkenwell EC1V 4JJ
e-mail: enquiries@themodernpantry.co.uk
web: www.themodernpantry.co.uk
dir: Nearest station: Farringdon, Barbican

Born in Canada, brought up in New Zealand, Anna Hansen has been at the forefront of fusion food in London since the early 1990s. Her current venture embraces a deli, external catering operation, ground-floor café and first-floor dining rooms in an impressive all-in-one enterprise. Overlooking St John's Square in Clerkenwell, the upstairs space is a sleekly designed environment for some vivid culinary pyrotechnics. Seared cuttlefish in curry leaves, tomato and ginger, with caramel coconut and vanilla cream, might begin things on a high. Eastern spices and seasonings electrify main courses such as roast monkfish with wasabi tobiko fish roe and a celery, sea beet and yuzu salad, or miso-marinated onglet steak, with cassava chips, and cherry tomatoes braised in lemongrass. Multi-layered desserts to make the head spin (in the nicest possible way) include orange and almond cake, with poached sour cherries, sumac, grapefruit, apricot, frozen rosewater mascarpone and pistachios.

Chef Anna Hansen **Owner** Anna Hansen **Times** 9am-11pm **Prices** Fixed L 2 course £17.50, Starter £4.50-£9.50, Main £14.50-£23.50, Dessert £5.50-£7.50, Service added but optional 12.5% **Wines** 64 bottles over £20, 12 bottles under £20, 17 by glass **Notes** Pre-theatre D available, Sunday L, Vegetarian available **Seats** 110, Pr/dining room 60 **Children** Portions **Parking** On street (meter)

Moro PLAN 3 F5

Islamic, Mediterranean

Vibrant home of Moorish food

☎ 020 7833 8336
34/36 Exmouth Market EC1R 4QE
e-mail: info@moro.co.uk
dir: Nearest station: Farringdon, Angel. 5 mins walk from Sadler's Wells theatre, between Farringdon Road and Rosebery Ave

It somehow doesn't seem as long ago as 1997 that Sam and Sam Clark opened Moro with the intention of bringing the food of the Moorish arc, from the eastern Mediterranean via North Africa to southern Spain, to Exmouth Market and beyond. It's been an exciting ride, with cookbooks scattered to right and left along the way. The place itself remains defiantly informal, loud and clattery when full, but plenty of fun, with tapas served all day, and some astonishingly vibrant dishes on the weekly-changing main menu. Cuttlefish, cauliflower and coriander salad with preserved lemon and capers, charcoal-grilled lamb with muhammara (Syrian hot pepper relish), fried aubergines, chilli and mint, and wood-roasted mackerel with asparagus escabèche in orange, thyme and garlic, are dishes to pique even the most jaded London palates, and are full of new taste discoveries. Dead-simple desserts such as a portion of Alfonso mango, or yoghurt cake with pistachios and pomegranate, round things off without cholesterol overload.

Times 12.30-2.30/7-10.30 Closed Xmas, New Year, BHs, Sun

St John PLAN 3 G4

British

No frills British food in a former smokehouse

020 7251 0848
26 St John St EC1M 4AY
e-mail: reservations@stjohnrestaurant.com
dir: Nearest station: Farringdon. 100yds from Smithfield Market, northside

It was back in 1994 that this former smokehouse up the road from Smithfield Market arrived on the London dining scene with its utilitarian look and menu full of not often seen cuts of meat. Others have followed the lead, few do it as well. It hasn't changed over the years: head through the large ground floor bar and up the narrow staircase to the raised dining room with its open plan kitchen (there's a bakery on the ground floor, too, where you can buy fresh bread or grab an Eccles cake). You'll find canteen-style tables covered with paper tablecloths, an absence of colour, and staff dressed in long aprons. It's noisy, convivial, great fun. The food has an unrivalled integrity, honesty and simplicity: roast bone marrow, for example, with parsley salad has become a signature dish, but there's ox heart with chicory and anchovy, too, and for main course, chitterlings and chips, or rabbit saddle with white beans and aïoli. It's not that there won't be a vegetarian dish on the menu (celeriac and baked eggs perhaps), it's just that it's not really the point. A superb French wine selection, with plenty available by the glass and bottles on sale to take away, is just another reason to come.

Chef Christopher Gillard **Owner** T Gulliver & F Henderson **Times** 12-3/6-11 Closed Xmas, New Year, Etr BH, L Sat, D Sun **Prices** Starter £6.20-£12.50, Main £13.50-£23, Dessert £5.90-£7.20, Service added but optional, Groups min 6 service 12.5% **Wines** 72 bottles over £20, 14 bottles under £20, 34 by glass **Notes** Sunday L, Vegetarian available **Seats** 100, Pr/dining room 18 **Parking** Meters in street

Smiths of Smithfield, Top Floor PLAN 3 F4

Modern British

City skyline views and passionate sourcing in a warehouse conversion

020 7251 7950
(Top Floor), 67-77 Charterhouse St EC1M 6HJ
e-mail: reservations@smithsofsmithfield.co.uk
dir: Nearest station: Farringdon, Barbican, Chancery Lane. Opposite Smithfield Meat Market

It's worth making the journey up to the fourth floor of this food and drink emporium in a former warehouse opposite Smithfield Meat Market. There you'll find John Torode's stylish fine-dining rooftop restaurant with its fantastic City views available to everyone thanks to its wall of windows. Sliding glass doors lead to a timber-decked terrace. Leather chairs and polished-wooden floors against linen-clothed tables make for a more refined look than the lower floors with their industrial chic sandblasted brickwork, industrial steel and reclaimed timber. The menu is the best of British with rare breed, organic and additive-free meat a focal point, although fish is also treated with due reverence. The kitchen doesn't need to muck about with ingredients of this quality. Start with mullet with chorizo, tomato and capers followed by a rare breed steak, or perhaps a big cut to share, or even roast spring chicken with turnip tops and lardons. For pudding, perhaps pancake parcels with citrus soup and blood orange sorbet.

Times 12-3.30/6.30-12 Closed 25-26 Dec, 1 Jan, L Sat, D Sun

LONDON EC2

L' Anima PLAN 6 C6

Italian

Classy regional Italian cooking in modish setting

020 7422 7000
1 Snowden St, Broadgate West EC2A 2DQ
e-mail: info@lanima.co.uk
dir: Nearest station: Liverpool Street

Owner Francesco Mazzei is a Calabrian (Italy's toe) and he's brought the soul of the south to the City of London. His restaurant deals in regional contemporary cooking served in a coolly modern room done out in limestone and marble, with white leather chairs adding to the sense of metropolitan chic. There's a bar separated from the main dining room by a glass wall and floor-to-ceiling windows let the light flood in. A crib sheet on the menu helps with some of the more unfamiliar terms (lagane is an egg-less, long-shaped pasta, for example) and the cooking achieves the holy grail of being both rustic and refined at the same time. Black Angus beef carpaccio is served with home-made pickles and in the pasta and risotto section might be a risotto with duck liver and Marsala, or native lobster linguine. From the wood oven comes monkfish with peppers and potatoes, or go for Sicilian rabbit, and save room for desserts such as liquorice zabayon or the Italian cheeses.

Chef Francesco Mazzei **Owner** Francesco Mazzei **Times** 11.45-3/5.30-10.30 Closed Xmas, New Year, BHs, Sun, L Sat **Prices** Fixed L 2 course £24.50, Service added but optional 12.5% **Wines** 200 bottles over £20, 2 bottles under £20, 13 by glass **Notes** Vegetarian available **Seats** 120, Pr/dining room 15 **Children** Portions **Parking** On street

Boisdale of Bishopsgate PLAN 6 C5

Traditional British

A great taste of Scotland in the heart of the City

020 7283 1763
Swedeland Court, 202 Bishopsgate EC2M 4NR
e-mail: katie@boisdale-city.co.uk
dir: Nearest station: Liverpool Street. Opposite Liverpool St station

Hidden down a Dickensian alleyway in the heart of the City, Boisdale comes decked out with enough clubby tartan, leather, and darkwood to soothe the soul of any ex-pat Scots doing business in the Square Mile. Like its Belgravia outpost (see entry), the set-up aims squarely at bulging city pockets with a butch, cigar-smoking vibe in the traditional champagne and oyster bar, a moody vaulted restaurant and a buzzy basement piano bar, where live jazz in the evenings gets the joint jumping. The kitchen has its supply lines north of the border to support a hearty modern menu that majors on the likes of game and Aberdeenshire dry-aged beef; typical offerings include smoked Finnan haddock fishcake with spinach and hot mustard sauce, or roast Macsween haggis with mash and bashed neeps.

Chef Neil Churchill **Owner** Ranald Macdonald **Times** 11-3/6-9 Closed Xmas, 31 Dec, BHs, Sat-Sun **Prices** Fixed L 2 course £12.50-£18.70, Fixed D 3 course £29.50-£38.50, Service added but optional 12.5% **Wines** 106 bottles over £20, 21 bottles under £20, 16 by glass **Notes** Vegetarian available, Dress restrictions, Smart casual **Seats** 100 **Parking** Middlesex St

Bonds PLAN 6 B4

Modern French NOTABLE WINE LIST

Grand setting for some slick, eye-catching modern cooking

020 7657 8088 & 7657 8090
Threadneedles, 5 Threadneedle St EC2R 8AY
e-mail: bonds@theetongroup.com
dir: Nearest station: Bank

Lofty classical columns, a high decorative ceiling and vast windows allude to Bonds' past life as a banking hall, and it oozes City style. Set in the swish, boutique Threadneedle Hotel, the makeover is less voluminous than some financial-institution conversions, smartly blending present-day fashion with Victorian grandeur. Thus its contemporary wood-veneered panels, glass, modern seating, low-slung lighting and polished-wood floors are in-vogue, while slick, informed service adds to the upbeat vibe. The client base may be deep-pocketed City suits, but there's a cracking-value lunch and early-evening Menu of the Day, while the succinctly scripted and keenly priced carte shows the true aspiration of chef Barry Tonks's talented kitchen. The modern French and European cooking is inventive and precise, with a lovely light, clean-cut delivery. Modern cooking methods abound, perhaps Peterhead cod (poached at 48 degrees C) accompanied by its own beignet, roasted chorizo and soft squid ink polenta, while a warm chocolate moelleux (with almond milk sorbet) might catch the eye at dessert.

Chef Barry Tonks **Owner** The Eton Collection **Times** 12-2.30/6-10 Closed 2 wks Xmas, 4 days Etr & BHs, Sat-Sun **Prices** Fixed L 3 course £15.50, Fixed D 3 course £17.50, Starter £7.95-£14.95, Main £12.50-£19.95, Dessert £6.50, Service added but optional 12.5% **Wines** 137 bottles over £20, 11 bottles under £20, 18 by glass **Notes** Tasting menu available, Vegetarian available, Dress restrictions, Smart casual **Seats** 80, Pr/dining room 16 **Parking** London Wall NCP

LONDON EC2 *continued*

Catch Restaurant PLAN 6 C5

Seafood, Modern European **NEW**

Fresh fish, shellfish and champagne in chic city hotel

020 7618 7200
ANdAZ London, 40 Liverpool St EC2M 7QN
e-mail: london.restres@andaz.com
dir: Nearest station: Liverpool Street On corner of Liverpool St & Bishopsgate, attached to Liverpool St station

This glamorous seafood and champagne joint has a buzzy location in the über-chic ANdAZ Hotel next to Liverpool Street station. Get in the mood with a glass of bubbly at the mosaic-covered horseshoe-shaped counter in the champagne bar, then watch the chefs deftly preparing fresh shellfish from a palate-tickling display amid the elegant Victorian splendour of the marble-clad dining room. Oysters are sourced from around the UK - Colchester, Falmouth Bay, and Loch Fyne - as Catch is committed to using sustainable materials and supporting small-scale fishermen. A creamy crab bisque and sorrel cream is a fine way to start, followed by steamed black bream with crushed new potatoes, broad beans and crab.

Times 12-2.30/6-10

Cinnamon Kitchen PLAN 6 C5

Modern Indian

Unusual Indian dishes in a one-time spice warehouse

020 7626 5000
9 Devonshire Square, LONDON EC2M 4YL
e-mail: info@cinnamon-kitchen.com
web: www.cinnamon-kitchen.com
dir: Nearest station: Liverpool Street. Off Bishopsgate Rd opposite Liverpool St Station

Occupying the former East India Company spice warehouse, not far from Liverpool Street station, this is the younger sibling of Cinnamon Club (see entry). When the sun shines, its raised decked terrace makes a fine alfresco venue, or else enter the industrial chic of the main restaurant, with its colossal spherical lights of silvered brass. Vivek Singh cooks an eclectic, highly appetising menu of unusual Indian dishes, from appetisers such as chargrilled Nile perch with lime leaf and chilli to roasted partridge with curried pear, or spice-crusted tilapia with kokum curry and citrus mash. Rabbit, venison and monkfish all turn up too, but there is also chicken and lamb biryani for the diehard traditionalists. Finish with spiced carrot cake served with cinnamon ice cream and rum-doused raisins.

Cinnamon Kitchen

Times 12-3.30/6-10.30 Closed 25-26 Dec, 1 Jan, some BHs, Sun, L Sat

Eyre Brothers PLAN 7 B2

Spanish, Portuguese

Vivid Iberian flavours from the brothers Eyre

020 7613 5346
70 Leonard St EC2A 4QX
e-mail: eyrebros@btconnect.com
dir: Nearest station: Old Street. Exit 4

The eponymous brothers grew up in Mozambique, thus grew their passion for the flavours of Portugal. It's a cool place, their restaurant, with a long counter overlooking the open kitchen, wood panelling, big, bold paintings, artful photographs and smart linen-clad tables. Inspiration comes from across the Iberian Peninsula, flavours are full-on and the charcoal grill works overtime. Hare soup with jamon, red wine and thyme is a full-blooded first course, or there's fritura gaditana (deep-fried baby cuttlefish, red mullet and whitebait with caper, gherkin and lemon mayonnaise) and for main course, perhaps arroz de pato (Portuguese baked rice with duck, chorizo, smoked bacon fat and ham), or grilled Mozambique tiger prawns piri piri. Toucinho do Céu or 'fat of heaven', is a soft egg custard made with crisp lemon pastry.

Chef Dave Eyre, Joao Cleto **Owner** Eyre Bros Restaurants Ltd **Times** 12-3/6.30-11 Closed Xmas-New Year, BHs, Sun, L Sat **Prices** Starter £6.50-£17, Main £10-£27.50, Dessert £5-£7, Service optional **Wines** 50 bottles over £20, 7 bottles under £20, 14 by glass **Notes** Vegetarian available **Seats** 100 **Parking** On street

Great Eastern Dining Room PLAN 7 B2

Pacific Rim

Pan-Asian food for the smart set

020 7613 4545
54-56 Great Eastern St, Shoreditch EC2A 3QR
e-mail: greateastern@rickerrestaurants.com
dir: Nearest station: Liverpool Street, Old Street.

King of Pan Asian food in London, Will Ricker's trendy Hoxton restaurant is a sleek, stylish and achingly cool place to eat, drink and be seen in the process. Minimalist in design, the black wooden floors and walls, leather seating and eye-catching chandeliers set the scene. The atmosphere is buzzy and excitable and the music is turned up high. It's not a case of all style and no substance though - the standard Pan-Asian dishes are treated with care and there's some off-centre options too. Dim sum might include white pepper tiger prawns or chicken and peanut spring roll, or how about a main of butternut squash and lychee green curry or whole crispy fried sea bass and three-flavour sauce? Sake or expertly made cocktails are the drinks of choice.

Chef Andrew Hearnden **Owner** Will Ricker **Times** 12-3/6-10.30 Closed Xmas & Etr, Sun, L Sat **Prices** Fixed L 2 course £15-£19, Fixed D 3 course £23-£39, Starter £3.75-£7.50, Main £8.50-£24.50, Dessert £4.50-£9, Service added but optional 12.5% **Wines** 40 bottles over £20, 10 bottles under £20, 10 by glass **Notes** Fixed L & D 2 course menu with wine available 12-3 & 6-7, Vegetarian available **Seats** 70, Pr/dining room 70 **Children** Portions, Menu

Mehek

PLAN 6 B5

Indian

Traditional and inventive Indian in East London

020 7588 5043 & 7588 5044
45 London Wall, Moorgate EC2M 5TE
e-mail: info@mehek.co.uk
dir: Nearest station: Moorgate, Liverpool Street Close to junct of Moorgate and London Wall

The London Wall once protected the city. Times have changed: Mehek welcomes all-comers. This Indian restaurant offers curry house favourites alongside some more inventive ideas. The long buzzy bar gives way to a choice of dining rooms designed by a Bollywood film-set designer and dotted with authentic artefacts. Taking inspiration from several Indian regions, the extensive menu lists familiar starters such as onion bhaji and fish tikka as well as kulfis for pudding. The chef's recommendations, though, bring on guinea fowl bilash (cooked on the bone Bengali style) or haash hyderabadi (duck with spices, sesame seeds, coconut, peanuts and mustard).

Chef A Matlib **Owner** Salim B Rashid **Times** 11.30-3/5.30-11 Closed Xmas, New Year, BHs, Sat-Sun **Prices** Fixed L 3 course £15.50-£22.90, Starter £3.90-£10.90, Main £8.50-£16.90, Dessert £3.20-£3.95, Service added but optional 10% **Wines** 23 bottles over £20, 5 bottles under £20, 9 by glass **Notes** Vegetarian available, Dress restrictions, Smart casual **Seats** 120 **Parking** On street, NCP

Miyako

PLAN 6 C5

Japanese **NEW**

Authentic cooking in buzzing Japanese restaurant

020 7618 7200
ANdAZ London, 40 Liverpool St EC2M 7QN
dir: Nearest station: Liverpool Street. On corner of Liverpool St & Bishopsgate, attached to Liverpool St station

Part of the ANdAZ hotel, this buzzing Japanese restaurant has its own separate entrance. Beyond the sushi bar, the restaurant is sleek and contemporary with bamboo-panelled walls and black lacquered tables and chairs. Not surprisingly popular with local office workers and also servicing them with takeaways, the menu offers authentic Japanese cooking with occasional European twists. A well made miso soup or selection of nigiri and maki sushi might be followed by chicken teriyaki and crab and avocado salad. Finish with a refreshing dessert of yuzu bavarois with sake macerated blueberries and green tea ice cream.

Times 12-2.15/6-10 Closed Sun, L Sat **Prices** Food prices not confirmed for 2011. Please telephone for details

1901 Restaurant

PLAN 6 C5

– see below

1901 Restaurant

LONDON EC2 PLAN 6 C5

Modern British **NEW**

21st-century style and classy, contemporary cooking

020 7618 7000
ANdAZ London, 40 Liverpool St EC2M 7QN
e-mail: london.restres@andaz.com
dir: Nearest station: Liverpool Street. On corner of Liverpool St & Bishopsgate, attached to Liverpool St station

The ANdAZ brand is designed to be funky and fashionable, in a sophisticated urban kind of way, and the Liverpool Street location appeals to City workers and anyone else who wants to bask in the cool, metropolitan chic. The vibe runs through everything from the typography of the logo to the Cocktail Bar, which takes pride of place in the centre of the 1901 Restaurant. It is a great location for a drink, but it would be a shame to miss the opportunity to sample the cooking of Dominic Teague. Despite the 21st-century embellishments, this is a Victorian building with a grand red-brick exterior, and the 1901 Restaurant is a room on a striking scale, with soaring pillars, a stained-glass dome, and well-spaced, cloth-less tables. Music adds to the buzz and the informally dressed staff fit the mood. The menu is suitably modern in its approach, with plenty of good ideas and well-judged flavours. A winter opener might be pot-roasted partridge with cauliflower purée, chanterelles and Madeira jus - spot on from concept to execution. Main-course roast cannon of lamb is equally well handled, served up with glazed sweetbread and a mini shepherd's pie made from the shoulder, and dessert might be a straightforward dish of plums roasted with Scottish honey, served with meringue and honeycomb ice cream. Cheese is a bit of a speciality, with a cheese and wine tasting table dominating one end of the room.

Chef Dominic Teague **Owner** Hyatt Hotels **Times** 12-2.30/6.30-10 Closed Xmas, New Year, BHs, Sun, L Sat **Prices** Fixed L 2 course £19, Starter £8-£12, Main £17-£22, Dessert £7, Service added but optional 12.5% **Wines** 500 bottles over £20, 11 bottles under £20, 12 by glass **Notes** Tasting menu 7 course, Vegetarian available, Civ Wed 160 **Seats** 100 **Parking** NCP London Wall

LONDON EC2 ***continued***

Rhodes Twenty Four PLAN 6 C5

@@@ – *see below*

Saf PLAN 7 C2

@ Vegan **NEW V**

Cutting-edge vegetarian and organic cooking

☎ 020 7613 0007
152-154 Curtain Rd, Shoreditch EC2A 3AT
e-mail: joe.mccanta@safrestaurant.co.uk
dir: Nearest station: Old Street. Exit 2 Old Street Station, towards Shoreditch High St, right Curtain Rd

Is there a restaurant more committed to organics and vegetarianism than Saf? Everything on the menu, down to the wine and cocktails, is organic, biodynamic and sustainable. An airy room with high ceilings and attractive artwork, this buzzy place also has an open kitchen so you can watch your food being prepared. Presentation of dishes is simple but very colourful - beetroot ravioli arrives with cashew herb ricotta, fennel carrot salad and balsamic figs, and might be followed by a creamy pumpkin risotto. Raw apple cake with hemp brittle and citrus frosting is a typical dessert.

Chef Faith Guven, Matt Downes **Owner** E Pamuksuzer, A Sezer, D Sanders & B Petterson **Times** 10.30-3.30/6-11 Closed 25 Dec, 1 Jan **Prices** Fixed D 3 course fr £30, Tasting menu £50-£75, Starter £7-£8.50, Main £13.50-£14.25, Dessert £4.25-£7.75, Service added but optional 12.5% **Wines** 50+ bottles over £20, 10 by glass **Notes** Tasting menu 7 course (with wine £75), Sunday L **Seats** 87, Pr/dining room 30 **Children** Portions, Menu

LONDON EC3

Addendum PLAN 6 C4

@@ Modern European

Appealing menu in slick City hotel

☎ 020 7977 9500 & 7702 2020
Apex City of London Hotel, 1 Seething Ln EC3N 4AX
e-mail: reservations@addendumrestaurant.co.uk
dir: Nearest station: Tower Hill, Fenchurch Street. Follow Lower Thames St, left onto Trinity Square, left onto Muscovy St, right onto Seething Ln, opposite Seething Ln gardens

Just a stone's throw from Tower Bridge, the Apex City of London Hotel's Addendum restaurant is in the heart of the Square Mile business district. Macho leather seats, wooden floors and subdued lighting create a relaxed atmosphere with the starched white tablecloths matching the sharp shirts and ties of the clientele. The modern European cooking, too, is business-like and confident, with menus offering seasonality and well-defined, clean flavours. A smoked trout fillet is served with horseradish, apple and watercress in a well-judged first course, or go for the traditional comforts of a roasted pork faggot with cider and sage. Main-courses might include calves' liver with spring onion mash and onion gravy, and pan-fried ling with green lentils and chervil butter sauce.

Times 12-2.30/6-10

Chamberlains Restaurant PLAN 6 C4

@@ Modern British, Seafood

Fresh fish in the heart of the City

☎ 020 7648 8690
23-25 Leadenhall Market EC3V 1LR
e-mail: info@chamberlains.org
dir: Nearest station: Bank, Monument.

Sitting pretty amid the Victorian splendour of Leadenhall Market, Chamberlains has quite a buzz from all those high-octane City workers. An upbeat seafood restaurant, it spreads over three floors and also has a terrace out front. Huge windows give views over the market and ensure the modern interior is light and bright during the day. There's a lively ground floor with a mezzanine balcony, a relaxed basement bar and a more formal upstairs room. Service zips along nicely. Fish and seafood come as fresh as it gets away from the coast, with dishes simply cooked without frills; take pan-fried John Dory (with capers and parsley butter), or chargrilled darne of Scottish halibut. It's not all fish, with a handful of meat options also available, however, side orders are a necessity and will push up the price.

Times 12-9.30 Closed Xmas, New Year & BHs, Sat-Sun

Rhodes Twenty Four

LONDON EC2 PLAN 6 C5

Modern British NOTABLE WINE LIST

Reinvented British food in the City sky

☎ 020 7877 7703
Tower 42, Old Broad St EC2N 1HQ
e-mail: reservations@rhodes24.co.uk
dir: Nearest station: Bank, Liverpool Street.

Named after its lofty eyrie on the 24th floor of Tower 42 - the Orwellian-sounding skyscraper better known as the NatWest Tower - Gary Rhodes' City of London restaurant quite literally hits the culinary heights. Once you have passed through airport-style security, a high-speed lift blasts you aloft for an unparalleled vista of the neighbouring Gherkin soaring from the heart of corporate moneyland. The neutral décor doesn't even attempt to compete with the view, and tables are spaced widely to allow the discreet conclusion of deals to the accompaniment of some pretty head-spinning gastronomic treats. A glance at the menu shows Gary Rhodes' trademark gutsy ingredients present and correct - mutton, suet pudding, oxtail, bone marrow - and you can expect them to have been impeccably sourced, cooked with top-level technical ability and brought together in thoughtful combinations. A meticulously-crafted starter teams a crispy breaded duck egg with wild mushrooms and Barkham blue cheese toasts. Next up, a succulent hunk of monkfish is a star turn alongside smoked bacon hash and the earthy flavours of salsify and trompette mushrooms. The meal finishes strongly with an iced blood orange mousse with chocolate jelly and a refreshing blood orange salad.

Chef Gary Rhodes, Adam Gray **Owner** Compass Group **Times** 12-2.30/6-9.15 Closed Xmas, New Year, BHs, Sat-Sun **Prices** Starter £9.80-£18, Main £16.50-£29.90, Dessert £8.95-£13.50, Service added but optional 12.5% **Wines** 243 bottles over £20, 21 by glass **Notes** Vegetarian available, Dress restrictions, Smart casual, no shorts **Seats** 75, Pr/dining room 30 **Parking**

Prism Brasserie and Bar PLAN 6 C4

◎◎ Modern European

Stylish brasserie and bar in impressive former banking hall

☎ 020 7256 3888
147 Leadenhall St EC3V 4QT
e-mail: prism.events@harveynichols.com
dir: Nearest station: Bank, Monument. Take exit 4 from Bank tube station, 5 mins walk

The grandly imposing surroundings of the former Bank of New York bring a touch of style to this Harvey Nichols-run operation. Soaring columns and lofty decorative ceilings offer a jaw-dropping backdrop to this upbeat, modern brasserie and bar. White linen, contemporary red leather chairs, flower displays and mood artwork bring colour to the dining quarter, while the large bar cranks-up the decibels and conceals a further narrow, conservatory-like dining area. The menu takes an accessible, something-for-everyone, modern brasserie approach, driven by fresh, quality produce. Classic grills, like 50-day aged Longhorn rib-eye, might rub shoulders with the more fashionable roasted Cornish pollock with borlotti beans, chorizo, lemon, chilli and parsley. The wine list is worth delving into, there's a smaller, club-like bar downstairs, while breakfast is served daily.

Chef Daniel Sherlock **Owner** Harvey Nichols
Times 11.30-2.30/6-10.30 Closed Xmas, BHs, Sat-Sun **Prices** Food prices not confirmed for 2011. Please telephone for details **Wines** 660 bottles over £20, 19 bottles under £20, 23 by glass **Notes** Vegetarian available **Seats** 120, Pr/dining room 40 **Children** Portions **Parking** On street & NCP

Restaurant Sauterelle PLAN 6 B4

◎◎ Modern French

Unfussy French cuisine in landmark building

☎ 020 7618 2483
The Royal Exchange EC3V 3LR
dir: Nearest station: Bank. In heart of business centre. Bank tube station exit 3

Sauterelle perches on the mezzanine floor of the historic Royal Exchange above an indoor courtyard awash with big-name designer boutiques and jet-set jewellers. Everything about this elegant restaurant fits the bill, from the swanky ambience to the well-oiled, professional service and the slick, French-accented modern cooking. The kitchen follows the seasons by choosing judiciously from the best materials available at London's markets, and delivering it in creative combinations of forthright flavours. Squid and black pudding is teamed with bulgar wheat, chorizo, lemon and parsley, ahead of brill with razor clams, red chard and Puy lentils. Cooking comes robust and rustic too, in the shape of 28-day aged Hereford beef fillet and ox cheek, with leek, bone marrow, tarragon and roasting juices. Considering the glam location, the set menu offering three choices at each course is a steal.

Chef Robin Gill **Owner** D & D London **Times** 12-2.30/6-10 Closed BHs, Sat-Sun **Prices** Fixed L 2 course £19.50, Fixed D 3 course £22.50, Tasting menu £45, Starter £8.75-£13.90, Main £17.50-£24, Dessert £7.50-£12, Service optional, Groups min 8 service 12.5% **Wines** 175 bottles over £20, 2 bottles under £20, 13 by glass **Notes** Tasting menu available L & D 5 course, Vegetarian available **Seats** 66, Pr/dining room 26 **Children** Portions

LONDON EC4

The Chancery PLAN 3 E3

◎◎ Modern British, French

Enjoyable brasserie-style dining in legal land

☎ 020 7831 4000
9 Cursitor St EC4A 1LL
e-mail: reservations@thechancery.co.uk
dir: Nearest station: Chancery Lane. Situated between High Holborn and Fleet St, just off Chancery Ln

There's a whiff of something Dickensian about the wig-wearing community in their chambers around Lincoln's Inn and Chancery Lane. But when the legal eagles want to pop out for some well-cooked modern European food, The Chancery is an antidote to the dry and dusty world of the law. It is a sleek, intimate bolt-hole - just a dozen tables in a modish monochrome décor: black leather chairs and white linen on burnished mahogany floors, with modern abstract art to add welcome colour. The kitchen goes about its business with a light touch, bringing a Mediterranean glow to the discreet neutral backdrop with dishes that paint an attractive picture on the plate: pan-roasted quail with white bean purée, and wild mushrooms and truffle jus sets the tone, ahead of main-course halibut partnered with wild garlic pommes purée, and tomato and mussel velouté. (The Clerkenwell Dining Room comes from the same stable, see entry.)

Chef Daniel Grurreio **Owner** Zak Jones
Times 12-2.30/6-10.30 Closed Xmas, Sun, L Sat **Prices** Food prices not confirmed for 2011. Please telephone for details **Wines** 12 bottles over £20, 5 bottles under £20, 3 by glass **Seats** 50 **Children** Portions **Parking** On street

Chinese Cricket Club PLAN 3 F2

◎ Chinese NEW V

Classic and modern Chinese in contemporary setting

☎ 020 7438 8051
Crowne Plaza London - The City, 19 New Bridge St EC4V 6DB
e-mail: loncy.ccc@ihg.com
dir: Nearest station: Temple, St Pauls, Blackfriars

Yes, China does have a national cricket team - it was formed in 2009, and this restaurant is named in honour of it. Part of the Crowne Plaza hotel near to Blackfriars Bridge, it is a sharp-looking contemporary space, all bare wood, neutral tones and Chinese calligraphy prints on the walls. Majoring in the dishes of Sichuan, the kitchen takes a modern tack, bringing a creative edge to the traditional repertoire; dim sum are a strong suit - lobster dumplings, black cod gow gee, honey-glazed pork puffs and steamed duck egg custard buns are all worth a try. Main courses bring the likes of crispy orange beef, 'hot and numbing' chicken, or for seafood fans, perhaps fried sea bass with garlic chives, or baby squid with broccoli and spiced oyster sauce.

Chef Brendan Speed **Owner** Intercon Hotel Group
Times 12-2.30/6-10 **Prices** Fixed L 2 course £15-£50, Fixed D 3 course £25-£45, Starter £4.50-£12, Main £7-£32, Dessert £5.50-£7.50, Service added 12.5%
Notes Vegetarian menu, Air con **Seats** 65

Lutyens Restaurant PLAN 3 F2

◎◎ Modern British, French NEW

Accomplished brasserie cooking in stylish setting

☎ 020 7583 8385
85 Fleet St EC4Y 1AE
e-mail: info@lutyens-restaurant.com
dir: Nearest station: Chancery Lane, St Pauls. Adjacent to St Bride's Church, opposite the former Daily Express building

Occupying what used to be the Reuters building on Fleet Street, it is easy to see the Conran stamp on this operation (the Prescott & Conran group is made up of Sir Terence, Vicki Conran and Peter Prescott). There's a large bar with a charcuterie counter, a shellfish bar where you can enjoy oysters and fruits de mer with a glass of wine, a members' club and private rooms, plus the coolly minimalistic restaurant, where neutral colours and smartly laid tables await. The cooking is modern British with a pronounced French accent. A starter of crèpe Parmentier with smoked eel and bacon might precede braised lamb and sweetbreads with roasted Jerusalem artichokes. Poached rhubarb with vanilla cream makes for a delightful finale.

Times 12-3/5.30-10 Closed Sat-Sun

LONDON EC4 ***continued***

Refettorio

PLAN 3 F2

◎◎ Italian

An Italian refectory in a City hotel

☎ 020 7438 8052 & 7438 8055
Crowne Plaza London - The City, 19 New Bridge St EC4V 6DB
e-mail: loncy.refettorio@ihg.com
dir: Nearest station: Blackfriars, Temple, St Paul's. Situated on New Bridge St, opposite Blackfriars underground (exit 8)

On the edge of the City proper, this branch of the Crowne Plaza hotel group boasts bright and contemporary décor behind an Edwardian façade. Lovers of innovative Italian cooking are drawn to Giorgio Locatelli's Refettorio, where a long communal table dominates a sleekly designed, smart space. Well-paced service might deliver one of the Convivium fixed-price selections of nibbles for sharing, but there is a full-dress menu of accomplished Italian dishes too. Generous portions of bresaola with rocket and parmesan, pork involtini with peperonata, and herb- and salt-crusted baked sea bass, the dish broached ceremonially at your table, and anointed with a balsamic dressing, are what to expect. Finish with tiramisù, served daringly with liquorice ice cream.

Chef Alessandro Bay **Owner** Crowne Plaza **Times** 12-2.30/6-10.30 Closed Xmas & BHs, Sun, L Sat **Prices** Fixed D 3 course £23-£25, Starter £7-£12, Main £16.75-£23.50, Dessert £6-£7.50, Service added but optional 12.5% **Wines** 59 bottles over £20, 6 bottles under £20, 8 by glass **Notes** Pre-theatre D menu £25, Bi-monthly seasonal menu £35, Vegetarian available, Dress restrictions, Smart casual, Civ Wed 100 **Seats** 100, Pr/dining room 33 **Children** Portions **Parking** NCP - Queen Victoria St

The White Swan Pub & Dining Room

PLAN 3 F3

◎ Modern, Traditional British

Upmarket gastro-pub with smart upstairs dining room

☎ 020 7242 9696
108 Fetter Ln EC4A 1ES
e-mail: info@thewhiteswanlondon.com
dir: Nearest station: Chancery Lane Tube Station

Holborn outpost of brothers Ed and Tom Martin's gastro-pub empire, The White Swan is certainly no mucky duck (as the pub was once called), with its lively, smartly remodelled wood-panelled bar and mezzanine floor, and dapper upstairs restaurant. The latter light, mirrored-ceiling room is where the real main culinary action kicks off - a fashionable confection of wood floor, leather seating and white linen. The kitchen's modern approach delivers clean-cut, clear-flavoured, well-presented dishes via a fixed-price lunch and evening carte. A starter of lobster and mushroom tortellini with salsify might precede poached Icelandic cod with squid and red pepper salad and saffron potatoes.

Times 12-3/6-10 Closed 25 Dec, 1 Jan and BHs, Sat-Sun (except private parties)

LONDON N1

Almeida Restaurant

PLAN 1 F4

◎◎ French V

French-inspired dishes in suave setting

☎ 020 7354 4777
30 Almeida St, Islington N1 1AD
e-mail: almeida-reservations@danddlondon.com
web: www.almeida-restaurant.co.uk
dir: Nearest station: Angel, Highbury & Islington. Turn right from station, along Upper St, past church

With the Almeida theatre opposite, and Sadler's Wells just up the road, this slick wine bar and restaurant has menus designed to dovetail with the performances. The wine bar section offers tapas-style grazing fodder to wash down with a great choice of wines by the glass or pichet, while eye-catching modern art against a cool backdrop of neutral cream and brown seems designed to appeal to Islington's chattering classes in the slick main restaurant. Gallic sophistication runs through the whole operation, from French-accented staff to a menu offering a light modern take on French classics; steaming and poaching are preferred cooking methods, rather than cream-based preparations. Sea bream might be partnered with herb gnocchi, warm cucumber and shellfish foam, while steamed sea trout could turn up with cockles and smoked bacon chowder. For something more gutsy, look no further than slow-braised suckling pig with caramelised apples, pommes purée, baby leeks and sauce aux épices.

Chef Alan Jones **Owner** D & D London **Times** 12-2.30/5.30-11 Closed 26 Dec, 1 Jan, L Mon, D Sun **Prices** Fixed L 2 course £15.95, Fixed D 3 course £32.50-£40, Starter £4.95-£9.50, Main £9.50-£15.50, Dessert £4.50-£8.50, Service optional, Groups min 8 service 12.5% **Wines** 195 bottles over £20, 5 bottles under £20, 21 by glass **Notes** Sunday L, Vegetarian menu, Civ Wed 120 **Seats** 80, Pr/dining room 20 **Children** Portions, Menu **Parking** On street

The Drapers Arms

PLAN 1 F4

◎ British **NEW**

Genuine gastro-pub with reassuringly robust seasonal cooking

☎ 020 7619 0348
44 Barnsbury St N1 1ER
e-mail: info@thedrapersarms.co.uk
dir: Nearest station: Highbury & Islington, Angel Just off Upper St, opposite town hall

Though discreetly tucked away in moneyed, residential Islington, the Drapers is no pretentious, counterfeit gastro-pub. Reborn back in 2009, it has pedigree; Karl Goward (former head chef at St John and St John Bread & Wine, see entries) heads up the kitchen, while Ben Maschler (son of *London Evening Standard* food critic Fay) is a partner. The restyled, pared-back Georgian interior is spread across two floors (with a restaurant upstairs), while the gutsy, no-nonsense British cooking cuts its cloth on seasonal ingredients and twice-daily changing menus that aren't afraid to use humbler ingredients. Grilled ox tongue comes with split peas and ham hock; braised veal cheeks with leeks, barley and aïoli; or there might be a sea bass dish for two to share. Informed, relaxed service, good wines, real ales and a courtyard garden add to the appeal.

Chef Karl Coward **Owner** Ben Maschler, Nick Gibson **Times** 12-3.30/6-10 **Prices** Fixed L 2 course £14-£23, Fixed D 3 course fr £25, Starter £4.50-£7.50, Main £9.50-£15.50, Dessert £5-£6.50, Service added 12.5% **Wines** 33 bottles over £20, 11 bottles under £20, 20 by glass **Notes** Sunday L, Vegetarian available **Seats** 60, Pr/dining room 45 **Children** Portions **Parking** On street

Fifteen London - The Dining Room

PLAN 3 H6

◎ Italian

A bootylicious chunk of Jamie delivered by fast-learning youngsters

☎ 020 3375 1515
15 Westland Place N1 7LP
dir: Nearest station: Old Street. Exit 1 from tube station, walk up City road, opposite Moorfields Eye Hospital

There can be very few who aren't aware of the raison d'être of Jamie Oliver's Fifteen, which represents a fine modern philanthropic venture, training up a new generation each year of young people in need of a better deal from life. The result is a growing international charitable enterprise, with JO's imprimatur stamped all over the heart-warming enthusiasm of the operation and the Italian-oriented menus. Beef carpaccio with truffled celeriac and the indispensable 'funky leaves' might start you off, before you step up to the plate with a 'wicked Sicilian fisherman's stew' comprised of salmon, cod, langoustine, squid, mussels and clams - not the easiest dish to bring off well. It all happens in a big converted warehouse.

Chef Andrew Parkinson **Owner** Jamie Oliver Foundation **Times** 12-2.45/6.30-9.30 Closed 25 Dec, 1 Jan **Prices** Fixed L 2 course fr £22.50, Tasting menu fr £60, Starter £9.50-£11.50, Main £20-£24, Dessert £6, Service added but optional 12.5% **Wines** 200+ bottles over £20, 12 by glass **Notes** Tasting menu, Sunday L, Vegetarian available **Seats** 68 **Children** Portions **Parking** On street & NCP

Frederick's Restaurant PLAN 1 F4

Modern European

Modern European cooking in Islington's antique quarter

020 7359 2888
Camden Passage, Islington N1 8EG
e-mail: eat@fredericks.co.uk
dir: Nearest station: Angel. From tube, 2 mins walk to Camden Passage. Restaurant among the antique shops

Hidden away in Islington's Camden Passage is this light and airy restaurant serving up modern European flavours. Sit in the main Garden Room with its spectacular vaulted glass roof or head outside to the patio when the weather is clement. Formally-laid tables and modern artwork on the walls provide the perfect backdrop to the simple and imaginative cooking. Start with dressed crab, tempura vegetables and beetroot coulis before pan-fried calves' liver, chargrilled polenta and Swiss chard and perhaps cinnamon beignets, praline cream and orange sauce to end. A decent selection of wines by the glass is another plus point.

Times 12-2.30/5.45-11.30 Closed Xmas, New Year, BHs, Sun (ex functions)

LONDON N7

Morgan M PLAN 1 E5

– see below

LONDON N17

The Lock Restaurant PLAN 1 F5

Modern British

Creative cooking in chic warehouse-style restaurant

020 8885 2829
Heron House, Hale Wharf, Ferry Ln N17 9NF
e-mail: thelock06@googlemail.com
dir: Nearest station: Tottenham Hale, Black Horse Station

Not the first place you might think of as a gastronomic destination, but step off the train at Tottenham Hale and head for this open-plan New York loft-style restaurant to puncture your prejudice. With its whitewashed walls, wooden floor and unclothed tables it has a relaxed vibe, which is added to by the open-plan kitchen and all round relaxed attitude. The menu delivers a broadly modern British repertoire with an open mind to the rest of the world. Savoury bread-and-butter pudding with sautéed foie gras, sliced poached beetroot and micro leaves is a first course with decidedly post-modern credentials. Follow that with pan-fried fillet of John Dory, served with citrus polenta cake and diver-caught scallop and sea urchin sauce. Deep-fried vanilla rice pudding bonbon and chocolate sauce is an equally creative finish.

Chef Adebola Adeshina **Owner** The Forerib Ltd **Times** 12-2/6.30-10 Closed Mon, L Sat (except match days), D Sun **Prices** Fixed L 2 course £11-£12.50, Fixed D 3 course £22.50-£25, Starter £4-£9.50, Main £9.50-£24.95, Dessert £5-£6, Service added but optional 10% **Wines** 10 bottles over £20, 15 bottles under £20, 12 by glass **Notes** Tasting menu available on request, Sunday L, Vegetarian available, Dress restrictions, Smart casual, no hats/caps **Seats** 60, Pr/dining room 18 **Children** Portions, Menu **Parking** 20

LONDON NW1

La Collina PLAN 1 E4

Italian

A taste of Italy in pretty Primrose Hill

020 7483 0192
17 Princess Rd, Chalk Farm NW1 8JR
dir: Nearest station: Chalk Farm, Camden Town

Sitting outside in the large rear garden at La Collina on a warm day, you could easily imagine yourself in Italy. The

continued

Morgan M

LONDON N7 PLAN 1 E5

Modern French V

Exemplary French cooking in relaxed, stylish setting

020 7609 3560
489 Liverpool Rd, Islington N7 8NS
dir: Nearest station: Highbury & Islington

In its Islington location, you might take the frosted glass and bottle-green frontage of Morgan M as a trendy gastro-pub, but a resolutely French enterprise lies within. The 'M' stands for Meunier, a chef-patron with pedigree, who has created his vision of an intimate Gallic restaurant. It is a civilised space, tables are immaculately set and well-spaced, the colour scheme is fresh and warm. The cuisine takes a thoroughly modern tack: anchored in the French classics, it bristles with luxury ingredients and respects the seasons. This is high-level, glossy cooking so you can expect foams, emulsions, purées, intriguing textures and curveball flavour combinations - push the boat out and go for the six-course tasting menu to try as many as you can. A winter menu might start with an unusual cream of chestnut with Stilton foam, ahead of seared John Dory fillet with braised Puy lentils, mushroom beignet and thyme beurre blanc. Pyrenean lamb is deconstructed as roast leg, confit shoulder, and grilled cutlet and served with Jerusalem artichoke soubise, braised potato and rosemary jus. Desserts maintain the same high standards, using only the best 70% Valrhona Guanaja in a dark chocolate moelleux with a mandarin drink and Grand Marnier ice cream. The excellent wine list focuses predictably enough on France, offering some massive vintages with prices to match.

Chef M Meunier, S Soulard **Owner** Morgan Meunier **Times** 12-2.30/7-10.30 Closed 24-30 Dec, Mon, L Tue, Sat, D Sun **Prices** Fixed L 2 course £22.50-£28.50, Fixed D 3 course £41-£46, Service added but optional 12.5% **Wines** 140 bottles over £20, 3 bottles under £20, 6 by glass **Notes** Tasting menu £50 (vegetarian £45), Sunday L, Vegetarian menu, Dress restrictions, Smart casual **Seats** 48, Pr/dining room 12 **Children** Portions **Parking** On Liverpool Rd

LONDON NW1 ***continued***

cooking is as authentic as you could wish for, and the Italian staff help complete the picture. There's an Italian feel to the place inside too, with its white-washed walls, linen-clothed tables, wooden chairs and stripped wooden floorboards. The menu - produced from an open kitchen - changes regularly but might offer the likes of creamy burrata with cherry tomatoes and basil to start, followed by braised rabbit with baby artichokes, or black potato dumplings with lobster ragu. The home-made Amaretto ice cream with baked peaches makes for a great early summer dessert.

Times 12-2.30/6-11 Closed Xmas wk, L Mon-Fri

Gilgamesh Restaurant Lounge PLAN 1 E4

Pan-Asian

Pan-Asian dishes in a psychedelic re-creation of ancient Babylon (in Camden)

☎ 020 7482 5757
Camden Stables Market, Chalk Farm Rd NW1 8AH
dir: Nearest station: Chalk Farm

Up an escalator in the Stables market in Camden Town, Gilgamesh takes its name from the earliest surviving epic narrative of ancient times. The Babylonian theme finds its elaboration in a series of mind-blowing interiors (sort of), where glass walls, trees and Near Eastern fabric design collide excitingly amid washes of psychedelic lighting. The food is pan-Asian, predominantly Japanese (good sushi, tempura and miso soup), but with admixtures of other culinary traditions too, in the shapes of Chinese dim sum, Thai salads and Malay specials like beef Penang with coconut rice. Finish with green tea brûlée with jasmine and white peach sorbet, accompanied perhaps by a tot of sweet sake, or go on to one of the fruity after-dinner cocktails.

Times 12-2.30/6

Melia White House

Spanish NEW

Modern and traditional Spanish cuisine in elegant surroundings

☎ 020 7391 3000
Albany Street, Regent's Park NW1 3UP

The Melia White House Hotel, an impressive art-deco hotel close to Regent's Park, is home to L'Albufera, an elegant fine-dining Spanish restaurant. Polished wooden floors, black clothed tables topped with fine glassware, cream upholstered chairs and subtle lighting make for a smart setting for an ambitious menu that features Spanish dishes of both old and new schools, and some broader Mediterranean influences. Some dishes are robust, others more refined, all are big on flavour and based on good quality ingredients. Slices of excellent Serrano ham carved from the bone kick things off, before a first course such as grilled squid, prawns and scallops on Parmentier foam with squid ink risotto; next up, main-course olive-crusted grilled tuna with truffled potatoes and olive consommé. Round things off with a spot-on lime and chocolate crème brûlée with basil ice cream.

Times 7-10.30 Closed Sun, L all wk

Megaro PLAN 3 C6

British

Modern cooking in smart city hotel

☎ 020 7843 2221 & 7843 2222
23-27 Euston Rd, St Pancras NW1 2SD
e-mail: gm@hotelmegaro.co.uk
dir: Nearest station: King's Cross St Pancras

Megaro Restaurant is a little oasis tucked away in the basement of a stylish boutique hotel close to King's Cross and St Pancras stations. Head down the staircase tiled with Italian granite and smooth Welsh slate into the smart, modern dining room with its red leather-style chairs and high quality beech-topped tables. Service is friendly and efficient and complemented by the kitchen team's modern menu. The dishes are very much driven by quality ingredients and simple yet appealing presentation; take gaspacho with tiger prawns, mint and coriander, beef fillet with bacon mash, Savoy cabbage and red onion marmalade, finishing with glazed lemon tart with raspberry sorbet.

Times 5-10 Closed L all week

Odette's Restaurant & Bar

LONDON NW1 PLAN 1 E4

Modern European V

Primrose Hill darling delivers modern British flavours

☎ 020 7586 8569
130 Regent's Park Rd NW1 8XL
e-mail: info@primrosehill.com
dir: Nearest station: Chalk Farm.

Step in off the chi-chi street in pretty Primrose Hill and you'd be forgiven for thinking you'd walked into a rather striking boudoir. Chef-patron Bryn Williams certainly hasn't gone the neutral route with his bold floral wallpaper and bright yellow leather chairs. Still, it's a look that works in this iconic neighbourhood restaurant, which first opened in 1978. A canvas awning provides shelter to the street-side diners and there's a small conservatory and bar area downstairs. Denbigh-born Williams' prestigious CV includes stints at Marco Pierre White's Criterion and Le Gavroche, while his TV career hit a high when he won the BBC's *Great British Menu* competition, cooking the starter for the Queen's 80th birthday celebration banquet. At Odette's, the modern European food is slick and technically impressive with great flavours guaranteed. It goes without saying that seasonal and regional produce play a starring role in the à la carte and tasting menu (veggies' get their own). You might find pig's head and black pudding terrine with sauce gribiche, watercress and toasted sourdough, followed by pan-fried turbot with braised oxtail, cockles and samphire. Finish with a confidently executed chocolate fondant, pistachio and tarragon ice cream.

Chef Bryn Williams **Owner** Bryn Williams
Times 12-2.30/6.30-10.30 Closed 25 Dec -1 Jan, Mon (incl BHs) **Prices** Fixed L 2 course £14, Starter £8-£12, Main £16-£21, Dessert £7-£11, Service added but optional 12.5% **Wines** 100 bottles over £20, 4 bottles under £20, 15 by glass **Notes** Tasting menu 7 course, Sunday L, Vegetarian menu **Seats** 75, Pr/dining room 25 **Children** Portions **Parking** On street

Mirrors Restaurant PLAN 3 C5

Modern European

Sleek modern hotel restaurant with a wide-ranging carte

☎ 020 7666 9080
Novotel London St Pancras, 100-110 Euston Rd NW1 2AJ
e-mail: h5309-fb@accor.com
dir: Nearest station: King's Cross, Euston, St Pancras International. 3 min walk from St Pancras International. Adjacent to the British Library

The bustle of Euston Road rumbles endlessly past the full-length picture windows of this natty contemporary restaurant within a busy outpost of the French Novotel chain. King's Cross, St Pancras and Euston railway stations and the British Library are all close neighbours. The curvy mirrors in question bounce your reflection around the entrance of the ground-floor venue, a sharply-dressed space of glass and pale wood, bold dark cherry and purple seating. A carvery and open kitchen are the focus of culinary endeavours delivering French-inflected modern European dishes on an eclectic menu. Carpaccio of venison with pickled walnuts and pomegranate molasses makes a good appetiser for main courses such as seared fillet of sea bass with tonnarelli pasta and tarragon-scented crab and clam velouté.

Chef Rees Smith **Owner** Accor UK Business & Leisure **Times** 12-2.30/6-10.30 Closed L Sat, Sun, BHs **Prices** Fixed L 2 course fr £16.50, Fixed D 3 course fr £22.50, Starter £5.75-£8.95, Main £13.50-£25.95, Dessert £6.25, Service added but optional 10% **Wines** 21 bottles over £20, 7 bottles under £20, 13 by glass **Notes** Vegetarian available **Seats** 89, Pr/dining room 250 **Children** Portions, Menu **Parking** Ibis Euston

Odette's Restaurant & Bar PLAN 1 E4

– see opposite page

St Pancras Grand PLAN 3 C6

British

Great British menu in art deco railway setting

☎ 020 7870 9900
St Pancras International NW1 9QP
dir: Nearest station: King's Cross St Pancras

At platform level of the grandly and expensively made-over St Pancras International, St Pancras Grand serves honest British cooking with aplomb. Reminiscent of the time when station dining was a romantic affair, the spacious restaurant benefits from art-deco styling with blue banquette seating, an old railway clock to keep tabs on the time 'til your train and a railway ticket for the cloakroom when you deposit your bags. An oyster bar at one end also offers charcuterie and cold fish for a quick bite. Open from breakfast to dinner and all eating occasions in-between, head chef Chris Dines has devised a very British menu of old favourites and modern inventions which does a fine job of convincing our French cousins that British food really is worth the Eurostar journey. Begin with English beetroot and watercress salad moving onto grilled Barnsley lamb chop, lamb's kidney and mint sauce and finish with burnt Cambridge cream and autumn fruits. Across the concourse lies sister operation the Champagne Bar (the longest in Europe, natch) for one last drink before you board that train.

Times 7am-11pm

Sardo Canale PLAN 1 E4

Italian

Classic Sardinian cuisine in a fashionable canalside setting

☎ 020 7722 2800
42 Gloucester Av NW1 8JD
e-mail: info@sardocanale.com
dir: Nearest station: Chalk Farm, Camden Town. Alongside Regents Canal, 5 min walk along the canal from Camden Market

Right on the Grand Union Canal, this modern Italian restaurant is in a listed building with a history that is part of the area's industrial heritage, with, amongst other things, the vaults once being used as tunnels where horses pulled goods from the yards to the canal. These days it looks very stylish with the vaulted ceiling exposed, the fixtures and fittings chosen with a keen eye and a smart contemporary feel. There're plenty of outside

continued

York & Albany

LONDON NW1

Modern British, European V

Classy, confident cooking in elegant Regency house

☎ 020 7387 5700
127-129 Parkway NW1 7PS
e-mail: yorkandalbany@gordonramsay.com
dir: Nearest station: Camden Town. Overlooking Regent's Park

There are some seriously grand buildings flanking Regent's Park and the York & Albany can hold its own, especially since the John Nash designed former coaching inn was given an invigorating refurbishment by Gordon Ramsay Holdings in 2008. It can't have looked so smart since its Regency heyday. It combines boutique hotel, vibrant bar, a tantalising deli called Nonni's (housed in the former stables), and a restaurant over two floors which is under the auspices of Angela Hartnett, with Colin Buchan heading up the kitchen team day-to-day. The look is smart and contemporary, the colours chosen from the muted modern palette, lighting is mellow and subdued, chairs are comfortable and tables are shorn of their cloths. A fair old buzz is generated at times. Hartnett has drawn on her favoured supply chain to deliver some superb produce. The focus is on a broadly modern European outlook, although with much evidence of her trademark Italian leanings, and a happy partnership of uncomplicated dishes and sharp technical skills. Confit duck leg tortellini with turnip purée and black cabbage is a well-judged first course; next up, perhaps pan-fried hake with crab and ginger risotto and pak choi, or braised lamb shank with kohlrabi fondant. Caramelised orange tart with chocolate and Amaretto ice cream is an enticing finish. The lunch and early supper menu is a bit of a steal.

Chef Angela Hartnett **Owner** Gordon Ramsay Holdings Ltd **Times** 12-3/6-11 **Prices** Fixed L 3 course £20, Fixed D 3 course £20, Starter £7.50-£12.50, Main £17-£46, Dessert £6-£12, Service added but optional 12.5% **Wines** 100 bottles over £20, 4 bottles under £20, 13 by glass **Notes** Sunday L, Vegetarian menu, Dress restrictions, Casual, no shorts or sportswear, denim OK, Civ Wed 40 **Seats** 85, Pr/dining room 70 **Children** Portions, Menu **Parking** On street

LONDON NW1 *continued*

tables, too, where there's a 300 year-old Sardinian olive tree to admire. Authentic, classy Sardinian food is the thing here and it adds up to an exciting dining experience. Start with baby octopus in a white wine and tomato sauce with pine kernels, move on to fresh crab meat linguine with extra virgin olive oil, parsley and fresh chillies, and for dessert, frozen panettone cream with dark chocolate sauce.

Chef Claudio Covino **Owner** Romolo & Bianca Mudu **Times** 12-3/6-11 Closed 25-26 Dec, Mon (ex BHs) **Prices** Starter £6.90-£8.90, Main £9.90-£17.50, Service added but optional 12.5% **Wines** 75 bottles over £20, 10 bottles under £20, 19 by glass **Notes** Sunday L **Seats** 100, Pr/dining room 40 **Children** Portions **Parking** On street

The Winter Garden

PLAN 2 F4

British, Mediterranean

Stunning atrium restaurant at Marylebone hotel

☎ 020 7631 8000 & 7631 8230
The Landmark London, 222 Marylebone Rd NW1 6JQ
e-mail: restaurants.reservation@thelandmark.co.uk
web: www.wintergarden-london.com
dir: Nearest station: Marylebone

A landmark by name and by nature, this Victorian Grande Dame was built during the Great Age of Steam when railways ruled the land. The old girl served for a while as the HQ of British Rail and is now restored to its full splendour as a five-star hotel. The central courtyard has been glassed over to become an amazing eight-storey atrium, where the Winter Garden restaurant sits centre stage beneath soaring palm trees. It's a splendid place to eat, light-drenched in the day, and romantic for dinner when a pianist plays a soundtrack to a menu of modern European themes. Pan-roasted scallops with squid ink risotto might appear as a starter, while main courses could see fillet of Irish beef served with oxtail ravioli, fondant potato, parsley and red wine sauce, alongside seared sea bass teamed with boulangère potatoes, braised fennel and tomato, and brown shrimp sauce. For a more casual menu, try the Cellars Bar and Restaurant.

Chef Gary Klaner **Owner** Khun Jatuporn Sihanatkathakul **Times** 11.30-3/6-10.45 **Prices** Fixed L 2 course fr £30, Starter £10-£16, Main £20-£38, Dessert fr £8.50, Service optional **Wines** all bottles over £20, 25 by glass **Notes** Sunday L, Dress restrictions, Smart casual **Seats** 90 **Parking** On street

York & Albany

– see page 245

LONDON NW3

Manna

International Vegetarian V

Trend-setting vegetarian in north London

☎ 020 7722 8028
4 Erskine Rd, Primrose Hill NW3 3AJ
e-mail: geninfo@mannv.com
dir: Nearest station: Chalk Farm

A forerunner of gourmet vegetarian and vegan dining when it opened in the 60s, Manna is still leading from the front with regard to ethical principles and organic values. The attractive shop front in a residential street in Primrose Hill gives way to a rather stylish interior where tables are neatly laid, colours are from the fashionable neutrally natural palette, and details such as branch-style light fittings give it a touch of class. Carefully-sourced produce is turned into dishes that take inspiration from far and wide whilst never losing focus. Expect the likes of spiced chole cake - a split chick pea, red lentil and cashew spiced pattie - with tamarind chutney and a herbed and ginger yoghurt curry and a main course of enchilada casserole with cashew 'cheese', black beans and rich mole sauce, or perhaps the speciality organic spaghetti with meatless balls.

Owner R Swallow, S Hague **Times** 12-3/6.30-11 Closed 25 Dec-1 Jan (open New Year's Eve), Etr Sun, Mon, L Tue-Fri **Prices** Food prices not confirmed for 2011. Please telephone for details **Wines** 20 bottles over £20, 8 bottles under £20, 8 by glass **Notes** Sunday L **Seats** 50 **Children** Portions **Parking** On street

XO

PLAN 1 E5

Pan-Asian

Asian variety act in well-heeled Belsize Park

☎ 020 7433 0888
29 Belsize Ln NW3 5AS
e-mail: xo@rickerrestaurants.com
dir: Nearest station: Swiss Cottage, Belsize Park. From Havistock Hill turn right into Ornan Rd (Before BP garage), restaurant on right

Another of London entrepreneur Will Ricker's pace-setting bar and restaurant group, XO is all pared-down sparseness, with booth-style seating, light fittings that look like Calderesque mobiles, and a lime green thing going on. The food ploughs several Asian furrows at once, offering Belsize Park's smart set the choice of seared tuna with miso aïoli, lamb Penang, or black cod with yuzu, with sides of bok choy in soy and ginger, or ho fun noodles. It's all great fun, the cultural collisions enhanced by some stirring cocktails at the bar. To end it all with banoffee pie seems almost prosaic in the circumstances.

Chef Jon Higgonson **Owner** Will Ricker **Times** 12-3/6-11 Closed 25-26 Dec **Prices** Fixed L 2 course fr £11, Fixed D 3 course £15-£36, Starter £5.50-£9.50, Main £9.50-£24.50, Dessert £4.75-£6, Service added but optional 12.5% **Wines** 60 bottles over £20, 12 bottles under £20, 14 by glass **Notes** Sunday L, Vegetarian available **Seats** 92, Pr/dining room 22 **Children** Portions, Menu **Parking** On street

LONDON NW4

Fringe Restaurant

PLAN 1 D5

British European

Dramatic setting for modern bistro cooking

☎ 020 8203 3341 & 8457 2502
Hendon Hall Hotel, Ashley Ln, Hendon NW4 1HF
dir: Nearest station: Hendon Central. M1 junct 2. A406. Right at lights onto Parson St. Next right into Ashley Lane, Hendon Hall is on right

Hendon Hall has been around since the 16th century, but while history looms large, there's nothing archaic about the food in the stylish Fringe Restaurant. A theatrical modern décor brings together plush tangerine high-backed seats and bare darkwood tables against a backdrop of gunmetal and damson walls, while staff make sure everything ticks over with friendly professionalism. A new chef came on board in 2009 and raised the kitchen's game, delivering a daily market menu to take advantage of the season's best produce in vibrant modern bistro-style cooking. Dishes are refined but never fussy, and flavours are fine-tuned so that they balance rather than compete with each other. Slow-cooked pork belly might be teamed in a first course with black pudding and apple purée and ham hock beignets, while mains might take in loin of venison with oxtail faggot, red cabbage, celeriac purée, Burgundy sauce and chocolate oil. Interesting dessert combinations include vanilla cheesecake with poached rhubarb, coconut gel and rhubarb sorbet.

Times 12-2.30/7-10

LONDON NW6

Singapore Garden Restaurant PLAN 1 E4

Singaporean, Malaysian

Well-established oriental restaurant with authentic flavours

020 7328 5314
83 Fairfax Rd, West Hampstead NW6 4DY
dir: Nearest station: Swiss Cottage, Finchley Road. Off Finchley Rd, on right before Belsize Rd rdbt

This classy neighbourhood oriental has been coming up with the goods among the chic boutiques near Finchley Road tube station since 1984, so lucky Swiss Cottagers can look forward to pukka renditions of Malaysian, Singaporean and Chinese specialities in an upmarket setting. The menu is huge, so it's probably best to seek satisfaction among the Singapore and Malaysian section, or the seasonal specials card, as the kitchen's repertoire is built on fresh materials. Watch out for the spicing that takes no prisoners, and go for prawns fried in the shell in a peanutty assam sambal sauce, hot-and-sour Singapore laksa soup, or otak otak fishcakes, grilled in a banana leaf over charcoal with kaffir lime leaf and chilli.

Chef Kok Sum Toh **Owner** Hibiscus Restaurants Ltd **Times** 12-2.45/6-10.45 Closed 4 days at Xmas **Prices** Food prices not confirmed for 2011. Please telephone for details **Wines** 39 bottles over £20, 4 bottles under £20, 6 by glass **Notes** Vegetarian available **Seats** 85 **Parking** Meters on street

LONDON SE1

The Anchor & Hope PLAN 5 F5

British

High octane gastro-pub with big-hearted cooking

020 7928 9898
36 The Cut SE1 8LP
e-mail: anchorandhope@btconnect.com
dir: Nearest station: Southwark, Waterloo

Except for Sunday lunch, you can't book to eat in this mega popular Waterloo gastro-pub: think of it as the height of democracy in action - everyone has to turn up and wait in the bar until called to table. Time to take in the décor, then, which is laid-back, informal and boldly coloured - no frills, in short, rather like the food really. Things can get loud too at peak times, with just a heavy curtain screening the high-decibel bar from the dining area. But the noise and wait are worth putting up with for the visceral, hearty dishes hewn from well-sourced seasonal materials. There's no need to do the three-course thing either: the flannel-free menu lists what's on for that meal sitting - you could go for several smaller portions or one big one. What arrives is heart-warming, rib-sticking British food - maybe ducks' hearts on toast to get the juices flowing, then roast saddle of hare with braised chicory and semolina gnocchi. Fish gets the same no-nonsense treatment - try hake and mussels in crab broth with rouille and Ogleshield cheese croûton. Puddings bring on treacle tart and clotted cream, all served with friendly gusto by clued-up young staff.

Chef Jonathon Jones **Owner** Robert Shaw, Mike Belben, Jonathon Jones, Harry Lester **Times** 12-2.30/6-10.30 Closed BHs, 25 Dec-1 Jan, L Mon, D Sun **Prices** Starter £4.60-£9, Main £10.80-£21, Dessert £2.40-£5, Service optional **Wines** 25 bottles over £20, 26 bottles under £20, 13 by glass **Notes** Sunday L, Vegetarian available **Seats** 58 **Parking** On street

Baltic PLAN 5 F5

Eastern European

Authentic Eastern European cooking in stylish, modern surroundings

020 7928 1111
74 Blackfriars Rd SE1 8HA
e-mail: info@balticrestaurant.co.uk
dir: Nearest station: Southwark. Opposite Southwark station, 5 mins walk from Waterloo

The minimally cool Baltic is the star in the capital's East European drinking and dining scene. The 18th-century coachbuilder's workshop certainly makes a striking statement - a free-form chandelier made of Baltic amber shards hangs from a 40-foot-high wooden-trussed ceiling with skylights flooding the long steel bar. Brain-numbing vodka cocktails, jazz and lots of hard surfaces add up to a lively vibe. Food-wise, the kitchen references the diverse pleasures of the Baltic and Adriatic in sharply-flavoured modern ideas. Tongue-twisting dishes are helpfully translated - start with krupnik (pearl barley and bacon soup) then try confit duck leg with bratwurst, bacon and butter beans, or kulebiak (salmon in pastry with wild mushrooms, kasza - buckwheat porridge - and spinach).

Times 12-3/6-11 Closed Xmas, 1 Jan, BHs

Canteen Royal Festival Hall PLAN 5 E5

British

Traditional British cooking beneath the Royal Festival Hall

0845 686 1122
Royal Festival Hall, Southbank Centre, Belvedere Rd SE1 8XX
e-mail: rfh@canteen.co.uk
dir: Nearest station: Waterloo

The runaway success of the Canteen family of restaurants has seen it mushroom into a mini-empire of four outposts, showing that there are plenty of willing takers for traditional British food done right. The operation in the basement of the Royal Festival Hall opens out onto a square for sunny day alfresco dining, but if the British summer sets in with its customary severity, this Canteen gives diners the culinary theatre of a busy open kitchen to provide distraction. The flag-waving food harks back to the schooldays comfort eating of yesteryear, based on wholesome, well-sourced British produce. Choosing from the all-day menu, you could kick off with a fish finger sandwich, or devilled kidneys on toast, before moving on to a daily-changing array of roasts, pies, stews and bakes - perhaps pork and cider pie, or sausages and mash with onion gravy.

Chef Cass Titcombe **Owner** Dom Lake, Patrick Clayton-Malone & Cass Titcombe **Times** 8am-11pm Closed 25 Dec **Prices** Starter £5.50, Main £8-£16.75, Dessert £4.50-£8.50, Service added but optional 12.5% **Wines** 27 bottles over £20, 9 bottles under £20, 33 by glass **Notes** Sunday L, Vegetarian available **Children** Portions

Cantina del Ponte PLAN 6 D2

Italian

Relaxed Italian dining by the Thames

020 7403 5403
The Butlers Wharf Building, 36c Shad Thames SE1 2YE
e-mail: cantinareservations@danddlondon.com
dir: Nearest station: Tower Hill, London Bridge. SE side of Tower Bridge, on river front

A corner of Mediterranean sunshine in Butlers Wharf, Cantina del Ponte offers the full Italian experience next to the Thames. Located on the wharfside promenade, and with views of Tower Bridge, the large heated terrace is a must for alfresco dining and inside the restaurant offers a modern twist on the traditional trattoria with clean lines and contemporary furnishings combined with terracotta floor tiles and a huge Italian market mural. The food is robust and packed with flavour, with classics like seafood linguine and beef carpaccio catching the eye. Fish might appeal given the waterside location; perhaps pan-fried sea bass with cannellini beans cooked with garlic and tomato with green herb sauce. Italian wines complete the picture.

Chef Brian Fantoni **Owner** D & D London **Times** 12-3/6-11 Closed 24-26 Dec **Prices** Fixed L 2 course £10.95, Fixed D 3 course £18.95, Starter £4.50-£9.50, Main £7.25-£19.50, Dessert £4.75-£7.95, Service optional, Groups min 8 service 12.5% **Wines** 33 bottles over £20, 5 bottles under £20, 11 by glass **Notes** Sunday L, Vegetarian available **Seats** 110 **Children** Portions **Parking** NCP Gainsford St

Cantina Vinopolis PLAN 6 A3

Modern European NOTABLE WINE LIST

Underneath the arches, London's wine tasting attraction

020 7940 8333
1 Bank End SE1 9BU
e-mail: info@cantinavinopolis.com
dir: Nearest station: London Bridge. 5 min walk from London Bridge on Bankside between Southwark Cathedral & Shakespeare's Globe Theatre

London's premier wine tasting attraction and adjoining restaurant are impressively located under the stunning arches of a Victorian railway viaduct near London Bridge Station. It's a vast space with high ceilings, exposed brickwork and displays of wine bottles to remind you of

continued

LONDON SE1 *continued*

your whereabouts. The theatre kitchen creates atmosphere, helped along by the subdued lighting, which also prevents the large room from feeling cavernous. The menu is largely pointed towards the Mediterranean and each dish comes with a wine recommendation. Follow spiced grilled squid with tomatoes, chorizo and olive salsa, with lamb rump with dauphinoise and lamb jus, leaving room for banana sticky toffee pudding.

Times 12-3/6-10.30 Closed BHs, D Sun

Champor-Champor PLAN 6 B2

® Modern Malay-Asian

Creative Malay-Asian fusion cooking in charming setting

☎ 020 7403 4600
62-64 Weston St SE1 3QJ
e-mail: mail@champor-champor.com
dir: Nearest station: London Bridge Joiner St exit. Left onto Saint Thomas St & 1st right into Weston St, restaurant 100yds on left

Tucked away on a side street behind London Bridge station, this quirky little Malay restaurant is something of a find. Step through the door and you enter a perfumed world of Asian treasures, with barely a space left uncovered by tribal masks, Buddhist statues, brightly coloured wall paintings and intricate carvings, and, if there's just two of you, try for the mezzanine table. Champor-Champor is a Malay expression, which loosely translates as 'mix and match' and the food, like the bohemian décor, reflects the theme, with Asian cuisines grafted onto distinctly Malay roots and given a modern, creative twist. Roasted sea bass fillet comes in a turmeric and galangal curry with salmon caviar, or there's ostrich fillet phad pet (a spicy stir-fry of thin beans, holy basil and lime leaves) with jasmine tea rice.

Times 6-10 Closed Xmas-New Year (7 days), Etr (5 days), BHs, Sun, L by appointment only

Chino Latino @ The Park Plaza Riverbank PLAN 5 D3

® Modern Pan-Asian

Pan-Asian menu in a stylish South Bank hotel

☎ 020 7769 2500
Albert Embankment SE1 7TJ
e-mail: avdwesthuizen@pphe.com
dir: Nearest station: Vauxhall

Chino Latino is an international brand with outposts in Nottingham, Leeds, Cologne, and here in a South Bank hotel facing the Palace of Westminster. Stylish décor is all cream leather and ruby-coloured glass panels, with sepulchral lighting, and the fusion indicated by the name embraces Latino cocktails and a Pan-Asian menu that is partly Chino, but more predominantly Japaneso. There are dim sum, tempura, sushi and sashimi sections on the menu, together with main dishes such as pork ribs in black bean and oyster sauce, or Chilean sea bass with choi sum cooked in shaoxing wine. The freshness and liveliness of it all are compelling, and the ideal way to finish is with green tea and mochi ice cream with chocolate sauce.

Chef Werner Seebach **Owner** Park Plaza Hotels **Times** 12-2.30/6-10.30 Closed 25-27 Dec, 1 Jan, L Sat-Sun **Prices** Food prices not confirmed for 2011. Please telephone for details **Wines** 45 bottles over £20, 9 bottles under £20, 8 by glass **Notes** Vegetarian available, Dress restrictions, Smart casual, no sportswear **Seats** 85 **Children** Portions **Parking** 60

The County Hall Restaurant PLAN 5 D5

® Modern European

Modern cooking in grand riverside setting

☎ 020 7902 8000
London Marriott Hotel, Westminster Bridge Rd SE1 7PB
e-mail: mhrs.lonch.fandb@marriott.com
dir: Nearest station: Waterloo, Westminster. Situated next to Westminster Bridge on the South Bank. Opposite side to Houses of Parliament

Once home to Greater London Council, this elegant crescent-shaped riverside dining room boasts stunning views of the London Eye, the Thames and the Westminster skyline and has even appeared in a James Bond film. The original oak panelling and high ceilings of what was the main reading room for County Hall workers make for an impressive setting for the modern European cooking which is rooted in classic French technique. A starter of five-spice Gloucestershire Old Spot pork belly with chorizo and Puy lentils might be followed by pan-seared John Dory with wilted kale and lemongrass foam.

Chef Christopher Basten **Owner** Marriott International **Times** 12.30-3/5.30-10.30 Closed 26 Dec **Prices** Fixed L 2 course fr £23.50, Fixed D 3 course fr £27, Starter £6-£10.50, Main £20-£28, Dessert £7-£9, Service optional **Wines** 89 bottles over £20, 16 by glass **Notes** Sunday L, Vegetarian available, Dress restrictions, Smart casual, Civ Wed 100 **Seats** 80, Pr/dining room 60 **Children** Portions, Menu **Parking** 8, Valet parking

Magdalen PLAN 6 C2

®® British, French

An absolute gem near London Bridge station

☎ 020 7403 1342 & 077961 77219
152 Tooley St SE1 2TU
e-mail: info@magdalenrestaurant.co.uk
web: www.magdalenrestaurant.co.uk
dir: Nearest station: London Bridge. 5 min walk from London Bridge. Restaurant opposite Unicorn Theatre, 300yds on right

Sheltering under the railway lines near London Bridge station, Magdalen is an absolute gem in an area not over-endowed with classy eating. The proximity of Borough Market helps, and much of the produce finds its way over from there to this chic, capably run venue with its varnished wood floors, paper-topped tables and gently tweaked French regional cooking. Accents of the South West can be heard in dishes such as duck confit salad with green beans and radishes, or baked saddle and belly of rabbit accompanied by roast fennel. The kitchen punches impressively above its weight with main courses like roast monkfish with Jerusalem artichokes and trompettes in red wine, and the closing deal may well be sealed by stickily British heritage fare such as treacle tart or steamed marmalade pudding and custard.

Chef James Faulks, Emma Faulks, David Abbott **Owner** Roger Faulks & James Faulks **Times** 12-2.30/6.30-10.30 Closed Xmas, BHs, 2wks Aug, Sun, L Sat **Prices** Fixed L 2 course £15.50, Starter £6-£12, Main £13.50-£22, Dessert £5-£6, Service added but optional 12.5% **Wines** 76 bottles over £20, 2 bottles under £20, 13 by glass **Notes** Vegetarian available **Seats** 90, Pr/dining room 30 **Parking** On street

The Oxo Tower Restaurant PLAN 3 F1

Modern British V

Great Thames views and creative, modern cooking

020 7803 3888
8th Floor, Oxo Tower Wharf, Barge House St SE1 9PH
e-mail: oxo.reservations@harveynichols.co.uk
dir: Nearest station: Blackfriars, Waterloo, Southwark. Between Blackfriars & Waterloo Bridge on the South Bank

The industrial heritage of the building is second to none on this part of the river, but the old girl has embraced modern times, no more so than up on the 8th floor, where the brasserie and restaurant pull in the punters for some diverting modern British cooking. There's something of the 1920s liner about the space, with its sleek glass frontage framing the Thames and sensational views across to St Paul's Cathedral. The terrace is much in demand for obvious reasons. There's a relaxed, unpretentious vibe here, with hardwood floors, leather tub-chairs and white linen filling the large space. The kitchen of this Harvey Nic's-run operation has a light touch, delivering creative combinations and making it all look very appealing on the plate. Start with salt-cod pasties with a suitably fiery harissa emulsion and fennel salad, before pan-fried skate fillet teamed with squid, red pepper and parsley salad and some clever chick pea chips, or perhaps Yorkshire Dales rabbit pie with Earl Grey prunes and pickled carrots. The wine list is a corker, too.

Chef Jeremy Bloor **Owner** Harvey Nichols & Co Ltd
Times 12-3/6-11.30 Closed 25-26 Dec, D 24 Dec
Prices Fixed L 2 course £26, Tasting menu £120, Starter £12.50-£17, Main £19.50-£32, Dessert £8-£15, Service added but optional 12.5% **Wines** 660 bottles over £20, 19 bottles under £20, 14 by glass **Notes** Sunday L, Vegetarian menu, Civ Wed 150 **Seats** 250
Children Portions, Menu **Parking** On street, NCP

Le Pont de la Tour PLAN 6 D2

Modern French V

Stylish Thames-side destination dining with unbeatable views

020 7403 8403
The Butlers Wharf Building, 36d Shad Thames SE1 2YE
e-mail: lepontres@danddlondon.com
dir: Nearest station: Tower Hill, London Bridge.

Translate the name and you have Tower Bridge, which is what fills your field of vision while you dine at this buzzing Thames-side brasserie-style restaurant. On a summer's day, the alfresco terrace is hard to beat for a touch of Riviera style, watching the waterborne bustle around Tower Bridge and le tout London strolling along the wharfside promenade. If the weather forces you indoors, the setting in the long dining room is suitably upmarket, with art-deco-style blue-and-white logos on the crockery, and plenty of luxury ingredients on the menu. Oysters are always a good way to start, either as nature intended or grilled with spinach, poitrine fumé (smoked bacon) and a parmesan crust. Follow with classic French dishes given a lighter spin - perhaps poached halibut with braised Swiss chard and champagne caviar sauce, while meat-eaters might go for herb-crusted rump of lamb with Provençal potatoes and basil dressing.

Chef Lee Bennett **Owner** Des Gunewardena
Times 12-3/6-11 **Prices** Fixed L 2 course £26.50, Fixed D 3 course £42.50, Service optional, Groups min 8 service 12.5% **Wines** All bottles over £20, 20 by glass
Notes Sunday L, Vegetarian menu, Dress restrictions, No trainers in main restaurant **Seats** 140, Pr/dining room 24
Children Portions, Menu **Parking** On street & car park

Roast PLAN 6 B3

British NOTABLE WINE LIST

Vibrant, upbeat restaurant set above Borough Market

020 7940 1300
The Floral Hall, Borough Market, Stoney St SE1 1TL
e-mail: info@roast-restaurant.com
dir: Nearest station: London Bridge

Perched above the foodie's favourite, Borough Market, Roast pays homage to its unique setting with a menu dedicated to British seasonal produce and the best of British cooking. Visit on a market day (Thursday to Saturday) and enjoy the hubbub below from the stylish, first-floor dining room and bar. A big, light, split-level, contemporary space, its huge windows also offer a glimpse of St Paul's from the upper tier. The large on-view kitchen delivers namesake roasts (rib of Welsh Black beef with Yorkshire pudding, creamed horseradish and mustard - for sharing) to grilled calves' liver with broad beans, peas and lovage, while puddings (perhaps strawberry trifle) offer best-of-Brit comfort. Breakfast, bar brunch and afternoon tea are also served, while the wine and cocktail lists are worth checking out.

Chef Lawrence Keogh **Owner** Iqbal Wahhab
Times 12-3/5.30-11 Closed D Sun **Prices** Starter £6-£15, Main £10-£30, Dessert £7, Service added but optional 12.5% **Wines** 100 bottles over £20, 6 bottles under £20, 10 by glass **Notes** Sunday L, Vegetarian available, Civ Wed 150 **Seats** 110 **Children** Portions, Menu

LONDON SE1 *continued*

RSJ, The Restaurant on the South Bank PLAN 5 F6

Modern

Unpretentious pre-theatre favourite

☎ 020 7928 4554
33 Coin St SE1 9NR
e-mail: sally.webber@rsj.uk.com
dir: Nearest station: Waterloo. Towards Waterloo Bridge & IMAX cinema. At rdbt, turn right into Stamford St. RSJ on the corner of Coin St, 2nd road on the right.

This long-established, unprepossessing little restaurant is popular with the South Bank's pre- and post-theatre and concert crowd, and is also handy for Waterloo Station. Friendly staff keep everything moving along with an eye on performance times, though the specialist Loire Valley wine list is a show-stopper in itself. The cooking keeps things simple and fresh and takes a mainstream modern European approach. Take Arborio risotto with lobster, brown shrimps, chorizo and tomatoes, or perhaps roast rump of English lamb served with French beans, spinach, dauphinoise and a red wine sauce. The décor - floorboards, neutral tones and simple blond-wood chairs - keeps things appropriately relaxed.

Times 12-2/5.30-11 Closed Xmas, 1 Jan, Sun, L Sat

LONDON SE3

Chapters All Day Dining PLAN 8 D1

Modern British

Laid-back all-day dining in smart Blackheath

☎ 020 8333 2666
43-45 Montpelier Vale, Blackheath Village SE3 0TJ
e-mail: chapters@chaptersrestaurants.co.uk
dir: Nearest station: Blackheath. 5 mins from Blackheath village train station

Chapters All Day Dining is the refurbished and reinvented version of the former fine-dining operation Chapter Two, the sister restaurant of the revered Chapter One in Bromley (see entry). The concept nowadays is more in tune with the casual vibe of trendy Blackheath village, offering breakfast, lunch, tea and dinner in an easygoing brasserie-style ambience. It is an unbuttoned space with bare brickwork, wooden floors and toffee-coloured banquette seating. You might start the day with eggs Benedict, or go for a more creative modern idea from the crowd-pleasing all-day menu - perhaps terrine of potted ham hock and black pudding with piccalilli and toasted sourdough, ahead of pan-fried sea bream with spiced couscous, rose harissa and almonds. Meat-lovers will find a slab of prime Black Angus fillet steak cooked on charcoal in the Josper oven an irresistible prospect, while the sweet of tooth will be similarly powerless when faced with Valrhona chocolate fondant with raisin purée and caramelised walnut ice cream.

Times 8am-11pm Closed 2-4 Jan

LONDON SE22

Franklins PLAN 1 F2

British

Hearty British cooking in Lordship Lane

☎ 020 8299 9598
157 Lordship Ln, East Dulwich SE22 8HX
e-mail: info@franklinsrestaurant.com
dir: Nearest station: East Dulwich. 0.5m S from station, along Dog Kennel Hill and Lordship Ln

Push on past the stripped floors and wooden benches of the convivial bar of this Dulwich Village neighbourhood bistro and all is revealed: behind a glass screen that partitions the kitchen, the chefs are hard at work producing unfussy British food, majoring on old-fashioned cuts of rare-breed meat delivered with refreshing honesty. A waffle-free menu of gutsy dishes delivers full-on flavours: smoked mackerel, paired simply with potatoes, cornichons and dill, to start, then venison haunch with barley, turnips and Chantenay carrots. End with creamed chocolate rice pudding. For astounding value, go for the daily set lunch menu offering three choices at each course. A farm shop next door sells the same Kentish fruit and vegetables and other produce that appears on the menu.

Chef Ralf Witting **Owner** Tim Sheehan & Rodney Franklin **Times** 12-12 Closed 25-26, 31 Dec, 1 Jan **Prices** Fixed L 2 course £13.50, Starter £5-£8, Main £11.50-£20, Dessert £5.25, Service optional, Groups min 6 service 10% **Wines** 23 bottles over £20, 13 bottles under £20, 9 by glass **Notes** Sunday L, Vegetarian available **Seats** 42, Pr/dining room 24 **Children** Portions **Parking** Bawdale Road

The Palmerston PLAN 1 F3

Modern British

Anglo-Mediterranean cooking in a Dulwich gastro-pub

☎ 020 8693 1629
91 Lordship Ln, East Dulwich SE22 8EP
e-mail: info@thepalmerston.net
dir: Nearest station: 10min walk from East Dulwich station

A revamped London corner boozer in East Dulwich, The Palmerston took its place firmly in the gastro-pub movement when it reopened in 2004. Free-range and organic produce form the backbone of the menus, and the ambience of terracotta floors and wood-panelled walls makes for a homely, welcoming feel. A touch of the Mediterranean is in evidence in a starter that looks like a small oblong pizza topped with capocollo (cured pork neck), fennel and taleggio. Mains might take in well-rendered, lightly floured whole lemon sole with cocoa beans and chorizo, with a pimento and basil relish and crème fraîche. Fine pastry work contributes to the enjoyment of a blackberry and almond tart, served with a no-holds-barred dollop of clotted cream.

Chef Jamie Younger **Owner** Jamie Younger, Paul Rigby, Remi Olajoyegbe **Times** 12-2.30/7-midnight Closed 25-26 Dec, 1 Jan **Prices** Fixed L 2 course fr £11.50, Starter £5-£10, Main £12.50-£22, Dessert £4.50-£6.50, Service added but optional 10% **Wines** 34 bottles over £20, 22 bottles under £20, 17 by glass **Notes** Sunday L, Vegetarian available **Seats** 70 **Children** Portions **Parking** On street

LONDON SE23

Babur PLAN 1 G2

Modern Indian

Modern Indian cuisine in a stylish brasserie setting

☎ 020 8291 2400 & 8291 4881
119 Brockley Rise, Forest Hill SE23 1JP
e-mail: mail@babur.info
web: www.babur.info
dir: Nearest station: Honor Oak Park. 5 mins walk from station

The life-size prowling Bengal tiger on its roof, makes this popular southeast London brasserie hard to miss. That, and the fact that Babur is something of a Forest Hill institution, having served the area for over 24 years. A far cry from the flock-wallpaper school of Indian restaurants, Babur's décor is clean-cut and stylish, with American walnut tables, chocolate brown banquettes and eye-catching Bengali artwork on exposed red-brick walls. The talented chefs remain as innovative as ever, working with traditional and more unusual ingredients - ostrich and buffalo, for example - to supply intense flavours. Watch out for the tiger head menu symbols flagging up dishes where eye-wateringly hot chillis lurk within. A vibrant starter pairs scallops encased in wafer thin pastry with a spicy tamarind sauce and dried plum chutney, followed by a Keralan dish of coconut lamb with mango purée, or 'Dum-cooked rabbit', pot-roasted in star anise and ginger broth.

Chef Jiwan Lal **Owner** Babur 1998 Ltd
Times 12.30-2.30/6-11.30 Closed 25-26 Dec **Prices** Food prices not confirmed for 2011. Please telephone for details **Wines** 16 bottles over £20, 24 bottles under £20, 14 by glass **Notes** Sunday L, Vegetarian available
Seats 72 **Parking** 15, On street

LONDON SW1

Al Duca PLAN 5 B6

@ Italian

Uncomplicated modern Italian cooking just off Piccadilly

☎ 020 7839 3090
4-5 Duke of York St SW1Y 6LA
e-mail: alduca@btconnect.com
dir: Nearest station: Piccadilly. 5 mins walk from station towards Piccadilly. Right into St James's, left into Jermyn St.

Affordable pricing, contemporary good looks and an upbeat atmosphere draw the crowds to this smart, friendly, ever-popular St James's Italian. The cooking is intelligently uncomplicated, clean-cut, and modern showing a light touch, driven by fresh, quality seasonal ingredients on fixed-price menus. Reginette (pasta) with Italian bacon and peas is a signature, while pan-fried sea bream might be teamed with basil mash and chargrilled courgette. A good all-Italian wine list and well-drilled service play their part, too, while neutral Mediterranean tones, etched glass, modern seating and closely-packed tables cut a dash. A feature wall wine rack catches the eye, too, while the glass frontage conveniently folds back for an alfresco summer vibe.

Chef Michele Franzolin **Owner** Cuisine Collection, Claudio Pulze **Times** 12-3/6-11 Closed Xmas, New Year, BHs, Sun **Prices** Fixed L 2 course £22.50-£29.50, Fixed D 3 course fr £27.50, Service added but optional 12.5% **Wines** 118 bottles over £20, 5 bottles under £20, 20 by glass **Notes** Pre & post theatre menu 2-4 course £15-£18, Vegetarian available, Dress restrictions, Smart casual **Seats** 56 **Children** Portions **Parking** Jermyn St, Duke St

Amaya PLAN 4 G4

@@ Indian

Ultra chic Knightsbridge Indian

☎ 020 7823 1166
Halkin Arcade, Motcomb St SW1X 8JT
e-mail: amaya@realindianfood.com
dir: Nearest station: Knightsbridge

Whether dining at Amaya by day or by night, the restaurant is visually quite stunning. Natural light floods in through a huge glazed atrium covering the dining area, highlighting the pink sandstone panels and shiny rosewood surfaces, and when night falls the place is transformed into a darkened arena backlit by the dramatically bright open kitchen. The menu is made up of various marinated meats, fish and vegetables, all cooked using one of three traditional methods - the tandoor (an extremely hot clay oven), sigri (a grill with a coal flame), and tawa (a thick iron hot-plate). The food is served as soon as it's ready, there are no conventional starters and main courses, and it's all designed for sharing. Try the tandoori venison seekh kebab, the griddled fillet of Dover sole with crust of coconut, coriander and mint, and, if you're feeling flush, splash out on the tandoori lobster.

Times 12-2.30/6-11.15 Closed 25 Dec

Apsleys at The Lanesborough PLAN 4 G5

@@@ – *see below*

Apsleys at The Lanesborough

LONDON SW1 PLAN 4 G5

Modern Italian NEW

Accomplished Italian cuisine in stunning atrium restaurant

☎ 020 7259 5599
The Lanesborough, Hyde Park Corner SW1X 7TA
e-mail: info@lanesborough.com
dir: Nearest station: Hyde Park Corner.

London is hardly short of impressive relics of empire, but this grand old mansion on Hyde Park Corner is in the Premier League. The Lanesborough is the kind of place offering a world-class level of luxury and service that's a magnet for celebs and oligarchs. But if you're not in the market for rooms starting at £500 a night - personal butler included - a keenly-priced menu del giorno gets you into the glass-roofed dining room for a taste of its jaw-dropping glamour: modern chandeliers hang above lavish artwork, exotic palms, and tables resplendent with top-class crystal and chinaware, while the staff-to-customer ratio delivers impeccable service. Recently relaunched as Apsleys under the aegis of stellar German chef Heinz Beck, modern Italian cuisine is the kitchen's thing, cooked with top-level skill and authenticity. The sheer quality of the ingredients makes for a superbly vibrant and colourful warm seafood salad, preceding suckling pig presented as roasted loin and braised shoulder, with crisp crackling and assured saucing bringing the dish triumphantly together. A huge, moist rum baba ends on a classic note.

Times 12-2.30/7-11.30

LONDON SW1 ***continued***

Avenue PLAN 5 B5

Modern British

Stylish modern bar-restaurant in St James's

☎ 020 7321 2111
7-9 St James's St SW1A 1EE
e-mail: avenuereservations@danddlondon.com
dir: Nearest station: Green Park. Turn right past The Ritz, 2nd turning into St James's St

A rolling programme of contemporary art exhibitions is among the lures at this stylish St James's restaurant, designed by Rick Mather. The menus have gradually evolved in the direction of a resolutely modern British idiom, with dishes such as gin and juniper salmon and rye bread, fish and chips served in paper with tartare sauce, and haunch of venison with pickled pear and black cabbage. Presentations are kept confidently simple, and the juxtapositions of ingredients, even when unfamiliar, work well. A typical example from the dessert menu might be raspberry cheesecake with black pepper ice cream.

Chef Mikko Kataja **Owner** D & D London
Times 12-3/5.45-11.30 Closed 25-26 Dec, 1 Jan, Sun, L Sat **Prices** Starter £6.50-£14, Main £12-£29.50, Dessert £7-£12, Service optional, Groups min 8 service 12.5% **Wines** 75 bottles over £20, 1 bottles under £20, 16 by glass **Notes** Vegetarian available, Civ Wed 150 **Seats** 150, Pr/dining room 20 **Children** Portions **Parking** Parking meters on streets

Bar Boulud

French NEW

Classic French bistro food in a fun and stylish setting

☎ 020 7201 3899
Mandarin Oriental Hyde Park, 66 Knightsbridge SW1X 7LA

Growing up on a farm near Lyon in France, Daniel Boulud developed a love of home cooking using fresh, seasonal produce, and it's his passion for simple French food and high quality ingredients that he aims to bring to London diners with his new restaurant within the Mandarin Oriental Hotel (there's also a separate street entrance). It's the second Bar Boulud after a successful first outing in Boulud's adopted hometown of New York, and it follows a similar format, with an open kitchen, a charcuterie bar, pictures of Lyon bistros and brasseries on the walls, and much use of wood, leather and cork designed to reflect the art of wine-making. An impressive zinc-topped bar dominates the entrance, along with a glass enclosed wine cellar. The bistro-style menu offers a selection of pates and terrines including a superb duck, foie gras and fig terrine (the fig cutting ably through the richness of the foie gras), plus main courses like volaille a l'ail printanier (roasted chicken breast with wild garlic, fingerling potatoes and artichokes), and a (nicely made) tarte au chocolat. The wine list focuses on Burgundy and the Rhone Valley, with an ample selection by the glass. Bar Boulud will soon be joined by Heston Blumenthal's first restaurant to open outside of the village of Bray. The restaurant remained unnamed as we went to print, but is due to open in late 2010 in the space previously occupied by Foliage, with Fat Duck former head chef Ashley Palmer-Watts at the helm.

Chef Dean Yasharian **Times** 6-11/12-3/6-11

Boisdale of Belgravia PLAN 4 H3

British

Highlandia heaven in a clubby Scottish Belgravia restaurant

☎ 020 7730 6922
15 Eccleston St SW1W 9LX
e-mail: info@boisdale.co.uk
dir: Nearest station: Victoria. Turn left along Buckingham Palace Rd heading W, Eccleston St is 1st on right

It is hard to imagine a more Caledonian clubby environment than the one found in this handsome Regency townhouse in Belgravia. The labyrinthine interior unfolds a mix of dining areas: the intimate Auld Restaurant; the wood panels, fancy mirrors and chandeliers of the Jacobite Room; the easygoing vibe of the back bar - all to the strains of laid-back live jazz. You can even light up a fat Cuban cigar on the heated cigar terrace. But Boisdale is more than a theme park for Americans in search of tartan-clad ancestors: the food is seriously good, showcasing Scotland's superb produce - caramelised diver-caught Shetland scallops with roast haggis, saffron mash, Ayrshire bacon and minted pea purée for starters, followed by a chargrilled fillet of Hebridean mutton with English asparagus, shallot and thyme mash and anchovy and caper dressing.

Chef Colin Wint **Owner** Mr R Macdonald
Times 12-3/7-11.15 Closed Xmas, New Year, Etr, BHs, Sun, L Sat **Prices** Fixed L 2 course £19.50, Fixed D 2 course £19.50, Starter £7.50-£21.50, Main £17.50-£45.50, Dessert £6-£6.50, Service added but optional 12.5% **Wines** 150 bottles over £20, 8 bottles under £20, 30 by glass **Notes** Pre-theatre 3 course £18.70, Vegetarian available, Dress restrictions, Smart casual **Seats** 140, Pr/dining room 34 **Parking** On street, Belgrave Sq

The Botanist PLAN 4 G2

British, French

Lively, stylish Chelsea eatery and bar

☎ 020 7730 0077
7 Sloane Square SW1W 8EE
e-mail: info@thebotanistonsloanesquare.com
dir: Nearest station: Sloane Square On the right as you exit the tube station

Brothers Ed and Tom Martin (well-known for their gastro-pub chain, which includes the White Swan and the Gun - see entries) are behind this highly popular, cool, relaxed modern venue in Sloane Square. The Botanist behind the name is one Sir Hans Sloane, and the décor reflects the theme, with a variety of coloured woods, neutral tones and imagery in a light open space. Dining tables are tightly packed, windows open on to the street and there's a lively bar, so it's high-octane decibels all round. The menu's brasserie-style dishes deliver a pleasingly light, simple modern British touch; take roast sea trout with pea purée and samphire, or perhaps a rack of Scottish Blackface lamb teamed with provençale vegetables, courgette flowers and basil jus. (Also open for breakfast and afternoon tea, plus there's a bar menu, too).

Times 12-3.30/6-10.30

Brasserie Roux PLAN 5 B6

French

Simple French brasserie food on Pall Mall

☎ 020 7968 2900
Sofitel St James London, 6 Waterloo Place SW1Y 4AN
e-mail: info@brasserieroux.com
dir: Nearest station: Piccadilly Circus. From Piccadilly turn right on to Haymarket, right on to Pall Mall & then right on to Regent St & Waterloo Place

Occupying a platinum-standard site on Pall Mall, the setting for the Albert Roux-inspired ground-floor brasserie in the St James's branch of the Sofitel chain is as prestigious as they come. Inside, yellow ochre walls mix with toffee-brown leather seats at bare darkwood tables in a classic brasserie look to go with the old favourites from the Gallic brasserie repertoire. Curry and parmesan-crusted scallops with capers, pine nuts and lemon butter shows the style, ahead of rack of lamb with roast garlic and ratatouille. End with a heritage dish like apricot clafoutis with vanilla ice cream.

Times 12-3/5.30-11

Brasserie Saint Jacques PLAN 5 A6

Traditional French

Classic French brasserie in the heart of St James's

020 7930 1007
33 St James's St SW1A 1HD
e-mail: brasseriestjacques@btconnect.com
dir: Nearest station: Green Park

Though set on one of the capital's most English of thoroughfares, this brasserie's red awning, name and pavement tables leave no doubt as to its charismatic French accent. The bright, high-ceilinged interior is a haven of joie de vivre, with eye-catching vintage French posters on yellow walls, while polished wooden floors and tables, red leather chairs and banquette booth seating add to the relaxed, upmarket buzz. Friendly service has bags of personality, while the kitchen reciprocates with a menu of French brasserie classics that come skilfully cooked with a light modern touch and bags of flavour. There's garlic and parsley buttered snails or Mediterranean fish soup with saffron rouille to get you in the mood, following on, perhaps, with centre-cut fillet of beef with pan-fried foie gras and Madeira truffle sauce. Wines are predominantly Francophile, while pricing is for deep St James's pockets.

Times 12-2.30/6-11 Closed BHs, Sun

Le Caprice PLAN 5 A6

Modern British, European V

Quality cooking in a restaurant that still brings out the stars

020 7629 2239
Arlington House, Arlington St SW1A 1RJ
e-mail: reservation@le-caprice.co.uk
dir: Nearest station: Green Park. Arlington St runs beside The Ritz. Restaurant is at end

Maybe it is the unrepentantly 1980s retro monochrome look that keeps Le Caprice close to the hearts of the Mayfair set who pack the place for lunch. The timeless New York Gordon Gekko cool has pulled in an endless procession of celebs - just check out the gallery of black-and-white David Bailey photographs - and still exerts enough of an attraction that you'll need to book well in advance to sample its repertoire of simple dishes done well. European brasserie comfort food best describes crowd pleasers such as smoked haddock tart with quail's eggs, or salmon fishcakes with spinach and sorrel sauce, while exotica such as yellowtail sashimi with tempura squid and ponzu also make an appearance.

Chef Lee Bull **Owner** Caprice Holdings Ltd
Times 12-3/5.30-12 Closed 25-26 Dec, 1 Jan, Aug BH, D 24 Dec **Prices** Food prices not confirmed for 2011. Please telephone for details **Wines** 120 bottles over £20, 5 bottles under £20, 22 by glass **Notes** Sunday L, Vegetarian menu **Seats** 80 **Children** Portions **Parking** On street, NCP

Le Cercle PLAN 4 F3

Modern French

Discreet basement restaurant offering modern French grazing food

020 7901 9999
1 Wilbraham Place SW1X 9AE
e-mail: info@lecercle.co.uk
dir: Nearest station: Sloane Square. Just off Sloane St

The Sloane outpost of the Club Gascon operation (see entry) occupies a swish, über-cool basement done out in understated neutral shades, with swathes of diaphanous gauze hung from a soaring ceiling to take the hard edges off the bare wooden tables and beige marble floor. The name is something of a clue to Le Cercle's style: the kitchen deals in dainty tapas-sized portions of Gallic invention, based loosely around the cooking of southwest France. The menu does away with the conventional starter/main course/dessert format, in favour of a more lyrical separation of dishes into categories such as 'vegetal', and on through 'marin' to 'fermier' and 'plaisirs'. The net result is a parade of small-but-perfectly-formed creations bursting with precise, well-balanced flavours. This is a kitchen that pairs sea bream tartare with pomegranate and verbena, braised ox cheek with Jerusalem artichoke gratin and liquorice jus, or squab pigeon with spicy caramel and pistachio pastilla. The Gascon group do wine with aplomb, so the sommelier's wine pairings are not to be ignored.

Times 12-3/6-11 Closed Xmas & New Year, Sun, Mon

The Cinnamon Club PLAN 5 C4

Modern Indian

Sophisticated modern Indian dining in former library

020 7222 2555
The Old Westminster Library, 30-32 Great Smith St SW1P 3BU
e-mail: info@cinnamonclub.com
dir: Nearest station: Westminster, St James's Park. Take exit 6, across Parliament Sq, then pass Westminster Abbey on left. Take 1st left into Great Smith St

The Grade II listed Old Westminster Library is the grand setting for this elegant Indian restaurant. The place buzzes with life from early morning - when it opens to serve breakfast with an Indian twist - until late at night when the last drinkers empty out of its two bars (one traditional, one modern). The dining room, which occupies two rooms, has a rather clubby, old-English colonial feel with its high ceilings, skylights, parquet floors, lots of darkwood, leather-backed chairs and books lining the walls. The food is modern Indian, using top quality seasonal British ingredients with plenty of fresh herbs and balanced spicing. Start, perhaps, with the wonderfully tender and moist hunter's style rabbit tikka with dill and mustard and hot garlic chutney, then be wowed by the size and freshness of the tandoori king prawns with coconut Malai curry. Lemon and coriander cake is a light and well-judged dessert.

Chef Vivek Singh **Owner** Indian Restaurant Limited
Times 12.30-2.30/6.30-10.30 Closed 25 Dec, 1 Jan, BHs, Sun **Prices** Fixed L 2 course fr £19, Fixed D 3 course fr £22, Tasting menu £75-£115, Starter £8-£12.50, Main £14-£37, Dessert £7-£8.50, Service added but optional 12.5% **Wines** 275 bottles over £20, 15 by glass **Notes** Vegetarian available, Dress restrictions, Smart casual, no jeans, T-shirts or trainers, Civ Wed 130 **Seats** 135, Pr/dining room 60 **Children** Portions **Parking** Abingdon St

City Café PLAN 5 C3

Modern European

Modern European in a modern, central hotel

020 7932 4600
City Inn Westminster, 30 John Islip St SW1P 4DD
e-mail: westminster.citycafe@cityinn.com
dir: Nearest station: Pimlico, Westminster. From Pimlico, follow signs for Tate Britain, just beyond rear entrance. From Westminster, head towards Millbank. Turn right at Millbank Tower

Part of the flagship City Inn hotel in the heart of Westminster, close to the River Thames and the Houses of Parliament and practically next door to Tate Britain. Not to be outdone, the striking contemporary glass building houses lots of regularly changing modern art throughout the public areas. The City Café restaurant benefits from plenty of natural light while the covered Art Street terrace is a novel way to dine alfresco. The main restaurant is vast but is split into several different areas with soft, neutral colours giving a clean, up-to-the minute feel. Potted ham with apple chutney and black sesame seed brioche buns, then pan-fried Gigha halibut, salsa verde and citrus dressing and a treacle tart with milk ice cream are the sort of things you'll find on the modern European menu. Meanwhile, the Millbank lounge is the place to go for a cocktail or to 'browse' the whisky library.

Times 12-3/5.30-10.30

LONDON SW1 ***continued***

Ebury PLAN 4 G2

British, French

Fashionable, buzzy Pimlico bar-brasserie

020 7730 6784
11 Pimlico Rd SW1W 8NA
e-mail: info@theebury.co.uk
dir: Nearest station: Sloane Sq, Victoria. From Sloane Sq Tube left into Holbein Place, then left at intersection with Pimlico Rd. The Ebury is on corner of Pimlico Rd & Ranelagh Grove

On a prominent corner site near to Sloane Square, the Ebury is home to a stylish brasserie and a cool lounge. Huge arching windows flood the interior with light - it's a good-looking contemporary space, all clean-cut lines, polished wooden floors and tables, chocolate-brown leather seats and low-slung copper dome lights around a huge island bar. The kitchen takes a modern British metropolitan approach to classic French and European ideas - expect goats' cheese beignets with bitter leaf salad, poached plums and hazelnut dressing, ahead of salmon fishcakes with baby spinach and hollandaise sauce, or meaty offerings such as sage-marinated pork fillet teamed with Welsh onion cake and cider jus. Finish with chocolate fondant and pistachio ice cream. A separate bar menu does modish wooden boards of Greek meze, Spanish charcuterie, farmhouse cheeses and small plates of grazing fodder.

Times 12-3.30/6-10.30 Closed 24-30 Dec

The Fifth Floor Restaurant PLAN 4 F4

French, European

Fashionable dining at landmark London store

020 7235 5250 & 7235 5000
Harvey Nichols, 109-125 Knightsbridge SW1X 7RJ
e-mail: reception@harveynichols.com
web: www.harveynichols.com
dir: Nearest station: Knightsbridge, Hyde Park Corner. Entrance on Sloane Street

Five floors up above the Knightsbridge traffic, Harvey Nic's impressive contemporary food hall - with restaurant, bar, café, wine shop and sushi bar - remains a perennial fixture on the see and be seen list. The funky bar cranks up the decibels for a drink before lunch or dinner with a look inspired by Russian 20th-century Constructivist art. The clinically white space of the flagship restaurant brings to mind retro '60's sci-fi, like a *Barbarella* film set with its fibre optic lighting, glass-domed ceiling and leather and chrome tubular chairs. As you'd expect, the kitchen's modern European brasserie dishes are easy on the eye, but there's no lack of substance here: the menu is based on exemplary ingredients, and prepared with sound skills. Take deep-fried langoustines with carrot purée and an apple, cucumber and hazelnut salad; venison with parsnip and white chocolate purée, parsnip gnocchi and juniper sauce; and frozen chestnut parfait with chocolate meringue.

The Fifth Floor Restaurant

Chef Jonas Karlsson **Owner** Harvey Nichols Ltd
Times 12-3/6-11 Closed Xmas, Etr Sun, D Sun
Prices Fixed L 2 course fr £19.50, Fixed D 3 course fr £27.50, Starter £8-£14, Main £16-£28, Dessert £6-£8, Service added but optional 12.5% **Wines** 700 bottles over £20, 30 bottles under £20, 30 by glass **Notes** Sunday L, Vegetarian available **Seats** 120 **Children** Portions, Menu **Parking** On street, NCP opposite

The Goring PLAN 4 H4

Traditional British

British heritage cooking in a suavely designed hotel dining room

020 7396 9000
Beeston Place SW1W 0JW
e-mail: reception@thegoring.com
dir: Nearest station: Victoria. From Victoria St turn left into Grosvenor Gdns, cross Buckingham Palace Rd, 75yds turn right into Beeston Place

The David Linley design flourishes, installed when the Goring reached its centenary in 2009, are something to see. Against a background of caramel and cream tones, the Swarovski light fitments look like frosted twigs that change colour with the light from outside. State-of-the-art, in other words, meets classic traditionalism, which one could say of the menus too. Beef Wellington, Dover sole with lobster sauce, cocktails of prawns and hard-boiled eggs in Marie Rose dressing are all gloriously unreconstructed British, but there are also tartare of venison with marinated beetroot and peppered sour cream, perhaps followed by roast haddock with braised red cabbage and parsnip sauce, for those in the mood to experiment. If you want to spend big, you could throw caution to the wind and start on the Beluga.

Times 12.30-2.30/6-10 Closed L Sat

Il Convivio PLAN 4 H2

Modern Italian

Chic modern Italian in Belgravia

020 7730 4099
143 Ebury St SW1W 9QN
e-mail: comments@etruscarestaurants.com
dir: Nearest station: Victoria, Sloane Square. 7 min walk from Victoria Station - corner of Ebury St and Elizabeth St

Roughly translated as 'banquet', there's plenty of opportunity for indulgence amid the four floors of this converted Georgian townhouse in the heart of upmarket Belgravia. A retractable conservatory-style roof is a great feature, bringing instant alfresco eating when the weather allows. Deep red walls are inscribed with quotes from Dante's *Il Convivio*. Imaginative cooking shows intelligent restraint and an understanding of flavour combinations. The seasonally-changing carte supplemented by twice weekly specials might feature antipasti of creamy crab soup with sautéed radishes or proper beef carpaccio with celery and basil infused olive oil, followed by, perhaps, black spaghetti with lobster and spring onions. Arctic black cod with aged balsamic and Muscat grapes is a typical main course, and don't miss out on the house speciality: white espresso ice cream. There's a new tasting menu with wine matches. Service is on the ball and charming with it.

Chef Lukas Pfaff **Owner** Piero & Enzo Quaradeghini
Times 12-3.15/6.30-11.15 Closed Xmas, New Year, BHs, Sun **Prices** Fixed L 2 course £17.50, Tasting menu £52, Starter £7.50-£16.50, Main £12.50-£28, Dessert £5.50-£8, Service added but optional 12.5% **Wines** 156 bottles over £20, 12 bottles under £20, 10 by glass **Notes** Tasting menu 7 course, Vegetarian available, Dress restrictions, Smart casual **Seats** 65, Pr/dining room 14 **Parking** On street

Inn the Park PLAN 5 C5

British

Relaxed all-day café and restaurant in city centre Royal park

020 7451 9999
St James's Park SW1A 2BJ
e-mail: info@innthepark.co.uk
dir: Nearest station: St James's Park, Charing Cross, Piccadilly. 200mtrs down The Mall towards Buckingham Palace

The grass-roofed, Scandinavian-style restaurant, with its floor-to-ceiling windows and glorious decked terrace, overlooks the duck lake and the rolling landscape of St James's Park, with the London Eye visible over the rooftops of Whitehall. An informal café by day, it morphs in the evening into a relaxed, romantic restaurant in one of the best spots in town. Expect straightforward, full-flavoured, brasserie-style dishes built on materials from artisan specialist producers. Start with coarse rabbit pâté with spicy apple chutney, followed by baked cod with braised leeks, cockles and samphire, and lemon posset with nutmeg shortbread for pudding.

Chef Amanda Wilson **Owner** Oliver Peyton
Times 12-3.30/5.30-9.30 **Prices** Starter £5.50-£9.50, Main £14.50-£19.50, Dessert fr £5.50, Service added but optional 12.5% **Wines** 38 bottles over £20, 8 bottles under £20, 17 by glass **Notes** Sunday L, Vegetarian available **Seats** 140 **Children** Portions, Menu **Parking** On street

JB's Restaurant PLAN 5 A3

Modern French, Mediterranean

Modern hotel brasserie dining

020 7769 9772 & 020 7769 9999
Park Plaza Victoria, 239 Vauxhall Bridge Rd SW1V 1EQ
e-mail: gfernando@pphe.com
dir: Nearest station: Victoria. 2 min walk from Apollo Victoria Theatre

The Park Plaza is a smart, modern hotel, handy for Victoria Station and the capital's major attractions. It has airy, stylish public areas that include an elegant bar and restaurant as well as a popular coffee bar. The restaurant itself (JB's) follows the contemporary theme, and has floor-to-ceiling windows and a lengthy, crowd-pleasing menu that offers something for everyone in its medley of modern and classics. Think simple, good-looking, well-executed dishes using quality produce like seared duck with watercress and pea shoot salad, followed by veal cutlet with spinach purée, caramelised shallots and anchovies. For dessert, perhaps an apple and crumble tart with cinnamon ice cream will catch the eye.

Times 6-10 Closed BHs, Sun, L all week

Just St James PLAN 5 B5

Modern British

Dining in high style in old St James's

020 7976 2222
12 St James's St SW1A 1ER
e-mail: bookings@juststjames.com
dir: Nearest station: Green Park. Turn right on Piccadilly towards Piccadilly Circus, then right into St James's St. Restaurant on corner of St James's St & King St

The former Lloyd's banking hall - one of the most expensive grand banking halls ever built back in the late 1800s - makes a jaw-dropping setting for this upbeat, modern restaurant and bar. Soaring Italian marble columns, huge arched windows, lofty decorative ceiling and a sweeping central staircase and glass lift (to a semi-private mezzanine floor) deliver the wow-factor. Softened with contemporary styling and furniture, 'Just' proves a vibrant and popular all-day venue. The menu's a crowd pleaser, too, blending British classics (mixed grill) with more innovative combinations (poached halibut with samphire, steamed cockles and a butter sauce), driven by fresh, quality, seasonal produce. There's breakfast, afternoon tea and an all-day bar menu, too, while the Just Oriental bar-brasserie is downstairs.

Times 12-3/6-11 Closed 25-26 Dec, 1 Jan, Sun, L Sat

Ken Lo's Memories of China PLAN 4 H3

Chinese

Upmarket Chinese delivering the real deal

020 7730 7734
65-69 Ebury St SW1W 0NZ
e-mail: memoriesofchina@btconnect.com
web: www.memories-of-china.co.uk
dir: Nearest station: Victoria. At junction of Ebury Street & Eccleston St

This smart, almost legendary Belgravia oriental restaurant certainly looks the part, with its sleek glass exterior oozing upmarket curb-appeal. Inside, the promised quality abounds, with subtle modern Chinese design - bamboo wallpaper, sandalwood screens and red lanterns and seating, backed by formally dressed but friendly staff. Reassuringly authentic Chinese cuisine is the kitchen's forte, delivered via a lengthy carte showcasing classic regional cooking and bolstered by a repertoire of set-menu options - take a 'Gastronomic Tour.' Dishes illustrate skilful handling of good ingredients, with the more humble (perhaps Peking lamb with ginger and spring onion) lining-up alongside luxury items (whole Szechuan crispy aromatic duck or Yu-Hsiang lobster).

Chef Kam Po But **Owner** A-Z Restaurants
Times 12-2.30/7-11 Closed BHs, L Sun **Prices** Fixed L 2 course £18.50-£21.95, Fixed D 3 course £31.50-£36, Starter £5.95-£17.50, Main £12.50-£39, Dessert £5-£6, Service added but optional 12.5%, Groups min 15 service 15% **Wines** 129 bottles over £20, 4 bottles under £20, 6 by glass **Notes** Sunday L, Vegetarian available, Dress restrictions, Smart casual **Seats** 120, Pr/dining room 20 **Children** Portions **Parking** On street

The Library PLAN 5 A4

Modern British

British food in a hotel with history

020 7834 6600
The Rubens at the Palace, 39 Buckingham Palace Rd SW1W 0PS
e-mail: bookrb@rchmail.com
dir: Nearest station: Victoria. From tube station head towards Buckingham Palace, hotel on right

Built as a house for debutants coming out at nearby Buckingham Palace in the early 1900s, the building was later used as the Polish Resistance headquarters during World War II. These days it's a thriving hotel serving modern British food with a commitment to sustainable ingredients. In the Library restaurant there's a traditional club-like vibe with rich fabrics on comfortable armchairs, crisp white linen on the tables and some quirky old sporting memorabilia on display. The menu might begin with mallard duck and foie gras terrine with Muscat grape and plum compôte, then perhaps the house special of whole grilled Dover Sole with chive and butter sauce, and to finish a dessert such as warm Valrhona chocolate and macadamia nut fondant with Seville orange marmalade ice cream. The Old Masters' offers a more informal buffet style carvery.

Chef Daniel Collins **Owner** Red Carnation Hotels
Times 7.30-10.30 Closed Xmas week, L all week
Prices Fixed D 3 course £35-£45, Starter £7.50-£14.50, Main £17.50-£35, Dessert £7.50-£10.50, Service added but optional 12.5% **Wines** 4 bottles over £20, 8 bottles under £20, 12 by glass **Notes** Vegetarian available, Dress restrictions, No shorts, tracksuits or trainers, Civ Wed 50 **Seats** 30, Pr/dining room 50 **Children** Menu **Parking** NCP at Victoria Coach Station

Marcus Wareing at The Berkeley

LONDON SW1 PLAN 4 G4

Modern French V NOTABLE WINE LIST

Stellar cooking from an immense talent

☎ 020 7235 1200
The Berkeley, Wilton Place, Knightsbridge SW1X 7RL
e-mail: marcuswareing@the-berkeley.co.uk
dir: Nearest station: Knightsbridge, Hyde Park Corner. 300mtrs from Hyde Park Corner along Knightsbridge

The term 'destination restaurant' is attributed to many places these days, some more deserving than others. Marcus Wareing at The Berkeley should be the goal, the objective, the target of every discerning foodie in the land, or indeed anyone who wants to find out what pleasures are to be found in the very best restaurants in the country. Designer David Collins has created an opulently timeless space with colours from the darker, warmer, cosseting end of the spectrum - leather seats of rich claret, deep-wood panelling - and lighting which keeps the occasion intimate. Tables are laid with the precision of a Swiss watchmaker, staff exude the right type of confidence, and trolleys bring forth petits fours, cheeses and ancient brandies to enhance further the sense of occasion. The food may look beautiful on the plate, the ingredients may be as good as money can buy, the cooking skills second to none, but the lasting impression of a visit chez Wareing is the sheer power of the flavours. This food tastes good. A first-course dish of veal sweetbreads, for example, roasted and glazed, with a sauce aigre-doux, salad of black radish and finished with toasted cashews is in these hands a triumph of balance and control, but, best of all, a delight to eat. There are plenty of luxury ingredients on show; foie gras, for example, pan-fried to perfection and served with pink pepper yoghurt, ginger crunch and a rhubarb muffin top. Main-course might see Dorset turbot with the subtle flavours of liquorice, the textures of carrot and lettuce hearts, and finished with a fennel dressing. Venison is smoked and roasted and served up with parsnips and heritage beetroots, and for dessert, perhaps a Granny Smith crème with spiced brioche crisps, popcorn and salted caramel ice cream. In amongst all this comes a cavalcade of canapes, amuses, pre-desserts and fantastic breads, and the wine list is a construction of considerable class that does justice to the food. As we go to press, the former Boxwood Café in the hotel has become the home of Pierre Koffmann; Koffmann's is not going down the fine-dining, haute cuisine route, rather focusing on the delights of provincial French cooking in a relaxed and informal setting. With these two under one roof, The Berkeley is the place to be in 2011.

Chef Marcus Wareing **Owner** Marcus Wareing Restaurants Ltd
Times 12-2.30/6-11 Closed 1 Jan, Sun, L Sat **Prices** Service added but optional 12.5% **Wines** 900 bottles over £20, 4 bottles under £20, 20 by glass
Notes ALC 3 course £75, Tasting menu 7 course, Gourmand 9 course, Vegetarian menu, Dress restrictions, Smart - jacket preferred, No jeans/trainers **Seats** 70, Pr/dining room 16
Children Portions **Parking** NCP and on street

LONDON SW1 *continued*

Mango Tree PLAN 4 H4

Thai V

Authentic Thai food in a stylish, modern setting

020 7823 1888
46 Grosvenor Place, Belgravia SW1X 7EQ
e-mail: reservations@mangotree.org.uk
dir: Nearest station: Victoria

This Belgravia Thai is located behind the best address in town, Buckingham Palace, and, like its sister venue Awana (a Malaysian restaurant in Chelsea - see entry), delivers an upmarket experience. The big, airy dining room uses materials sourced directly from Thailand to create a sleek, contemporary experience. Classic and creative Thai cuisine - with its subtle layering of flavours - takes in well-presented dishes such as sea bass fillet wrapped in banana leaves with cress salad and spicy lime and tamarind, or perhaps a yellow curry with monkfish and butterfish. Vegetarian and vegan, specials and tasting options add to the appeal.

Chef Mark Read **Owner** Eddie Lim **Times** 12-3/6-11 Closed Xmas, New Year **Prices** Fixed L 2 course £15-£18, Fixed D 3 course £35-£40, Starter £5.50-£7.50, Main £10.50-£18.50, Dessert £6.50-£8.50, Service added but optional 12.5% **Wines** 15 bottles over £20, 2 bottles under £20, 16 by glass **Notes** Tasting menu available, Sunday L, Vegetarian menu **Seats** 160 **Children** Portions, Menu **Parking** On Wilton St

Marcus Wareing at the Berkeley PLAN 4 G4

– see opposite page

Mint Leaf PLAN 5 C6

Modern Indian

Funky, subterranean Indian restaurant and cocktail bar

020 7930 9020
Suffolk Place, Haymarket SW1Y 4HX
e-mail: reservations@mintleafrestaurant.com
web: www.mintleafrestaurant.com
dir: Nearest station: Piccadilly, Charing Cross. At end of Haymarket, on corner of Pall Mall and Suffolk Place. Opposite Her Majesty's Theatre, 100mtrs from Trafalgar Square

A cross between a funky cocktail bar and a fine dining Indian restaurant, Mint Leaf is quite the cool hang-out. Mention the mezzanine champagne bar, DJs and live music at the weekend and the occasional fashion show, and you'll get the picture. If all that isn't your scene, rest assured the food is taken seriously. The kitchen uses high quality ingredients to create modern Indian dishes that are on the light side (that's down to careful use of ghee), and many are served up in small or large sizes. Start with crisp fried soft-shell crab with curry leaf and dry mango, following on with slow-roasted duck leg spiced with star anise and coriander.

Chef Vishal Rane **Owner** Out of Africa Investments **Times** 12-3/5.30-11 Closed 25-26 Dec, 1 Jan, L Sat, Sun **Prices** Fixed L 2 course fr £13.95, Fixed D 3 course fr £20, Starter £6-£12, Main £15-£25, Dessert £6-£8.50, Service added but optional 12.5% **Wines** 130 bottles over £20, 8 bottles under £20, 12 by glass **Notes** Pre-theatre menu 5-7pm 2 course £15, Vegetarian available, Dress restrictions, Smart casual, no scruffy jeans or trainers, Civ Wed 100 **Seats** 144, Pr/dining room 66 **Children** Portions **Parking** NCP, on street

Nahm

LONDON SW1 PLAN 4 G4

Thai

The very best Thai food in chic hotel

020 7333 1234
The Halkin Hotel, Halkin St, Belgravia SW1X 7DJ
e-mail: res@nahm.como.bz
dir: Nearest station: Hyde Park Corner. Halkin Street just off Hyde Park Corner

Hidden discreetly away in the high-rolling Belgravia Halkin Hotel, this top-flight Thai is a showcase for chef David Thompson's precise, harmonious, and thoroughly authentic take on the country's fragrant cuisine. The sleek bolt-hole is a perfect romantic venue for aficionados of South-East Asian cooking, flavours and textures, stylishly done out with shiny marble floors, slatted wooden screens, hardwood tables and shimmering tones of bronze and gold. You might as well buy into the glamour of the setting with a cocktail or glass of bubbly in the glitzy Halkin Bar before mulling over the palate-tingling ideas on the menu, which is helpfully translated so you can tell your yam king dong (squid and grilled pork salad with pickled ginger and chilli jam) from your dtum hang wua (double-steamed oxtail soup with mooli and Asian celery). Sourcing super-fresh esoteric ingredients is key to authenticity here, and the kitchen certainly has excellent supply lines to tip-top produce. If you want to do things the echt Thai way, the multi-course Nahm Arharn banquet is the way to go, or you might prefer to cherry pick your way through the à la carte. Taking the latter route, you might alight on a salad of grilled banana blossom with smoked fish, oysters and pork belly, then progress to a clear soup of chicken, squid, dried prawns and water chestnuts. Main courses involve the likes of quail in a red curry with ginger, peanuts and holy basil, or a green curry of crispy sea bass with white turmeric and Thai basil. As this is Belgravia, it's not one for a budget meal.

Chef David Thompson, Matthew Albert **Owner** Halkin Hotel Ltd **Times** 12-2.30/7-11 Closed 25 Dec & BHs, L Sat-Sun **Prices** Food prices not confirmed for 2011. Please telephone for details, Service added but optional 12.5% **Wines** 190 bottles over £20, 12 by glass **Notes** Traditional Nahm Arharn menu £60, Vegetarian available **Seats** 78, Pr/dining room 36 **Children** Portions **Parking** On street

LONDON SW1 ***continued***

Mitsukoshi
PLAN 3 B1

Japanese

Traditional Japanese eating in a department store

☎ 020 7930 0317
Dorland House, 14-20 Lower Regent St SW1Y 4PH
e-mail: restaurant@mitsukoshi.co.jp
web: www.mitsukoshi-restaurant.co.uk
dir: Nearest station: Piccadilly Circus

The restaurant of the Mitsukoshi department store, just off Regent Street, is a bright, welcoming place that offers a comprehensive range of Japanese eating and drinking styles. There's a long sushi counter serving impeccably fresh seafood, a shochu bar serving traditional Japanese spirits and single malts, and the main dining hall. Here, the range takes in seared salmon in spicy citrus dressing, sizzling-hot teriyaki beef, sukiyaki dishes cooked at your table, and shabu-shabu, the kind where you finish the noodles and broth after you've eaten the main item. It's all expertly presented, and comes with an array of little accessories and dipping sauces.

Chef Yuya Kikuchi **Owner** Mitsukoshi (UK) Ltd **Times** 12-2/6-10 Closed 25-26 Dec, 1 Jan, Etr **Prices** Food prices not confirmed for 2011. Please telephone for details **Wines** 3 bottles over £20, 4 bottles under £20, 4 by glass **Notes** Sunday L, Vegetarian available **Seats** 56, Pr/dining room 20 **Children** Menu **Parking** NCP

MU at Millennium Knightsbridge
PLAN 4 F4

Asian

Asian tapas in chic Knightsbridge hotel

☎ 020 7201 6330
17 Sloane St, Knightsbridge SW1X 9NU
e-mail: mu.knightsbridge@millenniumhotels.co.uk
dir: Nearest station: Knightsbridge, Victoria. 200yds from Knightsbridge Stn, near Harrods

Climb a chic white staircase to the first-floor restaurant at the Millennium Hotel, where a dramatic red and black room is the setting for what are billed as Asian tapas. Able waiting staff dispense advice freely, in case the menu confuses, although most of the eastern references are fairly familiar, notwithstanding the odd interpolation of French technique. Assorted sushi are zingingly fresh, and properly accompanied by pickled ginger and wasabi. If the crab spring roll lacks a little impact, despite its coriander and chilli, compensation is soon at hand in the form of chicken and foie gras dumplings topped with a pungent truffle dressing. Salt-and-pepper squid comes with good sweet chilli dipping sauce, and the eastern seasonings continue into desserts that take in a cocktail-glass layering of pineapple compôte, lemongrass mousse and chilli sorbet.

Times 5-10.30 Closed BH's, Sun-Mon, L all week

Nahm
PLAN 4 G4

– see page 257

One-O-One
PLAN 4 F4

– see below

One-O-One

LONDON SW1 PLAN 4 F4

French, Seafood V

Stunning seafood cookery in the heart of Knightsbridge

☎ 020 7290 7101
Sheraton Park Tower, 101 Knightsbridge SW1X 7RN
e-mail: darren.neilan@luxurycollection.com
dir: Nearest station: Knightsbridge. E from station, just after Harvey Nichols

Despite the landlocked grande luxe Knightsbridge location, every effort has been made here to transport you to the sea, from the oyster-shaped dining room to the sandy beach colour scheme and Breton chef Pascal Proyart's menu of upscale seafood dishes. The quality and freshness of raw materials are stunning, the more so in the central London setting. Start with twin towers of marine-fresh white crabmeat, served with a pancake full of unctuous crab risotto topped with parmesan cream, sauced with a lobster and tarragon reduction. It sounds complex, but the balance is flawless. Main course might deliver a piece of nervelessly timed halibut, accompanied by light, sweet tiger prawn dumplings, a 'cassoulet' of cocoa beans and truffle, a sliver of pork belly, and classical sauce Nantua. In lesser hands, the dish could be all over the place; here, it is an unqualified success. Dessert may not quite live up to the foregoing courses, but maintains the inventive pace, and there are French, English and Spanish cheeses served at peak maturity with membrillo.

Chef Pascal Proyart **Owner** Starwood Hotels & Resorts **Times** 12-2.30/6.30-10 **Prices** Fixed L 3 course £19, Fixed D 3 course £42, Starter £16-£24, Main £26-£37, Dessert £8-£12, Service optional **Wines** 200+ bottles over £20, 10 by glass **Notes** Tasting menu 6 course, Sunday L, Vegetarian menu, Dress restrictions, Smart casual preferred **Seats** 50, Pr/dining room 10 **Children** Portions **Parking** 60

One Twenty One Two PLAN 5 D5

◎◎ Modern, Traditional British **NEW**

Classic British cuisine on the Embankment

☎ 0871 376 9033
Royal Horseguards Hotel, 2 Whitehall Court SW1A 2EJ
e-mail: royalhorseguards@guoman.co.uk
dir: Nearest station: Embankment, Charing Cross. From Trafalgar Sq take exit to Whitehall. Turn into Whitehall Place then into Whitehall Court

In the days of black and white films, Whitehall 1212 was the telephone number of Scotland Yard, which stood upon this spot until the 1960s. The grand Thames-side Horseguards Hotel, a masterpiece of Empire-era pomp smack in the heart of town near Trafalgar Square and the Houses of Parliament, is the setting for One Twenty One Two. Inside, you might expect to eat in a clubby setting of leather and wood, so the glossy, plushly-upholstered décor of Royal blue, gold and beige is quite a surprise, as is the palpable buzz of on-the-ball staff serving a United Nations cast of diners. Classic British cooking informed by French techniques is the order of the day, as in a corn-fed chicken and quail terrine served with the sharp tang of rhubarb and kumquat compôte, followed by pan-fried sea bass with Jerusalem artichoke purée, samphire and ginger foam.

Times 12-3/5.30-10 Closed L Sun

L'Oranger PLAN 5 B5

◎◎ Modern French

Classic French cuisine amid impeccable elegance

☎ 020 7839 3774
5 St James's St SW1A 1EF
e-mail: loranger@londonfinedininggroup.com
web: www.loranger.co.uk
dir: Nearest station: Green Park. Access by car via Pall Mall

Swanky St James's Street is the right address for this elegant restaurant. Starting with the name, everything about L'Oranger is unmistakeably French: the beautifully warm interior is an exercise in faultless bourgeois taste - a glass atrium ceiling bathes mellow oak panels, plush gold damask and silk drapes, pale gold banquette seating and an abstract carpet in a flood of natural light. Modern artworks and exuberant flower displays throw contrasting splashes of colour into the mix, while service is discreet and efficient. Chef Laurent Michel's classic French cooking doesn't try to set any new trends: instead it brings the sunny lightness of Provençal cuisine to the table. Superbly fresh fish is big on a menu of intricate, immaculately-composed dishes - perhaps Dover sole with wild mushrooms, young leeks and a creamy truffled sauce; meat might appear as rack of lamb served in a croûte of winter fruits with citrus-flavoured eggplant and confit tomatoes.

Chef Laurent Michel **Owner** A to Z Restaurants Ltd **Times** 12-2.45/6.30-10.45 Closed Xmas, Etr, BHs, Sun, L Sat **Prices** Fixed L 2 course £27.50, Tasting menu £75, Starter £14-£26, Main £26-£29, Service added but optional 13.5% **Wines** 290 bottles over £20, 4 bottles under £20, 12 by glass **Notes** Tasting menu 6 course, Vegetarian available, Dress restrictions, Smart casual **Seats** 70, Pr/dining room 40 **Children** Portions **Parking** On street or NCP

Osteria Dell'Angolo PLAN 5 C3

◎ Italian

Vibrant Italian food near Parliament Square

☎ 020 3268 1077
47 Marsham St SW1P 3DR
e-mail: osteriadell_angolo@btconnect.com
dir: Nearest station: St James's Park, Westminster.

A cheering ambience has been created at this modern Tuscan restaurant not far from Parliament Square. Plain cream and terracotta walls and colourful Italian pictures lighten the décor, and the food offers plenty to think about. Pasta dishes such as scialatielli with white crabmeat and broccoli might be the curtain raiser for classic bistecca alla fiorentina (via Cumbria), 28-day-aged Lakeland beef with sautéed potatoes, or grilled tuna with roast agrodolce peppers and tapenade. Boozy Italian sweetness is the only way to finish, and there are tiramisù, zabaglione or rum baba doused in limoncello to choose from.

Chef Massimiliano Vezzi **Owner** Claudio Pulze **Times** 12-2.30/6.30-10.30 Closed Sun, L Sat **Prices** Fixed L 2 course £15, Starter £6.50-£10, Main £16.50-£36, Dessert £5-£8, Service added but optional 12.5% **Wines** 180 bottles over £20, 82 bottles under £20, 4 by glass **Notes** Vegetarian available **Seats** 60, Pr/dining room 20 **Parking** 6

Petrichor at The Cavendish PLAN 5 B6

◎ Modern British

Modern British food in a central London hotel

☎ 020 7930 2111
The Cavendish London, 81 Jermyn St SW1Y 6JF
e-mail: info@thecavendishlondon.com
dir: Nearest station: Green Park, Piccadilly. Situated directly behind Fortnum & Mason department store

The re-named restaurant at The Cavendish hotel in St James's is a traditional looking, light and bright room on the first floor, with large windows for looking out onto nearby attractions such as Fortnum & Mason and the temptations of Jermyn Street. It's popular with the pre-theatre brigade. Take a seat at a glass-topped table and sample the delights of the monthly-changing menu. Head chef Nitin Padwal takes sustainability seriously and attempts to source much produce regionally. Pan-fried Devon Rose chicken livers with dandelions and crispy Wicks Manor smoked bacon might kick things off, then perhaps chargrilled Welsh lamb cutlets with potato and watercress croquette and braised red onions. The cool and contemporary Lobby Bar offers a wide range of spirits and snacks.

Chef Nitin Padwal **Owner** Ellerman Investments Ltd **Times** 12-2.30/5.30-10.30 Closed 25-26 Dec, 1 Jan, L Sat-Sun & BH Mon **Prices** Food prices not confirmed for 2011. Please telephone for details **Wines** 20 bottles over £20, 10 bottles under £20, 10 by glass **Notes** Vegetarian available **Seats** 80, Pr/dining room 70 **Children** Portions, Menu **Parking** 60, secure on-site valet parking

Pétrus PLAN 4 G4

◎◎◎ – *see page 260*

LONDON SW1 ***continued***

Quaglino's PLAN 5 B6

French Brasserie

St James's glamorous mega-brasserie

☎ 020 7930 6767
16 Bury St, St James's SW1Y 6AJ
e-mail: saschak@danddlondon.com
dir: Nearest station: Green Park, Piccadilly Circus. Bury St is off Jermyn St

Descending the sweeping marble staircase from the mezzanine bar to the huge dining room - with its high glass ceiling, colourful supporting columns and serried ranks of tables - offers a hint of heyday ocean-liner glamour. Built on the site of the original society restaurant of the same name, the contemporary incarnation cuts quite a dash. A crustacea bar and live music add to the animated buzz in the room. The extensive, crowd-pleasing brasserie-style menu fits the bill, delivering uncomplicated, clean-cut dishes driven by quality seasonal ingredients. Humble classics like salmon fishcakes might rub shoulders with an indulgent plateau de fruits de mer or Chateaubriand, while more modern thinking could team spring lamb roast rump with tabouleh provençale and rosemary jus.

Times 12-3/5.30-mdnt Closed 24-25 Dec, 1 Jan, L 31 Dec

The Quilon PLAN 5 B4

Indian

Sophisticated Southern Indian cooking

☎ 020 7821 1899
41 Buckingham Gate SW1E 6AF
e-mail: info@quilonrestaurant.co.uk
web: www.quilon.co.uk
dir: Nearest station: St James's Park. Next to Crowne Plaza Hotel St James

Just down the road from Buckingham Palace, this upmarket Indian restaurant has some pretty smart neighbours, but with its own street entrance at the plush Crowne Plaza hotel and smart, broadly contemporary appearance, it can hold its own. The kitchen specialises in South Indian coastal cuisine, so seafood and vegetarian dishes are central to the menu, but there are plenty of meat options, too. Spicing is well judged and the dishes look great on the plate. Start with grilled scallops with mango and chilli, or spiced stir-fried oysters; next up, perhaps guinea fowl masala, baked black cod, or Koondapur fish curry. Vegetarians could choose from spinach poriyal (with mustard seeds, whole red chillies and freshly grated coconut) or mango curry.

Chef Sriram Aylur **Owner** Taj International Hotels Limited **Times** 12-2.30/6-11 Closed 25 Dec, L Sat **Prices** Fixed L 3 course £22-£40, Fixed D 3 course £40-£45, Starter £7-£9, Main £15-£28, Dessert £6-£7, Service added but optional 10% **Wines** 129 bottles over £20, 16 by glass **Notes** Sunday L, Vegetarian available, Dress restrictions, Smart casual **Seats** 90 **Children** Portions **Parking** On street, NCP

Quirinale PLAN 5 C3

Italian

Modern Italian cooking in Westminster

☎ 020 7222 7080
North Court, 1 Great Peter St SW1P 3LL
e-mail: info@quirinale.co.uk
dir: Nearest station: Westminster. From Parliament Sq to Lambeth Bridge take 2nd left into Great Peter St, restaurant on left

You can hobnob with the Westminster crowd in this intimate Italian restaurant discreetly secreted away in a pleasant side street a few minutes' from the Houses of

Pétrus

LONDON SW1 PLAN 4 G4

Modern French V NEW

Confident modern French cooking from Ramsay stable

☎ 020 7592 1609
1 Kinnerton St, Knightsbridge SW1X 8EA
e-mail: petrus@gordonramsay.com
dir: Nearest station: Knightsbridge

Gordon Ramsay has brought the Pétrus name back to life; perhaps more associated with Marcus Wareing than GR, nonetheless it was always part of Gordon Ramsay Holdings. So here is the 2010 incarnation, under the stewardship of Mark Askew (an established Ramsay aide-de-camp) and a young head chef, Sean Burbidge. It looks pretty swanky, as befits the Knightsbridge address, and no expense has been spared to turn the space into a contemporary, luxurious temple to 21st-century haute cuisine. There's a splendid wine cave taking centre stage in the room - about 1,500 bottles by all accounts - and the colours chosen are described, doubtless by the designer himself, as 'oyster, soft silver and copper', with splashes of claret in the fabrics and on the walls as a reminder of the eponymous wine. It is a suitably classy and opulent setting for some seriously good modern French food. Technical skills are razor sharp, as seen in a first course of pressed rabbit and foie gras mosaic, perfectly pointed up with carrot chutney and hazelnut salad. Produce is first-class, too, such as a superb piece of sea trout, pan-fried and served with sweetcorn, wild mushrooms and a sorrel sauce. Dessert is often a highlight in Mr Ramsay's establishments, and here it is again in the form of a chocolate sphere, which is covered by the waiter in a warm, rich chocolate sauce, and gives way to reveal pieces of honeycomb and a delicious milk ice cream.

Chef Sean Burbidge **Owner** Gordon Ramsay Holdings **Times** 12-2.30/6.30-10.30 Closed Sun **Prices** Fixed L 2 course £25, Fixed D 3 course £55, Service added but optional 12.5% **Wines** 800 bottles over £20, 12 by glass **Notes** Chef's menu 5 course £65 (Fixed L/D menu's ALC), Vegetarian menu, Dress restrictions, No sportswear **Seats** 45, Pr/dining room 6 **Children** Portions **Parking** On street

Parliament. David Collins, interior design wizard, has pulled off turning a basement dining room into a light, airy space, with cream leather upholstery, limestone panels, a large below-pavement window and limed oak flooring. The cooking and service is unashamedly Italian, a mix of classic and modern revolving around quality ingredients; lobster ravioli with broccoli (for the deeper wallets), or perhaps a breast of guinea fowl served with courgette and black summer truffle.

Times 12-3/6-12 Closed Xmas & New Year, 2 wks Aug, Sun

The Rib Room PLAN 4 F4

◎◎ British V

Classic roast beef dinners in the heart of Knightsbridge

☎ 020 7858 7250 & 7858 7181
Jumeirah Carlton Tower Hotel, Cadogan Place SW1X 9PY
e-mail: JCTinfo@jumeirah.com
dir: Nearest station: Knightsbridge

The Carlton Tower may be part of the international Jumeirah hotel group, but in the Rib Room it has a restaurant that is squarely in the tradition of hearty British dining. A ground-floor restaurant that looks out over Cadogan Gardens, it is furnished with clubby red seating, venetian blinds and high-quality table settings. Roast ribs of Aberdeen Angus from the Buccleuch estate are many people's main motivation for eating here, and the meat is reliably superb. Straying from the bovine trail, you might equally enjoy a fish dish such as roast halibut with wilted spinach in mussel and clam chowder. Loch Fyne mussels in cider, mustard and cream is a good bet among first courses, and desserts such as apple frangipane tart with cinnamon ice cream are richly satisfying.

Chef Simon Young **Times** 12.30-2.45/7-10.45 **Prices** Fixed L 2 course £28, Starter £16-£21, Main £29-£130, Dessert £9.50-£12, Service added but optional 15% **Notes** Fixed ALC D fr £28, British experience menu available, Sunday L, Vegetarian menu, Dress restrictions, Smart casual, Civ Wed 400 **Seats** 84, Pr/dining room 16 **Children** Portions, Menu **Parking** 70

Roussillon PLAN 4 G2

– see below

Sake No Hana PLAN 5 B5

◎ Traditional Japanese

Chic design and modern Japanese cooking in St James's

☎ 020 7925 8988
23 St James St SW1 1HA
e-mail: reservations@sakenohana.com
dir: Nearest station: Green Park, Piccadilly Circus. From Green Park Station, head towards Piccadilly Circus, first right St James St; restaurant situated half way down on right hand side

Recently refurbished to include a ground-floor lounge bar and sushi counter in the first-floor restaurant, this modern Japanese in St James's comes from acclaimed restaurateur Alan Yau, founder of Hakkasan. The stylish and striking interior boasts banquette seating and floor-to-ceiling windows in the spacious restaurant and bar serving Japanese-inspired cocktails as well as sake and wine. Attentive staff can guide you through the extensive menu, which includes sushi, sashimi and tempura in all its guises as well as plenty of less well-known Japanese classics. Try, perhaps Botan prawn tartare with tomato sorbet; sea bass usuzukuri with ponzu sauce or perhaps quail with sansho pepper from the robata grill.

Times 12-2.30/6-11.30 Closed 24-25 Dec, D Sun

Roussillon

Rosettes not confirmed at time of going to press

LONDON SW1 PLAN 4 G2

Modern French V

Changing of the guard in Pimlico

☎ 020 7730 5550
16 St Barnabas St SW1W 8PE
e-mail: michael.lear@roussillon.co.uk
dir: Nearest station: Sloane Square. Five minutes walk from Sloane Square, close to Peter Jones & near the Royal Hospital Chelsea

In a discreet location near the Royal Hospital, amid the antique shops of well-heeled Pimlico, the white-fronted, bay-windowed Roussillon is a fine-dining French restaurant of the old school. Flawlessly professional service from a youthful French team may extend to helping you in with any bags from the street, and the appointments are all top-drawer, from the spotless white linen to the ringing Riedel glassware and soft velour seating. Former chef-patron Alexis Gauthier left in the spring of 2010 to jointly run a new venture at Lindsay House, Soho, remaining as a partner at Roussillon, but no longer overseeing the kitchen (hence our unclassified rating for the time being). Expect deeply flavoured truffled seafood risotto with crisp-cooked purple basil, fantastically mature beef fillet with pommes Anna, green beans and a fine beef jus, and the Louis XV dessert, a soft praline bombe encasing a chocolate parfait interior, decorated with a little gold leaf bling. Incidentals are all comme il faut, from the amuse of sweetbreads and peas in chicken jus, to the vast array of breads with choice of salted or unsalted butter.

Chef D Gill **Owner** J & A Palmer **Times** 12-2.30/6.30-11 Closed Sun & BHs, L Sat **Prices** Fixed L 3 course £35, Fixed D 3 course £60, Tasting menu £65-£75, Service added but optional 12.5%, Groups min 10 service 15% **Wines** 500 bottles over £20, 20 bottles under £20, 20 by glass **Notes** Tasting menu & vegetarian tasting menu 8 course, Vegetarian menu, Dress restrictions, No shorts or flip flops **Seats** 50, Pr/dining room 28 **Children** Portions **Parking** NCP & on street 6.30 pm

Seven Park Place by William Drabble

LONDON SW1 PLAN 5 A5

Modern French NEW

Sophisticated setting for contemporary French cuisine

☎ 020 7316 1600
St James's Hotel and Club, 7-8 Park Place SW1A 1LS
e-mail: info@stjameshotelandclub.com
dir: Nearest station: Green Park. Off St James's St, close to Piccadilly

The appointment of executive chef William Drabble, after a decade winning plaudits at Aubergine (see entry), to work alongside head chef Philipp Vogel, and the launch of Seven Park Place, has jumped this striking-looking Victorian townhouse hotel into the Premier League of London dining. There is a second venue in the hotel - William's Bar and Bistro - but it is the fine-dining Seven Park Place that really catches the eye. The small, opulent restaurant has a high-end feel, with deep, rich colours, artful floral wallpaper and gold leaf inset in the ceiling, and the polished service fits the bill. The cooking is ostensibly modern French and based on tip-top ingredients, managing to maintain the integrity of the produce whilst delivering punchy flavours and avoiding over-embellishment. Baked fillet of red mullet is cooked perfectly, served with tender squid, a sage beignet and finished with a splendid mullet liver sauce, whilst main-course might be an assiette of veal with a Madeira jus, or fillet of turbot fricassée with langoustines, girolles and baby leeks. For dessert, perhaps a Bramley apple mousse, topped with a superb apple sorbet and complemented by a blackberry jelly.

Chef William Drabble **Times** 12-2/7-10 Closed D Sun-Mon **Prices** Food prices not confirmed for 2011. Please telephone for details **Wines** 14 by glass **Notes** Menu Gourmand available, Vegetarian available **Seats** 30, Pr/dining room 40 **Parking** On street and NCP

Zafferano

LONDON SW1 PLAN 4 F4

Italian

Smart modern Italian in Knightsbridge

☎ 020 7235 5800
15 Lowndes St SW1X 9EY
e-mail: info@zafferanorestaurant.com
web: www.zafferanorestaurant.com
dir: Nearest station: Knightsbridge. Located off Sloane St, behind Carlton Tower Hotel

Upmarket Italian cooking in the modern idiom is what Zafferano is about, and it has become one of that generation of London Italians that has helped redefine the gastronomy of that country for an adventurous clientele. The interior tone is refined but relaxed, with exposed brickwork, striped upholstery and orchids in vases making an uplifting setting. Service is highly praised for its professionalism and attention to detail, which also contributes powerfully to the air of class Zafferano exudes. The extensive menus - a carte at lunch, a fixed price with the odd supplement at dinner - offer a tour of new-wave Italian thinking, embracing a starter of warm octopus salad with purple potatoes and celery, pasta such as buckwheat pizzoccheri with leeks, sage and fontina, and mains like veal sweetbreads and kidney with artichokes and lentils. Presentation is very much in the contemporary style, and the counterpointing of flavours acts to give true depth to the dishes. Cherry and almond tart with mascarpone cream represents a satisfying conclusion to proceedings. A wine list packed with quality Italian growers makes for happy drinking.

Chef Andrew Needham **Owner** A-Z Restaurants-London Fine Dining Group **Times** 12-2.30/7-11 Closed 1 wk Xmas & New Year, L Etr Mon **Prices** Fixed D 3 course £45.80, Starter £10-£20, Main £10-£25, Dessert £8-£12.50, Service added 13.5% **Wines** 400 bottles over £20, 8 by glass **Notes** Seasonal truffle menu available. ALC L only, Sunday L, Vegetarian available, Dress restrictions, Smart casual **Seats** 85, Pr/dining room 20 **Children** Portions **Parking** NCP behind restaurant

LONDON SW1 *continued*

Salloos Restaurant PLAN 4 G4

◎ Pakistani

Pakistani cooking in Knightsbridge mews

☎ 020 7235 4444
62-64 Kinnerton St SW1X 8ER
dir: Nearest station: Knightsbridge. Kinnerton St is opposite Berkeley Hotel on Wilton Place

Upmarket and discreet, this venerable, genuine family business is located just across the road from The Berkeley hotel in a Knightsbridge mews house. Climb the stairs to the intimate first-floor dining room to enjoy some of London's most consistently sound Pakistani cooking. White linen, warm traditional colours and modern seating blend comfortably alongside polite (if old-school) service and atmosphere. The Mughlai cuisine delivers plenty of choice from the tandoor, with meats marinated 24-hours in advance (lamb shish kebab, perhaps), while house specialities might include chicken karahi (cooked with fresh tomatoes, ginger, green chillies and coriander), and curries could feature palak gosht (lamb and spinach cooked with fenugreek and ginger). Fat-wallet pricing reflects the location and clientele.

Chef Abdul Aziz **Owner** Mr & Mrs M Salahuddin **Times** 12-3/7-11.45 Closed Xmas, Sun **Prices** Food prices not confirmed for 2011. Please telephone for details **Wines** 40 bottles over £20, 3 bottles under £20, 2 by glass **Seats** 65 **Parking** Meters & car park Kinnerton St

Santini PLAN 4 H3

◎◎ Italian

Glamorous Italian in heart of Belgravia

☎ 020 7730 4094 & 7730 8275
29 Ebury St SW1W 0NZ
e-mail: info@santini-restaurant.com
dir: Nearest station: Victoria. Take Lower Belgrave St off Buckingham Palace Rd. Restaurant on 1st corner on left

A Belgravia favourite since 1984, this cool and confident Italian restaurant has a fabulous alfresco terrace framed by potted shrubs, glass screens and olive trees. Inside, though, is no less arresting, with light and bright pastel shades, large etched-glass windows, marble floors, leather banquettes and low-slung tub-style chairs. The carte offers an extensive selection of authentic regional Italian cooking with a Venetian accent. Dishes are simple with well-defined flavours and a good use of seasonal ingredients. The home-made pasta is a must; perhaps tagliolini with fresh Cornish crab, and to follow, grilled jumbo lobster tail with fresh tomato, chilli and rocket, or a classic bread-crumbed veal chop. The attentive, professional service is as Latin as the concise, all-Italian wine list.

Times 12-3/6-11 Closed Xmas, 1 Jan, Etr Sun & Mon, L Sat & Sun

Seven Park Place by William Drabble PLAN 5 A5

◎◎◎ – *see opposite page*

The Stafford London by Kempinski Hotel PLAN 5 A5

◎◎ British

Luxurious hotel dining in exclusive location

☎ 020 7493 0111
16-18 St James's Place SW1A 1NJ
e-mail: information@thestaffordhotel.co.uk
dir: Nearest station: Green Park

The Stafford is tucked away in a discreet cul-de-sac in London's St James's, just a short stroll from Green Park and Piccadilly. Not as well-known as the nearby Ritz, it is nonetheless a top-flight heritage hotel that exudes timeless luxury in a clubby country-house idiom. A Martini in the American bar, amid a quirky collection of club ties, sporting mementoes and signed celebrity photographs is de rigueur, and when it comes to dining, the grand restaurant has a real sense of occasion with its stucco pillars and candlelit tables dressed in crisp white linen. The menu is a stylish British affair with a clear classical pedigree and native produce at its heart. Expect a full complement of luxury ingredients - perhaps tartare of Wagyu beef with truffled toast and herb remoulade, followed by Cornish lamb noisette, best end and smoked lamb bacon Niçoise, or roast John Dory with saffron gnocchi, calamari and citrus vinaigrette. Finish with lemongrass pannacotta with blueberries. Wine buffs will be left open mouthed by the staggering wine list.

Times 12.30-2.30/6-10.30 Closed L Sat

Wheeler's PLAN 5 B6

◎◎ Seafood **NEW**

Renaissance of famous old name MPW style

☎ 020 7408 1440
72/73 St James's St SW1Y 6LB
e-mail: info@wheelersrestaurant.org
dir: Nearest station: Green Park

Marco Pierre White and Sir Rocco Forte have come together for the greater good to revive the iconic Wheeler's - a name synonymous with seafood since 1856. It's on the site of Marco's former Luciano restaurant and has been given a makeover of some pomp and circumstance. The cocktail bar remains a centrepiece with an eye-catching mosaic-tiled floor, while the restaurant behind is distinguished by its rich red walls, beautifully chosen fixtures and fittings and ordered rows of photos on the walls (some of them, ooh-err, on the titillating side). The brasserie-style menu deals in the classics, so there is langoustine cocktail and grilled Dover sole, or Wheeler's specialities like fish pie and steamed halibut à la sicilienne. There is a good showing of red meat, too - steaks from Scotland, calves' liver or Barnsley lamb chop. The ingredients are all tip-top and treated with skilful simplicity by a kitchen team led by Garry Hollihead. For dessert, follow the homely treacle tart, jam roly-poly route.

Times 12-3/5.30-11 Closed Sun, L Sat

Zafferano PLAN 4 F4

◎◎◎ – *see opposite page*

LONDON SW3

Awana PLAN 4 E2

◎◎ Traditional Malaysian V

Traditional Malaysian cooking and a warm welcome

☎ 020 7584 8880
85 Sloane Av SW3 3DX
e-mail: info@awana.co.uk
dir: Nearest station: South Kensington. Left out of South Kensington station onto Pelham Rd. Continue past Fulham Rd and onto Sloane Av

You don't often get the chance to sample Malaysian cuisine in the UK, so head to Awana for the real deal. The interior is inspired by traditional Malaysian teak houses, so think wooden floors and panelling and darkwood furniture. You can perch on a stool at the satay bar and watch the chef making Malaysian flatbreads, footage of which is relayed on TV screens around the restaurant. The friendly staff do a good job at explaining the dishes if required. Good quality and mostly authentic ingredients are used, as in a light salad of tiger prawns and crabmeat with pomelo (a South East Asian citrus fruit) and green mango. Cumin-spiced curried lamb shank is a good way to follow - the meat tender and the sauce a perfect balance of sweetness and spice. The Malaysian fruit durian - renowned for its noxious odour - turns up in an ice cream for dessert.

Chef Mark Read, Lee Chin Soon **Owner** Eddie Lim **Times** 12-3/6-11 Closed 25-26 Dec, 1 Jan, D 24 Dec **Prices** Fixed L 2 course £12.50-£15, Fixed D 3 course £20-£35, Tasting menu £45, Starter £5.20-£10.50, Main £9.50-£25, Dessert £6-£7.50, Service added but optional 12.5% **Wines** 98% bottles over £20, 2% bottles under £20, 12 by glass **Notes** Sunday L, Vegetarian menu, Dress restrictions, Smart casual **Seats** 110 **Children** Portions, Menu **Parking** Car park

LONDON SW3 ***continued***

Bibendum PLAN 4 E2

European V NOTABLE WINE LIST

Modern classics at a landmark Chelsea restaurant

☎ 020 7581 5817
Michelin House, 81 Fulham Rd SW3 6RD
e-mail: reservations@bibendum.co.uk
web: www.bibendum.co.uk
dir: Nearest station: South Kensington. Left out of South Kensington underground station on to Pelham Street and walk as far as the traffic lights; the Michelin building is opposite

The century-old Michelin building still looks timelessly immune from the vagaries of fashion, with the iconic wobble-bellied Michelin man, Bibendum, looking down from his azure stained-glass windows, while its '80's conversion to style-led restaurant (including street-level oyster bar and café) has become a design classic in its own right, too. Bright and airy, the stylish first-floor dining room looks sensational on sunny days with light streaming through that stained glass, while the atmosphere's pleasingly unstuffy. The cooking shows strong Gallic overtones with British influences on a menu of classic brasserie dishes shot through with flashes of contemporary verve. Clean-cut, skilful treatment of top-notch seasonal ingredients might deliver escargot de Bourgogne alongside roasted Anjou pigeon with cavolo nero, raisins and foie gras, or a Brit classic like deep-fried Haddock, chips and tartare. The wine list is a corker.

Chef Matthew Harris **Owner** Sir Terence Conran, Simon Hopkinson, Michael Hamlyn **Times** 12-2.30/7-11.30 Closed 25-26 Dec, 1 Jan, D 24 Dec **Prices** Fixed L 2 course £26, Starter £10.50-£24.50, Main £17-£29.50, Dessert £7-£9.50, Service added but optional 12.5% **Wines** 530 bottles over £20, 20 bottles under £20, 11 by glass **Notes** Sunday L, Vegetarian menu **Seats** 80 **Children** Portions **Parking** On street

The Capital PLAN 4 F4

Rosettes not confirmed at time of going to press
French

Chic landmark hotel with refined French cooking

☎ 020 7589 5171
22 Basil St, Knightsbridge SW3 1AT
e-mail: reservations@capitalhotel.co.uk
dir: Nearest station: Knightsbridge. Off Sloane St, beside Harrods

It's an impeccable address - Basil Street is a discreet little road with Harrods just around the corner - and this townhouse hotel meets all expectations from its unfettered, understated opulence to the refinement and professionalism of the service. The restaurant is a pleasingly contained space, consisting of a dozen or so tables, giving it the feel of a private club, but the soaring ceiling, big windows, blond-wood panelling and elegantly upholstered chairs inject the perfect amount of luxury. Eric Chavot has moved on after many years at the stoves and the kitchen is now headed up by Jérôme Ponchelle, a man well versed in French classical cooking. A starter of a terrine of duck, pork and foie gras is partnered with a rum jelly and toasted sourdough bread, while main-course grilled wild Scottish turbot (served on the bone) comes with béarnaise sauce and baby vegetables. The superb wine list includes bins from the owner's vineyard in the Loire.

Chef Jérôme Ponchelle **Owner** Mr D Levin **Times** 12-2.30/6.45-11 **Prices** Fixed L 2 course fr £27.50, Starter £14-£18, Main £22-£35, Dessert fr £12, Service added but optional 12.5% **Wines** All bottles over £20, 37 by glass **Notes** Dégustation menu 5 course £70, Sunday L, Vegetarian available, Dress restrictions, Smart casual **Seats** 35, Pr/dining room 24 **Parking** 10

Le Colombier PLAN 4 D2

French

Popular brasserie in Chelsea's heartland

☎ 020 7351 1155
145 Dovehouse St SW3 6LB
e-mail: lecolombier1998@aol.com
dir: Nearest station: South Kensington. Dovehouse St is just off the Fulham Rd S of South Kensington underground station

Le Colombier could not be more French if it wore a beret, except that its style is pitched rather more at the Parisian bourgeois end of the scale, in tune with its well-heeled Chelsea clientele. From the blue awning to the smart blue and cream décor and closely-packed tables, all the elements of a buzzing French neighbourhood bistro are present. Impeccably turned-out staff hit the same note of old-style Gallic correctness in their service, while the kitchen favours a classic style of comfort-food brasserie cooking, with starters such as snails with garlic cream sauce in puff pastry, followed by pig's trotters with sweetbreads and morels, or sole meunière.

Chef Philippe Tamet **Owner** Didier Garnier **Times** 12-3/6.30-10.30 **Prices** Fixed L 2 course £19-£23, Starter £6.90-£13.60, Main £16.20-£28.80, Dessert £6.70-£7.80, Service added but optional 12.5% **Wines** 200 bottles over £20, 12 bottles under £20, 10 by glass **Notes** Sunday L, Vegetarian available, Dress restrictions, Smart casual **Seats** 70, Pr/dining room 30 **Parking** Metered parking

Eight Over Eight PLAN 1 E3

Pan-Asian

Pan-Asian cooking in a chic Chelsea hangout

☎ 020 7349 9934
392 King's Rd SW3 5UZ
e-mail: eightovereight@rickerrestaurants.com
dir: Nearest station: Sloane Sq, South Kensington.

The über-trendy King's Road outpost of Will Ricker's oriental fusion empire brings in the bright young things who come to see and be seen while grazing through a Pan-Asian menu. But it's not all about posing and eyeballing here - the kitchen knows its way around the cuisines of Asia, sending out everything from dim sum to sashimi and sushi, tempura and roasts. Go for aromatic garlic duck with plum sauce, or black cod with sweet yuzu miso, and don't skip desserts like chocolate pudding with green tea ice cream. Eight is a lucky number in Chinese superstition, but the magic had an off-day in 2010: the restaurant was closed due to a fire at the time the guide went to press, but we can probably assume that it will open its doors with the sort of oriental-themed minimal chic look it had before the accident.

Times 12-3/6-11 Closed 24-29 Dec, Etr Sun, L Sun

Foxtrot Oscar PLAN 4 F1

Modern British

Gordon Ramsay's take on the neighbourhood bistro

☎ 020 7352 4448
79 Royal Hospital Rd SW3 4HN
e-mail: foxtrotoscar@gordonramsay.com
dir: Nearest station: Sloane Square

This local Chelsea bistro probably doesn't meet the public's perception of a Gordon Ramsay restaurant, but there is more to Gordon Ramsay Holdings than fine dining. The story goes that Ramsay and his team were fond of filling up at Foxtrot Oscar after a busy evening's service at the nearby flagship restaurant - so fond, in fact, that he added it to his portfolio. The enterprise shows his endorsement: simple, unpretentious, sound modern British bistro food, served in a relaxed, convivial ambience. The narrow room has a certain dapper style with its chocolate leather chairs, wood tables, slate-coloured flooring and black-and-white photos. The menu is an equally comforting mix of classic and modern; take chicken and ham hock terrine with piccalilli, and to follow, perhaps Goosnargh duck leg served with spring greens and beetroot chutney.

Times 12-3/6-10.30 Closed 1 wk Xmas, Mon-Tue, L Wed-Thu

Manicomio PLAN 4 F2

Italian

Buzzy, modern, informal Italian in stylish surroundings

☎ 020 7730 3366
85 Duke of York Square, Chelsea SW3 4LY
e-mail: manicomio@btconnect.com
dir: Nearest station: Sloane Square. Duke of York Sq 100mtrs along King's Rd from Sloane Sq

Although you're just a short hop away from the frenetic traffic of King's Road, Manicomio's expansive terrace overlooking the shops of the trendy Duke of York Square feels almost like dining alfresco in Italy, and the curvy glass roof and patio heaters keeps the elements at bay and the place busy. The indoor dining room looks sharp with a pared-back minimal look of bare bricks, wooden floors bright modern artworks on gun-metal grey walls, oak tables and red leather banquettes. The kitchen imports top-class ingredients from Italy and makes all its own pasta; expect creative modern Italian dishes such as chargrilled cuttlefish with chick peas, chilli, garlic and rosemary, or braised pig's cheeks with fennel, potato and truffle gratin. Hit the deli-café next door for simple snacky things and to take away authentic supplies. A second branch has opened in the City.

Times noon-3/6.30-10.30 Closed Xmas & New Year

Nozomi PLAN 4 E4

Japanese

Modern Japanese cuisine in cool Knightsbridge venue

☎ 020 7838 1500 & 7838 0181
14 - 15 Beauchamp Place, Knightsbridge SW3 1NQ
e-mail: info@nozomi.co.uk
dir: Nearest station: Knightsbidge

The front bar of this contemporary Japanese fairly buzzes with a see-and-be-seen crowd. Its fashionable good looks make it a favourite pre-club haunt, though the real draw is the dining room behind. Muted neutral tones, leather seating, subdued lighting, a big skylight and black-clad waiting staff combine with a trendy backing track to create an upbeat, modern space to enjoy some equally in-vogue Japanese cooking. The lengthy menu is flexible and ideal for sharing, with a good range of sushi, sashimi, tempura, maki rolls and temaki. Quality ingredients (including luxury ingredients such as Wagyu beef, lobster and foie gras) and skilful handling might deliver beef takikomi-gohan or lamb marinated in miso and mint and served with erangi mushrooms. Expect deep-pocket Knightsbridge price tags.

Times 12-3/6.30-11.30

Racine PLAN 4 E3

Traditional French

A touch of French verve close to the museums

☎ 020 7584 4477
239 Brompton Rd SW3 2EP
e-mail: bonjour@racine.com
dir: Nearest station: Knightsbridge, South Kensington. Restaurant opposite Brompton Oratory

It may be on the main drag in Knightsbridge, but this genuine bistrot de luxe - brimming with Gallic authenticity - wouldn't be out of place in Paris. A curtained entrance opens into a smart, retro setting, featuring chocolate-brown leather banquettes, wooden floors and mirror-lined walls, where waiters in black

continued on page 268

Rasoi Restaurant

LONDON SW3 PLAN 4 F2

Modern Indian V

Cutting-edge new Indian cuisine in lush Chelsea surroundings

☎ 020 7225 1881
10 Lincoln St SW3 2TS
e-mail: info@rasoirestaurant.co.uk
dir: Nearest station: Sloane Square. Near Peter Jones and Duke of York Sq

Entrance to the world of Rasoi Vineet Bhatia is gained by ringing the front door bell of a blue-chip townhouse on a Chelsea side street just off King's Road. Within lies an exotic fantasy of opulent silks, fragrant spices, the perfume of incense and interesting Indian objets d'art - all set in a classy contemporary décor of dark chocolate and cream. A blend of traditional and modern with plenty of wow factor, then, which is one way to describe Bhatia's cooking. This is highly-evolved food, steeped in classical tradition, but aimed squarely at waking up all the senses. A starter of lamb uttapam lasagne - Keralan lamb layered with rice flour pancakes, with coconut chutney and spicy sambhar - reworks a South Indian classic in a witty, East-meets-West style. Main courses bring on luxurious ingredients in a grilled ginger and chilli lobster, teamed with spiced lobster jus, curry leaf and spiced broccoli khichdi and spiced cocoa powder. Desserts conclude in the Euro-Indian fusion vein - perhaps a spiced tea 'chai' pannacotta with spiced orange and dry fruit cheesecake and pistachio biscuit. There are Western-style multi-course tasting menus too, and plenty to please vegetarians. Naturally, all of this comes priced to suit the SW3 postcode.

Chef Vineet Bhatia **Owner** Vineet & Rashima Bhatia **Times** 12-2.30/6-10.30 Closed Xmas, New Year, BHs, Sun, L Sat **Prices** Fixed L 2 course £21, Fixed D 3 course £58-£73, Tasting menu £83, Starter £20-£25, Main £28-£38, Dessert £10-£18, Service added but optional 12.5% **Wines** 250 bottles over £20, 4 bottles under £20, 10 by glass **Notes** Tasting menu 7 course, Degustation menu L 5 course £36, Vegetarian menu, Dress restrictions, Smart casual **Seats** 35, Pr/dining room 14 **Parking** On street

Restaurant Gordon Ramsay

LONDON SW3 PLAN 4 F1

French V NOTABLE WINE LIST

The mothership of the Gordon Ramsay empire

☎ 020 7352 4441
68 Royal Hospital Rd SW3 4HP
e-mail: reservations@gordonramsay.com
dir: Nearest station: Sloane Square. At junct of Royal Hospital Road & Swan Walk

The name needs no introduction and even if you've not eaten in one of the restaurants, you'll have come across *The F-Word, Hell's Kitchen* or *Kitchen Nightmares*. In these credit crunch times it may be that the era of super-chefs with global empires is in decline, but Ramsay Holdings still has interests in a dozen or so restaurants and a trio of pubs across London alone. It is worth noting that Ramsay is one of the best chefs the UK has produced, whose laudable goal was achieving nothing less than culinary perfection, and the Royal Hospital Road operation was where it all began back in 1998. It's a discreet place, nothing shouty or showy, just 15 tables in an intimate ivory and darkwood setting, and with Maître d' Jean-Claude Breton dealing suavely with the front-of-house, nothing distracts from the serious business of food. While the man himself isn't a fixture in his London flagship, it's good to see that it is still in capable hands. Under the guidance of executive chef Mark Askew, Clare Smyth interprets the Ramsay take on classic French Haute Cuisine. There's nothing that jars here - no misplaced attempts at innovation, just top-flight technical precision producing impeccable dishes of balance and refinement. So no surprises, then: it's a formula that works, and for most punters, still merits the stratospheric price tag. A perfectly-made king prawn tortellini is raised to a higher level when deft waiting staff pour on a delicate and subtle lemongrass consommé. Humble ingredients are used to great effect too: ox cheeks are braised to meltingly gelatinous perfection in a rich red wine sauce, and teamed with seasonal vegetables, polenta and mascarpone. Desserts, too, can be flawless - a textbook rum baba comes with caramelised mandarins and Chantilly cream. The wine list showcases the world's top producers, with a staggering presence from France, and commensurate prices.

Chef Gordon Ramsay, Mark Askew, Clare Smyth **Owner** Gordon Ramsay Holdings Ltd **Times** 12-2.30/6.30-11 Closed 1 wk Xmas, Sat-Sun **Prices** Fixed L 3 course £45, Fixed D 3 course £90, Tasting menu £120, Service added but optional 12.5% **Wines** 800+ bottles over £20, 2 bottles under £20, 13 by glass **Notes** Tasting menu 7 course, Seasonal menu 5 course £105, Vegetarian menu, Dress restrictions, Smart dress, no jeans or trainers **Seats** 45 **Children** Portions

Tom Aikens

LONDON SW3 PLAN 4 E2

Modern French V NOTABLE WINE LIST

Top of the league Chelsea dining

☎ 020 7584 2003
43 Elystan St SW3 3NT
e-mail: info@tomaikens.co.uk
web: www.tomaikens.co.uk
dir: Nearest station: South Kensington. Off Fulham Rd (Brompton Rd end)

'Give the people what they want' is an adage worth bearing in mind, especially during a recession. Tom Aikens has made a change to his menu with the addition of 'Tom's Classics', which is a range of more straightforward dishes available lunch and dinner alongside the complex, technically dextrous food that made his reputation. A sign of the times. The black-and-white frontage with a guard of perfectly trimmed shrubs is a lesson in refined understatement, a façade that inspires confidence rather than shouting 'look at me, look at me.' The theme continues on the inside, too, with the Anouska Hempel-designed space a lesson in cool minimalism with good use of natural materials to avoid any feeling of sterility. The front-of-house team are refreshingly lacking in pomposity, with the confidence to get the job done and maintain the right degree of charm and engagement. Tom's cooking is out of the top drawer and at this level the provenance of the ingredients is second to none. The tasting menu (with or without matched wines) will take you from roasted hand-dived scallop with spiced mango purée and confit duck, via John Dory with cauliflower purée, mint oil and pickled grapes to passionfruit jelly with vanilla pannacotta and passionfruit granité. Flavour combinations are unerringly well judged, presentation is out of the 'wow' school of design, and technical skills are as finely tuned as any Formula 1 pit crew. From the carte, sheep's cheese gazpacho with chervil cannelloni and Regent's Park honey is a compelling combination, while from the classics section is the joyous simplicity of tagliatelle with truffle. Main-course brings forth marinated pigeon, poached in cinnamon and coffee, and served with a pigeon confit, and from the classics perhaps a veal chop with lemon mash. Baked and poached meringue with salted popcorn and caramel ice cream is a well-judged dessert, or there is all the simplicity of a crème brûlée. The Premier League wine list is well worth exploring.

Chef Tom Aikens **Owner** Tom Aikens **Times** 12-2.30/6.45-11 Closed 2 wks Xmas & New Year, Etr, BHs, Sun, L Sat **Prices** Fixed L 2 course £39, Tasting menu £49-£80, Starter £10-£24, Main £21-£40, Dessert £8-£15, Service added but optional 12.5% **Wines** 250 bottles over £20, 1 bottle under £20, 10 by glass **Notes** Tasting menu L 6 course, D 8 course, Vegetarian menu **Seats** 60, Pr/dining room 10 **Children** Portions **Parking** Parking meters outside

LONDON SW3 ***continued***

waistcoats serve with verve and knowledge. Henry Harris is once again back at the helm, and his menu is a consummate example of classic cuisine bourgeoise - gutsy, rustic, big-hearted stuff. Think calves' brains with black butter and capers, followed by persillade of lamb with braised tarbais beans, or roasted skate with brown shrimps, lemon and croûtons. The high quality produce sings through at every turn, while daily specials are worth keeping an eye on. Appealing desserts and well-considered wines add to the experience.

Chef Henry Harris **Owner** Henry Harris, James Lee, George Bunnell **Times** 12-3/6-10.30 Closed 25 Dec **Prices** Fixed L 2 course £15, Fixed D 3 course £17.50, Starter £5.50-£16, Main £14.50-£26.25, Service added but optional 14.5% **Notes** Fixed D up to 7.30pm only, Sunday L **Seats** 60 **Children** Portions

Rasoi Restaurant PLAN 4 F2

@@@ – *see page 265*

Restaurant Gordon Ramsay PLAN 4 F1

@@@@ – *see page 266*

Sushinho PLAN 4 D1

@ Japanese, Brazilian

Contemporary Chelsea Japanese-Brazilian hybrid

☎ 020 7349 7496
312-314 King's Rd, Chelsea SW3 5UH
e-mail: info@sushinho.com
dir: Nearest station: Sloane Sq. On N side of King's Rd, Between Old Church St & The Vale

The name could belong to a Premiership footballer, but Sushinho is actually a stylish restaurant serving Brazilian-Japanese fusion cuisine (Brazil has the world's largest Japanese population outside of Japan, so it's not surprising to find a bit of cross-pollination between the two culinary cultures). The interior of this trendy King's Road venue goes for a contemporary oriental look involving bamboo screens, bare brickwork, moody lighting and hues of tobacco and café crème. The cocktail bar serves 'sakeirinhas' as a foretaste of the kitchen's fusion of gutsy, meat-and-beans Brazilian cooking with Japanese sushi and sashimi. Starters might include salmon sashimi pizza with anchovy aïoli and jalapeño, while main-course halibut might be teamed with razor clams, nameko mushrooms, and passionfruit and yuzu sauce. From the grill, comes US grain-fed sirloin robata with feijoada, romesco and farofa.

Times 12-3/6-10.30

Tom Aikens PLAN 4 E2

@@@@@ – *see page 267*

Tom's Kitchen PLAN 4 E2

@@ British, French

First-class brasserie food from top-class chef

☎ 020 7349 0202
27 Cale St, South Kensington SW3 3QP
e-mail: info@tomskitchen.co.uk
dir: Nearest station: South Kensington. Cale St (Parallel to Kings Rd), midway between Chelsea Green and St Lukes Church

'Food for everyone and anyone' is the mantra at Tom Aikens' fashionable all-day brasserie-style diner set over two floors in upmarket, residential Chelsea. It's in a handsome period building with the upbeat ground-floor brasserie looking good in an urban-rustic kind of way (white-tiled walls, wooden furniture, big black-and-white canvasses and an open-to-view kitchen. There's a first-floor bar, too, with lounge-style seating and white marble-top tables. The food (from breakfast to dinner) is based around English and French brasserie dishes, the cooking driven by quality seasonal produce. It is a lengthy, something-for-everyone roster, delivered by an accomplished crew. There's the familiar and comforting, like shepherd's pie or moules marinère to the more fashionable roasted fillet of line-caught sea bass with

Trinity Restaurant

LONDON SW4 PLAN 1 E3

British, French

Technically skilled modern cooking in the Clapham Polygon

☎ 020 7622 1199
4 The Polygon, Clapham SW4 0JG
e-mail: dine@trinityrestaurant.co.uk
dir: Nearest station: Clapham Common. 200 yds from tube opposite the Sun pub

To come across pace-setting food in the capital well away from the confines of the West End and City is always a thrill, and lucky Clapham has Adam Byatt to hug to its bosom. Situated in the Old Town, on the north edge of the Common, Trinity does a hearteningly brisk local trade. Cane-backed chairs at smartly dressed tables arranged with the quasi-military precision favoured nowadays set the scene, and there is a chef's table facility for those who like getting up close and personal. Modern Anglo-French cooking with high technical skill and improbable, but harmonious, juxtapositions is the stock-in-trade. A bunch of seasonal asparagus in spring is accompanied by smoked bacon, a crisp-fried pheasant egg and wild garlic mayonnaise, along with some salsify and cubes of crystal-clear apple jelly, for a stylish starter. Presentations refuse to gild the lily, allowing a piece of confit Loch Duart salmon to speak for itself, despite its backing chorus of broad bean ragoût, onion rings and lemon purée. Dessert capitalises on the alternative kinds of richness enjoyed these days, which might see toffee and caramel given a rest in favour of truffled honey parfait, ground podded cacao beans and pollen. It all comes at surprisingly un-horrifying prices, with gestures like treated tap water presented gratis instead of marked-up mineral water.

Chef Adam Byatt **Owner** Angus Jones & Adam Byatt **Times** 12.30-2.30/6.30-10.30 Closed 24-26 Dec, L Mon, D Sun **Prices** Fixed L 2 course £15, Fixed D 3 course £20, Starter £7-£12, Main £18-£28, Dessert £7-£9, Service added but optional 12.5% **Wines** 244 bottles over £20, 6 bottles under £20, 14 by glass **Notes** Fixed D Mon-Thu only, Tasting menu available, Sunday L, Vegetarian available **Seats** 63, Pr/dining room 12 **Children** Portions **Parking** On street

fennel, cherry tomato compôte and olive tapenade. And for pud, perhaps a vanilla pannacotta with passionfruit and mango.

Chef Richard Robinson **Owner** Tom Aikens
Times 12-3/6-11 Closed L 28 Dec **Prices** Starter £6-£15.50, Main £15-£29.50, Service added but optional 12.5% **Wines** 70 bottles over £20, 10 bottles under £20, 16 by glass **Notes** Fixed price menu not available all year round, Sunday L, Vegetarian available **Seats** 75, Pr/dining room 22 **Children** Portions **Parking** On street

Toto's

PLAN 4 F3

Italian

Innovative Italian food in smart Chelsea house

☎ 020 7589 2062 & 020 7589 0075
Walton House, Walton St SW3 2JH
e-mail: totos.restaurant@btconnect.com
dir: Nearest station: Knightsbridge

The location, just off Walton Street, is posh enough, but when you learn that the house was once the residence of Sir Winston Churchill's wife, Lady Clementine, it all feels even grander. The 17th-century fireplace and Murano chandelier are among the fittings to gaze at in wonder, but the innovative Italian cooking is absolutely of the moment. Start perhaps with tiger prawns and fennel in Sicilian citrus vinaigrette, or one of the pasta dishes, such as lobster linguini. Dishes show plenty of attention to detail, both in the quality of raw materials and their handling, with main courses like pecorino-crusted lamb cutlets and caponata full of vibrant flavour. Classic Italian desserts like pannacotta and tiramisù end things on a note of luxurious comfort.

Chef Paolo Simioni **Owner** Antonio Trapani
Times 12.15-3/7-11 Closed 25-27 Dec **Prices** Fixed L 2 course fr £23, Starter £9-£19, Main £12-£28, Dessert £7.50, Service added but optional 12.5% **Wines** 6 by glass **Notes** Sunday L, Vegetarian available, Dress restrictions, Smart casual **Seats** 90 **Children** Portions

LONDON SW4

Trinity Restaurant

PLAN 1 E3

– see opposite page

Tsunami

PLAN 1 E3

Japanese

Japanese fusion food at affordable prices

☎ 020 7978 1610
5-7 Voltaire Rd SW4 6DQ
e-mail: clapham@tsunamirestaurant.co.uk
dir: Nearest station: Clapham North. Off Clapham High Street

This cool minimalist operation offers Japanese-influenced fusion cooking in a side-street off Clapham High Street (Tsunami has a West End branch too). The décor ticks all the right style boxes - darkwood tables, funky modern art, mirrors, leather seating and a busy open-plan kitchen that sends out dishes made for sharing. The fashionable oriental hybrid cuisine turns out yellowtail sashimi jalapeño, or steamed crab and prawn shumai dumplings, then perhaps grilled marinated eel with rice, pickles and sansyo pepper, or foie gras Aberdeen Angus beef fillet served with sea urchin and foie gras butter.

Times 12.30-4/6-11 Closed 25 Dec-4 Jan, L Mon-Fri

LONDON SW5

Cambio De Tercio

PLAN 4 C2

Spanish

Contemporary Spanish cooking in vibrant atmosphere

☎ 020 7244 8970
163 Old Brompton Rd SW5 0LJ
dir: Nearest station: Gloucester Road. Close to junction with Drayton Gardens

Over 15 years Cambio De Tercio has confirmed its reputation as one of the capital's most loved Spanish restaurants. It may be decorated in colours redolent of an Iberian summer (a necessary tonic in this country, you might argue) and there may be a picture of a bull here and there, but this is no pastiche. The artworks are bold and modern, the floor covered in a cool black slate and the tables laid with crisp white linen. And the food is a happy blend of traditional and contemporary dishes, creatively presented, and with a ring of authenticity. Tapas or three-course convention are the options, the former delivering a ball of moist red tuna tartar, successfully paired with an avocado aïoli, salmon caviar, fresh herring roe and sweet tomato seeds. There's traditional prawns or skate wing with pig's ear from la plancha, plus black rice cooked with cuttlefish ink, squid and razor clams.

Times 12-2.30/7-11.30 Closed 2 wks at Xmas, New Year

New Lotus Garden

PLAN 4 B2

Chinese V

Snug neighbourhood Chinese handy for Earl's Court

☎ 020 7244 8984
15 Kenway Rd SW5 0RP
dir: Nearest station: Earl's Court

The locals flock to this cosy neighbourhood Chinese restaurant close to Earl's Court. It's an unassuming, intimate place with just a dozen or so tables, but the food punches above its weight. The menu offers a tried-and-tested repertoire of Chinese classics, using fresh, well-prepared ingredients in crowd-pleasing dishes such as light and well-spiced pork dumplings, and crispy salt and pepper squid; main courses offer exemplary versions of crispy duck or chicken with smoky black beans and green peppers. All accompanying dishes like fried rice and Singapore noodles are of an equally high standard.

Chef Hubert Jiang **Owner** Hubert Jiang
Times 12-3.30/5-11.30 **Prices** Fixed L 2 course £10-£25, Fixed D 3 course £13-£35, Starter £3-£7, Main £4-£9, Dessert £2-£3.80, Service added but optional 10% **Wines** 6 bottles over £20, 15 bottles under £20, 2 by glass **Notes** Sunday L, Vegetarian menu **Seats** 40 **Children** Portions

LONDON SW6

Blue Elephant

PLAN 1 D3

Traditional Thai

Truly extravagant Fulham Thai

☎ 020 7385 6595
3-6 Fulham Rd SW6 1AA
e-mail: london@blueelephant.com
dir: Nearest station: Fulham Broadway

Some might consider this extravagant, formidably-sized Thai restaurant (part of an international chain) somewhat passé these days, a piece of Thai bling or a bit footballers' wives, with its stage-set canopy of lush verdant plants, trickling fountains, bridges spanning carp-filled ponds and a 12-metre gilded bar resembling a royal barge, but it's enduringly popular because the food delivers. Candles twinkle while the scent of tropical flowers mingles with the heady aroma of exotic herbs and spices flown in fresh to service its equally flamboyant and lengthy menu. The set 'Royal Thai Banquette' repertoire offers a tasting-style experience, while house favourites appear under a 'Suggestions' section, otherwise expect mains like roasted duck curry, black pepper tiger prawns, lime sea bass or grilled lobster.

Times 12-2.30/7-12 Closed 25 Dec, 1 Jan

Deep

PLAN 1 E3

Seafood

Contemporary Thames-side surroundings for impressive seafood

☎ 020 7736 3337
8 The Boulevard, Imperial Wharf SW6 2UB
e-mail: info@deeplondon.co.uk
dir: Nearest station: Fulham Broadway. From underground station take Harwood Rd then Imperial Rd

Amid the upmarket Thames-side splendour of the Imperial Wharf development, Deep's name alludes to its intentions. A class act, the focus is on top-notch fish and seafood with a strong ecological ethos running right through. There are two lovely terraces overlooking the water and an open-plan kitchen to add to the appeal, plus floor-to-ceiling windows and an all round avant-garde feel. Expect some interesting combinations - with something of a Scandinavian accent reflecting the owner's Swedish roots. A signature dish of steamed halibut is served with egg, prawns and horseradish in warm butter, perhaps following a selection of herrings or seafood platter (for two), while a tasting menu and occasional meat offerings help broaden the appeal.

Times 12-3/7-11 Closed Mon, L Sat, D Sun

LONDON SW6 ***continued***

The Harwood Arms

PLAN 1 D3

@@ British V

Fulham gastro-pub with creative, seasonal cooking

☎ 020 7386 1847
27 Walham Grove, Fulham SW6 1QR
dir: Nearest station: Fulham Broadway. Located on the corner of Farm Lane & Walham Grove

You could almost imagine yourself transported to the home counties inside this posh Fulham gastro-pub: inside is a stripped-out contemporary décor - bare wooden tables and floors, walls in Shaker shades of battleship grey and cream, hung with huntin' and shootin' photos - nothing much to single it out from an army of pubs reworked with a contemporary look and food to match. But the Harwood Arms is the brainchild of the Ledbury's Brett Graham and the Pot Kiln's Mike Robinson (see entries): that should make foodies' ears prick up and pay attention. Chef Stephen Williams' inventive cooking is muscular stuff, backed by sound technique and fine-tuned to the seasons. His adventurous ideas involving top-grade English produce pull off riveting variations of flavour and texture - perhaps Hereford snails with oxtail braised in stout, with parsley crumbs and bone marrow. Game, perhaps, in the form of braised shoulder and grilled cutlet of fallow deer with crisp garlic potatoes, greens and mushroom ketchup, while fish turns up in the shape of roast Cornish cod with chanterelles, sea purslane, salsify fritters and garlic mayonnaise.

Chef Stephen Williams **Owner** Trieamain Harwood Ltd
Times 12-3/6.30-9.30 Closed 24-28 Dec, 1 Jan, L Mon
Prices Starter £6-£8, Main £14-£18, Dessert £5-£8, Service added 12.5% **Wines** 42 bottles over £20, 8 bottles under £20 **Notes** Sunday L, Vegetarian menu **Seats** 60
Children Portions **Parking** On street

Marco

PLAN 1 D3

@@ British

Classy modern brasserie at Chelsea FC

☎ 020 7915 2929
M&C Hotels At Chelsea FC, Stamford Bridge, Fulham Rd SW6 1HS
e-mail: info@marcorestaurant.org
dir: Nearest station: Fulham Broadway

Football fans are used to meat pies and burgers, but, courtesy of Marco Pierre White, at Chelsea Football Club's Stamford Bridge complex you can get braised oxtail and kidney pudding and roasted poulet noir with chipolata, roasting juices and bread sauce. This collaboration between MPW and club owner Roman Abramovich is a super-cool venue, elegant and glamorous (how about a striking golden pillar of Swarovski crystal?) with lots of subtle dark hues, low lighting, curved leather banquettes and white linen-clad tables. And with the addition of a sleek cocktail bar, you've got a Premier League venue. As you'd expect, the brasserie-style carte is an equally classy and typically Marco affair, driven by tip-top produce, clean flavours and skilful execution. Expect classics like grilled halibut garnished à la provençale, Scottish beef steaks and grilled calves' liver with bacon and creamed potatoes. There's carefully chosen English cheeses and for dessert, perhaps lemon tart or raspberry soufflé.

Chef Matthew Brown **Owner** Marco Pierre White & C.F.C
Times 6-10.30 Closed 2 wks Jul-Aug, Sun-Mon, L all week
Prices Fixed D 2 course £21.50-£24.50, Starter £8.50-£15.50, Main £16.50-£30, Dessert £6.50, Service added 12.5% **Wines** 40 bottles over £20, 6 bottles under £20, 8 by glass **Notes** Vegetarian available **Seats** 70
Children Portions **Parking** 10

Memories of India on the River

PLAN 1 E3

@ Indian

Sophisticated Indian restaurant in Chelsea Harbour

☎ 020 7736 0077
7 The Boulevard, Imperial Wharf, Townmead Rd, Chelsea SW6 2UB
dir: Nearest station: Fulham Broadway, Imperial Wharf. Close to Chelsea Harbour

This swish modern Indian on trendy Imperial Wharf looks the part, in keeping with its classy Chelsea location. Expect burnished wooden floors, toffee leather banquettes, white linen, wooden screens, and large vibrantly-coloured artworks giving off spicy, exotic warmth. The compendious menu is equally eye-catching: influences come from all across the sub-continent to play their part in a cocktail of regional classics and contemporary ideas. Murgh Karnataka brings together chicken with a smoky sauce, cut through with the citrus edge of lime and coriander - and who could pass over a Bengali Jhinga Macher Molai curry - lobster-sized prawns marinated in spices and coconut?

Chef Abdur Razzak **Owner** Mr Belal Ali & Mr Abdul Jalil
Times 12-3/5.30-11.30 Closed 25 Dec **Prices** Food prices not confirmed for 2011. Please telephone for details
Wines 25 bottles over £20, 20 bottles under £20, 6 by glass **Notes** Vegetarian available **Seats** 100, Pr/dining room 30 **Children** Portions, Menu **Parking** 50

Saran Rom

PLAN 1 E3

@@ Thai

Luxury Thames-side setting for authentic Thai cooking

☎ 020 7751 3111 & 7751 3110
The Boulevard, Imperial Wharf, Townmead Rd SW6 2UB
e-mail: info@saranrom.com
dir: Nearest station: Fulham Broadway. 1.5m from Stamford Bridge/Fulham Broadway tube station

In the striking new riverside development of Imperial Wharf, this lavish Thai restaurant fits the bill. The sumptuous colonial-style interior - with its silk hangings, 19th-century antiques, teak carvings, ornate fretwork panels and crisp white linen - certainly impresses, and owes more than a nod to Thailand's royal palaces. Add Thames views from all levels, a cocktail bar and two terraces and you have a grand setting (especially popular in summer) to enjoy some authentic Thai hospitality and skilfully-prepared cuisine. Chilli symbols on the menu flag-up dishes with attitude, like a high-octane classic green chicken curry (with freshly pounded green herbs, coconut and Thai aubergine), while tamarind duck (grilled breast served with seaweed and a sweet-and-sour tamarind sauce) offers more subtlety.

Times 6-11 Closed 25 Dec, 1-4 Jan

LONDON SW7

Baglioni Hotel

PLAN 4 C4

@ Italian, European **NEW**

Mediterranean cuisine in luxurious surroundings

☎ 020 7368 5900
60 Hyde Park Gate, Kensington Rd SW7 5BB
dir: Nearest station: Kensington High Street. Hotel entrance on Hyde Park Gate facing park & Kensington Palace

Opulence and decadence are the key words that describe the Brunello restaurant, set within the boutique Baglioni Hotel in the heart of Kensington and overlooking Hyde Park. Expect rich luxurious fabrics, a chic, grey and gold themed décor, and slick, attentive service delivered by friendly and professional staff. Classical Italian dishes are built round quality seasonal produce and presented in the traditional manner - antipasti, pasta, risotto, fish and meat courses. Dishes are authentic and not over complicated; take tender grilled squid with rocket and sweet chilli, halibut with Jerusalem artichokes and roasted tomatoes, roast duck with polenta, and Amaretto crème brûlée with blood orange. There's a list of classy Italian wines.

Chef Andrea Vercelli **Owner** Baglioni Hotels
Times 12.30-3/5.30-11 **Prices** Fixed L 2 course £20-£25, Fixed D 3 course £25, Starter £8.50-£17, Main £15.50-£32.50, Dessert £8-£12.50, Service added 12.5%
Wines 205 bottles over £20, 8 by glass **Notes** Sunday L, Vegetarian available, Dress restrictions, Smart casual, Civ Wed 60 **Seats** 60, Pr/dining room 60
Children Portions, Menu **Parking** 3, Kensington Road

L'Etranger

PLAN 4 C4

@@ French, Japanese NOTABLE WINE LIST

French food with a Japanese slant in a smart setting

☎ 020 7584 1118
36 Gloucester Rd SW7 4QT
e-mail: axelle@circagroupltd.co.uk
dir: Nearest station: Gloucester Rd. 5 mins walk from Gloucester Rd tube station at junct of Queens Gate Terrace and Gloucester Rd

L'Etranger is not a Camus-themed eatery where the menu presents diners with existential dilemmas, but an elegant fusion of East-meets-West. What chefs Jérome Tauvron and Kingshuk Dey aim to achieve here is not fusion cooking as such, but a happy marriage of two of the world's great cuisines. Sure, Asian style has quite a say in the kitchen's output, but the repertoire's basis is classic French dishes with Japanese flavours. The setting is aptly elegant and minimal, with oak floors and subtle shades of lilac and grey, and sleek well-polished service to match the five-star price tags. Scallops tartare with karasumi (air-dried salted mullet roe) and black truffles is a great way to start. Fishy mains might run to pan-seared Scottish halibut with sudachi lime beurre blanc and lobster claw, while Hampshire pork is showcased in the form of pot-roast cheeks and crispy belly, partnered by grilled squid and Granny Smith apple mash. For high-rollers, only Wagyu beef fillet Rossini with foie gras and black truffle will do. The wine list can go head to head with just about any of London's top-flight restaurants, and there's an expert sommelier to steer the way.

Times 12-3/6-11 Closed 25 Dec, 1 Jan, L Sat

Madsen PLAN 4 D3

European

Modern Scandinavian brasserie-style restaurant

020 7225 2772
20 Old Brompton Rd, South Kensington SW7 3DL
e-mail: reservations@madsenrestaurant.com
web: www.madsenrestaurant.com
dir: Nearest station: South Kensington. Outside tube station, opposite Lamborghini garage

Nordic cuisine is not generally seen as something to get excited about, but this stylish glass-fronted venue in Sloane-central near South Ken tube station is on a mission to put Scandinavian food on the map. As you'd expect from a part of the world known for design excellence, it's a clean-cut, contemporary space, all pale wood, whitewashed bare-brick walls, and iconic lamps by Poul Henningsen. Eco-ethics are big here, so materials used in the light, healthy dishes are sustainably-sourced and low on food miles. Classic sweet-cured herring with dill-marinated potatoes and mustard cream is a good way to start, ahead of pork meatballs teamed with red cabbage, gravy and pickled cucumber. If you can manage to say 'Kærnemælksfromage med kammerjunkere' you'll end with a delicious Danish buttermilk mousse with lemon sorbet and vanilla biscuit.

Chef Andre Friberg **Owner** Charlotte Kruse Madsen **Times** 12-4/6-10 Closed Xmas, D Sun **Prices** Fixed L 2 course £14-£16, Fixed D 3 course £23-£25, Starter £5-£7, Main £10-£15, Dessert £5-£7, Service optional, Groups min 5 service 12.5% **Wines** 35 bottles over £20, 7 bottles under £20, 10 by glass **Notes** Sunday L, Vegetarian available **Seats** 50, Pr/dining room 12 **Children** Portions, Menu **Parking** On street

Zuma PLAN 4 F4

Modern Japanese

Glamorous setting for sophisticated Japanese cuisine

020 7584 1010
5 Raphael St, Knightsbridge SW7 1DL
e-mail: info@zumarestaurant.com
dir: Nearest station: Knightsbridge. Brompton Rd west, turn right into Lancelot Pl & follow road to right into Raphael St

In the fickle world of the capital's dining scene, Zuma never seems to fall from favour or fashion. The posh Knightsbridge location helps, of course, as well as Zuma's creative take on the traditional Japanese isakaya style of informal eating. There's something very minimally Zen about the restaurant's hyper-modern textures of concrete, steel, glass, wood and stone, but it's not all calmness and meditation when the crowds turn up at the bar and the place starts to fizz. Japanese food is all about freshness of the ingredients, so the style of cooking messes with the materials as little as possible, and whether they are served from the sushi bar, the robata grill, or the main kitchen, dishes always paint a lovely picture on the plate. The tapas approach is the best way to go about a meal: ordering a string of dainty sharing dishes to turn up one after another will keep taste buds on high alert - if you're feeling minted, there's seared Wagyu beef sirloin tataki with black truffle ponzu, or more accessible ideas such as grilled sardines with sour shiso chilli butter, or fried soft-shelled crab with wasabi mayonnaise. Hot from the robata grill come saké-grilled chicken wings with sea salt and lime, or salt-grilled sea bass with burnt tomato and ginger relish. A saké sommelier is at hand to guide you through unfamiliar rice wine territory.

Chef Ross Shonhan **Owner** Rainer Becker & Arjun Waney **Times** 12-2.30/6-11 Closed 25-26 Dec, 1 Jan **Prices** Food prices not confirmed for 2011. Please telephone for details **Wines** 2 bottles under £20, 13 by glass **Notes** Sunday L, Vegetarian available **Seats** 147, Pr/dining room 14 **Children** Portions **Parking** Street parking

LONDON SW8

Tom Ilic PLAN 1 E3

Modern European

Robust flavours from seasoned chef in Battersea

020 7622 0555
123 Queenstown Rd SW8 3RH
e-mail: info@tomilic.com
dir: Nearest station: Close to Clapham Junct & Battersea Power Station

The shop-front façade of Tom Ilic's Battersea restaurant has the look of a simple neighbourhood bistro, but there's cooking of a rather higher order coming out of the kitchen. A cheerful porker smiles from the 'O' of the chef's name on the logo - a clue to the gutsy, turbo-charged flavours that are the signature of his operation. The vibe is unbuttoned and relaxing, confident staff know their way around the menu, and the venue has the warmth of wooden floors, terracotta and soft-pink coloured walls. The modern European cooking takes its cue from the more humble cuts of meat that take a bit more hard work and skill from the chef to make them sing in all their gluey, sticky, full-throttle glory - but the results Tom Ilic achieves are memorable indeed. Better still, his prices are extremely fair - this is not a restaurant that takes offal and tacks on a foie gras price tag. Braised pig's cheeks and chorizo with garlic and parsley mash and pork crackling sets the tone, ahead of cutlet, saddle and shoulder of lamb, teamed with gratin dauphinoise and spiced aubergine. Dark chocolate fondant with black pepper ice cream makes a suitably full-on finale.

Chef Tom Ilic **Owner** Tom Ilic **Times** 12-2.30/6-10.30 Closed last wk Aug, Xmas, Mon, L Tue, D Sun **Prices** Fixed L 2 course £14.50-£16.95, Fixed D 3 course £21.50, Starter £6-£8.50, Main £12.95-£16.50, Dessert £4.95-£7.50, Service added but optional 12.5% **Wines** 10 bottles over £20, 2 bottles under £20, 8 by glass **Notes** Sunday L, Vegetarian available **Seats** 58 **Children** Portions **Parking** On street

LONDON SW10

Aubergine PLAN 4 C1

– see page 272

Chutney Mary Restaurant PLAN 1 E3

Indian

Seductive, modern Indian offering refined cuisine

020 7351 3113
535 King's Rd, Chelsea SW10 0SZ
e-mail: chutneymary@realindianfood.com
dir: Nearest station: Fulham Broadway. On corner of King's Rd and Lots Rd; 2 mins from Chelsea Harbour

Chutney Mary opened in 1990, but it's certainly not stuck in the past. The restaurant has evolved over the years and while it still offers traditional cooking from various regions of India, its cuisine is also reflective of the modern food trends in Mumbai and other parts of the sub-continent. Moghul mirror-work murals lead to the classy split-level basement, moodily aglow with flickering candles, its walls lined with mirrors and antique Raj-era sketches. Fresh lobster in a tomato and brandy sauce, served in the shell with a separate lobster curry and rice, is an enduringly popular dish, as is the lamb pasanda cooked in the 'jewel of gravies'. Vegetarians get to choose from two different platters - a traditional North Indian version of vegetables and dhal, and a more unusual one with dishes such as stir-fried banana flower with coconut, and baby courgette masala. Every wine on the list has been chosen to complement the flavours of Indian food. (See entries for sister restaurants Veeraswamy and Amaya.)

Times 12.30-3/6.30-11.30 Closed L Mon-Fri, D 25 Dec

LONDON SW10 *continued*

The Painted Heron PLAN 1 E3

Modern Indian

Stylish, upmarket and impressive modern Indian

020 7351 5232
112 Cheyne Walk SW10 0DJ
e-mail: thepaintedheron@btinternet.com
dir: Nearest station: South Kensington

On the Chelsea embankment close to Battersea Bridge, a blue awning and glass frontage picks out this understated but thoroughbred contemporary Indian. Sleek minimalism delivers a stylish, modern edge to the deceptively roomy, split-level interior; think plain white walls adorned with modern art, blond-wood floors and black lacquered chairs. The high-quality modern Indian cooking follows suit, with traditional dishes given a contemporary spin and presentation, focusing on tip-top ingredients and vibrant, balanced spicing. There's tandoori-roasted rack of lamb with okra rice and tomato-tamarind chutney, or go for the catch-of-the-day - cod in a Keralan fisherman's curry for example. The creativity continues through desserts such as honey and cinnamon pudding. A small bar and lounge area, plus alfresco rear courtyard complete a class act.

Times 12-3/6.30-11 Closed Xmas & Etr, L Sat

Wyndham Grand London Chelsea Harbour PLAN 1 E3

International

Sophisticated waterside dining

020 7300 8443
Chelsea Harbour SW10 0XG
dir: Nearest station: Fulham Broadway

The Wyndham Grand Hotel overlooks the jet-set environs of Chelsea Harbour and its marina, and comes with a suitably style-driven contemporary interior. The restaurant's approach is one of constant reinvention: in 2010, it was named TwentyTen, but the name and concept will change each year. The look is suitably sharp and upmarket - wooden floors, constantly changing artworks, and linen-clad tables laid with designer glassware and cutlery. The alfresco decking terrace overlooks the marina, and is predictably in demand on warm summer days, but floor-to-ceiling glass panels in the restaurant mean everyone gets the view. The kitchen deals in modern European cooking founded on well-sourced ingredients combined with a creative spirit. Pan-fried scallops with Jerusalem artichokes, truffle foam and tapenade shows the style, ahead of a risotto of organic salmon fillet and smoked salmon with fresh dill.

Times All day

LONDON SW11

The Butcher & Grill PLAN 1 E3

Modern, Traditional

Meat-eaters' treat on an old Thames wharf

020 7924 3999
39-41 Parkgate Rd, Battersea SW11 4NP
e-mail: info@thebutcherandgrill.com
dir: Nearest station: Clapham Junction, Battersea

The former warehouse beside an old wharf near the Albert Bridge is a foodie paradise, from the butcher's shop and deli at the front to the cavernous, no-frills grill restaurant towards the rear. Top-quality cuts are the stars of the show, as in Highfields rack of lamb, or duck breast with spring greens, girolles and garlic. Go the whole hog by starting with some potted salt beef and gherkins, or beef tartare with pea shoots and lemon oil. Those in the market for something lighter might try sea bass with fennel, radishes and mange-tout. A range of sauce options may be added at no extra cost. Finish with vanilla pannacotta and fresh berries.

Times 12-3.30/6-11 Closed 25-27 Dec, D Sun

Aubergine

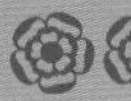

LONDON SW10 PLAN 4 C1

Modern French

Rarefied French cuisine in well-heeled Chelsea

020 7352 3449
11 Park Walk, Chelsea SW10 0AJ
e-mail: aubergine@londonfinediningroup.com
web: www.auberginerestaurant.co.uk
dir: Nearest station: South Kensington, Fulham Broadway. W along Fulham Rd

The aubergine brand is stamped throughout this polished stalwart of the Chelsea fine dining scene. You could play spot the aubergine, starting with the eggplant-shaped door handle and purple-hued canopy; once inside, there's the imperial purple carpet, hand-painted plates and motifs on the cutlery. In this well-heeled Chelsea location, a dining room has to look the part, and Aubergine has a suitably grown-up, soft-focus interior of French oak floors, muted shades and calm, correctly-formal service. Head chef Christophe Renou took over the reins in 2009, and has no plans to steer the kitchen into new territory; its mission is, and always has been, to deliver top-level contemporary French cuisine that follows the seasons. If you want to buy into this rarefied world at entry level prices, three-course set lunches are a steal. What you get is clear, precise flavours built on unimpeachable technique, rather than any attempt to chase the latest ephemeral trends. Snail ravioli with garlic and herb 'Aigo Bulido' is a real treat, a single pillowy pasta parcel filled with juicy snails and snail mousseline, supported by a silky sauce made from the cooking liquor, cream, garlic and fresh herbs. A turbot pot au feu with a big, full-on saffron bouillon sounds deceptively simple, but there's a lot more going on than the terse menu descriptions give away: this is a deeply satisfying dish of memorable intensity of flavour. Expert pastry skills wind up with a masterclass in tarte Tatin with vanilla ice cream.

Chef Christophe Renou **Owner** London Fine Dining Group **Times** 12-2.30/7-11 Closed Xmas, Sun-Mon (except BHs) **Prices** Fixed L 2 course fr £18.50, Fixed D 3 course fr £34, Service added but optional 12.5%, Groups min 8 service 15% **Wines** 500 bottles over £20, 3 bottles under £20, 10 by glass **Notes** Menu gourmand 7 course from £77, Vegetarian available, Dress restrictions, Smart casual preferred **Seats** 60 **Children** Portions **Parking** Local parking available

Ransome's Dock PLAN 1 E3

Modern British

Charming bistro-style restaurant by the Thames

020 7223 1611 & 7924 2462
35-37 Parkgate Rd, Battersea SW11 4NP
e-mail: chef@ransomesdock.co.uk
dir: Nearest station: Sloane Square, Clapham Junction. Between Albert Bridge & Battersea Bridge

Ransome's Dock is the neighbourhood restaurant everyone should be lucky enough to have in their neighbourhood. A former ice cream factory overlooking a former wharf close to Albert Bridge, inside it has an easy charm with cornflower blue walls, witty pictures and plenty of room between tables. It's all very relaxed, helped along by the laid-back staff. The outside terrace is the place to sit when the climate allows. The kitchen, led by owners Martin and Vanessa Lam, deals in appealing modern European dishes, based on top-notch ingredients and following the seasons; start, perhaps, with dressed Dorset crab with avocado and pink grapefruit salad, before tucking into Elizabeth David's spinach and ricotta gnocchi with butter and parmesan. Puddings include slow-poached quince with warm gingerbread and clotted cream or the lighter labneh (yoghurt) with orange blossom syrup, mango and pomegranate. The award winning wine list contains some rare treats.

Chef Martin & Vanessa Lam **Owner** Mr & Mrs M Lam **Times** 12-11 Closed Xmas, Aug BH, D Sun **Prices** Fixed L 2 course fr £15.50, Starter £5.50-£12.50, Main £11.50-£23, Dessert £5.50-£8.50, Service added but optional 12.5% **Wines** 360 bottles over £20, 22 bottles under £20, 10 by glass **Notes** Brunch menu Sat-Sun, Sunday L, Vegetarian available **Seats** 55 **Children** Portions **Parking** 20, Spaces in evenings & wknds only

LONDON SW12

Harrison's PLAN 1 E2

Modern British

Buzzy neighbourhood brasserie with crowd-pleasing menu

020 8675 6900
15-19 Bedford Hill SW12 9EX
e-mail: info@harrisonsbalham.co.uk
dir: Nearest station: Balham. Turn right from Balham High Rd opposite Waitrose, onto Bedford Hill. Restaurant on corner of Bedford Hill & Harberson Rd

This buzzy neighbourhood brasserie and bar in Balham was set up by Sam Harrison (of Sam's Brasserie & Bar in Chiswick - see entry) back in October 2007. The smart-casual modern vibe, eye-catching glass frontage and pavement tables, and unbuttoned trendy interior, is a winning formula. The cooking cuts its cloth to please local tastes, offering a solid, unfussy brasserie menu full of robust flavours, modern twists here and there, and at prices that won't sour the smiles. Take rabbit, foie gras and walnut terrine with pear chutney to start, then follow with roast rump of lamb, butternut purée, merguez sausage and harissa jus. A user-friendly wine list offers plenty by the glass and in 500ml carafes.

Chef Nick Stones **Owner** Sam Harrison **Times** 12-mdnt Closed 24-27 Dec, L 28 Dec **Prices** Food prices not confirmed for 2011. Please telephone for details **Wines** 50 bottles over £20, 15 bottles under £20, 21 by glass **Notes** Sunday L, Vegetarian available **Seats** 80, Pr/dining room 40 **Children** Portions, Menu **Parking** On street

Lamberts PLAN 1 E2

Modern British

Seasonal food from small producers

020 8675 2233
2 Station Pde, Balham High Rd SW12 9AZ
e-mail: bookings@lambertsrestaurant.com
dir: Nearest station: Balham. Just S of Balham station on Balham High Rd

Look for the pair of birds in white silhouette above the dark green frontage, and you've arrived at Balham's outstanding neighbourhood restaurant. A chic interior design has stripped-wood floors, unclothed tables and banquette seating, with gentle lighting and a murmur of unintrusive background music. The place is deservedly popular locally for its commitment to small food producers and an unimpeachably seasonal approach not necessarily expected in the south London hinterland. Soused mackerel with beetroot and horseradish, a main course of ovine variations (mutton, wether and lamb) with Lyonnaise potatoes, and desserts such as rhubarb tart with honeycomb ice cream, are the kinds of dishes to expect. An intelligent list of global wines is helpfully arranged by style.

Chef Andrew Bradford **Owner** Mr Joe Lambert **Times** 12-5/7-10.30 Closed 25 Dec, 1 Jan, BHs (except Good Fri), Mon, L Tue-Fri, D Sun **Prices** Fixed L 2 course £17-£20, Fixed D 3 course £20-£30, Service added but optional 12.5% **Wines** 51 bottles over £20, 14 bottles under £20, 14 by glass **Notes** Sunday L, Vegetarian available **Seats** 50 **Children** Portions, Menu **Parking** On street

LONDON SW13

Sonny's Restaurant PLAN 1 D3

Modern European

Accomplished cooking in popular neighbourhood restaurant

020 8748 0393
94 Church Rd, Barnes SW13 0DQ
e-mail: manager@sonnys.co.uk
dir: Nearest station: Barnes, Hammersmith. From Castelnau end of Church Rd on left by shops

The epitome of a modern, relaxed, neighbourhood restaurant (with food-store and deli next door), the ever-popular Sonny's is still pushing all the right buttons. A deceptively spacious, split-level space (given its setting in a parade of shops), it comes with a bar upfront and restaurant behind. Fashionable neutral colours are complemented by striking modern art, while white linen and modern wooden chairs (plus some banquette seating) continue the up-to-the-minute look. The cooking follows the well-dressed theme, taking a modern brasserie-style approach, with clean-cut, keenly priced dishes showing skilful restraint and a light touch combined with an eye for presentation. Tortellini of Dorset white crab meat with fennel purée, keta and burnt orange is a first course full of compelling flavours; next up, perhaps poached halibut accompanied by pancetta, Brussels sprouts, chestnuts and trompettes.

Chef Owen Kenworthy **Owner** Rebecca Mascarenhas, James Harris **Times** 12.30-2.30/7.30-11 Closed BHs, D Sun **Prices** Food prices not confirmed for 2011. Please telephone for details **Wines** 44 bottles over £20, 17 bottles under £20, 23 by glass **Seats** 100, Pr/dining room 26 **Children** Portions, Menu **Parking** On street

LONDON SW14

The Depot Waterfront Brasserie PLAN 1 D3

Modern British, European

Popular brasserie overlooking the Thames

020 8878 9462
Tideway Yard, 125 Mortlake High St, Barnes SW14 8SN
e-mail: info@depotbrasserie.co.uk
dir: Nearest station: Barnes Bridge. Between Barnes Bridge & Mortlake stations

Formerly the stables and coach houses for the Barnes Council refuse depot, this building now houses a cosy brasserie with a south-facing terrace ideal for a spot of alfresco eating. A breakfast-brunch menu Monday to Saturday is an attractive proposition in the stylish lounge bar and tables overlooking the Thames are sought after all year. Expect crowd-pleasing dishes in the vein of deep-fried goujons of plaice with tartare sauce and lemon, or perhaps chargrilled Cumberland sausages with mash and shallot gravy, and a baked vanilla cheesecake with caramelised bananas to finish. The set lunch and dinner menus are an attractive option.

Chef Gary Knowles **Owner** Tideway Restaurants Ltd **Times** 12-3.30/6-11 **Prices** Fixed L 2 course £12.50, Fixed D 3 course £18, Starter £5-£7.10, Main £10.50-£17.95, Dessert £5-£7.50, Service added but optional 12.5% **Wines** 32 bottles over £20, 19 bottles under £20, 20 by glass **Notes** Vegetarian available **Seats** 120, Pr/dining room 60 **Children** Portions, Menu **Parking** Parking after 6.30pm and at weekends

LONDON SW15

Enoteca Turi

PLAN 1 D3

Italian NOTABLE WINE LIST

Regional Italian cookery in Putney

☎ 020 8785 4449
28 Putney High St SW15 1SQ
e-mail: enoteca@tiscali.co.uk
dir: Nearest station: Putney Bridge. Opposite Odeon Cinema near bridge

This family-run restaurant close to the river and Putney Bridge, showcases regional Italian cuisine complemented by a great Italian wine list. The building was originally an undertakers but don't let that put you off - the modern restaurant with Mediterranean shades and abstract art on the walls has been pulling in the punters with its friendly vibe and efficient service since 1990. Italian regulars return for the authentic cuisine using well-sourced ingredients. Dishes from Puglia (head chef Giuseppe's home region) feature heavily but the menu also takes in Umbria and Marche. Start with warm salad of lamb's kidneys wrapped in pancetta with pecorino and mint before spaghetti with fresh crab, samphire, lemon, parsley and olive oil, and then breast of guinea fowl with ravioli of braised leg with butter and sage and Swiss chard with olive oil and lemon.

Chef G Turi, M Tagliaferri **Owner** Mr G & Mrs P Turi **Times** 12-2.30/7-10.30 Closed 25-26 Dec, 1 Jan, Sun, L BHs **Prices** Fixed L 2 course £15.50, Fixed D 3 course £29.50, Starter £7.50-£10.50, Main £11.50-£21.50, Dessert £5.50-£8.50, Service added but optional 12.5% **Wines** 300 bottles over £20, 16 bottles under £20, 11 by glass **Notes** Vegetarian available, Dress restrictions, Smart casual **Seats** 85, Pr/dining room 18 **Children** Portions **Parking** Putney Exchange car park, on street

Talad Thai Restaurant

PLAN 1 D3

Thai

Authentic Thai cooking in Putney

☎ 020 8789 8084
320 Upper Richmond Rd, Putney SW15 6TL
e-mail: info@taladthai.co.uk
dir: Nearest station: Putney, East Putney

If you can't find those esoteric specialist ingredients that you need for really authentic home-cooked Thai food, Talad Thai's specialist supermarket will sort you out. This Aladdin's cave of Thai produce started out 20 years ago, with Mrs Kriangsak holding cookery demonstrations on Sundays to share the art of Thai cooking with her customers. Nowadays, she preaches to the converted in the neighbouring restaurant, which has a convivial buzz among its tightly-packed simple wooden tables. The long menu covers a lot of ground, running through the Thai repertoire of soups, curries, stir-fries and noodle dishes, starting with old favourites like spicy fishcakes, or hot-and-sour tom yum soup and proceeding to duck curry with Thai aubergines and sweet basil.

Times 11.30-3/5.30-11 Closed 25-26 Dec, 1 Jan, Sat-Sun

LONDON SW17

Chez Bruce

PLAN 1 E2

– see below

Kastoori

PLAN 1 E2

Indian V

Vibrant Indian vegetarian cooking in Tooting

☎ 020 8767 7027
188 Upper Tooting Rd SW17 7EJ
dir: Nearest station: Tooting Bec, Tooting Broadway. Situated between two stations

The Thanki family's simply furnished Indian vegetarian restaurant in Tooting shows some African influences from

Chez Bruce

LONDON SW17 PLAN 1 E2

Modern NOTABLE WINE LIST

Seriously good cooking without pretence

☎ 020 8672 0114
2 Bellevue Rd, Wandsworth Common SW17 7EG
e-mail: enquiries@chezbruce.co.uk
dir: Nearest station: Wandsworth Common, Balham. Near Wandsworth Common station

Verdant plant boxes mark out Chez Bruce in a terrace overlooking Wandsworth Common. It is a neighbourhood restaurant in the same way an Aston Martin is a car - it gets you from A to B, but it is all about the quality of the ride. Putting the laboured simile aside for a moment, Bruce Poole has been cooking here since 1995 - that is cooking, by the way, with his own hands - and is greatly admired far beyond the boundaries of Wandsworth for his technical abilities and the unpretentious, fuss-free approach of his restaurant. Produce is sourced judiciously, less glamorous cuts of meat are not eschewed, and the classical principles of French cookery, and broader Mediterranean influences, lie at the heart of everything. Start with cod brandade, with a grilled brochette of seafood, chorizo, courgette and black olive, or mussel and leek soup, topped with a poached egg and chives, before main-course chump of lamb, served up with a kofta and stuffed aubergines, or Cornish black bream with Spanish bean casserole, stuffed gordal olives, razor clams and aïoli. Rhubarb and champagne trifle is a dessert to bring a warm glow to a cold February evening, and the cheeseboard warrants attention. White linen and neutral, natural tones make for a refreshingly unshowy setting, and the wine list has much of interest, including some regional French gems.

Chef Bruce Poole, Matt Christmas **Owner** Bruce Poole, Nigel Platts-Martin **Times** 12-2.15/6.30-10 Closed 24-26 Dec,1 Jan, L 27 Dec **Prices** Fixed L 2 course £19.50-£27.50, Fixed D 3 course fr £42.50, Service added but optional 12.5% **Wines** 700 bottles over £20, 5 bottles under £20, 15 by glass **Notes** Tasting menu available on request, Sunday L, Vegetarian available, Dress restrictions, Smart casual **Seats** 75, Pr/dining room 16 **Children** Portions, Menu **Parking** On street, station car park

the family's heritage as part of the Ugandan Asian diaspora. Typical might be kasodi, sweetcorn cooked in coconut milk in a sauce of ground peanuts, or the sesame-peanut sauce that forms the basis of the green pepper curry. Otherwise, it's vibrant, palate-awakening cuisine in the best south Asian manner, with puris to start, followed by one of the vegetable curries such as paneer pasanda, or a set-meal thali. Tomatoes play an even more significant part in the cooking than they usually do, outstandingly so in the special tomato curry, a signature dish. Finish with gulab jamun or ras malai.

Chef Manoj Thanki **Owner** Mr D Thanki
Times 12.30-2.30/6-10.30 Closed 25-26 Dec, L Mon-Tue
Prices Food prices not confirmed for 2011. Please telephone for details **Wines** 1 bottle over £20, 19 bottles under £20, 2 by glass **Notes** Sunday L **Seats** 82
Children Portions **Parking** On street

LONDON SW19

Cannizaro House — PLAN 1 D2

@@ British, European

Vibrant food in a glamorous country-house style hotel

☎ 020 8879 1464
West Side, Wimbledon Common SW19 4UE
e-mail: info@cannizarohouse.com
dir: Nearest station: Wimbledon. From A3 (London Rd) Tibbets Corner, take A219 (Parkside) right into Cannizaro Rd, then right into West Side

This elegant 18th-century country house, once home to the socialite Sicilian Duke of Cannizaro, has built up a colourful history during a long career playing host to London society. Named for its location overlooking Wimbledon Common, the restaurant's retro glamorous country-house vibe has acquired a funkier edge thanks to a recent redecoration incorporating fuchsia-pink flamingos on a grey background, and a changing cast of artworks on the walls. The kitchen clearly takes its business seriously, using classic French techniques to underpin a menu that presents dishes of vivid colours and clever textures, as in an eye-catching chicken liver pâté with Sauternes jelly and toasted sourdough, followed by confit salmon fillet with roasted beetroot risotto and liquorice. To finish, a Martini glass is layered with vanilla seed pannacotta, Pimm's jelly and mint syrup.

Chef Christian George **Owner** Bridgehouse Hotels
Times 12-3/7-10 **Prices** Fixed L 2 course fr £21.50, Fixed D 3 course fr £29.50, Starter £7-£11, Main £18-£21, Dessert £7-£9, Service optional **Wines** 110 bottles over £20, 20 bottles under £20, 14 by glass **Notes** Sunday L, Vegetarian available, Dress restrictions, No shorts, Civ Wed 100 **Seats** 46, Pr/dining room 120 **Children** Portions, Menu **Parking** 55

The Light House Restaurant — PLAN 1 D2

@ Modern International

Appealing modern cooking in SW19

☎ 020 8944 6338
75-77 Ridgway, Wimbledon SW19 4ST
e-mail: info@lighthousewimbledon.com
dir: Nearest station: Wimbledon. From station turn right up Wimbledon Hill then left at mini-rdbt onto Ridgway, restaurant on left

Light floods this aptly-named contemporary neighbourhood restaurant through its broad glass frontage. Inside, it's a bright and breezy, upbeat place fitted out with pale wood floors and tables, and abstract art on the walls. The menu delivers an appealing repertoire of modern European brasserie dishes - say seared scallops with Savoy cabbage and crème fraîche flan, and grilled chorizo. Mains range from roast pork belly with parsley mash, baby spinach and green peppercorn sauce, to baked salmon with potato and rosemary gratin, samphire, bouillabaisse and tarragon sauce. To finish, go for Tahitian vanilla pannacotta with poached rhubarb.

Chef Chris Casey **Owner** Mr Finch & Mr Taylor
Times 12-2.30/6-10.30 Closed 24-26 Dec, 1 Jan, D Sun
Prices Fixed L 2 course fr £11.50, Fixed D 3 course fr £18.50, Starter £5.50-£12.50, Main £12.50-£22.50, Dessert £5.50-£8.50, Service added but optional 12.5%
Wines 56 bottles over £20, 17 bottles under £20, 15 by glass **Notes** Fixed D Mon-Thu order before 7.30pm, Sunday L, Vegetarian available **Seats** 80
Children Portions, Menu

LONDON W1

Alain Ducasse at The Dorchester — PLAN 4 G6

@@@ – *see page 276*

The Albemarle — PLAN 3 A1

@@@ – *see page 277*

Alloro — PLAN 3 A1

@ Italian

Authentic Modern Italian cooking in Mayfair

☎ 020 7495 4768
19-20 Dover St W1S 4LU
e-mail: alloro@londonfinediningroup.com
web: www.londonfinediningroup.com
dir: Nearest station: Green Park. From Green Park station continue towards Piccadilly, Dover St is 2nd on left

This stalwart of the Mayfair dining scene has been serving up its style of modern Italian food since 2000. It suits the mood of the area, being confidently refined (leather banquettes and chairs, crisp white linen, cool neutral tones and sculptured laurel-leaf-themed artwork; alloro means bay leaf) and effortlessly charming service (bright and breezy staff add to the experience). The cooking style is simple, light and modern, taking its cue from the quality ingredients and delivering clean flavours. The fixed pricing keeps things reasonably accessible by Mayfair standards. Confit of rabbit leg is served with pan-fried polenta and girolles, while pan-fried cod fillet comes with spinach, beets and balsamic. Home-made pasta and breads, a cracking all-Italian wine list and an adjoining bar-bistro all add to the appeal.

Chef Daniele Camera **Owner** London Fine Dining Group
Times 12-2.30/7-10.30 Closed Xmas, 4 days Etr & BHs, Sun, L Sat **Prices** Fixed L 2 course £28, Fixed D 3 course £35, Service added but optional 12.5% **Wines** 200 bottles over £20, 2 bottles under £20, 16 by glass
Notes Vegetarian available, Dress restrictions, Smart casual **Seats** 60, Pr/dining room 16 **Children** Portions
Parking On street

Andrew Edmunds — PLAN 3 B2

@ Modern European NEW

Evergreen, rustic, Soho favourite

☎ 020 7437 5708
46 Lexington St, Soho W1F 0LW
dir: Nearest station: Oxford Circus

This ever-popular, quirky Soho stalwart - set in an old townhouse - has an endearingly unpretentious, Dickensian feel. Pint sized, its narrow ground floor and bijou basement rooms come hung with old prints, while closely-packed paper-clothed tables, old cottagey chairs and settles add to the Soho-fashion-police-be-damned character. Candlelight at night adds to the atmosphere,

continued

LONDON W1 *continued*

alongside its bohemian crowd and lunchtime suits. The kitchen takes a simple, honest approach, with light, seasonal, ingredient-led dishes on a handwritten daily-changing menu. Classics (dressed crab or goose rillettes) mix with more modern thinking (seared king scallops and calasparra pilaf with peas, chorizo and pancetta), while puds tow the chocolate brownie comfort line. The wine list's a corker.

Chef Rebecca St-John Cooper **Owner** Andrew Edmunds **Times** 12.30-3/6-10.45 Closed Xmas, Etr **Prices** Starter £3.50-£9, Main £10.50-£20, Dessert £4-£7, Service added but optional 12.5% **Wines** 190 bottles over £20, 10 bottles under £20, 4 by glass **Notes** Vegetarian available **Seats** 42

Aqua Kyoto PLAN 3 A2

Japanese NEW

Stylish Japanese food with breathtaking views of central London

☎ 020 7478 0540
240 Regent St W1B 3BR
dir: Nearest station: Oxford Street Opposite the London Palladium, just behind Regent St

The international Aqua restaurant group now has a firm foothold in London, on the top of the old Dickins & Jones building on Regent Street. Here, the space houses a Spanish tapas operation called Aqua Nueva and, in Aqua Kyoto, it has ventured into contemporary Japanese cuisine. Breathtaking views of central London amid the chic, ultra-designed red and black interiors are part of the lure, and the mix of sunken sushi bar, charcoal grill and gigantic, ornate light fittings make a combined modern statement, while the friendly, helpful staff are not too cool to advise on the menus. Visually striking dishes composed of top-notch ingredients are the business, including black pearl sushi rolls containing fatty tuna and tobiko flying-fish roe, served with soy and pickled ginger, tempura king prawns and sweet potato, classic chicken teriyaki, and green tea 'tiramisu' made with fresh, creamy mascarpone. High-rollers might push the boat out for marinated lobster served with seared foie gras and wasabi.

Chef Jordan Sclare **Times** 12-3/6-11.15 Closed Sun **Prices** Food prices not confirmed for 2011. Please telephone for details

Arbutus Restaurant PLAN 3 B2

– see page 278

Archipelago PLAN 3 B4

Modern, International

Unique, exotic, adventurous and romantic dining experience

☎ 020 7383 3346
110 Whitfield St W1T 5ED
e-mail: info@archipelago-restaurant.co.uk
dir: Nearest station: Warren Street. From tube, south along Tottenham Court Rd. 1st right into Grafton Way. 1st left into Whitfield St

The location is innocuous enough: an unremarkable Fitzrovia side street close to the bustle of Tottenham Court Road. But this small restaurant is anything but ordinary. Inside is a treasure trove of far-flung objet d'art, with golden Buddha's, primitive carvings, peacock feathers and colourful fabrics and seating among a riot of exotica that fills every inch of its green and red walls.

Alain Ducasse at The Dorchester

LONDON W1 PLAN 4 G6

Modern French NOTABLE WINE LIST

Culinary legend meets famous hotel

☎ 020 7629 8866 & 7629 8888
The Dorchester, 53 Park Ln W1K 1QA
e-mail: alainducasse@thedorchester.com
dir: Nearest station: Hyde Park Corner, Marble Arch

Alain Ducasse is a culinary big-hitter with a galaxy of global enterprises, so while you won't find him chopping garlic in the Dorchester's kitchen, his ethos, style and passion are firmly embedded in any restaurant bearing his name. The man heading up the crack kitchen brigade is Jocelyn Herland, a tried-and-trusted Ducasse protégé whose phenomenal technique is guaranteed to deliver the goods. The Patrick Jouin-designed dining room is a slick space, all shades of coffee and cream and neutrally timeless in a way that doesn't distract you from the business in hand, despite the Star Trek presence of the giant shimmering tent of lights that is the private table. Classical roots run deep in Ducasse's food. Some dishes are so retro that they seem lifted straight from the pages of Escoffier's *Guide Culinaire*; others fizz with modern presentation and technique, and luxury ingredients are employed with liberal abandon. Chestnut velouté is cleverly matched with petit gris snails and chicken sausage in a top-class first course, while main courses might include seared John Dory with citrus dressing and eggplant condiment. While Ducasse's rum baba is legendary, you might try a 'Girl from Ipanema' instead, an amazing demonstration of texture and technique uniting a vanilla brûlée with fresh and caramelised cubes of pineapple, vanilla emulsion and pineapple ice cream in a Martini glass. If you're feeling really flush, go for the seasonal tasting menu; and take a moment to compose yourself before looking at the prices on the heavyweight wine list (all 33 pages of it). Softly-spoken French staff deliver polished, attentive service.

Chef Jocelyn Herland, Bruno Riou, Angelo Ercolano **Owner** The Dorchester Collection **Times** 12-2/6.30-9.45 Closed 26-30 Dec, 1-5 Jan, Etr, Aug, Mon-Sun, L Sat **Prices** Fixed L 3 course £39.50, Fixed D 3 course £55, Tasting menu £95, Service added but optional 12.5% **Wines** 700 bottles over £20, 20 by glass **Notes** Tasting menu 7 course, Fixed price ALC L & D includes wine, Vegetarian available, Dress restrictions, Smart casual L, smart D **Seats** 82, Pr/dining room 26 **Parking** 20

It's dark, romantic and atmospheric, which is fitting for a restaurant that 'explores the exotic'. Even the menu arrives as a ribbon-bound scroll with an ancient map on the back, revealing an equally idiosyncratic safari of accomplished, vibrantly-flavoured and exotic-named dishes that might include crocodile, peacock or zebra. 'Hot Marsupial' is zhug-marinated kangaroo with water spinach and choi, or there's 'Swamp Fever' (wok-seared frogs' legs, cashew and callaloo with ginger and coriander rice). Fixed-price lunch is a steal, service knowledgeable and relaxed, and there's a tiny lounge-bar downstairs.

Chef Daniel Creedon **Owner** Bruce Alexander **Times** 12-2.30/6-10.30 Closed Xmas, BHs, Sun, L Sat **Prices** Food prices not confirmed for 2011. Please telephone for details **Wines** 45 bottles over £20, 3 bottles under £20, 4 by glass **Notes** Vegetarian available **Seats** 32 **Parking** NCP, on street

Artisan

PLAN 3 A2

Modern European

Ambitious cooking in the heart of Mayfair

☎ 020 8382 5450 & 7629 7755
The Westbury Hotel, Bond St W1S 2YF
e-mail: artisan@westburymayfair.com
dir: Nearest station: Oxford Circus, Piccadilly Circus, Green Park

Secreted inside one of Mayfair's swankiest hotels, Artisan is as glossy a set-up as you'd expect. With some of London's glitziest shopping on the doorstep, it pulls in well-heeled shoppers as well as residents to a luminous venue, all clean-cut lines and textures of velvet and wood buffed up with understated contemporary glamour. Chef Andrew Jones is a scholar of the Roux school, so has his roots in the French classics, underpinned by liberal use of luxury materials. The cooking aims high, and is not scared to throw in some off-the-wall combinations, as in a terrine of Vendée foie gras with Guanaja chocolate, marinated anchovies and toasted brioche. Main-course Dover sole with courgettes rejoins the mainstream, teamed with mussels, squid, dill and rye bread croûtons. Dessert could be an exotic cocktail of rum baba with spicy roasted pineapple and mango, coconut ice cream and jelly.

Chef Andrew Jones **Owner** Cola Holdings Ltd **Times** 12-2.30/6.30-10.30 Closed L Sat, D Sun **Prices** Fixed L 2 course £20, Fixed D 3 course £35, Tasting menu £75, Service added but optional 12.5% **Wines** 280 bottles over £20, 20 by glass **Notes** Fixed ALC 2 course £45, 3 course £55, Tasting menu 7 course, Sunday L, Vegetarian available, Dress restrictions, Smart casual, Civ Wed 20 **Seats** 65, Pr/dining room 20 **Children** Portions **Parking** 20

The Albemarle

LONDON W1 PLAN 3 A1

Traditional British V  

First-class British cooking in stylish landmark London hotel

☎ 020 7518 4004
Brown's Hotel, Albemarle St W1S 4BP
e-mail: thealbemarle@roccofortecollection.com
dir: Nearest station: Green Park. Off Piccadilly between Green Park tube station and Bond Street

Brown's is the capital's oldest five-star hotel, doing business in a swanky Mayfair terrace of Georgian townhouses since Victoria came to the throne in 1837. Rocco Forte took over in 2003 and unleashed his sister, designer Olga Polizzi, on the crusty interiors. After a megabucks facelift, the hotel sports a sharp-looking boutique interior, while the Albemarle - London's first hotel restaurant - retains its imperial grandeur, subtly tweaked with understated contemporary style: its clubby oak-panelled walls are hung with modern Brit art by the likes of Tracey Emin, Bridget Riley and photographer Rankin, and the austere oak columns are offset by linen-swaddled tables and soft mossy green chairs and banquettes. Under the guidance of Mark Hix, executive chef Lee Streeton produces a thoroughly British produce-driven menu, featuring classic pies, grills, hotpots and cuts of meat on the bone, as well as lighter fish and seafood dishes. There's no truck with foams and special effects cooking here: simplicity is king. Potted Morecambe Bay shrimps are the real buttery deal, while Cornish lamb's sweetbreads are served with wild boar bacon and ramsons (wild garlic). Mains come as earthy as oxtail braised in Hix Oyster Ale with horseradish mash, or as light as black bream with Orkney cockles and alexanders (a rarely seen indigenous vegetable). Roasts served from the carving trolley are a lunchtime fixture, and puddings bring more British institutions - Bramley apple crumble, or ginger parkin.

Chef Lee Streeton **Owner** The Rocco Forte Collection **Times** 12-3/5.30-11 **Prices** Fixed L 2 course fr £25, Fixed D 3 course £30, Starter £6.50-£16.50, Main £14.50-£34.75, Dessert £6.50-£12.50, Service optional **Wines** 340 bottles over £20, 18 by glass **Notes** Pre-theatre bookings 5.30-7.30pm Mon-Sat, Sunday L, Vegetarian menu, Dress restrictions, Smart casual, Civ Wed 70 **Seats** 80, Pr/dining room 70 **Children** Menu **Parking** Valet/Burlington St

LONDON W1 ***continued***

The Athenaeum Restaurant PLAN 4 H5

Modern British

Classic British cooking in sumptuous surroundings

☎ 020 7640 3333
116 Piccadilly W1J 7BJ
e-mail: info@athenaeumhotel.com
web: www.athenaeumhotel.com
dir: Nearest station: Hyde Park Corner, Green Park

The Edwardian Athenaeum delivers all the exclusivity you'd expect at this discreet Piccadilly address, but the ambience is more contemporary and unbuttoned in these informal times. The restaurant goes for a rather decadent art deco-influenced look that oozes glamour; check out the huge plush seats the size of fairground waltzers, and there are even mother of pearl buttons stitched like fish scales to one wall. The kitchen deals in European-accented modern cooking built from top-class seasonal ingredients. Try seared scallops with garlic purée and green apple, followed by wild bass with samphire, Cornish potatoes and fennel; lemon tart with seasonal English berries makes for a classic finish.

Chef David Marshall **Owner** Ralph Trustees Ltd **Times** 12.30-2.30/5.30-10.30 **Prices** Fixed L 2 course £19.50, Fixed D 3 course £27, Starter £8-£12, Main £18-£39, Dessert £7.50-£9, Service included **Wines** 41 bottles over £20, 1 bottle under £20, 15 by glass **Notes** All day dining menu 11am-11pm, Sunday L, Vegetarian available, Civ Wed 55 **Seats** 46, Pr/dining room 44 **Children** Portions, Menu **Parking** Close car park

L'Autre Pied PLAN 2 G3

– see opposite page

Avista PLAN 2 G1

Italian

Classic Italian cooking in glossy Mayfair restaurant

☎ 020 7596 3399 & 7629 9400
Millennium Hotel Mayfair, 39 Grosvenor Square W1K 2HP
e-mail: reservations@avistarestaurant.com
dir: Nearest station: Bond Street. Located on the south side of Grosvenor Square, 5 min walk from Oxford Street

As soon as head chef Michele Granziera - formerly of Zafferano - set up on his own at this swish Mayfair address, lovers of rustic regional Italian cooking beat a path to his door. And a very posh door it is too: the restaurant in the Millennium Hotel Mayfair has a separate entrance on Grosvenor Square, and comes buffed to a high gloss to suit the postcode, with a refined décor of herringbone marble floors, bare brickwork, fawn leather banquettes and soft-focus tones of ivory, honey and café crème; a granite-topped work station, where chefs primp and preen dishes ready for presentation, adds a touch of theatre. Granziera knows his way around his homeland's regional cuisine: a wide-ranging menu takes in classics such as aubergine parmigiana and beef bresaola with rocket, goats' cheese and walnuts, lifted to a high level by the quality of the raw materials; in the pasta department, expect gnocchi with Italian bacon, taleggio and parmesan cheese, or beef ravioli with red wine sauce, chestnuts and ceps. Mains might be loin of venison with black cabbage, roasted polenta and apple.

Arbutus Restaurant

LONDON W1 PLAN 3 B2

Modern French

Stunning but simple, affordable food and wine from Soho gem

☎ 020 7734 4545
63-64 Frith St W1D 3JW
e-mail: info@arbutusrestaurant.co.uk
dir: Nearest station: Tottenham Court Road. Exit Tottenham Court Road tube station, turn left into Oxford St. Left onto Soho St, cross over or continue around Soho Sq, restaurant is on Frith St 25mtrs on right

Five years on from its much-lauded opening, Arbutus is still firing on all cylinders. Anthony Demetre and Will Smith's Soho restaurant delivers earthy French-accented cooking, and at very reasonable prices considering it lives just off Soho Square, a location that is heavily populated with a clientele of expense-account film and TV execs. And don't forget the revolutionary wine policy: all of the wines are available in a 250ml carafe - a brilliant wheeze that lets you match a different wine to each course. The anonymous gunmetal façade typifies the unshowy, functional design within - a neutral, uncluttered bistro style with buttoned black banquettes and darkwood chairs. Anthony Demetre's gutsy cooking takes peasant ingredients and hits them with pedigree technique to wring out full-on visceral flavours in intelligent combinations. Intriguing dishes kick off with slow-cooked shoulder of English veal with pappardelle and pecorino, or a signature squid and mackerel 'burger' served with parsley emulsion, pea shoots, razor clams and finely sliced baby squid. Main courses bring a plat du jour option - perhaps pork caillettes (old-fashioned meatballs) with potato purée - or go for the Provençal speciality pieds et paquets - lamb's tripe parcels and trotters, served with Charlotte potatoes. To finish, try an unusual mango, vanilla and tapioca pannacotta.

Chef Anthony Demetre **Owner** Anthony Demetre, Will Smith **Times** 12-2.30/5-11.30 Closed 25-26 Dec, 1 Jan **Prices** Fixed L 3 course £16.95, Starter £6.95-£10.95, Main £13.50-£19.95, Dessert £5.95-£6.95, Service added but optional 12.5% **Wines** 40 bottles over £20, 10 bottles under £20, 50 by glass **Notes** Pre-theatre D 5-7pm 3 course £18.95, Sunday L, Vegetarian available **Seats** 75 **Children** Portions

Chef Michele Granziera **Owner** Milleniuim & Copthorne Hotels **Times** 12.30-2.30/6.30-10.30 Closed Xmas, Sun, L Sat **Prices** Fixed L 2 course £14.95, Fixed D 3 course £19.95, Starter £8.50-£22, Main £10-£26, Service added but optional 12.5% **Wines** 6 by glass **Notes** Fixed D available 6.30-7.30pm, Vegetarian available **Seats** 75, Pr/dining room 10 **Children** Portions **Parking** On street/NCP

Barrafina — PLAN 3 B2

Spanish

Barcelona-style tapas joint in the heart of Soho

☎ 020 7813 8016
54 Frith St W1D 4SL
e-mail: jose@barrafina.co.uk
dir: Nearest station: Tottenham Court Rd

Inspired by the iconic Cal Pep tapas bar in Barcelona, this simple, hugely authentic and traditionally casual tapas-style bar is a fun place to eat in the heart of Soho. With a no booking policy, arrive early or wait in the long, narrow room for one of the 23 high stools that run around the L-shaped, marble-topped bar counter in front of the open kitchen. The décor's modern - stainless steel, marble and glass - and the atmosphere is as upbeat as the quality, quick-turnover food, which delivers robust flavours and colourful presentation. Sip on a glass of Spanish wine or sherry while you soak up the action and aromas and wait for plates of ham and spinach tortilla, octopus with capers, chorizo Iberico or grilled quail, all driven by top-notch produce. There are bags of daily specials (including plenty of seafood) and staff are lively, informed and friendly.

Chef Nieves Barragan **Owner** Sam & Eddie Hart **Times** 12-3/5-11 Closed BHs **Prices** Food prices not confirmed for 2011. Please telephone for details **Wines** 25 bottles over £20, 4 bottles under £20, 29 by glass **Notes** Sunday L, Vegetarian available **Seats** 23 **Children** Portions **Parking** On street

Bar Trattoria Semplice — PLAN 2 H2

Italian

Authentic Italian cuisine in a smart modern space

☎ 020 7491 8638
22 Woodstock St W1C 2AR
dir: Nearest station: Bond Street

A rather good fun off-shoot of the fine-dining Italian Ristorante Semplice (see entry), the Bar Trattoria is tucked away between busy Oxford Street and Bond Street. Inside it's a rather contemporary space - all blond wood and sleek lines, with an old school meat slicing machine on the bar reminiscent of the old country. The food is predictable, but in all the right ways; classic regional Italian cooking using the finest Italian produce. Try some antipasti, a classic cured meat and cheese board, and then perhaps home-made spinach and potato gnocchi with truffle and cheese fondue, or braised lamb shank with mash potato.

Chef Marco Squillace **Times** 12-3/6-11 Closed Xmas, New Year & BHs **Prices** Fixed L 2 course £16.75, Starter £5.75-£11.25, Main £9.95-£18.95, Dessert £4.90-£5, Service added but optional 12.5% **Wines** 30 bottles over £20, 3 bottles under £20, 9 by glass **Notes** Sunday L, Vegetarian available **Seats** 70, Pr/dining room 30 **Children** Portions **Parking** Cavendish Square

Bellamy's — PLAN 2 H2

French

Classy French Mayfair brasserie and oyster bar

☎ 020 7491 2727
18-18a Bruton Place W1J 6LY
e-mail: gavin@bellamysrestaurant.co.uk
dir: Nearest station: Green Park, Bond St. Off Berkeley Sq, parallel with Bruton St

continued

L'Autre Pied

LONDON W1 — PLAN 2 G3

Modern European V

Confident and compelling cooking at Pied à Terre's stable mate

☎ 020 7486 9696
5-7 Blandford St, Marylebone Village W1U 3DB
e-mail: info@lautrepied.co.uk
dir: Nearest station: Bond St, Baker St

L'Autre Pied opened three years ago just off trendy Marylebone Road and, despite being a younger and less formal sibling to the much lauded Pied à Terre in Fitzrovia, has certainly made its mark in its own right. Also co-owned by Shane Osborn and David Moore, it stands serenely in a row of restaurants with a small strip of dining tables outside. Inside, polished wooden flooring, dark brown and red banquet seating and rosewood tables create a confidently contemporary space, while the staff perform with the perfect balance of relaxed professionalism. There's a good value set menu and a full-on tasting menu supporting the à la carte, providing different entry levels to the confident modern European cooking. Chef Marcus Eaves has shown a sure hand at the stoves; technically gifted and creative, his cooking shows precision and his menus are full of compelling ideas. Warm terrine of pig's head with brown shrimps, pak choi and preserved apricot purée is a well-judged first course, followed, perhaps, by poached sea trout, partnered perfectly with the flavours and textures of cauliflower cream, sea purslane, kaffir lime and lemongrass cream. With caramelised banana, gingerbread and pistachio financier and quince ice cream to finish, you're sure to leave on a high.

Chef Marcus Eaves **Owner** Marcus Eaves, Shane Osborn, David Moore **Times** 12-2.45/6-10.45 Closed 4 days Xmas, 1 Jan **Prices** Fixed L 2 course fr £17.95, Fixed D 4 course fr £44.95, Starter £9.50-£16.95, Main £21.95-£29.50, Dessert £7.50-£9.50, Service added but optional 12.5% **Wines** 10 by glass **Notes** Pre-theatre 2-3 course £17.95-£20.95, Sunday L, Vegetarian menu **Seats** 53, Pr/dining room 15

LONDON W1 ***continued***

Bellamy's is resolutely Mayfair, from its tucked-away mews location off Berkeley Square to its closely-set linen-clad tables, professional service and deep-pocket pricing. The appeal of this popular French brasserie, other than its buzzy lunchtime vibe, is the classic brasserie-style menu, which combines old-fashioned simplicity with a touch of luxury (oysters, caviar or scrambled egg with Périgord truffles for openers). For main course, try the sautéed John Dory and calamari or the beef entrecote with pommes frites, then follow with Tunisian orange and almond cake or pecan pie. Pale-yellow walls lined with French prints, posters and mirrors conform to the brasserie signature, the dining room accessed via its adjoining oyster bar and small food store. The wine list is patriotically French, too.

Chef Stephane Pacoud **Owner** Gavin Rankin and Syndicate **Times** 12-3/7-10.30 Closed Xmas, New Year, BHs, Sun, L Sat **Prices** Fixed L 2 course £24, Fixed D 3 course £28.50, Starter £6.50-£19.50, Main £17-£28, Dessert £6.50, Service added but optional 12.5% **Wines** 55 bottles over £20, 16 by glass **Notes** Vegetarian available **Seats** 70 **Children** Portions **Parking** On street, NCP

Benares Restaurant PLAN 2 H1

◎◎ Indian, British V

Assertive east-west fusion cooking on Berkeley Square

☎ 020 7629 8886
12a Berkeley Square W1J 6BS
e-mail: reservations@benaresrestaurant.com
dir: Nearest station: Green Park. E along Piccadilly towards Regent St. Turn left into Berkeley St and continue straight to Berkeley Square

In a suite of elegantly designed rooms above Berkeley Square, beginning with a bar where flowers and candles float in a chain of indoor ponds, Atul Kochhar's cutting-edge Indian restaurant mixes regional traditions with assertive Euro-modernism, underpinned by subtle spicing and demonstrable freshness. A fashionable grazing menu is one way of testing the range, with smaller-scale servings of menu items such as lobster rillettes with curry leaves and tarragon, tandoori rabbit in red chilli and yoghurt, roasted lamb rump on rosemary chick peas, and lemongrass cheesecake with yoghurt foam. These can be taken with optional wine pairings. A menu of more casual bar dishes is also available. Tandoori portobello mushrooms on garlic and leek risotto is among the vegetarian dishes.

Chef Atul Kochhar **Owner** Atul Kochhar
Times 12-2.30/5.30-11 Closed 23-26 Dec, L 27-31 Dec, Sat **Prices** Fixed L 2 course fr £19.95, Fixed D 3 course fr £24.95, Starter £12.95-£18.95, Main £19.50-£45, Dessert £8.50, Service included **Wines** Rest bottles over £20, 11 bottles under £20, 17 by glass **Notes** Fixed D available until 6.30pm Tasting menu available, Sunday L, Vegetarian menu, Dress restrictions, Smart casual **Seats** 120

Bentley's Oyster Bar & Grill PLAN 3 B1

◎◎ British, European

First-class classic seafood and grill

☎ 020 7734 4756
11-15 Swallow St W1B 4DG
e-mail: reservations@bentleys.org
web: www.bentleysoysterbarandgrill.co.uk
dir: Nearest station: Piccadilly Circus

Blue leather upholstery, wooden floors, beautiful William Morris wall coverings, and fine fish prints create a refined and civilised ambience in the elegant, Arts and Crafts style first-floor dining room, which is divided into Grill room, Rib room and Crustacea room. Home to Bentley's since 1916 and a West End institution for fish-eaters, the ground floor Oyster Bar and upstairs grill throng with diners, here for the buzzy, relaxed atmosphere and Richard Corrigan's exciting menu, which is crammed with incredibly fresh seafood. The food is modern British with Mediterranean influences and more than a hint of his native Ireland. Expect linguine of clams, chilli and garlic, skate wing with red wine and anchovy butter, roast cod with chorizo and rocket, and crab and wild mussel curry, with classic meat options like rib-eye steak with peppercorn sauce.

Chef Brendan Fyldes **Owner** Richard Corrigan
Times 12-3/6-11 Closed 25 Dec, 1 Jan, L Sat-Sun (Grill only), D Sun (Grill only) **Prices** Starter £7.50-£18.75, Main £17-£28.90, Dessert £4.50-£10.95, Service added but optional 12.5% **Wines** 150+ bottles over £20, 2 bottles under £20, 16 by glass **Notes** Oyster bar open Mon-Sat 12-12, Sun 12-10, Vegetarian available, Dress restrictions, Smart casual **Seats** 90, Pr/dining room 60 **Children** Portions **Parking** 10 yds away

Bocca di Lupo PLAN 3 B2

◎◎ Italian

Delicious authentic regional Italian cuisine at sensible prices

☎ 020 7734 2223
12 Archer St W1D 7BB
e-mail: info@boccadilupo.com
web: www.boccadilupo.com
dir: Nearest station: Piccadilly Circus. Turn left off Shaftesbury Ave into Gt Windmill St, then right into Archer St. Located behind the Lyric & Apollo theatres

Hidden down a Soho backstreet, Bocca di Lupo is a real find. The 'mouth of the wolf' is what Italian regional cooking is all about - inspirational, authentic food at wallet-friendly prices. There's a warm welcome as soon as you're through the door, and if you spot a free seat at the long marble eating bar, grab it: this is the fun place to be, watching the chefs at work an arms length away. You can do the starter-main course thing if you like - just order large portions - but the idea here is to take a grazing approach and order lots of dainty dishes. The food is all about big, gutsy flavours and top-class produce - rustic, authentic and delivered without effete presentations. Go for visceral nose-to-tail dishes such as ravioli Genovese - filled with braised beef, borage and brains, or spicy tripe stew with guanciale bacon, chilli and tomato. Meaty roasts include suckling pig with chicory, while fishy options could turn up grilled halibut and new potatoes with monksbeard, butter and lemon. Finish with sanguinaccio - a sweet pâté of pig's blood and chocolate with sourdough bread. A superb Italian wine list is an Aladdin's cave of new discoveries.

Chef Jacob Kenedy **Owner** Jacob Kenedy, Victor Hugo **Times** 12.30-3/5.30-12 Closed 24 Dec-4 Jan, D Sun **Prices** Starter £5.50-£12.50, Main £12-£25, Dessert £3-£7.50, Service added but optional 12.5% **Wines** 130 bottles over £20, 4 bottles under £20, 20 by glass **Notes** Pre-theatre menu available 5.30-7pm, Sunday L, Vegetarian available **Seats** 60, Pr/dining room 32 **Children** Portions **Parking** NCP Brewer St

Butler's PLAN 4 H6

@@ Traditional British

Traditional dining in the heart of Mayfair

☎ 020 7491 2622
Chesterfield Mayfair Hotel, 35 Charles St, Mayfair W1J 5EB
e-mail: restaurantch@rchmail.com
web: www.chesterfieldmayfair.com
dir: Nearest station: Green Park From N side exit underground station turn left & then first left into Berkeley St. Continue to Berkeley Sq & left towards Charles St

Liveried doormen greet you at the door of this Mayfair hotel, and the interior is a trip back to the Georgian period, furnished in a clubby style (perhaps the best way to describe the look of those elegant antiques, leather chairs and rich fabrics). Butler's restaurant goes for a bright look with bold hues of claret and tobacco and a suggestion of Africa. The service is traditional in its friendly formality and the use of carving trolleys, but what's on the plate is far from old hat. Top-class materials are used to good effect in accomplished cooking that brings together tradition - Dover sole is a signature dish here - with up-to-date British dishes. A delicate starter of pan-fried potato and goats' cheese terrine sits well with baby beetroot and horseradish dressing, while main courses might revert to classics in the form of a grilled veal chop with Parmentier potatoes, confit shallots and thyme and chervil sauce.

Chef Ben Kelliher **Owner** Red Carnation Hotels **Times** 12.30-2.30/5.30-10.30 **Prices** Fixed L 2 course £17.50, Fixed D 3 course £25.50, Starter £7.50-£17.50, Main £18.50-£39.50, Dessert £7.50-£10.50, Service added but optional 12.5% **Wines** 84 bottles over £20, 4 bottles under £20, 20 by glass **Notes** Pre-theatre menu available, Sunday L, Vegetarian available, Civ Wed 100 **Seats** 65, Pr/dining room 40 **Children** Portions, Menu **Parking** NCP 5 minutes

Caleya Restaurant PLAN 2 H4

@@ Modern Spanish **NEW**

Fine-dining Spanish restaurant, tapas bar and delicatessen of distinction

☎ 020 7636 8650
Iberica Food & Culture Ltd, 195 Great Portland St W1W 5PS
e-mail: info@ibericalondon.co.uk
dir: Nearest station: Great Portland St, Regent's Park. Top Great Portland Street, near Regent's Park

The fine-dining arm of Iberica, a slick outfit celebrating Spain's food culture, Caleya sits on a mezzanine above a lively tapas bar and eye-catching delicatessen. It's a classy, contemporary place, the big-windowed, double-height space flooded by light and dominated by a 15-metre bar serving an appealing range of tapas and pinchos. Upstairs, Caleya cranks up the ante, celebrating the contemporary cooking of Spain, with menus overseen by Nacho Manzano of acclaimed Casa Marcial restaurant in Spain's Astrurian mountains. Creative and modern - with a light, fresh, precise touch - dishes are driven by prime ingredients and clean flavours. As downstairs, innovation and tradition mix with classics (there's also a classics tasting option), so Iberica ham croquetes or fabada line up alongside grilled fillet of turbot with cauliflower purée and orange caramel and coca oil. A white-linen zone, Caleya's décor embraces the modern Spanish theme, while the all-Spanish wine list is worth exploring.

Chef Santiago Guerrero & Nacho Manzano **Owner** Iberica Food & Culture Ltd **Times** 11am-11.30pm Closed 25 & 31 Dec, BHs, D Sun **Prices** Starter £4.90-£9, Main £4.50-£38, Dessert £3.50-£4.50, Service added but optional 12.5% **Wines** 42 bottles over £20, 4 bottles under £20, 25 by glass **Notes** Sunday L, Vegetarian available **Seats** 120, Pr/dining room 30

Camerino PLAN 3 B3

@ Modern Italian

Neighbourhood-style Italian stamped with originality

☎ 020 7637 9900
16 Percy St W1T 1DT
e-mail: info@camerinorestaurant.com
dir: Nearest station: Tottenham Court Rd, Goodge St

It maybe perched on a side street just off the Tottenham Court Road, but Camerino has a neighbourhood vibe, its awning, glass frontage and pavement-side tables picking it out from the crowd. Inside is light and quirkily modish, with blond-wood flooring, informal chandelier-style lighting and a duo of skylights, while glitzy framed mirrors, old oils or cherubs decorate striped or swirling patterned wallpapers. Whatever the décor might be trying to say, the friendly, formally dressed staff, white linen and conventional Italian regional cooking - keeping things simple and fresh - takes a more traditional stance. Expect linguine with clams and sliced tomato, or perhaps fillets of lemon sole with artichokes and lemon sauce.

Times 12-3/6-11 Closed 1 wk Xmas, 1st Jan, Etr Day, most BHs, Sun, L Sat

Canteen Baker Street PLAN 2 G3

@ British

The best of British in a relaxed canteen-brasserie setting

☎ 0845 686 1122
55 Baker St W1U 8EW
e-mail: bakerstreet@canteen.co.uk
dir: Nearest station: Baker Street

The Canteen concept revolves around serving up traditional British comfort food with plenty of 21st-century attitude. It's clearly an idea that has caught fire, as this Baker Street outpost is now one of four. It goes for the same casual canteen-like vibe as its sibling in the Royal Festival Hall (see entry), with bare pale oak tables, banquettes and wooden chairs, and retro Bestlite lamps. It's a wallet-friendly format, but you can get free entertainment too if you bag a seat at the open kitchen to watch the chefs doing their thing. And that thing runs from all-day breakfasts to snacky stuff like potted duck with piccalilli and toast, to full-on roasts with all the trimmings, and nursery food desserts like steamed syrup sponge with custard.

Chef Cass Titcombe **Owner** Dom Lake, Patrick Clayton-Malone & Cass Titcombe **Times** 8am-11pm Closed 25 Dec **Prices** Starter £5.50, Main £8-£16.75, Dessert £4.50-£8.50, Service added but optional 12.5% **Wines** 27 bottles over £20, 9 bottles under £20, 33 by glass **Notes** Sunday L, Vegetarian available **Children** Portions

Cecconi's PLAN 3 A1

@@ Traditional Italian

Inspired Italian cooking near the Royal Academy

☎ 020 7434 1500
5a Burlington Gardens W1X 1LE
dir: Nearest station: Piccadilly Circus, Oxford Circus. Burlington Gdns between New Bond St and Savile Row

Mayfair has never been so egalitarian - it is fine to pop into Cecconi's for a light breakfast (a bacon sandwich), brunch (piadina filled with grilled aubergine and stracchino) or a few cichetti (Venetian tapas) at the bar counter, and you don't have to spend a fortune. But this is Mayfair and with green leather chairs and stools, velour banquettes and black-and-white tiled flooring, Cecconi's is smartly and fashionably dressed. Presentation is simple, precise and the produce first-class. Chicken liver crostini (off the cichetti section of the menu) is deliciously smooth, while from the 'pasta & risotto' selection might be risotto of asparagus and castelmagno, a fine dish with wonderfully balanced flavours. Lemon tart with mascarpone ice cream is as joyful as a Tuscan summer afternoon.

Times 7am-11.30pm Closed Xmas, New Year

LONDON W1 ***continued***

China Tang at The Dorchester PLAN 4 G6

Classic Cantonese

Sophisticated Chinese restaurant in legendary hotel

☎ 020 7629 9988
Park Ln W1K 1QA
e-mail: reservations@chinatanglondon.co.uk
dir: Nearest station: Hyde Park Corner

One gets to walk the entire length of The Dorchester's glittering Promenade before descending to this deluxe Chinese restaurant and cocktail bar in the basement. Lavishly opulent art-deco styling evokes a sense of colonial Shanghai or 1960's Hong Kong, with mirrored pillars, stunning glass-fronted fish-themed artworks, hand-carved seating and white linen and fabulous Chinoiserie. It's unashamedly decadent with high-rolling prices, but at lunch, the simple, optional fixed-price menu offers excellent value and some great people watching. The classic Cantonese cooking - driven by top-notch produce - parades on a dim sum menu and a carte dotted with luxuries. Classic Peking duck is a signature, while wok-fried squid or lobster in ginger spring onions might vie for attention with slow-braised pork belly with preserved vegetables.

Chef Yip Lam Law **Owner** Sir David Tang **Times** 11am-midnight Closed 25 Dec **Prices** Fixed L 2 course fr £15, Service added but optional 12.5% **Wines** 512 bottles over £20, 5 bottles under £20, 12 by glass **Notes** Sunday L, Vegetarian available, Dress restrictions, Smart casual **Seats** 120, Pr/dining room 80 **Children** Portions

C London PLAN 2 H2

Italian

Venetian elegance in Mayfair

☎ 020 7399 0500
25 Davies St W1E 3DE
dir: Nearest station: Bond Street

One of London's most famous Italian restaurants has been renamed after its founders lost a trademark battle with the owners of the Cipriani hotel in Venice. Arrigo Cipriani's father opened Hotel Cipriani in 1958, but it was later sold to Orient-Express Hotels. Following a legal ruling, the Cipriani family have been ordered to remove the name from their Mayfair restaurant. Although now known as C London, nothing else has changed at this popular celebrity haunt, sister to the famous Harry's Bar in Venice. The modern glass-fronted exterior leads to a large, stylish dining room, where impeccable art-deco style meets beautiful Murano chandeliers, and white-jacketed staff offer slick, discreet service. Settle into a low, leather-upholstered seat and watch the activity unfold before you. The people-watching is reason enough to go, while the classic, straightforward Italian cooking using prime quality ingredients hits the mark. Try the Dover sole with zucchini, or veal kidney with risotto alla Milanese, and do save room for the dessert selection of cakes.

Times 12-3/6-11.45 Closed 25 Dec

Cocoon PLAN 3 B1

Pan-Asian

Classic Pan-Asian cooking in an ultra-contemporary setting

☎ 020 7494 7600
65 Regent St W1B 4EA
e-mail: reservations@cocoon-restaurants.com
dir: Nearest station: Piccadilly Circus. 1 min walk from Piccadilly Circus on the corner of Regent St & Air St

Right in the heart of the West End, Cocoon is as funky as they come. It has the feel of a nightclub and has a champagne bar, cocktail lounge and a DJ doing his thing every Thursday, Friday and Saturday night. The six interconnecting rooms which make up the dining area include a sushi counter and some private rooms at which you might spot a famous face or two. The cooking is characteristically Pan-Asian, but the extensive menu does reveal some surprises alongside the familiar favourites. Try Guangzhou pork and radish dumplings with Thai sweet chilli, baked fillet of black cod with kinome miso and mirin glaze and to top it off, sample a delicious yoghurt cake with mango sorbet.

Chef Ricky Pang **Owner** Matt Hermer, Paul Deeming, Ignite Group **Times** 12-3/5.30-mdnt Closed 25-26 Dec, 1 Jan, Sun, L Sat **Prices** Food prices not confirmed for 2011. Please telephone for details **Wines** 100% bottles over £20, 14 by glass **Notes** Vegetarian available, Dress restrictions, Smart casual **Seats** 180, Pr/dining room 14 **Parking** NCP Brewer St

Corrigan's Mayfair

LONDON W1 PLAN 2 G1

Modern British V NOTABLE WINE LIST

The best of British and Irish produce cooked with flair

☎ 020 7499 9943
28 Upper Grosvenor St W1K 7EH
e-mail: reservations@corrigansmayfair.com
web: www.corrigansmayfair.com
dir: Nearest station: Marble Arch. Off Park Ln, main entrance via Upper Grosvenor St, 200 yds from American Embassy

Richard Corrigan's most recent culinary foray takes us into the heart of Mayfair to a pleasingly clubby dining room with the look of an art deco designer hunting lodge. Carved friezes of hunting scenes are a nod to the game that is dear to the chef's heart, while curvaceous blue leather seats, pale oak floors, shimmering silver wall panels, and bell-shaped light shades with a touch of gaslight about them complete the eye-catching décor. Corrigan is clearly a chef who likes to eat, and is known for an ethos that has as its bedrock the quality of the raw materials. His cooking is rustic, yet subtle, and not without understated sophistication. The menu aims straight at the heart of the British or Irish trencherman who loves the best produce these isles have to offer - how about suckling pig ravioli with roasted lobster, or tea-roasted veal sweetbreads and morels? Main courses could be as classic as sautéed veal liver with onion and leeks, as gutsy as shin of beef with peppered bone marrow and snails, or as modern as saddle of wild rabbit with Medjool dates, and orange and cumin carrots. Puddings deliver perfect pairings such as rhubarb soufflé with ginger ice cream, or you could end with exemplary British and Irish artisan cheeses.

Chef Richard Corrigan, Chris McGowan **Owner** Richard Corrigan Restaurants Ltd **Times** 12-2.30/6-11 Closed 23-27 Dec, L Sat **Prices** Fixed L 3 course £25-£27, Starter £9-£27, Main £22-£40, Dessert £6-£7.50, Service added but optional 12.5% **Wines** 400 bottles over £20, 4 bottles under £20, 12 by glass **Notes** Sunday L, Vegetarian menu **Seats** 85, Pr/dining room 30 **Children** Portions **Parking** On street

Corrigan's Mayfair
PLAN 2 G1

®®® – *see opposite page*

Dehesa
PLAN 3 A2

® Spanish, Italian

Vibrant, modern tapas dining just off Carnaby Street

☎ 020 7494 4170
25 Ganton St W1F 9BP
e-mail: info@dehesa.co.uk
dir: Nearest station: Oxford Circus. Close to underground station, half way along Carnaby St on corner of Ganton & Kingly St

This small and very popular walk-in charcuterie and tapas outfit is run by Sanja Morris and Simon Mullins, who also own the wonderful Salt Yard (see entry). With black awnings (sheltering outside tables), a copper-fronted bar, high-bench tables and tall, leather-cushioned stools (plus some cosier banquette seating), Dehesa has modern curb appeal. The food is an alluring mix of tapas imbued with the flavours of Italy and Spain, with clean-cut, unfussy, ingredient-driven dishes for sharing. Hand-sliced jambon iberico, or tapas like salt-cod croquetas with romesco sauce are based on high quality produce. Try grilled squid with chick peas, chorizo and mint or confit Gloucestershire Old Spot served with rosemary-scented cannellini beans. Bookings are now taken for some tables, but best to arrive early if you're just walking in.

Chef Giancarlo Vatteroni **Owner** Simon Mullins, Sanja Morris **Times** 12-3/5-11 Closed 10 days (Xmas & New Year), D Sun, BHs **Prices** Food prices not confirmed for 2011. Please telephone for details **Wines** 59 bottles over £20, 4 bottles under £20, 12 by glass **Notes** Sunday L, Vegetarian available **Seats** 40, Pr/dining room 12 **Parking** NCP

deVille
PLAN 2 G3

®® Traditional British

Stylish hotel and restaurant in chic central location

☎ 020 7935 5599
The Mandeville Hotel, Mandeville Place W1U 2BE
e-mail: info@mandeville.co.uk
dir: Nearest station: Bond St, Baker St. Just off Wigmore St; at end of Marylebone High St (3 mins walk from Bond St tube station)

The designers have been let loose on the interior of this boutique townhouse hotel in fashionable Marylebone village and pulled off a rather cool exercise in contemporary elegance. The Mandeville Hotel's deVille restaurant wears a smart look in shades of silver, tan and white, counterpointed by bold floral wallpaper, a bright pink wall at one end and Venetian mask wall lights. The food is pitched to suit the surroundings: vibrant, easy on the eye and put together with attention to detail. The brasserie-style offering of seasonal comfort food might start with ham hock terrine and port wine jelly, before calves' liver with bubble-and-squeak and onion gravy, or wild sea bass with saffron, clams and butter sauce. A strong green policy ensures that all ingredients are organic and food miles kept low.

deVille

Chef Matt Edmonds **Times** 12.30-3/7-11 Closed Sun **Prices** Food prices not confirmed for 2011. Please telephone for details **Wines** 80 bottles over £20, 6 bottles under £20, 20 by glass **Notes** Vegetarian available, Dress restrictions, Smart casual **Seats** 90, Pr/dining room 12 **Children** Portions **Parking** NCP nearby

Dinings
PLAN 2 E3

®® Japanese, European

Contemporary Japanese food in unpretentious surroundings

☎ 020 7723 0666
22 Harcourt St W1H 4HH
dir: Nearest station: Edgware Rd

Those in the know head for this discreet Georgian townhouse tucked away in the backwaters of Marylebone, where the owner, Tomonari Chiba (an ex-Nobu man), delivers small-but-perfectly-formed Japanese tapas dishes buzzing with inventiveness and memorable for their depth of flavour. Minimalist grey walls, concrete floors, bare tables and darkwood latticework make for a surprisingly spartan interior, but cheerful and clued-up staff add zing to the six-seat ground-floor sushi bar and 32-seat basement dining room. Food is Nobu-esque, but without the frightening price tag, and shows east-meets-west influences in dishes such as chargrilled Iberian pork in tomato lemon yuzu sauce, and intriguing sushi - fresh water eel and foie gras roll, or seared Wagyu beef with truffle salsa and ponzu jelly.

Chef Masaki Sugisaki **Owner** Tomonari Chiba **Times** 12-2.30/6-10.30 Closed Xmas, 31 Dec-1 Jan, L Sat-Sun **Prices** Starter £3.20-£19.80, Main £6.50-£19.80, Dessert £4.80-£6.90, Service added but optional 10% **Wines** 23 bottles over £20, 4 bottles under £20, 5 by glass **Notes** Fixed L menu available, Vegetarian available **Seats** 28

Dolada
PLAN 3 A1

®® Italian

New-wave Italian cooking in a Mayfair basement

☎ 020 7409 1011
13 Albemarle St W1S 4HJ
dir: Nearest station: Green Park

Lurking beneath the DKNY shop on Albemarle Street, Dolada is an Italian eatery for the style-conscious. A long narrow dining room with frieze mirrors, abstract prints and brash Murano glassware, it provides a voguish pit-stop for daytime shoppers, and a destination for the smart set, with food from a Veneto chef, Riccardo De Prà, who has also cooked in Japan. Supremely elegant, often spare, presentation and clarity of flavour combinations informs dishes such as venison fillet salad in pomegranate dressing, roasted monkfish with spinach in tomatoes and saffron, Angus beef barbecued over hazelnut wood, and platters of Venetian caramelised fruit. An extensive list of quality Italian wines adds to the excitement.

Times 12-2.30/6.30-10.45 Closed Sun, L Sat, Sun, Xmas, Etr, BHs

Embassy London
PLAN 3 A1

®® Modern European

Stylish Mayfair restaurant, bar and nightclub

☎ 020 7851 0956
29 Old Burlington St W1S 3AN
e-mail: embassy@embassylondon.com
dir: Nearest station: Green Park, Piccadilly Circus. Just off Burlington Gardens (between Bond St & Regent St)

With a basement members' nightclub, the Embassy is better known as a late-night celeb and partying hangout, but its smart and fashionable ground-floor restaurant - set behind a modern glass frontage and inviting pavement terrace - is worth a visit on its own merits. Backed by a darker-look bar, the dining room comes in soothing creams and browns, with mirrored walls, faux-stuccoed ceiling, chandeliers and leather seating. The accomplished modern European-vogue cooking hits just the right crowd-pleasing note, with clean flavours, neat presentation and quality produce. Pan-fried fillet of wild sea bass and scallops served with a sweet pepper sauce or rump of lamb with potato dauphinoise and thyme jus show the style. While evenings are buzzy, the fixed-price lunch offers amazing Mayfair value.

Chef David Landor **Owner** Mark Fuller
Times 12-3/6-11.30 Closed 25-26 Dec, 1 Jan, Good Fri, Sun-Mon, L Sat **Prices** Fixed D 3 course £19.95-£24.95, Starter £6.95-£11.95, Main £11.95-£22.95, Dessert £5.95-£10, Service added but optional 12.5%, Groups min 10 service 15% **Wines** 63 bottles over £20, 2 bottles under £20, 6 by glass **Notes** Vegetarian available, Dress restrictions, Smart casual, no trainers, smart jeans only **Seats** 140 **Parking** NCP opposite restaurant

LONDON W1 ***continued***

L'Escargot - The Ground Floor Restaurant

PLAN 3 C2

French

Long-established Soho pre-theatre favourite delivering accomplished French bistro fare

☎ 020 7439 7474
48 Greek St W1D 4EF
e-mail: sales@whitestarline.org.uk
web: www.lescargotrestaurant.co.uk
dir: Nearest station: Tottenham Court Rd, Leicester Square

A favourite with the West End theatre crowds, L'Escargot is a long-running Soho grandee. Fashioned from an elegant townhouse, today's incarnation - remodelled by design guru David Collins - has a light, classy retro vibe, with cut-glass mirrors and jaw-dropping original artwork by Miró, Chagall, Warhol, Hockney and Matisse. Add warm neutral colours, elegant leather seating and well-schooled service, and you have an upbeat, buzzy setting for classical French bistro cooking with a refined spin. Namesake snails (escargot en croquille Bordelaise) still find a place, while pan-fried daurade royale might be delivered with citrus fruits, braised endive and sauce vierge. A good-value, fixed-price lunch and pre-theatre offering bolsters the carte, while the upstairs Picasso Room is now private-dining only.

L'Escargot - The Ground Floor Restaurant

Chef Joseph Croan **Owner** Jimmy Lahoud
Times 12-2.30/5.30-11.30 Closed 25-26 Dec, 1 Jan, Sun, L Sat **Prices** Fixed L 2 course £15, Starter £7.50-£13.95, Main £10.50-£22.50, Dessert £7.95, Service added but optional 12.5% **Wines** 275 bottles over £20, 6 bottles under £20, 8 by glass **Notes** Pre/post theatre D 2 course £15, 3 course £18, Vegetarian available **Seats** 70, Pr/dining room 60 **Children** Portions **Parking** NCP Chinatown, on street parking

Fino

PLAN 3 B3

Spanish

Buzzing basement venue for top-notch tapas

☎ 020 7813 8010
33 Charlotte St W1T 1RR
e-mail: info@finorestaurant.com
dir: Nearest station: Goodge St, Tottenham Court Rd. Entrance on Rathbone St

Once you've found the place, down a narrow side road just off trendy Charlotte Street (it's just behind Roka), take the stairs down to the basement. But don't worry - it's a capacious, vibrant room that can generate quite a buzz. From the brothers Hart (Sam and Eddie), Fino serves tapas of the highest order, the authentic and inventive Spanish dishes made from top quality ingredients. Eat at the bar in front of the semi-open kitchen, or on red leather banquettes or rattan-backed chairs at one of the well-spaced tables. Expect the likes of ultra-fresh razor clams simply grilled on the plancha with herbs and garlic, fab deep-fried baby artichokes, and first-class tortilla, and finish with a traditional Santiago tart packed with coarsely chopped almonds and flavoured with orange and lemon juice. There is a good range of sherries and an all-Spanish wine list.

Chef Nieves Barragan Mohacho **Owner** Sam & Eddie Hart
Times 12-2.30/6-10.30 Closed Xmas, BHs, Sun, L Sat **Prices** Fixed L 2 course £14.95-£17.95, Starter £5-£18.50, Main £10.50-£24.50, Dessert £3.50-£7.50,

Galvin at Windows

LONDON W1 PLAN 4 G5

Modern French

Destination dining with majestic views and refined food

☎ 020 7208 4021
Restaurant & Bar, London Hilton on Park Ln, 22 Park Ln W1K 1BE
e-mail: reservations@galvinatwindows.com
dir: Nearest station: Green Park, Hyde Park Corner. On Park Lane, opposite Hyde Park

For a rare peek into the Queen's back garden go for a meal on the 28th-floor of the London Park Lane Hilton. Windows is aptly named: they are present in spades, from floor to ceiling, giving an unrivalled view over the capital. Glamour is all around: glossy darkwood floors counterpointing cream walls and sharply-styled leather chairs; slick staff are on the ball at all times, and clued-up when it comes to advising on both the menu and globetrotting wine list. But captivating as the view is, both inside and out of the dining room, your attention will be riveted on what appears at the table. Chef-patron Chris Galvin and head chef André Garrett deliver a French-influenced style of fine dining with a molecular spin so as to enhance textures and refine flavours. There is no room for dead weight with these creations: every element has to pay its way with a distinct presence. Terrine of foie gras opens in the company of blood orange purée, spiced salt and toasted brioche; next up, braised turbot is teamed with the fine-tuned flavours of lobster mousseline, crushed celeriac, trompette mushrooms and light shellfish jus. To finish, caramelised Williams pear tarte Tatin is fired up with Calvados crème fraîche and caramel sauce.

Chef André Garrett **Owner** Hilton International
Times 12-2.30/6-11 Closed BHs, 26 Dec, L Sat, D Sun **Prices** Fixed L 2 course £22, Fixed D 3 course £35-£65, Service added but optional 12.5% **Wines** 284 bottles over £20, 5 bottles under £20, 31 by glass **Notes** Tasting menu Dégustation available, Sunday L, Vegetarian available **Seats** 105 **Children** Portions **Parking** NCP

Service added but optional 12.5% **Wines** 118 bottles over £20, 7 bottles under £20, 9 by glass **Notes** Vegetarian available **Seats** 90 **Children** Portions

Galvin at Windows PLAN 4 G5

– see opposite page

Galvin Bistrot de Luxe PLAN 2 G3

French NOTABLE WINE LIST

Authentic French food in classy bistro setting

020 7935 4007
66 Baker St W1U 7DJ
e-mail: info@galvinrestaurants.com
dir: Nearest station: Baker Street. 5 min walk from Baker St underground station, on left near Dorset St

The Galvin brothers have brought la joie de vivre to Baker Street with a buzzing bistro that evokes the France that encouraged some half-a-million Brits to live over the other side of the Channel. It looks the part of a Parisian brasserie - a rather swanky one - with its masculine tones of darkwood and slate and ceiling fans turning indolently to blow away the imaginary smoke. The cooking grabs the Gallic bull by the horns as well, turning out exceptionally well-crafted and robust dishes. A classic soupe de poissons is full of rich, intense flavour, or there's escabèche of yellowfin tuna with saffron dressing. Main-course roasted calf's brain with a beurre noisette delivers on all counts, or go for tagine of lamb with couscous, root vegetables and harissa. The smart bar - Le Bar - is down in the basement.

Galvin Bistrot de Luxe

Chef Chris & Jeff Galvin **Owner** Chris & Jeff Galvin **Times** 12-2.30/6-10.30 Closed 25-26 Dec, 1 Jan, D 24 Dec **Prices** Fixed L 3 course £15.50, Fixed D 3 course £17.50, Main £11.50-£18.50, Service added but optional 12.5% **Wines** 110 bottles over £20, 5 bottles under £20, 25 by glass **Notes** Vegetarian available **Seats** 95, Pr/dining room 22 **Children** Portions **Parking** On street & NCP

Le Gavroche Restaurant PLAN 2 G1

– see below

Goodman PLAN 3 A2

British

Upmarket American-style steakhouse serving prime cuts

020 7499 3776
26 Maddox St W1S 1QH
dir: Nearest station: Oxford Circus

Goodman's mission is to 'bring the New York steakhouse to Mayfair', and the décor certainly looks manly enough for the red-blooded carnivorous activity taking place, with acreages of clubby darkwood and liver-brown leather seats and banquettes. Diners are introduced to the steaks in their raw splendour at the table, before the men at the grill go about their business, delivering big chargrilled flavours with spot-on accuracy. Starters include Russian-style (the group is Russian owned by the way) sweet herring with hot mustard, and if you're not up for the hot steak action, mains could be grilled rack of Devon lamb with mint jus, while desserts run to baked New York cheesecake with berry compôte.

Times noon-11 Closed Sun

Gordon Ramsay at Claridge's PLAN 2 H2

– see page 286

The Greenhouse PLAN 4 H6

– see page 287

Le Gavroche Restaurant

LONDON W1 PLAN 2 G1

French

Long-standing Mayfair outpost of haute cuisine

020 7408 0881 & 7499 1826
43 Upper Brook St W1K 7QR
e-mail: bookings@le-gavroche.com
dir: Nearest station: Marble Arch. From Park Lane into Upper Brook St, restaurant on right

The old ship sails on, its topsails gently fluttering in the breeze of London restaurant fashion, but negotiating the heaving billows with majestic ease. Indeed, there's even the slight feeling of sitting on a grand ocean liner in the stately basement dining room, which seems hardly to change from one season to the next. The Gavroche has been feeding princes, politicians and keen gastronomes since the 1960s, having helped to usher in a new era of aspirational dining in the capital when French cooking was still the height of exoticism. Michel Roux Jnr inherited from his father and uncle the mantle of awe-inspiring consistency, but has allowed a level of gradualist development in the menus that has been all to the good. The famous lobster mousse with caviar in champagne butter sauce is still there, but so too is stuffed pig's trotter with roasted vegetable salad, as well as red mullet in red wine and shallot sauce, alongside a croûton of beef marrow. Chick pea 'chips' and courgette cannelloni are the accompaniments for grilled turbot, a chive beurre blanc being the dish's only nod to tradition. Even these more novel dishes are creatively subsumed within the overarching context of haute cuisine, though, the commitment to which is probably more tenaciously observed here than at any other restaurant in London. Finish with the immaculate passionfruit soufflé with white chocolate ice cream, or more voguishly with pear millefeuille, served with salted caramel sauce and pistachios. Service is among the best in the country, full of punctilious courtesy, formal yes (jackets, please, gentlemen), but warmly engaging too. The wine list is a classic of the genre, a Francophile's dream read, but you will need to be handsomely resourced to get very far with it.

Chef Michel Roux Jnr **Owner** Le Gavroche Ltd **Times** 12-2/6.30-11 Closed Xmas, New Year, BHs, Sun, L Sat **Prices** Food prices not confirmed for 2011. Please telephone for details **Wines** 2000 bottles over £20, 21 bottles under £20, 20 by glass **Notes** Fixed L 3 courses, Tasting menu 8 courses, Dress restrictions, Jacket required, No jeans **Seats** 60 **Children** Portions **Parking** NCP - Park Lane

LONDON W1 ***continued***

The Grill (The Dorchester) PLAN 4 G6

Modern British NOTABLE WINE LIST

Palatial Scottish-themed grill room

☎ 020 7629 8888
The Dorchester, Park Ln W1K 1QA
e-mail: restaurants@thedorchester.com
dir: Nearest station: Hyde Park Corner. On Park Ln, overlooking Hyde Park

Be prepared for the Scottish theme at The Dorchester's Grill - plaid patterns carpet the floor and cover the chairs in the majestic formal dining room, while muscular kilted clansmen keep an eye on proceedings from hard-to-ignore murals. Head Chef Brian Hughson took over in 2009, bringing a long pedigree of stellar cooking, but the kitchen has no intention of deviating from its formula of modern-idiom classics alongside timeless dishes from the grill. A clever starter sees lemon sole fillets paired with de-boned and sautéed chicken wings, gem lettuce, pickled grapes and Véronique sauce, while main courses might go for an unexpectedly earthy peasant touch, as in slow-cooked pork belly, braised pig's cheek, black pudding spring roll and crackling. Five-star service keeps up the right tone throughout, courtesy of a well-drilled team of professional staff.

Times 12.30-2.30/6.30-10.30

Hakkasan PLAN 3 B3

Chinese NOTABLE WINE LIST

New-wave Chinese cooking in a see-and-be-seen basement setting

☎ 020 7927 7000
8 Hanway Place W1T 1HD
e-mail: mail@hakkasan.com
dir: Nearest station: Tottenham Court Rd. From station take exit 2, then 1st left, 1st right, restaurant straight ahead

With its black-lacquered design and marble flooring and its louche basement nightclub vibe, this elegant, modern Chinese restaurant is certainly a place to see and be seen, although the crepuscular lighting levels might make the latter task more of a challenge. An extensive menu of new-wave Chinese dishes, along with some Cantonese classics, provides plenty of compelling choices, and you might find choosing agonisingly difficult; one of everything not really being an option. From the 'small eat' list, kick off with salt and pepper squid or Jasmine tea-smoked organic pork ribs, and then follow with Dover sole with sea urchin and preserved black olive, stir-fried Mongolian-style venison, and steamed king crab claw with black bean sauce. Or, try one of the specialities (at a price) like Peking duck with Royal Beluga caviar and baby cucumber, orderable 24 hours in advance. Get into the vibrant mood with one of the exotic cocktails as an aperitif.

Chef Che Tong **Owner** Tasameem **Times** 12-5/6-1.30 Closed Xmas, New Year, 24-25 Dec, L 1 Jan **Prices** Fixed L 3 course £40-£108, Fixed D 3 course £50-£108, Starter £6.50-£19.50, Main £12.50-£58, Dessert £8-£13.50, Service added but optional 13% **Wines** 385 bottles over £20, 19 by glass **Notes** Sunday L, Vegetarian available, Dress restrictions, Smart elegant, no trainers or sportswear **Seats** 220 **Parking** Valet parking (from 6pm), NCP

Hélène Darroze at The Connaught PLAN 2 H1

– *see page 288*

Hibiscus PLAN 3 A2

– *see page 289*

Gordon Ramsay at Claridge's

LONDON W1 PLAN 2 H2

Modern European V NOTABLE WINE LIST

Sophisticated dining in legendary hotel

☎ 020 7499 0099
Brook St W1K 4HR
e-mail: reservations@gordonramsay.com
dir: Nearest station: Bond Street, Green Park

Claridge's is a byword for old-school glamour. Take your time passing through the foyer en-route to the restaurant to bask in the ambience of entitlement that its pre-war guests must have enjoyed. The dining room now flies the flag of the Gordon Ramsay brand, and thanks to a reworking by designer and architect Thierry Despont, pays homage to its 1930s heydays, albeit with a modernised, soft-edged opulence: lightshades resembling upturned pagodas hang from a high ceiling, and there are filigree-etched glass panels and claret-hued chairs set against a décor of toffee and gold. Top-drawer service is a vital element of the package, delivered adroitly by a battalion of well-drilled staff. The kitchen, led by Steve Allen, delivers confident modern European cuisine grounded in classical French technique with the focus on fine ingredients and balanced combinations. Seared and marinated Loch Duart salmon might open in the company of fennel, apple jelly, horseradish and beetroot ice cream, followed by steamed sea bass with scallop mousse, cucumber and apple and Oscietra caviar sauce. Meat dishes could be represented by roasted Creedy Carver duck with Périgord truffle jus, swede, hazelnut and wild mushrooms, and desserts finish with finesse - perhaps lemon pannacotta with basil ice cream, blackberry jus and honey madeleines. The wine list is a monumental tome.

Chef Steve Allen **Owner** Gordon Ramsay Holdings Ltd **Times** 12-2.45/5.45-11 **Prices** Fixed L 3 course fr £30, Fixed D 3 course fr £70, Service added but optional 12.5% **Wines** 800+ bottles over £20, 11 by glass **Notes** Prestige menu 6 course £80, Sunday L, Vegetarian menu, Dress restrictions, Smart, jacket preferred for gentlemen **Seats** 100, Pr/dining room 100 **Children** Portions **Parking** Mayfair NCP

The Greenhouse

LONDON W1 PLAN 4 H6

Modern French V 

Top-class Mayfair address

☎ 020 7499 3331
27a Hay's Mews, Mayfair W1J 5NY
e-mail: reservations@greenhouserestaurant.co.uk
dir: Nearest station: Green Park, Bond St. Behind Dorchester Hotel just off Hill St

The entrance in a wide Mayfair mews is as discreet as they come. One doesn't stumble upon The Greenhouse, for this is one of the leading destination restaurants in London, a place at the top of its game, where the refined, intelligent cooking of Antonin Bonnet is very much of the moment. Once you're in the mews, take a pathway through a modernist urban garden to the front door and enter the serene dining room, where the polished service plays its part in creating an extremely calm and suave oasis. Natural colours of beige complement the sleek Philippe Hurel furniture, while an artistic arrangement of branches and twigs on a feature wall brings nature's texture to the fore. As might be expected of a chef who trained under Michel Bras, Bonnet's cooking is based on supreme technical virtuosity and sound classical principles, with well-crafted creativity and occasional discreet Asian and Middle Eastern flavours leaving a lasting impression. An array of wonderful breads (a fabulous chestnut version among them), plus a creative canapé, kick things off, before a mightily impressive first-course of Limousin veal sweetbread, perfectly caramelised, with wild garlic caramel and glazed leek. Spot-on timing and high technical proficiency is evident in a main course dish of roast grouse, where coffee mashed potatoes and coffee foam are a perfect foil for the delicious meat. Chestnut surprise is an indulgent dessert, served with an ultra-thin molasses tuile and maple syrup, and the attention to detail remains all the way to the excellent coffee and dynamic petits fours. Call on the services of the sommelier to help you through the impressive wine list.

Chef Antonin Bonnet **Owner** Marlon Abela Restaurant Corporation
Times 12-2.30/6.45-11 Closed 23 Dec-5 Jan, BHs, Sun, L Sat **Prices** Fixed L 2 course fr £25, Fixed D 3 course fr £70, Tasting menu £70-£80, Service added but optional 12.5% **Wines** 3066 bottles over £20, 5 bottles under £20, 29 by glass **Notes** Cookery classes available 6 times a year, Vegetarian menu
Seats 65, Pr/dining room 10
Children Portions **Parking** NCP, Meter Parking

Hélène Darroze at The Connaught

LONDON W1 PLAN 2 H1

Modern French V

Dynamic French chef in an old London dining institution

☎ 020 3147 7200
Carlos Place W1K 2AL
e-mail: creservations@the-connaught.co.uk
dir: Nearest station: Bond Street, Green Park. Between Grosvenor Sq and Berkeley Sq in Mayfair

It doesn't seem that long ago that the Connaught was a bastion of Edwardian tradition in London, where time had stood still amid a fog of cigar smoke. The makeover of recent years has been a matter of letting daylight in on magic, but productively so. Paris-based designer India Mahdavi has introduced some eye-catching touches to the panelled dining room, now adorned with a pair of Damien Hirst's spin paintings, and Ducasse protégé Hélène Darroze was appointed on a cross-Channel brief to weave some of her own Parisian magic. The result has been sensational, making the old-timer suddenly one of the most happening of all the old five-star hotel dining rooms. Service remains as reassuringly formal as ever, impeccably correct in its ministrations. The Darroze style is a fascinating mix of high-flown refinement, top-drawer ingredients, and an almost rustic keenness for big, loud flavours. Great attention to detail distinguishes all dishes, with all the ancillary items registering strong, clean, precise impact on the palate, and timings spot-on throughout. The fixed-price lunch, at £42, seems a genuine bargain, including as it does two glasses of wine, water and coffee, especially when it comes in the form of a fish-lover's treat - scallop cappuccino with gnocchi, cockles, an oyster and trompette mushrooms in a lemongrass broth, followed by halibut roasted on the bone with fondant potato in saffron bouillabaisse. Add steamed Sicilian pistachio sponge with pink grapefruit and Greek yoghurt sorbet to finish, and one's cup runneth over. It all gets seriously involved at dinner, with main courses such as crisp-cooked rack of Pyrenean lamb, served with a confit of the leg, a skewer of the organ meats, and roasted seasonal vegetables, or truffled Basque pork chop with grilled fondant belly, mashed potatoes and braised romaine. The wine list is a huge, impressive tome, with mark-ups that may alarm but shouldn't surprise.

Chef Hélène Darroze **Owner** Maybourne Hotel Group **Times** 12-2.30/6.30-10.30 Closed 1 wk Jan, 2 wks Aug, Sun-Mon **Prices** Fixed L 3 course £35-£42, Fixed D 3 course £75, Tasting menu £85, Service added but optional 12.5% **Wines** 1100 bottles over £20, 6 by glass **Notes** Tasting menu 7 course, Vegetarian menu, Dress restrictions, Smart, no jeans or sportswear, Civ Wed 30 **Seats** 64, Pr/dining room 24 **Children** Portions **Parking** 2

Hibiscus

LONDON W1 PLAN 3 A2

Modern French V

Bold experimentation French-style, just off Regent Street

☎ 020 7629 2999
29 Maddox St W1S 2PA
e-mail: enquiries@hibiscusrestaurant.co.uk
dir: Nearest station: Oxford Circus

With the craziness of Oxford Circus just around the corner and the shopping opportunities on Regent Street just at the end of the road, Hibiscus could be described as an oasis amid the hustle-and-bustle of the West End. Though the room may be peaceful and tranquil enough to qualify as an oasis, what appears on the plate is best described as culinary fireworks. Claude Bosi's cooking is certainly innovative, leading you gently into his world where compelling flavours are wrought from top-class ingredients, but everything is supremely well judged, balance most certainly assured. The room has an air of calm about it, being neither over-egged nor lacking Mayfair sophistication; well-spaced tables, neutral and natural tones combine with a few lavish touches such as the opulent flower display and shimmering central chandelier. Bosi's Lyonnaise heritage and precocious technical skills, not to mention his desire to explore flavours and textures, result in menus of compelling combinations that are at the forefront of contemporary French cooking. A taste of the homeland starts things off - the excellent gougeres are as light and flavoursome as can be. Those sharp technical skills are evident in a first-course ravioli dish, the thin pasta having perfect bite, filled with spring onion and lime, with glazed broad beans, roast Cévennes onion, and a superb broad bean and mint purée that brings the whole dish together in perfect harmony. For main course, black bream from Cornwall is stuffed with morels and kaffir lime and served with polenta with wild mushrooms and coffee - an extremely well-judged and harmonious combination. Next up, a pre-dessert of serious refinement and invention: a combination of strawberries and celeriac delivering real impact on the palate. Dessert is no less impressive; a warm toasted rice soufflé - as good a one as you'll find anywhere - with pineapple sorbet and toasted rice syrup. This is a restaurant firing on all cylinders.

Chef Claude Bosi **Owner** Claude & Claire Bosi **Times** 12-2.30/6.30-10 Closed 10 days Xmas & New Year, Sun-Mon **Prices** Fixed L 3 course £29.50, Fixed D 3 course £75, Service added but optional 12.5% **Wines** 550 bottles over £20, 2 bottles under £20, 12 by glass **Notes** Tasting menu only Fri & Sat D, Vegetarian menu **Seats** 45, Pr/dining room 18 **Children** Portions **Parking** On street

LONDON W1 ***continued***

Hix PLAN 3 B2

Modern British **NEW** V

Cool Britannia and best of British dishes

☎ 020 7292 3518
66-70 Brewer St W1F 9UP
e-mail: reservations@hixsoho.co.uk
dir: Nearest station: Piccadilly. Located bottom Regent St, short walk from Piccadilly underground station

Mark Hix's Soho venture opened in October 2009 and immediately grabbed such a fat slice of the cool and arty bohemian pie that getting a table is a challenge in itself. Hix's culinary pedigree - Le Caprice, The Ivy, among other big names - speaks for itself: here, it appears in the company of a hefty dollop of Cool Britannia artwork by the likes of Damien Hirst and Sarah Lucas to funk up a dark, classically clubby British interior. Hix himself does not man the stoves - that's down to a team who successfully deliver the Hix concept of impeccable British materials in imaginative combinations. Dishes are defiantly unadorned: fresh, sweet scallops sit on a silky purée of whipped squash and hedgerow garlic; next comes Blythburgh pork chop with cockles and laverbread, and you could finish with Bakewell pudding with almond ice cream.

Chef Kevin Gratton **Owner** Mark Hix/Restaurants etc (Soho) Ltd **Times** 12-mdnt Closed 25-26 Dec, 1 Jan **Prices** Fixed D 3 course £19.95, Starter £6.50-£10.75, Main £14.50-£35, Dessert £3.50-£8, Service added but optional 12.5% **Wines** 130 bottles over £20, 7 bottles under £20, 23 by glass **Notes** Pre-theatre D menu 4.30-6.30pm Mon-Sat, Sunday L, Vegetarian menu, Air con **Seats** 80, Pr/dining room 12 **Children** Portions

Kai Mayfair PLAN 4 G6

Chinese

Excellent Chinese cooking in chic surroundings

☎ 020 7493 8988
65 South Audley St W1K 2QU
e-mail: reservations@kaimayfair.co.uk
dir: Nearest station: Marble Arch. From Marble Arch tube station along Park Ln toward Hyde Park Cnr, turn left after car showrooms into South St, continue to end & left into South Audley St. Restaurant on left

This established and deservedly popular Chinese restaurant is something of a hidden gem, located on a quiet street parallel to Park Lane. The lavish interior is certainly strikingly sophisticated throughout its two tiers, with mirrored pillars, granite flooring and colourful wall-coverings. The luxurious setting is gilded further by banquette seating, high-backed chairs and welcoming service. The extensive menu is a mix of authentic Chinese classics with some westernised specialties. Try scallop and tiger prawns with glass noodles, then perhaps Chilean sea bass fillet with chopped snow leaf and topped with shrimp crumble. Desserts include the Kai specialty of pumpkin cream with purple rice and coconut ice cream.

Chef Alex Chow **Owner** Bernard Yeoh
Times 12-2.15/6.30-11 Closed 25-26 Dec, 1 Jan
Prices Food prices not confirmed for 2011. Please telephone for details **Wines** 115 bottles over £20, 8 by glass **Notes** Sunday L, Vegetarian available **Seats** 85, Pr/dining room 12 **Parking** Directly outside

See advert on page 291

The Landau PLAN 2 H4

See below

The Landau

Rosettes not confirmed at time of going to press

LONDON W1 PLAN 2 H4

Modern European V NOTABLE WINE LIST

Inspirational grand dining in an historic hotel

☎ 020 7965 0165 & 7636 1000
The Langham London, Portland Place W1B 1JA
e-mail: reservations@thelandau.com
dir: Nearest station: Oxford Circus On N end of Regent St, by Oxford Circus

Built in 1865, The Langham was among the first of the grand hotels of Europe and an £80 million refurbishment a few years back has breathed new life into this magnificent pile at the north end of Regent Street. The Landau restaurant has its own entrance, via the Artesian Bar, an opulent and glamorous space, where a list of rum cocktails might well catch the eye. The oval Landau dining room, originally the hotel's ballroom, is no less eye-catching and elegant, with its equestrian sculptures, well-spaced tables, and tip-top service. A new chef arrived as we went to press. Expect the likes of a first course of pressed Landes foie gras and smoked duck terrine with parmesan marshmallows, pear chutney and brioche, followed by Guernsey sea bass with a light tiger prawn mousseline, courgettes and a Jacqueline sauce, and, for dessert, a white and dark chocolate mousse cake. Browse for your wine choice in the dramatically lit vaulted wine corridor beforehand.

Owner Langham Hotels International
Times 12.30-2.30/5.30-10.30 Closed BHs, Sun, L Sat
Prices Fixed L 2 course fr £21.50, Fixed D 3 course fr £28.50, Starter £12-£18, Main £18-£38, Dessert £8-£10, Service added but optional 12.5% **Wines** 135 bottles over £20, 20 by glass **Notes** Theatre menu 2-3 course, Grazing menu 5-8 course, Vegetarian menu, Dress restrictions, Smart casual, Civ Wed 230 **Seats** 100, Pr/dining room 18 **Children** Portions, Menu **Parking** On street & NCP

LONDON W1 *continued*

Latium PLAN 3 B3

Italian

Authentic Italian cuisine offering a taste of Lazio

020 7323 9123
21 Berners St W1T 3LP
e-mail: info@latiumrestaurant.com
dir: Nearest station: Goodge St, Oxford Circus

Chef-patron Maurizio Morelli's sleek Italian in Fitzrovia deals in the specialities of the Lazio region near Rome - Latium is the Roman name for Lazio - but also takes a wide-ranging approach to the rest of his country's regional and seasonal delights. The classy interior looks sharp with black leather banquettes against neutral walls jazzed up with stone mosaics and abstract Italian photography. Ravioli is raised to an art-form here: the little hand-made pasta parcels appear as starters, mains and desserts, and might encase anything from fish with sea bass bottarga, to veal with courgette and pecorino. Elsewhere there may be roast monkfish medallions wrapped in pancetta, served with Umbrian lentils and roast asparagus, and to finish, sweet chocolate ravioli filled with ricotta, candied fruit and pistachios, and orange sauce.

Chef Maurizio Morelli **Owner** Maurizio Morelli, Claudio Pulze **Times** 12-3/6-10.30 Closed BHs, Sun, L Sat **Prices** Fixed L 2 course £15.50-£22.50, Fixed D 3 course fr £33.50, Service added but optional 12.5% **Wines** 97 bottles over £20, 5 bottles under £20, 7 by glass **Notes** Vegetarian available **Seats** 50 **Children** Portions

Levant PLAN 2 G3

Lebanese, Middle Eastern

The scents and flavours of the Middle East

020 7224 1111
Jason Court, 76 Wigmore St W1H 9DQ
e-mail: info@levant.co.uk
dir: Nearest station: Bond Street. From Bond St station, walk through St Christopher's Place

Brimming with Eastern promise, Levant comes secreted away in a basement just off Wigmore Street and is great fun. Dimly lit, with lanterns, flickering candles, incense and rich colours and fabrics, it's like a scene from the *Arabian Nights*, the exotic atmosphere helped along mid-evening by nightly belly dancing. It's not the place for a cosy repas à deux, with a bar up front, high-decibel Middle Eastern music and dishes made for sharing. Choose from the fixed-price 'feast' or carte menu, with traditional meze (fatayer - baked pastries, perhaps filled with spinach - the star turn), and follow up with roasted sea bass fillet (served with citrus-scented rice) maybe washed down with Lebanese or North African wines.

Times 12-midnight Closed 25-26 Dec

Locanda Locatelli PLAN 2 F2

– see below

Maze PLAN 2 G2

See opposite page

Maze Grill PLAN 2 G2

Modern American NOTABLE WINE LIST

Classy grill room, part of the Ramsay stable

020 7495 2211
London Marriott Hotel Grosvenor Square, 10-13 Grosvenor Square W1K 6JP
e-mail: mazegrill@gordonramsay.com
dir: Nearest station: Bond St

Gordon Ramsay's sister restaurant to Maze (see entry) within the Marriott Hotel is modelled on the informal New York grill restaurants. It specialises in cooking outstanding quality steaks from different breeds of beef, some rare and expensive. This is modern fast food with a twist, with steaks quickly cooked on coals then under a unique grill at a high temperature. The impressive result is wonderfully full-flavoured steaks, say, an Aberdeen Angus grass- fed sirloin aged for 28 days, served on wooden boards with optional sauces, including a 'steak' sauce that's made at the table. Starters may take in confit tuna with white bean and tomato bruschetta, while

Locanda Locatelli

LONDON W1 PLAN 2 F2

Italian NOTABLE WINE LIST

High-quality Italian cooking of daring simplicity

020 7935 9088
8 Seymour St W1H 7JZ
e-mail: info@locandalocatelli.com
dir: Nearest station: Marble Arch. Opposite Marylebone police station

Still surely one of the most prestigious Italian restaurants in the capital, Giorgio Locatelli's ironically styled 'locanda' is to be found by the side of the Hyatt Regency Churchill Hotel in the temperate zone north of Oxford Street. Having escaped the madding crowd, you can escape central London altogether in the chic, low-lit interiors, with their variously pigmented and textured wood surfaces, leather-upholstered bucket chairs, and clever combination of rectilinear and curvaceous contours in the design. Locatelli made a noisy splash on TV a few years ago, but his food is unexpectedly understated in the best Italian manner. Dishes take time, which might feel surprising given that this is relatively low-intervention cooking, but the quality of the components is indisputable. A risotto of nettles and parmesan says it all, in its defiant simplicity, yet profound impact. Menu prices are certainly high, but the food looks and tastes the part, as when sea bass is crusted in herbs and salt, and served with a humble green salad. Kid isn't seen as often as it might be on London menus, but here it is, simply roasted and served with roasted vegetables. Side-dishes come at an extra cost, but don't miss the desserts, which may well be as richly complex as Locatelli's food ever gets. Chocolate and liquorice fondant with dried figs and rum ice cream is the sort of thing.

Chef Giorgio Locatelli **Owner** Plaxy & Giorgio Locatelli **Times** 12-3/6.45-11 Closed Xmas, BHs **Prices** Food prices not confirmed for 2011. Please telephone for details **Wines** 2 bottles under £20, 24 by glass **Notes** Sunday L, Vegetarian available **Seats** 70 **Children** Portions **Parking** NCP adjacent, parking meters

non-meat-eaters will be content with whole bay sea bass with spicy couscous and goats' cheese. The setting is a smart, modern, white linen-free zone; note the butcher's block table by the open kitchen that acts as a chef's table for 12.

Owner Gordon Ramsay Holdings Ltd
Times 12-2.30/5.45-11 **Prices** Food prices not confirmed for 2011. Please telephone for details **Wines** 100 bottles over £20, 17 by glass **Notes** Sunday L, Dress restrictions, Smart casual **Seats** 80, Pr/dining room 12
Children Portions

Mennula PLAN 3 B3

Modern Italian NEW

Authentic Sicilian cooking in medialand

☎ 020 7636 2833 & 7637 3830
10 Charlotte St W1T 2LT
e-mail: santino@mennula.com
dir: Nearest station: Goodge Street. 5 min walk from underground station

Décor-wise, this bijou Fitzrovia Sicilian venue is about as far from the old-school candles-in-Chianti-bottles stable as you can imagine: starkly-minimal white walls are stencilled with purple almond trees (mennula means almond, a staple of the Sicilian chef's arsenal), and there are vivid purple banquettes on walnut flooring. Chef-proprietor Santino Busciglio learned his trade while living in Sicily, before honing his skills in some of London's top Italians (Zafferano and Alloro, for example - see entries). What emerges from the kitchen has an authentic simplicity, but is refined and contemporary rather than staying slavishly rooted to rustic Sicilian home-cooking. A simple starter of burrata cheese with roasted beetroot and grilled courgettes shows the style, while pasta is represented by flat 'chitarra' spaghetti in a rustic combo with pan-fried sardines, crunchy fennel and pine nuts. Main-course delivers seared Cornish squid with tiny roasted peppers filled with cod and potato, and to finish, excellent Sicilian pasticceria arrives in the form of cannoli filled with sweet ewe's milk ricotta, and sfinci - a Sicilian take on profiteroles, filled with cinnamon, cream, honey and toasted sesame seeds.

Chef Santino Busciglio **Owner** Joe Martorana
Times 12-3/6-11 Closed Xmas, BHs, L Sat **Prices** Fixed L 2 course £17.50, Fixed D 3 course £19.50, Tasting menu £39.50, Starter £6.95-£11.50, Main £15.50-£25, Dessert £6.50-£11, Service added but optional 12.5% **Wines** 72 bottles over £20, 11 bottles under £20, 24 by glass **Notes** Tasting menu 6 course, Sunday L, Vegetarian available **Seats** 44, Pr/dining room 14 **Parking** On street

Mews of Mayfair PLAN 2 H2

European V

Crowd-pleasing cooking in Mayfair

☎ 020 7518 9388 & 7518 9395
10-11 Lancashire Court, New Bond St, Mayfair W1S 1EY
e-mail: info@mewsofmayfair.com
dir: Nearest station: Bond Street. Between Brook St & New Bond St. Opposite Dolce & Gabbana

This comfortably glamorous restaurant and cocktail bar is hidden away from the exclusive Bond Street shops and attracts a regular after work crowd for drinks in the cobbled outside area. After an expertly mixed drink there or in the clubby environs of the ground-floor bar, head upstairs to the restaurant - a light and airy room which makes the most of its intimate size with white and cream furniture against stripped wooden flooring. The simple menu owes much to British and French influences. Think classic starters such as crab and avocado cocktail or hand-cut steak tartare followed by sauté of tiger prawns, samphire, chilli and ginger or grilled calves' liver, ratte potatoes and crispy bacon.

Owner James Robson & Robert Nearn **Times** 12-4/6-12 Closed 25-26 Dec, 1 Jan, D Sun **Prices** Fixed L 2 course £10-£15, Fixed D 2 course £15-£20, Starter £6-£11, Main £14.50-£24, Dessert £5-£6, Service added but optional 12.5% **Wines** 30+ bottles over £20, 8 bottles under £20, 16 by glass **Notes** Sunday L, Vegetarian menu **Seats** 70, Pr/dining room 30 **Children** Portions, Menu **Parking** On street & NCP

Maze

Rosettes not confirmed at time of going to press

LONDON W1 PLAN 2 G2

French, Pacific Rim NOTABLE WINE LIST

Avant-garde cooking in famous West End square

☎ 020 7107 0000
London Marriott Hotel Grosvenor Square, 10-13 Grosvenor Square W1K 6JP
e-mail: reservations@gordonramsay.com
dir: Nearest station: Bond Street

Maze could be considered one of the brightest stars in the Ramsay firmament. Jason Atherton - who made his mark here - has moved on to pastures new in 2010 and the kitchen is now headed up by James Durrant. The David Rockwell design is certainly eye-catching, providing a multi-level space that really is something of a maze for first-time visitors (the Grill, for example, is near the entrance - see separate entry), with seating in dazzling yellow at clothless tables, plus a rosewood bar where you can eat or simply explore the cocktail list. The menu format centres on the lengthy list of tasting dishes, smaller (though by no means minuscule) compositions of arresting ingredients. These are supplemented by four-, five- or six-course lunch menus, and a seven-course chef's menu with a wealth of choice. The cooking is inventive and modern with plenty of appealing combinations; confit of wild mallard, for example, served with a raspberry gel, walnuts and compressed celery. There might also be braised octopus with an oxtail vinaigrette, dehydrated black olive, herbes fine and confit lemon, and among the sweet courses, the signature peanut butter and cherry jam sandwich, or slow-cooked 'tinned fruit' with condensed milk sorbet, fruit gel and apple salad. The wine list is an expensive cracker.

Chef James Durrant **Owner** Gordon Ramsay Holdings Ltd
Times 12-2.30/6-10.30 **Prices** Starter £9.50-£11.50, Main £12-£13.50, Dessert £4.50-£8.50, Service added but optional 12.5% **Wines** 600+ bottles over £20, 27 by glass **Notes** Chef menu 6 course £65, Sunday L, Vegetarian available, Dress restrictions, Casual, no shorts or sportswear **Seats** 100, Pr/dining room 40
Parking On street

LONDON W1 *continued*

Murano PLAN 4 H6

®®® – *see below*

Nicole's PLAN 3 A1

® Modern Mediterranean

Fashionable lunchtime retreat with careful cooking

☎ 020 7499 8408
158 New Bond St W1S 2UB
e-mail: nicoles@nicolefarhi.com
dir: Nearest station: Green Park, Bond St. Between Hermés & Asprey

As the Nicole in question is one Ms Farhi and the restaurant lies beneath the flagship Bond Street clothes store, you'd expect nothing less than a stylish modern setting to match the designer label. There's a small upper-deck bar area, while the main dining floor comes a few steps down, a fashionable blend of oak floors, tan leather seating and contemporary lighting. The cooking's light touch, simple handling and sunny Mediterranean flavours have broad appeal, from ladies-who-lunch to the suited deal makers; baked lemon sole fillets come with steamed baby vegetables and a lobster sauce, and hopefully you've time for a vanilla cheesecake (with blackberry compôte) before heading back out onto Bond Street. Breakfast and bar menus extend its usefulness even further.

Chef Francis Moore **Owner** Stephen Marks **Times** 12-3.30 Closed BHs, Sun, D all wk **Prices** Food prices not confirmed for 2011. Please telephone for details **Wines** 4 bottles over £20, 4 bottles under £20, 16 by glass **Notes** Vegetarian available **Seats** 65, Pr/dining room 80

Nobu PLAN 4 G5

®® Japanese

Legendary Japanese eatery perched above Park Lane

☎ 020 7447 4747
The Metropolitan, 19 Old Park Ln W1K 1LB
e-mail: london@noburestaurants.com
dir: Nearest station: Hyde Park Corner, Green Park. Located on 1st floor of Metropolitan Hotel

Ripples from the splash made by Nobu when it opened here in 1997 continue to spread, and somehow the place hasn't dated. A first-floor room overlooking Hyde Park is where the main action is (there's a cocktail bar on the ground-floor for those who want to linger on), and is packed with staff who cry out the traditional Japanese greeting, and also genteelly ensure you don't outstay your welcome at the strictly time-limited tables. There is the feeling of a blank canvas about the studiedly minimal décor, which only serves to focus attention on the pyrotechnical flavours and seasonings offered by the food. The raw fish morsels are prepared with consummate skill, perhaps best experienced in the form of a good-value lunchtime bento box, while the principal dishes remain undimmed. Rock shrimp tempura with ponzu is stunningly fresh, the miso-marinated black cod continues to impress, and accompaniments like oshitashi - Japanese spinach salad with roasted sesame seeds - are more than just makeweights. Diverting desserts include the whisky cappuccino, a small coffee-cup layered with coffee crème brûlée, crunchy coffee cacao, milk ice cream and a foam of Suntory Japanese whisky.

Chef Mark Edwards **Owner** Nobuyuki Matsuhisa **Times** 12-2.15/6-10.15 **Prices** Food prices not confirmed for 2011. Please telephone for details **Wines** 8 by glass **Notes** Vegetarian available, Dress restrictions, Smart casual **Seats** 160, Pr/dining room 40 **Parking** Car Park nearby

Nobu Berkeley Street PLAN 5 A6

®® Japanese

Traditional and modern Japanese food for the Mayfair set

☎ 020 7290 9222
15 Berkeley St W1J 8DY
e-mail: berkeley@noburestaurants.com
dir: Nearest station: Green Park

In the heart of Mayfair, the Berkeley Street branch of Nobu's London operations is spread over two floors, with a large ground-floor bar surmounted by the main restaurant upstairs. Black-clad staff look great against the backdrop of winter trees in the design, and the eating areas include a hibachi table where you can cook your

Murano

LONDON W1 PLAN 4 H6

Italian V NOTABLE WINE LIST

Italian inspiration in chic Mayfair

☎ 020 7592 1222
20 Queen St W1J 5PP
e-mail: murano@gordonramsay.com
dir: Nearest station: Green Park

Any temptation to push the Murano glass theme too far has been resisted, the glass instead used to great effect in specially commissioned blown glasswork light fittings. Angela Hartnett's restaurant - part of the Ramsay stable, the kitchen headed up by Diego Cardoso - is a chic room of neutral tones, the palette flowing from white to grey, splashes of colour arriving with the food on the plate. Service suits the confident Mayfair mood. Hartnett's cooking is driven by her Italian ancestry and the menu shows a willingness to embrace the rustic simplicity of the old country whilst delivering a contemporary sheen to proceedings as befitting the postcode. Truffled arancini is an amuse-bouche of unerring delight to get the ball rolling, ably supported by the excellent breads which come with an olive oil of judicious provenance. Set lunch, vegetarian and tasting menus support the carte, and there's the de rigeur chef's table if you want a view of the action. Start with caramelised sweetbreads, perfectly light and tender, supported by a rich cauliflower purée, plump golden raisins and sherry vinaigrette, before a main-course roasted monkfish tail served in a spring minestrone with lardo di colonnata and hand-rolled garganelli. Dessert might cast a wider net; ginger cake with Pineau des Charentes, Earl Grey ice cream and pickled ginger, perhaps. The wine list has Italian leanings but welcomes the rest of the world with open arms.

Chef Angela Hartnett **Owner** Gordon Ramsay Holdings **Times** 12-2.30/6-11 Closed 25-26 Dec, Sun **Prices** Fixed L 3 course fr £27, Fixed D 3 course fr £60, Tasting menu £75, Service added but optional 12.5% **Wines** 400 bottles over £20, 17 by glass **Notes** Tasting menu 8 course, Vegetarian menu, Dress restrictions, Smart **Seats** 46, Pr/dining room 10 **Children** Portions

own food, fondue-style. The thorough-going exploration of traditional and contemporary Japanese food includes signature dishes such as sashimi salad with the special Matsuhisa dressing (named after the founder), and the ever-popular grilled black cod with miso. There are some fine productions on the main menu, with crab leg tempura and ponzu sauce, lobster wasabi, and the fabled Wagyu beef all exerting their opulent influences. Fun desserts include the yuzu chocolate bar - a yuzu jelly encased in crunchy hazelnut chocolate, served with Alphons mango sorbet and goma toffee.

Chef Mark Edwards **Owner** Nobu Matsuhisa, Robert de Niro **Times** 12-2.15/6-1am Closed 25 Dec, Mon & BHs, L Sat-Sun **Prices** Food prices not confirmed for 2011. Please telephone for details **Wines** 10 by glass **Notes** Tasting menu called Omakase, Vegetarian available **Seats** 120 **Parking** Mayfair NCP

The Only Running Footman PLAN 4 H6

◎ Modern British

Renovated Mayfair pub with informal all-day dining

☎ 020 7499 2988
5 Charles St, Mayfair W1J 5DF
e-mail: manager@therunningfootmanmayfair.com
dir: Nearest station: Green Park, Bond St. Close to south end of Berkeley Sq

In the smart Mayfair environs of Berkeley Square, this red-brick corner pub has an all-day menu taking in the likes of pappardelle of wild rabbit, leeks and chanterelles alongside beer-battered fish and chips with home-made mushy peas and tartare sauce. That's in the buzzy ground-floor bar: move upstairs to the fine-dining restaurant - done out smartly in shades of café crème - and the kitchen cranks up a gear to offer smoked eel linguine with pancetta, roast shallots and Agen prunes, ahead of roast turbot with confit garlic mash, wilted Brussel tops and braised Puy lentils.

Chef Stephen Adams & Andrew Evans **Owner** Barnaby Meredith **Times** 12-2.30/6.30-10 Closed 25 Dec (bkgs only) **Prices** Starter £5.50-£8.50, Main £12.50-£22, Dessert £5.50-£11.95, Service added but optional 12.5% **Wines** 58 bottles over £20, 12 bottles under £20, 12 by glass **Notes** Sunday L, Vegetarian available **Seats** 30, Pr/dining room 40 **Children** Portions

Orrery PLAN 2 G4

◎◎ Modern European

Elegant dining room with confident cooking

☎ 020 7616 8000
55-57 Marylebone High St W1U 5RB
e-mail: oliviere@conran-restaurants.co.uk
dir: Nearest station: Baker St, Regent's Park. At north end of Marylebone High St

The Orrery is a long, galley-like room perched in a first-floor room above the Marylebone High Street branch of the Conran Shop, opposite the church gardens. Clothed tables and a relatively formal service approach give it a confident, thoroughbred feel, while the French-accented cooking has broad appeal. Start, perhaps, with peppered foie gras parfait with Madeira jelly and pain Poilâne, before coasting on to roasted sea bass, its skin crisped to golden, anointed sparingly with a champagne velouté and accompanied by earthy celeriac purée. To finish, a majestically risen blackberry soufflé, served with a matching sauce and a scoop of sour cream sorbet, does the trick.

Times 12-2.30/6.30-10.30

Ozer PLAN 3 A3

◎ Turkish, Middle Eastern

Authentic Turkish cuisine in the West End

☎ 020 7323 0505
5 Langham Place, Regent St W1B 3DG
e-mail: info@sofra.co.uk
dir: Nearest station: Oxford Circus. 2 min walk towards Upper Regent Street

Around the corner from the BBC and just up from Oxford Circus, Ozer has a steady stream of custom and a meal is usually a vibrant, frenetic, high decibel experience. This upmarket relation to the Sofra group has a pavement terrace and bustling bar upfront, and opens up at the back to reveal an expansive contemporary restaurant. Strikingly red walls combine with floaty white drapes and eye-catching lighting, while colour-coordinated leather seating and white linen provide the comforts. The menu is as big and confident as the room, listing a wide range of no-fuss, affordable traditional Turkish food with a few surprises along the way. Hot and cold meze (mujver, tabbouleh, duck roll, and kisir among them) are followed by main courses such as lamb fillet seasoned with oregano, sea bass wrapped in vine leaves, or venison tagine.

Times Noon-mdnt

Park Plaza Sherlock Holmes PLAN 2 F4

◎ Modern French **NEW**

Smart boutique-style hotel and contemporary grill

☎ 020 7486 6161
108 Baker St W1U 6LJ
e-mail: info@sherlockholmeshotel.com
dir: Nearest station: Baker Street. On Baker St, close to tube station (10 mins from Wembley by underground)

Where else could this modern hotel be located but Baker Street? A discreet entrance leads into the boutique-style hotel, where Sherlock's Grill, an intimate space with smart leather seating and white-clothed tables, brings forth a bit of culinary theatre as the chefs toil over the grills in the open-plan kitchen. The well-balanced menu focuses on grills and makes good use of the wood-burning oven. From the latter may come chicken marinated in thyme and garlic, with a classic rib-eye steak, served with chunky chips and pepper sauce, a firm favourite from the grill. Start with plump, juicy scallops with cauliflower purée and pancetta and finish with a delicious apple tarte Tatin.

Times 12-2.30/6-10.30 Closed D Sun

Patterson's PLAN 3 A2

◎◎ Modern European

Fine dining in family-run Mayfair restaurant

☎ 020 7499 1308
4 Mill St, Mayfair W1S 2AX
e-mail: info@pattersonsrestaurant.co.uk
dir: Nearest station: Oxford Circus. Located off Conduit St opposite Savile Row entrance

Since opening in 2003, this gem of a Mayfair restaurant has been run by the Patterson family with an immaculate combination of personable charm and top-level professionalism without a hint of hushed reverence. The understated elegant décor suits the swanky neighbourhood - oak flooring, chocolate leather chairs and matching banquettes with vibrant artwork and fish tanks to inject colour - and Maria Patterson works this arena in a relaxed way that lends it a neighbourhood buzz. A native of the fishing port of Eyemouth, Raymond Patterson has a life-long respect for top-flight produce, while a thorough grounding in the French classics has given him the razor-sharp technical skills and confidence to pull off inventive modern European dishes, with a flag-waving loyalty to fish and seafood sourced from Scotland. Fresh water crayfish might be sautéed and delivered with chicken wings and ceps, parmesan gnocchi and truffle butter in a well-conceived opener, followed by a dish steeped in the warmth of the Med: red mullet with squid ragoût, salt-cod brandade and bouillabaisse jus. Desserts are equally refined creations - perhaps chocolate fondant with liquid caramel, fleur de sel, milk sorbet and puffed rice.

Times 12-3/6-11 Closed 25-26 Dec, 1 Jan, Good Fri & Etr Mon, Sun, L Sat

LONDON W1 ***continued***

La Petite Maison
PLAN 2 H2

@@ French, Mediterranean NOTABLE WINE LIST

A touch of the Côte d'Azur in Mayfair

☎ 020 7495 4774
54 Brooks Mews W1K 4EG
e-mail: info@lpmlondon.co.uk
dir: Nearest station: Bond St

This London version of the namesake Niçoise restaurant - hangout of the international glitterati who roll up for its Mediterranean cuisine from Nice and Liguria - is ensconced in a quiet Mayfair mews behind Claridge's and shares a similar raison d'être. The light, diamond-shaped open-plan room has a breezily Mediterranean classy-casual vibe, and a jet-set Riviera-cool look with creamy walls, huge, discreetly-frosted windows, an open kitchen and slick service. The cooking's light, modern touch keeps things simple and fresh using top-notch ingredients in a procession of skilfully delivered dishes designed for sharing. There's salad of French beans and foie gras or home-made pasta with squid, prawns and chorizo, plus larger dishes like grilled lamb cutlets served with smoked aubergine. Be prepared for some Côte d'Azur-meets-Mayfair price tags.

Chef Raphael Duntoye **Owner** Raphael Duntoye, Arjun Waney **Times** 12-3/6-11 Closed 25-26 Dec **Prices** Food prices not confirmed for 2011. Please telephone for details **Wines** 150 bottles over £20, 16 by glass **Notes** Sunday L, Vegetarian available **Seats** 85 **Parking** On street

Pied à Terre
PLAN 3 B3

@@@@ – *see opposite page*

Plum Valley
PLAN 3 B2

@ Chinese **NEW**

Contemporary Chinatown trendsetter

☎ 020 7494 4366
20 Gerrard St W1D 6JQ
dir: Nearest station: Leicester Square

With its smart, contemporary appearance, Plum Valley certainly stands out from the crowd in bustling Chinatown. The multi-floored restaurant is stylishly decorated in darkwoods and slate, with modern furniture and subtle lighting helping to create an atmosphere of sophistication, but at the same time, fun. Staff are friendly and welcoming, and the place is a magnet for London's young Chinese population. Traditional Cantonese dishes - mostly served in authentic cooking pots - are given a modern makeover, with much use of organic produce. Expect excellent soft-shell crab with curry leaf and chilli, a selection of (well-made) dim sum, salt chilli ribs, and roasted chicken with satay sauce.

Times noon-mdnt

Polpo
PLAN 3 B2

@@ Italian **NEW V**

Busy Venetian 'bacaro' serving tapas-style 'chichetti'

☎ 020 7734 4479
41 Beak St W1F 9SB
e-mail: polporestaurant@optonline.net
dir: Nearest station: Piccadilly Circus

A fizzing little place in the heart of Soho, Polpo deals in Italian-style tapas called cichetti. The place takes its inspiration from the 'bacaros' of Venice - casual pubs where you drop in to meet friends, gobble down a few small plates of food and have a couple of drinks. Canaletto, the great painter of Venetian canal scenes once lived in this building, but there's nothing reverential in Polpo's style, which is rather metropolitan and pared-back, all bare-brick walls and bare blond-wood tables crammed in elbow-to-elbow. It's relaxed, unpretentious and noisy, and you can't book ahead but that's all part of the fun and funky vibe that makes Polpo a great place to hang out. The best way to go about the food is to order four or five dishes to share - it's all authentic, full-flavoured stuff, such as arancini rice cakes with mozzarella and courgette, salt-cod on grilled polenta, cured ham and split pea risotto, and some of the lightest fritto misto you're likely to find.

Chef Tom Oldroyd **Owner** Russell Norman, Richard Beatty **Times** 12-3/5.30-11 Closed 25 Dec-2 Jan, D Sun **Prices** Food prices not confirmed for 2011. Please telephone for details, Service added but optional 12.5% **Wines** 18 bottles over £20, 6 bottles under £20, 15 by glass **Notes** Small plate menu £1-£6.90, Sunday L, Vegetarian menu, Air con **Seats** 60, Pr/dining room 26 **Children** Portions

The Providores and Tapa Room
PLAN 2 G3

@@ International NOTABLE WINE LIST

Fashionable Marylebone venue delivering high-excitement fusion food

☎ 020 7935 6175
109 Marylebone High St W1U 4RX
e-mail: anyone@theprovidores.co.uk
dir: Nearest station: Bond St, Baker St, Regent's Park. From Bond St underground station cross Oxford St, down James St, into Thayer St then Marylebone High St

Here is a good location for a crash-course in fusion food, southern-hemisphere style. New Zealander Peter Gordon was one of the first to bring this vivid, hectically inventive cooking to London, and it's offered here on two floors - a café-like ground-floor room, and an only slightly more formal dining room upstairs. Rose-coloured lights lend softness to what might otherwise be a stark interior, but all the excitement is in the little dishes that turn up. Allow plenty of time to read through the menu descriptions, and you'll be rewarded by the freshness and intensity of compositions like tamarind, green peppercorn and coconut laksa, chicken and hijiki seaweed dumpling, green tea noodles and crispy coriandered shallots. Presentations might look a little rough-and-ready, but are convincing enough where it counts, on the palate. Somewhere underneath a pile of walnut crostini, pickled girolles, ginger-roasted grapes and pomegranate juice is a slice of velvet-smooth foie gras mousse - worth waiting for.

Chef Peter Gordon **Owner** P Gordon, M McGrath **Times** 12-2.30/6-10.30 Closed 24 Dec-3 Jan, Etr Mon **Prices** Starter £7.80-£13.20, Main £18-£26, Dessert £9.20-£9.80, Service added but optional 12.5% **Wines** 81 bottles over £20, 1 bottle under £20, 23 by glass **Notes** Tasting menu available 6 nights a week, Sunday L, Vegetarian available **Seats** 38 **Children** Portions

Quo Vadis
PLAN 3 B2

@@ Grill

Brasserie cooking in an old Soho stager

☎ 020 7437 9585
26-29 Dean St W1D 3LL
e-mail: info@quovadissoho.co.uk
dir: Nearest station: Tottenham Court Road, Leicester Square

It's hard to miss as you sashay up Dean Street, with its striped awnings and broad frontage. Older readers will have noticed that Quo Vadis has been here since the 1920s, but it was refurbished in 2008 by the partnership that owns Fino and Barrafina (see entries). Works by modern British artists add interest to the cream interiors, where back-to-back banquette seating divides up the space. The stained-glass windows are another treat, as is the brasserie-style cooking. From nibbly items like seasonal peas in the pod, or radishes with butter, you progress to globe artichoke vinaigrette, or a classic pasta dish such as crab linguine, before setting about the likes of grilled steak or rabbit pie. The pleasingly wide pudding selection includes nostalgic offerings such as Eton mess and rum baba.

Times 12-2.30/5.30-11 Closed 24-25 Dec, 1 Jan, BHs, Sun

Rasa Samudra
PLAN 3 B3

@ Indian

☎ 020 7637 0222
5 Charlotte St W1T 1RE
e-mail: dasrasa@hotmail.com
dir: Nearest station: Tottenham Court Road, Goodge Street

Rasa's flagship Charlotte Street branch is hard to miss with its signature shocking pink frontage. Inside is a warren of little rooms done out with exotic art, bright silks and wooden artefacts from the Sub-continent to put you in the right frame of mind for the kitchen's repertoire of authentic spice-rich Keralan cuisine. If you're not au fait with the style, relaxed staff will guide you through the lengthy menu. Kick off with an array of crispy, poppadom-type snacks with freshly-made pickles and chutneys. At Rasa Samudra, seafood sits alongside the vegetarian dishes that are its stock in trade. This is a world away

continued on page 298

Pied à Terre

LONDON W1 PLAN 3 B3

Modern French V NOTABLE WINE LIST

Beautifully refined, intelligent modern cooking in Fitzrovia

☎ 020 7636 1178 & 7419 9788
34 Charlotte St W1T 2NH
e-mail: info@pied-a-terre.co.uk
dir: Nearest station: Goodge Street. S of BT Tower and Goodge St

Between you and me, Pied à Terre has a lunch menu that is currently £24.50 per person. You get a choice of two starters (perhaps roasted saddle of rabbit with glazed carrot, rabbit livers, carrot and tarragon emulsion and liquorice powder), two main courses (poached and crumbed gilt head bream with cauliflower purée, caper and parsley coulis and red wine sauce maybe) and for a few quid more a choice of either cheese or dessert. Oh…and canapés to kick things off…for £24.50. It costs £23.95 for an Angus T-bone steak at the Aberdeen Angus Steak House. Enough said. David Moore and Shane Osborn's enduring professional association has proved something of a triumph - the combination of Shane's confident, intelligent cooking and David's abilities front-of-house and beyond has resulted in Pied à Terre sitting right at the top the London fine-dining firmament. The glass-fronted exterior of the restaurant is understated, easy to miss if you're not in the know, and if you are not in the know, you should be. Once across the threshold, the charming and professional greeting done with, take in the natural tones and colours, architectural glass, suede and rosewood furniture, and all round tasteful appearance of the place. It stretches over three floors these days, which consist of two downstairs dining areas, a bar on the first floor and private dining room up top. The service under David's guidance is as you would hope it to be - seemingly psychic. Shane, who hails from down under, cooks in the modern French vein, his dishes refined and classically inspired, but always delivering exciting flavour combinations and contemporary ideas without ever losing their way. There's a tasting menu, with a wine flight if you wish, and a carte packed with first-rate ingredients. Start with a wonderfully creative first course of native Colchester oysters with pickled black radish, samphire, nori jelly, pennywort and toasted Ryvita; next up, perhaps a main course with more Francophile leanings such as roasted breast of Anjou pigeon with the confit leg stuffed with foie gras and presented with braised turnip and a pain d'épice crumb. Desserts are no less thrilling; perhaps a warm carrot and pecan cake with Agen prunes, mandarin gel and Earl Grey ice cream. This is cooking of extraordinary ability, control and impact. The wine list is no weak link and does great justice to the food.

Chef Shane Osborn **Owner** David Moore & Shane Osborn **Times** 12-2.45/6.15-11 Closed 2 wks Xmas & New Year, Sun, L Sat **Prices** Fixed L 2 course £24.50-£57.50, Fixed D 3 course £71.50, Tasting menu £87, Service added but optional 12.5% **Wines** 620 bottles over £20, 11 bottles under £20, 15 by glass **Notes** Tasting menu 10 course, Pre/post theatre D 2 course £39.50, Vegetarian menu **Seats** 40, Pr/dining room 12 **Parking** Cleveland St

LONDON W1 ***continued***

from chicken tikka masala: you could delve into a seafood soup made with prawns, crab and squid, then move onto konju manga curry (king prawns cooked with turmeric, chillies, green mango and coconut), or kappayum meenum (kingfish in a sauce of onion, chillies, turmeric and ginger - served with cassava steamed in turmeric water. Make sure to order Malabar paratha (layered bread cooked on the griddle) to mop up the sauce - and finish with pal payasam, a Keralan take on rice pudding cooked with cardamom, cashew nuts and raisins.

Times 12-3/6-11 Closed 2 wks Dec, L Sun

The Red Fort PLAN 3 B2

◎◎ Indian V

Stylish contemporary Soho Indian

☎ 020 7437 2525 & 7437 2115
77 Dean St W1D 3SH
e-mail: info@redfort.co.uk
dir: Nearest station: Leicester Square. Walk N on Charing Cross Rd. At Cambridge Circus left into Shaftesbury Ave. Dean St 2nd right

This innovative Soho venue was in the vanguard of new-wave Indian cuisine back in the '80s, and is still in the business of pushing the boundaries and popping preconceptions about Sub-continental cuisine. After its neighbour went up in smoke in July 2009, the Red Fort got a top-to-toe refurb, so the interior looks the part; tastefully plush, with nods to Mughal art dovetailing with the cooking. The fashionably open kitchen deals in luxuriant 'Mughal court cooking' from Lucknow and Hyderabad, roping in prime British produce as a sound basis for dishes such as Scottish lobster chargrilled with saffron, garlic, cinnamon and nutmeg, or Herdwick lamb hit with an arsenal of exotic spices. Prices are - predictably, given the standard of cooking - a long way north of your average Indian.

Chef M A Rahman **Owner** Amin Ali
Times 12-2.30/5.30-11.30 Closed 25 Dec, L Sat-Sun
Prices Fixed L 2 course £12, Fixed D 3 course £40-£50, Starter £6-£10, Main £15-£36, Dessert £6-£12, Service added but optional 13% **Wines** 90 bottles over £20, 10 by glass **Notes** Pre-theatre 3 course meal £16, Vegetarian menu, Dress restrictions, Smart casual **Seats** 84

Rhodes W1 Brasserie and Bar PLAN 2 F2

◎ Modern British

Accomplished British cooking in lively modern brasserie

☎ 020 7616 5930
The Cumberland Hotel, Great Cumberland Place W1H 7DL
e-mail: brasserie@rhodesw1.com
dir: Nearest station: Paddington, Marble Arch

First: make sure you have the right venue - there are two Rhodes operations in the Cumberland Hotel, and we're dealing here with the entry-level brasserie, where feel good food is served in a lively setting of big brash colours and slick contemporary glamour, rather than the full-on fine-dining schtick in the Rhodes W1 Restaurant (see entry). Gary Rhodes's back-to-British-basics approach sticks to tried-and-tested territory - well-judged reworkings of crowd-pleasing brasserie classics. Truffled macaroni cheese with chestnut mushrooms shows the style, followed by grilled lemon sole with capers, shallots and lemon beurre noisette, or a hit of Gallic savoir-faire in an authentic coq au vin, served with creamy mash. Finish with true-Brit comfort food: spotted dick with caramel golden syrup and vanilla custard.

Chef Gary Rhodes, Darrel Wilde **Owner** Gary Rhodes **Times** 12-2.15/6-10.15 **Prices** Food prices not confirmed for 2011. Please telephone for details **Wines** 38 bottles over £20, 2 bottles under £20, 12 by glass **Notes** Sunday L, Vegetarian available **Seats** 150, Pr/dining room 30 **Children** Portions **Parking** NCP at Marble Arch

Rhodes W1 Restaurant PLAN 2 F2

◎◎◎ *– see opposite page*

Ristorante Semplice PLAN 2 H2

◎◎ Italian

Classy Italian with a passion for authenticity

☎ 020 7495 1509
10 Blenheim St W1S 1LJ
e-mail: info@ristorantesemplice.com
dir: Nearest station: Bond Street

Highly polished ebony walls with gold carvings, leather seating in brown and cream, blond-wood floors and linen-clad tables, set the classy, upbeat tone at this intimate Mayfair eatery. 'Semplice' means 'simple' in Italian and that's certainly the kitchen's ethos and exceptional ingredients form the foundation of the modern Italian menu, either garnered from the best British producers, or flown in from home (mozzarella arrives daily) - all are treated with due respect. An appealing variety of regional Italian dishes are delivered with assured self confidence and emphasis on flavour. Free-range Italian meat also wows, perhaps Italian rabbit with artichoke sauce, or roast squab pigeon with cheese fondue and sautéed Swiss chard, while fish options might see monkfish with Savoy cabbage and a balsamic and foie gras broth. Service is slick, well led and as Italian as the well-chosen wine list.

Times 12-2.30/7-10.30 Closed BHs, Sun

The Ritz London Restaurant PLAN 5 A6

◎◎ British NOTABLE WINE LIST

Luxurious five-star dining room with modernised menus

☎ 020 7493 8181 & 7300 2370
150 Piccadilly W1J 9BR
e-mail: enquire@theritzlondon.com
dir: Nearest station: Green Park. 10-minute walk from Piccadilly Circus or Hyde Park Corner

Be it ever so humble (and it ain't), there's no place like the Ritz. This is where the presiding genius of French haute cuisine, Auguste Escoffier, once cut his teeth, and even today, the sense of grandeur is a compelling asset. The huge dining room, with its chandeliers, its gilt statue of Poseidon and the swagged drapes at tall windows looking out over Green Park, is one of London's most beautiful gastronomic rooms, worth at least a summer lunch of anybody's money. John Williams has brought the menus into the 21st century with a gentle, reassuring touch, not forsaking the richness and splendour that grand hotel dining still mandate. There may now be sea bass with yuzu, but there's still a cheese trolley too. Start with native lobster with carrot purée in spiced coconut broth, then cannon and glazed rib of lamb with curried sweetbread and aubergine pain perdu, with quince soufflé and clove ice cream to finish.

Chef John T Williams MBE **Owner** The Ritz Hotel (London) Ltd **Times** 12.30-2.30/5.30-10 **Prices** Fixed L 3 course £39, Fixed D 3 course £48, Starter £17-£28, Main £30-£49, Dessert £14-£34, Service included **Wines** 400+ bottles over £20, 12 by glass **Notes** Pre-theatre D 3 course £47, Sunday L, Vegetarian available, Dress restrictions, Jacket & tie requested, No jeans or trainers, Civ Wed 60 **Seats** 90, Pr/dining room 14
Children Portions, Menu **Parking** NCP on Arlington Street

Roka PLAN 3 B3

◎◎◎ *– see page 300*

Salt Yard PLAN 3 B4

◎◎ Italian, Spanish

Top-notch tapas just off Tottenham Court Road

☎ 020 7637 0657
54 Goodge St W1T 4NA
e-mail: info@saltyard.co.uk
dir: Nearest station: Goodge St. Just off Tottenham Court Rd

A classy Fitzrovia tapas bar with an appealingly casual vibe and delightful staff who do their bit to keep it in fun and friendly mode. Great tapas is all about great ingredients and they are here in abundance; what's more, tapas Salt Yard-style is not quite as the Spanish would know it: this is tapas reworked with an earthy fusion of Italian, Spanish and English ingredients and ideas, so line-caught tuna carpaccio comes with baby broad beans and salsa verde, while braised oxtail is paired with tomato gnocchi and bone marrow; elsewhere, Umbrian lentils and Speck ham add depth and texture to roasted tiger prawns. Wine is a vital part of the tapas experience, and some interesting Italian and Spanish bottles, and splendid sherries by the glass, ensure that the choice does not disappoint.

Chef Benjamin Tish **Owner** Sanja Morris & Simon Mullins **Times** 12-3/6-11 Closed BHs, 25 Dec, 1 Jan, Sun, L Sat **Prices** Starter £3.75-£13, Main £4-£12, Dessert £4.75-£8.65, Service added but optional 12.5% **Wines** 50 bottles over £20, 6 bottles under £20, 15 by glass **Notes** Vegetarian available **Seats** 60 **Parking** NCP Cleveland St, meter parking Goodge Place

Rhodes W1 Restaurant

LONDON W1 PLAN 2 F2

Modern European NOTABLE WINE LIST

Glamour, glitz and fine dining at the Cumberland Hotel

☎ 020 7616 5930
The Cumberland Hotel, Great Cumberland Place W1H 7DL
e-mail: restaurant@rhodesw1.com
web: www.rhodesw1.com
dir: Nearest station: Paddington, Marble Arch

Gary Rhodes' culinary flagship in the Cumberland Hotel at Marble Arch is a real showstopper. A stylish high-rolling affair, it makes quite a style statement; think two-dozen dripping Swarovski chandeliers, ornate mirrors, antique French chairs and rich velvet fabrics in tones of purple, black and taupe. This Kelly Hoppen design offers another individual twist, too, courtesy of the bar seating, where Rhodes' recipes - in his own handwriting - are printed on the fabric. The cooking style delivers equal sparkle; modern, like the décor, British, smartly engineered and underpinned by classical French influence and top-notch produce. Soft duck egg served with chestnut mushrooms, watercress velouté and Roquefort and truffle 'soldiers' is a classy opener, while a saddle of venison teamed with spiced parsnip, pommes Anna, chestnuts, pancetta and a grand veneur jus makes a confidently flavoured main course. The sweet of tooth will find desserts impossible to pass up; perhaps warm ginger parkin with poached rhubarb, vanilla and hot-spiced syrup. The hotel also plays host to the more informal Rhodes W1 Brasserie (see entry).

Chef Gary Rhodes, Paul Welburn
Owner Gary Rhodes
Times 12-2.30/7-10.30 Closed 1st 2wks Aug, Sun-Mon, L Sat **Prices** Food prices not confirmed for 2011. Please telephone for details **Wines** 250 bottles over £20, 13 by glass **Notes** Vegetarian available, Dress restrictions, Smart dress, no torn jeans, no trainers
Seats 46 **Parking** NCP at Marble Arch

LONDON W1 ***continued***

Sartoria PLAN 3 A2

Italian

Elegant Italian dining amid the gents' outfitters

☎ 020 7534 7000 & 7534 7030
20 Savile Row W1S 3PR
e-mail: sartoriareservations@danddlondon.com
dir: Nearest station: Oxford Circus, Green Park, Piccadilly Circus. Oxford Circus tube exit 3, left down Regent St towards Piccadilly Circus, 5th right into New Burlington St, end of street on left

Taking its name from its upscale location amid the bespoke tailoring on Savile Row, Sartoria is an elegant Italian restaurant with linen-covered tables and a classically structured menu. Imported artisan produce and a keen feeling for seasonality inform the kitchen's outlook, on menus that might proceed from warm Tomino goats' cheese with green beans and sundried tomato, through a pasta dish such as lobster linguine, to something like braised venison with fried salsify and parsnip purée for main. A cheese-based dessert such as Neapolitan ricotta tart with vanilla ice cream brings things full circle.

Times 12-3/5.30-11 Closed 25-26 Dec, Sun (open for private parties only), L Sat

Scott's Restaurant PLAN 2 G1

Seafood V

Fashionable, glamorous seafood restaurant and oyster bar in the heart of Mayfair

☎ 020 7495 7309
20 Mount St W1K 2HE
dir: Nearest station: Bond Street. Just off Grosvenor Sq, between Berkeley Sq & Park Ln

This classic fish restaurant was resurrected with great hullabaloo at the end of 2007 by the people behind The Ivy, Le Caprice and J. Sheekey (see entries). Scott's was once Ian Fleming's favourite hangout, and it takes no great leap of the imagination to see 007 sipping Bollinger Grande Année among the Bond girl lookalikes perched at the spectacular onyx-topped crustacea bar. Like many a faded beauty, the oak-panelled interior of this Mayfair institution has received a facelift: it now looks rather glam in an art-deco-meets-1960s way, with burgundy leather seating, oak floors, a marble mosaic, and specially-commissioned modern British art. Super-fresh piscine produce gets the lightest of treatments in classics such as seafood platters or grilled Dover sole, but there are trips to the Med too, as in cod fillet with Padrón peppers and chorizo. Perhaps unsurprisingly it doesn't come cheap.

Chef Dave McCarthy **Owner** Caprice Holdings Ltd **Times** 12-10.30 Closed 25-26 Dec, 1 Jan **Prices** Starter £7.50-£22.50, Main £17.50-£39.50, Dessert £6.75-£8.50, Service added but optional 12.5% **Notes** Vegetarian menu, Dress restrictions, Smart casual **Seats** 125, Pr/dining room 40 **Children** Portions **Parking** Park Ln

Shogun, Millennium Hotel Mayfair PLAN 2 G1

Japanese

Traditional Japanese food in a Mayfair hotel

☎ 020 7629 9400
Grosvenor Square W1A 3AN
dir: Nearest station: Bond Street, Green Park.

The Georgian mansion house overlooking Grosvenor Square houses some sophisticated eating options, in the forms of Avista (see entry) and the Japanese venue Shogun, which is to be found at the far end of the hotel's rear courtyard, on the corner of Adam's Row. A stone-walled cellar feel and undressed tables are the context for a series of set menus offering traditional Japanese dining, whether based on main dishes such as chicken, beef or duck teriyaki, or sashimi and tempura variations. On the main menu, small appetisers such as grilled ox tongue with lettuce give way to dobin-mushi soups served in the traditional ceramic kettle, and specialities such as pork stir-fried with ginger, and grilled eel.

Times 6-11 Closed Mon, L all week

Roka

LONDON W1 PLAN 3 B3

Japanese

Dazzling Japanese robata cookery in voguish London quarter

☎ 020 7580 6464
37 Charlotte St W1T 1RR
e-mail: info@rokarestaurant.com
dir: Nearest station: Goodge St, Tottenham Court Rd. 5 min walk from Goodge St

A worldwide operation with branches in east Asia and Scottsdale, Arizona, as well as two in London (a new branch is in Canary Wharf), Roka has none of the feeling of a soulless corporate outfit. The décor helps enormously. Natural woods represent a cheering move away from the hard-edged minimalism of other modern Japanese eateries, and the full-drop windows allow for views out on the hive of activity that is Charlotte Street. The central focus is the robatayaki charcoal grill, and its square wood counter, where you can watch the chefs doing their pyrotechnical stuff at close quarters. Fish is, naturally, exquisitely fresh, and perfectly suited to rare cooking and sashimi. The tuna is beautifully deliquescent in the mouth, served with wasabi and fine soy in the classic manner. The robata-grilled sea bream, first marinated in miso and red onion, is again texturally wonderful, its crisp skin concealing curd-like creaminess within. Skewered dishes, such as teriyaki beef and asparagus, offer light, accurate cooking and spot-on seasoning, and even the vegetable side-dishes are overflowing with intense umami savouriness (try the aubergine in mirin, ginger and soy). Other Japanese favourites, such as tempura, gyoza dumplings and sour-dressed salads, fill out the options, and you might finish with fusion desserts such as sobacha (toasted buckwheat) crème brûlée with ginger ice cream.

Chef Nicholas Watt, Hamish Brown **Owner** Rainer Becker, Arjun Waney **Times** 12-2.30/5.30-11.30 Closed 25 Dec, 1 Jan **Prices** Food prices not confirmed for 2011. Please telephone for details **Wines** 9 by glass **Notes** Vegetarian available **Seats** 90 **Children** Portions **Parking** On street, NCP in Brewers St

Sketch (The Gallery) PLAN 3 A2

⊛⊛⊛ – *see below*

Sketch (Lecture Room & Library) PLAN 3 A2

⊛⊛⊛⊛⊛ – *see page 302*

So Restaurant PLAN 3 B2

⊛⊛ Japanese

Modern Japanese with European influences

☎ 020 7292 0767 & 7292 0760
3-4 Warwick St W1B 5LS
e-mail: info@sorestaurant.com
dir: Nearest station: Piccadilly Circus. Exit Piccadilly tube station via exit 1. Turn left along Glasshouse St. Restaurant next to The Warwick

Spread over two floors, a busy café-like ground floor and a more intimate, low-lit basement room, So brings informal Japanese eating to the hinterland just off Piccadilly Circus. Laminate tables, an open-plan kitchen and a yobanyaki grill, where items are cooked over volcanic rocks imported from the slopes of Mount Fuji, make the right design noises, and the food deals in the expected likes of tempura-battered seafood, sushi and maki rolls, as well as some more European-inspired dishes, such as tuna carpaccio with tapenade, seared foie gras in teriyaki sauce with rice, and fillet steak with roasted vegetables. Grilled lamb cutlets come with the fearsome-sounding Genghis Khan sauce.

Times 12-3/5-10.30 Closed Xmas-New Year, Sun

The Square PLAN 3 A1

⊛⊛⊛⊛ – *see page 303*

Sumosan Restaurant PLAN 3 A1

⊛ Japanese

Creative modern Japanese cooking in the heart of Mayfair

☎ 020 7495 5999
26 Albemarle St, Mayfair W1S 4HY
e-mail: info@sumosan.com
dir: Nearest station: Green Park

Albemarle Street is a swanky Mayfair address by any standards, with The Ritz and the Royal Academy just around the corner. Sumosan is a suitably classy and fashionable restaurant with a basement bar and some luxurious ingredients on the modern Japanese menu. There's a pleasing minimalism to the restaurant with its neutral colour tones, highly varnished darkwood tables and subtle lighting - smart and contemporary but not overworked. The open-plan kitchen produces precisely cooked dishes with some Western influence and showing a great deal of attention to detail. There's traditional sushi and sashimi, including clam, spicy cod roe, sweet shrimp, plus an extensive menu that runs to black cod with miso, tender beef tataki, or from the teppan-yaki, foie gras with wild berries or Wagyu beef with sweet potato purée.

Times 12-3/6-11.30 Closed Xmas, New Year, BHs, L Sat-Sun

Taman Gang PLAN 2 F2

⊛ Pan Asian

Upmarket Park Lane celeb haunt with enjoyable Pan-Asian cooking

☎ 020 7518 3160
141 Park Ln W1K 7AA
e-mail: info@tamangang.com
dir: Nearest station: Marble Arch. On the corner of Marble Arch & Oxford St end Park Lane

The setting may be a take on a fairytale Balinese temple - all Buddhas, colonial mahogany furniture, lanterns and low banquettes - but the food at this trendy Pan-Asian bar and restaurant takes you further afield on a far-flung tour of South-East Asian cuisine. The kitchen's repertoire cherry picks from the cuisines of Thailand, Japan, Korea and China, hopping from tempura to sashimi and sushi and main courses such as black cod with shiro miso, or Wagyu beef with honey teriyaki. Desserts are worth a bet too - warm chocolate pudding with green tea ice cream is

continued on page 304

Sketch (The Gallery)

LONDON W1 PLAN 3 A2

Modern European V NEW

Über-fashionable brasserie with exciting modern cooking

☎ 0870 777 4488
9 Conduit St W1S 2XG
dir: Nearest station: Oxford Street

The two expansive floors of a converted 18th-century house in Mayfair contain many wonders. Check out the entry for the Lecture Room & Library, which holds the maximum five Rosettes. That's up on the first floor of this impossibly glamorous venue, the brainchild of Mourad Mazouz and French super-chef Pierre Gagnaire. The Gallery brasserie is on the ground floor, with a wildly flamboyant décor including a magnificent domed ceiling and London scenes projected onto the walls. Denim-clad staff suit the über-fashionable vibe and are as keen as mustard and more than capable of advising on the menu. The food is less complex than upstairs, but still ambitious and confidently modern. The intriguingly named starter 'Kiki 10' is, in fact, Provencal-style rabbit rillettes with carrots, baby salad leaves and garlic. A main course of roast rib-eye arrives with black pepper jus and pistachios, Bolognese sauce, cherry tomatoes and celery, while, for dessert, chocolate cake with coffee syrup and ginger tuile is an extremely well-judged confection. A brasserie it may be, cheap it ain't.

Chef Roel Lintermans **Owner** Mourad Mazouz **Times** 7-11 Closed 25 Dec, BHs (excl Good Fri), Sun, L all week **Prices** Food prices not confirmed for 2011. Please telephone for details **Notes** Vegetarian menu **Seats** 150 **Children** Menu **Parking** On street

See advert on inside back cover

Sketch (Lecture Room & Library)

LONDON W1 PLAN 3 A2

Modern European V NOTABLE WINE LIST

A unique, dynamic and exciting dining experience

☎ 020 7659 4500
9 Conduit St W1S 2XG
e-mail: info@sketch.uk.com
web: www.sketch.uk.com
dir: Nearest station: Oxford Circus. 4 mins walk from Oxford Circus tube station, take exit 3, down Regent St. Conduit St 4th on right

Nothing can really prepare you for the Sketch experience. It has to be seen with your own eyes, to be explored, but most of all, to be tasted. It is a restaurant after all, in fact more than one restaurant: the full-set of five Rosettes goes to the Lecture Room & Library, though there are plenty of other options to sate the senses over these two floors in Conduit Street. It looks ordinary enough from the street; it is quite possible to walk right on by despite the scale of the premises and its history as the former headquarters of both the RIBA and Christian Dior. Look out for the doormen and, hopefully, they'll usher you inside. That's when the fun begins. Algerian-born restaurateur Mourad Mazouz has let loose his imagination to create a venue of opulent design and absolute ambition - a 'destination place for food, art and music' as he puts it. The association with French super-chef Pierre Gagnaire has been a fruitful partnership. The fine-dining Lecture Room & Library is on the first floor, forming two parts of the same space, and artfully and ostentatiously decorated in shades of orange, with ivory walls of studded leather and ornately plastered high ceilings; thick-piled, brightly coloured carpets and long dangling lampshades give it a somewhat Middle Eastern feel. Sit on richly upholstered armchairs at well-spaced tables and let the slick and confident service team look after you (you'll certainly need their assistance to help you through the menu). The menu bears the hallmark of the creative flair of its consultant chef, delivering a range of modern French dishes (if they can be classified at all) that are visually stunning, technically brilliant and hit the mark with their remarkable flavours and textures. It is worth mentioning at this point that prices are high, so brace yourself. The complexity of dishes is evident in the reading of the menu and in what arrives on the plate: 'Mr Boon' is a first-course filled with deftly controlled textures and flavours from a squid dim sum to a split-pea soup with green curry, and a buckwheat crêpe with avocado, coriander, fennel and manchego. The produce is as good as it gets, as with a main-course 'Pollock and cod', which consists of the former roasted with lemon butter and chicory, the cod braised in a Chablis nage and as brandade wrapped in lettuce. There's a lot going on, but this is a kitchen working with a Zen-like clarity of mind. For dessert, going for Pierre Gagnaire's Grand Dessert will remove the stress of trying to make a decision - it's a combination of five miniatures. Down on the ground floor there's the Gallery brasserie (bursting with art deco style; see entry), the cool Parlour (tea room by day, hyper-trendy bar by night) and The Glade, which focuses on the healthy side of life.

Chef Pierre Gagnaire, Jean Denis Le Bras **Owner** Mourad Mazouz
Times 12-2.30/6.30-11 Closed 18-29 Aug, 23-30 Dec, 1 Jan, BHs, Sun-Mon, L Sat **Prices** Fixed L 2 course £30, Starter £23-£44, Main £32-£53, Dessert £10-£27, Service added but optional 12.5%
Wines 709 bottles over £20, 6 bottles under £20, 29 by glass **Notes** Tasting menu 8 course, Vegetarian tasting menu 7 course, Vegetarian menu, Civ Wed 50 **Seats** 50, Pr/dining room 24
Children Portions **Parking** NCP Soho, Cavendish Sq

See advert on inside back cover

The Square

LONDON W1 PLAN 3 A1

Modern French

A class culinary act in the heart of Mayfair

☎ 020 7495 7100
6-10 Bruton St, Mayfair W1J 6PU
e-mail: info@squarerestaurant.com
web: www.squarerestaurant.com
dir: Nearest station: Bond Street, Green Park

After earning his spurs in a series of stellar kitchens, Philip Howard set up in business with Nigel Platts-Martin all the way back in 1991, since when The Square's status as one of London's top tables has never been in question. This is a team that understands what top-end dining is all about, and The Square delivers the complete package. First off, location matters: well, the discreet gloss of Mayfair's streets is hard to beat, and diners are screened from the road by a frontage of frosted glass. The décor is pitched just right too - striking abstract artworks on pearlescent walls, designer mirrors and smartly dressed tables spaced widely across the high-gloss parquet floor. Punctilious service from a team of real pros completes the picture. So far so very good, but all of this would be expensive window dressing without the astonishing food. Underlying the cooking is pitch-perfect classical French technique, and an instinctive understanding of how ingredients work together to knock diners socks off without ever needing to veer into the realm of outlandish combinations. Flavours and textures are unforgettably defined in superbly presented dishes, while the seasonality and incomparable quality of ingredients can be taken as read. Fixed-price lunch menus offer great value, but as food of this quality is a rare treat, why not go for broke with the epic nine-course tasting menu? A spring dinner might start with a sauté of Scottish langoustine tails with parmesan gnocchi and an emulsion of potato and truffle, or for addicts of unctuous poultry livers, there could be roast foie gras with a tarte fine of caramelised endive and burnt orange purée. Main courses deliver the likes of thinly-sliced grilled turbot with cauliflower purée, black truffle butter and a croquette of Beaufort cheese; simple yet intriguing to the end, dessert could be a Brillat-Savarin cheesecake with passionfruit and lime. Burgundy aficionados with an indulgent bank manager will encounter a head-spinning choice on a remarkable wine list brimming with classic French heavyweights, but the rest of the world gets a look in too, and there's a fair smattering of bottles coming in under the £50 mark.

Chef Philip Howard **Owner** Mr N Platts-Martin & Philip Howard
Times 12-2.30/6.30-10.30 Closed 24-26 Dec,1 Jan, L Sat-Sun, BHs **Prices** Fixed L 2 course fr £30, Fixed D 3 course fr £75, Tasting menu £100-£155, Service added but optional 12.5% **Wines** 1400 bottles over £20, 14 by glass
Notes Vegetarian available, Dress restrictions, Smart casual, jacket & tie preferred **Seats** 75, Pr/dining room 18
Children Portions

LONDON W1 *continued*

two flavours in perfect balance. Be warned that the restaurant morphs into a nightclub at 11pm.

Chef Ricky Pang **Owner** First Restaurant Group **Times** 6-12 Closed Xmas, Mon, L all week **Prices** Fixed D 2 course £15, Starter £4-£8, Main £11-£48, Dessert £5.50-£12.50, Service added 15% **Wines** 77 bottles over £20, 11 by glass **Notes** Fixed D 2 course available 6-7.30pm, Vegetarian available, Dress restrictions, Smart casual **Seats** 120 **Parking** NCP Marble Arch & street parking

Tamarind PLAN 4 H6

Traditional Indian

Classy contemporary Mayfair Indian

☎ 020 7629 3561
20 Queen St, Mayfair W1J 5PR
e-mail: manager@tamarindrestaurant.com
web: www.tamarindrestaurant.com
dir: Nearest station: Green Park. Towards Hyde Park, take 4th right into Half Moon St to end (Curzon St). Turn left, 1st right into Queen St

A stylish Indian restaurant tucked away in a quiet Mayfair street, Tamarind's basement dining room has an intimate, contemporary feel, with well-spaced tables and formally dressed, friendly staff adding to the appeal. A stunning floral display forms a centrepiece in the room, which is decked out in golds, browns and creams, with subdued modern lighting. A window into the kitchen is slightly obscured so as to give just a hint of what's going on within. And what is going on is some classy traditional Mogul-style north-west Indian cooking. Several dishes are cooked in the tandoor oven, although there are some European influences evident, too. For an authentic experience, try the lamb Chettinaad curry - full of wonderfully tender meat in a thick, medium-spiced sauce - or there's the more Western-styled grilled scallops delicately flavoured with spices, followed by pan-fried sea bass with a lightly-spiced tomato sauce.

Tamarind

Chef Alfred Prasad **Owner** Indian Cuisine Ltd **Times** 12-2.45/5.30-11.15 Closed 25-26 Dec, 1 Jan, L Sat **Prices** Fixed L 2 course £16.50, Fixed D 3 course £25, Starter £6.95-£26, Main £16.95-£21, Dessert £5.95-£7.75, Service added but optional 12.5% **Wines** 100 bottles over £20, 4 bottles under £20, 12 by glass **Notes** Pre-theatre D £24 5.30-7pm, Sunday L, Vegetarian available, Dress restrictions, No jeans or shorts **Seats** 90 **Parking** NCP

Texture Restaurant PLAN 2 F2

– see below

Time & Space PLAN 3 A1

Modern British

Modern British cooking at a scientific landmark

☎ 020 7670 2956
21 Albemarle St W1S 4BS
e-mail: timeandspace@ri.ac.uk
dir: Nearest station: Green Park. In the Royal Institute of Great Britain building close to underground

The 200-year-old building in the heart of Mayfair houses the venerable Royal Institution, which has a thoroughly absorbing museum outlining the history of scientific experimentation in the UK. In the restaurant (once the library), original features such as the fireplaces and ceiling frieze have been offset with glass cabinets with

Texture Restaurant

LONDON W1 PLAN 2 F2

Modern European V

Superb flavours and textures from Icelandic super-chef

☎ 020 7224 0028
Best Western Mostyn Hotel, 34 Portman St W1H 7BY
e-mail: info@texture-restaurant.co.uk

A room with all the elegance of its original Georgian proportions, including ornate plasterwork and hefty windows combined with polished wooden floors, darkwood tables and caramel leather chairs. If economic crisis and volcanic disturbances have created some tensions between the UK and Iceland of late, Agnar Sverrisson's cooking is a one-man entente cordiale capable of rebuilding love even between warring nations. There is an inkling of his Icelandic heritage in the cooking, but this is modern European food of flair and originality, the promised textures delivered in abundance on the plate alongside a lightness of touch and real depth of flavour. Poached Icelandic halibut is as ethereally cooked a piece of fish as you'll find, fresh light and delicious, served with Jerusalem artichoke textures which deliver well-judged flavours and, yes, superb textural contrasts. Main-course new season lamb from Skagafjördur is of superb quality, beautifully cooked and served in a broth of deep, satisfying flavour, with root vegetables and delicious herb purée. Flavour and texture are to the fore at dessert, too: fennel and quince cake, perhaps, with a spiced ice cream and citrus syrup.

Chef Agnar Sverrisson **Owner** Xavier Rousset & Agnar Sverrisson **Times** 12-2.30/6.30-11 Closed 2 wks Xmas, 2 wks Aug, Sun **Prices** Fixed L 2 course fr £18.50, Fixed D 4 course £52.50-£59, Starter £9.50-£18.50, Main £21.50-£27.50, Dessert £8.50, Service added but optional 12.5% **Wines** 110 bottles over £20, 12 by glass **Notes** Vegetarian menu, Dress restrictions, Smart casual **Seats** 55, Pr/dining room 16 **Parking** NCP Bryanston St

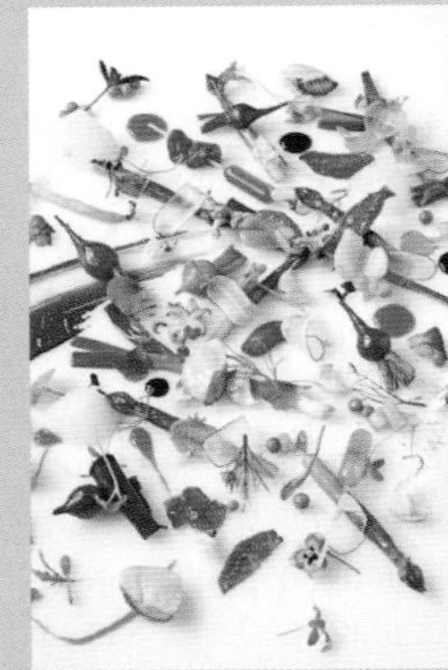

displays of scientific instruments. If you're expecting a mad-professor approach to the cooking, think again: the emphasis is on modern British dishes cooked with a certain panache. An omelette of Cornish crab seasoned with tarragon and chervil is a typical opener, with grilled steaks or whole lemon sole to follow. There are influences from further afield, to be sure, and creative energies are let off the leash when it comes to desserts such as pumpernickel summer pudding with thyme and wood sorrel ice cream.

Chef Julian Ward **Times** 12-3 Closed 24 Dec-3 Jan, Sat-Sun, D all week **Prices** Fixed L 2 course £15.95, Starter £5.50-£9.50, Main £9.95-£21, Dessert £5-£6, Service added but optional 12.5% **Wines** 33 bottles over £20, 2 bottles under £20, 12 by glass **Notes** Vegetarian available, Dress restrictions, Smart casual, Civ Wed 400 **Seats** 60, Pr/dining room 80 **Children** Portions **Parking** Berkeley Square

Trishna PLAN 2 G3

@@ Modern Indian V

Coastal Indian cuisine in Marylebone

☎ 020 7935 5624
15-17 Blandford St W1U 3DG
e-mail: info@trishnalondon.com
dir: Nearest station: Bond St, Baker St. 5th right off Baker St, 1st left at number 1 Marylebone High St

Sister restaurant to Trishna Mumbai, Trishna in Marylebone village serves up food influenced by the coastal part of south west India in a relaxed, informal atmosphere. The interior utilises smoked oak floors, brickwork and glass to create a clean and minimalist space. In the summer the doors open onto the street. A Koliwada or fisherman's table can also seat 10 and is handy for those without a booking or diners eating alone as well as groups. Head chef Ravi Deulkar, previously at Rasoi Restaurant (see entry), spent a year researching the latest coastal dishes to put on the menu along with more traditional offerings. Fish and seafood plays a starring role but there's plenty of meaty and veggie options too, all using the best of British produce. Begin with Aylesbury duck seekh kebab before seafood biryani or perhaps tandoori guinea fowl with masoor lentils. Desserts include mango rice pudding.

Chef Ravi Deulkar **Owner** Karam Sethi
Times 12-2.45/6-10.45 Closed 24-29 Dec, 1 Jan, Sun **Prices** Fixed L 2 course £14.50, Starter £5.75-£13.50, Main £13.50-£28, Dessert £6, Service added but optional 12.5% **Wines** 160 bottles over £20, 6 bottles under £20, 20 by glass **Notes** Early D 6-7pm, Post-theatre menu 2/5 course £14.50-£23.50, Vegetarian menu **Seats** 60, Pr/dining room 12 **Parking** On street/NCP

La Trouvaille PLAN 3 A2

@@ French

Modern approach to French bourgeois cooking in intimate surroundings

☎ 020 7287 8488
12a Newburgh St W1F 7RR
e-mail: contact@latrouvaille.co.uk
web: www.latrouvaille.co.uk
dir: Nearest station: Oxford Circus. Off Carnaby St by Liberty's

The name means a 'find', a spot-on description for this busy little bistro hidden among the cobbled pedestrian lanes off Carnaby Street. La Trouvaille offers a haven of French class amid the hurly-burly of Soho: its ground-floor wine bar might be first port of call for grazing with friends on tapas, charcuterie and cheeses with a glass of organic/biodynamic French wine. Upstairs lies a smart bijou restaurant with stripped pine floor, crisp white linen on the tables, and see-through Perspex chairs made for pert bottoms. Invention and well-sourced ingredients come together in intriguingly unconventional modern French dishes, as in smoked salmon and mascarpone crêpe with a cappuccino of scrambled egg and wasabi dressing. Mains might combine fillet of monkfish with a mushroom and Comté cheese risotto, parsley mousse and mango sauce.

Chef Mr Thierry Plaideau **Owner** T Bouteloup
Times 12-3/5.30-11 Closed Xmas, BHs, Sun, D Mon **Prices** Fixed L 2 course fr £17.50, Fixed D 3 course fr £35, Tasting menu £45-£70, Service added but optional 12.5% **Wines** 72 bottles over £20, 6 bottles under £20, 18 by glass **Notes** Pre-theatre 2/3 course £17.50-£21 5.30-7pm,Tasting 5 course, Vegetarian available **Seats** 45, Pr/dining room 30 **Children** Portions **Parking** NCP (off Broadwick St)

Umu PLAN 2 H2

@@@ – *see page 306*

Vanilla Restaurant & Bar PLAN 3 A4

@@ Modern European

Creative modern cooking in strikingly trendy basement

☎ 020 3008 7763
131 Great Titchfield St W1W 5BB
e-mail: info@vanillalondon.com
dir: Nearest station: Great Portland St, Oxford Circus

A few minutes from Oxford Street, tucked away in a basement restaurant, Vanilla is an über-cool lounge-bar-restaurant combo with an interior that could grace the pages of any style magazine. So, an ultra-contemporary space then, the bar a dazzling white, bathed in alternating blue and pink mood lighting, with a seriously good choice of cocktails and wines. The restaurant is a little more restrained: black leather seating, white walls and crisp linen. In tune with the setting the food is a little out of the ordinary, and the complexity of the cooking belies the simple menu descriptions. Typical of the style are foie gras and duck terrine with fig chutney; lobster tagliatelle with chilli and garlic; chocolate brownie with tonka bean ice cream and salted caramel mousse.

Chef Halim Merrir **Owner** David Alberto
Times 12-2.30/6.30-10.30 Closed BHs, 1 wk in Aug, Sun-Mon, L Sat **Prices** Fixed L 2 course fr £17.50, Fixed D 3 course £27-£37, Starter £7.50-£9.50, Main £12.50-£17.50, Dessert £7-£10, Service added but optional 12.5% **Wines** 70 bottles over £20, 8 bottles under £20, 6 by glass **Notes** Vegetarian available, Dress restrictions, Smart elegant, no sportswear/trainers **Seats** 55 **Children** Portions **Parking** NCP

Vasco & Piero's Pavilion Restaurant PLAN 3 B2

@@ Italian

Authentic Umbrian cooking in heart of Soho

☎ 020 7437 8774
15 Poland St W1F 8QE
e-mail: eat@vascosfood.com
dir: Nearest station: Oxford Circus. From Oxford Circus turn right towards Tottenham Court Rd, in 5min turn right into Poland St. Restaurant on corner of Great Marlborough St & Noel St

This stalwart of the Soho dining scene has been occupying this corner building since 1989. Authentic cooking from the Umbrian region of Italy is the name of the game and a warm welcome is pretty much guaranteed. Warm colours and subtle lighting add to the authenticity and many of the quality ingredients are imported from Italy, although sauces and, of course, pasta are home made. The handwritten menu changes after each serving; expect rustic, home-style cooking. Clear flavours leap out from dishes such as cured Tuscan ham with melon, asparagus tortellini, and main-courses such as grilled tagliata of rare sirloin beef with rosemary oil and sautéed kale, and sautéed calamari with garlic, chilli and cannellini beans. Finish with a textbook tiramisù.

Chef Vasco Matteucci **Owner** Tony Lopez, Paul Matteucci & Vasco Matteucci **Times** 12-3/5.30-11 Closed BHs, Sun, L Sat **Prices** Fixed L 2 course £15, Fixed D 2 course £19.50, Starter £5.50-£11.50, Main £12.50-£23.50, Dessert £6.50-£8.95, Service added but optional 12.5% **Wines** 40 bottles over £20, 6 bottles under £20, 4 by glass **Notes** Tasting menu if requested, Pre-theatre 2 course £19.50, Vegetarian available, Dress restrictions, No shorts **Seats** 50, Pr/dining room 36 **Children** Portions **Parking** NCP car park opposite

Umu

LONDON W1 PLAN 2 H2

Japanese NOTABLE WINE LIST

Authentic Kyoto cuisine in classy Mayfair setting

☎ 020 7499 8881
14-16 Bruton Place W1J 6LX
e-mail: reception@umurestaurant.com
dir: Nearest station: Green Park, Bond St. Off Bruton St & Berkeley Sq

Push a button to enter and like Mr Ben you're immediately transported away from the busy streets of Mayfair into another world. It's a world of top-quality authentic Japanese cooking. Staff greet in the traditionally respectful manner, but the service isn't overly formal overall. It looks pretty good: lots of darkwood - tables, banquettes, panelling - in a look put together by award winning designer Tony Chi, which includes an open kitchen so you can watch the chefs' expert knife work. The menu is extensive but staff are good at helping you pick your way through the classic and modern reworking of Kyoto dishes. A selection of kaiseki - traditional tasting menus of beautifully crafted and presented dishes influenced by Zen Buddhism - are a memorable way to proceed. Elsewhere sushi and sashimi are as fresh as you'll find anywhere in London and the range and quality of Wagyu beef is superb. Appetisers may include grilled aubergine Shigiyaki style, minced quail and sweet soy sauce, and mains perhaps monkfish tempura, veal jus and yuzu pepper. For something sweet try white miso ice cream. A decent wine list is on offer for those who don't fancy the vast array of sake.

Chef Ichiro Kubota **Owner** Marlon Abela Restaurant Corporation
Times 12-2.30/6-11 Closed between Xmas & New Year, Etr & BHs, Sun, L Sat
Prices Fixed L 3 course £25-£50, Tasting menu £65-£135, Starter £6-£20, Main £13-£57, Dessert £6-£12, Service added but optional 12.5%
Wines 834 bottles over £20, 20 by glass
Notes Kaiseki menu, Vegetarian available **Seats** 60, Pr/dining room 12
Parking NCP Hanover Hill, On street

LONDON W1 ***continued***

Veeraswamy Restaurant PLAN 3 B1

Indian

London's oldest Indian restaurant still going strong

020 7734 1401
Mezzanine Floor, Victory House, 99 Regent St W1B 4RS
e-mail: veeraswamy@realindianfood.com
dir: Nearest station: Piccadilly Circus. Entrance near junct of Swallow St & Regent St, in Victory House

For its 80th birthday in 2006, London's oldest Indian restaurant was fully restored to all its 1920s glory. The décor is rich and luxurious, designed to be evocative of the Maharajas' palaces of the '20s. Shimmering chandeliers and vibrant-coloured glass lanterns hang from the 10ft high silver-painted ceiling. Plush Moghul floral-design carpets sit on darkwood floors, along with gleaming black Indian granite speckled with gold. Classic pan-Indian dishes ride alongside more contemporary options on the pricey menu, all authentically and freshly prepared using high-quality ingredients. Try sholay chicken tikka - smoked chicken with garam masala cooked in the tandoor - or perhaps sea bream paturi, a classic Bengali dish where the fish is steamed in a banana leaf with a chilli and mustard sauce.

Times 12-2.30/5.30-11.30 Closed D Xmas

Via Condotti PLAN 3 A2

Italian

Traditional Italian cooking in moneyed Mayfair

020 7493 7050
23 Conduit St W1S 2XS
e-mail: info@viacondotti.co.uk
dir: Nearest station: Oxford Circus, Piccadilly Circus

The discreet lilac frontage is tucked in among the moneyed boutique shopping on Conduit Street (hence the name), and hides a narrow room that extends back from the street with a gentle pastel design tone and darkly upholstered seating. Sleekly presented Italian food is what it's about, dealing in tagliolini with crab, cherry tomatoes and chilli, baked fillet of red snapper with carrots, tomato and zucchini, or chicken breast Milanese-style with spinach. It's all served by immaculately attired waiting staff who know how to charm, as do the classic Italian torte, gelati and pannacotta that await at the finishing line.

Chef Giovanni Andolfi **Owner** Claudio Pulze
Times 12-3/5.45-11 Closed BHs, Sun **Prices** Fixed L 2 course £15, Fixed D 3 course £27.50, Starter £7.50-£10.50, Main £13.50-£19.50, Dessert £6-£9, Service added but optional 12.5% **Wines** 70 bottles over £20, 8 bottles under £20, 15 by glass **Notes** Vegetarian available **Seats** 90, Pr/dining room 18 **Children** Portions

Villandry PLAN 3 A4

French, European

Upbeat restaurant, café, bar and foodstore rolled into one

020 7631 3131
170 Great Portland St W1W 5QB
e-mail: contactus@villandry.com
dir: Nearest station: Great Portland Street, Oxford Circus. Entrance at 91 Bolsover St, between Great Portland St tube station & Oxford Circus

There's plenty going on at Villandry, whatever the time of day. The buzzy bar, café, restaurant and deli prizes the quality of its ingredients, while entering the restaurant through the foodstore is like an appetiser in itself. The glass-fronted dining room (also with rear access off Bolsover Street) is a light modern space, decked out in neutral tones with white-clothed tables and a mix of modern and country-style seating. The kitchen's crowd-pleasing brasserie-style repertoire takes an equally restrained, uncomplicated approach, with inspiration from French classics - coq au vin Bordelaise - to more modern thinking - seared black bream with sautéed potatoes, roasted tomato and olives.

Times 12-3/6-10.30 Closed 25 Dec, D Sun & BHs

Wild Honey PLAN 3 A2

– see below

Wild Honey

LONDON W1 PLAN 3 A2

Modern European

Refined and intelligently straightforward food in Mayfair

020 7758 9160
12 Saint George St W1S 2FB
e-mail: info@wildhoneyrestaurant.co.uk
dir: Nearest station: Oxford Circus, Bond St

This sister restaurant to Soho's Arbutus may well be in Mayfair, but it has no airs and graces, no pretentions. The winning formula of a French-style bistrot deluxe has been transported to this smarter part of town with the philosophy of reasonable prices intact, and delivering the same brand of highly appealing cooking, where luxury ingredients rub shoulders with more humble cuts of meat on a menu of flavour-packed dishes. Wines are available in 250ml carafes to add to the Gallic vibe, while service fits the bill (professional, of course, but not too stuffy with it). The premises was once a club and today's wood-panelled walls, intimate booths and banquettes would not have looked out of place back in the day. But there's a touch of modernity, too, with contemporary artworks, big lightshades and an onyx-topped front bar (grab a stool for bar dining). Daily-changing menus are full of appealing combinations and technique is as sharp as a knife; kick off with warm smoked eel with boneless chicken wings, a lusciously smooth sweetcorn purée and sour turnips, moving onto grilled salmon trout, elegantly presented with creamed cabbage and sautéed wild mushrooms. Wild honey ice cream with crushed honeycomb is an obvious choice at dessert, and there are excellent cheeses from La Fromagerie, too. A reasonably-priced fixed-price lunch menu is a daytime draw.

Chef Anthony Demetre **Owner** Anthony Demetre & Will Smith **Times** 12-2.30/6-11 Closed 25-26 Dec, 1 Jan **Prices** Fixed L 3 course £18.95, Starter £6.95-£11.95, Main £14.50-£22.50, Dessert fr £6.95, Service added but optional 12.5% **Wines** 40 bottles over £20, 10 bottles under £20, 50 by glass **Notes** Pre-theatre D £21.95 6-7pm, Sunday L, Vegetarian available **Seats** 65 **Children** Portions **Parking** On street

LONDON W1 *continued*

The Wolseley

PLAN 5 A6

European V

Bustling landmark brasserie offering stylish all-day dining

☎ 020 7499 6996
160 Piccadilly W1J 9EB
e-mail: reservations@thewolseley.com
dir: Nearest station: Green Park. 500mtrs from Green Park underground station

Along the same glitzy strip of Piccadilly as The Ritz, the art-deco glamour of The Wolseley offers an alternative riff on the grand tradition of the European café-restaurant. The buzz in this all-day venue never falters, all the way from morning porridge to post-dinner petits fours. Given that up to a thousand diners a day pass through, it's no surprise that there are hits and misses in cooking and service, but it remains a magnet for those who come to bask in the period splendour of it all. Battalions of slickly-orchestrated staff whisk crowd-pleasing brasserie staples from dumb waiters to tables; expect timeless dishes - oysters, steak tartare, or escargots à la bourguignonne to start, then Wiener schnitzels, roast Landaise chicken with Lyonnaise potatoes, or grilled halibut with béarnaise sauce to follow. Desserts such as apple strudel end with nursery comfort.

Chef Julian O'Neill **Owner** Chris Corbin & Jeremy King **Times** 7am-mdnt Closed 25 Dec, Aug BH, D 24 Dec, 31 Dec **Prices** Starter £6.50-£22.50, Main £10.75-£28.75, Dessert £5.50-£7.50, Service added but optional 12.5% **Wines** 58 bottles over £20, 3 bottles under £20, 32 by glass **Notes** Sunday L, Vegetarian menu **Seats** 150 **Children** Portions

Yauatcha

PLAN 3 B2

Chinese

Top-rate dim sum in seductive basement

☎ 020 7494 8888
15 Broadwick St W1F 0DL
e-mail: reservations@yauatcha.com
dir: Nearest station: Tottenham Ct Rd, Piccadilly, Oxford Circus. On corner of Broadwick St & Berwick St, Soho

Pulling in the crowds with its sexy interior and up-tempo buzz, the dim sum is still the star of the show at this super-cool all-day Soho hotspot. Behind the modern, blue-tinted glass frontage at street level there's a tea-house feel, while in the basement, it's a high-octane club-like space, seductively-lit with tightly packed tables, low-level seating, slender fish tanks, exposed brick and a glass-fronted kitchen. Dim sum is the thing and it's just about the best in town. The lengthy menu blends traditional Cantonese favourites alongside more esoteric pairings delivered dressed to thrill. Take scallop shu mai (open-top dumplings) or venison puffs, to larger plates like halibut with lotus root and pickled cabbage or stir-fry rib-eye beef in black bean sauce. Service zips along, while cocktails, numerous varieties of tea and stylish pastries and desserts are also worth exploring.

Chef Lee Che Liang **Owner** Hakkasan Limited **Times** Noon-11.30 Closed 24-25 Dec **Prices** Fixed L 3 course £40-£60, Fixed D 3 course £40-£60, Starter £3.50-£18, Main £11.50-£49, Dessert £7.50-£13.50, Service added but optional 12.5% **Wines** 107 bottles over £20, 10 by glass **Notes** Vegetarian available, Dress restrictions, Smart casual **Seats** 210 **Parking** Poland Street - 100 yds

YMing

PLAN 3 C2

Chinese V

Chinese regional specialities in theatreland

☎ 020 7734 2721
35-36 Greek St W1D 5DL
e-mail: cyming2000@blueyonder.co.uk
dir: Nearest station: Piccadilly Circus. From Piccadilly Circus tube station, head towards the Palace Theatre along Shaftesbury Avenue

Pronounced 'why ming', this classy Chinese keeps the frenetic bustle of Chinatown's heartlands at arms length from its location on the other side of Shaftesbury Avenue. After 20 years in business, the place has many fans, attracted by reliable cooking and service that lends a polite hand in steering diners through a biblical carte. The kitchen's repertoire is something of a Cook's tour of China, although its heart lies in the north. Big bold flavours are assured by traditional cooking techniques, while modern sensibilities are appeased by using lean, healthy ingredients and light oils. 'Firey' lean lamb with fresh hot chillis and lemongrass comes recommended, or try 'Village duck', cooked in the regional Hakka style with black mushrooms and lily flower.

Chef Aaron Wong **Owner** Christine Yau **Times** Noon-11.45 Closed 25-26 Dec, 1 Jan, Sun (ex Chinese New Year) **Prices** Food prices not confirmed for 2011. Please telephone for details **Wines** 15 bottles over £20, 19 bottles under £20, 7 by glass **Notes** Vegetarian menu, Dress restrictions, Clean and presentable **Seats** 60, Pr/dining room 25 **Parking** Chinatown car park

LONDON W2

Angelus Restaurant

PLAN 2 D2

Modern French NOTABLE WINE LIST

Chic French brasserie modernising the classics

☎ 020 7402 0083
4 Bathurst St W2 2SD
e-mail: info@angelusrestaurant.co.uk
dir: Nearest station: Lancaster Gate, Paddington Station. Opposite Royal Lancaster Hotel

Owner Thierry Tomasin, former head sommelier at Mayfair's Le Gavroche, has pulled out all the stops in this charming neighbourhood brasserie close to Hyde Park stables. With a true Parisian feel to it, the intimate 19th-century interior boasts period details such as stained glass and darkwood fittings combined with art-deco touches. Under ex-Savoy chef Martin Nisbet, French techniques are combined with the best of seasonal British ingredients in rustic dishes that deliver on flavour. After a signature starter of foie gras 'Angelus', caramelised almonds and toasted bread, go for roast rump of Cornish lamb with wild garlic pesto, white beans and Niçoise vegetables. Service is as polished as you'd expect under Tomasin, who proves himself a lively and enthusiastic host.

Chef Martin Nisbet **Owner** Thierry Tomasin **Times** 12-11 Closed 23 Dec-4 Jan **Prices** Food prices not confirmed for 2011. Please telephone for details **Wines** 800 bottles over £20, 11 bottles under £20, 4 by glass **Notes** Vegetarian available **Seats** 40, Pr/dining room 20 **Children** Portions

Assaggi

PLAN 2 A2

Italian

An Italian gem in Notting Hill

☎ 020 7792 5501
39 Chepstow Place W2 4TS
e-mail: nipi@assaggi.demon.co.uk
dir: Nearest station: Notting Hill Gate

On the first floor of a Georgian terraced building (downstairs is a pub), Assaggi provides a welcome burst of Italian sunshine in Notting Hill. From the Mediterranean colours, dozen well-spaced wooden tables and light-filled interior to the warmly welcoming staff on hand to, somewhat theatrically, translate the menu, this gem of a restaurant hits all the right notes. The to-the-point menu showcases honest Italian food, with a focus on Sardinia. Dig into gamberoni con carciofi (prawns cooked with artichokes) before a simple gnocchi al ragù di cinghiale (gnocchi with wild boar ragu) followed by the pesce del giorno (fish of the day). The all-Italian wine list is a cracker.

Chef Nino Sassu **Owner** Nino Sassu, Pietro Fraccari **Times** 12.30-2.30/7.30-11 Closed 2 wks Xmas, BHs, Sun **Prices** Starter £12.90-£16.90, Main £18.90-£26.90, Dessert £8, Service optional **Wines** All bottles over £20, 7 by glass **Notes** Vegetarian available **Seats** 35 **Children** Portions

Le Café Anglais

PLAN 2 B2

French

Art-deco beauty serving modern brasserie food

☎ 020 7221 1415
8 Porchester Gardens W2 4DB
e-mail: info@lecafeanglais.co.uk
dir: Nearest station: Bayswater, Queensway

Rowley Leigh's Bayswater restaurant may be on the first floor of Whiteley's shopping centre, but it does at least have a separate entrance. Once inside, the art deco magnificence of the dining room has the stately glamour of an old-school cruise liner with its white leather buttoned banquettes, tarnished mirrors and full-length leaded windows. Centre-stage in the open kitchen, a parade of sizzling meats turns on a vast rotisserie. The menu of modern brasserie dishes kicks off with the likes of classic fish soup with rouille or pike boudin with fines herbes, before roast squab pigeon with Seville orange and olive oil mash. Finish among a cast of classic desserts with a panettone bread-and-butter pudding.

Chef Rowley Leigh **Owner** Rowley Leigh & Charlie McVeigh **Times** 12-3.30/6.30-11.30 Closed 25-26 Dec, 1 Jan **Prices** Fixed L 2 course £16.50, Service added but optional 12.5% **Wines** 98 bottles over £20, 5 bottles under £20, 25 by glass **Notes** Sunday L, Vegetarian available **Seats** 170, Pr/dining room 26 **Children** Portions, Menu

Island Restaurant & Bar

Modern European

Unpretentious modern cooking with Hyde Park views

☎ 020 7551 6070
Lancaster London Hotel, Lancaster Ter W2 2TY
e-mail: eat@islandrestaurant.co.uk
dir: Nearest station: Lancaster Gate. Adjacent to Lancaster Gate underground station, 5 min walk to Paddington Station

Located within the Lancaster London Hotel, this hybrid lounge-bar-restaurant has its own entrance opposite Hyde Park. Diners can gaze through the huge plate glass windows over the park or stare at the sheer volume of traffic racing around Lancaster Gate. In contrast, the restaurant provides a chilled out atmosphere and the contemporary, uncluttered décor attracts a suitably smart set. The cooking in the open-plan kitchen takes in modern British classics with European influences, using quality materials presented without fuss. Kick off with pan-fried scallops with a golden glaze, served with butternut squash, pancetta and crisp sage, and move on to main-course Barbary duck breast and leg with sautéed root vegetables, red cabbage and blackberry jus.

Times 6.45am-10.30pm Closed Sun

Jamuna Restaurant PLAN 2 E3

Indian

Neighbourhood Indian delivering subtle, modern flavours

☎ 020 7723 5056 & 7723 5055
38A Southwick St W2 1JQ
e-mail: info@jamuna.co.uk
dir: Nearest station: Paddington, Edgware Road

Off the beaten track in a small leafy parade of shops in Paddington, Jamuna is a small neighbourhood restaurant in what was once a private house. Anything but your average Indian, the décor is stylish and minimalist with wooden floors, cream suede chairs and painted walls decorated with traditional and modern art (all for sale). The food is skilfully prepared using decent British produce and presented with clean, subtle flavours. The broad menu has a particular emphasis on north Indian dishes although other rare regional specialities also feature. Start with spinach and red cabbage cake and move onto Scottish Highland roe deer - grilled fillet of loin marinated with spices in tamarind sauce.

Times 12-2.30/6-11 Closed 25 Dec-1 Jan, 2 weeks in Aug, L all week (unless prior notice given)

Nipa

Thai

Genuine Thai cuisine with Hyde Park views

☎ 020 7551 6039
Lancaster London Hotel, Lancaster Ter W2 2TY
e-mail: nipa@lancasterlondon.com
dir: Nearest station: Lancaster Gate. Adjacent to Lancaster Gate underground station, 5 min walk to Paddington Station

A seriously authentic and rather classy Thai restaurant located on the first floor of the Thai-owned Lancaster London Hotel at Lancaster Gate. Expect impressive carved wood panelling, pukka Thai artefacts and exuberant orchid displays, which evoke the feel of its namesake restaurant in Bangkok's Landmark Hotel, although the views over Hyde Park bring you back to London pretty sharpish. Then there's the food: the wide-ranging carte and trio of set menus offer a good hit of the intense flavours that are the hallmark of the kitchen's regional specialities, peppered with herbs and seasonings flown in from Thailand. Go for soft-shell crab with spicy mango salad, chicken coconut soup, deep-fried sea bass with chilli sauce, or roast duck in red curry.

Times 12-2/6.30-10.30 Closed Sun, L Sat

Urban Turban PLAN 2 A2

Modern Indian V

Stylish Notting Hill Indian with dishes to share

☎ 020 7243 4200
98 Westbourne Grove W2 5RU
e-mail: info@urbanturban.uk.com
dir: Nearest station: Bayswater, Notting Hill.

Inspired by the street food of Mumbai, Urban Turban is Vineet Bhatia's latest initiative in weaning the British off their fixation with curry-house vindaloo. A range of Sub-continental 'tapas' options supplements a listing of platters for sharing, perhaps comprised of fried fish, lamb and vegetable samosas, red chicken tikka, chilli chicken, and tikki chaat. Even the more familiar Indian options, such as biryanis, are given a more authentic spin, with dried fruits and rosewater, while sweet things include a cardamom pannacotta with fresh berries, rose-petal coulis and basil. Drink sweet lassi or rose milk.

Chef Vineet Bhatia **Owner** Mr Vineet & Mrs Rashima Bhatia **Times** 12.30-3.30/5-11 Closed 25-26 Dec, 1 Jan, L Mon-Fri **Prices** Fixed L 2 course £9.99-£15, Fixed D 3 course £30-£40, Starter £6.50-£11.50, Main £11-£14, Dessert £6.50-£7, Service added but optional 12.5% **Wines** 50 bottles over £20, 10 by glass **Notes** Sunday L, Vegetarian menu, Dress restrictions, Smart casual **Seats** 140, Pr/dining room 75 **Children** Portions, Menu **Parking** On street

LONDON W4

High Road Brasserie PLAN 1 D3

European

All-day Chiswick brasserie with populist menu

☎ 020 8742 7474
162 Chiswick High Rd W4 1PR
e-mail: cheila@highroadhouse.co.uk
dir: Nearest station: Turnham Green

There are both indoor and outdoor seating at this chic west London joint all year round, and the place is open from breakfast until late evening, so it looks as though every possible need for sustenance is catered for. The eye-catching jumble of floor tiles is hard to miss, while the slate-coloured banquettes are supremely comfortable, and staff know what they're doing. Fish soup, goats' cheese and onion tart, leg of duck on white beans, and poached salmon with sorrel and lemon mayonnaise are the kinds of dishes to head for, with afters such as profiteroles, tiramisù and Tart of the Day to round things off. A well-chosen international wine list provides broad choice at no-nonsense prices.

Times 7am-mdnt

LONDON W4 *continued*

Sam's Brasserie & Bar

PLAN 1 C3

Modern European

Converted factory building housing a cool modern brasserie

020 8987 0555
11 Barley Mow Passage, Chiswick W4 4PH
e-mail: info@samsbrasserie.co.uk
dir: Nearest station: Chiswick Park, Turnham Green. Behind Chiswick High Rd, next to green, off Heathfield Terrace

Sam's is a very 21st-century kind of place, a big converted red-brick building (it was once the Sanderson wallpaper factory), which opens for business at nine every morning and stays open throughout the day. Breakfasts, brunches, light salads and serious roasts - it's all here, all cooked and served with panache. Special events such as tutored wine tastings enhance the appeal, and the place is always full of a cool, satisfied buzz. Truffle-oiled mushroom soup, deep-fried buffalo mozzarella with tomato chutney, rack of lamb with dauphinoise, and whole lemon sole with shrimp butter sauce give good indication of the brasserie style, as do desserts such as steamed ginger pudding with rum and raisin ice cream, and the international mix of wines.

Chef Ian Leckie **Owner** Sam Harrison **Times** 9am-10.30pm Closed 24-27 Dec, L 28 Dec **Prices** Fixed L 2 course £13.50, Fixed D 3 course £17, Starter £5.50-£8.50, Main £10.50-£18.50, Dessert £3.50-£8, Service added but optional 12.5% **Wines** 44 bottles over £20, 12 bottles under £20, 20 by glass **Notes** Fixed L Mon-Fri, Early bird D all week before 7.30 pm, Sunday L, Vegetarian available **Seats** 100 **Children** Portions, Menu **Parking** On street & car park

La Trompette

PLAN 1 C3

– see below

Le Vacherin

PLAN 1 C3

French

French classics in neighbourhood brasserie

020 8742 2121
76-77 South Pde W4 5LF
e-mail: malcolm.john4@btinternet.com
dir: Nearest station: Chiswick Park. From underground station turn left, restaurant 400mtrs on left

In a small parade of shops overlooking Chiswick Park, Le Vacherin is easy to spot by its smart black awning and large windows. The interior evokes the feel of a Parisian

La Trompette

LONDON W4 PLAN 1 C3

European

Confident modern European cooking in Chiswick

020 8747 1836
5-7 Devonshire Rd, Chiswick W4 2EU
e-mail: reception@latrompette.co.uk
dir: Nearest station: Turnham Green. From station follow Turnham Green Terrace to junct with Chiswick High Rd. Cross road & bear right. Devonshire Rd 2nd left

Behind its neat hedge in affluent Chiswick, La Trompette is one of the trio of high-achieving restaurants that also includes the Glasshouse in Kew and Wandsworth's Chez Bruce (see entries). It's a relaxing venue with deep windows that allow in plenty of light, banquette seating and lots of wood surfaces from the floor on up to the ceiling panels. James Bennington is a finely accomplished practitioner of the readily understandable modern European cooking in which all three members of the group trade. Pasta-work is fabulous, as in a raviolo of Middlewhite pork, a thin parcel of marjoram-seasoned meat sitting on top of a mound of lightly sautéed cabbage and sweetcorn purée. There is a feeling of precise balance about all dishes, as when a main-course fillet of sea bass on a pile of wilted spinach appears with half-a-dozen little pillows of golden-crumbed potato gnocchi, a cauliflower beignet and truffled jus. Desserts utilise lots of fruits, rather than just chocolate and toffee, but don't shy away from a robust approach that brings on violently green pistachio and polenta cake with pistachio parfait and cherry ice cream.

Chef James Bennington **Owner** Nigel Platts-Martin, Bruce Poole **Times** 12-2.30/6.30-10.30 Closed 25-26 Dec, 1 Jan **Prices** Fixed L 2 course £19.50-£24.50, Fixed D 3 course £19.50-£39.50, Service added but optional 12.5% **Wines** 500 bottles over £20, 30 bottles under £20, 15 by glass **Notes** Sunday L, Vegetarian available **Seats** 72 **Children** Portions **Parking** On street

bistro with its blond-wood floors, a mirror-frieze above banquette-lined cream walls, French-themed posters, smartly dressed and friendly staff clad in long white aprons and a backing track of Gallic music. The simple French brasserie fare is matched by an all-French wine list and the menu is packed with well-executed classics. Tuck into the likes of Bayonne ham and celeriac remoulade, or ox cheek bourguignon, Chantenay carrots and creamed potato, finishing off with a classic petit pot au chocolat.

Chef Malcolm John **Owner** Malcolm & Donna John **Times** 12-3/6-11 Closed 25 Dec, New Year & BHs, L Mon **Prices** Fixed L 2 course £14.95, Fixed D 3 course £22.50-£38, Starter £7.25-£13, Main £16-£23, Dessert £6.25-£9, Service added but optional 12.5% **Wines** 77 bottles over £20, 12 bottles under £20, 12 by glass **Notes** Sunday L, Vegetarian available **Seats** 72, Pr/dining room 36 **Children** Portions **Parking** On street (metered)

LONDON W5

Crowne Plaza London - Ealing PLAN 1 C4

Modern European NEW

Quality modern cooking in a smart chain hotel

☎ 020 8233 3278 & 8233 3200
Western Av, Hanger Ln, Ealing W5 1HG
e-mail: info@cp-londonealing.co.uk
dir: Nearest station: Hanger Lane. A40 from Central London towards M40. Exit at Ealing & North Circular A406 sign. At rdbt take 2nd exit signed A40. Hotel on left

This hulking monolithic hotel is refreshingly modern and stylish on the inside; an oasis on the notorious Hanger Lane. The staff are faultlessly efficient, too, and there's a team in the kitchen showing real commitment to delivering quality food. The unpretentious modern British repertoire ranges widely, taking in pasta and risotto, grills and classics. Seared Shetland scallops are teamed with sautéed pumpkin, crisp pancetta and apple jelly, ahead of a fine piece of 28-day aged Scottish sirloin with Lyonnaise potatoes. Dessert ends strongly with a home-made blackberry and almond frangipane tart with honey and vanilla custard.

Chef Ross Pilcher **Owner** Pedersen Hotels **Times** 12-9.45 Closed D 31 Dec **Prices** Starter £4.60-£8.45, Main £8.95-£17.95, Dessert £4.25-£6.25, Service optional **Wines** 22 bottles over £20, 23 bottles under £20, 11 by glass **Notes** Vegetarian available, Civ Wed 90, Air con **Seats** 106, Pr/dining room 60 **Children** Portions, Menu **Parking** 82

LONDON W6

Anglesea Arms, Ravenscourt Park PLAN 1 D3

British, French

Bustling gastro-pub with appealingly robust cooking

☎ 020 8749 1291
35 Wingate Rd W6 0UR
dir: Nearest station: Ravenscourt Park, Goldhawk Rd, Hammersmith. From Ravenscourt Park tube, walk along Ravenscourt Rd, turn left onto Paddenswick then right onto Wellesley Rd

This corner-sited gastro-pub in a residential street is a true classic of the genre - if only every neighbourhood could have one. Thriving, good humoured with a fashionably shabby-chic retro look, its low-lit dark-panelled bar is stocked with an array of well-kept ales, while the sky-lit dining area behind offers the theatre of an open kitchen. Menus change daily driven by seasonal produce to offer a modern European approach that's a cut above the norm, with gutsy, big-hearted cooking and some full-on flavours. Take poached skate wing with artichokes barigoule and aïoli, or perhaps salt marsh lamb breast and cutlet teamed with sprouting broccoli and parsnip purée. A winter fire and a front terrace up the year-round appeal.

Times 12.30-2.45/7-10.30 Closed 25-27 Dec

The River Café

LONDON W6 PLAN 1 D3

Italian

A taste of Italy by the Thames

☎ 020 7386 4200
Thames Wharf, Rainville Rd W6 9HA
e-mail: info@rivercafe.co.uk
dir: Nearest station: Hammersmith. Restaurant in converted warehouse. Entrance on S side of Rainville Rd at junct with Bowfell Rd

Iconic is a term much overused, but not in this instance: the River Café is an iconic restaurant by the Thames, oft imitated but seldom bettered. Run for 23 years by Ruth Rogers and, until her sad death in February 2010, Rose Gray, the business partners and friends were pioneers of putting the very best of Italian ingredients on a plate without a hint of fussiness at a time when the capital's experience of Italian food was limited to spaghetti Bolognese. Housed on the wharf with a terrace between the restaurant and the water, the converted warehouse's modern interior is as simple and striking as the food. The long room with a bar and kitchen taking up all of one wall is painted white against the petrol blue carpet, while silver mesh chairs are surprisingly comfortable. New additions include a private dining room seating up to 18, a cheese room and chef's table. Young, friendly and casually attired staff serve the room, which usually has quite a buzz about it. The roll call of chefs who've worked here includes Jamie Oliver (spotted by a TV crew) and Hugh Fearnley-Whittingstall. The menu is changed twice daily and the sourcing of first-rate produce knows no bounds. Dishes are biased towards northern Italy so expect the likes of chargrilled squid with fresh red chilli and rocket, a primi of pasta with nettles, nutmeg, butter and pecorino and secondi of turbot tranche wood-roasted with capers, rosemary branches and Vermontino with borlotti beans cooked with tomato and rocket. The signature chocolate nemesis is legendary, but for something different try pannacotta with grappa, vanilla and lemon peel. The food doesn't come cheap but you really are getting what you pay for. A good selection of regional Italian wines, plenty available by the glass, helps things along nicely.

Chef R Rogers, Sian Owen **Owner** Ruth Rogers **Times** 12.30-3/7-11 Closed 24 Dec-1 Jan, BHs, D Sun **Prices** Starter £13-£16, Main £25-£35, Dessert £7-£8, Service added but optional 12.5% **Wines** 155 bottles over £20, 6 bottles under £20, 18 by glass **Notes** Sunday L, Vegetarian available **Seats** 130, Pr/dining room 18 **Children** Portions **Parking** 29, Valet parking in evening & wknd/pay&display

LONDON W6 ***continued***

The Gate PLAN 1 D3

Modern Vegetarian V

Gourmet veggie embracing global influences

020 8748 6932
51 Queen Caroline St, Hammersmith W6 9QL
e-mail: hammersmith@thegate.tv
dir: Nearest station: Hammersmith. From Hammersmith Apollo Theatre, continue down right side for approx 40 yds

In a converted church in a quiet backstreet behind the Hammersmith Apollo stands one of the capital's most popular gourmet vegetarian restaurants. The modest interior belies the quality of the food - the dining room resembles a small school canteen with its basic fixtures and fittings and unadorned wooden tables and chairs. A 'secret' walled garden is a top spot when the weather allows. The influence of the owners' Indo-Iraqi Jewish grandmother is apparent on the menu that takes diners on an international tour without even a hint of worthiness. Try carciofini - baby artichoke stuffed with dolcelatte and wild mushroom duxelles served with a Puy lentil salsa and lemon and garlic aïoli or a main course of winter vegetable and chick pea tagine. End on a high with chocolate and hazlenut Eton mess with chocolate sauce and Tia Maria.

Chef Adrian Daniel, Mariusz Wegrodski **Owner** Adrian & Michael Daniel **Times** 12-2.30/6-10.30 Closed 23 Dec-3 Jan, Good Fri & Etr Mon, Sun, L Sat **Prices** Fixed D 3 course £23, Starter £5-£6.75, Main £10.50-£15.50, Dessert £5.50-£6, Service added but optional 12.5% **Wines** 35 bottles over £20, 9 bottles under £20, 12 by glass **Seats** 60 **Children** Portions **Parking** On street

The River Café PLAN 1 D3

– see page 311

Sagar PLAN 1 D3

Vegetarian, Indian V

Vegetarian Indian dining in the heart of Hammersmith

020 8741 8563
157 King St, Hammersmith W6 9JT
e-mail: info@gosagar.com
dir: Nearest station: Hammersmith. 10min from Hammersmith tube

The Sagar brand of South Indian vegetarian restaurants has spread its wings from the original operation in a row of shops in Hammersmith, to branches in the West End and Covent Garden. The formula is a simple one: a clean-cut modern blond-wood décor, with Indian brass figurines to remind you that we're here for Sub-continental cuisine, a bustling atmosphere kept simmering by a hard-working, friendly team, who are happy to guide you through the extensive menu. And last, but not least, the food: we're talking pukka South Indian cuisine, so expect veggie dishes that old hands from the India trail will be very familiar with: vast paper-thin dosas - rice and lentil pancakes filled with spicy combos of vegetables and cheese, and uthappam, an Indian lentil-based take on pizzas. For a good intro to a range of flavours, go for an udupi thali, a gut-busting traditional platter of various lentil and vegetable curries with rice, raitha, pappadam, puri and dessert. And it's good to know that all of this is easy on the wallet.

Times 12-2.45/5.30-10.45 Closed 25-26 Dec

LONDON W8

Babylon PLAN 4 B4

Modern British

Minimalist chic and extraordinary views

020 7368 3993
The Roof Gardens, 99 Kensington High St W8 5SA
e-mail: babylon@roofgardens.virgin.com
web: www.roofgardens.virgin.com
dir: Nearest station: High Street Kensington. From High St Kensington tube station, turn right, then right into Derry St. Restaurant on right

Looking out over the south London skyline from the seventh-floor decked terrace and sleek, glass-sided dining room - framed by the tree-top greenery from the famous Roof Gardens a level below - Richard Branson's Babylon is a venue with charisma. Understated, chic contemporary styling - pastel tones, silky wood flooring, leather seating and modern artwork - all blend together harmoniously, providing a great backdrop for view-gazing accompanied by slick, friendly service and accomplished modern cooking. Quality seasonal produce, a light touch and innovation drive the kitchen's well-dressed dishes. Take ravioli of Cornish crab served with violet potato, Périgord truffle and bisque dressing to open, while to follow, perhaps roasted calves' liver with herb crust, lardons, croûtons, lemon, nut-brown butter and red wine jus.

Chef Ian Howard **Owner** Sir Richard Branson **Times** 12-2.30/7-10.30 Closed Xmas, D Sun **Prices** Fixed L 2 course £17.50-£22, Starter £9-£16, Main £20-£26, Dessert £8-£16, Service added but optional 12.5% **Wines** 103 bottles over £20, 10 by glass **Notes** Sunday L, Vegetarian available, Dress restrictions, Smart casual, Civ Wed 28 **Seats** 120, Pr/dining room 12 **Children** Portions, Menu **Parking** 10, NCP car park on Young St

Belvedere PLAN 1 D3

British, French

Brasserie cooking in the middle of a famous London park

020 7602 1238
Abbotsbury Rd, Holland House, Holland Park W8 6LU
e-mail: sales@whitestarline.org.uk
web: www.belvedererestaurant.co.uk
dir: Nearest station: Holland Park. Off Abbotsbury Rd entrance to Holland Park

The 17th-century Belvedere was once the summer ballroom for the Jacobean mansion at the heart of Holland Park. The setting alone is reason enough to visit: the art-deco glamour of its mirrored walls, muslin drapes and geometric parquet floors gives any meal the gloss of a special occasion, particularly when the gardens are in full bloom. A modern brasserie menu showcases top-drawer British ingredients that speak with a clear French accent, kicking off with the likes of Jerusalem artichoke soup with truffle oil, or foie gras parfait with toasted Poilâne bread. Classic mains might include rump of lamb with Provençal vegetables and rosemary-scented jus, and desserts conclude in a similar vein - perhaps a tarte fine of apples with caramel sauce and Calvados ice cream.

Chef Gary O'Sullivan **Owner** Jimmy Lahoud **Times** 12-2.30/6-10.30 Closed 26 Dec, 1 Jan, D Sun **Prices** Fixed L 2 course £15, Starter £6.95-£12.95, Main £13.50-£22.50, Dessert £7.50, Service added but optional 12.5%, Groups min 13 service 15% **Wines** 129 bottles

over £20, 14 by glass **Notes** Sunday L, Vegetarian available, Dress restrictions, Smart casual **Seats** 90 **Parking** Council car park

Cheneston's Restaurant PLAN 4 B4

Modern British

International cuisine in luxurious surroundings

☎ 020 7917 1000
The Milestone Hotel, 1 Kensington Court W8 5DL
e-mail: bookms@rchmail.com
dir: Nearest station: High St Kensington. M4/ Hammersmith flyover, take 2nd left into Gloucester Rd, left into High St Kensington, 500mtrs on left

Opposite Kensington Palace and its Gardens, this one-time Victorian mansion, now classy, stylish townhouse hotel, provides the backdrop for the intimate Cheneston's Restaurant. Luxuriously ornate, its intricately plastered ceilings, statement fireplace and mahogany furniture fit the bill. The menu, dotted with deep-pocket luxury (think sturgeon caviar), offers a broadly modern British approach blended with international flavours and based around quality seasonal ingredients. Saddle of Shetland lamb is teamed with braised lentils and roasted salsify, pan-fried sea bass with confit ratte potatoes and lobster dressing. House favourites and grills complete the picture.

Chef Ryan O'Flynn **Owner** The Red Carnation Hotel **Times** 12-3/5.30-11 **Prices** Fixed L 2 course fr £21.50, Fixed D 3 course fr £26.50, Starter £14-£22, Main £19-£38, Dessert £9-£10, Service added but optional 12.5% **Wines** 250 bottles over £20, 12 by glass **Notes** Pre-theatre D £21.50, Tasting menu 7 course, Sunday L, Vegetarian available, Dress restrictions, Smart casual, Civ Wed 30 **Seats** 30, Pr/dining room 8 **Children** Portions, Menu **Parking** NCP Young Street off Kensington High Street

Clarke's PLAN 4 A5

British, Mediterranean  

Ground-breaking Kensington restaurant with simple culinary approach

☎ 020 7221 9225
124 Kensington Church St W8 4BH
e-mail: restaurant@sallyclarke.com
dir: Nearest station: Notting Hill Gate. Turn right out of Notting Hill Gate & then right into Kensingtson Church St. Restaurant on left

Sally Clarke's restaurant and deli are to be found up near the Notting Hill end of Church Street, the eatery divided over two floors, a sunny ground-floor room overlooking a back garden, and the gently lit basement, which had one of the first open-plan kitchens of any fine-dining restaurant in London. Conscientious buying and a wholeheartedly simple culinary approach have always distinguished Clarke's, and the no-choice dinner menus, based on impeccable seasonal raw materials, remain abidingly popular. Diners who rolled up on a Tuesday in February would have eaten grilled goats' cheese crostini with artichoke relish and toasted pine nuts, followed by Aylesbury duck breast with crackling and clementine glaze, accompanied by cavolo nero with chilli, and finished with dark chocolate mousse tart with raisins soaked in Jack Daniel's. It's all good, as they say, and served by knowledgeable, welcoming staff.

Chef Sally Clarke, Gabriele Marzo **Owner** Sally Clarke **Times** 12.30-2/7-10 Closed 8 days Xmas & New Year, D Sun **Prices** Food prices not confirmed for 2011. Please telephone for details **Wines** 86 bottles over £20, 10 bottles under £20, 8 by glass **Notes** Sunday L, Vegetarian available **Seats** 80, Pr/dining room 40 **Parking** On street

Kitchen W8

LONDON W8 PLAN 4 A4

Modern British NEW

Exciting addition to the W8 dining scene

☎ 020 7937 0120
11-13 Abingdon Rd, Kensington W8 6AH
e-mail: info@kitchenw8.com
dir: Nearest station: Kensington High Street. From High Street Kensington tube turn left onto High St for 500m & left into Abingdon Rd

Rebecca Mascarenhas and Philip Howard are names familiar to followers of the London restaurant scene and with Kitchen W8 they have brought to life their unified vision of a neighbourhood restaurant. The neighbourhood is W8, so it looks pretty fine: a cool, black canopied frontage with large plate-glass windows. Inside, the colours are natural (taupe, grey, olive and the like), the fixtures and fittings are well designed, a blend of old and new, giving it a smart but unpretentious contemporary look. Head chef Mark Kempson has worked under Howard at The Square and his menu has broad appeal, from the simplicity of a whole Dover sole with lemon and parsley butter to the boldly flavoured grilled ox tongue with shallot purée and foie gras baked potato. The cooking is broadly modern British, a bit English, a bit French, with evident dedication in the sourcing of produce. A risotto of butternut squash, enriched with chanterelles in a red wine sauce and topped with a soft poached egg is a tip-top first course, and to finish, perhaps a crème fraîche tart with lemon curd ice cream, or cheeses served with quince and raisin chutney. There's a set menu available lunchtime and early evening.

Chef Mark Kempson **Owner** Philip Howard & Rebecca Mascarenhas **Times** 12-2.30/6-10 Closed BHs **Prices** Fixed L 2 course £17.50, Fixed D 3 course £24.50, Starter £7-£10, Main £16.50-£22, Dessert £7.50-£9, Service added but optional 12.5% **Wines** 95 bottles over £20, 6 bottles under £20, 14 by glass **Notes** Sunday L, Vegetarian available **Seats** 75 **Children** Portions **Parking** On street, NCP High St

LONDON W8 ***continued***

Kensington Place PLAN 4 A6

Modern European

Buzzing brasserie, popular with the Notting Hill set

☎ 020 7727 3184
201-9 Kensington Church St W8 7LX
dir: Nearest station: Notting Hill Gate

Several years after long-standing chef Rowley Leigh exited its revolving doors, Kensington Place still packs them in. It sports a sharper look these days, without losing its casual, 80s vibe: floor-to-ceiling windows are still de rigueur for clocking who's passing by, while murals of water lilies, posh leather place mats on the tables and rather funky blue chairs all fit the relaxed style. The kitchen takes modern European classics and reconstructs them to add an extra dimension, as witnessed in an unusual starter of octopus sopressata - a cephalopod take on Italian dried sausage - with smoked paprika and shallot tempura. Tender rump of salt marsh lamb turns up with broad beans, wild garlic and potato gnocchi in a colourful main course.

Chef Daniel Phippard **Owner** D & D London
Times 12-3/6.30-10.30 **Prices** Fixed L 2 course £16.50-£19.50, Fixed D 3 course £25-£29, Service added but optional 12.5% **Wines** 123 bottles over £20, 5 bottles under £20, 16 by glass **Notes** Sunday L, Vegetarian available **Seats** 100, Pr/dining room 45 **Children** Portions, Menu **Parking** On street

Kitchen W8 PLAN 4 A4

– *see page 313*

Launceston Place Restaurant PLAN 4 C4

– *see below*

Min Jiang PLAN 4 B5

– *see opposite page*

Park Terrace Restaurant PLAN 4 B5

Modern European

Lively modern cooking overlooking Kensington Gardens

☎ 020 7361 0602
Royal Garden Hotel, 2-24 Kensington High St W8 4PT
e-mail: dining@royalgardenhotel.co.uk
dir: Nearest station: Kensington High Street. Next to Kensington Palace, Royal Albert Hall

The Park Terrace has had a makeover in the contemporary manner, so expect natural tones, clean lines and a few nice designer touches along the way; the hard surfaces are softened by the crisp white linen on the tables and splashes of colour from artful flower arrangements. The views overlooking Kensington Palace and its gardens are as good as ever, the floor-to-ceiling windows making the most of the vista and ensuring the room is light and bright during the day and atmospheric in the evening. The modern British menu draws on seasonal ingredients from trusted suppliers. Cromer crab ravioli with samphire and shellfish bisque makes for a vibrant starter and sets the stage for a well-executed lavender- and herb-crusted rump of Suffolk organic lamb with broad bean purée, French beans and confit potatoes. White coffee tart with mascarpone cream and coffee crisp is one of the beautifully presented desserts. Min Jiang (see entry) is up on the 10th floor.

Park Terrace Restaurant

Chef Steve Munkley **Owner** Goodwood Group
Times 12-3/6-10.30 **Prices** Fixed L 2 course £15-£19.50, Fixed D 3 course £31, Starter £5-£8, Main £10-£32, Dessert £5-£7.50, Service optional, Groups min 8 service 10% **Wines** 74 bottles over £20, 13 by glass **Notes** Pre-theatre menu available daily, Sunday L, Vegetarian available, Dress restrictions, Smart casual **Seats** 90, Pr/dining room 40 **Children** Portions, Menu **Parking** 160

Launceston Place Restaurant

LONDON W8 PLAN 4 C4

Modern British

Great modern British flavours in classy Kensington

☎ 020 7937 6912
1a Launceston Place W8 5RL
e-mail: lpr@egami.co.uk
dir: Nearest station: Gloucester Road, High Street Kensington Just south of Kensington Palace, 10 min walk from Royal Albert Hall

If it were true that the streets of London were paved with gold, this is a part of town where you might trip over a particularly large ingot, and in Launceston Place this leafy corner of Kensington has a restaurant worth its weight in bullion. But it is no golden temple (let's stop the metaphor now), rather a place with honest and serious intentions to deliver well-balanced, intelligent cooking based on the very best British produce. Tristan Welch worked at Pétrus and certainly knows a thing or two about attention to detail. It's an appealing space in shades of brown and coffee, with fibre-optic chandeliers and smart leather seats combining to give it the look of a cool, contemporary club. Service is spot on. The kitchen takes those top-notch ingredients and brings out the very best flavours, as in a first-course tartare of Cornish mackerel, the fish wrapped in nasturtium leaves, the flowers bringing splashes of colour, and main-course rose veal topped with their delectable sweetbreads, the richness perfectly pointed by some pickled mushrooms. Rice pudding soufflé with raspberry ripple ice cream epitomises the modern British approach, and everything from the excellent home-made breads to the carefully-chosen wine list assures no stone is left unturned.

Chef Tristan Welch **Owner** D & D London
Times 12.30-2.30/6-10.30 Closed Xmas, New Year, Etr, L Mon **Prices** Fixed L 3 course £20-£45, Fixed D 3 course £38-£45, Tasting menu £60, Service added but optional 12.5% **Wines** 87 bottles over £20, 5 bottles under £20, 13 by glass **Notes** Tasting menu 6 course, Early bird £38 (depart by 8pm), Sunday L, Vegetarian available, Dress restrictions, Smart casual, no T-shirts or caps **Seats** 60, Pr/dining room 10 **Children** Portions **Parking** Car park off Kensington High St

Min Jiang

LONDON W8 PLAN 4 B5

Chinese 

Imaginative modern Chinese cooking with 10th-floor views over London

020 7361 1988
Royal Garden Hotel, 2-24 Kensington High St W8 4PT
e-mail: reservations@minjiang.co.uk
web: www.minjiang.co.uk
dir: Nearest station: Kensington High Street. Next to Kensington Palace & gardens on 10th floor of Royal Garden Hotel

The view from the 10th floor of the Royal Garden Hotel makes Min Jiang a destination restaurant in its own right: beyond the treetops of Kensington Gardens and Hyde Park is a rollcall of London landmarks to tick off. It's a view that the muted creams and darkwood of the dining room doesn't try to compete with, although there's a scarlet-painted wall hung with black-and-white photos, and a collection of blue-and-white Chinese vases to catch the eye if you can tear your gaze from the cityscape. Contemporary Chinese food is the order of the day, on an extensive menu majoring in Cantonese and Szechuan flavours. Beijing-style duck is the restaurant's signature, roasted in an oven fired with apple wood, and presented in different ways - the crispy skin comes with sugar, or with garlic paste, radish and Tientsin cabbage, for example. Hand-made dim sum are worth checking out too - including rolls of that excellent crispy Beijing duck. Main courses take in everything from sautéed Gong Bao king prawns to braised pork belly in a rich sauce with Chinese buns, while desserts show an inventive streak, pairing cinnamon cheesecake with green tea ice cream, or chocolate coated lychees with ginger parfait. Service is well-drilled and knowledgeable throughout - useful in guiding you through the Chinese wine options.

Chef Lan Chee Vooi **Owner** Goodwood Group **Times** 12-3/6-10.30 **Prices** Fixed L 2 course fr £19.50, Fixed D 3 course £48-£68, Starter £6-£12.80, Main £14-£48, Dessert £6-£7.50, Service optional, Groups min 8 service 10% **Wines** 149 bottles over £20, 15 by glass
Notes Sunday L, Vegetarian menu, Dress restrictions, Smart casual, Civ Wed 80 **Seats** 100, Pr/dining room 20
Parking 160

LONDON W8 *continued*

Zaika

PLAN 4 B4

Indian V

Indian fusion cuisine opposite Kensington Palace

☎ 020 7795 6533
1 Kensington High St W8 5NP
e-mail: info@zaika-restaurant.co.uk
dir: Nearest station: Kensington High Street. Opposite Kensington Palace

Take a moment to appreciate the fine detailing in the original stonework both outside and in at Zaika, a former Kensington bank branch. The tall windows, rich panelling and outsized light fixture all combine to make for a stunning backdrop to the dining room, where Sanjay Dwivedi's highly individual menus subject the pick of British produce to some innovative Indian treatments. Battered soft-shell crab dusted with onion and sesame seeds and served with chilli jam and tamarind mayonnaise is an eye-catching starter. For main course, perhaps masala duck breast with crisped fat and pink meat in a sweet sauce of black lentils and tomatoes, with crisp-fried okra to add to the array of textures. The chocolate samosas, filled with pistachio-studded ganache, remain a popular way to finish.

Chef Sanjay Dwivedi **Owner** Claudio Pulze
Times 12-2.45/6-10.45 Closed BHs, Xmas, New Year, L Sat **Prices** Fixed L 2 course fr £20, Tasting menu fr £42, Starter £7.75-£11, Main £16.50-£25, Dessert £4-£12, Service added but optional **Notes** Gourmand menu 8 course £58, Tasting (incl veg) menu 6 course, Vegetarian menu **Seats** 84 **Children** Portions

LONDON W9

The Warrington

PLAN 2 C5

Modern British

Historic pub gets the Ramsay treatment

☎ 020 7592 7960
93 Warrington Crescent, Maida Vale W9 1EH
e-mail: warrington@gordonramsay.com
dir: Nearest station: Warwick Avenue, Maida Vale

Formerly the Warrington Hotel, this is now part of the Gordon Ramsay portfolio of gastro-pubs. The building dates back to the 1850s and now houses a buzzy locals pub on the ground floor with original marble pillars, a large mosaic fireplace and warm burgundy walls plus an eye-catching original mosaic floor. Bar snacks are above average - anyone for pork crackling and apple sauce or devilled whitebait? Upstairs the formal restaurant benefits from high ceilings with a cherub frieze, intricate ceiling roses and cornices. Food is British gastro-pub style so expect chicken and ham hock terrine with beetroot chutney, or a main of seared Longford Estate trout, spiced lentils and wild garlic gremolata and a pudding of bitter chocolate mousse with raspberry ripple ice cream.

Times 12-2.30/6-10.30 Closed L Mon-Thu

LONDON W11

E&O

PLAN 1 D4

Pan-Asian

Stylish Pan-Asian grazing for the Notting Hill crew

☎ 020 7229 5454
14 Blenheim Crescent, Notting Hill W11 1NN
e-mail: eando@rickerrestaurants.com
dir: Nearest station: Notting Hill Gate. From tube station turn right, at mini rdbt turn into Kensington Park Rd, restaurant 10min down hill

The denizens of achingly voguish Notting Hill show no sign of deserting this style-led Pan-Asian restaurant. The booming bar and minimally-decorated dining room - all slatted walls, brown leather banquettes, black lacquered chairs and darkwood floors - was never a case of style over substance. Its bijou tapas-sized dishes designed for grazing and sharing are put together with great skill and built on well-sourced ingredients. The trendy fusion menu yo-yos from East to West, cherry picking its way through Oriental cuisine. Dim sum - succulent crispy pork belly with black vinegar, perhaps - sit alongside lemon sole tempura, sea bass sashimi with yuzu and truffle oil, or classics such as black cod with sweet miso.

Chef Simon Treadway **Owner** Will Ricker **Times** 12-3/6-11 Closed 25-26 Dec, 1 Jan, Aug BH **Prices** Food prices not confirmed for 2011. Please telephone for details **Wines** 61 bottles over £20, 2 bottles under £20, 15 by glass **Notes** Sunday L, Vegetarian available **Seats** 86, Pr/dining room 18 **Children** Portions, Menu **Parking** On street

The Ledbury

LONDON W11 PLAN 1 D4

Modern French V

Highly accomplished cooking in fashionable, residential Notting Hill

☎ 020 7792 9090
127 Ledbury Rd W11 2AQ
e-mail: info@theledbury.com
dir: Nearest station: Westbourne Park, Notting Hill Gate. 5 min walk along Talbot Rd from Portobello Rd, on corner of Talbot and Ledbury Rd

As befits its fashionable Notting Hill beat, the Ledbury is a place to see and be seen in. This is the sort of classy neighbourhood restaurant you would happily move house for, if only the W11 postcode hadn't long ago hit the house price stratosphere. Nigel Platts-Martin and Philip Howard also own The Square in Mayfair (see entry) so know a thing or two about understated sophistication - the expansive dining room here is as smartly turned out as its voguish clientele, in beige and gold with a mirrored wall and plush leather seats at tables clothed in white linen. Heading a talented kitchen brigade is Brett Graham from Newcastle - the one in New South Wales - whose skilful French-accented contemporary cooking pulls off adventurous ideas with interesting mixes of flavour and texture and razor-sharp presentation. A 'risotto' of squid, for example, dices the squid minutely to resemble grains of rice, and teams it with pine nuts, a sherry reduction and a wafer-thin cauliflower tuile. Next up, an impeccable piece of roast turbot is pointed up with blood orange, broccoli on toast and crab. Desserts are a strong suit, delivering a caramelised banana galette with salted caramel and peanut ice cream. Naturally, none of this comes cheap, particularly if you go for broke with the tasting menu, but set lunch menus offer remarkable value. An exceptional wine list bristles with top-class stuff from the New and Old Worlds, and a talented sommelier is at hand to guide you to the right bottle.

Chef Brett Graham **Owner** Nigel Platts-Martin, Brett Graham & Philip Howard **Times** 12-2.30/6.30-10.30 Closed 24-26 Dec, 1 Jan, Aug BH wknd, L Mon **Prices** Fixed L 2 course fr £22.50, Fixed D 3 course fr £65, Tasting menu £75, Starter £12-£14, Main £23-£27, Dessert fr £7, Service added but optional 12.5% **Wines** 700 bottles over £20, 5 bottles under £20, 12 by glass **Notes** ALC available L only, Tasting menu 8 course, Sunday L, Vegetarian menu **Seats** 62 **Parking** Talbot Rd (metered)

Notting Hill Brasserie

LONDON W11 PLAN 1 D4

Modern European

Sophisticated food and luxurious surrounds in Notting Hill

☎ 020 7229 4481
92 Kensington Park Rd W11 2PN
e-mail: enquiries@nottinghillbrasserie.com
dir: Nearest station: Notting Hill Gate. 3 mins walk from Notting Hill station

Set apart from the famous bustling market in a cobbled street next to St Peter's Church is the elegant Notting Hill Brasserie. Three converted Edwardian houses make up this regency style building. Pull up a high leather-backed stool at the stylish bar before heading to a spacious table in one of the six interconnected dining rooms, where fine crockery, cutlery and glassware are set on top quality white linen - it makes for a luxurious feel. Cream and mushroom walls display old wooden artefacts and the ceiling features elegant cornicing. A good value lunch menu provides an entry point to chef Karl Burdock's refined modern Mediterranean menu. From the à la carte, start with a vibrant butternut squash soup with croque monsieur before pan-fried cod fillet with new potatoes, brown shrimps and watercress. Finish with a textbook warm chocolate fondant with vanilla ice cream. Service is formal but not stuffy. Families can enjoy Sunday lunch and live jazz while younger members of the party are entertained by a nanny in the brasserie playroom.

Chef Karl Burdock **Owner** Mitch Tillman **Times** 12-3/7-11 Closed 26 Dec, New Year, D Mon **Prices** Fixed L 2 course £17-£21, Starter £10.50-£16.50, Main £19-£30.50, Dessert £7.50-£8.50, Service added but optional 12.5% **Wines** 130 bottles over £20, 3 bottles under £20, 19 by glass **Notes** Sunday L, Vegetarian available **Seats** 110, Pr/dining room 44 **Children** Portions **Parking** On street

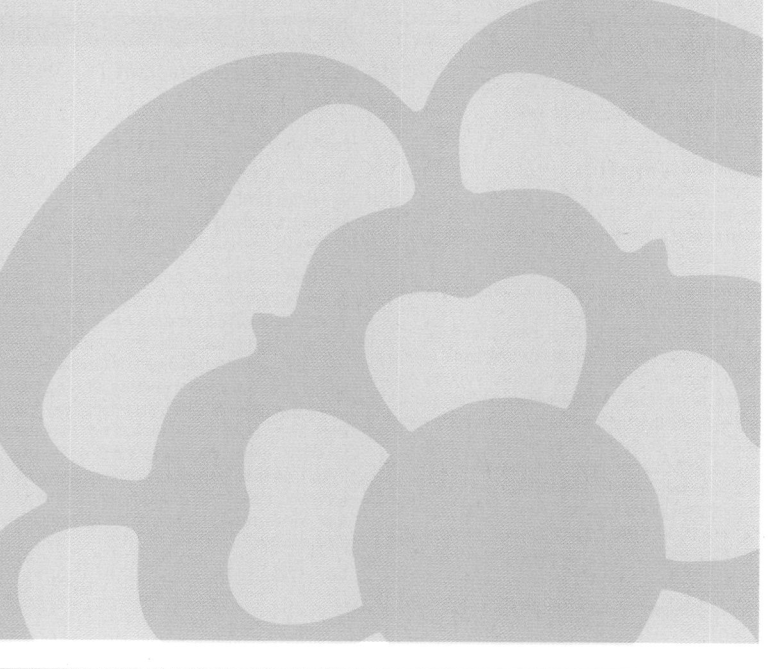

LONDON W11 *continued*

Edera PLAN 1 D4

◎◎ Modern Italian

Well-liked neighbourhood Italian in leafy Holland Park

☎ 020 7221 6090
148 Holland Park Av W11 4UE
e-mail: edera@btconnect.com
dir: Nearest station: Holland Park

This classy Italian plays up to the sensibilities of the well-heeled Holland Park neighbourhood with its fashionable Sardinian-accented cooking. Pavement tables have an obvious allure in this leafy postcode, while the split-level interior goes for a pared-back contemporary look with bare-wood floors, white walls hung with large mirrors, and linen-dressed tables. The kitchen keeps things simple, letting the main ingredients shine, so you're in safe hands with trattoria staples from the Italian mainland like bresaola with rocket and parmesan, or linguine with clams. But, it's not every day that Sardinia's delights are up for grabs, so go native with mullet roe carpaccio with artichokes and cherry tomatoes, or home-made semolina flour malloreddusu pasta with sausage, saffron, pecorino and tomato sauce. Mains might offer porceddu, a whole suckling pig cooked over embers, and to finish, seadas al miele - fried puff pastry stuffed with ricotta and honey.

Times 12-2.30/6.30-11 Closed 25-26 & 31 Dec

The Ledbury PLAN 1 D4

◎◎◎ – *see page 316*

Lonsdale PLAN 1 D4

◎ British, European

Trendy Notting Hill lounge-style eatery

☎ 020 7727 4080
48 Lonsdale Rd W11 2DE
e-mail: info@thelonsdale.co.uk
dir: Nearest station: Notting Hill, Ladbroke Grove. One street parallel to Westbourne Grove. Between Portobello Rd & Ledbury Rd

This hyper-trendy Notting Hill hangout might look pubby from the outside, but the buzzy evening-only venue has more in common with Manhattan once you're inside. Kicking off with cocktails served by a lively young team in the fun and funky vibe of the front cocktail bar is de rigueur, before moving into the lounge-style eating area. Scarlet banquettes and low-slung stools around low-level dark-wood tables, surrounded by purple-lit, mirrored walls make for a night-clubby ambience, while the modish modern British cooking fits the mood. Expect straightforward dishes such as seared scallops and chorizo with sweet potato purée, followed by roasted and rolled Tamworth pork belly with sage mash and apple purée.

Times 6-12 Closed 25-26 Dec, 1 Jan, L all week

Notting Hill Brasserie PLAN 1 D4

◎◎◎ – *see page 317*

LONDON W14

Cibo PLAN 1 D3

◎◎ Italian

Good honest Italian cooking in W14

☎ 020 7371 2085 & 7371 6271
3 Russell Gardens W14 8EZ
e-mail: ciborestaurant@aol.com
dir: Nearest station: Olympia, Shepherds Bush. Russell Gardens is a residential area off Holland Road

Local Italians and the odd celeb rub shoulders at this long-established neighbourhood Italian restaurant in West London. The draw is generous portions of simple, modern Italian cooking and a relaxed atmosphere. On smartly laid tables, fine linen tablecloths and napkins complement hand-made Italian crockery while abstract Renaissance-style nude paintings hang on the cream walls. In summer the full-length windows fold back giving the restaurant an alfresco vibe. Straightforward but imaginative cooking is driven by quality ingredients and seafood is the speciality. Try an antipasti of stuffed squid filled with crab, breadcrumbs and herbs with a light tomato sauce or move straight onto pasta filled with partridge in a wild mushroom sauce and a main course of baked monkfish with saffron and courgette flowers and home-made Amaretto ice cream to finish.

Times 12.15-2.30/7-11 Closed Xmas, Etr BHs, L Sat, D Sun

LONDON WC1

Acorn House Restaurant PLAN 3 D5

◎ Modern European

Eco-friendly cooking in King's Cross

☎ 020 7812 1842
69 Swinton St WC1X 9NT
e-mail: info@acornhouserestaurant.com
dir: Nearest station: King's Cross St Pancras

In a 1960s block close to King's Cross Station, the long dining room of Acorn House is cool and contemporary with an open kitchen and a takeaway counter for the locals. Sustainability and impeccable green credentials are the cornerstones of this environmentally friendly restaurant, which has its own urban vegetable garden, composting bins and sustainable energy. Not surprisingly, seasonality and provenance are key to the menu with fish endorsed by the Marine Stewardship Council and an emphasis on regional produce. The modern European menu could start with confit duck with blood oranges and sesame seeds, with venison ragoût with gnocchi and juniper and mint as a main course.

Times 12-3/6-10.30

Blue Door Bistro PLAN 3 C4

◎ Traditional British

Stylish hotel bistro with modern comfort classics

☎ 020 7612 8416 & 7637 1001
The Montague on the Gardens, 15 Montague St, Bloomsbury WC1B 5BJ
e-mail: bookmt@rchmail.com
dir: Nearest station: Russell Square. 10 minutes from Covent Garden, adjacent to the British Museum

In a quiet corner of Bloomsbury by the British Museum, the Blue Door Bistro of this chic boutique hotel is a modern, light-and-airy space. A gleaming brass name plaque and bowler-hatted doorman greet you at the door, setting the tone for top-notch friendly service throughout; inside, there's an upmarket country-house feel featuring mahogany panelling and a wall frieze of images showing London in Dickensian mode. The kitchen goes for an unfussy, comfort-oriented slant on modern British classics - chilled plum tomato soup with baby mozzarella and basil oil, for example, followed by herb-crusted rack of lamb with dauphinoise potatoes and tomato and basil jus.

Chef Martin Halls **Owner** Red Carnation Hotels
Times 12.30-2.30/5.30-10.30 **Prices** Fixed L 2 course fr £19.50, Fixed D 3 course fr £24.50, Starter £5.50-£10.50, Main £9.50-£25, Dessert £6.50-£10.50, Service added but optional 12.5% **Wines** 61 bottles over £20, 7 bottles under £20, 19 by glass **Notes** Pre-theatre, Business & Al fresco menu available, Vegetarian available, Civ Wed 90 **Seats** 45, Pr/dining room 100 **Children** Portions, Menu **Parking** On street, Bloomsbury Square

Pearl Restaurant & Bar PLAN 3 D3

◎◎◎ – *see opposite page*

Pearl Restaurant & Bar

LONDON WC1 PLAN 3 D3

Modern French 

Impressive cooking in opulent surroundings

☎ 020 7829 7000
Renaissance London Chancery Court Hotel, 252 High Holborn WC1V 7EN
e-mail: info@pearl-restaurant.com
web: www.pearl-restaurant.com
dir: Nearest station: Holborn. 200 mtrs from Holborn tube station

The marble banking hall of the erstwhile Pearl Assurance building was a restaurant waiting to happen. The designers were let loose on its Edwardian grandeur, adding string-of-pearl chandeliers, cappuccino leather seats and acres of walnut panels to create a glamorous city slicker hangout. Pearl is part of the slick Renaissance London Chancery Court Hotel, but feels like a stand-alone operation as it has its own separate revolving door entrance from the street. You might start off in the luminescent pearl-curtained bar with a glass of something a bit special from a choice of over 40 wines by the glass, before moving into the sleek surrounds of the restaurant. Chef Jun Tanaka (as seen on TV) started out in the kitchens of Marco Pierre White and Nico Ladenis, so his cooking bears their indelible modern French thumbprints. The menu wastes no breath on verbiage, headlining each dish with its main ingredient, followed by a terse list of the subsidiary items. Flavour profiles can be surprising - poached Maldon rock oysters are served with chicken-infused foam and a fruity julienne of fresh ginger, while rump of veal might be teamed with confit swordfish escabèche and carrot jelly. Main-course rabbit might be a play on Spanish tapas classics - the leg stuffed with paella, and served with baby red peppers, squid and chick peas. Desserts, too, are exquisite arrangements - perhaps a fromage frais pannacotta with rhubarb strudel and white chocolate ice cream, or a well-matched confection of caramelised apples with salted caramel mousse, thyme ice cream and honey jelly. The knowledgeable sommelier is at hand to lead you through a roll call of A-list wines.

Chef Jun Tanaka **Owner** Hotel Property Investors **Times** 12-2.30/6-10 Closed Dec, BHs, Sun, L Sat **Prices** Fixed L 2 course fr £26, Fixed D 3 course fr £58, Service added but optional 12.5% **Wines** 390 bottles over £20, 40 by glass **Notes** Fixed L 1 course £19, D £32, D 5 course £70, Tasting menu, Vegetarian available, Dress restrictions, Smart casual, no trainers **Seats** 74, Pr/dining room 12 **Parking** NCP Drury Lane or on street after 6.30 pm

LONDON WC2

L'Atelier de Joel Robuchon PLAN 3 C2

®®® – *see below*

Axis at One Aldwych PLAN 3 D2

®® Modern British

Classic and modern dining in London's theatreland

☎ 020 7300 0300 & 7300 1000
1 Aldwych WC2B 4RH
e-mail: axis@onealdwych.com
dir: Nearest station: Covent Garden, Charing Cross. At junct of Aldwych & The Strand opposite Waterloo Bridge

Intriguing contemporary styling makes for an engaging setting at this chic central London address. Curved cream walls, partly panelled in sea-green fabric, and well-spaced tables with chairs upholstered in an aubergine hue make a change from the anonymity of much urban restaurant design, and Tony Fleming's menus offer an eclectic mix of classic and modern dishes, with lighter offerings for the pre-theatre crowd. A serving of lightly crumbed ham hock fritters with smooth pease pudding and honey-mustard dressing offers a boost to the palate, as might a main of salmon fishcakes with horseradish velouté, or another of duck confit with colcannon and lentils in plum and port sauce. Finish with malt parfait, with liquorice ice cream and raspberry sauce.

Chef Tony Fleming **Owner** Gordon Campbell Gray **Times** 12-2.30/5.30-10.45 Closed Xmas, New Year, Etr, Sun-Mon, L Sat **Prices** Fixed L 2 course £16.75, Fixed D 3 course £19.75, Starter £7, Main £13-£21, Dessert £6-£11, Service added but optional 12.5% **Wines** 85 bottles over £20, 2 bottles under £20, 11 by glass **Notes** Pre & post theatre D & Fixed price L menu available, Vegetarian available, Civ Wed 60 **Seats** 120, Pr/dining room 40 **Children** Portions, Menu **Parking** NCP - Wellington St

Christopher's PLAN 3 D2

® Contemporary American

Modern American cooking in theatreland

☎ 020 7240 4222
18 Wellington St, Covent Garden WC2E 7DD
e-mail: coventgarden@christophersgrill.com
dir: Nearest station: Embankment, Covent Garden Just by Strand, overlooking Waterloo Bridge

In the heart of Covent Garden's theatreland, lies Christopher's American bar and grill with its buzzy atmosphere and great views over Waterloo bridge. Formerly a papier mache factory and then the city's first licensed casino, a sweeping stone staircase leads to an elegant dining room with high ceilings, original features and brightly painted walls. A lively martini bar downstairs is the perfect place to get waylaid before dinner (they even run martini master classes). The contemporary American menu offers well-executed classics such as cob salad with avocado, maple-cured bacon and blue cheese followed by steaks with a range of sauces or perhaps grilled Maine lobster with a sweetcorn pancake.

Times 12-3/5-11 Closed 24 Dec-2 Jan, 25-26 Dec, 1 Jan, D Sun

Clos Maggiore PLAN 3 C2

®®® – *see opposite page*

Great Queen Street PLAN 3 D3

® British

The best of British at bustling Covent Garden brasserie

☎ 020 7242 0622
32 Great Queen St WC2B 5AA
e-mail: greatqueenstreet@googlemail.com
dir: Nearest station: Covent Garden, Holborn

Informal, Bohemian Covent Garden brasserie that shares the same buzzy atmosphere and relaxed, unpretentious style to be found at its sister eateries, the Eagle and the Anchor & Hope, two of London's most iconic gastro-pubs. More importantly, expect the same robust, simple and straightforward modern British food, driven by top-notch ingredients, seasonality and clear, gutsy flavours. In a classic pub-style setting of wooden floors, blood-red walls and tightly packed unclothed tables, tuck into Jerusalem artichoke and scallop soup, pheasant pie, black bream with wild mushrooms, rib of Hereford beef

L'Atelier de Joel Robuchon

LONDON WC2 PLAN 3 C2

French

Slick, sexy sophistication from French super-chef

☎ 020 7010 8600
13-15 West St WC2H 9NE
e-mail: info@joelrobuchon.co.uk
dir: Nearest station: Leicester Sq, Covent Gdn, Tottenham Court Rd. Left off Cambridge Circus & Shaftesbury Av

Joel Robuchon, acclaimed as one of the superstars of the French culinary universe, came up with his 'Atelier' concept to bring diners up close and personal with the sharp end of kitchen business. The name means 'workshop', so this glamorous Covent Garden operation seats diners on high stools at a long sushi-style counter to watch the chefs at work in an open kitchen, turning out small-but-perfectly-formed tapas-sized hits of turbocharged flavours. It is clearly a concept that works, as the Atelier stable now runs to 10 outposts spanning the globe's big cities. The London operation is a place to see and be seen in: done out in the signature décor of red and black, the Japanese influence is tangible - it is a self-consciously glamorous venue, where glossy staff in designer black thread slickly through the animated ruck of grazers, who clearly feel at ease amid the futuristic décor of lacquer, glass and black granite. But when all of the style is shorn away, the food is what counts, and Robuchon's style has its roots deep in French classical techniques. The culinary cultures of Spain and Japan have a lot to say too, and the whole thing relies on peerless raw materials, with a fair turnout of luxury ingredients. Foie gras ravioli in warm chicken broth delivers head-spinning depth of flavour, but it is given a good run for its money by veal medallions with morel mushrooms and white asparagus. At dessert stage, a warm yuzu soufflé served with vanilla-infused raspberry sorbet goes head to head for intensity and creativity. If you prefer your surroundings more traditional, the La Cuisine dining room on the first floor goes for a clean-cut monochrome chequerboard look - the menu is the same wherever you choose.

Chef Olivier Limousin **Owner** Bahia UK Ltd **Times** 12-3/5.30-11 **Prices** Fixed D 2 course fr £22, Service added but optional 12.5% **Wines** 250 bottles over £20, 10 bottles under £20, 26 by glass **Notes** Tasting menu 9 course, Pre-theatre 2/3 course, Vegetarian available **Seats** 43 **Children** Portions **Parking** Valet parking service

with chips and béarnaise, or lamb's neck with red cabbage and sour cream, leaving room for steamed prune pudding or rhubarb and prosecco jelly.

Chef Tom Norrington-Davies, Sam Hutchins **Owner** R Shaw, T Norrington-Davies, J Jones, M Belben **Times** 12-2.30/6-10.30 Closed last working day in Dec-1st working day in Jan, BHs, D Sun **Prices** Starter £4-£9, Main £10-£25, Dessert £4-£8, Service optional **Wines** 20 bottles over £20, 25 bottles under £20, 13 by glass **Notes** Sunday L, Vegetarian available **Seats** 70

Incognico PLAN 3 C2

French, Italian

Handsome interior and vibrant Franco-Italian food

☎ 020 7836 8866
117 Shaftesbury Av, Cambridge Circus WC2H 8AD
e-mail: incognicorestaurant@gmail.com
dir: Nearest station: Leicester Sq. Off Cambridge Circus at crossing with Charing Cross Rd, opposite Palace Theatre

In the heart of theatreland, this David Collins designed restaurant has the look of a brasserie while the food is focused on Franco-Italian flavours. Enter through the discreet grey frontage on Shaftesbury Avenue into a striking interior featuring red leather chairs and banquettes, stripped wooden floors and darkwood panelling. Attractively presented dishes utilise high quality produce, ranging from the traditional to the flamboyant. The pre-theatre menu served five days a week is a popular draw, supported by the broad choice from the à la carte. Start perhaps with creamy pappardelle with Parma ham and crispy parmesan before calves' liver with sage butter and cauliflower purée.

Times 12-3/5.30-11 Closed 10 days Xmas, 4 days Etr, BHs, Sun

Indigo PLAN 3 D2

Modern European

Lively brasserie fare at the stylish One Aldwych

☎ 020 7300 0400 & 7300 1000
One Aldwych WC2B 4RH
e-mail: indigo@onealdwych.com
dir: Nearest station: Covent Garden, Charing Cross. At Aldwych & The Strand junct, opposite Waterloo Bridge

An infectiously buzzy restaurant venue overlooking the Lobby Bar at One Aldwych, Indigo is a good informal alternative to the same venue's Axis (see entry). Starched table linen and chairs upholstered in an umber hue maintain the sense of style, and the menu deals in contemporary brasserie fare rendered with great gusto. Start with smoked eel served warm, alongside potato and celeriac remoulade and an apple and red wine purée, before going on to monkfish osso buco, or braised beef short ribs with trompette mushrooms and horseradish foam. Mixing and matching your own bespoke salads and dressings is fun, and afters might include something novel like coriander-marinated pineapple with mandarin sorbet and a mint tuile.

Chef Tony Fleming **Owner** Gordon Campbell Gray **Times** 12-3/5.30-11.15 **Prices** Fixed D 3 course £19.75, Starter £6.50-£13.50, Main £15-£23.50, Dessert £6.50-£8, Service added but optional 12.5% **Wines** 40 bottles over £20, 1 bottle under £20, 11 by glass **Notes** Sat & Sun brunch menu, Pre/post-theatre D available, Vegetarian available, Civ Wed 60 **Seats** 62 **Children** Portions, Menu **Parking** Valet parking

The Ivy PLAN 3 C2

British, International V

Ever-popular Theatreland legend with brasserie-style menu

☎ 020 7836 4751
1-5 West St, Covent Garden WC2H 9NQ
dir: Nearest station: Leicester Square. Leave Leicester Square tube station by exit 3 & turn right, along Charing Cross Rd & take 2nd right into Litchfield St. Restaurant entrance is around the left hand corner on West St, opposite St Martin's Theatre

It is 20 years since the relaunched Ivy burst onto the scene and won the heart of seemingly every celebrity in the land. And quite a few of us regular folk, too. The room has a calming dignity about it, nothing showy or in yer face, just a calm club-like room with oak panelling,

continued

Clos Maggiore

LONDON WC2 PLAN 3 C2

Modern French V NOTABLE WINE LIST

An intimate oasis in the heart of Covent Garden

☎ 020 7379 9696
33 King St, Covent Garden WC2E 8JD
e-mail: enquiries@closmaggiore.com
dir: Nearest station: Covent Garden. 1 min walk from The Piazza & Royal Opera House

An intimate restaurant and blossom-filled courtyard provide a romantic oasis in the heart of Covent Garden. The interior is influenced by the stylish country inns of Provence and Tuscany - so oak panels, fireplaces and warm colours add to the cosseted feel. The courtyard has a fully retractable roof, roaring fires in the winter, box hedging and flowers and is candlelit by night. The food lives up to the wonderful surroundings. Modern French dishes underpinned by head chef Marcellin Marc's classical training are the thing here. Dishes are well-judged, the main ingredient given room to shine through. Start perhaps with a braised shoulder of Loire Valley rabbit with sweet-and-sour black radish and wholegrain mustard mousseline - a dish of superbly balanced tastes and textures. Follow on with slow-cooked fillet of Cornish cod with a ricotta cheese and chive glaze, broccoli, cauliflower and celeriac casserole and smoked haddock velouté. There are imaginative vegetarian dishes, too, while dessert might bring forth poached conference pear and gingerbread biscuit, served with a chestnut ice cream. Seasonal and vegetarian tasting menus are an option. A wine list of considerable scope and class is a good reason to linger a little longer in what has to be one of the capital's most romantic restaurants.

Chef Marcellin Marc **Owner** Tyfoon Restaurants Ltd **Times** 12-2.30/5-11 Closed 24-25 Dec **Prices** Fixed L 2 course £19.50-£24.50, Fixed D 3 course £19.50-£24.50, Starter £6.50-£13.50, Main £16.50-£19.50, Dessert £6, Service added but optional 12.5% **Wines** 2000 bottles over £20, 11 bottles under £20, 19 by glass **Notes** Tasting menu 6 course, Post-theatre menu 2 course, Sunday L, Vegetarian menu, Dress restrictions, Smart casual **Seats** 70, Pr/dining room 23 **Children** Portions **Parking** NCP, on street

LONDON WC2 *continued*

smart green leather seating, wooden floors and harlequin-like stained glass to keep out prying eyes. There can be quite a buzz about the place (there's a private room upstairs as well) and the staff cope with it all with aplomb. The large brasserie-style menu does what it does very well, and can take you from grilled squid, chorizo and parsley salad, via Middlewhite pork belly with Goldrush apples and creamed cider sauce, to goats' curd cheesecake, or deliver traditional comforts in the likes of breaded scampi with tartare sauce, eggs Benedict and steak and kidney pudding.

Chef Gary Lee **Owner** Caprice Holdings
Times 12-3/5.30-12 Closed 25-26 Dec, 1 Jan, D 24 Dec
Prices Starter £6.25-£16.75, Main £13.75-£28.75, Dessert £6.75-£8, Service added but optional 12.5%
Notes Sunday L, Vegetarian menu, Dress restrictions, Smart casual **Seats** 100, Pr/dining room 60
Children Portions **Parking** NCP, on street

J. Sheekey & J Sheekey Oyster Bar PLAN 3 C2

Seafood V

Renowned theatreland fish restaurant

☎ 020 7240 2565
St Martin's Court WC2N 4AL
dir: Nearest station: Leicester Square. Leave underground station by Exit 1 & turn left onto Charing Cross Rd. St Martin's Court is the 2nd road on the left

If this legendary theatreland fish restaurant seems old fashioned, remember that there has been a restaurant on the site since 1896, when Josef Sheekey's oyster bar set up shop. Over the decades the place has sprawled sideways, taking over the neighbours in a quartet of congenial, clubby wood-panelled dining rooms, plus a seafood and oyster bar. It's something of a celeb haunt, as shown by black and white photos of the thesps and entertainers who have frequented the place for decades. The kitchen also works from a well-rehearsed script, majoring in simply-prepared fish and seafood, but the menu doesn't turn its back on hardcore carnivores. Fresh seafood platters are one way to go, but there's also pan-fried skate with capers and brown butter, a cracking haddock and chips with mushy peas, or herb-roasted gilt head bream.

Chef Richard Kirkwood **Owner** Caprice Holdings
Times 12-3/5.30-12 **Prices** Food prices not confirmed for 2011. Please telephone for details **Notes** Vegetarian menu **Seats** 105 **Children** Portions **Parking** On street

Mon Plaisir PLAN 3 C2

French

A Francophile's delight in theatreland

☎ 020 7836 7243 & 7240 3757
19-21 Monmouth St WC2H 9DD
e-mail: monplaisirrestaurant@googlemail.com
dir: Nearest station: Covent Garden, Leicester Square. Off Seven Dials

Amid the bustle of the West End, there is a restaurant that will be forever France. This Gallic stalwart has been in business since the '40s, when De Gaulle held court here in exile; one assumes he did not say 'non' to the French onion soup and authentic Burgundian coq au vin. This is about as French as it gets north of Calais: a zinc-topped bar salvaged from a Lyonnaise bordello, waiters with extreme French accents - all that's missing is Edith Piaf singing in the background. Its classic bistro-style main dining room has the elbow-to-elbow joie de vivre of a Lyonnaise bouchon, while other convivial rooms are decorated with Picasso-esque mirrors, classic French posters and modern abstract art. The brasserie and à la carte menus take in everything from timeless snails in garlic and parsley butter to a more modern pan-fried cod with orange juice, rosemary and black olive tapenade. To finish, it just has to be a plate of pungently melting cheeses.

Chef Franck Raymond **Owner** Alain Lhermitte
Times 12-2.15/5.45-11.15 Closed Xmas, New Year, BHs, Sun **Prices** Fixed L 2 course £14.95, Fixed D 3 course £15.95, Starter £5.95-£9.95, Main £16.95-£28.50, Dessert £4.95-£8.95, Service added but optional 12.5%
Wines 70 bottles over £20, 19 bottles under £20, 13 by glass **Notes** Fixed D pre-theatre menu inc. glass of house wine/coffee, Vegetarian available, Dress restrictions, Smart casual **Seats** 100, Pr/dining room 28
Children Portions

Orso Restaurant PLAN 3 D2

Modern Italian

Italian food in a lively basement

☎ 020 7240 5269
27 Wellington St WC2E 7DA
e-mail: info@orsorestaurant.co.uk
dir: Nearest station: Covent Garden

While the street entrance could easily be missed, savvy crowds have been flocking downstairs to this relaxed, all-day Covent Garden Italian since the mid-'80s. The big basement dining room (a one-time orchid warehouse) reverberates with the buzz of conversation, clinking glasses and friendly, quick-fire service. Herringbone-patterned wood floors, white tiled walls, pastel shades and black-and-white photos add further atmosphere, with their nod to Milan of the '50s. The menus are equally crowd pleasing, showcasing simple regional Italian cooking with bags of choice. Pasta (tagliatelle with aubergine, oven-dried tomatoes, basil and pecorino) and pizza sit alongside main courses such as grilled calves' liver with red onions, spinach and balsamic. Pre-theatre fixed-price menus, a bar and all-Italian wines complete the package.

Times noon-midnight Closed 24-25 Dec, L Sat-Sun (Jul-Aug)

The Portrait Restaurant & Bar PLAN 3 C1

Modern British

Sleek, contemporary, buzzy dining with rooftop views

☎ 020 7312 2490
National Portrait Gallery, St Martins Place WC2H OHE
e-mail: portrait.reservation@searcys.co.uk
dir: Nearest station: Leicester Square, Charing Cross. Just behind Trafalgar Square

The jaw-dropping view from the sleek, light and contemporary restaurant on the top floor of the National Portrait Gallery certainly pulls in the crowds. A wall of windows means everyone gets an outlook across the London landscape, including Nelson's-eye views up Whitehall to Westminster, while an otherwise minimalist grey, cream and black colour scheme is interrupted only by the warmth of red leather high-back banquettes and a blond-wood floor. The modern bistro-style fare takes an equally light, simple, clean-lined approach, perhaps featuring lamb cutlets with confit lamb hash, aubergine, tomato and sultana relish, or maybe organic salmon with purple sprouting broccoli and blood orange hollandaise. Be warned though, the hard surfaces and a bar up front ratchet up the decibels.

Chef Katarina Todosijevic **Owner** Searcys
Times 11.45-2.45/5.30-8.30 Closed 24-26 Dec, 1 Jan, D Sat-Wed **Prices** Fixed L 2 course £20-£30, Fixed D 3 course £25-£35, Starter £5-£10, Main £13.50-£22, Dessert £5.50-£8, Service added but optional 12.5%
Wines 35 bottles over £20, 9 bottles under £20, 14 by glass **Notes** Pre-theatre menu D Thu & Fri only, Sunday L, Vegetarian available **Seats** 100 **Children** Portions, Menu
Parking NCP - Orange St

The Strand PLAN 3 C1

French, European

Contemporary cooking in a grand Victorian railway hotel

020 7747 8410
Charing Cross Hotel, The Strand WC2N 5HX
e-mail: vidur.kapur@guoman.co.uk
dir: Nearest station: Charing Cross. Adjacent to Charing Cross station

This Grande Dame of the Victorian railway era still puts on a fine show in the 21st century. The Charing Cross Hotel is quite literally at the centre of London, since the railway station is the point from which all road distances are measured. The views from the Victorian-styled dining room's incredibly high and ornate windows across the busy Strand to Trafalgar Square are among London's finest. The kitchen deals in contemporary British dishes with forays into an international repertoire. A starter of pigeon foie gras and ham hock terrine is served with mesclun salad, then followed by roast rack of Southdown lamb with French beans, glazed parsnips and dauphinoise potatoes. Finish with the comfort of walnut and date sticky toffee pudding with vanilla sauce.

Chef Franck Siblas **Owner** Guoman Hotel Ltd
Times 12-3/5-10 **Prices** Fixed L 2 course £25.95, Fixed D 3 course £29.95, Starter £7.50-£13, Main £16.50-£25, Dessert £7-£10.95, Service added but optional 12.5% **Wines** 40 bottles over £20, 15 by glass **Notes** Pre-theatre meals 2 course £16.95, 3 course £24, Vegetarian available, Dress restrictions, Smart casual, Civ Wed 120 **Seats** 30 **Children** Portions

Terroirs PLAN 3 C1

French NOTABLE WINE LIST

Rustic French cooking in the heart of London

020 7036 0660
5 William IV St, Covent Garden WC2N 4DW
e-mail: enquiries@terroirswinebar.com
dir: Nearest station: Covent Garden, Charing Cross

If you're thinking the term wine bar is a bit passé, think again. Terroirs has given the genre a shot in the arm with its determination to source interesting organic and bio-dynamic wines from small artisan producers (mostly from France and Italy), matched by a passion for the provenance of ingredients, and some great cooking. The décor is very French, rustic, with the split-level ground-floor dominated by a zinc-topped bar, and a deep, deep basement providing more tables and nooks and crannies. Broadly speaking you go for small plates upstairs and the more traditional starter-main format in the basement, but they're flexible, and the relaxed attitude makes for a happy buzz all round. All the food - from the charcuterie (delicious ventrêche or duck rillette) to the excellent cheeses, small plates such as Cheltenham beetroot with fresh goats' curd, and main courses like line-caught cod with brown shrimps, cucumber and dill - allows the ingredients to speak for themselves, delivering top-notch flavours.

Chef Ed Wilson **Owner** Ed Wilson, Nigel Sutcliffe, Eric Nariod **Times** 12-11 Closed Xmas, Etr, Sun **Prices** Food prices not confirmed for 2011. Please telephone for details, Service added but optional 12.5% **Wines** 248 bottles over £20, 14 bottles under £20, 24 by glass **Notes** Fixed 1 course L £10, Pre/post theatre menu available, Vegetarian available **Seats** 120
Children Portions

12 Temple Place Restaurant PLAN 3 E2

Modern British

Innovative modern British cooking in individually styled hotel

020 7836 3555 & 7300 1700
Swissotel The Howard, London, Temple Place WC2R 2PR
e-mail: 12templeplacerestaurant.london@swissotel.com
dir: Nearest station: Temple. Opposite tube station

The modish restaurant of Thames-side Swissôtel The Howard, 12 Temple Place, is a fusion of splendid Regency ceilings garlanded with fancy plasterwork, and a chic designer ensemble of boldly-patterned upholstery and wallpaper, funky candelabras in kaleidoscopic colours, and quirky cloth-wrapped teapots for vases on darkwood tables. The cooking is as fashionable as the décor, based around a broadly modern British repertoire of tersely-described dishes that rely on top-class raw materials to make their point. Chervil and juniper-cured pollock might open in the company of sloe gin dressing and pollock rillettes, while main courses bring chargrilled Scottish halibut teamed with beetroot purée, brown shrimps, tarragon and horseradish, alongside roast beef fillet with oxtail pie, shallot purée and baby leeks. As a change to wine, flavoured beers and artisan British lagers are matched with the food.

Chef Brian Spark **Owner** New Ray Ltd
Times 12-2.30/5.45-10.30 Closed 1st wk Jan, BHs, Sun, L Sat **Prices** Food prices not confirmed for 2011. Please telephone for details **Wines** 120 bottles over £20, 10 by glass **Notes** Vegetarian available, Dress restrictions, Smart casual, Civ Wed 100 **Seats** 56 **Parking** 30

GREATER LONDON

BARNET Map 6 TQ29

Savoro

Modern European

Contemporary good looks and well-judged menu

020 8449 9888
206 High St EN5 5SZ
e-mail: savoro@savoro.co.uk
web: www.savoro.co.uk
dir: M25 junct 23 to A1081, continue to St Albans Rd, at lights turn left to A1000

Set back from Barnet's bustling high street, the traditional façade of this restaurant with rooms belies the snazzy modern dining areas and bedrooms found within. The restaurant has been kitted out with contemporary design - glass screens, tiled floor, concealed lighting - and is a very modern kind of neighbourhood restaurant. The kitchen aims for 'simple execution of good technique', and it is demonstrable in the eclectic range of dishes to be found on the set dinner menu. Start with chargrilled calamari marinated in lime and chilli, before roast belly pork with celeriac mash and braised red cabbage, and perhaps chocolate and hazelnut brownie to finish.

Times 12-3/6-11 Closed 1 Jan, 1 wk New Year, D Sun

BECKENHAM

Mello PLAN 1 G1

Modern European

Fashionable dining in the suburbs

020 8663 0994
2 Southend Rd BR3 1SD
e-mail: info@mello.uk.com
dir: 0.5m from Beckenham town centre, directly opposite Beckenham train station

Prepare to ditch postcode preconceptions: suburban Beckenham may not be on the hot-list of the foodie radar, but Mello is the exception that proves the rule. Emerge from the station, and the Victorian building catches the eye; once inside, it's a smart venue done out in shades of burgundy and caramel, with smart high-backed leather and suede chairs and modern artwork to peruse. The kitchen draws its inspiration from classical themes, which it plays out using well-sourced materials on a

continued

BECKENHAM ***continued***

menu that hikes its way around the Mediterranean. Pan-fried red mullet with escabèche dressing and parmesan crisps is a good way to get off the mark, then you might follow with pot-roasted partridge with sautéed curly kale, parsnip purée, truffled potato fondant and thyme jus. Finish with hot chocolate fondant with pistachio ice cream.

Times 12-2.30/6-10 Closed D Sun

BROMLEY

Chapter One PLAN 1 H1

@@@@ – *see opposite page*

ENFIELD Map 6 TQ39

Royal Chace Hotel

@ Modern British

Brasserie dining in Middlesex

☎ 020 8884 8181
162 The Ridgeway EN2 8AR
e-mail: reservations@royalchacehotel.co.uk
dir: 3m from M25 junct 24, 1.5m to Enfield

Located in six acres of rolling countryside, this Middlesex hotel offers great views while still being close to London. The Chace Brasserie is at the back of the hotel and so enjoys panoramic views of the surrounding countryside. Traditional and contemporary furnishings are melded in some style and tables are formally presented with starched white linen. For more informal dining, head to the King's Bar & Lounge. A variety of modern and classic British dishes characterise the menu, all made using mainly local ingredients. White crab cocktail combines white crabmeat with baby gem lettuce, pink grapefruit and Bloody Mary sauce. For mains there's chicken Kiev, champ, fricassée of peas, bacon and fine beans and rhubarb crumble and custard pannacotta to finish.

Chef Peter Leggat **Owner** B Nicholas **Times** 12-2/6-9.30 Closed Xmas, BH Mon **Prices** Starter £5.25-£6.95, Main £9.95-£21.95, Dessert £6.95, Service added but optional 10% **Wines** 13 bottles over £20, 23 bottles under £20, 7 by glass **Notes** Sunday L, Vegetarian available, Dress restrictions, Smart casual, Civ Wed 220 **Seats** 60, Pr/dining room 50 **Children** Portions, Menu **Parking** 220

HADLEY WOOD Map 6 TQ29

The Mary Beale Restaurant

@ Modern British

Solid British cooking in tranquil country-house hotel

☎ 020 8216 3900
West Lodge Park Hotel, Cockfosters Rd EN4 0PY
e-mail: westlodgepark@bealeshotels.co.uk
dir: On A111, 1m S of M25 junct 24

An impressive Regency-style country house set in 35 acres of grounds that include an arboretum and lake. Just 12 miles from central London and conveniently located close to the M25 (exit 24), this charming, family-run hotel makes a peaceful rural base. The contemporary restaurant, named after the artist Mary Beale and displaying many of her original paintings, provides a convivial setting for some enjoyable modern British cooking. Typical dishes may include seared scallops with pea and mint purée, sea bass with braised leeks and gribiche sauce, and milk chocolate crème brûlée.

Chef Wayne Turner **Owner** Beales Ltd **Times** 12.30-2.30/7-9.30 **Prices** Fixed L 2 course £15, Fixed D 3 course £25, Starter £7-£11, Main £15-£24, Dessert £8, Service optional **Wines** 51 bottles over £20, 24 bottles under £20, 7 by glass **Notes** Sunday L, Vegetarian available, Dress restrictions, Smart casual, jacket & tie recommended, Civ Wed 72 **Seats** 70, Pr/dining room 54 **Children** Portions **Parking** 75

HARROW ON THE HILL

Incanto Restaurant PLAN 1 B5

@ Modern Italian

Authentic southern Italian cooking in historic village

☎ 020 8426 6767
41 High St HA1 3HT
e-mail: info@incanto.co.uk
web: www.incanto.co.uk

Opposite the village green in Harrow on the Hill, the 19th-century former post office is these days a sleek and modern Italian restaurant. The Grade II listed building has been lovingly restored and has a coolly minimal interior that includes full-length glass skylights, a sweeping staircase, comfortable leather banquettes and wooden beams. There is a genuine interest in authentic and contemporary southern Italian cooking here. Try home-made ravioli filled with free-range egg and black truffle, followed by pan-fried wild sea bass, razor clams, wild garlic and cauliflower purée, and finish with fresh rhubarb with cinnamon mascarpone, or go for one of the home-made gelati.

Chef Marcus Chant **Owner** David & Catherine Taylor **Times** 12-2.30/6.30-11 Closed 25-26 Dec, 1 Jan, Etr Sun, Mon, D Sun **Prices** Fixed L 2 course fr £15.95, Fixed D 3 course fr £22.50, Starter £6.25-£7.95, Main £14.25-£18.70, Dessert £6.95-£7.90, Service added but optional 12.5% **Wines** 76 bottles over £20, 10 bottles under £20, 8 by glass **Notes** Sunday L, Vegetarian available **Seats** 64, Pr/dining room 30 **Children** Portions, Menu **Parking** On street

HARROW WEALD

Grim's Dyke Hotel PLAN 1 B6

@@ Modern British

Peaceful country-house conveniently close to London

☎ 020 8385 3100
Old Redding HA3 6SH
e-mail: reservations@grimsdyke.com
dir: 3m from M1 between Harrow & Watford

Sir William Gilbert, the writing half of the Gilbert & Sullivan partnership, lived for 20 years in this elegant Victorian mansion wrapped in 40 acres of heavenly gardens and parkland. Memorabilia of famous G&S productions are thick on the ground, and many years of artistic tenure mean that the house is a highly individual place, bristling with original features. Gilbert's former billiard room looks more or less as it did in 1880, except it is now an atmospheric restaurant slathered with hand-painted wallpapers, ceramic tile friezes, cathedral-like windows, and ornate plasterwork ceilings. Expect modern British cooking with classical undertones from a kitchen that follows the seasons and makes fine use of produce from the hotel's kitchen garden. A meal could begin with smoked eel with beetroot tart and horseradish cream, followed by tournedos of 18-hour-braised mutton served with crushed potatoes and barley broth.

Chef Daren Mason **Owner** Skerrits of Nottingham Holdings **Times** 12.30-2/7-9.30 Closed 24 Dec, 1 Jan, L Sat, D 25-26 Dec **Prices** Fixed L 2 course £9.95-£12.95, Fixed D 3 course £22-£30, Tasting menu £40, Starter £6.50-£9.50, Main £13.95-£25, Dessert £6.50-£9.50, Service optional **Wines** 70 bottles over £20, 10 bottles under £20, 10 by glass **Notes** Tasting menu 6 course Fri-Sat, Sunday L, Vegetarian available, Dress restrictions, No jeans or trainers (Fri-Sat), Civ Wed 88 **Seats** 60, Pr/dining room 88 **Children** Portions **Parking** 100

Chapter One

BROMLEY PLAN 1 H1

Modern European NOTABLE WINE LIST

Sumptuous contemporary design with food to match

☎ 01689 854848
Farnborough Common, Locksbottom BR6 8NF
e-mail: info@chaptersrestaurants.com
dir: On A21, 3m from Bromley. From M25 junct 4 onto A21 for 5m

The mock-Tudor building that is home to Chapter One has become a beacon for local foodies. While there's nothing cutting edge about the restaurant's façade, the door opens onto a realm of striking contemporary design and top-level culinary experience. This may be suburban Kent on the outer fringes of the metropolis, but Andrew McLeish's cooking is straight out of the big city's style book. The blocks of dark chocolate, cream and cherry colours in the glamorous dining room are rather like sitting in a box of very posh chocolates, subtly back-lit through shimmery curtains of beads, while the striking bar is hewn from German alabaster and volcanic rock, and food-related art helps to titillate the taste buds. Andrew McLeish started out his culinary career with Nico Ladenis, so classical ways are deeply ingrained in his consummate technical skills, enlivened by a leaning for modish ingredients and wow-factor presentation. An eye-catching opener of warm smoked eel with smoked eel brandade, pickled beetroot and celeriac remoulade might set the tone, ahead of a tasting of veal rump, sweetbread and cheek with gratin potatoes, parsnip purée and baby kale, or roast cod with orange-braised chicory, roasted gnocchi and pancetta. Meals climax with desserts that have a definite X factor, such as pavé of Valrhona chocolate with sugared pistachio, honeycomb and caramelised pear purée, or organic lemon tart with crème fraîche sorbet and passionfruit millefeuille. What's more, this is all priced very keenly. There is also an informal brasserie area with bare tables and a pared-back menu.

Chef Andrew McLeish **Owner** Selective Restaurants Group
Times 12-2.30/6.30-10.30 Closed 1-4 Jan **Prices** Fixed L 3 course fr £18.50, Starter £7.50, Main £17, Dessert £7.50, Service added but optional 12.5%
Wines 133 bottles over £20, 17 bottles under £20, 10 by glass **Notes** Sunday L, Vegetarian available, Dress restrictions, No shorts, jeans or trainers **Seats** 120, Pr/dining room 55 **Children** Portions
Parking 90

HEATHROW AIRPORT (LONDON)

Sheraton Skyline Hotel PLAN 1 A3

Italian, International

Classy modern Italian cooking in chic hotel

020 8564 3300 & 020 8759 2535
Bath Rd, Hayes UB3 5BP
e-mail: jirayr.kececian@sheraton.com
dir: M4 junct 4 towards Terminals 1,2 & 3. Follow signs for A4 London entering Bath Rd, hotel 1m on left

This upmarket hotel may not win many awards for its looks from the outside but inside it is modern, stylish and very well presented. Similarly, the Al Dente Ristorante is a light and airy space with a clean-cut contemporary look and warm lighting to soften the edges. Modern Italian cuisine is the name of the game and the menu offers all the old favourites, with a few modern ideas from the Piedmontese chef. A starter of open ravioli with confit duck, roasted pumpkin, spinach and foie gras might be followed by slow-braised short rib of beef with broad bean purée, stuffed cabbage, soft polenta and Merlot jus. For dessert, perhaps a warm clementine sponge with rosemary and raspberry sorbet.

Chef Marco di Tullio **Owner** Host Hotels & Resorts TRS UK Holdings Ltd **Times** 12-3/6-10.45 **Prices** Fixed L 2 course fr £16, Fixed D 3 course fr £26, Starter £6.95-£10.95, Main £14.95-£17.95, Dessert £5.50 **Wines** 30+ bottles over £20, 15 by glass **Notes** Vegetarian available, Civ Wed 300 **Seats** 80, Pr/dining room 10 **Children** Portions, Menu **Parking** 300

KEW

The Glasshouse PLAN 1 C3

– *see below*

KINGSTON UPON THAMES

Frère Jacques PLAN 1 C1

French

Popular Thames-side brasserie with authentic French cooking and ambience

020 8546 1332
10-12 Riverside Walk, Bishops Hall KT1 1QN
e-mail: john@frerejacques.co.uk
web: www.frerejacques.co.uk
dir: 50 mtrs S of Kingston side of Kingston Bridge, by the river

A bastion of the riverfront prom since the mid '90s, Jacques offers a refreshing respite from the crowd of pubs and chain eateries. On lazy summer days there isn't a better pitch in town, while in less clement weather, a permanent awning with heaters offers rustic charm, or move inside to the modern dining room. Wherever you sit, red tablecloths and a backing track of Gallic music offer bags of unpretentious joie de vivre. The kitchen's repertoire plays to the passing gallery, mixing straightforward French brasserie staples (crispy fried frogs' legs to moules marinière) with more modish dishes (grilled sea bass fillet with black truffle mash, seafood bisque and piperade). In winter it's not quite as colourful, but friendly service and value ensures year-round appeal.

Frère Jacques

Times 12-11 Closed 25-26 Dec, 1 Jan, D 24 Dec

The Glasshouse

KEW PLAN 1 C3

Modern European

Local favourite with confident, modern cooking

020 8940 6777
14 Station Pde TW9 3PZ
e-mail: info@glasshouserestaurant.co.uk

Part of the Nigel Platts-Martin and Bruce Poole stable of restaurants (together with Chez Bruce and La Trompette - see entries), The Glasshouse is a buzzy neighbourhood bolt-hole that gets everything right. Lucky residents of posh Kew, then, who can rely on this light-flooded, uncluttered contemporary eatery next to Kew Gardens tube station to come up with the goods: seasonally-driven modern European food that doesn't try any fancy trickery. Expect accurate, confident cooking with spot-on flavours in imaginative yet unfussy combinations. A warm salad of wood pigeon is given extra depth with the addition of a deep-fried truffled egg and balsamic vinegar, while foie gras ballottine comes with the contrasting textures of duck pastilla, lentils, green beans and quince jelly. Main course might bring together pot-roast rabbit leg with gnocchi, wild mushrooms, Bayonne ham and tarragon, and to finish there's superb cheeses and classic puddings with a modern twist - Black Forest trifle with toasted almonds, perhaps. The wine list is a serious piece of work with some top-notch stuff from France, and ample choice available by the glass.

Owner Larkbrace Ltd **Times** 12-2.30/6.30-10.30 Closed Xmas, New Year **Prices** Fixed L 2 course £18.50-£24.50, Fixed D 3 course £39.50, Service added but optional 12.5% **Wines** 376 bottles over £20, 4 bottles under £20, 16 by glass **Notes** Tasting menu Mon-Fri D on request, Sunday L, Vegetarian available **Seats** 60 **Children** Portions, Menu **Parking** On street; metered

PINNER

Friends Restaurant PLAN 1 B5

Modern British

Modernised classics in a period building

020 8866 0286
11 High St HA5 5PJ
e-mail: info@friendsrestaurant.co.uk
dir: In centre of Pinner, 2 mins walk from underground station

A long-standing locals' favourite, this traditional black-beamed 400-year-old building with whitewashed exterior is an oasis at the bottom of historic Pinner High Street. Dining rooms over two floors have low wooden beams in predominantly black-and-white surroundings while a single flower stem on each smartly dressed table gives just a soupçon of colour. The cooking makes use of good British ingredients in modern dishes that are soundly based in classical thinking: a winning formula. Start with a pan-fried haggis cake with a soft poached egg, whisky sauce and pancetta, followed by an inventive main of medallions of red deer with chocolate and chilli sauce, chestnuts and lardons with rum baba and spiced plums to finish. The predominantly French wine list offers a good selection by the glass.

Friends Restaurant

Chef Terry Farr **Owner** Mr Farr **Times** 12-3/6.30-10.30 Closed 25 Dec, BHs, Mon in summer, D Sun **Prices** Fixed L 2 course fr £18.95, Fixed D 3 course £31.50, Service added but optional 10% **Wines** 40 bottles over £20, 8 bottles under £20, 17 by glass **Notes** Sunday L, Vegetarian available **Seats** 40, Pr/dining room 30 **Children** Portions **Parking** Nearby car parks

RICHMOND UPON THAMES

Bacco Restaurant Italiano PLAN 1 C3

Italian NEW

Smart and welcoming neighbourhood Italian

020 8332 0348
39-41 Kew Rd TW9 2NQ
e-mail: bookings@bacco-restaurant.co.uk
dir: A316 towards Richmond Station or town centre, 2 min walk from tube

A smart independent Italian (which makes a nice change in chain-filled Richmond) with a loyal local following and a lively atmosphere. Bacco occupies two adjoining buildings, with the dining room split into two distinctly separate areas, both decked out in neutral shades with closely packed tables. A library of all-Italian wines lines the walls, and there are regular wine dinners. The cooking is contemporary Italian (no spaghetti Bolognese or pizza in sight), with pasta and breads made in-house. Tuna and black pearl scallops are accurately cooked and served with braised chicory and orange vinaigrette to start, while tagliatelle with duck ragu and crunchy vegetables makes a fine main course.

Chef Vincenzo Indelicato **Owner** Stefano Bergamin **Times** 12-2.30/5.45-11 Closed Xmas, New Year, BHs, Sun **Prices** Fixed L 2 course £14.50, Fixed D 2 course £14.50-

continued

Bingham

RICHMOND UPON THAMES PLAN 1 C2

Modern British

Thameside luxury and skilful flavour combinations

020 8940 0902
61-63 Petersham Rd TW10 6UT
e-mail: info@thebingham.co.uk
dir: On A307

This boutique hotel, which was originally built as two Georgian houses, has been renovated and refurbished to the max. The superb position by the Thames, tucked away from the main hustle and bustle of Richmond town centre, with its own delightful gardens, is these days as delightful as when the house was first built. The lavish interior features statement chandeliers and mirrored walls for a luxurious feel, plus fifteen sensuous bedrooms boast art-deco inspired furniture and high comfort levels. In the restaurant, well-spaced tables, soft light and caramel tones combine with surprisingly comfortable seating creating an understated air of opulence. Chef Shay Cooper's modern British menu is full of stunning combinations of flavours and textures. Start perhaps with brill fillet with ricotta gnocchi, seared scallop, poached grapes and light bread sauce. Move on to salt marsh lamb, the breast crisp and tender, served with artichoke barigoule, confit garlic and ratte potato purée. A delicious hazelnut and chocolate marquise, sugared hazelnuts, yoghurt jelly and mandarin sorbet rounds things off. That said, great petits fours and a selection of cheeses from small suppliers are worth lingering over, particularly if you bagged a table on the terrace overlooking the river.

Chef Shay Cooper **Owner** Ruth & Samantha Trinder **Times** 12-2.30/7-10 Closed D Sun **Prices** Fixed L 2 course fr £19.50, Fixed D 3 course fr £45, Service added but optional 12.5% **Wines** 178 bottles over £20, 5 bottles under £20, 14 by glass **Notes** Tasting menu 8 course, Sunday L, Vegetarian available, Civ Wed 90 **Seats** 50 **Children** Portions, Menu **Parking** 8

RICHMOND UPON THAMES *continued*

£19, Starter £6.50-£10, Main £9.50-£20, Dessert £4.50-£6, Service added 12.5% **Wines** 45 bottles over £20, 12 bottles under £20, 16 by glass **Notes** Fixed L 2/3 course pre-theatre, D 5 course with wine £65, Vegetarian available, Dress restrictions, Smart casual, Air con **Seats** 50, Pr/dining room 27

Bingham PLAN 1 C2

@@@ – *see page 327*

La Buvette PLAN 1 E3

@ French, Mediterranean

Charming French bistro serving up simple classics

☎ 020 8940 6264
6 Church Walk TW9 1SN
e-mail: info@labuvette.co.uk
dir: 3 mins from train station, opposite St Mary Magdalene Church

When the citizens of Richmond need a shot of cross-channel cuisine, La Buvette is at hand. The York stone building was once the refectory of the Saxon church in whose shadow it sits; outside there's a secluded walled courtyard for open air dining, while the interior is pleasing in an unshouty way - split into two intimate dining areas with elbow-to-elbow tables, dark beams, and big sash windows letting in plenty of light. Reliable old-school French bistro cooking is the kitchen's stock in trade. A tarte fine of red onion and goats' cheese is a good way to start, followed by a rib-sticking main course of braised belly pork with choucroute and smoked sausage. French staff are friendly and charming, and the icing on the cake: prices are gentle - the lunchtime set menu is a steal.

Chef Buck Carter **Owner** Bruce Duckett **Times** 12-3/6-10 Closed 25-26 Dec, 1 Jan, Good Fri **Prices** Fixed L 2 course £13.25, Fixed D 3 course £19.75, Service added but optional 12.5% **Wines** 21 bottles over £20, 7 bottles under £20, 14 by glass **Notes** Sunday L, Vegetarian available **Seats** 50 **Children** Portions, Menu **Parking** NCP - Paradise Road

Petersham Nurseries PLAN 1 C2

@@ Modern

English domestic produce with Italian overtones in a verdant setting by the Thames

☎ 020 8605 3627
Church Ln, Off Petersham Rd TW10 7AG
e-mail: cafe@petershamnurseries.com
dir: Adjacent to Richmond Park & Petersham Meadows. Best accessed on foot or bicycle along the river

Here is one of the south's more diverting destinations. It's the café at a garden centre by the Thames, where weathered old tables are set out in the glasshouse among the trailing plants, and your waiter will probably be wearing wellies. Suffice it to say gentlemen don't require a jacket and tie. Skye Gyngell has been at the forefront of seasonal cooking in the UK, and offers a menu gently inflected with Italian modes, but hawkishly following the seasons for domestic produce from week to week. Expect crab with kohlrabi dressed in verjus, or white bean soup trickled with Capezzana olive oil, for starters, before going on to main courses that are simplicity itself, perhaps matching mackerel with Swiss chard and horseradish cream. A winter dinner might conclude with blood oranges dressed in rosemary honey. Good drinking includes a fine selection of teas, including China's rarely seen bai ling gong fu, a mellow, caramelly red tea.

Chef Skye Gyngell **Owner** Franceso & Gael Boglione **Times** 12-2.45 Closed Etr Sun, 25 Dec, Mon-Tue, D all week **Prices** Fixed L 2 course £27.50, Starter fr £10, Main fr £19, Dessert £7-£8, Service added but optional 12.5% **Wines** 27 bottles over £20, 4 bottles under £20, 11 by glass **Notes** Vegetarian available **Parking** Town Centre, Paradise Road or The Quadrant

Restaurant at the Petersham PLAN 1 C2

@@ British, European

Elegant hotel with accomplished cooking

☎ 020 8940 1084 & 020 8940 7471
The Petersham Hotel, Nightingale Ln TW10 6UZ
e-mail: restaurant@petershamhotel.co.uk
dir: From Richmond Bridge rdbt (A316) follow Ham & Petersham signs. Nightingale Lane off Petersham Rd, hotel on left

For dining with one of the best rural views in London, look no further than this grand Victorian mansion on Richmond Hill: the vista sweeps across cows grazing Petersham meadow to a bend in the River Thames, immortalised by Joshua Reynolds and JMW Turner, and it's all protected from developers by an Act of Parliament. Chef Alex Bentley cooks in tune with the surroundings, pulling together the best of classic and contemporary styles, in an elegant setting of walnut panelling, ornate mirrors and well-spaced tables, with full-length windows opening up the river views. Expect classic, well-executed cooking updated in a contemporary British style with sharp flavours and some intriguing combinations. Pigeon and sweetbreads are paired with sautéed mushrooms, button onions and date sauce; to follow there might be grilled sea bass with piquillo peppers, caper polenta, anchovy and courgette beignet, and smoked aubergine.

Chef Alex Bentley **Owner** The Petersham Hotel Ltd **Times** 12.15-2.15/7-9.45 Closed 25-26 Dec, 1 Jan, D 24 Dec **Prices** Fixed L 2 course £18.50, Starter £7.50-£13, Main £14.50-£26.50, Dessert £7, Service added but optional 10% **Wines** 100 bottles over £20, 4 bottles under £20, 11 by glass **Notes** Degustation menu (6 course) £60, Sunday L, Vegetarian available, Civ Wed 40 **Seats** 70, Pr/dining room 26 **Children** Portions, Menu **Parking** 60

Richmond Gate Hotel - Gates on the Park PLAN 1 C3

@@ Modern British **NEW**

Elegant restaurant in a prestigious hotel

☎ 020 8940 0061
152-158 Richmond Hill TW10 6RP
e-mail: richmondgate@foliohotels.com
dir: From Richmond to top of Richmond Hill. Hotel on left opposite Star & Garter home at Richmond Gate exit

At the top of Richmond Hill, close to the 2,500-acre Royal Park, there are magnificent views over the River Thames from this elegant former Georgian country house. The hotel is more extensive than its frontage of a few 18th-century houses might suggest, with beautifully refurbished period day rooms and bedrooms, a smart leisure club, and the intimate Gates on the Park Restaurant. Light and airy, it mixes an air of Georgian formality with contemporary style, complemented by friendly and attentive service. The seasonal menu is characterised by modern interpretations of classically-based ideas and the kitchen makes sound use of quality ingredients in dishes that deliver satisfying, clear flavours. Seared scallops with caramelised apple, pork belly and veal jus, halibut with grilled polenta, white onion purée and red wine salsify, and chocolate fondant with white chocolate and orange mousse show the style.

Chef Simon Borough **Owner** Folio Hotels **Times** 7-9.30 Closed L all week (rest only) **Prices** Food prices not confirmed for 2011. Please telephone for details **Wines** 37 bottles over £20, 17 bottles under £20, 8 by glass **Notes** Sunday L, Vegetarian available, Dress restrictions, Smart casual, Civ Wed 70 **Seats** 30, Pr/dining room 70 **Children** Portions, Menu **Parking** 50

Richmond Hill Hotel PLAN 1 C3

@ Modern European **NEW**

Thameside location for all-day dining

☎ 020 8939 0265
144-150 Richmond Hill TW10 6RW
e-mail: restaurant.richmondhill@foliohotels.com
dir: A316 for Richmond, hotel at top of Richmond Hill

The Richmond Hill Hotel, where Pembrokes Restaurant is situated, overlooks the River Thames and Richmond Park where herds of red and fallow deer roam. This 17th-century Grade II listed Georgian manor has been sensitively restored and modernised, so expect grand period details and bags of character among the essentially contemporary interior. The bar area leading into the restaurant sports comfortable leather sofas and pastel tones. Pembrokes itself is divided into two parts and tables are simply dressed with proper napkins and quality tableware. The all-day menu of brasserie crowd-pleasers features a grill and favourites section. Go for 'posh' creamy garlic mushrooms or a main of slow-cooked lamb shank in rosemary and merlot with a creamed mash.

Chef William Morvan **Owner** Folio Hotels **Times** 10.30am-10.30pm **Prices** Food prices not confirmed for 2011. Please telephone for details **Wines** 8 bottles over £20, 16 bottles under £20, 9 by glass **Notes** Sunday L, Vegetarian available, Dress restrictions, Smart casual, Civ Wed 80 **Seats** 85, Pr/dining room 30 **Children** Portions, Menu **Parking** 150

RUISLIP

Hawtrey's Restaurant at the Barn Hotel PLAN 1 A5

◎◎ Modern French

Imaginative, sophisticated cuisine in a smart hotel

☎ 01895 636057 & 679999
The Barn Hotel, West End Rd HA4 6JB
e-mail: info@thebarnhotel.co.uk
dir: From M40/A40 exit at Polish War Memorial junct onto A4180 towards Ruislip. In 2m turn right at mini rdbt into hotel entrance

This design-led boutique-style hotel has at its heart the humble origins of a farm dating from the 17th century. There are few clues to its age until you arrive in Hawtrey's restaurant, which goes for the grand ambience of a Jacobean-style baronial hall with oak beams supporting a coffered ceiling, and gilt-framed oil paintings on mahogany-panelled walls. The kitchen team show their mettle on a modern Anglo-French repertoire that runs to an inventive six-course tasting menu. The focus is on showing off good raw materials brought together in dishes such as roasted duck foie gras with essence of coffee and hazel. Main courses might team sea bass with the textures of asparagus spears and purée, forest mushrooms, spinach and truffle gnocchi and truffle dressing.

Times 12-2.30/7-10.30 Closed L Sat, D Sun

SURBITON

The French Table PLAN 1 C1

◎◎ French, Mediterranean

Modern French cuisine in exemplary neighbourhood restaurant

☎ 020 8399 2365
85 Maple Rd KT6 4AW
e-mail: enquiries@thefrenchtable.co.uk
dir: 5 min walk from Surbiton station, 1m from Kingston

Local Surbiton residents know they have it lucky with The French Table. It is the epitome of a classy neighbourhood restaurant, going quietly and competently about its business in a leafy suburban parade of shops and pubs. The glass-fronted room has a good sense of space, boosted by a glass atrium roof at the rear, and a warm, laid-back look with aubergine-hued banquettes, simple pale wood chairs, a slate-tiled floor and modern art. Service is pitched just right - switched-on, attentive yet relaxed. Chef-patron Eric Guignard's earthily creative output is rooted in France and the Mediterranean, and presented with flair. Expect terrine of pheasant, ham hock and lentils to be served with date purée and toasted walnut bread, and pan-fried cod with ratatouille pickle, smoked aubergine purée and gremolata.

Chef Eric Guignard **Owner** Eric & Sarah Guignard **Times** 12-2.30/7-10.30 Closed 25-26 Dec, 1-3 Jan, Mon, D Sun **Prices** Fixed L 2 course £16.50-£19.50, Starter £5.80-£9.80, Main £11.80-£22.50, Dessert £6.50-£9.50, Service added but optional 12.5% **Wines** 102 bottles over £20, 7 bottles under £20, 9 by glass **Notes** Sunday L, Vegetarian available, Dress restrictions, Smart casual **Seats** 48, Pr/dining room 26 **Children** Portions **Parking** On street

TWICKENHAM

A Cena PLAN 1 C2

◎ Modern Italian

Italian domestic cooking by Richmond Bridge

☎ 020 8288 0108
418 Richmond Rd TW1 2EB
dir: 100 yds from Richmond Bridge

Brave the contortions of Richmond's one-way system to find this attractive, black-fronted Italian restaurant just near Richmond Bridge on the Twickenham side. Wood panelling and mirrors create a light, contemporary feel within, and the whole place, while run by a British team, is an extended homage to Italian domestic cooking. Radicchio frittelle with parmesan and lemon is one of the simplest antipasti, following on perhaps with a bowl of chillied-up cannellini bean and chicory soup. Mains include classic whole roast sea bass served on the bone, or veal cutlet with capers, lemon and parsley, before chocolate tartufo with honeycomb and cream.

Chef Nicola Parsons **Owner** Camilla Healy **Times** 12-2.30/7-10.30 Closed Xmas & BHs, L Mon, D Sun **Prices** Starter £6-£11, Main £12.50-£22, Dessert £3.50-£8.50, Service optional, Groups min 6 service 12.5% **Wines** 80 bottles over £20, 9 bottles under £20, 12 by glass **Notes** Sunday L, Vegetarian available **Seats** 55

MERSEYSIDE

BIRKENHEAD Map 15 SJ38

Fraiche

◎◎◎ – *see page 330*

LIVERPOOL Map 15 SJ39

The London Carriage Works

◎◎ British, International

Confident cooking in the heart of Liverpool

☎ 0151 705 2222 & 709 3000
Hope Street Hotel, 40 Hope St L1 9DA
e-mail: eat@hopestreethotel.co.uk
dir: Follow Cathedral & University signs on entering city, at the centre of Hope St between the two cathedrals

On the famous Liverpool street that joins the Anglican and Catholic cathedrals and which also houses the Royal Philharmonic, this stylish restaurant is part of the classy Hope Street Hotel. Occupying a former 19th-century carriage builders, the décor goes in for lots of bare oak and exposed brickwork, dramatic modern art and glass sculptures. The cooking is modern in style with a focus on local and organic materials, and a high level of skill is evident. To start, braised Saddleback pork cheek comes with cauliflower and organic cider jus. Next, a main course confit of Suffolk lamb is served with curly kale, carrot and potato rösti and roasted garlic jus, and for pud, all the indulgence of a chocolate bread-and-butter terrine with mascarpone ice cream.

Chef Paul Askew **Owner** David Brewitt **Times** 12-3/5-10 Closed D 25 Dec **Prices** Fixed L 2 course £15, Fixed D 3 course £20, Starter £4.95-£10.50, Main £15.50-£29, Dessert £5.50-£9.50, Service optional, Groups min 8 service 10% **Wines** 164 bottles over £20, 10 bottles under £20, 14 by glass **Notes** Prix Fixe menu, Pre theatre & tasting menus available, Sunday L, Vegetarian available, Dress restrictions, Smart casual, Civ Wed 60 **Seats** 100, Pr/dining room 60 **Children** Portions, Menu **Parking** On street, car park opposite

Malmaison Liverpool

◎ Modern British

Contemporary brasserie cuisine in on the Mersey waterfront

☎ 0151 229 5000
7 William Jessop Way, Princes Dock L3 1QZ
e-mail: liverpool@malmaison.com
dir: Located on Princes Dock near the Liver Building

The first purpose-built hotel in this design-led chain of hotels stands beside the Mersey in the regenerated Princes Dock area of the city. It has a sharp style with all the hallmarks of the brand: in-your-face colours, a dark, Manhattan-esque nightclub feel, glitzy champagne and cocktail bar, with exposed brickwork, air vents and pipe work continuing the trendy, modern theme in the stylish

continued

LIVERPOOL *continued*

waterfront Brasserie. The menu takes in classic and contemporary dishes, ranging from Gloucestershire Old Spot pork belly with apple galette and trotter jus for a starter, to mains such as pan-fried bream with spring vegetable broth, or straight-up grilled steaks.

Times 12-2.30/6.30-10.30

Simply Heathcotes

Modern British

Sophisticated British cooking near the Liverpool waterfront

☎ 0151 236 3536
Beetham Plaza, 25 The Strand L2 0XL
e-mail: liverpool@heathcotes.co.uk
dir: Opposite pier head, on The Strand near Princes Dock

There are views of the fine period dockland buildings that make up the heart of Liverpool's maritime past from the full-length windows at this Merseyside branch of the Heathcote empire. Relaxing, friendly service creates the right tone for the menus of rejuvenated British classics, which are founded on carefully cultivated local supply lines. Not just any old duck livers, but the livers of corn-fed ducks from Goosnargh go into the pâté that comes with sharp rhubarb chutney, while the chump of lamb hails from Curwen Hill and is served with bouncy dumplings and seasonal spring greens. Star of the show might well be one of the crowd-pleasing desserts, such as golden-glazed orange cream tart with chocolate brownie ice cream.

Chef Carl Noller **Owner** Heathcotes Restaurants
Times 12-2.30/6-10 Closed Xmas, BHs (except Good Fri)
Prices Fixed L 2 course fr £15.50, Fixed D 3 course fr £20, Starter £4.30-£10.50, Main £11.50-£26, Dessert £4.50-£7.95, Service optional, Groups min 8 service 10%
Wines 40 bottles over £20, 18 bottles under £20, 10 by glass **Notes** Sunday L, Vegetarian available **Seats** 75, Pr/dining room 30 **Children** Portions, Menu **Parking** On street

60 Hope Street Restaurant

Modern British V

Minimalist setting for smart modern dining

☎ 0151 707 6060
60 Hope St L1 9BZ
e-mail: info@60hopestreet.com
web: www.60hopestreet.com
dir: From M62 follow city centre signs, then brown tourist signs for cathedral. Hope St near cathedral

In the heart of Liverpool's creative quarter, near to Philharmonic Hall and within sight of the two cathedrals, 60 Hope Street is a popular venue for the city's foodies and culture vultures. The elegant Georgian townhouse sports a modishly minimal interior of pale wood and white walls, jazzed up by a regularly changing cast of modern artworks. It is a place of two halves, made up of a buzzy ground-floor dining room with stripped floors and huge mirrors, and an informal basement bistro. Whichever you go for, the kitchen delivers confident up-to-date cooking full of muscular flavours. Take button mushroom and chestnut risotto, brimful of the earthy tones of autumn, while pan-fried halibut with pancetta lentils is paired with a more delicate herb and butter velouté.

60 Hope Street Restaurant

Chef Sarah Kershaw **Owner** Colin & Gary Manning
Times 12-2.30/6-10.30 Closed BHs, Sun, L Sat
Prices Fixed L 3 course £19.95, Fixed D 3 course £19.95, Starter £5.95-£13.95, Main £12.95-£29.95, Dessert £5.95-£8.95, Service optional, Groups min 8 service 10%
Wines 70 bottles over £20, 18 bottles under £20, 6 by glass **Notes** Pre-theatre Mon-Sat 5-7pm, Vegetarian menu, Civ Wed 50 **Seats** 90, Pr/dining room 40
Children Portions **Parking** On street

Fraiche

BIRKENHEAD **Map 15 SJ38**

Modern French, European V NOTABLE WINE LIST

Wirral star displaying dazzling originality

☎ 0151 652 2914
11 Rose Mount, Oxton CH43 5SG
e-mail: contact@restaurantfraiche.com
dir: M53 junct 3 towards Prenton. In 2m left towards Oxton. Fraiche on right

It still comes as quite a jolt to find a restaurant of this level of ambition in a little village on the Wirral peninsula. We intend no disrespect to the people of Oxton in saying this; indeed, we can only be green with envy. Marc Wilkinson is the prime mover of the whole venture in every sense. He designed the discreet interior of deep brown and sand tones to reflect the nearby coastal views, while the menus, offered in a number of fixed-price formats, bear evidence of one of the most productively restless culinary talents in the country. A determined targeting of originality has seen Fraiche move away from today's high-fashion techniques, and towards an ever more sharply defined clarity of flavours. The simplest menu, Elements, might offer tuna sashimi with wild rice and watercress, followed by loin of lamb with chervil root purée and shimeji mushrooms, and apple soup to finish. Trade up to Signature, and a five-course affair comes into play, ringing the changes from mussels with cauliflower and passionfruit, through foie gras with smoked olive and apple, sea bass with aubergine yoghurt and verjus, and Gressingham duck in chervil cream, to alight gently at lemongrass pannacotta, the breathtakingly scenic journey complete. The whole drill, right down to service that demonstrates as much precision as a Japanese tea ceremony, is quite an experience. A fabulous, broadly based wine list only adds to the thrill of it all.

Chef Marc Wilkinson **Owner** Marc Wilkinson
Times 12-1.30/7-9.30 Closed 25 Dec, 1 Jan, Mon-Tue, L Sun, Wed-Thu **Prices** Fixed L 3 course £23.50-£45, Fixed D 3 course fr £38, Service optional **Wines** 270 bottles over £20, 24 bottles under £20, 6 by glass **Notes** Bespoke menu available £65, Vegetarian menu **Seats** 20, Pr/dining room 20 **Children** Portions **Parking** On street

SOUTHPORT Map 15 SD31

Bistrot Vérité

French NEW

Authentic rustic French bistro

01704 564199
7 Liverpool Road, Birkdale PR8 4AR

This delightful rustic-style bistro is very much a family affair, with Marc Vérité at the stoves, wife Michaela running front of house and Marc's dad Claude taking care of the pâtisserie. In case the name isn't enough of a clue, this vibrant operation is French to the core: onions hang from the kitchen's extractor hood which is painted in the colours of the French flag, and tables are packed elbow-to-elbow in the intimate manner of a Lyonnaise bouchon. All of this adds up to a charming convivial ambience for dining on classic bistro dishes wrought from an entente cordiale of ingredients - fresh local produce bolstered by specialist stuff delivered weekly from across the Channel. An authentic soupe de poisson with gruyère and rouille kicks off in true Gallic style, followed by pan-roasted cod wrapped in Bayonne ham, served with a light Provençal sauce and Parmentier potatoes.

Chef Marc Vérité **Owner** Marc Vérité **Times** 12-1.30/5.30-10 Closed Sun, Mon

V-Café & Sushi Bar

Modern International

Modern international dining in a chic designer hotel

☎ 01704 883800
Vincent Hotel, 98 Lord St PR8 1JR
e-mail: norbert@thevincenthotel.com
dir: M58 junct 3, follow signs to Ormskirk & Southport. Hotel on Lord St

Don't be surprised if you spot the odd Liverpool footballer - past or present - on a neighbouring table in the V-Cafe. Since opening its doors in 2008, the trendy Vincent Hotel has become a bit of a mecca for the fashionable set of Southport and nearby Formby. With its glass and stone frontage, it certainly stands out from the crowd of traditional Victorian buildings, while inside it is all super-chic shiny marble, curvaceous creamy leather and polished herringbone parquet floors. When the weather's fine you can dine alfresco while watching life go by on leafy Lord Street, otherwise there's plenty going on inside, with the open kitchen and sushi bar presided over by a specialist Asian chef. The all-day menu is broadly international and offers the likes of red onion and goats' cheese tart with rocket leaves, Atlantic cod with shrimp and lemon butter and bubble-and-squeak, and vanilla cheesecake with fresh raspberries.

Times 7am-9pm

Warehouse Kitchen & Bar

International NEW

Buzzy warehouse conversion with eclectic, fun menu

☎ 01704 544662
30 West St PR8 1QN
e-mail: info@warehousekitchenandbar.com
dir: Please telephone for directions

Southport's coolest restaurant has undergone a makeover, and is now a joint-venture partnership owned by local hotelier Paul Adams and Liverpool FC captain Steven Gerrard. The same vibe that made the place locally noted has been retained, with a glassed-in area at the front leading to a spacious, buzzy, mirrored room within. The menu is eclectic and fun, making more than passable attempts at a range of international dishes. Start with Chinese-style battered squid in chilli salt, before heading towards north Africa for a cumin- and cinnamon-scented lamb shank, served with smoked aubergine and couscous studded with raisins and chick peas. The money dessert has to be the dark mocha tart with vanilla cream.

Chef Tom Lowe **Owner** Paul Adams, Steven Gerrard **Times** 12-2/5.30-10 Closed 25-26 Dec, 1 Jan, Sun **Prices** Starter £3.95-£7.95, Main £9.95-£24.95, Dessert £4.95-£8.50 **Wines** 43 bottles over £20, 11 bottles under £20, 8 by glass **Notes** Early D menu available Mon, Tue-Thu 5.30-7pm, Vegetarian available **Seats** 85, Pr/dining room 18 **Children** Portions **Parking** NCP - Promenade

THORNTON HOUGH Map 15 SJ38

The Lawns Restaurant

Modern British

Historic country-house hotel with modern cooking

☎ 0151 336 3938
Thornton Hall Hotel, Neston Rd CH63 1JF
e-mail: reservations@thorntonhallhotel.com
dir: M53 junct 4 onto B5151 & B5136, follow brown tourist signs (approx 2.5m) to Thornton Hall Hotel

Formerly the billiard room of this former Victorian manor turned country-house hotel, the elegant Lawns Restaurant is the fine-dining option at Thornton Hall. Overlooking the gardens, the dining room is the setting for confident modern British cooking driven by clear flavours and the freshest ingredients, sourced from local suppliers. Take a fillet of Welsh Black beef with horseradish rösti, celeriac purée and wilted spinach or pan-fried fillet of halibut with sautéed potatoes, chorizo, carrot and vanilla purée and red wine jus. Finish with coffee pannacotta with poached pear, Baileys ice cream and almond croquant.

Chef David Gillmore **Owner** The Thompson Family **Times** 12-2/7-9.30 Closed 1 Jan **Prices** Food prices not confirmed for 2011. Please telephone for details. **Wines** 36 bottles over £20, 11 bottles under £20, 10 by glass **Notes** Sunday L, Vegetarian available, Dress restrictions, Smart casual, no T-shirts or jeans, Civ Wed 400 **Seats** 45, Pr/dining room 24 **Children** Portions **Parking** 250

NORFOLK

ALBURGH Map 13 TM28

The Dove Restaurant with Rooms

Modern European V

Family-run restaurant with a classic menu

☎ 01986 788315
Holbrook IP20 0EP
e-mail: thedovenorfolk@freeola.com
dir: On South Norfolk border between Harleston & Bungay, by A143, at junct of B1062

The Dove models itself on the style of a French country auberge and has been run by the Oberhoffer family since 1980. Robert is the fifth generation chef in the family, and together with wife Conny, is now in charge at the stoves, deploying his sound culinary pedigree to produce unpretentious classic dishes from the best local and home-grown produce. The dining room has a clean-cut modern look with pale wooden floors, cerise walls and high-backed wooden chairs at smartly linen-clothed tables. When the weather's good, the outdoor terrace is an inviting place to dine. Starters might offer home-made game and pistachio terrine with cranberry compôte, while mains run to pan-fried Blythburgh pork tenderloin on sweet potato purée with grain mustard butter sauce.

Chef Robert Oberhoffer **Owner** Robert & Conny Oberhoffer **Times** 12-2/7-9 Closed Mon-Tue, L Wed-Sat, D Sun **Prices** Fixed L 2 course £14.45-£16.70, Starter £4.45-£6.25, Main £14.95-£17.95, Dessert fr £5.25, Service optional **Wines** 6 bottles over £20, 25 bottles under £20 **Notes** Sunday L, Vegetarian menu, Dress restrictions, Smart casual **Seats** 50 **Children** Portions **Parking** 20

ATTLEBOROUGH Map 13 TM09

The Mulberry Tree

Modern International

Trendy eatery with relaxed atmosphere and superb bedrooms

☎ 01953 452124
NR17 2AS
e-mail: relax@the-mulberry-tree.co.uk
dir: Exit A11 to town centre. Continue on one-way system. Restaurant on corner of Station Rd

Expect a contemporary, brasserie feel at this stylish gastro-pub with rooms on the main road into Attleborough. Darkwood floors, chunky wooden tables, smart, high-backed wicker chairs and quality table settings set the informal scene, and the relaxed service from the smartly turned out team fits the bill. Cooking is consistent and modern, resulting in simple dishes with decent flavours, the short menu perhaps listing a crayfish and pea risotto starter, followed by sea bass with citrus butter, griddled Mediterranean vegetables, gremolata mash and fish velouté, and mango, pineapple and raspberry Pavlova with passionfruit coulis and mascarpone.

Times 12-2/6.30-9 Closed 25-26 Dec, Sun

BARNHAM BROOM Map 13 TG00

Flints Restaurant

Modern British, European

Creative cooking in a modern golfing hotel

01603 759393
Barnham Broom Hotel, Golf & Country Club, Honingham Rd NR9 4DD
e-mail: enquiry@barnhambroomhotel.co.uk
dir: A47 towards Swaffham, turn left onto Honingham Rd, hotel 1m on left

A golfing hotel in unruffled Norfolk, Barnham Broom is sited in 250 acres, not all of it golf course. Flints, the main restaurant with its arches and wall of windows, is where the fine-dining action takes place, and the kitchen deals in fine produce fashioned into assured, creative dishes. Start with Cromer crab tian, with avocado purée and sauce vierge, or chicken liver parfait with curried pickled vegetables, before going on to Dingley Dell belly pork with saffron potatoes and aïoli. A finisher of treacle tart with honeycomb ice cream displays good pastry work, or you might opt for a plate of local cheeses with quince jelly. The Sports Bar and Café offer more informal eating.

Chef John Batchelor **Owner** Barnham Broom Hotel **Times** 7-9.30 **Prices** Food prices not confirmed for 2011. Please telephone for details. **Wines** 14 bottles over £20, 16 bottles under £20, 9 by glass **Notes** Vegetarian available, Dress restrictions, Smart casual, no trainers, Civ Wed 120 **Seats** Pr/dining room 50 **Children** Portions, Menu **Parking** 500

BLAKENEY Map 13 TG04

The Blakeney Hotel

Traditional British

Quayside restaurant with sublime North Norfolk coastal views

01263 740797
The Quay NR25 7NE
e-mail: reception@blakeneyhotel.co.uk
dir: From A148 between Fakenham & Holt, take B1156 to Langham & Blakeney

When the sun is out, dining alfresco on the quayside terrace of this charming flint-faced Norfolk hotel is balm to the soul: a soft-focus Impressionist's landscape beneath ever-changing skies, serenaded by the gentle cries of wading birds. Work up an appetite walking the North Norfolk coastal path through salt marshes and across the tidal estuary to Blakeney Point, then put the tempting menu of modern British dishes through its paces. Local mussels in white wine with a shallot and garlic cream sauce are a good way to start, given the area's superb fish and seafood, then go for something local and meaty, such as roast loin of Norfolk Black pork with roast potatoes, crackling and apple sauce. Finish with a lemony Norfolk treacle tart with cream.

Chef Martin Sewell **Owner** Michael Stannard **Times** 12-2/6.30-8.45 **Prices** Fixed L 2 course £13.90-£18.45, Fixed D 3 course £27.50, Service optional **Wines** 36 bottles over £20, 35 bottles under £20, 11 by glass **Notes** ALC 3 course £27.50-£42, Sunday L, Vegetarian available, Dress restrictions, Smart casual for D **Seats** 100, Pr/dining room 80 **Children** Portions **Parking** 60

Morston Hall

– see below

BRANCASTER STAITHE Map 13 TF74

The White Horse

Modern British

Marsh views and modern British grub

01485 210262
PE31 8BY
e-mail: reception@whitehorsebrancaster.co.uk
dir: On A149 (coast road) midway between Hunstanton & Wells-next-the-Sea

Built in 1934, the White Horse is a traditional inn with a relaxed conservatory restaurant and sundeck at the back overlooking the North Norfolk marshes across to Scolt Head Island and beyond to the sea - the perfect spot to watch the sun set. Scrubbed pine furniture, old

Morston Hall

BLAKENEY Map 13 TG04

Modern British, French V

Confident cooking in attractive country hotel

01263 741041
Morston, Holt NR25 7AA
e-mail: reception@morstonhall.com
dir: On A149 (coast road) between Blakeney & Stiffkey

A couple of miles from Blakeney on the North Norfolk coast, and handy for trips to the royal residence at Sandringham, Morston is a 17th-century country house with many comforts and attractions, not least of which is the sunny conservatory dining room and the inspired cooking of ex-Lakelander Galton Blackiston. The daily-changing, no-choice menu format pioneered in the Lakes is on offer here, in a style of food that allies country-house richness with a keen sense of the seasons. An autumn menu might deliver unctuously smooth duck liver parfait with black fig chutney to start, followed by sea bass on a rich mushroom duxelle with champagne nage. The tendency is towards complexity, with lots of elements in a dish, such as a main course of local beef rib-eye with aubergine caviar, fine ratatouille, tapenade, puréed basil and Madeira jus. There is no stinting on quality of ingredients, and there are plenty of interesting little extras throughout. A broadly based international wine list is fully in keeping.

Chef Galton Blackiston **Owner** T & G Blackiston **Times** 12.30-7.30 Closed 2 wks Jan, L Mon-Sat (ex party booking) **Prices** Fixed D 4 course £56, Service optional **Wines** 160 bottles over £20, 8 bottles under £20, 15 by glass **Notes** Sunday L, Vegetarian menu, Dress restrictions, Smart casual **Seats** 50, Pr/dining room 26 **Children** Portions, Menu **Parking** 40

photographs on the walls and an open log fire confirm its rustically appealing credentials. The landscaped sunken garden with marsh style shrubbery offers a natural alfresco environment, although with the benefit of heating. Expect modern British food with Mediterranean and sometimes Asian influences, served up by unhurried staff that set the relaxed and friendly tone of the place. Given the location, it would be madness not to use the fantastic local seafood and use it they do, though not to the exclusion of meat and veggie options. Go for Cyril's Brancaster Staithe mussels poached in white wine, cream and parsley followed by the White Horse fish stew with rouille. There's a good 'young person's' menu too.

Chef Rene Llupar **Owner** Clifford Nye **Times** 12-2/6.30-9 **Prices** Starter £5.25-£7.50, Main £10.95-£17.50, Dessert £4.95-£5.95, Service optional **Wines** 28 bottles over £20, 29 bottles under £20, 16 by glass **Notes** Sunday L, Vegetarian available **Seats** 100 **Children** Portions, Menu **Parking** 85

BRUNDALL — Map 13 TG30

The Lavender House

Modern British V

Cooking with finesse in a 16th-century cottage

01603 712215
39 The Street NR13 5AA
e-mail: lavenderhouse39@aol.com
dir: A47 E, 4m from Norwich city centre

The light, modern interior belies the age of this 16th-century thatched cottage turned restaurant and cookery school. The heavy oak beams alone date the space, which has been carefully restored and extended to include a bar with comfortable sofas and high-backed wicker dining chairs and crisp white table settings in the restaurant. Artisan local suppliers feature heavily on the modern British menu created by a small team of chefs headed up by chef-owner Richard Hughes. Start perhaps with terrine of Shropham pork, Granny Smith and crispy pig's ears before tucking into a main of pan-fried stone bass with ratte potatoes, leek and truffle oil. For dessert, there might be buttermilk pannacotta with blood orange granita and warm ginger madeleines. Diners keen to get a closer look at the action can book the Willi Opitz room with its kitchen theatre table and nine-course tasting menu.

Chef Richard Hughes, Richard Knights **Owner** Richard Hughes **Times** 12-4/6.30-12 Closed Mon, L Tue-Sat, D Sun **Prices** Food prices not confirmed for 2011. Please telephone for details. **Wines** 50 bottles over £20, 16 bottles under £20, 8 by glass **Notes** Sunday L, Vegetarian menu **Seats** 50, Pr/dining room 36 **Children** Portions **Parking** 16

BURNHAM MARKET — Map 13 TF84

Hoste Arms Hotel

Modern British, Pacific Rim NOTABLE WINE LIST

Refined old inn with confident cooking

01328 738777
The Green PE31 8HD
e-mail: reception@hostearms.co.uk
dir: 2m from A149 between Burnham & Wells

Burnham Market is a charming small town, the jewel, perhaps, in North Norfolk's crown. At the heart of it stands the Hoste Arms, sating the needs of residents and visitors for so long that even Lord Nelson propped up the bar. The 17th-century coaching inn has surely never looked so smart, although not a jot of its character has been lost, the décor blending antiquity with modern trappings in the copious diverse rooms. The bar, conservatory, various dining areas and Indian and Moroccan-styled walled garden mean there really is somewhere to suit every mood, and with breakfast, lunch, afternoon tea and dinner on offer, every appetite, too. The menu could be described as modern-British-gone-global, so tempura black pudding with a poached egg, crispy shallots and a devilled sauce might precede seared sea bass with Thai-spiced potatoes, or home-made steak and kidney pudding. Finish with an espresso tart (with coffee sauce and vanilla ice cream) or the laudable selection of British cheeses.

Chef Aaron Smith **Owner** Jeanne Whittome **Times** 12-2/6-9 Closed D 25 Dec **Prices** Starter £5.25-£12.75, Main £11.75-£20, Dessert £6.95-£13.25, Service optional **Wines** 153 bottles over £20, 14 bottles under £20, 21 by glass **Notes** Sunday L, Dress restrictions, Smart casual **Seats** 140, Pr/dining room 24 **Children** Menu **Parking** 45

CROMER — Map 13 TG24

See also **Sheringham**

Frazers, Sea Marge Hotel

Modern British

Assured local cooking on a Norfolk clifftop

01263 579579
16 High St, Overstrand NR27 0AB
e-mail: info@mackenziehotels.com
dir: A140 to Cromer, B1159 to Overstrand, 2nd left past Overstrand Church

A clifftop mansion commissioned in the Edwardian era by a German banker, when such a thing was still imaginable, the Sea Marge sits in timbered splendour on the North Norfolk coast. The largely buff-coloured Frazers dining room makes a gentle setting for some assured cooking that delivers the bounty of East Anglia in the manner best suited to show it off. Spanking-fresh Cromer crab bound in mayonnaise comes with vivid avocado purée and sweetcorn sorbet, while the fine local lamb is served in two cuts - saddle and shoulder - with aubergine caviar, pancetta and a well-reduced jus. Hare served three ways should be a strong lure (especially when we hardly ever see it served in one), but fish dishes too may combine productively with meat, as in the ham cassoulet that partners halibut. Finish with good cinnamon doughnuts and pear purée.

Chef Andy Hill **Owner** Mr & Mrs Mackenzie **Times** 12-2/6.30-9.30 **Prices** Food prices not confirmed for 2011. Please telephone for details. **Wines** 10 bottles over £20, 21 bottles under £20, 6 by glass **Notes** Sunday L, Vegetarian available, Dress restrictions, Smart casual **Seats** 80, Pr/dining room 40 **Children** Portions, Menu **Parking** 50

White Horse Overstrand

Modern British

Great Norfolk produce cooked with real flair

01263 579237
34 High St, Overstrand NR27 0AB
e-mail: enquiries@whitehorseoverstrand.co.uk
dir: From A140, before Cromer, turn right onto Mill Rd. At bottom turn right onto Station Rd. After 2m, bear left onto High St, pub on left

This family-run Victorian inn in the village of Overstrand is a short walk from the glorious beaches of North Norfolk, and there's a great cliff-top walk to Cromer to work up an appetite. The revitalised interior looks smart, but still retains a welcoming pubby feel, while the kitchen serves up an appealing line in modern British dishes. Chef Nathan Boon is a local lad with good supply lines to Norfolk's best producers, particularly fresh fish and seafood such as Thornham oysters and Cromer crab - the day's catch is spelled out on chalkboards to supplement a menu of pub classics perked up with creative touches, as in a starter of skate rillettes with poached duck's egg, salt beef and morels. Mains deliver the likes of steamed

continued

CROMER *continued*

cod fillet with Morston cockles, brown butter and creamed leeks. End with apple pannacotta with toffee jelly, or a plate of fine Norfolk cheeses.

Chef Nathan Boon **Owner** Darren Walsgrove
Times 12-3/6-9.30 Closed D 25 Dec **Prices** Food prices not confirmed for 2011. Please telephone for details. **Notes** Sunday L, Vegetarian available **Seats** 80, Pr/dining room 40 **Children** Portions, Menu **Parking** 6, On street

FRITTON Map 13 TG40

Fritton House

Modern British NEW

Lakeside dining in smart surroundings

☎ 01493 484008
Church Ln NR31 9HA
e-mail: frittonhouse@somerleyton.co.uk

Set within the grounds of the Somerleyton Estate on the banks of a lake, Fritton House is an elegant 15th-century property that has been transformed into a boutique-style hotel by Adnams of Southwold. The dining room is contemporary in style with plain dark tables, wooden floors and smart leather chairs. The same menu is also available in the large open-plan lounge bar and outside on the terrace. Using the best of local produce, you might start with stilton, walnut and pear tart with red onion marmalade, moving on to chargrilled sirloin steak with dauphinoise potatoes, fine beans and béarnaise.

GREAT BIRCHAM Map 13 TF73

The Kings Head Hotel

Modern British

Great food in stylish village hotel

☎ 01485 578265
PE31 6RJ
e-mail: welcome@the-kings-head-bircham.co.uk
dir: A148 to Hillington through village, take next left B1153 signed Great Bircham & CITB Construction College. Continue along B1153 into village of Great Bircham. Hotel located on left

When the owners of the Kings Head decided to refurbish their 19th-century inn in a tranquil village near Sandringham they went for a radical contemporary look. In the brasserie-style restaurant are unclothed darkwood tables on chrome pedestals, curvy chairs and pyjama-striped banquettes that could pass muster in any big city, plus there's a secluded courtyard for alfresco dining in summer. A straightforward menu of Mediterranean-accented British dishes has heaps of great Norfolk produce to inject local flavour – go for a velouté of local asparagus to start, then follow with baked cod fillet with Mediterranean vegetables and pesto, and wrap things up with a double chocolate brownie with chocolate ice cream and lavender shortbread.

Times 12-2/7-9

GREAT YARMOUTH Map 13 TG50

Andover House

Modern British

Relaxed modern brasserie in smart restaurant with rooms

☎ 01493 843490
28-30 Camperdown NR30 3JB
e-mail: info@andoverhouse.co.uk
dir: Opposite Wellington Pier, turn onto Shadingfield Close, right onto Kimberley Terrace, follow onto Camperdown. Property on left

A lovely listed Victorian house totally transformed by the current owners, Andover House has dashing contemporary good looks that blend in with the original features. The Lounge is a chic bar and modern brasserie with chunky wooden tables and dark leather chairs on a polished wood floor, and it sets the scene for some confident modern British cooking with some Asian flavours on show. Take a starter of pan-fried scallop and black pudding with white truffle, and a main dish of beef fillet with tiger prawns, poached potato in garlic soy sauce and cauliflower purée. Puddings might include coconut cream and lime pannacotta. On warm days, eat outside on the smart terrace.

Chef Patrick Moore **Owner** Mr & Mrs Barry Armstrong **Times** 12-2/6-9.30 Closed Sun-Mon **Prices** Starter £6.90-£9, Main £14.50-£24.50, Dessert £6-£9, Service optional **Wines** 22 bottles over £20, 23 bottles under £20, 8 by glass **Notes** Vegetarian available **Seats** 37, Pr/dining room 40 **Parking** On street

Café Cru Restaurant

Modern British

Contemporary cooking by the sea

☎ 01493 842000
Imperial Hotel, North Dr NR30 1EQ
e-mail: reception@imperialhotel.co.uk
web: www.cafecru.co.uk
dir: follow signs to seafront, turn left. Hotel opposite tennis courts

Bright and modern, Café Cru in the Imperial Hotel is a useful address on Great Yarmouth's seafront. It's got a younger, more contemporary vibe than the rest of the hotel, with the neutral tones, funky chrome lighting, banquette seating and cloth-covered tables bringing a bit of metropolitan chic. A daily specials board complements the à la carte of simply cooked, clearly defined modern British dishes. There might be steamed Morston mussels, for example, in white wine, cream and tarragon, followed by slow-cooked skirt of beef. An impressive wine list has a decent selection by the glass. The refurbished and renamed Bar Fizz is open all day for drinks and snacks.

Chef Simon Wainwright **Owner** Mr N L & Mrs A Mobbs **Times** 12-2/6.30-10 Closed 24-28 & 31 Dec, L Sat-Mon, D Sun **Prices** Fixed L 2 course £14, Starter £4.50-£8.50, Main £9.50-£22, Dessert £5.50-£8.50, Service optional **Wines** 25 bottles over £20, 68 bottles under £20, 12 by glass **Notes** Sunday L, Vegetarian available, Dress restrictions, Smart casual, No shorts or trainers, Civ Wed 140 **Seats** 60, Pr/dining room 140 **Children** Portions **Parking** 45

GRIMSTON Map 12 TF72

Congham Hall Country House Hotel

Modern British V

Georgian country house with excellent local British food

☎ 01485 600250
Lynn Rd PE32 1AH
e-mail: info@conghamhallhotel.co.uk
dir: 6m NE of King's Lynn on A148, turn right towards Grimston. Hotel 2.5m on left (do not go to Congham)

Elegant and tastefully decorated, this 18th-century Georgian manor is set amid 30 acres of landscaped gardens and surrounded by parkland. There are over 700 varieties of herbs in the herb garden - they're picked daily for use in the kitchen as well as providing a wonderful aroma when strolling around the grounds. The terracotta-coloured Orangery restaurant has large French windows giving panoramic views and leads out onto a pretty terrace. Classy modern British food is the name of the game and the kitchen goes as far as to smoke its own fish, make its own honey and preserves as well as growing several speciality fruit and vegetable varieties and sourcing meat and fish locally. Ballottine of foie gras with golden raisins, Muscat jelly and caramelised jelly kicks things off, before moving onto slow-cooked pork belly served with the fillet pan-roasted, sticky red cabbage, turnip and potato gratin, apple and cinnamon purée. There's also an inventive vegetarian menu.

Chef David Hammond **Owner** von Essen Hotels **Times** 12-2/7-9 **Prices** Fixed L 2 course £16.25, Fixed D 3 course £35, Starter £9-£12, Main £22.25-£26.50, Dessert £8.25-£9.50, Service optional **Wines** 60 bottles over £20, 10 bottles under £20, 10 by glass **Notes** Gourmand menu L £35, D £65, Sunday L, Vegetarian menu, Dress restrictions, Smart casual, Civ Wed 100 **Seats** 50, Pr/dining room 18 **Children** Portions, Menu **Parking** 50

HETHERSETT Map 13 TG10

Park Farm Hotel

British

☎ 01603 810264
NR9 3DL
e-mail: enq@parkfarm-hotel.co.uk
dir: 6m S of Norwich on B1172

This Georgian farmhouse in 200 acres of lovely Norfolk countryside just south of Norwich has evolved over the years into a smart modern hotel with impressive spa and leisure facilities. The orangery-style restaurant, done out in a clean uncluttered style, with bright artworks on plain white walls, and full-length windows overlooking landscaped gardens, is the setting for appealing modern European cooking using the best of the local larder. Chicken, ginger and coconut soup makes a fine starter, before rosemary and garlic-scented rump of lamb arrives on colcannon mash with glazed carrots and redcurrant jus. Pear and almond tart with home-made ice cream wraps things up nicely.

Times 12-2/7-9.30

HOLKHAM Map 13 TF84

The Victoria at Holkham

British, French

Norfolk gem with a colonial feel

☎ 01328 711008
Park Rd NR23 1RG
e-mail: victoria@holkham.co.uk
dir: 3m W of Wells-next-the-Sea on A149. 12m N of Fakenham

Guarding the gates of the Earl of Leicester's Holkham Estate, the Victoria was built in smart brick and Norfolk flint at the height of the Empire's glory. Inside, you could be forgiven for thinking that the days of the Raj were not yet numbered, as colonial-chic Rajasthani furniture and latticed doors combine in an idiosyncratic bohemian décor. While echoes of the Sub-continent are never far away, the food comes from much closer to home: the Norfolk larder supplies seafood from Brancaster and Cromer, while venison, beef, game and eel come from the Holkham Estate itself – it's all top-notch stuff and the kitchen knows better than to fiddle about with it. A menu of unfussy modern Anglo-French classics opens with smoked mackerel pâté, home-made piccalilli and horseradish dressing, then proceeds to a local rib-eye steak with a tried-and-tested combo of crisp French fries, confit tomatoes, Portobello mushrooms, onion rings and a rich red wine jus.

Times 12-2.30/7-9.30

HOLT Map 13 TG03

Butlers Restaurant

Modern European

Unpretentious bistro where Norfolk meets Italy

☎ 01263 710790
9 Appleyard NR25 6BN
e-mail: eat@butlersrestaurants.com
dir: Just off High Street, signed Appleyard

Every market town should have one - a relaxed, unpretentious bistro serving good fresh food, cooked with care and a lack of fuss. Few do. Lucky old Holt has Butlers, a light and bright space leading onto a pretty courtyard where garden tables and an abundance of potted plants make for a tranquil spot, shaded by a 200-year-old copper beech tree. There's a large oak bar and an open-to-view kitchen adding to the happy hubbub, and a menu which makes the best of the Norfolk larder and duly follows the seasons. Grab a snack during the day like soft herring roes on brown toast, or tuck into the full menu, with its mostly British and Italian influences. Ribolata (Tuscan bean soup), for example, followed by slow-cooked pork belly with wilted winter greens and creamed butter beans. Butlers has a sister restaurant in Norwich, see entry for Tatlers.

Chef Sean Creasey **Owner** Sean & Ruth Creasey **Times** 12-3/6-9 Closed 25-26 Dec, Sun **Prices** Starter £4.50-£6.95, Main £9.95-£16.95, Dessert £3.95-£5.25, Service optional **Wines** 13 bottles over £20, 20 bottles under £20, 12 by glass **Notes** Monthly events with special menu, Vegetarian available **Seats** 50 **Children** Portions **Parking** On street (free after 6pm)

The Lawns Wine Bar

Modern European

Classic comfort food in a peaceful setting

☎ 01263 713390
26 Station Rd NR25 6BS
e-mail: mail@lawnsatholt.co.uk
dir: A148 (Cromer road). 0.25m from Holt rdbt, turn left, 400yds along Station Rd

A smart Georgian townhouse in the heart of the historic market town of Holt, The Lawns is these days a restaurant with rooms with a stylish bar (complete with plush leather sofas) and a restaurant that extends into a conservatory. You can eat in the bar or restaurant and, if you're lucky, on the outside terrace and in the pretty garden. There is a relaxed and convivial air about the place. The seasonal menu contains lots of crowd-pleasers and plenty of choice, whether you're after a full meal or something lighter (sandwiches at lunchtime, for example). Start with goats' cheese and red onion marmalade tart, before moving onto a classic rib-eye steak with chips, mushrooms and deep-fried onion rings and end with a comforting stem ginger pudding.

Chef Leon Brookes, Jenner Hilton **Owner** Mr & Mrs Daniel Rees **Times** 12-2/6-9 **Prices** Starter £4.75-£6.95, Main £9.95-£16.95, Dessert £5, Service optional **Wines** 6 bottles over £20, 29 bottles under £20, 9 by glass **Notes** Wine tasting D available, Sunday L, Vegetarian available **Seats** 24 **Children** Portions **Parking** 18

The Pigs

British

Cheery Norfolk pub with porcine theme

☎ 01263 587634
Edgefield NR24 2RL
e-mail: info@thepigs.org.uk
dir: On B1149

The Pigs is a proper Norfolk pub, complete with local cask ales, bar billiards and quizzes. A much-extended, white-painted building, it is also some kind of homage to one of our more versatile farm animals, with braised cheeks, crispy ears, hand-carved ham and all-day pig-based breakfasts on offer. It's all good, including a starter of potted pork with cornichons and a cold pork pie. Depart from the theme, and you may equally enjoy a slow-cooked duck leg with lentils, baby onions and, er, lardons, or even fish and chips with tartare sauce. Afters could be lardy cake (but of course), or perhaps a ginger beer ice cream float with warm parkin.

Chef Tim Abbott **Owner** Iain Wilson & Richard Hughes **Times** 11-2.30/6-11 **Prices** Starter £2.50-£4.95, Main £9.95-£17.50, Dessert £2.50-£5 **Wines** 11 bottles under £20, 10 by glass **Notes** Sunday L, Vegetarian available **Seats** 80 **Children** Portions, Menu **Parking** 40

HUNSTANTON Map 12 TF64

The Neptune Restaurant with Rooms

– see below

ITTERINGHAM Map 13 TG13

Walpole Arms

Modern European

Village gastro-pub serving modern British cuisine

☎ 01263 587258
NR11 7AR
e-mail: goodfood@thewalpolearms.co.uk
dir: Between Norwich & north Norfolk coast. Towards Aylsham & Blickling, then 1st right to Itteringham approx 1m after Blickling Hall. Walpole Arms on right on entering village

Close to Blickling Hall, this unspoilt 18th-century brick and timber cottage overlooks the River Bure on the edge of the village. Its attractive restaurant delivers modern British cooking, featuring high-quality produce, much of it locally sourced, such as mussels from Morston or venison from nearby Gunton Hall. Expect dishes with lots of flavour and considered combinations of ingredients. Start with chicken, ham and pepper terrine with cherry tomato salad, followed by grilled leg of lamb steak with Spanish-style chick pea and spinach salad, and chocolate and almond torte. The same menu is served in the oak-beamed bar.

Times 12-2.30/7-9 Closed D Sun

KING'S LYNN Map 12 TF62

Bank House Hotel

Modern British

Quality brasserie cooking in historic townhouse

☎ 01553 660492
King's Staithe Square PE30 1RD
e-mail: info@thebankhouse.co.uk
dir: Alongside quay, opposite Custom House, through floodgates, hotel on right (Kings Lynn Old Town)

In the heart of the historical quarter of King's Lynn, right on the quayside and looking out over the River Ouse, you'll find this Grade II listed townhouse. Originally a wine merchants, it was turned into Gurney's bank in the 18th century (Gurney's eventually became Barclays), and now it's a hotel and brasserie-style restaurant serving up some good food with, appropriately enough, a good cellar. Head Chef Ed Lewis formerly headed up Fergus Henderson's renowned St John (see entry) and as you might expect a simple style informs the skilful cooking here. On the locally-sourced menu might be calves' liver with mash, baked onion and horseradish, roasted local cod with chorizo stew and curly kale, or the banker - a steak ciabatta with balsamic red onion and chips.

Chef Stuart Deuchars **Owner** Jeannette & Anthony Goodrich **Times** 12-2/6.30-9 **Prices** Starter £4.95-£7.95, Main £9.50-£16.50, Dessert £4.25-£5.75, Service optional, Groups min 8 service 10% **Wines** 10 bottles over £20, 20 bottles under £20, 6 by glass **Notes** Pre/post theatre menu available on request, Sunday L, Vegetarian available **Seats** 60, Pr/dining room 40 **Children** Portions, Menu **Parking** 5, On quayside or Baker Lane car park

NORTH WALSHAM Map 13 TG23

Beechwood Hotel

Modern British, Mediterranean

Norfolk's best produce in popular hotel

☎ 01692 403231
Cromer Rd NR28 0HD
e-mail: info@beechwood-hotel.co.uk
dir: From Norwich on B1150, 13m to N Walsham. Left at lights, next right. Hotel 150mtrs on left

Agatha Christie once had a soft spot for the genteel Georgian elegance of this charming house - her letters to

The Neptune Restaurant with Rooms

HUNSTANTON Map 12 TF64

Modern British

A Georgian inn with classy design and serious culinary appeal

☎ 01485 532122
85 Old Hunstanton Rd PE36 6HZ
e-mail: reservations@theneptune.co.uk
dir: On A149

Kevin and Jacki Mangeolles moved to this creeper-swathed 18th-century inn in 2007 after a decade at the George Hotel on the Isle of Wight (see entry). First job was to give the place a makeover: the dining room now sports a biscuit-hued, clean-cut décor with white-painted wood-clad walls and Lloyd Loom chairs evoking the jaunty, nautical style of New England. Kevin's reputation precedes him, and he carries on where he left off, delivering seriously good, modern British dishes bursting with invention and technical ability. Getting off to a flying start is a cleverly-constructed tian-style tower of flavour-packed grilled fillet of mackerel with compressed watermelon, and crab with horseradish cream. Local ingredients star in a main course of Sedgfield lamb with sautéed sweetbreads, broad beans, silky potato purée and a superb meaty jus. Desserts often bring on an exotic influence, as seen in milk chocolate mousse with ras el hanout caramel and dark chocolate sorbet. Add in great breads, an amuse such as plaice fish finger coated with poppy seeds with Marie Rose sauce, and pre-desserts of orange and ginger jelly with tahini cream, and it's clear that this a top-class foodie bolt-hole.

Chef Kevin Mangeolles **Owner** Kevin & Jacki Mangeolles **Times** 12-2/7-9 Closed 2 wks Nov & Jan, Mon, L Tue-Sat (except by arrangement) **Prices** Fixed L 2 course £20.50, Starter £9.25-£12.50, Main £22.50-£26.50, Dessert £9.50, Service optional **Wines** 55 bottles over £20, 13 bottles under £20, 10 by glass **Notes** Tasting menu available on request when booking, Sunday L, Vegetarian available, Dress restrictions, Smart casual **Seats** 24 **Children** Portions **Parking** 6, On street

the family who once lived here are framed in the hallway. The Beechwood is one of those intimate small hotels that gets everything right, from its graceful traditional interior, to the exemplary attentive service, and a kitchen with real passion for its work. Intelligent modern British dishes with a touch of Mediterranean warmth are the deal here. Superb Norfolk ingredients are the mainstay of the menus - most notably in daily 'ten-mile' dinners, which garner materials - Cromer crab, Morston mussels, Thornham oysters, Sheringham lobster and local meat and veg - from within 10 miles of the hotel. You might start with Walsingham cheese tartlet with bacon and mustard ice cream, ahead of pork tenderloin on sage and onion mash with spring green cabbage, crispy parsnips, glazed apples and brandy jus, and finish with vanilla pannacotta and the zing of rhubarb compôte.

Chef Steven Norgate **Owner** Don Birch & Lindsay Spalding **Times** 12-1.45/7-9 Closed L Mon-Sat **Prices** Fixed L 3 course fr £21, Fixed D 4 course fr £35, Service optional **Wines** 220 bottles over £20, 10 bottles under £20, 8 by glass **Notes** Sunday L, Vegetarian available, Dress restrictions, Smart casual **Seats** 60, Pr/dining room 20 **Children** Portions **Parking** 20

NORWICH **Map 13 TG20**

Arlington Grill & Brasserie

Modern British

Friendly hotel serving unfussy dishes

☎ 01603 617841
BW George Hotel, 10 Arlington Ln, Newmarket Rd NR2 2DA
e-mail: reservations@georgehotel.co.uk
web: www.arlingtonhotelgroup.co.uk
dir: From A11 follow city centre signs. Newmarket Rd towards centre. Hotel on left

Tucked away in a peaceful conservation area a short stroll from Norwich city centre, the George is a welcoming, smartly-modernised hotel in a grand Victorian house. The Arlington Brasserie goes for a classic French brasserie look, with its caramel leather banquettes, darkwood panelling, mirrored walls, and polished wooden floors and tables. The kitchen takes an uncomplicated approach with well-sourced local produce - a Greek salad does what it says on the tin, using good-quality ingredients, then Cajun chicken continues the simple style, teamed with a fresh salsa and thick hand-cut chips.

Times 12-2/6-10

Best Western Annesley House Hotel

Modern British, European

Impressive cuisine overlooking tranquil water garden

☎ 01603 624553
6 Newmarket Rd NR2 2LA
e-mail: annesleyhouse@bestwestern.co.uk
dir: On A11, close to city centre

It is hard to believe that this handsome Grade II listed Georgian hotel in three acres of tranquil landscaped grounds, including a peaceful water garden and waterfall, is just a short stroll from the bustling historic heart of Norwich. The Mediterranean-style conservatory restaurant makes the most of this peaceful retreat, giving diners a lovely garden view to go with a wide-ranging repertoire of modern European-accented British dishes. Top-quality ingredients are key in starters such as pan-seared diver scallops with garlic and chive new potatoes and shallot and thyme dressing, or a main-course pan-seared chump of lamb with fondant potato, aubergine caviar, chargrilled Mediterranean vegetables and rosemary jus. Finish with a croissant and sultana bread-and-butter pudding with coffee anglaise.

Chef Steven Watkin **Owner** Mr & Mrs D Reynolds **Times** 12-2/6-9 Closed Xmas & New Year, L Sun **Prices** Fixed D 3 course £29.50, Starter £6, Main £19.50, Dessert £6, Service optional **Wines** 6 bottles over £20, 19 bottles under £20, 9 by glass **Notes** Pre-theatre menu available from 6pm by arrangement, Vegetarian available **Seats** 30, Pr/dining room 18 **Children** Portions **Parking** 25

Brummells Seafood Restaurant

International, Seafood

Great seafood cookery in historic Norwich

☎ 01603 625555
7 Magdalen St NR3 1LE
e-mail: brummell@brummells.co.uk
web: www.brummells.co.uk
dir: In city centre, 2 mins walk from Norwich Cathedral, 40yds from Colegate

A blue-fronted, beamed, 17th-century building in the historic heart of Norwich is home to Andrew Brummell's high-achieving seafood restaurant. Regulars appreciate the venerable atmosphere, with flickering candles enhancing the exposed beams and stonework, but most of all it's the highly capable fish and shellfish cookery that brings people back. Grilled sardines in chilli oil, or fried breaded oysters with horseradish mayonnaise, might set the ball rolling, and be followed by sea bass with leeks and ginger in a shellfish butter sauce, or chargrilled tuna with curried marmalade. If you're not feeling fishy, choose a steak, or perhaps the richly sauced Argyll venison. Peppered strawberries in orange and rum is a good way to finish. It's all served with appreciable warmth and hospitality.

Chef A Brummell, J O'Sullivan **Owner** Mr A Brummell **Times** 12-2/6-9.30 **Prices** Starter £6.50-£16, Main £17-£29.95, Dessert £6, Service optional, Groups min 7 service 10% **Wines** 56 bottles over £20, 27 bottles under £20, 3 by glass **Notes** Sunday L, Vegetarian available, Dress restrictions, Smart casual or jacket & tie **Seats** 25 **Children** Portions **Parking** On street after 6.30pm & Sun, Car park nearby

De Vere Dunston Hall

British, French

Modern cooking in impressive setting

☎ 01508 470444
Ipswich Rd NR14 8PQ
e-mail: dhreception@devere-hotels.com
dir: On A140 between Norwich & Ipswich

Dating back to 1869 and originally built by a wealthy Victorian family with a taste for Elizabethan style, Dunston Hall is surrounded by 170 acres of wooded parkland with its own 18-hole golf course. And it's only a short drive from the centre of Norwich. La Fontaine restaurant majors on classic British and French dishes utilising contemporary skills and much of the produce is sourced from within a 30-mile radius of the kitchen. Cromer crab with fresh potato gnocchi, chilli, parmesan and sorrel might start you off, followed by roast fillet of beef with horseradish hash, oxtail and Guinness raviolo and swede purée.

Chef Paul Murfitt, Rob Everitt **Owner** De Vere Hotels **Times** 7-10 Closed BH's, Sun, L all week **Prices** Starter £5.95-£10.95, Main £15.50-£24.50, Dessert £5.95-£8.50, Service added but optional 10% **Wines** 40 bottles over £20, 1 bottle under £20 **Notes** Vegetarian available, Dress restrictions, Smart, No jeans **Seats** 45 **Children** Portions, Menu **Parking** 300

NORWICH *continued*

The Dining Room at the Old Rectory

Modern British V

Country-house style in a city location

01603 700772
103 Yarmouth Rd, Thorpe St Andrew NR7 0HF
e-mail: enquiries@oldrectorynorwich.com
dir: From A47 take A1042 to Thorpe, then A1242. Hotel right after 1st lights

Everything about this charming ivy-clad Georgian rectory is more akin to a classic country house than its location on the outskirts of Norwich would suggest. Secluded in an acre of neatly-coiffed gardens alive with birdsong in magnificent mature trees, and with sweeping views over the Yare Valley, it's easy to see why the Entwistle family settled here in 1995 to run the house as an easy going bolt-hole. Chef James Perry can be found wandering the fields of Norfolk foraging fresh goodies to go with garden vegetables, herbs and other local materials that are the foundation of his French-accented modern British cooking. A menu of good ideas includes an eye-catching coarse terrine of local pork, chicken and Agen prunes with mustard courgette pickle and gooseberry chutney, ahead of roasted Shropham lamb fillet with a powerfully-flavoured pesto dressing and a rich sauce of chick peas and chorizo in tomato.

Chef James Perry **Owner** Chris & Sally Entwistle
Times 7-9 Closed Xmas & New Year, Sun-Mon, L all week
Prices Fixed D 3 course £27-£30, Service optional
Wines 14 bottles over £20, 8 bottles under £20, 5 by glass **Notes** Vegetarian menu **Seats** 18, Pr/dining room 16 **Children** Portions **Parking** 16

Elm Hill Brasserie

French

Relaxed brasserie in Norwich's historic heart

01603 624847
2 Elm Hill NR3 1HN
e-mail: reservations@elmhillbrasserie.co.uk

This welcoming contemporary brasserie at the medieval heart of Norwich provides a fix of classic French cooking for deprived francophiles. It is a crisp, uncluttered, intimate venue kitted out with stripped pine floors and dark wood tables - get one by the huge picture window and you can spot the tip of the cathedral spire peeking above the jumbled buildings of the old town. Materials are sourced with the greatest of care by chef-proprietor Simon Turner, reaching the plate in the form of 'moules piquantes' - Brancaster mussels in a light broth spiked with chilli, garlic, parsley, peppers and shallots. Main courses might include a bouillabaisse stew of local fish and shellfish, or a bavette steak with brandy and tarragon butter sauce. It's worth the wait while apple tarte Tatin is cooked to order and served with cinnamon ice cream.

Chef Simon Turner **Owner** Simon Turner
Times 12.30-2.30/5.45-10.30 Closed Xmas, Mon
Prices Fixed L 2 course £12, Fixed D 3 course £15.50, Starter £6.50-£8.95, Main £11.95-£16.95, Dessert £6.95, Service optional, Groups min 6 service 10% **Wines** 25 bottles over £20, 15 bottles under £20, 6 by glass
Notes Fixed D menu only available pre-theatre 5.45-6.45pm Mon-Fri, Sunday L, Vegetarian available
Seats 24 **Parking** On street & car park

The Maids Head Hotel

Modern NEW

Sound modern cooking in characterful old hotel

01603 209955
Tombland NR3 1LB
dir: A147 to north of the city. At rdbt for A1151, signposted Wroxham, follow signs for Cathedral and Law Courts along Whitefriars. Hotel is approx 400 mtrs on right along Palace St

The red-brick and timber Maids Head is a Norwich institution at the heart of the city opposite the Norman cathedral. Legend has it that Elizabeth I slept here, but while she might find that the Jacobean Maids Head bar has a comfortingly familiar look, this historic gem has moved with the times when it comes to food. The old courtyard where horse-drawn carriages used to pull in has been glassed over and laid with terracotta tiles to become the relaxed brasserie-style restaurant. The kitchen hauls in fine Norfolk produce as the basis for its unfussy comfort-oriented repertoire. Ham hock and parsley terrine with piccalilli is a good way to start, then follow with roasted skate wing with spinach and caper jus, or roast rump of lamb with Mediterranean vegetables. For pudding, treacle tart and clotted cream should hit the spot, or go for a plate of Norfolk cheeses.

Marriott Sprowston Manor Hotel

Modern British

Good cooking in a luxurious country house

01603 410871
Sprowston Park, Wroxham Rd NR7 8RP
e-mail: mhrs.nwigs.frontdesk@marriotthotels.com
dir: From A47 take Postwick exit onto Norwich outer ring road, then take A1151. Hotel approx 3m and signed

Sprowston Manor is a striking gabled country manor and club set in neat well kept grounds which has a picturesque lake and a golf course among its many features. The interior overflows with period charm and is very well kept; courteous staff set the right mood, including in the formal dining room, which excels in relaxed and attentive service. The talented kitchen team play their part, too, serving up imaginative modern British and European dishes. Start, perhaps, with cod cheeks deep-fried in lemonade and chilli batter, served with sweet potato chips and minted peas, then move on to oak-smoked fillet of beef with baby vegetables, potato cake and essence of shiraz. Deep-fried rice pudding with raspberry jam makes a comforting finale. Other dining options are the more informal 1559 bar and Zest café bar and grill.

Chef Andrew Barrass **Owner** Marriott International Inc
Times 12.30-3/6.30-10 Closed L Mon-Sat, D Sun
Prices Fixed L 3 course £25, Starter £5.95-£8.95, Main £15.50-£29.50, Dessert £6.95, Service optional **Wines** 29 bottles over £20, 12 bottles under £20, 12 by glass
Notes Sunday L, Vegetarian available, Dress restrictions, Smart casual, no shorts, Civ Wed 300 **Seats** 70, Pr/dining room 150 **Children** Portions, Menu **Parking** 170

1 Up @ The Mad Moose

Modern British

Intimate restaurant and modern food above trendy pub

01603 627687
The Mad Moose Arms & 1Up, 2 Warwick St NR2 3LD
e-mail: madmoose@animalinns.co.uk
dir: A11 onto A140. Turn right at lights onto Unthank Rd, then left onto Dover/Warwick St

Chic chandeliers, luxurious velvet curtains and striking wall coverings provide a touch of sophistication for evening diners (plus Sunday lunch) in the fine-dining, upstairs restaurant at this trendy, bustling gastro-pub located close to the University. The atmosphere is intimate and unpretentious and helped along by the professional yet relaxed service. Modern menus make much of high quality Norfolk produce. Expect the likes of potted Suffolk pork with celeriac remoulade; roast line-caught cod with white beans, salsify, chorizo and crispy leeks; daube of beef with horseradish mash. Go for dark chocolate terrine with glazed bananas, praline anglaise and liquorice ice cream for dessert. In addition, a substantial bar menu is offered downstairs.

Chef Nick Andeise **Owner** Mr Henry Watt
Times 12-3/7-9.30 Closed 25-26 Dec, 1 Jan, L Mon-Sat, D Sun **Prices** Fixed D 3 course fr £27.50, Starter £5.50-£8.50, Main £10.50-£18.50, Dessert £5.50-£6.50, Service optional **Wines** 32 bottles over £20, 24 bottles under £20, 11 by glass **Notes** Sunday L, Vegetarian available
Seats 48 **Children** Portions **Parking** On street

St Benedicts Restaurant

Modern British

Imaginative cooking in the heart of Norwich

01603 765377
9 St Benedicts St NR2 4PE
e-mail: jayner@talktalk.net
dir: Just off inner ring road. Turn right by Toys-R-Us, 2nd right into St Benedicts St. Restaurant on left by pedestrian crossing

On a bustling street in Norwich city centre, St Benedicts is very much a neighbourhood restaurant with the heart and soul of a French bistro. With its grey and green colour scheme, panelled walls, closely-packed tables and banquette seating, it looks the part too. The emphasis is on good, clean flavours and seasonal produce with a genuine desire to make the most of excellent local supply lines. Start with home-made rabbit sausage with Savoy cabbage, Jerusalem artichokes and macerated prunes moving onto a main course such as 24-hour cooked brisket of beef, which comes with carrot purée, and finish with a lemon buttermilk pudding, shortbread and lemon sauce.

Chef Nigel Raffles **Owner** Nigel & Jayne Raffles **Times** 12-2/7-10 Closed 25-31 Dec, Sun-Mon **Prices** Fixed L 2 course fr £8.95, Fixed D 2 course fr £16.95, Groups min 10 service 10% **Wines** 15 bottles over £20, 34 bottles under £20, 8 by glass **Notes** Vegetarian available **Seats** 42, Pr/dining room 24 **Children** Portions **Parking** On street, Car parks nearby

St Giles Restaurant

Modern British

Relaxed dining in stylish city-centre hotel

01603 275180 & 275182
St Giles House Hotel, 41-45 St Giles St NR2 1JR
e-mail: reception@stgileshousehotel.com
web: www.stgileshousehotel.com
dir: A11 into central Norwich. Left at rdbt signed Chapelfield Shopping Centre. 3rd exit at next rdbt. Left onto St Giles St. Hotel on left

Expect quirky and sumptuous individuality at this stylish city-centre hotel housed within an impressive Grade II listed building, designed by distinguished Norwich architect George Skipper in 1906. Beyond the grand pillared façade, period features - note the original wood panelling, ornamental plasterwork and elegant marble floors - blend effortlessly with the modern design and eclectic décor. Served within the stunning art-deco dining room, sound modern cooking utilises quality local ingredients, the monthly-changing menu perhaps offering scallops with braised oxtail and pea purée, or confit duck leg with spiced plums, followed by Norfolk venison with dauphinoise and blackberry vinegar jus, or sea bass with cockle and herb cream, and quince and ginger crème brûlée.

Chef Stewart Jefferson **Owner** Norfolk Hotels Ltd **Times** 11-10 **Prices** Fixed L 2 course £14.95, Fixed D 3 course £18.95, Starter £7.50, Main £22, Dessert £7.50, Service optional **Wines** 38 bottles over £20, 25 bottles under £20, 9 by glass **Notes** Sunday L, Vegetarian available, Civ Wed 60 **Seats** 50, Pr/dining room 48 **Children** Portions, Menu **Parking** 30

Shiki

Modern Japanese

Smart little Japanese place near the cathedral

01603 619262
6 Tombland NR3 1HE
e-mail: bookings@shikirestaurant.co.uk
dir: City centre. From Castle Meadow onto Upper Kings St, straight onto Tombland, restaurant on left

A smart little Japanese restaurant in the old heart of the city near the cathedral, Shiki incorporates a sushi bar just inside the entrance, as well as a more full-dress dining room with rosewood tables and high chairs. Service by T-shirted staff keeps things moving, and the menu of traditional Japanese eating includes full-flavoured miso soup with wakame seaweed, tofu and spring onions, deep-fried dishes such as pork tonkatsu (breaded fillet), and fun selections of Japanese 'tapas' in either omnivorous or veggie versions, the former including seafood tempura, minced pork pot-sticker dumplings, and chicken yakitori.

Times 12-2.30/5.30-10.30 Closed Xmas, Sun

Stower Grange

Traditional British, European

Small hotel restaurant with garden views

01603 860210
40 School Rd, Drayton NR8 6EF
e-mail: enquiries@stowergrange.co.uk
dir: Norwich ring road N to ASDA supermarket. Take A1067 (Fakenham road) at Drayton, right at lights into School Rd. Hotel 150yds on right

Set in mature grounds on the outskirts of Norwich, this attractive 17th-century ivy-clad hotel attracts business people and the wedding brigade but the restaurant also has a good local following. Intimate and traditionally set up with neat, crisp clothed tables and cloth napkins, the fine-dining restaurant looks out onto the gardens. New head chef Lee Parrette presides over a monthly-changing menu, which uses local and home-grown produce to good effect. You might find beetroot cured salmon with chopped duck's egg, wild rocket and orange dressing and a main course of corn-fed chicken breast with baby gem, button onion and peas. There's also a good choice of vegetarian options.

Chef Lee Parrette **Owner** Richard & Jane Fannon **Times** 12-2.30/7-9.30 Closed 26-30 Dec, D Sun **Prices** Fixed L 3 course £23.50, Starter £6.50-£7.95, Main £12.50-£18.50, Dessert £6.50, Service optional **Wines** 15 bottles over £20, 28 bottles under £20, 8 by glass **Notes** Sunday L, Vegetarian available, Civ Wed 100 **Seats** 25, Pr/dining room 100 **Children** Portions **Parking** 40

The Sugar Hut

Thai

Tingling Thai cuisine in the city centre

01603 766755
4 Opie St NR1 3DN
e-mail: lhongmo@hotmail.co.uk
dir: City centre next to Castle Meadow & Castle Mall car park

The Norwich branch of this dynamic little restaurant group opened in 2002 to bring the tingling flavours of Thai cuisine to a staid, bank-laden part of the city centre. Staff dressed in the house uniform are friendly and efficient, and the menu deals in the expected sweet, hot-and-sour currents of classic Thai cooking. King prawn spring rolls with plum dipping sauce, spare ribs in garlic and peppercorns, stir-fried rump steak in sweet wine with bamboo shoots, mushrooms and spring onions, and drunken prawn and noodle stir-fry with beans, basil and rice wine all hit the mark.

Times 12-2.30/6-10.30 Closed Sun

Tatlers

Modern British V

Dependable neighbourhood restaurant by the Cathedral

01603 766670
21 Tombland NR3 1RF
e-mail: info@tatlers.com
dir: In city centre in Tombland. Next to Erpingham Gate by Norwich Cathedral

The historic Tombland area nudging the splendid medieval cathedral makes a characterful location for this neighbourhood restaurant in a Victorian townhouse. Tatlers is a stalwart of the Norwich dining scene, its trio of rooms done out in a fetching mix of claret walls, scrubbed pine floors and bare rustic tables. The kitchen takes an uncomplicated modern British line in its cooking that has earned a strong local following. The menus change daily to make the most of what's good in the season, so braised oxtail pasty with creamed horseradish might appear among starters, followed by haunch of local estate venison with curly kale, buttered carrots, fondant potato and blueberry jus. Finish with a Tunisian orange and almond cake, natural yoghurt and citrus salad. There's a sister restaurant in Holt, (see entry for Butlers).

Chef Adam Jarvis **Owner** Sean Creasey & Charles Butler **Times** 12-2/6-9 Closed 25-26 Dec, Sun **Prices** Fixed L 2 course £12, Fixed D 3 course £16, Starter £4.25-£6.95, Main £9.95-£16.95, Dessert £5.95-£7.95, Service optional, Groups min 6 service 10% **Wines** 34 bottles over £20, 14 bottles under £20, 15 by glass **Notes** Vegetarian menu **Seats** 75, Pr/dining room 33 **Children** Portions **Parking** Law courts, Elm Hill, Colegate, St Andrews

NORWICH *continued*

Thai Cuisine Restaurant

Thai V

Top Thai cuisine in Norwich

☎ 01603 700444
9 Ring Rd, Thorpe St Andrew NR7 0XJ
e-mail: richardakidd@aol.com
dir: From Southern bypass, follow airport signs. Located at top of hill past Sainsburys

Just off the ring road in a huge white painted detached house is this traditional Thai restaurant, which has been pulling in Norwich regulars since it opened 24 years ago. Female staff look the part in traditional Thai garb and the men look smart in black trousers and bow ties. The tables are equally well presented, chairs are dark bamboo-style and, to help customers imagine they're in more exotic climes, pictures of Thailand adorn the walls. The authentic food is skilfully made using top quality produce. Familiar dishes such as crispy spring rolls, chicken satay and king prawn tempura give way to the likes of beef musaman and chicken with garlic. And as the saying goes, book early to avoid disappointment.

Owner Richard & Onuma Kidd **Times** 12-3/6-10 Closed 25 Dec, L Sat-Mon **Prices** Food prices not confirmed for 2011. Please telephone for details. **Notes** Vegetarian menu, Dress restrictions, Smart casual **Seats** 55 **Parking** 25

RINGSTEAD Map 12 TF74

The Gin Trap Inn

Modern British

Charming 17th-century inn turned gastro-pub

☎ 01485 525264
6 High St PE36 5JU
e-mail: thegintrap@hotmail.co.uk
dir: A149 from King's Lynn towards Hunstanton. After 15m turn right at Heacham for Ringstead

The last two miles of the Roman Peddars Way run past this 17th-century pub's doorstep to join the sea on the splendid North Norfolk coast. In a tranquil village on the fringes of Hunstanton, the Gin Trap is a buzzy place with ploughshares above the door of its whitewashed exterior, opening into a rustic bar with a blazing log burner, bare bricks and beams, and light fittings made from vicious-looking gin traps. Eat in either the cosy bar, the posher restaurant, where tables are laid with linen and candles, or the conservatory. Whichever you choose, the deal is unfussy modern British food from a kitchen that hunts down the best local produce - oysters from nearby Thornham, for starters, followed by Arthur Howell's pork sausages with mash and red onion gravy, or something more involved, such as roast pheasant breast with stuffed Savoy cabbage, cocotte potatoes, parsnip purée, and Madeira and thyme gravy.

Chef Darren Smith **Owner** Steve Knowles & Cindy Cook **Times** 12-2/6-9 **Prices** Starter £5-£8.50, Main £9-£14.50, Dessert £6-£6.50, Service optional **Wines** 13 bottles over £20, 19 bottles under £20, 7 by glass **Notes** Sun L not available during school summer holidays, Sunday L, Vegetarian available **Seats** 60, Pr/dining room 18 **Children** Portions, Menu **Parking** 20, On street

SHERINGHAM Map 13 TG14

Marmalade's Bistro

British, International V

Relaxed, family-run bistro serving simply cooked local produce

☎ 01263 822830
5 Church St NR26 8QR
dir: A149 into town centre then left at clock tower

This Tudor-beamed former fishing cottage is now a friendly, rustic bistro run by a charming husband-and-wife-team. Plain pine tables, cream paintwork, wood floors and chalkboard menus make for an informal, relaxed mood, and it's comforting to see that the kitchen is governed by what's local and seasonal, including fish delivered daily. The cooking is intelligently simple and flavours are well-defined. Potted Sheringham crab with Thai spices might precede a main course of roast local pheasant with caramelised apples and sage with cider sauce. Bread and butter pudding with toffee sauce may round things off.

Chef Ben Mutton **Owner** Mr & Mrs B Mutton **Times** 12-2/6-9 Closed Wed, L Mon, D Sun **Prices** Starter £4.75-£5.95, Main £10.95-£18.95, Dessert fr £5.25, Service optional **Wines** 3 bottles over £20, 17 bottles under £20, 6 by glass **Notes** Pre-theatre D available, Sunday L, Vegetarian menu, Dress restrictions, Smart casual **Seats** 30 **Children** Portions **Parking** On street & town car parks

Upchers Restaurant

British, European

Country-house dining in delightful parkland surroundings

☎ 01263 824555
Dales Country House Hotel, Lodge Hill NR26 8TJ
e-mail: dales@mackenziehotels.com
dir: On B1157, 1m S of Sheringham. From A148 Cromer to Holt road, take turn at entrance to Sheringham Park. Restaurant 0.5m on left

Hidden away in extensive grounds, adjacent to the National Trust parkland of Sheringham Park, this stylishly refurbished Victorian country-house hotel retains its period charm. Follow drinks and canapés in the Kings Bar, or on the lawn in summer, with an enjoyable dinner in the relaxed and smart, traditionally-styled Upchers Restaurant, with its inglenook fireplace and fine oak panelling. Using game from local estates, fish from the North Norfolk coast and locally-reared meats, the kitchen delivers simple, accomplished dishes that yield excellent flavours. From the short, imaginative carte, follow roast beetroot soup with roast duck with apple tarte Tatin, creamed Savoy cabbage and duck liver jus, or choose from the 'fish board' options, perhaps local mussel and crayfish chowder, followed by pan-fried halibut with herb butter sauce. To finish, try the lemon sabayon tart.

Chef Nick Parker **Owner** Mr & Mrs Mackenzie **Times** 12-2/7-9.30 **Prices** Food prices not confirmed for 2011. Please telephone for details. **Wines** 16 bottles over £20, 28 bottles under £20, 8 by glass **Notes** Sunday L, Vegetarian available, Dress restrictions, No shorts or sportswear **Seats** 70, Pr/dining room 40 **Children** Portions **Parking** 50

SNETTISHAM Map 12 TF63

Rose & Crown

Modern British **NEW**

Bustling local with global dishes and British classics

☎ 01485 541382
Old Church Rd PE31 7LX
e-mail: info@roseandcrownsnettisham.co.uk
dir: From King's Lynn take A149 N towards Hunstanton. After 10m into Snettisham to village centre, then into Old Church Rd towards church. Hotel 100yds on left

Set in the smart village of Snettisham, this 14th-century country village pub is a textbook warren of nooks and crannies, gnarled beams, wobbly floors and log fires, but it also boasts a clean-cut modern beachcomber look, with vibrant hues here and there. On the wide-ranging menu are pub classics, such as gammon steak, eggs and hand-cut chips or steak burger with bacon, cheese, tomato ketchup and fries, and more contemporary ideas spiced up with global influences, all built on tip-top locally-sourced ingredients. Expect the likes of home-smoked Norfolk pigeon breast with baby beetroot, pancetta and pine nut salad followed by whole baked plaice, new potatoes, curly kale and salsa verde. There's a flexible approach here, so you can choose to eat in the bar, restaurant, cellar bar or the garden room.

Chef Keith McDowell **Owner** Anthony & Jeanette Goodrich **Times** 12-2/6.30-9 **Prices** Starter £4.95-£7.95, Main £9.50-£16.50, Dessert £4.25-£5.75, Service optional, Groups min 8 service 10% **Wines** 10 bottles over £20, 27 bottles under £20, 10 by glass **Notes** Sunday L, Vegetarian available **Seats** 60, Pr/dining room 30 **Children** Portions, Menu **Parking** 70

STOKE HOLY CROSS Map 13 TG20

The Wildebeest Arms

Modern British

Exotic take on a traditional pub with enticing menus

☎ 01508 492497
82-86 Norwich Rd, Stoke Holy Cross NR14 8QJ
e-mail: wildebeest@animalinns.co.uk
dir: From A47 take A140, left to Dunston. At T-junct turn left, Wildebeest Arms on right

Three miles south of Norwich, this traditional looking village local has been tastefully modernised inside, taking on a contemporary rustic-chic look with a touch of African exoticism, as its name suggests. Thick, chunky wooden tables, wooden floors, vases of fresh lilies, open log fires and a quirky, African-inspired décor (spears, masks, motifs and rugs) make a good first impression. Cooking is mostly Anglo-French, as seen in appealing set-price menus du jour, and the accomplished kitchen uses quality local seasonal produce to good effect. Food is fresh and vibrant with strong clear flavours. Take a simple but well-executed starter of truffled goats' cheese with goats' cheese beignet, local asparagus and home-made bread, and moist, well-seasoned chargrilled chicken breast served with charred Mediterranean vegetables and a chorizo and caper vinaigrette for main course.

Chef Eden Derrick **Owner** Henry Watt
Times 12-3.30/6-11.30 Closed 25-26 Dec **Prices** Fixed L 2 course fr £14.95, Fixed D 3 course fr £21.50, Starter £4.95-£8.50, Main £12.50-£21.50, Dessert £4.95-£7.50, Service optional **Wines** 70 bottles over £20, 41 bottles under £20, 13 by glass **Notes** Sunday L, Vegetarian available **Seats** 75 **Children** Portions **Parking** 40

SWAFFHAM Map 13 TF80

Best Western George Hotel

British, International V

Enjoyable food in historic hotel overlooking market square

☎ 01760 721238
Station Rd PE37 7LJ
e-mail: georgehotel@bestwestern.co.uk
dir: Located on main X-roads in Swaffham

The 300-year-old George sits on the crossroads at the heart of local life in the venerable market town of Swaffham, which telly addicts might know as 'Market Shipborough', its stage name when it stars as the location for the *Kingdom* series. The kitchen puts faith in the quality of Norfolk produce as the mainstay of its crowd-pleasing modern European menu, served on linen-clothed tables in the traditional setting of the Green Room restaurant. Norfolk potted shrimps with granary toast is a classic, unfussy starter, while mains could see honey-glazed chicken teamed with cider and rosemary, Lyonnaise potatoes and roasted squash, alongside a timeless roast beef with Yorkshire pudding, gravy and all the trimmings.

Chef Pete Crundwell **Owner** David Easter
Times 12-2.30/6.30-9.30 Closed 25 Dec **Prices** Food prices not confirmed for 2011. Please telephone for details. **Wines** 5 bottles over £20, 20 bottles under £20, 7 by glass **Notes** Sunday L, Vegetarian menu **Seats** 40, Pr/dining room 18 **Children** Portions, Menu **Parking** 80

THETFORD Map 13 TL88

Elveden Café Restaurant

Modern

Relaxed café-style dining on the Elveden Estate

☎ 01842 898068
London Rd, Elveden IP24 3TQ
e-mail: estate.shop@elveden.com
dir: On A11 between Newmarket & Thetford, 800 mtrs from junct with B1106

This smart café on the Elveden Estate near Center Parcs is set in a large courtyard of converted red-brick farm buildings that also house a range of shops. There's an open-plan alfresco barbecue zone and large outdoor dining area too, all tastefully set out with patio heaters. Inside it's equally light and airy with vaulted ceiling and beams, natural-wood floors, cream walls and black marble-topped tables partnered by modern-style wooden chairs. Regularly-changing menus range from restaurant-style meals and daily specials to lovely home-made sandwiches and cakes, all using local produce. Expect chicken and ham pie and Elveden Estate burger (made from 21-day hung beef) with perhaps a rum truffle cake to finish.

Chef Chris Allen **Owner** The Earl of Iveagh **Times** 9.30-5 Closed 25-26 Dec,1 Jan, D all week **Prices** Starter £4.50-£6.75, Main £6.75-£12.95, Dessert £3.50-£4.75, Service optional **Wines** 2 bottles over £20, 4 bottles under £20, 6 by glass **Notes** Sunday L, Vegetarian available **Seats** 70 **Children** Portions, Menu **Parking** 200

THORNHAM Map 12 TF74

Lifeboat Inn

Traditional British

Beautifully situated historic North Norfolk inn

☎ 01485 512236
Ship Ln PE36 6LT
e-mail: reception@lifeboatinn.co.uk
dir: A149 from Hunstanton for approx 6m. 1st left after Thornham sign

The rambling, 16th-century smugglers' inn, situated on the edge of an expanse of salt marsh, is a short stroll from vast sweeping beaches and bracing coastal path rambles. Inside, it seems some previous incumbents had a nice line in architectural salvage: there's a splendid baronial fireplace, exposed brickwork and ancient oak beams for classic pub character, and a smart restaurant, with white-clothed, candlelit tables for romantic dinners. The daily specials board features 'what's been caught, shot, picked or dug locally each day'. Fish is high on the agenda, with starters such as seared scallops with bonne femme sauce, then, to keep the carnivores happy, lamb cutlets with ratatouille and minted garlic gravy.

Times 12-2.30/7-9.30

THURSFORD Map 13 TF93

The Old Forge Seafood Restaurant

Seafood V

Locally-caught seafood in a family-run restaurant with rooms

☎ 01328 878345
Fakenham Rd NR21 0BD
e-mail: sarah.goldspink@btconnect.com
dir: On A148

700 years ago, when the Old Forge was a coaching station with the requisite horseshoe maintenance facilities, pilgrims on their way to Walsingham Abbey would make a pitstop for a breather and a bite to eat. This excellent tradition is still going strong in the 21st century: a homely rustic-styled dining room with York stone floors and the original horse-tethering hooks still embedded in the walls is the venue for travellers who turn up for chef-patron Colin Bowett's confident, unfussy treatment of spanking fresh fish and seafood. Spanish and French influences have plenty of say in what leaves the kitchen – seafood platters, fish and seafood zarzuela cooked with white wine, cream and tomatoes, monkfish in Provençal sauce, being cases in point. Otherwise, dressed Cromer crab, a half-dozen Blakeney oysters, or roasted cod topped with melted potted shrimps have a strictly local flavour.

Chef Colin Bowett **Owner** Colin & Sarah Bowett
Times 12-2/6.30-9.30 Closed Mon **Prices** Fixed L 2 course fr £16.50, Fixed D 3 course fr £21.50, Starter £3.95-£7.50, Main £12.95-£28.95, Dessert £3.95-£4.95, Service optional **Wines** 5 bottles over £20, 10 bottles under £20, 5 by glass **Notes** Vegetarian menu **Seats** 28 **Children** Portions **Parking** 12

TITCHWELL Map 13 TF74

Titchwell Manor Hotel

Modern European

Charming hotel with classy conservatory restaurant

☎ 01485 210221
PE31 8BB
e-mail: margaret@titchwellmanor.com
dir: On A149 (coast road) between Brancaster & Thornham

A delightful country hotel with a boutique feel, Titchwell Manor has views towards the coast over the RSPB reserve

continued

NORWICH ***continued***

of Titchwell Marsh. It's a classic North Norfolk setting, and chef Eric Snaith ensures the region's produce, especially the excellent seafood, gets a good showing on the menu. The house is done out in today's favoured muted contemporary tones, while the restaurant is in a splendid green-framed conservatory, giving views over the charming garden, from whence some of the vegetables and herbs come. A new brasserie is the latest addition to the set up, underway as we go to press. In the restaurant, the cooking is in the modern European vein, with plenty of good ideas, eye-catching presentations, and delivering some top-drawer flavours. A refined start might be foie gras ballottine with prunes and spiced streusel; next up, perhaps a top-notch rib-eye, or chargrilled halibut with aubergine pickle and curried celeriac.

Chef Eric Snaith **Owner** Margaret & Ian Snaith **Times** 12-2.30/6-9.30 **Prices** Fixed L 2 course fr £12, Fixed D 4 course £40, Starter £4-£8, Main £7-£25, Dessert £6-£10, Groups min 8 service 10% **Wines** 27 bottles over £20, 25 bottles under £20, 9 by glass **Notes** Sunday L, Vegetarian available, Dress restrictions, Smart casual, Civ Wed 85 **Seats** 80 **Children** Portions, Menu **Parking** 50

WIVETON **Map 13 TG04**

Wiveton Bell

Modern British NEW

Refurbished traditional pub serving up good local produce

☎ 01263 740101
The Green, Blakeney Rd NR25 7TL
e-mail: enquiries@wivetonbell.co.uk
dir: 1m S of Blakeney on the Holt road

On the village green and close to the salt marshes of North Norfolk, this traditional 18th-century inn turned gastro-pub stays true to its roots with a large bar area for locals. Heavily beamed it may be, with an open inglenook fire, but recent refurbishment has brought it bang up to date. Cream walls, contemporary art and natural wooden tables are very much in the modern pub idiom. Quality local produce simply prepared drives the expansive seasonal menus – think Morston mussels, Blakeney crabs or Holkham game. Expect classics such as bangers and mash or fisherman's pie or a tender main course of Briston slow-cooked belly pork served with black pudding mash and Bramley apple and cider jus. Friendly staff are casually dressed in black while alfresco dining in the well-maintained garden is popular in good weather.

Chef Nick Anderson **Owner** Berni Morritt & Sandy Butcher **Times** 12-2.15/6-9 Closed 25 Dec **Prices** Food prices not confirmed for 2011. Please telephone for details. **Wines** 6 bottles over £20, 28 bottles under £20, 21 by glass **Notes** Sunday L, Vegetarian available **Seats** 60 **Children** Portions, Menu **Parking** 5, village green 50yds away

WROXHAM **Map 13 TG31**

Traffords

Traditional British NEW

Elegant country house in Broadland setting

☎ 01603 783567
Broad House Hotel, The Avenue NR12 8TS
e-mail: info@broadhousehotel.co.uk

A beautiful Queen Anne property, Broad House is a country hotel in the Norfolk Broads set in 24 acres of grounds, including a kitchen garden that provides plenty of seasonal produce. The rooms are traditionally and formally decorated to a high standard, the dining room is a rich, warming red, its tables dressed in crisp white linen. Norfolk produce figures large on the ambitious, fine-dining menu where a salad of garden beetroot is partnered with Green Farm goats' cheese, and a loin of local venison is served with dauphinoise potatoes, braised red cabbage, roast parsnips and finished with a red wine sauce. Rum baba is a traditional finish.

Times 12-2/7-9

WYMONDHAM **Map 13 TG10**

Number Twenty Four Restaurant

Modern British

Relaxed dining and market fresh produce

☎ 01953 607750
24 Middleton St NR18 0AD
dir: Town centre opposite war memorial

Grade II listed 18th-century cottages in the centre of the historic market town of Wymondham are home to this smart, family-run restaurant. The dining room has plenty of period charm and warm, soothing colours on the walls; neatly clothed, well-spaced tables and genuinely welcoming staff complete the picture. Dishes change daily depending on what's in season so the compact menu, showing modern British sensibilities, might feature seared king prawns with crispy pork belly served on Thai-spiced cauliflower and sweet chill dressing, or perhaps seared fillet of beef served on Lyonnaise potatoes, wild mushroom stout and peppercorn gravy topped with rocket and aoïli dressing. Vanilla crème brûlée with roast spiced pineapple and passionfruit sorbet or a hot dark chocolate and orange pudding make for a difficult choice at dessert.

Chef Jonathan Griffin **Owner** Jonathan Griffin **Times** 12-2/7-9 Closed 26 Dec, 1 Jan, Mon, L Tue, D Sun **Prices** Fixed L 2 course £14.95-£17.95, Fixed D 3 course £24.95-£30 **Wines** 10 bottles over £20, 26 bottles under £20, 6 by glass **Notes** Sunday L, Vegetarian available, Dress restrictions, Smart casual, No shorts **Seats** 60, Pr/dining room 55 **Children** Portions **Parking** On street opposite. In town centre car park

NORTHAMPTONSHIRE

COLLYWESTON **Map 11 SK90**

The Collyweston Slater

Modern British

Stylish village inn serving modern British food

☎ 01780 444288
87-89 Main Rd PE9 3PQ
e-mail: info@thecollywestonslater.co.uk
dir: 4m S of Stamford, A43, 2m off A1

With splendid views over the Wetland Valley and Fineshade Woods, this traditional 17th-century inn has been sympathetically remodelled by new owners, yet retains the old fabric and character of the inn. Original oak beams, stone walls and slate floors blend well with lightwood tables and leather chairs in the rambling bar and brasserie-style restaurant. Serving modern British food, with a focus on seasonal, local produce, the emphasis is on quality and flavour. Take a starter of local game terrine with Cumberland jelly, or goats' cheese parfait with figs, sour pear sorbet and fig jelly, and inventive main courses, perhaps braised shoulder of lamb with roast onions, ceps, pancetta and haggis ravioli, or roast salmon with Puy lentils, basil pomme purée, red wine jus and baby leeks. For pudding, try the chocolate tart with mascarpone sorbet.

Chef Dameon Clarke **Owner** Dameon Clarke & Philip Robson **Times** 11.30-9.30 **Prices** Starter £6.75-£9.95, Main £13.95-£22.95, Dessert fr £5.95, Service optional **Notes** Tasting menu on request, Sunday L **Seats** 34, Pr/dining room 10 **Children** Portions, Menu **Parking** 32

DAVENTRY **Map 11 SP56**

Equilibrium

– see opposite page

FOTHERINGHAY Map 12 TL09

The Falcon Inn

British, European

Modern cooking in rural Northamptonshire

01832 226254
Main St PE8 5HZ
e-mail: info@thefalcon-inn.co.uk
dir: From A605 at Warmington follow signs to Fotheringhay. Situated centre of village

In the heart of the sleepy village famous as the birthplace of Richard III, and the place where Mary, Queen of Scots was imprisoned, this historic pub overlooks the Church of St Mary. The Falcon is a proper local with a smart restaurant attached. The modern British classics on offer aim straight for the comfort zone, ranging from bar menu dishes such as pan-fried salmon with new potatoes, mixed leaf salad and tartare sauce, to European-influenced dishes on the restaurant menu. Tuck into a main course such as braised rabbit with champ mash, baby carrots and turnips, shallots, pancetta and a prune and Armagnac reduction.

Times 12-2.15/6.15-9.15

KETTERING Map 11 SP87

Langberrys Restaurant

Modern British

Kettering branch of reliable hotel chain

01536 416666
Kettering Park Hotel & Spa, Kettering Parkway NN15 6XT
e-mail: kpark.reservations@shirehotels.com
dir: Off A14 junct 9

The restaurant at this spa hotel, a member of the Shire group, is split over two floors, and features a terraced area for outdoor dining. Dishes in Langberrys restaurant are the same as those offered elsewhere within the chain, with conscientious use of local supplies and simple, unpretentious presentation. You might start with crispy duck spring rolls and pickled cucumber, before setting about a trio of Stamford lamb cutlets with salsa verde. The top of the crème brûlée shatters properly at the tap of a spoon, and reveals a rich, vanilla-speckled custard beneath, but perhaps you've got your eye on the pedigree English cheeses.

Chef Stephen Robinson **Owner** Shire Hotels **Times** 12-1.45/7-9.30 Closed Xmas & New Year (ex residents), L Mon-Sat **Prices** Starter £6-£10, Main £13-£23, Dessert £6-£8, Service optional **Wines** 69 bottles over £20, 5 bottles under £20, 15 by glass **Notes** Sunday L, Vegetarian available, Civ Wed 120 **Seats** 90, Pr/dining room 40 **Children** Portions, Menu **Parking** 200

Tresham Restaurant, Rushton Hall Hotel & Spa

Modern European

Highly accomplished cooking in magnificent surroundings

01536 713001
Rushton NN14 1RR
e-mail: enquiries@rushtonhall.com
web: www.rushtonhall.com
dir: A14 junct 7. A43 to Corby, A6003 to Rushton, turn off after bridge

continued

Equilibrium

DAVENTRY Map 11 SP56

Modern British V

Exhilarating cooking in characterful country house

01327 892000
Fawsley Hall, Fawsley NN11 3BA
e-mail: info@fawsleyhall.com
dir: A361 S of Daventry, between Badby & Charwelton. Follow signs to Fawsley Hall along single track lane

Expect to be swept away by the grandeur of the impressive 14th-century Fawsley Hall country-house hotel, set in 2,000 acres of rolling hills and parkland. Its medieval splendour is plain for all to see as you enter the Tudor Great Hall with its lofty oak-vaulted ceiling - a striking place to take drinks. Deep squashy sofas, cavernous period fireplaces and a myriad of pictures on the walls make it a memorable place to wile away the time. Georgian and Victorian wings have also been added to the property and now house comfortably luxurious bedrooms. Equilibrium is one of two restaurants - Bess's Brasserie provides a more informal option - and it's a neutral canvas for a host of period touches. Gothic-style chairs covered in Rossini linen and lime stripes, tables dressed with table skirts and striking cutlery and glassware. Exemplary raw ingredients are put through their paces with the highest level of technical expertise - this is modern British food majoring in the wow factor. Excellent canapés, including a 'Cornetto' cheese shortbread precede a smartly presented 24-hour suckling pig served with marbled terrine and crispy crackling. Succulent Pyrenean milk-fed lamb with sweetbreads, kidney, wild garlic, new season peas and broad beans punches above its weight while an unusual dessert of artichoke crème, toasted oats, truffle ice cream and olive oil gel is one way to end the meal. Those in need of a sweeter hit can tuck into the caramel salted chocolate popcorn served with tea and coffee.

Chef Nigel Godwin **Owner** Bahram Holdings **Times** 7-9.30 Closed Xmas, Sun-Mon, L all week **Prices** Tasting menu £79-£119, Service added but optional 12.5% **Wines** 160+ bottles over £20, 10 bottles under £20, 20 by glass **Notes** Fixed D 5 course £59, Tasting menu 7 course with wine £119, Vegetarian menu, Dress restrictions, Smart casual **Seats** 30, Pr/dining room 20 **Parking** 140

KETTERING *continued*

Rushton is everything you'd expect in a grand country-house hotel dating from 1438, set in acres of parkland and seriously overhauled with Victorian wealth. Walk-in stone fireplaces, delicate plasterwork and stained glass abound, and the tone continues into the magnificent oak linenfold-panelled dining room. In the kitchen, however, we're in a modern European realm, with a confident team delivering classically-influenced cuisine of a high order. Noteworthy depth of flavour impresses, and simple menu descriptions belie the technical skill that has gone into dishes such as Blythburgh pork belly with barbecue sugar and sweetcorn. The style is typified in a main course of turbot with parsley risotto, clams, garlic purée and red wine jus, or Angus beef fillet with ox cheek and smoked horseradish mash, and a pudding like peanut butter parfait with salt caramel and peanut brittle.

Times 12-2/7-9

OUNDLE — Map 11 TL08

Oundle Mill

◎◎ Modern European NEW V

Modern European food in a classy, converted watermill

☎ 01832 272621
Barnwell Rd PE8 5PB
e-mail: info@oundlemill.co.uk
dir: Located just outside Oundle off A605

A large old watermill on the banks of the River Nene, on the outskirts of a charming Northamptonshire market town, has been sensitively converted into a modern boutique hotel. The contemporary design job incorporates some very classy features, not least the glass floor in the restaurant that straddles the rushing water below. Light stone walls, original oak beams and undressed tables with sleek Italian seating all add up to a nicely relaxed air, and the small kitchen brigade under Jeremy Medley produces some intricately detailed modern European food. Clarity of flavours and properly defined seasoning distinguish dishes such as cured mackerel and scallops with beetroot and lemon risotto, or rump of local lamb with chilli vinegar, smoked garlic and capers, but even the less adventurous options - chicken liver parfait with brioche toast, or grilled rib steak with chips - are brought off with great aplomb.

Chef Jeremy Medley **Owner** Mark & Sarah Harrod **Times** 12-2.30/6.30-9.30 **Prices** Fixed L 2 course £12, Fixed D 3 course £20, Starter £4.50-£14.50, Main £10.50-£26, Dessert £5.50-£11, Service optional **Wines** 138 bottles over £20, 4 bottles under £20, 14 by glass **Notes** Sunday L, Vegetarian menu, Civ Wed 100 **Seats** 50, Pr/dining room 45 **Children** Portions, Menu **Parking** 60

ROADE — Map 11 SP75

Roade House Restaurant

◎ Modern French

Well loved village restaurant with rooms with well-judged menu

☎ 01604 863372
16 High St NN7 2NW
e-mail: info@roadehousehotel.co.uk
dir: M1 junct 15 (A508 Milton Keynes) to Roade, left at mini rdbt, 500yds on left

Sandwiched between the M1 and Silverstone race track - although seemingly a million miles away when you're in the delightful village - this restaurant with rooms has an easy charm. It may have been a pub in a former life, but these days it has an appealing understated elegance, the beamed dining room done out in natural, muted tones, thus setting the scene for some refreshingly fuss-free cooking based on excellent seasonal produce. Chris Kewley's cooking puts the focus on flavour, so simple ideas are based on sound principles and pack a punch; start with a salad of lentils with artichokes and mint, or perhaps a gratin of knuckle of ham with peas and horseradish. Fillet of halibut is grilled and served with fine beans, white wine, mussel and prawn sauce, and for dessert, how about the comfort of profiteroles with hot chocolate sauce?

Chef Chris Kewley **Owner** Mr & Mrs C M Kewley **Times** 12-2/7-9.30 Closed 1 wk Xmas, L Sat, D Sun **Prices** Fixed L 2 course £20, Fixed D 3 course £31, Service optional **Wines** 40 bottles over £20, 30 bottles under £20, 4 by glass **Notes** Sunday L, Vegetarian available, Dress restrictions, No shorts **Seats** 50, Pr/dining room 16 **Children** Portions **Parking** 20

TOWCESTER — Map 11 SP64

Vine House Hotel & Restaurant

◎◎ Modern, Traditional British

Rural setting for daily-changing menu of local produce

☎ 01327 811267
100 High St, Paulerspury NN12 7NA
e-mail: info@vinehousehotel.com
dir: 2m S of Towcester, just off A5

Marcus and Julie Springett run their restaurant with rooms with a personal touch that has won a strong fan base since they started in business back in 1991. The rambling 300-year-old creeper-clad cottage in a lovely village setting sits well with the traditional, relaxed feel within - there's also a whimsical garden folly for romantic dining à deux. The fixed-price menu keeps focus by offering three choices at each stage, plus a slate of artisan British cheeses. The food is full-bodied and rustic, but stays in touch with modern trends: a starter of local black pudding comes with mushroom mousse and truffle sauce, followed by the likes of Middlewhite pork fillet with braised leeks, mustard and shallots. Homely desserts follow the lines of honey and apricot bread pudding with clotted cream.

Chef Marcus Springett **Owner** Mr M & Mrs J Springett **Times** 12-2/6-10 Closed 1 wk winter, Sun, L Mon **Prices** Fixed L 2 course £26.95-£29.95, Fixed D 2 course £26.95-£29.95, Service added 12.5% **Wines** 47 bottles over £20, 26 bottles under £20, 2 by glass **Seats** 26, Pr/dining room 10 **Parking** 20

WHITTLEBURY — Map 11 SP64

Murrays at Whittlebury Hall

◎◎ British, European

Fine-dining restaurant dedicated to Formula 1 commentator Murray Walker

☎ 01327 857857 & 0845 4000001
Whittlebury Hall Hotel NN12 8QH
e-mail: sales@whittleburyhall.co.uk
web: www.whittleburyhall.co.uk
dir: A43/A413 to Whittlebury, through village, hotel at far end on right within Westpark grounds

Whittlebury Hall lies just a Ferrari's roar away from Silverstone. The much-loved Formula 1 commentator Murray Walker lends his name to the sophisticated fine dining restaurant of this plush neo-Georgian hotel with a Rolls Royce of a spa. Some of his celebrated gaffes are immortalised on the walls, together with F1 memorabilia. While the slick front-of-house team ensures diners can relax in the slow lane, the kitchen shifts into top gear with its modern British cooking. Finely-tuned classical techniques underpin dishes such as confit leg and home-smoked breast of duck with Hellidon Farm cider and pear pickle, and toasted walnut bread, followed by aged fillet of beef with morel and oyster mushroom casserole and horseradish foam. Full-throttle desserts might feature dark chocolate fondant with passionfruit and orange essence and cardamom ice cream.

Chef Craig Rose **Owner** Macepark (Whittlebury) Ltd **Times** 7-10 Closed 24-26, 31 Dec, 1-7 Jan, Sun-Mon, L all week **Prices** Food prices not confirmed for 2011. Please telephone for details. **Notes** Sunday L, Vegetarian available, Dress restrictions, Smart casual, No jeans, trainers or shorts **Seats** 32, Pr/dining room 10 **Children** Portions, Menu **Parking** 460

NORTHUMBERLAND

BAMBURGH Map 21 NU13

Grays Restaurant at Waren House Hotel

Modern British NEW

Traditional country-house dining with local flavour

01668 214581
Waren Mill NE70 7EE
e-mail: enquiries@warenhousehotel.co.uk
dir: Exit A1 on B1342, follow signs to Bamburgh. Hotel in 2m in village Waren Mill

Tradition is the watchword at this charming small Georgian country-house hotel in six acres of lovely gardens near to Lindisfarne Island and Bamburgh Castle. Its restaurant is a textbook example of classic country-house style, all elegant restraint in its colour scheme, antique tables polished to a mirror finish and walls hung with prints and paintings. The kitchen sources its raw materials from within a 40-mile radius to produce a repertoire that extends to first-course baked Doddington cheese soufflé with a simple beetroot and grain mustard chutney; then, perhaps, monkfish wrapped in cured ham and teamed with parsley mash, tartlet of lemon-roasted vegetables and vermouth velouté.

Times 6.30-8.30

CORNHILL-ON-TWEED Map 21 NT83

Tillmouth Park Country House Hotel

Traditional British

Splendid Northumbrian mansion with country-house cooking

01890 882255
TD12 4UU
e-mail: reception@tillmouthpark.force9.co.uk
dir: A698, 3m E from Cornhill-on-Tweed

The mists of time are somewhat hazy on the origins of this country mansion, but what is sure is that its Victorian inhabitants rebuilt it in the 1880s in grandiose style using the stones from the ruined Twizel Castle. The setting by the River Till in peaceful border country is glorious, and the interior is packed with plenty of Victorian Gothic romance - oak panelling, beautiful stained glass and an amazing galleried lounge. The kitchen takes a ground-up approach to sourcing the freshest local materials, and cooks in a classic country-house style, but with an eye to current trends. Eyemouth mussels steamed in herbs and vermouth cream are a fine way to start, then you might proceed to loin of venison en croûte with beetroot and horseradish purée, potato confit and red wine jus.

Chef Piotr Dziedzic **Owner** Tillmouth Park Partnership **Times** 12-2/7-8.45 Closed 26-28 Dec, Jan-Mar, L Mon-Sat **Prices** Fixed L 3 course fr £22, Fixed D 3 course fr £37, Service optional **Wines** 50 bottles over £20, 7 bottles under £20, 6 by glass **Notes** Sunday L, Vegetarian available, Dress restrictions, Smart casual, No jeans, Civ Wed 50 **Seats** 40, Pr/dining room 20 **Children** Portions **Parking** 50

HEXHAM Map 21 NY96

Dukes Grill

Modern British

Fine dining in a grand Edwardian mansion

01434 673350
De Vere Slaley Hall, Slaley NE47 0BX
e-mail: slaley.hall@devere-hotels.com
dir: A1 from S to A68. Follow signs for Slaley Hall. From N A69 to Corbridge then take A68 S and follow signs to Slaley Hall

From its elevated position, the imposing Edwardian pile that is Slaley Hall looks out over 1,000 acres of parkland, and beyond to the wild and rugged Northumberland countryside. These days a hotel owned by the De Vere chain, Slaley has a lot to offer - luxury accommodation, two championship golf courses, and a spa and fitness centre. The Dukes Grill is in the original Edwardian drawing room and it's here that you can tuck into the theatre of dishes prepared at your table, plus prime cuts cooked on the Josper grill. The kitchen takes great care to source local, seasonal produce, and dishes are well-executed. Expect seared scallops with squid ink, celeriac and watercress as an opener, then follow with rump of lamb, potato and fennel Parmentier and aubergine confit.

Times 1-3/6.30-9.45 Closed Mon

Josephine Restaurant

Modern British

Innovative cuisine in a medieval castle

01434 688 888
Langley Castle Hotel, Langley on Tyne NE47 5LU
e-mail: manager@langleycastle.com
web: www.langleycastle.com
dir: From A69 take A686 S, restaurant 2m on right

Langley Castle Hotel is a 14th-century pile nestling in the South Tyne valley in Northumbria in its own 10 acres of woodland. Built during the reign of Edward III, amazing original details such as stained glass windows, rich furnishings and roaring log fires abound in the Josephine Restaurant while high-backed chairs and solid tables add to the air of luxury. The small kitchen team produces outstanding food - beautifully presented and not overly complicated - and makes the most of local produce such as game in season. Start with red breast of local pigeon, black pudding bonbon, Jerusalem artichoke purée and liquorice froth followed by pan-fried South Tyne salmon with seared scallops, sautéed cucumber, baby gem and chorizo foam. 'Orange' – tangerine cheesecake, star anise soup, orange sorbet and shortbread 'Jaffa cake' makes for an inventive finish.

Chef Andy Smith **Owner** Dr S Madnick **Times** 12-2.30/7-9 **Prices** Fixed L 2 course £15.95, Fixed D 3 course £27.50-£39.50, Service optional **Wines** 19 bottles over £20, 20 bottles under £20, 7 by glass **Notes** Sunday L, Vegetarian available, Dress restrictions, Smart casual, Civ Wed 120 **Seats** 48 **Children** Portions, Menu **Parking** 57

LONGHORSLEY Map 21 NZ19

Dobson Restaurant

Modern International

Grade II listed country property set in extensive parkland

01670 500000
Macdonald Linden Hall, Golf & Country Club NE65 8XF
e-mail: general.lindenhall@macdonald-hotels.co.uk
dir: 7m NW of Morpeth on A697 off A1

There's plenty of scope for working up an appetite at Linden Hall; the late-Georgian mansion sits in 450 acres of park and mature woodland with its own golf course. At its culinary heart is the Dobson Restaurant, a plush, upmarket venue, elegantly laid out in warm autumnal tones of russet and brick-red, with linen-clothed tables and relaxed service that sets diners at ease. The kitchen takes a modern approach to dishes built on first-class raw materials, and its strengths lie in the fact that it sticks to tried-and-tested themes. Expect the likes of roast scallops with pea purée, pancetta and pea shoots, followed by roasted loin and braised shoulder of Scottish lamb with potato gratin, spring vegetables and red wine jus, or a modish fish and meat pairing of pan-fried halibut with braised chicken wings with chervil gnocchi and wild mushrooms. More informal brasserie-style dishes are served in the hotel's Linden Tree Pub.

Times 12-2.30/6.30-9.30 Closed L Mon-Sat

MATFEN Map 21 NZ07

Matfen Hall

Modern British

Elegant dining in a Victorian library

01661 886500 & 855708
NE20 0RH
e-mail: info@matfenhall.com
dir: A69 signed Hexham, leave at Heddon on the Wall. Then B6318, through Rudchester & Harlow Hill. Follow signs on right for Matfen

Matfen Hall was built to impress by Victorian forebears of its owners, the Blackett family. It is a truly stately home, set in 300 acres of parkland handy for exploring

continued

MATFEN *continued*

Hadrian's Wall or the wild and windy Northumberland coast - or if you prefer your landscapes more managed, there's a 27-hole golf course to tackle. The spectacular Library makes a memorable setting for dining among walls lined with leather-bound tomes, or there's an inviting alfresco terrace for sunny days. The menus have a seasonal impetus and an emphasis on imaginative modern British re-inventions of the classic country-house idiom. Pressed ham hock terrine with pease pudding is a hearty opener, while main-course pan-seared venison comes with fig tarte Tatin and boulangère potatoes. Desserts are a strong suit: a perfectly-cooked blackcurrant soufflé with liquorice and Sambuca parfait.

Chef Phil Hall **Owner** Sir Hugh & Lady Blackett **Times** 12.15-2.30/6.45-9.15 Closed L Mon-Sat **Prices** Fixed L 3 course fr £19.95, Starter £7.25-£7.95, Main £19.95-£24.95, Dessert £7.95-£8.25, Service optional **Wines** 56 bottles over £20, 37 bottles under £20, 20 by glass **Notes** Sunday L, Vegetarian available, Dress restrictions, Smart casual, Civ Wed 160 **Seats** 90, Pr/dining room 120 **Children** Portions, Menu **Parking** 120

OTTERBURN **Map 21 NY89**

Otterburn Hall Hotel

Modern British NEW

Modern British food in the wilds of Northumberland

☎ 01830 520663
NE19 1HE
e-mail: info@otterburnhall.com
dir: A696 to Otterburn

Otterburn Hall is a squat red-brick Victorian country house set in 500 acres of elemental Northumberland National Park landscapes. After you have honed your appetite walking in one of England's last remaining areas of wilderness, or exploring Hadrian's Wall country, the restaurant offers relaxed dining in a setting that blends hints of Victorian elegance with an uncluttered modern feel - widely-spaced tables float like islands of white linen sprinkled across a burnished pine floor, flanked by two antique horses. The kitchen takes a broadly modern British approach, rooted in the classics, and with good use of local materials - boudin of Borders mallard with spiced plum and apple chutney, for example, followed by noisettes of local lamb, teamed with lamb croquette, mint pea purée and dark mint jus.

Times 6.30-9

The Otterburn Tower Hotel

Modern British NEW

Modern British cooking on the site of a medieval castle

☎ 01830 520620
NE19 1NS
e-mail: info@otterburntower.com
dir: On A696 in centre of Otterburn

Saturated in history, the Otterburn Tower was originally a castle built in the 11th century by a cousin of William the Conqueror, as is referenced by its crenellated roofline. Its restaurant dates back merely to the 16th century, and is all oak panelling and stained-glass windows. A fairly formal approach is taken, as well it might be in the surroundings, although the cooking sounds more contemporary notes in its modern British way. Accurate handling of fine raw materials produces successful dishes such as a partnership of scallops and belly pork in a butternut squash and ginger velouté, and main courses like locally-shot roe deer with beetroot and spiced red cabbage, sauced with juniper-scented roasting juices. Great visual impact, as well as clear, uncluttered flavours are the distinguishing hallmarks. Finish with a diverting ensemble of almond parfait, olive oil cake and roasted figs, which is full of clever flavour contrasts.

Chef Craig Nellis **Owner** John Goodfellow **Times** 12-3/6-9.30 **Prices** Fixed L 2 course fr £11, Starter £5-£6.95, Main £13.95-£21.50, Dessert £5-£6, Service optional **Wines** 18 bottles over £20, 20 bottles under £20, 6 by glass **Notes** Sunday L, Vegetarian available **Seats** 50, Pr/dining room 250 **Children** Portions, Menu **Parking** 70

PONTELAND **Map 21 NZ17**

Café Lowrey

British, French

Relaxed bistro-style food and a warm welcome

☎ 01661 820357
33-35 The Broadway, Darras Hall NE20 9PW
web: www.cafelowrey.co.uk
dir: From A696, follow signs for Darras Hall. Left at mini rdbt, restaurant in 200yds

Café Lowrey is a popular bistro in the well-to-do residential estate of Ponteland, close to Newcastle airport. You can see the hustle-and-bustle of the kitchen pass from the relaxed brasserie-style restaurant, and there is a friendly vibe going-on which makes it an especially great place to bring children. The food is much as you'd expect from the style of the place: simple accomplished cooking using fine local produce. Evocative of this style are dishes like chilli-salted squid, loin of venison with goats' cheese mash, red cabbage and griottine cherry sauce and to finish, perhaps a lemon tart with blackcurrant sorbet.

Chef Ian Lowrey **Owner** Ian Lowrey **Times** 12-2/5.30-10 Closed BHs, Mon, L Tue-Fri, D Sun **Prices** Fixed L 2 course fr £13.95, Fixed D 3 course fr £16.95, Starter £5.50-£9.50, Main £12.95-£22.95, Dessert £5.50-£6, Service optional, Groups min 10 service 10% **Wines** 12 bottles over £20, 18 bottles under £20, 6 by glass **Notes** Early evening menu 5.30-7pm, Sunday L, Vegetarian available, Dress restrictions, Smart casual **Seats** 68 **Children** Portions **Parking** 15

NOTTINGHAMSHIRE

GUNTHORPE **Map 11 SK64**

Tom Browns Brasserie

Modern International

Modern British food in bustling riverside brasserie

☎ 0115 966 3642
The Old School House, Trentside NG14 7FB
e-mail: info@tombrowns.co.uk
dir: A6097, Gunthorpe Bridge

If the name Tom Brown conjures an image of Victorian-era schooldays, the observation is spot-on: this busy bar-brasserie is indeed housed in a converted Victorian schoolhouse. But that is where the 19th-century stops: exposed brick walls, wooden floors and high-backed leather seats are the hallmarks of a classy contemporary venue; on fine days, go for a table on the decking terrace overlooking the River Trent. The menu fits the bill, offering well-balanced modern British dishes focused on local materials combined for maximum flavour. To start, crispy duck egg is teamed with home-made wild mushroom sausage, tomato compôte, pancetta brittle and Tom Brown's sauce (available to take away if it hits the spot). Mains might bring on pan-fried turbot with black truffle and seafood mousse, asparagus and Romesco sauce. Don't skip dessert - perhaps a Toblerone parfait with milk chocolate fudge and toffee sauce.

Chef Peter Kirk **Owner** Adam & Robin Perkins **Times** 12-2.30/6-9.30 Closed D 25-26 Dec **Prices** Food prices not confirmed for 2011. Please telephone for details. **Wines** 37 bottles over £20, 19 bottles under £20, 19 by glass **Notes** Sunday L, Vegetarian available, Dress restrictions, Smart casual **Seats** 100, Pr/dining room 20 **Children** Portions **Parking** 28, On street

LANGAR Map 11 SK73

Langar Hall

Modern British

An avenue of limes leading to adept modern British cooking

01949 860559
Church Ln NG13 9HG
e-mail: info@langarhall.co.uk
web: www.langarhall.com
dir: Signed off A46 & A52 in Langar village centre (behind church)

The original grand house at Langar having burned down some time in the early 19th century, the present Hall arose phoenix-like at around the time of the accession of Queen Victoria. An elegant approach along an avenue of lime trees prepares the visitor for the luxurious refinement within. Antiques and oil paintings abound, and dining goes on in a pillared dining room, as well as a conservatory. The cooking is an adept version of modern British, built around considered combinations and skilled classical technique. Braised pig cheek and ox tongue make a good duo for a starter, along with celeriac remoulade and a quail's egg. Different ways with local lamb might form the centre pieces for a meat main course, or there may be sea bass in vermouth with saffron potatoes and braised fennel. Friendly service enhances the appeal.

Chef Gary Booth **Owner** Imogen Skirving **Times** 12-2/7-10 **Prices** Fixed L 2 course £15-£20, Fixed D 3 course £25-£35, Starter £5-£20, Main £12.50-£30, Dessert £5-£10, Service added but optional 10% **Wines** 40 bottles over £20, 10 bottles under £20, 10 by glass **Notes** Sunday L, Vegetarian available, Civ Wed 50 **Seats** 30, Pr/dining room 20 **Children** Portions **Parking** 40

MANSFIELD Map 16 SK56

Lambs at the Market

Modern British

Smart family restaurant with local flavour

01623 424880
Cattle Market House, Nottingham Rd NG18 1BJ
e-mail: troylamb2003@yahoo.co.uk

A Grade II listed converted tavern once joined to the town's original cattle market, Lambs at the Market is a rather handsome red-brick Victorian building beneath a pepperpot turret. In keeping with its foodie heritage, this family-run restaurant sources the best local produce from named suppliers. Inside, exposed brick and aubergine-painted walls combine with darkwood and creamy leather to give a contemporary vibe. The kitchen's stock-in-trade is very much British cuisine, but done with flair and style; smoked haddock chowder with sweetcorn, tomatoes and fresh herbs might start, followed by blade of local beef with mash, bashed roots and buttered kale. Finish in traditional fashion with ginger parkin, poached forced rhubarb and stem ginger custard.

Chef Troy Lamb **Owner** Ted & Brenda Dubowski, Alison & Troy Lamb **Times** 12-2.30/6.30-9.30 Closed 25 Dec & 1 Jan, 1 wk Jan, 1 wk summer, Mon, L Tue, D Sun **Prices** Food prices not confirmed for 2011. Please telephone for details. **Wines** 31 bottles over £20, 21 bottles under £20, 8 by glass **Notes** Tasting menu available, Early bird available Tue 5.30-7.30pm, Sunday L, Vegetarian available **Seats** 56 **Children** Portions **Parking** 4, Public car parks adjacent or on street

NEWARK-ON-TRENT Map 17 SK75

Cutlers at The Grange

Modern British

Good, honest cooking in an elegant Victorian setting

01636 703399
The Grange Hotel, 73 London Rd NG24 1RZ
e-mail: info@grangenewark.co.uk
dir: From A1 follow signs for Balderton, the hotel is opposite the Polish War Graves

As far as the name goes, the penny should drop when you see the display cabinets and prints of antique cutlery that provide the visual distraction in the vibrant red, blue and gold, high-ceilinged Victorian dining room. The emphasis on the refreshingly waffle-free menu is on plain, honest food without affectation, focusing on seasonal and natural flavours, as in a coarse country pâté with a fruity Victorian chutney, followed by main-course pan-fried lamb cutlets with crushed potatoes and a ginger and grape jus. Dessert might be a cappuccino crème brûlée with amaretti biscuits.

Chef Tamas Lauko **Owner** Tom & Sandra Carr **Times** 12-2/6.30-9 Closed 25 Dec-5 Jan, L Mon-Sat **Prices** Fixed L 2 course £13.95-£18.50, Starter £5-£9.50, Main £12.50-£21, Dessert £5.95-£7, Service optional **Wines** 30 bottles over £20, 10 bottles under £20, 6 by glass **Notes** Sunday L, Vegetarian available **Seats** 40 **Children** Portions **Parking** 17

NOTTINGHAM Map 11 SK53

Cockliffe Country House

Modern, European

Modern European cooking in an elegant country house

0115 968 0179
Burntstump Country Park, Burntstump Hill, Arnold NG5 8PQ
e-mail: enquiries@cockliffehouse.co.uk
web: www.cockliffehouse.co.uk
dir: M1 junct 27, follow signs to Hucknall (A611), then B6011, right at T-junct, follow signs for Cockliffe House

This small but perfectly-formed country house has sat for three centuries in its landscaped grounds, peacefully-cushioned from the industrial bustle of Nottingham and Mansfield. A brace of intimate dining rooms provides heaps of period atmosphere, in the form of parquet floors, gilt-framed mirrors and antiques, while diners sit on modish black leather high-backed seats at tables clothed in traditional white. Thus is the scene set for modern cooking that brings a certain artistic presence to the table. Chicken liver and foie gras parfait is partnered with apple and fig chutney, followed, perhaps, by pan-fried cod with spiced Puy lentils, pea and mint purée and home-made tartare sauce. Inventive desserts might turn up the likes of a Baileys crème brûlée with cinder toffee and blood orange jelly.

Chef Andrew Wilson **Owner** Dane & Jane Clarke **Times** 12-2/6-9.30 Closed L Mon-Wed, D Sun **Prices** Food prices not confirmed for 2011. Please telephone for details. **Wines** 25 bottles over £20, 14 bottles under £20, 11 by glass **Notes** Early evening menu Sun-Fri 6-7pm, Sunday L, Vegetarian available, Dress restrictions, Smart casual, Civ Wed 50 **Seats** 50, Pr/dining room 30 **Children** Portions **Parking** 50

Hart's Restaurant

Modern British V

Modern cooking in elegant city restaurant

0115 988 1900
Hart's Hotel, Standard Court, Park Row NG1 6FN
e-mail: ask@hartsnottingham.co.uk
dir: At junct of Park Row & Ropewalk, close to city centre

Hart's ranks among the best dining venues in the city, a stylish modern restaurant just a stone's throw from Tim Hart's chic boutique hotel built on the ramparts of the

continued

NOTTINGHAM ***continued***

city's medieval castle. Visually appealing and occupying a fine building, the former A&E department of the nearby general hospital is a busy and hugely comfortable restaurant, drawing foodies from afar for its vibrant, contemporary décor (oak floor, crushed velvet banquettes, brightly coloured walls hung with abstract paintings), and skilfully cooked modern British food. The focus of the kitchen is on clear, accurately cooked dishes that are packed with flavour through sound use of quality locally-sourced produce. A typical meal may kick off with a texturally impressive guinea fowl ballottine served with an intense raisin purée and game sauce, followed by succulent, well-seasoned chump of lamb accompanied by broccoli purée, tomato, black olives and mini balls of deep-fried goats' cheese, and a classic lemon tart with raspberry sorbet. Super breads and excellent coffee complete the picture.

Chef Tom Earle **Owner** Tim Hart **Times** 12-2/6-10.30 Closed 1 Jan, L 31 Dec, D 25 Dec **Prices** Food prices not confirmed for 2011. Please telephone for details. **Wines** 57 bottles over £20, 23 bottles under £20, 6 by glass **Notes** Sunday L, Vegetarian menu, Civ Wed 100 **Seats** 80, Pr/dining room 100 **Children** Portions **Parking** 15

Merchants

Modern European NOTABLE WINE LIST

Great brasserie menu in eye-catching surroundings

☎ 0115 958 9898 & 852 3232
Lace Market Hotel, 29-31 High Pavement NG1 1HE
e-mail: restaurant@lacemarkethotel.co.uk
dir: Follow city centre signs for Galleries of Justice, entrance is opposite

The two Georgian townhouses forming this stylish boutique hotel were once used as a mill for making lace, a snippet of local history which is recognised in panels of lace woven into the décor. Otherwise, the interior has a rather more eye-catching contemporary glamour - toffee-hued leather banquettes, chainmail light fittings and shimmering back-lit wall panels as a classy backdrop for the kitchen's creative modern brasserie dishes. A starter of braised local pork belly teamed with carrots, pickled shimeji mushrooms and sweetbread ravioli shows serious intent, ahead of mains that might bring on a butter poached fillet of Derbyshire beef with ox cheek, and beef 'ham' faggots with cumin-scented carrots. Granny Smith apple stars in a finale - served as a millefeuille, parfait and roasted, together with cider sorbet and heather honey madeleines.

Chef Dean Crews **Owner** Finesse Hotels
Times 12-2.30/6-10 Closed 26 Dec, 1 Jan, Sun-Mon **Prices** Fixed L 2 course £13.95-£14.95, Tasting menu fr £55, Starter £5-£9, Main £16-£24, Dessert £4.50-£8.50, Service added but optional 10% **Wines** 70+ bottles over £20, 5 bottles under £20, 12 by glass **Notes** Tasting menu 6 course, Vegetarian available, Civ Wed 60 **Seats** 50, Pr/dining room 20 **Children** Portions, Menu **Parking** On street. NCP adjacent

Restaurant Sat Bains with Rooms

– *see opposite page*

Tonic

Modern British NEW

Chic modern dining showcasing local produce

☎ 0115 941 4770
6B Chapel Quarter, Chapel Bar NG1 6JS
e-mail: info@tonic-online.co.uk
dir: W of city centre at junct of Maid Marian Way & Upper Parliament St

You have to head up to the third floor to reach the restaurant at Tonic (on the first two levels it's all about cocktails and bar food). When you do, you'll find a dramatically modern dining room with some striking artwork, booth seating, funky swivel armchairs and cool lighting. From the open-plan kitchen comes some accomplished modern British cooking. Spiced scallops with confit duck leg and tempura cauliflower makes a superb starter, its varying flavours and textures all singing in harmony. Follow up with pot-roasted chicken with sweet potato, lemon and thyme dumplings and oyster mushrooms, and round things off nicely with a delicate praline pannacotta with orange sherbet and Irn Bru sorbet.

Chef Andrew Brookes **Owner** The Brasserie Business Ltd **Times** 12-2/6-10 Closed 25-26 Dec, 1 Jan, Sun **Prices** Fixed L 2 course £12.95-£16.45, Fixed D 3 course £15.95-£19.45, Starter £4.95-£9.95, Main £11.95-£16.95, Dessert £5.95-£6.95, Service added but optional 10% **Wines** 28 bottles under £20, 34 by glass **Notes** Gourmet menu 6 course £27.50 last Thu mth, Pre-theatre menu, Vegetarian available, Air con **Seats** 90 **Children** Portions **Parking** NCP Mount St (5 min walk)

World Service

Modern British

Exotic surroundings and confident cooking

☎ 0115 847 5587
Newdigate House, Castle Gate NG1 6AF
e-mail: enquiries@worldservicerestaurant.com
web: www.worldservicerestaurant.com
dir: 200mtrs from city centre, 50mtrs from Nottingham Castle

This chic fine-dining restaurant and lounge bar housed in the historic Newdigate House has a colonial interior that looks like the abode of an eccentric traveller, with exotic artefacts at every turn. There's a slightly moody, luxury clubby feel to the place. Entry is through an oriental garden into a lounge of gilt armchairs, a roaring fire and coconut shell tables. On into the restaurant and its darkwood dining tables, brown leather seating and low-level mirrors along the walls. Previously the food style was heavily fusion but a new head chef - Gareth Ward from Hart's down the road (see entry) - is more focused on the individual flavours of quality ingredients. You might find roast scallops with carrot, pumpkin and hazelnut followed by roast cod with Indian-spiced red lentils, chicory, olives and cherry tomatoes. Puddings include the imaginative Turkish delight mousse and lime sorbet. The wine list is a joy to behold.

Chef Gareth Ward, Garry Hewitt **Owner** Daniel Lindsay, Phillip Morgan, Ashley Walter, Chris Elson **Times** 12-2.15/7-10 Closed 25-26 Dec, 1-7 Jan **Prices** Fixed L 2 course £13, Starter £5.50-£14.95, Main £16-£23.95, Dessert £6-£8.50, Service added but optional 10% **Wines** 170 bottles over £20, 34 bottles under £20, 17 by glass **Notes** Sunday L, Vegetarian available, Civ Wed 50 **Seats** 80, Pr/dining room 34 **Children** Portions, Menu **Parking** NCP

OLLERTON **Map 16 SK66**

Thoresby Hall Hotel and Spa

Modern British NEW

Grand dining in a magnificent Victorian country house

☎ 01623 821000
Thoresby Park NG22 9WH
e-mail: thoresbyhall.reception@bourne-leisure.co.uk

This mightily impressive Grade I listed Victorian country-house hotel is set in rolling parklands on the edge of Sherwood Forest. A spa session or simply a stroll around the beautiful gardens will set you up nicely for a meal (there are three restaurants to choose from). The architecturally stunning Blue Room restaurant is an impressive place to dine, thanks to its high, ornately decorated ceilings, chandeliers and grandly elegant furnishings. Local ingredients get name-checked on the carte of classically inspired dishes; start with Manor Farm oxtail with blade of beef faggot, curly kale and horseradish oil, before red mullet fillets with a risotto of langoustine and chorizo Iberico and warm salad of broccoli and radish. A simple dessert of baked lemon tart, clotted cream and strawberries is a winner.

Chef Tim Doolan **Owner** Burne Leisure **Times** 6.30-9.30 Closed Tue-Wed, L all week **Prices** Starter £5.75-£8, Main £16.75-£20, Dessert £5.75-£6.75, Service optional **Wines** 17 bottles over £20, 8 bottles under £20, 14 by glass **Notes** Vegetarian available, Dress restrictions, Smart Dress, Civ Wed 90 **Seats** 60, Pr/dining room 25 **Parking** 120

Restaurant Sat Bains with Rooms

NOTTINGHAM **Map 11 SK53**

Modern British V 

Culinary alchemy at one of the UK's highest-achieving restaurants

☎ 0115 986 6566
Lenton Ln, Trentside NG7 2SA
e-mail: info@restaurantsatbains.net
dir: M1 junct 24, A453 for approx 8m. Through Clifton, road divides into 3 - take middle lane signed 'Lenton Lane Industrial Estate', then 1st left, left again. Follow brown Restaurant Sat Bains sign

The location, just off the A52, not far from an industrial estate, is the only prosaic aspect of Sat Bains's restaurant with rooms. Inside the place looks as though it could be dropped seamlessly into London's West End, with its high-toned design, all frosted-glass panelling, smartly laid tables and discreet classical music. The fact that you aren't in London, though, says much about the development of British dining in the new millennium. For make no mistake: this is one the UK's highest-achieving kitchens. The willingness to interact with customers, via a Tasting Room, the tantalising glimpses of the brigade at work, kitchen tours, and the offering of a Bespoke Menu deal, in which you get to eat a few of your favourite things Sat Bains-style, mark a creative departure from the old routine of simply feeding you luxuriously and taking your money. Bains determines on getting the best out of every ingredient, whatever its official culinary status, lobster or mackerel, pork cheek or roe deer. Even at the entry-level set menu, there are challenges, innovations and intensities of many kinds. Lemon sole with apple, celery and 'sea vegetables' is the prelude to a serving of belly pork with sweetcorn and thyme. Cornish brill with leek, hazelnut, potato and cucumber is the principal business, before the first of two desserts, comprising chocolate, liquorice and lime, and the concluding vanilla cheesecake with sweet-and-sour cherries. These bare ingredient listings scarcely do justice to the artful layering of technique and presentation, where flavours, textures and temperatures all play their intriguing parts. From the first nibble of bread, perhaps a superb treacle roll served hot with Lincolnshire Poacher butter, the standard is set for an experience that will endure in the memory.

Chef Sat Bains **Owner** Sat Bains, Amanda Bains **Times** 7-8.30 Closed 2 wks Jan,1 wk May, 2 wks Aug, Sun-Mon, L all week **Prices** Food prices not confirmed for 2011. Please telephone for details. **Wines** 120 bottles over £20, 6 bottles under £20, 30 by glass **Notes** Vegetarian menu **Seats** 34, Pr/ dining room 14 **Parking** 22

OXFORDSHIRE

ARDINGTON Map 5 SU48

The Boar's Head

◎◎ Modern British

Peaceful village pub serving up good food

☎ 01235 833254
Church St OX12 8QA
e-mail: info@boarsheadardington.co.uk
web: www.boarsheadardington.co.uk
dir: 2 m E of Wantage on A417, next to village church

The Boar's Head pub has kept the idyllic Downland village of Ardington's community well fed and watered for over 150 years. The scene is impossibly chocolate-box pretty: a black-and-white half-timbered pub tucked among trees by the village church. Inside, there's a well-groomed yet cosy bar or a posher restaurant with chunky bare wooden tables and the glowing hues of Provence in its walls. Food is taken seriously here under the guidance of chef Bruce Buchan, with a deserved reputation for serving up the best the region's farms and suppliers can offer. Breast of Gressingham duck could come with wild rabbit croustade, or snails in garlic might partner trout in a pastry puff. Fish is prominent on the menu, and comes up daily from Cornwall to star in dishes such as seared red mullet with spinach fettuccine. Excellent desserts include the likes of praline soufflé with iced nougat.

Chef Bruce Buchan **Owner** Boar's Head (Ardington) Ltd **Times** 12-2/7-10 **Prices** Fixed L 2 course £15, Starter £6.50-£10.50, Main £15-£24, Dessert £6.50-£8.50, Service optional **Wines** 70 bottles over £20, 30 bottles under £20, 12 by glass **Notes** Gastronomic menu 6 course £39.50, Sunday L, Vegetarian available **Seats** 40, Pr/dining room 24 **Children** Portions **Parking** 20

ASTON ROWANT Map 5 SU79

Lambert Arms

◎ Modern British

Comfortably upgraded old inn just two minutes from M40

☎ 0845 459 3736
London Rd OX49 5SB
e-mail: info@lambertarms.com
dir: M40 junct 6, at T-junct right towards Chinnor (B4009), back under motorway. 1st left to Postcombe/ Thame (A40)

This pretty black-and-white timbered old coaching inn has been dressed inside with the 21st-century customer in mind: the heart and soul of the building remains intact, with the addition of some smart fixtures and fittings. Service is on the informal side and the customer-comes-first attitude extends to the dining options: you can choose to eat in the spacious, wood-floored main dining area, bar or cosy lounge. Simple earthly flavours abound on the menu; poached smoked haddock and leek risotto, perhaps, preceding pan-fried lambs' liver with streaky bacon, sweetbreads and mashed potato. Finish with vanilla and mascarpone cheesecake with warm chocolate sauce and vanilla ice cream, or maybe the excellent selection of British cheeses. They also serve familiar favourites ('classics') such as fish and chips and shepherd's pie.

Times 12-2.30/6.30-9

BANBURY Map 11 SP44

Restaurant 1649

◎ Modern British

Picturesque village hotel with sound modish cooking

☎ 01295 730777
Wroxton House Hotel, Silver St, Wroxton OX15 6QB
e-mail: reservations@wroxtonhousehotel.com
dir: From M40 junct 11 follow A422 (signed Banbury, then Wroxton). After 3m, hotel on right

The inn dates in part from the mid-17th century, and stands in a picturesque village of thatched houses a little to the west of Banbury. Original oak beams and feature fireplace are part of the package, with fresh flowers adorning the tables. The cooking keeps things relatively simple but effective, with chicken and leek terrine and red onion marmalade, stone bass tossed in black linguine with chorizo in lemon butter sauce, and lemon tart with mixed berry compôte to finish. Coffee is served with Cornish fudge.

Chef Steve Mason-Tucker **Owner** John & Gill Smith **Times** 12-2/7-9 **Prices** Fixed L 2 course fr £13.75, Fixed D 3 course fr £31, Service optional **Wines** 25 bottles over £20, 26 bottles under £20, 9 by glass **Notes** Sunday L, Vegetarian available, Dress restrictions, Smart casual, Civ Wed 60 **Seats** 60, Pr/dining room 45 **Children** Portions, Menu **Parking** 70

BICESTER Map 11 SP52

Bignell Park Hotel & Restaurant

◎ Modern British V

Modern British cooking in relaxed country setting

☎ 01869 326550
Chesterton OX26 1UE
e-mail: enq@bignellparkhotel.co.uk
dir: M40 junct 9, follow A41 towards Bicester, turn off at Chesterton and hotel is signed at turning

Built in the 16th century, this former farmhouse is set in landscaped gardens in Oxfordshire, close to Blenheim Palace and Bicester outlet village, depending on your inclination. The Oaks restaurant has oak beams aplenty and the look of a great hall, including minstrels' gallery. On Sundays, there is jazz from the resident band. The modern British menu features the likes of sorrel soup and soft hen's egg, followed by pan-fried chicken supreme with chorizo and herb risotto and parmesan crisp. Finish with a flavoursome fig tartlet and pistachio ice cream.

Chef Chris Coates **Owner** Caparo Hotels **Times** 12-2/7-9.30 Closed D Sun **Prices** Fixed L 3 course £12, Fixed D 3 course £19.95, Service optional **Wines** 16 bottles over £20, 30 bottles under £20, 4 by glass **Notes** Sunday L, Vegetarian menu, Civ Wed 60 **Seats** 60, Pr/dining room 20 **Children** Portions **Parking** 50

BRITWELL SALOME Map 5 SU69

The Goose

Modern British

Serious cooking in former village pub

01491 612304
OX49 5LG
e-mail: info@thegoosebritwellsalome.com
dir: M40 junct 6 take B4009 to Watlington, then towards Benson. Restaurant on left 1.5m

The Goose sounds like a pub, but it's actually a smart rural restaurant with a good pedigree, in a gorgeous corner of the Chilterns. Inside, the original 18th-century beams and fireplaces blend with a country chic décor of polished wood tables, banquette seats, and horsey polo prints on olive green walls. The new chef has a CV listing stints at Raymond Blanc's Le Manoir aux Quat' Saisons and L'ortolan (see entries). The cooking now takes an eminently sound modern British path, with maximum use of local materials. A slow-cooked fillet of Orkney salmon with thinly-sliced cauliflower and ratte potato mousse is an opener of serious intent. Next comes belly pork from the Red Lion Farm over the road, teamed with purées of potato and apple and Savoy cabbage 'choucroute', and for dessert, there's an inventive banana tarte Tatin with peanut butter ice cream and lime caramel.

Chef John Footman **Owner** Paul Castle **Times** 12-3/7-9.30 Closed 5 days Xmas/New Year, 1st 2 wks Jan, 1st 2 wks Aug, Mon, D Sun **Prices** Fixed L 2 course £14.95, Fixed D 3 course £17.95, Starter £7-£11, Main £14-£25, Dessert £6-£8.50, Service optional, Groups min 8 service 12.5% **Wines** 35 bottles over £20, 3 bottles under £20, 8 by glass **Notes** Tasting menu on request, Sunday L, Vegetarian available **Seats** 40 **Children** Portions **Parking** 35

BURFORD Map 5 SP21

The Angel at Burford

Modern European V

Cotswold coaching inn with eclectic cooking

01993 822714
14 Witney St OX18 4SN
e-mail: paul@theangelatburford.co.uk
dir: From A40, turn off at Burford rdbt, down hill 1st right into Swan Lane, 1st left to Pytts Lane, left at end into Witney St

A stone-built 16th-century coaching inn on the high street of this peaceful Cotswold town, the Angel is an agreeably old fashioned place, complete with a walled garden and courtyard. Oak beams and unclothed tables set the scene, while the cooking draws influences from hither and yon, with game a strong suit in the season. Start perhaps with duck confit terrine, served with redcurrant, orange and port jelly. Butterflied sea bass is a well-timed main course, stuffed with spiced pepper julienne and coriander, while desserts tend to the flamboyant, as in black cherry bread-and-butter pudding with almond ice cream.

Chef David Latter **Owner** Paul Swain **Times** 12-2/7-9 Closed Early Jan-15 Jan, Mon, D Sun **Prices** Starter £5.50-£7.50, Main £15-£19, Dessert £5.50-£7.50, Service optional **Wines** 15 bottles over £20, 20 bottles under £20, 11 by glass **Notes** Sunday L, Vegetarian menu, Dress restrictions, Smart casual **Seats** 28, Pr/dining room 18 **Children** Portions **Parking** On street

The Bay Tree Hotel

Traditional British

Stylish Cotswold retreat with skilful kitchen

01993 822791
Sheep St OX18 4LW
e-mail: info@baytreehotel.info
web: www.cotswold-inns-hotels.co.uk/baytree
dir: A40 or A361 to Burford. From High St turn into Sheep St, next to old market square. Hotel on right

Draped with streamers of wisteria, this honeystone 16th-century inn is a Cotswolds classic. All the elements of pub paradise are present and correct: in the Woolsack bar are flagged floors and comfy armchairs by a sizzling log fire in a walk-in inglenook - but this is no spit-and-sawdust boozer, it's rather more gentrified than that, particularly if you trade up to the classy restaurant, which hits the spot for romantic dining by candlelight amid a setting of country-house chic. There's a confident, creative spirit at work in the kitchen, turning super local produce into unpretentious modern British dishes, such as pressed ham hock and foie gras terrine with Parma ham and grain mustard dressing, followed by pan-fried beef sirloin with chorizo dauphinoise, béarnaise sauce and rosemary velouté.

Chef Brian Andrews **Owner** Cotswold Inns & Hotels **Times** 12-2/7-9.30 **Prices** Fixed L 2 course £10, Fixed D 3 course £29.95, Service optional **Wines** 40 bottles over £20, 23 bottles under £20, 5 by glass **Notes** Sunday L, Vegetarian available, Dress restrictions, No jeans or trainers, Civ Wed 80 **Seats** 70, Pr/dining room 24 **Children** Portions **Parking** 55

The Lamb Inn

Traditional British

Imaginative modern cooking in classic village inn

01993 823155
Sheep St OX18 4LR
e-mail: info@lambinn-burford.co.uk
web: www.cotswold-inns-hotels.co.uk/lamb
dir: Exit A40 into Burford, downhill, take 1st left into Sheep St, hotel last on right

Just a stroll from the main street of the delightful Cotswold village of Burford, this 15th-century inn was originally a row of weavers' cottages. Within its wisteria-clad Cotswold-stone walls, an enchanting jumble of steps, corridors, flagstone floors, antiques, log fires, copper and brass and comfy sofas makes for a classic English country inn. In summer, the stone-walled courtyard is the place to be, but the elegant, airy restaurant is a charming place all year round with its cerise and cream walls, mullioned windows and frosted skylights. The vibrant food is simply conceived, carefully prepared and well presented. Pressed ham hock terrine with pease pudding and crisp bread wafers might turn up among starters, then perhaps pan-fried cod with squid ink risotto and baby leek with truffle froth.

Chef Sean Ducie **Owner** Cotswold Inns & Hotels **Times** 12-2.30/7-9.30 **Prices** Fixed D 3 course fr £35, Service added but optional 10% **Wines** 37 bottles over £20, 17 bottles under £20, 9 by glass **Notes** Sunday L, Vegetarian available, Dress restrictions, Smart casual, no jeans or T-shirts **Seats** 55 **Children** Portions **Parking** Care of The Bay Tree Hotel

CHECKENDON Map 5 SU68

The Highwayman

British, International

Good food in traditional country inn

01491 682020
Exlade St RG8 0UA
dir: Exlade St signed off A4074 (Reading/Wallingford road), 0.4m

A top to bottom refurbishment has turned this Highwayman into a 21st-century local that stands and delivers. With an appetite suitably sharpened by walking in the lovely Chiltern beechwoods, the 17th century inn awaits: expect a fetching blend of tradition - in the form

continued

CHECKENDON *continued*

of head-grazing beams, stripped wooden floors and furniture - and a good dash of contemporary style. The food is the kind of unshowy stuff with a seasonal accent and plenty of local connections that appeals to the heart - go for home-made corned beef and piccalilli with crusty bread for starters, ahead of cockle-warming mains such as braised pork belly on bashed swede and carrot with thyme sauce, or lamb stew with black pudding, root vegetables and mash. Round it off with bread-and-butter pudding with ginger cream and orange sauce.

Chef Paul Burrows **Owner** Mr Ken O'Shea **Times** 12-2.30/6-10 Closed 26 Dec, 1 Jan, D Sun **Prices** Food prices not confirmed for 2011. Please telephone for details. **Wines** 15 bottles over £20, 25 bottles under £20, 5 by glass **Notes** Sunday L, Vegetarian available, Dress restrictions, No work clothes or vests **Seats** 55, Pr/dining room 60 **Children** Portions, Menu **Parking** 30

CHINNOR Map 5 SP70

Sir Charles Napier

British, French NOTABLE WINE LIST

Pace-setting cookery in the upper reaches of the Chilterns

☎ 01494 483011
Sprigg's Alley OX39 4BX
e-mail: info@sircharlesnapier.co.uk
web: www.sircharlesnapier.co.uk
dir: M40 junct 6 to Chinnor. Turn right at rdbt, up hill for 2m to Sprigg's Alley

The best way to arrive at this charismatic country pub high in the Chiltern Hills - and simultaneously work up an appetite for its seductive cooking - is on foot from Chinnor Village, a two-mile hike through dense beech woods, where the chefs forage for wild garlic, fennel, nettles and fungi. It is at its most idyllic on summer days, dining outside on the vine-entwined terrace taking in the menagerie of animal sculptures in the delicious garden; indoors is as relaxed and inviting as you could ask for, with more sculptures to entertain. Chef Sam Hughes treats the best seasonal materials with due respect and without affectation, whether it is the bounty of fungi forays in the woods, game in winter, or wild asparagus in spring. Polished classical French technique underpins dishes such as roasted foie gras with gingerbread and poached rhubarb, followed by wild sea bass with pistachio and lemon verbena quinoa, girolles and trompette mushrooms, or a winter's dish of roast mallard with confit leg, beetroot, quince purée and elderberry jus.

Chef Sam Hughes **Owner** Julie Griffiths **Times** 12-3.30/6.30-10 Closed 25-27 Dec, Mon, D Sun **Prices** Fixed L 2 course £14.50, Fixed D 2 course £15.50-£16.50, Starter £8.50-£13.50, Main £17.50-£35, Dessert £8.50, Service added but optional 12.5% **Wines** 200 bottles over £20, 23 bottles under £20, 9 by glass **Notes** Tasting menu available, Sunday L, Vegetarian available **Seats** 75, Pr/dining room 45 **Children** Portions, Menu **Parking** 60

CHOLSEY Map 5 SU58

The Sweet Olive

French

French restaurant in charming pub

☎ 01235 851272
Baker St OX11 9DD

The best elements of cross-channel cultures join forces in the Sweet Olive: the archetypal English country pub is run with panache and a certain Gallic je ne sais quoi by the French team of chef-patron Olivier Bouet and Stéphane Brun, who takes care of front-of-house and sommelier duties. Inside, it's an unpretentious, rustic place with old wine cases decorating the bar, and chalkboards that change from day to day to take advantage of the seasonal bounty. The kitchen's focus is on quality materials, so local produce is bolstered by reinforcements such as foie gras and superb cheeses from France in a repertoire of crowd-pleasing dishes that are big on flavour. Sautéed lamb's sweetbreads with grain mustard, spinach and wild mushrooms is a typical opener, while mains might bring oxtail in puff pastry with mash and red Burgundy sauce.

Times 12-2/7-9 Closed Feb, 1 wk Jul, Sun, Wed

DEDDINGTON Map 11 SP43

Deddington Arms

Modern British

Modern menu in an old coaching inn on the village square

☎ 01869 338364
Horsefair OX15 0SH
e-mail: deddarms@oxfordshire-hotels.co.uk
web: www.deddington-arms-hotel.co.uk
dir: From S: M40 junct 10/A43. 1st rdbt left to Aynho (B4100) & left to Deddington (B4031). From N: M40 junct 11 to hospital & Adderbury on A4260, then to Deddington

The erstwhile coaching inn overlooks the medieval village square, where Deddington's farmers' market takes place. Inside are all the accoutrements you could wish for, from a bar with a log fire and real ales to a limestone-floored, white-walled informal restaurant, where modern British food is built around some of the produce from that market. Breast of pigeon with black pudding, wild mushrooms and soy and ginger dressing is a robust way to start, and might be the prelude to one of the well-conceived fish dishes, such as fillet of salmon with crab and vegetable risotto and chive beurre blanc. Finish with orange-glazed bread-and-butter pudding.

Chef Nick Porter **Owner** Oxfordshire Hotels Ltd **Times** 12-2.30/6.30-9.45 **Prices** Fixed L 2 course fr £10, Fixed D 3 course fr £19.95, Starter £6.15-£6.65, Main £10.25-£17.75, Dessert £3.88-£6.50, Service optional, Groups min 6 service 10% **Wines** 19 bottles over £20, 24 bottles under £20, 10 by glass **Notes** Sunday L, Vegetarian available **Seats** 60, Pr/dining room 30 **Children** Portions, Menu **Parking** 36

DORCHESTER (ON THAMES) Map 5 SU59

White Hart Hotel

British, French

Simple but effective cooking in historic old coaching hotel

☎ 01865 340074
High St OX10 7HN
e-mail: whitehart@oxfordshire-hotels.co.uk
web: www.oxfordshire-hotels.co.uk
dir: Village centre. Just off A415/ A4074. 3m from Wallingford, 6m from Abingdon

A timbered old coaching house with some parts dating back to 1691, the White Hart is unmissable in this beautiful Thameside village, noted for its winding lanes and fashionable shops. The unexpectedly high-ceilinged restaurant is done out in homely style, with staff offering a warm welcome, and modern cooking that keeps things reasonably simple. Seared scallops with chorizo and dressed leaves, and pan-fried duck breast with sweet braised red cabbage, pak choi and cherry sauce, are the kinds of dishes to expect. Round off with cappuccino crème brûlée.

Times 12-2.30/6.30-9.30

GORING Map 5 SU68

The Leatherne Bottel

Modern European NOTABLE WINE LIST

Global fusion food in a Wind in the Willows setting

01491 872667
RG8 0HS
e-mail: leathernebottel@aol.com
dir: M4 junct 12 or M40 junct 6, signed from B4009 towards Wallingford

Perched on the riverbank along the upper reaches of the Thames, the Bottel is a fine place for outdoor terrace eating, as well as a pleasant stopover to break a river journey (the inn has its own quayside moorings). Well-spaced tables dressed in their white linen best make for a relaxing experience, and the food describes an arc from modern European gleanings to the Pan-Asian stylings of New Zealand, where chef Julia Abbey (née Storey) lived for 17 years. Ideas are bold and good: try steak tartare with horseradish ice cream for starters, or rolled rabbit loin with leg confit, shiso leaves and Jerusalem artichoke crisps. Japanese technique may surface in a main course of tempura-battered vegetables with coriander and parsley cream, or there could be roast sea bass with lobster risotto and sweet chilli jam. End things fruitily with caramelised passionfruit and lemon tart with raspberry sorbet.

Chef Julia Abbey **Owner** John Madejski
Times 12-2.30/7-9.30 Closed D Sun **Prices** Fixed L 2 course £14.95-£24.95, Starter £8.50-£14.50, Main £16-£24.50, Dessert £7.95, Service added 10% **Wines** 175 bottles over £20, 15 by glass **Notes** Tasting menu available, Sunday L, Vegetarian available **Seats** 45 **Children** Portions **Parking** 40, extra parking available

The Miller of Mansfield

Modern British, European

Chiltern country inn with ultra-modern makeover

01491 872829
High St RG8 9AW
e-mail: reservations@millerofmansfield.com
dir: M40 junct 7, S on A329 towards Benson, A4074 towards Reading, B4009 towards Goring. Or M4 junct 12, S on A4 towards Newbury. 3rd rdbt onto A340 to Pangbourne. A329 to Streatley, right at lights onto B4009 into Goring

Don't worry about the name: this Miller of Mansfield is nowhere near Nottinghamshire. Behind its traditional Virginia creeper-swathed red-brick frontage, the 18th-century Chilterns coaching inn has gone all 'boutique' after a top-to-toe facelift. The bar is a modern reincarnation, all stripped wood, buffed-up oak panels and beaten-up clubby leather armchairs, while the chic restaurant goes for sleek cream chairs and tables, walls done in white and metallic foil, and shining darkwood floors. The kitchen cooks a modern British repertoire, liberally sprinkling its upbeat dishes with European influences and giving due credit to the suppliers whose superb produce is its basis. Chicken liver and foie gras parfait is served with apricot and tomato chutney and home-made toasted brioche to start; you might follow with oven-roasted cod loin, curried lentils, fine beans and bacon and brown shrimp beurre noisette.

Times 12-3/6-9.30 **Prices** Food prices not confirmed for 2011. Please telephone for details. **Notes** Vegetarian available **Seats** 75, Pr/dining room 14 **Children** Portions, Menu **Parking** 4, Car park

GREAT MILTON Map 5 SP60

Le Manoir aux Quat' Saisons

– *see page 354*

HENLEY-ON-THAMES Map 5 SU78

Hotel du Vin Henley-on-Thames

British, French

An old riverside brewery given the Hotel du Vin makeover

01491 848400
New St RG9 2BP
e-mail: info@henley.hotelduvin.com
dir: M4 junct 8/9 signed High Wycombe, take 2nd exit and onto A404 in 2m. A4130 into Henley, over bridge, through lights, up Hart St, right onto Bell St, right onto New St, hotel on right

Wherever the Hotel du Vin has sprung up, it has made its home in a sensitively converted historic building, and Henley is no exception. Housed in what was once the Brakspear brewery, the hotel has been formed from a cluster of redbrick buildings around the old brewery yard, close by the Thames. Varnished wood floors, wine-related paraphernalia and the island of banquettes in the centre of the room reference the house design style, and not surprisingly, the menus are also structured along similar lines as elsewhere in the group. Simple Classics such as moules marinière, and steak and chips with béarnaise, are supplemented by a repertoire of European-influenced dishes like roast cod with crushed Spanish beans in tomato velouté, or confit duck with gnocchi, beetroot purée and honey.

Times 12-2.30/6-10

KINGHAM Map 10 SP22

Mill Brook Room at The Mill House Hotel

British, French

Straightforward modern British cooking in a rustic idyll

01608 658188
OX7 6UH
e-mail: stay@millhousehotel.co.uk
dir: Just off B4450, between Chipping Norton & Stow-on-the-Wold. On southern outskirts of village

The hotel is a rustic idyll in the Cotswolds, with 10 acres of grounds full of weeping willows, rushing brooks, little bridges and a riot of flowers. Its restaurant, the Mill Brook Room, is an appealing place in which to enjoy some essentially straightforward, uncontroversial modern British cooking, along the lines of confit duck and foie gras terrine with orange and thyme chutney, sea bass with cockles, mussels and seashore vegetables, and pear poached in red wine accompanied by gingerbread ice cream. The cheeses are a selection of modern England's finest.

Times 12-2/6.30-10

Le Manoir aux Quat' Saisons

GREAT MILTON Map 5 SP60

Modern French V NOTABLE WINE LIST

As good as it gets

☎ 01844 278881
Church Rd OX44 7PD
e-mail: lemanoir@blanc.co.uk
dir: M40 junct 7 follow A329 towards Wallingford. After 1m turn right, signed Great Milton and Le Manoir aux Quat' Saisons

'The devil is in the detail' says the nation's favourite Frenchman: that, in short is Raymond Blanc's culinary manifesto. And a visit to Le Manoir aux Quat' Saisons is indeed characterised by meticulous attention to detail on every level. After arrival at the splendid mellow stone, 15th-century manor-house hotel, an introductory amble around the gardens is de rigueur: not only are they exquisite in their own right, with their statues, huge bronze sculptures of globe artichokes, plus a Japanese tea garden, but they supply much of the kitchen's produce, running to well over 150 varieties of organically-grown vegetables and esoteric herbs. Pause to take in the mullioned windows and soaring chimneys of the dignified old house. The original dining room has expanded into a series of interconnecting rooms and a luminous conservatory to take on board hordes of foodie pilgrims who have bought a few hours of nirvana. Exemplary service is an intrinsic part of the experience - staff are hard to fault, ever-watchful, but without crossing over to intrusiveness, and not too haughty to indulge in a bit of friendly chat. Gary Jones has run the kitchen with Raymond since 1999, and, although the modern French cooking has evolved continually, the insistence on the very finest, seasonal organic produce has always been a bedrock. Blanc's rustic roots and self-taught classical pedigree underpin a restless contemporary inventiveness that sometimes amazes with revelatory combinations of flavour and texture, but dishes are never overwrought for flashy effect. The kitchen's focus these days is on surprising and exciting diners with multi-course menus, so the carte is pruned back to three or four choices at each stage, running alongside a five-course 'Les Classiques' menu, and the bells-and-whistles 10-course 'Menu Découverte'. With a meat-free menu du jour, vegetarians are not marginalised. Smoked haddock soup with native oyster and Oscietra caviar starts with irreproachable clarity of flavour, followed, perhaps by a risotto of seasonal vegetables and Sicilian tomatoes. Top-class fish and seafood is showcased next - Cornish red mullet, fricassée of squid, salt-cod brandade and bouillabaisse jus - ahead of an assiette of suckling pig in its roasting juices. You're in the safe hands of an expert chef pâtissier for dessert, who might wrap things up with caramelised Braeburn apples in exemplary croustade pastry with honey and ginger ice cream. Having already dug deep into your pockets for food of this level, go for broke and pay the supplement for world-class cheeses too. A biblically thick wine list brims with judiciously-sourced wines from France's top appellations, and also acknowledges that wine is produced elsewhere in the world; expert sommeliers know their way around the back roads of its staggering 1,000 bins.

Chef Raymond Blanc, Gary Jones **Owner** Mr R Blanc & OE Hotels **Times** 12-2.30/7-10 **Prices** Fixed L 3 course £52.50-£57.50, Starter £36-£45, Main £40-£45, Dessert £21-£23, Service optional **Wines** 1100 bottles over £20, 15 by glass **Notes** Menu Classiques 5 course daily, Menu Découverte Sat-Sun, Sunday L, Vegetarian menu, Dress restrictions, No jeans, trainers or shorts, Civ Wed 50 **Seats** 100, Pr/dining room 50 **Children** Portions, Menu **Parking** 60

MURCOTT **Map 11 SP51**

The Nut Tree Inn

◎◎ Modern European

Confident cooking in a pretty village inn

☎ 01865 331253
Main St OX5 2RE
dir: M40 junct 9. A34 towards Oxford, take 2nd exit for Islip. At Red Lion pub turn left, then 3rd right signposted Murcott

You can prop up the bar of this whitewashed and thatched 14th-century inn surveying the village pond, supping on a pint of local ale. But it's the food that is the big draw. Those Gloucestershire Old Spot and Tamworth pigs roaming the acreages of garden are destined for the table, in the company of excellent raw materials from local artisan producers. Chef-proprietor Michael North delivers skilful modern European cooking that satisfies with deep flavours and satisfying textures. A starter ballottine of foie gras with Yorkshire rhubarb and ginger beer jelly has clear, well-defined flavours; next up, a fillet of 28-day-aged Oxfordshire beef is served with triple-cooked chips, baked tomato, onion rings and tarragon butter. To finish, tangy passionfruit soufflé comes with its own sorbet. A refurbishment is underway as we go to press, including the addition of a new purpose-built dining room.

Chef Michael North **Owner** Michael North, Imogen Young **Times** 12-2.30/7-9 Closed Mon, D Sun (Winter) **Prices** Fixed L 2 course £15, Fixed D 3 course £18, Starter £7.50-£12, Main £15.50-£25, Dessert £6-£7.50, Service optional, Groups min 6 service 10% **Wines** 43 bottles over £20, 7 bottles under £20, 12 by glass **Notes** Tasting menu available Tue-Sat eve, Sunday L, Vegetarian available **Seats** 60, Pr/dining room 20 **Children** Portions **Parking** 30

OXFORD **Map 5 SP50**

Gee's Restaurant

◎ Modern European NEW

Modern cooking in handsome Victorian conservatory

☎ 01865 553540
61 Banbury Rd OX2 6PE
e-mail: info@gees-restaurant.co.uk
dir: N of city centre off A4165, close to the Radcliffe Infirmary

A couple of minutes' walk from St Giles on the Banbury Road, this well-established restaurant is located in a splendid Victorian conservatory. Needless to say it has a light and airy feel, with chequered tiled flooring, wicker chairs and tables turned out in their best whites. Staff - kitted out in smart aprons - do a good job at keeping it all friendly and relaxed. The modern brasserie food is underpinned by classics such as smoked eel, devilled kidneys and potted shrimps. Good fresh produce combines with simple presentation and accurate cooking in a first course of lamb's sweetbreads with pearl barley and parsley, and in main-course calves' liver, which is cooked nice and pink and comes with bacon and sage. There's live jazz on Sunday evenings.

Chef Ben Aslin, Martin Curr **Owner** Jeremy Mogford **Times** 12-2.30/5.45-10.30 Closed 25 Dec **Prices** Fixed L 2 course £13.50, Fixed D 3 course £25, Starter £4.50-£10, Main £14.50-£23.50, Dessert £6.95-£7.95, Service optional, Groups min 5 service 12.5% **Wines** 4 bottles over £20, 4 bottles under £20, 16 by glass **Notes** Pre-theatre menu 5.45-6.45pm, Sunday L, Vegetarian available, Dress restrictions, Smart casual **Seats** 85 **Children** Portions, Menu **Parking** On street

High Table Brasserie & Bar

◎ Modern British, French

Buzzy brasserie close to the action

☎ 0870 400 8201 & 01865 248332
Mercure Eastgate Hotel, 73 High St OX1 4BE
e-mail: h6668-fb1@accor.com
dir: A40 into Oxford. At Headington rdbt follow signs to city centre. Cross Magdalen Bridge & stay in the inside lane. Continue past lights then turn left into Merton St

A short stroll from the city centre, this hotel occupies the site of the city's medieval East Gate. Originally a 17th-century inn, the interior is as contemporary as the outside is historic, with the brasserie-style restaurant appealing to a mixed crowd. The menu can be as traditional as deep fried haddock with chips or there are more ambitious things such as a starter of duck rillettes served with onion chutney and main-course sea bass fillet served on herb risotto with a red pepper reduction. Finish with pineapple tarte Tatin with rum and vanilla ice cream. The setting is informal, children have their own menu, and service is relaxed and upbeat.

Chef Mehdi Amiri **Owner** MREF Trade Co **Times** 12-2.30/6-9.30 **Prices** Fixed L 2 course £9.95, Tasting menu £49.95, Starter £6.50-£8.95, Main £14.50-£22.95, Dessert £5.95-£6.95, Groups min 6 service 12.5% **Wines** 19 bottles over £20, 16 bottles under £20, 11 by glass **Notes** Tasting menu 6 course, Sunday L, Vegetarian available, Dress restrictions, Smart casual **Seats** 70, Pr/dining room 8 **Parking** 40, Parking charges apply

Macdonald Randolph

◎◎ Traditional British

Classic Oxford dining experience

☎ 0844 879 9132 & 01865 256400
Beaumont St OX1 2LN
e-mail: foodservice.randolph@macdonald-hotels.co.uk
web: www.macdonaldhotels.co.uk
dir: M40 junct 8, A40 towards Oxford, follow city centre signs, leads to St Giles, hotel on right

The Randolph is a much-loved Oxford institution, and one which will look rather familiar to fans of Colin Dexter's world-famous cerebral detective Inspector Morse. It is a glorious Victorian Gothic confection of oak-panels, vaulted ceilings and a grand staircase sweeping aloft from the lobby. The restaurant never lacks for well-heeled parents treating their student offspring to something rather more upmarket than beans on toast amid the opulence of a soaring ceiling covered with college crests, and huge full-length windows looking over the Ashmolean Museum. The kitchen duly delivers British classics, done well, thanks to well-sourced ingredients and a fuss-free approach that leaves the flavours to shout out loud. A seasonal menu might deliver goats' cheese mousse with beetroot purée and melba toast to set the ball rolling, followed by confit pork belly teamed with braised red cabbage, Anna potato and roasted parsnip. Puddings offer the nursery comfort of warm treacle sponge.

Macdonald Randolph

Chef Tom Birks **Owner** Macdonald Hotels **Times** 12-2.30/6.30-10 **Prices** Fixed L 2 course fr £19, Fixed D 3 course fr £29.50, Starter £6.75-£8.95, Main £17.50-£26.50, Dessert £7.95-£11.50, Service optional **Wines** 100 bottles over £20, 15 bottles under £20, 15 by glass **Notes** Sunday L, Vegetarian available, Dress restrictions, Smart casual, Civ Wed 300 **Seats** 90, Pr/dining room 30 **Children** Portions, Menu **Parking** 50, (Chargeable - pre-booking essential)

Malmaison Oxford

◎ Modern European

Modern European menu in former prison canteen

☎ 01865 268400
Oxford Castle, 3 New Rd OX1 1AY
e-mail: oxford@malmaison.com
dir: M40 junct 9 (signed Oxford/A34). Follow A34 S to Botley Interchange, then A420 to city centre

The Oxford branch of the boutique hotel chain was once not so boutique. It used to house the city's prison, as will be apparent from the interior architecture, and what is now the basement brasserie was formerly its canteen. Rest assured the bill of fare is a little more cheering these days, with a modern European menu to lift the spirits. The Spanish charcuterie platter with shaved manchego is an appetising way to start, or it might be twice-baked French cheese soufflé, before main dishes of the order of slow-cooked Gressingham duck leg with beans, or herb-crusted halibut with pig's cheek and chorizo. Crème brûlée is reliably on hand to round it all off.

continued

OXFORD ***continued***

Chef Russell Heeley **Owner** MWB **Times** 12-2.30/6-10.30 **Prices** Fixed L 2 course £10, Fixed D 3 course £44.95, Starter £5.95-£8.95, Main £10.95-£22.95, Dessert £5.95-£8.95, Service added but optional 10%, Groups min 6 service 10% **Wines** 120 bottles over £20, 20 bottles under £20, 18 by glass **Notes** Pre-theatre menu available, Sunday L, Vegetarian available, Civ Wed 50 **Seats** 100, Pr/dining room 35 **Children** Portions, Menu **Parking** Worcester St, Westgate

Old Parsonage Restaurant

Modern British

Bohemian setting for rejuvenated British classics

01865 292305
The Old Parsonage Hotel, 1 Banbury Rd OX2 6NN
e-mail: restaurant@oldparsonage-hotel.co.uk
web: www.mogford.co.uk
dir: M40 junct 8, A40. Right onto ring road, 1st left into Banbury Rd. Hotel & restaurant on right just before St Giles Church

Close to St John's and Keble colleges, and dating from the 17th century, one of this quintessentially Oxford hotel's former guests was a certain Oscar Wilde, and it is easy to imagine him feeling right at home in the clubby, bohemian atmosphere of the current incarnation. The restaurant is full of character with its Russian red walls hung with original cartoons and portraits and elegantly laid tables. The concise menu relies on high quality produce to showcase British classics with a modern touch here and there. The crowd-pleasing menu might kick off with chicken soup with dumplings, then move on to salmon fishcake with spinach and sorrel sauce, and for pudding perhaps a lemon pot.

Chef Simon Cottrell **Owner** Jeremy Mogford **Times** 12-10.30 **Prices** Fixed L 2 course £13.50, Fixed D 3 course £32, Starter £4.50-£9.50, Main £13.50-£23.50, Dessert £6.95-£7.95, Service optional, Groups min 5 service 12.5% **Wines** 40 bottles over £20, 5 bottles under £20, 10 by glass **Notes** Early supper menu available, Sunday L, Vegetarian available, Civ Wed 20 **Seats** 75, Pr/dining room 15 **Children** Portions, Menu **Parking** 16, Metered parking in road opposite

Quod Brasserie & Bar

British, European

All-day brasserie menu in a former bank

01865 202505
Old Bank Hotel, 92-94 High St OX1 4BN
e-mail: quod@oldbank-hotel.co.uk
web: www.quod.co.uk
dir: Approach city centre via Headington. Over Magdalen Bridge into High St. Hotel 75yds on left

This brasserie is housed in what was once Barclays Bank in the centre of Oxford. Owned by the people behind the Old Parsonage and Gee's (see entries), Quod is a trendy joint with a relaxed vibe and contemporary décor, including an eclectic collection of modern pictures and photographs by British artists. A spacious outdoor heated terrace is popular in the summer months and live jazz provides the soundtrack on Sunday evenings. The all-day menu changes seasonally with daily specials like Jersey crab bruschetta or navarin of Rofford Farm spring lamb as well as variations on burgers and chips, steaks and pizzas.

Chef Michael Wright **Owner** Mr J Mogford **Times** 7am-11pm **Prices** Fixed L 2 course £9.95, Starter £5.95-£10, Main £9.95-£19.95, Dessert £5.95-£6.95, Service optional, Groups min 5 service 10% **Wines** 6 bottles over £20, 6 bottles under £20, 17 by glass **Notes** Early supper & Fixed L menus available Mon-Fri, Sunday L, Vegetarian available **Seats** 164, Pr/dining room 24 **Children** Portions, Menu **Parking** 50

STADHAMPTON — **Map 5 SU69**

The Crazy Bear

Modern British

Charming 16th century inn with some fine cooking

01865 890714
Bear Ln OX44 7UR
e-mail: enquiries@crazybear-oxford.co.uk
dir: M40 junct 7, A329. In 4m left after petrol station, left into Bear Lane

The popular Crazy Bear is a country inn that manages to combine modern elegance and old-world character. There's a great garden to spread out in, or a dining area filled with an array of wine bottles racked up on the ceiling. Such is the scale of the operation that there's a Thai restaurant here too (see entry below). If you're in the mood for something more local, though, and a little bit modern perhaps, the English restaurant may float your boat; flavours come from across Europe, ingredients are sourced judiciously, and the menu can keep you going from breakfast through to dinner. Start with pan-seared foie gras on a glazed puff-pastry tart, flavoured with Manuka honey, moving onto fillets of sea bass with spiced mussels, then comes all the indulgent comfort of a treacle tart with Jersey milk ice cream to finish.

The Crazy Bear

Chef Martin Picken **Owner** Jason Hunt **Times** 12-10 **Prices** Fixed L 2 course fr £15, Fixed D 3 course fr £19.50, Starter £6.50-£45, Main £12-£42, Dessert £6.70-£9.50, Service added but optional 12.5% **Wines** 130 bottles over £20, 12 bottles under £20, 16 by glass **Notes** Sunday L, Vegetarian available, Civ Wed 100 **Seats** 40, Pr/dining room 140 **Children** Portions **Parking** 100

Thai Thai at the Crazy Bear

Modern Thai

Thai cooking in an old coaching inn

01865 890714
The Crazy Bear, Bear Ln OX44 7UR
e-mail: enquiries@crazybear-oxford.co.uk
dir: M40 junct 7, A329. In 4m left after petrol station, left into Bear Lane

A 16th-century coaching inn south of Oxford isn't exactly the location you might expect to find a Thai restaurant dressed up like a Moroccan Bedouin tent. But here it is, complete with mirror-panelled ceiling, luxurious velvet walls and shiny gold tables. If these decadent furnishings get a bit too much for you, there is also the option of dining alfresco in the pretty gardens. The food is a mix of authentic Thai dishes and some oriental twists on western classics. Typical of the style are chargrilled marinated beef sirloin wrapped in cha poo leaf with sauce Sam Ross or slow-roasted pork belly flavoured with star anise, cinnamon, cloves, coriander, garlic and gai lan. See entry above for the other dining possibility at the Crazy Bear.

Chef Chalao Mansell **Owner** Jason Hunt **Times** 12-3/6-12 Closed L Sun **Prices** Starter £6-£9, Main £7.50-£18.50, Dessert £6.70-£9.50, Service added but optional 12.5% **Wines** 130 bottles over £20, 12 bottles under £20, 16 by glass **Notes** Vegetarian available, Civ Wed 100 **Seats** 30, Pr/dining room 140 **Children** Portions **Parking** 100

SWERFORD Map 11 SP33

The Mason's Arms

Modern British

Country gastro-pub with local flavour

☎ 01608 683212
Banbury Rd OX7 4AP
e-mail: admin@masons-arms.com
dir: On A361 between Banbury & Chipping Norton

Set in three acres of lovely gardens overlooking the Swere Valley, the Mason's Arms is a Cotswolds classic. The 300-year-old stone-built inn has had a stylish facelift to pull in the diners for Bill Leadbeater's interesting modern cooking, but locals drop in for a pint of well-kept real ale too - it is still the village pub, after all. Inside are cheery colour-washed walls, rugs on stripped wooden floors and rustic pine tables - an unpretentious décor that suits the food. A menu sprinkled with European and Asian accents champions locally-sourced meat - shoulder of Gloucestershire Old Spot pork, for example, is slow cooked and teamed with chorizo and olive mash, tea-soaked sultanas and rich gravy; fish dishes might take in seared fillet of pollock with crushed potatoes with lemon and thyme, and creamy caper sauce.

Chef Bill Leadbeater **Owner** B & C Leadbeater, Tom Aldous **Times** 12-3/7-11 Closed 25-26 Dec, D 24 Dec **Prices** Fixed L 2 course £15, Fixed D 3 course £26, Starter £4-£10, Main £10-£19, Dessert £6, Service optional, Groups min 10 service 10% **Wines** 18 bottles over £20, 34 bottles under £20, 16 by glass **Notes** Sunday L, Vegetarian available **Seats** 75, Pr/dining room 40 **Children** Portions, Menu **Parking** 60

SWINBROOK Map 10 SP21

The Swan Inn

Modern British NEW

Sound modern cooking in the tranquil Windrush valley

☎ 01993 823339
OX18 4DY
e-mail: swaninnswinbrook@btconnect.com
dir: A40 towards Cheltenham, turn left to Swinbrook

The Orr-Ewings added a second feather to their country-pub cap (see also King's Head Inn, Bledington, Stow-on-the-Wold) when they took over the running of this wisteria-clad inn owned by the Dowager Duchess of Devonshire. Sitting serenely by the River Windrush, it makes the most of its tranquil surroundings, and offers sandwiches and chips to bar diners, as well as a more upscale menu in the restaurant. Organic local ingredients are the emphasis; fish is delivered daily from Cornwall, Angus beef comes from the chef's uncle and an array of regional cheeses are available. Upton smoked beef fillet is served carpaccio fashion for an impressive opener, traditionally dressed in parmesan and rocket. Mains might run to a whole roast quail stuffed with chorizo and sage in a port-enriched gravy, while local clotted cream and soft fruits should not be missed when in season.

Chef Giles Leigh **Owner** Archie & Nicola Orr-Ewing **Times** 12-2/7-9 Closed 25-26 Dec **Prices** Starter £5-£8, Main £10-£22, Dessert £5-£7, Service optional, Groups min 8 service 10% **Notes** Sunday L, Vegetarian available **Seats** 70 **Children** Portions **Parking** 12, On road

TOOT BALDON Map 5 SP50

The Mole Inn

Modern European

Big flavours at a top-class dining pub

☎ 01865 340001
OX44 9NG
e-mail: info@themoleinn.com
dir: 5m S of Oxford

It is clear from the moment you arrive that the 300-year-old Mole Inn has taken the path of quality since a smart refurbishment put it firmly on the map for foodies around Oxford. The punters now travel out from the city centre to the wonderfully-named hamlet of Toot Baldon for its exciting modern cooking, but the place still keeps a finger on the pulse of village life. A clean-cut modern look pulls together the best of ancient and modern styles in the various dining rooms, blending gnarled timbers, wood and terracotta floors, bare stone and bricks, with chunky rustic tables, leather chairs and chocolate-brown sofas. There's no pretension in the kitchen, just skilled modern cooking based on tried-and-tested combinations and well-sourced ingredients. Wild mushrooms en croûte might get the thumbs up to start, while venison steak with lardon and truffle potatoes, juniper carrots, and port and redcurrant jus is a typically hearty main course.

Chef Gary Witchalls **Owner** Gary Witchalls **Times** 12-2.30/7-9.30 Closed 25 Dec **Prices** Food prices not confirmed for 2011. Please telephone for details. **Notes** Sunday L, Vegetarian available **Seats** 70 **Children** Portions, Menu **Parking** 40

WALLINGFORD Map 5 SU68

Lakeside Restaurant

Modern British

Gentle country-house cooking with lovely lakeside views

☎ 01491 836687 & 0845 365 2697
The Springs Hotel & Golf Club, Wallingford Rd, North Stoke OX10 6BE
e-mail: info@thespringshotel.com
dir: Edge of village of North Stoke

The Victorian mock-Tudor house deep in the Oxfordshire countryside is now the setting for a peaceful golfing hotel, with attractive grounds, luxurious interiors and a professional, unobtrusive service approach. Gentle pastoral views, including the lake of course, are offered from the elegantly done-out dining room, as is an equally gentle style of country-hotel cooking, in which locally-sourced produce is put to productive use. Pigeon breast with caramelised apple and black pudding in redcurrant jus, seared salmon with spinach and wild mushroom cream, and white and dark chocolate terrine with berry compôte should leave everybody feeling happy.

Times 12-2/6.30-9.45

WALLINGFORD *continued*

The Partridge

Modern French

Top quality gastro-pub offering refined modern food

01491 825005
32 St Mary's St OX10 0ET
e-mail: contact@partridge-inn.com

Given the pedigree of the chef-proprietor, who has served time in the kitchens of the Roux brothers, Raymond Blanc and Nico Ladenis, it isn't perhaps surprising that this particular Partridge is more slick country restaurant than cosy boozer. A makeover worthy of *Homes and Gardens* magazine deploys the full arsenal of contemporary restaurant design strokes - creamy carpet and polished wood underfoot, contrasting with boldly patterned wallpaper, bare brick walls and leather sofas. José Cau has wonderful technique in the kitchen, teasing deep flavours from top-grade British produce. Start with a wood pigeon breast with parsnip mash and chocolate sauce, followed by fillet of lemon sole with pork rillettes, confit potato and caviar broth.

Chef José Cau **Owner** José Cau **Times** 12-2.30/6-9.30 Closed D Sun **Prices** Fixed L 2 course fr £13.95, Fixed D 3 course fr £17.95, Starter £5.50-£10.50, Main £12.50-£22.75, Dessert fr £6.50, Groups min 6 service 10% **Wines** 85 bottles over £20, 23 bottles under £20, 9 by glass **Notes** Sunday L, Vegetarian available, Dress restrictions, Smart casual **Seats** 50 **Children** Portions

WOODCOTE **Map 5 SU68**

Woody Nook at Woodcote

British, International V

Modern British food and pedigree Australian wines

01491 680775
Goring Rd RG8 0SD
e-mail: info@woodynookatwoodcote.co.uk
dir: Opposite village green

Overlooking the village green, the white-fronted house offers a simple, homely dining room and outdoor terrace tables in a setting of bucolic calm. Modern British menus deal in the likes of Chinese-spiced duck terrine with a crispy wonton, spring onions and hoisin, followed by haddock with herbed mash, a poached egg and saffron cream, or roast best end of lamb with ratatouille in Madeira jus. Dessert might be an Australian take on Pavlova, with kiwi slices and a mango coulis. The owners have a vineyard in the highly regarded Margaret River region of Western Australia, so expect some big, sunny flavours from the wine list.

Chef Stuart Shepherd **Owner** Jane & Peter Bailey **Times** 12-2.30/7-9.30 Closed Xmas, Mon & Tue, D Sun **Prices** Fixed L 2 course £12.95-£14.95, Fixed D 3 course £21.45-£25.25, Starter £6.95-£8.25, Main £15.25-£22.50, Dessert £6.25-£7.25, Service optional, Groups min 6 service 10% **Wines** 23 bottles over £20, 5 bottles under £20, 8 by glass **Notes** Sunday L, Vegetarian menu **Seats** 50 **Children** Portions **Parking** 25

WOODSTOCK **Map 11 SP41**

Feathers Hotel

Modern British

Accomplished modern British cuisine at a sophisticated townhouse hotel

01993 812291
Market St OX20 1SX
e-mail: enquiries@feathers.co.uk
dir: from A44 (Oxford to Woodstock), 1st left after lights. Hotel on left

The Feathers has been at the heart of Woodstock since the 17th century. It has always been an elegant place to stay, but, not one for resting on its laurels, it kicked off 2010 with a top-to-toe makeover. The original wood panelling and low-beamed ceilings are timeless and need no fixing, but bold designer fabrics and eye-catching colour schemes have jazzed the place up with a sharper contemporary edge. As a prelude to dining in the elegantly-panelled environs of the restaurant, aficionados of the G&T should note that the Gin Bar lists over 50 examples - try them out in the pretty courtyard garden, which has also had a facelift. Perhaps inspired by the new look, the kitchen is firing on all cylinders to bring a creative modern spin to classic themes. A starter of beef tartare teamed with fluffy potato mousse, caviar, fried quail's egg and horseradish cream is a real success, while main-course sea bass is served with the contrasting flavours and textures of crisp smoked bacon, confit fennel, cardamom cream and saffron butter.

Feathers Hotel

Chef Marc Hardimon **Owner** Empire Ventures Ltd **Times** 12.30-2/7.10-9.30 Closed D Sun **Prices** Food prices not confirmed for 2011. Please telephone for details. **Wines** 150+ bottles over £20, 20 bottles under £20, 8 by glass **Notes** Sunday L, Vegetarian available, Dress restrictions, No shorts or T-shirts **Seats** 40, Pr/dining room 24 **Children** Portions, Menu **Parking** On street

See advert below

Macdonald Bear Hotel

◎◎ Modern European

Gentle modern European cooking in ancient inn

☎ 0844 879 9143
Park St OX20 1SZ
e-mail: bear@macdonald-hotels.co.uk
web: www.bearhotelwoodstock.co.uk
dir: M40 junct 9 follow signs for Oxford & Blenheim Palace. A44 to town centre, hotel on left

An ivy-clad former coaching-inn, the Bear dates all the way back to the 13th century, while part of its premises once housed a glove factory. It all adds up to one of the more architecturally fascinating places in the Home Counties. The period charm is maintained in a low-ceilinged trio of dining rooms with their original beams and stone walls. A gentle take on modern European food is presented via fixed-price menus of two or three courses, with the option at dinner of a sorbet after the starter. Start with seared red mullet with caponata and aubergine caviar. Main courses offer cod with creamed leeks in dill sauce, or herb-crusted lamb rump with couscous in minted jus, and desserts run to cherry and almond clafoutis with vanilla ice cream.

Chef Adrian Court **Owner** Macdonald Hotels
Times 12.30-2/7-9.30 **Prices** Fixed L 2 course £18, Fixed D 3 course £32-£36, Service optional **Wines** 70 bottles over £20, 18 bottles under £20, 12 by glass **Notes** Sunday L **Seats** 80, Pr/dining room 30 **Children** Portions, Menu **Parking** 45

RUTLAND

CLIPSHAM — Map 11 SK91

The Olive Branch

◎◎ British, European V

Rural pub with gastro credentials

☎ 01780 410355
Main St LE15 7SH
e-mail: rooms@theolivebranchpub.com
dir: 2m from A1 at Stretton junct, 5m N of Stamford

Deep in rural Rutland, yet just a handy couple of miles off the A1, the name may suggest a trendy country restaurant, but the Olive Branch is a real pub that acquired its name when a row of worker's cottages were joined together in the 19th century to become the local watering hole. Inside, books are stacked higgledy-piggledy and logs climb ceiling-high to fuel a roaring fire. Sit at one of the pine farmhouse tables to sample the wide-ranging choice of skilfully-cooked modern pub staples, from the simplicity of a pork and Stilton pie with home-made piccalilli, to the more avant-garde loin of swordfish with chorizo gnocchi, Mediterranean vegetables and tomato coulis. Treat yourself to a finale of apple tarte Tatin with blackberry compôte and clotted cream, or croissant-and-butter pudding with marmalade ice cream.

Chef Sean Hope **Owner** Sean Hope, Ben Jones
Times 12-2/7-9.30 Closed D 25 Dec **Prices** Fixed L 2 course fr £17.25, Fixed D 3 course fr £27.50, Starter £5.50-£11.50, Main £14.50-£24.50, Dessert £5.50-£8.50, Service optional, Groups min 12 service 10% **Wines** 30 bottles over £20, 20 bottles under £20, 10 by glass **Notes** Sat afternoon menu available 2.30-5.30, Sunday L, Vegetarian menu **Seats** 45, Pr/dining room 20 **Children** Portions, Menu **Parking** 15

OAKHAM — Map 11 SK80

Barnsdale Lodge Hotel

◎ Modern British

Modern European cooking in an 18th-century farmhouse

☎ 01572 724678
The Avenue, Rutland Water, North Shore LE15 8AH
e-mail: enquiries@barnsdalelodge.co.uk
dir: Turn off A1 at Stamford onto A606 to Oakham. Hotel 5m on right. (2m E of Oakham)

On the north shore of Rutland Water and close to Oakham and Stamford, Barnsdale Lodge Hotel was converted from a farmhouse by owner Thomas Noel in 1989. The building has been in his family since 1760 and formed part of the adjoining Exton Park, seat of the Earls of Gainsborough. The décor is cosy, country-house style with squashy sofas and stone floors. Dine on modern British dishes created from a good amount of local produce, in the main dining room, conservatory or outside in the courtyard. Expect the likes of pork rillettes with home-made piccalilli and watercress salad followed by pan-fried fillet of Rutland water trout with saffron fondant potato, champagne and smoked salmon sabayon.

Chef Adam Dowdy **Owner** The Hon Thomas Noel
Times 12-2.15/7-9.30 **Prices** Fixed L 2 course fr £12.95, Starter £4.25-£7.50, Main £12.95-£21.95, Dessert £4.95-£6.95, Service added but optional 10% **Wines** 45 bottles over £20, 33 bottles under £20, 10 by glass **Notes** Sunday L, Vegetarian available, Civ Wed 100 **Seats** 120, Pr/dining room 50 **Children** Portions, Menu **Parking** 250

Hambleton Hall Hotel

◎◎◎◎ *– see page 360*

Nick's Restaurant at Lord Nelson's House

◎◎ Modern European

Characterful setting for modern European cooking

☎ 01572 723199
11 Market Place LE15 6HR
e-mail: simon@nicksrestaurant
dir: Off A606 in town centre

The name sounds very grand, but this is a charming small-scale boutique-style restaurant with rooms ensconced in a corner of Oakham's market square. The dining room is cosy, and full of period character, glowing with warm hues of ochre and terracotta, and kitted out with unclothed dark wood antique tables and chairs. The kitchen takes a modern European approach, producing ambitious dishes founded on top-grade seasonal materials. The line-up might start with pistachio-crusted foie gras teamed with balsamic jelly, roasted pear and red wine reduction, then move on to roast duck breast with duck and potato hash, Puy lentil vinaigrette, duck and foie gras ravioli, roast beetroot and port jus. Finish with apple and raisin crumble soufflé with cider sorbet. A concise, well-chosen list of around 30 bins offers a good selection by the glass.

Times 12-2.30/6-9.30 Closed 25-26 Dec, Mon, D Sun

UPPINGHAM — Map 11 SP89

The Lake Isle

◎◎ British, French

Confident cooking in elegant townhouse hotel

☎ 01572 822951
16 High Street East LE15 9PZ
e-mail: info@lakeisle.co.uk
web: www.lakeisle.co.uk
dir: From A47, turn left at 2nd lights, 100yds on right

In the beautiful Rutland market town of Uppingham, this former shop and townhouse dates back more than 350

continued on page 361

Hambleton Hall Hotel

WINE AWARD OF THE YEAR

OAKHAM Map 11 SK80

Modern British V NOTABLE WINE LIST

Magisterial cooking in a setting of great refinement

☎ 01572 756991
Hambleton LE15 8TH
e-mail: hotel@hambletonhall.com
web: www.hambletonhall.com
dir: 8m W of A1 Stamford junct (A606), 3m E of Oakham

The house was built in the Victorian era by a brewing magnate who wanted a base in the middle of fox-hunting country. In later years, it served as a refuge for the sharp-tongued bright young things of the Noël Coward set. To be knee-deep in witticisms was one thing, but the location of Hambleton must have exerted almost as powerful a pull. Overlooking Rutland Water, and set amid glorious gardens, it's a supremely graceful pile, which has been maintained in high style by Tim and Stefa Hart since 1980. The interiors are pastorally pretty, with much use of gentle light green in the lounge, and shimmering deep red in the dining room. Here, service is as slick and spot-on as can be, without being in the least starchy, while table settings, with their fine stemware, wine cradles and crisp linen, are the last word in refinement. Aaron Patterson has taken the cooking here to the highest levels over the years. His style is not one of technological wizardry; dishes are not about foams and dusts so much as the coaxing of magisterial depth from ingredients whose integrity is respected. An assiette of duck to start delivers a timbale of confit topped with orange jelly, together with a mousse of duck foie gras and Earl Grey coated in crumbled pistachio, as well as shards of crisp crackling. Whissendine veal from a local supplier might star at main course, a tender cut from the leg, together with a raviolo of the sweetbread, the whole assemblage gaining depth from garnishes of pak choi and morels, and unified with a deeply rich Madeira sauce. Fish might crop up on one of the set menus in the form of fillet of sea bream with fennel purée and olives. Dessert compositions impress as forcefully as the preceding courses, never more so than in the ginger-crumbed gingerbread parfait that accompanies a poached pear, alongside sorbets of pear and of lime, and a scattering of blackberries. A gargantuan wine list has all the comprehensive reach one expects in the context.

Chef Aaron Patterson **Owner** Mr T Hart **Times** 12-1.30/7-9.30 **Prices** Fixed L 2 course £20, Fixed D 3 course £37-£46, Starter £14-£22, Main £25-£38, Dessert £13-£16, Service added but optional 12.5% **Wines** 375 bottles over £20, 10 bottles under £20, 10 by glass

Notes Tasting menu available, Sunday L, Vegetarian menu, Dress restrictions, Smart dress, no jeans, T-shirts or trainers, Civ Wed 64 Seats 60, Pr/dining room 20 **Children** Portions, Menu **Parking** 40

UPPINGHAM *continued*

years. The original mahogany fittings and panelled walls can still be seen in what is now a delightful restaurant and elegant bar, complete with a first-floor guest lounge and bedrooms. The British- and French-influenced cooking makes good use of local produce in dishes such as a first-course pan-roasted breast of wood pigeon wrapped in pancetta and served with a salad of watercress, hazelnuts, baked beetroot and finished with blackberry vinegar dressing. Follow on with a main course of twice-roasted belly of pork with pak choi, carrot and ginger purée and a five spice honey jus, and finish with steamed rhubarb sponge with orange and whisky ice cream.

Chef Stuart Mead **Owner** Richard & Janine Burton **Times** 12-2.30/7-9 Closed L Mon, D Sun **Prices** Fixed L 2 course £9.25-£15, Fixed D 3 course £23.90-£32.85, Starter £4.95-£6.95, Main £12.95-£18.95, Dessert £6-£7.50, Service optional **Wines** 190 bottles over £20, 15 bottles under £20, 15 by glass **Notes** Fixed menu can be served pre-theatre by arrangement, Sunday L, Vegetarian available, Dress restrictions, Smart casual **Seats** 40, Pr/dining room 16 **Children** Portions **Parking** 7, Car park adjacent

WING Map 11 SK80

Kings Arms Inn & Restaurant

Modern British

Supplier-led cooking in a traditional inn

☎ 01572 737634
13 Top St LE15 8SE
e-mail: info@thekingsarms-wing.co.uk
dir: 1m off A6003, between Oakham & Uppingham

This 17th-century traditional village inn has a lot going for it. There's the setting in the pretty village just a couple of miles from Rutland Water, a rustic, country interior (flagstone floors, two roaring fires and low-beamed ceilings), and, best of all, a serious attitude towards good, fresh food. The commitment to real food runs deep: ice creams and sorbets are home-made, they produce their own charcuterie, have their own smokehouse, bake the bread and make the stocks, chutneys, jams etc. Eat in the bar or the dining room and expect to tuck into the likes of cold-smoked Rutland trout served with a blini, herbed mascarpone mousse and a potato vinaigrette, followed by a fragrant Thai-style fish stew or cannon of Melton lamb with crisp sweetbreads, fondant potato and rhubarb.

Chef James Goss **Owner** David, Gisa & James Goss **Times** 12-2.30/6.30-9 Closed Mon, L Tue (Nov - Apr), D Sun **Prices** Starter £6-£10, Main £9-£25, Dessert £3-£7.50, Service optional, Groups min 7 service 10% **Wines** 20 bottles over £20, 28 bottles under £20, 20 by glass **Notes** Sunday L, Vegetarian available **Seats** 38, Pr/dining room 24 **Children** Portions **Parking** 30

SHROPSHIRE

BRIDGNORTH Map 10 SO79

Old Vicarage Hotel and Restaurant

– see below

CHURCH STRETTON Map 15 SO49

The Pound at Leebotwood

Modern British

Local produce cooked with flair in a popular country inn

☎ 01694 751477
Leebotwood SY6 6ND
e-mail: info@thepound.org.uk
dir: On A49, 9m S of Shrewsbury

Set beside the A49 between Shrewsbury and Church Stretton and backed by stunning rural views, the thatched 15th-century former drovers' inn has been transformed into a vibrant gastro-pub. Modern artwork and oak furniture are set against exposed beams, real fires, and woodblock and carpeted floors in an appealing

continued

Old Vicarage Hotel and Restaurant

BRIDGNORTH Map 10 SO79

Modern European

Delicious Shropshire views and intricate seasonal cooking

☎ 01746 716497
Hallow, Worfield WV15 5JZ
e-mail: admin@the-old-vicarage.demon.co.uk
dir: Off A454, approx 3.5m NE of Bridgnorth, 5m S of Telford on A442, follow brown signs

In a rural Shropshire setting in the village of Worfield, the Old Vicarage is an Edwardian house sitting in a modest couple of acres, with lush pastoral views all around. The main dining goes on in the spacious Orangery, where daylight pours in from above and around, and where a loyal local following also pours in for the highly skilled classical cooking. This isn't the place for avant-garde ingredient collisions, but that doesn't mean that the cooking isn't quite intricate and cleverly wrought in its own way. Start enterprisingly with a piece of roasted organic salmon alongside a helping of salmon rillettes, served with Avruga caviar, fennel-seed bread and a dollop of mascarpone (a nice spin on the cured fish and sour cream theme). Seafood generally shows well, as witness a main course of beautifully timed Canadian halibut with a crab fishcake, wild sea beets and a brilliant shellfish butter sauce. Meats ring the changes on the usual offerings, in the shapes of pigeon breasts or roast veal topside, the latter served with ravioli, garlic-buttered mushrooms and Madeira sauce. Lightness is the key to desserts such as properly made vanilla pannacotta, in a soup of peach blended with champagne and scented with basil.

Chef Simon Diprose **Owner** Mr & Mrs D Blakstad **Times** 12-2.30/7-9.30 Closed L Mon-Tue, Sat-Sun (by reservation only), D 24-26 Dec **Prices** Fixed L 2 course £19.50, Fixed D 3 course £35, Service optional **Wines** 77 bottles over £20, 27 bottles under £20, 10 by glass **Notes** Sunday L, Vegetarian available, Dress restrictions, Smart casual **Seats** 64, Pr/dining room 20 **Children** Portions, Menu **Parking** 30

CHURCH STRETTON *continued*

blend of old and new. Outside, there is a screened area for alfresco dining. The atmosphere is relaxed and unpretentious and the food is modern British and freshly prepared from local ingredients. A typical meal may take in tomato risotto with courgette fritter, parmesan and pesto to start, followed by lamb confit with roasted root vegetables, mustard mash and Madeira sauce, with rhubarb clafoutis for pudding.

Times 12-2.30/6.30-9.30 Closed 25 & 26 Dec

The Studio

British, French

Modern British cooking and an art collection too

☎ 01694 722672
59 High St SY6 6BY
e-mail: info@thestudiorestaurant.net
dir: Off A49 to town, left at T-junct onto High St, 300yds on left

Once an artist's studio, as attested by the swinging palette sign, this stylish restaurant displays a diverting collection of artworks and ceramics. The comfortable, smart interior is supplemented by outdoor tables under parasols for fine-weather dining, and the Martlands run the place deftly and sympathetically. Traditional British dishes with some modern tweaks are to be found on menus that might run from a tian of prawns, crayfish and smoked salmon, through seared Mortimer Forest venison with pickled pears in blackberry and red wine sauce, to bread-and-butter pudding served with brandied apricots and vanilla ice cream.

Chef Tony Martland **Owner** Tony & Sheila Martland **Times** 7-9 Closed 2 wks Jan, 1 wk Apr, 1 wk Nov, Sun-Tue, L all week **Prices** Fixed D 3 course £26.50, Service optional **Wines** 13 bottles over £20, 27 bottles under £20, 6 by glass **Notes** Vegetarian available, Dress restrictions, Smart casual **Seats** 34 **Children** Portions **Parking** On street parking available

HADNALL **Map 15 SJ52**

Saracens at Hadnall

Modern British

Confident cooking at smart restaurant with rooms

☎ 01939 210877
Shrewsbury Rd SY4 4AG
e-mail: reception@saracensathadnall.co.uk
dir: M54 onto A5, at junct of A5/A49 take A49 towards Whitchurch. Follow A49 to Hadnall, diagonally opposite church

Set on the main road, this delightful restaurant with rooms occupies a handsome former Georgian coaching inn. There are two dining rooms, the Georgian-style front room, with its polished-wood floor, panelled walls and stone fireplace, or the conservatory, which features a capped well; there's a traditional bar, too. The owner has a share in a local farm which secures the journey from farm to fork, the tip-top ingredients put to good use on the modern British menu. Timbale of smoked haddock with leek and potato broth is an imaginative starter full of complementary flavours, while main-course honey-glazed breast of corn-fed Goosnargh duckling with potato fondant, buttered spinach and beetroot reduction is an equally well-judged dish.

Chef David Spencer **Owner** Ben & Allison Christie **Times** 11.30-2.30/6.30-9.30 Closed Mon, L Tue, D Sun **Prices** Fixed L 2 course fr £11.95, Fixed D 3 course fr £15, Starter £4.50-£7, Main £13-£19.50, Dessert £5.50-£5.95, Service optional **Wines** 20 bottles over £20, 26 bottles under £20, 8 by glass **Notes** Early eve menu Tue-Fri before 7.30pm, Sunday L, Vegetarian available, Dress restrictions, Smart casual **Seats** 45 **Children** Menu **Parking** 20

IRONBRIDGE **Map 10 SJ60**

Restaurant Severn

Modern French

Country cooking beside the Ironbridge gorge

☎ 01952 432233
33 High St TF8 7AG
web: www.restaurantsevern.co.uk
dir: Travelling along High St, pass Restaurant Severn on right, to mini rbdt, take 3rd exit onto Waterloo St, continue 50 mtrs to car park on left

In a parade of period shops adjacent to the heritage site of the world's first iron bridge, this informal neighbourhood restaurant is a relaxed, welcoming place. Making do without coverings on tables or floor, it aims for a modern brasserie ambience, backed up by the sound practice of growing some of the produce on their own local plot. 'Simplicity at its best' is one way of summing up dishes such as a starter of seared king scallops and sweet-cure bacon with leaves dressed in the pan juices. Traditional fruity accompaniments with duck breast extend to both orange sauce and a caramelised white peach, while fish might be Scottish halibut cooked in Chablis. Beb Bruce is in charge of desserts, and is justly proud to present the pick of June's strawberries alongside a pannacotta also flavoured with them.

Chef Eric & Beb Bruce **Owner** Eric & Beb Bruce **Times** 12-2/6.30-8.30 Closed BHs, Mon-Tue, L Wed-Sat, D Sun **Prices** Fixed D 3 course £25.95-£28.95, Service optional, Groups min 8 service 10% **Wines** 15 bottles over £20, 25 bottles under £20, 5 by glass **Notes** Sunday L, Vegetarian available, Dress restrictions, Smart casual **Seats** 30 **Children** Portions **Parking** On street & car park opposite

LUDLOW **Map 10 SO57**

La Bécasse

– *see opposite page*

The Clive Bar and Restaurant with Rooms

Modern British

Bright, modern restaurant in renovated Shropshire farmhouse

☎ 01584 856565 & 856665
Bromfield SY8 2JR
e-mail: info@theclive.co.uk
web: www.theclive.co.uk
dir: 2m N of Ludlow on A49, near Ludlow Golf Club, racecourse & adjacent to Ludlow food centre

The Clive in question is Clive of India, who once lived in this 18th-century red-brick farmhouse converted stylishly into a contemporary bar, bistro and restaurant with rooms. It looks good: pale wood tables and floors and exposed beams contrasting with walls in modish shades of dove grey and oxblood, and violet upholstered chairs. Shropshire and the Welsh Marches are a good place to be for sourcing fresh, seasonal materials, deployed here in French-influenced modern British dishes. A meal might kick off with ham hock and rabbit confit terrine with cranberry and orange relish, before Barbary duck with truffled Lyonnaise potatoes, braised endive and beetroot sauce. End with a smile on your face, courtesy of desserts such as bread-and-butter pudding with clementine marmalade and iced white chocolate parfait.

Chef Martin Humphries **Owner** Paul & Barbara Brooks **Times** 12-3/6.30-10 Closed 25-26 Dec **Prices** Starter £5.25-£8.50, Main £9.95-£18.95, Dessert £4.50-£5.95, Service optional **Wines** 31 bottles over £20, 35 bottles under £20, 9 by glass **Notes** Sunday L, Vegetarian available **Seats** 90 **Children** Portions **Parking** 80

Dinham Hall Hotel

Modern British

Accomplished cooking in a smart country-house setting

☎ 01584 876464
By the Castle, Dinham SY8 1EJ
e-mail: info@dinhamhall.com
dir: Town centre, off Market Place, opposite Ludlow Castle

Face-to-face with the ramparts of Ludlow Castle above the coils of the River Teme, Dinham Hall is in the thick of the action in Shropshire's foodie mecca. It is a handsome Georgian place, all oak floors, high plasterwork ceilings and period pastels - until, that is, you enter the glass-roofed brasserie, which goes for a pared-back contemporary look with unclothed tables. The casually-dressed staff know a thing or two about the menu. The sound supply lines to the cornucopia of Shropshire produce are backed by a skilled team to cook it all up into impressively crafted creations with an unmistakable French accent. A pressing of confit duck and foie gras with celeriac cream might precede a modish combo of fish and meat, with sea bream and braised oxtail served up with roasted salsify and artichoke. A deeply rich chocolate tart with honeycomb and vanilla ice cream makes a satisfying finish.

Chef Wayne Vickarage **Owner** Metzo Hotels Ltd **Times** 12.30-2.30/6.30-9.30 **Prices** Fixed L 2 course fr £10, Service added but optional 10% **Wines** 98 bottles over £20, 9 bottles under £20, 8 by glass **Notes** ALC 2 course £27.50, 3 course £35, Pre-theatre menu, Sunday L **Seats** 36, Pr/dining room 60 **Parking** 16, On street

The Feathers Hotel

European

Traditional cooking in beautiful timber-framed hotel

☎ 01584 875261
Bull Ring SY8 1AA
e-mail: enquiries@feathersatludlow.co.uk
dir: from A49 follow town centre signs to centre. Hotel on left

Mentioned by Pevsner in *The Buildings of England*, The Feathers Hotel is internationally recognised for its stunning Jacobean architecture and Medieval heritage. Situated in the heart of this ancient market town, the extravagantly timber-framed exterior is matched by rough-cast stone walls in the dining room and good table linen. The kitchen uses as much local produce as possible, including venison from Mortimer Forest. Start perhaps with pan-fried breast of wild wood pigeon, braised onion and bacon tart and beetroot purée, moving on to confit shoulder and rack of new season lamb with thyme jus. Finish with lavender sablé with honey crème fraîche and fresh raspberries.

Chef Martin Jones **Owner** Ceney Developments **Times** 7-9 Closed L all week **Prices** Fixed D 3 course £39.50, Service optional, Groups min 12 service 10% **Wines** 19 bottles over £20, 17 bottles under £20, 10 by glass **Notes** Vegetarian available, Dress restrictions, Smart casual, Civ Wed 80 **Seats** 50, Pr/dining room 30 **Children** Portions, Menu **Parking** 36

La Bécasse

LUDLOW **Map 10 SO57**

French V

Experimental Anglo-French cooking of high ambition

☎ 01584 872325
17 Corve St SY8 1DA
e-mail: info@labecasse.co.uk
web: www.labecasse.co.uk
dir: In town centre opposite Feathers Hotel, at bottom of hill

Ludlow's time in the culinary spotlight continues, despite some high profile departures in recent years. Alan Murchison of L'ortolan in Shinfield (see entry) opened here in 2007, leaving the kitchen in the formidably-talented hands of Will Holland. Inside, it has burnished oak panelling, exposed brickwork and understated touches of contemporary style in a warren of intimate interconnecting rooms. La Bécasse is French for 'woodcock' - an immediate nod to the classically-rooted fine dining that is dear to the restaurant's heart. Interpreting the classic French repertoire with modern British creative flair, Holland is adept at bringing together big bold flavours in perfect balance, for compelling results. He's also a keen supporter of the 'Local to Ludlow' movement promoting the cornucopia of produce from within 30 miles of the town. A starter of Scottish surf clams with parsley pasta, cauliflower carpaccio, prune purée and lemon and caper salsa reveals superb technical skills in a triumph of clear flavours and textures. A main course of roast Mortimer Forest venison loin is wrapped in smoked bacon, and teamed with turnip rösti, fig purée and bitter chocolate sauce. Dinner reaches its climax with desserts that might play a lemon and aniseed savarin off with lemon rice pudding, pineapple carpaccio, fennel ice cream and 'spice of angels' fennel pollen. While the kitchen is firing on all cylinders, praise must also go to excellent front-of-house staff.

Chef Will Holland **Owner** Alan Murchison Restaurants Ltd **Times** 12-2/7-9.30 Closed Xmas, New Year, Mon, L Tue, D Sun **Prices** Fixed L 2 course fr £25, Fixed D 3 course fr £55, Tasting menu fr £60, Starter fr £15, Main fr £30, Dessert fr £15, Service added but optional 10% **Wines** 123 bottles over £20, 4 bottles under £20, 20 by glass **Notes** Tasting menu 7 course, surprise menu 10 course £85, Sunday L, Vegetarian menu **Seats** 40 **Children** Portions **Parking** 6

LUDLOW *continued*

Fishmore Hall

◎◎ Modern European

Clever cooking in a boutique hotel

☎ 01584 875148
Fishmore Rd SY8 3DP
e-mail: reception@fishmorehall.co.uk
dir: A49 from Shrewsbury, follow Ludlow & Bridgnorth signs. 1st left towards Bridgnorth, at next rdbt left onto Fishmore Rd. Hotel 0.5m on right after golf course

This beautifully restored Georgian property on the outskirts of Ludlow is now a privately owned boutique country-house hotel. The elegant and contemporary restaurant boasts French windows that afford views over the beautiful Shropshire countryside, or get even closer on warm days with a table on the terrace. Head to the attractive lounge and small bar area for pre- and post-dinner drinks. Creative use of great quality local produce from the Shropshire Marches makes for modern and exciting food. There's a seven-course Shropshire Tasting Menu and a ten-course Menu Gourmand alongside the à la carte; try, perhaps, lamb's sweetbreads with violet artichokes, wild mushrooms and eucalyptus and a flavoursome line-caught sea bass, braised gem lettuce, oxtail ravioli and crayfish consommé. Finish with a rich chocolate delice, mango and passionfruit flavours.

Times 12-2.30/7-9.30

Mr Underhills

◎◎ Modern International

Individual and tasteful restaurant with rooms

☎ 01584 874431
Dinham Weir SY8 1EH
dir: From Castle Square: with castle in front, turn immediately left, proceed round castle, turn right before bridge, restaurant on left

A stalwart of the local foodie scene for a dozen years, Chris and Judy Bradley's idyllic restaurant with rooms has been a jewel in Ludlow's crown since its earliest days as a centre of gastronomy. With the River Teme meandering past the foot of the garden to tumble over Dinham Weir, and Ludlow Castle's battlements peeking through a screen of mature trees, the serene setting is an English idyll. Inside, the charming dining room is run with effortless efficiency by Judy, while Chris gets on with the serious business of preparing his seven-course daily menus, which can be tailored to the needs of individual diners. Dishes are put together with the sort of confidence that keeps full-on flavours working in perfect harmony, and only the very best local produce finds its way into this kitchen. An Autumn menu could parade the likes of toasted almond velouté with orange zest oil and dust, then duck liver custard with quince cream and five spice glaze. Fish comes next – perhaps brill with lime, coconut, ginger and coriander – then the main event might be slow-roasted fillet of Mortimer Forest venison with caper and raisin sauce, sprouts with chestnuts and pancetta, baked potato and shallot mash.

Chef Christopher Bradley **Owner** Christopher & Judy Bradley **Times** 7.30-8.30 Closed 1 wk Jan, 1 wk Jul, Mon-Tue, L all week **Prices** Food prices not confirmed for 2011. Please telephone for details. **Wines** 90 bottles over £20, 35 bottles under £20, 12 by glass **Notes** Dress restrictions, Smart casual **Seats** 30 **Children** Portions **Parking** 7

Overton Grange Country House & Restaurant

◎◎ Modern British, European

Anglo-French cooking in a splendid Edwardian house

☎ 01584 873500
Old Hereford Rd SY8 4AD
e-mail: info@overtongrangehotel.com
dir: M5 junct 5. On B4361 approx 1.5m from Ludlow towards Leominster

A white-fronted, wood-panelled Edwardian house in the countryside outside Ludlow, Overton is a picture of unruffled elegance. Spa treatments are on offer for the guests, and in the aubergine-coloured dining room, the cooking is in the hands of Christophe Dechaux-Blanc, who trained at France's much-acclaimed La Pyramide. He brings, as one would expect, a contemporary French sensibility to what is essentially modern British cooking, and achieves a high degree of dazzle in the process. Roasted andouillette may seem entirely French rural, but serve it on buckwheat blinis with puréed celeriac, and sauce it with a reduction of apples and cider and it all starts to feel closer to home. Mains might embrace sea bream with smoked pancetta and celery risotto in a sauce of star anise, or more mainstream Herefordshire beef fillet in Madeira jus. Tasting menus of seven courses plus trimmings are an alluring way to try the range.

Chef Christophe Dechaux-Blanc **Owner** Metzo Hotels Ltd **Times** 12-2.30/7-10 **Prices** Fixed D 3 course £42.50, Service added 10%, Groups min 10 service 10% **Wines** 150 bottles over £20, 20 bottles under £20, 12 by glass **Notes** Pre-theatre meal available from 5.30pm, Sunday L, Vegetarian available, Dress restrictions, Smart casual, Civ Wed 50 **Seats** 40, Pr/dining room 24 **Parking** 50

MARKET DRAYTON **Map 15 SJ63**

The Cottage Restaurant at Ternhill Farm House

◎ Modern International

Ambitious cooking in homely Georgian farmhouse

☎ 01630 638984
Ternhill TF9 3PX
e-mail: info@ternhillfarm.co.uk
dir: On x-rds of A41 & A53, 3m W of Market Drayton

Originally part of a working farm, this red-brick Georgian farmhouse was completely refurbished by chef-proprietors Mick and Jo Abraham to begin a new lease of life as the Cottage Restaurant. They have gone for a clean-cut modern look, blending chocolate leather seats and bare wooden tables with yellow ochre walls and ancient oak beams. An extensive menu of modern classics offers something to keep everyone happy - smoked mackerel and horseradish fishcakes are a good way to start, ahead of an Aga-roasted pork fillet studded with garlic and glazed with apricot and wholegrain mustard. After that, banana marmalade sponge pudding comes with butterscotch sauce and home-made banana ice cream.

Chef Michael Abraham **Owner** Michael & Joanne Abraham **Times** 6.30-mdnt Closed Sun & Mon, L all week **Prices** Fixed D 3 course £15.95, Starter £4.50-£6.25, Main £10.25-£17.95, Dessert £4.50-£6.25, Service optional, Groups min 8 service 10% **Wines** 4 bottles over £20, 20 bottles under £20, 6 by glass **Notes** Fixed D Tue-Fri, Vegetarian available, Dress restrictions, Smart casual **Seats** 22, Pr/dining room 12 **Parking** 16

Goldstone Hall

◎◎ Modern British

Accomplished modern cooking in a charming Shropshire country house

☎ 01630 661202
Goldstone Rd, Goldstone TF9 2NA
e-mail: enquiries@goldstonehall.com
dir: 4m S of Market Drayton off A529 signed Goldstone Hall Hotel. 4m N of Newport signed from A41

A more attractive image of understated English charm is hard to conjure than this elegant Georgian country-house hotel set in lovely gardens and woodland. A snooker room, conservatory and oak-panelled dining room complete the genteel picture. Service fits the overall ambience - well-organised and attentive. Thanks to a well-stocked kitchen garden, abundant local ingredients, and a kitchen team that knows what to do with them, there's nothing quaint about the food. Menus offer a wide-ranging choice of dishes in a hearty modern British vein: take seared pigeon breast with caramelised onion, port syrup and pear crisp to start, then main-course cinnamon apple pork belly with mulled cider, red cabbage and glazed apple that delivers gutsy, clearly-defined flavours.

Chef John Thompson **Owner** Mr J Cushing & Mrs H Ward **Times** 12-2.30/7.30-11 **Prices** Fixed L 3 course fr £24.90, Starter £7-£16, Main £10.50-£24.90, Dessert £6.75-£8.50, Service included **Wines** 65 bottles over £20, 22 bottles under £20, 11 by glass **Notes** Sunday L, Vegetarian available, Dress restrictions, Smart casual, Civ Wed 100 **Seats** 40, Pr/dining room 14 **Children** Portions **Parking** 60

MUCH WENLOCK Map 10 SO69

Raven Hotel

British, Mediterranean

Modern cooking in characterful old coaching inn

☎ 01952 727251
30 Barrow St TF13 6EN
e-mail: enquiry@ravenhotel.com
dir: 10m SW from Telford on A4169, 12m SE from Shrewsbury. In town centre

The Raven Hotel has been looking after visitors to the small town of Much Wenlock for centuries, and although it has been modernised in recent years, it still retains bags of original features, including exposed beams and open fires. The hotel incorporates several 15th-century almshouses and a medieval great hall, with a restored 17th-century coaching inn at its heart. The bright, attractive restaurant overlooks an inner courtyard where you can eat outside on warm summer evenings. The food is unfussy and uses plenty of local produce, with classic dishes given a modern twist. A starter of home-cured gravad lax with beetroot salsa and basil and goats' cheese mousse might be followed by pavé of Morville beef served with a mushroom and blue cheese fricassée and parsley purée. Finish with a light raspberry mousse with liquorice and blackcurrant ice cream dressed with a raspberry coulis.

Times 12-2.30/6.45-9.30 Closed 25 Dec

MUNSLOW Map 10 SO58

Crown Country Inn

Modern British

Historic country inn with superior cooking

☎ 01584 841205
SY7 9ET
e-mail: info@crowncountryinn.co.uk
dir: On B4368 between Craven Arms & Much Wenlock

This Grade II listed quintessential country inn is right in the heart of Shropshire, near to the market towns of Bridgnorth, Ludlow and Shrewsbury. The Corvedale restaurant, with its grand open fire place, was once the local courtroom and erstwhile home of the notorious Judge Jefferies (known rather forebodingly as the hanging judge). But don't let any gruesome stories put you off, for the cooking here has much to offer, serving up classic English dishes in a refined, modern style, utilising the array of local produce in the area. From the seasonal menu, start with crostini of local black pudding and tomato topped with Wenlock Edge farm bacon, then home-smoked breast of Shropshire farm chicken with red onion confit. Finish with warm spiced apple and cinnamon cake with Calvados caramel sauce.

Chef Richard Arnold **Owner** Richard & Jane Arnold **Times** 12-2/6.45-8.45 Closed Xmas, Mon, D Sun **Prices** Fixed L 2 course fr £13, Fixed D 2 course fr £13, Starter £4.95-£6.95, Main £13.50-£17.95, Dessert £5.50-£6.95, Service included **Wines** 13 bottles over £20, 29 bottles under £20, 5 by glass **Notes** Sunday L, Vegetarian available **Seats** 65, Pr/dining room 42 **Children** Portions **Parking** 20

NORTON Map 10 SJ70

Hundred House Hotel

British, European

Hands-on family hotel where quirky charm meets skilled modern cuisine

☎ 01952 580240 & 580265
Bridgnorth Rd TF11 9EE
e-mail: reservations@hundredhouse.co.uk
web: www.hundredhouse.co.uk
dir: Midway between Telford & Bridgnorth on A442. In village centre

There's a sense of fun shot through this old Georgian coaching inn, starting with the stained glass Temperance Hall panels at the front door. And, should you be staying overnight to loosen your belt a notch in the restaurant, the bedrooms come complete with a swing suspended from the ancient beams. The hands-on family who run the hotel have packed the warren of rooms making up the bar, brasserie and main restaurant with mildly-eccentric character that says 'relax, make yourself at home' - think quarry-tiled floors, oak panels, baskets of pumpkins and squashes, and bunches of dried herbs hanging from oak rafters. These herbs - plucked from a profusion of over a hundred types grown in the kitchen garden - also turn up in the company of top-drawer Shropshire produce on a creative modern British menu that's big on flavour. A starter of griddled scallops with cauliflower purée, black pudding, crispy pancetta and cumin dressing shows the style, before roast rack and braised shoulder of Shropshire lamb with gratin potato and rosemary jus.

Chef Stuart Phillips **Owner** Mr H Phillips, Mr D Phillips, Mr S G Phillips **Times** 12-2.30/6-9.30 Closed 26 Dec, D 1 Jan **Prices** Fixed L 2 course £13-£15, Starter £4.95-£7.95, Main £12.95-£21.95, Dessert £4.95-£7.95, Service optional, Groups min 7 service 10% **Wines** 30 bottles over £20, 15 bottles under £20, 10 by glass **Notes** Sunday L, Vegetarian available, Dress restrictions, Smart casual, Civ Wed 100 **Seats** 60, Pr/dining room 30 **Children** Portions, Menu **Parking** 30

OSWESTRY Map 15 SJ22

Pen-y-Dyffryn Country Hotel

Modern British

Confident cooking in a hillside hotel on the Welsh border

☎ 01691 653700
Rhydycroesau SY10 7JD
e-mail: stay@peny.co.uk
dir: 3m W of Oswestry on B4580

On the last hill in Shropshire along the historic Offa's Dyke, this handsome Georgian rectory makes a fine hideaway. Whether you're here for some of the finest hill walking in Britain, or happy simply to look at the scenery while sipping tea on the terrace, a civilised time is on the cards; log fires keep things cosy, and confident contemporary Anglo-Welsh cuisine awaits at the end of the day. Local, often organic produce is to the fore on daily-changing menus, that might kick off with king scallops with parsnip purée, apple and a curried butter sauce, then move on to Welsh beef sirloin, Parmentier potatoes, wild mushrooms, smoked bacon, watercress salsa and red wine jus. A silky vanilla pannacotta with fresh raspberries and biscotti makes a delightful end to the meal.

Chef David Morris **Owner** MJM & AA Hunter **Times** 6.45-11 Closed 20 Dec-21 Jan, L all week **Prices** Fixed D 3 course £30-£35, Service optional **Wines** 30 bottles over £20, 40 bottles under £20, 3 by glass **Notes** Vegetarian available **Seats** 25 **Children** Portions, Menu **Parking** 18

OSWESTRY *continued*

Sebastian's Hotel & Restaurant

@@ French

Qualité française à Oswestry

☎ 01691 655444
45 Willow St SY11 1AQ
e-mail: sebastians.rest@virgin.net
dir: Follow town centre signs. Take road towards Selattyn & Llansilin for 300yds into Willow St, hotel on left

The hotel occupies a 16th-century house in the old town centre, where oak-panelled walls make an atmospheric backdrop for food-themed artworks and a charming cartoon portrait of your hosts, the Fishers. The culinary approach is classical French, with the bilingual menus of another era bestowing a warm glow of nostalgia over the enterprise. That said, the dishes themselves can be surprisingly up-to-date in their thinking, with starters such as a pairing of braised belly pork and deep-fried mussels, which works persuasively well. Proceed with halibut wrapped in Parma ham in an assertive grain mustard sauce, or lamb loin with smoked aubergine purée, sauced with tomato and tarragon. Modern Brit desserts include 'brownie au chocolat, glace Nutella', probably no translation needed, served with griottines.

Chef Mark Sebastian Fisher, Richard Jones **Owner** Mark & Michelle Fisher **Times** 6.30-9.30 Closed 25-26 Dec, 1 Jan, Sun-Mon, L all week **Prices** Fixed D 3 course fr £19.95, Service optional **Wines** 16 bottles over £20, 38 bottles under £20, 6 by glass **Notes** ALC fixed menu 5 course £37.50, Vegetarian available **Seats** 35 **Children** Portions **Parking** 25, On street

Wynnstay Hotel

@@ Modern European

Classic dishes in a red-brick Georgian inn

☎ 01691 655261
Church St SY11 2SZ
e-mail: info@wynnstayhotel.com
dir: In town centre, opposite church

The immaculately maintained red-brick Georgian inn once stood at a crossroads on the Liverpool-to-Cardiff and London-to-Holyhead routes, and now makes a stolidly handsome all-mod-cons hotel, complete with indoor pool and spa facilities. An elegant dining room with good napery, subtle lighting and fine art prints is attended by formally trained staff, and makes a fitting context for the sophisticated classical cooking. The fixed-price menus (with supplements) deal in the likes of smoked haddock and chive risotto, pork tenderloin with black pudding, cider cream sauce and apple crisps, and tiger prawns in garlic butter. Simple desserts include a citrus tart served with raspberry sauce, or zabaglione. A pair of lounge bars offer alternative eating spaces.

Chef Chris Ridges **Owner** Mr N Woodward **Times** 12-2/7-9.30 Closed 25 Dec, L Mon-Sat, D Sun **Prices** Fixed D 3 course fr £12, Starter £4.95-£6.25, Main £10.95-£23.95, Dessert £4.95-£7.25, Service optional **Wines** 20 bottles over £20, 36 bottles under £20, 7 by glass **Notes** Early bird menu 3 course Mon-Fri 6-7.30pm, Sunday L, Vegetarian available, Dress restrictions, Smart casual, Civ Wed 90 **Seats** 46, Pr/dining room 200 **Children** Portions, Menu **Parking** 80

SHIFNAL Map 10 SJ70

Park House Hotel

@ European

Modern European menu in singular market town hotel

☎ 01952 460128
Park St TF11 9BA
e-mail: reception@parkhousehotel.net
dir: From M54 J4 take A464 through Shifnal; hotel 200yds after railway bridge

Two Regency country houses, one red-brick, one white-fronted, have been bolted elegantly together to make this singular market town hotel. Dramatic red colour schemes within are enhanced by original artworks, and there is a refined service ethos to the front-of-house approach. Butlers restaurant deals in modern European cooking presented straightforwardly, without excess flounce. Take in grilled halloumi in sherry, or crayfish and salmon risotto in lemongrass and coconut bisque, to start, and then move on to roast venison loin with spinach, a black pudding beignet and juniper jus. Chips cooked in goose fat are among the possible side orders, and meals might conclude with a galvanising assemblage of citrus posset, blood orange snow and lemon shortbread.

Chef Les Tait **Owner** Andrew Hughes **Times** noon-10 **Prices** Fixed L 2 course £12.95, Fixed D 3 course £16.95, Starter £6.95-£8.95, Main £12.95-£17.45, Dessert £5-£6.95, Service optional **Wines** 33 bottles over £20, 31 bottles under £20, 6 by glass **Notes** Sunday L, Vegetarian available, Dress restrictions, Smart casual preferred, Civ Wed 150 **Seats** 50, Pr/dining room 180 **Children** Portions, Menu **Parking** 80

SHREWSBURY Map 15 SJ41

Albright Hussey Manor Hotel & Restaurant

@@ Modern British

Romantic Tudor manor with refined and contemporary cooking

☎ 01939 290571
Ellesmere Rd, Broad Oak SY4 3AF
e-mail: info@albrighthussey.co.uk
dir: 2.5m N of Shrewsbury on A528, follow signs for Ellesmere

It may be a much-used phrase, but you really do step back in time as you cross the stone bridge to this delightful medieval timbered manor house. It is a building of two halves: the Hussey family's original beamed Tudor house stands shoulder to shoulder with a brick and stone 16th-century wing. Set in beautiful landscaped gardens, it is a seductive place, with an authentic interior of oak beams and panels, leaded windows and a huge walk-in inglenook. There's nothing archaic about the kitchen's modern cooking, though, which raids the Shropshire larder to create clean, clear flavours and textures. Beetroot gets a workout in a starter, coming smoked and as a sorbet with goats' cheese crostini, followed by a well-balanced teaming of seared sea bass fillet with tomato ratatouille, orzo rice pasta and aubergine caviar. High standards extend to desserts - vanilla pannacotta with pistachio purée and rose praline tuile - and you could be tempted by an array of Shropshire artisan cheeses.

Chef Michel Nijsten **Owner** Franco, Vera & Paul Subbiani **Times** 12-2.15/7-10 **Prices** Food prices not confirmed for 2011. Please telephone for details. **Wines** 53 bottles over £20, 43 bottles under £20, 5 by glass **Notes** Dress restrictions, No jeans, trainers or T-shirts, Civ Wed 200 **Seats** 80, Pr/dining room 40 **Children** Portions **Parking** 100

Mad Jack's Restaurant & Bar

@ Modern British **NEW** V

Vibrant atmosphere and modern dining

☎ 01743 358870
15 St Mary's St SY1 1EQ
e-mail: info@madjacks.uk.com
dir: In Shrewsbury town centre, on the one way system, almost opposite St Mary's Church

You're probably wondering who Mad Jack was, and why he got his name: well, John 'Mad Jack' Mytton was a Regency rake who blew his inherited wad on boozing and hellraising. Cartoon sketches celebrate his antics in this smart modern restaurant with rooms, hung from cappuccino and cerise walls above sparkly black marble tables, and terracotta-tiled floors. It's a buzzy, stylish setting for modern cooking from a kitchen well-supplied with good ideas and local Shropshire produce. Starters of seared scallops with local Wenlock Edge black pudding, pea purée, and port and girolle mushroom jus set the tone, before roast loin of local spring lamb teamed with garlic and thyme stuffing, fondant potato and butter bean purée. You could end on a boozy note with a 'dessert cocktail' - such as a Bakewell Tartini - that Mad Jack would surely have gone for.

Chef Daniel Silcock **Owner** Ann & Danny Dirella
Times 12-10 Closed 25-26 Dec **Prices** Starter £4.95-£7.95, Main £9.95-£22, Dessert £4.95-£6.95
Notes Sunday L, Vegetarian menu **Seats** 60
Children Portions

Mytton & Mermaid Hotel

Modern British V

Riverside setting and a true Shropshire flavour

01743 761220
Atcham SY5 6QG
e-mail: admin@myttonandmermaid.co.uk
dir: Just outside Shrewsbury on B4380 (old A5). Opposite Attingham Park

In an idyllic riverside setting by the Atcham Bridge on the River Severn, this ivy-clad Grade II listed former coaching inn is a handsome red-brick affair. The brasserie-style restaurant has plenty of period features alongside antique oak tables topped with fresh flowers and candles. The cooking shows some ambition and creative touches in an essentially modern British repertoire with excellent use of local seasonal produce. Start, perhaps, with a terrine of Muckleton ham knuckle with spiced pineapple pickle, potato foam and root vegetable crisps, before moving onto 'Shropshire Lad' fish and chips (served with mushy peas, hand-cut chips and tartare sauce) or braised Shropshire venison with Shropshire Blue dauphinoise. Dessert serves up pannacotta flavoured with local honey, warm figs with balsamic, and black pepper shortbread.

Chef Adrian Badland **Owner** Mr & Mrs Ditella
Times 12-2.30/6.30-10 Closed 25 Dec, D 26 Dec, 1 Jan
Prices Fixed L 2 course £13.95, Fixed D 3 course £24.95-£29.95, Starter £4.95-£7.25, Main £10.50-£27.50, Dessert £4.95-£6.95, Service optional **Wines** 26 bottles over £20, 30 bottles under £20, 12 by glass **Notes** Sunday L, Vegetarian menu, Civ Wed 90 **Seats** 100, Pr/dining room 12 **Children** Portions, Menu **Parking** 80

Rowton Castle Hotel

Modern British

Modern cooking in restored 17th-century castle

01743 884044
Halfway House SY5 9EP
e-mail: post@rowtoncastle.com
dir: From Birmingham take M6 west. Then M54 & A5 to Shrewsbury. Exit A5 at 6th rdbt. A458 to Welshpool. Hotel 4m on right

A castle has stood on this site in the Welsh Marches for 800 years. Demolished by the marauding Llewellyn, Prince of Wales, then rebuilt and much added-to over the years, most of what you see nowadays dates from the 17th century, and comes with heaps of period character. The Cedar Restaurant is darkly atmospheric with its carved oak fireplace, liver-brown oak panelling and pink pyjama-striped velvet chairs, while the kitchen takes a modern British line with its seasonal menus. You might start with a terrine of confit chicken wrapped in ham, served with pea shoot salad and beetroot dressing, followed by slow-roasted pork shoulder with white bean casserole, deep-fried sage leaves and cider sauce. Rich chocolate torte with passionfruit sorbet and mango purée is an indulgent way to finish.

Times 12-2/7-9.30

TELFORD — Map 10 SJ60

Best Western Valley Hotel & Chez Maw Restaurant

Modern British

Modern British food near the Ironbridge

01952 432247
TF8 7DW
e-mail: info@thevalleyhotel.co.uk
dir: M6/M54 from junct 6 take A5223 to Ironbridge for 4m. At mini island right, hotel 80yds on left

The hotel is perfectly placed for tourists to the Ironbridge world heritage area (there are nine museums to get through), sitting on the banks of the River Severn not far from the first piece of iron civil engineering in the world. Indeed, it once belonged to a local industrialist, and is an elegant place on a human scale. The peach-toned dining room is enhanced by well-chosen artworks and generously spaced tables, and staff are both amiable and knowledgeable. Local produce is enthusiastically celebrated in starters like Severn and Wye smoked salmon with pickled fennel and beetroot purée, and mains such as braised lamb shoulder, sweet-and-sour red cabbage, fondant potato and braising juices. To finish, consider tangy passionfruit pannacotta with pineapple carpaccio and basil ice cream.

Times 12-2/7-9.30 Closed 26 Dec-2 Jan, L Sat & Sun

Hadley Park House

Modern British

01952 677269
TF1 6QJ
e-mail: info@hadleypark.co.uk
web: www.hadleypark.co.uk
dir: M54 junct 5, A5 (Rampart Way), at rdbt take A442 towards Hortonwood, over double rdbt, next rbdt take 2nd exit, hotel at end of lane

You could easily imagine yourself right out in the countryside - not just a few minutes from the centre of Telford - while strolling in the three acres of mature grounds surrounding elegant Hadley Park House. Built by Thomas Telford's chief engineer, the Georgian house has been sympathetically restored and the attractive conservatory restaurant has well-spaced, smartly dressed tables, serviced by friendly, informed staff. The cooking is broadly modern British with some French and Eastern influences, making full use of carefully-sourced seasonal produce. Start, perhaps, with natural smoked haddock tartare with sauce gribiche and a honey and mustard dressing, followed by cumin-crusted lamb loin wrapped in garlic leaves and pastry with smoked aubergine and garlic purée, and a spicy masala sauce.

Times 12-2/7-9.30 Closed L Sat (subject to availability), D Sun (subject to demand)

SOMERSET

BATH Map 4 ST76

Barcelo Combe Grove Manor Hotel

International

Georgian country-house hotel with fine-dining restaurant

☎ 01225 834644
Brassknocker Hill, Monkton Combe BA2 7HS
e-mail: combegrovemanor@barcelo-hotels.co.uk
dir: Exit A36 at Limpley Stoke onto Brassknocker Hill. Hotel 0.5m up hill on left

Close to Bath in impressive grounds, this country-house hotel has a brasserie and a classy fine-dining restaurant. The latter, the Georgian Room, has wonderful views over the delightful Limpley Stoke valley alongside well-dressed tables and plenty of Georgian charm. Service is by a confident young team of staff. Local produce, including game, are used to good effect on the regularly-changing menu which combines classical techniques with some modern touches. Start with salad of wood pigeon with beetroot, Puy lentils and hazelnut dressing, then maybe a main-course wood mushroom and parmesan risotto and truffle foam, or salmon and crayfish tortellini. Mocha chocolate fondant pudding and pistachio nut cream is a thrilling finish. The Eden Brasserie and bar in the vaulted cellars offers lighter menu options and atmosphere.

Times 12-2/7-9.30

The Bath Priory Hotel, Restaurant & Spa

– see below

Cavendish Restaurant

Modern British

Assured modern cooking in impressive Georgian townhouse hotel

☎ 01225 787960 & 787963
Dukes Hotel, Great Pulteney St BA2 4DN
e-mail: info@dukesbath.co.uk
dir: M4 junct 18, A46 to Bath. At lights left towards A36, at next lights right, & right again into Gt Pulteney St

Located on a magnificent avenue just a short walk from the city's iconic Pulteney Bridge, Dukes Hotel is a shining example of Bath's Georgian splendour. The Cavendish Restaurant occupies the lower ground floor of the Grade I listed Palladian-style townhouse, but employs a well-lit, airy and refined décor to avoid any hint of basement claustrophobia; it also helps that there's a charming secluded walled patio garden for alfresco eating. The cooking is ambitious, well-presented stuff, which majors on seasonality and local - largely organic - suppliers. Smoked duck breast, artichoke pannacotta and mustard fruit shows the kitchen's contemporary style; follow on with pork - roast fillet and slow-braised cheek - with apple and sage, and black pudding croquette, and finish with the lively textural contrasts of rhubarb and apple crumble, vanilla pannacotta and apple sorbet.

Chef Fran Snell **Owner** Alan Brookes, Michael Bokenham **Times** 12-2.30/6.30-10 Closed L Mon-Thu **Prices** Fixed L 2 course fr £12.95, Starter £6.95-£9.95, Main £13.95-£23.95, Dessert £6.95-£8.95, Service optional **Wines** 28 bottles over £20, 10 bottles under £20, 16 by glass **Notes** Sunday L, Vegetarian available **Seats** 28, Pr/dining room 16 **Children** Portions **Parking** On street (with permits)

The Dower House Restaurant

Modern British V

Contemporary fine dining in Georgian splendour

☎ 01225 823333
The Royal Crescent Hotel, 16 Royal Crescent BA1 2LS
e-mail: info@royalcrescent.co.uk
dir: From A4, right at lights. 2nd left onto Bennett St. Continue into The Circus, 2nd exit onto Brock St

Bath's Royal Crescent is one of the UK's most magnificent legacies from the Georgian era, and an unbeatable setting for the upper-crust elegance of the eponymous luxury hotel's Dower House Restaurant. Lovely landscaped gardens are secreted away behind the hotel for idyllic summertime alfresco dining. Inside, there's a subtly opulent décor in hues of toffee and lime green, bathed in light through French windows. The kitchen produces a creative menu in a modern British vein, based on

The Bath Priory Hotel, Restaurant & Spa

BATH Map 4 ST76

Modern European V

Skilful country-house cooking in grand Georgian hideaway

☎ 01225 331922
Weston Rd BA1 2XT
e-mail: mail@thebathpriory.co.uk
dir: Adjacent to Victoria Park

An elegant Georgian house not far from the centre of Bath, the Priory is owned by the Brownswords, who also have Gidleigh Park (see entry, Chagford, Devon) to their credit. Michael Caines, one of the premier division of country-house chefs, oversees the kitchen business at both locations, and the same sense of style, charm and white-hot skill is evident here too. Produce is assiduously locally sourced, much of it from the hotel's own kitchen garden, and the level of achievement that chef Sam Moody brings to the realisation of the Caines idiom is high. A fashionable pairing of meat and fish for a first course brings together braised ox cheek and brill poached in truffle butter, with mushroom duxelles and a ceps foam for company. Combinations are not always out to surprise, as witness a main course of roast venison loin with spiced pear compôte and braised salsify in a red wine jus, which delivers excellent meat and a fine balance of flavours. Meals end with a flourish, perhaps juxtaposing the molten richness of chocolate fondant with a sharp blood orange sorbet. Extras do the jobs expected of them, from the little cup of foamy parsnip soup to the wonderful breads.

Times 12-2.30/7-9.30

seasonal local materials, and backed by sound technical skills. A modish fish and meat pairing of millefeuille of Loch Duart salmon with crisp belly pork and caramelised baby onions could start things off; next, pan-fried stone bass might be teamed with sautéed langoustine, confit frogs' legs and warm saffron jelly. Desserts such as rhubarb and vanilla mousse with gingerbread ice cream are equally refined.

Chef Luke Richards **Owner** von Essen Hotels
Times 12.30-2/7-9.30 **Prices** Fixed L 2 course fr £15.50, Fixed D 3 course fr £60, Service optional **Wines** 270 bottles over £20, 10 by glass **Notes** Tasting & pre-theatre menus available, Sunday L, Vegetarian menu, Dress restrictions, Smart casual, No denim, Civ Wed 60
Seats 50, Pr/dining room 40 **Children** Portions, Menu
Parking 17

Four Seasons Restaurant

Traditional International

Accomplished cooking in traditional country-house setting

☎ 01225 723226
Best Western The Cliffe Hotel, Cliffe Dr, Crowe Hill, Limpley Stoke BA2 7FY
e-mail: cliffe@bestwestern.co.uk
dir: A36 S from Bath for 4m. At lights left onto B3108 towards Bradford-on-Avon. Before rail bridge right into Limpley Stoke, hotel 0.5m on right

Originally a private gentleman's residence, The Cliffe Hotel sits in three and a half acres of peaceful grounds just to the south of Bath, with stunning views across the Avon Valley. The original billiard room is these days home to the traditional-styled Four Seasons Restaurant, overlooking the well-tended gardens. Fresh, locally-sourced produce is the mainstay of the seasonally-changing menu, which serves up classic cooking with a few twists along the way. Start, perhaps, with smoked chicken with poached smoked quail's eggs and hollandaise sauce, before moving on to fillet of beef with a stilton and port reduction, and finish with amaretti baked Alaska.

Chef Martin Seccombe **Owner** Martin & Sheena Seccombe
Times 12-2.30/7-9.30 **Prices** Fixed L 2 course £11.50-£15, Fixed D 3 course £25-£30, Starter £4.95-£7, Main £15.50-£22, Dessert £4.55-£8, Service optional **Wines** 30 bottles over £20, 10 bottles under £20, 6 by glass
Notes Sunday L, Vegetarian available, Dress restrictions, Smart casual **Seats** 50, Pr/dining room 15
Children Portions, Menu **Parking** 30

Jamie's Italian

Italian

Jamie's winning rustic Italian formula

☎ 01225 510051
10 Milsom Place BA1 1BZ

Jamie Oliver's ever-expanding empire of rustic Italian restaurants (10 at the last count) operates a no-booking policy, which is either commendably democratic or very frustrating, depending on your point of view. Don't get impatient though: the rustic Italian food is worth any wait. The Bath branch occupies an elegant Georgian building smack in the city centre, its interior done out in a suitably unaffected style with well-worn wooden floors and a mish-mash of wooden and red metal chairs. Expect authenticity built on top-quality produce - and celebrity has given him the clout to serve his own mozzarella and olive oil. All in all, it's a cracking formula: a great choice at sensible prices, starting with antipasti served on planks for sharing; pasta is made in-house daily for classics such as spaghetti vongole, while mains take in sea bass with mussels and clams steamed in their own juices and served with smashed fennel, capers, arrabbiata sauce and Amalfi lemon.

Times 12pm-11pm

Macdonald Bath Spa Hotel, Vellore Restaurant

Traditional British, International

Traditional grand-hotel cuisine amid the spa treatments

☎ 0844 879 9106
Sydney Rd BA2 6JF
e-mail: sales.bathspa@macdonald-hotels.co.uk
dir: A4 and follow city-centre signs for 1m. At lights turn left towards A36. Turn right after pedestrian crossing then left into Sydney Place. Hotel 200yds on right

The city of Bath has been about spa treatments and self-indulgence since Roman times, and the Bath Spa hotel provides a whole array of facilities for those so inclined. Its majestic Georgian façade establishes the tone of affable grandeur that prevails throughout, and nowhere more so than in the Vellore Restaurant, once the ballroom, where a canopied outdoor terrace opens off the main room. Well-sourced ingredients play their part in a fairly traditional style of opulent hotel cuisine, starting with a smoked salmon pancake garnished with caviar crème fraîche and a dressing of roasted beetroot, moving onto exemplary blade of Scottish beef, slow-braised, glazed in horseradish and served with luxuriously smooth mash, and finishing with a proudly risen strawberry soufflé, offset with tangy raspberry and balsamic sorbet.

Times 12-2/6.15-10 Closed L Mon-Sat

Marlborough Tavern

Modern British **NEW**

Accomplished cooking in a contemporary city pub

☎ 01225 423731
35 Marlborough Buildings BA1 2LY
e-mail: info@marlborough-tavern.com
dir: Short stroll from the city centre, close to The Royal Crescent & station

Revamped from a faded alehouse to a vibrant, contemporary gastro-pub, this 18th-century corner pub is rammed with local diners, business-types and the foot-weary from the city's tourist trail. The appeal is the rustic-chic bars - think stripped floors, muted tones, striking wall coverings, and church candles on scrubbed tables - the raft of decent wines by the glass, tip-top Butcombe Bitter on tap, and a classy menu that delivers gutsy, full-flavoured dishes prepared from quality local and seasonal produce. Simple, generously served dishes may include pressed Wiltshire lamb and caper terrine with home-made chutney, Neston Park organic sirloin steak with thyme, tomato and pink peppercorn dressing and hand-cut chips, and rhubarb crème brûlée.

Times 12.30-2.30/6-9.30 Closed D Sun

The Olive Tree at the Queensberry Hotel

– see page 370

Woods Restaurant

Modern British, French

Bistro cooking in Georgian Bath

☎ 01225 314812 & 422493
9-13 Alfred St BA1 2QX
e-mail: claude@woodsrestaurant.fsnet.co.uk

Extending over the ground-floors of five contiguous Georgian townhouses, opposite the famous Assembly Rooms and the Costume Museum, Woods has been a family-run restaurant since 1979. Horse racing prints abound, and the ambience is enhanced by well-spaced, smartly laid tables and attentive service. The French-oriented food is at the richer end of bistro eating, with main dishes such as breast of guinea fowl sauced with cream cheese, lemon, herbs and garlic, or seared beef fillet in port, but simpler, lighter dishes impress too, as in tasty celeriac, butternut squash and onion soup, or grilled goats' cheese salad with balsamic-dressed leaves. To finish, the orange sorbet comes in a meringue nest with passionfruit coulis.

Times 12-2.30/5.30-10 Closed 25-26 Dec, Sun (open for special request)

The Olive Tree at the Queensberry Hotel

BATH Map 4 ST76

Modern British

First-class contemporary cooking in chic, boutique-style Georgian townhouse hotel

☎ 01225 447928
4-7 Russell St BA1 2QF
e-mail: reservations@thequeensberry.co.uk
web: www.thequeensberry.co.uk
dir: 100mtrs from the Assembly Rooms

We can thank the 8th Marquess of Queensberry for the row of terrace townhouses. Everything else we owe to Laurence and Helen Beere. Their tenure of the building has seen it develop into a top-ranking boutique hotel, one that fulfills all the cool style expectations without ever going overboard or losing its way. The whole place is impeccably chic, including the Olive Tree restaurant, which is a series of interconnecting rooms in the basement, done out in natural tones with subtle lighting and mellow contemporary art on the walls. If we're handing out plaudits, then chef Nick Brodie deserves his fair share. The kitchen team is turning out some impressive food with evident sharp technical skills on show, plenty of care taken in the sourcing of local and regional produce, and an eye for thrilling presentations. There are vibrant and well-judged flavours in a first-course risotto of Cornish cock crab, served with a velouté of the dark meat and a crisp soft-shell crab tempura. Next up, a brochette of Creedy Carver duck breast, liver and kidney comes with the confit leg meat in a spring roll, along with potato fondant and assorted vegetables - a first-class main course. Banana tarte Tatin with a Valrhona chocolate sorbet brings things to a close in style. The young and knowledgeable service team assure everything goes along nicely.

Chef Nick Brodie **Owner** Mr & Mrs Beere **Times** 12-2/7-10 **Prices** Fixed L 2 course £16.50, Starter £7.75-£12, Main £16.50-£27.75, Dessert £8.50-£9.50, Service added but optional 10%, Groups min 10 service 10% **Wines** 270 bottles over £20, 30 bottles under £20, 34 by glass **Notes** Sunday L, Vegetarian available **Seats** 60, Pr/dining room 30 **Children** Portions, Menu **Parking** On street pay/display

BRIDGWATER Map 4 ST43

The Lemon Tree Restaurant

Modern British

Cheerful hotel restaurant with a touch of ambition

☎ 01278 662255
Walnut Tree Hotel, Fore St, North Petherton TA6 6QA
e-mail: reservations@walnuttreehotel.com
web: www.walnuttreehotel.com
dir: M5 junct 24, A38, hotel 1m on right opposite St Mary's Church

The Walnut Tree Hotel started out in the 17th century as a cider house and coaching inn catering to travellers heading to the West Country, a function it still carries out today, since the M5 is but a few minutes away. Its Lemon Tree restaurant looks spruce in shades of lemon and blue, while service comes with sincere friendliness, courtesy of an experienced team of local staff. The kitchen knows its stuff too, delivering a soundly-cooked repertoire of modern British staples, taking in chicken and tarragon tortellini, followed by herb-crusted cod with tartar potato cake, green beans and caviar lemon butter sauce. After that, consider a hot apple and ginger charlotte with vanilla ice cream.

Chef Luke Nicholson, Debbie Palmer **Owner** Kristine & Stephen Williams **Times** 12-2.30/6.30-9.30 **Prices** Fixed L 2 course £25-£30, Fixed D 3 course £31-£36, Service optional **Wines** 18 bottles over £20, 16 bottles under £20, 10 by glass **Notes** Sunday L, Vegetarian available, Civ Wed 100 **Seats** 40, Pr/dining room 100 **Children** Portions **Parking** 70

DULVERTON Map 3 SS92

Tarr Farm Inn

Modern British

Beautifully situated historic inn with focus on good food

☎ 01643 851507
Tarr Steps, Exmoor National Park TA22 9PY
e-mail: enquiries@tarrfarm.co.uk
dir: 4m NW of Dulverton. Off B3223 signed Tarr Steps, signs to Tarr Farm Inn

Dating back to the 16th century, this remote inn hides away in a forested valley where the famous Tarr Steps, a rare clapper bridge made of flat stones, crosses the River Barle. The cosily rustic bar is exactly what you hope for inside - eat here by the fireside, or park at a high-backed leather seat in the classy candlelit restaurant. This is deepest huntin', shootin', fishin' country on Exmoor, so the kitchen stocks its larder with the best of what's available locally, putting an up-to-date spin on hearty classic dishes. Duck, pork belly and corn-fed chicken make a well-matched partnership in a terrine served with quail's eggs and wild mushrooms à la Grecque. Next, fillet of Devon Ruby Red beef might be teamed with roasted potatoes and shallots, watercress purée, pancetta crisps and red wine jus.

Chef Paul Webber **Owner** Richard Benn & Judy Carless **Times** 12-3/6.30-12 Closed 1-10 Feb **Prices** Fixed L 2 course fr £10, Fixed D 2 course fr £20, Starter £5-£8, Main £12-£22, Dessert £5-£7, Service optional **Wines** 53 bottles over £20, 40 bottles under £20, 8 by glass **Notes** Sunday L, Vegetarian available **Seats** 50, Pr/dining room 20 **Children** Portions **Parking** 40

Woods Bar & Dining Room

Modern British, French

French food at a West Country hostelry exuding bonhomie

01398 324007
4 Banks Square TA22 9BU
e-mail: woodsdulverton@hotmail.com

It is indeed, as described, a bar with dining rooms, in which eating and drinking occur simultaneously and harmoniously. The place feels relaxed and engagingly lived-in, and is reliably full of the burble of contented punters. A French chef bestows a little Gallic magic on dishes such as silky-smooth duck liver parfait with red onion marmalade, crisp-skinned seared sea bass on a saffron and basil risotto cake, served with ratatouille and fennel pollen velouté, and decently rich crème brûlée, served with a perhaps under-powered rhubarb parfait. Owner Paddy Groves is an enthusiastic wine-lover, whose recommendations can be acted on with confidence.

Chef Olivier Certain **Owner** Paddy Groves **Times** 12-2/7-9.30 Closed 25 Dec **Prices** Starter £6.50-£8.50, Main £10.50-£16.50, Dessert £5.50-£6.50, Service optional **Notes** Sunday L, Vegetarian available **Seats** 38 **Parking** On street

EXFORD Map 3 SS83

Crown Hotel

Modern British

Daring cooking in a tranquil Somerset inn

01643 831554
Park St TA24 7PP
e-mail: info@crownhotelexmoor.co.uk
web: www.crownhotelexmoor.co.uk
dir: From Taunton take A38 to A358. Turn left at B3224 & follow signs to Exford

The rather handsome village inn at a road junction in the midst of greenest Somerset is smartly appointed within. High-backed leather chairs in the smart, red-walled dining room add to the comfort factor, as does the occasional clip-clopping of a passing horse outside. The cooking tries out some more speculative turns than you might be expecting in the surroundings, with starters such as tempura-battered langoustines with minted peas and lemon oil, and mains like roast Gressingham duck with pineapple tarte Tatin and a host of other accompaniments. Dessert like frangipane tart topped with marinated strawberries, served with good yoghurt sorbet, should not be missed.

Crown Hotel

Owner Mr C Kirkbride & S & D Whittaker **Times** 7-9 Closed L all wk **Prices** Food prices not confirmed for 2011. Please telephone for details. **Wines** 25 bottles over £20, 16 bottles under £20, 19 by glass **Notes** Sunday L, Vegetarian available, Dress restrictions, Smart casual, no jeans, T-shirts, swimwear **Seats** 45, Pr/dining room 20 **Children** Portions **Parking** 30

Homewood Park

HINTON CHARTERHOUSE Map 4 ST75

Modern British, European

Accomplished modern British cooking in an understated Georgian house

01225 723731
Homewood Park, Abbey Ln BA2 7TB
e-mail: info@homewoodpark.co.uk
dir: 6m SE of Bath on A36, turn left at 2nd sign for Freshford

Enjoying views over sumptuous Limpley Stoke valley, not far from Bath, Homewood Park is a fine, largely Georgian house with some Victorian add-ons. It sits in 10 acres of splendid lawns and parkland, and is decorated inside with a lighter touch than many such places. You won't feel suffocated in chintz as you progress to the dining room with its garden views. Daniel Moon has set the kitchen operation on a firm upward course, heading up a small brigade that seems strong in all areas, delivering consistently accomplished modern British cooking. Start with deeply satisfying and moreish confit belly pork with a stick of crackling, a mousse of black pudding and white onion cappuccino, a memorable exercise in textural contrasts. Main course could be a seared tranche of monkfish, presented with a varied array of carrot treatments and pancetta crisps. Excellent pastry work is the hallmark of the superbly intense bitter chocolate tart, served with silky-textured pistachio ice cream. A lot of work has also gone into the imaginative extras, helping to earn Homewood its deserved third Rosette.

Chef Daniel Moon **Owner** von Essen Hotels **Times** 12-1.45/6.30-9.30 **Prices** Food prices not confirmed for 2011. Please telephone for details. **Wines** 130 bottles over £20, 15 bottles under £20, 6 by glass **Notes** Sunday L, Vegetarian available, Dress restrictions, Smart casual, No jeans or trainers, Civ Wed 50 **Seats** 60, Pr/dining room 40 **Children** Portions, Menu **Parking** 50

HINTON CHARTERHOUSE Map 4 ST75

Homewood Park

– see page 371

HOLFORD Map 4 ST14

Combe House Hotel

Modern British

Complex modern cuisine in a characterful Somerset hotel

01278 741382
TA5 1RZ
e-mail: info@combehouse.co.uk
dir: From A39 W left in Holford then left at T-junct. Left at fork, 0.25m to Holford Combe

In a secluded wooded valley in the heart of the Quantock Hills, Combe House sprawls through a converted tannery and terrace of workers' cottages with the original waterwheel still in place. Its four acres of gardens are a delightful haven for wildlife, and an invaluable source of fresh seasonal produce for the kitchen. And with Exmoor on the doorstep, there's no excuse for not bringing a keen appetite to dinner in the intimate beamed restaurant. Top-grade materials from West Country suppliers form the backbone of the kitchen's skilfully-cooked, often elaborate, modern repertoire. Start with seared scallops pointed up with the sharpness of poached and puréed rhubarb, and pistachios, both toasted and in praline form. At main-course stage, pan-fried duck breast might be partnered by rolled confit leg, dauphinoise potatoes, pancetta lardons and Cassis sauce.

Times 12-2.30/7-9

HUNSTRETE Map 4 ST66

Hunstrete House Hotel

Modern European

Confident cooking in classic country-house hotel

01761 490490
BS39 4NS
e-mail: info@hunstretehouse.co.uk
dir: On A368 - 8m from Bath

A splendid Georgian mansion within 92 acres of rambling deer park on the edge of the beautiful Mendip Hills, Hunstrete House is the archetypal English country-house hotel. Inside, period detail abounds, with walls and public areas packed with antiques and oil paintings. The main Popham's restaurant is classical in style with beautiful arched windows looking out onto the courtyard. The modern English cooking rises to the occasion, making good use of local, seasonal produce, including much from the hotel's own Victorian walled garden. The kitchen shows a sure hand in dishes that reveal some contemporary sensibilities; roasted quail, for example, served with boudin noir, beetroot and horseradish crème fraîche. Follow on with sautéed fillet of sea bream with smoked mash potato, Jerusalem artichoke purée and fennel foam. Round things off with dark chocolate and passionfruit fondant with fennel sorbet and coconut jelly.

Chef Tom Bally **Owner** von Essen hotels
Times 12-2/7-9.30 **Prices** Fixed L 2 course £18-£23, Fixed D 3 course £50, Tasting menu fr £80, Service added but optional 10% **Wines** 92 bottles over £20, 17 bottles under £20, 7 by glass **Notes** Sunday L, Vegetarian available, Dress restrictions, No jeans, smart casual, Civ Wed 60 **Seats** 50, Pr/dining room 50 **Children** Portions, Menu **Parking** 50

LOWER VOBSTER Map 4 ST74

The Vobster Inn

British, European

Lovely rural English setting and carefully-sourced ingredients

01373 812920
BA3 5RJ
e-mail: info@vobsterinn.co.uk
dir: 4m W of Frome, between Wells & Leigh upon Mendip

King James II and his army dropped into the Vobster before the Battle of Sedgemoor in 1685. These days things are much calmer: sit outside to eat in four acres of grounds in rolling Somerset countryside, or inside, which is just as inviting, having been brought smartly up to date with a tastefully contemporary décor. Fresh fish comes most days from Cornwall, and the owners are keen advocates of West Country produce, so sourcing is diligent; as much as possible is made in-house. Seared Cornish scallops with smoked tomato sauce and polenta, or foie gras crème brûlée might start things off, ahead of roast duck breast with spiced red cabbage, roast pear and Cassis sauce. Desserts such as baked ginger parkin are supplemented by superb home-made ice creams.

Chef Mr Rafael F Davila **Owner** Mr Rafael F Davila
Times 12-3/6.30-11 Closed 25 Dec, L Mon, D Sun
Prices Starter £5-£7, Main £9.50-£22.50, Dessert £5.25, Service optional **Wines** 9 bottles over £20, 18 bottles under £20, 12 by glass **Notes** Sunday L, Vegetarian available **Seats** 40, Pr/dining room 40 **Children** Portions, Menu **Parking** 60

MIDSOMER NORTON Map 4 ST65

The Moody Goose At The Old Priory

Modern British V

Historic setting for well-balanced modern cooking

01761 416784 & 410846
Church Square BA3 2HX
e-mail: info@theoldpriory.co.uk
dir: Along High St, right at lights, right at rdbt in front of church

A 12th-century priory in a place called Midsomer Norton sounds like a good basis for a murder mystery TV series, but this one is home to the Moody Goose restaurant. The priory is a warren of a place, all flagstones, inglenooks and oak beams in its tiny rooms, while the restaurant surprises with its simple modern look of smart pyjama-striped chairs, and walls of claret and exposed stone. The kitchen garden provides herbs, fruit and vegetables, together with quality local and seasonal materials; the kitchen focuses on sound classical technique to deliver sharp flavours in intelligent combinations - as in a layered terrine of ham hock, guinea fowl and foie gras with pickled beetroot. Classy presentation and clear flavours are the hallmarks of main courses such as roasted monkfish with artichokes, crayfish and a light white wine cream, while a cob nut pannacotta might be teamed with praline and coffee ice cream.

Chef Stephen Shore **Owner** Stephen Shore
Times 12-1.30/7-9.30 Closed Xmas, New Year, BHs, Sun-Mon **Prices** Food prices not confirmed for 2011. Please telephone for details. **Wines** 81 bottles over £20, 13 bottles under £20, 9 by glass **Notes** Vegetarian menu, Dress restrictions, Smart casual **Seats** 34, Pr/dining room 22 **Children** Portions **Parking** 12

PORLOCK Map 3 SS84

The Oaks Hotel

Traditional British

Honest, homely cooking with fantastic sea views

01643 862265
TA24 8ES
e-mail: info@oakshotel.co.uk
dir: At bottom of Dunstersteepe Road, on left on entering Porlock from Minehead

From its elevated position on a Somerset hillside this charming Edwardian country-house hotel offers distant views of Porlock Bay. It's run with consummate aplomb by the Rileys - he reigns out front, she cooks. The mustard-coloured dining room, with its grandfather clock, has an appealing domestic feel, and is the setting for the classically-based cooking. From the four-course dinner menu there might be hot cheese soufflé or pear and watercress soup, followed by an intermediate refresher of smoked haddock mousse, before a main course of Exmoor venison with redcurrant and juniper. End on a comforting note with apple and almond pudding with clotted cream.

Times 7-8 Closed Nov-Mar

PORTISHEAD Map 4 ST47

The Lockhouse

Modern British NEW

Creative cooking at the regenerated Portishead marina

☎ 01275 397272
Portishead Marina BS20 7AF
e-mail: info@thelockhouseportishead.co.uk
dir: M5 junct 19 Portishead. Follow signs for marina. Restaurant opposite marina control centre

Working docks are an endangered species these days: no longer the province of horny-handed workmen, we flock to them up and down the land in their regenerated form to eat and drink in stylish hangouts. And Bristol's reinvented Portishead docks are no exception since the arrival of the Lockhouse Restaurant, a sharp-looking contemporary conservatory venue grafted onto the old lock keeper's cottage. The minimal décor goes for modern art hanging on exposed red-brick walls and high-backed Lloyd loom chairs at darkwood tables - tasteful but nothing to distract from the view across the marina through walls of glass. The cooking takes an inventive modern tack, using well-chosen local produce in appealing flavour combinations - grilled red mullet with watercress, blood orange and gazpacho vinaigrette, say, and mains of braised belly pork teamed with colcannon galette, caramelised apple and mustard velouté.

Times 12-3/6-10 Closed 26 Dec

SHEPTON MALLET Map 4 ST64

Thatched Cottage

Modern British, European

Vibrant European cooking in stylish Somerset inn

☎ 01749 342058
Thatched Cottage, 63-67 Charlton Rd BA4 5QF
e-mail: david@thatchedcottage.info
dir: 0.6m E of Shepton Mallet, at lights on A361

Cider and perry connoisseurs will find plenty to put a smile on their faces at this 400-year-old roadside inn - a specialist in these fine Somerset traditions. Within the ancient stone-built hostelry are all the oak beams, log fires and panelled walls you would expect, but it's all spruced up with a smart contemporary edge. In the Rendezvous Restaurant, the kitchen sources its ingredients well for a hearty repertoire of modern pub staples sprinkled with European influences. Expect Somerset-style mussels steamed in cider with chorizo, garlic, onion and parsley, then main courses such as a straight-up rib-eye steak with mushrooms, cheese-topped tomato and chips, or lamb navarin stew with rosemary and root vegetables, and braised red cabbage. End with a chocolate fondant with salted caramel heart.

Thatched Cottage

Chef David Pledger **Owner** David Pledger **Times** 12-2.30/6.30-9.30 **Prices** Fixed L 2 course £10, Starter £4.50-£7.95, Main £10.25-£20.95, Dessert £4.50-£6.50, Service optional, Groups min 8 service 9% **Wines** 7 bottles over £20, 27 bottles under £20, 23 by glass **Notes** Sunday L, Vegetarian available **Seats** 56, Pr/dining room 35 **Children** Portions, Menu **Parking** 35

The Three Horseshoes Inn

Modern, Traditional

☎ 01749 850359
Batcombe BA4 6HE
dir: Signed from A359 Bruton/Frome

It would be hard to find a more peaceful spot than this. Tucked away down a myriad of country lanes, the 17th-century Three Horseshoes is a haven of tranquility - the perfect antidote to the frenzied pace of modern life. That's not to say it hasn't moved with the times - the cooking is pretty much up-to-the-minute at least - but the old inn is certainly full of period charm, with its vast inglenook fireplace in the bar, low beamed ceilings and traditional furnishings. You can eat in one of several cosy rooms, or out in the garden if the weather allows. The kitchen uses local, organic and often home-grown produce in dishes such as asparagus with pea purée, crispy poached egg and parmesan shavings; honey-roasted belly pork with sweet potato mash, sautéed broccoli and cider gravy; and rhubarb crumble with a light custard.

Chef Mike Jones, Bob Wood **Owner** Bob Wood & Shirley Greaves **Times** 12-2/7-9 Closed 25 Dec, Mon, D Sun **Prices** Food prices not confirmed for 2011. Please telephone for details. **Wines** 8 bottles over £20, 28 bottles under £20, 8 by glass **Notes** Sunday L, Vegetarian available, Dress restrictions, Smart casual **Seats** 40, Pr/dining room 40 **Children** Portions **Parking** 30

SOMERTON Map 4 ST42

The Devonshire Arms

Modern British

Gastro-pub menu in a former village hunting lodge

☎ 01458 241271
Long Sutton TA10 9LP
e-mail: mail@thedevonshirearms.com
dir: Off A303 onto A372 at Podimore rdbt. After 4m, left onto B3165, signed Martock and Long Sutton

The rather grand greystone inn with porticoed entrance derives its lofty air from its former role as a hunting lodge. Sitting on a pretty village green not far from Somerton, it's a relaxing place with an appealing air of informality. Wood floors and tables and a blackboard menu give the feel of a gastro-pub, and the extensive menus reinforce the impression. Cornish mussels steamed over the local cider, and seasoned with chilli, garlic and thyme, are one way to start, local asparagus in the season another - delicious when dressed in black truffle and parmesan. Quantock duck confit with spring onions and Puy lentils is an eye-catching main course, and meals might end with rhubarb clafoutis and orange marmalade ice cream.

Chef Sasha Matkevich **Owner** Philip & Sheila Mepham **Times** 12-2.30/7-9.30 Closed 25-26 Dec, 1 Jan **Prices** Starter £5.95-£7.95, Main £10.50-£16.20, Dessert £5.50-£6.40, Service optional **Wines** 10 bottles over £20, 17 bottles under £20, 10 by glass **Notes** Sunday L, Vegetarian available **Seats** 40 **Children** Portions, Menu **Parking** 6, On street

STON EASTON Map 4 ST65

Ston Easton Park

Modern British

Top-end dining in a gorgeous Palladian mansion

☎ 01761 241631
BA3 4DF
e-mail: info@stoneaston.co.uk
dir: A39 from Bath for approx 8m. Onto A37 (Shepton Mallet). Hotel in next village

A superb example of a Palladian mansion in a lush West Country estate, Ston Easton is an iconic slice of perfectly preserved British architectural heritage. With grounds by the great landscape gardener Humphry Repton, it's clear you'll lack for nothing to admire here. In the Sorrel Restaurant, panelled in pastel-hued limed oak, it also has a top-end dining space, overseen by the creatively talented Matthew Butcher. Dishes here are dressed to impress, served on irregular plates for maximum visual impact. Torchon of foie gras with maple, watercress and damsons is a good way to start, the richness and acidity complementing each other well, while main courses might see sea bass teamed with baby squid and crisp-fried sweetbreads, alongside pak choi and candied beetroot. Desserts keep up the pace with hazelnut and butterscotch millefeuille, served with caramelised pear and mascarpone sorbet.

Times 12-2/7-9.30

TAUNTON Map 4 ST22

Farthings Country House Hotel and Restaurant

Traditional British

Country-house hotel cuisine built on sound local ingredients

☎ 01823 480664
Village Rd, Hatch Beauchamp TA3 6SG
e-mail: info@farthingshotel.co.uk
dir: M5 junct 25 towards Ilminster, Yeovil, Chard on A358. From A303 turn towards Taunton & M5. Hatch Beauchamp is clearly signposted off A358

A quintessentially English village in Somerset makes the perfect setting for this Georgian country-house hotel. Picturesque grounds, a relaxed ambience and on-the-ball service in the smart traditional restaurant complete the picture. Local produce treated simply and presented without ostentation is the cornerstone of the kitchen's output; the menu name-checks suppliers for each course. Duck eggs from the hotel's own flock are scrambled with smoked eel in a typical starter, followed by pan-seared Dunster Estate venison with smoked bacon, apricots and wild mushrooms. Comforting classics such as bread-and-butter pudding and tarte au citron make a fine finish.

Chef Simon Clewlow **Owner** John Seeger, Kevin Groves **Times** 12-3/6.30-9.15 **Prices** Fixed L 2 course £24-£29, Fixed D 3 course £29-£39, Starter £6-£9, Main £15-£25, Dessert £8-£9, Service optional **Wines** 48 bottles over £20, 3 bottles under £20, 4 by glass **Notes** Sunday L, Vegetarian available, Civ Wed 50 **Seats** 60, Pr/dining room 30 **Children** Portions **Parking** 25

The Mount Somerset Hotel

British, French

Proficient locally-based food in smartly formal surroundings

☎ 01823 442500
Henlade TA3 5NB
e-mail: info@mountsomersethotel.co.uk
dir: M5 junct 25, A358 towards Chard/Ilminster; right in Henlade (Stoke St Mary), left at T-junct. Hotel 400yds on right

Much refurbishment has been going on at the Mount Somerset, with a new spa facility set to launch as we go to print, but the surroundings remain serenely unruffled, nestled as the place is between the Blackdown and Quantock hills. The interior features are pretty head-turning too, not least the majestic sweeping staircase that's just made for grand entrances. The kitchen is plentifully supplied with choice local produce, from Brixham seafood to Exmoor lamb and Quantock chickens, and the smartly formal style suits the context. Start with a refined pairing of smoked salmon and a smoked haddock soufflé in Dijon dressing, before moving on to some of that Exmoor lamb, perhaps served as the roasted rack, with Savoy cabbage purée and tomato relish, or a fillet of John Dory with sautéed squash in vermouth cream. Sticky date pudding with vanilla mousse and toffee milk ice cream, or a fine selection of local cheeses, make grand finales.

Times 12-2/7-9.30

The Willow Tree Restaurant

Modern British

Accomplished locally-based cooking in a waterside location

☎ 01823 352835
3 Tower Ln, Off Tower St TA1 4AR
e-mail: willowtreefood@aol.com
dir: 200yds from Taunton bus station

Tucked away down a little lane in a charming waterside setting, the Willow Tree is worth seeking out. It was once the Taunton moathouse, and retains its inglenook fireplace (complete with wine rack) and oak beams. Run with great authority and aplomb front-of-house, the place also offers some highly accomplished Anglo-French cooking using quality local ingredients. Carefully constructed, aesthetically pleasing dishes might include roast pigeon breast to start, accompanied by butternut squash and truffled potato in a black cherry reduction, or a soufflé of Montgomery cheddar dressed in a cream sauce combining walnut and celery. Superb handling of fish distinguishes a main course of red mullet, served on haricot cassoulet seasoned with smoked paprika, while desserts deliver indulgence in the form of warm chocolate and peanut cake with muscovado ice cream and salted caramel sauce.

Chef Darren Sherlock **Owner** Darren Sherlock & Rita Rambellas **Times** 6.30-9.30 Closed Jan, Aug, Sun-Mon, L all week **Prices** Fixed D 3 course £24.50-£29.95, Service optional, Groups min 7 service 10% **Wines** 20 bottles over £20, 25 bottles under £20, 4 by glass
Notes Vegetarian available, Dress restrictions, Smart casual **Seats** 25, Pr/dining room 15 **Parking** 20 yds, 300 spaces

TINTINHULL Map 4 ST41

Crown & Victoria

British

Handsome village pub serving good local produce

☎ 01935 823341
14 Farm St BA22 8PZ
e-mail: info@thecrownandvictoria.co.uk
dir: Westbound off A303 follow signs for Tintinhull

Famished A303 travellers should take note of this refurbished stone inn, set in a charming village a minute's drive south of the dual carriageway. The attractive gardens make eating outside a popular choice in the summer. The décor is comfortable and inviting, and the traditional pub food - unpretentious and entirely in keeping with the surroundings - is made using the best of local and regional organic produce. Start with mussels cooked in a cider, pancetta and parsley cream sauce, followed by pan-fried duck breast with Madeira jus, and finish with hot chocolate fondant with hazelnut ice cream or a plate of West Country cheeses.

Times 12-2.30/6.30-9.30

WELLS Map 4 ST54

Best Western Swan Hotel

Traditional British

Sound modern cooking in historic inn

☎ 01749 836300
Sadler St BA5 2RX
e-mail: info@swanhotelwells.co.uk
dir: A39, A371, on entering Wells follow signs for Hotels & Deliveries. Hotel on right opposite Cathedral

After 500 years in the shadow of Wells cathedral, this ancient coaching inn was due for a facelift. A top-to-toe makeover in recent years has brought in smart contemporary style, blending immaculately with all the period character you would expect from five centuries of history. The classic dining room offers a memorable setting with its antiques and beautifully-sculpted linen-fold oak panelling; when alfresco dining is on the cards, you can sit outside in a secluded walled garden. Well thought out, daily-changing menus are full of good ideas, founded on top-notch materials from Somerset suppliers - perhaps brown onion and Butcombe ale soup to start, followed by a roasted fillet of Devon hake teamed with curried risotto, buttered spinach and black pudding.

Chef Leigh Say **Owner** Kevin Newton **Times** 12-2/7-9.30 **Prices** Fixed L 2 course £14.50, Starter £4.95-£6.75, Main £12.50-£17.50, Dessert £5.75-£5.95, Service optional **Wines** 20 bottles over £20, 16 bottles under £20, 7 by glass **Notes** Sunday L, Vegetarian available, Civ Wed 70 **Seats** 50, Pr/dining room 100 **Children** Portions, Menu **Parking** 25

Goodfellows

Modern European

Confident cooking in the heart of Wells

☎ 01749 673866
5 Sadler St BA5 2RR
e-mail: goodfellows@btconnect.com
dir: Town centre near Market Place

Behind its mulberry-coloured shop front, Goodfellows serves the local community from breakfast to dinner with a range of tantalising options. Lucky old Wells. There's the informal patisserie and coffee shop at the front part of the ground floor, where you can have lunch or simply a coffee and a cake, and, at the back (and upstairs), a stylish restaurant with an open-plan kitchen delivering some technically accomplished modern European cooking with an emphasis on top-notch fish and seafood. The style here is light and vibrant, with a use of light flavoured oils and vinaigrettes for added oomph. Start with a tian of hand-picked Brixham crab with avocado purée and keta caviar, or chilled gazpacho with crayfish tails and bay artichoke, moving on to roast fillet of halibut with black pudding and Puy lentils, red wine and crème de Cassis sauce. This is confident cooking with precise skills and presentations. The on-site patisserie means puddings and bread are ace, and a six-course tasting menu is available if you want to push the boat out.

Goodfellows

Chef Adam Fellows **Owner** Adam & Martine Fellows **Times** 12-2/6.30-9.30 Closed 25-27 Dec, 1 Jan, Sun-Mon, D Tue **Prices** Fixed L 2 course £16.50, Fixed D 3 course £35, Tasting menu £55, Starter £6.50-£11, Main £11.50-£23, Dessert £6.50-£8.50, Service optional, Groups min 8 service 8% **Wines** 45 bottles over £20, 16 bottles under £20, 16 by glass **Notes** Tasting menu 6 course, Vegetarian available **Seats** 35, Pr/dining room 20 **Children** Portions

The Old Spot

European

Superior bistro in the shadow of the cathedral

☎ 01749 689099
12 Sadler St BA5 2SE
dir: On entering village, follow signs for Hotels & Deliveries. Sadler St leads into High St, Old Spot on left opposite Swan Hotel

This may be our only restaurant entry named after a pig breed, in this case the fabled Gloucestershire Old Spot (as per the signboard). The location is appetising enough in itself, as the place occupies a historic building facing the west front of Wells cathedral. Stripped wooden floors are offset with smartly clothed tables, but the atmosphere is bistro-buzzy, and the cooking quite something. Ian Bates was formerly at Bibendum (see entry, London) and it shows, in dishes such as convincingly rich chicken confit terrine with mustard-dressed leeks and the plangent note of tarragon. Follow that with a superbly mature hanger steak, lightly grilled and sweetly sauced with bone marrow, shallots and red wine, accompanied by powerful, garlicky dauphinoise. Good fish dishes may include pollock fillet with samphire and a tomato and saffron beurre blanc, before simple desserts such as chocolate mousse with praline, or red wine jelly with strawberries and elderflower cream.

Chef Ian Bates **Owner** Ian & Clare Bates **Times** 12.30-2.30/7-10.30 Closed 1 wk Xmas, Mon, L Tue, D Sun **Prices** Food prices not confirmed for 2011. Please telephone for details. **Wines** 56 bottles over £20, 11 bottles under £20, 15 by glass **Notes** Sunday L, Vegetarian available **Seats** 50 **Children** Portions **Parking** On street, Market Square

WEST CAMEL **Map 4 ST52**

The Walnut Tree Hotel

British, French

Hearty food in friendly village hotel

☎ 01935 851292
Fore St BA22 7QW
e-mail: info@thewalnuttreehotel.com
dir: Just off A303 between Sparkford & The RNAS Yeovilton Air Base

Even in a quiet Somerset village hotels have to move with the times, so the Walnut Tree combines the essential easygoing charm and cheerful ambience of a small family-run hotel with a spruce modern look. Stylish claret and cream leather high-backed seats blend tastefully with oak beams and exposed brickwork in the wood-panelled Rosewood restaurant, where exceptionally friendly service is the norm. The kitchen's output focuses on simple hearty cuisine, with a wide-ranging, meat-oriented menu backed by daily-changing specials. Smoked haddock topped with a Welsh rarebit crust is a good way to get going, before moving on to rump of lamb with red wine and rosemary sauce, or fillet of beef Rossini with a rich red wine and Madeira sauce.

Chef Peter Ball **Owner** Mr & Mrs Ball **Times** 12-2/6-8.45 Closed 25-26 Dec, 1 Jan, L Mon, D Sun **Prices** Starter £4.95-£6.95, Main £13.95-£22.95, Dessert £4.95-£5.95, Service optional **Wines** 25 bottles over £20, 20 bottles under £20, 5 by glass **Notes** Sunday L, Vegetarian available, Dress restrictions, Smart casual **Seats** 40 **Children** Portions **Parking** 40

WESTON-SUPER-MARE **Map 4 ST36**

The Cove

Modern British NEW

Stylish seafront dining with a Mediterranean influence

☎ 01934 418217
Marine Lake, Birnbeck Rd BS23 2BX
e-mail: info@the-cove.co.uk
dir: From Grand Pier on Royal Parade N onto Knightstone Rd. Left into Birnbeck Rd. Restaurant on left

Times they are a-changing in Weston-super-Mare, as the northern seafront heads upmarket with an ongoing programme of redevelopment and general sprucing up. Fitting in nicely with this smart new image is this stylishly revamped bistro-style restaurant on the seafront near Birnbeck Pier. Large windows flood the room with light, bare tables are angled cleverly so that no-one has to sit with their back turned to the sea views, and the whole ambience would not feel out of place in a trendy hotspot such as Padstow. Nor would the Mediterranean-accented menu, which deals in cracking fresh produce treated simply and brought together in hard-to-resist flavour combinations. Take lime and chilli crab with white radish and bean sprouts with soy and sesame dressing for starters, then follow with pan-seared sea bass with chorizo, white beans, purple basil and baby squid tempura.

Chef Kieran Lenihan **Owner** Heath Hardy & Gemma Stacey **Times** 12-3/7-9.30 Closed 25 Dec, Mon, D Sun **Prices** Fixed L 3 course fr £14.95, Fixed D 3 course fr £19.95, Starter £4.95-£7, Main £9.95-£18.95, Dessert £4.75-£5, Service optional **Wines** 26 bottles over £20, 21 bottles under £20, 11 by glass **Notes** Fixed D Tue-Thu only, Sunday L, Vegetarian available **Seats** 65 **Children** Portions, Menu **Parking** On street/car park

WINCANTON **Map 4 ST72**

Holbrook House Hotel & Spa

British, French

Versatile modern food in elegant Somerset house

☎ 01963 824466
Holbrook BA9 8BS
e-mail: enquiries@holbrookhouse.co.uk
web: www.holbrookhouse.co.uk
dir: From A303 at Wincanton, turn left on A371 towards Castle Cary & Shepton Mallet

In the 14th century, Holbrook was the home of a Speaker of the House of Commons, indicating something of both the gentility and longevity of the place. It sits today, a creeper-covered, elegant house, amid 20 acres of woodland and pasture, with spa facilities and a range of dining options in the modern way. The Cedar restaurant is the top-notch venue, where orange-papered walls and swagged curtains make a handsome setting for Callum Keir's versatile contemporary cooking. A raviolo of smoked eel with crushed peas and a marjoram-scented sauce is a good opener, while mains are balanced between fish - perhaps turbot with braised red cabbage and a potato and salsify gâteau, sauced with gin - and meats such as Charlton Musgrove beef from a local estate, or loin of venison in red wine. Appealingly presented desserts such as a layered assemblage of lemongrass bavarois, green apple jelly and stewed Agen prunes, end things on a high note.

continued

WINCANTON ***continued***

Chef Callum Keir **Owner** Mr & Mrs J McGinley **Times** 12.30-2/7-9 Closed D Sun **Prices** Food prices not confirmed for 2011. Please telephone for details. **Wines** 86 bottles over £20, 20 bottles under £20, 10 by glass **Notes** Sunday L, Vegetarian available, Dress restrictions, Smart casual, Civ Wed 160 **Seats** 70, Pr/dining room 140 **Children** Portions **Parking** 100

WOOKEY HOLE **Map 4 ST54**

Wookey Hole Inn

Modern European

Vibrant cooking in quirky Somerset inn

☎ 01749 676677
High St BA5 1BP
e-mail: mail@wookeyholeinn.com

The unexpectedly quirky style of this village inn opposite the eponymous caves is a refreshing antidote to the herd of identikit gastro-pubs. The colourful interior is crammed with nods to the Mediterranean, North Africa and hippy-trippy Glastonbury, plus its array of local ales, ciders and perries, and head-banging Belgian beers on tap is an Aladdin's cave for beer and cider fans. True to the décor, the eclectic menu trawls the Mediterranean and further afield for ideas, and it's all made from soundly-sourced, often local materials. Crispy tempura tiger prawns are served with coriander crème fraîche and chilli jam; to follow, roast chicken breast stuffed with haloumi cheese and wrapped in Parma ham is teamed with olive oil and chive mash and leek and chorizo sauce.

Chef Ivan Keable, Michael Davey **Owner** Michael & Richard Davey **Times** 12-2.30/7-9.30 Closed 25 & 26 Dec **Prices** Starter £6-£7, Main £13.25-£23.50, Dessert £4-£6, Service optional **Wines** 6 by glass **Notes** Sunday L, Vegetarian available **Seats** 60, Pr/dining room 12 **Children** Portions, Menu **Parking** 12

YEOVIL **Map 4 ST51**

The Helyar Arms

British

Unpretentious country cooking in a charming medieval inn

☎ 01935 862332
Moor Ln, East Coker BA22 9JR
e-mail: info@helyar-arms.co.uk
dir: 3m from Yeovil. Take A37 or A30. Follow signs for East Coker. Helyar Arms 50mtrs from church

The Helyar Arms is a gem of a 15th-century country inn that relies on crackling log fires, a traditional skittle alley and good honest food to bring in the customers. Friendly young staff keep things ticking over nicely in the dining room - a cosy, rustic chic place with bare-wood tables and leather sofas - while the kitchen takes a fiercely local, seasonal approach to its materials - in fact, if you have a brace of pheasant or basket of home-grown veg to trade, they are happy to do a deal. Expect pub classics such as beer-battered cod with chips and home-made tartare sauce, or sausages with champ mash and onion gravy, alongside rack of lamb with dauphinoise potatoes, braised red cabbage and cardamom jus. Finish with apple and blackberry crumble with vanilla bean custard.

Times 12-2.30/6.30-9.30 Closed 25 Dec

Lanes

Modern British

Crowd-pleasing brasserie cuisine in a striking modern venue

☎ 01935 862555
West Coker BA22 9AJ
e-mail: stay@laneshotel.net
dir: 2m W of Yeovil, on A30 towards Crewkerne

At first sight, this mellow-stone Edwardian rectory looks like a classic country-house hotel. On closer inspection, it is clear that the old place has been transformed into a stylish contemporary venue guaranteed to appeal to design-savvy city slickers looking for a boutique bolt-hole for the weekend. The restaurant makes a striking architectural statement: the modern extension is built of structural plate glass, while vibrant modern artworks hang on white walls, in a sleek designer look involving classy wooden floors, cream leather chairs and unclothed wooden tables. The cooking suits the modish setting:

Little Barwick House

YEOVIL **Map 4 ST51**

Modern European NOTABLE WINE LIST

Tranquil restaurant with rooms serving food of powerful simplicity

☎ 01935 423902
Barwick Village BA22 9TD
e-mail: reservations@barwick7.fsnet.co.uk
dir: Turn off A371 Yeovil to Dorchester opposite Red House rdbt, 0.25m on left

The West Country is full of tranquil getaways and peaceful retreats, but Little Barwick stands out from the crowd. It's hidden away down a little lane in a village not far from Yeovil, with acres of gardens for wandering in, acres of tactile fabrics and comfy sofas inside, and staff who are willing to chat if you so wish. An elegant dining room with well-spaced tables and candles manages to avoid any suggestion of starchiness, thanks to Emma Ford's serene professionalism. Husband Tim cooks a finely judged version of modern European food, achieving depths of flavour without ambiguity and without undue delegation. Witness a grilled fillet of red mullet, generous in size, sublimely flavoured, with carrot and orange escabèche to add bite, and a sesame dressing to bind the whole dish together. Saddle of wild venison with beetroot purée and braised red cabbage is a tour de force, its resonance all the more astonishing for being conjured out of such economy of means. That note of powerful simplicity is sustained in a dessert such as dark chocolate and cherry tart, with silky dark chocolate sauce and fine vanilla ice cream. An excellent wine list only adds to the sense of occasion.

Chef Timothy Ford **Owner** Emma & Timothy Ford **Times** 12-2/7-9.30 Closed New Year, 2wks Jan, Mon, L Tues, D Sun **Prices** Food prices not confirmed for 2011. Please telephone for details, Service optional **Wines** 179 bottles over £20, 21 bottles under £20, 6 by glass **Notes** ALC L 2/3 course fr £20.95/fr £24.95, D 3 course £39.95, Sunday L, Vegetarian available **Seats** 40 **Children** Portions **Parking** 25

dishes range from unfussy brasserie classics along the lines of lamb's liver and bacon, or posh burgers made with smoked Applewood cheddar, through to more ambitious ideas that see scallops appearing with artichoke purée, wild mushrooms and Madeira velouté, ahead of hake fillet with yoghurt mash, wilted samphire and lobster bisque. A helpful approach to wine sees the list divided according to style, so you can home in on anything from fresh and zesty to heavy, rich and powerful.

Times 12-2.30/7-9.30 Closed L Sat

Little Barwick House

®®® – *see opposite page*

Yeovil Court Hotel & Restaurant

®® Modern European

Family-run hotel with appealing menu

☎ 01935 863746
West Coker Rd BA20 2HE
e-mail: unwind@yeovilhotel.com
dir: On A30, 2.5m W of town centre

It's hard to believe, but back in the '80s this welcoming, family-run hotel was a broken down B&B. Since then, it has gone from strength to strength, and after a recent makeover, it sports a smart contemporary look. Clean-cut modern style defines the restaurant too, with an eye-catching décor in shades of chocolate, cream and black against a neutral white backdrop. The food matches the setting: modern, confident, understated dishes founded on judiciously-sourced seasonal ingredients are the kitchen's stock in trade - perhaps a hearty British classic such as slow-braised lamb shank with creamed potato, carrots and swede with onion gravy, or fresh market fish in the shape of pan-fried lemon sole with garlic butter, rocket and parmesan salad, and French fries. Desserts are equally fuss-free - steamed spotted dick with honey custard is a good way to finish.

Chef Simon Walford **Owner** Brian Devonport **Times** 12-1.45/7-9.30 Closed 26-30 Dec, L Sat **Prices** Fixed L 2 course £9-£12, Starter £4-£7.90, Main £11-£19.90, Dessert £4.25-£6, Service optional **Wines** 12 bottles over £20, 27 bottles under £20, 8 by glass **Notes** Sunday L, Vegetarian available **Seats** 50, Pr/dining room 80 **Children** Portions **Parking** 65

STAFFORDSHIRE

BURTON UPON TRENT — Map 10 SK22

The Grill Room

® Modern British

Central location, ambitious kitchen team

☎ 01283 523800
Three Queens Hotel, 1 Bridge St DE14 1SY
e-mail: restaurant@threequeenshotel.co.uk
dir: On A511, at junct of High St & Bridge St

In the centre of the town close to the river, this smart, comfortable hotel dates back to 1531 and is a great base for touring the area. The Grill Room is an intimate dining room, reminiscent of a Victorian gentlemen's dining club with its hardwood panelling and screens. The food is based around traditional preparations, with a contemporary eye for presentation and delivering some big flavours. Expect sautéed scallops on black pudding served with chilli salsa, perhaps followed by steaks from the grill or slow-roasted loin of Staffordshire pork with potatoes and a Jack Daniels and marmalade jus.

Chef Craig Tyrell **Owner** Three Queens Hotel Ltd **Times** 6.15-10 Closed L all week **Prices** Fixed D 3 course £17.50, Starter £4.25-£6.50, Main £12.95-£18.95, Dessert £4.95-£5.95, Service optional **Wines** 17 bottles over £20, 18 bottles under £20, 8 by glass **Notes** Gourmet D £39.50, Vegetarian available **Seats** 36, Pr/dining room 60 **Children** Portions, Menu **Parking** 40

LEEK — Map 16 SJ95

Peak Weavers Rooms & Restaurant

® Modern British

Fresh local ingredients treated with due diligence

☎ 01538 383729
21 King St ST13 5NW
e-mail: info@peakweavershotel.co.uk
dir: In town centre behind St Mary's Church, off A53

This charming guest house and intimate restaurant has certainly had a varied career: built originally in the Regency period as a local mill owner's residence, it then served as a Catholic convent for 120 years before abandoning its life of abstinence. Nick Bettany presides over front-of-house, while wife Emma rules the culinary domain, letting first-class local and seasonal produce speak for itself in accurately-cooked dishes. Her style is straightforward, honest cooking refreshingly shorn of affectation - expect medallions of wild venison with red wine and morello cherry jus, or roasted cod with salsa verde, rocket and basil oil, and end with date bread-and-butter pudding with boozy toffee sauce.

Chef Emma Bettany **Owner** Nick & Emma Bettany **Times** 6.45-9 Closed Xmas & New Year, Sun-Wed **Prices** Starter £3.95-£6.95, Main £11.95-£18.95, Dessert £3.50-£5.95, Service optional, Groups min 10 service 7.5% **Wines** 15 bottles over £20, 30 bottles under £20, 4 by glass **Notes** Vegetarian available, Dress restrictions, Smart casual **Seats** 40 **Children** Portions **Parking** 18

Three Horseshoes Inn & Country Hotel

®® Modern British, Thai V

Well-cooked Thai and British cuisine in traditional inn

☎ 01538 300296
Buxton Rd, Blackshaw Moor ST13 8TW
e-mail: enquiries@threeshoesinn.co.uk
dir: M6 junct 15 or 16 onto A500. Exit A53 towards Leek. Turn left onto A50 (Burslem)

It is worth the trip to this sprawling creeper-clad inn in the Peak District National Park just for the views of the Staffordshire Moorlands and Tittesworth reservoir from its lovely gardens. Inside are all the ancient beams, gleaming brass and chunky rustic furniture you'd expect in a classic country inn, while you can eat beneath the oak-truss roof of the bustling brasserie or in the more formal restaurant. The menu deals in gutsy modern British cooking with a Thai accent, while the chefs do their stuff in the open, glass-walled kitchen for a bit of culinary theatre. Start with shredded duck salad with hoi sin and sesame, followed by local beef served as a fillet with parmesan cream, and a daube infused with oriental spicing, and partnered with roasted shallots and shallot sauce.

Chef Mark & Stephen Kirk **Owner** Bill, Jill, Mark & Stephen Kirk **Times** 6.30-9 Closed 26-30 Dec, L Mon-Sat **Prices** Starter £4.95-£8.95, Main £9.95-£18.95, Dessert £4.50-£6 **Wines** 30 bottles over £20, 50 bottles under £20, 10 by glass **Notes** Tasting menu available, Vegetarian menu, Dress restrictions, Smart casual, Civ Wed 150 **Seats** 50, Pr/dining room 150 **Children** Portions, Menu **Parking** 100

LICHFIELD — Map 10 SK10

The Four Seasons Restaurant

®® Modern British

Modern British menu in a handsome Georgian mansion

☎ 01543 481494
Swinfen Hall Hotel, Swinfen WS14 9RE
e-mail: info@swinfenhallhotel.co.uk
dir: 2m S of Lichfield on A38 between Weeford rdbt & Swinfen rdbt. Follow A38 to Lichfield, hotel 0.5m on right

The handsome neo-classical house dates from the time of George III, with the south wing added in Edwardian times by a Swinfen who had married into Eno's Liver Salts money. Inside is fittingly grand, with oak panelling, many

continued

LICHFIELD *continued*

fine paintings and swagged curtains in the Four Seasons dining room, and there's also a tiled terrace for clement days. The cooking plots a modern British course, with fruit and veg grown in the Hall's own walled garden and deer from the park providing the venison. Start with red mullet on tagliatelle, dressed at the table with tomato and saffron consommé, and continue with honeyed, spiced Gressingham duck breast, served with a large raviolo of the confit leg meat, alongside pak choi from the garden.

Chef Adam Thomson **Owner** Helen & Vic Wiser **Times** 12.30-2.30/7.30-9.30 Closed L Sat, D Sun **Prices** Fixed L 2 course fr £19.95, Fixed D 3 course £45, Service optional **Wines** 108 bottles over £20, 9 bottles under £20, 6 by glass **Notes** Sunday L, Vegetarian available, Dress restrictions, No trainers or jeans, Civ Wed 120 **Seats** 50, Pr/dining room 20 **Parking** 80

STAFFORD **Map 10 SJ92**

Moat House

Modern British

Conservatory dining in a Staffordshire village

☎ 01785 712217
Lower Penkridge Rd, Acton Trussell ST17 0RJ
e-mail: info@thelewispartnership.co.uk
dir: M6 junct 13 towards Stafford, 1st right to Acton Trussell, hotel by church

This 14th-century moated manor house in the heart of Staffordshire has developed from a village pub into a sizeable hotel and restaurant popular for weddings and business conferences. The Conservatory restaurant is a contemporary, airy and stylish affair where you can expect to indulge in creative British food with French roots. Kick things off with ravioli of lobster and Loch Duart salmon, leeks à la crème, shellfish bisque and lemon oil then move onto loin of Windsor estate venison cooked in Lapsang Souchong tea, with slow-cooked belly pork, baby turnips, Savoy cabbage, Jerusalem artichoke purée and a port wine sauce. Finish with hot bittersweet chocolate fondant served with a bay leaf ice cream and chocolate 'soil'.

Chef Matthew Davies **Owner** The Lewis Partnership **Times** 12-2/6.30-9.30 Closed 25 Dec **Prices** Fixed L 2 course £15.50, Fixed D 3 course £30, Service optional **Wines** 94 bottles over £20, 41 bottles under £20, 16 by glass **Notes** Tasting & early doors menu available, Sunday L, Vegetarian available, Dress restrictions, No jeans, Civ Wed 120 **Seats** 120, Pr/dining room 150 **Children** Portions, Menu **Parking** 200

STOKE-ON-TRENT **Map 10 SJ84**

The Manor at Hanchurch

Modern Italian

Authentic Italian cuisine in tranquil surroundings

☎ 01782 643080 & 07703 744479
Newcastle Rd, Hanchurch ST4 8SD
e-mail: info@hanchurchmanor.co.uk
dir: M6 junct 15, 3rd exit at rdbt & 3rd exit onto Clayton Rd A519 through lights. After driving under M6 mtrwy bridge hotel is on right

The thatched and half-timbered Manor at Hanchurch was designed by Sir Charles Barry who was normally engaged on rather weightier commissions, such as the Houses of Parliament. It's in a handy spot for the M6, but remains unruffled by the presence of this mighty artery, screened by tranquil wooded gardens. The dining room is still the same clean-cut place it always was - neutral tones of mushroom and beige, crisp white linen draping down to herringbone parquet floors - but the culinary concept has changed radically, rebranding itself as Maldini's and dealing in a wide-ranging Italian repertoire. The kitchen turns out plenty of uncomplicated old favourites - start with baked mushrooms stuffed with gorgonzola and wrapped in Parma ham, and follow with pan-seared scallops with spring onion and chive risotto. A classic tiramisu makes a fitting finale to a simple, flavoursome meal.

Times 12-2.30/7-10

UTTOXETER **Map 10 SK03**

Restaurant Gilmore at Strine's Farm

Modern British

Confident cooking in charming converted farmhouse

☎ 01889 507100
Beamhurst ST14 5DZ
e-mail: paul@restaurantgilmore.com
dir: 1.5m N of Uttoxeter on A522 to Cheadle. Set 400yds back from road along fenced farm track

Paul and Dee Gilmore's three-storey converted farmhouse is in Staffordshire spa country, a short drive outside Uttoxeter. The house is full of rustic charm and country comforts, the dining room decorated in warm natural tones. The kitchen takes considerable care with the sourcing of produce, with the local suppliers getting a good look in; a kitchen garden supplies much of the fresh stuff. Menus change monthly, and the cooking style follows a modern British path with solid classical foundations. Ham hock and roast vegetable terrine with piccalilli is a nicely contemporary opener, or go for chestnut mushroom velouté finished with a wild mushroom oil. Main-course roast loin of Staffordshire venison comes with sweet and sour cabbage, and for dessert, perhaps a garden rhubarb and vanilla brûlée.

Chef Paul Gilmore **Owner** Paul & Dee Gilmore **Times** 12.30-2.30/7.30-9.30 Closed 1 wk Jan, 1 wk Etr, 1 wk Jul, 1 wk Oct, Mon-Tue, L Sat & Wed, D Sun **Prices** Fixed L 2 course £24, Fixed D 3 course £42.50, Service optional, Groups min 8 service 10% **Wines** 33 bottles over £20, 14 bottles under £20, 10 by glass **Notes** Sunday L, Vegetarian available, Dress restrictions, Smart casual **Seats** 24 **Children** Portions **Parking** 12

SUFFOLK

ALDEBURGH **Map 13 TM45**

Best Western White Lion Hotel

Modern British

Suffolk's bounty cooked without fuss by the sea

☎ 01728 452720
Market Cross Place IP15 5BJ
e-mail: info@whitelion.co.uk
dir: A12 onto A1094, follow signs to Aldeburgh at junct on left. Hotel on right

Freshly-landed fish is sold from wooden huts on Aldeburgh's shingle beach, so it is fitting that the village's oldest hotel still places a firm emphasis on serving great food. The White Lion dates from the 16th century, and has plenty of character from period features - a beautifully-carved inglenook in the bar, and oak panels in the restaurant - blending seamlessly with a smart modern refurbishment. Fantastic Suffolk produce - including fish from the beach, of course - drives the kitchen's unfussy British cooking. Expect appealing dishes that stay in touch with modern trends - deep-fried crab and ginger cakes with aïoli and rocket, say, followed by roast chicken with herb rösti and purple-sprouting broccoli, and lemon tart with crushed raspberries to finish.

Times 12-2.30/6.30-9.30

Brudenell

Modern European

Mediterranean style on the Suffolk coast

☎ 01728 452071
Brudenell Hotel, The Parade IP15 5BU
e-mail: info@brudenellhotel.co.uk
dir: A12/A1094, on reaching town, turn right at junct into High St. Hotel on seafront adjoining Fort Green car park

Just a step away from the beach of this delightful Suffolk town, this gracious Edwardian seaside hotel enjoys stunning sea and coastal views from refurbished bedrooms and The Bru, the hotel's modern and bright split-level restaurant. Expect stripped wooden tables with modern settings, colourful seating, soothing pastel colours, and big picture windows that frame the sea views; go for a table on the terrace if the weather allows. Weekly menus showcase unpretentious contemporary European dishes, which are skilfully prepared using quality seasonal produce, notably seafood landed by local fishermen. Start with crab and tomato risotto with ginger and herbs, followed by roast cod with sorrel and spinach velouté, or rabbit with tortellini and roast morel sauce.

Chef Justin Kett **Owner** Thorpeness & Aldeburgh Hotels Ltd **Times** 12-2.30/6.30-9.30 **Prices** Starter £5.95-£9, Main £9.50-£22, Dessert £5.50, Service optional **Wines** 56 bottles over £20, 26 bottles under £20, 21 by glass **Notes** Sunday L, Vegetarian available, Dress restrictions, Smart casual **Seats** 100, Pr/dining room 14 **Children** Portions, Menu **Parking** 15

152 Aldeburgh

Modern British, European

Unpretentious food in friendly beachside brasserie

☎ 01728 454594
152 High St IP15 5AX
e-mail: info@152aldeburgh.co.uk
web: www.152aldeburgh.co.uk

The feel of summer pervades this simple, sunny brasserie in a busy corner site by an archway linking the high street to the beach. The relaxed contemporary vibe is right in tune with the arty Aldeburgh vibe, and the place is a magnet for locals and festival-goers. Given the location, it's no surprise that fish and seafood are a strong suit on its to-the-point menus of seasonal modern European dishes. Take potted shrimps in lemon and dill butter with rustic granary bread for a joyously simple starter, then locally-landed cod and chips with home-made tartare sauce for a superior version of a classic. Carnivores aren't marginalised either, as shown in main-course confit duck.

Chef Christopher Easters **Owner** Andrew Lister **Times** 12-3/6-10 **Prices** Starter £4.95-£9.95, Main £9.95-£17.95, Dessert £4.50-£5.95, Service optional **Wines** 13 bottles over £20, 24 bottles under £20, 7 by glass **Notes** Sunday L, Vegetarian available **Seats** 56 **Children** Portions, Menu **Parking** On street parking on High St & Kings St

Regatta Restaurant

Modern British

Buzzy bistro where local fish is the star

☎ 01728 452011
171 High St IP15 5AN
e-mail: rob.mabey@btinternet.com
dir: Middle of High St, town centre

Recently refurbished with comfortable banquettes, clean lines and a stylish décor, this lively and contemporary bistro is renowned for its freshly-caught local fish and seafood. Look to the chalkboard for the day's offerings, perhaps bruschetta of crayfish with wild mushrooms, trio of smoked salmon with smoked prawns and brandon rost, or tempura of sole with saffron fricassée. Carnivores will not be disappointed with crispy duck confit on mustard mash with roast garlic and bacon sauce, while puddings may include warm treacle tart with vanilla ice cream. Food comes simply cooked and presented with clear flavours from the wonderfully fresh ingredients. Lookout for the special gourmet evenings.

Chef Robert Mabey **Owner** Mr & Mrs R Mabey **Times** 12-2/6-10 Closed 24-26 Dec, D Sun (Nov-Feb) **Prices** Starter £4-£7.50, Main £10-£18, Dessert £4-£5.50 **Wines** 6 bottles over £20, 40 bottles under £20, 6 by glass **Notes** Sunday L, Vegetarian available **Seats** 90, Pr/dining room 30 **Children** Portions, Menu **Parking** On street

Wentworth Hotel

Modern British

Great local seafood in a delightful seafront hotel

☎ 01728 452312
Wentworth Rd IP15 5BD
e-mail: stay@wentworth-aldeburgh.co.uk
dir: From A12 take A1094 to Aldeburgh. In Aldeburgh straight on at mini rdbt, turn left at x-roads into Wentworth Rd. Hotel on right

Tucked away at the peaceful end of Aldeburgh's seafront, tradition is the watchword at the Wentworth - it has, after all, been managed by the Pitt family for 90 years. Perhaps this long line of family involvement is why the hotel's trio of plush lounges have the feel of a stylish private residence. The cocktail bar is a pleasant spot for an aperitif before moving into the classy dining room, where you get sea views, claret walls hung with oval-framed portraits, and candlelit tables swathed in linen. The kitchen cooks in a style that suits the Aldeburgh mood - traditional Anglo-French, perked up with a modern edge, and paying due attention to the seasons on daily-changing menus. Pan-fried fishcake with sweet chilli dressing is a good way to get going, followed, perhaps, by fillet of sea bream with cannellini bean and tomato casserole, and rounding off with a good old plum and almond sponge with custard.

Chef Tim Keeble **Owner** Wentworth Hotel Ltd/Michael Pritt **Times** 12-2/7-9 **Prices** Fixed L 2 course £10-£18, Fixed D 3 course £19-£23, Service optional **Wines** 40 bottles over £20, 23 bottles under £20, 9 by glass **Notes** Sunday L, Vegetarian available **Seats** 90, Pr/dining room 20 **Children** Portions, Menu **Parking** 33

BILDESTON Map 13 TL94

The Bildeston Crown

– *see page 380*

BRANDESTON Map 13 TM26

The Queen's Head Inn

Modern British NEW

Friendly village inn with hearty modern cooking

☎ 01728 685307
The Street IP13 7AD
e-mail: thequeensheadinn@btconnect.com
dir: Signed from A1120 at Earl Soham, follow signs to village, on left hand side

The Suffolk village of Brandeston oozes history and a real sense of community, and at its heart is this smartly-refurbished inn that hosts the village fete, beer festivals and summertime hog roasts. Mind you, things weren't always this peaceful: among the skeletons rattling in its historical cupboard are witchfinding trials and involvement in the smuggling trade. Nowadays you're welcomed with a fine pint of Adnams and forthright modern British cooking with full-on flavours. Starters might offer chicken liver parfait with apple chutney and toasted brioche; meaty mains include the likes of saddle of venison served with its own 'cottage pie' and braised red cabbage, or twice-cooked pork belly with bacon and cabbage mash and leek and mustard cream.

Chef Alan Randall, Daniel Bryant **Owner** Alan Randall **Times** 12-2/6.30-9 Closed Mon, D Sun **Prices** Starter £4-£7, Main £9-£17, Dessert £4-£7, Service optional **Wines** 10 bottles over £20, 12 bottles under £20, 9 by glass **Notes** Sunday L, Vegetarian available **Seats** 65 **Children** Portions, Menu **Parking** 25, On street

The Bildeston Crown

BILDESTON Map 13 TL94

Modern British NOTABLE WINE LIST

Classic culinary reinterpretations in an ancient timbered inn

☎ 01449 740510
104 High St IP7 7EB
e-mail: hayley@thebildestoncrown.co.uk
web: www.thebildestoncrown.co.uk
dir: A12 junct 31. B1070 to Hadleigh, B1115 to Bildeston

The buttery-yellow half-timbered 15th-century exterior of The Bildeston Crown says classic old inn; once inside, however, you're greeted with a distinctly contemporary wow factor, by a voguish fusion of medieval fireplaces and head-skimming ancient beams with bare wooden tables and high-backed seats. The kitchen takes a similar attitude with its modern British output: a menu of classics sits alongside some rather more adventurous contemporary offerings. Whichever you go for, local produce sits at the heart of the kitchen's ethos - beef is invariably of the Suffolk rare breed Red Poll variety, while lamb travels but a few miles from nearby Semer, and pork from Nedging. Be prepared for some interesting, inventive takes on traditional ideas: a watercress velouté comes with tikka frog's leg and garlic, while a main-course cod is accompanied by its confit cheek, ham and a kick of fennel. If you're in a less experimental frame of mind, the 'Crown Classics' menu offers the comfortable familiarity of braised Red Poll faggot with artichoke mash, followed by Semer mutton hotpot with red cabbage. When it comes to dessert, a classic tarte Tatin is reworked with goats' milk and a sage and apple doughnut, while the menu of fine British cheeses tempts with the likes of Sussex Dammer, Bosworth Ash and Barkham Blue.

Chef Chris Lee **Owner** Mrs G Buckle, Mr J K Buckle **Times** 12-7/3-10 Closed D 25-26 Dec, 1 Jan **Prices** Food prices not confirmed for 2011. Please telephone for details. **Wines** 118 bottles over £20, 18 bottles under £20, 17 by glass **Notes** Sunday L, Vegetarian available, Civ Wed 24 **Seats** 100, Pr/dining room 16 **Children** Portions **Parking** 36, Market Sq

BUNGAY Map 13 TM38

Earsham Street Café

Modern British, Mediterranean

Anglo-Mediterranean cooking in an unpretentious café

☎ 01986 893103
13 Earsham St NR35 1AE
e-mail: www.earshamstcafe@aol.com
dir: In village centre

Every town should have a café like this: a real café you can pop into for a cake, snack or a full-on meal from an eclectic modern brasserie-style menu, served with unstuffy professionalism. Although, popping in off the cuff might mean disappointment - this place is so popular that booking is the best bet to avoid being turned away. They are not trying to reinvent the wheel here - menus take a tried-and-tested modern British route, sexed up with a fair sprinkling of Mediterranean ideas, as in an appealing combination of tagliatelle with walnuts, wild mushrooms, lime and parmesan shavings, or baked sea bass with chick peas, fine beans and chorizo. Meat dishes are hearty stuff - perhaps best end of lamb with dauphinoise potato, celeriac purée and sticky red cabbage, while desserts range from bread-and-butter pudding with vanilla custard, to chilled elderflower rice pudding with vodka stewed rhubarb.

Chef Stephen David **Owner** Rebecca Mackenzie, Stephen David **Times** 9.30-4.30/7-9 Closed Xmas, New Year, BHs, D ex last Fri & Sat of month **Prices** Starter £5-£10, Main £10-£18, Dessert £6, Service optional **Wines** 27 bottles over £20, 22 bottles under £20, 16 by glass **Notes** Pre-concert lunches available, Vegetarian available **Seats** 55, Pr/dining room 16 **Children** Portions, Menu **Parking** Parking opposite

BURY ST EDMUNDS Map 13 TL86

Angel Hotel - The Eaterie

Modern British

Carefully-sourced menu in grand old coaching inn

☎ 01284 714000
Angel Hill IP33 1LT
e-mail: staying@theangel.co.uk
dir: Town centre, right from lights at Northgate St

With a prime position overlooking the cathedral and the old abbey walls, The Angel meets all initial expectations of an old Georgian coaching inn; its façade is on the grand side and creepers have had plenty of time to work their way across the brickwork. Inside, the generous Georgian spaces have a more contemporary feel, especially in The Eaterie, where artworks, light-wood tables and designer high-backed chairs make for a pleasingly up-to-date setting. The kitchen shows 21st-century sensibilities for sourcing tip-top local produce and a keen eye for appealing flavour combinations along with a lack of unnecessary embellishment. Seared scallops with black pudding, cauliflower purée and sweet cured bacon is a worthy signature starter, followed, perhaps, with a roast loin of venison with pearl barley and a wild mushroom risotto.

Chef Simon Barker **Owner** Robert Gough **Times** 7am-9.30pm **Prices** Fixed L 2 course fr £12.50, Starter £4.50-£9.50, Main £9.95-£24.50, Dessert £4-£9.95, Service optional **Wines** 49 bottles over £20, 21 bottles under £20, 34 by glass **Notes** Sunday L, Vegetarian available, Dress restrictions, Smart casual/dress, Civ Wed 85 **Seats** 85, Pr/dining room 80 **Children** Portions, Menu **Parking** 30

Clarice House

Modern European

Upmarket health and beauty spa with modern menu

☎ 01284 705550
Horringer Court, Horringer Rd IP29 5PH
e-mail: bury@claricehouse.co.uk
dir: From Bury St Edmunds on A143 towards Horringer and Haverhill, hotel 1m from town centre on right

Pampering in the spa is foremost in the minds of most visitors to Clarice House. After a serious detox session and a walk around the gorgeous landscaped gardens of the Jacobean-style country house, take a table in the oak-panelled restaurant, a smartly traditional venue with well-spaced tables laid with pristine white linen. The kitchen deals in modern European cuisine on a wide-ranging menu that has something for everyone, including, of course, some light and healthy options. You might start with prosciutto served with chargrilled courgettes, pine nuts, parmesan and basil, followed by a more substantial smoked Suffolk ham hock with roasted root vegetables and pease pudding. Dessert? - oh go on then - how about baked chocolate hazelnut mousse cake with crème fraîche.

Chef Steve Winser **Owner** King Family **Times** 12-2/7-9 Closed 25-26 Dec, 1 Jan **Prices** Fixed L 2 course £18.95, Fixed D 3 course £26.95, Starter £5-£7, Main £10-£19, Dessert £5-£7, Service optional **Wines** 29 bottles over £20, 10 bottles under £20, 10 by glass **Notes** Sunday L, Vegetarian available, Dress restrictions, Smart casual D, Civ Wed 100 **Seats** 70, Pr/dining room 20 **Parking** 82

The Leaping Hare Restaurant & Country Store

Modern British

Picturesque vineyard restaurant serving modern British dishes

☎ 01359 250287
Wyken Vineyards, Stanton IP31 2DW
e-mail: info@wykenvineyards.co.uk
dir: 8m NE of Bury St Edmunds, 1m off A143. Follow brown signs at Ixworth to Wyken Vineyards

Recorded long ago in the Domesday book, the ancient Wyken estate has its roots set deep into heavenly Suffolk countryside. Ancient woodland, an Elizabethan manor, and a working vineyard all have their attractions, but none so pressing for foodies than the café and restaurant in a 400-year-old timbered barn. The leaping hare monicker is celebrated in paintings and tapestries, while wood-burning stoves, exposed beams, wooden floors and expansive windows opening onto fields and woodlands make an inviting setting for Mediterranean-influenced modern British fodder. Much of what's on the menu comes from the estate - including award-winning wines from the vineyard. Slow-cooked Suffolk pork belly with Charentais melon salad is a good prelude to main-course Sutton Hoo chicken breast with summer vegetables.

Chef Jon Ellis **Owner** Kenneth & Carla Carlisle **Times** 12-2.30/7-9 Closed 2 wks Xmas, D Sun-Thu **Prices** Fixed L 2 course fr £15.95, Starter £5.95-£8.95, Main £12.95-£23.95, Dessert £5.95-£7.95, Service optional, Groups min 6 service 10% **Wines** 16 bottles over £20, 22 bottles under £20, 17 by glass **Notes** Sunday L, Vegetarian available **Seats** 55 **Children** Portions **Parking** 50

Maison Bleue

Modern French

Upbeat modern French seafood brasserie

☎ 01284 760623
30-31 Churchgate St IP33 1RG
e-mail: info@maisonbleue.co.uk
dir: A14 junct 43 (Sugar Beet, Central exit) to town centre. Follow signs to the Abbey Gdns, Churchgate St is opposite cathedral

Centrally located in Bury St Edmunds, on a quiet street close to the cathedral, this stylish modern French restaurant is worth seeking out for its fresh fish and seafood. The setting is sleek, contemporary and intimate, with cream leather seating, original artwork on warm, pastel-painted walls, and linen-clad tables adorned with candles and quality glassware. Cooking is accomplished and pleasingly straightforward. The excellent value lunchtime 'plat du jour with coffee' is a real winner - booking is advisable. Fresh, clear flavours shine through in dishes like seared scallops with chorizo-infused potato mousseline and tomato dressing and halibut with cauliflower and Dijon mustard tapenade and green olive sauce. Carnivores are not forgotten - try the beef fillet with mushroom sauce - and puddings may include dark chocolate and raspberry tart.

Chef Pascal Canevet **Owner** Regis Crepy **Times** 12-2.30/7-9.30 Closed Jan, 2 wks summer, Sun-Mon **Prices** Fixed L 2 course £16.95, Fixed D 3 course £28.95, Starter £6.50-£14.95, Main £14.50-£26.95, Dessert £5.95, Service optional **Notes** Vegetarian available, Dress restrictions, Smart casual recommended **Seats** 65, Pr/dining room 35 **Children** Portions **Parking** On street

BURY ST EDMUNDS *continued*

Priory Hotel

Modern European

Modern European food in characterful building

01284 766181
Mildenhall Rd IP32 6EH
e-mail: reservations@prioryhotel.co.uk
dir: From A14 take Bury St Edmunds W slip road. Follow signs to Brandon. At mini-rdbt turn right. Hotel 0.5m on left

The Grade II listed Priory Hotel was built on the remains of a 13th-century priory on the outskirts of the town centre. The recently updated and restyled Garden Room restaurant is modern and comfortable and is located by the manicured gardens. Modern European and British dishes showcase local produce and are presented on good quality white china by the well-drilled staff. Start with something like pan-seared pigeon breast served in a warm salad of pear, pancetta and new potatoes or a main course of slow-cooked belly of Suffolk pork with bubble-and-squeak and creamed cabbage and onion marmalade. Finish with dark chocolate torte, iced banana parfait and coconut sorbet.

Chef Graham Smith **Owner** Priory Hotel
Times 12.30-2/7-10 Closed L Sat **Prices** Food prices not confirmed for 2011. Please telephone for details.
Wines 20 bottles over £20, 12 bottles under £20, 6 by glass **Notes** Sunday L, Vegetarian available, Civ Wed 55 **Seats** 74, Pr/dining room 26 **Children** Portions **Parking** 60

Ravenwood Hall Country Hotel & Restaurant

Modern British

Tudor charm and confident cooking

01359 270345
Rougham IP30 9JA
e-mail: enquiries@ravenwoodhall.co.uk
dir: 3m from Bury St Edmunds, just off A14 junct 45 signed Rougham

Hidden away inside seven acres of woodland and expansive lawns, Ravenwood Hall dates from the reign of Henry VIII, so you can expect character in spades, in the shape of ornately carved oak beams, original Tudor wall paintings, antique furniture and roaring log fires in walk-in inglenooks. The classy formal dining room - a romantic candlelit place with sculpted timbers - was once the main living hall, and makes a fitting venue for traditional British cooking liberally sprinkled with modern touches. The kitchen relies on first-class seasonal materials, including meat and fish smoked in-house and home-preserved fruits and vegetables; carpaccio of Denham Estate venison with air-dried bresaola with truffle dressing and parmesan might start things off, followed by a steamed beef and ale suet pudding with braised ox cheeks, celeriac purée and ale jus that the Tudors wouldn't have found too alien a concept. Finish right back in the 21st century with a zingy organic lime and lemon tart with a millefeuille and gel of passionfruit.

Chef Saurav Kumar **Owner** Craig Jarvis
Times 12-2/7-9.30 **Prices** Food prices not confirmed for 2011. Please telephone for details. **Wines** 54 bottles over £20, 32 bottles under £20, 11 by glass **Notes** Sunday L, Vegetarian available, Civ Wed 130 **Seats** 50, Pr/dining room 50 **Children** Portions, Menu **Parking** 150

CHILLESFORD — Map 13 TM35

The Froize Freehouse Restaurant

Traditional British, European

Rustic flavours in a red-brick inn

01394 450282
The Street IP12 3PU
e-mail: dine@froize.co.uk
dir: On B1084 between Woodbridge & Orford

This charming Suffolk country inn combines old-fashioned hospitality and contemporary style with great success. Always busy, a bustling atmosphere is guaranteed. On the menu there's English and French rustic dishes using local seafood and game in season. To start, perhaps terrine of hare and chestnuts with cider and orange jelly. Mains, including honey-roast lamb shank with caramelised shallots are then all served from the high quality hot buffet. Desserts are treated with reverence and there's a decent selection – try upside down ginger pudding or mango, papaya and passionfruit Pavlova.

Chef David Grimwood **Owner** David Grimwood
Times 12-2/7 Closed Mon (ex BHs) **Prices** Fixed L 2 course fr £18.50, Fixed D 3 course fr £26, Service optional **Wines** 6 bottles over £20, 14 bottles under £20, 14 by glass **Notes** Sunday L, Vegetarian available **Seats** 48 **Children** Portions

DUNWICH — Map 13 TM47

The Ship Inn

Traditional British NEW

Traditional British cooking in idyllic village pub

01728 648219
St James St IP17 3DT
e-mail: info@shipatdunwich.co.uk
dir: From N: A12, exit at Blythburgh onto B1125, then left to village. Inn at end of road. From S: A12, turn right to Westleton. Follow signs for Dunwich

Once the haunt of smugglers, The Ship is located in a peaceful village surrounded by nature reserves, heathland and beaches. This traditional old inn has bags of charm and character and after a pint in the bar with its real fire, move into the attractive conservatory or covered courtyard overlooking the landscaped garden. There is a choice of dining options here but the restaurant has the benefits of comfortable padded chairs and a wood burner at one end. The food is pleasingly straightforward British cooking – chicken liver pâté might be followed by fresh plaice and chips, with Bakewell tart rounding things off.

Times 6-9 **Prices** Food prices not confirmed for 2011. Please telephone for details.

EYE — Map 13 TM17

Lexington

Modern British

Charming country-house dining

01379 870326
The Cornwallis Hotel, Rectory Rd, Brome IP23 8AJ
e-mail: reservations.cornwallis@ohiml.com

A long drive lined with beautiful lime trees leads you up to the Cornwallis Hotel, with its timbered façade and gardens filled with topiary. There are 23 acres of grounds to explore, plus plenty of interest inside the Grade II listed house, including ancient beams, open fireplaces and wood carvings. The Lexington restaurant is a romantic setting for some straightforward modern British cooking. Pan-fried scallops with cauliflower purée, black pudding and crispy bacon makes a fine opener, followed by rib-eye of Scottish beef with hand-cut chips, wilted rocket and Madeira jus, and mango pannacotta with thyme syrup to finish.

Times 12-3/6-9 Closed L Mon-Sat

FRESSINGFIELD — Map 13 TM27

Fox & Goose Inn

Modern British

Historic Tudor village restaurant and bar with ambitious modern cooking

01379 586247
Church Rd IP21 5PB
e-mail: foxandgoose@uk2.net
dir: A140 & B1116 (Stradbroke) left after 6m - in village centre by church

The 500-year-old Fox & Goose was built as a timber-framed Tudor guildhall next to the village's medieval church. While the scene presents a quintessentially English tableau, the place has been made over inside with a clean-cut modern look, and although real ales are tapped straight from the barrel in the bar, it is the ambitious restaurant that drives the operation. The beamed dining room is the setting for the kitchen's thoroughly contemporary food - expect intricately-woven flavour profiles and some bold marriages in dishes such as tian of crab with lemongrass and smoked salmon 'cannelloni', red pepper purée and coriander tuiles. Local meat fans might go for a main course starring rump of lamb with a supporting cast of apple, mint and butternut squash chutney, mustard gnocchi, salsify, spinach and lamb jus.

Chef P Yaxley, M Wyatt **Owner** Paul Yaxley
Times 12-2/7-8.30 Closed 27-30 Dec, 2nd wk Jan for 2 weeks, Mon **Prices** Fixed L 2 course fr £13.50, Tasting menu £42, Starter £4.95-£8.25, Main £11.95-£18.95, Dessert £4.50-£6.50, Service optional **Wines** 26 bottles over £20, 28 bottles under £20, 7 by glass **Notes** Tasting menu 7 course, Sunday L, Vegetarian available **Seats** 70, Pr/dining room 35 **Children** Portions **Parking** 15

GREAT GLEMHAM Map 13 TM36

The Crown Inn

Traditional British, Mediterranean

Relaxed, classic country inn serving locally-sourced produce

01728 663693
The Street IP17 2DA
e-mail: crown-i.cottle@btconnect.com
dir: A12 (N) left at Marlesford signed Gt Glemham. In 3m, pub 250yds after church on left. A12 (S), right at Stratford St Andrew, follow Crown Inn signs

Expect to find tip-top Suffolk ales tapped from the cask, wooden pews and sofas fronting crackling log fires, and a warm and friendly welcome at this 17th-century brick-built village local, just a short drive inland from the A12 and Heritage Coast. Better still, the food is admirably put together from producers as local as the neighbouring Great Glemham estate. The kitchen steers an uncomplicated course, letting the food speak for itself and delivering clear, fresh flavours. Expect the likes of smoked haddock and pea fishcake, served with lemon crème fraîche, then slow-roasted belly pork with dauphinoise potatoes, with apple pie with clotted cream ice cream for dessert.

Times 11.30-2.30/6.30-9 Closed Mon (ex BHs)

HINTLESHAM Map 13 TM04

Hintlesham Hall

Modern European V

Classic cuisine in an Elizabethan manor

01473 652334
IP8 3NS
e-mail: reservations@hintleshamhall.com
web: www.hintleshamhall.com
dir: 4m W of Ipswich on A1071

Set in 175 acres of grounds and landscaped gardens, this magnificent Grade I listed Elizabethan Manor is a country-house hotel with all the trimmings, and then some. The Georgian inhabitants broke the bank giving the place a serious makeover, but the oak staircase and ornate plaster ceilings date back to Stuart times. Three dining rooms have got the lot when it comes to grandeur - ornate mirrors, chandeliers, oil paintings and antique rugs on oak boards - but the elegant Salon restaurant wins by a head with its high domed ceiling with gold leaf and ornate cornices - the sort of old-school formal setting that requires jackets to be worn at dinner. After 20 years at the stoves, chef Alan Ford has his repertoire buffed to a high polish - classic stuff with a tweak of modernity here and there, and bristling with top-notch produce. A textbook chicken liver parfait appears in a tried-and-tested pairing with melba toast, and pear and fig compôte, ahead of chilli-roasted supreme of cod with bok choy and vegetable noodles perked up with chilli butter sauce. An exemplary vanilla crème brûlée with a rhubarb crumble shot makes a perfect finale.

Hintlesham Hall

Chef Alan Ford **Owner** Ms Dee Ludlow
Times 12-2.30/7-10 Closed L Sat **Prices** Fixed L 3 course fr £33.50, Fixed D 3 course fr £33, Service optional **Wines** 200 bottles over £20, 65 bottles under £20, 12 by glass **Notes** Sunday L, Vegetarian menu, Dress restrictions, Tailored jacket at D, smart casual at L, Civ Wed 100 **Seats** 80, Pr/dining room 80 **Children** Portions **Parking** 80

HORRINGER Map 13 TL86

The Ickworth Hotel

Modern British

Modern cooking in family-friendly National Trust-owned hotel

01284 735350
IP29 5QE
e-mail: info@ickworthhotel.co.uk
dir: From A14 take 1st exit for Bury St Edmunds (junct 42). Follow signs for Westley & Ickworth Estate

The National Trust-owned East Wing of Ickworth is run as a luxurious hotel with a child-friendly ethos by the team behind Woolley Grange (see entry). With 1,800 acres of grounds to run around and ride horses and bikes in, kids are, of course, in their element. But as it's mum and dad who are paying for all of this, the grown-ups are assured of a child-free time when it's time for dinner in the slick contemporary surroundings of Frederick's, the adults-only dining room. The food is unmistakably modern stuff that draws its influences from Europe as well as the domestic larder, so seared scallops could be teamed in a first course with local black pudding, cauliflower purée and apple jelly, while mains might take in pan-roasted monkfish with saffron, lemon and spinach risotto, or 28-day aged beef teamed with smoked garlic mash, braised ox cheek and seared foie gras.

Times 12-2/6-9.30

IPSWICH Map 13 TM14

Best Western Claydon Country House Hotel

Modern British

Modern British menu close to Ipswich

01473 830382
16-18 Ipswich Rd, Claydon IP6 0AR
e-mail: enquiries@hotelsipswich.com
dir: A14, junct 52 Claydon exit from rdbt, 300yds on left

Situated to the north west of Ipswich, this small hotel is popular for golf breaks and also with the business brigade. Originally two old village houses, the hotel houses a smart Victorian-style dining room, which overlooks the gardens. Smartly uniformed staff are professional and welcoming. Modern British food is created by a small team of chefs who use local produce wherever possible. Expect simple dishes along the lines of wild mushroom bruschetta, tempura battered cod and a properly runny chocolate fondant. Decent home-made rolls and a good range of coffee show attention to detail all round.

Times 12-2/7-9.30

Mariners

French, Mediterranean V

Sound brasserie cooking on a vintage Belgian gunboat

01473 289748
Neptune Quay IP4 1AX
e-mail: info@marinersipswich.co.uk
dir: Situated on Wherry Quay, accessed via Key St. follow brown tourist signs to waterfront

Regis Crepy has relaunched his floating French eatery (formerly Il Punto), introducing a new name and a stylish new look to the 110-year-old Belgian gunboat that commands splendid river views from its mooring at Neptune Quay in the heart of Ipswich. The handsome interior is certainly shipshape, decked out with brass rails, polished mahogany, a chic white and grey colour scheme and crisp white linen, or eat outside up on the deck. The food is rooted firmly in the French brasserie style, with modern French dishes and simple classics cooked with well-executed precision; start on a suitably maritime note with tuna and sea bass carpaccio with salsa verde, moving on to leg of lamb confit with chestnut mushroom and tarragon sauce.

Chef Frederic Lebrun **Owner** Mr R Crepy
Times 12-2.30/6.30-9.30 Closed Jan, Sun-Mon
Prices Fixed L 2 course £12.95, Fixed D 3 course £24.95, Service optional, Groups min 10 service 10% **Wines** 124 bottles over £20, 48 bottles under £20, 8 by glass
Notes Pre-theatre D available 2 course £15.95, Vegetarian menu, Dress restrictions, Smart casual
Seats 80, Pr/dining room 20 **Children** Portions, Menu
Parking On street, NCP

IPSWICH *continued*

Salthouse Harbour Hotel, The Eaterie

Modern British

Smart and funky hotel with commendable food

01473 226789
No 1 Neptune Quay IP4 1AX
e-mail: staying@salthouseharbour.co.uk
dir: A14 junct 53, A1156 to town centre & harbour, off Key St

Part of Ipswich's revitalised waterfront, overlooking Neptune harbour, this former dockside warehouse has risen like a phoenix to become a stylish hotel with a penchant for pop art and a vibrant brasserie delivering a lively menu of well-judged dishes. The name of the restaurant - The Eaterie - reflects the unpretentious intentions of chef Simon Barker, and the focus is on clear, well defined flavours, and the considered use of excellent local produce (80% of ingredients are from the region, they say). Start with something simple such as salt beef with rocket, parmesan, cornichons and Suffolk mud mayo, before a traditional steak and ale pie, or go for roast loin of Denham Estate venison, served with fondant potato, celeriac purée, wild mushrooms and a game jus. Glazed lemon tart is a sparkily flavoured dessert and top-notch British cheeses come from Neal's Yard.

Chef Simon Barker **Owner** Robert Gough **Times** 12-6/6-10 **Prices** Fixed L 2 course fr £12.50, Starter £4.50-£9.50, Main £9.95-£24.50, Dessert £4-£9.95, Service optional **Wines** 49 bottles over £20, 21 bottles under £20, 34 by glass **Notes** Sunday L, Vegetarian available **Seats** 70 **Children** Portions, Menu **Parking** 30

IXWORTH Map 13 TL97

Theobalds Restaurant

Modern British

Charming village restaurant serving accomplished classical dishes

01359 231707
68 High St IP31 2HJ
web: www.theobaldsrestaurant.co.uk
dir: 7m from Bury St Edmunds on A143 (Bury to Diss road)

Husband-and-wife-team Simon and Geraldine Theobald's 16th-century timber-framed restaurant is a long-standing institution on the pretty village of Ixworth's high street. Inside, a huge inglenook fireplace and ancient oak beams make for heaps of traditional character, while local artists' work adds splashes of colour. When the weather plays ball, the delightful patio garden is just made for pre-dinner drinks. The cooking has a solidly classical basis that brings out good, clear flavours from the season's best produce, as in a summery dinner of potted dressed crab and smoked salmon, with avocado and cucumber, served with lime juice and walnut oil dressing, followed by roast best end of lamb with candied aubergines and a jus laced with rosemary and sherry.

Chef Simon Theobald **Owner** Simon & Geraldine Theobald **Times** 12.15-1.30/7-9 Closed 10 days in Spring/Summer, Mon, L Tue, Thu, Sat, D Sun **Prices** Fixed L 2 course fr £24, Fixed D 3 course fr £30, Starter £6.75-£8.95, Main £14.95-£18.50, Dessert £6.95, Service optional **Wines** 34 bottles over £20, 18 bottles under £20, 7 by glass **Notes** Fixed L menu available Wed & Fri, Fixed D midweek, Sunday L, Vegetarian available **Seats** 42, Pr/dining room 16 **Children** Portions **Parking** On street

KESGRAVE Map 13 TM24

Milsoms Kesgrave Hall

Modern

Relaxed dining in a contemporary country bistro

01473 333741
Hall Rd IP5 2PU
e-mail: reception@kesgravehall.com
dir: A12 N of Ipswich/Woodbridge, rdbt onto B1214

Once a Georgian family home set in a thickly-wooded area north of Ipswich, Kesgrave Hall has met the 21st century in impeccable style after a boutique makeover in 2008. At its culinary heart is a buzzy bistro with a scrubbed-up modern look combining oak floors, pine tables, leather chairs and tasteful shades of cream and sage. The chefs toiling all day in the open kitchen champion Suffolk produce on a wide-ranging menu of brasserie dishes. Tomato and courgette tart with peppered goats'cheese bavarois and rocket pesto might start things off; next comes a crispy escalope of pork Holstein, served with creamy mash, wilted spinach, a fried egg on top and caper beurre noisette. For dessert, treacle tart is partnered satisfyingly with lemon and cinnamon cream and crème anglaise.

Chef Stuart Oliver **Owner** Paul Milsom **Times** 12-9.30 **Prices** Starter £4.95-£8.95, Main £9.75-£26.95, Dessert £5.95, Service optional **Wines** 33 bottles over £20, 18 bottles under £20, 15 by glass **Notes** Sunday L, Vegetarian available **Seats** 80, Pr/dining room 24 **Children** Portions, Menu **Parking** 150

LAVENHAM Map 13 TL94

The Angel

Traditional English, Modern British

Traditional English cooking in timeless setting

01787 247388
Market Place CO10 9QZ
e-mail: angel@maypolehotels.com
dir: Between Bury St Edmunds & Sudbury on A1141. In town centre, Market Place just off High St

This historic trading inn has been just that since the year 1420 and even if the food is somewhat more modern these days, there are plenty of reminders of the provenance of the building. As such the interior is much as you'd expect: exposed beams and brickwork, bare tables and a log fire create a timeless mood. The seasonal menu is all about refined versions of classic English dishes; begin with a duck and orange parfait with toast, followed by slow-roast belly pork with caraway infused carrots and plum and apple compôte, and, to finish, a pear and ginger steamed pudding with custard.

Chef Michael Pursell **Owner** Mr Alastair McEwen **Times** 12-2.15/6.45-9.15 **Prices** Starter £4.50-£6.50, Main £7.95-£16.95, Dessert £4.95-£6.25, Service optional, Groups min 10 service 10% **Wines** 15 bottles over £20, 26 bottles under £20, 10 by glass **Notes** Sunday L, Vegetarian available, Dress restrictions, Smart casual **Seats** 100, Pr/dining room 16 **Children** Portions, Menu **Parking** 5, Car park (40)

Lavenham Great House Restaurant with Rooms

Modern French

East Anglian produce in a light, airy setting

01787 247431
Market Place CO10 9QZ
e-mail: info@greathouse.co.uk
dir: In Market Place (turn onto Market Lane from High Street)

Opposite the village cross sits the Great House, its trim Georgian façade concealing a succession of smart, fresh, airy interiors. The place is run with infectious cheer, and the dining room suits the mood, with its bare-boarded floor and cornflower-blue seating, and a cutting-edge style of cooking that gives East Anglian produce star billing. Expect Suffolk pork rillettes with pickled vegetables to start, with mains running from coriander-marinated breast of local chicken with black olive sauce and red pepper jelly, or pigeon served on stewed red cabbage in a light brandy sauce. It all gets rather more elaborate towards the end of the week, when foie gras and truffled turbot may be the order of the day. Finish with nougat glacé in red fruit coulis.

Chef Regis Crepy **Owner** Mr & Mrs Crepy **Times** 12-2.30/7-9.30 Closed Jan & 2 wks summer, Mon, L Tue, D Sun **Prices** Fixed L 2 course fr £16.95, Fixed D 3 course fr £31.95, Starter £6.95-£12.95, Main £15-£23.50, Dessert £5.95, Service optional, Groups min 10 service

10% **Wines** 65 bottles over £20, 75 bottles under £20, 10 by glass **Notes** Sunday L, Vegetarian available **Seats** 40, Pr/dining room 15 **Children** Portions **Parking** Market Place

The Swan Hotel

British, European V

Modern dining in medieval splendour

☎ 01787 247477
High St CO10 9QA
e-mail: info@theswanatlavenham.co.uk
dir: From Bury St Edmunds take A134 (S) for 6m. Take A1141 to Lavenham

The Tudor market town of Lavenham grew rich on the wool trade 600 years ago, and that's just how long the Swan has been in business. This is a textbook ancient inn, sagging black timbers outside, and rich in history within: its brick floor is ballast taken from wool ships, and the gnarled beams, oak panels and cosy nooks and crannies could tell many a tale from the Second World War, when RAF pilots from Lavenham airfield dropped by to let off steam. You couldn't ask for a better setting for crowd-pleasing pub grub classics, but you might trade up to the fine-dining Gallery Restaurant, a barn-sized medieval-style great hall complete with a minstrels' gallery. There's nothing archaic about the food: a thoughtful menu of modern British and European dishes takes in the likes of pan-seared scallops with Savoyard potato, salsify purée and apple crisp, followed by braised shin of Red Poll beef bourguignon teamed with parsnip mash, glazed carrots and spring greens.

Chef Nicholas Wilson **Owner** Thorpeness & Aldeburgh Hotels Ltd **Times** 12-2.30/7-9.30 **Prices** Fixed L 2 course £14.95, Fixed D 3 course £35.95, Starter £9-£12, Main £20-£24, Dessert £6-£9.50, Service optional **Wines** 80 bottles over £20, 20 bottles under £20, 14 by glass **Notes** Sunday L, Vegetarian menu, Dress restrictions, No jeans or trainers, Civ Wed 100 **Seats** 90, Pr/dining room 32 **Children** Portions, Menu **Parking** 50

See advert below

LONG MELFORD **Map 13 TL84**

Scutchers Restaurant

British

Creative bistro cooking in former pub

☎ 01787 310200
Westgate St CO10 9DP
e-mail: info@scutchers.com
web: www.scutchers.com
dir: Approx 1m from Long Melford towards Clare

Look for the striking vertical sign and you've found the Barretts' professionally run country bistro, once a pub that served the local linen-workers' community. The low ceilings, exposed beams and bare-wood tables retain that pubby ambience, but the cooking is several cuts above the norm. If you're in the mood to put on a little Ritz, you might start with a serving of 30g of caviar with sour cream, or sautéed foie gras, the latter juxtaposed with more ostentatiously humble ingredients such as black pudding, mushy peas and port gravy. The cooking imports influences creatively in main dishes such as pork stroganoff with basmati, or fishcakes and chips with spicy tomato sauce, while dessert may take you to Italy for pannacotta with rhubarb compôte, or Derbyshire for Bakewell tart and vanilla ice cream.

Chef Nicholas Barrett **Owner** Nicholas & Diane Barrett **Times** 12-2/7-9.30 Closed 25 Dec, Sun-Mon **Prices** Food prices not confirmed for 2011. Please telephone for details. **Wines** 90 bottles over £20, 7 bottles under £20, 17 by glass **Notes** Vegetarian available **Seats** 70 **Children** Portions **Parking** 12

LOWESTOFT **Map 13 TM59**

The Crooked Barn

Modern European

Great seafood-led cookery in a converted barn

☎ 01502 501353
Ivy House Country Hotel, Ivy Ln, Oulton Broad NR33 8HY
e-mail: aa@ivyhousecountryhotel.co.uk
web: www.ivyhousecountryhotel.co.uk
dir: A146 into Ivy Lane

continued

LOWESTOFT *continued*

This converted 18th-century thatched barn is as higgledy-piggledy as its name suggests, with wonky beams and creaking floorboards adding to the character of the place. Adorned with local artists' work, and with soothing views over gardens and lily ponds, it's also a restful venue. East Anglian seafood is a strong suit, with dishes such as green Thai curry fishcakes with chilli jam to start, and complex main assemblages like grilled sea bass with Cromer crab risotto, Norfolk samphire and lemon dressing to follow. Precision timing and impeccable sourcing ensure the success of these dishes. Those of meatier appetites might try Telmara Farm duck with celeriac and kale in red wine sauce, while desserts bring down the curtain with a flourish with Tia Maria-laced coffee mousse and dark chocolate sauce.

Chef Martin Whitelock **Owner** Caroline Coe **Times** 12-1.45/7-9.30 Closed 24 Dec-8 Jan **Prices** Fixed L 2 course £15.95, Fixed D 3 course £18.95-£27.50, Starter £5.50-£9.95, Main £14.75-£25.95, Dessert £4.50-£9.95, Service optional **Wines** 20 bottles over £20, 17 bottles under £20, 4 by glass **Notes** Sunday L, Vegetarian available, Dress restrictions, Smart casual, No shorts, Civ Wed 80 **Seats** 45, Pr/dining room 24 **Children** Portions **Parking** 50

Hotel Victoria

British

Hotel dining with views of the sea

☎ 01502 574433
Kirkley Cliff NR33 0BZ
e-mail: info@hotelvictoria.co.uk

The attractive Victorian building on the esplanade overlooking the sea has direct access onto the beach from its location on Kirkley Cliff. Coast is a modern restaurant and lounge bar benefitting from those sea views, as well as a refurbishment which has made the most of its period features and added some contemporary comforts. Modern British food is complemented by a good wine list with about a dozen available by the glass. Expect local ingredients to crop up in the likes of local cod, mushy pea fishcake, lemon and chervil dressing, followed by Suffolk venison and Flixton mushroom suet pudding with roasted baby vegetables, red wine and thyme reduction.

Times 12-2/6.30-9

MILDENHALL **Map 12 TL77**

The Olde Bull Inn

Modern British

Old meets new in historic coaching inn

☎ 01638 711001
The Street, Barton Mills IP28 6AA
e-mail: bookings@bullinn-bartonmills.com
dir: Off A11 between Newmarket & Mildenhall, signed Barton Mills. Hotel by Five Ways rdbt

Queen Elizabeth I spent a night at this charming 16th-century coaching inn in the days when her romance with the Earl of Leicester was in full flower. Although lovingly refurbished, the pub retains much of its original charm with its picturesque courtyard, stagecoach archway, quaint gables and dormer windows. There is a choice of bars, lounge area and a smart brasserie-style restaurant, the Oak Room. Many ingredients come from local suppliers and are used to good effect in a mix of traditional and modern dishes. Pan-fried Denham Estate lamb steak is served with new potatoes, green beans and cherry tomatoes and Gressingham duck confit arrives with red cabbage, Madeira sauce and fondant potatoes.

Chef Cheryl Hickman, Matthew Cooke, Shaun Jennings **Owner** Cheryl Hickman & Wayne Starling **Times** 12-9 Closed 25 Dec **Prices** Starter £5.50-£7.50, Main £13-£23, Dessert £6-£7, Service optional **Wines** 15 bottles over £20, 15 bottles under £20, 8 by glass **Notes** Sunday L, Vegetarian available **Seats** 60, Pr/dining room 30 **Children** Portions, Menu **Parking** 60

See advert below

MONKS ELEIGH **Map 13 TL94**

The Swan Inn

British, Mediterranean

Unfussy bistro cooking in rural Suffolk

☎ 01449 741391
The Street IP7 7AU
e-mail: carol@monkseleigh.com
dir: On B1115 between Sudbury & Hadleigh

Not far from the historic wool town of Lavenham in the Suffolk countryside, the village of Monks Eleigh boasts this thatched 16th-century inn. The inviting modern bar has oak floors, beamed ceilings and an open fire, but there are slightly more formal dining rooms too. An intelligent, unfussy bistro approach to local food supplies brings dishes such as dressed Cromer crab with lemon and mayonnaise, and Italian-style agrodolce duck leg with rosemary potatoes, to the blackboard menus. Natural flavours are left to speak for themselves in a terrine of pork, apricot and pistachio with a sharp accompanying chutney, or well-timed tempura-battered cod with tartare sauce and chips. Desserts might include summer fruit Pavlova with red berry coulis.

Chef Nigel Ramsbottom **Owner** Nigel Ramsbottom **Times** 12-2/7-9.30 Closed 25-26 Dec, Mon (except BHs), D Sun **Prices** Fixed L 2 course fr £13.75, Fixed D 3 course fr £17.75, Starter £4.75-£8, Main £8.75-£20, Dessert £5.50-£7.50, Service optional **Wines** 10 bottles over £20, 30 bottles under £20, 10 by glass **Notes** Sun L winter only, Sunday L, Vegetarian available **Seats** 30, Pr/dining room 24 **Children** Portions **Parking** 12

NEWMARKET Map 12 TL66

Bedford Lodge Hotel

Modern International

Accomplished cooking in hotel close to Newmarket races

☎ 01638 663175
Bury Rd CB8 7BX
e-mail: info@bedfordlodgehotel.co.uk
dir: From town centre take A1304 towards Bury St Edmunds, hotel 0.5m on left

Horse-related artwork and a colourful collection of racing silks are a nod to this Georgian hunting lodge's long connection with Newmarket's racing heritage. Its three acres of flower-filled gardens rub shoulders with the paddocks and training stables, and even if you're not in town for a flutter on the races, there's a classy health and fitness club to raise the heartbeat without losing your shirt. The relaxed Orangery Restaurant is the venue for the kitchen's ambitious modern repertoire built on produce that never travels far from producer to plate - dairy produce and vegetables, for example, come from the Elveden Estate just a few miles away. Starters could range from confit Norfolk duck leg and cured foie gras terrine with pineapple and chilli jam, to Cromer crab with baby gem and tomato jelly. Progressing to main course, halibut steak might appear in a modish fish and meat pairing with braised oxtail, saffron pommes purée, confit onions and a pea and Avruga caviar nage.

Times 12-2/7-9.30 Closed L Sat

Carriages Restaurant at The Rutland Arms

British, Mediterranean

Former coaching inn serving up brasserie-style food

☎ 01638 664251
The Rutland Arms Hotel, 33 High St CB8 8NB
e-mail: reservations.rutlandarms@ohiml.com
dir: In town centre at top of High St

With its own entrance within this former coaching inn – these days The Rutland Arms Hotel - Carriages restaurant and bar does well with passing trade, particularly on race days, as well as proving popular with hotel residents. The street-facing dining room sports unclothed tables and exposed brickwork – the perfect backdrop to its simple brasserie-style food. British and Mediterranean seasonal influences are apparent in dishes such as a classic moules marinière or roast cod, celeriac remoulade and hazelnut emulsion and a well-made lemon tart.

Times 12-2.30/7-9.30

Tuddenham Mill

Modern European

Relaxed, rustic-chic brasserie in former watermill

☎ 01438 713552
High St, Tuddenham St Mary IP28 6SQ
e-mail: info@tuddenhammill.co.uk

Tuddenham is a 17th-century watermill converted into a sleek boutique hotel in 12 acres of idyllic grounds amid rolling Suffolk countryside. The original wooden mill wheel is illuminated to dramatic effect in the rustic-chic restaurant, a super-stylish venue where massive gnarled beams blend with contemporary prints, charcoal-lacquered tables and brown suede chairs; switched-on staff in long black aprons complete the picture. The kitchen takes a modern European route, using the best the local larder has to offer, with terse descriptions belying food cooked with skill and presented with impact. Pig's head terrine with chorizo, apple and soy is one way to start, then mains could deliver rump and braised shoulder of lamb with clam escabèche, courgette, and Pink Fir potatoes, or perhaps lemon sole well-matched by pork belly, asparagus, broad beans and pickled mushrooms.

Times 12-2.30/6.30-10.30

ORFORD Map 13 TM45

The Crown & Castle

Modern V

Unpretentious cooking in an inn by the Castle

☎ 01394 450205
IP12 2LJ
e-mail: info@crownandcastle.co.uk
dir: Off A12, on B1084, 9m E of Woodbridge

Once an integral part of the outer walls of Orford Castle, but now separated from it by a bit of road, the Watsons' medieval inn is a relaxing bolt-hole not far from Aldeburgh and its festival. Most of the ground floor is given over to eating in various areas, and it's all hugely comfortable, a great place to linger. And a great place to eat too, as might be expected given Ruth Watson's reputation - you might have seen her on the telly. The menu is divided into hot and cold dishes, with fish and seafood featuring strongly. Crab and saffron soufflé, potted shrimps, or smoked trout with beetroot and horseradish crème fraîche are among the appetisers, while locally-landed sea bass with Asian slaw and mint and coriander dressing makes a grand main course. Meatier appetites may be assuaged by rump of local lamb with dauphinoise and seasonal greens in red wine sauce. Finish with hot bitter chocolate mousse.

Chef Ruth Watson, Nick Thacker **Owner** David & Ruth Watson, Tim Sunderland **Times** 12.15-2.15/7-9.30 Closed 6-9 Jan, L 31 Dec **Prices** Starter £4.95-£11.50, Main £13.95-£21, Dessert £6.95, Service optional, Groups min 8 service 10% **Wines** 98+ bottles over £20, 25 bottles under £20, 16 by glass **Notes** Sunday L, Vegetarian menu **Seats** 60, Pr/dining room 10 **Children** Portions, Menu **Parking** 19, Market Sq, on street

SOUTHWOLD Map 13 TM57

The Blyth Hotel

Modern British NEW

Stylishly-restored seaside inn with modern British repertoire

☎ 01502 722632
Station Rd IP18 6AY
e-mail: reception@blythhotel.com
dir: Follow A1095 from the A12, signed Southwold. Hotel on left after bridge

This handsome Edwardian building sits at a crossroads on the way into Southwold, Suffolk's superstar resort. There's a lovely summery seaside feel to the interior: an airy bar in the modern vein, with stripped floors, natural wood tables and chunky wicker chairs, Adnams ales (what else in Southwold?) on tap, and a stylish contemporary restaurant. The kitchen's output has oodles of flair, wrought from a sound foundation of solid technique and well-sourced produce, some of which comes from the kitchen garden and local organic allotments. To start, locally-reared pork belly is served with apple and frisée salad, crackling and apple purée, followed by baked cod with herb-crushed potatoes, cockle chowder and vegetable ribbons.

Chef Shaun Doig, Chris Fairs **Owner** Richard & Charlie Ashwell **Times** 12-2/6.30-9 **Prices** Fixed L 2 course £11.95, Fixed D 3 course £27.95, Service optional **Wines** 30 bottles under £20, 2 by glass **Notes** Sunday L, Vegetarian available **Seats** 38 **Children** Portions, Menu **Parking** 8, On street

The Crown

Modern British NOTABLE WINE LIST

Modern big-city cooking at Adnams' in-crowd hotel

☎ 01502 722275
90 High St IP18 6DP
e-mail: crown.reception@adnams.co.uk
dir: A12 onto A1095 to Southwold. Hotel on left in High Street

continued

SOUTHWOLD *continued*

The Crown is the hip option of Adnams' hotels in its Southwold HQ - the other being the flagship Swan Hotel (see entry). When weekenders descend on the place, the heaving bar-brasserie generates quite a buzz, or if you prefer a less jostling ambience, there's a relaxed dining room. Wherever you choose, the kitchen sends out modern metropolitan food tailor-made for the incoming clientele, but proudly bursting with Suffolk ingredients. Smoked carp is not something you see very often, teamed here in a starter with kedgeree cake and curried crème fraîche. Fish always makes a strong showing - perhaps pan-roasted halibut with potato, fennel and saffron boulangère, and olive salsa verde, or for fans of local meat, there might be slow-braised Dingley Dell pork belly with sweet potato purée, black pudding and wild garlic.

Chef Robert Mace **Owner** Adnams plc
Times 12-2/6.30-9.30 **Prices** Starter £4.50-£7.95, Main £9.95-£19.95, Dessert £5-£7, Service optional **Wines** 144 bottles over £20, 73 bottles under £20, 14 by glass **Notes** Vegetarian available **Seats** 65, Pr/dining room 30 **Children** Portions, Menu **Parking** 15, Free car parks within 5 mins walking distance

Sutherland House

Modern British

Trendy dining in an ancient townhouse

01502 724544
56 High St IP18 6DN
e-mail: enquiries@sutherlandhouse.co.uk
dir: A1095 into Southwold, on High St on left after Victoria St

The pink-washed façade of this elegant townhouse on Southwold's High Street belies the grandeur of its interior. Once a residence of James II, it has impressive pargetted plasterwork ceilings, foot-wide elm floorboards, ancient beams and huge fireplaces, which blend effortlessly with opulent modern fabrics and designer furniture. The two classy dining areas, decked out with modish darkwood tables and plush purple chairs, are served by easy-going but efficient staff. Local produce is the bedrock of the kitchen's innovative modern output; food miles are taken seriously enough that they even appear on the menu. From the carte, go for a starter of beef tartare with smoked shallot purée and pickled radish, followed by pan-fried sea bass with salsify chips, herb gnocchi and spinach sauce, and lemon curd mousse with rhubarb and vanilla foam. The lunchtime set-price menu is great value.

Chef Dan Jones **Owner** Peter & Anna Banks
Times 12-3/7-9.30 Closed 25 Dec, Mon (off season only), D Sun **Prices** Fixed L 2 course £15, Fixed D 3 course £24, Starter £4.50-£7, Main £10.95-£18, Dessert £4.50-£5.50, Service optional **Wines** 35 bottles over £20, 15 bottles under £20, 10 by glass **Notes** Sunday L, Vegetarian available **Seats** 50, Pr/dining room 60 **Children** Portions, Menu **Parking** 1, On street

Swan Hotel

Modern British

Contemporary British cooking at the Adnams flagship

01502 722186
High St, Market Place IP18 6EG
e-mail: swan.hotel@adnams.co.uk
dir: A1095 to Southwold. Hotel in town centre. Parking via archway to left of building

The pretty seaside town of Southwold is the epicentre of the Adnams empire, a company which embraces the trades of brewer, publican, wine merchant and hotelier. The Swan is at the heart of the operation (the brewery is at the back), right in the centre of town, with an elegant Victorian façade concealing its 17th-century origins. There's a bar menu, but head to the traditional dining room with its bold red walls for some confident contemporary cooking, rooted in traditional British and classical French cuisine. Roast pigeon breast is perfectly pointed up with rhubarb and ginger in a first course, and finished with a port dressing, while main-course slow-cooked Label Anglais chicken comes with a confit of the leg, mushroom and cauliflower lasagne and smoked cheddar gratin. Norfolk and Suffolk cheeses make a good alternative to desserts such as apple beignets with compôte and sorbet, unless you've room for both.

Chef Rory Whelan **Owner** Adnams plc
Times 12-2.30/7-9.30 **Prices** Fixed L 2 course fr £15.95, Starter £5.50-£7.95, Main £13.95-£19.25, Dessert £6.75, Service optional **Wines** 60 bottles over £20, 60 bottles under £20, 13 by glass **Notes** Pre-theatre picnic hampers & D (summer only), Sunday L, Vegetarian available, Dress restrictions, Smart casual - no jeans, Civ Wed 40 **Seats** 65, Pr/dining room 36 **Children** Portions, Menu **Parking** 36

STOKE-BY-NAYLAND Map 13 TL93

The Crown

Modern British

Boutique hotel and village inn in one

01206 262001
CO6 4SE
e-mail: info@crowninn.net
dir: A12 junct 30 towards Higham for 1m. At village green left & left again towards Stoke by Nayland. Hotel on right approx 3m

Perfectly placed for exploring Constable country and with unspoilt views across the peaceful Box Valley, the classy 16th-century Crown has been spruced up with style and panache, becoming a classy boutique inn with the addition of 11 swish bedrooms in 2008. The rambling beamed bar and dining areas sport a soothingly contemporary look, with relaxing easy chairs, big log fires, cosy corners, and an in-house wine shop. Monthly-changing modern British menus, supplemented by daily fish dishes on the chalkboard, reflect the seasons and show flair, imagination, and sound use of quality local ingredients. Take a starter of pork, rabbit, prune and pistachio terrine, followed by braised shoulder of lamb with curly kale and spring onion mash, or cod with samphire, mussels, red onion and pancetta. Leave room for steamed jam pudding or a plate of artisan British cheeses.

Chef Mark Blake **Owner** Richard Sunderland
Times 12-2.30/6-9.30 Closed 25-26 Dec **Prices** Starter £4.50-£7.50, Main £9.95-£18.95, Dessert £3.20-£9.25, Service optional **Wines** 160 bottles over £20, 41 bottles under £20, 29 by glass **Notes** Sunday L, Vegetarian available, Dress restrictions, No baseball caps or head gear **Seats** 130, Pr/dining room 12 **Children** Portions, Menu **Parking** 49

STOWMARKET Map 13 TM05

The Shepherd and Dog

Modern European

Smart gastro-pub with confident cooking

01449 711361 & 710464
Forward Green IP14 5HN
e-mail: marybruce@btinternet.com
web: www.theshepherdanddog.com
dir: On A1120 between A14 & A140

Expect a fresh, contemporary feel - deep leather sofas, high-backed chairs and lightwood furnishings - at this smartly refurbished gastro-pub in a hamlet beside the A1120 east of Stowmarket. The kitchen's modern approach to simply cooking quality local ingredients might deliver starters of chicken liver and red wine pâté with white onion chutney, and crispy duck salad with watercress and orange, followed by lamb rump with rosemary cream sauce, or grilled sea bass with red pepper dressing, with dark chocolate and ginger cheesecake and tiramisù with Marsala and coffee sauce for pudding.

Chef Christopher Bruce & Daniela Bruce **Owner** Christopher & Mary Bruce **Times** 12-2/7-11 Closed mid Jan, Mon, D Sun **Prices** Fixed L 2 course £14.50-£17.50, Fixed D 3 course £17.50-£19.50, Starter £5.50-£8, Main £14-£24, Dessert £5.75-£6.75, Service optional **Wines** 28 bottles over £20, 25 bottles under £20, 19 by glass **Notes** Sunday L, Vegetarian available **Seats** 50, Pr/dining room 24 **Children** Portions **Parking** 35

WALBERSWICK Map 13 TM47

The Anchor

Modern British

Gastro-pub with equal passion for food and drink

01502 722112
Main St IP18 6UA
e-mail: info@anchoratwalberswick.com
dir: On entering village The Anchor on right, immediately after MG garage

The traditional pub-turned-gastro-pub in the 1920s Arts and Crafts style boasts great sea views, a relaxed atmosphere and unpretentious cooking. Plenty of the original fixtures and fittings remain with food offered throughout the pub and a separate restaurant with stripped pine tables and chairs. As well as the modern menu, simpler comfort food is also available. The owners' vast knowledge of beer and wine is apparent with each dish matched with one or the other. The kitchen deals in the freshest local and seasonal produce with many ingredients from the owners' allotment. Start, perhaps, with caramelised scallops served on a bed of artichoke purée, followed by deep-fried local cod with a crisp golden beer batter, home-made fat chips, pease pudding and jalapeno tartare sauce. Service is professional but not formidable.

Chef Sophie Dorber **Owner** Sophie & Mark Dorber **Times** 11-4/6-11 Closed 25 Dec **Prices** Food prices not confirmed for 2011. Please telephone for details. **Wines** 22 by glass **Notes** Vegetarian available **Seats** 55, Pr/dining room 26 **Children** Portions, Menu **Parking** 60

WESTLETON Map 13 TM46

The Westleton Crown

Modern British

Vibrant modern cooking in an ancient Suffolk inn

01728 648777
The Street IP17 3AD
e-mail: info@westletoncrown.co.uk
dir: A12 N, turn right for Westleton just after Yoxford. Hotel opposite on entering village

The charming rustic inn dates back partly to the 12th century, and is a handy base for visitors to the Aldeburgh festival or historic Southwold. All the benefits of a traditional village inn are on show, from the hand-pumped ales to the cheering log fires in chilly weather, and the food is in plentiful supply, starting at the breakfast hour. Traditional roasts on Sundays don't lack for supporters, but the main menu deals in vibrant European and British dishes presented with panache. Start by dipping tiger prawns in chilli sauce and aïoli, before kicking on with lamb loin, goats' cheese and lavender, or cod fillet with crab and spring onion rösti, served with fennel tempura, red pepper purée and lemongrass sauce. Rhubarb and ginger crumble tart with yoghurt sorbet makes a stylish finale.

Chef Richard Burgewell **Owner** Agellus Hotels Ltd **Times** 12-2.30/7-9.30 **Prices** Starter £5.50-£7.50, Main £11.75-£23, Dessert £5.85-£7.25, Service optional **Wines** 29 bottles over £20, 22 bottles under £20, 9 by glass **Notes** Sunday L, Vegetarian available **Seats** 85 **Children** Portions, Menu **Parking** 50

WOODBRIDGE Map 13 TM24

The Crown at Woodbridge

Modern European

Boutique-style inn with relaxed dining

01394 384242
2 Thoroughfare IP12 1AD
e-mail: info@thecrownatwoodbridge.co.uk
dir: A12 follow signs for Woodbridge onto B1438 after 1.25m from rdbt turn left into Quay Street & hotel on right, approx 100 yds from junct

A dramatic no-expense-spared facelift in 2009 relaunched the Crown as a stylish 21st-century inn. The look is now decidedly boutique, combining original 16th-century features with a fresh, New England-style contemporary design ethos in several dining areas - one has glowing paprika red walls, another is done out in cool shades of grey and features an etched glass mural screen with views of Woodbridge, while a Windermere skiff hangs above the long grey bar. The vibe is suitably urbane and relaxed, and the kitchen raids the Suffolk larder for its unfussy, big-hearted modern British cooking. Local fish and seafood make a good showing - dressed Orford crab with lime-pickled cucumber and sorrel mayonnaise, for example, ahead of roasted sea bass with samphire, lentils and anchovy vinaigrette, while the likes of roast loin and braised leg of rabbit with girolles, fondant potato and Aspall's cider jus should keep the carnivores happy.

Chef Stephen David, Luke Bailey **Owner** Thorpness & Aldeburgh Hotels **Times** 12-2.15/6.15-9 Closed D 25 Dec (available for residents only) **Prices** Starter £6-£9, Main £10-£22, Dessert £4.50-£7, Service optional **Wines** 70 bottles over £20, 10 bottles under £20, 14 by glass **Notes** Sunday L, Vegetarian available **Children** Portions, Menu

Seckford Hall Hotel

Modern British

Sound cooking amid Elizabethan splendour

01394 385678
IP13 6NU
e-mail: reception@seckford.co.uk
dir: Hotel signed on A12 (Woodbridge bypass). Do not follow signs for town centre

The Seckford family's ancestral home has all the history you'd expect of a 16th-century Tudor manor that was home to the same family for 500 years until it stood on the verge of demolition in the mid 20th-century. This is a much-loved house with an interior steeped in medieval drama. Pass through the massive oak entrance door, and 60 carved faces peer out from timbers; panelling and doors, combined with armour and oil paintings, are worthy of a historical drama film set. An imaginative modern British menu is put together with an impressive level of skill, delivering accurate cooking and great flavour combinations from excellent local materials.

continued

WOODBRIDGE ***continued***

Brandade of smoked haddock with blinis and lime crème fraîche might precede a main-course rack of lamb teamed with Parma ham-wrapped foie gras and apricot boudin with white wine sauce. Go for cheeses such as Shipcord cheddar or Blackstick Blue as a savoury alternative to roast fig and chocolate fondant with bitter chocolate ice cream.

Chef Mark Archer **Owner** Mr & Mrs Bunn
Times 12.30-1.45/7.30-9.30 Closed 25 Dec, L Mon
Prices Fixed L 2 course £12.50-£15.50, Fixed D 3 course £27.50-£32.50, Service included **Wines** 40 bottles over £20, 45 bottles under £20, 11 by glass **Notes** Sunday L, Vegetarian available, Dress restrictions, Smart casual, No jeans or trainers, Civ Wed 120 **Seats** 70, Pr/dining room 100 **Children** Portions, Menu **Parking** 100

YAXLEY **Map 13 TM17**

The Auberge

◎◎ International

Family-run restaurant with rooms

☎ 01379 783604
Ipswich Rd IP23 8BZ
e-mail: deestenhouse@fsmail.net
dir: 5m S of Diss on A140

The Auberge dates back to the 16th century and was once a rural public house providing basic food and drink. Things have changed for the good. Lovingly converted by its owners into a smart restaurant with rooms, the inn's charm has been retained - the original exposed brickwork and oak beams add a certain cosiness. The extended dining room is still intimate; tables are crisply laid with linen, embellished with bowls of fresh lemons and lit by candles. Service fits the bill. The kitchen guarantees consistency because if chef John Stenhouse isn't there, the kitchen ain't open. Fresh local produce is used to excellent effect in classic dishes with European and Far Eastern ingredients sometimes thrown into the mix. So you might find yellow split pea and smoked sausage soup and lemon sole on a rich Provençal tomato sauce served on fettucine with pak choi.

Chef John Stenhouse **Owner** John & Dee Stenhouse
Times 12-2/7-9.30 Closed 1 Jan, Sun & Mon, L Sat
Prices Fixed L 2 course £14.95-£16.95, Fixed D 3 course £26.50-£28.50, Starter £5-£8, Main £18-£23, Dessert £6-£8.50, Service optional **Wines** 35 bottles over £20, 25 bottles under £20, 13 by glass **Notes** Vegetarian available **Seats** 60, Pr/dining room 20 **Children** Portions **Parking** 25

YOXFORD **Map 5 TM36**

Satis House

◎◎ Modern British

Rural country house dishing up some contemporary flavours

☎ 01728 668418
Main Rd IP17 3EX
e-mail: enquiries@satishouse.co.uk
dir: off A12 between Ipswich & Lowestoft. 9m E Aldeburgh & Snape

Name-checked in Charles Dickens' *Great Expectations*, Satis House is an 18th-century Grade II listed country house offering a peaceful Suffolk retreat with some serious food to boot. Outside there's three acres of parkland while inside among the impressive period features is original York paving in the hallway. That's not to say that Satis is living in the past though. It's been brought firmly up to date with all mod cons in the rooms and the contemporary restaurant is miles away from a stuffy country-house affair. Unclothed tables are set against bold wallpaper providing the backdrop to modern British food with Asian and European notes using the best of Suffolk's larder. So whipped goats' cheese with tempura aubergine and onion syrup might start things off; next up, steamed hare suet pudding with medlar gravy, bubble-and-squeak, braised cabbage and hare gravy and a delicious strawberry and almond tart to finish.

Chef David Little, David Potter **Owner** David Little, Kevin Wainwright **Times** 12-3/6.30-11 Closed L Mon-Tue **Prices** Food prices not confirmed for 2011. Please telephone for details. **Wines** 20 bottles over £20, 10 bottles under £20, 6 by glass **Notes** Sunday L, Vegetarian available, Civ Wed 30 **Seats** 30, Pr/dining room 30 **Children** Portions **Parking** 30

See advert below

SURREY

ABINGER HAMMER Map 6 TQ04

Drakes on the Pond

Modern British

Skilful cooking in a classy village restaurant

01306 731174
Dorking Rd RH5 6SA
dir: On A25 between Dorking & Guildford

Tucked away in the sticks, Drake's sits beside a pond of grand enough proportions to count as a small lake. The cottagey exterior is deceptively rustic, since there's nothing unsophisticated about what's going on in the kitchen. Once inside, it's clear that there's a strong local fan base attracted by the friendliness of the owners, the stylish but unaffected décor of beechwood furniture and yellow ochre walls, and the appealing modern British food. Chef-proprietor John Morris draws on a deep well of classical cooking which he brings bang up to date with thought-provoking ideas - but there's no gimmickry involved, just exciting palate-tingling dishes built on top-class local materials. A starter of tempura scallops with pan-fried squid and chorizo, dressed leaves and orange salad ticks all the right boxes for taste, texture and timing. Slow-cooked belly pork might follow, in the rib-sticking company of fondant potato, black pudding, crackling and pancetta cream sauce; end with a trio of chocolate brûlées, chocolate brownie and Nutella ice cream.

Chef John Morris **Owner** John Morris & Tracey Honeysett **Times** 12-2/7-10 Closed 2 wks Aug-Sep, Xmas, New Year, BHs, Sun (except Mothering Sun), Mon **Prices** Fixed L 2 course fr £21.50, Starter £12-£16, Main £23-£29.50, Dessert fr £8, Service optional, Groups min 8 service 10% **Wines** 65 bottles over £20, 9 bottles under £20, 9 by glass **Notes** Vegetarian available, Dress restrictions, Smart casual **Seats** 32 **Parking** 20

BAGSHOT Map 6 SU96

The Brasserie

Modern British

Classy brasserie in spa hotel

01276 471774
Pennyhill Park Hotel & Spa, London Rd GU19 5EU
e-mail: enquiries@pennyhillpark.co.uk
dir: M3 junct 3, through Bagshot, left onto A30. 0.5m on right

Not many top hotels deserve a separate entry for their understudy restaurants (see also The Latymer for the hotel's destination restaurant), still less one with two Rosettes, but The Brasserie at Pennyhill Park is a hugely classy operation in its own right. Reached via the ground-floor entrance, it overlooks the outdoor swimming pool and manicured gardens, and is an eye-catching venue with brightly coloured upholstery, marble floor-tiles, and quality table settings. Seafood specialities are worth a look, perhaps potted crab with heritage potato salad, while a range of grills takes in half-pound rump steaks with sauce variations, as well as pork and lamb chops. Otherwise, lamb might come in three cuts (saddle, breast and shoulder) with dauphinoise and puréed shallots for an intense and labour-intensive main course.

Chef Iain Inman **Owner** Exclusive Hotels **Times** 12-2.30/6-10 **Prices** Fixed L 3 course £30-£37, Fixed D 3 course £21 (earlybird price), Starter £7.50-£9.50, Main £16.50-£26.50, Dessert £8.50-£11, Service added but optional **Wines** 220 bottles over £20, 20 by glass **Notes** Sunday L, Vegetarian available, Dress restrictions, Smart casual, Civ Wed 160 **Seats** 120, Pr/dining room 30 **Children** Menu **Parking** 500

The Latymer

– *see page 392*

BANSTEAD Map 6 TQ25

Post

Modern

First-class Post arrives in leafy Banstead

01737 373839
28 High St SM7 2LQ
e-mail: enquiries@postrestaurant.co.uk

The former Post Office on the High Street delivers the backdrop for TV chef Tony Tobin's cosmopolitan-style coffee shop, brasserie and restaurant package; sister venue to The Dining Room in Reigate (see entry). Contemporary design and buzzy atmosphere is the remit in the airy brasserie on street level (separate menu), while the intimate Tony Tobin @ POST restaurant upstairs is the operation's fine-dining arm. Here, cream leather banquettes, swivel leather tub chairs, staggered mirrors and a small bar complete the upbeat modern setting. The appealing fixed-price menus include a good-value carte and tasting option driven by quality produce, accurate technical skills and a light modern approach; think pan-fried scallops and chorizo with lemon aïoli, and to follow, perhaps monkfish wrapped in Parma ham with fennel and tomato sauce and gnocchi potato.

Times 11am-10pm

CAMBERLEY Map 6 SU86

Macdonald Frimley Hall Hotel & Spa

Modern European

Smart country-house dining

0844 879 9110
Lime Av GU15 2BG
e-mail: gm.frimleyhall@macdonald-hotels.co.uk
dir: M3 junct 3, A321 follow Bagshot signs. Through lights, left onto A30 signed Camberley & Basingstoke. To rdbt, 2nd exit onto A325, take 5th right

'Where there's muck there's brass' is a dictum that made a fortune out of dirt for the Wright Coal Tar Soap family, who built this elegant ivy-clad Victorian manor. Nowadays, Frimley Hall is an upmarket country-house hotel with a snazzy spa and health club that brings together tasteful contemporary themes with period grandeur, epitomised in the fine-dining Linden Restaurant. It's a fresh-looking, expansive venue with well-spaced tables - romantically candlelit at dinner - and delightful views over the woodland garden. The kitchen takes a modern European approach, placing a welcome emphasis on sourcing quality, seasonal ingredients. Smoked chicken with grilled vegetables and raspberry dressing is a typical starter, followed by the likes of pan-fried Gressingham duck breast with sauté potatoes, honey and cranberry sauce.

Owner Macdonald Hotels **Times** 12.30-2/7-9.45 Closed L Sat **Prices** Fixed L 2 course fr £19, Fixed D 3 course fr £29.50, Service added but optional 12.5% **Wines** 50 bottles over £20, 9 bottles under £20, 12 by glass **Notes** Sunday L, Vegetarian available, Civ Wed 120 **Seats** 70, Pr/dining room 200 **Children** Portions, Menu **Parking** 100

CHARLWOOD

For restaurant details see under Gatwick Airport (London), (Sussex, West)

COBHAM Map 6 TQ16

The Old Bear

Modern British NEW

Welcoming pub with a serious attitude to British food

01932 862116
Riverhill KT11 3DX
e-mail: www.theoldbearcobham.co.uk
dir: M25 junct 10, follow A3 towards London, exit A245 signed Cobham. Over 1st rdbt, 2nd exit next rdbt, the pub is located on the left, past Waitrose

On the main road through the town, the white-painted Old Bear catches the eye with its parasol-bedecked front terrace, neat white-painted façade, the woodwork picked out in fashionable charcoal grey, and window boxes which bring flashes of seasonal colour. The sympathetic remodelling, embracing contemporary sensibilities, continues on the inside, too, so chunky beams, winter fires, parquet and oak boards sit alongside a few well-chosen fixtures and fittings, creating an unfettered rusticity that is matched by the output from the kitchen. The bar serves up classics like lamb hotpot, but the dining room digs a little deeper to deliver a little more refinement. The kitchen's buying skills are finely tuned and there is good use of more humble cuts - pig's trotter stuffed with morels and served with potato purée and autumn truffles, for example. The chef has served time at Soho's acclaimed Arbutus (amongst others) and there is an honest, robust integrity to the keenly British cooking. Wild sea bream comes with crushed potatoes, Savoy cabbage and shrimp beurre noisette, and there is traditional rice pudding or British cheeses to finish.

Chef Nathan Green **Owner** Simon Anderson, Richard Turner, Andy Stevens & Nathan Green **Times** 12-3/5-12 **Prices** Fixed L 2 course £12.50, Fixed D 3 course £15.50, Starter £6.50-£10, Main £10.50-£20, Dessert £6.50, Service added but optional 10% **Wines** 77 bottles over £20, 9 bottles under £20, 13 by glass **Notes** Fixed menus Mon-Sat 12-3pm L, 6-7pm D, Sunday L, Vegetarian available **Seats** 80, Pr/dining room 22 **Parking** 18

The Latymer

BAGSHOT Map 6 SU96

Modern European V

Innovative modern European cooking in plush hotel

☎ 01276 471774
Pennyhill Park Hotel & Spa, London Rd GU19 5EU
e-mail: enquiries@pennyhillpark.co.uk
dir: M3 junct 3, through Bagshot, left onto A30. 0.5m on right

Home to wealthy bankers and industrialists since the 19th century, this splendid Victorian country house is still the playground of well-heeled bankers and industrialists in the 21st century. You approach Pennyhill Park down an impressively long driveway through 123 acres of verdant parkland in green-and-pleasant Surrey countryside, to emerge at an imposing creeper-clad stone manor. Naturally enough, there's a nine-hole golf course and Premier League spa to put everyone in a suitably unwound frame of mind for the gastronomic indulgence at hand in The Latymer restaurant. Since head chef Michael Wignall took the reins in 2007, this has become a top-flight dining destination in its own right, spruced up with a completely new, lighter, more contemporary look. The sombre Victoriana of dark beams, carved panelling and leaded windows is now leavened by the addition of moss-green chairs and banquettes and white linen. Service is appropriately professional and well-informed, but not so buttoned up as to preclude a friendly touch. Michael Wignall takes a highly technical, modern approach to his craft: dishes are complex, but based on classical themes, delivering light, elegant food with clear, intense flavours and exciting textures. Menu descriptions introduce the star ingredient in a one-word headline, then flesh out in greater depth what's involved - 'pigeon' is slow-poached Anjou pigeon in a Pedro Ximenez consommé, delivered with boudin noir croquant, spring truffles, apple gel, artichoke and sourdough crisp. There's lots going on, but Wignall's technique is on top form, making each element stand to attention - and it's all dressed to thrill. Main course might bring slow-cooked suckling pig, teamed with pork popcorn, creamed cabbage scented with mustard seed, and honey-glazed parsnips. Desserts are equally involved, labour-intensive works - perhaps 'rhubarb', an assemblage of fromage blanc, poached rhubarb and jelly, basil powder, rhubarb and custard, lemongrass and palm sugar, and lemongrass ice cream. Breads, canapés, and all intermediate nibbles and pre-desserts are equally fine-tuned. Lunch menus offer serious value for cooking of this standard, or at the opposite end of the budget spectrum, eight lucky diners can book the chef's table for a bespoke tasting menu. Unusually, the impressive wine list offers over 200 fine wines by the glass.

Chef Michael Wignall **Owner** Exclusive Hotels **Times** 12.30-2/7-9.30 Closed 1-14 Jan, Mon & Sun (Open Sun BHs but closed following Tue), L Sat **Prices** Fixed L 2 course fr £25, Fixed D 3 course fr £58, Tasting menu £79-£90, Service added but optional 12.5% **Wines** 220 bottles over £20, 20 by glass **Notes** Tasting menu L 8 course £58, Tasting menu D 10 course, Vegetarian menu, Dress restrictions, Smart casual, Civ Wed 160 **Seats** 50, Pr/dining room 30 **Parking** 500

DORKING Map 6 TQ14

Mercure Burford Bridge Hotel

Modern European

Historic hotel offering contemporary design and creative modern cooking

01306 884561
Burford Bridge, Box Hill RH5 6BX
e-mail: h6635@accor.com
dir: M25 junct 9, A245 towards Dorking. Hotel within 5m on A24

Sitting at the foot of Box Hill, with the Mole River running by at the bottom of the pretty garden, the Burford Bridge Hotel has a romantic setting. How very appropriate, then, that it was in this 16th-century building that Lord Nelson and Lady Hamilton reputedly met for the last time before the Battle of Trafalgar. These days it's a smart, contemporary hotel, with an elegant restaurant with low ceilings and candlelit tables overlooking the garden. There's a clear classical foundation to the modern cooking, which uses prime produce to craft a menu of sharply-flavoured, beautifully-presented dishes. Smoked eel with liquorice ash foie gras and Waldorf bits is an inventive starter, and main-course roast loin of lamb with braised breast, sweetbread popcorn and goats' cheese foam carries things on in the same vein. Hot lemon curd with thyme biscotti and 'marshmallows to toast' rounds things off nicely.

Times 12-2.30/7-9.30 Closed Mon, L Tue-Fri, D Sun

Two To Four

Modern V

Stylish town-centre venue with creative cookery

01306 889923
2-4 West St RH4 1BL
e-mail: eliterestaurants@hotmail.com
web: www.twotofourrestaurant.com
dir: M25, exit at Leatherhead junct, follow signs to town centre

Extending over three floors in what were once three cottages, this stylish venue with its cream-painted, latticed façade has played a proactive role in Surrey's dining scene. Undressed tables and a supplementary blackboard menu give notice that informality is the name of the game, and Rob Gathercole's cooking mixes influences creatively in the modern way. Crisp pork belly with Bramley apple and parsnip purée offers good textural contrasts to kick things off, while main courses such as seared bream with Lyonnaise potatoes, bacon and red pepper, or confit free-range chicken with creamy mash and pickled red cabbage, show a neat understanding of flavour composition. Hard-to-resist desserts include a crème brûlée made with figs and mascarpone, served with fig purée and a cinnamon biscuit.

Chef Rob Gathercole **Owner** Elite Restaurants **Times** 12-2.30/6.30-10 Closed Xmas, Etr, BHs, 2 wks Aug, Sun-Mon **Prices** Fixed L 2 course £12-£15, Fixed D 2 course £16-£19, Starter £7.50-£8.95, Main £15.95-£18.95, Dessert £7.50, Service optional, Service added but optional 10% **Wines** 23 bottles over £20, 9 bottles under £20, 4 by glass **Notes** Vegetarian menu **Seats** 70, Pr/dining room 12 **Children** Portions **Parking** West St car park

EGHAM Map 6 TQ07

The Oak Room at Great Fosters

– see page 394

GODALMING Map 6 SU94

La Luna

Modern Italian NOTABLE WINE LIST

Modern Italian with Sicilian and Tuscan influences

01483 414155
10-14 Wharf St GU7 1NN
e-mail: info@lalunarestaurant.co.uk
dir: In town centre, at junct of Wharf St & Flambard Way

A contemporary Italian restaurant in the centre of town with a well-earned reputation, the dining room at La Luna is a light and airy space with a striking caramel, chocolate and black colour scheme and oak tables. The menu - written in Italian with translations (plus there's help from the charming Italian waiters) - features modern Italian dishes simply presented. Antipasti might include arancini (risotto balls), panelle (chick pea pancakes) or crostini with rosemary and cannellini bean pâté. Gnocchi comes with gorgonzola, Sicilian pistachio pesto and rocket, while poached red gurnard is served with clam guazzetto (fish soup) and sprouting broccoli. The over 150 wines span Italy's regions.

Chef Valentino Gentile **Owner** Daniele Drago & Orazio Primavera **Times** 12-2/7-10 Closed early Jan, 2 wks in Aug, Sun-Mon **Prices** Fixed L 2 course £11.95, Starter £3.50-£8.95, Main £9.95-£18.50, Dessert £4.50-£6.50 **Wines** 136 bottles over £20, 12 bottles under £20, 8 by glass **Seats** 58, Pr/dining room 24 **Children** Portions **Parking** Public car park behind restaurant

HASLEMERE Map 6 SU93

The Restaurant at Lythe Hill

Modern British

Unfussy cooking in charming hotel with gardens

01428 651251
Petworth Rd GU27 3BQ
e-mail: lythe@lythehill.co.uk
dir: 1m E of Haslemere on B2131

This privately-owned hotel stands in 30 acres of attractive parkland on the border of Hampshire and West Sussex. The hotel has been created from a small hamlet of old farm buildings, some of which date back to the 15th century. The oak-panelled restaurant is located in a timbered Tudor farmhouse and is split into two rooms of contrasting styles - one with darkwood panels and an open fireplace, the other lighter and more modern with views across the gardens and lake. The simple modern British cooking uses a mix of traditional and contemporary cooking styles, so expect the likes of roulade of ham hock and foie gras with macerated prunes and toasted brioche, followed by fillet of sea bream with oven-dried tomatoes, baby fennel and tagliatelle on basil butter sauce.

Chef Michael Graham **Owner** Lythe Hill Hotel Ltd **Times** 12.30-2.15/7.15-9.30 **Prices** Food prices not confirmed for 2011. Please telephone for details. **Wines** 100 bottles over £20, 8 bottles under £20, 10 by glass **Notes** Vegetarian available, Dress restrictions, Smart casual, Civ Wed 128 **Seats** 60, Pr/dining room 35 **Children** Portions, Menu **Parking** 150

HORLEY

For restaurant details see Gatwick Airport (London), (Sussex, West)

The Oak Room at Great Fosters

EGHAM Map 6 TQ07

Modern British V NOTABLE WINE LIST

Regal Elizabethan setting for highly accomplished cuisine

☎ 01784 433822
Stroude Rd TW20 9UR
e-mail: enquiries@greatfosters.co.uk
dir: From A30 (Bagshot to Staines), right at lights by Wheatsheaf pub into Christchurch Rd. Straight on at rdbt (pass 2 shop parades on right). Left at lights into Stroude Rd. Hotel 0.75m on right

Built as a hunting lodge in the 16th century, this magnificent Elizabethan manor sits in exuberant gardens framed by a Saxon moat. The great Windsor Forest where the nobles once hunted has all but gone, but the house opens a window onto how they feasted amid dark oak panelling, splendid Jacobean fireplaces, and ornate ceilings. But enough history - after all, Great Fosters is no museum: this is a top-flight country house with bags of character and a very modern approach to dining. The fine dining Oak Room restaurant is a real one-off: an intricate spider's web of vaulted oak beams spans the roof above an understated modern décor involving a bright contemporary tapestry and high-backed chairs at linen-clad tables. Head chef Simon Bolsover made a name for himself at Linthwaite House (see entry) and is living up to his new surroundings in style; he leads a talented kitchen team along a route of light, modern cooking, underpinned by classical roots, that sees crab risotto teamed with parmesan, crisp chicken wing and poultry jus. A main course of Cumbrian lamb rump cooked at 60 degrees is served with the Mediterranean flavours of ricotta dumplings, black olives, fennel and basil jus, while dessert is a knockout dark chocolate sphere with a heart of salted caramel, served with white chocolate mousse and confit lemon.

Chef Simon Bolsover **Owner** Great Fosters (1931) Ltd
Times 12.30-2/7-9.30 Closed L Sat
Prices Fixed L 2 course £23, Fixed D 3 course £39, Starter £12, Main £30, Dessert £9, Service added but optional 12.5% **Wines** 285 bottles over £20, 2 bottles under £20, 14 by glass
Notes Sunday L, Vegetarian menu, Civ Wed 170 **Seats** 60, Pr/dining room 20
Children Portions, Menu **Parking** 200

OCKLEY Map 6 TQ14

Bryce's Seafood Restaurant & Country Pub

Modern British, Seafood V

Great local fish and seafood in beamed pub-restaurant

01306 627430
The Old School House, Stane St RH5 5TH
e-mail: fish@bryces.co.uk
dir: From M25 junct 9 take A24, then A29. 8m S of Dorking on A29

A former gymnasium of a boys' boarding school dating from 1750 is these days home to a restaurant and pub with a passion for the fruits of the sea. It has retained much of its character with beams in abundance and a friendly, informal atmosphere. The menu offers tip-top fresh fish and seafood, much of it sent up from Shoreham, an hour away on the Sussex coast. Typical dishes from the fixed-price menu included natural smoked haddock with potato purée and a pancetta and mushroom cream sauce, and fillet of sea bream with prawn and basil risotto. Daily specials feature some non-fish alternatives including meat from local farms.

Chef B Bryce, Ashley Sullivan **Owner** Mr B Bryce **Times** 12-2.30/7-9.30 Closed 25-26 Dec, 1 Jan, D Sun (Nov & Jan-Feb) **Prices** Fixed L 2 course fr £12.50, Fixed D 3 course £15.50, Service optional, Groups min 8 service 10% **Wines** 13 bottles over £20, 22 bottles under £20, 16 by glass **Notes** Set ALC 2 course £29, 3 course £34 Fixed L & D Mon-Thu only, Sunday L, Vegetarian menu **Seats** 50 **Children** Portions **Parking** 35

REDHILL Map 6 TQ25

Nutfield Priory - Cloisters Restaurant

Modern European

Stylish modern cooking in a Victorian Gothic setting

0845 0727486
Nutfield Rd RH1 4EL
e-mail: nutfieldpriory@handpicked.co.uk
dir: On A25, 1m E of Redhill, off M25 junct 8 or M25 junct 6, follow A25 through Godstone

The name and the look might fool you, but Nutfield was never a priory before it morphed into a grand country-house hotel: it's a classic piece of Victorian Gothic whimsy, inspired by Pugin's design for the Houses of Parliament. Still, shame to waste a good theme, so the Cloisters restaurant is a convincing bit of period fakery with its oak ceilings, vaulted archways and mullioned windows giving inspirational views across the South Downs. Blue-chip ingredients from Sussex and Surrey form the backbone of a menu that brings the country-house repertoire into the 21st century using foams and other modish techniques. Seasons are respected, as witnessed in a summer menu starter of duck rillettes with vanilla and orange foam. Main-course spring lamb is an accomplished showing too, delivered as a noisette, confit belly crumbed and deep-fried, and braised kidneys with basil fondant and ratatouille-style Provençal vegetables.

Chef Neil Davison **Owner** Hand Picked Hotels **Times** 12-2.30/7-9.30 Closed L Sat **Prices** Fixed L 2 course £21-£25, Fixed D 2 course £36-£42, Starter £10-£12, Main £20-£30, Dessert £10-£12, Service optional **Wines** 90 bottles over £20, 2 bottles under £20, 18 by glass **Notes** Tasting menu available, Sunday L, Vegetarian available, Dress restrictions, No jeans or trainers, Civ Wed 80 **Seats** 60, Pr/dining room 100 **Children** Portions, Menu **Parking** 130

REIGATE Map 6 TQ25

The Dining Room

Modern British V

Creative cooking from TV chef

01737 226650
59a High St RH2 9AE
dir: 1st floor restaurant on Reigate High St

Tony Tobin continues to be a regular on our TV screens and his Reigate showcase restaurant continues to pull in the punters. It's an elegant space, tastefully decorated with sumptuous curtains, artworks and mirrored walls; tables are suitably formally dressed with white linen and smart crockery. Tobin's modern British menu is full of good ideas and inspiration is global. There's a Tasting Menu (with optional wine selections) if you want to let the kitchen spread its wings. Start with tea-smoked king prawns with cumin-scented vegetables and lemon crème fraîche, or spiced lamb empanada with fragrant tomato kasundi, before moving on to roasted monkfish tail with chorizo, couscous and spicy tomato jus. Finish with an Amaretto and espresso parfait with almond biscotti and vanilla coffee syrup.

Chef Tony Tobin **Owner** Tony Tobin **Times** 12-2/7-10 Closed Xmas & BHs, L Sat, D Sun **Prices** Fixed L 2 course £12.50, Fixed D 3 course £19.50, Tasting menu fr £42, Starter £12-£15.50, Main £18-£27.50, Dessert £7.95, Service added but optional 12.5% **Wines** 61 bottles over £20, 16 bottles under £20, 10 by glass **Notes** Tasting menu available, Sunday L, Vegetarian menu, Dress restrictions, Smart casual **Seats** 75, Pr/dining room 28 **Children** Portions **Parking** On street, car park

The Westerly

Modern

First-class bistro with great food at fair prices

01737 222733
2-4 London Rd RH2 9AN

The Westerly is the sort of unbuttoned modern bistro that every town should have. Chef-patron Jon Coomb, with his wife Cynthia taking care of front-of-house, have hit on a formula that ticks all the boxes. The bistro is classy, yet unpretentious, with its pale wooden floors, red high-backed banquettes, chocolate leather chairs and modern artwork. And in keeping with the quietly stylish, unfussy setting, the confident modern cooking is well-thought-out and in tune with customers who want high-quality food at fair prices. Mediterranean warmth infuses the menu in starters such as Catalan-style pork rillettes with green olive tapenade, or there might be a gutsy croquette of pig's trotter and hock with sauce gribiche. Main courses deliver crisp pork belly partnered by morcilla and potato hotpot and Granny Smith purée, or roast cod with mash and salsa verde.

Times 12-2.30/7-10 Closed Sun, Mon, L Tue, Sat

RIPLEY Map 6 TQ05

Drake's Restaurant

– see page 396

The Talbot Inn

British

Charming historic inn and modern British food

01483 225188
High St GU23 6BB
e-mail: info@thetalbotinn.com
dir: Exit A3 signed Ripley, on left on High St

This recently remodelled 15th-century coaching inn on Ripley's high street now boasts a contemporary restaurant alongside its old-school bar. While the real-ale serving bar is all low, dark beams and timbers, the restaurant and conservatory revels in its modernity - think quirky lighting, a copper-covered ceiling, sandblasted exposed brickwork and light oak furniture and floorboards. Quality local ingredients shine through in the simple modern British cooking. Start perhaps with West Coast scallops with parsnip purée, caramelised apple and crispy coppa di Parma moving onto pork medallions with Bramley mash and apple jus. A selection of British cheeses makes for a patriotic ending.

Chef Gavin Chilcott **Owner** Merchant Inns **Times** 12-2.30/6.30-9.30 Closed D Sun (Winter only) **Prices** Starter £4.50-£8.20, Main £9.95-£19.95, Dessert £5.70-£5.95, Service optional, Groups min 6 service 7% **Wines** 25 bottles over £20, 8 bottles under £20, 8 by glass **Notes** Sunday L, Vegetarian available, Civ Wed 120 **Seats** 100, Pr/dining room 80 **Children** Portions, Menu **Parking** 60, On Street

SHERE Map 6 TQ04

Kinghams

Modern British

Local produce showcased in attractive cottage restaurant

☎ 01483 202168
Gomshall Ln GU5 9HE
e-mail: paul.kinghams@googlemail.com
dir: M25 junct 10. On A25 between Guildford & Dorking

The setting couldn't be more delightful - a picture-book 17th-century brick-and-timber cottage festooned with rambling roses and tucked away in the perfect English village. With its head-cracking low beams, glowing fires and intimate small rooms, Kinghams oozes charm and character, and the colourful garden, replete with statues, fountains and a heated gazebo, is a great spot for summer alfresco dining. Classic British cooking is imaginative with good presentation and sound use of local produce on seasonal menus and daily fish specials. Typically, start with seared scallops with yellow pepper compôte, parmesan wafers and saffron crème fraîche, move on to marinated lamb rump on slow-roasted aubergines with sun-dried tomato and basil jus, and round off with a medley of chocolate desserts.

Chef Paul Baker **Owner** Paul Baker
Times 12.15-2.30/7-9.30 Closed 25 Dec-4 Jan, Mon, D Sun **Prices** Fixed L 2 course £16.95, Fixed D 2 course £16.95, Starter £6.95-£10.95, Main £14.95-£20.95, Dessert £5.95-£6.95, Service optional, Groups min 8 service 10% **Wines** 12 bottles over £20, 26 bottles under £20, 6 by glass **Notes** Sunday L, Vegetarian available **Seats** 48, Pr/dining room 24 **Children** Portions **Parking** 16

STOKE D'ABERNON Map 6 TQ15

Oak Room @ Woodlands Park Hotel

Modern British, French

Grand Victorian house with cooking to match

☎ 01372 843933
Woodlands Ln KT11 3QB
e-mail: woodlandspark@handpicked.co.uk
dir: A3 exit at Cobham. Through town centre & Stoke D'Abernon, left at garden centre into Woodlands Lane, hotel 0.5m on right

The imposing red-brick mansion was built in the 1880s by William Bryant, heir to the Bryant and May matchstick fortune. At its heart is the Oak Room restaurant, where the view over the gardens through majestic bay windows is serene enough to aid digestion, and your dinner arrives on silver trays in the manner of the service on a luxury liner. It all makes a fitting backdrop for the country-house British cuisine, which trades in dishes such as smoked duck and foie gras roulade in apple dressing, sea bass with mussels and clams in garlic and saffron, and perhaps pecan nougat glacé with matching ice cream and maple syrup to finish.

Chef Matthew Ashton **Owner** Hand Picked Hotels
Times 12-2.30/7-10 Closed Mon, L Tue-Sat, D Sun **Prices** Fixed D 3 course £46, Service optional **Wines** 125 bottles over £20, 4 bottles under £20, 10 by glass **Notes** Sunday L, Vegetarian available, Dress restrictions, No jeans or trainers, Civ Wed 200 **Seats** 35, Pr/dining room 150 **Children** Portions, Menu **Parking** 150

Drake's Restaurant

RIPLEY Map 6 TQ05

Modern British V

Innovative, classy cooking in elegant house

☎ 01483 224777
The Clock House, High St GU23 6AQ
e-mail: info@drakesrestaurant.co.uk
web: www.drakesrestaurant.co.uk
dir: M25 junct 10, A3 towards Guildford. Follow Ripley signs. Restaurant in village centre

Chef-patron Steve Drake continues to wow diners at his elegant restaurant in a smart Georgian town house. First impressions count, and the interior affects an understated boutique style with local art on the walls. Steve describes his work as 'artisan cooking', but there's not a hint of the rough-and-ready peasant approach this might imply. The term 'artisan' might, however, be applied to the suppliers who furnish the kitchen with top-class materials, but the cooking is sophisticated, labour-intensive, inventive and fizzing with technical prowess. Dishes are often superlative exercises in flavours and textures - perhaps rabbit with crispy carrot, tarragon cream and Parma ham, ahead of roasted brill teamed with chorizo, piccalilli and baby gem lettuce. Duck with chestnut, satsuma, turnip and cromesqui, shows an eclectic mind at work, while desserts continue the theme of dazzling with unlikely combinations - beetroot parfait with mandarin sorbet, chocolate crumbs and star anise gel, for example, or go for a more orthodox crème renversée, a French-accented pannacotta with Granny Smith sorbet and dried apple tuile.

Chef Steve Drake **Owner** Steve & Serina Drake
Times 12-1.30/7-9.30 Closed 2 wks Jan, 2 wks Aug, Sun-Mon, L Sat **Prices** Fixed L 2 course fr £21, Fixed D 3 course fr £46, Tasting menu £60, Service added but optional 12.5% **Wines** 180 bottles over £20, 5 bottles under £20, 11 by glass **Notes** Tasting menu & vegetarian tasting menu available, Vegetarian menu **Seats** 34, Pr/dining room 12 **Parking** 2

SUSSEX, EAST

ALFRISTON Map 6 TQ50

Harcourts Restaurant

Modern British

Seasonal modern cooking in the heart of the Sussex countryside

☎ 01323 870248
Deans Place Hotel, Seaford Rd BN26 5TW
e-mail: mail@deansplacehotel.co.uk
dir: off A27, signed Alfriston & Drusillas Zoo Park. Continue south through village

Deans Place is a welcoming hotel set amongst the attractive gardens of what used to be an agricultural estate. The building has been a prominent feature of the pretty village of Alfriston for hundreds of years. Most produce is sourced locally from both farm and sea and the kitchen puts these ingredients to good use in classic dishes with a few modern twists along the way. Start with pan-fried scallops with avocado mash and sauce vierge before moving onto pink roasted duck breast with pommes Anna, spring greens, confit carrots and rhubarb jus. For dessert, perhaps a baked chocolate tart with mocha ice cream.

Chef Stuart Dunley **Times** 12.30-2.30/6.30-9.30 **Prices** Food prices not confirmed for 2011. Please telephone for details. **Wines** 52 bottles over £20, 27 bottles under £20, 10 by glass **Notes** Sunday L, Vegetarian available, Dress restrictions, Smart casual, Civ Wed 140 **Seats** 60, Pr/dining room 50 **Children** Portions, Menu **Parking** 100

BATTLE Map 7 TQ71

Powder Mills Hotel

Modern British V

Modern menu in an attractive conservatory dining room

☎ 01424 775511
Powdermill Ln TN33 0SP
e-mail: powdc@aol.com
dir: M25 junct 5, A21 towards Hastings. At St Johns Cross take A2100 to Battle. Pass abbey on right, 1st right into Powdermills Ln. 1m, hotel on right

In the heart of 1066 country, this elegant Georgian mansion sits in 150 acres of beautiful Sussex countryside, complete with lakes and woodland. The site was originally a gunpowder factory whose products helped keep Napoleon at bay; nowadays it is given over to more serene pursuits, chief among which is dining in the luminous Orangery Restaurant, where Italian statuary, huge potted plants, marble floors, and wicker chairs create a summery vibe. Materials from the hotel's kitchen gardens and on-site farm make a fair showing alongside Sussex's bounty in refreshingly uncomplicated modern British dishes. You might start with smoked haddock risotto and shaved parmesan, then move on to slow-roasted pork belly with caramelised apples and cider sauce. Finish in homely style with bread-and-butter sauce with crème anglaise, and there are fine Sussex cheeses.

Chef Lee Griffin **Owner** Mr & Mrs D Cowpland **Times** 12-2/7-9 **Prices** Fixed L 3 course £17.50-£21.50, Fixed D 3 course £29.50, Service added but optional 10%, Groups min 10 service 10% **Wines** 38 bottles over £20, 32 bottles under £20, 4 by glass **Notes** Sunday L, Vegetarian menu, Dress restrictions, Smart casual, no jeans, shorts or T-shirts, Civ Wed 100 **Seats** 90, Pr/dining room 16 **Children** Portions, Menu **Parking** 100

BRIGHTON & HOVE Map 6 TQ30

Chilli Pickle

Indian NEW

Indian cooking with heart and soul

☎ 01273 323 824
42 Meeting House Ln BN1 1HB
e-mail: enquiries@thechillipicklebistro.co.uk
web: www.thechillipicklebistro.co.uk
dir: In the heart of South Lanes. At the entrance of Meeting House Ln between The Pumphouse & The Druids Head

There's a lot more going on down the narrow and winding Laines of Brighton than the buying and selling of jewellery. The Chilli Pickle deals in the food of the Indian sub-continent and it does so with an attention to detail, passion and verve that puts many a local curry house to shame. It looks the part for Brighton – unpretentious, urban-rustic, with colourful pictures on the walls depicting cliché-free scenes of India and Sanskrit writing that is probably not a quote from the forearm of a Premiership footballer. At lunchtime the deal is Indian street food – uttapam, medu vada, pakora, plus dosas and thalis. In the evening, the menu treads a more traditional starter, main course format, the dishes plated up in the Western manner. Ingredients are sourced with due diligence, the cooking is careful, well-judged and flavours are powerful but not overpowering. Moilly mussels and scallops is a starter that delivers plump and beautifully fresh mussels simmered in a delicious coconut and ginger broth, topped with perfectly seared scallops, while main-course oxtail Madras has won awards, don't you know.

Chef Alun Sperring **Owner** Alun & Dawn Sperring **Times** 12-3/6.30-10.30 Closed 25-26 Dec, 1 Jan, Mon-Tue **Prices** Starter £3.95-£7.95, Main £9.50-£16.95, Dessert £4.50, Service optional **Wines** 15 bottles over £20, 14 bottles under £20, 7 by glass **Notes** Vegetarian available **Seats** 50, Pr/dining room 12 **Children** Portions **Parking** Laines car park

Drakes

British, European

Fashionable boutique hotel with creative, destination restaurant

☎ 01273 696934
43-44 Marine Pde BN2 1PE
dir: From A23 at Brighton Pier rdbt. Left into Marine Pde towards marina. Hotel on left before lights (ornate water feature at front)

A beautiful bow-fronted Georgian house on the seafront road, not a million miles from the pier, Drakes is a boutique hotel with an über-cool cocktail bar and a restaurant that has gained itself a reputation as a serious dining destination in the city. The bar gets the views out to sea, while the restaurant is down in the basement, but no matter, for it is stylishly kitted out and the subterranean setting helps create an appealing intimacy. Striking photographs adorn the walls and the tables are formally dressed in preparation for Andrew MacKenzie's well-crafted modern European cooking. Tempura frogs' legs are paired with garlic purée and a hazelnut salad in a creative starter that draws inspiration from further afield than just across the water, while 21-day aged fillet of Irish beef, with shin and pork faggot, is finished with a bone marrow and truffle sauce. For dessert, lemon meringue pie with mascarpone custard should hit the spot.

Chef Andrew MacKenzie **Owner** Andy & Gail Shearer **Times** 12.30-2.30/7-10 **Prices** Fixed L 2 course £25-£32, Fixed D 3 course £37-£42, Tasting menu fr £50 **Wines** 55 bottles over £20, 10 by glass **Notes** 5 course tasting menu available D, Sunday L, Vegetarian available, Civ Wed 42 **Seats** 42, Pr/dining room 12 **Parking** On street

BRIGHTON & HOVE *continued*

Due South

Modern British

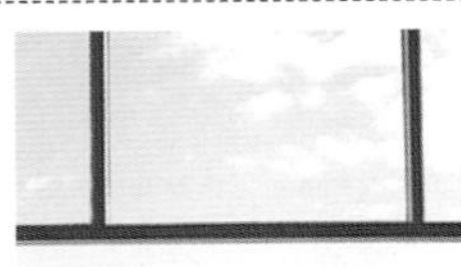

Seaside dining with genuine commitment to organic and local produce

☎ 01273 821218
139 Kings Road Arches BN1 2FN
e-mail: eat@duesouth.co.uk
web: www.duesouth.co.uk
dir: On seafront, beneath cinema

Due South is Brighton's seafront shop window for small-scale Sussex producers. On a sunny day, the location on the terrace along the beachfront strip takes some beating, but even on bad days, the mezzanine level slotted into the Victorian arches beneath Brighton's prom is tops for sea views. Inside, it's a simple, contemporary space with pine tables, boarded floors and banquettes. In tune with the vibe of the UK's first officially Green constituency, the kitchen has a heartfelt commitment to the environment, sourcing the lion's share of its ingredients from organic, free-range and biodynamic producers within a 35-mile radius of the pebbles. The roll call of imaginative combinations kicks off with wild rabbit terrine with pickled Sussex apples and organic cider jelly; fish and seafood is naturally a strong suit - perhaps pan-roasted brill with sautéed pak choi, crab gnocchi and tomato and cinnamon broth. Sussex wines appear on an English and European-only list inspired by minimising food miles.

Chef Michael Bremner **Owner** Robert Shenton **Times** 12-3.30/6-9.45 Closed 25 Dec **Prices** Fixed L 2 course £10-£15, Starter £5-£12, Main £7.50-£32, Dessert £6-£12, Service added but optional 10%, Groups min 10 service 10% **Wines** 8 bottles over £20, 25 by glass **Notes** Sunday L, Vegetarian available, Civ Wed 55 **Seats** 55, Pr/dining room 12 **Children** Portions, Menu **Parking** NCP behind Grand Hotel

The Gingerman Restaurant (Norfolk Square)

Modern British

Original branch of a classy Brighton restaurant group

☎ 01273 326688
21A Norfolk Square BN1 2PD
e-mail: info@gingermanrestaurants.com
dir: A23 to Palace Pier rdbt. Turn right onto Kings Rd. At Art Deco style Embassy building turn right into Norfolk Sq

The original progenitor of Ben McKellar's still-growing restaurant family in and around Brighton remains an appealing spot in the city centre, just off the seafront. Classy, often arresting, cooking has been going on here now since 1998. It's a low-ceilinged former tea room, run by friendly, interested staff, and the food is a recognisable version of modern British modes, based on sound, locally-sourced ingredients. Sautéed Rye Bay cuttlefish with chorizo and rosemary, flamed with brandy, makes a change from the ubiquitous scallops, and may be followed by olive-crusted rump of lamb with a potato galette, aubergine and puréed roasted garlic. Finish with mango and honeycomb trifle and passionfruit sauce, or with elderflower jelly, mixed berries and vanilla ice cream.

Times 12.30-2/7-10 Closed 2 wks Xmas, Mon

Graze Restaurant

Modern British V

Classy tapas-style modern European food

☎ 01273 823707
42 Western Rd BN3 1JD
e-mail: bookings@graze-restaurant.co.uk
dir: A23/A259 Brighton Pier. E for 1.5m onto Lansdowne Place. Restaurant on Western Rd on right

On the bustling Western Road, just around the corner from the splendid Brunswick Square, Graze has hit on a winning formula with its grazing dishes, which give diners the chance to explore a multitude of flavours. The glass windows open onto the pavement to give the place a French feel in warm weather, while inside the theme is Regency, in homage to the city's famous Royal Pavilion. The menu takes its inspiration from Europe, with local, seasonal produce to the fore, and note it is possible to have a traditional three-course meal if you prefer. Tuck into gazpacho with peas and crab or courgette flower tempura with goats' cheese, ratatouille and pesto, while a main-course option might be steamed line-caught sea bass with spiced fishcake, coconut lentils and greens. Tasting menus are a great way to explore the repertoire, and they come with wine recommendations, too.

Chef Gethin Jones **Owner** Kate Alleston, Neil Mannifield **Times** 12-2/6.30-10 Closed 25-26 Dec, 1 Jan, Mon, D Sun **Prices** Fixed L 2 course £14, Fixed D 2 course £16, Starter £5.50-£8, Main £13.50-£18, Dessert £6.50-£8, Service added but optional 12% **Wines** 35 bottles over £20, 13 bottles under £20, 11 by glass **Notes** Tasting menu 7 course & vegetarian tasting menu, Sunday L, Vegetarian menu, Dress restrictions, Smart casual **Seats** 50, Pr/dining room 24 **Children** Portions

Hotel du Vin Brighton

French, European

Urbane brasserie dining in stylish contemporary hotel

☎ 01273 718588
2-6 Ship St BN1 1AD
e-mail: info@brighton.hotelduvin.com
dir: A23 to seafront, at rdbt right, then right onto Middle St, bear right into Ship St, hotel at sea end on right

Perfectly situated in Brighton's famous Laines area and a pebble's throw from the beach is the city's buzzy outpost of the Hotel du Vin chain. The fun ambience in the busy wine bar and laid-back vibe in the brasserie restaurant gel nicely with the mood of the seaside resort that invented the dirty weekend. The wine-themed decor is the ideal backdrop for the kitchen's classic Anglo-French bistro repertoire built around seasonal ingredients. A good honest starter of ham hock terrine with apple and vanilla chutney and toasted sourdough sets the tone, while main-course sea bass is seared and served with courgette, pea and herb risotto, and gremolata. The Hotel du Vin stable is known for its excellent wine list, with clued-up sommeliers on hand to guide you in the right direction.

Chef Rob Carr **Owner** M.W.B **Times** 12-2/7-10 Closed 31 Dec D **Prices** Food prices not confirmed for 2011. Please telephone for details. **Wines** 300 bottles over £20, 50 bottles under £20, 12 by glass **Notes** Sunday L, Vegetarian available, Civ Wed 90 **Seats** 85, Pr/dining room 90 **Children** Portions, Menu **Parking** The Laines NCP

The Meadow Restaurant

British

Local ingredients the star of the show

☎ 01273 721182
64 Western Rd BN3 2JQ
e-mail: info@themeadowrestaurant.co.uk

A former bank on Hove's main thoroughfare is now a bright and airy restaurant with the focus firmly set on seasonal Sussex produce. Chef-owner Will Murgatroyd namechecks his local suppliers (or 'friends') on the menu including his own parents, whose garden contributes vegetables, herbs and flowers. The vibrant space with its high ceilings, white walls and blond wooden tables and chairs is presided over by easy-going and friendly staff. Meanwhile, the intelligently-constructed menu allows the quality ingredients to speak for themselves in modern British dishes touched by the hand of Europe. Think organic Jerusalem artichoke soup with truffle oil and goats' curd or slow-cooked shoulder of Middlewhite pork with crackling and home-made Bramley apple sauce and a finale of crème fraîche tart with boozy prunes and rhubarb ripple ice cream.

Chef Will Murgatroyd **Owner** Will Murgatroyd **Times** 12-2.30/6-9.30 Closed 25-26 Dec, BH's, Mon, D Sun **Prices** Fixed L 2 course £12, Fixed D 3 course £15, Service added but optional 10% **Wines** 15 bottles over £20, 8 bottles under £20, 18 by glass **Notes** Fixed D only available before 7.30pm, Sunday L, Vegetarian available **Seats** 70 **Children** Portions, Menu **Parking** On street

Sam's of Brighton

Modern British NEW

Unpretentious global cooking just off Kemp Town seafront

☎ 01273 676222
1 Paston Place, Kemptown BN2 1HA
e-mail: info@samsofbrighton.co.uk
dir: Between Brighton Pier & Marina

The second arm of Sam Metcalfe's Brighton operation (see entry, Sevendials), this light, airy, cream-coloured room is situated just off the seafront in Kemp Town. Casting the culinary net wide, the menu has the laid-back feel of a gastro-pub about it, and dishes can impress. Tender tempura-battered squid with green beans and red onion salsa is a fresh, enlivening starter, and might be followed by roast noisette of South Downs lamb with ratatouille, garlicky potato gratin and crisp-fried sweetbreads. Vegetarians might proceed from artichoke gnocchi to vegetable tagine with couscous and Greek yoghurt, while meals end well with the likes of lemon tart, served with crème fraîche and raspberry coulis.

Chef Simon Dunlan, Sam Metcalfe **Owner** Sam & Laura Metcalfe **Times** 12-3/6-10 Closed Mon **Prices** Fixed L 2 course £12.50, Starter £4.50-£8, Main £10-£17.95, Dessert £5-£7, Service optional, Groups min 6 service 12.5% **Wines** 17 bottles over £20, 13 bottles under £20, 15 by glass **Notes** Sunday L, Vegetarian available, Air con **Seats** 52 **Children** Portions, Menu **Parking** On street

Sevendials

Modern British

Lively modern British menu with lots of local flavour

☎ 01273 885555
1-3 Buckingham Place BN1 3TD
e-mail: info@sevendialsrestaurant.co.uk
dir: From Brighton station turn right 0.5m up hill, restaurant at Seven Dials rdbt

The Seven Dials area of Brighton, just north of the station, is a residential quarter of the city with a mix of Georgian and Victorian housing and a nice line in delis and chilled out cafés and bars around the busy intersection. The Sevendials restaurant has a prime position in a converted bank, the generous proportions of the building suiting the relaxed, brasserie vibe of the place - bare darkwood tables, large windows, lofty ceilings and a neutral colour scheme. There's a decked terrace allowing for some outside eating. The kitchen makes everything in-house and walks a broadly modern British path. A ragout of Sussex lamb comes in a first course with home-made potato gnocchi, or there's all the simplicity of a half-dozen Carlingford oysters. Main course brings forth fillet of local wild sea bass (with crushed ratte potatoes and Shetland rope-grown mussels) and braised leg of rabbit (with carrot and swede purée and buttered Savoy cabbage). Sam's of Brighton (see entry) is an offshoot.

Chef Sam Metcalfe, Mark Kinzel **Owner** Sam Metcalfe **Times** 12-3/6-10.30 Closed 25 Dec, 1 Jan, D Sun **Prices** Fixed L 2 course £10, Fixed D 3 course £21, Tasting menu fr £40, Starter £4.75-£7, Main £10-£17.95, Dessert £5-£7, Service optional, Groups min 6 service 12% **Wines** 15 bottles over £20, 20 bottles under £20, 12 by glass **Notes** ALC menu 6-7pm £10-£15, Tasting menu available Sat D, Sunday L, Vegetarian available, Civ Wed 80 **Seats** 60, Pr/dining room 20 **Children** Portions, Menu **Parking** 3, 2 mins from restaurant on street

Terre à Terre

Modern Vegetarian V

Bold and exciting vegetarian and vegan cooking

☎ 01273 729051
71 East St BN1 1HQ
e-mail: mail@terreaterre.co.uk
web: www.terreaterre.co.uk
dir: Town centre, close to Brighton Pier & The Laines

It seems fair enough, after more than 17 years of ground-breaking innovative vegetarian cooking, to refer to Terre à Terre as an iconic restaurant. With a reputation that goes far beyond Brighton, it continues to confound the expectations of cynical carnivores. Close to the seafront and just a short stroll from the pier, it is a surprisingly spacious place, with colourful walls, light wooden tables, comfortable chairs and enthusiastic staff, smartly dressed in black, who can give you the lowdown on the menu. The food is famously innovative, flavour combinations are bold, influences global and menu descriptions detailed and somewhat esoteric. Start with a 'Pea Shooter', which is a baked ash Crottin (goats' cheese) served with roasted violet garlic, a shot glass filled with minted pea purée and topped with a lemon thyme cream, and finally 'big linseed parchment shards' (a crisp flatbread). For main course there might be 'Sodden Socca' (hot chick pea chubby pancakes with warm piquant caponata), and to finish, 'Perky Pear and Choccy tart'. The ingredients are first-rate, seasonality drives the menu and vegan and gluten-free dishes are marked as such.

Chef Dino Pavledis, A Powley, P Taylor **Owner** Ms A Powley & Mr P Taylor **Times** 12-10.30 Closed 25-26 Dec, 1 Jan **Prices** Starter £4.85-£8.65, Main £11.50-£20, Dessert £3.95-£7.85, Service optional, Groups min 6 service 10% **Wines** 45 bottles over £20, 15 bottles under £20, 25 by glass **Notes** Promotional fixed price L & D menus available **Seats** 110 **Children** Portions, Menu **Parking** NCP, on street

EASTBOURNE — Map 6 TV69

Conservatory at Langhams

British

Good British cooking in seafront terrace restaurant

☎ 01323 731451
Langham Hotel, 43-49 Royal Pde BN22 7AH
e-mail: neil@langhamhotel.co.uk
dir: A22 follow signs for seafront Sovereign Centre take 3rd exit onto Royal Pde. Hotel on corner Royal Pde & Cambridge Rd

Langhams Hotel is a classic white-painted Edwardian seaside hotel smack on Eastbourne's seafront. Sea views towards the pier and Beachy Head are glorious, and there's no better place to take them in than the fine-dining restaurant in the sunny conservatory, where vast windows look out from a sleek modern space with wooden floors and coffee-hued high-backed chairs. The kitchen puts an imaginative contemporary spin on classic British dishes with a clear French influence. Take feuillettes of scallops in a grapefruit and champagne sauce to start, and follow with rack of South Downs lamb teamed with rosemary, Parma ham and redcurrant jus, or brill fillet cooked in a pot with cockles and tarragon.

Chef Michael Titherington **Owner** Neil Kirby **Times** 12-2.30/6-9.30 **Prices** Food prices not confirmed for 2011. Please telephone for details. **Wines** 4 bottles over £20, 16 bottles under £20, 18 by glass **Notes** Vegetarian available, Civ Wed 120 **Seats** 24 **Children** Portions, Menu

Grand Hotel (Mirabelle)

Modern, Classic NOTABLE WINE LIST

Grand seafront hotel with confident cooking

☎ 01323 412345 & 435066
King Edward's Pde BN21 4EQ
e-mail: reservations@grandeastbourne.com
dir: Western end of seafront, 1m from Eastbourne station

Built in 1875 and dominating one end of Eastbourne's seafront, this magnificent Victorian hotel enjoys stunning sea views and has welcomed many of the great and the good over the years including Winston Churchill, Charlie

continued

EASTBOURNE *continued*

Chaplin and Elgar. Affectionately known as 'The White Palace', the Grand Hotel integrates late 19th-century charm and grandeur with modern comforts. Tastefully restored to its former glory, it is suitably palatial and comes complete with spacious lounges, luxurious health club and a Grand Hall, where afternoon tea is served amid marble-columned splendour. The Mirabelle is the light-and-airy fine-dining restaurant and its décor and atmosphere follows the traditional theming, though the kitchen takes a more modern approach. Pike soufflé with smoked salmon and dill sauce, perhaps, followed by roast duck with caramelised salsify Tatin and shiraz sauce. Finish with apple and rhubarb parfait with ginger foam and rhubarb tuile.

Grand Hotel (Mirabelle)

Chef Keith Mitchell, Gerald Roser **Owner** Elite Hotels **Times** 12.30-2/7-10 Closed 2-16 Jan, Sun-Mon **Prices** Fixed L 2 course £19.50-£23.50, Fixed D 3 course £38-£42, Starter £5.95-£9.95, Main £7.50-£14.50, Dessert £2.50-£3.95, Service optional **Wines** 268 bottles over £20, 11 by glass **Notes** Tasting menu 5 course, Vegetarian available, Dress restrictions, Jacket or tie for D, Civ Wed 200 **Seats** 50 **Parking** 70

FOREST ROW — Map 6 TQ43

Anderida Restaurant

British, European V

Grand hotel dining in an upmarket country-house

☎ 01342 824988
Ashdown Park Hotel, Wych Cross RH18 5JR
e-mail: reservations@ashdownpark.com
dir: A264 to East Grinstead, then A22 to Eastbourne. 2m S of Forest Row at Wych Cross lights. Left to Hartfield, hotel on right 0.75m

The swanky Ashdown Park Hotel and Country Club is a slick operation squirrelled away in the silent depths of Ashdown Forest. With 186 acres of landscaped gardens and parkland to roam in, plus an 18-hole golf course and a fitness and spa complex, you should have no trouble working up an appetite to give the Anderida Restaurant a good workout. The culinary hub of the whole Ashdown Park set up is a grandly formal old-school dining experience, where discreetly amiable staff show off polished silver service skills. This is flamboyantly-presented classical cuisine, perhaps a contemporary spin here and there, but nothing too radical. Luxury ingredients make an early showing in a starter of pan-seared pigeon breast with foie gras, pear, cherry sorbet and chocolate gel. Local venison comes next as loin and 'Wellington' with smoked garlic and herbs, roasted root vegetables, and a port and blackberry jus.

Anderida Restaurant

Chef Roger Gadsden **Owner** Elite Hotels **Times** 12-2/7-10 **Prices** Fixed L 2 course fr £16.95, Fixed D 3 course fr £37.50, Tasting menu fr £79.95, Starter £8-£12, Main £27-£30, Dessert £9-£11.50, Service optional **Wines** 334 bottles over £20, 14 bottles under £20, 12 by glass **Notes** Sunday L, Vegetarian menu, Dress restrictions, Jacket or tie for gentlemen after 7pm, Civ Wed 150 **Seats** 120, Pr/dining room 160 **Children** Portions, Menu **Parking** 120

HASTINGS & ST LEONARDS — Map 7 TQ80

Jali Restaurant at Chatsworth Hotel

Indian

Modern Indian cooking by the sea

☎ 01424 457300 & 720188
7-11 Carlisle Pde TN34 1JG
e-mail: info@chatsworthhotel.com
dir: On Hastings seafront, near railway station

Jali is a stylishly contemporary Indian restaurant in a friendly hotel in pole position on Hastings seafront - a pleasant backdrop as you ponder a menu that ranges more widely than the usual offerings from the Indian sub-continent. The waiters know their stuff, so let them guide you to pastures new - perhaps try the old Bombay favourite starter, bhel puri - puffed rice flour crisps with potatoes, mint, mango chutney, gram flour vermicelli and a pungent kick of coriander. Then go for a creamy murgh tikka makhani that marries tandoori chicken tikka with dried fenugreek leaves and a rich tomato gravy. In tune with the modern trends of Indian cuisine, the kitchen tries to cut the fat and salt content of their cooking.

Times 6.30-11 Closed L all week

JEVINGTON — Map 6 TQ50

Hungry Monk Restaurant

British, French

Ancient flint building, the home of banoffee pie

☎ 01323 482178
BN26 5QF
web: www.hungrymonk.co.uk
dir: A22, turn towards Wannock at Polegate x-rds. Continue for 2.5m, restaurant on left

A stalwart of the Sussex dining scene, the Hungry Monk is a delightfully intimate venue in a 14th-century flint building. The best way to start is with a fireside aperitif in one of the cosy, richly-coloured sitting rooms, before moving into the low-beamed dining room. The cooking is comfort-oriented, full-flavoured stuff, with local supply lines forming the mainstay of fixed-price lunch and dinner menus. Dinner might begin with a classic duck liver parfait with red onion marmalade and toasted brioche, followed, perhaps, by rabbit roasted in prosciutto with leek and ricotta and mild mustard sauce. To finish, aficionados of the banoffee pie have no choice, since the dish was invented here.

Times 12-2/6.45-9.45 Closed 24-26 Dec, BHs, Mon, Tue (Jan-May)

NEWICK Map 6 TQ42

Newick Park Hotel & Country Estate

@@ Modern European

Accomplished cooking in elegant country house

☎ 01825 723633
BN8 4SB
e-mail: bookings@newickpark.co.uk
dir: Exit A272 at Newick Green, 1m, pass church & pub. Turn left, hotel 0.25m on right

When it comes to elegant country-house dining, Newick Park is the real deal. With a 250-acre estate taking in peaceful parkland, a couple of lakes, and fabulous views towards the South Downs, all the elements of the classic English country house are present and correct. Add to this a gorgeous interior with plush fabrics and tasteful antiques, and a panelled dining room with high ceilings, exuberant flower displays, and floor-to-ceiling windows looking over the lake, and culinary expectations are certainly set high. And it delivers. Game comes from the estate, and much of the fruit and veg is grown in the walled kitchen garden and used creatively in well-thought-through daily menus. The kitchen takes a modern tack, opening with a characterful combo of pig's cheeks scented with five spice and paired with pineapple, lobster and ginger sauce. Main-course Newick Park rabbit comes with the punchy flavours of its kidneys and a pâté, together with Maxim potatoes, bacon pressé, apricots and pistachio crumbs. Dessert works a riff on blackberries, in the form of crumble, brûlée and parfait. Well-drilled staff deliver correctly formal service in keeping with the venue, and know their onions when it comes to recommending wines by the glass or from an interesting array of bins.

Chef Chris Moore **Owner** Michael & Virginia Childs **Times** 12-2/7-9 Closed 31 Jan **Prices** Fixed L 2 course £21.50, Fixed D 3 course £42.50, Service optional **Wines** 85 bottles over £20, 25 bottles under £20, 9 by glass **Notes** Sunday L, Vegetarian available, Civ Wed 120 **Seats** 40, Pr/dining room 74 **Children** Portions, Menu **Parking** 100

RYE Map 7 TQ92

The George in Rye

@ Modern Mediterranean

Modern restaurant in historic town

☎ 01797 222114
98 High St TN31 7JT
e-mail: stay@thegeorgeinrye.com
dir: M20 junct 10, then A2070 to Brenzett then A259 to Rye

Dating back to 1575, the George hotel in the centre of Rye has an impressive original Georgian ballroom and a rather more modern intimate restaurant following a sympathetic refurbishment which blends antiques with contemporary style. Seating 28, the relaxed and welcoming restaurant has low lighting, cream walls hung with local artwork and clothed candlelit tables. On the menu, Mediterranean flavours complement the local fish and seafood in the likes of a starter of Rye Bay scallops with parmesan crust, cauliflower purée and crispy speck. Or try a main course of Romney Marsh lamb noisettes with roast garlic, Lyonnaise potatoes and churrasco sauce. A Kent and Sussex cheese board provides a fitting finish. The George Tap is a popular bar, which serves a selection of wines from East Sussex and Kent vineyards.

Chef Rod Grossmann **Owner** Alex & Katie Clarke **Times** 12-3/6.30-9.30 **Prices** Fixed L 2 course £12.50, Starter £5.25-£8, Main £14-£16.75, Dessert £4.50-£6.50, Service optional **Wines** 31 bottles over £20, 10 bottles under £20, 12 by glass **Notes** Sunday L, Vegetarian available, Civ Wed 100 **Seats** 30, Pr/dining room 100 **Children** Portions, Menu **Parking** On street

Mermaid Inn

@ Traditional British & French V

Classical and modern dishes in a venerable setting

☎ 01797 223065 & 223788
Mermaid St TN31 7EY
e-mail: info@mermaidinn.com
dir: A259, follow signs to town centre, then into Mermaid St

Members of the Royal Family, as well as Hollywood royalty such as Johnny Depp and Pierce Brosnan, have put their heads round the door of this medieval Sussex hostelry in historic Rye. The location on a cobbled street, the panelled dining room and the bar with its display of antique weaponry above the great fireplace all look the part. A mix of old and new informs the cooking style, which extends to a separate vegetarian menu. Otherwise, it's seared scallops with figs and balsamic reduction dressing, red mullet with fennel and endive salad and ratatouille vinaigrette, or grilled sirloin steak with horseradish mash. Desserts such as two-tone parfait of raspberry and white chocolate aim to please.

Chef Roger Kellie **Owner** Mrs J Blincow & Mr R I Pinwill **Times** 12-2.30/7-9.30 **Prices** Fixed L 2 course £20, Fixed D 3 course £35, Starter £9.50-£11, Main £24.50-£32, Dessert £7, Service added but optional 10% **Wines** 48 bottles over £20, 6 bottles under £20, 15 by glass **Notes** Sunday L, Vegetarian menu, Dress restrictions, Smart casual, no jeans or T-shirts **Seats** 64, Pr/dining room 14 **Children** Portions, Menu **Parking** 26

Webbes at The Fish Café

@ Modern British

Modern seafood cooking in converted warehouse

☎ 01797 222226 & 222210
17 Tower St TN31 7AT
e-mail: info@thefishcafe.com
dir: 100mtrs before Landgate Arch

This converted warehouse in the middle of Rye once housed a toy factory. Tasteful renovation has kept many of the old warehouse-style features of the original building - the exposed brickwork and high ceilings are particularly impressive. Today's fish restaurant is laid out over three floors with a lively café on the ground floor, a more formal first floor dining room and a private function room up on the second. The open-plan kitchen takes an appealing modern approach to local seafood: ceviche of scallop and salmon with fennel, caviar and lime dressing, and loin of monkfish wrapped in prosciutto with crushed new potatoes, pan-fried leeks and sage sauce showing the style. Under the same ownership as The Wild Mushroom in Westfield (see entry).

Chef Paul Webbe, Mathew Drinkwater **Owner** Paul & Rebecca Webbe **Times** 12-2.30/6-9.30 Closed 25-26 Dec, 2-11 Jan, Mon (winter only) **Prices** Starter £5-£7.50, Main £11-£19, Dessert £5.50-£6.95, Service optional **Wines** 52 bottles over £20, 16 bottles under £20, 9 by glass **Notes** Sunday L, Vegetarian available **Seats** 52, Pr/dining room 70 **Children** Portions, Menu **Parking** Cinque Port Street

TICEHURST Map 6 TQ63

Dale Hill Hotel & Golf Club

Modern European

Countryside and golf course views with modern British food

01580 200112
TN5 7DQ
e-mail: info@dalehill.co.uk
dir: M25 junct 5/A21. 5m after Lamberhurst turn right at lights onto B2087 to Flimwell. Hotel 1m on left

High on the Sussex Weald with breathtaking views of the East Sussex countryside, Dale Hill has two 18-hole golf courses, an indoor heated pool and gym, plus a choice of two restaurants. The fine-dining Wealden restaurant is spacious and decked out in a country-club style with views out across the course. Expect modern European dishes using classic flavour combinations such as mosaic of farmed rabbit wrapped in pancetta, Meaux mustard cream, apple chutney and pistachio brioche, followed by seared sea bass on sorrel infused crushed potatoes, lobster ravioli, leek and noilly Pratt velouté. There's the more casual Eighteenth Restaurant, too.

Times 12-2.30/6.30-9 Closed L Mon-Sat

UCKFIELD Map 6 TQ42

The Dining Room

Modern, Traditional V

Skilful cooking in elegant country-house hotel

01825 733333 & 0845 458 0901
Buxted Park Hotel, Buxted Park, Buxted TN22 4AY
e-mail: buxtedpark@handpicked.co.uk
dir: Exit A22 Uckfield bypass (London-Eastbourne road), take A272 to Buxted. Cross lights, hotel entrance 1m on right

In over 300 acres of private grounds and parkland, which includes large lakes, a deer park and walled gardens, the Palladian Georgian façade of this grand manor house makes a good first impression. Built in 1722, the house has played host to society's movers and shakers including William Wordsworth, Winston Churchill and Marlon Brando. The restaurant, located in the original Victorian orangery, retains many original features but still feels modern and bright. It's a stylish and relaxing place in which to dine, with views over the gardens. Accomplished modern British and European cuisine blends classic and modern ideas and is based around top-quality ingredients. Lobster and salmon ravioli on caramelised fennel with Pernod velouté might be followed by local venison with truffled dauphinoise, braised red cabbage and bitter chocolate.

Chef Lucy Hyder **Owner** Hand Picked Hotels **Times** 12-2/7-9.30 **Prices** Fixed L 2 course fr £15, Fixed D 3 course fr £32, Service optional **Wines** 130 bottles over £20, 8 bottles under £20, 20 by glass **Notes** ALC 3 course £42, Degustation 7 course £54, Vegetarian menu, Dress restrictions, Smart casual, Civ Wed 120 **Seats** 40, Pr/dining room 120 **Children** Portions, Menu **Parking** 100

East Sussex National Golf Resort & Spa

Modern European NEW

Modern golf-oriented hotel with sound contemporary cooking

01825 880088
Little Horsted TN22 5ES
e-mail: reception@eastsussexnational.co.uk
dir: M25 junct 6/A22 towards Eastbourne. After rdbt with A22/A26 hotel off next rdbt on A22

This vast modern golf-centric hotel complex looks over the green expanses of two championship golf courses towards the South Downs. As well as the obvious core attractions of its fairways and spa treatments, the hotel's Pavilion Restaurant delivers a repertoire of well-executed modern British ideas in an upmarket setting with sweeping views across the undulating countryside through a wall of floor-to-ceiling windows. With producers of superb Sussex produce on its doorstep, the kitchen is spoilt for choice. An excellent starter teams lobster tortellini with wilted samphire and a saffron and shellfish sauce, ahead of main-course rack of lamb with red pepper and aubergine caviar, mashed potato dumplings and pistachio sauce.

Chef Andrew Wiles **Times** 12.30-2/7-9 Closed L (may close if no advance bookings) **Prices** Food prices not confirmed for 2011. Please telephone for details.

Horsted Place

Modern British NEW

Elegant country-house dining amid magnificent grounds

01825 750581
Little Horsted TN22 5TS
e-mail: hotel@horstedplace.co.uk
dir: 2m S on A26 towards Lewes

The landscaped gardens at Horsted Place include a tennis court and croquet lawn if you're feeling competitive, or there are tranquil pathways to explore if you prefer. It is a striking 17th-century Gothic-style country house which serves up a formal dining experience. Tables are well-spaced in the elegantly traditional restaurant, so good for intimate conversation whether business or pleasure, and there are views over the impressive estate if words fail you. Pre-dinner drinks can be taken in the drawing room or garden terrace. The chef has been ensconced here for nearly 20 years and produces tried-and-tested dishes using excellent quality produce. Start with rillette of goose with tomato chutney and toasted brioche, before perhaps a seared wild sea bass on basil and pancetta risotto. Finish on a high with hot chocolate fondant.

Chef Allan Garth **Owner** Perinon Ltd **Times** 12-2/7-9.30 Closed 1st wk Jan, L Sat **Prices** Fixed L 2 course £16.95, Starter £9.50, Main £20, Dessert £8.50, Service optional **Wines** 120 bottles over £20, 6 bottles under £20, 8 by glass **Notes** Sunday L, Vegetarian available, Dress restrictions, No jeans, Civ Wed 100 **Seats** 40, Pr/dining room 80 **Children** Portions **Parking** 50

WESTFIELD Map 7 TQ81

The Wild Mushroom Restaurant

Modern British

Confident cooking in a converted Victorian farmhouse

01424 751137
Woodgate House, Westfield Ln TN35 4SB
e-mail: info@wildmushroom.co.uk
dir: From A21 towards Hastings, left onto A28 to Westfield. Restaurant 1.5m on left

On the ground floor of a converted red-brick 19th-century farmhouse near historic Hastings, the L-shaped dining room at the Wild Mushroom is done out in mellow natural tones with starched white linen-clad tables, and cream-painted beams. There's a conservatory-style bar and charming garden for you to choose between depending on the weather. High quality ingredients are transformed into beautifully presented yet simple dishes by a kitchen that demonstrates good technical skills. Foie gras presse with rhubarb jam might be followed by grilled fillet of Loch Duart salmon with rock oyster and watercress sauce. Finish with iced carrot parfait with carrot cake and whisky custard. Webbes at The Fish Café in Rye (see entry) is a sister establishment.

Chef Paul Webbe, Christopher Weddle **Owner** Mr & Mrs P Webbe **Times** 12-2.30/7-10 Closed 25 Dec, 2 wks at New Year, Mon, D Sun **Prices** Fixed L 2 course £15.95, Tasting menu fr £32, Starter £5.50-£8.50, Main £12-£19, Dessert £6-£6.95, Service optional **Wines** 46 bottles over £20, 33 bottles under £20, 6 by glass **Notes** Tasting menu available 6 course, Sunday L, Vegetarian available, Dress restrictions, Smart casual **Seats** 40 **Children** Portions **Parking** 20

WILMINGTON Map 6 TQ50

Crossways

Modern British

Relaxed and welcoming country-house dining

01323 482455
Lewes Rd BN26 5SG
e-mail: stay@crosswayshotel.co.uk
dir: On A27, 2m W of Polegate

Whether you're down in the Cuckmere valley for Glyndebourne or walking the beautiful South Downs Way, this delightful Georgian country-house restaurant is worth seeking out. It has an unimpeachable culinary heritage, since it was once home to Elizabeth David's parents, and has been run by the same owners with welcoming, easy-going charm for 22 years. Ms David would surely nod her appreciation of the kitchen's sourcing ethos: many ingredients - South Downs lamb, obviously - come from local farms and butchers within a few miles' radius. A set, monthly-changing menu might kick off, perhaps, with a seafood pancake, then a home-made curried parsnip soup, before main-course rack of local lamb served with port, rosemary and redcurrant sauce. Don't skimp on pudding: ice cream is home-made, and the sorbet might be made from damsons plucked from the garden.

Chef David Stott **Owner** David Stott, Clive James **Times** 7.30-8.30 Closed 24 Dec-24 Jan, Sun-Mon, L all week **Prices** Fixed D 4 course £37.95, Service optional **Wines** 18 bottles over £20, 25 bottles under £20, 10 by glass **Notes** Vegetarian available **Seats** 24 **Parking** 20

SUSSEX, WEST

ALBOURNE Map 6 TQ21

The Ginger Fox

 Modern European 

Classy country cousin of Brighton's Gingerman Restaurant

01273 857888
Muddleswood Rd BN6 9EA
dir: On A281 at the junction with B2117

Part of a small Brighton-based group that includes a smart local restaurant (see entry for Gingerman) and a couple of dining pubs, the Ginger Fox is the rural outpost. It is properly in the country, with the South Downs on its doorstep, and it even has a thatched roof to add to its rustic charm. It has been done out in the contemporary manner and is very much a dining pub, with an open-plan layout and smart fixtures and fittings. The food is certainly a cut above, showing a broadly modern European focus and turning out some imaginative dishes whilst keeping its feet on the ground. Mushrooms and duck egg on toast is a comforting way to start, before perhaps a stuffed saddle of rabbit or roast skate wing with spiced chick pea purée, warm aubergine and a chilli lime dressing. There's a classy three cheese ploughman's and a small garden for the ultimate country pub experience.

Chef Ben McKellar, David Keats **Owner** Ben & Pamela McKellar **Times** 12-2/6.30-10 Closed Xmas Day **Prices** Fixed L 2 course £10, Starter £4.50-£8.50, Main £9.50-£18, Dessert £5, Service optional, Groups min 6 service 10% **Notes** Fixed L 2 course Mon-Fri until 7pm, Sunday L, Vegetarian available **Seats** 50, Pr/dining room 24 **Children** Portions, Menu **Parking** 60

AMBERLEY Map 6 TQ01

Amberley Castle Hotel

– *see below*

Amberley Castle Hotel

AMBERLEY Map 6 TQ01

Modern European V

Ambitious cooking in a one-off historical setting

01798 831992
BN18 9LT
e-mail: info@amberleycastle.co.uk
dir: Off B2139 between Storrington & Houghton

Castle by name and castle by nature; even arriving here transports you back 900 years to a bygone age. After the sweeping drive, marvel at the twin-tower gatehouse and garderobe tower with gun loops. Inside, the bedrooms are sumptuous with four-poster beds and bags of character. Arms and weapons adorn the walls and the lounges and restaurant simply ooze history. Make no mistake, this is a grand place to dine but there's nothing snooty about the service, all are welcomed with open arms – except that is, those wearing jeans or trainers. The kitchen brigade is skilled at delivering big flavours in a contemporary European style with lots of twists along the way and a strong commitment to seasonal and local produce. Begin with rabbit and black pudding terrine with a beautifully flavoured Muscat jelly and pea purée. Next up, a main-course cutlet of Cornish lamb with the braised breast, sweetbreads, shallot purée and glazed potatoes. Finish with a poshed-up banoffee pie with chestnuts, toffee shards, salt caramel and banana sorbet, decorated with gold leaf. The experience includes all the intermediate extras such as amuse-bouche and pre-dessert, while the wine list is ably represented by the excellent sommelier.

Chef James Dugan **Owner** Amberley Castle Hotel Ltd **Times** 12-2/7-9.30 **Prices** Food prices not confirmed for 2011. Please telephone for details. **Wines** 155 bottles over £20, 4 bottles under £20, 14 by glass **Notes** Sunday L, Vegetarian menu, Dress restrictions, Smart casual, jacket or tie, Civ Wed 55 **Seats** 70, Pr/dining room 40 **Children** Portions **Parking** 30

ARUNDEL Map 6 TQ00

The Townhouse

@@ Modern British

Elegant Regency townhouse with assured modern cooking

☎ 01903 883847
65 High St BN18 9AJ
e-mail: enquiries@thetownhouse.co.uk
dir: Follow A27 to Arundel, onto High Street, establishment on left at top of hill

There's some confident culinary goings on at this charming Regency building opposite Arundel's castle. It looks warmly inviting with its high-backed chairs covered in black fabric, formally-laid tables and large mirrors on the neutral walls. Look up and behold the ceiling - it's a stunning original 16th-century gilded Florentine number that predates the house. The kitchen turns out some modern British cooking of considerable poise and craft. Start with hand-dived scallops, beautifully seared, and served with an admirable caramelised shallot tart, before a grilled supreme of guinea fowl, the leg served up as confit, plus lentils braised with pearl barley and bacon. Tip-top pastry skills are confirmed in a cinnamon, apple and frangipane tart, with a silky caramel ice cream. Breads are made daily, service is personable and effective.

Chef Lee Williams **Owner** Lee & Kate Williams **Times** 12-2.30/7-9.30 Closed 2 wks Oct, Xmas, 2 wks Feb, Sun-Mon **Prices** Fixed L 2 course £14, Fixed D 3 course £27.50, Service optional **Wines** 29 bottles over £20, 15 bottles under £20, 6 by glass **Notes** Vegetarian available **Seats** 24 **Children** Portions **Parking** On street or nearby car park

BOSHAM Map 5 SU80

Millstream Hotel and Restaurant

@@ Modern British

Idyllic setting and warm hospitality

☎ 01243 573234
Bosham Ln PO18 8HL
e-mail: info@millstream-hotel.co.uk
web: www.millstream-hotel.co.uk
dir: 4m W of Chichester on A259, left at Bosham rdbt. After 0.5m right at T-junct signed to church & quay. Hotel 0.5m on right

In the picturesque setting of the harbourside village of Bosham, near Chichester, is the Millstream Hotel. Part malt house and part manor house, the interior is traditional and comfortable. Wicker chairs in the cosy bar make an inviting place to take a pre- or post-dinner drink or, in clement weather, go through the doors and take a seat on the manicured lawns where the soundtrack of quacking ducks provides a back-to-nature atmosphere. In the restaurant, well-groomed staff serve imaginatively presented dishes made using high-quality local ingredients. Dinner might include gammon terrine with fried quail's egg and spiced pineapple pickle, breast of guinea fowl with a watercress risotto and carrot purée, with dark chocolate and hazelnut brownie and hot chocolate foam and orange sorbet to finish.

Chef Neil Hiskey **Owner** The Wild family **Times** 12.30-2/6.45-9.15 **Prices** Fixed L 2 course £19-£26, Fixed D 3 course £30-£40, Service optional **Wines** 60 bottles over £20, 12 bottles under £20, 11 by glass **Notes** Sunday L, Vegetarian available, Dress restrictions, Smart casual, no jeans in the evenings, Civ Wed 97 **Seats** 60, Pr/dining room 97 **Children** Portions, Menu **Parking** 40

BURPHAM Map 6 TQ00

George & Dragon

@ British, French

Classic pub food in an idyllic spot on the South Downs

☎ 01903 883131
BN18 9RR
e-mail: info@gdinn.co.uk
dir: Off A27 1m E of Arundel, signed Burpham, 2.5m pub on left

When you're striding out across the beautiful South Downs Way, make sure to schedule in a pitstop at the George & Dragon in the idyllic village of Burpham, just a few miles upstream of Arundel on the River Arun - but ring ahead for a table, as this is a popular place. Once inside, it's clear why: stone floors, ancient beams and well-kept ales from the Arundel brewery help foster a chatty ambience, and the kitchen turns out a sound line in unpretentious rustic pub grub that stays in touch with today's trends. Top-notch Sussex produce is too good to mess about with, so it appears in simple starters such as Golden Cross goats' cheese with beetroot and walnut salad and a red wine reduction, followed by a duo of guinea fowl - confit leg on bean cassoulet and chargrilled breast wrapped in pancetta and thyme with celeriac mash and confit garlic jus. Blackboard specials supplement the short carte.

Times 12-2/7-9 Closed 25 Dec, D Sun

CHICHESTER Map 5 SU80

Comme Ça

@ French

Popular restaurant serving classical French cuisine

☎ 01243 788724 & 536307
67 Broyle Rd PO19 6BD
e-mail: comme.ca@commeca.co.uk
dir: On A286 near Festival Theatre

If you need a fix of French cooking, save yourself the ferry trip from Portsmouth to Cherbourg and head to this charmingly-restored Georgian inn just a short stroll from Chichester's Festival Theatre. Normandy-born chef-proprietor Michel Navet may have been in business on this side of la manche for over 20 years, but his culinary heart is staunchly Gallic. Classic French country cooking is the deal here, presented on a helpfully-translated menu of regional French dishes, as in a trademark moules marinières made Normandy-style with Cornish mussels cooked in cider, shallots and cream. A main course of duck leg confit in a rich Armagnac and orange sauce might take you on a trip down to Gascony, while roast breast of corn-fed chicken with grilled aubergines, peppers and olives with sauce vierge glows with the sunshine of Provence.

Chef Michel Navet, Mark Howard **Owner** Mr & Mrs Navet **Times** 12-2/6-10.30 Closed Xmas & New Year weeks, BHs, Mon, L Tue, D Sun **Prices** Food prices not confirmed for 2011. Please telephone for details. **Wines** 60 bottles over £20, 60 bottles under £20, 7 by glass **Notes** Sunday L, Dress restrictions, Smart casual **Seats** 100, Pr/dining room 14 **Children** Portions, Menu **Parking** 46

Croucher's Country Hotel & Restaurant

@@ British, International

Sound cooking in smart former farmhouse

☎ 01243 784995
Birdham Rd PO20 7EH
e-mail: crouchers@btconnect.com
dir: From A27 Chichester bypass onto A286 towards West Wittering, 2m, hotel on left between Chichester Marina & Dell Quay

Homely, unpretentious conviviality is the strength at this refurbished former farmhouse, situated in open countryside south of Chichester and a short drive from the harbour. That said the approach to cooking is very serious from a kitchen team who deliver simply presented modern British dishes that make sound use of quality local ingredients and display good balance of flavours. Take a starter of roasted scallops with garden pea purée and a scallop and chive velouté, followed by pork three ways - crisp belly, braised cheek and tenderloin - with sage mousse, apple compôte and creamed shallots, and perhaps vanilla and rhubarb cheesecake with poached rhubarb for pudding. The smart restaurant overlooks the landscaped grounds and there are splendid terraces at the rear and front.

Chef G Wilson, N Markey **Owner** Mr L van Rooyen & Mr G Wilson **Times** 12.30-2.30/7-11 Closed 26 Dec, 1 Jan **Prices** Food prices not confirmed for 2011. Please telephone for details. **Wines** 29 bottles over £20, 18 bottles under £20, 6 by glass **Notes** Dress restrictions, Smart casual, Civ Wed 50 **Seats** 80, Pr/dining room 20 **Children** Portions, Menu **Parking** 60

Earl of March

British

Former Ritz chef in Sussex country pub

☎ 01243 533993
Lavant Rd PO18 0BQ
e-mail: info@theearlofmarch.com
dir: On A286, 2m N of Chichester towards Midhurst, on the corner of Goodwood Estate

This charming Sussex country pub would be worth visiting just for its vista out onto the South Downs and cosy interior, but the presence of top London chef Giles Thompson is the real draw these days. Thompson earned his spurs at The Connaught and then The Ritz and, having moved out to the sticks, brings his classic French experience to bear on the menu, daily specials and bar snacks. The pub dates back to the 18th century when it was a coaching inn and it's said that William Blake wrote the words to *Jerusalem* here. These days you'll find a restaurant area with wooden tables and leather chairs and a more relaxed bar area and open fireplace. From April to September a 'Seafood Shack' opens out onto the lawn. Local produce is given the Thompson touch and what emerges is cleanly executed food where you can taste each component part. Try a lovely terrine maison; duck, pistachios and field mushrooms, fig chutney and toasted soda bread, then Gressingham duck breast with braised rhubarb, spring greens, rösti potato and Madeira jus. A simple vanilla pannacotta and mulled summer berries rounds things off nicely.

Chef Mathias Thumshirn **Owner** Giles Thompson **Times** 12-2.30/6.30-9.30 Closed D Sun **Prices** Fixed L 2 course £20-£30, Fixed D 3 course £25-£35, Starter £6.50-£9.50, Main £14-£21, Dessert £6.75, Service optional, Groups min 11 service 12.5% **Wines** 33 bottles over £20, 16 bottles under £20, 18 by glass **Notes** Pre-theatre menu 2 course £18, 3 course £22, Sunday L, Vegetarian available **Seats** 60, Pr/dining room 12 **Children** Portions, Menu **Parking** 30

Hallidays

Modern British

Carefully-sourced produce cooked with flair

☎ 01243 575331
Watery Ln, Funtington PO18 9LF
e-mail: hallidaysdinners@aol.com
dir: 4m W of Chichester, on B2146

Three 13th-century flint and thatched cottages at the foot of the South Downs have been transformed to create this intimate restaurant. The Grade II listed building, clad with wisteria and roses, is popular locally for its quiet charm and impeccable service. Family-run, the chef-proprietor changes the menus weekly depending on the local produce available and sources from local farmers, day boats and smallholders, as well as foraging for his own wild food. Start with home-smoked local sea trout with watercress, following on with 21-day aged Adsdean Farm sirloin steak with ceps, cream and Madeira or confit of Barbary duck with celeriac mash and crab apple jelly. Finish with lemon verbena crème brûlée.

Chef Andrew Stephenson **Owner** Mr A & Mrs J Stephenson **Times** 12-2.15/7-10.15 Closed 1 wk Mar, 2 wks Aug, Mon-Tue, L Sat, D Sun **Prices** Fixed L 2 course £13, Fixed D 3 course £25-£35, Starter £6-£8, Main £14-£19, Dessert £5.50-£8, Service optional **Wines** 65 bottles over £20, 25 bottles under £20, 5 by glass **Notes** Sunday L, Vegetarian available, Dress restrictions, No shorts **Seats** 26 **Children** Portions **Parking** 12

West Stoke House

CHICHESTER Map 5 SU80

Modern British, French

Fine dining in a beautifully restored South Downs house

☎ 01243 575226
Downs Rd, West Stoke PO18 9BN
e-mail: info@weststokehouse.co.uk
dir: 3m NW of Chichester. Off B286 to West Stoke, next to St Andrew's Church

The painstakingly restored white Georgian mansion overlooking the luscious South Downs (now elevated to National Park dignity) is a testament to the single-minded tenacity of Rowland and Mary Leach, who rescued it from stasis a few years ago. It's now a breathtaking country-house hotel with many fine features. Guests who make it to the attic bedrooms will find the exposed beams of the original medieval house, while the old ballroom, with its ornate mouldings and chandelier, and the no less fabulous Blue Room, make fine backdrops for a candlelit dinner. Darren Brown once cooked at the Lanesborough in London, and brings a fine dining sensibility to proceedings here, which seems only fitting in the surroundings. A meal might start with a very glossy spin on Niçoise salad, with tuna, fine beans, quail's egg, ratte potatoes, capers and olives all present and more than correct, before main course anatomises lamb in the modern way, but more comprehensively than usual, with the roasted loin and braised shoulder accompanied by a faggot and kidneys, alongside aubergine caviar, creamed potato and wild garlic. An Anglo-French cheese selection offers the savoury alternative to a compact choice of three desserts, including variations on impeccably fashionable rhubarb.

Chef Darren Brown **Owner** Rowland & Mary Leach **Times** 12-2/7-9 Closed Xmas, 1 Jan, Mon-Tue **Prices** Fixed L 2 course £22.50, Fixed D 3 course £46.50, Service optional, Groups min 8 service 12.5% **Wines** 100 bottles over £20, 14 bottles under £20, 10 by glass **Notes** Sunday L, Vegetarian available, Civ Wed 70 **Seats** 40, Pr/dining room 26 **Children** Portions **Parking** 20

CHICHESTER *continued*

Royal Oak Inn

◉ Modern British

Broad gastro-pub menu in old Sussex inn

☎ 01243 527434
Pook Ln, East Lavant PO18 0AX
e-mail: info@royaloakeastlavant.co.uk
web: www.royaloakeastlavant.co.uk
dir: From Chichester take A286 towards Midhurst, 2m to mini rdbt, turn right signed East Lavant. Inn on left

A white-fronted Sussex pub in a village not far from Chichester, the Royal Oak is a mix-and-match amalgam of rustic buildings, including what was once a barn. Tables polished to a high gloss and a refreshing absence of the usual knick-knacks make the place feel hearteningly modern, and the food does the rest. Expansive menus of quality fare mix culinary influences enthusiastically, taking in pigeon breast and black pudding on braised Puy lentils, and free-range local pork loin with dauphinoise, wilted greens and Calvados cream. Go eastern perhaps with monkfish and tiger prawns in lemongrass and coconut cream, served with stir-fried pak choi and noodles, and finish with warm Scotch pancakes layered with apple confit, teamed with subtle ginger ice cream.

Chef Steven Ferre **Owner** Charles Ullmann
Times 10-3/6-10.30 **Prices** Starter £5-£11, Main £9-£24, Dessert £3.50-£7.50, Service optional, Groups min 6 service 10% **Wines** 45 bottles over £20, 12 bottles under £20, 20 by glass **Notes** Pre-theatre menu from 5.30pm, Sunday L, Vegetarian available **Seats** 55 **Children** Portions **Parking** 25

See advert below

West Stoke House

◉◉◉ *– see page 405*

CHILGROVE **Map 5 SU81**

The Fish House

◉◉ Modern British **NEW** V

Fabulous fish up on the Downs

☎ 01243 519444
PO18 9HX
e-mail: info@thefishhouse.co.uk
dir: 7m N of Chichester on B2141. W of A286 onto B2141. From Lavant restaurant 4m on right

With the Sussex Downs National Park as its backdrop, the Fish House is a smartly refurbished 18th-century building, just a short drive from the centre of Chichester. If the name isn't enough of a giveaway, once through the door the crustacean counter reveals the passion for the fruits of the sea that lies within. There's a bar serving a menu of modern classics from Carlingford oysters to skate with caper beurre noisette, and a more formal restaurant decked out with crisp linen-covered tables on oak and limestone flooring. A fixed-price menu in the restaurant (supported by a tasting menu) delivers a sensibly balanced choice of five dishes at each course. Expect superbly fresh seafood with well-balanced flavour combinations and some creative touches (there are one or two meaty alternatives). Roasted scallops from Skye are beautifully glazed and come with a carrot and vanilla purée, followed by butter-poached Dover sole with a risotto of Jerusalem artichokes and girolles. Excellent bread and well-drilled service show this to be a quality operation from top to bottom.

Chef Alan Gleeson **Owner** David & Jackie Barnard **Times** 12-2.30/6-9.30 **Prices** Fixed L 2 course £17.50-£19.50, Fixed D 3 course £19.50-£35, Tasting menu £59, Starter £7.50-£18.50, Main £14.50-£38, Dessert £5.95-£7.95, Service added but optional 10% **Wines** 220 bottles over £20, 30 bottles under £20, 30 by glass **Notes** Early bird menu 6-7pm 2 course £17, 3 course £22, Sunday L, Vegetarian menu, Dress restrictions, Smart casual **Seats** 100 **Children** Portions **Parking** 50, On street

CLIMPING Map 6 SU90

Bailiffscourt Hotel & Spa

Modern British

Medieval-effect manor house with modern European food

01903 723511
BN17 5RW
e-mail: bailiffscourt@hshotels.co.uk
dir: From A27 (Arundel) take A284 towards Littlehampton. Take A259. Hotel signed towards Climping Beach

A scion of the Guinness family built Bailiffscourt in the 1920s, as some kind of homage to medieval England, with mullioned windows, flagstoned floors and wooden beams. The fact that it's all only a stone's throw from the beach at Climping makes it more surreal. These days, up-to-the-minute spa facilities are laid on thick, and once you've been enveloped in nourishing mud, it must surely be time for a look-in at the restaurant. Here, an impeccably fashionable modern British menu deals in the likes of crumbed scallops with cauliflower purée and spiced pork belly, roasted lamb rump with smoked baby plum tomatoes, green beans and goats' cheese, and desserts such as apple, blackberry and pecan crumble with honey ice cream and pear fool.

Times 12-1.30/7-9.30

COPTHORNE

For restaurant details see Gatwick Airport (London), (Sussex, West)

CRAWLEY

For restaurant details see Gatwick Airport (London), (Sussex, West)

CUCKFIELD Map 6 TQ32

Ockenden Manor

– see below

EAST GRINSTEAD Map 6 TQ33

Anise

Modern European

Glamorous contemporary restaurant with creative cuisine to match

01342 337768 & 337700
The Felbridge Hotel & Spa, London Rd RH19 2BH
e-mail: sales@felbridgehotel.co.uk
web: www.felbridgehotel.co.uk
dir: A22 (southbound), 200mtrs beyond East Grinstead boundary sign

The classy Felbridge Hotel and Spa's Anise restaurant is a stylish exercise in crepuscular shades of black, cream and grey, high-backed leather chairs, crisp white linen and gleaming silverware. The kitchen raids the larders of Sussex, Kent and Surrey, throwing oodles of flair and

continued

Ockenden Manor

CUCKFIELD Map 6 TQ32

Modern French V 

Creative cuisine in an elegant manor house

01444 416111
Ockenden Ln RH17 5LD
e-mail: reservations@ockenden-manor.com
web: www.hshotels.co.uk
dir: Village centre

Wander down a skinny lane off Cuckfield's charming high street and you arrive at Ockendon, a vision of bucolic English lovelinesss secreted away in nine acres of idyllic grounds complete with a walled garden. The Elizabethan manor house is the sort of place where afternoon tea on the terrace with views across verdant meadows to the spine of the South Downs is an absolute must, but if the weather keeps you indoors, rest assured it is an uplifting place, done out with bright and summery shades of yellow to lighten the load of its gnarled Tudor beams, oak panelling and stone fireplaces. Delightful staff play their part with aplomb, always solicitous, friendly and welcoming. In the panelled dining room, heraldic stained-glass windows and a wonderful painted ceiling all add to a sense of occasion for chef Stephen Crane's seriously accomplished French-oriented cooking. The fields and coastline of Sussex are first ports of call for much of the kitchen's materials, which are handled with panache and a creative approach, within the confines of the country-house idiom. Dinner could take you from hot and cold Selsey crab with sweet potato tempura and oriental salad through to a saddle and pasty of Balcombe venison with buttered kale, braised turnips and swede and carrot purée, or grilled red mullet teamed with buttered courgettes, tapenade, confit tomatoes and mussels; to finish, go for hazelnut dacquoise and chocolate ice cream. Classic French appellations abound on a list of serious bottles at equally serious prices.

Chef Steve Crane **Owner** The Goodman & Carminger family **Times** 12-2/7-9 **Prices** Fixed L 2 course £14.95-£17, Tasting menu £70, Service optional, Groups min 10 service 10% **Wines** 207 bottles over £20, 11 by glass **Notes** ALC 3 course £53, Sunday L, Vegetarian menu, Dress restrictions, No jeans, T-shirts, Civ Wed 100 **Seats** 40, Pr/dining room 95 **Parking** 45

EAST GRINSTEAD ***continued***

flourishes into the mix, to come up with a French-inflected modern European menu conceived with imagination and realised with a serious level of technical expertise. Portland scallops star in a first course that delivers them seared with ginger moulis, finely chopped in a spring roll, and as tartare with wasabi and coriander. At main course stage, roast loin of English rose veal is partnered with potato and bacon 'cannelloni', bone marrow beignet and curly kale. Finally, an ultra-rich dark chocolate fondant comes with sour cherry sorbet and a quenelle of sour cherries and violets.

Chef Frederick Tobin **Owner** New Century, East Grinstead Ltd **Times** 12-2/6.30-10 **Prices** Fixed L 3 course £32-£45, Fixed D 3 course £32-£45, Service optional **Wines** 64 bottles over £20, 6 bottles under £20, 12 by glass **Notes** Vegetarian available, Civ Wed 200 **Seats** 34, Pr/dining room 20 **Children** Portions, Menu **Parking** 200

See advert below

GATWICK AIRPORT (LONDON) Map 6 TQ24

La Brasserie

British, French

Good food in stylish airport restaurant

☎ 01293 567070 & 555000
Sofitel London Gatwick, North Terminal RH6 0PH
e-mail: h6204-re@accor.com
dir: M23 junct 9, North Terminal at Gatwick Airport

One of the closest hotels to Gatwick airport and only minutes from the terminals, it may not be the first place that springs to mind on the list of culinary destinations, but Sofitel has brought a bit of Gallic flair here. The airy and contemporary brasserie restaurant is clean-cut with lots of wood, chrome and glass but what stands out is the professional and friendly service and relaxed atmosphere. The modern British cooking has a French accent but uses the best local and seasonal produce. A starter of home-cured and oak-smoked Sussex wood pigeon breast with beetroot, pickled wild mushrooms and pigeon consommé might precede slow-braised veal cheeks in red wine with caramelised onion mash and girolles.

Chef David Woods **Owner** S Arora **Times** 6.30-10.30 Closed L all week **Prices** Starter £6-£10.95, Main £16.75-£24.95, Dessert £5.75-£7.50, Service added but optional 12.5% **Wines** 36 bottles over £20, 2 bottles under £20, 15 by glass **Notes** Vegetarian available, Dress restrictions, Smart casual **Seats** Pr/dining room 40 **Children** Portions, Menu **Parking** 100

Langshott Manor

Modern British V

Impressive cooking in elegant manor house

☎ 01293 786680
Langshott Ln, Horley RH6 9LN
e-mail: admin@langshottmanor.com
dir: From A23 take Ladbroke Rd, off Chequers rdbt to Langshott, after 0.75m hotel on right

It's hard to believe that the 21st-century hurly-burly of Gatwick Airport is just five minutes away from this calm Elizabethan manor house built of timber and herringbone brick. The Mulberry restaurant looks through leaded windows over three acres of pampered gardens, from a setting of period ancient beams and oak panelling blending with an understated smart modern décor. The hotel's own garden plays its part in supplying the kitchen with the top-class materials that are the foundation of its dishes - skilfully crafted stuff in a creative modern British vein. Braised rhubarb and Sauternes jelly are a perfect foil for a foie gras 'sandwich' - a clever take on a classic pairing. Mains might go down the local Sussex route: braised shoulder and cutlet of Romney Marsh lamb, or an assiette of rabbit with spring greens, red wine sauce and mustard cream.

Chef Phil Dixon **Owner** Peter & Deborah Hinchcliffe **Times** 12-2.30/7-9.30 **Prices** Fixed L 2 course £15-£25, Fixed D 3 course £42-£46.50, Tasting menu £55-£80, Service added but optional 12.5% **Wines** 120 bottles over £20, 5 bottles under £20, 17 by glass **Notes** Tasting menu 7 course, with wine £80, Sunday L, Vegetarian menu, Dress restrictions, Smart casual, no jeans or shorts, Civ Wed 60 **Seats** 55, Pr/dining room 22 **Children** Portions **Parking** 25

The Old House Restaurant

Traditional

Sound cooking in charming old cottage

☎ 01342 712222
Effingham Rd, Copthorne RH10 3JB
e-mail: info@oldhouserestaurant.co.uk
dir: M23 junct 10, A264 to East Grinstead. 1st left at 2nd rdbt, left at x-rds, restaurant 0.75m on left

Just a few minutes' drive from Gatwick Airport, this delightful beamed 16th-century house on the edge of Copthorne village oozes rustic period charm. It features a collection of cosy lounges with intimate lighting and comfortable seating, and the sunny, elegant dining room is suitably grand, in gold, cream and navy, without being over-bearing. The emphasis is on good quality ingredients, locally sourced wherever possible; from the essentially traditional menu, begin with smoked haddock, prawn and mussel cocktail with grain mustard mayonnaise and move on to chump of lamb with sweet potato dauphinoise, spicy ratatouille and basil jus. Round off with rhubarb and ginger crème brûlée.

Times 12.15-2/6.30-9.30 Closed Xmas, New Year, Mon, L Sat, D Sun

Restaurant 1881

Modern French, Mediterranean

Good views and sound European cooking

☎ 01293 862166
Stanhill Court Hotel, Stanhill Rd, Charlwood RH6 0EP
e-mail: enquiries@stanhillcourthotel.co.uk
dir: N of Charlwood towards Newdigate

Originally built as a family home by a Scottish Victorian gentleman who did rather well for himself as an underwriter for Lloyds, Stanhill Court Hotel sits in 35 acres of wooded grounds on Stan Hill amid the buxom folds of the South Downs. This ex-pat clearly missed the mists and glens of home, as the house is built in Scottish baronial style, and comes with intricately-carved pine panelling, a minstrels' gallery and a barrel-vaulted roof with stained-glass windows. The house's dining room was designed to get the best views, and now that it trades as Restaurant 1881, lucky diners get glowing wood panelling and a romantic ambience to go with the kitchen's European-accented cooking. You might start with a straightforward tomato and mozzarella salad with basil oil and red onion compôte, then follow with confit duck leg with cherry jus, or pan-fried hake with sweet garlic and sage oil.

Times 12-3/7-11 Closed L Sat

GOODWOOD **Map 6 SU80**

The Richmond Arms, The Goodwood Hotel

Traditional French

Good food on the Goodwood Estate

☎ 01243 775537
PO18 0QB
e-mail: reservations@goodwood.com
dir: Just off A285, 3m NE of Chichester. Follow signs for Goodwood.

Much of the activity in the Goodwood Estate centres around speed: galloping gee gees, fast cars, vintage aircraft bombing around; thankfully, fast food is not on the agenda in the 18th-century Richmond Arms. The culinary heart of the 12,000-acre estate's classy contemporary hotel and country club complex occupies a contemporary conversion of an old stable block, where skylights and high timbers make for an airy, barn-like venue. The kitchen subjects sound local materials to modern British treatments, using well-judged flavour combinations. Begin with ham hock and honey-roasted chicken terrine with sweet rhubarb compôte, ahead of slow-roast pork belly with champ mash, Savoy cabbage and apple jus. Desserts such as dark chocolate delice with white chocolate sauce and bitter chocolate candy close the show.

Chef Lee Holland **Owner** The Goodwood Estate Company Ltd **Times** 6.30-10.30 Closed L Mon-Sat **Prices** Fixed D 3 course £25, Starter £5.50-£9.50, Main £12.95-£23, Dessert £6.50, Service optional **Wines** 47 bottles over £20, 9 bottles under £20, 10 by glass **Notes** Sunday L, Vegetarian available, Civ Wed 120 **Seats** 85, Pr/dining room 120 **Children** Portions, Menu **Parking** 350

HAYWARDS HEATH **Map 6 TQ32**

Jeremy's at Borde Hill

Modern European

Modern European cooking in idyllic garden setting

☎ 01444 441102
Balcombe Rd RH16 1XP
e-mail: reservations@jeremysrestaurant.com
dir: 1.5m N of Haywards Heath. From M23 junct 10a take A23 through Balcombe

It is hard to imagine a more idyllic setting for summer dining than this contemporary restaurant on the magnificent Borde Hill Estate. Jeremy's occupies a stable block conversion overlooking the Victorian walled garden and a dreamy south-facing terrace basking in the Sussex sun. Indoors, it's a wide-open, bright space with wooden floors, smart high-backed leather chairs and modern art on the walls. Chef Jeremy Ashpool knows his way around the modern European repertoire, raiding the Sussex larder for an assiette of local rabbit with pea and tarragon risotto. Next, pan-fried brill turns up with braised gem lettuce, potted langoustine, and a mussel and clam ragoût. Finish with chocolate and orange tart with crème fraîche.

Chef J & V Ashpool, Richard Cook **Owner** Jeremy & Vera Ashpool **Times** 12-2.30/7-9.30 Closed 1st 2 wks Jan, Mon, D Sun **Prices** Fixed L 2 course £17.50, Fixed D 3 course £25, Tasting menu £35-£55, Starter fr £8, Main £14.50-£24, Dessert £6.50, Service optional, Groups min 8 service 10% **Wines** 70 bottles over £20, 18 bottles under £20, 20 by glass **Notes** Tasting menu Tue evening (with wine £55), Sunday L, Vegetarian available, Civ Wed 55 **Seats** 55 **Children** Portions **Parking** 20

HORSHAM Map 6 TQ13

Restaurant Tristan

Modern British, French

Adventurous modern cooking in a late-medieval hall

☎ 01403 255688
3 Stan's Way, East St RH12 1HU
e-mail: info@restauranttristan.co.uk

A chef who trained with Marco Pierre White is always a good basis for an ambitious modern restaurant; an interesting building helps too - in this case a 500-year-old tangle of beams tucked away just off Horsham's high street. The dining room brings together vaulted medieval oak timbers with blocks of modern art and panels of wall painted burnt orange in a nod, perhaps, to Mondrian's designs - a stylish setting to suit the modern Anglo-French food. Sound technical ability is on display in a starter of foie gras trifle with eggy bread - the fat liver layered with creamy truffle topping and a sweet Sauternes jelly - while more gutsy dishes such as pheasant and wild mushroom Pithiviers (or pie, in plain English) also turn up. A passionfruit soufflé of perfect consistency paired with lemon sorbet brings things to a refreshing close.

Chef Tristan Mason **Owner** Tristan Mason **Times** 12-2.30/6.30-9.30 Closed Sun-Mon **Prices** Fixed L 2 course fr £12, Fixed D 3 course fr £36, Service added but optional 12.5% **Wines** 44 bottles over £20, 6 bottles under £20, 7 by glass **Notes** Tasting menu 5 course £50, with wine £76, Vegetarian available, Dress restrictions, Smart casual **Seats** 40

LEWES

Jolly Sportsman

Modern European NEW

Serious attitude to food in country-pub setting

☎ 01273 890400
Chapel Lane, East Chiltington BN7 3BA

dir: A23/M23 towards Brighton, A27 towards Lewes. Take A275, East Grinstead road, left onto the B2116 Offham, second right Novington Lane. In approx 1m first left Chapel Lane

There's not much to the South Downs village of East Chiltington, but down the narrow dead-end lane that leads to the church you'll find this gem of a country pub. You can sit out back and sip a pint of real ale while nibbling on the excellent bar snacks, or get a table on the wonderful terrace with its tiled tables and pergola. It still qualifies as a pub with its small bar stocked with excellent regional beers, a good wine list and a fantastic range of bottled Belgian beers, but food is the main business in hand. The series of knocked-through rooms are rustic in a smart sort of way, with lots of bold local art on view and for sale. Daily specials are listed on the blackboard in support of the carte; expect a menu of confidently robust, modish dishes along the lines of braised beef cheek with horseradish mash, almond-crusted brill with crispy polenta and, for dessert, perhaps a custard tart with apricot compôte.

Chef Alistair Doyle **Owner** Bruce Wass **Times** 12-3/6-11 **Children** Menu

LOWER BEEDING Map 6 TQ22

The Camellia Restaurant at South Lodge Hotel

British, Mediterranean V

Traditional comforts and modern cooking

☎ 01403 891711
South Lodge Hotel, Brighton Rd RH13 6PS
e-mail: enquiries@southlodgehotel.co.uk
dir: On A23 left onto B2110. Turn right through Handcross to A281 junct. Turn left, hotel on right

In need of a quiet break away from it all? Then this grand, wisteria-clad Victorian lodge, set in 90 acres of well-tended gardens and parkland with wonderfully therapeutic views over the rolling South Downs, is a good bet. A sense of opulent luxury pervades throughout, no more so than in the traditional and elegant Camellia Restaurant, with its twinkling chandeliers, wooden panelling, fine oil paintings, ornate table lamps, crisp white napery and sparkling glasses. Work up an appetite with an escorted stroll through the grounds, which

The Pass Restaurant at South Lodge Hotel

LOWER BEEDING Map 6 TQ22

Modern European V

Modern fine dining in the heart of the kitchen

☎ 01403 891711
South Lodge Hotel, Brighton Rd RH13 6PS
e-mail: enquiries@southlodgehotel.co.uk
dir: From A23 turn left onto B2110 & then right through Handcross to A281junct. Turn left hotel on right

We are all familiar with the chef's table concept that has been in vogue over the last few years: well, South Lodge has taken the theme a step further and inserted a whole restaurant into the kitchen. The pass is the part of the kitchen where the head chef gives the final okay to dishes before waiting staff whisk them away. Here, it's all decked out in hyper-modern style - lime green and cream leather seats at tables running along the edge of the pass, with the industrial stainless steel of the kitchen as a backdrop and plasma screens to zoom in on the action out of view. The format is tasting menus only - either five, six or eight courses, with a dedicated vegetarian option. The cooking takes a modern European tack, full of lively invention, based on first-class produce and sent out dressed to thrill. The five-course deal might kick off with cauliflower velouté with pine nuts, bacon and goats' cheese, ahead of ballottine of mackerel, smoked eel, Jerusalem artichoke and buttered leeks. The main event might feature pork - slow-cooked loin and spiced belly - with creamed baby onions, chorizo cream and button mushrooms. Full marks for desserts too - perhaps lemon pannacotta with yoghurt sorbet, popcorn and candied olive, and a second visit to the sweetie department for peanut parfait with salted caramel, prune compôte and rhubarb sorbet. For those not familiar, South Lodge is a top-flight country-house hotel, whose other classy restaurant is The Camellia (see entry).

Chef Matt Gillan **Owner** Pecorelli family **Times** 12-2/7-9 Closed 1st 2 wks Jan, Mon-Tue **Prices** Food prices not confirmed for 2011. Please telephone for details, Service added but optional 10% **Wines** 200 bottles over £20, 200 by glass **Notes** Fixed L 4/6 course £28-£38, D 6/8 course £60-£70, Sunday L, Vegetarian menu **Seats** 22 **Children** Menu **Parking** 200

contain over 260 varieties of camellia and rhododendron, returning to enjoy some classic country-house cooking, which balances excellent flavours and showcases quality local ingredients. Refreshingly unpretentious menus may highlight a starter of scallops with crab ravioli and braised fennel, with roast poussin with lemon and thyme risotto and Dijon jus for main course, and lemon cheesecake with pecan ice cream for pudding. The Pass (see entry) is the hotel's avant-garde take on the chef's table concept - an actual mini-restaurant in the kitchen.

Chef Lewis Hamblet **Owner** Pecorelli family **Times** 12-2.30/7-10 **Prices** Fixed L 2 course fr £15, Starter £9-£18, Main £16-£38, Dessert £8-£11, Service added but optional 10% **Wines** 250 bottles over £20, 4 bottles under £20, 250 by glass **Notes** Sunday L, Vegetarian menu, Civ Wed 130 **Seats** 75, Pr/dining room 140 **Children** Portions, Menu **Parking** 200

The Pass Restaurant at South Lodge Hotel

@@@ *– see opposite page*

MANNINGS HEATH **Map 6 TQ22**

Goldings Restaurant

@ Modern British

Impressive cooking against a background of serious golf

☎ 01403 210228
Mannings Heath Golf Club, Hammerpond Rd RH13 6PG
e-mail: enquiries@manningsheath.com
dir: From Horsham A281, for 2m. Approaching Mannings Heath turn left at Dun Horse continue to T-junct then left past village green. At next T-junct turn right & right again

The Mannings Heath Golf Club might not be the first place that springs to mind when you're looking to dine on fine Sussex produce, but so it goes. Goldings Restaurant occupies a clubby old lodge full of rustic beams, and the kitchen knows where to source the region's best ingredients, putting them together in simple, hearty combinations. The 'Taste of Sussex' menu showcases South Downs pheasant sausage, teamed with buttered spinach and field mushrooms, and port jus, ahead of slow-roasted local belly pork on Puy lentils, apple compôte and sage fondant. Keep things local to the end with Sussex cheeses, or a sweet alternative such as tarte fine of Granny Smith apple and marmalade with cinnamon sorbet.

Chef Robbie Pierce **Owner** Exclusive Hotels **Times** 12-3/7-9 **Prices** Fixed L 2 course £14.50, Service added but optional 10% **Wines** 32 bottles over £20, 3 bottles under £20, 4 by glass **Notes** Sunday L, Vegetarian available, Dress restrictions, Smart casual, collared shirt required, Civ Wed 100 **Seats** 43, Pr/dining room 12 **Children** Portions, Menu **Parking** 120

MIDHURST **Map 6 SU82**

Spread Eagle Hotel and Spa

@@ Modern British

Up-to-the-minute cooking in a Tudor house

☎ 01730 816911
South St GU29 9NH
e-mail: reservations@spreadeagle-midhurst.com
dir: Town centre

Prepare for a journey back in time as you step into the Spread Eagle, which once accommodated Elizabeth I, and has been serving the public since around the time of the Restoration. The beamed interiors are a pleasing antithesis to today's geometric lines, and the inglenook fireplace and stained-glass windows of the dining room evoke that bygone era too. The cooking, on the other hand, could hardly be more up-to-the-minute in its clever balancing of classical technique and modern ideas. Start perhaps with truffle-oiled risotto enriched with pecorino and topped with a poached egg, and follow up with grilled salmon, crisp-fried squid and mash, with spinach and chive sauce. The cheese trolley contains some interesting choices, or you might opt to finish with something as unreconstructedly homely as steamed syrup pudding and custard.

Chef Gary Moreton-Jones **Owner** The Goodman family **Times** 12.30-2/7-9.30 **Prices** Fixed L 2 course £14.95-£24.95, Fixed D 3 course £39.50, Service optional **Wines** 100 bottles over £20, 20 bottles under £20, 15 by glass **Notes** Fixed ALC £39.50, Sunday L, Vegetarian available, Dress restrictions, Smart casual, Civ Wed 120 **Seats** 50, Pr/dining room 12 **Children** Portions, Menu **Parking** 75

ROWHOOK **Map 6 TQ13**

The Chequers Inn

@ Traditional British

Great British cooking in rural pub

☎ 01403 790480
RH12 3PY
e-mail: thechequersrowhook@googlemail.com
dir: From Horsham A281 towards Guildford. At rdbt take A29 signed London. In 200mtrs left, follow Rowhook signs

With oak beams, flagstone floors, rustic wooden tables, welcoming open fires and a battery of real ales kept in tip-top condition, there's a lot to like about this welcoming 15th-century country inn. And that's not all: chef-proprietor Tim Neal shows a talent for tracking down peerless Sussex produce - whether it's from the pub's own garden, game from local shoots, or mushrooms and truffles foraged in nearby woodlands. It all turns up in food that stretches well beyond the usual pub standard, ranging from Harveys beer-battered haddock with chunky chips and mushy peas from a hearty, no-nonsense bar menu, or something more serious from an intelligent restaurant menu. Get going with sautéed breast of wood pigeon served with chestnut polenta, wild mushroom fricassée and crispy pancetta, and follow with slow-braised pork belly, home-made black pudding and apple and celeriac purée.

Chef Tim Neal **Owner** Mr & Mrs Neal **Times** 12-2/7-9 Closed 25 Dec, D Sun **Prices** Starter £5.50-£9.75, Main £8.75-£17.95, Dessert £5.50-£7.95, Service optional, Groups min 8 service 10% **Wines** 22 bottles over £20, 29 bottles under £20, 8 by glass **Notes** Vegetarian available **Seats** 40 **Children** Portions **Parking** 40

RUSPER **Map 6 TQ23**

Ghyll Manor Hotel & Restaurant

@ Modern British

Appealing, unfussy cooking in a charming country hotel

☎ 0845 345 3426
High St RH12 4PX
e-mail: reception@ghyllmanor
web: www.ghyllmanor.co.uk
dir: M23 junct 11, join A264 signed Horsham. Continue to 3rd rdbt, take 3rd exit towards Faygate and Rusper

The 16th-century manor house in one of Sussex's many picture-postcard villages is overflowing with period styling, and stands in 40 acres of grounds. Start a sunny evening with an aperitif on the terrace overlooking the lake and gardens, and eat either in the conservatory or in the charming main dining room. Appealing cooking with a minimum of fuss is what the kitchen is all about, seen in the form of flavour-packed smoked chicken terrine with girolles and walnut bread, crisped pork belly with celeriac purée and sautéed potatoes, and rich orange crème brûlée with mocha cream.

Chef Alec Mackins **Owner** Civil Service Motoring Association **Times** 12-2/6.30-9.30 **Prices** Starter £4-£11.45, Main £12.95-£18.95, Dessert £5-£7, Service optional **Wines** 76 bottles over £20, 16 bottles under £20, 8 by glass **Notes** Sunday L, Vegetarian available, Dress restrictions, Smart casual, Civ Wed 120 **Seats** 40, Pr/dining room 30 **Children** Portions **Parking** 100

SIDLESHAM **Map 5 SZ89**

The Crab & Lobster

British, Mediterranean

Stylishly-renovated waterside hideaway with switched-on menu

☎ 01243 641233
Mill Ln PO20 7NB
e-mail: enquiries@crab-lobster.co.uk
dir: A27 S onto B2145 towards Selsey. At Sidlesham turn left onto Rookery Ln, continue for 0.75m

The Crab and Lobster sounds like a pub, and the 350-year-old inn on the waterside of Pagham Harbour Nature Reserve might even look like one, but that's as far as it goes. This chic restaurant with rooms is a thoroughly contemporary take on the inn concept; its sleek modern dining room pulls together the tones of mushroom, cerise and ivory with darkwood tables, age-old flagstone floors and oak beams. The kitchen cooks in step with the décor - bang up to date, its menus brimming with peerless Sussex produce. Given the watery location, it's no surprise that fish and seafood is a strong suit: start with clam and red mullet chowder, ahead of halibut poached in thyme and milk, served with wild mushroom risotto and baby fennel. Finish with deep-fried ice cream with butterscotch sauce.

Chef Sam Bakose **Owner** Sam & Janet Bakose **Times** 12-2.30/6-10 **Prices** Starter £5.75-£12.50, Main £14.50-£27, Dessert £6.25, Service optional, Groups min 7 service 10% **Wines** 44 bottles over £20, 11 bottles under £20, 17 by glass **Notes** Sunday L, Vegetarian available **Seats** 54 **Children** Portions **Parking** 12

See advert below

TILLINGTON **Map 6 SU92**

The Horse Guards Inn

Traditional British **NEW**

Relaxed pub dining with a local flavour

☎ 01798 342332
GU28 9AF
e-mail: info@thehorseguardsinn.co.uk
dir: On A272, 1m west of Petworth, take road signposted Tillington. Restaurant 500mtrs opposite church

A delightful little pub made up of three converted cottages, the 350-year-old Horse Guards Inn has lovely views over the Rother Valley. Period fireplaces, exposed wooden beams in low ceilings, candles burning and unclothed wooden tables lend a homely air, as does the gaggle of locals propping up the bar. Drinkers are welcomed, but it would be a shame to miss out on the good quality, honest cooking. All ingredients are sourced locally and bread is baked in-house (and you can buy it to take home, too). A well-balanced plate of Indian-spiced scallops with butternut purée might precede South Downs venison haunch with Cheltenham beets, red cabbage and parsnip mash. Finish with a plum tarte Tatin with double dairy ice cream and caramel sauce.

Chef Andrew Kilburn **Owner** Sam Beard & Michaela Hohrkoua **Times** 12-2.30/6.30-9.00 Closed D Sun **Prices** Starter £5-£9, Main £8-£20, Dessert £5-£12, Service optional, Groups min 12 service 12% **Wines** 23 bottles over £20, 12 bottles under £20, 9 by glass **Notes** Sunday L, Vegetarian available **Seats** 55, Pr/dining room 20 **Children** Portions, Menu **Parking** On street

TROTTON **Map 5 SU82**

The Keepers Arms

British, Mediterranean **NEW**

Upmarket country pub with appealing menu

☎ 01730 813724 & 07710 678297
Love Hill, Terwick Ln GU31 5ER
e-mail: nick@keepersarms.co.uk
dir: A272 towards Petersfield after 5m, restaurant on right just after narrow bridge. From Midhurst follow A272 for 3m, restaurant on left

A well groomed 17th-century country inn sitting up above the A272, the Keepers Arms makes a good first impression. The terrace is a big draw for a spot of fair-weather eating, while in cooler times welcoming log fires seduce all who cross the threshold. Though an opened-up affair, the bar retains bags of beamed-and-timbered charm, while in contrast, the lighter restaurant delivers easy-on-the-eye modernity with its pastel tones and mellow tartan fabrics. Blackboard classics such as Cumberland sausages with mash and onion gravy will satisfy traditionalists, while the carte ups the ante with some unthreatening contemporary thinking. Warm tartlet of goats' cheese and onion marmalade might precede roasted pheasant breast with fondant potato, curly kale and winter berry sauce. Well-chosen wines or good real ales accompany.

Chef Charlie Piper-Hodgkins **Owner** Nicholas Troth **Times** 12-2/6.30-9 Closed 25-26 Dec **Prices** Starter £5-£9, Main £10-£22, Dessert £5-£7, Service optional **Wines** 30 bottles over £20, 8 bottles under £20, 8 by glass **Notes** Sunday L, Vegetarian available **Seats** 36, Pr/dining room 8 **Children** Portions **Parking** 25

TURNERS HILL Map 6 TQ33

AG's Grill Room

Traditional British

Traditional grill room menu in fine country-house hotel and spa

01342 714914
Alexander House Hotel, East St RH10 4QD
e-mail: info@alexanderhouse.co.uk
web: www.alexanderhouse.co.uk
dir: On B2110 between Turners Hill & East Grinstead; 6m from M23 junct 10

Alexander House is a grand 17th-century country mansion set in 170 acres of beautiful grounds, and now operates as a chic boutique hotel and spa. It has been sensitively restored and it combines understated luxury with original character. AG's Grill Room, the main restaurant, is in the oldest part of the hotel and its opulent furnishings and impressive works of art are country-house grandeur to a tee. The cooking is based on the traditional style of a grill room and champions aged Sussex beef, Cornish seafood and fish fresh from the south coast. Expect potted shrimps or duck liver and foie gras parfait to start, then perhaps grilled sole with herb sauce or sirloin steak with red wine sauce. Puddings may include peanut butter parfait with white chocolate and praline mousse.

Chef Paul Nixon **Owner** Alexander Hotels Ltd **Times** 12-3/7-10 Closed Mon-Tue **Prices** Food prices not confirmed for 2011. Please telephone for details. **Wines** 130 bottles over £20, 4 bottles under £20, 18 by glass **Notes** Sunday L, Vegetarian available, Dress restrictions, No jeans or trainers, Civ Wed 100 **Seats** 40, Pr/dining room 20 **Children** Portions **Parking** 100

Reflections at Alexander House

Modern International V

Modern, relaxed hotel dining option

01342 714914
Alexander House Hotel, East St RH10 4QD
e-mail: admin@alexanderhouse.co.uk
dir: On B2110 between Turners Hill & East Grinstead; 6m from M23 junct 10

With 170 acres of gardens and parkland, Alexander House is an imposing, early 17th-century mansion turned boutique hotel and destination spa (see entry, above). The more casual dining option is Reflections, a sleek, contemporary space that overlooks the central courtyard and comes complete with its own champagne bar. The kitchen's straightforward brasserie-style output plays to the hotel's leisure market, offering something for everyone; from light bites (pumpkin and sage tortellini) to salads (chicken Caesar) and veggie options (wild mushroom risotto). Classics range from rib-eye steak and chunky chips to more adventurous dishes like halibut with pumpkin purée, celeriac foam and sautéed ceps.

Chef Paul Nixon **Owner** Peter & Deborah Hinchcliffe **Times** 12-3/6.30-10 **Prices** Starter £5-£14, Main £10-£24, Dessert £7.50-£9, Service added but optional 12.5% **Wines** 47 bottles over £20, 2 bottles under £20, 12 by glass **Notes** Sunday L, Vegetarian menu, Civ Wed 100 **Seats** 70, Pr/dining room 12 **Children** Portions **Parking** 100

TYNE & WEAR

GATESHEAD Map 21 NZ26

Eslington Villa Hotel

Modern British V

Period features and a local flavour

0191 487 6017 & 420 0666
8 Station Rd, Low Fell NE9 6DR
e-mail: home@eslingtonvilla.co.uk
dir: off A1(M) exit for Team Valley Trading Estate. Right at 2nd rdbt along Eastern Av. Left at car show room, hotel 100yds on left

A calm home-from-home ambience prevails at this rambling Victorian house with beautiful gardens in a leafy Gateshead district close to, but a world apart from, the industry of the Team Valley. Family owned and run, the stunning venue has retained many features from the 19th century, particularly in the traditional dining room with its antler chandeliers, old fireplaces and shooting lodge-style tartan floor. The more contemporary conservatory has impressive views across to Newcastle. The classic cooking with some imaginative touches is based on seasonal Northumberland produce; start with brown ale risotto with local black pudding and crisp parsley, then move onto seared salmon with artichokes or duck two ways.

Chef Andy Moore **Owner** Mr & Mrs N Tulip **Times** 12-2/7-9.45 Closed 25-26 Dec, 1 Jan, BHs, L Sat, D Sun **Prices** Fixed L 2 course fr £18.95, Fixed D 3 course fr £25.50, Service optional **Wines** 17 bottles over £20, 24 bottles under £20, 8 by glass **Notes** Sunday L, Vegetarian menu **Seats** 80, Pr/dining room 30 **Children** Portions **Parking** 30

NEWCASTLE UPON TYNE Map 21 NZ26

Blackfriars Restaurant

Traditional, Modern British

Modern dining in historical setting

0191 261 5945
Friars St NE1 4XN
e-mail: info@blackfriarsrestaurant.co.uk
web: www.blackfriarsrestaurant.co.uk
dir: Take only small cobbled road off Stowell St (China Town). Blackfriars 100yds on left

Originally a refectory used by Dominican friars from around 1239 AD, this atmospheric restaurant claims to be the oldest dining room in the UK. It revels in its antiquity: the Gothic stone-walls, venerable timbers, carved wooden chairs, and ranks of church candles echo medieval scenes when Henry III caroused here. The food has fast-forwarded quite a few centuries to feature modern British dishes with robust, hearty flavours built on fresh local ingredients. There might be Cumbrian rabbit and confit apple terrine with spiced carrot chutney to start, ahead of braised North Sea halibut with tomato and mussel broth, and wilted pak choi. End with dark chocolate cake and Lindisfarne mead marmalade ice cream. A grassy courtyard makes a great summer-season setting.

Chef Troy Terrington **Owner** Andy & Sam Hook **Times** 12-2.30/6-12 Closed Good Fri & BHs, D Sun **Prices** Fixed L 2 course £12, Starter £5-£10, Main £9-£21, Dessert £5-£8, Service added but optional 10% **Wines** 26 bottles over £20, 17 bottles under £20, 8 by glass **Notes** Sunday L, Vegetarian available **Seats** 80, Pr/dining room 50 **Children** Portions, Menu **Parking** Car park next to restaurant

NEWCASTLE UPON TYNE *continued*

Brasserie Black Door

Modern British

Brasserie dining in a stylish commercial art gallery

0191 260 5411
The Biscuit Factory, 16 Stoddart St, Shieldfield NE2 1AN
e-mail: info@blackdoorgroup.co.uk

The modern artworks on display are food for thought at this classy brasserie in the old Biscuit Factory, Britain's largest commercial art gallery. Like much of Newcastle's industrial heritage, this expansive space has been modishly dressed up, in this case with chunky wooden tables, leather chairs and warm colours beneath a soaring warehouse ceiling. The vibe is busy and convivial, the cooking hearty and unfussy, with its heart in the French classics and its supply lines local, as evidenced in starters such as a warm salad of Craster kippers with potatoes and herb dressing, or a North Shields fish soup. For mains, go for the big flavours of venison loin with butternut squash, braised red cabbage and scallop.

Chef David Kennedy **Owner** David Ladd & David Kennedy **Times** 12-3/7-10 Closed 25-26 Dec, D Sun **Prices** Fixed L 2 course £10, Fixed D 3 course £18.95-£24.95, Starter £4.50-£8.95, Main £11-£20, Dessert £3.95-£8.95, Service added but optional 10% **Wines** 7 bottles over £20, 7 bottles under £20, 8 by glass **Notes** Sunday L, Vegetarian available **Seats** 70, Pr/dining room 24 **Children** Portions **Parking** 20, On street

Café 21 Newcastle

Modern V

Modern bistro eating by the revamped quayside

0191 222 0755
Trinity Gardens, Quayside NE1 2HH
e-mail: enquiries@cafetwentyone.co.uk

The regenerated quayside quarter is home to Terry Laybourne's slick Café 21, a location that is tailor-made for this contemporary urban brasserie. The expansive, elegant room has been done out in an understated modern style - restful slate-grey with splotches of lime green, a dark wooden floor and buttoned banquettes. The style of cooking suits the venue, offering bistro dishes that take their cue from French classics, dipping into Spain and Italy here and there. Tried-and-tested combinations begin with a warm salad of ham knuckle with soft-poached egg and mustard dressing, before a hearty sauté of Northumbrian venison with winter fruits and vegetables, or whole lemon sole with maître d'hotel butter. Laybourne's trademark sourcing of top-notch local produce lies at the heart of the kitchen's efforts.

Chef Chris Dobson **Owner** Terry Laybourne **Times** 12-2.30/5.30-10.30 Closed 25-26 Dec, 1 Jan, Etr Mon, D 24 Dec **Prices** Fixed L 2 course £16, Fixed D 3 course £19.50, Starter £5.50-£13.80, Main £14.80-£30, Dessert £6.50-£9, Service added but optional 10% **Wines** 81 bottles over £20, 7 bottles under £20, 14 by glass **Notes** Sunday L, Vegetarian menu **Seats** 90, Pr/dining room 40 **Parking** NCP

Hotel du Vin Newcastle

Modern British NEW NOTABLE WINE LIST

Stylish urban French bistro dining in designer hotel

0191 229 2200 & 0191 229 2205
Allan House, City Rd NE1 2BE
e-mail: reception.newcastle@hotelduvin.com
dir: A1 junct 65 slip road to A184 Gateshead/Newcastle, Quayside to City Rd

If anyone is still unfamiliar with the brand, the HdV formula converts historical or interesting buildings into

Jesmond Dene House

NEWCASTLE UPON TYNE Map 21 NZ26

European V NOTABLE WINE LIST

Brilliant, innovative food in a splendid Georgian house

0191 212 3000
Jesmond Dene Rd NE2 2EY
e-mail: info@jesmonddenehouse.co.uk
dir: From city centre follow A167 to junct with A184. Turn right towards Matthew Bank. Turn right into Jesmond Dene Rd

The expansive late-Georgian house was built with shipbuilding and armaments money in the 1820s. It's a veritable Arcadia, set in grounds that encompass waterfalls, bridges, manicured lawns, and the ruins of a mill, the more extraordinary for its being so close to the centre of Newcastle (albeit in a district that can fairly consider itself Tyneside's Kensington). It's run with formality and warmth in the old-school manner, and regularly hosts special evenings for jazz aficionados, as well as dinners addressed by food and wine experts. Within the oak-panelled and garden-view dining rooms, the cooking has set and maintains a cracking pace, offering creativity and skill in its contemporary approach to classic dishes. A meal might open with steamed Lindisfarne oysters, alongside watercress jelly, Avruga, and a gin and grapefruit granité, or sea bass served in carpaccio style, with clementine and coriander salad. Much use is made of fine local materials for main courses that take in Steve Ramshaw's beef fillet with bone marrow, girolles and truffled sauce, or veal from New Moor Farm with braised lettuce, sweetbreads and mash. The innovative vein continues in architecturally complex desserts such as chocolate and salted caramel sphere, or a millefeuille of apple and popcorn with apple sorbet.

Chef Pierre Rigothier **Owner** Peter Candler **Times** 12-2.30/7-10.30 **Prices** Fixed L 3 course £25-£26, Fixed D 3 course £27-£35, Starter £11-£18, Main £14-£40, Dessert £4.50-£10, Service added but optional 10% **Wines** 187 bottles over £20, 6 bottles under £20, 17 by glass **Notes** Tasting menu available, Sunday L, Vegetarian menu, Dress restrictions, Smart casual, Civ Wed 100 **Seats** 60, Pr/dining room 18 **Children** Portions, Menu **Parking** 64

style-oriented contemporary hotels, each with its own unique character. The red-brick warehouse of the Tyne Tees Steamship Company, built in 1908, was a natural candidate for transformation into the chain's Geordie outpost. In a glorious riverside location, it revels in grand views along the Tyne to the iconic arching bridge. Remaining true to the brand's ethos, the restaurant is decked out in retro French bistro style, or there's an inviting alfresco patio for summer dining. The menu majors on the classics, sticking to simple, tried-and-tested combinations of gutsy flavours. A starter of bone marrow served with tomato salad and roasted garlic sets out the kitchen's style; to follow, shin of beef with carrots and oyster mushrooms is a master class in precise flavours, while fine local materials turn up in Craster smoked haddock with a poached egg and mustard beurre blanc.

Chef Graeme Cuthell **Owner** MWB Holdings PLC **Times** 12-2/6-10 Closed L 1 Jan, D 25 Dec **Prices** Fixed L 2 course £20-£30, Fixed D 3 course £30-£40, Starter £6-£10, Main £12-£25, Dessert £6.75-£10, Service added but optional 10% **Wines** 370 bottles over £20, 30 bottles under £20, 20 by glass **Notes** Sunday L, Vegetarian available, Civ Wed 40, Air con **Seats** 85, Pr/dining room 20 **Children** Portions **Parking** On street

Jesmond Dene House

– see opposite page

Malmaison Newcastle

French

Good brasserie dining in trendy location

☎ 0191 245 5000
Quayside NE1 3DX
e-mail: newcastle@malmaison.com
dir: Follow signs for city centre, then for Quayside/Law Courts. Hotel 100yds past Law Courts

The Newcastle outpost of the boutique Malmaison chain of hotels stands in the upbeat revitalised quayside quarter overlooking the Millennium Bridge. The former warehouse has all the hallmarks of the 'Mal' brand: boudoir-chic shades of deep purple, crimson and plum, and textures of velvet, chrome, wood and leather. The moodily-lit bar has high stools and aubergine-coloured leather sofas and views of the River Tyne. Move into the brasserie, where the kitchen deals in classics with a modern spin – take duck liver parfait with fig chutney, followed by roast cod with chorizo and mussels, and Amaretto praline mousse. The 'Home Grown and Local' menu showcases produce from Tyneside and Northumbria.

Times 12-2.30/6-11

Vermont Hotel

British, French

Landmark views and modern menu

☎ 0191 233 1010
Castle Garth NE1 1RQ
e-mail: info@vermont-hotel.co.uk
dir: City centre by high level bridge & castle keep

Plumb in the city centre next to the castle and sharing the same courtyard as the Moot Hall (Law Courts), the Vermont is a highly distinctive building. Built of Portland stone in 1910, and Grade II listed, it has the look of a Manhattan-style tower block about it. The aptly named Bridge Restaurant is on the 6th floor, looking directly out onto the Tyne and Millennium Bridges. Smart leather chairs, banquette seating and white-clothed tables set the scene for some carefully prepared modern British cooking. Begin with confit chicken terrine, moving on to rib-eye steak with smoked bone marrow butter and chunky chips, or black bream with pommes purée and horseradish cream.

Times 12-2.30/6-11

WARWICKSHIRE

ALCESTER — Map 10 SP05

Essence

Modern British

Modern cuisine and style to match in a 17th-century cottage

☎ 01789 762764 & 07900 210552
50 Birmingham Rd B49 5EP
e-mail: info@eatatessence.co.uk
dir: From town centre towards Birmingham & M42. Restaurant is opposite Alcester Grammar School

A 17th-century cottage on the outside, Essence opens onto a scene of clean-cut contemporary style that mixes up ancient oak beams with cream-washed walls, modern art and leather chairs, darkwood tables and slate placemats. Essence has a strong local fan base, and no wonder: the kitchen deals in cooking to suit the surroundings - unpretentious modern British dishes that are big on flavour, cooked accurately and without fuss, using a rock-solid base of locally-sourced produce. Set-price menus offering superb value might start with a risotto of brie and walnuts, followed by chicken breast with mustard mash and mushroom cream sauce; desserts such as minted chocolate Gascony mousse with a home-made cookie end in the comfort zone.

Chef Chris Short **Owner** Chris Short **Times** 10-3/6.30-10 Closed Mon, D Sun **Prices** Fixed L 2 course £13.50-£31, Fixed D 3 course £16.50-£39, Starter £4.25-£8.50, Main £10.50-£22.50, Dessert £5.50-£8, Service optional **Wines** 20 bottles over £20, 10 bottles under £20, 6 by glass **Notes** Early D deal Tue-Fri 6.30-8pm, Sunday L, Vegetarian available **Seats** 42 **Children** Portions, Menu **Parking** 19

ALDERMINSTER — Map 10 SP24

Ettington Park Hotel

British, French

Fine-dining venue in a jaw-dropping Gothic mansion

☎ 01789 450123
CV37 8BU
dir: M40 junct 15/A46 towards Stratford-upon-Avon, then A439 into town centre onto A3400 5m to Shipston. Hotel 0.5m on left

Arising in the midst of rural Warwickshire, the jaw-dropping neo-Gothic mansion stands in 40 acres of parkland and gardens. It comes as no surprise to learn the place is licensed for weddings. Crammed with antiques and artworks, it's a sight for sore eyes inside as well as out, and in the Oak Room, has a deeply comfortable, high-end dining venue. Service here is refreshingly friendly and attentive without being overbearing, and the food focuses on traditional juxtapositions teased gently into the modern era. A bowl of superb river Exe mussels is cooked in Lady Godiva ale as a spin on the wine-based moules marinière, while Gressingham duck comes as crisp-skinned breast and confit leg, alongside sautéed kale and beetroot fondant, in a pan gravy sweetened with elderberries. Finish with assertive basil pannacotta and poached rhubarb.

Chef Gary Lissemore **Owner** Hand Picked Hotels **Times** 12-2/7-9.30 Closed L Mon-Fri **Prices** Food prices not confirmed for 2011. Please telephone for details. **Wines** 52 bottles over £20, 6 bottles under £20, 12 by glass **Notes** Civ Wed 96 **Seats** 50, Pr/dining room 80 **Children** Portions, Menu **Parking** 80

Mallory Court Hotel

LEAMINGTON SPA (ROYAL) Map 10 SP36

Modern British V 

Imaginative cooking in a grand country retreat

☎ 01926 330214
Harbury Ln, Bishop's Tachbrook CV33 9QB
e-mail: reception@mallory.co.uk
dir: M40 junct 13 N'bound. Left, left again towards Bishop's Tachbrook. 0.5m, right into Harbury Ln. M40 junct 14 S'bound, A452 for Leamington. At 2nd rdbt left into Harbury Ln

It's not hard to see why Mallory Court is in the Premier League of country bolt-holes: the creeper-swathed manor house is secluded in 10 acres of primped gardens on the edge of Royal Leamington Spa, and comes with all the bells and whistles you'd expect in a hotel of this standing. Sure, the gardens are idyllic, but they also serve a more utilitarian purpose, providing the kitchen with year-round supplies of herbs, vegetables and fruit. The oak-panelled Dining Room makes a suitably opulent setting for the hotel's fine dining operation, or if you're lucky with the weather, a terrace is the place to be for alfresco dining to a background of gently verdant Warwickshire countryside. The kitchen pulls together classically-inclined technique with modern themes in a well-considered style of country-house cooking. Menus are not weighed down by verbosity: each dish is described with economy on a daily-changing carte that makes the most of the best produce the region has to offer. A foie gras 'bonbon' with smoked duck salad and duck pastilla is one way to kick-start the taste buds, before main-course breast of wood pigeon with venison bolognaise and red wine sauce; fish might be represented by pan-fried John Dory with dressed crab and a bisque-style sauce, while masterful desserts run to a chocolate and hazelnut rocher with mascarpone ice cream and bergamot apricots. There's something to suit all occasions and pockets on the compendious list of fine wines. The less formal Brasserie is listed separately (see entry).

Chef Simon Haigh **Owner** Sir Peter Rigby **Times** 12-1.45/6.30-8.45 Closed L Sat **Prices** Fixed L 2 course fr £25.50, Fixed D 3 course £42.50-£59.50, Service optional **Wines** 2 bottles under £20, 7 by glass **Notes** Sunday L, Vegetarian menu, Dress restrictions, No jeans or sportswear, Civ Wed 160 **Seats** 56, Pr/dining room 14 **Children** Portions, Menu **Parking** 100

ATHERSTONE Map 10 SP39

Chapel House Restaurant with Rooms

British, French

Elegant surroundings and French-accented cooking

01827 718949
Friar's Gate CV9 1EY
e-mail: info@chapelhouse.eu
dir: Off Market Sq in Atherstone, behind High St

This tranquil restaurant with rooms set in secluded walled gardens in a corner of the market square was once the dower house to Atherstone Hall, visited by no less a personage than Florence Nightingale. Built in 1728, Chapel House has been extended over the years, but retains plenty of period charm, particularly in the elegant Georgian dining room. The cooking has its roots firmly in the French classics, lightened to suit modern tastes, and with an eye to prime local ingredients. Expect the likes of local Grendon lamb served with shallot and green Chartreuse sauce, and potato rösti, or fish dishes such as monkfish fillets in lobster and brandy sauce with king prawns.

Chef Richard Henry Napper **Owner** Richard & Siobhan Napper **Times** 12-2/7-9.30 Closed 24 Dec-3 Jan, Etr wk, late Aug-early Sep, Sun, L Mon-Tue **Prices** Starter £4.95-£8.95, Main £17.95-£21.25, Dessert £5.95-£8.95, Service optional **Wines** 61 bottles over £20, 44 bottles under £20, 9 by glass **Notes** Vegetarian available, Dress restrictions, Smart casual **Seats** 24, Pr/dining room 12 **Children** Portions **Parking** On street

LEA MARSTON Map 10 SP29

The Adderley Restaurant

Modern British V

Smart modern Midlands hotel with good contemporary dining

01675 470468
Lea Marston Hotel, Haunch Ln B76 0BY
e-mail: info@leamarstonhotel.co.uk
dir: From M42 junct 9/A4097 signed Kingsbury Hotel, 2nd turning right into Haunch Lane. Hotel 200yds on right

Lea Marston Hotel is a sharp-looking contemporary hotel in 54 acres of grounds in green-and-pleasant Warwickshire countryside. As it's not far from the relentless thunder of the main Midlands motorway network and the business hub of Brum, conferences and events are naturally a big thing here. Leisure travellers will also find much to praise in its friendly ambience, plus there's a whizzo spa and fitness club to hone both body and appetite for relaxed dining in the smartly-minimal Adderley Restaurant. The kitchen deals in classic British cooking brought up to date with imagination, and prepared with respect for the basic culinary rules: fresh local ingredients cooked accurately to achieve well-defined, balanced flavours. Rabbit with black pudding and red wine jus starts strongly, followed by more gutsy flavours in duck three ways - breast, confit leg, and liver, teamed with fondant potato and cabbage.

Chef Richard Marshall **Owner** Blake Family **Times** 7-9.30 Closed L Mon-Sat, D Sun **Prices** Starter £3.95-£7.25, Main £13.50-£18.50, Dessert £4.95-£6.25, Service optional **Wines** 18 bottles over £20, 16 bottles under £20, 6 by glass **Notes** Sunday L, Vegetarian menu, Dress restrictions, Smart dress, Civ Wed 100 **Seats** 100, Pr/dining room 30 **Children** Portions, Menu **Parking** 200

LEAMINGTON SPA (ROYAL) Map 10 SP36

The Brasserie at Mallory Court

Modern British

The simpler dining option in opulent Mallory Court

01926 453939
Harbury Ln, Bishop's Tachbrook CV33 9QB
e-mail: thebrasserie@mallory.co.uk
web: www.mallory.co.uk
dir: M40 junct 13 N'bound left, left again towards Bishops Tachbrook, right onto Harbury Ln after 0.5m. M40 junct 14 S'bound A452 to Leamington, at 2nd rdbt left onto Harbury Ln

The Brasserie is the relaxed and less formal eating option in the luxurious Mallory Court Hotel (see separate entry). Décor is muted black and cream with nods to art-deco styling. A garden for outdoor dining and a very chic cocktail bar come as part of the package too. The menu of straightforward brasserie classics is cooked with confidence, and takes in pigeon with date purée, lentils and roasted hazelnuts, crisp pork belly with curly kale and chorizo, skate wing with capers and lemon, and sirloin steak with hand-cut chips and confit tomatoes. Desserts to write home about include a hot chocolate and orange cake with mandarin sorbet and spiced tangerines, or a vanilla pannacotta with rhubarb and orange compôte.

Times 12-2.30/6.30-9.30 Closed D Sun

Mallory Court Hotel

– see opposite page

Restaurant 23

Modern European

Smart modern European cooking opposite the bandstand

01926 422422
23 Dormer Place CV32 5AA
e-mail: info@restaurant23.co.uk
dir: M40 junct 13 onto A452 towards Leamington Spa. Follow signs for town centre, opposite band stand

Genteelly positioned opposite the bandstand at the bottom of Leamington Spa's parade, the smart, white-fronted restaurant is a magnet for pre-theatre diners, as well as for those with more time to spare. Modern European cooking of great acuity is Peter Knibb's style, and the informal ambience and open-plan kitchen suit the mood perfectly. Pork belly with crackling has found its way on to starter listings these days, and appears here with a fennel salad and spiced pineapple to make a stimulating assemblage of flavours. Meat and fish juxtapositions are directly in line with modern thinking too, as represented by a carefully composed main course of grey mullet with chorizo and mussels. Add potato confit and broad beans, and there is evidence here of real culinary intelligence. Poached fruits and satisfyingly crunchy coconut macaroons are the accompaniments to an unabashedly acidic frozen passionfruit mousse. A good wine list leads off with some unusually imaginative French selections.

Chef Peter Knibb **Owner** Peter & Antje Knibb **Times** 12.15-2.30/6.15-9.45 Closed 25 Dec, 2 wks Jan, 2 wks Aug, Sun-Mon **Prices** Fixed L 2 course £17, Fixed D 3 course £23.50, Starter £9.50-£14.50, Main £20, Dessert £8.50, Service optional, Groups min 7 service 10% **Wines** 120 bottles over £20, 14 bottles under £20, 7 by glass **Notes** Pre-theatre 2 or 3 course menu Tue-Fri 6.15-7pm, Vegetarian available **Seats** 24 **Parking** On street opposite

SHIPSTON ON STOUR Map 10 SP24

The Red Lion

British NEW

Attractive Cotswolds pub serving well-cooked local produce

01608 684221
Main St CV36 5JJ
e-mail: info@redlion-longcompton.co.uk
dir: 5m S of Shipston on Stour on A3400

Take a classic Cotswolds coaching inn dating from 1748, kit out the interior with a neatly contemporary rustic-chic look that blends leather armchairs with ancient oak beams and an open fire in a huge inglenook, and you have the delightful Red Lion. Five classy bedrooms mean you can stay over and put the menu and wine list through their paces. The draw here is fuss-free modern British cuisine made from as much local produce as the kitchen can lay its hands on. The well-thought-out menu offers an appealing choice of good hearty dishes such as a warm poached egg salad with apple, black pudding, crisp bacon and mustard mayonnaise, followed by a whole roasted sea bass with wilted spinach, spicy red peppers and garlic and chive butter. Finish in the comfort zone with rhubarb and ginger crumble with custard.

Chef Sarah Keightley **Owner** Lisa Phipps
Times 12-2.30/6-9 **Prices** Food prices not confirmed for 2011. Please telephone for details. **Notes** Sunday L, Vegetarian available **Seats** 50, Pr/dining room 20 **Children** Portions, Menu **Parking** 70

STRATFORD-UPON-AVON Map 10 SP25

The Legacy Falcon Hotel

British

Atmospheric hotel with ambitious cooking

0844 411 9005
Chapel St CV37 6HA
e-mail: res-falcon@legacy-hotels.co.uk
dir: M40 junct 15, follow town centre signs towards Barclays Bank on rdbt. Turn into High Street, between Austin Reed & WH Smiths. Turn 2nd right into Scholars Lane & right again into hotel

You couldn't get more picture-postcard Stratford than the Falcon, with its black-and-white Tudor façade with leaded-light windows. The interior is a successful blend of period features and modern furnishings. Will's Place restaurant (there's a bistro, too) delivers modern British food such as warm goats' cheese on toasted brioche with a grape dressing to start, followed by tomato and paprika chicken breast with cucumber relish, fondant potato and a tomato and tarragon sauce. Dessert could be chocolate fudge sundae with chocolate sauce and vanilla ice cream.

Times 12.30-2/6-9

Macdonald Alveston Manor

Modern British

Atmospheric old house with confident cooking

01789 205478
Clopton Bridge CV37 7HP
e-mail: events.alvestonmanor@macdonald-hotels.co.uk
dir: 6m from M40 junct 15, (on edge of town) across Clopton Bridge towards Banbury

In peaceful grounds, not far from Stratford, the striking red-brick and timbered façade of Alveston Manor delivers a hearty dose of Elizabethan charm. The Manor restaurant has all the original oak beams and mullioned windows you might hope for, and makes an appealing setting for the confident modern British cooking. Start with roast ceps and onion tart with Madeira jus, then move on to Highland lamb neck fillet with spiced aubergine and pickled carrot. Alveston Manor's pineapple cheesecake makes for a great finale. Those who are taking in some of the Bard's work during their stay may be interested to know that the hotel's cedar tree is rumoured to have witnessed the first ever performance of *A Midsummer Night's Dream*.

Chef Jason Buck **Owner** Macdonald Hotels plc
Times 12-2.30/6-9.30 Closed L Mon-Sat **Prices** Fixed L 2 course £12-£22, Fixed D 3 course £25-£32, Starter £5-£9, Main £13-£31, Dessert £5-£9, Service included **Wines** 69 bottles over £20, 14 bottles under £20, 15 by glass **Notes** Pre-theatre menu available, Sunday L, Vegetarian available, Civ Wed 120 **Seats** 110, Pr/dining room 40 **Children** Portions, Menu **Parking** 120

Menzies Welcombe Hotel Spa and Golf Course

Modern, Traditional

Traditional manor house serving seasonal food

01789 295252
Warwick Rd CV37 0NR
e-mail: welcombe@menzieshotels.co.uk
dir: M40 junct 15, A46 to Stratford-upon-Avon. 1st rdbt left onto A439, hotel 3m on right

Built by Victorians in Jacobean style, this red-brick manor-house hotel sits in 157 acres of landscaped parkland with colourful Italian gardens. A golf course, plus a glitzy spa and health club offer ample opportunity to hone the appetite for dining in the Trevelyan restaurant, a traditional place with glamorous French glass chandeliers that suits the style of cooking. Appealing menu options stick to tried-and-tested combinations, tweaked here and there to add an extra level of interest - home-smoked chicken and sweetcorn risotto with deep-fried chicken wings, for example, followed by pan-fried hake with crushed potatoes and leek and clam chowder. Dessert unites strawberry pannacotta with rosewater cream and oat biscuits to good effect.

Chef Robin Smith **Owner** Menzies Hotels
Times 12.30-2/7-9.30 Closed L Sat **Prices** Fixed L 2 course fr £15.95, Fixed D 3 course fr £30, Starter £9.50-£11, Main £21-£28, Dessert £6.50-£10.50, Service optional **Wines** 125 bottles over £20, 5 bottles under £20, 16 by glass **Notes** Pre-theatre D menu available, Sunday L, Vegetarian available, Dress restrictions, Smart casual, shirt with collar, Civ Wed 180 **Seats** 70, Pr/dining room 150 **Children** Portions, Menu **Parking** 150

Mercure Shakespeare

Traditional British

Historic English setting for vibrant European cooking

01789 294997
Chapel St CV37 6ER
e-mail: h6630@accor.com
dir: Follow signs to town centre. Round one-way system, into Bridge St. At rdbt turn left. Hotel 200yds on left

One of the oldest in town, this historic hotel was reputedly the first (but not the last) to cash in on the Shakespeare name. The classic tudor façade certainly fits the bill, but step into the dining area of 'Othello's Brasserie' and you'll find a more contemporary space warmed up by a roaring log fire in the winter. The menu is full of European flavours, so expect pan-seared pigeon breast served on toasted brioche and thyme-infused chicory, then sautéed tuna with a chorizo and butternut squash risotto with tomato and herb salsa. Lemon meringue pie with cranberry sorbet and sablé biscuit is a grandstand finale.

Chef Paul Harris **Owner** Mercure Hotels **Times** 12-10 **Prices** Fixed L 2 course £13.50, Fixed D 3 course £25, Starter £3.95-£9.95, Main £10.50-£23.50, Dessert £4.95-£6.50, Service included **Wines** 22 bottles over £20, 16 bottles under £20, 15 by glass **Notes** Pre-theatre menu 2 course £12.95, 3 course £16.50, Sunday L, Vegetarian available, Civ Wed 100 **Seats** 80, Pr/dining room 90 **Children** Portions, Menu **Parking** 35

The Stratford

Modern European

Comforting classics in modern hotel

01789 271000
Arden St CV37 6QQ
e-mail: thestratfordreservations@qhotels.co.uk
dir: A439 into Stratford. In town follow A3400/ Birmingham, at lights left into Arden Street, hotel 150yds on right

At first sight, the Stratford Victoria hotel looks every inch the smart contemporary hotel, but it was originally a Victorian workhouse and hospital. Beneath its exposed beams, the Quills restaurant is an expansive space, with a clean-cut modern décor making a suitable backdrop for the kitchen's crowd-pleasing repertoire of unpretentious comfort food that will appeal to fans of both traditional and modern cooking. You might start with pan-seared tiger prawns teamed with garlic, saffron and lime cream sauce and risotto cake, then follow with duck confit with bubble-and-squeak and red wine sauce, or something fishy like poached haddock on pea and bacon risotto with chive velouté.

Times 12.30-2/6-9.45

Stuart Restaurant

Modern British

Modern cooking in historic manor house

01789 279955 & 767103
Barcelo Billesley Manor Hotel, Billesley, Alcester B49 6NF
e-mail: billesleymanor@barcelo-hotels.co.uk
dir: M40 junct 15, A46 S towards Stratford/Worcester. E over three rdbts. 2m then right for Billesley

Billesley is a mellow stone 16th-century manor in 11 acres of English country gardens that would surely have had Bill Shakespeare reaching for a quill and parchment to knock out a quick ode. The house was built to impress, with oak panelling, huge stone fireplaces and mullioned windows, and the regal décor of old leather chairs, chandeliers and tapestries boosts the sense of occasion. The kitchen doesn't intend to scare the horses and uses the best seasonal ingredients in dishes such as a homely, flavour-packed chorizo and pepper tart with parmesan salad. Next up, confit shoulder of lamb is as tender as you could ask of it, and comes with roasted vegetables, fondant potatoes and sweet garlic jus. Finish with a deeply-flavoured chocolate mousse with the textural contrasts of honeycomb and Tia Maria sabayon.

Chef Ian Buckle **Owner** Barcelo Hotels
Times 12.30-2/7-9.30 **Prices** Fixed L 3 course £37.50, Fixed D 3 course £37.50, Service optional **Wines** 46 bottles over £20, 8 bottles under £20, 14 by glass **Notes** Sunday L, Vegetarian available, Dress restrictions, Smart Casual, Civ Wed 100 **Seats** 42, Pr/dining room 100 **Children** Portions, Menu **Parking** 100

THURLASTON Map 11 SP47

Draycote Hotel

Modern British V

Golfing hotel with modern British menu

01788 521800
London Rd CV23 9LF
e-mail: info@draycotehotel.co.uk
dir: M1 junct 17 onto M45/A45. Hotel 500mtrs on left

A golfing hotel that's equally well placed for the Shakespeare circuit and the motorways, the Draycote is an all-mod-cons place with a light contemporary dining venue in the Papaveri Restaurant. The cooking style here is unimpeachable modern British, with that fondness for mixing elements of different cuisines to productive effect. Either curried parsnip pannacotta with an onion bhaji and coriander raita, or smoked salmon and dill risotto topped with the yolk of a poached egg, might lead the way to fillet of hake with chorizo crushed potatoes and aubergine caviar, with apple crumble and clove ice cream to finish.

Chef Glyn Jackson **Owner** Draycote Hotel Ltd **Times** 7-9.30 **Prices** Starter £5.25-£7.95, Main £11.95-£18.95, Dessert £5.25, Service optional **Notes** Open for L all day, Vegetarian menu, Dress restrictions, Smart casual, Civ Wed 180 **Seats** 100, Pr/dining room 60 **Children** Portions

WARWICK Map 10 SP26

The Lodge Restaurant at Ardencote Manor Hotel

British, International

Waterside restaurant with ambitious modern menu

01926 843111 & 843939
The Cumsey, Lye Green Rd CV35 8LT
e-mail: hotel@ardencote.com
dir: Off A4189. In Claverdon follow signs for Shrewley & brown tourist signs for Ardencote Manor, approx 1.5m

Patio doors open on to a waterside terrace at the Lodge Restaurant, which stands on the lake shore a short stroll from the main hotel building. Standing in 90 acres of glorious Warwickshire countryside, The Lodge is done out in a contemporary manner, with dark brown leather partitions and wine-themed pictures adorning the room. Dishes on seasonal menus are bang up to date, with good combinations such as smoked ham hock, ox cheek and quail's egg terrine with home-made piccalilli for starters, and John Dory with samphire and surf clam and tomato broth. There are grilled dishes from La Plancha, too. The wine list features plenty of New World treats.

Times 12-3/6-11

WELLESBOURNE Map 10 SP25

Barcelo Walton Hall

British

Cooking with an avante-garde edge in ritzy Warwickshire hotel

01789 842424
Walton CV35 9HU
e-mail: waltonhall.mande@barcelo-hotels.co.uk
dir: A429 through Bradford towards Wellesbourne, right after watermill, follow signs to hotel

Not 10 minutes off the A40, and yet enjoying 65 acres of prime Warwickshire to itself, Walton Hall is a member of the Barcelo hotel group. Parts of the building date back to the 16th century, while the main dining room, the Moncreiffe Restaurant, is attired in ritziest style, all swagged drapes and chandeliers. The cooking style brings things right up to date, with an avant-garde approach as seen in dishes such as a pigeon bonbon starter, accompanied by pancetta and green beans, dressed in honey and garlic. Main courses run from an engaging assemblage of sea bass and scallops with salsify and cucumber in vanilla cream to a beef duo (braised cheek and roasted fillet) with carrot purée and thyme jus. Espresso crème brûlée offers a new spin on that much-modified dessert, and comes with Agen prunes and almond caramel.

Chef Darren Long **Owner** Barcelo Hotels & Resorts **Times** 7-9.30 **Prices** Food prices not confirmed for 2011. Please telephone for details. **Wines** 49 bottles over £20, 8 bottles under £20, 14 by glass **Notes** Vegetarian available, Civ Wed 125 **Seats** 60, Pr/dining room 22 **Children** Portions, Menu **Parking** 240

WEST MIDLANDS

BALSALL COMMON Map 10 SP27

Oak Room

Modern

Delightful cooking in an attractive country house

024 7646 6174
Nailcote Hall, Nailcote Ln, Berkswell CV7 7DE
e-mail: info@nailcotehall.co.uk
dir: On B4101 towards Tile Hill/Coventry, 10 mins from NEC/Birmingham Airport

A Jacobean half-timbered manor with tall chimneys, Nailcote Hall delivers period character in spades, bolstered by a modern spa and a nine-hole championship golf course in its 15 acres of grounds. The dark-beamed Oak Room restaurant is the setting for the kitchen's ambitious contemporary food – expect confit pork belly with cauliflower purée, black pudding crumble and poached egg yolk, ahead of pan-fried sea bass with saffron and chorizo risotto and roasted cherry tomatoes. If you're in the market for a bit of dining room theatre, steak Diane is flambéed at the table, as are traditional crêpes Suzette to finish.

Times 12-2.30/7-9.30 Closed L Sat, D Sun

BARSTON Map 10 SP27

The Malt Shovel at Barston

British

Reliable village gastro-pub

01675 443223
Barston Ln B92 0JP
web: www.themaltshovelatbarston.com
dir: M42 junct 5, take turn towards Knowle. 1st left on Jacobean Ln, right at T-junct (Hampton Ln). Sharp left into Barston Ln. Restaurant 0.5m

A trim village pub-restaurant not far from Birmingham, the Malt Shovel will tempt you in with log fires in the winter chill and a garden terrace in the summer. Efficient service from a well-drilled team enhances the professionalism of the operation, and the menu of appealing gastro-pub fare is capably cooked. Cosmopolitan starters range from chick pea falafels on grilled pitta to Jamaican spiced chicken with sugared mango, while mains maintain the pace with locally-reared chicken presented three ways (a braised thigh on

continued

BARSTON ***continued***

mash, a goujon with barbecue dip and crisp-skinned fried breast). Properly runny dark chocolate fondant with vanilla ice cream concludes things in style.

The Malt Shovel at Barston

Chef Max Murphy **Owner** Caroline Furby & Chris Benbrook **Times** 12-2.30/6-9.30 Closed D Sun **Prices** Fixed D 3 course £25.50-£28.50, Starter £4.50-£9.50, Main £12.95-£18.95, Dessert £5.50-£6.95, Service optional, Groups min 6 service 10% **Wines** 12 bottles over £20, 14 bottles under £20, 6 by glass **Notes** Sunday L, Vegetarian available **Seats** 40 **Children** Portions **Parking** 30

BIRMINGHAM **Map 10 SP08**

Birmingham Marriott

Modern British, French

Modern brasserie in smart city-centre hotel

☎ 0121 452 1144
12 Hagley Rd, Five Ways B16 8SJ
dir: Leebank Middleway to Five Ways rdbt, 1st left then right. Follow signs for hotel

Recently refurbished to the tune of a cool million, this impressive city-centre hotel sits at the heart of Five Ways, within easy walking distance of all the bars and action of the trendy Gas Street Basin area and Brum's theatre and concert venues. The West 12 restaurant and bar is a boldly-styled contemporary venue, done out with funky scarlet leather and stripy banquette seating, unclothed tables and vibrant modern artworks. A contemporary brasserie-style menu plays to the crowd, opening with the likes of Thai beef salad with julienne vegetables and coriander lime dressing, while main-course options see pan-seared sea bass paired with crushed lemon new potatoes and sauce vierge, alongside pan-fried rump of lamb served with mustard and mint mash and caramelised red onion jam. Finish with hot chocolate fondant and honeycomb ice cream.

Times 12-2.30/6-10 Closed L Sat

City Café

Modern European

Modern cooking in the heart of Birmingham

☎ 0121 643 1003
City Inn Birmingham, 1 Brunswick Square, Brindley Place B1 2HW
e-mail: birmingham.citycafe@cityinn.com
dir: M6 junct 6, A38M, follow signs for A456, right into Sheepcote St, hotel straight ahead

Close to the city centre in the popular Brindley Place, this large modern chain hotel's contemporary City Café gives the option of outside eating on the terrace. Neutral beige, grey and white tones combined with banquettes and chairs, make for a relaxed, comfortable feel. Well-sourced seasonal ingredients reign across the menus including the good value market menu. On the à la carte you might find pan-fried breast of quail with honey and five spice, pea and mint risotto cake and balsamic dressing followed by trio of Middlewhite pork - confit belly, roast fillet and pork sausage - served with sweet red cabbage and crackling.

Chef Neil Peers **Owner** City Inn Ltd **Times** 12-2.30/6-10 **Prices** Fixed L 2 course £9.95-£16.95, Fixed D 3 course £16.50-£21.95, Starter £4.95-£7.95, Main £9.95-£19.95, Dessert £3.50-£9.50, Service optional **Wines** 36 bottles over £20, 12 bottles under £20, 29 by glass **Notes** Pre-theatre menu available, Sunday L, Vegetarian available, Dress restrictions, Smart casual, Civ Wed 100 **Seats** 110, Pr/dining room 50 **Children** Portions, Menu **Parking** 24, NCP behind hotel

Loves Restaurant

BIRMINGHAM **Map 10 SP08**

Modern British V NEW

High class cuisine in the canal district

☎ 0121 454 5151
The Glasshouse, Canal Square, Browning St B16 8FL
e-mail: info@loves-restaurant.co.uk
dir: Turn off Broad St towards NEC & Sherbourne Wharf then left to Grosvenor St West & right into Sherbourne St at end take right into Browning St

The thriving Birmingham dining scene has been enriched further by the arrival of Steve and Claire Love's eponymous restaurant. With a good measure of experience between them - Steve a sure hand in the kitchen and Claire a calm presence front-of-house - the Loves have created a fine-dining venue of considerable class. The setting is surprisingly idyllic given the urban location, with the sleek, minimalist décor creating a comfortable, contemporary atmosphere for the modern, refined cooking. Produce is king here, with high quality local ingredients starring alongside top-notch stuff from further afield. In true fine-dining fashion there's a tasting menu, plus a good-value lunch and early evening menu alongside the fixed-price carte; there's also an inspired vegetarian menu, which can entice with the likes of parmesan risotto with wild mushrooms, kaffir lime and lemongrass sauce. Steve's cooking displays considerable technical ability and each dish makes a strong visual impact. A first-course wood pigeon - slow-cooked breast and braised leg (perfectly tender) - is partnered with pink praline brittle and sour blackberries, the plate finished with a swipe of chocolate, while main-course Herefordshire beef comes as rump, cheek and tongue, served with smoked potato mash and celeriac choucroute. Finish with apple in the form of a financier and crumble, sublimely paired with rosemary ice cream and a shot glass of custard espuma. Everything, including the bread, amuse-bouche and pre-dessert, show precision when it comes to balancing flavours and textures.

Chef Steve Love **Owner** Steve & Claire Love **Times** 12-2.15/6-10 Closed 2 wks Xmas & Aug, 1 wk Etr, Sun-Mon **Prices** Fixed L 2 course fr £20, Fixed D 3 course fr £25, Tasting menu £58.50, Service added 10% **Wines** 171 bottles over £20, 19 bottles under £20, 20 by glass **Notes** Fixed ALC 2 course £34, 3 course £38.50, Vegetarian menu **Seats** 32, Pr/dining room 8 **Children** Portions **Parking** Brindley Place car park

Hotel du Vin Birmingham

Mediterranean, French

Chic hotel with a winning bistro menu

0121 200 0600
25 Church St B3 2NR
e-mail: info@birmingham.hotelduvin.com
dir: M6 junct 6/A38(M) to city centre, over flyover. Keep left & exit at St Chads Circus signed Jewellery Quarter. At lights & rdbt take 1st exit, follow signs for Colmore Row, opposite cathedral. Right into Church St, across Barwick St. Hotel on right

The Victorian grandeur of the erstwhile Birmingham eye hospital in the trendy regenerated Jewellery Quarter was a perfect platform for conversion into the Brum outpost of this style-driven boutique hotel brand. This HdV has plenty of period style - a sweeping main staircase, granite pillars, and rooms around a central courtyard done out in a cool, contemporary manner. Kick off with something fizzy in the sleek champagne bar, before settling into the easygoing bistro-style restaurant for modern Anglo-French dishes along the lines of ham hock and parsley terrine with home-made piccalilli, followed by poached smoked haddock with ventrèche bacon, pea risotto, crispy leeks and chive velouté, or something meaty like a chargrilled rib-eye steak with slow-roast tomatoes, snail and garlic butter and hand-cut chips. True to HdV form, the wine list is a cracker.

Times 12-2/6-10

Loves Restaurant

– see opposite page

Malmaison Bar & Brasserie

Traditional, Modern NEW

Stylish city-centre brasserie in regenerated Royal Mail building

0121 246 5000
1 Wharfside St, The Mailbox B1 1RD
e-mail: birmingham@malmaison.com
dir: M6 junct 6, follow the A38 (city centre), via Queensway underpass. Left to Paradise Circus, 1st exit Brunel St, right T-junct, Malmaison directly opposite

Housed in the former Royal Mail sorting office, the groovy Mailbox development is a flagship of Brum's sexy new image. And with designer boutiques and a branch of Harvey Nic's as neighbours, the Birmingham outpost of this stylish metropolitan hotel and brasserie chain has bagged the ideal location. The Mal brasserie pulls off its trademark butch look using a classic clubby blend of darkwood and chocolate leather, while old pictures of Birmingham's canal heritage give a sense of place. Staff are on the ball - there are no airs and graces here; the menu matches the mood with unfussy modern brasserie classics. A braised leek and Fourme d'Ambert tart is a typical starter, followed by a manly, 35-day aged rump steak served freshly striped from the chargrill with crispy home-made fries and béarnaise sauce.

Chef Brian Neath **Owner** Malmaison Ltd
Times 12-2.30/6-10.30 **Prices** Fixed L 2 course £14.50-£16.50, Fixed D 3 course £16.50-£18.50, Starter £4.95-£8.95, Main £10.50-£27.50, Dessert £5.95-£10.50, Service added but optional 10% **Wines** 250 bottles over £20, 20 bottles under £20, 26 by glass **Notes** Fixed 2-3 course home grown & local menu, Vegetarian available, Civ Wed 120 **Seats** 155, Pr/dining room 120
Children Portions, Menu **Parking** 300, Mailbox car park chargeable

Opus Restaurant

Modern British V

Stylish contemporary design showcasing quality produce

0121 200 2323
54 Cornwall St B3 2DE
e-mail: restaurant@opusrestaurant.co.uk
dir: Close to Birmingham Snow Hill railway station in the city's financial district

Opus has broad appeal, from Birmingham's business crowd meeting up for leisurely lunches to well-heeled shoppers ending a day of retail therapy. The boldly-designed brasserie is the epitome of cosmopolitan cool, all clean lines and banquettes in a cavernous light-flooded expanse of bare tables; centre-stage is a chef's table if you're up for a special tasting menu put together before your very eyes. Birmingham's excellent wholesale

continued

Purnell's

BIRMINGHAM **Map 10 SP08**

Modern British NOTABLE WINE LIST

Stellar cooking with bags of local pride

0121 212 9799
55 Cornwall St B3 2DH
e-mail: info@purnellsrestaurant.co.uk

Glynn Purnell's talent at the stoves has raised Brum's culinary scene to a rather high plane these days. After making his name in leafy Edgbaston, he now plies his trade in the financial quarter in a handsomely-converted Victorian warehouse, designed with post-industrial cool - buttery yellow leather, exposed metalwork, bare darkwood tables, and arty photos of the cityscape in moody blues and monochrome are flooded with light from huge windows looking over the street bustle. Purnell's cooking takes the modernist 'molecular' path, bringing advanced techniques to bear on top-class materials in dishes bursting with invention and fun. The food arrives dressed to thrill, and hits the taste buds with an astounding array of tastes and textures designed either to harmonise or contrast. A starter of roast duck liver is partnered with a vibrant orange duck egg yolk, Jerusalem artichoke purée, crisp buttery brioche and morel vinaigrette. Due homage to the city's Asian chefs is paid in a main-course roasted brill, teamed with Indian lentils, cumin and toffee carrots, coconut milk and coriander. Desserts hold true to form with a masterful Pavlova that nails the crisp and chewy textures of meringue with perfectly-balanced temperatures of warm griottine cherries, crunchy pistachios and iced vanilla yoghurt.

Chef Glynn Purnell **Owner** Glynn Purnell
Times 12-2/7-9.30 Closed Xmas, New Year, 1 wk Etr, 2 wks end Jul-beg Aug, Sun-Mon, L Sat **Prices** Fixed L 2 course fr £21, Fixed D 3 course £42-£47, Tasting menu £68, Service added but optional 12.5% **Wines** 391 bottles over £20, 3 bottles under £20, 20 by glass **Notes** Tasting menu 8 course, Vegetarian available, Dress restrictions, Smart casual **Seats** 45, Pr/dining room 15 **Parking** On street, Snow Hill car park nearby

BIRMINGHAM *continued*

markets supply the chefs with the best the British Isles have to offer - fish from the West Country, grass-fed beef from Aberdeenshire, free-range Blythburgh pork, for example - championed in a great-value market menu. Starters might be brasserie classics such as leek and haddock fishcake with poached egg and beurre blanc, ahead of steamed fillet of turbot with vegetable and clam chowder, and braised fennel; desserts could run to a spiced carrot cake cheesecake with toasted walnuts.

Chef David Colcombe **Owner** Ann Tonks, Irene Allan, David Colcombe **Times** 12-2.15/6-9.30 Closed between Xmas & New Year, Sun, L Sat **Prices** Fixed L 3 course £18.50, Fixed D 3 course £18.50-£27.50, Starter £6.50-£10.50, Main £14-£26, Dessert £6.50-£7, Service added but optional 12.5% **Wines** 74 bottles over £20, 6 bottles under £20, 21 by glass **Notes** Tasting menu for chef's table 6 course, Vegetarian menu **Seats** 85, Pr/dining room 64 **Children** Portions, Menu **Parking** On street

Pascal's

Modern French

Confident cooking with a leafy aspect

☎ 0121 455 0999
1 Montague Rd, Edgbaston B16 9HN
e-mail: info@pascalsrestaurant.co.uk

Expect an unexpectedly countrified outlook from this restaurant in the grounds of Asquith House, although it is only a short hop into the city centre. There are lovely views over the garden from the conservatory-style dining room, where tables are laid with white linen and the service is on the ball. There is a decidedly Anglo-French approach in the kitchen, displaying good technique, respect for the classical ways, and plenty of good British produce. Staffordshire cheddar soufflé with creamed leeks and a tomato compôte might start things off, following on with crisp pork belly with braised trotter, black pudding and an apple and vanilla purée, the dish finished with an apple reduction. Finish with a marinated pineapple baked Alaska with a coulis of exotic fruits.

Chef Andrew Wilde **Owner** P Cuny **Times** 12-2/7-10 Closed 1 wk Xmas, 1 wk Etr, last wk Jul & 1st wk Aug, Mon-Tue, L Sat, D Sun **Prices** Fixed L 2 course £15.50, Fixed D 3 course £34.95, Service added but optional 12.5% **Wines** 50 bottles over £20, 7 bottles under £20, 8 by glass **Notes** Sunday L, Vegetarian available, Dress restrictions, Smart casual **Seats** 40 **Children** Portions **Parking** 10, On street

Purnell's

– see page 421

Simpsons

– see below

Thai Edge Restaurant

Thai

Modern setting for the flavours of Thailand

☎ 0121 643 3993
7 Oozells Square, Brindley Place B1 2HS
e-mail: birmingham@thaiedge.co.uk
dir: Brindley Place just off Broad St (approx 0.5m from B'ham New Street station)

Thai cuisine in a contemporary oriental setting is the name of the game at this small-chain restaurant. The open-plan space is divided up by glass and wooden screens and Thai artefacts engage the eye. Thai music plays softly and tables are dressed with linen and orchids. Authentically attired staff are attentive and helpful, but there's also a much-needed food glossary to help explain the lengthy menu. Choose a greaseless 'gai ho bai tloy' (deep-fried marinated chicken wrapped and baked in pandanus leaves and served with sweet chilli sauce), or 'hoi shell pad celery' (stir-fried scallops with celery, ginger and spring onion). There's Thai whisky and Asian beer to explore, too.

Chef Mit Jeensanthia **Owner** Harish Nathwani **Times** 12-2.30/5.30-11 Closed 25-26 Dec, 1 Jan **Prices** Food prices not confirmed for 2011. Please telephone for details. **Wines** 14 bottles over £20, 26 bottles under £20, 6 by glass **Seats** 100 **Parking** Brindley Place

Simpsons

BIRMINGHAM **Map 10 SP08**

Modern French V NOTABLE WINE LIST

Breathtaking cooking in an elegant boutique hotel

☎ 0121 454 3434
20 Highfield Rd, Edgbaston B15 3DU
e-mail: info@simpsonsrestaurant.co.uk
dir: 1m from city centre, opposite St Georges Church, Edgbaston

A former private dwelling in Edgbaston, Simpsons is a picture of boutique-hotel elegance. With a private dining area, as well as a small bar in which to sip a glass of champagne, the dining room proper is comprised of a conservatory and glassed-in verandah. Outside tables with large parasols look the part in warmer weather, and there is a summer-house in the garden. Service is highly polished and old-school, with courses arriving at the table on a vast tray. A hierarchy of culinary intelligences is responsible for the frequently changing menus, which aim for excellence from the superb breads (including a moreish blue cheese focaccia) to the labour-intensive petits fours. In between, some breathtakingly skilled, ambitious cooking will come your way, drawing on European techniques to highly imaginative effect. A risotto is the best for miles around, flawlessly timed, deepened with wild garlic, peas and lettuce, and served with crisp sweetbread fritters and aged parmesan. Main course might be Indian-spiced cod fillet with coconut basmati and puréed cauliflower, alongside an apple and coriander salad, or there could be a duo of Aberdeen beef, roasted fillet and braised cheek raviolo, with toasted peanuts and a foam of Bathams bitter ale. A witty spin on the chocolate éclair idea sees a torpedo of choux pastry covered in nibbed almonds and filled with espresso granité, served with orange sauce. Add in a no less imaginative wine list, and here we have one of the Midlands' high achievers.

Chef Luke Tipping **Owner** Andreas & Alison Antona **Times** 12-2.30/7-9.30 Closed BHs, D Sun **Prices** Fixed L 3 course £30, Fixed D 3 course £32.50, Tasting menu fr £70, Starter £11-£14, Main £20-£27.50, Dessert £8.50-£11.50, Service added but optional 12.5% **Notes** Sunday L, Vegetarian menu, Dress restrictions, Smart casual **Seats** 70, Pr/dining room 22 **Children** Portions, Menu **Parking** 12, On Street

Turners of Harborne

®® Modern French

Classy French-influenced food in Brum suburb

☎ 0121 426 4440
69 High St, Harborne B17 9NS
e-mail: info@turnersofharborne.com

Opened in a suburb of Birmingham three years ago by chef Richard Turner and business partner Nick Cruddington, Turners of Harborne serves modern European cuisine with classical French influences. Inside the cosy restaurant, original quarry tiles line the floor while striking dark logoed mirrors adorn the walls. The small kitchen team produces a tasting menu and set lunch alongside the regularly changing à la carte. The complex and confident dishes might include a pigeon starter of carpaccio and pastilla served with a foie gras ballottine, beetroot, hazelnuts and horseradish, followed by venison cannon with black pudding, Savoy cabbage, butternut squash, pickled pear and sauce Grand Veneur. Finish with prune soufflé, Armagnac and Earl Grey tea ice cream.

Chef Richard Turner **Times** 12-2/6.45-9.30 Closed Mon-Sun, L Sat **Prices** Fixed L 2 course £17.50-£36.50, Fixed D 3 course fr £45, Tasting menu fr £59, Service optional **Wines** 65 bottles over £20, 5 bottles under £20, 14 by glass **Notes** Vegetarian available **Seats** 30 **Parking** 50

DORRIDGE Map 10 SP17

The Forest

®® Modern European

Stylish boutique setting for classy, modern cooking

☎ 01564 772120
Station Approach B93 8JA
e-mail: info@forest-hotel.com
dir: M42 junct 5, through Knowle right to Dorridge, left before bridge

This late Victorian building opposite the train station in Dorridge town centre has been trading as a hotel ever since the station opened. Nowadays, though, it has boutique credentials, with a chic, contemporary look in both the bar and brasserie-style restaurant. The simple-yet-refined food makes good use of fresh produce and brings classic flavours together with a good degree of skill. Kick off with goats' cheese and red onion tart or potted shrimps with smoked salmon and pickled cucumber, followed by slow-roasted rack of lamb flavoured with cumin and orange and served with a fondant potato and ratatouille. Finish with a decadent white chocolate fondant with banana caramel and peanut butter ice cream. There's a great value menu du jour.

Chef Dean Grubb **Owner** Gary & Tracy Perkins **Times** 12-2.30/6.30-10 Closed 25 Dec, D Sun **Prices** Fixed L 2 course £13, Fixed D 3 course £15.50, Starter £4.50-£7.95, Main £10.50-£18.50, Dessert £4.75-£6.50, Service added but optional 10% **Wines** 12 bottles over £20, 30 bottles under £20, 9 by glass **Notes** Fixed L Mon-Sat, D Mon-Fri, Sunday L, Vegetarian available, Civ Wed 100 **Seats** 70, Pr/dining room 150 **Children** Portions, Menu **Parking** 40

HOCKLEY HEATH Map 10 SP17

Nuthurst Grange Country House Hotel

®® British, French

Fine dining with bags of imagination and country-house style

☎ 01564 783972
Nuthurst Grange Ln B94 5NL
e-mail: info@nuthurst-grange.com
dir: Off A3400, 0.5m south of Hockley Heath. Turn at sign into Nuthurst Grange Lane

Nuthurst Grange sits in seven acres of immaculate gardens and woodland in verdant Warwickshire countryside - a handy spot for accessing Brum's shopping and business pursuits. First impressions are rather good - the creeper-swathed country house lies along a tree-lined drive, and there's a helipad for the airborne guest. The luminous dining room continues the upmarket vibe, with romantic candlelight, sparkling crystal and roses on well-spaced linen-clothed tables. The skilled kitchen team delivers an eclectic mix of refined modern French and British cuisine, taking in classics as well as more creative ideas. A pressed terrine of ham hock, goats' cheese and carrots is teamed with pain d'épice crumbs, soaked raisins and prune purée in a well-balanced starter; next comes a riff on lamb - a thick slice of rump, confit shoulder and caramelised liver, pointed up with the Mediterranean flavours of mint couscous, yoghurt and feta cheese crumble. A spot-on blueberry soufflé with lemon curd iced cream and shortbread finishes on a high note.

Nuthurst Grange Country House Hotel

Times 12-2/7-9.30 Closed 25-26 Dec, L Sat

See advert below

MERIDEN Map 10 SP28

The Regency @ Manor Hotel

Modern British, French

Modern British menu in a Midlands manor

01676 522735
Main Rd CV7 7NH
e-mail: reservations@manorhotelmeriden.co.uk
dir: M42 junct 6, A45 towards Coventry then A452 signed Leamington. At rdbt take B4102 signed Meriden, hotel on left

A sympathetically extended Georgian manor house in a country setting not far from Birmingham, the hotel boasts the spacious fine-dining Regency restaurant, where fresh flowers and plenty of artworks make a refined setting for the appealing modern British cooking. Starters might include grilled red mullet with glazed fennel in an orange and chive butter sauce, or pressed terrine of chicken and confit duck with spiced apple chutney. Carefully timed black bream dressed with lemon oil is one main course, or there may be braised blade of beef en croûte with foie gras in Madeira sauce. Well-made rhubarb crumble comes with matching ice cream.

Chef Darion Smethurst **Owner** Bracebridge Holdings **Times** 12-2/7-9.45 Closed 27-30 Dec, L Sat **Prices** Fixed L 2 course £17.95-£18.95, Fixed D 3 course £20.95-£21.95, Starter £3.95-£8.95, Main £12.95-£19.95, Dessert £4.95-£5.50, Service optional **Wines** 25 bottles over £20, 19 bottles under £20, 6 by glass **Notes** Sunday L, Vegetarian available, Civ Wed 120 **Seats** 150, Pr/dining room 220 **Children** Portions, Menu **Parking** 180

SUTTON COLDFIELD Map 10 SP19

The Bridge Restaurant, New Hall

Modern British

Modern fine-dining in historic house

0121 378 2442
Walmley Rd B76 1QX
e-mail: sales@newhall.co.uk
dir: On B4148, E of Sutton Coldfield, close to M6 & M42

Reputedly the oldest inhabited moat house in the country at 800 years old, New Hall has been sympathetically restored to combine medieval charm with 21st-century mod cons. There are beautiful grounds to explore (26 acres of them), home to plentiful wildlife. The imposing building's public areas retain traditional panelling and stunning stained glass windows, including in the Bridge Restaurant, which is an intimate, elegant room, where meals are served at a leisurely pace. Expect a classy fining-dining experience, beginning with dishes such as braised oxtail faggot with parsnip purée, bacon and frisée salad and red wine dressing (a hearty winter starter), and move on to Brixham cod with curly kale, butternut squash, chorizo and squid daube. Expect lots of little extras in the form of canapés, amuse-bouche and pre-desserts. There's an informal brasserie, too.

Chef Wayne Thomson **Owner** Hand Picked Hotels **Times** 12.30-2.30/7-9.30 Closed L Sat, D Sun-Mon **Prices** Food prices not confirmed for 2011. Please telephone for details. **Wines** 65 bottles over £20, 14 bottles under £20, 14 by glass **Notes** Sunday L, Vegetarian available, Dress restrictions, No jeans or trainers, Civ Wed 150 **Seats** 30, Pr/dining room 50 **Children** Portions, Menu **Parking** 60

Mint Restaurant

Modern NEW

Impressive modern British cooking

0121 353 0488
52 Thornhill Rd, Little Aston B74 3EN
e-mail: dan@mint-restaurant.com
dir: A51, B4138 Thornhill Road

Mint is a modern and bright neighbourhood restaurant located in a small row of shops overlooking Sutton Park. Set on two floors and decorated in contemporary style, with trendy motif wall coverings, wooden floors and polished wooden tables topped with quality cutlery and glassware, it delivers accomplished modern British cooking from an ambitious chef – Matt Warburton – on innovative daily-changing menus. The food that arrives on the plate far outweighs the simple descriptions, so expect some wonderful combinations, clear, concise flavours and interesting textures. Take a smooth goats' cheese parfait starter, served with pickled beetroot, beetroot sorbet, a goats' cheese crisp and horseradish, or a well-executed main dish of pork fillet with Parma ham and crispy pork belly with black pudding crumble and apple sauce. Leave room for a delicious caramelised banana mousse with a creamy, nutty and smooth peanut butter ice cream.

Chef Matt Warburton **Owner** Dan Ralley **Times** 12-2.30/6.30-9.30 Closed Mon **Prices** Food prices not confirmed for 2011. Please telephone for details. **Notes** Sunday L

WALSALL Map 10 SP09

Fairlawns Hotel and Spa

Modern British V

Smart hotel with sound modern cooking

01922 455122
178 Little Aston Rd, Aldridge WS9 0NU
e-mail: reception@fairlawns.co.uk
web: www.fairlawns.co.uk
dir: Outskirts of Aldridge, 400yds from junction of A452 (Chester Rd) & A454

In a handy spot for accessing the Midlands motorway network, but well insulated from the urban sprawl by nine acres of landscaped gardens, this busy family-run hotel occupies a smartly-updated and extended Victorian building complete with spa and fitness centre. The kitchen team turns out a nice line in modern British cooking with international influences, based on a solid foundation of excellent, soundly-sourced seasonal produce. A fish cake starter is made from Craster smoked haddock flavoured with chives, and served with prawn beurre blanc; next up, Royal Balmoral Estate venison comes with carrot purée, baby turnip and fondant potato. End on a note of soothing familiarity, with Victoria plum crème brûlée and home-made fig roll.

Chef Neil Atkins **Owner** John Pette **Times** 12-2/7-10 Closed 25-26 Dec, 1 Jan, Good Fri, Etr Mon, May Day, BH Mon, L Sat **Prices** Fixed L 2 course £16.50, Fixed D 3 course £29.50, Service optional **Wines** 36 bottles over £20, 30 bottles under £20, 12 by glass **Notes** Sunday L, Vegetarian menu, Dress restrictions, No jeans, trainers, sports clothing, Civ Wed 100 **Seats** 80, Pr/dining room 100 **Children** Portions, Menu **Parking** 120

WOLVERHAMPTON Map 10 SO99

Bilash

Bangladeshi

Inventive modern regional cuisine from the Indian sub-continent

01902 427762
2 Cheapside WV1 1TU
e-mail: m@thebilash.co.uk
dir: Opposite Civic Hall & St Peter's Church

Tucked away in a quiet corner of the pedestrianised Civic Centre square overlooking St Peter's church, Bilash has stood head and shoulders above the herd of local sub-continental eateries for over 20 years - and there's no lack of competition in the West Midlands. The modishly pared-back interior is as different to run-of-the-mill curry houses as the kitchen's approach is to its inventive repertoire of Bangladeshi and regional Indian cuisine. The much-abbreviated menu steers clear of the usual lengthy roll call: although there are familiar tandoori and biryani dishes, you will strike gold among the dishes you haven't heard of before. The freshly-made pickles start off on the right foot, then you might get things under way with maacher shami kebab - a spicy fishcake served with sour tamarind sauce; main courses take in a luxurious Hyderabadi biryani and a Bengali maacher jhool fish curry.

Chef Sitas Khan **Owner** Sitas Khan **Times** 12-2.30/5.30-10.30 Closed 25-26 Dec, Sun **Prices** Fixed L 2 course £9.50-£12.90, Fixed D 3 course £20.90-£35.90, Starter £5.90-£11.90, Main £9.90-£29.90, Dessert £4.90-£7.90 **Notes** Pre-theatre D, tasting menu with wine, Vegetarian available, Dress restrictions, No tracksuits & trainers **Seats** 48, Pr/dining room 40 **Children** Portions, Menu **Parking** 15, Civic car park

WIGHT, ISLE OF

RYDE Map 5 SZ59

Lakeside Park Hotel

Modern European NEW

Bold, creative, modern cooking in lakeside hotel

01983 882 266
High St PO33 4LJ
e-mail: info@lakesideparkhotel.com
dir: A3054 towards Newport. Hotel on left after crossing Wotton Bridge

The lake in question is a 20-acre tidal one, which makes a peacefully picturesque backdrop for this luxurious hotel, where conferences can be held and the spa facilities will likely sooth away any stresses and strains. It's all very modern and open inside, with a smart bar and brasserie offering all-day dining. The highlight, though, is The Oyster Room, where head chef Luke Holder is cooking up a storm with a thoroughly modern menu of European sensibilities, based on excellent produce, using up-to-the-minute cooking techniques and with an eye for thrilling visual presentations. The room - open only for dinner - is small but not overcrowded, smartly done out, while the service is on the informal side. Great balancing of flavours and high technical competence are on display in a first-course seared and smoked foie gras, partnered with caramelised rosemary-scented pineapple and brioche, while a main-course fillet of stone bass comes with a crab filled gnocchi, grape 'semi-gel' and pickled grapes. The creative flair continues to dessert (assiette of chocolate with mango, Szechuan pepper and salt, perhaps) and through all the intermediate courses. One to watch.

Chef Luke Holder **Times** 12-2.30/6.30-9.30 **Prices** Food prices not confirmed for 2011. Please telephone for details.

The St Helens

Modern British

Unfussy food using the best local produce

01983 872303 & 0771 7175 444
Lower Green Rd, St Helens PO33 1TS
e-mail: sthelensrestaurant@hotmail.co.uk
dir: Follow B3330 to St Helens

The jaunty blue and white décor, wooden floor and tables, and seaside-themed artwork might transport you to New England, but the huge swathe of village green outside is unmistakably Blighty. It's a heavenly spot for eating alfresco when the sun shines, and a clear inspiration for the kitchen's relaxed, rustic approach to dishes founded on the pick of the Isle of Wight's seasonal larder. Local crabcakes with sweet chilli sauce get things under way; considering the island location, meat makes a surprisingly strong showing among main courses - slow-cooked pork belly with crackling, grain mustard mash, cabbage and black pudding being a typically hearty offering. Clotted cream crème brûlée with Garibaldi biscuits is a real treat to finish.

Chef Jason West **Owner** Mr & Mrs West **Times** 12-2.30/6.30-9.30 Closed Mon (Nov-Mar), L Mon-Sat **Prices** Starter £4.95-£5.95, Main £12-£22.50, Dessert £5, Service optional, Groups min 8 service 10% **Wines** 16 bottles over £20, 10 bottles under £20, 4 by glass **Notes** Sunday L, Vegetarian available, Dress restrictions, Shirt & shoes must be worn **Seats** 42 **Children** Portions, Menu **Parking** On street, car park 100yds

SEAVIEW Map 5 SZ69

Priory Bay Hotel

Modern

Peaceful location, great views and confident cooking

01983 613146
Priory Dr PO34 5BU
e-mail: enquiries@priorybay.co.uk
dir: B3330 towards Seaview, through Nettlestone. (Do not follow Seaview turn, but continue 0.5m to hotel sign)

An aura of peacefulness persists at this creeper-clad 14th-century former priory. Set in 70 acres of woodlands and private gardens, the hotel is a popular wedding venue, and has a restaurant that is making a mark in its own right. The fine-dining Island Room is done out in elegant Regency style, complemented by murals of local sea views, though in the summer you can look out over the grounds to the real thing. Seafood is a speciality on the à la carte and tasting menu with British and French influences, although there's plenty for the carnivores and herbivores too. Start perhaps with warm Puy lentil salad with braised veal cheeks, grain mustard dressing and shallots, before moving on to whole red mullet stuffed with samphire and spinach, braised and creamed leeks, white wine and saffron fish jus.

Chef Carlos Garcia Rodreguez **Owner** Mr R Palmer & Mr J Palmer **Times** 12.30-2.15/7-9.30 **Prices** Fixed L 2 course £22-£32, Fixed D 3 course fr £38, Service added but optional 12.5%, Groups min 8 service 12.5% **Wines** 29 bottles over £20, 14 bottles under £20, 8 by glass **Notes** Tasting menu available, Sunday L, Vegetarian available, Dress restrictions, Smart casual recommended, Civ Wed 100 **Seats** 70, Pr/dining room 50 **Children** Portions, Menu **Parking** 50

The Restaurant at The Seaview

Modern European

Charming hotel with confident cooking

01983 612711
High St PO34 5EX
e-mail: reception@seaviewhotel.co.uk
dir: Take B3330 from Ryde to Seaview, left into Puckpool Hill, follow signs for hotel

On the east side of the island, the Seaview is a charmingly sited hotel with a thoroughgoing nautical theme in the décor. The fine-dining venue is the Front Restaurant, a small, intimate room with a mix of differently shaped tables with elegant settings, and walls done in two tones – sea-blue and lobster-pink. The cuisine keeps things relatively simple with the likes of deeply flavoured roast salmon and spinach en croûte with lemon hollandaise for main course, preceded perhaps by chicken liver parfait with truffle butter and red onion jam. Good pastry and a properly zesty filling distinguish the lemon tart, which is offset with passionfruit syrup, caramelised hazelnuts and vanilla ice cream.

Times 12-2/6.30-9.30 Closed 21-26 Dec, Mon, L weekdays during winter, D Sun

VENTNOR Map 5 SZ57

The Leconfield

Traditional British V

Wonderfully situated hotel with traditional menu

01983 852196
85 Leeson Rd, Upper Bonchurch PO38 1PU
e-mail: enquiries@leconfieldhotel.com
dir: Upper Bonchurch on A3055, 1m from Ventnor, 2m from Shanklin opposite turning, Bonchurch Shute

Basking in a balmy microclimatic zone of the Isle of Wight, the Leconfield looks across the English Channel from its perch on St Boniface Down, above the lovely village of Bonchurch. The aptly-named Seascape dining room takes in those sweeping views through large picture windows, as a backdrop to an appealing menu of traditional dishes built on locally-farmed meat and freshly-landed fish. Confit duck and caramelised onion ravioli teamed with red cabbage purée and duck consommé is a good way to start, followed by roast silverside of Island beef with Yorkshire pudding, creamed mash and pan juices.

Chef Jason Lefley **Owner** Paul & Cheryl Judge **Times** 6.30-8.15 Closed 24-26 Dec, 3 wks Jan, L all week (except by prior arrangement) **Prices** Fixed D 4 course £22-£29, Starter £3.95-£5.95, Main £14.75-£18.50, Dessert £4.50-£5.95, Service optional **Wines** 13 bottles over £20, 20 bottles under £20, 15 by glass **Notes** Vegetarian menu, Dress restrictions, Smart casual **Seats** 26 **Parking** 14

Robert Thompson The Hambrough

VENTNOR Map 5 SZ57

Modern European V NOTABLE WINE LIST

Innovative modern cooking in hotel with sea views

☎ 01983 856333
Hambrough Rd PO38 1SQ
e-mail: info@thehambrough.com
web: www.thehambrough.com

The hillside position ensures this attractive Victorian villa has terrific views out to sea and over Ventnor's harbour, and the vista can be fully appreciated through the large bay windows in the restaurant. A stylish makeover has made the most of the features of the hotel, bringing sophisticated natural tones to the restaurant, which occupies the two rooms at the front; a comfortable lounge at the rear is the place for a pre-dinner drink. Chef-patron Robert Thompson's brand of intelligent modern European cooking takes first class produce, much of it from the local environs, and delivers vibrant, well-judged dishes. Sharp technical skills are evident right from the off: a divine amuse-bouche of white bean velouté and summer truffle gets things off to a flying start. A first-course ravioli of lobster with braised veal shin, young vegetables and lobster cappuccino is a happy marriage of flavours, while good skill is again to the fore in a main-course pan-roasted lemon sole with croquettes of local crab and rock samphire. A light and fluffy cherry and almond soufflé with almond ice cream ends things on a high.

Chef Robert Thompson **Owner** Robert Thompson **Times** 12-1.30/7-9.30 Closed 2 wks New Year & Jan, Apr & Nov, Sun-Mon **Prices** Fixed L 2 course £22, Fixed D 3 course £55, Tasting menu £70-£110, Service optional **Wines** 158 bottles over £20, 6 bottles under £20, 21 by glass **Notes** Tasting menu 7 course, Vegetarian menu, Dress restrictions, Smart casual, No sportswear **Seats** 45, Pr/dining room 22 **Children** Portions **Parking** On street

VENTNOR *continued*

The Pond Café

Modern Mediterranean

Accomplished seasonal cooking by the pond

01983 855666
Bonchurch Village Rd, Bonchurch PO38 1RG
e-mail: info@thepondcafe.com

This small but smart modern restaurant in Bonchurch has an outdoor terrace overlooking the pond. Simple, fresh décor - clothless tables and unadorned walls - makes an understated backdrop for some confident, seasonally-based cooking, with the daily catch of fish a strong suit. The local sea bass in summer is amazingly fresh, and served on crushed new potatoes, zested lemon and tender artichoke, to make a thoroughly satisfying main course. Prior to that, there could be vibrantly presented chargrilled squid with chilli, lime and coriander, or a trattoria-style serving of prosciutto with black figs and port. A triumphant rendition of treacle tart with rich vanilla ice cream represents the self-indulgent way to finish. Home-made tomato bread with extra-virgin olive oil is an equally pleasing way to kick things off. The Pond is a sister establishment to The Hambrough at Ventnor (see entry).

Chef Emma Ayres **Owner** Robert Thompson **Times** 12-2.30/6.30-9.30 Closed 2 wks Jan, 1 wk Apr, 1 wk Nov **Prices** Fixed L 2 course £16-£26, Starter £7-£11, Main £13-£19, Dessert £6-£10, Service optional **Wines** 27 bottles over £20, 8 bottles under £20, 6 by glass **Notes** Sunday L, Vegetarian available **Seats** 26 **Children** Portions **Parking** On street

Robert Thompson The Hambrough

– see opposite page

The Royal Hotel

Modern British V

Sophisticated cuisine in a timelessly elegant setting

01983 852186
Belgrave Rd PO38 1JJ
e-mail: enquiries@royalhoteliow.co.uk
dir: On A3055 (coast road) into Ventnor. Follow one-way system, left at lights into Church St. At top of hill left into Belgrave Rd, hotel on right

Purpose-built as a hotel when Queen Victoria was a slip of a girl, the Royal is a classic period piece that suits the mood of the traditional Isle of Wight. Delicious sub-tropical gardens overlooking the sea enfold a timeless English hotel replete with high plasterwork ceilings, parquet floors, decorative ironwork and crystal chandeliers. The dining room too is a grand old dame, all heavily swagged drapes and oil paintings. But the cooking fast-forwards to the 21st century: modern British stuff delivering inventive, well-presented ideas using the best of seasonal, local ingredients. Chicken liver and foie gras parfait with pain d'épice starts things off, ahead of home-made venison faggots with mashed potatoes and caramelised onion gravy, and to finish up, perhaps vanilla pannacotta with caramelised pears and mulled wine figs.

Chef Alan Staley **Owner** William Bailey **Times** 12-1.45/6.45-9 Closed 2 wks Jan or 2 wks Dec, L Mon-Sat **Prices** Fixed D 3 course fr £38, Tasting menu fr £48, Service optional **Wines** 57 bottles over £20, 18 bottles under £20, 6 by glass **Notes** Tasting menu 7 course, Sunday L, Vegetarian menu, Dress restrictions, Smart casual, no shorts or trainers, Civ Wed 150 **Seats** 100, Pr/dining room 40 **Children** Portions **Parking** 50

YARMOUTH Map 5 SZ38

Brasserie at The George Hotel

British, Mediterranean

The flavours of the Mediterranean with Solent views

01983 760331
The George Hotel, Quay St PO41 0PE
e-mail: res@thegeorge.co.uk
web: www.thegeorge.co.uk
dir: Between castle & pier

This delightful 17th-century colour-washed hotel enjoys a wonderful location at the water's edge, adjacent to the castle and the quay, and only a short stagger from the ferry terminal. The bright, contemporary and sunny brasserie enjoys stunning Solent views and offers a vibrant Mediterranean-inspired menu. Top-notch local ingredients, especially fish, are used to create simple, unfussy dishes that allow the freshness and flavours to shine through. From fishy starters like grilled sardines with salsa verde, or chargrilled squid with fresh chilli and rocket, the menu extends to fillet of wild Isle of Wight sea bass stuffed with herbs with olives and a tomato and caper dressing, and new season lamb with truffle mash, broad beans, peas and courgettes. Desserts include summer cherry tart with vanilla ice cream.

Chef Jose Graziosi **Owner** John Illsley, Jeremy Willcock **Times** 12-3/7-10 **Prices** Food prices not confirmed for 2011. Please telephone for details. **Wines** 40 bottles over £20, 20 bottles under £20, 10 by glass **Notes** Sunday L, Vegetarian available, Dress restrictions, Smart casual **Seats** 60, Pr/dining room 20 **Children** Portions, Menu **Parking** The Square

WILTSHIRE

BRADFORD-ON-AVON Map 4 ST86

The Tollgate Inn

Modern British

Classically-based cooking in a 16th-century inn

01225 782326
Ham Green BA14 6PX
e-mail: alison@tollgateholt.co.uk
web: www.tollgateholt.co.uk
dir: 2m E on B3107, at W end of Holt

The 16th-century West Country inn looks a little like two different buildings joined at the hip, reflecting its origins as a weaving shed and workers' Baptist chapel. Inside is furnished in simple country-pub fashion, the front-of-house run by a young, enthusiastic team. Alex Venables' cooking style is clearly based on British and European classics, but rendered in a modern vein, with menus progressing perhaps from foie gras parfait to beef Wellington, with chocolate fondant and liquorice anglaise to finish. There is plenty of evidence of sound technique in a starter, say, of pink-cooked pigeon breasts served with a gamey risotto, and in a generous piece of milky-white, herb-crusted cod, served with tomato confit in a light mustard sauce. A lighter way to finish might be with properly tremulous pannacotta, served with citrus fruits in champagne syrup.

Chef Alexander Venables **Owner** Alexander Venables, Alison Ward-Baptiste **Times** 11-2.30/5.30-11 Closed 25-26 Dec, Mon, D Sun **Prices** Fixed L 2 course fr £10.95, Fixed D 3 course fr £19.95, Starter £4.50-£8.50, Main £12.50-£18.95, Dessert £4.50-£5.95, Service optional, Groups min 6 service 10% **Wines** 12 bottles over £20, 23 bottles under £20, 9 by glass **Notes** Sunday L, Vegetarian available **Seats** 60, Pr/dining room 38 **Children** Portions **Parking** 40

BRADFORD-ON-AVON *continued*

Widbrook Grange

Modern British

Confident cooking in elegant country house

01225 864750
Trowbridge Rd, Widbrook BA15 1UH
e-mail: stay@widbrookgrange.com
dir: 1m S of Bradford-on-Avon on A363

Built in the early 1700s, Widbrook was originally a model farm and its architectural heritage is reflected by low walls containing bee bowls on both sides of the house. An elegant property sitting peacefully amid 11 acres of grounds on the outskirts of the ancient town of Bradford-on-Avon, close to the Kennet and Avon Canal, the hotel has a relaxed atmosphere. A casual style of dining is offered in the Bee Bowl Conservatory, while the intimate fine-dining Medlar Tree Restaurant offers British classics using plenty of local produce, some from the hotel's garden. Roasted Cornish scallops, for example, come with a minted pea purée and home-cured venison ham; follow on with braised brisket of Lackham beef with celeriac purée, grilled oyster, baby carrots and fried horseradish bread with bone marrow butter.

Chef Phil Carroll **Owner** Peter & Jane Wragg **Times** 11.30-2.30/7-11 Closed 24-30 Dec **Prices** Food prices not confirmed for 2011. Please telephone for details. **Wines** 16 bottles over £20, 11 bottles under £20, 6 by glass **Notes** Vegetarian available, Dress restrictions, Smart casual, Civ Wed 50 **Seats** 45, Pr/dining room 12 **Children** Portions, Menu **Parking** 50

Woolley Grange

Modern British V

Child-friendly atmosphere and excellent dining in Jacobean manor

01225 864705
Woolley Green BA15 1TX
e-mail: info@woolleygrangehotel.co.uk
dir: A4 onto B3109. Bradford Leigh, left at x-roads, hotel 0.5m on right at Woolley Green

The whole family is catered for with panache at this classy Jacobean manor house. The ethos that drives Woolley Grange is that parents don't have to renounce the good life when children come along, so there's a full programme of kids stuff to keep them happy, while mum and dad zone out in a stylishly made-over country-house hotel. Once the offspring are taken care of by trained nannies and baby-listening services, the restaurant is strictly adults-only territory at dinner. Without being too ambitious, the chefs at Woolley Grange deal in characterful modern British cooking, wrought from top-class materials – the hotel's home-grown organic vegetables, fruits and herbs from the walled garden, for example. Sauté of quail with green cabbage and red shallot jus precedes main-course sea bass, pan-fried and served with light vermouth cream and crushed potatoes. A textbook pannacotta with cardamom-poached pears finishes on a high note.

Chef Mark Bradbury **Owner** Luxury Family Hotels & von Essen Hotels **Times** 12-2/7-9.30 **Prices** Fixed L 2 course £10.50-£14.50, Fixed D 3 course £37.50, Service optional **Wines** 75 bottles over £20, 7 bottles under £20, 8 by glass **Notes** Sunday L, Vegetarian menu, Dress restrictions, Smart casual, Civ Wed 50 **Seats** 40, Pr/dining room 22 **Children** Portions, Menu **Parking** 45

CALNE Map 14 ST97

Shelburne Restaurant & Bar

Modern British NEW V

Newly-built spa hotel with classy cooking

01249 822228
Bowood Hotel, Spa & Golf Resort, Derry Hill SN11 9PQ
e-mail: resort@bowood.org
dir: M4 junct 17, 2.5m W of Calne off A4

Bowood is a sizeable and grand estate with a beautiful house and gardens at its heart, developed to include a championship golf course and the Bowood Hotel and Spa. The hotel's Shelburne Restaurant makes the best of the sweeping views over the estate through large French windows and the kitchen delivers some equally eye-catching food. The estate provides some of the produce in dishes that might include a starter of crisp pork belly

continued on page 430

The Bybrook at the Manor

CASTLE COMBE Map 4 ST87

Modern British V NOTABLE WINE LIST

Dazzling cooking in a grand West Country manor

01249 782206
Manor House Hotel SN14 7HR
e-mail: enquiries@manorhouse.co.uk
dir: M4 junct 17, follow signs for Castle Combe via Chippenham

Legend has it that the real-life model for Shakespeare's immortal Sir John Falstaff once ruled the roost at this estate and, even in its modern incarnation, the place certainly looks worthy of his grandiloquence, but also of his zest for life. A sweeping drive through hundreds of acres establishes the tone, and the approach on a winter's night when all the lights are blazing in the tall windows is a breath-catcher. Inside, ancient rugs, leather chesterfields, tapestries and mood lighting are all in keeping, and yet the service tone is refreshingly straightforward, helping out knowledgeably with any queries you may have. Richard Davies has honed a culinary style that is cleverly balanced between classical and modern ways, in dishes that can dazzle throughout a meal. A meaty terrine hardly seems an innovation, but its technically flawless composition of organic chicken, duck and foie gras is something else, and it gains further from well-thought accompaniments of prune and Armagnac purée and segments of blood orange. Progress towards a main course of slow-cooked Brecon venison loin with truffled potato in spiced redcurrant jus, and the whole experience deepens as it should, with fabulous meat the principal focus. A fish dish might deliver roast gilt head bream in a clam chowder with lemon mash, while a dessert such as Valrhona chocolate fondant with tonka ice cream and chocolate liqueur jelly show a willingness to find new, exciting ways of serving up your chocolate fix. Incidentals are all of a high order, including a fine wine list and equally fine sommelier.

Chef Richard Davies **Owner** Exclusive Hotels **Times** 12.30-2.30/7-9.30 Closed L Sat **Prices** Fixed L 2 course £21, Fixed D 3 course £30-£57, Service added but optional 12.5% **Wines** 305 bottles over £20, 12 by glass **Notes** Tasting menu 7 course, Sunday L, Vegetarian menu, Dress restrictions, Smart casual, Civ Wed 120 **Seats** 60, Pr/dining room 120 **Children** Portions, Menu **Parking** 100

The Park Restaurant

COLERNE Map 4 ST87

Modern British V

Technical virtuosity amid Palladian splendour in 500 acres

☎ 01225 742777
Lucknam Park Hotel & Spa SN14 8AZ
e-mail: reservations@lucknampark.co.uk
dir: M4 junct 17, A350 to Chippenham, then A420 towards Bristol for 3m. At Ford left towards Colerne. In 4m right into Doncombe Ln, then 300yds on right

The present house at Lucknam was begun in the 18th century, gradually extended, and given a major interior refit in the Victorian era, by which time it had taken on the splendid form we see today. Standing proud amid 500 acres of grounds, it is one of the grander of England's grand country-house hotels, only minutes away from Bath. Principal dining goes on in The Park Restaurant, where all the decorative accoutrements of fine dining - swagged curtains, chandelier, double-layered napery and ornately framed mirrors - are on display. In Hywel Jones, Lucknam has a wondrously gifted chef who has proved a major talent at marrying modern British modes with French technical virtuosity. The menu takes some reading, as dishes are complex and there are plenty of them. Expect a thorough-going culinary journey, perhaps starting out with a duo of thinly sliced Norfolk eel and grilled Cornish mullet, served with a potato and horseradish risotto, watercress purée and pancetta in red wine vinaigrette, as a prelude to fillet of English Rose veal with Savoy cabbage and bacon, baby artichokes, salsify and leeks, in a truffled reduction of Madeira. The pace is maintained impressively in desserts too, perhaps a pineapple croustillant with rum and raisin pannacotta, coconut sorbet and macadamia toffee.

Chef Hywel Jones **Owner** Lucknam Park Hotels Ltd **Times** 6.30-10 Closed Sun-Mon, L all week **Prices** Fixed D 3 course fr £66, Service optional **Wines** 450 bottles over £20, 15 by glass **Notes** Gourmand menu available, Vegetarian menu, Dress restrictions, Jacket required & tie preferred, no jeans, Civ Wed 110 **Seats** 80, Pr/dining room 30 **Children** Portions, Menu **Parking** 80

CALNE *continued*

with a succulent langoustine, crushed peas and balsamic. The modern British bent continues in a main course assiette of new season lamb - the rump, shoulder and sweetbread, all beautifully cooked, served with buttered vegetables, potato purée and thyme sauce - and a dessert of a faultless caramel pannacotta with poached strawberries.

Chef Chris Dawson **Owner** The 9th Marquis of Lansdowne **Times** 12-2/7-9.30 Closed 25 Dec, L Mon-Sat **Prices** Fixed L 2 course fr £19, Starter £5.50-£10.50, Main £15.50-£21.50, Dessert £5.50-£9, Service optional **Notes** Sunday L, Vegetarian menu, Dress restrictions, Smart casual **Seats** 64, Pr/dining room 180 **Children** Portions **Parking** 200

CASTLE COMBE Map 4 ST87

The Bybrook at the Manor

®®® – *see page 428*

COLERNE Map 4 ST87

The Brasserie

® Modern European NEW

Informal stylish brasserie at five-star country-house hotel

☎ 01225 742777
Lucknam Park Hotel & Spa SN14 8AZ
dir: M4 junct 17, A350 towards Chippenham, then A420 towards Bristol for 3m. At Ford left to Colerne, 3m, right at x-rds, entrance on right

Lucknam Park is a truly five-star country house that stints on nothing when it comes to pampering its guests. The handsome Palladian mansion dates from 1720, and not content with an interior of decadent opulence, it has sprouted a megabucks state-of-the-art spa complex to boost the feelgood factor further still. Fine dining is very much at the forefront of Lucknam Park's top-drawer package, but as well as the formal Park Restaurant in the former ballroom (see entry), a stylish new brasserie offers a more unbuttoned ambience, with a pared-back contemporary décor - cream leather seats and bare tables on a gleaming tiled floor - to suit its flavour-driven modern cooking. A wood oven is put to good use in grilling a starter of red mullet with beetroot and apple purée and sour cream, ahead of wood-roast loin of local pork, teamed with crushed sweet potato, sprouting broccoli and apple sauce.

Chef Hywel Jones, Hrishikesh Desai **Times** 7.30am-10pm **Prices** Food prices not confirmed for 2011. Please telephone for details. **Children** Menu

The Park Restaurant

®®® – *see page 429*

HINDON Map 4 ST93

The Lamb at Hindon

® Traditional British

Historic inn with a taste of Wiltshire and Scotland

☎ 01747 820573
High St SP3 6DP
e-mail: info@lambathindon.co.uk
dir: M3 junct 8 onto A303. Exit towards Hindon 4m after Salisbury exit & follow signs to Hindon

Part of the Boisdale group (see London SW1 and EC2), this 17th-century inn deep in Wiltshire's huntin', shootin' and fishin' country overflows with character. Bursting with inglenook fireplaces, heavy beams, flagged floors and rich red walls, it's a place to enjoy good ales and extensive wine and whisky lists, as well as good food. Local produce is abundant on the menu, alongside a scattering of Scottish produce and influences - pickled Orkney herring and Loch Carrnon hot-smoked salmon, for example. Wiltshire rarebit is made with real ale and Longman mature cheddar, while local Stourhead pork sausages come with mashed potato, broccoli and beer and onion gravy.

Chef Andrzej Piechocki, Christopher Kendall **Owner** Ranald Macdonald (Boisdale Plc) **Times** 12-2.30/6.30-9.30 **Prices** Starter £3.80-£8.50, Main £8-£18.90, Dessert £5.45-£6.50, Service added but optional 10% **Wines** 68 bottles over £20, 21 bottles under £20, 9 by glass **Notes** Sunday L, Vegetarian available, Civ Wed 70 **Seats** 52, Pr/dining room 32 **Children** Portions, Menu **Parking** 16

HORNINGSHAM Map 4 ST84

The Bath Arms at Longleat

®® Modern, Traditional British

Home-grown food on the historic Longleat Estate

☎ 01985 844308 & 07770 268359
Longleat Estate BA12 7LY
e-mail: enquiries@batharms.co.uk
dir: A36 Warminster. At Cotley Hill rdbt 2nd exit (Longleat), Cleyhill rdbt 1st exit. Through Hitchcombe Bottom, right at x-rds. Hotel on the green

This ivy-covered traditional stone-built country inn can be found in the quintessential English village of Horningsham in the heart of the Longleat estate. Step inside and you'll find a chic, quirky interior, with the option of eating in the informal public bar or opulent dining room with its dramatic chandeliers, ornate wallpaper and enormous candlesticks. The kitchen cooks honest British food often using home-grown produce from the vegetable garden and their own home-reared pigs. Typical of the unpretentious output are a salad of conference pears with blue cheese, chicory and walnuts, belly pork with a faggot, glazed apples and mash, and stuffed saddle of rabbit with rabbit shepherd's pie and pickled vegetables.

Chef Chris Gregory **Owner** Hillbrooke Hotels **Times** 12-2.30/7-9 **Prices** Food prices not confirmed for 2011. Please telephone for details. **Wines** 21 bottles over £20, 10 bottles under £20, 8 by glass **Notes** Vegetarian available **Seats** 45, Pr/dining room 60 **Children** Portions, Menu **Parking** 8, On street

LITTLE BEDWYN Map 5 SU26

The Harrow at Little Bedwyn

®®® – *see opposite page*

LOWER CHICKSGROVE Map 4 ST92

Compasses Inn

® Modern British

Modern cooking in attractive country inn

☎ 01722 714318
SP3 6NB
e-mail: thecompasses@aol.com
dir: Off A30 signed Lower Chicksgrove, 1st left onto Lagpond Ln, single-track lane to village

Located within easy reach of Bath, Salisbury, Glastonbury and the Dorset coast, this handsome 14th-century thatched inn has a timeless quality about it. Accessed via winding lanes deep in rolling Wiltshire countryside, an old cobbled path leads to the low latch door and the charmingly unspoilt bar, which overflows with rustic character - worn flagstones, low beams, soft candlelight and intimate booth seating. Cooking is modern and champions local, seasonal produce. Look to the chalkboard for ham hock and prune terrine with potato and mustard salad followed by local calves' liver, bacon and bean casserole.

Chef Dave Cousin, Damian Trevett **Owner** Alan & Susie Stoneham **Times** 12-3/6-11 Closed 25-26 Dec

Prices Starter £5-£8.50, Main £9.50-£17, Dessert £5.50, Service optional **Wines** 10 bottles over £20, 20 bottles under £20, 8 by glass **Notes** Sunday L, Vegetarian available **Seats** 50, Pr/dining room 14 **Children** Portions, Menu **Parking** 35

MALMESBURY **Map 4 ST98**

Best Western Mayfield House Hotel

Modern British

Modern cooking with good use of local produce

01666 577409
Crudwell SN16 9EW
e-mail: reception@mayfieldhousehotel.co.uk
dir: M4 junct 17, A429 to Cirencester. 3m N of Malmesbury on right in Crudwell

This congenial country-house hotel in a quiet village is a good base for exploring Wiltshire and the Cotswolds. There's a convivial bar with snug, a comfortable lounge and traditional restaurant, as well as a spacious walled garden. Seasonal menus use locally-sourced ingredients and herbs from the hotel's own gardens. Starters might include grilled asparagus with poached egg and chive hollandaise, while roast chump of lamb with apricot purée, dauphinoise potatoes and rosemary jus is a typical main course. Finish with chocolate and orange tart with coffee cream.

Chef Nick Batstone **Owner** David Beeson & Frank Segrave-Daly **Times** 12-2/6.45-12 **Prices** Starter £3.95-£6, Main £12.50-£21, Dessert £5-£6.50, Service optional **Wines** 17 bottles over £20, 18 bottles under £20, 10 by glass **Notes** Sunday L, Vegetarian available, Dress restrictions, Smart casual **Seats** 60, Pr/dining room 40 **Children** Portions **Parking** 40

Old Bell Hotel

Modern British, French

Venerable setting for a modern British menu

01666 822344
Abbey Row SN16 0BW
e-mail: info@oldbellhotel.com
dir: M4 junct 17, follow A429 north. Left at 1st rdbt. Left at T-junct. Hotel next to Abbey

Purpose-built hotels can sometimes be a touch bland, but not this one: the Old Bell lays claim to be England's oldest, having been in the business of taking paying guests since 1220. Wisteria-clad honey-hued Cotswold stone on the outside, and deeply comforting within, the décor bathes guests in rich autumnal colours, while staff add an extra feelgood glow of welcoming service. Accomplished modern British food with classical French influences and inventive flavour combinations forms the backbone of the up-to-date menu. Starters could be sautéed scallops, their juicy sweetness pointed up by smoked bacon, cauliflower, apple and curry oil, while line-caught sea bass with poached rock oyster, Avruga caviar, linguine and champagne sauce shows fine ingredients all singing in harmony.

Chef Tom Rains **Owner** The Old Bell Hotel Ltd **Times** 12.15-2/7-9.30 Closed D Sun-Mon **Prices** Fixed D 3 course £37.50, Service optional **Wines** 109 bottles over £20, 8 bottles under £20, 9 by glass **Notes** Tasting menu 7 course available, Sunday L, Vegetarian available, Dress restrictions, Smart dress preferred, Civ Wed 80 **Seats** 60, Pr/dining room 48 **Children** Portions, Menu **Parking** 35

Whatley Manor

– see page 432

The Harrow at Little Bedwyn

RESTAURANT OF THE YEAR

LITTLE BEDWYN **Map 5 SU26**

Modern V

Accomplished cooking in stylish restaurant with fabulous wine list

01672 870871
SN8 3JP
e-mail: reservations@harrowinn.co.uk
dir: Between Marlborough & Hungerford, well signed

What sounds like a village pub, in a little hamlet near the Kennet and Avon canal in deepest Wiltshire, is actually a top-flight country restaurant. Make no mistake, the Harrow Inn is a class act: for 12 years, Roger and Sue Jones have put heart and soul into building a rock solid reputation for supremely accomplished food, supported by a world-class wine list. All the details in the sharp-looking restaurant are right: dark leather high-backed chairs, wooden floor, colourful Villeroy & Boch ceramics, and the finest Riedel glasses to do justice to those wines. Sue Jones leads a super team of enthusiastic and clued-up staff with an easygoing style, while Roger directs the kitchen's output. Passion about the freshness, sourcing and quality of raw materials is the cornerstone here; fish and seafood come from Brixham, Lyme Bay and the Scilly Isles; meat and game is from specialist farmers and butchers, and you might be treated to locally-foraged English truffles. Put together in subtle combinations with top-level technical skill and allowed to do their own talking, the results are memorable. A ceviche of langoustine, turbot and sea bass is set on nori seaweed, its flavours framed with a salpicon of cucumber, carrot and red pepper. Next up, the game season kicks off with roast grouse, celeriac crisps and purée, and a Wiltshire truffle jus served in a shot glass. The house's exceptional wine list is big on rare old iconic bottles from Down Under, and currently going through a love affair with New Zealand.

Chef Roger Jones, John Brown, Jaillin Argent **Owner** Roger & Sue Jones **Times** 12-3/7-11 Closed Xmas & New Year, 2 wks Aug, Mon-Tue, D Sun **Prices** Tasting menu fr £40, Starter £12-£15, Main £24-£28, Dessert £8-£10, Service optional **Wines** 900 bottles over £20, 10 bottles under £20, 20 by glass **Notes** Fixed L 5 course & wine £30, Gourmet menu 8 course £70, Vegetarian menu, Dress restrictions, Smart casual **Seats** 34 **Children** Menu **Parking** On street

Whatley Manor

MALMESBURY Map 4 ST98

Modern French NOTABLE WINE LIST

Technically brilliant contemporary French food in a luxury spa hotel

☎ 01666 822888
Easton Grey SN16 0RB
e-mail: reservations@whatleymanor.com
web: www.whatleymanor.com
dir: M4 junct 17, follow signs to Malmesbury, continue over 2 rdbts. Follow B4040 & signs for Sherston, hotel 2m on left

Whatley Manor is the kind of place you choose for a weekend of pampering and generally spoiling yourself, particularly if you're an aficionado of sybaritic Swiss La Prairie spa treatments. First impressions are, well, very impressive indeed: you arrive in the absolute peace of 12 acres of meadows, woodland and splendid gardens, while huge gates worthy of a castle open onto the immaculate cobbled courtyard of the old stone manor house. Whatley is one of the UK's Premier League country-house hotels, a place with its own intrinsic splendour, and an opulently reworked interior that strikes a fine balance between contemporary and classic. The Dining Room is the fine dining venue, made over in recent years to look quietly dignified with pale wood floors, buttermilk walls hung with bright splashes of modern art, and Italian silks providing more colour. The service is pitched just right - friendly and knowledgeable, and without a trace of starched formality. Chef Martin Burge heads up the kitchen, delivering top-level Anglo-French cooking with a modern spin that keeps diners on the edge of their seats. This is cooking with the utmost confidence, total respect for the ingredients and high style. Whether you choose to go for the à la carte or full-on seven-course tasting menu, every atom of flavour is teased out in inventive combinations to keep you on your toes. While there's plenty of drama on the plate, nothing is done for effect. Braised snails are set in garlic cassonade and teamed with red wine sauce infused with veal kidney in an opening course where every ingredient pulls its weight. An elaborately worked main course of squab pigeon delivers the bird poached and roasted, and served with coffee and sherry gel, roasted foie gras and young turnips - a triumph of stunning technique that's made to look effortless. Desserts show a similarly sound mastery of what works with what: an unusual black truffle ice cream with lightly creamed Roquefort, deep-fried goats' cheese and candied walnuts, for example, or a slightly more orthodox treacle tart with poached pineapple and coconut gel. The wine list is a serious piece of work, bringing together modern and classic bottles from the Old and New worlds. The hotel's less formal option is the Swiss chalet-styled brasserie, Le Mazot, which has a divine alfresco patio.

Chef Martin Burge **Owner** Christian Landolt & Alix Landolt **Times** 7-10 Closed Mon-Tues, L all week **Prices** Food prices not confirmed for 2011. Please telephone for details. **Wines** 265 bottles over £20, 5 bottles under £20, 18 by glass **Notes** Vegetarian available, Civ Wed 120 **Seats** 40, Pr/dining room 30 **Children** Portions **Parking** 120

MELKSHAM Map 4 ST96

Beechfield House Hotel & Restaurant

Modern British

Contemporary country-house dining in elegant surroundings

01225 703700
Beanacre SN12 7PU
e-mail: reception@beechfieldhouse.co.uk
web: www.beechfieldhouse.co.uk
dir: M4 junct 17, A350 S bypass Chippenham, towards Melksham. Hotel on left after Beanacre

There are period details galore at Beechfield House, a late-Victorian country house built of Bath stone but in a decidedly Venetian style. It makes a refined and traditional setting for some equally diverting cooking, albeit of more modern sensibilities, based on sound local produce and delivered via a daily-changing carte. It's a restful dining room with an open fire, crystal chandelier, prints on the walls and richly upholstered chairs at tables laid with crisp white linen. A simple starter might be a salad of poached pears with chicory leaves and Cornish Yarg, or try the half-dozen frogs' legs with parsley velouté and garlic purée. Main-course West Country grey mullet is served with sautéed potatoes, purple sprouting broccoli and a caper and anchovy dressing, and, to finish, there might be vanilla pannacotta with poached rhubarb.

Chef Tony Thurlby **Owner** Chris Whyte **Times** 7-9 Closed D Sun **Prices** Starter £5.25-£5.95, Main £15.95-£23.50, Dessert £5-£8.50, Service optional **Wines** 29 bottles over £20, 16 bottles under £20, 5 by glass **Notes** Sunday L, Vegetarian available, Dress restrictions, Smart casual, Civ Wed 70 **Seats** 22, Pr/dining room 20 **Children** Portions, Menu **Parking** 70

OAKSEY Map 4 ST99

The Wheatsheaf @ Oaksey

Modern British

Confident cooking in relaxed village gastro-pub

01666 577348
Wheatsheaf Ln SN16 9TB
e-mail: info@thewheatsheafatoaksey.co.uk
dir: Off A429 towards Cirencester, near Kemble

On the margins of the Cotswolds and within striking distance of Malmesbury and Cirencester, this classic stone pub dates back to the 14th century. No surprise, then, that it is crammed with character: local lore has it that the Wheatsheaf was once the local slaughterhouse, the massive lintel over the inglenook fireplace is reckoned to be a Roman coffin lid, and crosses carved into the beams and chimney are there to ward off witches. The restaurant area, though, goes for a modern look with a sisal carpet and bare wooden tables. Modern British pub food is the kitchen's stock-in-trade, with menus designed to make the most of what's local and in season. Lunchtimes keep things simple and pubby, but dinner runs to braised lamb and chicken liver terrine, followed by slow-roast Gloucestershire Old Spot pork with black pudding cake and smoked apple sauce.

Chef Tony Robson-Burrell & Jack Robson-Burrell **Owner** Tony & Holly Robson-Burrell **Times** 12-2/6.30-9.30 Closed Mon, D Sun **Prices** Starter £4-£7, Main £4.50-£9, Dessert £5.50-£7, Service optional **Wines** 12 bottles over £20, 16 bottles under £20, 9 by glass **Notes** Sunday L, Vegetarian available **Seats** 50, Pr/dining room 8 **Children** Portions, Menu **Parking** 15

PURTON Map 5 SU08

The Pear Tree at Purton

Modern British

Former vicarage majoring on ethically sourced ingredients

01793 772100
Church End SN5 4ED
e-mail: stay@peartreepurton.co.uk
dir: From M4 junct 16, follow signs to Purton. Turn right at Bestone shop, hotel 0.25m on right

The Pear Tree's conservatory restaurant certainly makes the most of its glorious setting in the Vale of the White Horse: the 15th-century Cotswold-stone former vicarage overlooks landscaped Victorian gardens, wildflower meadows and a vineyard. The hotel lives by a strong green ethos, nurturing the wildlife that visits the grounds, and carefully sourcing local and fairtrade produce - its coffee, for example is bought in from a village on the slopes of Mount Kilimanjaro. The kitchen delivers it all in well-considered, inventive combinations on menus that shift with the seasons, backed up by daily specials to capitalise on whatever is good at the time. The ambitious approach could produce starters of marinated lemon sole with pesto dressing and ratatouille chutney, while main courses bring on tenderloin and braised belly of Wiltshire pork with apricot and brioche croûtons and braised white cabbage. A luscious selection of desserts might include orange and thyme syrup cake with blueberry ice cream.

Chef Alan Postill **Owner** Francis & Anne Young **Times** 12-2/7-9.15 **Prices** Fixed L 2 course fr £14.50, Fixed D 4 course fr £34.50, Service optional **Wines** 76 bottles over £20, 24 bottles under £20, 11 by glass **Notes** Sunday L, Vegetarian available, Dress restrictions, No shorts, Smart casual, Civ Wed 50 **Seats** 50, Pr/dining room 50 **Children** Portions **Parking** 70

ROWDE Map 4 ST96

The George & Dragon

Modern British V

Charming old inn with a relaxed gastro-pub atmosphere

01380 723053
High St SN10 2PN
e-mail: thegandd@tiscali.co.uk
dir: On A342, 1m from Devizes towards Chippenham

Fish and seafood arrives daily from Cornwall to star on the menu at the George & Dragon, a pukka 16th-century coaching inn complete with open fires and venerable beams carved with a Tudor rose. Modern gastro-pub sensibilities are catered for in the restaurant, where wooden furniture and floors strewn with antique rugs and simple unclothed tables work a pared-back rustic chic look. As the catch decides the day's specials there might be whole grilled crab or lobster served simply with garlic butter or lemon mayonnaise, while the à la carte menu delivers traditional comfort in the shape of roast monkfish with green peppercorn cream sauce, or slow-roast belly pork with grain mustard mash. Puddings head straight for the comfort zone with chocolate orange croissant bread-and-butter pudding with Jersey cream.

Chef Christopher Day **Owner** Christopher Day, Philip & Michelle Hale **Times** 12-3/7-11 Closed D Sun **Prices** Food prices not confirmed for 2011. Please telephone for details. **Wines** 35 bottles over £20, 13 bottles under £20, 9 by glass **Notes** Vegetarian menu **Seats** 35 **Children** Portions, Menu **Parking** 14

SALISBURY Map 5 SU12

Best Western Red Lion Hotel

Modern European

Modern cooking in an ancient inn

01722 323334
Milford St SP1 2AN
e-mail: reception@the-redlion.co.uk
dir: In city centre close to Guildhall Square

Reputedly the oldest purpose-built hotel in England, the Red Lion once played host to workers building Salisbury Cathedral. Don't miss the Virginia creeper that adorns the courtyard: even that's been there since the 18th century. The spacious dining room is done in dark blues and reds, with a partly exposed wattle-and-daub wall dating from the original edifice. Knick-knacks abound, and the staff add a mustard-keen sense of professionalism to the whole enticing package. The cooking is in a modern idiom, wrapping monkfish in nori and setting it on artichoke purée, accompanying venison with a sauce of chilli and chocolate, and offering warm rhubarb compôte and raspberry sorbet with crème brûlée.

Chef Jamie Holmes **Owner** Maidment Family **Times** 12.30-2/6-9.30 Closed L Mon-Sat **Prices** Starter £4-£9, Main £9-£18, Dessert £4-£8, Service included **Wines** 4 bottles over £20, 22 bottles under £20, 12 by glass **Notes** Sunday L, Vegetarian available, Civ Wed 80 **Seats** 85, Pr/dining room 80 **Children** Portions **Parking** Brown St. Pay & display car park

Salisbury Seafood & Steakhouse

Modern

Classy brasserie focusing on seafood and steaks

01722 417411 & 424111
Milford Hall Hotel, 206 Castle St SP1 3TE
e-mail: simonhughes@milfordhallhotel.com
dir: From A36 at rdbt on Salisbury ring road, right onto Churchill Way East. At St Marks rdbt left onto Churchill Way North to next rdbt, left in Castle St

Milford Hall, a Grade II listed red-brick Georgian mansion, lies just a short stroll from Salisbury's historic market square. Inside, a recent facelift blends period elegance with a sharp contemporary look, used to impressive effect in the very 21st-century Seafood and Steakhouse restaurant - cream and brown leather high-backed chairs sit on wooden floors, and the walls are lined with wine bottles and padded with leather. The menu 'does what it says on the tin' – top-grade meat, fresh fish and seafood are treated with a pleasing lack of fuss – but that's not to say that the food lacks style. Kick off with a retro prawn cocktail '70s style', and follow with an up-to-date idea like pan-seared scallops with pea purée and crispy pancetta.

Chef Chris Gilbert **Owner** Simon Hughes **Times** 12-2/6-10 Closed 26 Dec **Prices** Fixed L 2 course £15-£20, Starter £5.50-£7.75, Main £9.95-£25, Dessert £5.25-£7, Service optional, Groups min 8 service 10% **Wines** 9 bottles over £20, 22 bottles under £20, 10 by glass **Notes** Sunday L, Vegetarian available, Civ Wed 50 **Seats** 55, Pr/dining room 20 **Children** Portions, Menu **Parking** 60

STANTON ST QUINTIN Map 4 ST97

Stanton Manor Hotel

Modern European

Intimate restaurant in a country house with a past

01666 837552 & 0870 890 02880
SN14 6DQ
dir: M4 junct 17 onto A429 Malmesbury/Cirencester, in 200yds 1st left signed Stanton St Quintin. Hotel entrance on left just after church

The original building that stood here goes back to the time of the Domesday Book and was once owned by Elizabeth I's treasurer, Lord Burghley, but it was rebuilt just after Queen Victoria came to the throne. A relative stripling then, although the fireplaces were salvaged from the old house. These days, the refurbished Gallery Restaurant is the setting for some enterprising modern cooking served in a relaxed, intimate ambience. Much of the produce is grown in the hotel's own kitchen garden, and finds its way into dishes such as rabbit rillettes with golden beetroot and candied walnuts in lime and maple dressing, or wild sea bass with purple potatoes, baby fennel and orange butter.

Times 12-2.30/7-9.30

SWINDON Map 5 SU18

The Brasserie at Menzies Swindon

Modern British

Modern brasserie in centrally-located hotel

01793 528282
Fleming Way SN1 1TN
e-mail: swindon@menzieshotels.co.uk
dir: Just off Whalbridge rdbt next to Debenhams

The modern Menzies Swindon hotel is right in the heart of the town so accordingly popular with business travelers, plus families looking to explore the attractions of Wiltshire and the Cotswolds. The Brasserie is fittingly relaxed and modern in design, with plenty of darkwood and muted tones of white, yellow and brown. There's a small bar area or you can head straight to the table and tuck into the likes of spring onion potato cake scented with wild garlic and served with a fried duck's egg, or pressed ham terrine with juniper-pickled cucumber. The brasserie-style cooking continues into main courses such as crispy pork belly and braised red cabbage with a honey and five-spice jus on rösti potato.

Times 7-9.30 Closed Sun, L all week

Chiseldon House Hotel

Modern European

Creative cooking in Regency manor house

01793 741010 & 07770 853883
New Rd, Chiseldon SN4 0NE
e-mail: info@chiseldonhousehotel.co.uk
dir: M4, junct 15, A346 signed Marlborough. After 0.5m turn right onto B4500 for 0.25m, hotel on right

Well-placed for Swindon centre and the M4, Chiseldon is an elegant Regency manor house in immaculate lawned gardens. Inside, it is a comfy traditional hotel done out in cheerful pastel shades, with a welcoming and relaxed ambience in the intimate Orangery restaurant overlooking the garden. The kitchen team sources its materials well, and puts them together in well-balanced, imaginative combinations. The à la carte menu might start with a braised lamb, onion and mint terrine paired with beetroot chutney, while mains might offer up pan-fried sea bass with pea purée, chorizo, smoked garlic potato purée and sorrel hollandaise. Finish with rhubarb, delivered as a brûlée, sorbet, and with apple as a compôte.

Chef Robert Harwood **Owner** John & Sarah Sweeney **Times** 12-5.30/7-9.30 **Prices** Fixed D 3 course £24.95-£31.50, Service optional **Wines** 7 bottles over £20, 24 bottles under £20, 11 by glass **Notes** Sunday L, Vegetarian available, Civ Wed 120 **Seats** 65, Pr/dining room 25 **Children** Portions **Parking** 85

TROWBRIDGE Map 4 ST85

Red or White

Italian NEW

Fantastico Italian wines and food

01225 781666
46 Castle St BA14 8AY
e-mail: vito@vsvino.co.uk
dir: A361 or B3106 Trowbridge

Italian brothers Vito and Salvo Scaduto are passionate about their country's food and wine, so it's no surprise to see them converting a former wine warehouse into a restaurant and wine shop. The building, in the heart of Trowbridge, has kept its name from its previous life, and there are still plenty of wine racks on view, displaying bottles of fine wines from first-class, mainly Italian, producers. It's all available to buy, or to drink with your meal in the spacious restaurant. The food is simple, authentic Italian cooking at its best, using seasonal, mostly local, ingredients. A spring lunch might begin with a slice of ricotta, pea and pancetta tart, and some excellent home-made breads. Braised leg of chicken comes in a flavour-packed tomato and olive sauce with gnocchi, and for dessert don't miss the faultless tiramisù, served appropriately in a wine glass.

Chef Marc Salmon **Owner** Vito & Salvo Scaduto **Times** 12-2/6.30-10 Closed Sun **Prices** Food prices not confirmed for 2011. Please telephone for details.

WARMINSTER **Map 4 ST84**

Bishopstrow House Hotel

◎◎ Modern British V

Skilled cooking in sleek 21st-century country-house surroundings

☎ 01985 212312
Boreham Rd BA12 9HH
e-mail: info@bishopstrow.co.uk
dir: From Warminster take B3414 (Salisbury). Hotel signed

Bishopstrow is every inch the Georgian country mansion, ivy-clad and set in 27 acres of landscaped 18th-century grounds. Once indoors, however, it becomes clear that this is no hidebound, old-school country house. A recent makeover marries the best of the 19th and 21st centuries in a modern take on the luxury hotel, blending heaps of period grandeur with a touch of modern chic. The Mulberry restaurant is a slick exercise in understated contemporary style - all darkwood floors and tables, neutral tones of taupe and stone, and glass walls that open the room to the gardens and terrace for fine weather alfresco dining. In such a setting, anything other than a modern British menu would look a touch out of place: so a superb layered terrine of ham hock, pressed chicken and foie gras kicks off a menu of highly-skilled and creative cooking. Next up, butter-baked halibut is teamed with a white bean and mussel cassoulet, sugar-cured tomatoes and lemon oil to cut through the richness of the beans. Finish with Seville orange cheesecake with macerated oranges and Grand Marnier sabayon.

Chef Ben Streak **Owner** von Essen Hotels
Times 12-2.30/7-9.30 **Prices** Food prices not confirmed for 2011. Please telephone for details. **Wines** 220 bottles over £20, 12 by glass **Notes** Tasting menu 7 course, Sunday L, Vegetarian menu, Dress restrictions, Smart casual, Civ Wed 70 **Seats** 65, Pr/dining room 28 **Children** Portions, Menu **Parking** 100

The Dove Inn

◎ Modern, Traditional British NEW

Country inn with an appealing menu

☎ 01985 850109
Corton BA12 0SZ
e-mail: info@thedove.co.uk
dir: A303 off A36, Salisbury to Bath road

In a tranquil Wiltshire village close to the River Wylie, the Dove is a quintessentially English country pub that feels warmly welcoming as soon as you're through the door. The recently refurbished bar is the heart of the place, focused around a dramatic central fireplace. As is the case with many thriving inns these days, food is taken seriously, and the kitchen here takes classic pub staples and throws in a tweak here and there to up the interest factor, so a starter of fat scallops is served with Chinese-spiced confit duck leg and a chilli and ginger dressing. Next up, a whole roast partridge comes with local bacon, sautéed onions and wild mushrooms; finally, a sticky toffee date pudding with home-made custard keeps things firmly in crowd-pleasing mode.

Chef Paul Kinsey **Owner** William Harrison-Allan
Times 12-3/6-11 Closed D Sun **Prices** Starter £4.95-£8.95, Main £9.95-£19.95, Dessert £4.50-£5.50, Service optional **Wines** 6 bottles over £20, 20 bottles under £20, 6 by glass **Notes** Sunday L, Vegetarian available **Seats** 60 **Children** Portions, Menu **Parking** 30

WHITLEY **Map 4 ST86**

The Pear Tree Inn

◎◎ Modern British

Beautiful old inn with classy modern menu

☎ 01225 709131
Top Ln SN12 8QX
e-mail: peartreeinn@maypolehotels.com
dir: Turn into Top Lane from B3353

If the misuse of the gastro-pub label is getting you down, head to the Pear Tree to have your faith restored: It is a pub. It has a restaurant. It has a bar. It serves real ale. The food is good, very good. What's in a name? It's a real good looker, too, built of Wiltshire stone, with a pretty garden and creepers weaving their way around the doorway. The restaurant is in a gorgeous room with floor-to-ceiling glass bringing forth verdant views of the garden, and stripped wooden tables and a spruce, natural décor suit the mood to a tee. The kitchen seeks out a good amount of local produce and takes inspiration from modern European cookery. Starters could offer a simple but very flavoursome parsnip soup topped with pumpkin oil; next up a crispy skinned chicken breast with truffle mash potatoes and spring greens, or roast fillet of red gurnard with crushed saffron potatoes, pesto, tomato jam and prosciutto. The ambition and contemporary leanings continue with dessert; perhaps a tonka bean crème brûlée with spiced prune compôte.

Chef Karl Penny **Owner** Maypole Group plc
Times 12-2.30/6.30-9.30 **Prices** Fixed L 2 course £12.50, Starter £4.50-£7.95, Main £12.95-£18.95, Dessert £5.95-£6.95, Service optional, Groups min 10 service 10% **Wines** 34 bottles over £20, 22 bottles under £20, 15 by glass **Notes** Sunday L, Vegetarian available **Seats** 80 **Children** Portions, Menu **Parking** 60

WORCESTERSHIRE

ABBERLEY **Map 10 SO76**

The Elms Hotel

◎◎ Modern, Traditional British V

English country elegance and fine dining in family-friendly hotel

☎ 01299 896666
Stockton Rd WR6 6AT
e-mail: info@theelmshotel.co.uk
dir: On A443 near Abberley, 11m NW of Worcester

The stern exterior of this Queen Anne mansion belies the easygoing family-friendly ethos that runs through The Elms. The unbuttoned 21st-century approach extends to the contemporary design tweaks softening the edges of the opulent interior's ornate ceilings, sculpted fireplaces and stained-glass windows. Although this all adds up to a stylish bolt-hole for well-heeled families, grown-ups will also appreciate a bit of me-time in the swish spa and the child-free oasis at dinner in the Brooke Restaurant. Confident, up-to-date cooking with creative flavour juxtapositions is what to expect. Pan-fried sea bass served with crab broth, apple and celery leaf might sit alongside a classic roast cannon of Shropshire lamb with new season's garlic, olives and parsley.

Chef Daren Bale **Owner** von Essen Hotels
Times 12-2.30/7-9.30 **Prices** Food prices not confirmed for 2011. Please telephone for details. **Wines** 111 bottles over £20, 21 bottles under £20, 10 by glass **Notes** ALC 3 courses, Sunday L, Vegetarian menu, Dress restrictions, Smart casual, no jeans, no T-shirts, Civ Wed 70 **Seats** 50, Pr/dining room 50 **Children** Portions, Menu **Parking** 100

BEWDLEY **Map 10 SO77**

The Mug House Inn

◎ Modern British

Sound British cooking on the banks of the Severn River

☎ 01299 402543
12 Severnside North DY12 2EE
e-mail: drew@mughousebewdley.co.uk
dir: B4190 to Bewdley. On river, just over bridge on right

First the history lesson: a mug house is an old word for an alehouse. Next the reassurance: the restaurant may be called the Angry Chef, but all is calm and tranquil. Part

continued

BEWDLEY *continued*

of a terrace of 19th-century properties on the banks of the River Severn, there's a traditional bar and smart restaurant, where you will find subtle lighting, linen-clad tables and attentive service. Plenty of local ingredients turn up on the menu, which contains lots of good, well-judged dishes. Local black pudding comes with bubble-and-squeak and a coarse grain mustard cream (a great gastro-pub dish to be sure), then perhaps a slow-cooked pheasant and sausage casserole with chervil dumplings. The British cheese plate is a stunner.

Chef Drew Clifford, Martin Warner **Owner** Drew Clifford **Times** 12-2.30/6.30-9 Closed D Sun **Prices** Starter £3.95-£6.95, Main £10.95-£26, Dessert £4.95-£6.95, Service optional **Wines** 6 bottles over £20, 23 bottles under £20, 9 by glass **Notes** Sunday L, Vegetarian available, Dress restrictions, Smart casual **Seats** 26, Pr/dining room 16 **Parking** Car park 100mtrs along river

Royal Forester Country Inn

Modern European NEW

Stylishly-refurbished 15th-century inn with modern cuisine

☎ 01299 266286
Callow Hill DY14 9XW
e-mail: royalforester@btinternet.com

This ancient inn, a few miles outside Bewdley in the heart of the Wyre Forest, dates back to 1411, so there's plenty of ancient character in its gnarled beams and tiled floors, which blends in tastefully with a stylish contemporary facelift. The kitchen's ethos of using fresh seasonal food is pushed to its limits here: customers are encouraged to bring their own home-grown produce, which is deducted from the food bill under a barter system. Name-checked local suppliers form the backbone of a menu of unfussy, full-flavoured dishes, as in a starter of crispy pork belly and black pudding with caper mayonnaise and wood sorrel, and main-course lamb - tender cannon and confit shoulder - with broad beans, pea purée and port jus.

Times 12-6/6-9.30

BROADWAY Map 10 SP03

Barcelo The Lygon Arms

Anglo-French

Modern Anglo-French cooking in grandiose setting

☎ 01386 852255 & 854400
High St WR12 7DU
e-mail: info@thelygonarms.co.uk
dir: A44 to Broadway

A Cotswold classic in the honeypot village of Broadway, the Lygon Arms sees a fair share of celebrities pass through its historic rooms. There's something impressive about staying in a room where Charles I slept, or where Cromwell ate dinner before the Battle of Worcester, a cachet that has lifted the Lygon from its roots as a simple inn to a full-on manor house, where the Great Hall's barrel-vaulted ceiling and minstrels' gallery makes a suitably striking venue for the kitchen's skilled modern Anglo-French cooking. Terrine of rabbit, mustard, leeks and hazelnuts with fig and plum jam might appear ahead of mains such as fillet of Tamworth pork with apple faggot, roasted pear, Savoy cabbage and cider jus. End with a classy orange and Cointreau bread-and-butter pudding with vanilla custard.

Chef Peter Manner **Owner** Barceló Hotels & Resorts **Times** 12-2/7-9.30 Closed L Sat **Prices** Fixed L 2 course £19-£25, Fixed D 3 course £37.50, Starter £8.50-£12.50, Main £29.50-£35, Dessert £8.50-£12.50, Service optional **Wines** 107 bottles over £20, 16 by glass **Notes** Sunday L, Vegetarian available, Dress restrictions, Smart casual, no jeans, T-shirts or trainers, Civ Wed 80 **Seats** 80, Pr/dining room 110 **Children** Portions, Menu **Parking** 150

Dormy House Hotel

Modern British

Imaginative flavours at luxurious Cotswold retreat

☎ 01386 852711
Willersey Hill WR12 7LF
e-mail: reservations@dormyhouse.co.uk
dir: 2m E off A44, top of Fish Hill, turn for Saintbury picnic area. After 0.5m left, hotel on left

A tastefully converted 17th-century farmhouse, this attractive, honey-stoned hotel stands in manicured grounds high above pretty Broadway, with stunning views across the Vale of Evesham. Flagged floors, stone walls, beamed ceilings, deep sofas and crackling log fires create a cosy and relaxed country-house atmosphere, yet modern-day expectations of classy rooms and a high level of customer care are fulfilled. Attentive service is equally matched by the impressive cooking from a skilled and technically sound kitchen brigade. Dishes are tightly focused and punchy, with an emphasis on depth of flavour, texture and harmony of ingredients. The well-presented dishes are prepared from top-notch local produce; a well conceived starter of mackerel tartare, for example, with carpaccio of scallop, cucumber, horseradish and fennel, followed by a dry-aged rump steak with smoked beef marrow, caramelised cauliflower and pickled carrots. To finish, there may be coffee mousse with cinnamon doughnuts and vanilla foam.

Chef Andrew Troughton **Owner** Mrs I Philip-Sorensen **Times** 12-2/7-9.30 Closed 24-27 Dec, L Mon-Sat **Prices** Food prices not confirmed for 2011. Please telephone for details. **Wines** 70 bottles over £20, 10 bottles under £20, 10 by glass **Notes** Sunday L, Vegetarian available, Dress restrictions, No jeans, Civ Wed 150 **Seats** 80, Pr/dining room 170 **Children** Portions, Menu **Parking** 80

Russell's

Modern British

Fine dining in a chic restaurant with rooms

☎ 01386 853555
20 High St WR12 7DT
e-mail: info@russellsofbroadway.co.uk
dir: A44 follow signs to Broadway, restaurant on High St opposite village green

In the honeypot Cotswolds town of Broadway, this mellow 16th-century Cotswold-stone house was once the HQ of world-famous furniture designer George Russell. A boutique makeover in the mid-noughties turned the almost derelict building into a classy restaurant with rooms blending period features, such as a grand stone fireplace used as a fine wine store, with an understatedly chic décor. Glass doors open out from the L-shaped dining room onto a secluded courtyard that's much in demand for alfresco eating - particularly on sunny days when the fixed-price lunch menu offers remarkable value. The kitchen's business is unfussy modern brasserie cooking sprinkled with Mediterranean and Asian influences; the menu roams from lamb fillet spring roll with nori seaweed and sesame salad, to pan-fried venison with haggis mash, maple-glazed beetroot, Chantenay carrots and game jus, or fishy options such as grilled lemon sole with new potatoes, market vegetables and lemon and herb hollandaise.

Chef Matthew Laughton **Owner** Andrew Riley, Barry Hancox **Times** 12-2.30/6-9.30 Closed D Sun & BH Mon **Prices** Fixed L 2 course £12, Fixed D 3 course £15-£22.95, Starter £8-£12, Main £12-£26, Dessert £7, Service optional **Wines** 38 bottles over £20, 12 bottles under £20, 12 by glass **Notes** Sunday L, Vegetarian available **Seats** 55, Pr/dining room 14 **Children** Portions **Parking** 16

CHADDESLEY CORBETT **Map 10 SO87**

Brockencote Hall Country House Hotel

Modern French V

Divine French cooking in an elegant manor house

☎ 01562 777876
DY10 4PY
e-mail: info@brockencotehall.com
dir: On A448 just outside village, between Kidderminster & Bromsgrove

A smart Victorian country house in 70 acres of landscaped grounds, with its own gatehouse, dovecote and lake, Brockencote Hall is built to impress. Outside it has the look of a French château; inside you sink into sumptuous country-house opulence with eager-to-please staff on hand to help you relax in style. The dining room fits the bill, with grand chandeliers, elegant pastel hues and views through vast picture windows to go with the modern French menu. Among starters, classic ideas such as foie gras and smoked goose are brought up to date with the addition of green apple, celery sorbet and fig brioche. Main courses might pair loin of lamb and confit neck fillet with a minestrone of vegetables, borlotti beans and basil gnocchi, or Cornish lemon sole with vanilla pommes purées, beets, wild mushrooms, hazelnut oil and sherry vinegar.

Chef John Sherry **Owner** Mr & Mrs Petitjean **Times** 12-1.30/7-9.30 **Prices** Fixed L 2 course fr £17, Fixed D 3 course £36.30, Starter £10.50-£13.50, Main £18.50-£24.50, Dessert £8.50-£10.50, Service included **Wines** 160 bottles over £20, 26 bottles under £20, 13 by glass **Notes** Dégustation menu with wine 6 course £85, Sunday L, Vegetarian menu, Dress restrictions, Smart casual, no jeans, Civ Wed 80 **Seats** 60, Pr/dining room 30 **Children** Portions, Menu **Parking** 45

EVESHAM **Map 10 SP04**

Northwick Hotel

Modern British

Traditional dining in welcoming riverside hotel

☎ 01386 40322
Waterside WR11 1BT
e-mail: enquiries@northwickhotel.co.uk
dir: M5 junct 9, A46 Evesham, follow town centre signs. At River Bridge lights turn left, hotel 50yds on left

The Northwick Hotel started life in the 18th century as a coaching inn overlooking the River Avon and just a short stroll from the town centre. Things have not stood still since then: the building has been smartly modernised to take on the appetites of the 21st century in its contemporary-styled Courtyard Restaurant. The kitchen applies sound technical skills to locally-sourced produce to deliver an uncomplicated repertoire of simple, well-presented traditional dishes with clear flavours. Take pea and ham risotto with a poached egg to start, followed by grilled fillet of sea bass with baby new potatoes and pesto sauce. Pudding might be a simple mango pannacotta and strawberry compôte made memorable by its impressive depth of flavour.

Times 12-2/7-9.30 Closed Xmas

KIDDERMINSTER **Map 10 SO87**

The Granary Hotel & Restaurant

Modern British

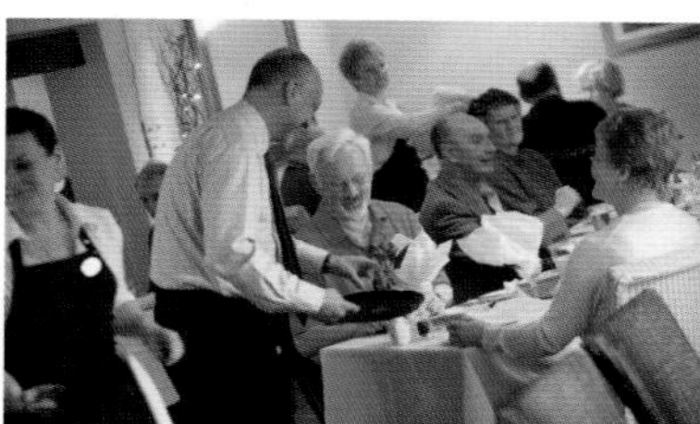

Modern British food in rural Worcestershire

☎ 01562 777535
Heath Ln, Shenstone DY10 4BS
e-mail: info@granary-hotel.co.uk
web: www.granary-hotel.co.uk
dir: On A450 between Worcester & Stourbridge. 2m from Kidderminster

In the Worcestershire countryside, on the outskirts of Kidderminster, the Granary boasts a gradually expanding market garden. Thus is the kitchen supplied with produce that has the very best claim of all to traceability. The minimal modern décor is enhanced by fine artworks, and the restaurant is furnished with well-spaced tables and subtle lighting to create a calm ambience. A modern British cooking style, with admixtures of European and Asian influences, aims for a unified, uncluttered approach. Begin perhaps with smoked haddock risotto topped with a poached egg, as a prelude to braised blade of beef with borlotti bean casserole, or slow-cooked pork belly and creamed Savoy cabbage with bacon. Banana Tatin with toasted almonds and honeycomb is one of the more unusual desserts.

Chef Tom Court **Owner** Richard Fletcher **Times** 12-2.30/7-11 Closed L Mon & Sat, D Sun **Prices** Fixed L 2 course £9.75-£12.25, Fixed D 3 course £18.50, Starter £5.25-£7.50, Main £14.50-£20.50, Dessert £4.50-£5.25, Service optional **Wines** 14 bottles over £20, 29 bottles under £20, 11 by glass **Notes** Sunday L, Vegetarian available, Civ Wed 200 **Seats** 60, Pr/dining room 40 **Children** Portions **Parking** 95

Stone Manor Hotel

British NEW

Romantic hotel with modern cuisine

☎ 01562 777555
Stone DY10 4PJ
e-mail: enquiries@stonemanorhotel.co.uk
dir: 2.5m from Kidderminster on A448, on right

Built in the 1920s in the style of a timbered Tudor manor, this rambling country-house hotel sits in 25 acres of lovely landscaped gardens. A romantic feel means it does a roaring trade in weddings, while a classy fitness and leisure complex plus easy access to the Midlands motorway arteries makes it a top spot for doing business. The beamed and pillared Fields restaurant is the venue for good-looking modern cooking, delivered by a kitchen that believes in keeping things simple to accentuate the quality of the raw materials. Tried-and-tested flavour combinations certainly hit home in a starter of pan-seared scallops with local black pudding, pancetta and pea purée, followed by pan-roasted guinea fowl with potato and black pudding torte, root vegetables and thyme jus.

Chef Adam Saville **Prices** Food prices not confirmed for 2011. Please telephone for details.

MALVERN **Map 10 SO74**

L'Amuse Bouche

Traditional French

French-style cooking in a quintessentially English setting

☎ 01684 572427
The Cotford Hotel, 51 Graham Rd WR14 2HU
e-mail: reservations@cotfordhotel.co.uk
dir: From Worcester follow signs to Malvern on A449. Left into Graham Rd signed town centre, hotel on right

In 1851, the Bishop of Worcester had this dramatic Gothic mansion built as his summer residence in landscaped gardens tucked beneath the voluptuous Malvern Hills. Nowadays it is a charming family-run hotel, and the old private chapel is a place of culinary contemplation as the Amuse Bouche Restaurant. The clue is there in the name, but this kitchen takes a contemporary Anglo-French route with the best seasonal, often organic, produce it can lay its hands on. Starters could be as classic as a crème vichyssoise leek and potato soup, or chicken liver and Cognac parfait, while main courses might bring apple-braised belly with a pistachio crust, served with black pudding with a cider, sage, cream and honey sauce.

Times 12-1.30/6-8

MALVERN *continued*

Holdfast Cottage Hotel

Traditional, Modern British

Sound cooking in delightfully peaceful setting

☎ 01684 310288 & 311481
Marlbank Rd, Welland WR13 6NA
e-mail: enquiries@holdfast-cottage.co.uk
dir: On A4104 midway between Welland & Little Malvern

At the foot of the Malvern Hills, this delightful, wisteria-covered hotel dates from the 17th century and stands in attractive, manicured grounds, with magnificent views. There are two acres of gardens and woodland to explore before (or after) taking your seat in the elegant dining room, with its oak tables, fresh flowers and views over the garden. The modern British cuisine is simply presented and makes good use of seasonal produce; pan-fried fillet of sea bass, for example, served with a pea risotto and pea velouté, and main-course cannon of English lamb with a cumin crust, sautéed potatoes and a cauliflower purée.

Chef Adam Cambridge **Owner** Guy & Annie Dixon **Times** 12.30-2.30/7-8.30 **Prices** Fixed L 2 course £19.95, Fixed D 3 course £27.50, Service optional **Wines** 11 bottles over £20, 24 bottles under £20, 2 by glass **Notes** Sunday L, Vegetarian available **Seats** 30 **Children** Portions **Parking** 15

Outlook Restaurant

Modern British

Ambitious cooking in charming hotel with sensational views

☎ 01684 588860
The Cottage in the Wood Hotel, Holywell Rd, Malvern Wells WR14 4LG
e-mail: reception@cottageinthewood.co.uk
web: www.cottageinthewood.co.uk
dir: 3m S of Great Malvern off A449, 500yds N of B4209, on opposite side of road

First things first: the view. High on a wooded hillside in the Malvern Hills, the Severn Valley opens up below this Georgian former dower house, giving a spectacular vista. The Outlook Restaurant has floor-to-ceiling windows - anything else would be a waste - and an elegant countenance. The food is based around fine produce from good local suppliers, prepared in a modern British or European manner; ham hock and duck egg terrine, for example, with celeriac remoulade and parsley juices, followed by sea bass with a crab and mussel bisque. Dessert might be glazed passionfruit tart with mango sorbet, or there is the plate of British cheeses (including local varieties). The wine list is a gem, too, with transparent mark-ups and packed with well-chosen bins.

Outlook Restaurant

Chef Dominic Pattin **Owner** The Pattin family **Times** 12.30-2/7-9.30 **Prices** Starter £4.95-£7.95, Main £9.50-£19.45, Dessert £5.25-£6.50, Service optional **Wines** 331 bottles over £20, 52 bottles under £20, 11 by glass **Notes** Pre-theatre D from 6pm, Sunday L, Vegetarian available **Seats** 70, Pr/dining room 20 **Children** Portions **Parking** 40

Seasons Restaurant at Colwall Park Hotel

Modern British

Excellent modern British cooking in the Malvern Hills

☎ 01684 540000
Walwyn Rd, Colwall WR13 6QG
e-mail: hotel@colwall.com
dir: On B4218, off A449 from Malvern to Ledbury

Built in the early 20th century to serve the local racetrack, today this independent country-house hotel has broad appeal. At the foot of the Malvern Hills, it is a house of generous proportions and the service keeps things relaxed and friendly. Seasons Restaurant is a light and bright space and feels contemporary thanks to some modern works of art and the smart fixtures and fittings (two wrought-iron chandeliers, for example), and well-dressed tables. The small kitchen brigade makes good use of quality seasonal ingredients in accurately cooked dishes in the modern British vein. Home-made bread is a great start to proceedings, before crispy pig's trotters with a ham hock mousseline and pea purée or duo of Middlewhite pork with sage and onion mash, cabbage and bacon, apple fondant and red wine jus. If you don't fancy fine dining, the hotel's Lantern Bar serves light meals and snacks.

Chef James Garth **Owner** Mr & Mrs I Nesbitt **Times** 12-2/7-9 Closed L all week (ex by arrangement) **Prices** Starter £7.15-£8.15, Main £18.95-£23.95, Dessert £6.50-£8.50, Service included **Wines** 55 bottles over £20, 19 bottles under £20, 9 by glass **Notes** Sunday L, Vegetarian available **Seats** 40, Pr/dining room 100 **Children** Portions, Menu **Parking** 40

OMBERSLEY **Map 10 SO86**

The Venture In Restaurant

British, French

Historic building with skilfully prepared Anglo-French food

☎ 01905 620552
Main Rd WR9 0EW
dir: From Worcester N towards Kidderminster on A449 (approx 5m). Left at Ombersley turn. Restaurant 0.75m on right

Set in the hushed village of Ombersley in a period black-and-white building (dating from the 1430s), step inside the former draper's to find a modern restaurant which embraces the character of its past. The 30-seater restaurant boasts bare topped wooden tables brightened by fresh flowers, comfortable high-backed brown leather chairs and cream walls hung with good quality prints, plus the regulation old beams. The accurate and simple cooking draws on good quality local produce; start with home-smoked free-range chicken with wholegrain mustard and celeriac remoulade and seasonal leaves. Move onto seared calves' liver with onion chutney, creamed potato and smoked belly bacon and bring down the curtain with a caramelised orange tart with chocolate sorbet. Keep your eyes peeled too for the restaurant's resident ghost.

Chef Toby Fletcher **Owner** Toby Fletcher **Times** 12-2/7-9.30 Closed 25 Dec-1 Jan, 2 wks summer & 2 wks winter, Mon, D Sun **Prices** Fixed L 2 course £23, Fixed D 3 course £37, Service optional **Wines** 40 bottles over £20, 20 bottles under £20, 6 by glass **Notes** Sunday L, Vegetarian available, Dress restrictions, Smart casual **Seats** 32, Pr/dining room 32 **Parking** 15, on street

STONEHALL **Map 10 SO84**

The Inn at Stonehall

Modern British NEW

Modern cooking in a smart country inn

☎ 01905 820462
Stonehall Common WR5 3QG
e-mail: info@theinnatstonehall.com
dir: M5 junct 7 towards Worcester, then onto the A440 at next rdbt towards Norton. Straight on at next rdbt then first left. Restaurant located on left

This smartly-restored Victorian Inn has all the ingredients of a successful contemporary foodie pub. The interior looks the part: leather seats, darkwood tables and an open log fire set the scene for pre-dinner drinks in the grand bar, and a clean-cut modern restaurant with flagstoned floors awaits. Cheerful staff inject a good buzz into the place, and the kitchen team produce a nice line in accurately-cooked, simply-presented modern dishes. Pea and ham hock soup is a typical no-nonsense starter, followed, perhaps, by home-made pork faggots with thyme sauce, dauphinoise potatoes and green beans or the Inn's pork, pear and perry sausage with mash, roasted root vegetables and onion gravy.

Chef Dwight Clayton **Owner** Joanna Coull **Times** 12-2.30/6.30-9.30 Closed 26-30 Dec, Mon, D Sun **Prices** Starter fr £5.50, Main fr £12, Dessert fr £5.50, Service optional, Groups min 10 service 10% **Wines** 10 bottles over £20, 12 bottles under £20, 7 by glass **Notes** Sunday L, Vegetarian available **Seats** 60, Pr/dining room 12 **Children** Portions, Menu **Parking** 30

TENBURY WELLS Map 10 SO56

Cadmore Lodge

Modern British

Contemporary cooking in idyllic lakeside location

01584 810044
Berrington Green, St Michaels WR15 8TQ
e-mail: reception.cadmore@cadmorelodge.com
dir: Off A4112 from Tenbury Wells to Leominster. 2m from Tenbury Wells, turn right opposite St Michael's Church

With its lakeside spot in a 70-acre private estate and nature reserve, it's no surprise that this family-run hotel was once a fishing lodge. In fact, fishing is still on the agenda for many guests - or perhaps a round on the 9-hole golf course. A log-burning fire and soothing colours in the rustic restaurant provide an easygoing ambience for straightforward, attractively-presented dishes, with local suppliers duly name-checked on daily-changing menus. Smoked salmon and pea risotto is a good way to open, followed by crispy braised local belly pork with wholegrain mustard mash and black pudding, or suprême of chicken wrapped in pancetta and Cadmore Valley wild garlic leaves, with morel mushroom sauce.

Chef Moustafa Molla Achmet, Chris Bushell **Owner** Mr & Mrs J Weston **Times** 12-2/7-9.15 Closed 25 Dec, L Mon **Prices** Fixed L 2 course £11.50-£12.95, Starter £2.50-£7.50, Main £13-£20, Dessert £4.50-£6.25 **Wines** 3 bottles over £20, 13 bottles under £20, 6 by glass **Notes** Sunday L, Civ Wed 100 **Seats** 50, Pr/dining room 50 **Children** Portions, Menu **Parking** 100

UPTON UPON SEVERN Map 10 SO84

White Lion Hotel

Modern British

Historic hotel with contemporary feel and flavour

01684 592551
21 High St WR8 0HJ
e-mail: info@whitelionhotel.biz
dir: From A422 take A38 towards Tewkesbury. After 8m take B4104 for 1m, after bridge turn left to hotel

Dating back to 1510, the White Lion in the heart of Upton has a colourful history and was home to author Henry Fielding during the writing of *Tom Jones*. In the Pepperpot Brasserie, named after the town's landmark church spire, its venerable beams and lathe and plaster walls now rub shoulders with an updated interior design with fresh flowers on chunky oak tables. The kitchen's modern British output focuses on seasonal, local produce to deliver clearly-defined flavours. Typically, start with confit duck and beetroot terrine with celeriac remoulade, then follow with roast cod wrapped in Parma ham with pea purée and roasted cherry tomatoes. For pudding, try the crème brûlée with brandied stewed dates.

Times 12-2/7-9.15 Closed 31 Dec-1 Jan, L few days between Xmas & New Year

WORCESTER Map 10 SO85

Brown's Restaurant

Modern International V

Seasonal ingredients and fabulous views

01905 26263
The Old Cornmill, 24 Quay St, South Quay WR1 2JJ
e-mail: enquiries@brownsrestaurant.co.uk
dir: From M5 junct 7 to city centre, at lights turn into Copenhagen St

This Victorian former corn mill enjoys an idyllic location by the River Severn – a dreamy setting for Brown's accomplished seasonal cooking. After a dramatic entrance through two large glass doors, suspended lighting and metal rafters continue to wow. Head downstairs, via black diamond patterned carpeted stairs to the dining room with its well-spaced and dressed tables, each of which feature a large black oil candle. If views of the river aren't romantic enough, there's a swan sanctuary to boot. Attentive staff are smartly dressed in black uniforms and aprons. Simple, honest seasonal cooking with straightforward presentation is the order of the day; expect mosaic of chicken, Caesar salad and croutons, then seared calves' liver with creamed potatoes, onion rings, shallot jus and crispy bacon.

Chef Darren Cornish **Owner** Mr & Mrs R Everton **Times** 12-2.30/6-9.30 Closed 26 Dec, 1 Jan, Mon, D Sun **Prices** Fixed L 2 course £11.95, Tasting menu £47.50, Starter £5.95-£11.50, Main £12.95-£26.95, Dessert £5.95-£7.50, Service optional **Wines** 10 bottles over £20, 10 bottles under £20, 15 by glass **Notes** Vegetarian tasting menu available on request, Sunday L, Vegetarian menu, Civ Wed 100 **Seats** 100 **Children** Portions, Menu **Parking** 6, NCP (parking on site after 5pm)

The Glasshouse

Modern British

Bustling town-centre brasserie with cathedral views

01905 611120
Danesbury House, 55 Sidbury WR1 2HU
e-mail: eat@theglasshouse.co.uk
dir: M5 junct 7 towards Worcester. Continue straight over 2 rdbts, through 2 sets of lights. At 3rd lights left into car park, restaurant opposite

This upbeat metropolitan brasserie spreads over three floors of a landmark custom-built venue in the centre of Worcester, with great views of the cathedral from the upstairs 'glass box' dining room. The interior designers have done their stuff, giving the place a clean-cut, modish contemporary look with grey slate floors, stripy banquettes and leather chairs. It has a cool, unbuttoned vibe, alive with the thrum of happy diners chatting over great food. The kitchen deals in unpretentious brasserie favourites, taken up a notch or two by the sheer quality of the ingredients, and presented without airs and graces. Steamed woodpigeon pudding stuffed with morels, crisp sage and bacon offers deeply-flavoured comfort, ahead of glazed crisp belly pork with braised cheeks and black pudding, caramelised onions and potato purée. Add in a serious kid's menu and a snappy line in cocktails, and it's clear that the Glasshouse has a wide appeal.

Chef Duncan Mitchell **Times** 12-2.30/5.30-10 Closed 26 Dec, 1 Jan & BHs, Sun **Prices** Fixed L 2 course £12.50, Fixed D 3 course £16.95, Starter £4.95-£8.95, Main £13.50-£25, Dessert £5.50-£6.50, Service optional, Groups min 8 service 10% **Wines** 21 bottles over £20, 10 bottles under £20, 13 by glass **Notes** Pre-theatre menu available, Vegetarian available **Seats** 100, Pr/dining room 16 **Children** Portions, Menu **Parking** Pay & display 100yds

YORKSHIRE, EAST RIDING OF

BEVERLEY Map 17 TA03

Beverley Tickton Grange

Modern British

Period charm and fine local produce

01964 543666
Tickton HU17 9SH
e-mail: info@ticktongrange.co.uk
dir: From Beverley take A1035 towards Bridlington. After 3m hotel on left, just past Tickton

A stone-built Georgian house amid four acres of private grounds and gardens, Tickton Grange has a great deal of period charm. An aperitif in the library lounge will get you in the mood, before progressing to the 1920s-fashioned dining room, where crisply clothed tables and candlelight create a soothing scene. Attractively presented modern British dishes are the order of the day, with local supply lines in heartening evidence on the menus. Start with pan-fried pigeon with quince and raisin marmalade, and move on to crisp pork belly with braised shoulder, pan-fried loin, black pudding sausage and smoked garlic purée, or cod with saffron fondant potato and braised lentils. Finish with hot chocolate and hazelnut pudding, or there are the regional cheeses to consider.

Chef David Nowell **Owner** Mr & Mrs Whymant **Times** 12-2/7-9.30 Closed 26 Dec **Prices** Fixed L 2 course fr £19.50, Fixed D 3 course fr £30, Service optional **Wines** 33 bottles over £20, 32 bottles under £20, 8 by glass **Notes** Sunday L, Vegetarian available, Civ Wed 150 **Seats** 45, Pr/dining room 20 **Children** Portions, Menu **Parking** 75

BEVERLEY *continued*

The Pipe and Glass Inn

Modern British V

Well-cooked local produce in stylish country inn

01430 810246
West End, South Dalton HU17 7PN
e-mail: email@pipeandglass.co.uk
dir: Just off B1248

Dating right back to the 15th-century, the Pipe and Glass stands on the site of the original gatehouse to Dalton Park, still the residence of Lord Hotham. This rambling building is the perfect example of a charming traditional country inn run with modern style and great attention to detail all round. Grab a seat by the fire in the traditional beamed snug bar and enjoy a pint of local ale or a table in the stylish modern conservatory and dining area for a menu packed with locally-sourced produce. James Mackenzie's innovative modern British repertoire includes some interesting combinations; take honey-smoked duck breast with a mini confit duck Scotch egg, blood orange dressing and celery cress, or venison and juniper suet pudding with wild mushrooms, butter braised Chantenay carrots, crispy smoked bacon and clapshot.

Chef James Mackenzie **Owner** James & Kate Mackenzie **Times** 12-2/6.30-9.30 Closed 25 Dec, 2 wks Jan, Mon (except BH), D Sun **Prices** Starter £4.25-£9.95, Main £9.95-£23.50, Dessert £4.95-£8.95, Service optional **Wines** 71 bottles over £20, 26 bottles under £20, 15 by glass **Notes** Sunday L, Vegetarian menu **Seats** 70, Pr/dining room 26 **Children** Portions, Menu **Parking** 60

WILLERBY **Map 17 TA03**

Best Western Willerby Manor Hotel

Modern European

Modern, brasserie-style food and décor in peaceful setting

01482 652616
Well Ln HU10 6ER
e-mail: willerbymanor@bestwestern.co.uk
dir: M62/A63, follow signs for Humber Bridge, then signs for Beverley until Willerby Shopping Park. Hotel signed from rdbt next to McDonald's

Originally created for a wealthy shipping merchant and set in well-tended gardens, Willerby Manor has a brasserie - Figs - that blows away any traditional preconceptions, with its smart, contemporary styling, which includes a bar and heated alfresco terraces. Modern lighting, unclothed tables and a crowd-pleasing menu catch the eye, while service is appropriately informal, with diners ordering from the menu via table notepads or at the bar. The kitchen's good-value repertoire mixes classics like beer-battered Whitby haddock with more current thinking, perhaps slow-cooked pork belly with roasted baby potatoes, creamy garlic peas, spring onions and parsley. A few dishes are available as either starters or mains, like goujons of sole or salmon Niçoise.

Chef David Roberts, Ben Olley **Owner** Alexandra Townend **Times** 10am-10pm Closed 25 Dec **Prices** Starter £5-£5.45, Main £8.50-£17.40, Dessert £3.60-£4.40, Service optional **Wines** 4 bottles over £20, 10 bottles under £20, 14 by glass **Notes** Sunday L, Vegetarian available, Civ Wed 300 **Seats** 40, Pr/dining room 40 **Children** Portions, Menu **Parking** 200

YORKSHIRE, NORTH

ASENBY **Map 19 SE37**

Crab and Lobster Restaurant

British, European

Brimming with quirky charm and a seafood-focused menu

01845 577286
Dishforth Rd YO7 3QL
e-mail: enquiries@crabandlobster.co.uk
web: www.crabandlobster.co.uk
dir: From A19/A168 take A167. Through Topcliffe, follow signs for A1. Restaurant on left 8m from Northallerton

An informal atmosphere, charming, professional service and a style which is nothing if not individual, contribute to the appeal of this thatched restaurant. Inside and out it is festooned with everything from old advertising signs to fishing nets, and barely an inch of wall space is free from some memorabilia or other. Those nets hint at the main passion in the kitchen - seafood. Eat in the bar or go through to the conservatory-style restaurant - either way you'll get seriously good produce cooked with flair. Pressed terrine of duck confit, ham shank and foie gras with Yorkshire rhubarb compôte, followed by twice-baked Ribblesdale and Wensleydale cheese soufflé demonstrate the ambition and technical dexterity of the chefs, while a large haddock fillet in local beer batter comes with all the trimmings among the seafood choices. There are outside areas for drinking and eating.

Crab and Lobster Restaurant

Chef Steve Dean **Owner** Vimac Leisure
Times 12-2.30/7-9.30 **Prices** Fixed L 2 course fr £14.50, Fixed D 3 course fr £35, Starter £5-£11.50, Main £11.50-£30, Dessert £5-£12, Service optional **Wines** 8 bottles over £20, 8 bottles under £20, 8 by glass **Notes** Sunday L, Vegetarian available, Civ Wed 75 **Seats** 85, Pr/dining room 24 **Children** Portions **Parking** 80

AUSTWICK Map 18 SD76

The Austwick Traddock

Traditional British V

Popular hotel with local and organic sensibilities

☎ 015242 51224
Settle LA2 8BY
e-mail: info@austwicktraddock.co.uk
dir: From Skipton take A65 towards Kendal, 3m after Settle turn right signed Austwick, cross hump back bridge, hotel 100yds on left

In the heart of the Dales, this winsome hotel and restaurant was once a trading paddock for the local horse trade. The handsome exterior is matched by the traditionally elegant furnishings and décor on the inside, where a handful of open log fires add a welcoming glow in the cooler months. The menu has a simple ethos: local, seasonal, flavoursome and, where possible, organic. Combinations on the plate are distinct, showing a skilled hand in the kitchen; first courses might bring forth a pigeon breast marinated in dandelion and burdock, served with a pearl barley risotto. Follow that with a poached haddock stuffed with crab and spinach mousse served with sautéed salsify and spinach beurre blanc, and finish with an inventive and gratifying Yorkshire champagne rhubarb pannacotta with a ginger snap basket and rhubarb sorbet.

Chef John Pratt **Owner** The Reynolds Family
Times 12-3/6.30-11 **Prices** Starter £4.95-£6.50, Main £14.50-£17.50, Dessert £5.25-£7.95, Service optional **Wines** 35 bottles over £20, 19 bottles under £20, 9 by glass **Notes** Sunday L, Vegetarian menu **Seats** 36, Pr/dining room 16 **Children** Portions, Menu **Parking** 20

BOLTON ABBEY Map 19 SE05

The Burlington Restaurant

– *see page 442*

BOROUGHBRIDGE Map 19 SE36

The Crown Inn

Modern British NEW V

Refurbished gastro-pub firing on all cylinders

☎ 01423 322300
Roecliffe YO51 9LY
e-mail: info@crowninnroecliff.com
dir: A1M junct 48, follow brown sign

The Crown in Roecliffe was in a sad state until new owners gave the place a top-to-toe makeover. All the elements of a top-class foodie pub are now present and correct: the mood is upbeat and the place already has an army of local fans, the bar is the real McCoy with flagstones, open fires, cosy armchairs and an array of well-kept real ales, and the Green Room and posher dining room are equally inviting. Local produce is name-checked - kippers, salmon and haddock are smoked in-house - and put to fine use on a clearly-focused modern British menu, backed up by daily chalkboard specials. Everything is home-made, such as velvety smooth leek and potato soup, ahead of pan-fried calves' liver served with fondant potato, caramelised swede, rhubarb chutney and port jus.

Chef Stephen Ardern **Owner** Karl Mainey
Times 12-2.45/6-9.45 **Prices** Fixed L 2 course fr £14.95, Fixed D 2 course fr £14.95, Starter £4.50-£7.95, Main £9.95-£19.95, Dessert fr £6.50, Service optional **Wines** 33 bottles over £20, 21 bottles under £20, 19 by glass **Notes** Sunday L, Vegetarian menu **Seats** 60, Pr/dining room 20 **Children** Portions, Menu **Parking** 30

The Dining Room

British, French

Assured cooking in stylish neighbourhood restaurant

☎ 01423 326426
20 St James Square YO51 9AR
e-mail: chris@thediningrooms.co.uk
dir: A1(M), Boroughbridge junct, follow signs to town. Opposite fountain in town square

Husband-and-wife-team Christopher and Lisa Astley run their popular neighbourhood restaurant with hands-on verve - chef Chris calling the shots in the kitchen while Lisa takes care of the front-of-house team. The eponymous Dining Room at the heart of the bow-fronted Grade II listed Queen Anne building is a bright white contemporary affair, with artworks to inject colour, or when the weather plays ball, you can move outside to the walled terrace for relaxed alfresco dining or pre-dinner drinks. The cooking steers well clear of over-complication, sticking to a repertoire of well-thought-out combinations that leave the top-class local materials tasting honestly and forthrightly of themselves. Loch Fyne oak roast salmon with Morecambe Bay shrimps and chive butter is a typical starter, followed by free-range belly pork with baby apples, black pudding mash and cider sauce. Finish with a seasonal rhubarb and pink champagne jelly with home-made liquorice ice cream.

Chef Christopher Astley **Owner** Mr & Mrs C Astley
Times 12-2/7-9.30 Closed 26-28 Dec, 1 Jan, BHs, Mon, L Tue-Sat, D Sun **Prices** Fixed L 2 course fr £22.50, Fixed D 3 course fr £28.50, Starter £5.95-£8.95, Main £13.95-£19.95, Dessert £4.95-£7.95, Service optional **Wines** 81 bottles over £20, 20 bottles under £20, 9 by glass **Notes** Sunday L, Vegetarian available, Dress restrictions, Smart casual, no T-shirts **Seats** 32 **Children** Portions **Parking** On street/Private on request

The Burlington Restaurant

BOLTON ABBEY Map 19 SE05

Modern French V NOTABLE WINE LIST

Top-flight cooking on a beautiful Yorkshire estate

☎ 01756 718111
The Devonshire Arms, Country House Hotel & Spa BD23 6AJ
e-mail: res@devonshirehotels.co.uk
dir: On B6160 to Bolton Abbey, 250 yds N of junct with A59 rdbt

The Duke and Duchess of Devonshire's Bolton Abbey Estate consists of 30,000 acres in the beautiful Yorkshire Dales and there is no better base for exploring the area, and indulging in a bit of pampering, than the Devonshire Arms. The building started life in the 17th century as a coaching inn, but these days it is best described as a country mansion hotel, where stunning flower displays, antiques and oil paintings from the Devonshires' Chatsworth House collection lend an atmosphere of luxury. As well as lavish spa facilities and handsomely decorated rooms there are two dining options: the relaxed and decidedly funky brasserie, and the main attraction, the elegant Burlington Restaurant, with its designer silverware, fine crystal and polished, but by no means over-bearing, service. The cooking of Stephen Smith and his team does justice to the surroundings, delivering complex, contemporary cooking based on first-rate ingredients, a good percentage of which come from the kitchen garden and estate. An amuse-bouche of pea velouté with parmesan ice cream gets things off to a finely-judged start, before first-course 'Scallops' (menu descriptions are to the point), which brings forth a stunningly presented dish with plump and wonderfully fresh scallops, perfectly pointed with smoked eel, celeriac, apple and truffle. Main-course 'Veal' comes as sirloin, belly, braised shin and sweetbread, with sweetcorn in various forms, morels and finished with a veal jus. The superb technique continues at dessert, from the Earl Grey pannacotta taster (with lemon jelly and thyme foam) through to the main event, 'Apple', perhaps, as a caramelised apple pie mousse and a nicely tart sorbet, served with blackberry jelly and a filo crisp. The premier-league wine list is a sight to behold, reading as a who's who of top-class producers.

Chef Stephen Smith **Owner** Duke & Duchess of Devonshire **Times** 7-10 Closed Xmas, 3-10 Jan, Mon, L all week **Prices** Tasting menu £65, Service added but optional 12.5% **Wines** 2300 bottles over £20, 30 bottles under £20, 12 by glass **Notes** ALC menu 3 course £60, Tasting menu 6 course, Vegetarian menu, Dress restrictions, Smart dress, no jeans or T-shirts, Civ Wed 90 **Seats** 70, Pr/dining room 90 **Children** Menu **Parking** 100

BURNSALL **Map 19 SE06**

Devonshire Fell

Modern British NEW

Bold modern cooking in a chic Yorkshire conservatory

01756 729000
BD23 6BT
e-mail: manager@devonshirefell.co.uk
dir: On B6160, 6m from Bolton Abbey rdbt A59 junct

To help you get your geographical bearings, the Devonshire Fell is in a Yorkshire Dales village, the name being derived from its acquisition by the Duke and Duchess of Devonshire. The Duchess oversaw the refurbishment, and did a fine job with it too. Contemporary artworks and smartly set tables look good, as do the views over the Fell afforded by the conservatory windows. A bold style of modern British food is fully in keeping with the surroundings, delivering a signature starter of slow-cooked pig cheek with smoked potato, black pudding croquette and apple purée, a winning combination of ingredients. Mains take in good local lamb, hake with cassoulet, and an enterprising reworking of osso buco using pork. Excellent pastry work shines through in a zinger of a lemon curd tart with orange ice cream.

Chef Daniel Birk **Times** 12-2.30/6.30-9.30 **Prices** Fixed L 2 course £14-£26, Fixed D 3 course £18-£32, Main £8.50-£9.95 **Wines** 35 bottles over £20, 8 bottles under £20, 11 by glass **Notes** Tasting menu available on request - must be pre-booked, Sunday L, Vegetarian available, Civ Wed 70 **Seats** 18, Pr/dining room 70 **Children** Portions, Menu **Parking** 40

BYLAND ABBEY **Map 19 SE57**

The Abbey Inn

Modern British

Hearty food in fabulously situated romantic inn

01347 868204
YO61 4BD
e-mail: info.appletreeinn@virgin.net
dir: From A19 Thirsk/York follow signs to Byland Abbey/ Coxwold

This characterful inn sits next to the romantic ruins of Byland Abbey on the edge of the North York Moors. Parts of the medieval monastic buildings were converted to a pub in the 20th century, and it's now fully refurbished in a rustic-chic blend of bare-stone walls, flagstone floors and oriental rugs. A trio of charming dining rooms have drink-related names - Abbey Cider, Brown Brothers and Louis Roederer. The modern British food wrought from top-class local produce focuses on flavour in confidently rustic dishes. Expect Yorkshire game terrine with damson chutney and toasted croûtons, ahead of pheasant breast - courtesy of the local shoot - teamed with chestnuts, bacon and lentils and a red wine reduction. Finish with the deep indulgence of prune and Armagnac brioche bread-and-butter pudding with date and walnut ice cream.

Chef Dave Robbins **Owner** Melanie Drew & Dave Robbins **Times** 12-9.30 Closed Xmas, New Year, Tue **Prices** Starter £4.75-£9.50, Main £12-£19.50, Dessert £1.50-£7.50, Service optional **Wines** 104 bottles over £20, 50 bottles under £20, 13 by glass **Notes** Sunday L, Vegetarian available, Civ Wed 80 **Seats** 45 **Children** Portions **Parking** 40

CRATHORNE **Map 19 NZ40**

Crathorne Hall Hotel

British

Edwardian country house with impressive contemporary cuisine

01642 700398
TS15 0AR
e-mail: crathornehall@handpicked.co.uk
dir: Off A19, 2m E of Yarm. Access to A19 via A66 or A1, Thirsk

Crathorne Hall is a grandiose Edwardian pile, the largest and last to be built in North Yorkshire in the swan-song years of stately homes. The Leven Valley and Cleveland Hills are the backdrop wherever you are in its magnificent interior, including the Leven Restaurant, where oak panels, gold-framed oil paintings and gilt coffered ceilings, combine in an opulent setting. The cuisine tends towards modern British sensibilities, with plenty of sound, classical technique on display. Tip-top produce, much of it sourced locally, is put to good use in well-considered dishes such as pork belly (from Happy Trotter Farm, no less), served with two plump langoustines, an apple salad and purée. Main-course fillet of turbot is partnered with the flavours and textures of cauliflower, trompette mushrooms, and finished with a pea dressing. End on a high with a stonkingly good sticky toffee pudding.

Chef Paul Soczowka **Owner** Hand Picked Hotels **Times** 12.30-2.30/7-9.30 **Prices** Fixed L 2 course £16.50-£19.50, Fixed D 3 course £35-£40, Starter £12.50-£17, Main £19-£29, Dessert £10.50-£13.50, Service included **Wines** 98 bottles over £20, 1 bottle under £20, 18 by glass **Notes** Sunday L, Vegetarian available, Civ Wed 90 **Seats** 45, Pr/dining room 26 **Children** Portions, Menu **Parking** 80

EASINGTON **Map 19 NZ71**

The Grinkle Park Hotel

British & French

Country estate setting, modern British cuisine

01287 640515
TS13 4UB
e-mail: info.grinklepark@classiclodges.co.uk
dir: 9m from Guisborough, signed off A171 Guisborough-Whitby road

Grinkle Park has a lot going for it - 35 acres of beautiful grounds and a grand, Baronial-style Victorian house full of period features. In Conyers Restaurant there are elegantly dressed tables, views over the lawns, and modern British cooking based around top-notch Yorkshire produce, including fish from Whitby and game from Grinkle Park's own estate. The 'Yorkshire tapas' is a fun way to begin - a mini Yorkshire pudding and roast sirloin with horseradish, mini fish and chips with tartare sauce, and Mrs Bells' Yorkshire blue and red onion tart. For the main event try the roast crab-crusted loin of cod with lemon-scented mashed potato and roasted cherry tomatoes on the vine, and finish with the rich dark chocolate marquise with cappuccino sauce and walnut ice cream.

Times 12.15-7.15

ESCRICK **Map 16 SE64**

The Parsonage Country House Hotel

Modern British

Artfully presented dishes in a Yorkshire village hotel

01904 728111
York Rd YO19 6LF
e-mail: sales@parsonagehotel.co.uk
dir: From A64 take A19 Selby. Follow to Escrick. Hotel on right of St Helens Church

Built in the early Victorian era, the Parsonage is a village hotel only a few miles outside York. Its six acres of gardens are worth a potter in summer, and the dining goes on in the vibrantly decorated golden-yellow Lascelles restaurant, as well as a conservatory extension. Painstakingly presented dishes utilise local and home-grown produce, and the cooking is agreeably straightforward. A bowl of thick, velvety vegetable and blue cheese soup might be the prelude to braised neck fillet of lamb with mixed beans, capers and mint, with a labour-intensive dessert of peach parfait wrapped in peach slices, alongside a sorbet of the same, and a syrup of jasmine tea and vanilla.

Times 12-2/6.30-9 Closed L Sat

GRASSINGTON **Map 19 SE06**

Grassington House

Modern British NEW

Stylish Georgian hotel with a creative take on Yorkshire's finest produce

01756 752406
5 The Square BD23 5AQ
e-mail: bookings@grassingtonhousehotel.co.uk
dir: A59 into Grassington, in town square opposite post office

Smack on the cobbled square of this lovely Yorkshire Dales village, Grassington House is a stylishly-refurbished Georgian building run with hands-on charm by owners John and Sue Rudden. John is a leading light on the Yorkshire culinary scene, and now brings his exceptional talents to bear on the best local produce he can lay his hands on at the stoves of the 5 The Square restaurant - and that goes as far as raising his own pigs

continued

GRASSINGTON *continued*

as part of a passionate 'field to fork' ethos. There's nothing affected about what leaves this kitchen - just top-class ingredients that taste honestly and forthrightly of themselves, brought together in creative modern marriages. Take home-smoked beef fillet carpaccio with tempura oyster and watercress foam to start, and follow with loin of that home-bred Saddleback pork, teamed with home-made black pudding boudin, braised cabbage and cider jus, or roast loin and leg of rabbit with honey bacon potatoes and liquorice jus. Excellent northern cheeses are hard to resist, but Valrhona chocolate and salted nut caramel delice with Horlicks ice cream offers serious temptation.

Chef John Rudden **Owner** Susan & John Rudden **Times** 12-2.30/6-9.30 Closed 25 Dec **Prices** Fixed L 2 course £12, Fixed D 4 course £35.50, Starter £4.50-£6.95, Main £12.50-£21.50, Dessert £5.25-£8.25, Service optional **Wines** 16 bottles over £20, 14 bottles under £20, 12 by glass **Notes** Fixed D 4 course available Sun-Tue, £35.50 per couple, Sunday L, Vegetarian available **Seats** 40 **Children** Portions, Menu

GUISBOROUGH **Map 19 NZ61**

Macdonald Gisborough Hall

Modern British

Creative fine dining at an elegant country-house hotel

☎ 0844 879 9149
Whitby Ln TS14 6PT
e-mail: general.gisboroughhall@macdonald-hotels.co.uk
dir: A171, follow signs for Whitby to Waterfall rdbt then 3rd exit into Whitby Lane, hotel 500yds on right

Gisborough Hall is an ivy-clad Victorian mansion sitting in peaceful landscaped grounds on the edge of the North Yorkshire Moors. Its period charms are many, and Tockett's restaurant, in the Edwardian billiards room, has its fair share of original features. It's an elegant space, candlelit at night, with open fires and large windows looking out over the gardens. The cooking is classically-based, though with an undoubted modern slant. Take home-cured gravad lax with sweet pickled courgette and chervil crème fraîche, followed by trio of pork - slow-cooked belly, pan-seared fillet and braised cheek with home-made black pudding, spinach and confit potato. Make room for desserts such as steamed treacle sponge with pickled walnut ice cream.

Times 12.30-2.30/6.30-9.30

HAROME **Map 19 SE68**

The Star Inn

Traditional British V Notable Wine List

Creative cuisine at a popular village inn

☎ 01439 770397
YO62 5JE
e-mail: jpern@thestaratharome.co.uk
dir: From Helmsley take A170 towards Kirkbymoorside, after 0.5m turn right towards Harome. After 1.5m, inn 1st building on right

Originally a 14th-century longhouse, the thatched Star Inn is picture-postcard pretty outside and equally delightful within, with low beams, wonky walls, cosy candlelit tables and the aroma of wood smoke and bees wax. Rescued from dereliction by Andrew and Jacquie Pern in 1996, it is now one of the finest pub-restaurants in Britain. The tightrope between gastro and pub is a hard balancing act to pull off, but it works here and a new state-of-the-art kitchen and the recent extension to the contemporary dining room have proved a boon as Andrew Pern's creative cooking draws foodies from afar - booking is essential. His food is robust, seasonal, packed with bold and vibrant flavours, and what Andrew calls 'Yorkshire with a twist'. Making full use of home-grown ingredients from the kitchen garden and top-drawer produce from a select network of local suppliers, menus work with the seasons, with a typical winter meal kicking off with a salad of langoustines with pork belly, spiced pickled pears and Waldorf vinaigrette. To follow, perhaps rack of Ryedale lamb with lamb neck hotpot, pickled red cabbage and pearl barley juices, with dark chocolate and rosemary pudding with local raspberries to finish. Don't miss the Pern's Corner Shop deli opposite.

Chef Andrew Pern **Owner** A & J Pern **Times** 11.30-3/6.30-11 Closed 1 Jan, L Mon, D Sun **Prices** Starter £5-£12, Main £16-£26, Dessert £5-£12, Service optional **Wines** 81 bottles over £20, 8 bottles under £20, 14 by glass **Notes** Chef's table for 6-8 people, 6-8 course, Sunday L, Vegetarian menu, Civ Wed 50 **Seats** 70, Pr/dining room 10 **Children** Portions **Parking** 30

HARROGATE **Map 19 SE35**

The Boar's Head Hotel

British V

Charming old coaching inn with creative kitchen team

☎ 01423 771888
Ripley Castle Estate HG3 3AY
e-mail: reservations@boarsheadripley.co.uk
dir: On A61 (Harrogate/Ripley road). In village centre

If you somehow feel that you've travelled back to the 16th century in the village of Ripley, that might be because the whole shebang goes back to the feudal era, owned by the Ingilby family for 26 generations. Sir Thomas and Lady Ingilby live in Ripley Castle, while the Boar's Head is the old coaching inn, a smartly traditional place in a hunting-shooting-fishing kind of way. Oil paintings of Ingilby ancestors preside over a comfy wonky-floored, woodsmoke-scented interior, with a choice of restaurant or bistro when hunger strikes. The kitchen, however, is not in any way hidebound or held back by tradition: intelligent modern cooking is the deal here, beginning with slow-cooked Yorkshire oxtail ravioli with spinach, cooking jus and horseradish air; continue with a fashionable meat and fish combo: rare-breed pork and cod cheeks with fondant potatoes, apple and vanilla purée and thyme jus. Dessert serves up poached Yorkshire rhubarb with vanilla pannacotta. Lord Ingilby takes upon himself the arduous chore of putting together the rather good wine list.

Chef Kevin Kindland **Owner** Sir Thomas Ingilby & Lady Ingilby **Times** 12-2/7-9 **Prices** Fixed L 2 course £16-£20, Fixed D 3 course £25-£35, Starter £5-£9, Main £12-£20, Dessert £4.50-£7, Service optional **Wines** 50 bottles over £20, 20 bottles under £20, 22 by glass **Notes** Tasting menu available, Sunday L, Vegetarian menu, Civ Wed 150 **Seats** 40, Pr/dining room 40 **Children** Portions, Menu **Parking** 45

Clocktower

Modern British V

Yorkshire Food Heroes celebrated in style

☎ 01423 871350
Rudding Park Hotel & Golf, Follifoot HG3 1JH
e-mail: reservations@ruddingpark.com
web: www.ruddingpark.co.uk
dir: A61 at rdbt with A658 follow signs 'Rudding Park'

Handy for Leeds and York, the Clocktower restaurant in the splendidly handsome Rudding Park Hotel has a bespoke 'Yorkshire Food Heroes Menu', ensuring the best regional produce gets the attention it deserves. The interior designer has pushed the boat out here to create vibrant, colourful spaces, from the bar with its limestone counter, to the grand conservatory with a 400-year-old olive tree, and the dining room with its eye-catching chandelier. That local heroes menu might see Lowna goats' cheese and red onion tartlet with confit tomatoes and sauce vierge (40 miles travelled) preceding roast Easingwold pork cutlet served with thyme-roast potatoes, Moss House rhubarb compôte, crackling, and cider jus (35 miles). From the carte, perhaps an Asian-inspired grilled sea bass, followed by orange and chocolate fondant with an orange compôte and Grand Marnier sorbet.

Chef Jerome Gaudre **Owner** Simon Mackaness **Times** 12-2.30/7-9.30 **Prices** Fixed L 2 course £26, Fixed

D 3 course £34, Starter £9-£12.50, Main £19-£25, Dessert £8.50-£14.50, Service optional **Wines** 60 bottles over £20, 15 bottles under £20, 20 by glass **Notes** Sunday L, Vegetarian menu, Civ Wed 180 **Seats** 170, Pr/dining room 240 **Children** Portions, Menu **Parking** 250

Hotel du Vin Harrogate

British, Mediterranean

Fine food and wine in famous spa town

☎ 01423 856800
Prospect Place HG1 1LB
e-mail: info.harrogate@hotelduvin.com
dir: A1(M) junct 47, A59 to Harrogate, follow town centre signs to Prince of Wales rdbt, 3rd exit, remain in right lane. Right at lights into Albert St, right into Prospect Place

The senses have always been well catered for by the renowned tea shops and Victorian spa in Harrogate, a tradition continued 21st-century-style by the local outpost of the HdV chain in a luxuriously-converted terrace of eight Georgian townhouses opposite the 200-acre Stray common. As its name makes abundantly clear, the Hotel du Vin brand takes a serious approach to wine, so head for the Champagne and Claret bar for a snifter of one of the impressive array of wines available by the glass, then settle into the slick Gallic-style bistro. The kitchen makes a virtue of simplicity and restraint, leaving the quality and freshness of the ingredients to speak for themselves. Home-made pork pie with apple piccalilli is one way to start, or there could be grilled sardines on garlic crostini with basil and tomato confit. Main-course pork belly comes with onion tarte Tatin, red cabbage purée and apple boulangère potato.

Times 12-2/6.30-10

Nidd Hall Hotel

Modern British **NEW**

Modern dining in an impressive stately home

☎ 01423 771598
Nidd HG3 3BN
dir: A1M junct/A59 follow signs to Knaresborough. Continue through town centre & at Bond End lights turn left, then right onto B6165 signed Ripley & Pateley Bridge. Hotel on right in approx 4m

Romantics will revel in the idea that Edward VIII and Wallis Simpson first met amid the Tuscan columns, stained glass, wrought-iron balustrades and wedding-cake plasterwork of this grand Regency fantasy. The fine dining Terrace Restaurant has been recently jazzed up to lend a more contemporary feel - a lavish marble fireplace is still its centrepiece, but the floor is polished wood and tables are fashionably bare. The kitchen has tracked down the best local suppliers, and menus reflect the seasons. The modern British style opens with a well-judged teaming of roast king scallops, caramelised cauliflower and caper and sultana dressing, then moves on to sticky Easingwold pork with parmesan creamed potatoes, pointed up with a tangy apple fondant and cider jus.

Chef Jason Wardill **Owner** Warner Leisure
Times Closed Tue-Wed, L all week **Prices** Starter £5.50-£7.95, Main £12-£19.95, Dessert £5.50-£6.95, Service optional **Notes** Sunday L, Vegetarian available, Dress restrictions, Smart dress **Seats** 42

Orchid Restaurant

Pacific Rim

Modern cooking in stylish hotel

☎ 01423 560425
Studley Hotel, 28 Swan Rd HG1 2SE
e-mail: info@orchidrestaurant.co.uk
dir: Opposite Mercer Art Gallery

Close to the centre of town within the Studley Hotel, this stylish, modern restaurant has a deserved reputation for its dynamic and authentic approach to Asian and Pacific Rim cuisine. The elegant lacquered tables, rattan bamboo steamers and Asian clay pots are mirrored by the high-quality traditional and unusual ingredients used with good effect to produce well-flavoured dishes. A typical starter might be Szechuan bang bang chicken, followed by a main course of Cantonese black pepper sizzling beef or Thai red duck curry. For dessert, Vietnamese coconut crème brûlée or chilled mango pudding from Hong Kong will do nicely.

Chef Kenneth Poon **Owner** Bokmun Chan
Times 12-2/6.30-10 **Prices** Fixed L 2 course £10.95, Fixed D 4 course £21.95-£30.95, Starter £4-£7.50, Main £7.50-£20.50, Dessert £4.90-£5, Service added but optional 10% **Wines** 13 bottles over £20, 15 bottles under £20, 8 by glass **Notes** Tue D sushi & sashimi, Sunday L, Vegetarian available **Seats** 72, Pr/dining room 18 **Parking** 18

van Zeller

Modern British

Home-coming chef making a splash in Harrogate

☎ 01423 508762
8 Montpellier St HG1 2TQ
e-mail: info@vanzellerrestaurants.co.uk

This intimate modern restaurant in Harrogate's trendy Montpellier Quarter bears the name of chef Tom van Zeller who jumped ship from the Hotel du Vin in 2009, and walked up the road to set up on his own. He brings with him a stellar CV, starting out from good old Betty's Tea Rooms to globetrot around big names in big cities before returning to his native town. The interior is done in a classy, understated contemporary style, with darkwood floors, and cream walls jazzed up with abstract artworks; relaxed but knowledgeable staff get service pitch perfect. In his own kitchen, van Zeller has all the room he needs to express himself, but his restraint is admirable. What appears on the table is confident, well-grounded, unpretentious cooking, on menus - including a five-course tasting workout - that work with the seasons. A starter of seared foie gras with mango and Yorkshire cobble makes a virtue of simplicity, followed by a main course that is similarly shorn of embellishment: roast loin and braised leg of hare, teamed with Savoy cabbage, juniper and glazed turnips. Finish with iced Yorkshire rhubarb parfait. Wine, too, is done well here, with themed tasting evenings and an excellent choice offered by the glass.

Chef Tom van Zeller **Owner** Tom van Zeller
Times 12-2.30/6-10 Closed Mon, D Sun **Prices** Fixed D 4 course £20, Tasting menu £40, Starter £7.50-£15.50, Main £16.50-£35, Dessert £6.50-£10.50, Service optional, Groups min 8 service 10% **Wines** 85 bottles over £20, 8 bottles under £20, 9 by glass **Notes** Fixed L & pre-theatre menu available, Tasting menu 6 course, Sunday L, Vegetarian available, Dress restrictions, Smart casual **Seats** 34 **Children** Portions **Parking** Montpellier Hill

HAWNBY **Map 19 SE58**

The Inn at Hawnby

Traditional British, French **NEW**

Hearty, honest cooking at a welcoming village inn

☎ 01439 798202
YO62 5QS
e-mail: info@innathawnby.co.uk
dir: From the S, A1 to Thirsk & Teeside exit A19/A168 for Scarborough onto A170. 1st left through Felixkirk. Through Boltby into Hawnby

Step out of the door of this welcoming Victorian village inn and the North York Moors National Park lies before you. Hawnby is a real village with real people that brings in walkers and cyclists for its unspoilt authenticity. The Inn's owners are a hands-on couple, always around and always welcoming and helpful. Expect great food, simply cooked with top-notch local ingredients. Take a seat in the rustic dining room (after a pint in the cosy bar, of course) and kick off with a hearty ham hock with braised Puy lentils. Pause to watch rabbits, squirrels, pheasants and a robin in the garden, then continue with seared sea bass, citrus couscous, chive dressing, roasted vine tomatoes and smoked pancetta.

Chef Andrew Holt **Owner** Kathryn & David Young
Times 12-2/7-9 Closed 25 Dec, L Mon-Tue (Feb-Mar) **Prices** Starter £3.65-£6.50, Main £10.75-£16.50, Dessert £4.50-£4.95, Service optional **Wines** 19 bottles over £20, 15 bottles under £20, 12 by glass **Notes** Sunday L, Vegetarian available **Seats** 32, Pr/dining room 30 **Children** Portions **Parking** 22

HELMSLEY Map 19 SE68

Black Swan Hotel

Modern British V

Charming hotel with first-class food

☎ 01439 770466
Market Place YO62 5BJ
e-mail: enquiries@blackswan-helmsley.co.uk
dir: A170 towards Scarborough, on entering Helmsley hotel at end of Market Place, just off mini-rdbt

The Black Swan sits proudly on the market square of one of the North York Moors' prettiest villages. The hotel has had a makeover in recent years, and the décor blends its Georgian and Elizabethan pedigree with a contemporary look. They like their cakes up in Yorkshire, so the tea room is a hugely popular addition. The kitchen too has upped its game: the Rutland restaurant overlooking the secluded walled garden is the setting for its well-executed contemporary ideas that take their inspiration from the county's fine produce, and arrive dressed to thrill. Seared scallops appear in the company of parmesan gnocchi and shallot, truffle and smoked chicken sauce, while main-course Dales beef fillet is partnered by slow-braised rib, oxtail, truffle risotto, shallot, spinach and truffle jus and onion soubise.

Chef Paul Peters **Owner** John Jameson
Times 12.30-2.30/7-9.15 Closed L Mon-Sat **Prices** Fixed L 2 course £19.95, Fixed D 3 course £33-£50, Starter £8-£12, Main £17-£25, Dessert £8-£12 **Wines** 158 bottles over £20, 8 bottles under £20, 14 by glass **Notes** Tasting menu 7 course, Sunday L, Vegetarian menu, Dress restrictions, Smart casual, Civ Wed 100 **Seats** 85, Pr/dining room 30 **Children** Portions, Menu **Parking** 40

Feversham Arms Hotel & Verbena Spa

Modern British V

Stylish boutique hotel with high-achieving kitchen

☎ 01439 770766
1-8 High St YO62 5AG
e-mail: info@fevershamarmshotel.com
dir: A1 junct 29 follow A170 to Helmsley, at mini-rdbt turn left then right twice. Hotel just past church on right

Within striking distance of York and many of the county's heritage sites, the Feversham Arms is a perfect base for travellers who like to return each day to generous dollops of contemporary style, plus pampering treatments in the Verbena Spa. Within its classic Yorkshire stone walls, the owners have refurbished the old place with a lavish boutique look, and under the stewardship of Simon Kelly, the kitchen has stayed solidly on track. The skilled modern British cooking takes its cue from French classics in creative dishes wrought from Yorkshire's finest produce, handled with precision and restraint, and brought together in intelligent combinations. The modish marriage of pan-fried scallops and pork belly is pointed up with salsify and caper dressing in a flavour-packed opener, while main course Goosnargh duck breast is teamed with veal sweetbreads, swede purée, foie gras and red wine salsify.

Chef Simon Kelly **Owner** Simon Rhatigan
Times 12-2/7-9.30 **Prices** Fixed D 3 course £36-£45, Starter £7.50-£12.50, Main £18-£25, Dessert £7.50-£9.50, Service optional **Wines** 215 bottles over £20, 5 bottles under £20, 11 by glass **Notes** Tasting menu available, Sunday L, Vegetarian menu, Dress restrictions, Smart casual, Civ Wed 80 **Seats** 55, Pr/dining room 35 **Children** Portions, Menu **Parking** 35

HETTON Map 18 SD95

The Angel Inn

Modern British NEW

Classic Yorkshire inn serious about food

☎ 01756 730263
BD23 6LT
e-mail: info@angelhetton.co.uk
dir: 6m N Skipton, follow B6265 towards Grassington, left at duck pond & again at T-junct. The Angel up the hill on right

The creeper-covered Angel was at the forefront of the food revolution that has taken place in British inns and pubs and it remains as dedicated as ever to satisfying diners with first-rate produce and careful, intelligent cooking. The series of inter-linked rooms includes the bar-brasserie, where the likes of Bolton Abbey mutton and Hetton ale pie are supported by both vegetarian and children's menus. The restaurant brings out the linen tablecloths and smartly upholstered chairs to create a refined but still unpretentious and relaxed space. The good value 'early bird' menu is deservedly popular, with its three choices at each course, while the full carte might start with ballottine of foie gras with Sauternes jelly, served with a toasted brioche. This is creative modern British cooking, based on well-sourced produce, such as a main-course wild sea bass fillet with braised fennel, red kale, crayfish tortellini and citrus foam. A wine cave is well worth exploring.

Chef Bruce Elsworth, Mark Taft **Owner** Juliet Watkins
Times 12-2.30/6-10 Closed 25 Dec & 1wk in Jan, L Mon-Sat, D Sun **Prices** Fixed D 3 course fr £18.95, Starter £6.25-£6.95, Main £12.95-£26.95, Dessert £6.50, Service optional **Wines** 172 bottles over £20, 4 bottles under £20, 26 by glass **Notes** Sunday L, Vegetarian available, Civ Wed 40 **Seats** 65 **Children** Portions, Menu **Parking** 40

KNARESBOROUGH Map 19 SE35

General Tarleton Inn

Modern British

Confident cooking in restored coaching inn

☎ 01423 340284
Boroughbridge Rd, Ferrensby HG5 0PZ
e-mail: gti@generaltarleton.co.uk
dir: A1(M) junct 48 at Boroughbridge, take A6055 to Knaresborough. 4m on right

This tastefully restored coaching inn on the outskirts of Harrogate is now a popular foodie destination in its own right. The original beamed ceilings and rustic walls are all present and correct, and duly complemented by upholstered high-backed chairs and subtle lighting to create an intimate atmosphere. The menu comes under the heading of 'food with Yorkshire roots' and local produce does indeed form the backbone of the daily-changing menus and specials. Start with Whitby crab spring rolls with mango and coriander salsa, then, perhaps, slow-braised shoulder of Dales lamb with crushed haricot beans, cracked coriander, confit garlic, lemon, parsley and mint. Comforting desserts include freshly baked plum tarte Tatin with vanilla ice cream or the signature sticky toffee pudding.

Chef John Topham **Owner** John & Claire Topham
Times 12-1.45/6-9.15 Closed 25 Dec, L Mon-Sat, D Sun, 26 Dec, 1 Jan **Prices** Fixed L 2 course £10.95, Starter £4.95-£9, Main £11.50-£19.50, Dessert £4.95-£6.95, Service optional, Groups min 6 service 10% **Wines** 70 bottles over £20, 9 bottles under £20, 11 by glass **Notes** Sunday L, Vegetarian available, Dress restrictions, Smart casual, Civ Wed 50 **Seats** 64, Pr/dining room 42 **Children** Portions, Menu **Parking** 40

MALTON Map 19 SE77

Burythorpe House Hotel

Modern European

Smart boutique hotel with appealing menu

☎ 01653 658200
Burythorpe YO17 9LB
e-mail: burythorpe.house@realyorkshirepubs.co.uk
dir: 4m S of Malton & 4m from A64 (York to Scarborough road)

This creeper-covered country house near to York has recently been on the receiving end of a smart refurbishment that has delivered lovely lounge areas to relax in and thumb through the pages of a magazine with an apéritif in hand. The oak-panelled Priory restaurant looks the part too, its romantic period style nicely updated with stripped floors and subtly-lit modern art as a backdrop to the kitchen's seasonally-driven output of full-flavoured modern ideas. Calves' liver and foie gras appear in a terrine served with apple and grape chutney, while pork is presented as braised shoulder, crisp-skinned belly and loin and comes with fondant potato and rich pan juices. To finish, a perfectly gooey chocolate fondant is pointed up by a tangy orange and Cointreau ice cream.

Times 7-9.30 Closed L all week

MASHAM **Map 19 SE28**

Samuel's at Swinton Park

– see below

Vennell's

Modern British

Electrifying cooking in a smart village restaurant

01765 689000
7 Silver St HG4 4DX
e-mail: info@vennellsrestaurant.co.uk
dir: 8m from A1 Masham exit

The aubergine-coloured frontage looks discreet enough, but make no mistake: Vennell's is a real gem. Smartly decorated within, with quality furniture and good artworks, the place inspires confidence. But then Jon Vennell is a confident chef, producing electrifying results from food that is nearly all sourced locally, including game from virtually on the back doorstep, all the way to fine Yorkshire farmhouse cheeses. The short menu is confined to four choices at each course, which is often a sound way of concentrating the effort and energy into truly memorable dishes. Start with seared mackerel with celeriac remoulade and sardine dressing, and follow with roasted roe deer, served with wilted spinach, cep risotto and a port jus. The asking price, particularly on weekdays, is remarkably modest for the quality, and nobody can say they aren't looked after when there's ginger pudding and gingerbread ice cream to round things off.

Chef Jon Vennell **Owner** Jon & Laura Vennell **Times** 12-2/7.15-mdnt Closed 26-29 Dec, 1-14 Jan, 1 wk Sep, BHs, Mon, L Tue-Sat, D Sun **Prices** Fixed L 3 course fr £19.95, Fixed D 3 course fr £25, Service optional **Wines** 54 bottles over £20, 18 bottles under £20, 8 by glass **Notes** Sunday L, Vegetarian available **Seats** 30 **Children** Portions **Parking** On street and in Market Sq

OLDSTEAD **Map 19 SE57**

The Black Swan at Oldstead

Modern British V

Impressive cooking in lovely country inn

01347 868387
YO61 4BL
e-mail: enquiries@blackswanoldstead.co.uk
web: www.blackswanoldstead.co.uk
dir: A1 junct 49, A168, A19 S (or from York A19 N), then Coxwold, Byland Abbey, Oldstead

After a day's hiking in the elemental landscapes of the North York Moors National Park, you couldn't hope for a better refuelling stop than this thoroughbred Yorkshire 16th-century inn. The Banks family have lived in the village of Oldstead for generations, and know what keeps

continued

Samuel's at Swinton Park

MASHAM **Map 19 SE28**

Modern British, French

Grandiose stately home with classic dining

01765 680900
Swinton HG4 4JH
e-mail: enquiries@swintonpark.com
dir: A1 take B6267, from Masham follow brown signs for Swinton Park

Swinton Park is virtually self-sufficient thanks to its 20,000-acre estate where game, lamb, beef and venison is reared, wild foods are foraged, and four acres of walled kitchen garden sort out the fruit, veg and herbs. The old house dates from the 17th century, with dollops of Regency and Victorian Gothic added on by the current owners' ancestors. The dining room is resplendent beneath its gold leaf ceiling, with oceans of space between linen-clad tables and views over the grounds through floor-to-ceiling windows. Chef Simon Crannage cooks in a classic French vein, sexed-up with modern British influences on a menu that follows the seasons, starting, perhaps, with foie gras pressed with truffle oil and served with Madeira jelly, hazelnuts and rosemary toast. Main courses continue the creative theme - honey-glazed breast and confit leg of duck is teamed with carrot purée, braised kohlrabi, soused cabbage, cumin fudge and red port jus. To end, pure indulgence comes in the form of praline and chocolate parfait, mousse and biscuit.

Chef Simon Crannage **Owner** Mr and Mrs Cunliffe-Lister **Times** 12.30-2/7-9.30 Closed L Mon-Tue (Only Castle menu in bar) **Prices** Fixed D 4 course £45-£55, Starter £6-£8.50, Main £8.95-£15.50, Dessert £4.95-£6.50, Service optional **Wines** 121 bottles over £20, 18 bottles under £20, 9 by glass **Notes** Tasting & signature menu available, Sunday L, Vegetarian available, Civ Wed 100 **Seats** 60, Pr/dining room 20 **Children** Portions, Menu **Parking** 80

OLDSTEAD *continued*

customers coming: a classic bar - all flagstoned floors, oak tables and chairs and a real fire - is the place to sink a pint; then head upstairs to the smart restaurant, where a Persian rug-strewn oak floor and antique tables and chairs make a classy setting. Ingredients from name-checked farms form the backbone of the menu, and are treated with a careful and confident hand to produce skilled modern British dishes. Hand-dived king scallops with sweetcorn purée, parsley essence and crispy pancetta might be followed by haunch of venison with red cabbage choucroute, fondant potato and star anise-spiced carrot purée. Leave room for a lemon and mascarpone cream with blackberry and fig salad and blackberry ice cream.

Chef Adam Jackson **Owner** The Banks family **Times** 12-2/6-9 Closed 2 wks Jan, L Mon-Wed **Prices** Tasting menu £49.95-£79.95, Starter £6-£12, Main £16-£22, Dessert £6-£8, Service optional **Wines** 54 bottles over £20, 22 bottles under £20, 19 by glass **Notes** Tasting menu 7 course (with wine £79.95), Sunday L, Vegetarian menu **Seats** 30, Pr/dining room 20 **Children** Portions, Menu **Parking** 25

PICKERING — Map 19 SE78

Fox & Hounds Country Inn

@ Modern British

Traditional country inn with imaginative cooking

☎ 01751 431577
Main St, Sinnington YO62 6SQ
e-mail: foxhoundsinn@easynet.co.uk
dir: In Sinnington centre, 3m W of Pickering, off A170

A traditional sandstone country inn in the ancient village of Sinnington in the North York Moors, The Fox & Hounds has a serious-yet-relaxed approach to eating and drinking that suits the pubby surroundings. Eat in the bar-lounge or the dining room and tuck into some British favourites alongside some more left-field dishes that reveal the ambitions in the kitchen. Good quality produce, some of it local, is used throughout. Start perhaps with smoked haddock roasted with pancetta (a happy partnership) with eggs florentine and a gruyère and spinach bake, moving onto trio of guinea fowl (confit leg, roasted breast, Pithiviers) with asparagus, orange and shallots, mushroom and tarragon roasted potatoes, then finish with lemon tart with raspberry coulis and clotted cream.

Times 12-2/6.30-9 Closed 25-26 Dec

The White Swan Inn

@ British V

Traditional market-town inn with well-judged menu

☎ 01751 472288
Market Place YO18 7AA
e-mail: welcome@white-swan.co.uk
dir: Just beyond junct of A169/A170 in Pickering, turn right off A170 into Market Place

Run with genuine enthusiasm by the Buchanan family for over 25 years, this 16th-century coaching inn stands at the heart of this charming market town below the North York Moors. Old-fashioned courtesy is the style in the intimate snug bar and elegant lounge, replete with deep, comfy sofas and blazing log fire. Using fresh Whitby fish, local meats, game and vegetables, cooking is simple, contemporary, but unpretentious - Yorkshire dishes given a modern twist. Take potted Whitby crab with celeriac remoulade, rack of Ryedale lamb with caper sauce, Holme Farm venison with wild mushrooms, and glazed lemon tart with mixed berry compôte, all served informally at unclothed tables in the cosy rear dining room, with its warm red painted walls, flagged floors and open fire.

Chef Darren Clemmit **Owner** The Buchanan family **Times** 12-2/6.45-9 **Prices** Starter £4.95-£11.25, Main £10.95-£19.95, Dessert £3.65-£10.95, Service optional **Wines** 61 bottles over £20, 16 bottles under £20, 11 by glass **Notes** Sunday L, Vegetarian menu, Civ Wed 50 **Seats** 50, Pr/dining room 18 **Children** Portions, Menu **Parking** 45

PICKHILL — Map 19 SE38

Nags Head Country Inn

@@ Modern British V

Charming countryside inn with great food, fine wines and real ales

☎ 01845 567391 & 567570
YO7 4JG
e-mail: reservations@nagsheadpickhill.co.uk
dir: 1m E of A1, 4m N of A1/A6 junct

One part of Edward and Janet Boynton's business is making sure that visitors are welcomed with a smile and waved off well fed from their 17th-century coaching inn in a tranquil village just off the A1 near Thirsk - the family have been at it for over 30 years, so you can expect Yorkshire hospitality at its warmest. Another strand of the Boynton portfolio is as a wine merchant, so you can be certain of a good glass or two to go with the kitchen's hearty and imaginative cooking. Settle into either the classic Tap Room bar, where a tie collection festoons the dark timbers, or the beamed and comfortably-furnished main restaurant. Local game and seafood turn up in gutsy, full-flavoured dishes, starting with pan-fried lamb's kidneys with shallots, mustard and brandy, ahead of leg of jugged hare with wild mushroom stuffing and pickled red cabbage.

Owner Edward & Janet Boynton **Times** 12-2/6-9.30 Closed 25 Dec **Prices** Food prices not confirmed for 2011. Please telephone for details. **Wines** 30 bottles under £20, 8 by glass **Notes** Sunday L, Vegetarian menu **Seats** 40, Pr/dining room 24 **Children** Portions **Parking** 50

RICHMOND — Map 19 NZ10

The Frenchgate Restaurant & Hotel

@@ Modern British

Cosy dining room in a Georgian hotel amid cobbled streets

☎ 01748 822087
59-61 Frenchgate DL10 7AE
e-mail: info@thefrenchgate.co.uk
web: www.thefrenchgate.co.uk
dir: From A1 Scotch Corner take A6108 to Richmond. After schools on left, straight over rdbt, past petrol station on left, through lights & 1st left into Lile Close

The Frenchgate is a classic Georgian townhouse in the cobbled tangle of old Richmond, brought stylishly up to date with a neat blend of contemporary elegance and period grandeur. With just seven tables, the restaurant certainly offers an intimate dining experience, while changing exhibitions of local artists' work sit well with an eclectic mix of bare oak tables on the original foot-wide floorboards - it's a welcoming place, where friendly service and sound cooking go hand-in-hand. Seasonal Yorkshire produce is a big part of the appeal too, put together along modern lines, as in a daily special starter bringing together pan-seared Scottish scallops with Pickering asparagus tips and purée, and Cumbrian air-dried ham. Main courses can get quite involved - a 'pot au feu' of squab pigeon delivers the bird's leg stuffed with light forcemeat in a consommé of pearl barley, with braised vegetables, a ravioli-style offal dumpling, and Jerusalem artichoke purée.

Times 12-2.30/7-9.30

SCARBOROUGH — Map 17 TA08

Best Western Ox Pasture Hall Country Hotel

@ Modern French

Inventive cooking amid landscaped splendour

☎ 01723 365295
Lady Edith's Dr, Raincliffe Woods YO12 5TD
e-mail: oxpasture.hall@btconnect.com
dir: A171, left onto Lady Edith's Drive, 1.5m, hotel on right

Set amid 17 acres of landscaped grounds only a couple of miles from the seaside at Scarborough, the stone-built Hall is a beguiling country bolt-hole. The beamed restaurant with its light walls and soft lighting is a well-run dining room offering some ambitious cooking. Deep-fried monkfish cheeks are hardly a run-of-the-mill starter, their tender batter and good home-made tartare dressing working well. A more classic main-course offering might be accurately cooked calves' liver with sage-scented mash and red wine sauce, while desserts may well be the high point, as when creamed rice pudding flavoured with mango and served in a martini glass with passionfruit sorbet ends things with an impressive flourish.

Times 12-2.45/6.30-10.15 Closed Sun-Mon

SCAWTON **Map 19 SE58**

The Hare Inn

Modern British

Hearty British food in traditional village inn

☎ 01845 597769
YO7 2HG
e-mail: info@thehareinn.co.uk
web: www.thehareinn.co.uk
dir: From A170 Sutton Bank take 1st left signed Rievaulx Abbey. Restaurant in 1.5m along road

Not far from the famous abbey, this charming 13th-century rural village inn in the Rievaulx Valley has all the low ceilings and doorways, log fires and real ales you would hope to find in such a traditional pub. The restaurant - done out with William Morris wallpaper, pine tables and church candles - is the perfect setting for simple, hearty British cooking that showcases local and seasonal produce. Lunch is as traditional as grilled Cumberland sausages and mash or a classic ploughman's, while the carte cranks up the ante to bring on roast fillet of cod with spinach, poached egg and hollandaise, or tender seared calves' liver. Warm treacle tart has well-made pastry and comes with local vanilla pod ice cream.

Chef Geoff Smith **Owner** Geoff & Jan Smith **Times** 12-2/6-9.30 Closed 4 days Feb, Mon, D Sun **Prices** Food prices not confirmed for 2011. Please telephone for details. **Wines** 15 bottles over £20, 10 bottles under £20, 10 by glass **Notes** Sunday L, Vegetarian available **Seats** 70, Pr/dining room 16 **Children** Portions **Parking** 12

See advert under Asenby

SKIPTON **Map 18 SD95**

The Bull at Broughton

Traditional British **NEW**

Terrific food in Yorkshire portions

☎ 01765 792065
Broughton BD23 3AE
e-mail: enquiries@bullatbroughton.com
dir: M65/A6068 (Vivary Way) for 1m, turn left onto A56 (Skipton Rd) for 7m, then right onto A59. Restaurant on right

Two Lancastrians, Nigel Haworth and Craig Bancroft of Northcote Manor (see entry) have taken over this Yorkshire gastro-pub near Skipton. Instead of re-igniting the Wars of the Roses, the venture has brokered a gastronomic entente cordiale between the combatant counties. There's good beer in The Bull, as well as a classic 21st-century look - cosy flagstones and oak panels for sure, but in clean-cut, freshly-decluttered rooms. The kitchen turns out good local food - look at the back of the menu: a map marks 27 suppliers who provide the raw materials for the Bull's skilfully-cooked, big-hearted modern pub grub, served in proper Yorkshire-sized portions. In a delicious starter, Yellinson goats' cheese comes with beetroot relish, a herb salad and crumpets slathered with melting butter. The best of the two counties is united in a hearty (Lancastrian) Goosnargh duck pie teamed with slow-cooked Yorkshire rhubarb, chunky chips and duck gravy.

Chef Richard Upton **Owner** Craig Bancroft & Nigel Haworth **Times** 12-2/6-9 Closed 25 Dec **Prices** Starter £3.50-£8.50, Main £8.50-£21, Dessert £3.50-£5.50, Service optional **Wines** 24 bottles over £20, 18 bottles under £20, 12 by glass **Notes** Sunday L, Vegetarian available **Children** Portions, Menu

SUTTON-ON-THE-FOREST **Map 19 SE56**

The Blackwell Ox Inn

British

Cosmopolitan dining in a picturesque North Yorkshire village

☎ 01347 810328
Huby Rd YO61 1DT
e-mail: enquiries@blackwelloxinn.co.uk
dir: Off A1237, onto B1363 to Sutton-on-the-Forest. Left at T-junct, 50yds on right

You only need to drive a short distance out of York to find this charming inn in the heart of the pretty village of Sutton-on-the-Forest. It was built in the 1820s and takes its name from a famous Shorthorn Teeswater ox which stood six foot tall and was butchered in 1779. As well as five individually designed bedrooms and a traditional bar, there's a country-style restaurant serving up mostly French-accented food with a few international influences. The menu changes daily and might offer confit duck leg and trompette mushroom pressing with orange jelly to start with, followed, perhaps, by fillet of sea bream with sweet chilli bok choy, surf clams and pickled wild mushrooms.

Chef Thomas Kingston **Owner** Blackwell Ox Inns (York) Ltd **Times** 12-2/6-9.30 Closed 25 Dec, 1 Jan, D Sun **Prices** Food prices not confirmed for 2011. Please telephone for details. **Wines** 36 bottles over £20, 32 bottles under £20, 20 by glass **Notes** Sunday L, Vegetarian available **Seats** 50, Pr/dining room 20 **Children** Portions, Menu **Parking** 19

Rose & Crown

Modern British

Locally-based food in a charming Yorkshire pub

☎ 01347 811333
Main St YO61 1DP
e-mail: ben@rosecrown.co.uk
web: www.rosecrown.co.uk
dir: 8m N of York towards Helmsley on B1363

A textbook charming country inn in a village just outside York, the 200-year-old Rose & Crown is all rustic appeal. Enter to the left to find the spacious dining area, where an endearing jumble of furniture, an oak floor and open fires provide the kind of ambience that encourages relaxation. The cooking is firmly based on local supplies, seen in dishes such as Yorkshire beef carpaccio with truffled potato salad, parmesan and pesto, chicken breast on the bone with bok choy, creamy mash, wild mushrooms and red wine jus, and properly rich sticky toffee pudding with fudge ice cream and butterscotch sauce.

Chef Russell Johnson **Owner** Ben & Lucy Williams **Times** 12-2/6-9.30 Closed 1st wk Jan, Mon, D Sun **Prices** Fixed L 2 course fr £14.95, Fixed D 3 course fr £19.95, Starter £4.50-£7.95, Main £10.50-£16.95, Dessert £5.95-£6.50, Service optional **Wines** 50 bottles over £20, 20 bottles under £20, 12 by glass **Notes** Early bird 2 course & glass wine £14.95, Sunday L, Vegetarian available, Civ Wed 80 **Seats** 80 **Children** Portions **Parking** 12

THIRSK Map 19 SE48

Carlton Bore at Carlton Husthwaite

Modern British NEW

Country pub serious about good food

01845 501265
Main St, Carlton Husthwaite YO7 2BW
e-mail: chefhessel@aol.com

From the team that run the Old Bore in Rishworth (see entry), comes another bore, this one in a splendid village a few miles south of Thirsk. The red-brick inn is geared up for dining, which is not surprising given the pedigree of owner Scott Hessel as a Roux scholarship winner. Set on the main road through the village, there is a decidedly country feel to the place, with a quirky character embodied by four boars' heads on the wall, each given the name of a celebrity chef (Gordon, Jamie, Delia and Rick). Uncomplicated but not uninteresting food comes in generous Yorkshire portions, so a risotto is flavoured with roast pumpkin and Yorkshire blue cheese, and roast wild duck gets a traditional treatment with honey-roast vegetables, bread sauce and game chips. Service is polished.

Chef Zoë Moore **Owner** Scott Hessel **Times** 12-2.15/6-9.30 Closed 3-21 Jan, Mon-Tue **Prices** Starter £4.75-£5.95, Main £8.95-£19.95, Dessert £4.75-£5.95 **Wines** 8 bottles over £20, 18 bottles under £20 **Notes** Sunday L, Vegetarian available **Seats** 100, Pr/dining room 14 **Children** Portions, Menu

WEST WITTON Map 19 SE08

The Wensleydale Heifer

Modern British, seafood V

Top-notch seafood in the heart of the Yorkshire Dales

01969 622322
Main St DL8 4LS
e-mail: info@wensleydaleheifer.co.uk
dir: On A684 (3m W of Leyburn)

Landlocked in the middle of cow-freckled Yorkshire Dales country is perhaps an unexpected place to find a top-class fish specialist. But the Heifer has a maverick spirit that injects this 17th-century coaching inn with a healthy streak of eccentricity. Chef-proprietor David Moss moved up the road from the Crab and Lobster in Asenby (see entry) to set up a buzzy operation here comprising a rather classy restaurant with smart chocolate leather chairs, linen-clothed tables and Doug Hyde artwork, and a more casual fish bar with seagrass matting, rattan chairs and pale wood tables; pictures of seafaring cows add to the heifer theme. The kitchen team has serious intent in its modern British approach to seafood. On the à la carte you might find prawn cocktail with Jack Daniel's Marie Rose sauce, classic lobster thermidor, an Asian-influenced sweet chilli sea bass with crab and prawn stuffing, and a trip to the sunny Med, in the shape of steamed mussels and clams with white wine, garlic and cream.

Chef David Moss **Owner** David & Lewis Moss **Times** 12-2.30/6-9.30 **Prices** Fixed L 2 course £16.75, Fixed D 3 course £19.50, Starter £5.50-£11.50, Main £13.50-£21, Dessert £5.50-£8.50, Service added but optional 10% **Wines** 68 bottles over £20, 23 bottles under £20, 14 by glass **Notes** Sunday L, Vegetarian menu **Seats** 70 **Children** Portions, Menu **Parking** 30

WHITBY Map 19 NZ81

The Cliffemount Hotel

British NEW

Flavour-driven British cuisine in modern clifftop hotel

01947 840103
Bank Top Ln, Runswick Bay TS13 5HU
e-mail: info@cliffemounthotel.co.uk
dir: Exit A174, 8m N of Whitby, 1m to end

Boredom is an unknown concept at this newly-refurbished modern hotel on the cliffs above Runswick Bay: you could beachcomb for fossils down on the beach, the expanses of the North York Moors are on the doorstep, and Dracula fans can sink their teeth into nearby Whitby. The restaurant shares the same clean-cut modern look as the rest of the hotel, and its clifftop perch means an unforgettable panorama of the sea as a backdrop to skilled modern British cooking. Regular hauls from local boats and produce from moorland farms drive the kitchen's work - both meat and fish might end up home-smoked or cured, and bread is baked fresh daily. The specials board tells you what has been landed that day - a seafood special is a good starter, combining a classic fish soup with crab mayonnaise, fishcake and smoked sea trout. Main-course sage and parmesan-crumbed pork loin with a cassoulet of tomato, chorizo and haricot beans might catch the carnivore's eye.

Chef David Spencer **Owner** Ian & Carol Rae **Prices** Starter £5.75-£9.95, Main £16.50-£26.50, Dessert £6.50, Service optional **Notes** Sunday L, Vegetarian available **Seats** 50 **Children** Portions

Dunsley Hall

Modern, Traditional V

Enticing cooking on the Yorkshire coast

01947 893437
Dunsley YO21 3TL
e-mail: reception@dunsleyhall.com
dir: 3.5m from Whitby off A171(Teeside road)

If you were a Victorian shipping magnate with a blank cheque to create your dream home, what would you want? First, a stunning location perched above the North Yorkshire coast, maybe; next, build a mansion imposing enough that there's no argument about your status. And finally, furnish it with the height of (Victorian) taste - oak panelling and plasterwork ceilings that say you're a man of substance. That's Dunsley Hall - except for the tasteful updates in décor and facilities to pander to modern sensibilities. Knowledgeable, self-assured staff help too, and a kitchen team with its feet on the ground, top-class Yorkshire produce in the larder, and the sound technical skills to turn it into well-balanced modern dishes. Take seared hand-dived scallops with glazed pork belly, shallot purée with vanilla and air-dried ham to start, and follow with Whitby pollock with saffron mash, sun-blushed tomato and basil risotto, steamed mussels and prawn cream chervil sauce.

Chef Graham Hughes **Owner** Mr & Mrs W Ward **Times** 12-2/7.30-9.30 **Prices** Food prices not confirmed for 2011. Please telephone for details. **Wines** 10 bottles over £20, 10 bottles under £20, 10 by glass **Notes** Sunday L, Vegetarian menu, Dress restrictions, Smart casual, no jeans or shorts, Civ Wed 100 **Seats** 85, Pr/dining room 30 **Children** Portions, Menu **Parking** 30

Estbek House

Modern British NOTABLE WINE LIST

Pretty Yorkshire coastal setting for fresh seafood

01947 893424
East Row, Sandsend YO21 3SU
e-mail: info@estbekhouse.co.uk
dir: From Whitby follow A174 towards Sandsend. Estbek House just before bridge

In an appealing coastal village near Whitby, the Georgian house was once the headquarters of the local alum-mining industry, which constitutes some sort of USP. Creatively refitted as a country hotel, it retains a cosy domestic feel, with a wood floor and simple table settings in the dining room. The daily-changing menu is big on fish and seafood, as befits the location, with starters embracing crab and brown shrimp ravioli, griddled prawns, and kipper pâté with melba toast. Fresh fish, served with a choice of accompaniments that are intended not to interfere with your simple enjoyment of the principal components, are the backbone of the main-course choice, but there are also classics like lobster Thermidor, and meats such as beef fillet glazed with Shiraz. Finish with rhubarb and ginger trifle.

Times 6-9

See advert opposite

YARM Map 19 NZ41

Judges Country House Hotel

– ***see opposite page***

Judges Country House Hotel

YARM **Map 19 NZ41**

Modern British NOTABLE WINE LIST

Aspirational and inspirational cooking in charming hotel

☎ 01642 789000
Kirklevington TS15 9LW
e-mail: enquiries@judgeshotel.co.uk
dir: 1.5m from junct W A19, take A67 towards Kirklevington, hotel 1.5m on left

Set back from the twisting road, this grand Victorian country-house hotel is highly regarded in North Yorkshire and for good reason. A sense of tranquillity infuses the well-tended 22 acres of landscaped gardens with a stream running through them - ideal for a pre- or post-prandial stroll. Judges takes its name from the period in the 1970s when judges on circuit to Middlesbrough courts used it as a residency, but it was originally built in 1881 for the Richardson's of Hartlepool and has only been a privately owned hotel since 1994. The sense of history is maintained inside through traditional fixtures and fittings and a delightful bar. The service throughout is attentive and staff genuinely care about looking after their guests. It's the food that's the big draw though. The kitchen brigade, led by John Schwarz, is passionate about the finer details so expect top-notch ingredients, skilful pairings and impressive presentation. Served in the conservatory restaurant to make the most of the views across the grounds, things might begin with a perfectly cooked risotto with superb ceps, white asparagus and summer truffle. Follow that with wild turbot, served with Morteau sausage and a seafood chowder containing spectacular mussels, scallop and clams. For dessert, an adventurous passion for pineapple brings forth a pineapple cocktail, ravioli and frozen soufflé. The wine list showcases a good selection of quality bins.

Chef John Schwarz **Owner** Mr M Downs
Times 12-2/7-9.30 **Prices** Fixed L 2 course £17.50, Fixed D 3 course £32.50, Starter £8.95-£14.95, Main £28.50-£36.50, Dessert £8.95, Service optional **Wines** 117 bottles over £20, 45 bottles under £20, 12 by glass **Notes** Early bird menu available, Sunday L, Vegetarian available, Dress restrictions, Jacket & tie preferred, No jeans or trainers, Civ Wed 200 **Seats** 60, Pr/dining room 50 **Children** Portions, Menu **Parking** 110

YORK Map 16 SE65

D.C.H at the Dean Court Hotel

Modern European

High quality ingredients and stunning views of York Minster

01904 625082
Duncombe Place YO1 7EF
e-mail: sales@deancourt-york.co.uk
dir: City centre, directly opposite York Minster

Built in the 1850s to house the clergy at York Minster, D.C.H enjoys unrivalled views of the said landmark - if you're not lucky enough to bag a table with a view you can still get a sense of history every time the bells chime. There's formal table service in the modern dining room which features digital wallpaper with enlarged photos of, yup, you've guessed it, the minster and its carvings and impressive stone features. It's worth putting aside the view for long enough to concentrate on the food though as it hits the spot with its modern British-European style. Good quality ingredients shine through in retro classics such as smoked salmon terrine served with a red pepper sauce, herb and pepper salad or a main of roast loin of Fountains Abbey Farm venison with creamed potato, caramelised red cabbage and honey-roast root vegetables. Iced Armagnac parfait finishes things off nicely.

Chef Jamie Cann **Owner** Mr B A Cleminson **Times** 12.30-2/7-9.30 Closed L 31 Dec, D 25 Dec **Prices** Food prices not confirmed for 2011. Please telephone for details. **Wines** 112 bottles over £20, 17 bottles under £20, 15 by glass **Notes** Vegetarian available, Dress restrictions, No T-Shirts, Civ Wed 50 **Seats** 60, Pr/dining room 40 **Children** Portions, Menu **Parking** Pay & display car park nearby

Hotel du Vin York

European, French

Luxury bistro with exciting food and wine to match

01904 557350
89 The Mount YO24 1AX
e-mail: info.york@hotelduvin.com
dir: A1036 towards city centre, 6m. Hotel on right through lights

In typical Hotel du Vin style, creating stylish boutique hotels in characterful old buildings, the York outpost occupies a beautiful Grade II listed early 19th-century property close to the city centre. It's a dynamic place with a vibrant contemporary bistro - all bare wood, chocolate leather chairs, French-style prints and wine memorabilia. Clued-up staff are happy to recommend from an outstanding wine list, and a menu of simple classic dishes delivers the likes of smoked haddock chowder to start, then perhaps confit duck leg with Puy lentils, or halibut with butter bean ragoût and rosemary sauce, finishing with a crème brûlée.

Chef Nico Cecchella **Owner** MWB **Times** 12-2.30/6.30-10.30 **Prices** Food prices not confirmed for 2011. Please telephone for details. **Wines** 21 bottles over £20, 18 by glass **Notes** Sunday L, Vegetarian available **Seats** 80, Pr/dining room 24 **Children** Portions, Menu **Parking** 18

The Ivy

Modern

Classy brasserie close to York Minster

01904 644744
The Grange Hotel, 1 Clifton YO30 6AA
e-mail: info@grangehotel.co.uk
dir: A19 (York/Thirsk road), approx 400yds from city centre

Ideally located for exploring the city, this bustling Regency town house is just a few minutes' walk from the centre and a brief stroll from the Minster. A handsome porticoed construction, it was built in the 1830s for a lucky local clergyman. The hotel's Ivy brasserie offers ambitious, creative cooking in a lavishly decorated room with painted murals, deep red fabric wall coverings and modern furniture and contemporary art on the walls. The innovative food is well presented and makes good use of local and seasonal produce, as in a starter of ham hock with fried egg and hazelnut and apple salad. Follow on with an open lasagne of pickled wild mushrooms, confit garlic purée and mascarpone chive cream, and end with a coconut tart, as pretty as a picture, with Thai rice pudding, mango and chilli salsa.

Chef Andrew Birch **Owner** Jeremy & Vivien Cassel **Times** 12-2/6.30-10.30 **Prices** Fixed L 2 course £13.50-£15.50, Tasting menu fr £54.95, Starter £5.75-£8.95, Main £12.95-£18.75, Dessert £5.85-£7.75, Service added but optional 10% **Wines** 23 bottles over £20, 20 bottles under £20, 8 by glass **Notes** Tasting menu 8 course, Sunday L, Vegetarian available, Civ Wed 60 **Seats** 60, Pr/dining room 60 **Children** Portions, Menu **Parking** 26

Melton's

Modern European

Bustling bistro with appealing modern European menu

01904 634341
7 Scarcroft Rd YO23 1ND
e-mail: greatfood@meltonsrestaurant.co.uk
web: www.meltonsrestaurant.co.uk
dir: South from centre across Skeldergate Bridge, restaurant opposite Bishopthorpe Road car park

A stalwart of the York dining scene for two decades, Melton's continues to operate at a high standard to keep packing in a strong local following. The Victorian terraced venue looks smart in the mode of a French neighbourhood bistro, and shares the same sort of buzzy vibe inside: tables and floors are bare wood, and walls are covered with mirrors and large murals of the chef playing to his audience. The cooking takes an unfussy modern European line and is strong on local sourcing: buckwheat blini with beetroot and crème fraîche is a simple combination that works well, while a rustic dish of confit pork belly with smoked oil dressing, butternut squash and pease pudding provides hearty comfort. Cheerful, relaxed service is the icing on the cake.

Chef Michael Hjort **Owner** Michael & Lucy Hjort **Times** 12-2/5.30-10 Closed 23 Dec-9 Jan, Sun-Mon **Prices** Starter £6.30-£8.80, Main £14-£18.50, Dessert £5.80-£6.90, Service optional **Wines** 85 bottles over £20, 20 bottles under £20, 6 by glass **Notes** Pre-theatre D, early evening 2 course £19, 3 course £22.50, Vegetarian available **Seats** 30, Pr/dining room 16 **Children** Portions **Parking** Car park opposite

Middlethorpe Hall & Spa

Modern British

Classical cooking in elegant country house

☎ 01904 641241
Bishopthorpe Rd, Middlethorpe YO23 2GB
e-mail: info@middlethorpe.com
dir: A64 exit York West. Follow signs Middlethorpe & racecourse

Homes don't come much more stately than Middlethorpe Hall, a handsome William and Mary country house just a short canter away from York racecourse. Perhaps the ultimate accolade for its splendour is that it became part of the National Trust in 2008 - but that's not to say Middlethorpe is a museum preserved in aspic - this is a grand hotel complete with a 21st-century luxury spa, and a restaurant that aims high and moves with the times. The elegant, candlelit, oak-panelled dining room fits the bill for accomplished cooking, as seen in a starter of roast pumpkin risotto with ceps, Madeira jelly and chive mascarpone. Main courses dip into Yorkshire's seasonal larder for roast loin of venison with parsnip purée, poached pear, red cabbage, fondant potato and bitter chocolate sauce.

Chef Nicholas Evans **Owner** The National Trust **Times** 12.30-2/7-9.45 **Prices** Starter £9.50-£15.50, Main £16.50-£24.50, Dessert £7.50-£12.50, Service included **Wines** 221 bottles over £20, 17 bottles under £20, 9 by glass **Notes** Gourmet 6 course menu £65, Sunday L, Vegetarian available, Dress restrictions, Smart, no trainers, tracksuits or shorts, Civ Wed 56 **Seats** 60, Pr/dining room 56 **Children** Portions **Parking** 70

One 19 The Mount

British

Elegant dining in a popular hotel

☎ 01904 619444
Mount Royale, The Mount YO24 1GU
e-mail: info@mountroyale.co.uk
dir: W on B1036, towards racecourse

Part of the classy Mount Royale hotel, this airy contemporary restaurant mixes the period elegance of a Regency townhouse with a smart modern look involving claret-hued walls and high-backed seats, unclothed darkwood tables and chequerboard floors. It sits in a quiet spot away from the hurly burly of the town centre, and has soothing views of lovely gardens to go with an imaginative menu of Mediterranean-accented ideas made with top-drawer British materials. The kitchen keeps things simple to let natural flavours shine – try the chicken liver pâté, flavoured with garlic, brandy and thyme and served with red onion marmalade, and follow with medallions of pork fillet in Calvados sauce with caramelised apples.

Times 12-2.30/6-9.30 Closed 1-6 Jan, Sun

The Piano Restaurant

Modern British

Mansion house hotel with creative kitchen team

☎ 01904 644456
The Churchill Hotel, 65 Bootham YO30 7DQ
e-mail: info@churchillhotel.com
web: www.churchillhotel.com
dir: Along Bootham from York Minster, hotel on right

A late-Georgian mansion house, the Churchill Hotel plays homage to the Great British Prime Minister, although don't go thinking it is stuck in the past. The majestic staircase hung with portraits may be reminiscent of Number 10, but much of the hotel has a more contemporary look and feel, including the Piano Bar, with its mood lighting and fashionable colours. The dining room has the fine proportions and huge windows the Georgians are famous for and the accompanying pianist on the baby grand adds to the sense of occasion. The food is ostensibly modern British, inasmuch as it is based on good British ingredients and inspiration is drawn from the UK and classical European preparations. Rillettes of wild rabbit, for example, is wrapped in Parma ham and comes with pea mousse in an attractively presented first course, and main-course rump of Yorkshire lamb is roasted and served with aubergine cannelloni, sautéed sweet potatoes, pancetta and pine nuts.

Times 11-2.30/6-9.30

YORKSHIRE, SOUTH

CHAPELTOWN — Map 16 SK39

Greenhead House

European

Accomplished, seasonal cooking in country-style restaurant

☎ 0114 246 9004
84 Burncross Rd S35 1SF
dir: 1m from M1 junct 35

In the distinctly suburban outpost of Sheffield that is Chapeltown, this 300-year old house has a homely elegance. Comfort can be found in the cosy lounge with quirky knitted cushions and warming fireplace or, if the sun's out, in the pretty walled garden. There's a strong Mediterranean influence on the menu, the dishes put together with a degree of finesse. Start, perhaps, with a classic tartiflette, or a chicken and morel terrine, then move on to sautéed fillet steak with shallots, red wine and Dijon mustard sauce, and for dessert, try an authentic baked amaretti and caramel custard, flavoured with Marsala.

Chef Neil Allen **Owner** Mr & Mrs N Allen **Times** 12-1/7-9 Closed Xmas-New Year, 2wks Etr, 2wks Aug, Sun-Tue, L Wed, Thu & Sat **Prices** Fixed L 3 course £20-£24, Fixed D 4 course £41-£45.50, Service included **Wines** 30 bottles over £20, 13 bottles under £20, 20 by glass **Notes** Vegetarian available **Seats** 32 **Children** Portions **Parking** 10

ROSSINGTON — Map 16 SK69

Best Western Premier Mount Pleasant Hotel

Modern British

Sound country-house cooking in tip-top hotel

☎ 01302 868696 & 868219
Great North Rd, Rossington DN11 0HW
e-mail: reception@mountpleasant.co.uk
dir: S of Doncaster, adjacent to Robin Hood Airport, on A638 between Bawtry & Doncaster

This charming 18th century country-house hotel is set in 100 acres of picturesque woodland. It is a grand old house with an interior designed for comfort (sink into a leather chair in the cosy lounge) and set up with the full range of conference and leisure facilities. The Garden Restaurant is a formally-dressed room, providing the full country-house comforts, and delivering a traditional menu of well-judged dishes. Start with the contemporary combination of seared scallops with honey-spiced belly of pork and a white onion purée, moving onto rack of lamb with pistachio crust and artichoke purée. Finish in the comfort zone with a hot blackberry roly-poly.

Chef Dave Booker **Owner** Richard McIlroy **Times** 12-2/6.45-9.30 Closed 25 Dec **Prices** Starter £6.50-£8.95, Main £15.50-£24.95, Dessert £6.95, Service included **Wines** 38 bottles over £20, 15 bottles under £20, 7 by glass **Notes** Sunday L, Vegetarian available, Dress restrictions, Smart casual preferred, Civ Wed 150 **Seats** 72, Pr/dining room 200 **Children** Portions, Menu **Parking** 140

SHEFFIELD **Map 16 SK38**

Copthorne Hotel Sheffield

Modern British NEW

Ambitious contemporary cuisine in a modern urban hotel

☎ 0114 252 5480
Sheffield United Football Club, Bramhall Ln S2 4SU
e-mail: orla.watt@millenniumhotels.co.uk
dir: M1 junct 33, A57 Sheffield, A61 Chesterfield Rd, follow brown tourist signs for Bramall Lane

Tucked into a quiet corner of Sheffield United's football ground, the 1855 Restaurant is a stylish affair in the contemporary idiom and steers clear of any football clichés. Expect plenty of darkwood, neutral earthy tones of mushroom and stone and soft lighting, and a modern British menu to match. The restaurant is building a strong local following for the consistently interesting combinations and impressive depth of flavour that the kitchen teases out of top-notch local produce. Among starters might be a salad of pan-fried monkfish cheeks and smoked eel with roasted pear and a honey and dill dressing; a main-course grilled fillet of sea bass is served with leek and mussel risotto, braised fennel and saffron-vanilla sauce. A baked walnut and date pudding with brandy syrup and honey and cinnamon ice cream wraps things up nicely.

Chef Ernst Van Zyl **Owner** Millennium Copthorne Group **Times** 12-2/5.30-10 Closed 24 Dec-4 Jan **Prices** Starter £5.25-£7.95, Main £8.95-£17, Dessert £5.75-£6.95, Service optional **Wines** 25 bottles over £20, 10 bottles under £20, 9 by glass **Notes** Sunday L, Vegetarian available **Seats** 100 **Children** Portions, Menu **Parking** 225

Nonnas

Modern Italian V NOTABLE WINE LIST

Italian mini-chain offering authentic cooking

☎ 0114 268 6166
535-41 Ecclesall Rd S11 8PR
e-mail: info@nonnas.co.uk
dir: Large red building on Ecclesall Rd

A proper Italian café-bar with high stool seating looking on to the street, and a constant lively bustle, Nonna's is a life-affirming place to stop and sip espresso, as well as to eat good Italian home cooking. Many of the ingredients are imported, and help to give edge to dishes such as bollito misto served as a terrine with tricolore dressings. Accurately cooked chicken breast is full of flavour, helped on by garlic and rosemary gnocchi and wild mushroom cream. You might be surprised to find a steamed sponge pudding among desserts, but flavour it with orange and cloves and serve it with bayleaf custard, and it becomes an altogether different proposition. An almost entirely Italian wine list is only fitting.

Chef Jamie Taylor **Owner** Gian Bohian, Maurizio Mori **Times** 12-3.30/5-9.45 Closed 25 Dec, 1 Jan **Prices** Fixed L 2 course £15, Fixed D 3 course £24.95, Starter £4.95-£6.95, Main £8.95-£17.95, Dessert £3.95-£5.95, Service optional, Groups min 6 service 10% **Wines** 80 bottles over £20, 20 bottles under £20, 18 by glass **Notes** Pre-theatre menu available, Sunday L, Vegetarian menu **Seats** 75, Pr/dining room 32 **Children** Portions, Menu **Parking** On street

Rafters Restaurant

Modern European

Modern cuisine in a relaxed neighbourhood venue

☎ 0114 230 4819
220 Oakbrook Rd, Nethergreen S11 7ED
e-mail: marcus.lane@tiscali.co.uk
dir: 5 mins from Ecclesall road, Hunters Bar rdbt

The eponymous woodwork that gives this neighbourhood restaurant its name is a venerable set of oak beams dating from the time of the Battle of Waterloo. Perched above a corner shop in a leafy suburb of Sheffield, Rafters goes for a comforting rustic look - exposed brickwork, hand-blown Italian glass lamps - and a cooking style that sends out plates of bold modern British flavours with plenty of international pizzazz. Roast butternut squash soup with crisp slow-roasted belly pork sets out in a hearty way, ahead of pan-fried Angus beef fillet with roast sweet potatoes, crisp pancetta and béarnaise sauce. They like their puddings in Yorkshire, and the bread-and-butter pudding with dried winter fruits, butterscotch sauce and vanilla ice cream is a cracking example.

Chef Marcus Lane **Owner** Marcus Lane **Times** 7-10 Closed 25-26 Dec, 1wk Jan, 2 wks Aug, Sun, Tue, L all week **Prices** Fixed D 3 course fr £36, Service optional, Groups min 8 service 10% **Wines** 20 bottles over £20, 25 bottles under £20, 7 by glass **Notes** Fixed D 2 course with glass wine available Mon,Wed,Thu, Sunday L, Vegetarian available, Dress restrictions, Smart casual, no jeans **Seats** 38 **Children** Portions **Parking** 15

Sheffield Park Hotel

Modern, Traditional

Modern brasserie dishes in an efficiently run hotel

☎ 0114 282 9988
Chesterfield Road South S8 8BW
e-mail: info.sheffield@pedersenhotels.com
dir: From N: M1 junct 33, A630 Sheffield. A61 Chesterfield. After Graves Tennis Centre follow A6/Chesterfield/M1 South signs. Hotel 200yds on left

A member of the Pedersen hotel group, the Sheffield Park is a chic modern establishment a little to the south of the city. The atmosphere in the restaurant is that of a buzzy city brasserie with efficient service and classic modern dishes. Start with pancetta, chestnut and cranberry tart with cranberry vinaigrette, and move on to a pasta or risotto dish, or chargrilled tuna with braised chicory in pink grapefruit dressing, before rounding things off in homely style with ginger parkin and caramel ice cream, or perhaps a trio of Yorkshire cheeses served with chutney.

Chef Paul Thompson **Owner** Park Hotel (Sheffield) Ltd **Times** 12.30-2/6.30-9.45 Closed L Sat **Prices** Fixed D 3 course £17.95, Starter £4.95-£9.50, Main £9.95-£17.50, Dessert £4.95-£5.50, Service included **Wines** 12 bottles over £20, 31 bottles under £20, 13 by glass **Notes** Sunday L, Vegetarian available, Civ Wed 475 **Seats** 140, Pr/dining room 280 **Children** Portions, Menu **Parking** 260

Staindrop Lodge Hotel

Modern British

Art-deco style brasserie in a smart hotel

☎ 0114 284 3111
Lane End, Chapeltown S35 3UH
e-mail: info@staindroplodge.co.uk
dir: M1 junct 35, take A629 for 1m, straight over 1st rdbt, right at 2nd rdbt, hotel approx 0.5m on right

Staindrop Lodge sits in lovely gardens in a spot that is perfect both for doing business in Sheffield or striding out into the Peak District. The lodge has its origins in the early 19th century, but is much extended and brought smartly up to date. Served in a sharp-looking split-level brasserie inspired by the clean lines of art-deco style, the cooking takes a suitably modern route, using soundly-sourced local produce in a wide-ranging globally-influenced repertoire. Hearty fare such as a pie of the day, sausages and mash, or steaks from the grill sit alongside roast partridge with baked butternut squash and wild mushroom and shallot jus. Desserts are homespun classics like warm Yorkshire parkin with toffee sauce.

Times 12-9.30

Whitley Hall Hotel

Modern British

Seasonal local produce in a 16th-century country house

☎ 0114 245 4444
Elliott Ln, Grenoside S35 8NR
e-mail: reservations@whitleyhall.com
dir: A61 past football ground, then 2m, right just before Norfolk Arms, left at bottom of hill. Hotel on left

Expect high levels of comfort at this 16th-century ivy-clad hotel, which stands in 20 acres of landscaped grounds with lakes and immaculate gardens. The comfortable oak-panelled restaurant serves up a menu of traditional and contemporary dishes utilising the best of local produce from South Yorkshire, all thoroughly in tune with the seasons. The enthusiastic young kitchen team create imaginative and flavoursome food (Sunday lunch is particularly popular). From the à la carte, choose ham hock and apricot terrine with shallot jam to start, move on to seared Shetland salmon with shrimp bisque, and leave room for iced peanut butter parfait with banana ice cream and ginger sablé.

Times 12-2/7-9.30 Closed D 25-26 Dec,1 Jan

WORTLEY **Map 16 SK39**

Montagu's at the Wortley Arms

◎◎ Modern British

Intimate restaurant serving imaginative modern food

☎ 0114 288 8749
Halifax Rd S35 7DB
e-mail: thewortleyarms@aol.com
dir: M1 junct 36. Follow Sheffield North signs, right at Tankersley garage, 1m on right

While this renovated traditional village inn on the Wharncliffe Estate serves carefully prepared, informal meals daily (nothing so unusual there), its fine-dining Montagu's restaurant upstairs really ups the ante. Bookings are essential at Montagu's though, as there are just 40 covers in this formally set, upmarket venue. The skilful kitchen's modern approach shows flair and innovation, and takes its cue from prime local produce on a fixed-price, three-course menu. So expect stylishly presented dishes such as scallops with chorizo, cauliflower purée and port reduction to start, perhaps an iced lemon parfait with tequila sorbet to finish, and in-between, rack of lamb with ratatouille and pesto, or sea bass with braised baby fennel and red wine shallot.

Chef Andy Gabbitas **Owner** Andy Gabbitas **Times** 7-9 Closed Mon, L Tue-Sat, D Sun **Prices** Food prices not confirmed for 2011. Please telephone for details. **Wines** 34 bottles over £20, 19 bottles under £20, 7 by glass **Notes** Sunday L, Vegetarian available **Seats** 40, Pr/dining room 10 **Children** Portions **Parking** 30

YORKSHIRE, WEST

CLIFTON **Map 16 SE12**

Black Horse Inn Restaurant with Rooms

◎ British, Mediterranean

Welcoming Yorkshire village inn with hearty modern cooking

☎ 01484 713862
HD6 4HJ
e-mail: mail@blackhorseclifton.co.uk
dir: M62 junct 25, Brighouse, follow signs

Dating from the 17th century, the Black Horse has resisted the gastro trend in favour of a more traditional pubby vibe. A real fire and - more importantly - real ales from Yorkshire stalwarts Timothy Taylor and Black Sheep make a good impression in the beamed bar - eat here for a more casual experience, or go for the smart restaurant kitted out with leather chairs and linen-clad tables. On a summer's day, the courtyard makes an inviting spot too. Wherever you choose, the food is locally sourced, unfussy modern British stuff sprinkled with Mediterranean sunshine - warm black pudding and bacon salad with rocket and grain mustard dressing sits alongside pan-fried scallops with spiced prunes and crispy pig's ear. Mains can be as traditional as roast beef with all the trimmings, or as modern as noisettes of Swaledale lamb with spiced chick pea and carrot cassoulet and coriander foam.

Times 12-3/5.30-9.30 Closed 25-26 Dec

See advert on page 456

HALIFAX **Map 19 SE02**

Holdsworth House Hotel

◎◎ Modern British

Grand Yorkshire manor house with extensive menu

☎ 01422 240024
Holdsworth HX2 9TG
e-mail: info@holdsworthhouse.co.uk
dir: From Halifax take A629 (Keighley road), in 2m right at garage to Holmfield, hotel 1.5m on right

A stately greystone Jacobean manor in the moors to the north of Halifax, Holdsworth House is a grand country-house hotel with all the trimmings. Lovely, secluded gardens shut out prying eyes - this is perhaps why so many celebrities have passed through, particularly during the '60s when Cliff, Cilla and the Fab Four all stayed. They would still recognise the period features - low, beamed ceilings, and the oak-panelled restaurant, but the grey food of the Swinging Sixties is, thankfully, consigned to history. An eclectic modern menu dips into European influences, ranging from starters such as Whitby crab tortellini with citrus fennel and herb oil, to a pressing of house-smoked Goosnargh chicken and foie gras with roast pears and watercress, before moving on to rabbit Pithiviers with a cassoulet of beans and game sausage; fish might turn up as pan-roasted sea bass with chive mash, roasted asparagus and crayfish velouté. A detailed cheese menu is an alternative to dessert.

Chef Lee Canning **Owner** Gail Moss, Kim Wynn **Times** 12-2/7-9.30 Closed Xmas (open 25-26 Dec L only) **Prices** Fixed L 2 course fr £15.95, Fixed D 3 course fr £19.95, Starter £5-£8, Main £16.50-£19.95, Dessert £6, Service optional, Groups min 10 service 10% **Wines** 40 bottles over £20, 32 bottles under £20, 13 by glass **Notes** Tasting menu 5 course, Sunday L, Vegetarian available, Dress restrictions, Smart casual, No shorts, Civ Wed 120 **Seats** 45, Pr/dining room 120 **Children** Portions **Parking** 60

The Old Bore at Rishworth

◎ British

Trad British with continental flourishes in a Yorkshire inn

☎ 01422 822291
Oldham Rd, Rishworth HX6 4QU
e-mail: chefhessel@aol.com
dir: M62 junct 22, A672 towards Halifax, 3m on left after reservoir

A 200-year-old coaching inn in a Yorkshire village, the Old Bore boasts three separate eating areas. Wherever you choose to pitch camp, you'll find the ambience cosy and welcoming, and the cooking centred on classic British pub fare, overlaid with the odd continental flourish. Smoked horseradish risotto topped with devilled kidneys is an imaginative way to start, and you might follow with beer-battered fish and chips, or lamb shank braised in red wine with root veg, red cabbage and creamy mash. Sunday roasts are a strong draw, as are puddings like rhubarb crumble with custard.

Chef Scott Hessel **Owner** Scott Hessel **Times** 12-2.15/6-9.30 **Prices** Starter £5.95-£7.95, Main £10.95-£19.95, Dessert £4.95-£6.95, Service optional **Wines** 30 bottles over £20, 15 bottles under £20, 9 by glass **Notes** Sunday L, Vegetarian available **Seats** 80, Pr/dining room 20 **Children** Portions **Parking** 20

HEBDEN BRIDGE Map 19 SD92

Moyles

Modern British

Confident cooking in stylish small hotel

☎ 01422 845727
6-10 New Rd HX7 8AD
e-mail: enquire@moyles.com
dir: M62 junct 24. A646 Halifax to Burnley through Hebden Bridge. Located in the centre of town opposite marina

Formerly a rundown guesthouse, built in Victorian times, Moyles has been fully refurbished in recent years and turned into a smart boutique restaurant with rooms. The light and airy restaurant is informal and relaxed with muted duck-egg blue colours, a stone floor and an abundance of wood and natural materials. The modern British menu changes with the seasons and might offer a starter of hand-dived scallops with braised pig's cheek, crispy ear and sweetcorn puree, followed by rack and neck of lamb with peas and mint and an olive oil mash. Moyles banana split - with toffee parfait, poached banana ice cream and vanilla espuma – is a contemporary interpretation of an old favourite.

Times 12-3/6-10

ILKLEY Map 19 SE14

Best Western Rombalds Hotel & Restaurant

Modern European

Charming hotel restaurant by Ilkley Moor

☎ 01943 603201
11 West View, Wells Rd LS29 9JG
e-mail: reception@rombalds.demon.co.uk
dir: From Leeds take A65 to Ilkley. At 3rd main lights turn left & follow signs for Ilkley Moor. At junct take right onto Wells Rd, by HSBC bank. Hotel 600yds on left

Situated on the edge of Ilkley Moor in an elegant Georgian townhouse, this traditional hotel and restaurant offers a relaxed atmosphere and a warm welcome. Indeed this Yorkshire country house started off life in 1835 as a rooming house. Skilfully prepared, imaginative menus show a commitment to local produce delivering a modern European menu of some style. Expect carpaccio of Yorkshire beef with celeriac coleslaw and Cow and Calf ale syrup, and a main course of pan-fried fillet of hake with braised pak choi and curried clam broth, and rum and raisin rice pudding brûlée with a nutmeg tuile to finish.

Chef Paul Laidlaw **Owner** Colin & Jo Clarkson
Times 12-2/6.30-9 Closed 28 Dec-2 Jan **Prices** Fixed L 2 course £12.95, Fixed D 3 course £19.95, Starter £5.95-£6.75, Main £10.95-£18.95, Dessert £5.50-£6.75, Service optional **Wines** 46 bottles over £20, 58 bottles under £20, 6 by glass **Notes** Sunday L, Vegetarian available, Civ Wed 70 **Seats** 34, Pr/dining room 50 **Children** Portions **Parking** 22

Box Tree

– see below

Box Tree

ILKLEY Map 19 SE14

British, French NOTABLE WINE LIST

Yorkshire institution on top form

☎ 01943 608484
37 Church St LS29 9DR
e-mail: info@theboxtree.co.uk
dir: On A65 from Leeds through Ilkley, main lights approx 200yds on left

The Box Tree has earned its place in the UK's gastronomic history: after Elizabeth David told us that olive oil wasn't necessarily something one bought from the chemist for ear problems, the country shook off the grey shroud of the 1950s and started to enjoy food - and the Box Tree was in the forefront of the revolution. In the '70s, Marco Pierre White first made a name for himself here. Since chef Simon Gueller took over, the kitchen has been firing on all cylinders once again. The interior of the Georgian stone farmhouse is a class act, done out with taste and restraint, while front-of-house staff take care of proceedings with due diligence. Well-sourced ingredients put together in intelligent combinations are the basic principle of the kitchen's skilled contemporary cooking, as in a starter of roast scallops with butternut purée, Alsace bacon and beurre noisette, or there might be a velouté of potato, presented with potato foam, roast foie gras and baby leeks. Respect for the classics still runs deep in this kitchen - main-course roast fillet and slow-cooked daube of beef with baby vegetables, pommes purées, and red wine being a case in point. Desserts hold form to the end, when caramelised pear tarte Tatin comes with the citrus twist of lime-scented ice cream, Medjool date purée, crème patissière and orange sorbet. Prix-fixe dinners offer a more accessible option to the pricey à la carte menu.

Chef Mr S Gueller **Owner** Mrs R Gueller
Times 12-2/7-9.30 Closed 27-31 Dec, 1-7 Jan, Mon, L Tue-Thu, D Sun **Prices** Fixed L 2 course fr £22, Fixed D 3 course fr £32, Starter £11-£18.50, Main £28-£32, Dessert £10-£12, Groups min 8 service 10% **Wines** 256 bottles over £20, 7 by glass **Notes** Sunday L, Vegetarian available, Dress restrictions, Smart casual **Seats** 50, Pr/dining room 16 **Parking** NCP

LEEDS Map 19 SE23

Anthony's Restaurant

@@@ – *see below*

The Calverley Grill

@@ British

Delightful hotel offering confident British cuisine

☎ 0113 282 1000
De Vere Oulton Hall, Rothwell Ln, Oulton LS26 8HN
e-mail: oulton.hall@devere-hotels.com
dir: 2m from M62 junct 30, follow Rothwell signs, then 'Oulton 1m' sign. 1st exit at next 2 rdbts. Hotel on left. Or 1m from M1 junct 44, follow Castleford & Pontefract signs on A639

Oulton Hall is an imposing Grade II listed mansion sitting in beautiful gardens and with wonderful views across the Yorkshire Dales, although it's just 15 minutes' drive from the centre of Leeds. The house successfully combines the traditional with the modern, and the Calverley Grill - named after one of Oulton Hall's earliest owners, John Calverley - is a striking and elegant room in black and crimson, with rich fabrics, leather banquettes and an abundance of darkwood. Grills and classic brasserie dishes are the order of the day and the kitchen places great emphasis on local produce. Start, perhaps, with a Caesar salad prepared at your table, or seared scallops with Lishman's black pudding and roast apple purée, and move on to a grass-fed, 28-day hung fillet or sirloin steak (from farmer Stephen Knox) with your choice of sauces. Finish with symphony of Oldroyd's rhubarb with Yorkshire parkin, or for a more savoury option, Yorkshire rarebit on brioche.

Times 12.30-2/7-10

Casa Mia Grande

@ Modern Italian **NEW**

An authentic taste of Italy in Leeds

☎ 0113 239 2555 & 0845 688 3030
33-37 Harrogate Rd, Chapel Allerton LS7 3PD
e-mail: francesco@casamiaonline.com

This bustling restaurant is just the ticket for an authentic taste of Italy. Italian-owned and staffed, it has an open-plan kitchen to let the chefs add their efforts to the evening's entertainment. There's a real Mediterranean buzz and friendly ambience throughout the three sprawling floors. Kick off in the champagne bar with a glass of fizz before moving up to the second-floor à la carte restaurant, where the kitchen pulls out the stops to produce its best work. Fish and seafood is a speciality, so go for a 'nozze di mare' starter of tiger prawns and scallops roasted with garlic, white wine, lemon juice, olive oil and fresh ginger. The house speciality pasta is fettuccine leccabaffi (meaning 'moustache-licking') - scampi and mango in cream and white wine sauce - or fishy main courses might offer bream fillets treated simply by roasting in a herb-crusted potato casing with white wine and lemon zest.

Times 12-3/6-10.30 Closed 26 Dec, 1 Jan, L Mon-Sat

City Inn Leeds

@ Modern European **NEW**

Skilled modern cooking in smart canalside venue

☎ 0113 241 1000
Granary Wharf, 2 Wharf Approach LS1 4BR
e-mail: leeds.citycafe@cityinn.com
dir: M1 junct 43 right onto M621 (follow Leeds (Centre)/ M621 signs). At junct 3 exit towards Holbeck. Merge onto A653/Dewsbury Rd follow until filter onto Neville St. 1st left at lights into Water Ln. 2nd right into Canal Wharf, over bridge, continue to hotel, on right

The Leeds branch of this smart contemporary hotel chain has a brilliant location in the regenerated Granary Wharf area, right in the thick of the theatre, ballet, opera and shopping action. The light-flooded contemporary restaurant makes the most of the canalside setting through floor-to-ceiling windows, or in good weather you can grab a seat outside on the terrace overlooking the water. But first, make sure to do as the Leeds in-crowd do, and pop up to the 13th-floor Sky Lounge for cocktails and step onto the balcony beyond the glass walls for

Anthony's Restaurant

LEEDS Map 19 SE23

Modern European

A shining star of the north

☎ 0113 245 5922
19 Boar Ln LS1 6EA
e-mail: anthonys@anthonysrestaurant.co.uk
dir: 500 yds from Leeds Central Station towards The Corn Exchange

Anthony Flinn's empire has expanded apace across the city to encompass a pâtisserie, the Flannels Restaurant (in a clothing store, get it?), and most recently, Piazza by Anthony, a statement brasserie in the glorious old Corn Exchange. By comparison, the flagship Boar Lane venue sits on a busy, unglamorous high street, but once inside, a chic minimalism takes over in the cool ground-floor bar; you then drop down a level into the basement dining room, where shades of café crème twinned with clever lighting make for a remarkably luminous space, considering there's no natural light. Nothing to distract from the food, then, and it would be remiss not to point out that Anthony Flinn did a stint at Catalan maestro Ferran Adria's El Bulli, global HQ of the school of molecular gastronomy, an experience which informs rather than dominates his approach. His cuisine takes a left-field approach that is all his own, and never less than exciting, creative and awash with originality. Not that you'd know that from the tersely-written menus, but all formulas buzz with intrigue and seductive combinations. Great-value lunch offerings might include potato velouté with crab and chestnut dumpling, followed by poached baby chicken hotpot - nothing outside the box there, but the sure-handed control over the balance of flavours raises these dishes to a serious level. The inspirational wizardry kicks in with the à la carte menu - take the flavour juxtapositions and gentle cooking techniques in a starter of olive oil-poached quail with toasted rice and green tea consommé. Main-course belly pork comes with pig's ear and tail and sushi prawns; fish in eye-opening company - as in John Dory with whelks, chorizo and squash. Presentation, too, is an experience, involving swashes, streaks and dollops of pure essential flavours.

Chef Anthony Flinn **Owner** Anthony Flinn
Times 12-2/7-9.30 Closed Xmas-New Year, Sun, Mon
Prices Food prices not confirmed for 2011. Please telephone for details. **Wines** 110 bottles over £20, 10 bottles under £20, 16 by glass **Notes** Vegetarian available **Seats** 40 **Children** Portions **Parking** NCP 20 yds

views across the cityscape to the Yorkshire hills. Back down in the restaurant, the kitchen takes an unaffected modern European tack, showcasing the region's top seasonal bounty in a market menu to supplement the à la carte. A starter of pork belly confit with pan-fried scallop, pea purée and quail's egg is right on the money, while a main-course 21-day aged Buccleuch steak follows suit with crispy frites, watercress and béarnaise sauce.

Chef Scott MacDonald **Times** 1-3.00/5.30-10.30 **Prices** Food prices not confirmed for 2011. Please telephone for details. **Notes** Supplements may apply to fixed price menu, Sunday L

Malmaison Leeds

British, French

Vibrant cooking in stylish city brasserie

☎ 0113 398 1000
1 Swinegate LS1 4AG
e-mail: leeds@malmaison.com
dir: City centre. 5 mins walk from Leeds railway station. On junct 16 of loop road, Sovereign St & Swinegate

Close to the waterfront and five minutes from the city's upmarket fashion boutiques and department stores, the Leeds outpost of this stylish hotel group was once a bus and tram company office. The popular, candlelit brasserie boasts an impressive vaulted ceiling, leather booths and a funky glass fireplace. Choose between the carte or the 'home grown and local' set menu for unpretentious British and European favourites, where flavour is to the fore. Open ravioli of scallops and cauliflower velouté is a starter with a contemporary flavour, while venison Wellington comes with a home-made black pudding. Chocolate marquise with milk ice cream is a typical dessert.

Chef James Key **Owner** Malmaison **Times** 12-2.30/6.30-9.30 Closed D 25 Dec **Prices** Fixed L 2 course £10-£30.45, Fixed D 3 course £15.95-£36, Starter £5.25-£7.95, Main £10.50-£22.50, Dessert £5.95, Service added but optional 10% **Wines** 90% bottles over £20, 10% bottles under £20, 25 by glass **Notes** Sunday L, Vegetarian available, Civ Wed 40 **Seats** 85, Pr/dining room 12 **Children** Portions, Menu **Parking** Criterion Place car park

Thorpe Park Hotel & Spa

Modern British

Chic modern dining showcasing local produce

☎ 0113 264 1000
Century Way, Thorpe Park LS15 8ZB
e-mail: thorpepark@shirehotels.com
dir: M1 junct 46, follow signs off rdbt for Thorpe Park

Not to be confused with the white-knuckle thrills and spills of Thorpe Park in Surrey, this classy modern hotel on the outskirts of Leeds offers a rather more civilised form of leisure. Whether you prefer to pamper or punish yourself, the glitzy state-of-the-art spa should help hone the appetite – luckily, the terrace and courtyard venues will sort you out with contemporary grazing and snacking food throughout the day. When it comes to dining of a more serious order, the sleek open-plan restaurant goes for a modish look involving pale wood, black leather and abstract art. Yorkshire's larder is proudly showcased on a crowd-pleasing menu of modern British ideas – pan-seared scallops and black pudding from Lishman's of Ilkley, with pea and mint purée, say, ahead of slow-cooked belly pork with Savoy cabbage and Bramley apple.

Times 12-2/6.45-9.30 Closed L Sat & Sun

LIVERSEDGE Map 16 SE12

Healds Hall Hotel & Restaurant

Modern British

Charming 18th-century hotel with modern bistro and restaurant

☎ 01924 409112
Leeds Rd WF15 6JA
e-mail: enquire@healdshall.co.uk
dir: M1 junct 40, A638. From Dewsbury take A652 signed Bradford. Left at A62. Hotel 50yds on right

Not only does this 18th-century mill owner's mansion have connections to the Brontë family, but it looks the part too; its creeper-swathed stone walls could easily serve as a film set for a period drama. The contemporary bistro is another story: a stylish, relaxed place done out in pale wood, curvy leather seats and diaphanous cerise voile drapes; alternatively, there's the more formal setting of Harringtons Restaurant. A daily specials menu gives the kitchen free rein to make the most of what its local sources can come up with, in a range of unfussy bistro dishes taking in pan-fried scallops with crispy pork belly, pig's cheek, apple and vanilla purée, or slow-braised lamb shank with creamy mash, roasted root vegetables and rich red wine jus.

Chef Andrew Ward, David Winter **Owner** Mr N B & Mrs T Harrington **Times** 12-2/6-10 Closed 1 Jan, BHs, L Sat, D Sun (ex residents) **Prices** Fixed L 2 course £8.95, Fixed D 3 course £16.95-£22.95, Starter £4.50-£8.50, Main £10-£25, Dessert £4.95-£8, Service optional **Wines** 21 bottles over £20, 31 bottles under £20, 8 by glass **Notes** Sunday L, Vegetarian available, Civ Wed 100 **Seats** 46, Pr/dining room 30 **Children** Portions **Parking** 90

MARSDEN Map 16 SE01

The Olive Branch Restaurant with Rooms

Modern French

Victorian roadside inn with sound Anglo-French cooking

☎ 01484 844487
Manchester Rd HD7 6LU
e-mail: eat@olivebranch.uk.com
dir: On A62 between Slaithwaite & Marsden

The warren of cosy, intimate little rooms at the Olive Branch invites exploration. It's a welcoming Victorian roadside inn, now run as a modern restaurant with rooms. Old pine tables and rugs establish the appealing domestic ambience, and the cooking looks to both sides of the Channel for inspiration. Foie gras and Armagnac terrine with Riesling jelly is one way to start, with breadcrumbed monkfish tail and tapenade, or Gressingham duck breast with truffled mash in port and peppercorn sauce, to follow. A good little selection of dessert wines waits to accompany something like banana cheesecake with caramel sauce.

Chef Paul Kewley **Owner** Paul Kewley & John Lister **Times** 6.30-9.30 Closed 26 Dec, 1st 2 wks Jan, L Mon-Sat **Prices** Fixed D 3 course £18.95, Starter £5.95-£9.95, Main £13.95-£29.95, Dessert £5.95-£7.50, Service optional **Wines** 100 bottles over £20, 30 bottles under £20, 16 by glass **Notes** Sunday L, Vegetarian available **Seats** 65, Pr/dining room 40 **Children** Portions **Parking** 20

PONTEFRACT Map 16 SE42

Wentbridge House Hotel

Modern British V

Classical cuisine in elegant country-house hotel

01977 620444
The Great North Rd, Wentbridge WF8 3JJ
e-mail: info@wentbridgehouse.co.uk
dir: 4m S of M62/A1 junct, 0.5m off A1

There's a blue-blooded pedigree to this well-established country-house hotel: it was once home to the Bowes-Lyon family and the Leathans who founded Barclays Bank. A short drive from the A1, it is secluded within expansive grounds in the picturesque Went Valley. The Fleur de Lys restaurant - aptly named for the profusion of the said motif throughout - is an elegant, traditional venue for candlelit dining; some dishes are even cooked at the table for that touch of old-school culinary theatre. Top-class produce, locally sourced where possible, forms the backbone of the kitchen's modern British repertoire. Start with seared king scallops with minted garden peas and local smoked streaky bacon, followed by pan-seared pheasant breast with pumpkin and spinach pie and blackberry and juniper jus.

Chef Steve Turner **Owner** Mr G Page **Times** 7.15-9.30 Closed L Mon-Sat, D Sun, 25 Dec **Prices** Starter £8.50-£12, Main £18.50-£29.95, Dessert £6.95-£9.50, Service optional **Wines** 100 bottles over £20, 30 bottles under £20, 10 by glass **Notes** Sunday L, Vegetarian menu, Civ Wed 130 **Seats** 60, Pr/dining room 24 **Children** Portions **Parking** 100

SHIPLEY Map 19 SE13

Marriott Hollins Hall Hotel & Country Club

Traditional British

Classic flavour combinations in a Victorian pile

01274 530053
Hollins Hill, Baildon BD17 7QW
e-mail: mhrs.lbags.frontdesk@marriotthotels.com
dir: From A650 follow signs to Salt Mill. At lights in Shipley take A6038. Hotel 3m on left

In 200 acres of grounds with stunning views of the Pennines, Victorian Hollins Hall is a good base for exploring the area and has easy access to both Bradford and Leeds. The hotel is geared up for business travellers, but the leisure facilities (pool, sauna, that sort of thing) give it broad appeal, as do the two restaurants. Leave your jeans at home for Heathcliff's Restaurant in the original drawing room and expect simple traditional and modern ingredients with tried-and-tested flavour combinations. Smoked haddock and dill risotto with a soft-poached egg makes way for 6oz fillet steak with Yorkshire blue cheese crust, thyme potato cake, crisp bacon and carrots. Zest Bar and Restaurant is the more informal option for breakfast, lunch or dinner.

Chef Uwe Range **Owner** Marriott International **Times** 12-2/7-10 Closed L Sat, D BHs **Prices** Food prices not confirmed for 2011. Please telephone for details. **Wines** 32 bottles over £20, 8 bottles under £20, 14 by glass **Notes** Sunday L, Vegetarian available, Dress restrictions, Smart casual, Civ Wed 120 **Seats** 120, Pr/dining room 30 **Children** Portions, Menu **Parking** 250

WAKEFIELD Map 16 SE32

Waterton Park Hotel

Modern European **NEW**

Aspirational cooking by a Yorkshire lake

01924 257911 & 249800
Walton Hall, The Balk, Walton WF2 6PW
e-mail: info@watertonparkhotel.co.uk
dir: 3m SE off B6378. Exit M1 junct 39 towards Wakefield. At 3rd rdbt right for Crofton. Right at 2nd lights & follow signs

They don't come much more eye-catchingly sited than this. Walton Hall is a Georgian mansion sitting on an island in the midst of a Yorkshire lake, reached by an iron footbridge. The hotel accommodation is split between that and the purpose-built Waterton Park on the mainland, which also houses the restaurant. Done in neutral hues with well-spaced tables and crisp linen, it makes a refined environment for the aspirational contemporary cooking. Meals might start with beautifully presented wild mushroom risotto, garnished with truffle, parmesan crisps and herb oil, its savoury intensity mightily impressive. Proceed with a seared, well-timed venison steak, which comes with pearl barley, glazed parsnips and Madeira gravy, and finish with a crème brûlée loaded with blackberries grown in the hotel's own garden.

Chef Armstrong Wgabi **Owner** The Kaye Family **Times** 7-9.30 Closed D Sun **Prices** Food prices not confirmed for 2011. Please telephone for details. **Wines** 10 bottles over £20, 50 bottles under £20, 10 by glass **Notes** Civ Wed 200 **Seats** 50, Pr/dining room 35 **Children** Portions **Parking** 130

WETHERBY Map 16 SE44

Wood Hall Hotel

Modern British

Contemporary cuisine in classic country house

01937 587271
Trip Ln, Linton LS22 4JA
dir: From Wetherby take A661 (Harrogate road) N for 0.5m. Left to Sicklinghall/Linton. Cross bridge, left to Linton/Woodhall, right opp Windmill Inn, 1.25m to hotel (follow brown signs)

Cromwell's army chucked the original Norman manor into the nearby River Wharfe, so Wood Hall was resurrected in glorious Georgian splendour in 1750. And it was built to impress, perched on a hillside among 100 acres of delicious woodland, with a working Carmelite monastery on the estate. Of course, it's not preserved in aspic - the interior has been reworked in a smart modern style, and a new wing houses an excellent beauty spa. The Georgian dining room also has a sleek contemporary look in neutral shades of coffee and cream to suit the modern cooking. The kitchen team takes local sourcing so seriously that a new kitchen garden is under way, and they have started to breed cattle in the grounds - the rest comes from the Wharfe Valley or top UK suppliers. A summer dinner opens with an eye-catching sardine Niçoise sandwich with asparagus and a shot of tomato, then moves on to a cutlet of Dales lamb with Lishman's black pudding, broad beans and onion shells.

Chef Norman McKenzie **Owner** Hand Picked Hotels **Times** 12-2.30/7-9.30 Closed L Mon-Sat **Prices** Fixed D 3 course £35, Starter £12-£16, Main £18-£29, Dessert £6.50-£12, Service optional **Wines** 112 bottles over £20, 2 bottles under £20, 8 by glass **Notes** Sunday L, Vegetarian available, Dress restrictions, Smart casual, no jeans or trainers, Civ Wed 100 **Seats** 40, Pr/dining room 100 **Children** Portions, Menu **Parking** 100

CHANNEL ISLANDS

GUERNSEY

CASTEL Map 24

Cobo Bay Restaurant

European

Wonderful sea views and confident cooking

☎ 01481 257102
Cobo Coast Rd, Cobo GY5 7HB
e-mail: reservations@cobobayhotel.com
dir: From St Peter Port follow Castel/Cobo/West Coast signs. At coast road turn right, hotel 100mtrs on right

The sunsets across the bay are truly spectacular and can be fully appreciated from the dining room, but the view is pretty special even if the red glow is absent. A beach terrace with its own à la carte menu is a new development at the hotel. The main restaurant - to which the Rosettes apply - is designed to make the most of the view through large windows and is decorated in natural colours (shades of brown and cream) with a natural stone floor, all of which blend seamlessly with the sand and stone visible through the windows. Tables are well spaced and elegantly set. The cooking is in the modern European vein with plenty of seafood on offer, so a seafood platter or smoked chicken and avocado stack might precede local brill with hollandaise sauce, with perhaps a lime and basil cheesecake to finish.

Chef John Chapman **Owner** Mr D Nussbaumer **Times** 12-2/6.30-9.30 Closed Jan & Feb, L Mon-Sat **Prices** Fixed L 3 course £18.95, Fixed D 3 course £27.50, Starter £5.95-£7.95, Main £9.95-£25, Dessert £5.95-£7.95 **Wines** 21 bottles over £20, 24 bottles under £20, 6 by glass **Notes** Sunday L, Vegetarian available, Dress restrictions, Smart casual **Seats** 110 **Children** Portions, Menu **Parking** 50

La Grande Mare Hotel Golf & Country Club

Modern

Welcoming resort hotel restaurant serving accomplished cuisine

☎ 01481 256576
The Coast Rd, Vazon Bay GY5 7LL
e-mail: simon@lagrandemare.com
dir: From airport turn right. 5 mins to reach Coast Rd. Turn right again. Hotel 5 min drive

To be found on Guernsey's west coast with seaward aspects over the broad sweep of Vazon Bay, La Grande Mare has 120 acres of land, complete with an 18-hole golf course and health suite. The friendly restaurant has oak floors, granite fireplaces and several arches. Dishes are based on the wealth of fabulous local produce available, from organic vegetables and Guernsey cheese to freshly caught seafood; specialities of the house include flambé and rotisserie dishes. Start with confit duck and chorizo terrine with spiced rhubarb chutney, follow on with brill with chive beurre blanc, or venison with juniper and chocolate sauce.

Times 12-2/7-9.30

ST MARTIN Map 24

The Auberge

Modern European

Imaginative cooking with jaw-dropping marine views

☎ 01481 238485
Jerbourg Rd GY4 6BH
e-mail: dine@theauberge.gg
web: www.theauberge.gg
dir: End of Jerbourg Rd at Jerbourg Point

The stylish Auberge perches on a lofty clifftop a few miles outside St Peter Port, basking in sweeping views through vast windows towards neighbouring islands. Inside there's a contemporary cosmopolitan vibe: a swish long bar, unclothed blond wood tables and clued-up staff to make sure things tick over effortlessly. The kitchen works with a lively, imaginative approach using plenty of local produce, particularly fresh fish and seafood. Marinated red mullet escabeche comes with pink grapefruit, pickled cucumber and avocado cream. Vibrant combinations are found among main courses too: sea bass is presented with roast cherry tomatoes, artichoke and shallot salad, pesto and herb crème fraîche. Impressive desserts unite classic combinations such as a decadently gooey chocolate fondant with home-made coffee ice cream.

Chef Daniel Green **Owner** Lapwing Trading Ltd **Times** 12-2/7-9.30 Closed 25-26 Dec, D Sun **Prices** Fixed L 2 course fr £14.95, Fixed D 3 course fr £18.95, Starter £5.50-£8.50, Main £13.50-£22, Dessert £5.50-£7.50, Service optional **Wines** 19 bottles over £20, 16 bottles under £20, 12 by glass **Notes** Sunday L, Vegetarian available **Seats** 70 **Children** Portions, Menu **Parking** 25

La Barbarie Hotel

British, French

Tranquil Guernsey hotel with a strong local reputation

☎ 01481 235217
Saints Rd GY4 6ES
e-mail: reservations@labarbariehotel.com
dir: At lights in St Martin take road to Saints Bay. Hotel on right at end of Saints Rd

An extended 16th-century former priory enjoying a peaceful rural location and retaining all the charm and character of the original building. Guernsey's coasts and meadows supply a cornucopia of fresh fish, seafood, meat, cream and butter for La Barbarie's kitchen team, whose French influences are obvious in the simply cooked and presented dishes. Typical dishes are ham hock terrine with home-made piccalilli for starters, followed by slow-roasted shoulder of lamb with broad beans in garlic and boulangère potatoes, or sea bass with Niçoise salad, with baked vanilla cheesecake with raspberry compôte for pudding.

Times 12-1.45/6-9.30 Closed 2 Nov-13 Mar

ST PETER PORT Map 24

The Absolute End

Mediterranean, International V

Fresh seafood in a harbourside cottage

☎ 01481 723822
St Georges Esplanade GY1 2BG
e-mail: absoluteendrestaurant@hotmail.com
dir: Less than 1m from town centre. N on seafront road towards St Sampson

Super-fresh fish and seafood is the name of the game at this unpretentious restaurant overlooking the harbour just outside St Peter Port - fittingly so, since the whitewashed house was once a fisherman's cottage. Inside, bright white half-panelled walls hung with interesting artwork and pale wood floors combine in a crisp modern look. The chef-proprietor is Italian, so the menu deals mainly, but not exclusively, in simply-cooked Italian seafood classics. Crab cakes with sweet chilli sauce, or a fritto misto of whitebait, prawns and calamari might feature among starters, followed by pan-seared sea bass with spicy mashed potatoes and fried courgettes; end with zingy lemon tart.

Chef Giuseppe Cerciello Rega **Owner** Giuseppe Cerciello Rega **Times** 12-2.30/6.30-10 Closed Sun **Prices** Fixed L 3 course fr £15, Fixed D 3 course fr £20, Starter £5.50-£8.50, Main £10.50-£20, Dessert £5.50-£8 **Wines** 17 bottles over £20, 35 bottles under £20, 3 by glass **Notes** Vegetarian menu, Civ Wed 50 **Seats** 55, Pr/dining room 22 **Children** Portions **Parking** On street

ST PETER PORT ***continued***

Governor's

Traditional French

Seafood-focused cooking in grand harbourside restaurant

01481 738623
Old Government House Hotel, St Ann's Place GY1 2NU
e-mail: governors@theoghhotel.com
dir: At junct of St Julian's Ave & College St

Affectionately known locally as the OGH, the white Victorian building was once the official residence of the Governor of Guernsey. Overlooking the harbour and the old town, it is naturally rather a majestic place, but is now full of modern hotel accoutrements and is run with great warmth and efficiency. Its principal dining room, Governor's, with its voluptuous burgundy tones, textured wallpaper and pictures of bygone incumbents, is something of a gem. The cooking is in the hands of a Breton chef, Jérôme Barbançon, who isn't of course that far from home, and is naturally strong in seafood. Roast monkfish with dried tomato, artichoke and aubergine croustillante raises the curtain with a flourish, and could be followed exotically by turbot poached in coconut milk with tempura prawns and squid ink risotto, or perhaps beef fillet with oxtail ravioli, pomme purée and asparagus in red wine jus. A separate vegetarian menu is offered, and desserts will tempt everybody in with the likes of strawberries given no fewer than five treatments – jelly, tartlet, sorbet, parfait and samosa.

Times 12-2/7.30-10 Closed L Sat, Sun, D Mon

Mora Restaurant & Grill

Traditional European

Contemporary cooking overlooking the marina

01481 715053
The Quay GY1 2LE
e-mail: eat@mora.gg
dir: Facing Victoria Marina

Occupying two floors of a vaulted, 18th-century cellar on the historic seafront, this combined brasserie and more formal restaurant overlooks the marina and the islands of Sark and Herm. Downstairs, Little Mora is perfect for a lighter meal, but go upstairs for the full dining experience and views of the open-plan kitchen. Soft lighting and black-and-white photographs of local fishermen add to the ambience and the cooking is simple with plenty of local produce on show. Mora crab and prawn fritters with saffron and tomato mayonnaise might be followed by poached brill with local oysters and mussels with basil butter sauce, or medallion of fillet steak with stilton rarebit and truffle potatoes.

Chef Trevor Baines **Owner** Nello Ciotti
Times 12-2.15/6-10 **Prices** Fixed L 2 course fr £12.50, Fixed D 3 course fr £13.95, Starter £4.75-£7.95, Main £12.50-£19.50, Dessert £5.80-£6.15, Service optional **Wines** 31 bottles over £20, 29 bottles under £20, 12 by glass **Notes** Fixed D 3 course only available 6-7pm, Sunday L, Vegetarian available **Seats** 90
Children Portions **Parking** On pier

ST SAVIOUR Map 24

The Farmhouse Hotel

Modern International

Creative cooking in stylishly refurbished hotel

01481 264181
Route des bas Courtils GY7 9YF
e-mail: admin@thefarmhouse.gg
web: www.thefarmhouse.gg
dir: From airport, left to 1st lights, left then left again. After 1m left at x-rds. Hotel 100mtrs on right

The same family have run this classily-refurbished hotel for nigh on half a century, so expect every detail to be just so, plus slick, polished service to match. The place has come a long way since it was a farmhouse in the 15th century: nowadays there are five individual restaurant areas within the sophisticated set-up, while in the summer months you can dine by the pool, on the terrace, or in one of the gazebos in the sprawling gardens. Local Guernsey produce - particularly the island's superb fish and seafood - is the cornerstone of the kitchen's imaginative dishes. Taking inspiration from the Continent, start with pan-seared Guernsey scallops with a velouté of celery and pesto oil, followed by steamed turbot with truffled mash and verjus butter sauce.

The Farmhouse Hotel

Chef Ankur Biswas **Owner** David & Julie Nussbaumer
Times 12-2/6.30-9.30 **Prices** Starter £5.50-£9.25, Main £9.95-£19.50, Dessert £5.50-£6.95, Service optional
Wines 35 bottles over £20, 20 bottles under £20, 8 by glass **Notes** Sunday L, Vegetarian available, Dress restrictions, Smart casual **Seats** 100, Pr/dining room 25
Children Portions, Menu **Parking** 70

See advert below

HERM

HERM Map 24

White House Hotel

Traditional British

Escape to a timeless hotel with simple fresh food

☎ 01481 722159
GY1 3HR
e-mail: hotel@herm-island.com
dir: Close to harbour. Access by regular 20 min boat trip from St Peter Port, Guernsey

Just 20 minutes by ferry from St Peter Port in Guernsey, safe, clean and pollution-free, with no cars, no crowds and no stress; how many hotels can boast an island as their garden? Every table in the bright and airy restaurant has a sea view, but the laid-back ethos stops short of letting men off the requirement to wear a jacket and tie for dinner. The kitchen team keeps things simple on its concise menu, with daily specials to take advantage of what has just been landed. Table d'hôte menus might kick off with a leek and potato soup with chive cream, then follow with beef medallions with green peppercorn sauce and confit shallots, and wild berry cheesecake with apricot sorbet for pudding. Check out one of the best wine lists in the Channel Islands.

Chef Nigel Waylen **Owner** Herm Island **Times** 12.30-2/7-9 Closed Nov-Apr **Prices** Fixed L 3 course £25, Service optional **Wines** 74 bottles over £20, 101 bottles under £20, 7 by glass **Notes** Sunday L, Vegetarian available, Dress restrictions, No jeans or trainers, Civ Wed 100 **Seats** 100 **Children** Portions

JERSEY

GOREY Map 24

Suma's

Modern Mediterranean

The pick of the Jersey larder on Gorey harbourfront

☎ 01534 853291
Gorey Hill JE3 6ET
e-mail: info@sumasrestaurant.com
dir: From St Helier take A3 E for 5m to Gorey. Before castle take sharp left. Restaurant 100yds up hill on left (look for blue & white blind)

With majestic views over the harbour, Suma's is the younger sibling of Longueville Manor (see entry). The marine scene can be enjoyed from most tables, and the outdoor area is a treat on warm days. Inside, contemporary artworks divert the eye. The culinary emphasis on an extensive menu is on top-quality local produce, with seafood featuring strongly. A half-lobster served in the shell, topped with white crabmeat and prawns, is a recipe for main-course happiness, simply served with seasonal Jersey Royals and saladings. Substantial starters might include an assemblage of crackled pork belly with confit pig cheeks and black pudding, dressed with maple syrup, or scallops with minted risotto and pink grapefruit. Presentations are neat and professional, all the way through to desserts such as chocolate and peanut brownie with cherries and Jamaican pepper ice cream. Other ice creams such as peach, and sorbets such as raspberry or passionfruit, all have the requisite concentration of flavour.

Chef Daniel Ward **Owner** Mrs Bults & Mr M Lewis **Times** 12-2.30/6.15-10 Closed late Dec-mid Jan (approx), D Sun **Prices** Fixed L 2 course fr £16.50, Starter £5.50-£14, Main £11.75-£22.50, Dessert £5.25-£9.75, Service included **Wines** 42 bottles over £20, 20 bottles under £20, 12 by glass **Notes** Sunday L, Vegetarian available, Dress restrictions, Smart casual **Seats** 40 **Children** Portions, Menu **Parking** On street

ROZEL Map 24

La Chaire Restaurant

Traditional British, French V

Local seafood in a Victorian retreat

☎ 01534 863354
Chateau La Chaire, Rozel Bay JE3 6AJ
e-mail: res@chateau-la-chaire.co.uk
dir: From St Helier NE towards Five Oaks, Maufant, then St Martin's Church & Rozel; 1st left in village, hotel 100mtrs

Tucked away amid the leafy scenery of the Rozel Valley, this charming 19th-century hotel and former gentlemen's residence is well worth seeking out. Fresh fish and seafood are the focus of the Anglo-French menu, although there's also a separate vegetarian version. Portions are hearty so bring a good appetite to the oak-panelled restaurant. The adjacent conservatory and terrace are appealing dining options. Kick off with grilled scallops wrapped in pancetta with carrot purée, pesto and pea shoots before moving on to fillet of local brill with woodland mushroom and white wine sauce. For dessert, perhaps an unusual take on a classic in the form of caramelised white chocolate rice pudding with cinnamon and orange ice cream.

Chef Marcin Ciehomski **Owner** The Hiscox family **Times** 12-3/7-10 **Prices** Fixed L 3 course £14.95, Starter £6.95-£10.95, Main £16.95-£26.95, Dessert £7.95, Service added but optional 10% **Wines** 51 bottles over £20, 18 bottles under £20, 12 by glass **Notes** Fixed D 6 course £29.95, Sunday L, Vegetarian menu, Dress restrictions, Smart casual, Civ Wed 60 **Seats** 60, Pr/dining room 28 **Children** Portions, Menu **Parking** 30

ST AUBIN Map 24

The Boat House

Modern European

Seafood-based cookery in a spacious harbourside venue

☎ 01534 744226 & 747141
One North Quay JE3 8BS
e-mail: enquiries@jerseyboathouse.com

Overlooking busy St Aubin harbour, this spacious, airy, two-storey restaurant is bright and modern, with laminate tables and topical artwork in the first-floor Sails brasserie. (The ground-floor Quay Bar offers simpler fare.) The kitchen knows its constituency, and offers up plenty of marine bounty, in the form of cumin-scented scallops with butternut squash purée and ginger cream sauce, and mains such as a lobster and crab pairing, served with saffron mayonnaise, a basket of great chips and salad. Meat eaters might go for rack of lamb with potato gratin and rosemary jus. Finish with feather-light, biscuit-based cheesecake with peach purée.

Times 12-2/6-9.30 Closed 25 Dec & Jan, Mon-Tue (Winter), L Wed-Thu & Sat (Winter), D Sun (Winter)

The Salty Dog Bar & Bistro

Modern International V

Globetrotting seafood dishes in a picture-perfect location

☎ 01534 742760
Le Boulevard, St Aubins Village JE3 8AB
e-mail: info@saltydogbistro.com
web: www.saltydogbistro.com
dir: Walking from centre of St Aubin Village along harbour, approx halfway along, slightly set back

A charming seaside restaurant located on the west coast of Jersey, right at the heart of St Aubin's picturesque harbour, the plain wooden floors and simple wooden tables of the Salty Dog help create a rustic vibe which is neatly matched by the relaxed service. As you'd expect, the seafood is the star and there's a comprehensive selection of shellfish and super-fresh fish on offer. Expect accomplished cooking and some appealing Asian influences on the globetrotting menu; start with scallops in a light ginger and spring onion sauce with a rocket and toasted sesame dressing, and follow on with sea bass wrapped in banana served with Thai hot-and-sour

continued

ST AUBIN *continued*

sauce, or organic salmon with chive beurre blanc and red pepper pesto.

Chef Damon James Duffy **Owner** Damon & Natalie Duffy **Times** 12.30-6/6-1.30am Closed 2 wks Xmas, Mon (Jan-Feb), L Tue-Fri (Jan-Mar) **Prices** Fixed L 3 course £18.50-£23.50, Fixed D 3 course £30, Starter £7.45-£9.50, Main £11.95-£28, Dessert £3.95-£5.50, Service added but optional 9.71% **Wines** 24 bottles over £20, 23 bottles under £20, 7 by glass **Notes** Sunday L, Vegetarian menu **Seats** 60 **Children** Portions, Menu **Parking** Car parks & on street parking nearby

Somerville Hotel

@@ Modern International

A romantic setting for local seafood

☎ 01534 741226
Mont du Boulevard JE3 8AD
e-mail: somerville@dolanhotels.com
dir: From village follow harbour, then take Mont du Boulevard

The Tides Restaurant is the place to head for when you want to sample Jersey's superb fish and seafood at its absolute freshest. From its position on the hillside above the yachting harbour, the spectacular views of St Aubin's Bay are none too shabby either - this is a superbly romantic setting for dinner at simply-laid tables lit by modern oil lamps. Fish and crustaceans may be the main draw, but local meat puts in a healthy showing too in dishes that are influenced by the proximity of France. Start with a warm tart of local crab thermidor with cucumber and chive crème fraîche, followed by grilled sea bass fillet with chorizo, piperade, chargrilled fennel and pesto. Finish with the island's fine dairy produce in a soufflé of Jersey black butter with white chocolate ice cream and honey crème anglaise.

Chef Wayne Pegler **Owner** Mr W Dolan **Times** 12.30-2/7-9 **Prices** Fixed L 2 course £12.50, Fixed D 3 course £29.50, Starter £8.50-£10, Main £18.50-£22, Dessert £8.50, Service optional **Wines** 42 bottles over £20, 23 bottles under £20, 6 by glass **Notes** Sunday L, Vegetarian available, Dress restrictions, Smart casual at D, Civ Wed 40 **Seats** 120, Pr/dining room 40 **Children** Portions **Parking** 30

ST BRELADE Map 24

L'Horizon Hotel and Spa

@@ British, French V

Accomplished cooking and a touch of luxury on Jersey

☎ 01534 743101
La Route de la Baie JE3 8EF
e-mail: lhorizon@handpicked.co.uk
dir: 3m from airport. From airport right at rdbt towards St Brelades & Red Houses. Through Red Houses, hotel 300mtrs on right in centre of bay

This relaxed and luxurious hotel overlooks the golden sands of one of Jersey's most stunning beaches and has an almost Mediterranean feel (when the sun is shining at least). Built in 1850 by George Hicks, a Colonel in the Bengal army, the interior is all Victorian elegance, space and light. A choice between The Grill restaurant, Brasserie, Lounge & Bar and elegant Crystal Room restaurant means there's something to suit all moods (there's a large beach-facing terrace, too). Food is light and contemporary with evident classic influences. The Grill menu is focused heavily on local seafood with the likes of Jersey crab and lobster cocktail with avocado and Marie Rose sauce, and sea bass fillet with purple sprouting broccoli and asparagus. To finish, Baked Alaska with cider and black butter ice cream makes for an innovative dessert.

Chef Nicholas Valmagna **Owner** Hand Picked Hotels **Times** 7-9.45 Closed Xmas, Sun-Mon, L all week **Prices** Fixed D 3 course £42.50, Service optional **Wines** 75 bottles over £20, 14 bottles under £20, 8 by glass **Notes** Vegetarian menu, Civ Wed 200 **Seats** 46, Pr/dining room 240 **Children** Portions, Menu **Parking** 150

Ocean Restaurant at the Atlantic Hotel

@@@ *– see opposite page*

ST CLEMENT Map 24

Green Island Restaurant

@ Mediterranean

Great local seafood in bustling beach café

☎ 01534 857787
Green Island JE2 6LS
e-mail: greenislandrestaurant@jerseymail.co.uk

There's a real emphasis on fish and shellfish at this relaxed and very popular beachside café and restaurant, which has a distinct Mediterranean influence. Expect an informal, laid-back approach, with half the tables outside when the weather is fine (it's advisable to book). The views out over Green Island are well worth lingering over, as is the stylish modern cooking. Expect fresh grilled sardines, crab and lobster to be on the menu when available. Smoked haddock, crevettes and mascarpone risotto might be followed by brill with pea purée, shaved fennel and crab bisque, or monkfish with tomato tapenade, olive and feta potato mash and aubergine caviar.

Times 12-3/7-10 Closed 21 Dec-Mar, Mon, D Sun

ST HELIER Map 24

Bohemia Restaurant

@@@@ *– see page 466*

Grand, Jersey

@@@ *– see page 467*

Hotel Savoy

@ Modern British

Seafood delights in a modernised hotel dining room

☎ 01534 727521
37 Rouge Bouillon JE2 3ZA
e-mail: info@thesavoy.biz
dir: From airport 1st exit at rdbt. At next rdbt take 2nd exit right, down Beaumont Hill. At bottom turn left, along coast onto dual carriageway. At 3rd lights turn 1st left. Right at end. Remain in right lane, into left lane before hospital. Hotel on left opp police station

On the outskirts of St Helier, this intimate family-run hotel was originally a 19th-century manor house and has recently been refurbished to a high standard. In its own grounds, the shops and nightlife of the town centre are only a short stroll away. Seafood and fish from the Jersey coast play a starring role in the small but comfortable Montana dining room, where service is on the formal side. On the menu, expect the likes of Jersey mussel and smoked paprika chowder, then roasted sea bass, thyme and garlic, buttered Jersey royals, Vichy carrots and almond Calabrese. Save room for Guernsey Gache bread-and-butter pudding and custard. Roberto's jazz bar is a draw on Friday evenings when live music plays and tapas is served.

Times 6.30-9 Closed L ex by prior arrangement

La Petite Pomme

@@ Modern European V

Local seafood in landmark hotel with views

☎ 01534 880110
Pomme d'Or Hotel, Liberation Square JE1 3UF
e-mail: enquiries@pommedorhotel.com
dir: 5m from airport, 0.5m from ferry terminal

Known affectionately by its fans as the 'Pomme', the historic Pomme d'Or Hotel has been a stalwart of the St Helier dining scene for more than 175 years. The occupying German navy took advantage of its hospitality when it was their HQ during World War II, and its location on Liberation Square puts it at the epicentre of the annual liberation celebrations on May 9th. La Petite Pomme - a plush venue with plenty of breathing space between tables - has great views across the square to St Helier marina to go with a menu of creative contemporary dishes built on intuitive combinations of local materials. Fillet of salmon rillettes with cucumber salad and chive and lime crème fraîche, followed by pan-fried fillet of

continued on page 468

Ocean Restaurant at the Atlantic Hotel

ST BRELADE Map 24

Modern British V 

Outstanding cooking to match the views

☎ 01534 744101
Le Mont de la Pulente JE3 8HE
e-mail: info@theatlantichotel.com
web: www.theatlantichotel.com
dir: A13 to Petit Port, turn right into Rue de la Sergente & right again, hotel signed

With exotic palm trees, white louvred shutters and a deep blue pool straight out of a Hockney painting, this could be Miami, but luckily the Atlantic Hotel overlooks the stunning Jersey coast. There's a whiff of art deco in the clean lines of its low-slung white façade; inside, the feel is suitably cool, white and neutral in the Ocean Restaurant, where the exciting cooking of Mark Jordan has turned this place into a real Channel Islands destination. Having served his time with a stellar cast of mentors in top-drawer restaurants, he brings a wealth of effervescent ideas, backed by masterful techniques, to produce good-looking results. There's a mix of classic and visionary dishes here, all headlined with their main ingredient: a simple risotto of summer truffle with parmesan tuile marries classic flavours and knows when to leave a good thing alone; pan-seared duck foie gras is raised to another level with the sweet-and-sour addition of mango, passionfruit and salted caramel. Mains offer the finest from Jersey's fields and the ocean in some stimulating combinations, as witnessed in citrus-roasted halibut with morel mushrooms, herb gnocchi, and garden peas with a hint of truffle. Desserts display the same thought-provoking flavours spiked with a sense of fun - marshmallow comes with vanilla ice cream, strawberries, mint jelly and rich dark chocolate leaves. The sommelier is a real pro too, pointing you in the right direction with a globetrotting list that offers a good choice by the glass.

Chef Mark Jordan **Owner** Patrick Burke
Times 12.30-2.30/7-10 Closed Jan
Prices Fixed L 2 course £20, Fixed D 3 course £50, Tasting menu £70, Service included **Wines** 392 bottles over £20, 8 bottles under £20, 12 by glass
Notes Fixed ALC 2 course £50, 3 course £60, Sunday L, Vegetarian menu, Dress restrictions, Smart dress, Civ Wed 80
Seats 60, Pr/dining room 20
Children Portions, Menu **Parking** 60

Bohemia Restaurant

ST HELIER Map 24

Modern British, French V NOTABLE WINE LIST

Pace-setting contemporary cooking in a smart spa hotel

☎ 01534 880588 & 876500
The Club Hotel & Spa, Green St JE2 4UH
e-mail: bohemia@huggler.com
dir: In town centre. 5 mins walk from main shopping centre

Jersey's smart set hotfoots it after work to the heaving bar of the hyper-trendy Club Hotel and Spa. On a busy street away from the town centre, it's the place to check out the local beau monde, before moving on to the swish restaurant where chrome, leather and wood come together in an exercise in luxurious modern chic. Blending Gallic and Anglo Saxon influences is what Jersey is all about, so Shaun Rankin's cooking fittingly unites Jersey's top-class lobster and turbot with the likes of Scottish beef, Yorkshire venison, French foie gras and Anjou pigeon. For those who want to get up close and personal with the workings of a kitchen in full flight, there's a six-seater chef's table - the only one currently operating on the island. Fixed-price lunch is the way to go for top value, but whatever your budget or appetite, menus are built to showcase Jersey's world-class produce - so you can certainly expect the Jersey Royals to be on fine form. The kitchen's style is modern Anglo-French, and Rankin gets it right at every stage, nailing precise, big and bold flavours with polished technique, and bringing them together in refreshingly clever ways. Nibbles such as anchovy sticks, risotto balls, and beetroot and parsnip crisps with balsamic foam show that you're in safe hands from the off, then a tuna and sashimi scallop salad gets the meal off to a flying start, offering lime-scented chunks of fish with wafer-thin scallop slices with Bloody Mary jelly, cucumber sorbet, avocado purée and vanilla dressing. Marriages of meat and fish put in an appearance as a classic combo of turbot and oxtails, the former grilled to perfection, the latter braised to gluey richness, and matched with light horseradish gnocchi and chestnut purée. Desserts show the same precision and attention to detail, organic carrot cake with vanilla cheese frosting appearing with carrot jelly, poached carrots, and cinnamon ice cream with crushed walnuts. An entente cordiale of British and French farmhouse cheeses brought to perfect ripeness by Mr Blanchard offers serious temptation away from the sweet stuff. Punctuated by exemplary amuses such as goats' cheese cake with beetroot sorbet, and a pre-dessert of lemon posset with tequila granité, this is virtuoso cooking at every step.

Chef Shaun Rankin **Owner** Lawrence Huggler **Times** 12-2.30/6.30-10 Closed 25-28 Dec, Sun **Prices** Fixed L 2 course £18.50, Fixed D 3 course £49.50-£58, Tasting menu £75-£116, Starter £17.50, Main £27.50-£36, Dessert £7.50-£12.50, Service added but optional 10% **Wines** 180 bottles over £20, 4 bottles under £20, 28 by glass **Notes** Tasting menu 11 course, Fixed L 2/3 course Sat £15-£18.50, Vegetarian menu, Dress restrictions, Smart casual, Civ Wed 80 **Seats** 60, Pr/dining room 24 **Children** Portions **Parking** 20, Opposite

Grand, Jersey

ST HELIER Map 24

Modern European 

High-class modern cooking in landmark hotel

☎ 01534 722301
The Esplanade JE2 3QA
e-mail: reservations@grandjersey.com
dir: Located on St Helier Seafront

Overlooking St Aubin's Bay, a few minutes up from the beach, the Grand is one of the landmarks of St Helier. Stylish understatement is the decorative tone throughout most of the public rooms, although an exception has been made for the principal dining room, Tassili, which has swathes of black chiffon, dark walls and dim lighting, together with light fittings that look like little stalactites. It certainly makes for an arresting experience. The same could be said of Richard Allen's cooking, which draws on local day-boats and island farmers, as well as handpicked wild flowers and shoots from the coastal paths, for its raw materials. A trio of scallops from the bay are briefly sautéed, classically teamed with smoked belly pork, and offset with a tart apple jelly. Lamb two ways - roast best end and braised shoulder - comes in its own roasting juices, with potato cannelloni and puréed garlic for an impeccably contemporary main course, while dessert might hark back productively to earlier eras for texturally perfect caramelised lemon tart with poached raspberries and yoghurt ice cream. Incidentals, from breads to petits fours, all confirm the class.

Chef Richard Allen **Owner** Hilwood Resorts & Hotels **Times** 7-9.30 Closed Sun-Wed, L Thu-Sat **Prices** Fixed D 3 course fr £49.50, Tasting menu £65, Service optional **Wines** 200 bottles over £20, 6 bottles under £20, 15 by glass **Notes** Tasting menu 7 course, Vegetarian available, Dress restrictions, Smart casual, Civ Wed 180 **Seats** 36 **Parking** 32, NCP

ST HELIER *continued*

black bream with a Niçoise garnish show the style. Turn up on Friday evening for the legendary seafood buffet.

Chef James Waters, Martin Black **Owner** Seymour Hotels of Jersey **Times** 7-10 Closed 26-30 Dec, Sun, L all week **Prices** Fixed D 3 course fr £59.85, Service optional **Wines** 34 bottles over £20, 41 bottles under £20, 12 by glass **Notes** Vegetarian menu, Dress restrictions, Smart casual **Seats** 50, Pr/dining room 50 **Children** Portions, Menu **Parking** 100 yds from hotel

Restaurant Sirocco @ The Royal Yacht

Modern British

Serious modern cooking overlooking the harbour

☎ 01534 720511
The Weighbridge JE2 3NF
e-mail: reception@theroyalyacht.com
dir: Adjacent to Weighbridge Park overlooking Jersey Harbour

The Royal Yacht Hotel has been around in St Helier in one form or another since the Regency period, although a classy makeover in recent years has brought the old girl firmly into the 21st century. The best views in town across the bustling marina and steam dock are to be had from its fine-dining venue, the slick-looking contemporary Sirocco Restaurant. The pick of the island's seasonal and organic produce is hauled in by a sure-footed kitchen to deliver food full of impact, both to look at and taste. Seared scallops with cauliflower purée are perked up with the left-field addition of pickled apple and blue cheese beignets. Main courses might be a modish meat and fish pairing involving pan-roasted Jersey turbot with fondant potato, oxtail bourguignon and glazed salsify, or the old-school luxury of fillet steak Rossini, teamed with seared foie gras, pommes Anna, sautéed spinach, wild mushrooms and Madeira jus. To finish, perhaps Amaretto parfait with lemon curd, almond ice cream and biscotti.

Chef Steve Walker **Owner** Lodestar Group
Times 12-4/7-10 Closed L Mon-Sat **Prices** Fixed D 3 course £25, Starter £8.50-£10, Main £14.50-£29, Dessert £9-£10.50, Service optional **Wines** 126 bottles over £20, 16 bottles under £20, 19 by glass **Notes** Sunday L, Vegetarian available, Dress restrictions, Smart casual, Civ Wed 300 **Seats** 65, Pr/dining room 20
Children Portions **Parking** Car park

Seasons

British, International

Modern British food served with a smile

☎ 01534 726521
Best Western Royal Hotel, 26 Davids Place JE2 4TD
e-mail: manager@royalhoteljersey.com
dir: Follow signs for Ring Rd, pass Queen Victoria rdbt keep left, left at lights, left into Piersons Rd. Follow one-way system to Cheapside, Rouge Bouillon, at A14 turn to Midvale Rd, hotel on left

In a great location in the heart of St Helier is the Best Western Royal Hotel and its charming Seasons restaurant. Attentive service from friendly staff helps generate a relaxed atmosphere in the intimate dining room with its formal table appointments and wooden floorboards. Modern British cuisine with tip-top local ingredients is the name of the game. Start with pan-fried quail's breast with potato galette and port and juniper berry jus. Next up, maybe a confidently cooked fillet of sea bass with shellfish risotto, chive beurre blanc and buttered fennel. Leave room for plum fritters with lemon rice pudding. Lighter snacks are available in the lounge.

Times 12-2/6.30-9 Closed L Mon-Sat (unless by prior arrangement)

ST LAWRENCE — Map 24

Indigos

Modern, International

Vibrant, modern cooking in hotel with sweeping views

☎ 01534 758024
Hotel Cristina, Mont Felard JE3 1JA
e-mail: cristina@dolanhotels.com
dir: A10 to Mont Felard Exit, hotel on left

Perched in splendid gardens on a hillside with sweeping views over St Aubin's Bay, the Hotel Cristina has superb beaches and some of Jersey's unique heritage sites on its doorstep. On a summer's evening you can take in the vista from the sea view terrace, but the smart bistro-style restaurant has picture windows, so the view is available all year. Uncomplicated Mediterranean-influenced dishes are based on good quality produce, perhaps pan-fried local scallops in a starter with sweetcorn purée, parmesan crisp, a salad of pea shoots and sauce vierge. Main courses include the likes of pan-fried fillet of sea bass with tortellini of crab, sauté of pak choi, spring onion and ginger, tomato and coriander broth.

Chef Mark Rowan **Owner** W G Dolan
Times 12-2/6.30-8.30 Closed Nov-Mar **Prices** Fixed D 3 course £21.50-£25, Starter £6.50-£10.50, Main £16-£23.50, Dessert £6.50-£10.50, Service optional **Wines** 7 bottles over £20, 24 bottles under £20, 10 by glass **Notes** Vegetarian available, Dress restrictions, Smart casual, Civ Wed 60 **Seats** 120 **Children** Portions **Parking** 60

ST PETER — Map 24

Greenhills Country Hotel

Traditional, European

Fine dining in peaceful period surroundings

☎ 01534 481042
Mont de L'Ecole JE3 7EL
e-mail: reserve@greenhillshotel.com
dir: A1 signed St Peters Valley (A11). 4m, turn right onto E112

This stone-built 17th-century country-house hotel in the leafy tranquillity of St Peter's Valley is a real find. Owned by the Seymour family, you can expect the whole experience to be polished, intimate and attentive. The sun-trap gardens are a mass of colour in the summer months, and the restaurant provides a soothing, soft-focus setting for sampling fine local produce. The kitchen brings together some quite elaborate modern combinations - smoked chicken breast is served with new potato salad, gherkins and quail's egg with a mustard dressing in a well-balanced starter, ahead of pan-fried local sea bass with potatoes, asparagus, tomato concasse, tarragon vinegar and a zesty champagne sauce.

Chef Marcin Dudek **Owner** Seymour Hotels
Times 12.30-2/7-9.30 Closed 20 Dec-6 Feb **Prices** Fixed L 2 course £12.50, Fixed D 4 course £28-£30, Starter £5.95-£12.95, Main £19-£26.50, Dessert £5.95-£8.25, Service added 10% **Wines** 37 bottles over £20, 46 bottles under £20, 8 by glass **Notes** Sunday L, Vegetarian available, Dress restrictions, Smart casual, Civ Wed 40 **Seats** 90, Pr/dining room 40 **Children** Portions, Menu **Parking** 45

ST SAVIOUR — Map 24

Longueville Manor

– see opposite page

Longueville Manor

ST SAVIOUR Map 24

Modern British 

Refined country-house dining in Jersey

☎ 01534 725501
JE2 7WF
e-mail: info@longuevillemanor.com
web: www.longuevillemanor.com
dir: From St Helier take A3 to Gorey, hotel 0.75m on left

The Lewis family have run their beautiful 14th-century Norman manor-house hotel for half a century. And who can blame them for wanting to stay put? Secluded in 15 acres of woodland with black swans gliding across a lake, you could hardly ask for a more romantic setting. The five 'C's - character, courtesy, calmness, charm and cuisine - epitomise the ethos with which the hotel is run. The last, but not least, of these comes in the form of refined contemporary country-house cuisine, the result of the garden and kitchen pulling together - self-sufficiency in fruit, vegetables and herbs grown in the walled kitchen gardens and Victorian glasshouses is the aim, backed up by the best fish and meat the chefs can lay their hands on. Take your pick of two dining rooms: the oak-panels of the atmospheric Oak Room are from carved oak chests taken from the Spanish Armada, while the Garden Room is a luminous space with French windows opening into a lovely flower garden. Beautiful presentation adds a wow factor at each course, starting with a paella of sauté tiger prawns, rabbit cutlets and a deeply-flavoured shellfish reduction. A light touch backed by skilled French technique is evident in suprême of turbot with champagne beurre blanc, ginger, spring onions and galette Bretonne. Dessert brings on vanilla crème brûlée with garden mint and a strawberry float.

Chef Andrew Baird **Owner** Malcolm Lewis **Times** 12.30-2/7-10 **Prices** Fixed L 2 course fr £17, Fixed D 3 course £55-£68.75, Service included **Wines** 300+ bottles over £20, 20 bottles under £20, 23 by glass **Notes** Sunday L, Vegetarian available, Dress restrictions, Smart casual, jacket required, Civ Wed 40 **Seats** 65, Pr/dining room 22 **Children** Portions, Menu **Parking** 45

continued

SARK

SARK Map 24

Hotel Petit Champ

British NEW

Tranquil setting for an appealing menu

01481 832046
GY9 0SF
e-mail: info@hotelpetitchamp.co.uk
dir: 20 min walk from village, signed from Methodist Chapel

Set in the beautiful countryside of Sark's west coast, you can expect a warm welcome at this secluded and peaceful hotel with well-tended grounds. Once a private home, boatyard and even a German observation post, the only thing guests come to watch out for these days are the magnificent views across the sea, which are particularly stunning at sunset. The restaurant delivers a menu of traditional and modern British dishes with a good use of ingredients sourced from the island: local lobster and crab platter, for example, or pan-seared Sark scallops and confit belly of pork with minted pea purée. Finish with a caramelised fig tart with a mulled wine coulis.

Times 12-2/7-10.30 **Prices** Fixed L 2 course £9-£15, Fixed D 3 course £20-£28, Starter £4.50-£9, Main £13.50-£23, Dessert £3.75-£5, Service optional **Wines** 8 bottles over £20, 69 bottles under £20, 4 by glass **Notes** Fixed D 5 course £25, Sunday L, Vegetarian available, Dress restrictions, Smart casual **Seats** 50 **Children** Portions, Menu **Parking** No cars on Sark

La Sablonnerie

Modern, Traditional International

Uniquely remote dining with home-grown ingredients

01481 832061
Little Sark GY9 0SD
e-mail: lasablonnerie@cwgsy.net
web: www.lasablonnerie.com
dir: On southern part of island. Horse & carriage transport to hotel

Visiting this charming whitewashed 400-year old former farmhouse on the tiny island of Sark is like stepping back in time. Even the journey there is medieval, thanks to cars being banned from the island. The hotel's answer is to send a vintage horse-drawn carriage to pick up guests and bring them down the single lane track to this peaceful retreat. Beautifully maintained gardens are perfect for eating outdoors and taking in the unpolluted air. Inside extremely low beams, exposed stone walls and a coal fire make for a cosy dining experience echoed by the genuinely warm welcome from proprietor of 20 years standing, Elizabeth Perrée. Expect modern international dishes with a strong French influence from this practically self-sufficient kitchen. Fresh Sark lobster done any way you can imagine is a specialty, otherwise try ravioli of Sark crab and scallops with fennel velouté and lime oil, followed by ballottine of rabbit leg with caramelised lemon-shredded chicory and cherry dressing. Chocolate truffle ravioli with rum and sultana ice cream brings things to a close.

Chef Martin Cross **Owner** Elizabeth Perrée
Times 12-2.30/7-9.30 Closed mid Oct-Etr **Prices** Fixed L 2 course £17.80-£23.30, Fixed D 3 course £23.60-£30.10, Starter £6.80-£8.80, Main £12-£15.50, Dessert £6.80-£7.80, Service added 10% **Wines** 9 bottles over £20, 41 bottles under £20, 6 by glass **Notes** Sunday L, Vegetarian available **Seats** 39 **Children** Portions, Menu

ISLE OF MAN

DOUGLAS Map 24 SC37

Sefton Hotel

Modern European

Fine food in a Victorian seafront hotel

01624 645500
Harris Promenade IM1 2RW
e-mail: info@seftonhotel.co.im
dir: From sea terminal, hotel 1m along Promenade

A fine restored Victorian hotel is one thing but when it comes with a new extension set around a unique Atrium water garden and a restaurant with uninterrupted views out to sea, yet just a five-minute stroll from the town centre, you know you're onto a winner. The Gallery restaurant (with plenty of art on the walls) is popular with theatregoers who can opt for some theatrics of their own by ordering the flambé service tableside. The à la carte delivers a mix of modern European and classic French dishes; expect wafer thin Szechuan pepper-crusted venison carpaccio with plum jelly, horseradish cream and port-marinated beetroot, and a very fresh roasted halibut with butterbean purée, garlic, chorizo and salsa verde. Caramelised lemon tart with ginger beer granité, fresh strawberries and mint sugar provides a refreshing finish.

Times 12-2/6-10 Closed L Sun

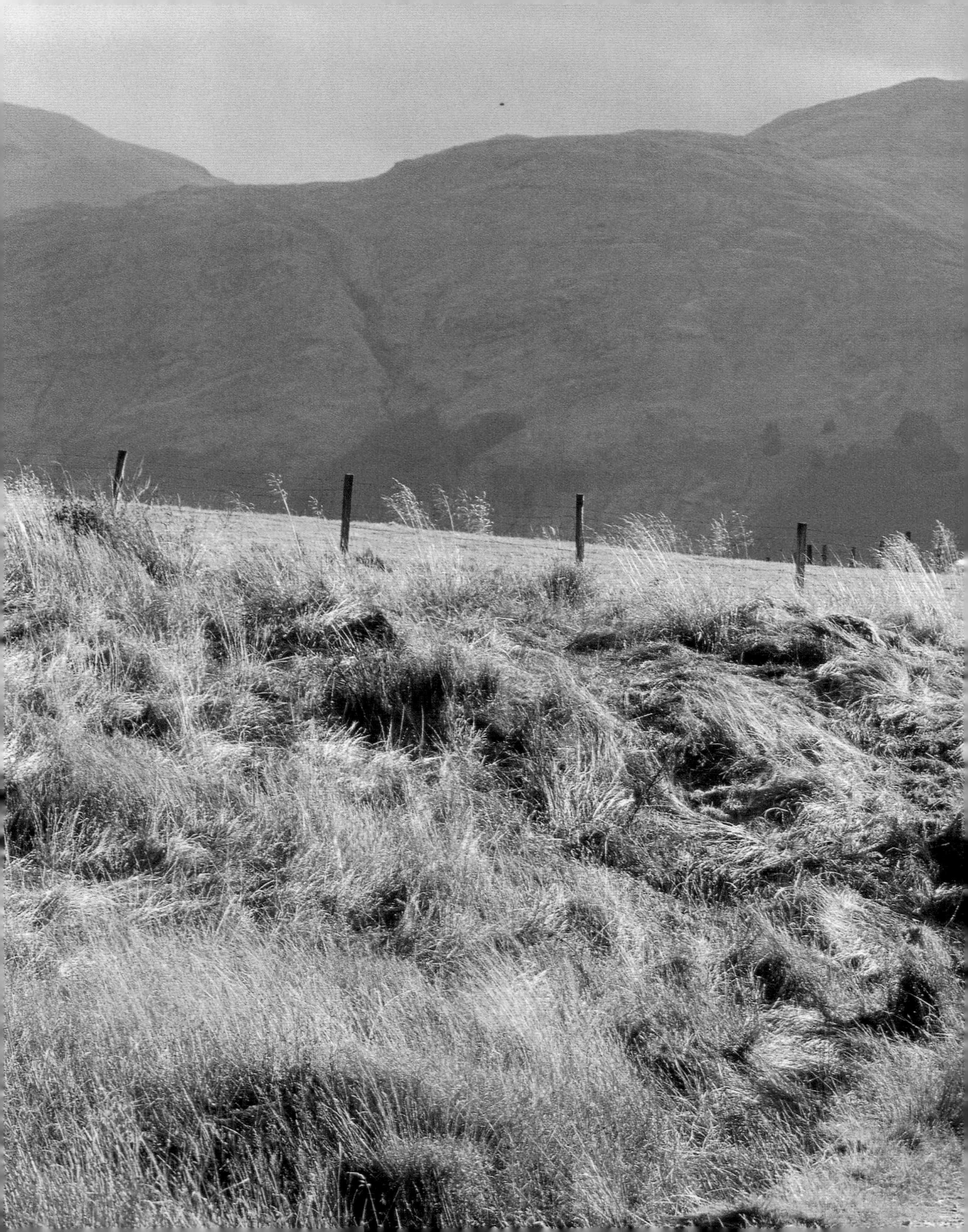

Scotland
West Highland Way

SCOTLAND

CITY OF ABERDEEN

ABERDEEN **Map 23 NJ90**

Atlantis at the Mariner Hotel

Modern British, Seafood V

Nautical décor and local seafood in Aberdeen's West End

☎ 01224 588901
349 Great Western Rd AB10 6NW
e-mail: info@themarinerhotel.co.uk
dir: From S, 400yds right off A90 at Great Western Rd lights

This charming family-run hotel and restaurant is popular with the locals lured to the west of the city centre by its ample seafood platters. Around for over 30 years, the restaurant started off life in an Aberdeen basement but has since moved to the stylish Mariner Hotel. The split-level room showcases maritime antiques, while panelled walls and a wooden floor give a traditional feel. Daily specials supplement the fish-biased à la carte, which includes simply prepared seafood from triple salmon roulade and Cullen skink to monkfish and pancetta brochette on a mixed bean casserole.

Chef George Bennett **Times** 12-2.30/6-9.30 Closed 26 Dec, 1-2 Jan, L Sat **Prices** Fixed L 2 course £16.50, Fixed D 3 course £20, Starter £3.95-£10, Main £14-£30, Dessert £5-£5.50, Service optional **Wines** 34 bottles over £20, 12 bottles under £20, 10 by glass **Notes** Sunday L, Vegetarian menu **Seats** 50 **Children** Portions, Menu **Parking** 50

Malmaison Aberdeen

Modern British

Stylish brasserie with theatre kitchen serving modern Scottish cuisine

☎ 01224 327370
49-53 Queens Rd AB15 4YP
e-mail: info.aberdeen@malmaison.com
dir: A90, 3rd exit onto Queens Rd at 3rd rdbt, hotel on right

The deliciously flouncy art nouveau canopy over the entrance of the Granite City's branch of the Malmaison chain hints that what lies within the revamped Queen's Hotel has nothing to do with its stern grey façade. Balmoral staff were once housed here, but they would recognise nothing inside: the interior is all about decadent fun - sensual textures and in-your-face colours combined in a theatrical look that is the Mal brand signature. Exceptional wine has always been a key note of the Malmaison experience: here you walk through - and on top of - the wine cellar displayed in the glass tunnel and floor leading to the Brasserie restaurant. Surrounded by funky tartan seats, the chefs are at work manning the Josper grill. The 'home-grown and local' section of the modern brasserie menu flies the flag for the fine Scottish produce that forms the backbone of the kitchen's output. Smoked mackerel with horseradish potato salad and beetroot syrup should bring your taste buds to attention, while main course could bring forth sea bass with fennel pesto and shellfish bouillabaisse.

Chef Guy Gallister **Owner** Malmaison **Times** 12-2.30/5.30-10.30 Closed D 25 Dec **Prices** Food prices not confirmed for 2011. Please telephone for details **Wines** 161 bottles over £20, 7 bottles under £20, 13 by glass **Notes** Sunday L, Vegetarian available **Seats** 90, Pr/dining room 30 **Children** Portions, Menu **Parking** 50

Maryculter House Hotel

Scottish

Contemporary Scottish cooking in historic house

☎ 01224 732124
AB12 5GB
e-mail: info@maryculterhousehotel.com
dir: Off A90 to S of Aberdeen and onto B9077. Hotel is located 8m on right, 0.5m beyond Lower Deeside Caravan Park

Dating from 1225 and with past associations with the Knights Templar, this imposing mansion is set in grounds that extend to the banks of the River Dee. The elegant Priory restaurant is in the oldest part of the building, where an open fire, stone walls and wood panels combine with quality table settings and candles to create a romantic setting. Local produce gets a good showing, especially fish and seafood, and some modern cooking techniques bring a gloss to traditional dishes. Start with house-cured organic Shetland salmon with soft quail's egg, baby herbs, shallot and sherry vinaigrette, and move on to the likes of roast loin of wild Highland venison, fine ratatouille vegetables, creamed Savoy cabbage, pommes dauphinoise and bitter chocolate jus.

Chef David Bell **Owner** James Gilbert **Times** 7-9 Closed L all week **Prices** Starter £5.95-£7.95, Main £16.95-£25.95, Dessert £5.95-£7.95, Service optional **Wines** 23 bottles over £20, 18 bottles under £20, 3 by glass **Notes** 8 course gourmet menu available Fri-Sun, Vegetarian available, Dress restrictions, Smart casual, no jeans or T-shirts, Civ Wed 132 **Seats** 40, Pr/dining room 18 **Children** Portions **Parking** 150

Norwood Hall

British, European

Comforting modern food in a splendid Victorian mansion

☎ 01224 868951
Garthdee Rd, Cults AB15 9FX
e-mail: info@norwood-hall.co.uk
dir: From S, exit A90 at 1st rdbt, cross bridge, left at rdbt into Garthdee Rd, hotel in 5m

Built in the 1880s on the site of 15th-century Pitfodels Castle, near Aberdeen, Norwood is all porticoed splendour from the outside, and grand Victorian décor within. Sweeping staircases and log fires are what you might expect to see, and you will not be disappointed. Attentive, amiable service ensures the right tone is set when it comes to eating, in a dining room that is hung with old tapestries. The food is comforting modern British, along the lines of seared scallops with pea and parmesan risotto, baked cod with chorizo, black olives and sun-blushed tomatoes, and correctly made crème brûlée.

Chef Russell R Robertson **Owner** Monument Leisure **Times** 12-2.30/6.30-9.45 Closed L Mon-Fri **Prices** Food prices not confirmed for 2011. Please telephone for details **Wines** 43 bottles over £20, 23 bottles under £20, 9 by glass **Notes** Vegetarian available, Dress restrictions, Smart casual, Civ Wed 180 **Seats** 28, Pr/dining room 180 **Children** Portions **Parking** 100

The Silver Darling

French, Seafood

Fresh seafood dishes with panoramic sea views

☎ 01224 576229
Pocra Quay, North Pier AB11 5DQ
e-mail: silverdarling@hotmail.co.uk
dir: At Aberdeen Harbour entrance

The quayside building looks a little like a miniaturised castle with its crenellated walls, but one surmounted by a many-windowed viewing gallery housing what turns out to be a highly impressive seafood restaurant. There's nothing like a panoramic sea view to enhance the appetite for fish and shellfish, and the cooking fully lives up to its promise, with freshness and sensitive handling at a premium. Expect to begin with a bowl of mussel soup garnished with brandade gnocchi, stewed leeks and deep-fried squid, before going on to seaweed-crusted steamed halibut with emmental potato mousseline, or rock turbot with oysters and clams, alongside a smoked salmon and cucumber risotto. Desserts are in the modern style, with multi-flavoured crèmes brûlées, or sorbets served in shot glasses.

Chef Didier Dejean **Owner** Didier Dejean & Karen Murray **Times** 12-1.45/6.30-9.30 Closed Xmas-New Year, Sun, L Sat **Prices** Fixed L 2 course fr £15.50, Starter £9.50-£14.50, Main £19.50-£25.50, Dessert £7.50-£10.50, Service added but optional 10% **Wines** 51 bottles over £20, 8 by glass **Notes** Vegetarian available **Seats** 50, Pr/dining room 8 **Children** Portions **Parking** On quayside

ABERDEENSHIRE

BALLATER Map 23 NO39

The Auld Kirk

Modern Scottish

Ex-village church with modern Scottish dining

☎ 01339 755762 & 07918 698000
Breamar Rd AB35 5RQ
e-mail: info@theauldkirk.com
dir: From Braemar on A93, on the right before entering village

This stylish modern restaurant with rooms was previously a village church and retains plenty of original features and charm. A fine example of a Victorian Scottish Free Church building, Auld Kirk was sensitively converted in 1986. The Spirit Restaurant certainly has the all-important wow factor: high vaulted ceilings, cathedral windows and ornate chandeliers blend seamlessly with modern artwork and seating. The modern Scottish menu might start with two cold birds – sliced confit of local organic goose and Deeside smoked pheasant breast, served with sweet pickled kale and lightly soused winter vegetables and their own mustard oatcakes. A more classic bouillabaisse could follow. The Kirk Bar is fashioned from ancient pew ends and serves a decent selection of Scottish single malt whiskies.

Times 6.30-9 Closed Xmas, 1st 2 wks Jan, Tue & Wed (winter), D Sun (summer)

Darroch Learg Hotel

– *see below*

The Green Inn

– *see page 476*

Loch Kinord Hotel

Modern British

Victorian hotel with imaginative cooking

☎ 013398 85229
Ballater Rd, Dinnet AB34 5JY
e-mail: stay@lochkinord.com
dir: From Aberdeen take A93 W towards Braemar, hotel on A93 between Aboyne & Ballater

Conveniently close to the salmon fishing beats of the River Dee and the malt-lover's mecca of Speyside, this impressive, stone-built Victorian hotel in Royal Deeside sits in an ideal spot for raiding the regional larder's peerless produce. Inside, the place is snugly Scottish, but brought smartly up-to-date both in its décor and in the straightforward modern Scottish approach that is brought to bear on the food. Pan-fried scallops partnered by cauliflower purée and caper and apple dressing shows a kitchen that keeps abreast of current trends; next up, roast saddle and confit leg of local rabbit might arrive with spring cabbage, dauphinoise potato and prune essence, while desserts such as sticky toffee pudding with butterscotch sauce finish in the comfort zone.

Times 6.30-9 Closed L all week

BALMEDIE Map 23 NJ91

Cock & Bull

Modern Scottish

Distinctive country inn with appealing menu

☎ 01358 743249
Ellon Rd, Blairton AB23 8XY
e-mail: info@thecockandbull.co.uk
dir: 6m N of Aberdeen on A90

An atmospheric former coaching inn, just north of Aberdeen, the Cock & Bull has enough beams to satisfy traditionalists and a serious approach to food that separates it from the crowd. There's a lounge bar where

continued

Darroch Learg Hotel

BALLATER Map 23 NO39

Modern Scottish NOTABLE WINE LIST

Stunning Dee Valley views and modern Scottish cooking

☎ 013397 55443
56 Braemar Rd AB35 5UX
e-mail: enquiries@darrochlearg.co.uk
web: www.darrochlearg.co.uk
dir: On A93 at the W end of village

Perched in an elevated position overlooking the Dee Valley and surrounding hills, this small period hotel has been in the Franks family for some 40 years. It has a charmingly confident traditional feel, with cosy lounges warmed by roaring fires and well-chosen furniture and fabrics throughout. The restaurant opens up into a light and bright conservatory-style space with views over the pretty wooded grounds and wild landscape beyond. Carefully lit original Scottish artwork, linen-clad tables, fine silverware and small lamps make for a smart setting. On the menu, classical French influences are given a Highland touch thanks to the wealth of produce from the local larder. A tasting menu offers the chance to work your way through appealing, flavourful courses. Start perhaps with pan-fried Isle of Skye scallops with confit of Scottish free-range pork. Move onto fillet of prime Scottish beef with beetroot, horseradish relish, pommes gratin and shallot and red wine sauce. Puddings can be as classic as a lemon tart or as indulgent as sticky toffee pudding with caramel sauce and bananas. The wine list is well worth exploring, with a fixed mark-up at the top end of the spectrum making it pretty good value, too.

Chef David Mutter **Owner** The Franks family
Times 12.30-2/7-9 Closed Xmas, last 3wks Jan, L Mon-Sat **Prices** Fixed L 3 course £25, Fixed D 3 course £35-£50, Tasting menu fr £55, Service included **Wines** 130 bottles over £20, 4 by glass **Notes** Sunday L, Vegetarian available, Dress restrictions, Smart casual **Seats** 48 **Children** Portions, Menu **Parking** 15

BALMEDIE *continued*

you can cut loose in front of a log fire, an airy conservatory if you're feeling open-hearted, and if you want something a little more formal, there's the newly refurbished main restaurant. The menu will satisfy a multitude of desires from classic pub dishes, Scottish specialities and some more outré offerings. Cullen skink with leek crisps and bacon powder is one way to go, or there is the chef's tapas platter; next up, perhaps breaded scampi with rustic chips, Thai-style chicken, or roasted halibut with Savoy cabbage and pancetta served with pommes dauphinoise.

Chef Ross Cochrane **Owner** Rodger Morrison **Times** 12-2.30/5.30-late Closed 25-26 Dec, 1-2 Jan **Prices** Food prices not confirmed for 2011. Please telephone for details **Wines** 13 bottles over £20, 15 bottles under £20, 7 by glass **Notes** Sunday L, Vegetarian available, Civ Wed 150 **Seats** 80 **Children** Portions, Menu

BANCHORY Map 23 NO69

Banchory Lodge Hotel

Modern British

Great Scottish produce in a tranquil setting

01330 822625 & 822681
AB31 5HS
e-mail: enquiries@banchorylodge.co.uk
dir: Off A93 18m W of Aberdeen

With its idyllic location beside Salmon Leap Falls at the confluence of the Rivers Dee and Heugh, it's no wonder that the kitchen team of Banchory Lodge have salmon, game and Aberdeen Angus beef as a permanent fixture of the menu. The historic 16th-century coaching inn has a traditional, Victorian-style dining room where the best local and seasonal produce forms the backbone of its modern British cooking. The sheer quality of the materials is what makes a starter of smoked venison, venison salami and smoked pheasant with rowan jelly something special; next, a sure hand at the stoves is evident in a baked fillet of halibut with pesto, seared scallops and tomato butter sauce.

Chef Jeff Purvis **Owner** Mrs M Jaffray **Times** 12-2.30/6.30-9 **Prices** Fixed L 2 course £22-£26, Fixed D 3 course £30-£35, Service optional **Wines** 46 bottles over £20, 14 bottles under £20, 5 by glass **Notes** Sunday L, Vegetarian available, Dress restrictions, Smart casual, Civ Wed 50 **Seats** 90, Pr/dining room 20 **Children** Portions, Menu **Parking** 50

CRATHES Map 23 NO79

The Milton Restaurant

Modern Scottish

Contemporary Scottish dining at the gateway to Royal Deeside

01330 844566 & 844474
AB31 5QH
e-mail: jan@themilton.co.uk
web: www.themilton.co.uk
dir: On the A93, 15m W of Aberdeen, opposite Crathes Castle

You're never at a loss for things to help work up an appetite in Crathes. Apart from its own castle, art galleries and craft shops are thick on the ground here in

The Green Inn

BALLATER Map 23 NO39

Modern British V

Precision cooking bursting with seasonal flavours in a family-run restaurant

013397 55701
9 Victoria Rd AB35 5QQ
e-mail: info@green-inn.com
dir: In village centre

The foursquare stone building overlooking the village green was once a temperance hotel, but in the hands of the O'Hallorans it is a smart and stylish restaurant with rooms firmly focused on the epicurean side of life. There's an agreeably domestic, lived-in feel to this family-run operation: dinners are an intimate affair in a stylish dining room glowing with rich scarlet walls, and furnished with curvaceous blond wood tables and chairs on a tartan carpet to remind you where you are - plus there's a conservatory extension. Dad Trevor orchestrates front-of-house duties at an unbuttoned pace, while chef Chris O'Halloran - ably assisted by mum, Evelyn - delivers the goods in the kitchen. A spell spent training chez Raymond Blanc helped to fine tune the French classical techniques that underpin Chris's modern cooking, while nurturing a passion for sourcing the best local ingredients available. An eye-catching starter brings pan-seared West Coast scallops topped with a soft-fried quail's egg, sweetcorn purée and truffle cream, while Angus beef fillet stars in a slickly-presented main course, with a supporting cast of buttered spinach, smoked pommes purées, glazed baby shallots, wild mushrooms, seared foie gras and red wine jus. A dessert of roasted banana and rum soufflé with caramel sauce scores full marks for big flavours and light-as-air textures.

Chef Chris & Evelyn O'Halloran **Owner** Trevor & Evelyn O'Halloran **Times** 7-9 Closed 2 wks Nov, 2 wks Jan, Sun-Mon, L all week **Prices** Fixed D 3 course fr £33.50, Service optional **Wines** 62 bottles over £20, 3 bottles under £20, 7 by glass **Notes** Vegetarian menu, Dress restrictions, Smart casual **Seats** 30, Pr/dining room 24 **Parking** On street & car park nearby

the gateway to Royal Deeside. The Milton restaurant is at the hub of local goings-on, playing host to the opening of the River Dee fishing season, and making the odd TV appearance. It is a good-looking, softly-lit space with rustic bare beams, jazzed up with artworks on whitewashed walls. There's a light-flooded conservatory for dining too. The kitchen deals in modern Scottish cuisine built on a wealth of superb Scots ingredients, as in Loch Creran hand-dived scallops with chorizo and Puy lentil ragoût and chorizo froth. Mains might offer seared fillet and slow-roasted belly of pork with cider fondant potato and warm apple compôte.

The Milton Restaurant

Chef David Littlewood **Owner** Neil Rae **Times** 9.30am-9.30pm Closed D Sun, (Mon-Tue, Feb-Mar) **Prices** Fixed L 2 course £11-£19, Fixed D 3 course £17-£27, Starter £5-£10, Main £16-£24, Dessert £5-£14, Service optional **Wines** 14 bottles over £20, 17 bottles under £20, 11 by glass **Notes** Early D available 5-6.30pm 2/3 course £13.25-£17.50, Sunday L, Vegetarian available, Civ Wed 120 **Seats** 90 **Children** Portions **Parking** 70

See advert below

OLDMELDRUM Map 23 NJ82

Meldrum House Hotel Golf & Country Estate

Modern Scottish

Elegant dining in a splendid country mansion

01651 872294
AB51 0AE
e-mail: enquiries@meldrumhouse.co.uk
dir: 11m N of Aberdeen (from Aberdeen to Dyce), A947 towards Banff, through Newmachen along outskirts of Oldmeldrum, main entrance large white archway

Meldrum House can trace an unbroken line of history back to the 13th century. It certainly looks rooted into the landscape, baronial turrets soaring out of 350 acres of wooded parkland with a golf course that is a big part of the attraction for many visitors to this deeply traditional country-house hotel. The cooking is Scottish country-house classics with a European edge, built on well-sourced local materials, which might see starters like seared West Coast scallops served with cauliflower purée, beignets, curry oil and crisp bacon. Mains might involve stuffed saddle and confit leg of wild rabbit with macaroni cheese, braised onions and white bean purée.

Chef Peter Conlin **Owner** Sylvia Simpson **Times** 12-2/6.30-9 **Prices** Starter £4.50-£12, Main £11.50-£30, Dessert £5-£8, Service optional **Wines** 46 bottles over £20, 25 bottles under £20, 4 by glass **Notes** Sunday L, Vegetarian available, Dress restrictions, Smart casual, Civ Wed 80 **Seats** 40, Pr/dining room 16 **Children** Portions, Menu **Parking** 60

PETERHEAD Map 23 NK14

The Grill Room at Buchan Braes Hotel

Modern Scottish

Stylish modern hotel serving top-notch local produce

01779 871471
Boddam AB42 3AR
e-mail: info@buchanbraes.co.uk
dir: From Aberdeen take A90, follow Peterhead signs. 1st right in Stirling signed Boddam. 50mtrs, 1st right

This modern hotel opened in 2008 and got off to a flying start with a reputation for good food in its Grill Room restaurant. The open-plan space has an upbeat, colourful modern look, and the chefs at work in the open kitchen add a touch of culinary theatre to proceedings. This is a kitchen that has a passion for top-notch local materials - meat comes from farms around Buchan, smoked fish comes from the venerable Ugie smokehouse, and fresh fish from the local boats. Simple, straightforward modern Scottish cooking is typified in a starter of pan-fried squid with chilli, ginger and coconut, and Boddam crab risotto. Mains might involve unfussy combinations such as roast monkfish wrapped in pancetta with wilted greens and crushed potatoes.

Chef Gary Christie, Paul McLean, Michael Watt **Owner** Kenneth Watt **Times** 11.45-2.30/6-9.30 **Prices** Food prices not confirmed for 2011. Please telephone for details **Wines** 16 bottles over £20, 16 bottles under £20, 7 by glass **Notes** Sunday L, Vegetarian available, Civ Wed 250 **Seats** 70, Pr/dining room 80 **Children** Portions, Menu **Parking** 100

STONEHAVEN Map 23 NO88

Carron Art Deco Restaurant

Modern Scottish

Modern Scottish menu in tribute to art-deco movement

01569 760460
20 Cameron St AB39 2HS
e-mail: jacki@cleaverhotels.eclipse.co.uk
dir: From Aberdeen, right at town centre lights, 2nd left onto Ann St, right at road end, 3rd building on right

This glass-fronted restaurant dating back to 1937 has been beautifully restored to its former glory as an impressive example of art-deco design. Many of the original features have been restored with objets d'art such as the risqué 'Picasso mystery mirror' - nine feet of mirror etched with a naked lady and decorated with tiny silver mosaic tiles. On warm days dine on the terrace overlooking the sunken garden. Seafood features heavily on the modern Scottish menu and daily specials board; perhaps hot-smoked salmon hash served with a sweet red pepper and sour cream dressing followed by a signature dish of haunch of venison slowly braised and served in a port and orange sauce on ciabatta crostini.

Chef Robert Cleaver **Owner** Robert Cleaver **Times** 12-2/6-9.30 Closed 24 Dec-10 Jan, Sun-Mon **Prices** Starter £3.75-£5.85, Main £10.50-£17.95, Dessert £5.50-£6.50, Service optional **Wines** 12 bottles over £20, 15 bottles under £20, 5 by glass **Notes** Vegetarian available **Seats** 80, Pr/dining room 30 **Children** Portions, Menu **Parking** Town Square

Tolbooth Restaurant

Modern British, Seafood

Quayside restaurant serving seafood straight off the boats

01569 762287
Old Pier, Stonehaven Harbour AB39 2JU
e-mail: enquiries@tolbooth-restaurant.co.uk
dir: 15m S of Aberdeen on A90, located in Stonehaven harbour

Smack on the quayside with stunning views across Stonehaven's pretty harbour, this 400-year-old former prison and excise house is the place to come for local fish and seafood. Reached by climbing outside stone steps, the first-floor restaurant has a light, modern atmosphere, with local artwork on whitewashed stone and panelled walls, wooden floors, classy table settings, and a picture window that makes the most of the harbour view. Expect wonderfully fresh seafood on the menu and blackboard, all served with light aromatic sauces and dressings that don't overpower the delicate fish flavours. Typical dishes may include crab soup, olive-crusted cod on pumpkin risotto with herb oil, and roast monkfish wrapped in Parma ham with a raisin, caper and saffron sauce.

Chef Craig Somers **Owner** J Edward Abbott **Times** 12-4/6-12 Closed 2 wks Xmas & Jan, Sun (Oct-Apr) & Mon **Prices** Fixed L 2 course £12.95-£17.95, Starter £4.25-£7.95, Main £13.95-£22.95, Dessert £5.95-£6.95, Service optional, Groups min 10 service 10% **Wines** 24 bottles over £20, 8 bottles under £20, 3 by glass **Notes** Sunday L, Vegetarian available **Seats** 46 **Children** Portions **Parking** Public car park, 100 spaces

STRATHDON Map 23 NJ31

The Glenkindie Arms

French, Scottish NEW

Modern Scottish cuisine in a 16th-century drover's inn

019756 41288
Glenkindie AB33 8SX
e-mail: iansimpson1873@live.co.uk
dir: On A97 between Alford & Strathdon

Shooting and fishing is high on the agenda at this 400-year-old drover's inn, so the kitchen has no problems tapping into a rich vein of field- and river-fresh local produce. Hands-on owners Ian Simpson and Aneta Olechno took over the Glenkindie Arms in 2009, bringing with them a relaxed and friendly attitude, and - in Ian's case - an enviable culinary pedigree, having served a stint at Gordon Ramsay's operation in Claridge's. Dishes are kept unfussy and put together with attention to detail and well-balanced flavours, as witnessed in a starter of pan-seared scallops with cauliflower and pea purée and smoked bacon crisp. Main course turbot is cooked spot-on and comes with samphire and lemon velouté; to end, go for a hazelnut and crowdie (that's a type of cream cheese to non-Scots) torte with Cointreau-baked apricots.

Chef Ian Simpson **Owner** Ian Simpson & Aneta Olechno **Times** 12-10 Closed 3 wks Nov, Mon-Tue (Nov-Mar) **Prices** Fixed L 2 course £13.95-£19.95, Fixed D 3 course £23.95, Starter £4.50-£7.50, Main £8.50-£21.50, Dessert £4.50-£7.25, Service optional **Wines** 1 bottle over £20, 16 bottles under £20, 5 by glass **Notes** Sunday L, Vegetarian available **Seats** 40, Pr/dining room 20 **Children** Portions, Menu **Parking** 22

ANGUS

CARNOUSTIE Map 21 NO53

Dalhousie Restaurant

Traditional British

Fine dining in a championship location

01241 411999
Carnoustie Golf Hotel, The Links DD7 7JE
e-mail: reservations.carnoustie@ohiml.com
dir: From A92 exit at Upper Victoria junct, follow signs for town centre, then signs for golf course

Gourmet golf fans can combine two of their dearest pastimes with a stay at the impressive modern Carnoustie Golf Hotel. Its Dalhousie Restaurant looks over the ball-whacking action on the infamously tricky golf course that hosted the 2007 British Open - an airy setting flooded with light from huge windows, and a clean-cut contemporary décor. Attentive and personable staff make meals go with a swing, while the unfussy traditional cooking built on top-class local produce is more than just par for the course. Expect to find chicken liver parfait with brioche and chutney - all made in-house - ahead of baked salmon fillet with green-lipped mussels and herb butter sauce, or beef bourguignon with roasted root vegetables and rich red wine jus.

Times 7-9.30 Closed L all week

INVERKEILOR Map 23 NO64

Gordon's

Modern British

Confident modern cooking in charming family-run restaurant

01241 830364
Main St DD11 5RN
e-mail: gordonsrest@aol.com
dir: From A92 exit at signs for Inverkeilor (between Arbroath & Montrose)

In the very small village of Inverkeilor near picturesque Lunar Bay, this friendly restaurant is a real family operation. The eponymous Gordon runs the kitchen alongside his son, Garry, while wife (and mother) Maria handles front-of-house. They are a welcoming trio and this friendly mood continues in the rustic dining room with its wood-burning stove and colourful stained glass windows. The kitchen makes good use of Scottish seasonal produce in impressively imaginative and accomplished dishes. Twice baked soufflé, for example, with Strathdon blue cheese, walnuts, pear and crisp cured ham might precede Scotch lamb with lavender crust, a confit of the shoulder, Jerusalem artichoke, cassoulet, greens and a goats' cheese dauphinoise. Baked set lemon custard with gingerbread, white chocolate and an orange crisp is a sweet finish.

Chef Gordon Watson, Garry Watson **Owner** Gordon & Maria Watson **Times** 12-1.45/7-9 Closed 1st 2 wks Jan, Mon, L Sat, D Sun (in Winter) **Prices** Fixed L 3 course fr £27, Fixed D 4 course fr £45, Service optional **Wines** 19

bottles over £20, 25 bottles under £20, 3 by glass **Notes** Sunday L, Vegetarian available, Dress restrictions, Smart casual **Seats** 24, Pr/dining room 8 **Parking** 6

ARGYLL & BUTE

ARDUAINE Map 20 NM71

Arduaine Restaurant

Modern Scottish V

Tip-top ingredients and stunning views

☎ 01852 200233
Loch Melfort Hotel PA34 4XG
e-mail: reception@lochmelfort.co.uk
dir: On A816, midway between Oban & Lochgilphead

The view out over the Sound of Jura to the surrounding islands is really quite special. The backdrop of woodland and the mountains of Argyll is no slouch either. But there are many more reasons to come to Loch Melfort than the view, not least the refined and intelligent modern Scottish cooking, served up in the traditional dining room with large windows framing the spectacular vista. There's an abundance of first-class produce around these parts and they get a good showing on the daily-changing dinner menus, starting perhaps with Inverawe smoked Loch Etive trout, served with horseradish ice cream, rocket and baby capers. Main course sees Gigha turbot pan-fried and served up with Puy lentils, chargrilled asparagus and a saffron mussel sauce, or go for rack of Barbreck lamb. Lunch is available in the hotel's informal bistro.

Chef Colin McDonald **Owner** Calum & Rachel Ross **Times** 7-9 Closed 1st 2 wks Jan, L all week **Prices** Fixed D 4 course £39-£45, Service optional **Wines** 25 bottles over £20, 40 bottles under £20, 8 by glass **Notes** Vegetarian menu, Dress restrictions, Smart casual, no jeans, Civ Wed 100 **Seats** 60, Pr/dining room 14 **Children** Portions, Menu **Parking** 65

BARCALDINE Map 20 NM94

Barcaldine House

Modern NEW

Great food in a real Highland retreat

☎ 01631 720219
PA37 1SG
e-mail: enquiries@barcaldinehouse.co.uk
dir: Located on A828 (North Argyll), between Oban and Fort William

Tired of living in the damp and draughty family castle, Patrick Campbell IV of Barcaldine moved into the more modest new house in 1709. The grand stone manor is a romantic place to stay, with just eight bedrooms and acres of enchanting gardens and forest all around to lose your fellow guests in. The charming restaurant is a winner, blending period features - oak floors, rococo plasterwork and grand fireplaces - with a classy modern décor. The kitchen is a crucial part of the show, turning out deftly-cooked modern Scottish dishes founded on outstanding raw materials - game and meat from the hills all around, fish and seafood from nearby Oban. A lovely amuse-bouche of star anise-flavoured oyster in puff pastry hits the mark, before a crab cake starter served with tomato, spring onions and ginger salsa. Pan-seared halibut appears as a main course, in the company of sea-fresh cockles, pickled mussels, roast salsify and gazpacho dressing, while dessert finishes with a sticky toffee soufflé with toffee ice cream.

Chef Craig Ferguson **Times** 7-9 **Prices** Food prices not confirmed for 2011. Please telephone for details **Notes** Civ Wed 40

Isle of Eriska

ERISKA Map 20 NM94

Traditional British

Luxurious island retreat with first-class team in the kitchen

☎ 01631 720371
Benderloch, By Oban PA37 1SD
e-mail: office@eriska-hotel.co.uk
dir: Exit A85 at Connel, onto A828, follow for 4m, then follow hotel signs from N of Benderloch

When you cross the iron bridge linking this 300-acre island estate to the mainland, you leave the humdrum world behind and enter a little realm of romance. The wild beauty of Scotland is all around the 'Big House', a Victorian baronial mansion in the guise of a fantasy castle. This is a special place: a top-drawer country-house hotel that has stayed elegantly traditional, while cherry-picking the best ideas from the contemporary world - a luxurious spa, for starters, and a classily-refurbished and air-conditioned restaurant. The same could be said of the highly-accomplished cooking: Robert MacPherson has headed the kitchen team for over 20 years, and while his style is firmly grounded in the classics, he dips freely into contemporary ideas and techniques. Peerless Scottish materials - some from no further away than the hotel's kitchen garden - form the foundations of concise, daily-changing menus fizzing with interest. You might start with Loch Linnhe brown crab kedgeree with chilli and coriander, and the silky textures of avocado purée and mango emulsion, then move on to Argyll lamb, which is presented as best end, shin cake, and neck bonbon, teamed with rosemary fondant and broad bean jus. Finely-tuned desserts might include bitter chocolate fondant with fresh cherry jelly and vanilla bean ice cream - alternatively you could finish on a savoury note with Kentish rarebit, or explore the trolley of well-kept cheeses. The extensive wine list is a treasure trove of quality.

Chef Robert MacPherson **Owner** Mr Buchanan-Smith **Times** 7.30-9 Closed Jan **Prices** Fixed D 4 course £42, Service optional **Wines** 236 bottles over £20, 60 bottles under £20, 10 by glass **Notes** Vegetarian available, Civ Wed 110 **Seats** 50, Pr/dining room 20 **Children** Portions, Menu **Parking** 50

The Ardanaiseig Hotel

KILCHRENAN Map 20 NN02

Modern Scottish V 

Excellent food in peaceful hotel with stunning views

☎ 01866 833333
PA35 1HE
e-mail: info@ardanaiseig.com
dir: From A85 at Taynuilt onto B845 to Kilchrenan. Left in front of pub (road very narrow) signed 'Ardanaiseig Hotel' & 'No Through Road'. Continue for 3m

Hidden away down a single-track road, Ardanaseig is ensconced in the sort of jaw-dropping scenery that has graced a million shortbread tins. Such seclusion means tranquility is guaranteed at this Victorian baronial country house. Set in miraculously lush gardens where Ben Cruachan rises from the clear waters of Loch Awe, the interior is tailor-made for holing up over a weekend amid antiques and fine art - but this is no starchy mausoleum. The colour scheme is bold and funky designer-Gothic and staff are young and the opposite of stuffy. And this gem of a hotel is a sanctuary for food-lovers. Gary Goldie is the driving force in the kitchen, and knows what's available in his own backyard - superlative local fish and seafood, and fresh ingredients from the hotel's own gardens, put together with skill and creativity. Dinner is a full-on five-course workout, kick-started by a vibrant velouté of purple sprouting broccoli with earthy wild mushrooms, then progressing via a robust braised pig's head with parsley root purée, spicy black pudding and apple, to a main event of pan-roasted turbot with wild garlic, sautéed langoustine tails and tortellini of claw meat in a foamy shellfish essence. Desserts are also full of excellent fresh flavours, as witnessed in an Amalfi lemon tart with fromage frais sorbet.

Chef Gary Goldie **Owner** Bennie Gray **Times** 12-2/7-9 Closed 2 Jan-10 Feb **Prices** Fixed L 2 course £25, Fixed D 2 course £50, Service optional **Wines** 94 bottles over £20, 4 bottles under £20, 16 by glass **Notes** Sunday L, Vegetarian menu, Dress restrictions, Smart casual, no jeans or trainers, Civ Wed 50 **Seats** 36 **Children** Portions, Menu **Parking** 20

CARRADALE **Map 20 NR83**

Dunvalanree

Modern Scottish

Superb seafood (and more) in stunning coastal location

01583 431226
Port Righ PA28 6SE
e-mail: stay@dunvalanree.com
dir: On B879. In Carradale turn right at x-rds, restaurant at end of road

There are stunning views from Dunvalanree across the Kilbrannan Sound to the hills of Arran beyond and it's the perfect place from which to explore the Mull of Kintyre. This is a genuine family-run operation with mum in the kitchen and father and daughter welcoming guests in the traditional restaurant. There is one sitting, which adds to the dinner party feel. Skilful Scottish cuisine is conjured from the very best local ingredients in a daily-changing menu that might include Campbeltown haggis with neeps and whisky cream, followed by monkfish wrapped in pancetta with lemon cream, and raspberry crème brûlée.

Times 7 Closed Jan-Feb, L all week

ERISKA **Map 20 NM94**

Isle of Eriska

– see page 479

KILCHRENAN **Map 20 NN02**

The Ardanaiseig Hotel

– see opposite page

Taychreggan Hotel

Modern British V

Modern British cooking with sublime loch views

01866 833211 & 833366
PA35 1HQ
e-mail: info@taychreggan.co.uk
dir: W from Crianlarich on A85 to Taynuilt, S for 7m on B845 (single track) to Kilchrenan

Loch Awe could hardly be more felicitously named, as the waterside setting of this 17th-century former drovers' inn amply attests. Those much-travelled companions, Johnson and Boswell, once pitched up here, and doubtless appreciated the beauty and tranquility of the place as readily as we still can today. French-influenced modern British cooking is on offer in the simply appointed dining room, and the format is a four-course dinner with appetiser and coffee, with a pair of choices for starter, main and dessert. Begin with a serving of prosciutto with celeriac remoulade and sweetcorn sorbet, and continue, via a bowl of truffle-oiled cauliflower velouté, to rack of lamb with aubergine purée and olive and caper jus, or potato-scaled sea bass in mussel and saffron nage. Apple crumble soufflé with crème anglaise is an ingenious dessert.

Chef Colin Cairns **Owner** North American Country Inns **Times** 7-8.45 Closed 24-26 Dec, 2 Jan-10 Feb **Prices** Food prices not confirmed for 2011. Please telephone for details **Wines** 33 bottles over £20, 22 bottles under £20, 2 by glass **Notes** Fixed D 5 course £45, Vegetarian menu, Dress restrictions, Smart casual, Civ Wed 70 **Seats** 45, Pr/dining room 18 **Children** Portions **Parking** 40

LOCHGILPHEAD **Map 20 NR88**

Cairnbaan

British, European

Canal views and local ingredients

01546 603668
Crinan Canal, Cairnbaan PA31 8SJ
e-mail: info@cairnbaan.com
dir: From Lochgilphead 2m N to Cairnbaan on A83, hotel 1st on left

Halfway along the nine-mile Crinan Canal, views of the water are guaranteed at this hotel and dining room. Built in the latter part of the 18th century as a coaching inn for fishermen and puffers on the canal, the restaurant is now a split-level room with alfresco dining in the summer. Muted tones are enlivened by colourful artwork and, of course, those views. Top-quality local seafood and meat take centre stage on the menu of well-executed classics. Start, maybe, with seared scallops with Stornoway black pudding and pea purée, before a main of Argyll game pie with chestnuts in a rich port gravy with chive mash.

Times 12-2.30/6-9.30

LUSS **Map 20 NS39**

Colquhoun's

Modern British

Idyllic Loch Lomond location for fine dining

01436 860201
The Lodge on Loch Lomond G83 8PA
e-mail: res@loch-lomond.co.uk
dir: N of Glasgow on A82

It is hard to believe that this lodge sitting with its toes in the waters of Loch Lomond is just a half-hour drive from Glasgow. Even the nearby village of Luss seems a world away once you sink into the embrace of dense pine woods all around. Naturally, the hotel is designed to bask in these world-class views, particularly in the fine dining Colquhoun's restaurant, where full-length windows wrap around a Scotland-meets-Scandinavia décor of pine walls and pillars. When the sun shines, the balconied terrace is the place to be for dining in the open. The kitchen sources prime Scottish ingredients on which its menu of modern brasserie-style dishes is based. You might start with smoked salmon cannelloni with caramelised lemon, then follow the fishy mood with grilled sea bass with potato galette, broad bean fricassée and shallot dressing. If that doesn't tempt, twice-cooked rump of Perthshire lamb with dauphinoise potatoes, minted peas and red wine jus doubtless will.

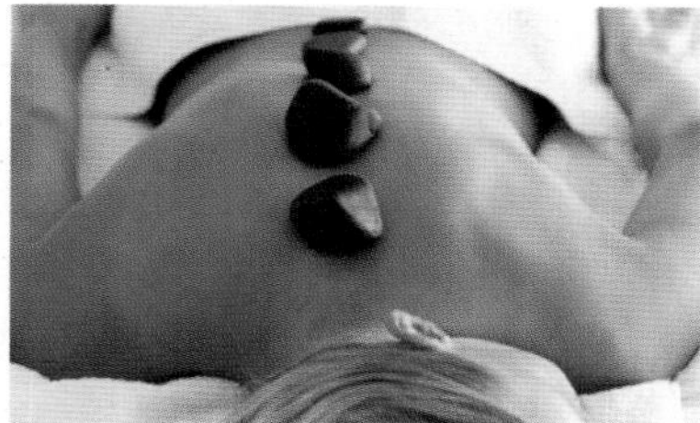

Chef Donn Eadie **Owner** Niall Colquhoun **Times** 12-5/6-9.45 **Prices** Fixed L 2 course fr £12.95, Fixed D 3 course £18.95-£29.95, Starter fr £6.95, Main £16.95, Dessert £6.95, Service optional **Wines** 29 bottles over £20, 20 bottles under £20, 7 by glass **Notes** Sunday L, Vegetarian available, Civ Wed 100 **Seats** 100, Pr/dining room 40 **Children** Portions, Menu **Parking** 70

OBAN Map 20 NM82

Coast

Modern

Contemporary design and fabulously fresh local seafood

☎ 01631 569900
104 George St PA34 5NT
e-mail: coastoban@yahoo.co.uk
web: www.coastoban.co.uk
dir: On main street in town centre

From the exterior, Coast has the solid granite face of the high street bank that it once was before morphing into a sleek modern restaurant. Inside, its clean-cut metropolitan styling stands out from the fish-and-chips eateries all around like a peacock among pigeons, looking sharp in shades of cream and cappuccino, and textures of pale wood, designer fabrics and modern abstract art. The kitchen embraces modern and international influences to deliver imaginative food that fits the setting: unpretentious dishes are driven by the purity of local raw materials - super-fresh fish and seafood landed over the way on Oban's quayside, and meat and game from the hills all around. Starters might bring potted Isle of Mull crab with watercress salad and melba toast, followed by Oban scallops with Parmentier potatoes, artichoke purée and chive sauce.

Chef Richard Fowler **Owner** Richard & Nicola Fowler **Times** 12-2/5.30-9.30 Closed 25 Dec, 2 wks Jan, Sun (Nov-Mar), L Sun **Prices** Fixed L 2 course £12, Fixed D 3 course £15, Starter £4.50-£8.95, Main £12.50-£22.50, Dessert £5.95, Service optional, Groups min 8 service 10% **Wines** 19 bottles over £20, 22 bottles under £20, 5 by glass **Notes** Fixed D available early eve, Vegetarian available **Seats** 46 **Parking** On street

Manor House Hotel

Traditional European

Elegant Georgian dower house with quality local produce

☎ 01631 562087
Gallanach Rd PA34 4LS
e-mail: info@manorhouseoban.com
web: www.manorhouseoban.com
dir: follow MacBrayne Ferries signs, pass ferry entrance for hotel on right

The combination of the beautiful views over Oban Bay, across to the Isle of Kerrera, and the Georgian charm of the hotel, make for an ideal spot to get a real taste of Argyll. Originally built for the Duke at the end of the 18th century, the hotel is traditionally decorated, so expect rich, dark colours on the walls and, in the dining room, a tartan carpet. A pre-dinner drink on the terrace is a fair-

Airds Hotel and Restaurant

PORT APPIN Map 20 NM94

Modern British V Notable Wine List

Splendid Argyll views and first-class cooking

☎ 01631 730236
PA38 4DF
e-mail: airds@airds-hotel.com
web: www.airds-hotel.com
dir: On A828 (Oban to Fort William road) follow signs for Port Appin. 2.5m, hotel on left

The sense of anticipation grows as you head along the narrow road from Port Appin to Airds, where awaits an Argyll gem: country-house comforts on an intimate scale, views down to Loch Linnhe and across to the Morven Mountains, and superb local produce cooked with confidence by chef Paul Burns. Once a ferry inn for those heading to market, dating from the 1700s, the white-painted house is confidently understated, while within are richly furnished rooms and a traditionally elegant dining room, its windows enlarged in homage to the magnificent vista. The provenance of ingredients is second to none, the changing seasons duly embraced, and the modern British dishes imbued with Scottish and French influences. Creamed local smoked haddock with a poached hen's egg and leeks is enriched with the flavour of truffles, followed by a middle course (cappuccino of mushroom and truffle), and then the main event, perhaps sautéed sea bass and hand-dived Mull scallop with a cauliflower and parmesan risotto. Lemon curd mousse with champagne rhubarb is a signature finish. The service is refreshingly unstuffy and the wine list is well worthy of a dalliance.

Chef J Paul Burns **Owner** Mr & Mrs S McKivragan **Times** 12-1.45/7.30-9.30 **Prices** Fixed L 2 course fr £21.95, Fixed D 4 course £53, Service optional **Wines** 165 bottles over £20, 10 bottles under £20, 12 by glass **Notes** Sunday L, Vegetarian menu, Dress restrictions, Smart casual at D, no jeans/trainers/T-shirts, Civ Wed 40 **Seats** 32 **Children** Portions, Menu **Parking** 20

weather treat, but it is no hardship spending time in the bar and elegant drawing room if the weather won't allow. The daily-changing five-course dinner menu deals in European-influenced cuisine with a Scottish flavour and a few twists along the way. Scottish brie is turned into a first-course soufflé (served with a poached pear and lemon and hazelnut dressing) and supreme of guinea fowl is a typical main course served with fine beans, Parisienne potatoes and a jus flavoured with white truffle oil.

Chef Patrick Freytag, Shaun Squire **Owner** Mr P L Crane **Times** 12-2.30/6.45-8.45 Closed 25-26 Dec **Prices** Starter £3-£9, Main £15-£25, Dessert £7, Service optional **Wines** 23 bottles over £20, 32 bottles under £20, 8 by glass **Notes** Fixed D 5 course £38, Vegetarian available, Dress restrictions, Smart casual, Civ Wed 30 **Seats** 34 **Children** Portions **Parking** 18

PORT APPIN **Map 20 NM94**

Airds Hotel and Restaurant

◎◎◎ *– see opposite page*

The Pierhouse Hotel

◎ Seafood **NEW**

Top-notch fish and seafood with stunning views

☎ 01631 730302 & 730622
PA38 4DE
e-mail: reservations@pierhousehotel.co.uk
dir: M8/A82 to Crianlarich & Fort William. At Ballachulish take A828 towards Oban. Turn right in Appin for Port Appin & Lismore Ferry

Tucked away on a quiet arm of Loch Linnhe where the little foot passenger ferry shuttles across to Lismore Island, this waterside restaurant specialises in fish and seafood. The brasserie-style restaurant is a simple white-painted room - after all, there's no point getting tied up in interior design when all eyes are turned towards the array of islands marching across the skyline above the loch. Oysters are hand-picked from the Lismore oyster beds, mussels and langoustines come from Loch Linnhe and lobsters are kept in creels at the end of the pier where fishermen land their catch. The kitchen keeps it all simple: classic starters such as moules marinières let the freshness of the shellfish do the talking, while main-course blackboard specials and seafood platters show off the pick of the day's catch.

Chef Derek McLean **Owner** Nicholas & Nicolette Horne **Times** 12.30-2.30/6.30-9.30 Closed 25-26 Dec **Prices** Starter £4.95-£9.95, Main £14.95-£34.99, Dessert £4.95-£6.95, Groups min 10 service 15% **Wines** 10 bottles over £20, 21 bottles under £20, 5 by glass **Notes** Vegetarian available, Civ Wed 100 **Seats** 45, Pr/dining room 20 **Children** Portions, Menu **Parking** 25

STRACHUR **Map 20 NN00**

Creggans Inn

◎◎ British, French

Fine food in a breathtaking lochside setting

☎ 01369 860279
PA27 8BX
e-mail: info@creggans-inn.co.uk
dir: A82 from Glasgow, at Tarbet take A83 towards Cairndow, left onto A815 to Strachur Or by ferry from Gourock to Dunoon onto A815

Creggans' Inn overlooks Loch Fyne, in a heaven-sent location that is perfect, not only for striding out into remote and unspoilt Scottish landscapes, but also for the kitchen to source the Loch's finest fish and seafood and game from the hills all around. Views from the dining room's huge picture windows are to die for, while its bleached wood floors, rich red walls and crackling log fires in winter make for an upmarket, cosseting ambience. Scottish cuisine is most emphatically what the kitchen is all about, with a menu that offers the likes of chicken liver and foie gras parfait, pointed up with a lightly-spiced apple chutney, and mains of roast loin of Balagowan venison with butternut squash purée, potato gratin and red wine sauce. For dessert, the flavours of a dark chocolate and orange tarte with Cointreau ice cream are perfectly in tune.

Chef Gordon Smilie **Owner** The MacLellan Family **Times** 7-9 Closed 25-26 Dec, L all week **Prices** Fixed D 4 course fr £37, Service optional **Wines** 32 bottles over £20, 33 bottles under £20, 6 by glass **Notes** Sunday L, Vegetarian available, Dress restrictions, Smart casual, Civ Wed 80 **Seats** 35 **Children** Portions, Menu **Parking** 25

TARBERT LOCH FYNE **Map 20 NR86**

Stonefield Castle Hotel

◎ Modern British

Plenty of local flavours in an old baronial keep

☎ 01880 820836
PA29 6YJ
e-mail: reservations.stonefieldcastle@ohiml.com
dir: From Arrochar follow signs for A83 through Inveraray & Lochgilphead, hotel on left 2m before Tarbert

Perched high on the Kintyre peninsula in 60 acres of mature woodland and gardens, this Scottish baronial pile is the very image of a Highland laird's retreat. The magnificent Victorian castle was built in 1837, so expect heaps of period grandeur in the restaurant, plus endlessly distracting views over Loch Fyne through sweeping picture windows. The kitchen treads a line between classical and modern British cooking, with a focus on local produce and a strong line in fish and seafood landed at Tarbert and game from local estates. Start with peat-smoked haddock, leek and potato chowder with parsley oil, before a duo of smoked and slow-roasted pork belly with lentil cassoulet and cider foam. Don't skip dessert - there might be sticky gingerbread pudding with butterscotch sauce and spiced date ice cream.

Chef Oscar Sinjorgo **Owner** Oxford Hotels & Inns **Times** 12-9 **Prices** Fixed D 3 course fr £25, Starter £5-£15, Main £15-£35, Dessert £5-£9.50, Service optional **Wines** 23 bottles over £20, 38 bottles under £20, 6 by glass **Notes** Sunday L, Vegetarian available, Dress restrictions, Smart casual, Civ Wed 120 **Seats** 120, Pr/dining room 40 **Children** Portions, Menu **Parking** 65

AYRSHIRE, EAST

SORN **Map 20 NS52**

The Sorn Inn

◎◎ Modern British

Contemporary-styled coaching inn with modern cuisine

☎ 01290 551305
35 Main St KA5 6HU
e-mail: craig@sorninn.com
dir: From A77 take A76 to Mauchline. Take B743, 4m to Sorn

Run with great flair and an impressive hands-on approach by the Grant family, this former 18th-century coaching inn stands deep in the Ayrshire countryside on the old road between Kilmarnock and Edinburgh - so best to stay over in one of the comfortably refurbished bedrooms. Inside, expect modern styling and a warm rustic-chic décor. The restaurant offers an impressive medley of fine dining and brasserie-style dishes, whether you choose to eat in the cosier pub-style Chop House or the rather classy fine-dining restaurant. Seasonally-changing menus are well thought out, produce is of the highest quality and cooking is accurate, be it the popular steaks and well-established favourites or one of the more innovative dishes. Kick off with smoked haddock croquette with mushy peas, before pheasant with braised red cabbage and a leek and wild mushroom sauce, and round off with apricot crème brûlée.

Chef Craig Grant **Owner** The Grant Partnership **Times** 12-2.30/6-9 Closed 2 wks Jan, Mon **Prices** Fixed L 2 course £14.95, Fixed D 3 course £23.95, Starter £4-£5.50, Main £8.50-£23.50, Dessert £4.50-£5.50, Service optional, Groups min 8 service 10% **Wines** 37 bottles over £20, 25 bottles under £20, 12 by glass **Notes** Sunday L, Vegetarian available **Seats** 42 **Children** Portions, Menu **Parking** 9

AYRSHIRE, NORTH

DALRY Map 20 NS24

Braidwoods

Modern Scottish

Creative flair from a talented husband-and-wife-team

☎ 01294 833544
Drumastle Mill Cottage KA24 4LN
e-mail: keithbraidwood@btconnect.com
dir: 1m from Dalry on Saltcoats road

Braidwoods is a charming converted miller's cottage tucked away down a path and surrounded by fields – look for the signs off the Saltcoat road south-west of Dalry. It's run by two very talented and passionate chef-patrons, husband-and-wife-team Keith and Nicola Braidwood, who have impressive CVs and deliver a level of culinary expertise way beyond what you might expect from its rustic whitewashed cottage exterior. The two dining areas within are a natty mix of dark beams and exposed stone with a modern décor of jaunty stripes, hues of blue and white and stylish high-backed metal chairs. The Braidwoods know that any good kitchen has to start by getting the basics right, so their approach to local sourcing is of the highest order. This painstaking preparation pays off in delivering top-quality modern Scottish dishes of intense flavour and clarity. Four-course dinners might start with whole roast quail stuffed with black pudding, then proceed via an Arbroath smokie and saffron soup to baked turbot on smoked salmon risotto, and warm dark chocolate soufflé for pudding.

Times 12-1.45/7-9 Closed 25-26 Dec, 1st 3 wks Jan, 1st 2 wks Sep, Mon, L Tue (Sun Etr-Sep), D Sun

AYRSHIRE, SOUTH

AYR Map 20 NS32

Browne's @ Enterkine

Modern British V

The best of Scottish produce in an art deco country house

☎ 01292 520580
Enterkine Country House, Annbank KA6 5AL
e-mail: mail@enterkine.com
dir: 5m E of Ayr on B743

Romantics and fans of 1930s period style will swoon over this art deco country-house hideaway in 350 acres of woodland and meadows lording it over the Ayr Valley. The recently-redesigned Browne's restaurant sports a smart contemporary look with a cosy log fire in winter. The kitchen aims high with a menu of creative French-influenced modern country house cooking. Perfectly-judged combinations and seriously-skilful technique are present from start to finish, in dishes that might include a terrine of veal cheeks and Buccleuch oxtail with shallot relish, ginger muffin and pear purée, followed by rump and kidneys of organic Borders lamb with goats' cheese emulsion, baby leeks and olive jus. Intriguing desserts such as pecan nut and honey parfait, bee pollen, toffee lemon curd, nougat and gingerbread are a hallmark.

Chef Paul Moffat **Owner** Mr Browne **Times** 12-2/7-9 Closed Mon-Tue **Prices** Fixed L 2 course £16.50, Starter £6.95-£10.50, Main £9.95-£23.95, Dessert £5.50-£12.95, Service optional **Wines** 36 bottles over £20, 14 bottles under £20, 4 by glass **Notes** Tasting menu available, Sunday L, Vegetarian menu, Dress restrictions, Smart casual, Civ Wed 70 **Seats** 40, Pr/dining room 14 **Children** Portions, Menu **Parking** 20

Fairfield House Hotel

British

Modern Scottish cooking in hotel with sea views

☎ 01292 267461
12 Fairfield Rd KA7 2AS
e-mail: reservations@fairfieldhotel.co.uk
dir: From A77 to Ayr South. Follow signs for town centre. Left into Miller Rd. At lights turn left, then right into Fairfield Rd

The Glasgow tea merchant who built his mansion just off the esplanade certainly had an eye for a good location. In Fairfield House you wake to unforgettable views across an open green to the Firth of Clyde and the Isle of Arran. The Victorian pile has been stylishly brought up-to-date without sacrificing its period charm - Martin's Bar and Grill has kept its high ceilings and fancy plasterwork, blending tastefully with a clean-cut, neutral modern look. Although the kitchen's heart is in Scotland and its peerless produce, it embraces modern and international influences in starters such as a Ballantrae tian of crab and langoustine with lemon crème fraîche and remoulade, followed by a main-course such as seared fillet and braised belly of pork with Stornoway black pudding and celeriac purée.

Owner G Martin **Times** 11am-9.30pm **Prices** Fixed L 2 course £12.50-£19.50, Fixed D 3 course £19.50-£25, Starter £4.95-£7.95, Main £10.95-£25, Dessert £4.95-

£7.95, Service optional **Wines** 34 bottles over £20, 16 bottles under £20, 6 by glass **Notes** Sunday L, Vegetarian available, Civ Wed 150 **Seats** 80, Pr/dining room 12 **Children** Portions, Menu **Parking** 50

See advert on opposite page

Fouters

French, Scottish

Intimate basement restaurant with ambitious cooking

☎ 01292 261391
2A Academy St KA7 1HS
e-mail: chef@fouters.co.uk
dir: Town centre, opposite Town Hall

There's a certain synergy going on in Ayr: this cosy basement restaurant tucked down a cobbled lane has as its neighbour a well-reputed wine merchant. The atmospheric setting is an 18th-century bank vault, complete with the old bank counter and document box; a vaulted ceiling, flagstone floor and modern art inject character and colour. Good ingredients, including a fair showing of local game and fish, play a big part in its French-influenced Scottish menus. Crab cakes with tomato salsa make a simple but effective starter; a well-put-together main course features medallions of fillet beef with wild mushrooms, dauphinoise potatoes and a red wine and thyme jus, while a dark chocolate and honeycomb terrine with burnt caramel sauce and fresh raspberries closes on an indulgent note.

Chef Adele Wylie, Victoria Semple **Owner** Barry Rooney **Times** 12-2/6-9 Closed 2 wks Feb, 2 wks Nov, 1 Jan, Sun-Mon **Prices** Fixed L 2 course £11-£15, Fixed D 3 course £23-£38, Starter £4.50-£6.95, Main £13.95-£23.95, Dessert £4.95-£5.25, Service optional **Wines** 22 bottles over £20, 10 bottles under £20, 3 by glass **Notes** Pre-theatre D Tue-Sat 6-7pm 2/3 course £14.95-16.95, Vegetarian available **Seats** 36, Pr/dining room 22 **Children** Portions **Parking** On street

The Western House Hotel

Traditional Scottish

Traditionally based cooking within the grounds of Ayr racecourse

☎ 0870 055 5510
2 Craigie Rd KA8 0HA
e-mail: msimpson@ayr-racecourse.co.uk
dir: From Glasgow M77 then A77 towards Ayr. At Whitletts rdbt take A719 towards town centre

A modern, two-storey, cream-coloured hotel within the grounds of the Ayr racecourse, Western House is all about celebrating the sport of kings. Its Jockey Club restaurant is adorned with equestrian pictures harking back to the good old days, and Duncan McKay cooks a menu of Scottish dishes, with the emphasis on tradition. Creamy Cullen skink, rich with Finnan haddock, is one way to prime the taste buds, or there is oak-smoked salmon with capers, shallots and lemon. A breast of corn-fed chicken is stuffed with skirlie (oatmeal) and served with honeyed carrots in a sauce of heather ale, while Scots cheeses take their proud place alongside one or two French items, or there might be champagne and lemon cheesecake with citrus syrup.

Times 12-2/7-9.30

BALLANTRAE — Map 20 NX08

Glenapp Castle

– see below

TROON — Map 20 NS33

Barcelo Troon Marine Hotel

Modern NEW

Modern Scottish cuisine in historic golfing hotel

☎ 01292 314444
Crosbie Rd KA10 6HE
e-mail: marine@barcelo-hotels.co.uk
dir: A77, A78, A79 onto B749. Hotel on left after golf course

Panoramic views from the stylish split-level Fairways Restaurant at this handsome Victorian hotel extend over the 18th fairway of Royal Troon golf course to the coast and beyond to Arran. It's a stunning spot in which to savour sound modern Scottish cooking. Daily set-price

continued

Glenapp Castle

BALLANTRAE — Map 20 NX08

Modern Scottish V

Accomplished cooking in stunning Scottish hideaway

☎ 01465 831212
KA26 0NZ
e-mail: info@glenappcastle.com
dir: S through Ballantrae, cross bridge over River Stinchar, 1st right, castle gates in 1m, use entry system

A romantic, luxurious retreat in 36 acres of exquisite grounds, Glenapp Castle is framed by the wild Ayrshire coast, with views over the Isle of Arran and the granite crag of Ailsa Craig. The opulent interior includes enough oak panels to build an Armada, plus chandeliers, antiques and atmospheric oil paintings - and the kitchen team and attentive waiting staff manage to rise to the stately surroundings. The modern Scottish food is underpinned by innovative, accurate and, when necessary, highly technical cooking and utilises the very best Scottish produce, including fruit, veg and herbs from the castle's gardens. A well-executed starter of haggis with neep and saffron purée, crispy tatties and a pan-fried foie gras ravioli is a modern take on a Scottish classic. The pace continues with a fish course - tartare of scallops with salt-cod brandade, cucumber essence and caviar, then a choice appears at the main course - perhaps poached and roast Stanhope Estate young grouse with blackberries and bread sauce. Perfectly-ripened Scottish cheeses come before dessert, perhaps Castle garden summer fruit pudding soufflé with blackcurrant sorbet.

Chef Adam Stokes **Owner** Graham & Fay Cowan **Times** 12.30-2/7-10 Closed 2 Jan-25 Mar, Xmas **Prices** Fixed L 3 course fr £35, Service optional **Wines** 200 bottles over £20, 8 by glass **Notes** D 6 course £60, Gourmet D £60, Sunday L, Vegetarian menu, Civ Wed 40 **Seats** 34, Pr/dining room 20 **Children** Portions, Menu **Parking** 20

TROON *continued*

dinner menus make good use of quality local produce and combine simple classic dishes with more adventurous things, such as a starter of chicken liver parfait with grape and apple chutney, followed by pan-fried sea bass on citrus couscous with spinach, aubergine relish and braised fennel. Puddings may include spiced carrot and ginger pudding with orange yoghurt ice cream.

Chef Kevin McGillivray **Times** 7-9.45 Closed L all week **Prices** Food prices not confirmed for 2011. Please telephone for details

Lochgreen House Hotel

®®® – *see below*

MacCallums of Troon

® Seafood

Appropriately straightforward seafood cookery by the harbour

☎ 01292 319339
The Harbour KA10 6DH

Watch the waves crash over the harbour wall and the fishing fleet land their catch from this stunningly located harbourside restaurant, formerly a hydraulic pump station. In the suitably rustic dining room, a high-raftered, wooden-floored room filled with plain wood furnishings and maritime memorabilia, fish-fanciers flock to savour the squeaky fresh seafood listed on a simple menu that changes with what has been landed on the quayside opposite. A confident kitchen takes a simple approach and the freshness and flavour of the seafood shines through. Tuck into grilled langoustines with garlic butter, perhaps followed by seared sea bass and scallops with crab mash and Pernod cream, or a bowl of bouillabaisse. Service is informal and friendly.

Chef Philip Burgess, Neil Marriot **Owner** John & James MacCallums **Times** 12-2.30/6.30-9.30 Closed Xmas, New Year, Mon, D Sun **Prices** Starter £3.85-£8.95, Main £9.95-£27.50, Dessert £4.85-£5.85, Service optional, Groups min 12 service 10% **Wines** 9 bottles over £20, 17 bottles under £20, 4 by glass **Notes** Sunday L **Seats** 43 **Children** Portions **Parking** 12

TURNBERRY **Map 20 NS20**

Malin Court

® Scottish

Straightforward cooking in a golf hotel with fine coastal views

☎ 01655 331457
KA26 9PB
e-mail: info@malincourt.co.uk
dir: on A74 to Ayr, take A719 to Turnberry & Maidens

A modern golfing hotel on the edge of the all-star goings-on at Turnberry, Malin Court also boasts fine views of the Ayrshire coastline and the Isle of Arran, for those who can bear to take their eye off the ball for a moment. Cotters restaurant has a smart corporate feel, with a menu that ranges from game terrine with mulled wine dressing, through seared salmon in red wine and orange, or herb-crusted lamb chops in Madeira jus, to minted chocolate mousse with Shrewsbury biscuits. The Friday Fare menu offers top value.

Times 12.30-2/7-9

Turnberry Resort

®® Traditional

Fine dining with views to match at luxury golf resort

☎ 01655 331000
KA26 9LT
e-mail: turnberry@westin.com
dir: from Glasgow take A77/M77 S towards Stranraer, 2m past Kirkoswald, follow signs for A719/Turnberry. Hotel 500mtrs on right

The 1906 Restaurant of this luxurious golf-centric hotel is named after the year it opened. But before we get to food, there's a lot more to take in: the Turnberry sits on the glorious Ayrshire coast, with sweeping views across greens and fairways to the hump of Ailsa Craig. And this is not any old golf course: the world-class Ailsa has hosted the Open four times. For those not bitten by the golfing bug, a recent multi-million pound revamp has provided pampering in a top-notch spa, and the Grand

Lochgreen House Hotel

TROON **Map 20 NS33**

Modern British V

Grand restaurant in grand golf hotel

☎ 01292 313343
Monktonhill Rd, Southwood KA10 7EN
e-mail: lochgreen@costley-hotels.co.uk
dir: From A77 follow Prestwick Airport signs, take B749 to Troon, hotel on left, 1m from junct

Say 'Troon' and golf probably springs to mind. Lochgreen House pays due homage to the sport from its setting in 30 acres of spotlessly-kept gardens and woodland looking over the famous Royal Troon links and out to sea along the glorious Ayrshire coastline. Lochgreen House is as immaculately-presented as its grounds, carefully restored and sympathetically extended to provide oceans of space in the Tapestry restaurant, an expansive venue with a lofty beamed roof, drenched with light from huge windows, and smartly done out with plush high-backed chairs and tables dressed in their best whites. Head chef Andrew Costley likes to wave the flag for Scotland's peerless produce, which he puts to good use in his thoroughly accomplished modern cooking. Expect punchy, clearly-delineated flavours and clever texture contrasts in starters like grilled red mullet teamed with smoked paprika and vegetable tart, beech-smoked anchovies, pecorino cheese and aged balsamic. Scottish materials remain at the heart of things for the main event – perhaps medallions of Ayrshire beef with red wine shallots, squash remoulade, toasted hazelnuts and goats' cheese, and charcuterie sauce, or Loch Duart salmon and scallops served with purple potatoes, asparagus wrapped in smoked salmon and beurre blanc. Overt complexity continues to the end in a trio of citrus desserts – lime crème brûlée, lemon curd ice cream and orange marmalade sponge. A well-drilled team seals the deal with correctly-pitched formal service.

Chef Andrew Costley **Owner** Mr W Costley **Times** 12-2/7-9 **Prices** Fixed L 2 course fr £17.95, Fixed D 3 course £39.95-£44.95, Service optional **Wines** 82 bottles over £20, 27 bottles under £20, 9 by glass **Notes** Fixed D 5 course £42.50, Sunday L, Vegetarian menu, Dress restrictions, Smart casual, Civ Wed 100 **Seats** 80, Pr/dining room 30 **Children** Portions, Menu **Parking** 60

Tea Lounge is resurrected for genteel afternoon teas. For the full-on dining experience, however, it's back to 1906, where the kitchen puts a luxury modern spin on Escoffier's classics. Foie gras gets its own section – perhaps pan-seared and served with Calvados caramelised apple, gingerbread and jus gras, while mains could involve poached and pan-seared Scottish grouse with 'reconstructed' Brussels sprouts, cauliflower cheese purée and foie gras. For more informal dining there's the Tappie Toorie restaurant in the golf clubhouse.

Times 7-10 Closed Xmas, L Mon-Sun

DUMFRIES & GALLOWAY

AUCHENCAIRN — Map 21 NX75

Balcary Bay Hotel

@@ Modern French

Top-notch food on the idyllic Solway coast

☎ 01556 640217 & 640311
Shore Rd DG7 1QZ
e-mail: reservations@balcary-bay-hotel.co.uk
dir: on A711 between Dalbeattie & Kirkcudbright. In Auchencairn follow signs to Balcary along shore road for 2m

The 17th century gang of smugglers who used to operate from this genteel country house on Balcary Bay certainly had an eye for a top location: the dramatic views across the Solway coast to the far peaks of Cumbria are priceless - who says crime doesn't pay? And when you're done hiking the coastline or browsing the art galleries in neighbouring Kircudbright, the kitchen is ready with its impressive menu of modern Scottish-accented French cuisine. The Dumfries & Galloway area is a cornucopia of top-drawer produce, which a sound technical hand at the stoves turns into lively combinations of precise, crisp flavours. A warm duck rillette starter is served with soused cucumber, confit cherry tomatoes and port syrup, while a main course poached saddle of rabbit is perfectly partnered with artichoke risotto, wild mushrooms and black truffle foam. It would be a shame to forgo either the enticing Scottish cheeses - how about Dunsyre Blue or local ewe's milk Cairnsmore? - or puddings such as white chocolate mousse in a dark chocolate tear with Kirsch-soaked griottine cherries.

Times 12-2/7-8.30 Closed early Dec-early Feb, L prior booking only Mon-Sat

GATEHOUSE OF FLEET — Map 20 NX55

Cally Palace Hotel

@ Traditional V

Formal dining on the Solway coast

☎ 01557 814341
Cally Dr DG7 2DL
e-mail: info@callypalace.co.uk
dir: From A74(M) take A75, at Gatehouse take B727. Hotel on left

Built in 1763, this traditional hotel on the Solway coast has extensive leisure facilities and is set in 150 acres of forest and parkland, incorporating its own golf course. Marble pillars flank the entrance hall and the opulence continues throughout the interior. In the restaurant, formally laid tables look out onto the golf course and grounds. Gentlemen should remember to pack a jacket and tie for the formal dinner service, when a pianist usually plays requests. The Scottish menu might include asparagus, Galloway smokehouse smoked chicken and rocket risotto followed by Castle of Mey beef fillet, celeriac purée, fondant potato, green beans and beef jus.

Chef Jamie Muirhead **Owner** McMillan Hotels
Times 12-1/6.45-9 Closed 3 Jan-early Feb **Prices** Fixed D 4 course £29.50, Service optional **Wines** 34 bottles over £20, 48 bottles under £20, 11 by glass **Notes** Sunday L, Vegetarian menu, Dress restrictions, Jacket and tie **Seats** 110 **Children** Portions, Menu **Parking** 70

GRETNA — Map 21 NY36

Smiths at Gretna Green

@ Modern British, International

Contemporary hotel with modern, globally-inspired menu

☎ 01461 337007
Gretna Green DG16 5EA
e-mail: info@smithsgretnagreen.com
web: www.smithsgretnagreen.com
dir: From M74 junct 22 follow signs to Old Blacksmith's Shop. Hotel opposite

Opposite the famous Old Blacksmith's Shop that put the place on the map, Smiths brings a touch of contemporary gloss to the home of the runaway wedding. With its open-plan bar-brasserie styling - think polished darkwood tables, spotlights, leather tiled walls and laid-back ambience - it has the look of a big-city venue in the nicest possible way. Locally-sourced produce gets a good look-in on the modern British menu, with due diligence shown to the seasons. Thai chicken soup or honey-glazed pork ribs with ham hock salad and piccalilli lay bare the kitchen's modish ambitions, following on with a traditional chargrilled rib-eye with all the trimmings or Smiths risotto, flavoured with tomato confit and caramelised gooseberries.

Chef Sumit Chakrabarty **Owner** Alasdair Houston
Times 12-9.30 Closed 25 Dec **Prices** Food prices not confirmed for 2011. Please telephone for details
Notes Sunday L, Vegetarian available, Civ Wed 150
Seats 60, Pr/dining room 18 **Children** Portions, Menu
Parking 115

KIRKBEAN — Map 21 NX95

Cavens

@ British, French

Simple seasonal cooking in a home-from-home country hotel

☎ 01387 880234
DG2 8AA
e-mail: enquiries@cavens.com
dir: From Kirkbean, follow signs for Cavens

A white-walled house standing in six acres of impeccably maintained gardens, Cavens is close by the expansive Galloway Forest Park. It's run with the intent of creating a home-from-home feel, the effect reinforced by the hands-on ministrations of chef-patron Angus Fordyce, who cooks a three-course menu with a pair of alternatives at each stage. His soundly rendered seasonal dishes might take in an asparagus tartlet with beautifully soft pastry and a rich, quiche-like filling, breast of corn-fed chicken with well-executed dauphinoise and a classical creamy mushroom and tarragon sauce, or sea bass in lemon butter. Finish with Scottish cheeses and oatcakes, or perhaps a zingy lemon crème brûlée.

Times 7-8.30 Closed Dec-1 Mar, L all week

MOFFAT — Map 21 NT00

Annandale Arms Hotel

@ Traditional Scottish NEW

250-year-old inn serving well-cooked local produce

☎ 01683 220013
High St DG10 9HF
e-mail: simon@annandalearmshotel.co.uk
dir: M74 junct 15/A701. Hotel on west side of central square that forms High St

The Annandale Arms has been at the heart of life in Moffat for 250 years, and still enjoys a strong local fan base, attracted by its sincere welcome and flag-waving Scottish food. It's what a proper inn should be: the ambience is easygoing, there's a battalion of real ales and malts to take on in the oak panelled bar, and a sharp-looking modern restaurant with bare darkwood tables and imperial purple velvet seats. On the food front,

continued

MOFFAT ***continued***

the kitchen keeps things pretty traditional, pulling in meat and game from local farms and estates, injected with a modern tweak here and there to grab your attention. Pan-fried scallops with smoked pancetta and horseradish cream kicks off with well-balanced flavours, followed by loin of local estate venison with crushed potatoes, roasted carrots and parsnips and redcurrant jus.

Chef Margaret Tweedie **Owner** Mr & Mrs Tweedie **Times** 12-2/6-8.30 **Prices** Food prices not confirmed for 2011. Please telephone for details **Notes** Civ Wed 120

Hartfell House & The Limetree Restaurant

Modern British

Well-judged cooking in fine Victorian guest house

☎ 01683 220153
Hartfell Crescent DG10 9AL
e-mail: enquiries@hartfellhouse.co.uk
dir: Off High St at war memorial onto Well St & Old Well Rd. Hartfell Crescent on right

High above the town (but not an arduous walk away), a handsome Victorian guest house is home to the Limetree Restaurant, where the high ceilings, ornate cornicing and shimmering chandeliers make for a comfortingly traditional setting. Tables are neatly dressed in white linen and the work of home-grown artists on the walls adds a local flavour. The cooking shows considerable flair and a happy mix of traditional and modern ideas, all based on good quality produce. A risotto of Jerusalem artichokes, bacon and parsley is further invigorated by foie gras butter, and main-course roast rump of Cumbrian lamb is served up with fondant potato, creamed parsnips, red cabbage, rosemary and baby caper sauce.

Chef Matt Seddon **Owner** Robert & Mhairi Ash **Times** 12.30-2.30/6.30-9 Closed Xmas, Mon, L Tue-Sat, D Sun **Prices** Fixed L 2 course £19.50, Fixed D 3 course £27.50, Service optional, Groups min 6 service 10% **Wines** 12 bottles over £20, 12 bottles under £20, 5 by glass **Notes** Sunday L, Vegetarian available **Seats** 26 **Children** Portions **Parking** 6

NEWTON STEWART — Map 20 NX46

Kirroughtree House

Modern European

High quality cooking in historic Scottish mansion

☎ 01671 402141
Minnigaff DG8 6AN
e-mail: info@kirroughtreehouse.co.uk
dir: From A75 take A712, entrance to hotel 300yds on left

Dating from the early 1700s, this handsome country mansion is rich in history, the most auspicious visitor being poet Robert Burns, who sat on the grand staircase to recite his poetry. Located on the edge of Galloway Forest Park, it is built in the Scottish baronial style, with various Victorian add-ons. Dinner, in the opulent dining room, is a formal affair with attentive service at tables set with good quality china, linen and glassware. The chef makes good use of the abundant local produce, using local lobster, salmon, Kirroughtree venison and Cairnsmore cheeses in his modern European output. Expect starters such as Solway scallops wrapped in pancetta with maple syrup and chive sauce to precede loin of Scottish lamb, dauphinoise potatoes, stuffed vegetables and thyme sauce.

Chef Rolf Mueller **Owner** Mr D McMillan **Times** 12-1.30/7-9 Closed 2 Jan-mid Feb **Prices** Fixed D 4 course £35, Service optional **Wines** 73 bottles over £20, 21 bottles under £20, 5 by glass **Notes** Sunday L, Vegetarian available, Dress restrictions, Jacket must be worn after 6.30pm **Seats** 45 **Parking** 50

PORTPATRICK — Map 20 NW95

Knockinaam Lodge

– see opposite page

SANQUHAR — Map 20 NS70

Blackaddie House Hotel

Modern British **NEW**

Traditional country house with imaginative modern cuisine

☎ 01659 50270
Blackaddie Rd DG4 6JJ
e-mail: ian@blackaddiehotel.co.uk
dir: 300 mtrs off A76 on north side of Sanquhar

This honey-hued stone hotel in a gorgeous tranquil spot overlooking the River Nith started life as a 16th-century rectory and is now in the hands of experienced owners who have grand plans for the old girl. The chef-proprietor was once the youngest Englishman to win a Michelin star, has written bestselling cookery books and certainly knows his way around the stoves. Food will only ever be as good as the raw ingredients, so we're off to a flying start here with superb produce from name-checked local suppliers. It's clear that there's some serious work going on in the kitchen to produce a menu that buzzes with good ideas. Dishes are presented to impress: take roasted breasts of quail with Parma ham scrambled eggs and tomato fondue to start, then lamb with seared scallops teamed with warm lamb terrine, asparagus and dauphinoise potatoes. To finish, a clever assiette of apple presents the fruit in the form of crumble, sorbet, cake, purée, and dust, together with ginger custard.

Chef Ian McAndrew **Owner** Ian McAndrew **Times** 12-2/6.30-9 **Prices** Fixed L 2 course £20.50, Starter £5-£12.50, Main £14-£28, Dessert £8.50-£9.50, Service optional **Wines** 61 bottles over £20, 10 bottles under £20, 11 by glass **Notes** Sunday L, Vegetarian available, Civ Wed 25 **Seats** 20, Pr/dining room 20 **Children** Portions, Menu **Parking** 20

DUNBARTONSHIRE, WEST

BALLOCH — Map 20 NS38

The Cameron Grill

British

Low-lit brasserie venue at the Cameron House

☎ 01389 755565
Cameron House on Loch Lomond G83 8QZ
e-mail: reservations@cameronhouse.co.uk
dir: M8 (W) junct 30 for Erskine Bridge. A82 for Crainlarich. 14m, at rdbt signed Luss, hotel on right

This is one of the subsidiary dining rooms in the Cameron House hotel (see entry, Martin Wishart). It's a singular-looking venue in its own right, with smart leather-upholstered winged armchairs facing leather banquettes in a long, low-lit space, where the main visual cue is a spotlit mural of a group of merry old souls carousing at the table. And indeed there's nothing to prevent a spot of carousing via the brasserie menu on offer here, which runs the range from Orkney scallops with spiced Bramley apple and a fennel and herb salad, to sea bass dressed in pesto, via a slate of steak variations cooked on the Josper grill. Finish with almond and granola crumble with poached rhubarb.

Times 5.30-9.30 Closed L all week

Martin Wishart at Loch Lomond

– see opposite page

Knockinaam Lodge

PORTPATRICK **Map 20 NW95**

Modern Scottish V NOTABLE WINE LIST

Modern Scottish cooking in an unbeatable coastal location

☎ 01776 810471
DG9 9AD
e-mail: reservations@knockinaamlodge.com
dir: From A77, follow signs to Portpatrick, follow tourist signs to Knockinaam Lodge

The wild Galloway coastline stretches away from 30 acres of woodland and gardens enfolding this greystone Victorian hunting lodge. Better still, everything you see around is yours to explore, as the neatly-trimmed apron of lawn leading down to the pocket-sized beach is part of the lodge's own private inlet. In fact, the seclusion here is so complete that Sir Winston Churchill and General Eisenhower met here safe from prying eyes in wartime. The scene is easy to picture in the clubby oak-panelled whisky bar, although the fog of cigar smoke is consigned to the past. The dining room wears unchallenging pastel hues matched with antique chairs and classic country-house toile de jouy fabrics - a decorative idiom that suits the classically influenced style of cooking. Prime Scottish ingredients treated with respect are what form the foundations of the daily-changing four-course set menus. Chef Tony Pierce cooks with the confidence to know that less really is more, as in a simply grilled fillet of salmon, perked up with a simple pink grapefruit emulsion. Next up, a cappuccino of butterbean and parsley with a poached quail's egg, and then the main - usually meaty - event, perhaps roast fillet of Speyside Angus beef with potato rösti, shallot purée, garlic beignet and truffle and Madeira jus. Finally, it's make your mind up time - hot passionfruit soufflé and its sorbet, or exemplary British and French cheeses with walnut and sultana bread? Or both.

Chef Anthony Pierce **Owner** David & Sian Ibbotson **Times** 12.30-2/7-9 **Prices** Food prices not confirmed for 2011. Please telephone for details, Service optional **Wines** 335 bottles over £20, 18 bottles under £20, 9 by glass **Notes** Fixed L 4 course £39.50, Fixed D 5 course £55, Sunday L, Vegetarian menu, Dress restrictions, No jeans, Civ Wed 40 **Seats** 32, Pr/dining room 18 **Children** Menu **Parking** 20

Martin Wishart at Loch Lomond

BALLOCH **Map 20 NS38**

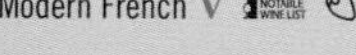

Modern French V NOTABLE WINE LIST

The very best Scottish produce in the hands of a talented kitchen team

☎ 01389 722504
Cameron House on Loch Lomond G83 8QZ
e-mail: info@mwlochlomond.co.uk
dir: From A82, follow signs for Loch Lomond. Restaurant 1m after Stoneymullan rdbt on right

Cameron House has Caledonian charm and five-star appeal in spades, so a link-up with Martin Wishart, a man leading the Scottish culinary vanguard from his eponymous Leith restaurant (see entry), has unsurprisingly proven to be a happy union. Wishart has installed a team here, on the lapping shores of Loch Lomond, under head chef Stewart Boyles. A Canadian of Scottish descent, Boyles faithfully produces Wishart's style of refined, intelligently modern cooking, based around French classicism and the superb natural larder of the surrounding country. The interior designer has picked out warm natural tones reminiscent of heather-covered hillsides, with sumptuous banquette seating, grandly comfortable leather chairs and tables dressed to kill. Precision runs through the place, from the delights of a haggis bonbon among the canapés to the charmingly poised service. Superb produce and well-judged flavours are a hallmark, thus three beautiful langoustines, poached to perfection in butter, sit atop goats' cheese gnocchi in a first-class first course. Again, top-notch technical skill is on display in a main-course fillet of turbot (a superb piece of fish), dressed in a Café de Paris butter, and served with crisp potato rösti, spinach and finished with a light red wine sauce. End on a sweet note with banana soufflé with caramel ice cream or go for the cheese (at a supplement on the fixed-price carte).

Chef Stewart Boyles **Owner** Martin Wishart **Times** 12-2.30/6.30-10 Closed 25-26 Dec, 1 Jan, Mon-Tue, L Wed-Fri **Prices** Fixed L 3 course £35, Fixed D 3 course £60, Tasting menu £45-£65, Service added but optional 10% **Wines** 190 bottles over £20, 12 by glass **Notes** Sunday L, Vegetarian menu, Dress restrictions, Smart casual **Seats** 40 **Children** Portions **Parking** 150

CLYDEBANK Map 20 NS47

Arcoona at the Beardmore

British

Modern British cooking on the site of an old shipyard

☎ 0141 951 6000
Beardmore Hotel, Beardmore St G81 4SA
e-mail: info@beardmore.scot.nhs.uk
dir: M8 junct 19, follow signs for Clydeside Expressway to Glasgow road, then A814 (Dumbarton road), then follow Clydebank Business Park signs. Hotel on left

On the banks of the River Clyde, not far out of Glasgow, the Beardmore is a business-oriented conference hotel on the site of what was once a shipyard. Recent changes have resulted in a newly designed principal restaurant, the Waterhouse, which looks over the river towards the Renfrewshire hills beyond. Well-spaced, smartly dressed tables and bright décor establish an uplifting tone, and the modern British cooking strikes some vibrant chords. A dish of West Coast scallops has its accompanying light ham broth poured over it at the table. Mains run the range from rib-eye and sirloin steaks with your choice of sauces, through roast pork chop with black pudding mash and apple purée, to a generous tranche of roast halibut with crushed potatoes in crab bisque. Properly fragile pannacotta is flavoured with white chocolate, and comes with a hazelnut crisp and coffee syrup.

Chef Iain Ramsay **Owner** Scottish Executive **Times** 7-10 Closed L all week **Prices** Food prices not confirmed for 2011. Please telephone for details **Wines** 39 bottles over £20, 30 bottles under £20, 12 by glass **Notes** Vegetarian available, Civ Wed 174 **Seats** 60, Pr/dining room 16 **Children** Portions, Menu **Parking** 400

CITY OF EDINBURGH

EDINBURGH Map 21 NT27

Apex International Hotel

Modern Scottish

Accomplished cooking and magnificent castle views

☎ 0845 365 0002 & 0131 300 3456
31-35 Grassmarket EH1 2HS
e-mail: heights@apexhotels.co.uk
dir: Into Lothian Rd at west end of Princes St, then 1st left into King Stables Rd, leads into Grassmarket

The aptly-named Heights Restaurant takes up the fifth floor of the contemporary boutique-style Apex International Hotel, and comes with some of the best views in town of Edinburgh Castle through a full-length wall of windows. The setting is minimalist and modern, with textures of wood and marble, glass and chrome, while the succinct, up-to-date menu fizzes with good ideas and top-notch seasonal Scottish ingredients. Expect clear, clean flavours and textures in dishes like monkfish with confit duck leg and Puy lentil vinaigrette. Main courses might bring wild venison loin teamed with salsify, candied pear and sloe gin jus, or pan-fried John Dory with roast garlic, fennel purée and bordelaise sauce. High standards extend to desserts such as dark chocolate and orange marquise with kumquat jam.

Chef John Newton **Owner** Norman Springford **Times** 7-9.30 Closed Sun-Wed, L all week **Prices** Fixed D 3 course £23.50, Tasting menu £45, Starter £5.50-£10.50, Main £14-£18.95, Dessert £5.50-£5.90, Service optional **Wines** 15 bottles over £20, 8 bottles under £20, 6 by glass **Notes** Scottish tasting menu 5 course, Vegetarian available, Civ Wed 100 **Seats** 85, Pr/dining room 120 **Parking** 65, On street, NCP

The Atholl at The Howard

Modern Scottish

Stylish Georgian townhouse with intimate dining room

☎ 0131 557 3500
34 Great King St EH3 6QH
e-mail: reception@thehoward.com
dir: E on Queen St, 2nd left, Dundas St. Through 3 lights, right, hotel on left

A short stroll from the main drag of Princes Street in the heart of Edinburgh, a trio of elegant Georgian townhouses have been tastefully converted into the exemplary small-scale luxury of The Howard. The Howard sticks to the classic Georgian opulence of plush fabrics, paintings and antiques, as typified in the intimate Atholl dining room. With room for just 14 diners, the setting amid hand-painted murals dating from the 1820s and a handsome marble fireplace is akin to a dinner party in a period drama. There's nothing old hat about the cooking though - expect classically-influenced dishes brought up to date with lively creativity, and plenty of Scottish flourishes. Seared West Coast scallops come in a thoroughly modern combination with slow-cooked pork belly, lemongrass foam and pea shoots, while mains could team fillet of Buccleuch Estate beef with braised oxtail, garlic and thyme rösti and pan jus.

Times 12-2/6-9.30

Atrium

Modern Scottish NOTABLE WINE LIST

Good, clear flavours from the best of Scottish produce

☎ 0131 228 8882
10 Cambridge St EH1 2ED
e-mail: eat@atriumrestaurant.co.uk
dir: Restaurant to left of Usher Hall. Shares entrance with Blue Bar Café & Traverse Theatre

The clean-cut contemporary look of Atrium is tailor-made for its location at the hub of Edinburgh's financial district, sporting a minimal décor of chunky darkwood tables, wooden floors and mellow lighting that is guaranteed to appeal to city slickers and urban style fans. Atrium shares the ground floor with the Traverse Theatre, but the stars of this show are Scottish artisan producers who take top billing on a menu of modern Scottish dishes. The kitchen knows the virtue of simplicity, and builds each dish around a few core ingredients, as in a starter of seared Campbeltown scallops, Stornoway black pudding (the best there is, according to its devotees) and apple purée. Follow with Gressingham duck breast, fondant potato, roast butternut squash and pan jus, and round things off with apple tarte Tatin, crème fraîche and star anise ice cream.

Chef Neil Forbes **Owner** Andrew Radford **Times** 12-2/5.30-10 Closed 25-26 Dec, 1-2 Jan, Sun, L Sat **Prices** Fixed L 2 course £15, Fixed D 3 course £24.50, Tasting menu £60, Starter £8-£13.50, Main £19-£26, Dessert £7.50-£8, Service optional, Groups min 5 service 10% **Wines** 200 bottles over £20, 6 bottles under £20, 200 by glass **Notes** Tasting menu 5 course (with matching wines add £35 pp), Vegetarian available, Civ Wed 190 **Seats** 70 **Children** Portions **Parking** Castle Terrace car park

Channings Bar and Restaurant

Modern British

Quirky Edinburgh hotel with neighbourhood bistro eating

☎ 0131 315 2225
12-15 South Learmonth Gardens EH4 1EZ
e-mail: restaurant@channings.co.uk
dir: From Princes St follow signs to Forth Bridge (A90), cross Dean Bridge, 4th right into South Learmonth Ave. Follow to bottom of hill

One of the five Edinburgh townhouses from which Channings has been assembled was once the home of Antarctic explorer Sir Ernest Shackleton. A determined quirkiness imbues the whole place with charm, and extends to the wood-floored restaurant downstairs, which functions as neighbourhood bistro as well as hotel dining room. A starter of pressed terrine is comprised of game bird and hazelnut, with apple chutney, while mains run from saddle of venison with chocolate jus to tapenade-crusted sea bream. Finish with cranachan parfait and raspberry compôte.

Chef Karen MacKay **Owner** Mr P Taylor **Times** 11.30-2.30/6-10 **Prices** Starter £4-£6.50, Main £6.50-£27.50, Dessert £5.50-£7, Service optional, Groups min 10 service 10% **Wines** 27 bottles over £20, 12 bottles under £20, 7 by glass **Notes** Boozy snoozy menu £69.95, Sunday L, Vegetarian available **Seats** 40, Pr/dining room 30 **Children** Portions **Parking** On street

Chop Chop

Chinese **NEW**

Thriving restaurant serving authentic Northern Chinese cuisine

☎ 0131 221 1155
248 Morrison St EH3 3DT
e-mail: info@chop-chop.co.uk
dir: From Haymarket Station, restaurant 150 yds up Morrison St

The exterior is unlikely to draw you in if you happen to be passing. Catching sight of the functional wooden tables and chairs may not fill you with confidence either, but rest assured, there is some great cooking going on here, and it is accompanied by genuinely friendly service. And be sure to get here early as it gets rammed. The punchy Northern Chinese cooking is designed to be shared, coming out of the kitchen as and when. The dumplings such as guo tie (fried versions) and jiao zi (steamed) are spot on, such as the fried beef and chilli variety, full of zinging flavour. There's tender fried lamb with cumin seeds, too, or a broth of pork belly with sauerkraut and fine glass noodles, and unusual noodle dishes such as a version flavoured with peanut and mustard sauce. Service is candid and more than happy to help you through the menu and grapple with how much you should order.

Chef Jian Wang **Owner** Jian Wang **Times** 12-2/5.30-10 Closed Mon, L Sat-Sun **Prices** Fixed L 2 course £7.50, Groups min 5 service 10% **Wines** 12 bottles under £20, 10 by glass **Notes** Unlimited banquet £18.50 12/15 dishes (min 4 people), Vegetarian available, Air con **Seats** 60

Dungeon Restaurant

Modern European

Creative cuisine in a truly unique setting

☎ 01875 820153
Dalhousie Castle & Aqueous Spa, Bonnyrigg EH19 3JB
e-mail: info@dalhousiecastle.co.uk
dir: From A720 (Edinburgh bypass) take A7 south, turn right onto B704. Castle 0.5m on right

You know you're in for a bit of a special experience when the venue is a barrel-vaulted dungeon beneath a 13th-century castle in tracts of wooded parkland on the banks of the River Esk. But before you get down to the foodie business, there's sybaritic pampering to be had in the glitzy hydro-spa. The Dungeon Restaurant is exactly as you'd expect: suits of armour and enough medieval weaponry to equip the cast of *Braveheart*, within an authentic stone dungeon - all romantically candlelit, naturally. Menus are rooted in the French classics, ingredients are top-class - and pretty luxurious to boot - but a questing creativity reworks it all in a contemporary vein. Take smoked boudin of venison with bitter chocolate mayonnaise, followed by pan-fried halibut with truffle and salsify velouté, pommes Maxim and spinach.

Chef Francois Graud **Owner** von Essen Hotels **Times** 7-10 Closed L all week **Prices** Fixed D 4 course £47, Service optional **Wines** 100 bottles over £20, 23 bottles under £20, 15 by glass **Notes** Sunday L, Civ Wed 100 **Seats** 45, Pr/dining room 100 **Children** Portions **Parking** 150

La Favorita

Italian, Mediterranean NEW

Authentic pizzas from a wood-fired oven

☎ 0131 554 2430
325-331 Leith Walk EH6 8SA
e-mail: info@la-favorita.com

There's only one way to cook a pizza for that perfect taste and texture you find in Italy - and that's in the authentic wood-burning ovens that are at the heart of La Favorita's kitchen. The place gets it right at every level: top-class produce, a shiny modern vibe with funky artworks on white walls and friendly Italian staff. The menu brims with good ideas from the modern Italian repertoire, with a sprinkling of Sicilian specialities. Try bucatini alla Norma - long pasta tubes in spicy tomato sauce filled with fresh basil, aubergine, smoked and fresh ricotta and topped with shaved parmesan. And the pizzas are the real deal, including pizza ai due salami - topped with mozzarella and tomato sauce, rocket and Neapolitan and Milanese salamis - or folded calzone pizzas.

Chef Japeck Splawski **Owner** Tony Crolla **Times** 12-11 Closed Xmas **Prices** Fixed L 2 course £10-£15, Fixed D 3 course £22-£26, Starter £2.95-£6.95, Main £8.95-£20.45, Dessert £2.95-£5.95, Service added but optional 10%, Groups min 10 service 10% **Wines** 15 bottles over £20, 25 bottles under £20, 7 by glass **Notes** Sunday L, Vegetarian available **Seats** 120, Pr/dining room 30 **Children** Portions, Menu **Parking** On street

La Garrigue

Traditional French

☎ 0131 557 3032
31 Jeffrey St EH1 1DH
e-mail: reservations@lagarrigue.co.uk
web: www.lagarrigue.co.uk
dir: Halfway along Royal Mile towards Holyrood Palace, turn left at lights into Jeffrey St

La Garrigue is the name given to a beautiful and arid stretch of land in the Languedoc region of France and this neighbourhood restaurant certainly brings a truly Gallic flavour to Edinburgh's old town. It's a rustic restaurant with blue walls and chunky wooden tables and chairs made by the woodcarver and artist Tim Stead. The authentic regional cooking style delivers homely rustic dishes showing great balance of flavour, using good local produce and specialist ingredients sourced by the chef. To start there's pan-fried scallops with pistachio and apple purée or crispy spinach and snails parcel with wild garlic pesto, followed by a classic daube of beef shin in red wine sauce, and, to finish, the likes of warm lemon soufflé with raspberry sauce.

Chef Jean Michel Gauffre **Owner** Jean Michel Gauffre **Times** 12-3/6.30-10.30 Closed 25-26 Dec, 1-2 Jan, Sun **Prices** Fixed L 2 course £13.50-£16, Fixed D 3 course £26-£28, Service added but optional 10% **Wines** 24 bottles over £20, 10 bottles under £20, 11 by glass **Notes** Vegetarian available **Seats** 48, Pr/dining room 11 **Children** Portions **Parking** On street, NCP

Hadrian's

Modern European

Buzzy, stylish brasserie with a cosmopolitan menu

☎ 0131 557 5000
The Balmoral Hotel, 1 Princes St EH2 2EQ
e-mail: hadrians@roccofortehotels.com
dir: Follow city centre signs. Hotel at E end of Princes St, adjacent to Waverley Station

The landmark Balmoral Hotel's polished urban brasserie occupies one of Edinburgh's prime spots on Princes Street. It's a stylish, trendy venue sporting a slick, art-deco influenced interior, with walnut floors and walls in shades of lime and violet; staff in classic black waistcoats and long white aprons set the right tone for its European-accented menu. The Scottish larder provides its finest ingredients for classic brasserie dishes using tried-and-tested combinations. A quirky starter reworks the cooked breakfast using Musk's chipolata sausages wrapped in bacon with a fried quail's egg and slice of black pudding, while main-course Shetland salmon with spiced lentils and coriander yoghurt shows good natural flavours.

Chef Jeff Bland **Owner** Rocco Forte Hotels **Times** 12-2.30/6.30-10.30 **Prices** Fixed L 2 course fr £15, Service optional, Groups min 8 service 10% **Wines** 42 bottles over £20, 8 by glass **Notes** Sunday L, Vegetarian available, Dress restrictions, Smart casual, Civ Wed 60 **Seats** 100, Pr/dining room 26 **Children** Portions, Menu **Parking** 40

Harvey Nichols Restaurant

Modern, International NEW

Slick modern dining with skyline views

☎ 0131 524 8350 & 524 8388
30-34 St Andrew Square EH2 2AD
e-mail: forthfloor.reservations@harveynichols.com
dir: Located on St Andrew Square at the east end of George Street, 2 min walk from Princes Street

Harvey Nic's classy restaurants tend to take the names of the floor numbers on which they are located - in London there's the legendary original Fifth Floor, up here in Edinburgh, it's known as the Forth Floor so as to inject a little local character. And with good reason: the glass walls of this modishly minimal hangout give wraparound views of the Edinburgh cityscape from the castle to the

continued

EDINBURGH *continued*

Firth of Forth and all points in between. The fourth floor is an open-plan mecca for foodies, taking in the food hall, brasserie, restaurant and cocktail bar. It's the sort of place where the style conscious of Edinburgh refuel on the kitchen's polished modern Scottish cooking, kicking off, perhaps, with a white onion and parmesan velouté with a twist of toasted almonds and Amaretto cream. Main-course grilled halibut is cooked just-so, and teamed with a saffron nage, roast capers and grapes, and salt and vinegar mash.

Chef Stuart Muir **Owner** Harvey Nichols **Times** 12-3/6-10 Closed 25 Dec, 1 Jan, D Sun-Mon, 24 & 26 Dec, 2 Jan **Prices** Fixed L 2 course £20-£28, Tasting menu £55, Starter £9-£10, Main £20-£25, Dessert £7-£8, Service added but optional 10% **Wines** 300 bottles over £20, 2 bottles under £20, 12 by glass **Notes** Tasting menu 7 course (with wine £90), Vegetarian available, Air con **Seats** 65 **Children** Portions, Menu **Parking** 20

Hotel du Vin Edinburgh

European V NOTABLE WINE LIST

Modern brasserie cooking in trendy boutique hotel

☎ 0131 247 4900
11 Bristo Place EH1 1EZ
dir: M8 junct 1, A720 (signed Kilmarnock/W Calder/ Edinburgh W). Right at fork, follow A720 signs, merge onto A720. Take exit signed A703. At rdbt take A702/ Biggar Rd. 3.5m. Right into Launceston Pl which becomes Forrest Rd. Right at Bedlam Theatre. Hotel on right

A former lunatic asylum in the Old Town is the setting for Hotel du Vin's Edinburgh outpost. The interior goes for the group's timeless clubby look - scuffed leather armchairs and tartans to suit a Highland laird in the whisky snug, while a buzzing mezzanine bar overlooks the bistro with its wooden floors, unclothed tables and wine-related memorabilia on the walls. Waiting staff know their stuff, and there's a commendable degree of Scottish inflection to the trademark HdV French bistro-style menu. Pain d'épice and Dunsyre Blue terrine with celery chutney is a typically fusion starter, while for main course you can go as Gallic as duck à l'orange, or as Scottish as baked dandelion and burdock ham hock with curly kale and sweetcorn pudding.

Chef Matt Powell **Owner** Hotel du Vin & Malmaison **Times** 12-2.30/5.30-10.30 Closed D 25 Dec **Prices** Fixed L 2 course fr £10, Fixed D 3 course fr £10, Starter £4.95-£7.95, Main £12.50-£21, Dessert £2.50-£8.50, Service added but optional **Wines** 600 bottles over £20, 5 bottles under £20, 12 by glass **Notes** Sunday L, Vegetarian menu **Seats** 82, Pr/dining room 26 **Children** Portions

Iggs

Spanish

Vibrant Spanish cooking close to the Royal Mile

☎ 0131 557 8184
15 Jeffrey St EH1 1DR
e-mail: info@iggs.co.uk
dir: In heart of Old Town, 0.5m from castle, just off Royal Mile

Handy for the city's Royal Mile, this modern glass-fronted restaurant is the more formal dining option to the next-door tapas bar (Barioja), run by the same owners. It's a popular place, bringing a taste of the Mediterranean to the city, with its warm shades of terracotta complemented by large cast-iron candlesticks and antique dressers, not to mention oil paintings and mirrors adorning the walls. The Spanish-influenced cooking shows a good deal of thought and imagination and the menu evolves all the time. Traditional bacalao, cod fritters with saffron aioli, is an appealing first course, before a main such as roasted chicken supreme with jamon, sun-blushed tomato and chorizo oil. The wine list is equally patriotic.

Times 12-2.30/6-10.30 Closed Sun

The Indian Cavalry Club

Indian

Fine-dining Indian restaurant in Edinburgh's West End

☎ 0131 220 0138
22 Coates Crescent EH3 7AF
e-mail: shahid@indiancavalryclub.co.uk
dir: 3 mins walk from Haymarket Railway Stn

There are four dining spaces to choose from in Edinburgh's most stylish pan-Indian restaurant, with quality prints and art objects cleverly used to elevate the tone throughout into the fine-dining bracket. Formally drilled staff are willing to offer advice, and the cooking achieves a high level of precision and impact. A tandoori mixed kebab of five different meat preparations is a great appetiser, and may be followed by gobi dilruba, a South Indian vegetarian speciality involving cauliflower and spinach in a sweet-sour medium, with tamarind and mango sauce. Pile on the style with a show-stopping seafood platter, combining chargrilled tuna and tandoori salmon tikka with barbecued jumbo prawns in green chilli, garlic, tamarind and cumin.

Chef Muktar Miah, M D Qayum **Owner** Shahid Choudhury **Times** 12-4/5.30-11.30 **Prices** Fixed L 3 course fr £10, Fixed D 3 course £25-£36, Service added but optional 10% **Wines** 15 bottles over £20, 16 bottles under £20, 2 by glass **Notes** Vegetarian available **Seats** 120, Pr/dining room 50 **Parking** On street

The Kitchin

– *see opposite page*

Locanda de Gusti

Italian NEW

Contemporary Italian cuisine with a Neapolitan accent

☎ 0131 558 9581
7-11 East London St EH7 4BN

While the name clearly says 'Italian', you won't find a run-of-the-mill menu of Italian staples at this contemporary city-centre restaurant. Forget melted candles in Chianti bottles: the décor here is of the moment, a pared-back minimal look of terracotta floors, whitewashed brick walls splashed with vibrant artworks, and bare darkwood tables. The kitchen team comes from four different regions of Italy, so authenticity can be taken as read, while the overriding theme is modern Italian cooking with a strong streak of Neapolitan style. Fish and seafood is the bedrock of the menu, starting with pan-cooked tiger prawns done with garlic, olive oil, white wine and cream, and paired unusually with cream of butternut squash. Linguine pescatora marries super-fresh prawns, mussels, clams and langoustines with freshly-made pasta and a punchy cherry tomato sauce.

Chef Rosario Sartore **Owner** Rosario Sartore **Times** 12-2.30/5-11 Closed Xmas & New Year, Sun, L Mon **Prices** Fixed L 2 course £8.95-£13.95, Starter £4.95-£6.95, Main £9.95-£14.95, Dessert £3.95-£5.95, Service optional **Wines** 50% bottles over £20, 50% bottles under £20, 24 by glass **Notes** Vegetarian available **Seats** 70, Pr/dining room 30 **Children** Portions **Parking** On street

The Kitchin

WINE AWARD OF THE YEAR

EDINBURGH Map 21 NT27

Scottish, French 

Nature-to-plate cooking of a very high order in fashionable Leith

☎ 0131 555 1755
78 Commercial Quay, Leith EH6 6LX
e-mail: info@thekitchin.com
dir: In Leith opposite Scottish Executive building

The name is no reflection on the declining standards of literacy in the UK - chef Tom Kitchin's name lends itself to his restaurant as naturally as the regenerated spaces of the Leith Dockyards lend themselves to funky drinking and dining venues. The Kitchin rises several notches above the rank and file of the Leith scene, with a modishly functional interior of grey and silver foil walls, bare walnut tables and chairs, and moody lighting. Front-of-house staff are largely French, clued-up and courteous, in fact there's a strong French foundation to the whole operation: Tom Kitchin trained with Alain Ducasse and Pierre Koffmann, so razor-sharp French technique underpins his modern European style of cooking. Kitchin is obsessive about seasonal Scottish ingredients - there's a clear penchant towards seafood, offal and unusual ingredients, while meat and game arrives resplendent in fur and feathers so chefs can ensure butchery is up to the house's exacting standards (proof that the restaurant's byline 'From nature to plate' is not mere marketing flannel). And it's good to see the man himself in his natural element, working away behind a glass screen that allows diners to see Kitchin in the kitchen. Pig's head 'fromage de tête' sets the ball rolling, a rustic slab of terrine, served with a classic garnish of celeriac remoulade and sauce gribiche with mustard dressing. Main course delivers a vibrant hit of spring in a dish of baby squid from Scrabster stuffed with spinach and shellfish, with razor clams and a white wine and tarragon sauce, or meat fans might go for roasted saddle of roe deer teamed with an endive Tatin, celeriac fondant and pepper sauce. Desserts end with full-throttle flavours - spiced chocolate gâteau with sea buckthorn sorbet and candied kumquats, or a classic rhubarb crumble with amaretti ice cream. The set lunch menu offers staggering value for money.

Chef Tom Kitchin **Owner** Tom & Michaela Kitchin
Times 12.30-2.30/6.45-10 Closed Xmas, New Year, 1st wk Jan, Sun-Mon
Prices Fixed L 3 course £24.50-£29.50, Tasting menu £65, Starter £15-£17, Main £27-£34, Dessert £9-£10.50, Service optional, Groups min 8 service 10% **Wines** 239 bottles over £20, 21 by glass **Notes** Tasting menu 6 course, Vegetarian available **Seats** 50
Children Portions **Parking** On site parking eve. Parking nearby daytime

EDINBURGH *continued*

Malmaison Edinburgh

British, French

Unpretentious, well cooked food in waterfront brasserie

☎ 0131 468 5000
One Tower Place, Leith EH6 7DB
e-mail: edinburgh@malmaison.com
dir: A900 from city centre towards Leith, at end of Leith Walk through 3 lights, left into Tower St. Hotel on right at end of road

The location, in a former seamen's mission on the banks of the Forth, is an echo of old Leith, but these days the run-down dockyards buzz with new life, as Edinburgh's cool young things head for its trendy bars and restaurants. The characterful castellated building was prime material for a chic Mal makeover, and its brasserie now looks the business, kitted out with chocolate leather banquettes, darkwood, ornate ironwork and moody candlelight. Straightforward brasserie classics are built on local materials: choosing from the 'Homegrown and Local' menu, you might start with pan-fried mackerel with rhubarb compôte, ahead of venison haggis from Findlays of Portobello, teamed with good old neeps and tatties.

Times 12-2.30/6-10.30 Closed D 25 Dec

Marriott Dalmahoy Hotel & Country Club

Modern, Traditional

Stylish Scots cooking in Georgian splendour

☎ 0131 333 1845
Kirknewton EH27 8EB
e-mail: mhrs.edigs.frontdesk@marriotthotels.com
dir: Edinburgh City Bypass (A720) turn onto A71 towards Livingston, hotel on left in 2m

You don't have to be bitten by the golf bug to stay at this majestic Georgian mansion in a thousand acres of sylvan grounds, but many visitors are here for a round on one of its two courses. The Pentland hills wrap this upmarket country club in a green embrace, but you're close enough to Edinburgh to see the castle in the distance. The smartly classical Pentland restaurant is where the serious cooking happens, showcasing splendid Scottish produce in imaginative dishes; try oatmeal-crumbed haggis with red cabbage, port and plum sauce for starters, and follow with lamb chump partnered with caramelised red onion, polenta and salsa verde. Well-kept regional cheeses and quince jelly make a fine finish, or go for something sweet - perhaps chocolate and orange Pithiviers with Chantilly cream.

Chef Alan Matthew **Owner** Marriott Hotels Ltd **Times** 7-10 **Prices** Starter £5.95-£8.50, Main £18.50-£29.50, Dessert £6-£8.50, Service optional **Wines** 19 bottles over £20, 10 bottles under £20, 8 by glass **Notes** Vegetarian available, Dress restrictions, Smart casual, Civ Wed 300 **Seats** 120, Pr/dining room 16 **Children** Portions, Menu **Parking** 350

North Bridge Brasserie

Modern British, Scottish

Stylish setting for relaxed, modern fine dining

☎ 0131 622 2900 & 556 5565
The Scotsman, 20 North Bridge EH1 1YT
e-mail: northbridge@tshg.co.uk
dir: Town centre, next to railway station, 1 min from Royal Mile & 2 mins to Princes St

When the Scotsman newspaper moved to a whizzo new home near the Scottish Parliament building, its grand Victorian offices on North Bridge, straddling the medieval Old Town and the Georgian New Town, were ripe for transformation into a top-ranking hotel. After a megabucks redevelopment, the Scotsman Hotel blends glorious period features with sharp contemporary design. In the hierarchical old days, only the editors were allowed to use the superb marble staircase leading to the bustling brasserie, where marble pillars, fancy plasterwork and oak panelling abound in an imposing space with a dramatic mezzanine galleried area. The kitchen takes a classic brasserie approach, creating intelligent food that meets the demands of traditionalists and modernists. Beetroot-cured salmon is served with pickled cucumber and the kick of horseradish cream, followed by rump of lamb with crushed peas and fondant potato. Dessert delivers punchy flavours in a citrus jelly with banana and passionfruit sorbet.

Times 12-2.30/6-10.30

Norton House Hotel

EDINBURGH **Map 21 NT27**

Modern British, French

Sophisticated fine-dining restaurant in elegant hotel

☎ 0131 333 1275
Ingliston EH28 8LX
e-mail: nortonhouse@handpicked.co.uk
dir: M8 junct 2, off A8, 0.5m past Edinburgh Airport

Norton House still goes about the business for which it was intended when it was built by the wealthy Usher brewing family at the start of Victoria's reign: providing a bolt-hole from the commotion of Edinburgh. The realities of 21st-century life may be nearby - Edinburgh Airport is just two miles away - but 55 acres of lovely grounds are an ample buffer, and the sybaritic delights of this opulent contemporary country-house hotel include a smart spa and some serious dining. The interior sports a slick contemporary look to offset its period grandeur: a sleek metropolitan-style brasserie done out in black leather and darkwood is the entry-level option to see what the kitchen can do, but all the stops are pulled out in Ushers, the sophisticated fine-dining venue. Its edible colour scheme of cappuccino, toffee and chocolate seems chosen specifically to provoke the appetite, and with just eight well-spaced tables to cater for, the kitchen and front-of-house teams have no trouble delivering Rolls Royce service. Head chef Greg Anderson has perfected a culinary style that is unmistakably rooted in the French classics, but shot through with modern flourishes and painstaking attention to detail. Naturally, top-class ingredients underpin everything, put together in some thought-provoking combinations, delivered by a team that has the technical skills and intelligence to pull it off. Tortelloni of Scottish langoustine come with the full-throttle flavours of pig's head, parsnip purée and shellfish foam, ahead of perfectly-cooked sea bass with broad beans, chorizo and chicory. Masterful desserts are also imbued with deep, complex flavours - crisp rice pudding beignets counterpointed by the sharp citrus zing of blood orange sorbet and contrasting textures of blood orange and Amaretto jellies.

Chef Graeme Shaw, Greg Anderson, Glen Bilins **Owner** Hand Picked Hotels **Times** 7-9.30 Closed 26 Dec, 1 Jan, Sun-Mon, L all week **Prices** Fixed D 3 course fr £30, Starter £7.95-£12.50, Main £22.95-£28.50, Dessert £8.50, Service optional **Wines** 168 bottles over £20, 12 by glass **Notes** Tasting menu £80 incl wine, Vegetarian available, Civ Wed 140 **Seats** 22, Pr/dining room 40 **Children** Portions **Parking** 100

Norton House Hotel

@@@ – *see opposite page*

Number One, The Balmoral Hotel

@@@ – *see below*

Plumed Horse

@@@ – *see page 496*

The Restaurant at the Bonham

@@ Modern Scottish

Stylish urban setting for lively, modern cooking

☎ 0131 274 7445 & 274 7400
35 Drumsheugh Gardens EH3 7RN
e-mail: restaurant@thebonham.com
dir: At W end of Princes St

Peer behind the sober Victorian façade of this elegant townhouse in Drumsheugh Gardens, and the spiralling crimson sofa makes it clear that something out of the ordinary is going on inside. The boutique Bonham is in the Premier League of interior style statements, pulling together the period detail of burnished hardwood floors, oak panelling and fancy plasterwork with an ever-changing exhibition of modern art in an explosion of vibrant colour. The restaurant décor seems designed to provoke the appetite with shades of apricot, chocolate and coffee, and textures of polished woods and leather. Classy, then, and the polished service and refined, creative cooking, built on high-quality Scottish ingredients, match the setting. Chef Michel Bouyer's cooking is rooted in French classics with a modern feel. A top-value market menu reaches for what's good on that day and turns it into simple full-flavoured dishes, such as wood pigeon casserole with chive mash, while full-on dinner dishes run to a more adventurous seared fillet of sea bass with leek and potato Parmentier, mussels and brown shrimp broth.

Chef Michel Bouyer **Owner** Peter Taylor, The Town House Company **Times** 12-2.30/6.30-10 **Prices** Fixed L 2 course £14.50-£20, Fixed D 3 course £18-£25, Starter £7-£13, Main £15-£28.50, Dessert £6.50-£8.50, Service added but optional 10%, Groups min 6 service 10% **Wines** 38 bottles over £20, 8 bottles under £20, 9 by glass **Notes** Sunday L, Vegetarian available **Seats** 60, Pr/dining room 26 **Children** Portions **Parking** 20, NCP

Restaurant Martin Wishart

@@@@ – *see page 497*

Rhubarb - the Restaurant at Prestonfield

@@ Traditional British

Opulent surroundings for high-impact cooking

☎ 0131 225 1333
Prestonfield House, Priestfield Rd EH16 5UT
e-mail: reservations@prestonfield.com
web: www.rhubarb-restaurant.com
dir: Exit city centre on Nicholson St, onto Dalkeith Rd. At lights turn left into Priestfield Rd. Prestonfield on left

continued on page 498

Number One, The Balmoral Hotel

EDINBURGH **Map 21 NT27**

Modern Scottish, French

Highly refined haute cuisine at the heart of the Scottish capital

☎ 0131 557 6727
1 Princes St EH2 2EQ
e-mail: numberone@roccofortecollection.com
dir: follow city centre signs. Hotel at E end of Princes St, adjacent to Waverley Station

The Balmoral could hardly be better placed to impress. A short trot from Waverley railway station, it sits at the start of the most prestigious shopping street in Scotland. Nor does it disappoint once you're through the doors, with rich red lacquered walls, carpets to sink into, and well-spaced tables all looking the part in the Number One restaurant. Menus, under the executive direction of Jeff Bland, continue to ply an essentially classical line, with discreet modern embellishments throughout. A starter of crab millefeuille, the fresh brown meat sandwiched between wafer-thin biscuits, is accompanied by an intense pannacotta of crab, and mayonnaise dressing gently teased with wasabi. Seafood is highly reliable in main courses too, as in a partnership of well-timed John Dory and langoustine with morels, asparagus and peas in an opulently buttery shellfish sauce. Meat options may include the celebrated Borders beef fillet with oxtail ravioli, puréed squash and braised leeks. Desserts end proceedings on a high, with the likes of small but perfectly formed lemon savarin, teamed with crème caramel, strawberry ice cream and streaks of balsamic syrup.

Chef Jeff Bland, Craig Sandle **Owner** Rocco Forte Hotels **Times** 6.30-10 Closed 1st 2 wks Jan, L all week **Prices** Fixed D 3 course £59, Tasting menu fr £65, Service optional, Groups min 6 service 12.5% **Wines** 350 bottles over £20, 8 by glass **Notes** 8 course tasting menu, Vegetarian available, Dress restrictions, Smart casual preferred, Civ Wed 60 **Seats** 50, Pr/dining room 50 **Children** Portions **Parking** NCP: Greenside/St James Centre

Plumed Horse

EDINBURGH Map 21 NT27

Modern European

Imaginative cuisine served in Georgian grandeur

☎ 0131 554 5556 & 05601 123266
50-54 Henderson St, Leith EH6 6DE
e-mail: plumedhorse@aol.com
web: www.plumedhorse.co.uk
dir: From city centre N on Leith Walk, left into Great Junction St & 1st right into Henderson St. Restaurant 200mtrs on right

Leith has gathered critical mass as a foodie destination in recent years, with some heavyweight venues not far from the Plumed Horse. The unassuming Georgian building doesn't stand out from the neighbours, but the wow factor takes off once you're through the door. A smart, understated décor blends with grand period plasterwork and a monthly-changing exhibition of art on the walls in a rather classy, intimate ambience. A small team delivers correctly formal service in a way that suits the French-influenced cooking of chef-proprietor Tony Borthwick. Only the best local ingredients make it into the kitchen to form the backbone of his imaginative output. Menus are tightly focused - just four choices at each course - and conceived to deliver some surprising taste and texture combinations, as seen in a ballottine of smoked foie gras with confit duck leg bonbon, its richness offset by a robustly-flavoured quenelle of brandy-soaked cherries. Main course brings a roast fillet of halibut with olive and Arran Victory potato mash, a subtle swipe of fennel purée, vanilla foam and red pepper butter sauce. Rich flavours and textural contrasts continue in a glossy chocolate and peanut pavé with banana sherbet and marshmallows.

Chef Tony Borthwick **Owner** The Company of The Plumed Horse Ltd **Times** 12.30-1.30/7-9 Closed Xmas, New Year, 2 wks Summer, l wk Easter, Sun-Mon **Prices** Fixed L 3 course £25, Fixed D 3 course £46, Tasting menu £57, Service optional **Wines** 165 bottles over £20, 24 bottles under £20, 10 by glass **Notes** ALC menu 5 courses £50 **Seats** 36, Pr/dining room 10 **Parking** On street

Restaurant Martin Wishart

EDINBURGH Map 21 NT27

Modern French V NOTABLE WINE LIST

Imaginative, memorable French cooking in intimate, fashionable waterfront venue

☎ 0131 553 3557
54 The Shore, Leith EH6 6RA
e-mail: info@martin-wishart.co.uk
dir: Please telephone for directions/map on website

The reinvention of the UK's redundant dockyards has been a phenomenon of our age. Not that long ago, Leith was a place to avoid; now the thriving cluster of trendy bars and restaurants are one of Edinburgh's hot tickets, and Martin Wishart's operation is at the top of the pile. Over the last decade, Martin Wishart has gone from strength to strength in his culinary vision. Immaculate attention to detail from start to finish characterises the ethos in the flagship Leith restaurant, where he delivers a high-art take on classical French traditions, without resorting to gimmicks. The cooking demonstrates an innate understanding of how ingredients work together, pulling off some surprisingly left-field combinations of flavour and texture; first-class Scottish produce can be taken as read. The room is super-cool and contemporary, done out in unshowy style-magazine tones of caramel, chocolate and cream, with contemporary artworks and oceans of space between tables dressed in their best whites. The fixed-price menu format involves a keenly-priced daily set-lunch, an à la carte option with a choice of five or six dishes at each stage, and the full-works six-course tasting extravaganza; vegetarians need not feel marginalised – they get a six-course taster too, plus bespoke à la carte choices. As soon as the first of a stream of canapés turns up, it is clear that presentation is superb and evidently the result of serious time spent on each dish. This is a kitchen that might send out a pressé of foie gras with praline, apricot purée, black olive tapenade and Madeira cream to kick-start the palate, or a gratin of Kilbrannon langoustine with Devon snails, parsley and grain mustard. Cooking treatments deliver a light touch, as in a main-course fillet of steamed sea bass, accompanied by a gratin of white asparagus, pommes soufflée, and a morel and rosemary jus, while other combinations could see a more avante-garde pairing of Dover sole with braised pig's trotter and mushrooms, served with wheat cracker, mushroom vinaigrette and braising jus. Classy desserts also aim for lightness – perhaps a cylinder of dark chocolate with Jivara milk chocolate mousse, lemon cream and Earl Grey ice cream. With one member of staff for every two guests, service is attentive beyond reproach, without being overly intrusive, and the expert sommelier is a match for the exemplary wine list, which excels in classic French regions without neglecting the rest of the world. For equally refined dining on the bonny, bonny banks of Loch Lomond, Martin Wishart has a second operation in Cameron House (see entry).

Chef Martin Wishart **Owner** Martin Wishart **Times** 12-2/6.30-10 Closed 25-26 Dec, 1 Jan, 2 wks Jan, Sun-Mon **Prices** Fixed L 3 course £24.50, Fixed D 3 course £60, Service optional, Groups min 6 service 10% **Wines** 200+ bottles over £20, 2 bottles under £20, 12 by glass **Notes** Vegetarian menu, Dress restrictions, Smart casual **Seats** 50, Pr/dining room 10 **Children** Portions **Parking** On street

EDINBURGH ***continued***

The story goes that Bonnie Prince Charlie, stopping in at Prestonfield, once stabbed the table with his fork in a bit of a tantrum - explaining why the forks at the table settings in the Rhubarb restaurant today are all turned respectfully tines-down. Not that there need be any tantrums today. The place is a haven of luxurious elegance, next to Holyrood Park on the outskirts of Edinburgh. Ruby-red furnishings and high-class table settings with flickering tea-lights set the elevated tone, and the cooking rarely disappoints. An opulent opener of roast pheasant with black pudding is sweetly offset with roasted quince and red cabbage purée, while lightly smoked Loch Duart salmon is teamed with its own caviar, horseradish and wood sorrel. Dishes look smart and deliver real impact, as when crisp-skinned sea bream is partnered with squat lobster risotto, spiced pumpkin and coconut.

Rhubarb – the Restaurant at Prestonfield

Chef John McMahon **Owner** James Thomson OBE **Times** 12-2/6-11 **Prices** Fixed L 2 course £16.95, Fixed D 3 course £30, Starter £10-£16, Main £15-£33, Dessert £6.50-£8.95, Service optional, Groups min 8 service 10% **Wines** 500+ bottles over £20, 12 by glass **Notes** Theatre D 2 course £16.95, Sunday L, Vegetarian available, Civ Wed 500 **Seats** 90, Pr/dining room 500 **Children** Portions **Parking** 200

The Royal Terrace Hotel

Modern British

Brasserie fare in a luxurious Georgian townhouse

☎ 0131 557 3222
18 Royal Ter EH7 5AQ
dir: A8 to city centre, follow one-way system, left into Charlotte Sq. At end right into Queens St. Left at rdbt. At next island right into London Rd, right into Blenheim Place leading to Royal Terrace

Combining traditional charm with contemporary luxury this recently refurbished hotel is in a prime and peaceful spot a short walk from the centre of Edinburgh. Part of a terrace of prestigious Georgian townhouses, the Royal Terrace enjoys views over the Firth of Forth and its own landscaped gardens. In the Terrace Brasserie, or looking out over those gardens in the conservatory, expect roast cannon of rabbit wrapped in pancetta with sautéed kidneys and bacon lardons, and a homely main of oven-roasted Borders' lamb with minted mash potato and rosemary jus. A retro pud of vanilla banana split parfait with chocolate strawberries rounds things off nicely.

Chef Steven Scutt **Owner** Liam Walshe **Times** 5-9.30 **Prices** Fixed L 2 course £12-£18, Fixed D 3 course £28-£30 **Wines** 50 bottles over £20, 6 bottles under £20, 10 by glass **Notes** Pre-theatre menu 2 course 5-7pm, Vegetarian available, Civ Wed 75 **Seats** 40, Pr/dining room 24 **Parking** On street (charged)

Santini Restaurant

Italian **NEW**

Authentic Italian flavours in a stylish bistro and restaurant

☎ 0131 221 7788 & 229 9131
Sheraton Grand Hotel & Spa, 8 Conference Square EH3 8AN
e-mail: info@santiniedinburgh.co.uk
dir: From west end of Princes St, turn onto Lothian Rd. 1st right at lights onto West Approach Rd. 1st left to the Sheraton Grand Hotel & Spa, restaurant on right

Santini makes a flamboyantly Italian splash next to the Sheraton Grand's glitzy One Spa building. A vibrant cocktail bar is the place to start off before moving into either the bistro to perch at one of the high black leather bar stools, or the restaurant, decked out in glass, chrome and neutral shades. The Sicilian head chef brings a touch of authentic Italian flair to the cooking, uniting the best Scottish fish and meat with tip-top supplies brought in from Milan and across Italy. A classic zuppa di pesce is a big gutsy dishful, ahead of home-made black tagliolini pasta with prawns scallops and vanilla sauce. Main course might offer steamed sea bass with mixed herbs and balsamic or grilled Scotch beef fillet wrapped in smoked bacon with lentils.

Chef Malcolm Webster, Marco Terranova **Owner** Sheraton Grand Hotel & Spa **Times** 12-2.30/6.30-9.30 Closed 27 Dec-8 Jan, Sun, L Sat **Prices** Fixed L 2 course £9.50, Fixed D 3 course £18.50, Starter £4-£11, Main £8-£28, Dessert £5.50-£6.50, Service added but optional 10% **Wines** 45 bottles over £20, 8 bottles under £20, 7 by glass **Notes** Vegetarian available, Dress restrictions, Smart casual **Seats** 100 **Children** Portions, Menu **Parking** 50

Stac Polly

Modern Scottish

Scottish cuisine in city centre

☎ 0131 229 5405
8-10 Grindlay St EH3 9AS
e-mail: bookings@stacpolly.com
dir: In city centre beneath castle, near Lyceum Theatre

Just a few minutes' walk from the Princes Street shops, this popular restaurant is one of three in the city; the others are in Dublin Street (see next entry) and St Mary's Street. Beyond the unprepossessing exterior is an intimate and colourful basement restaurant of two softly lit rooms, furnished with tartan chairs and curtains, and prints on the walls. The menu delivers quality Scottish cuisine, with traditional dishes given a modern twist using top-notch local and seasonal produce. Expect accurate cooking and a good balance of flavours as seen in a thick and creamy smoked haddock and potato chowder and tender venison with pickled walnuts, turnip purée and a robust port sauce.

Chef Steven Harvey **Owner** Roger Coulthard **Times** 12-2/6-10 Closed Xmas, New Year, Sun, L Sat **Prices** Fixed L 2 course £12.95, Fixed D 3 course £20-£33, Starter £5.95-£7.95, Main £15.95-£19.95, Dessert £6.55-£8.25, Service added but optional 10% **Wines** 50 bottles over £20, 6 bottles under £20, 6 by glass **Notes** Pre-theatre menu 6-7pm 2 course £15, 3 course £20 **Seats** 98, Pr/dining room 50 **Children** Portions **Parking** NCP - Castle Terrace

Stac Polly

Modern Scottish

Scottish cuisine in fashionable city centre venues

☎ 0131 556 2231
29-33 Dublin St EH3 6NL
e-mail: bookings@stacpolly.com
dir: On corner of Albany St & Dublin St

This popular Edinburgh mini-chain has a trio of restaurants dotted around the city centre in St Mary's Street, Grindlay Street and Dublin Street. All are set in characterful old buildings fitted out in tasteful contemporary style - the Dublin Street venue occupies a warren of cosy stone-walled cellars in the basement of a 200-year-old building. The kitchen deals in a modern Scottish repertoire with a judicious spicing of international influences, and one or two off-piste dishes here and there. Start with a robust pressed partridge and duck liver terrine with a pear cider jelly, then stay in game mode for a main-course breast of pheasant with apricot and black pudding farce with caramelised root vegetables and a cassis and juniper berry game reduction.

Chef Andre Stanislas **Owner** Roger Coulthard **Times** 12-2/6-10 Closed L Sat-Sun **Prices** Fixed L 2 course £10-£12.95, Fixed D 3 course £20-£35, Starter £5.95-£8.25, Main £15.95-£20.95, Dessert £6.25-£6.95, Service added but optional 10% **Wines** 40+ bottles over £20, 12 bottles under £20, 8 by glass **Notes** Pre-theatre menu 2 course £15, 3 course £20, Vegetarian available **Seats** 100, Pr/dining room 54 **Children** Portions **Parking** On street - after 6.30pm

The Stockbridge Restaurant

Modern European

Well-sourced produce cooked with flair

0131 226 6766
54 St Stephen St EH3 5AL
e-mail: jane@thestockbridgerestaurant.com
web: www.thestockbridgerestaurant.com
dir: From A90 towards city centre, left Craigleith Rd B900, 2nd exit at rdbt B900, straight on to Kerr St, turn left onto St Stephen St

Down a cobbled street in the cosmopolitan area of Stockbridge, a large Georgian building is home to this characterful basement restaurant; white fairy lights lead the way. Dramatic black walls, bold Scottish prints and copious mirrors give a Gothic impression, with flickering candles and formally set tables completing the picture. The kitchen certainly isn't upstaged by the sumptuous décor, delivering well-sourced seasonal produce, cooked with flair and showing sound technique. The modern European dishes are not unduly complicated and deliver some great flavours. Take a spiced pigeon breast with roasted beetroot, crisp pork belly and jus or the fashionable partnership of seared scallops with cauliflower purée, raisin and caper dressing. Main course might bring on seared sea bass with sautéed ratte potatoes, ratatouille, parmesan crackling and basil pesto, and to finish, banana tarte Tatin with butterscotch sauce and vanilla ice cream.

Chef Jason Gallagher **Owner** Jason Gallagher & Jane Walker **Times** 12.30-2.30/7-9.30 Closed 1st 2 wks Jan after New Year, Mon, L Tue-Fri **Prices** Fixed L 2 course £13.95, Fixed D 3 course £21.95, Starter £4.95-£12.95, Main £16.95-£23.95, Dessert £4.95-£6.95, Service optional, Groups min 6 service 10% **Wines** 34 bottles over £20, 19 bottles under £20, 5 by glass **Notes** Pre-theatre menu available in Aug, Vegetarian available **Seats** 40 **Children** Portions **Parking** On street

Tower Restaurant & Terrace

Modern British NOTABLE WINE LIST

Views of the Edinburgh skyline and creative cooking

0131 225 3003
National Museum of Scotland, Chambers St EH1 1JF
e-mail: reservations@tower-restaurant.com
web: www.tower-restaurant.com
dir: Above Museum of Scotland building at corner of George IV Bridge & Chambers St, on level 5

The views from Tower Restaurant, on the roof of the 20th-century Museum of Scotland, are phenomenal. If the weather's on your side, head for the terrace and look out over Edinburgh's skyline, across the chimneys and spires, past the castle and beyond. Inside the décor is clubby - think cool modern furniture, tactile furnishings, shades of violet and orange and a mosaic bar. The seasonal menu

continued

21212

EDINBURGH **Map 21 NT27**

Modern French NOTABLE WINE LIST

0131 523 1030 & 0845 22 21212
3 Royal Ter EH7 5AB
e-mail: reservations@21212restaurant.co.uk
dir: Calton Hill, city centre

Manchester's loss is Edinburgh's gain: after leaving Altrincham in the suburbs of the north-western English city, chef Paul Kitching and front-of-house Katie O'Brien are now based in a splendid-looking townhouse in a smart part of Edinburgh. Those in the know will expect the unexpected, starting perhaps with the name of the restaurant (not the rhythms of a military march, but rather the number of dishes to choose from at each course); the four coolly modern bedrooms are in on the joke, too, numbered, 1, 2, 12 and 21. Paul's cooking has long defied classification: modern French is a good starting point, with a personal stamp that pretty much makes his cooking unique. Those familiar with Juniper will find this a much bolder and more ambitious operation, the building restored to its former elegance, the colours and tones suiting the traditions of the building whilst satisfying contemporary sensibilities. There's private dining, too, and an elegant drawing room. The open-plan design of the dining room gives a view of the kitchen alchemy from which emerges dishes bursting with creative ideas and tantalising combinations of flavours; at lunch the choice is 2, 3, 4, or 5 courses, but for dinner it is in for a penny in for pound with the full 5-courses. A soup in the hands of Paul Kitching could be expected to contain a surprise or two, and so it is with yellow-split pea with confit and caramelised onion, roasted garlic and chestnut, the dish a thrilling combination of textures and flavours. Both an impressive talent for maintaining balance on the plate and a ready playfulness are evident in chicken and cheesy chips, haggis, bacon, prunes, walnuts, girolles, mustard and blue cheese flapjack. The cheese course is first-rate and desserts such as baked lemon curd with cumin wild cherries and sticky rice are impressive. With Katie directing the top-notch service and an intelligently selected wine list, 21212 is 1 2 visit post-haste.

Chef Paul Kitching **Owner** P Kitching, K O'Brien, J Revle **Times** 12-1.45/6.30-9.30 Closed 2 wks Jan, Sun-Mon **Prices** Fixed L 2 course fr £25, Fixed L 5 course £55, 5 course D £65, Service optional **Wines** 8 by glass **Notes** Vegetarian available **Seats** 36, Pr/dining room 8 **Parking** On street

EDINBURGH ***continued***

points up Scottish ingredients in imaginatively prepared fare. There's prosciutto with mini Scotch egg and celeriac remoulade or sea trout with cauliflower purée and barley risotto, and berry Pavlova with whisky cream for pud.

Tower Restaurant & Terrace

Chef Gavin Elden **Owner** James Thomson OBE **Times** 12-11.30 Closed 25-26 Dec **Prices** Fixed L 2 course £13.95, Fixed D 3 course £30, Starter £7-£14, Main £16-£32, Dessert £6.50, Service optional, Groups min 8 service 10% **Wines** 150+ bottles over £20, 14 by glass **Notes** Theatre supper £13.95, Sunday L, Vegetarian available **Seats** 96, Pr/dining room 90 **Parking** On street

21212

◎◎◎ – *see page 499*

The Vintners Rooms

◎◎ Mediterranean, French

Candlelit restaurant with vintage charm

☎ 0131 554 6767
The Vaults, 87A Giles St, Leith EH6 6BZ
e-mail: enquiries@thevintnersrooms.com
dir: At end of Leith Walk, left into Great Junction St, right into Henderson St. Restaurant in old warehouse on right

Housed in an old wine merchants' auction room within a 16th-century former warehouse, this atmospheric candlelit restaurant is exquisitely adorned with hand-worked stucco and set over historic vaults which have stored barrels of fine wines since the 12th century. Expect refined, confident modern French cooking, presented with great flair, the dishes based on high quality Scottish produce. Duck 'four ways' makes for a deliciously indulgent start, with a generous lobe of seared foie gras, punchy duck liver parfait, smoked duck prosciutto and crackling. Follow on, perhaps, with a perfectly cooked seared halibut, served with a potato galette and mussel and vegetable fricassée, and to finish, perhaps a warm pancake stuffed with pastry cream and roasted quinces, or a chocolate tart with vanilla ice cream. The 200 bin wine list is worth delving into, plus there's a whisky tasting room with over 100 malts to get to know.

Chef David Spanner **Owner** Lonico Ltd **Times** 12-2/7-10 Closed 24 Dec-6 Jan, Sun-Mon **Prices** Fixed L 2 course £19, Starter £8.50-£13.50, Main £22-£30, Dessert £6-£7.80, Service added but optional 10%, Groups min 5 service 10% **Wines** 160 bottles over £20, 12 bottles under £20, 6 by glass **Notes** Vegetarian available **Seats** 64, Pr/dining room 34 **Children** Portions **Parking** 4

The Witchery by the Castle

◎ Modern Scottish NOTABLE WINE LIST

Historic, atmospheric restaurant with confident cooking

☎ 0131 225 5613
Castlehill, The Royal Mile EH1 2NF
e-mail: mail@thewitchery.com
web: www.thewitchery.com
dir: Top of Royal Mile at gates of Edinburgh Castle

Established more than 25 years ago and still a destination for in-the-know foodies and many celebrities visiting the city, this popular restaurant stands in a historic building at the gates of Edinburgh Castle. The Witchery takes its name from the many hundreds of witches burned at the stake on Castlehill during the 16th and 17th centuries. The décor in the dining rooms is darkly opulent: tapestry-hung walls, oak panelling, flagged floors and magnificent candelabra conjure a moody, gothic setting in the Witchery, while the Secret Garden, reached via a stone staircase from the courtyard, is much lighter and has lovely painted ceiling panels. First-rate Scottish produce provides a rock-solid base for a menu of simple contemporary classics. Herb-baked Kilbrannan scallops come with smoked Iberico pancetta and garlic, while roast breast and stuffed confit thigh of chicken comes with leek risotto and oyster mushrooms.

Chef Douglas Roberts **Owner** James Thomson OBE **Times** 12-4/5-11.30 Closed 25-26 Dec **Prices** Fixed L 2 course £13.95, Fixed D 3 course £30, Starter £8-£12, Main £15-£30, Dessert £7-£9, Service optional, Groups min 8 service 10% **Wines** 700+ bottles over £20, 20 bottles under £20, 14 by glass **Notes** Theatre supper 2 course £13.95, Sunday L, Vegetarian available **Seats** 120, Pr/dining room 70

FALKIRK

BANKNOCK — Map 21 NS77

Glenskirlie House and Castle

◎◎ Modern British

Fashionable Scottish castle with terrific food

☎ 01324 840201
Kilsyth Rd FK4 1UF
e-mail: macaloneys@glenskirliehouse.com
dir: Follow A803 signed Kilsyth/Bonnybridge, at T-junct turn right. Hotel 1m on right

Expect understated Edwardian elegance alongside modern innovative Scottish cuisine at this classical fine-dining restaurant. Long established and located in a spruced-up country house, set in glorious parkland beside a stunning castle offering sumptuous, boutique-style bedrooms, it is a finely tuned operation, with knowledgeable, welcoming staff. Luxury fabrics, striking wall coverings, plush seating and crisp linen-clothed tables create the intimate, formal setting in which to sample some accomplished cooking conjured from the high quality seasonal ingredients. The seasonally-changing menus may take in smoked crayfish and salmon ravioli with scallops and shellfish consommé to start, followed by roast venison with celeriac dauphinoise, beetroot purée, braised red cabbage and port jus, or wild halibut with crab and basil vinaigrette. Desserts appear on a trolley.

Chef Daryl Jordan **Owner** John Macaloney, Colin Macaloney **Times** 12-2/6-9.30 Closed 26-27 Dec, 1-4 Jan, D Mon **Prices** Fixed L 2 course fr £17.50, Starter £7.25-£11.75, Main £18.50-£26.50, Dessert £8.25, Service optional **Wines** 117 bottles over £20, 17 bottles under £20, 11 by glass **Notes** Sunday L, Vegetarian available, Dress restrictions, Smart casual, Civ Wed 150 **Seats** 54, Pr/dining room 150 **Children** Portions, Menu **Parking** 100

FIFE

ANSTRUTHER — Map 21 NO50

The Cellar

◎◎◎ – *see opposite page*

CUPAR Map 21 NO31

Ostlers Close Restaurant

Modern British V

Local stalwart serving unfussy, full-flavoured cooking

01334 655574
Bonnygate KY15 4BU
dir: In small lane off main street, A91

Ostler's Close is not the easiest place to find, hidden away in a narrow alley off Cupar's high street - but ask any local, and they will point you in the right direction - after all this restaurant in a 17th-century former temperance hotel has been a fixture of the local foodie scene for three decades. Top-grade raw materials are key to this operation, so fresh fruit, veg and herbs proceed directly from the garden to the kitchen; James Graham is passionate about wild mushrooms, foraged from the woods, and a well-established network of local suppliers provides the rest. Handwritten menus typify the unfussy, honest-to-goodness approach taken in the kitchen - there's no pretension here, just classic flavour pairings, and a clear preference for punchy stocks, reductions and olive oil rather than dairy produce. Breast of woodcock is served with braised leg meat on Stornoway black pudding mash with beetroot sauce in a full-throttle starter, while main courses might see wild halibut teamed with hot-smoked salmon risotto and parsley sauce. Desserts hold true to form - perhaps steamed Seville orange marmalade syrup sponge with cream custard and orange ice cream.

Chef James Graham **Owner** James & Amanda Graham **Times** 12.15-1.30/7-9.30 Closed 25-26 Dec, 1-2 Jan, 2 wks Oct, 2 wks Apr, Sun-Mon, L Tue-Fri **Prices** Starter £7.50-£13, Main £18-£22, Dessert £7.50-£8.50, Service optional **Wines** 60 bottles over £20, 31 bottles under £20, 6 by glass **Notes** Vegetarian menu **Seats** 26 **Children** Portions **Parking** On street, public car park

DUNFERMLINE Map 21 NT08

Cardoon

Modern, Traditional

Scottish cooking in relaxed conservatory restaurant

01383 736258
BW Keavil House Hotel, Crossford KY12 8QW
e-mail: events@keavilhouse.co.uk
dir: M90 junct 3, 7m from Forth Road Bridge, take A985, turning right after bridge. From Dunfermline, 2m W on A994

Dating from the 16th-century, this former manor house is set in gardens and parkland. Expect contemporary, brasserie-style cooking in the stylish conservatory restaurant with its rich colours and airy, relaxed atmosphere. Dishes on the well-balanced menu are accurately cooked and the kitchen tries to use as much locally sourced produce as possible, as witnessed in a starter of oatmeal-crusted haggis with Dundee marmalade and Drambuie cream. A main course of fillet of grey mullet served with roast salsify, mashed potato and red wine gravy might be followed by warm apple lattice pie with vanilla ice cream.

Chef Phil Yates **Owner** Queensferry Hotels Ltd **Times** 12-2/6.30-9.30 Closed 1 Jan **Prices** Starter £3.95-£6.95, Main £9.95-£18.95, Dessert £4.50, Service optional **Wines** 18 bottles over £20, 15 bottles under £20, 9 by glass **Notes** Sunday L, Vegetarian available, Dress restrictions, No football colours, Civ Wed 200 **Seats** 80, Pr/dining room 22 **Children** Portions, Menu **Parking** 250

Pitfirrane Hotel

Modern, Traditional Scottish NEW

Top-notch Scottish ingredients given due respect

01383 736132
27 Main St, Crossford KY12 8NJ
e-mail: reservations@pitfirranehotel.co.uk
dir: A994 Dunfermline, Crossford is 2nd village from rdbt, hotel is on right after traffic lights

In an area rich with famous golf courses, the wood-panelled walls of the Pitfirrane Hotel's restaurant play host to artworks which depict many of them. Warm, traditional colours and unclothed darkwood tables give a comfortingly unpretentious feel to the restaurant, with the service pitched perfectly to maintain the happy mood. The proudly Scottish menu puts prime Scottish produce rightly at the top of the agenda. This translates into the likes of smoked haddock chowder with fresh shredded

continued

The Cellar

ANSTRUTHER Map 21 NO50

Seafood

Excellent fish and seafood cooking in a former smokery

01333 310378
24 East Green KY10 3AA
dir: Behind Scottish Fisheries Museum

This cracking little restaurant tucked away behind the Scottish Fisheries Museum may not get the waterside views of Anstruther's harbour front, but its romantic intimacy is more than ample compensation. A lovely cobbled courtyard leads into the 17th-century building, where stone walls and ancient beams are lit by the soft-focus glow of candles and a sizzling fire. Susan Jukes is a welcoming front-of-house presence, clued-up about husband Peter's food and which wines will best suit the day's dishes. It is fitting that the Cellar is now a fish restaurant, as it was a cooperage and smokery back in the days when Scotland's herring industry was alive and wriggling. Peter Jukes cooks with spot-on technical skills and the quiet confidence to keep things simple: dishes are never overworked, just kept unfussy and beautifully presented. The quality of the produce speaks for itself in a starter trio of salmon - oak-smoked, gravad lax and hot-smoked, served with dill and sweet mustard dressing. Halibut could star in a main course with greens, pine nuts, smokey bacon and hollandaise sauce, or there might be seared monkfish with scallops (diver-caught, naturally) and steamed mussels with herb and garlic butter and couscous. After all that light and healthy fish, there's no excuse for skipping dessert - go for date and ginger sponge with hot butterscotch sauce, or a terrine of layered chocolate mousses with orange liqueur custard.

Chef Peter Jukes, Mathew Thomas **Owner** Susan & Peter Jukes **Times** 12.30-1.30/6.30-9.30 Closed Xmas, Sun (Sun & Mon Winter), L Mon-Tue **Prices** Fixed L 2 course £19.50, Fixed D 3 course fr £37.50, Service optional **Wines** 300 bottles over £20, 20 bottles under £20, 5 by glass **Seats** 38 **Children** Portions **Parking** On street

DUNFERMLINE *continued*

leeks and truffle oil or a main course of best end of lamb with Stornoway black pudding and pea mash. A perfectly set Drambuie crème brûlée with home-made shortbread discs makes for a fine finish.

Chef Garry Noble **Owner** Scott Adamson
Times 12-2.30/6-9 **Prices** Fixed L 2 course £10.95, Fixed D 3 course £40-£100, Starter £3.25-£7.95, Main £10.95-£24.95, Dessert £3.95-£4.95, Service optional **Wines** 8 bottles over £20, 15 bottles under £20, 10 by glass **Notes** Sunday L, Vegetarian available **Seats** 70, Pr/dining room 20 **Children** Portions, Menu **Parking** 40

ELIE **Map 21 NO40**

Sangsters

Modern British

Modern cooking in relaxed surroundings

☎ 01333 331001
51 High St KY9 1BZ
e-mail: bruce@sangsters.co.uk
dir: From St Andrews on A917 take B9131 to Anstruther, right at rdbt onto A917 to Elie. (11m from St Andrews)

To the less savvy, Sangsters could appear like just any other small seaside village restaurant, but the place has pedigree and something of a 'destination' draw. Chef-patron Bruce Sangster's cooking is precise and accomplished and displays bags of imagination and flair; take seared Ross-shire scallops teamed with slow-cooked pork belly, Chinese five spice and an orange dressing as an opener. The modern approach reigns, driven by quality local, seasonal ingredients; confit of Loch Duart salmon, perhaps, accompanied by wilted leeks with pine kernels and pancetta and a beetroot, red wine and port reduction, while catching the eye at dessert might be warm pear and almond financier with ginger custard, butterscotch sauce and pear sorbet. The intimate dining room and comfortable lounge are bright and comfortable, the halls hung with local art.

Times 12.30-1.30/7-9.30 Closed 25-26 Dec, early Jan, mid Feb/Oct, mid Nov, Mon, L Tue & Sat, D Sun

MARKINCH **Map 21 NO20**

The Orangery

British

Accomplished cuisine in imposing Georgian mansion

☎ 01592 610066
Balbirnie House, Balbirnie Park KY7 6NE
e-mail: info@balbirnie.co.uk
dir: M90 junct 13 follow signs for Glenrothes & Tay Bridge, right onto B9130 to Markinch & Balbirnie Park

Set in 400 acres of stunning landscaped parkland, this gorgeous honey-hued Georgian mansion dates from 1777, and is one of Scotland's most important historic buildings of its era. The luxuriously refurbished building - complete with its own golf course and state-of-the-art spa - epitomises the luxurious Scottish country-house hotel experience. The romantic Orangery restaurant, with floor-to-ceiling lunette windows and a glass roof, looks good enough to eat in warm hues of silver, toffee and tobacco. On the menu is cooking that keeps to the country-house idiom: classically influenced dishes from a kitchen that conscientiously sources prime Scottish materials. Home-smoked Bradan Rost salmon with celeriac remoulade and dill crème fraîche shows the style, ahead of main courses that range from roast loin and braised neck of lamb with parmesan polenta and root vegetables to fillet of bream with basil mash, pak choi, mussels and chorizo velouté.

The Orangery

Chef Mark Lindsey **Owner** The Russell family
Times 12-2/7-9.30 Closed Mon-Tue **Prices** Fixed L 2 course £12, Fixed D 3 course £33, Starter £4.95-£6.50, Main £10.50-£19.50, Dessert £5.50-£6.50, Service optional **Wines** 56 bottles over £20, 42 bottles under £20, 12 by glass **Notes** Sunday L, Vegetarian available, Civ Wed 216 **Seats** 65, Pr/dining room 216 **Children** Portions, Menu **Parking** 150

The Peat Inn

RESTAURANT OF THE YEAR

PEAT INN **Map 21 NO40**

Modern British

Classy cooking using first-class local produce

☎ 01334 840206
KY15 5LH
e-mail: stay@thepeatinn.co.uk
dir: At junction of B940/B941, 6m SW of St Andrews

Geoffrey and Katherine Smeddle have been running the Peat Inn since 2006, taking the baton from the celebrated David Wilson, and they have created a restaurant with rooms more than worthy of its glorious past. An inn since the 1700s, today's incarnation is elegantly kitted out, with roaring fires and old beams rubbing shoulders with well-chosen furniture and objets d'art. There's a comfortable lounge, while in the three intimate dining rooms smartly laid, linen-clad tables await. Service sets a nice tone of relaxed professionalism. Geoffrey mans the stoves, cooking up a storm with the carefully-sourced produce, much of it from the region, delivering well-judged dishes where flavour is paramount and contemporary sensibilities combine with classical technique. Pumpkin and parmesan soup comes with a poached quail's egg, ricotta gnocchi and pumpkin seed oil in a first course, while John Dory might turn up in a main course with a gratin of razor clams, creamed Swiss chard, glazed salsify and a shellfish velouté. The food is as pretty as a picture, including desserts such as lemon tart with poached rhubarb and pistachio ice cream.

Chef Geoffrey Smeddle **Owner** Geoffrey & Katherine Smeddle **Times** 12.30-2/7-9.30 Closed 25-26 Dec, 1-14 Jan, Sun-Mon **Prices** Fixed L 3 course fr £16, Fixed D 3 course fr £32, Starter £10-£13, Main £18-£28, Dessert £9-£10, Service optional **Wines** 250 bottles over £20, 3 bottles under £20, 9 by glass **Notes** Tasting menu 6 course, Vegetarian available **Seats** 40, Pr/dining room 14 **Parking** 24

PEAT INN Map 21 NO40

The Peat Inn

@@@ – *see opposite page*

ST ANDREWS Map 21 NO51

Fairmont St Andrews

@@ Modern European NEW V

Luxurious golf hotel with inventive Mediterranean-accented food

☎ 01334 837000
KY16 8PN
e-mail: standrews.scotland@fairmont.com
dir: 1.5m outside St Andrews on A917 towards Crail

The Fairmont St Andrews is a luxurious golf and spa hotel on an epic scale, with two golf courses in its 520-acre coastal estate in St Andrews Bay, and the sort of glamorous spa set-up you'd expect in a hotel of this stature. Overlooking the atrium, the Esperante restaurant is the fine-dining option, a Mediterranean-influenced space done out in shades of terracotta, earthy browns and olive greens, with a huge mural to evoke the fields of Tuscany. While the kitchen also takes its inspiration from the sunny climes of Southern Europe, its raw materials come from closer to home - expect to find Scotland's finest produce treated with skill in an inventive modern European approach. Roasted quail is served with rich, sticky oxtail and blueberry jus, followed by a well-balanced main course of sustainably-sourced halibut teamed with bourgogne sauce, pancetta and potato confit. A chocolate marquise with cherries ends with a flourish of masterful presentation.

Chef Adam Handling **Owner** Apollo European Real Estate **Times** Closed Seasonal, L all week **Prices** Food prices not confirmed for 2011. Please telephone for details **Wines** 67 bottles over £20, 3 bottles under £20, 6 by glass **Notes** Operating hours fluctuate seasonally, Vegetarian menu, Dress restrictions, Semi formal, no denim, trainers or shorts, Civ Wed 600 **Seats** 60, Pr/dining room 80 **Parking** 250

Inn at Lathones

@@ Modern European

Imaginative cooking in a characterful coaching inn

☎ 01334 840494
Largoward KY9 1JE
e-mail: lathones@theinn.co.uk
dir: 5m SW of St Andrews on A915. In 0.5m before Largoward on left, just after hidden dip

Set on the back roads into St Andrews, surrounded by rolling countryside, this charming old coaching inn close to the golf course houses an intimate restaurant serving traditional dishes with modern interpretations. Parts of the pub date back 400 years and the whitewashed walls and bare brick fireplaces are complemented by contemporary artwork and objet d'art. Although tables are formally laid, the friendly staff and colourful interior give it a laidback vibe, enough, hopefully, to allay any fears about meeting the resident ghost. Excellent local ingredients and imaginative cooking combine in dishes such as crab fritters with mango salsa and a wasabi mayonnaise. Main-courses such as game suet pudding with roasted root vegetable mash, Stornoway black pudding and port wine sauce might precede dessert of iced whisky heather honey parfait with raspberries.

Chef Richard Brackenbury **Owner** Mr N White **Times** 12-2.30/6-9.30 Closed 26 Dec, 1st 2 wks Jan **Prices** Food prices not confirmed for 2011. Please telephone for details. **Wines** 89 bottles over £20, 13 bottles under £20, 5 by glass **Notes** Sunday L, Vegetarian available, Dress restrictions, Smart casual, Civ Wed 40 **Seats** 40, Pr/dining room 40 **Children** Portions, Menu **Parking** 35

Macdonald Rusacks Hotel - Rocca

@@ Italian, Scottish

Modern Italian cooking in world-famous golf hotel

☎ 0844 879 9136
Pilmour Links KY16 9JQ
e-mail: general.rusacks@macdonald-hotels.co.uk
dir: M90 junct 8, A91 to St Andrews. Hotel on left on entering town

There's been a bit of a change at the Macdonald Rusacks Hotel. It's still one of the most famous golfing hotels on the planet, with fantastic views across the world-famous Old Course, but its main restaurant - which benefits from those views through huge windows - has been relaunched as a modern Italian bar and grill. Called Rocca, it's all about top-notch Scottish produce prepared in the Italian style. Think fritto misto - crispy tempura squid, red mullet and prawns with a tartare dressing - to start, followed by sirloin of beef tagliata, carved pink with rosemary potatoes and a rocket salad. There's a good selection of pasta and risotto dishes (available as a starter or main) and a range of grills served with a classic garnish. Dessert might be vanilla pannacotta with home-grown rhubarb and elderflower syrup, or a classic tiramisù with espresso cream and cappuccino ice cream.

Chef Liam McKenna **Owner** Macdonald Hotels/APSP Restaurants Ltd **Times** 12-2.30/6.30-9 Closed L all week, D Sun (Oct-Mar) **Prices** Fixed L 2 course £15-£20, Fixed D 3 course £25-£35, Starter £4.50-£10.90, Main £9.95-£26.95, Dessert £5.95-£7.95, Service optional **Wines** 35 bottles over £20, 15 bottles under £20, 13 by glass **Notes** Vegetarian available, Dress restrictions, Smart casual, Civ Wed 60 **Seats** 80, Pr/dining room 30 **Children** Portions, Menu **Parking** 23

The Road Hole Restaurant

@@@ – *see page 504*

Rufflets Country House & Terrace Restaurant

@@ Modern Scottish, Mediterranean NOTABLE WINE LIST

Scottish cuisine in friendly country-house hotel

☎ 01334 472594
Strathkinness Low Rd KY16 9TX
e-mail: reservations@rufflets.co.uk
dir: 1.5m W of St Andrews on B939

continued

ST ANDREWS *continued*

Ten acres of award-winning formal gardens and woodland make a splendid setting for this turreted Edwardian country house located a mile west of St Andrews. The Garden Restaurant is contemporary in style, with bold rich fabrics, colourful artwork and views of the delightful terraced gardens, and makes a civilised setting in which to enjoy lunch and dinner. Expect careful Scottish cooking with Mediterranean influences and imaginative use of top-notch local produce. Dishes on the weekly-changing carte may include carpaccio of venison with beetroot and horseradish pesto, loin of Fife lamb with rosemary potatoes and roast garlic gravy, scallops with pancetta risotto and Jerusalem artichoke purée, and dark chocolate fondant with milk and honey ice cream.

Chef Mark Nixon **Owner** Ann Murray-Smith **Times** 12.30-2.30/7-9 Closed L Mon-Sat **Prices** Fixed L 3 course £22.50-£25, Starter £4.75-£7.75, Main £14.50-£22, Dessert £6.50-£9, Service optional, Groups min 20 service 10% **Wines** 88 bottles over £20, 18 bottles under £20, 9 by glass **Notes** Sunday L, Vegetarian available, Dress restrictions, No shorts, Civ Wed 130 **Seats** 80, Pr/dining room 130 **Children** Portions, Menu **Parking** 50

Russell Hotel

Scottish, International

Imaginative cooking in an intimate setting

☎ 01334 473447
26 The Scores KY16 9AS
e-mail: russellhotel@talk21.com
dir: From A91 left at 2nd rdbt into Golf Place, right in 200yds into The Scores, hotel in 300yds on left

The views across St Andrews Bay from this family-run Victorian townhouse hotel are quite stunning. What's more, the Russell is only two minutes' walk from the first tee of the world-famous Old Course. On the dining front, the Russell offers imaginative Scottish cooking in its cosy candlelit restaurant. High-quality local ingredients are put to good use in dishes such as seared West Coast scallops with dressed rocket, red pepper salsa and crispy chorizo, and roast loin of Highland roe deer with wild mushrooms and bacon and a porcini mushroom foam. Save room for the home-made sticky toffee pudding with butterscotch sauce and vanilla ice cream.

Russell Hotel

Times 12-2/6.30-9.30 Closed Xmas

Sands Grill

International

Stylish restaurant within upmarket golf-resort hotel complex

☎ 01334 474371 & 468228
The Old Course Hotel, Golf Resort & Spa KY16 9SP
e-mail: reservations@oldcoursehotel.co.uk
dir: M90 junct 8 then A91 to St Andrews

With views of the bay, the city, the Highlands and 17th fairway of the legendary golf course, The Old Course Hotel is one of the most famous golfing hotels in the world.

The Road Hole Restaurant

ST ANDREWS **Map 21 NO51**

Modern Scottish V

Confident creative cooking with views of the golf

☎ 01334 474371
Old Course Hotel, Golf Resort & Spa KY16 9SP
e-mail: reservations@oldcoursehotel.co.uk
dir: M90 junct 8 then A91 to St Andrews

There can be few more relaxing sports to spectate than golf, which is why the layout of the Road Hole restaurant, adjacent to the whisky-laden bar of the same name, makes a virtue of its views over the 17th hole of the world-famous Old Course. From his open-plan kitchen, Paul Hart offers an opulent style of high-gloss modern Scottish cooking. There is confident creativity in abundance on the menus, and the results can be breathtaking. As well as visual appeal, dishes deliver seductive aromatic impact on arrival, as is the case with a starter of roasted scallops with braised artichokes and shallots, and an overlay of smoked anchovy foam. Seasonal game is another strong point, never more so than in a serving of Perthshire grouse in the lightest buttery puff pastry, alongside pickled red cabbage and kohlrabi gratin. Eye-catching desserts marshal seasonal fruits to great effect, perhaps an autumn crumble of Victoria plums, with plum jelly, vanilla-speckled custard and a little doughnut.

Chef Paul Hart **Owner** Kohler Company **Times** 7-10 Closed Jan, Sun-Mon, L all week **Prices** Food prices not confirmed for 2011. Please telephone for details **Wines** 400 bottles over £20, 11 by glass **Notes** Tasting menu & vegetarian tasting menu available, Vegetarian menu, Dress restrictions, Smart, no jeans/trainers, collared shirt req, Civ Wed 200 **Seats** 70, Pr/dining room 20 **Parking** 100

Newly renamed, the informal Sands Grill is one of the dining options and sports a classy look reminiscent of a luxury ocean-going liner of yesteryear, with lots of darkwood and black leather. Specialising in local seafood and steaks, the Mediterranean influenced menu offers accurately cooked yet unpretentious brasserie-style dishes. Chicken liver pâté with apple chutney, roast cod with chorizo, mussels and borlotti beans, rib-eye steak with peppercorn sauce, grilled lobster, and sticky toffee pudding with vanilla ice cream are typical examples. Service is attentive and professional.

Chef Simon Whitely **Owner** Kohler Company **Times** 12-2.30/6-10 **Prices** Food prices not confirmed for 2011. Please telephone for details **Wines** 60 bottles over £20, 11 by glass **Notes** Vegetarian available, Dress restrictions, Smart casual, Civ Wed 400 **Seats** 75, Pr/dining room 40 **Children** Portions, Menu **Parking** 100

The Seafood Restaurant

– see below

ST MONANS **Map 21 NO50**

The Seafood Restaurant

Modern Scottish, Seafood

Impeccably fresh seafood by the harbour

☎ 01333 730327
16 West End KY10 2BX
e-mail: info@theseafoodrestaurant.com
dir: Take A959 from St Andrews to Anstruther, then W on A917 through Pittenweem. In St Monans to harbour then right

When the Seafood Restaurant opened in the late-1990s the maxim was locally-landed seafood, much of it from up the road at Pittenweem. But things have changed over the last decade; the number of local fisherman has dramatically reduced, with over-fishing and climate change playing a part, and the industry is in crisis. With that in mind, sustainability is today's focus. The 800-year-old former fisherman's cottage has wonderful views across the town and harbour and over the Firth of Forth towards Edinburgh, and with its light beech wood and Rennie Mackintosh-style chairs, it cuts a contemporary dash. A modern approach to presentation sees sweetcorn velouté topped with a crab beignet and scattered with micro herbs, while main-course stone bass (aka wreckfish for its tendency to hang around wrecks and rocks) is pan-fried and comes with a mix of peas and beans flavoured with bacon, potato gnocchi and finished with a chorizo cream. Finish with a blueberry and vanilla friande or a selection of mature cheeses. Note a meat option is always on the menu.

Chef Craig Millar, Roy Brown **Owner** Craig Millar, Tim Butler **Times** 12-2.30/6-9.30 Closed 25-26 Dec, 1-2 Jan, Mon-Tue (Sep-Jun) **Prices** Fixed L 2 course £22, Fixed D 3 course £40, Service optional **Wines** All bottles over £20, 6 by glass **Notes** Oct-1 Apr fixed L/D menu 3 course £14.95-£19.95 Wed-Fri, Sunday L, Vegetarian available **Seats** 44 **Children** Portions **Parking** 10

CITY OF GLASGOW

GLASGOW **Map 20 NS56**

La Bonne Auberge

French, Mediterranean

Confident French cooking in contemporary hotel

☎ 0141 352 8310
Holiday Inn Theatreland, 161 West Nile St G1 2RL
e-mail: info@higlasgow.com
dir: M8 junct 16, follow signs for Royal Concert Hall, hotel opposite

With the city's theatres and shops close at hand, this popular and relaxed French brasserie-style restaurant in the contemporary Holiday Inn is a useful address. The kitchen has a wide repertoire with the range of accomplished, honest, French- and Mediterranean-inspired dishes playing to the crowds. Menus take in a

continued

The Seafood Restaurant

ST ANDREWS **Map 21 NO51**

Modern Seafood

Seriously good seafood in a dramatic setting

☎ 01334 479475
The Scores KY16 9AS
e-mail: reservations@theseafoodrestaurant.com

The sleek cubist installation of glass, metal and wood perched on the sea wall above the waves of St Andrews Bay reels in a healthy catch of eager fish aficionados. The Seafood Restaurant makes a defiant style statement in this conservative tweed-and-Pringle golfing Mecca and couldn't be better placed for a restaurant that exploits the cream of the local catch. The slickly minimal décor is the most modern thing in St Andrews by a clear century or so, and doesn't even try to fight with the view outside for diners' attention - particularly if the RAF flyboys from Leuchars are putting the fighters through their paces. The chefs work within the gleaming glass and steel arena of their open-plan kitchen, floating tantalising aromas across the dining room. Fresh fish and shellfish are the big stars here, but the supporting cast of ingredients is also chosen with care and imagination, and combined with an eye for what's fashionable. Take a starter of smoked haddock rarebit pointed up with punchy hits of pancetta, mustard and creamed leeks. Next up, cod with Parmentier potatoes, chorizo, sun-dried tomatoes, green and white beans and olives is a colourful assemblage of sharp flavours and interesting textures. For pudding, try an indulgent warm pecan tart with ginger ice cream and poached apple.

Chef Craig Millar **Owner** Craig Millar, Tim Butler **Times** 12-2.30/6.30-10 Closed 25-26 Dec, Jan 1 **Prices** Fixed L 2 course £22, Fixed D 3 course £45, Service optional **Wines** 180 bottles over £20, 5 bottles under £20, 8 by glass **Notes** Sunday L, Vegetarian available **Seats** 60 **Children** Portions **Parking** 50mtrs away

GLASGOW *continued*

fixed-price pre-theatre option, while lunch might deliver simple classics like French onion soup or steak frites, and dinner cranks up the ante with five-spiced duck breast, sesame wok-fried vegetables and aromatic Asian sauce, or slow-cooked belly and loin of pork with pan-roasted loin, parsnip purée and pork jus.

Chef Gerry Sharkey **Owner** Chardon Leisure Ltd **Times** 12-2.15/5-10 **Prices** Fixed L 2 course £14.95, Starter £4.95-£7.50, Main £13.95-£25.95, Service added but optional 12.5% **Wines** 32 bottles over £20, 15 bottles under £20, 10 by glass **Notes** Sunday L **Seats** 90, Pr/dining room 100 **Children** Portions, Menu **Parking** NCP opposite

Brian Maule at Chardon d'Or

French V NOTABLE WINE LIST

Confident cooking in a classy city-centre venue

☎ 0141 248 3801
176 West Regent St G2 4RL
e-mail: info@brianmaule.com
dir: 10 minute walk from Glasgow central station

Brian Maule returned to his homeland in 2001 after a stint as head chef at Le Gavroche, and set up the Chardon d'Or in a city-centre Victorian townhouse. Inside it is light and modern in an understated neutral way - expect suede and leather banquettes, high-backed chairs, wooden floors, cream walls and glass panels. Brian Maule's name is above the door, so he is in the kitchen overseeing every dish of his classically French-driven modern Scottish output before it makes it onto the table. Tuna and crab with potato salad and a Madeira truffle dressing delivers fresh, clear flavours to start, before a perfectly-grilled sea bream with a purée of caramelised parsnips and a light thyme and lamb jus.

Chef Brian Maule **Owner** Brian Maule at Chardon d'Or **Times** 12-2/6-10 Closed 25-26 Dec, 1-2 Jan, 1 wk Jan, BHs, Sun, L Sat **Prices** Fixed L 2 course £16.50, Fixed D 3 course £19.50, Starter £6.50-£12.25, Main £21.50-£26.75, Dessert £8.50-£11.75, Service optional, Groups min 8 service 10% **Wines** 170 bottles over £20, 2 bottles under £20, 9 by glass **Notes** Tasting menu 6 course, Pre-theatre 6-6.45pm, Vegetarian menu, Dress restrictions, Smart casual **Seats** 90, Pr/dining room 60 **Children** Portions **Parking** On street (metered)

City Café

Modern European

Modern cuisine beside the Clyde

☎ 0141 227 1010 & 240 1002
City Inn Glasgow, Finnieston Quay G3 8HN
e-mail: glasgow.citycafe@cityinn.com
dir: M8 junct 19 follow signs for SECC. Hotel on left 200yds before entrance to SECC

Right by the 'squinty bridge' over the Clyde, the City Inn's relaxed and informal bistro has great views of Queen's Dock and the vast hammerhead of the Finnieston Crane. The alfresco riverside terrace is the place to head for when the weather plays ball, but funky artwork on the walls and stylish modern chairs and banquettes make for an equally attractive interior. Scotland's peerless produce is well represented on an appealingly eclectic menu of contemporary dishes. Start with pan-fried quail breast with honey and five spice, and pea and mint risotto cake, before a main-course trio of Middlewhite pork delivers confit belly, roast fillet and sausage with crackling and sweet red cabbage.

Chef Scott MacDonald, Charles Hilton **Owner** City Inn Limited **Times** 12-2.30/5.30-10.30 **Prices** Fixed L 2 course £9.95-£16.95, Fixed D 3 course £16.50-£21.95, Starter £4.95-£7.95, Main £9.95-£19.95, Dessert £5.50-£9.50, Service optional **Wines** 35 bottles over £20, 12 bottles under £20, 28 by glass **Notes** Pre-theatre menu from 5pm 2 course £16.95, 3 course £19.95, Sunday L, Vegetarian available, Dress restrictions, Smart casual, Civ Wed 60 **Seats** 80, Pr/dining room 60 **Children** Portions, Menu **Parking** 120

Gamba

Scottish, Seafood

Vibrant fish and seafood in the West End

☎ 0141 572 0899
225a West George St G2 2ND
e-mail: info@gamba.co.uk
dir: On the corner of West Campbell St & West George St, close to Blythswood Sq

The clue to where Gamba's heart lies is in the name: gamba is Spanish for king prawn. This perennial favourite enjoys a well-deserved reputation as the place to go for top-notch fish and seafood. A basement restaurant in the heart of the fashionable West End of the city, its warm colours, terracotta floor tiles, stylish fish-themed artwork and polished-wood tables create a decidedly warm feel - perfect for the Mediterranean and Asian influenced cooking. Top-quality produce is used to great effect in starters such as a well-judged fish soup, enriched with crabmeat, stem ginger and prawn dumplings, and main-course roast monkfish with chorizo, chick pea and prawn stew. Desserts like bitter chocolate tart with peanut butter ice cream show the ambition and sound technique remains to the end. There's a meat and vegetarian option to satisfy those on either side of the divide.

Chef Derek Marshall **Owner** Mr A C Tomkins & Mr D Marshall **Times** 12-2.30/5-10.30 Closed 25-26 Dec, 1-2 Jan, L Sun **Prices** Food prices not confirmed for 2011. Please telephone for details **Wines** 60 bottles over £20, 8 bottles under £20, 8 by glass **Notes** Vegetarian available **Seats** 66 **Parking** On street

Hotel du Vin Bistro at One Devonshire Gardens

– see opposite

Killermont Polo Club

Traditional Indian

Creative Indian cooking in a setting fit for a maharaja

☎ 0141 946 5412
2022 Maryhill Rd, Maryhill Park G20 0AB
e-mail: info@killermontpoloclub.com

Not your run-of-the-mill curry house by any stroke of the imagination, with its décor inspired by the sub-continent's centuries-old fascination with the sport of princes, while Dum Pukht is the culinary speciality originating from the Indian Moghul emperors. Subtle spices are blended with others brought from the Silk Road city of Samarkand in Uzbekistan to create slow-cooked dishes where quality fresh produce isn't overpowered. The kitchen's lengthy roster also takes in Club Specials (chicken rogan josh) and popular dishes (chicken dhansak), but the Dum Pukht dishes are the star turn; perhaps murgh laziz – a Punjabi dish of chicken tikka, braised in a spicy masala of garlic, ginger, onions and tomatoes, tempered with crushed coriander seeds and crisp red-hot chillies.

Times 12-2.30/5-11.30

the left bank

International

Great value global food in vibrant urban setting

☎ 0141 339 5969
33-35 Gibson St, Hillhead G12 8NU
e-mail: contact@theleftbank.co.uk
dir: M8 junct 17, A82. After Kelvinbridge turn left onto Otago St, left onto Gibson St. Restaurant on right

There's a pleasantly hang-loose vibe to this funky modern eatery in Glasgow's dynamic West End. The stripped-out urban look uses textures of wood, bare brick, glass and metal in its split-level layout, with plenty of corners and crannies to find your own breathing space. Local artists have pitched in too: the Timorous Beasties designed the wallpaper and lights, and sculptor Chris Bannerman did the one-off concrete bar. There are no eating rules here: an eclectic menu will come up with just about whatever you want whenever you want it, from brunch to lunch to all-day mains and evening specials. A globetrotting cast of flavours is built from as much Scottish produce as the kitchen can lay its hands on, and you're never far from the fragrances of Southeast Asia. Start with sticky pork ribs in maple, star anise, sesame and chilli before main-course cod in white wine and mussel broth with fennel, capers, tomato and olive oil.

Chef Liz McGougan **Owner** Catherine Hardy, Jacqueline Fennessy, George Swanson **Times** 9am-mdnt Closed 25 Dec, 1 Jan **Prices** Fixed L 2 course £7.45-£10.95, Starter £3.50-£5.50, Main £7.25-£24.95, Dessert £2.95-£4.75,

Service optional, Groups min 6 service 10% **Wines** 5 bottles over £20, 12 bottles under £20, 16 by glass **Notes** Vegetarian available **Seats** 75 **Children** Portions **Parking** On street

Malmaison Glasgow

Modern French, Scottish

Fine-dining brasserie using locally-sourced produce

☎ 0141 572 1001
278 West George St G2 4LL
e-mail: glasgow@malmaison.com
dir: From George Square take St.Vincent St to Pitt St. Hotel on corner with West George St

The city's rendition of the smart boutique hotel chain doesn't disappoint on contemporary styling or atmosphere – not least as it was formerly a Greek Orthodox church. Its chic restaurant is set in the vaulted crypt and comes decked out in dark, robust colours and furnished with leather banquettes and chairs and subtle lighting that lend an intimate, relaxed buzz. The kitchen's modern, brasserie-style output comes in praise of quality regional produce (Donald Russell Aberdeenshire beef for the steak and frites, for example), while mains like sea trout with crushed peas, broad beans and crème fraîche offer a lighter touch. Finish with a maple pecan cheesecake or cherry clafoutis. There's a classy bar, too.

Times 12-2.30/5.30-10.30

La Parmigiana

Italian, Mediterranean

Family-owned intimate Italian amid the Glasgow bustle

☎ 0141 334 0686
447 Great Western Rd G12 8HH
e-mail: sgiovanazzi@btclick.com
web: www.laparmigiana.co.uk
dir: Opposite Hillhead underground station

On the bustling Great Western Road, surrounded by shops and restaurants of all provenances, this Glasgow Italian is something of an institution. Done in robust red and soothing cream inside, it's a small, comfortable place, with close-set tables creating a feeling of cosy intimacy. The menu represents an entente cordiale between Scots produce and classical Italian cooking, with starters such as lobster ravioli in tomato and basil sauce, and main dishes like venison medallions with salsiccia and porcini on fried polenta. Tender, moist guinea-fowl is a winner, served in a reduction of roasting juices with rosemary and grappa.

Times 12-2.30/5.30-10.30 Closed 25-26 Dec, 1 Jan, Sun

Shish Mahal

Modern Indian, European

Long-standing Indian restaurant in a quiet part of the city

☎ 0141 339 8256
60-68 Park Rd G4 9JF
e-mail: reservations@shishmahal.co.uk
dir: From M8/A8 take exit towards Dumbarton. On Great Western Rd 1st left into Park Rd

A Kelvinbridge institution for half a century, the Shish Mahal is almost as Glaswegian as Rangers and Celtic,

continued

Hotel du Vin Bistro at One Devonshire Gardens

GLASGOW **Map 20 NS56**

French, European

Fine dining in sophisticated townhouse hotel

☎ 0141 339 2001
1 Devonshire Gardens G12 0UX
e-mail: bistro.odg@hotelduvin.com
dir: M8 junct 17, follow signs for A82 after 1.5m turn left into Hyndland Rd

Just off the main artery of Glasgow's West End near the Botanic Gardens, the operation at One Devonshire Gardens has the edge on its siblings in the ever-growing HdV stable of hotel brasseries. The Victorian terrace of five honey-hued sandstone townhouses embodies the trendy chain's boutique styling, without losing any of the original period charm of the building, giving a rather masculine gentlemen's club vibe. Kick off with an impressive range of aperitif firewaters in the bar-lounge, before heading into the bistro. The style here is something of a surprise - a bistro, but not as we know it. The oak-panelled warren of rooms have a plush formality and tables clothed decorously in floor-length swathes of linen - more the hushed arena of fine-dining than the buzzy clatter of a bistro. In the kitchen, Paul Tamburrini has clearly set his cheffy sights high: excellent raw materials are delivered with impressive technical skill on a menu that runs the spectrum from classics, such as straight-up 28-day-aged steaks, to more complex stuff. Picturesque presentation is a trademark here, as in a starter of sweet langoustine tails served on a patty of confit pig's cheek with soy marshmallows, smoked mussel velouté and braised baby carrots. Main-course reverts to classic territory with a caramelised fillet of veal with ventrèche bacon, pommes Maxim, garlic fondue, caramelised onion and sauce béarnaise. Dessert concludes with a more avante-garde display - an organic carrot soufflé with a citric kick of lime coulant at its heart, a tarragon and chocolate lollipop, and chocloate-coated Space Dust 'Rice Krispies'. There's a helpful sommelier to guide you through the trademark first-rate wine list.

Chef Paul Tamburrini **Owner** MWB/Hotel Du Vin **Times** 12-2.30/6-10 Closed L Sat **Prices** Fixed L 2 course fr £17.50, Service added but optional 10% **Wines** 600 bottles over £20, 12 bottles under £20, 12 by glass **Notes** 5 course D £55, Sunday L, Vegetarian available, Dress restrictions, Smart casual, Civ Wed 70 **Seats** 78, Pr/dining room 70 **Children** Portions **Parking** Nearby

GLASGOW *continued*

and retains a massive, loyal following. It's not hard to see why. Knowledgeable, friendly service, crisp table linen and an extensive menu of regional dishes elevate it well above the formula curry-house norm. Shorba (soup) is a different way to kick things off, perhaps combining spiced lentils, lemon and coconut milk, while chicken cooked on the bone in fresh garam masala, tomatoes and ginger is a tender treat. Proper jalfrezi based on stir-fried peppers, sweet-sour pathia, and rogan josh alive with Kashmiri chillies are among the favourites, as well as a good listing of vegetarian dishes. Roti and naan breads are freshly baked, and you might finish with crisp chocolate and smoked cashew samosa with coconut ice cream.

Chef Mr I Humayun **Owner** Ali A Aslam, Nasim Ahmed **Times** 12-2/5-11 Closed 25 Dec, L Sun **Prices** Fixed L 3 course £5.95-£7.50, Fixed D 3 course £18.50-£23.50, Starter £3.25-£7.50, Main £9.50-£16.95, Dessert £2.50-£3.95, Service optional, Groups min 5 service 10% **Wines** 3 bottles over £20, 13 bottles under £20, 1 by glass **Notes** Fixed L 4 course, Vegetarian available **Seats** 95, Pr/dining room 14 **Children** Portions **Parking** Side street, Underground station car park

Stravaigin

Modern International

The global larder comes to Glasgow

0141 334 2665
28 Gibson St, Kelvinbridge G12 8NX
e-mail: stravaigin@btinternet.com
web: www.stravaigin.com
dir: Next to Glasgow University. 200yds from Kelvinbridge underground

Taking up the three floors of a city tenement, this popular outfit takes an informal approach. Eat in the laid-back bar-café split across two floors, or in the basement restaurant; the same high standards apply throughout. The kitchen makes fine use of the fab Scottish larder on an appealing modern menu with a nod to the Med and far beyond; think West Coast langoustine and stuffed baby squid with Vietnamese carrot and sesame salad and kaffir lime caramel to open. In between, perhaps a Tuscan braised shoulder of lamb with cavolo nero, roast red onion polenta and fig compôte, while to finish, Andalucian lemon and mascarpone tart served with brown butter ice cream might catch the eye.

Stravaigin

Chef Andrew Mitchell **Owner** Colin Clydesdale **Times** 12-3.30/5-12 Closed 25-26 Dec, 1 Jan, L Mon-Fri **Prices** Starter £3.65-£11.95, Main £8.95-£22.95, Dessert £4.25-£10.95, Service optional **Wines** 34 bottles over £20, 26 bottles under £20, 22 by glass **Notes** Pre-theatre menu 2 course £12.95, 3 course £15.95, Vegetarian available **Seats** 76 **Children** Portions, Menu **Parking** On street, car park 100yds

Ubiquitous Chip

Traditional Scottish NOTABLE WINE LIST

Reliable Scottish cuisine in a unique setting

0141 334 5007
12 Ashton Ln G12 8SJ
e-mail: mail@ubiquitouschip.co.uk
dir: In West End, off Byres Rd. Adjacent to Hillhead underground station

The kitchen's drive to showcase the finest Scottish produce has helped ensure the popularity of this West End stalwart for 40 years. Throw in a glass canopy sheltering a cobbled courtyard with a jungly tangle of greenery beneath a mezzanine gallery, plus factor in a more formal skylit dining room, a brasserie and trio of pubby venues, and it is little wonder the Chip has endured so successfully. The cooking takes a fiercely Scottish line but comes peppered with imagination; hand-dived seared scallops, for example, teamed with Rothesay black pudding, candied and sour apples, vanilla oil and a hazelnut and dill tuile for openers. Main courses might feature the conventional (Aberdeen Angus fillet steak au poivre) to the more ambitious, perhaps a trilogy of Ardnamurchan venison with contrasting sauces.

Chef Ian Brown **Owner** Ronnie Clydesdale **Times** 12-2.30/5.30-11 Closed 25 Dec, 1 Jan **Prices** Food prices not confirmed for 2011. Please telephone for details **Wines** 295 bottles over £20, 35 bottles under £20, 35 by glass **Notes** Sunday L, Vegetarian available, Civ Wed 60 **Seats** 200, Pr/dining room 45 **Children** Portions, Menu **Parking** Lilybank Gardens (50m)

Urban Bar and Brasserie

Modern French

Confident brasserie cooking in grand old building

0141 248 5636
23/25 St Vincent Place G1 2DT
e-mail: info@urbanbrasserie.co.uk
dir: In city centre between George Sq & Buchanan St

This sleek and modern bar-brasserie has monopolised on the handsome architecture of this ex-bank (the former Scottish HQ of the Bank of England). It's a grand building, as you might expect, and the décor has been put together with a good deal of panache; brown leather banquettes and chairs flank smartly laid tables, and huge canvases of modern art bring vibrant splashes of colour. Good quality Scottish produce turns up on the menu of skilfully rendered dishes. Grilled sardines with caper, lemon and garlic olive oil is a Mediterranean classic, whilst main courses might see peppered loin of Buccleuch served up with chestnut mushrooms and chips, or West coast plaice steamed in paper with Chinese greens, garlic and black beans.

Chef Derek Marshall & John Gillespie **Owner** Alan Tomkins, Derek Marshall **Times** Noon-10 Closed 25-26 Dec, 1-2 Jan **Prices** Fixed L 2 course £16.95, Fixed D 3 course £19.95, Starter £6-£10, Main £12-£22, Dessert £6-£8, Service optional, Groups min 6 service 10% **Wines** 40 bottles over £20, 20 bottles under £20, 10 by glass **Notes** Pre-theatre menu 5-6pm £16.95 incl wine, Sunday L, Vegetarian available **Seats** 110, Pr/dining room 20 **Children** Portions **Parking** NCP West Nile St

HIGHLAND

ACHILTIBUIE **Map 22 NC00**

The Summer Isles Hotel

Modern British

Tranquil surroundings, superb sea views and top class Scottish ingredients

01854 622282
IV26 2YG
e-mail: info@summerisleshotel.co.uk
dir: 10m N of Ullapool. Left off A835 onto single track road. 15m to Achiltibuie. Hotel 100yds after post office on left

Visitors to this hotel, in a wilderness of islands and mountains in the far north west of Scotland, should pack their wellies and work up an appetite for some fine Scots produce in refined surroundings. Run by Terry and Irina Mackay, these white cottages overlooking the Summer Isles and out to the Hebrides have escaped modernisation, instead the superlative sea views take precedence. The result of all that stress-relieving sea air is a relaxed atmosphere. Refined yes, stuffy no. The neutrally-decorated dining room features smartly dressed tables and makes for a civilised space to enjoy just about the finest produce the Highlands have to offer. Typical dishes include warm scallop mousse with a light jus and home-made herb and tomato loaf, or grilled fillet of Lochinver halibut with local mussels steamed in saffron and white wine. Don't skip dessert – it's worth it for the old fashioned sweet trolley. Coffee also comes accompanied by traditional Scottish tablet.

Times 12.30-2/8 Closed mid Oct-Etr

ARISAIG **Map 22 NM68**

Cnoc-na-Faire

Modern Scottish NEW

Relaxed dining showcasing the best of the west

☎ 01687 450249
Back of Keppoch PH39 4NS
e-mail: cnocnafaire@googlemail.com
dir: A830/B8008 at sign for establishment, after 1m, left into driveway

The name means 'Hill of Vigil' in Gaelic, an apt title for this small inn that sits in a dreamy location atop a small knoll with postcard-perfect views taking in a white sand beach and the Inner Hebridean isles of Rhum and Eigg. When you have the Mallaig fishing fleet moored nearby, it would be remiss not to make full use of their world-class catch. Thankfully, Cnoc-na-Faire's kitchen knows a good thing when it sees it, making full use of the local seafood in modern interpretations of classic dishes, such as Cullen skink - this hearty Scottish chowder made with smoked Mallaig haddock, cream and potatoes - or main-course cod, which comes with a langoustine and brioche crumb coating, creamy leek mash and curly kale.

Chef Allan Ritchie **Owner** D & J Sharpe **Times** 12-2/6-9 Closed 23-27 Dec **Prices** Starter £4.15-£6.15, Main £10.45-£19.45, Dessert £5.15-£7.95, Service optional **Wines** 4 bottles over £20, 8 bottles under £20, 4 by glass **Notes** Sunday L, Vegetarian available, Civ Wed 20 **Seats** 20 **Children** Portions, Menu **Parking** 20

BOAT OF GARTEN **Map 23 NH91**

Boat Hotel - Osprey Bistro

Modern Scottish

Modern bistro classics in a majestic Cairngorm setting

☎ 01479 831258
Deshar Rd PH24 3BH
e-mail: info@boathotel.co.uk
dir: Turn off A9 N of Aviemore onto A95. Follow signs to Boat of Garten

A short drive from the winter sports at Aviemore, in the heart of the Cairngorms, the Boat is a sumptuously located Victorian hotel. With such a majestic setting, it would be natural enough to expect a full-dress formal restaurant, and yet the approach taken here is refreshingly laid-back. To be sure, the panelled bar and bistro look smart enough, but the ambience is much more relaxed than the silver-service, Scots baronial norm. The quality of the cooking is a draw to match the views, with a repertoire of modern classics bringing on duck and wild mushroom terrine with roast pepper chutney and brioche, followed perhaps by ragout of scallops and monkfish in tarragon and vanilla nage with lemon and herb basmati. Indulge yourself at the close with white chocolate and pear cheesecake, served with dark chocolate sauce.

Chef Peter Woods **Owner** Mr J Erasmus & Mr R Drummond **Times** 12-3.30/7-9.30 Closed Dec-Feb (bookings only) **Prices** Starter £3.50-£9.95, Main £10.95-£22.50, Dessert £5.95-£7.50, Service optional **Wines** 40 bottles over £20, 6 bottles under £20, 8 by glass **Notes** Vegetarian available **Seats** 70, Pr/dining room 40 **Children** Portions, Menu **Parking** 36

BRACHLA **Map 23 NH53**

Loch Ness Lodge

French, Scottish

Spectacular Loch Ness views and locally-produced ingredients

☎ 01456 459469
Loch Ness-Side IV3 8LA
e-mail: escape@lodgeatlochness.com
dir: A9/A82 Fort William/Loch Ness Rd. On right hand side after Clansman Hotel

No expense has been spared at this Loch Ness-side purpose-built restaurant which manages to retain something of the more formal country houses of old. Expect a cosy lounge and more formal sitting room, open fires, lots of books and magazines and fresh flowers throughout. The modern restaurant's best seats are by the window where you can gaze over Loch Ness in search of the elusive beast of the water. The finest tableware, linen and original artwork complement the restaurant's bold colour combinations. Artisan producers supply organic as well as local ingredients for the Franco-Scottish menu. Pace yourself, as dinner is a relaxed affair of five courses. Start perhaps with braised belly of Morayshire pork with poached hen's egg and walnut dressing before wild brill poached in red wine with langoustine and boulangère potatoes. The grounds are carefully landscaped and there's also an indoor hot tub, sauna and treatment room should further pampering be required.

Times 7-11.30 Closed 2-31 Jan, L all week (except by arrangement)

BRORA **Map 23 NC90**

Royal Marine Hotel, Restaurant & Spa

Modern Scottish

Traditional Highland hotel with reliable cooking

☎ 01408 621252
Golf Rd KW9 6QS
e-mail: info@royalmarinebrora.com
dir: off A9 in village towards beach & golf course

This smartly refurbished Edwardian country-house hotel plays to the gallery with a choice of three dining venues. It's a popular 19th hole for the golfing fraternity, too, with Brora's renowned golf course smack on the doorstep. There's the more informal Garden Room, a buzzy modern Bistro Bar and the traditional, formally attired Lorimers Restaurant, which serves up clear-flavoured dishes in the modern Scottish vogue. Tee off with hand-dived seared king scallops, perhaps served with peas and basil oil, and to follow, seared saddle of Achentoul venison with a caraway seed crust accompanied by confit potatoes, Umbrian lentil and smoked bacon broth and a redcurrant and walnut jus.

Times 12-2/6.30-8.45 Closed L (pre booking only)

CONTIN **Map 23 NH45**

Coul House Hotel

Modern Scottish V

Magically located Georgian hotel with a range of dining styles

☎ 01997 421487
IV14 9ES
e-mail: stay@coulhousehotel.com
dir: A835 signed Ullapool, 12m Contin. Hotel drive 100yds right after petrol station

A fine, late-Georgian country house in the Ross-shire hills, surrounded by magical scenery, Coul House stands on the banks of the River Blackwater. The ornate dining room with its swagged drapes makes a stylish setting for Garry Kenley's ambitious cooking, which comes in three styles – gourmet, 'more traditional' and vegetarian. The traditional options might take in haggis with neeps and potato bridie, or sirloin steak with dauphinoise and a choice of sauces, but there is no stinting on imaginative presentations. A skirlie and potato crust may be applied to a fillet of halibut, which is then accompanied by a casserole of cockles, borlotti beans and spinach. Intriguing desserts have included butterscotch and date turnover with caramelised rhubarb ice cream and saffron vanilla sauce.

Chef G Kenley **Owner** Stuart MacPherson **Times** 12-2.30/6.30-9 Closed 24-26 Dec **Prices** Starter £5-£8.95, Main £11-£22.50, Dessert £6-£6.50, Service optional **Wines** 67 bottles over £20, 15 bottles under £20, 7 by glass **Notes** Sunday L, Vegetarian menu, Civ Wed 120 **Seats** 70, Pr/dining room 40 **Children** Portions, Menu **Parking** 60

DORNOCH Map 23 NH78

Dornoch Castle Hotel

⊛ Scottish, Fusion

Country-house cooking in a restored medieval castle

☎ 01862 810216
Castle St IV25 3SD
e-mail: enquiries@dornochcastlehotel.com
dir: 2m N of Dornoch Bridge on A9, turn right to Dornoch. Hotel in village centre

Sitting on the market square opposite the 12th-century cathedral, the old stone castle and tower make a highly individual country hotel. The main dining room, with its 11-foot fireplace, was once the bishop's kitchen, and there is also a Garden Room looking out over the formal walled garden. An uncontroversial take on country-house cookery sees the likes of mussels from Dornoch Firth cooked marinière-style in white wine, garlic and cream, with main courses such as roast loin of Highland venison with creamy mash, chicory and Madeira jus. Finish with coconut pannacotta and mango coulis.

Times 12-3/6-9.30 Closed 25-26 Dec

FORT AUGUSTUS Map 23 NH30

The Lovat

⊛⊛ Modern Scottish

Imaginative fine dining in a charming period house

☎ 0845 450 1100 & 01456 459250
Loch Ness PH32 4DU
e-mail: info@thelovat.com
dir: A82 between Fort William & Inverness

With a prominent position overlooking the scenic town of Fort Augustus and nearby Loch Ness, this country-house hotel in a Victorian building houses a smart, contemporary style brasserie and the more traditional Loch Ness restaurant. For the latter, the kitchen conjures up creative modern Scottish treats using the vast Highland's larder at its disposal. A well-flavoured watercress velouté may be followed by a sea-fresh main of baked fillet of halibut with Torridon pink fur apple potatoes, West Coast mussels and saffron sauce. A stunningly presented blackberry tart with vanilla sauce anglaise, blackberry jelly and raspberry sorbet makes a fresh and light finish.

Owner David, Geraldine & Caroline Gregory **Times** 7-9 Closed Hogmanay (Jan) - guests only, Nov-Mar, Sun-Mon **Prices** Fixed D 3 course £35-£40, Starter £4.25-£7.50, Main £9.95-£22.95, Dessert £5.25-£7.50, Service optional, Groups min 8 service 10% **Wines** 20 bottles over £20, 20 bottles under £20, 10 by glass **Notes** Vegetarian available, Civ Wed 150 **Seats** 27, Pr/dining room 50 **Children** Portions, Menu **Parking** 30

FORT WILLIAM Map 22 NN17

Inverlochy Castle Hotel

⊛⊛⊛ – *see below*

Lime Tree Hotel & Restaurant

⊛ Modern European

Modern cooking in charming restaurant and art gallery

☎ 01397 701806
Lime Tree Studio, Achintore Rd PH33 6RQ
e-mail: info@limetreefortwilliam.co.uk
web: www.limetreefortwilliam.co.uk

In the heart of Fort William, this charming small hotel, restaurant and art gallery has dramatic views of Loch Linnhe and the mountains beyond. An old stone manse, it is now fresh and modern thanks to the original artwork on display and the stylish décor, but real fires and natural

Inverlochy Castle Hotel

FORT WILLIAM Map 22 NN17

Modern British V NOTABLE WINE LIST

Classic country-house hotel in the foothills of Ben Nevis

☎ 01397 702177
Torlundy PH33 6SN
e-mail: info@inverlochy.co.uk
dir: 3m N of Fort William on A82, just past Golf Club, N towards Inverness

Looking up at the UK's highest mountain - Ben Nevis - stands this 1860s fortress serving up fantastic Scottish produce in grand surroundings. Queen Victoria is said to have deemed it 'one of the loveliest and most romantic spots' and she had a point. Dramatic backdrop aside, the hotel sits in 600 acres of beautifully landscaped gardens and even has its very own loch. Inside, expect a host of original features and opulence aplenty. While the lavish main hall and lounge are the perfect setting for afternoon tea or a post-prandial cocktail, you may prefer to head for the terrace when the weather is kind. In the three formal dining rooms (gentlemen are asked to don a jacket and tie), guests are in safe hands with service that manages to be both accomplished and also friendly. Don't overindulge in the excellent canapés and bread straight out of the oven, instead save room to explore the imaginative modern British menu which makes the best of local Scottish ingredients as well as some sourced even closer to home in the castle's own garden. Start with caramelised scallop with a pig's head beignet and cauliflower salad, followed by roasted sea bass with caramelised chicory, Loch Linnhe prawns and truffle. Finish off with a creative lime parfait with cream cheese beignet, lime jelly, apple and coriander.

Chef Philip Carnegie **Owner** Inverlochy Hotel Ltd **Times** 12.30-1.45/6.30-10 **Prices** Fixed L 2 course £28, Fixed D 4 course £65, Service added but optional **Wines** 283 bottles over £20, 8 by glass **Notes** Vegetarian menu, Dress restrictions, Jacket & tie for D, Civ Wed 80 **Seats** 40, Pr/dining room 20 **Children** Portions, Menu **Parking** 20

materials are reminders of the past. The menu is a blend of local ingredients and modern European ideas: terrine of guinea fowl, duck and pigeon is served with walnut brioche and raisin purée and might be followed by braised blade of beef with crispy snails, truffle and red wine jus. Finish with pink rhubarb jelly with vanilla ice cream.

Chef Ross Sutherland **Owner** David Wilson & Charlotte Wright **Times** 12-2.30/6.30-9 Closed Nov **Prices** Fixed L 2 course £9.95-£15.95, Starter £4.25-£8.50, Main £12.95-£20, Dessert £5-£8.75, Service optional **Wines** 14 bottles over £20, 17 bottles under £20, 5 by glass **Notes** Sunday L, Vegetarian available, Civ Wed 50 **Seats** 30 **Children** Portions **Parking** 10

Moorings Hotel

Modern, Traditional

Popular Highland hotel with accomplished cooking

☎ 01397 772797
Banavie PH33 7LY
e-mail: reservations@moorings-fortwilliam.co.uk
web: www.moorings-fortwilliam.co.uk
dir: From A82 take A830 W for 1m. 1st right over Caledonian Canal on B8004, signed Banavie

The Jacobite steam train - aka Hogwarts Express when it starred in the Harry Potter films - steams past this relaxed traditional hotel in a glorious location on the Caledonian Canal with Ben Nevis as a backdrop. There's no lack of Highland entertainment here - you could watch the boats toiling up the flight of locks known as Neptune's Staircase, and the Great Glen Way is on the doorstep to work up a keen appetite for dinner in the beamed Jacobean Restaurant. The kitchen raids the local larder, hauling in top-class West Coast seafood and game for its well-prepared British and European dishes. Local mussels star in classic moules marinières, followed by baked monkfish on Puy lentils with pak choi, sweet-and-sour sauce and prawn tempura.

Chef Paul Smith **Owner** Mr S Leitch **Times** 7-9.30 Closed 24-26 Dec, L all week **Prices** Fixed D 4 course £30, Starter £5-£8, Main £12-£23, Dessert £5-£6.50, Service optional **Wines** 17 bottles over £20, 28 bottles under £20, 7 by glass **Notes** Vegetarian available, Dress restrictions, Smart casual, Civ Wed 120 **Seats** 60, Pr/dining room 120 **Children** Portions **Parking** 50

GLENFINNAN Map 22 NM98

The Prince's House

Modern British

Welcoming old coaching inn with fine Scottish produce

☎ 01397 722246
PH37 4LT
e-mail: princeshouse@glenfinnan.co.uk
dir: From Fort William N on A82 for 2m. Turn left on to A830 Mallaig Rd for 15m to hotel

Highland scenery doesn't come more romantic than the wild mountains and forests of the 'Road to the Isles' running through the heart of Bonnie Prince Charlie country from Fort William to the fishing port of Mallaig. A great setting, then, to base yourself in this charming 17th-century family-run coaching inn renowned for its sincere welcome. Better still, the chef-proprietor is well-tuned in to local supply lines for excellent fish and seafood, beef and lamb, and game from neighbouring estates. It is all about the quality of the ingredients here, with the sensibly concise menus kicking off with a risotto of West Coast crab served with marinated fennel wafers and fennel mascarpone 'ice cream'. Follow that with medallion of Kinlochmoidart venison with celeriac and potato rösti, roast root vegetables and redcurrant jus, and finish with Granny Smith apple flan with butterscotch sauce and wild bramble and Drambuie ice cream.

Chef Kieron Kelly **Owner** Kieron & Ina Kelly **Times** 7-9 Closed Xmas, Jan-Feb, Low season - booking only, L all week **Prices** Fixed D 3 course £35-£40, Service included **Wines** 70 bottles over £20, 6 bottles under £20, 8 by glass **Notes** Vegetarian available **Seats** 30 **Children** Portions **Parking** 18

GRANTOWN-ON-SPEY Map 23 NJ02

The Glass House Restaurant

Modern British V

Homely but smart cooking in a conservatory in whisky country

☎ 01479 872980
Grant Rd PH26 3LD
e-mail: info@theglasshouse-grantown.co.uk
dir: Turn off High St between the bank and Co-op into Caravan Park Rd. First left onto Grant Rd, restaurant on right

The low-roofed stone house with its conservatory attachment is to be found in one of the headquarter towns of the malt whisky industry. With its solid oak tables and log fire in the chilly season, it's a welcoming place, and the Robertsons ensure it is run with proper Highland hospitality. A starter consisting of a big field mushroom topped with smoked brie and bacon is full of the kind of richness you hope for in autumn, or there might be home-cured Shetland salmon marinated in orange, chilli, ginger and thyme. Main courses are substantial but well-judged, as when pigeon breast arrives with venison patties in a rosemary cream alongside a version of bashed neeps and chunky chips. The homely puddings might take in syrup sponge and custard, or a great apple crumble with a scoop of lemon curd ice cream that perfectly balances tartness and creaminess.

Chef Stephen Robertson **Owner** Stephen and Karen Robertson **Times** 12-1.45/7-9 Closed 2 wks Nov, 1 wk Jan, 25-26 Dec, 1-2 Jan, Mon, L Tue, D Sun **Prices** Fixed L 2 course £15, Fixed D 3 course £37, Starter £3.95-£8.75, Main £17.95-£21.50, Dessert £6.95-£8.75, Service optional **Wines** 14 bottles over £20, 15 bottles under £20, 5 by glass **Notes** Fixed price D available on Sat only, Sunday L, Vegetarian menu **Seats** 30 **Children** Portions **Parking** 10

INVERGARRY Map 22 NH30

Glengarry Castle

Scottish, International

Stunning views and traditional Scottish food

☎ 01809 501254
PH35 4HW
e-mail: castle@glengarry.net
dir: 1m S of Invergarry on A82

Loch Oich on one side, mountains on the other, this Victorian country-house hotel, with the ruins of Invergarry Castle in the grounds, has the best of Highland views. The landscaped gardens look pretty good too, as do the period features in the traditional dining room. Service from a young team is smiley and genuine. No twists here - the food is Scottish and proud of it. The menu changes daily and features local produce; warm oak-smoked salmon parcel, perhaps, filled with chive-scented scrambled eggs, or a main course of baked fillet of sea bass with a fennel, white wine and cream sauce.

Times 12-1.45/7-8.30 Closed mid Nov to mid Mar, L all week

INVERGORDON Map 23 NH76

Kincraig Castle Hotel

Modern Scottish V

Fine dining in a lovingly restored period house

☎ 01349 852587
IV18 0LF
e-mail: info@kincraig-castle-hotel.co.uk
web: www.kincraig-castle-hotel.co.uk
dir: Off A9, past Alness towards Tain. Hotel is 0.25m on left past church

continued

INVERGORDON ***continued***

If you'd like to live like a Laird, try a stay in this pocket-sized castle, which was once the seat of the MacKenzie clan. The Baronial country house with decorative mini turrets and stepped gables sits in delightful landscaped grounds with stunning views over the Cromarty Firth and Black Isle. There's plenty of feelgood factor in its period features, antiques and plush furnishings - a decorative style that continues in the fine-dining restaurant with a stone fireplace, cherry-red walls, and tables swathed in crisp linen. The cooking takes a restrained Franco-Scottish path, giving excellent local produce an unfussy modern workout in dishes such as Isle of Skye scallops with pork belly, sautéed potato, and sweetcorn and mango salsa. Mains might involve pan-roasted sea bass teamed with samphire, mussels, Jersey Royal potatoes and coral foam.

Chef Mark Fairgrieve **Owner** Kevin Wickman **Times** 12.30-2/6.45-9 **Prices** Fixed L 2 course £12.95, Fixed D 4 course £35, Tasting menu fr £45, Starter £3.95-£7.95, Main £11.95-£22.95, Dessert £5.95-£7.95, Service optional **Wines** 29 bottles over £20, 23 bottles under £20, 4 by glass **Notes** Sunday L, Vegetarian menu, Dress restrictions, Smart casual, Civ Wed 50 **Seats** 30, Pr/dining room 40 **Children** Portions, Menu **Parking** 40

INVERNESS **Map 23 NH64**

Abstract Restaurant & Bar

– see below

Bunchrew House Hotel

Modern, Traditional

Quality ingredients in a spectacular Highland location

☎ 01463 234917
Bunchrew IV3 8TA
e-mail: welcome@bunchrewhousehotel.com
dir: 3m W of Inverness on A862 towards Beauly

On the shores of the haunting Beauly Firth, a short drive out of Inverness, Bunchrew House is a 17th-century baronial mansion with bits that date back to the early 1500s. It's the sort of setting at which you might fancy staging your wedding celebrations, and many do, but it's also a destination address for some seriously fine dining. The restaurant is panelled in mahogany, with a great fireplace and commanding marine views, and the cooking suits the surroundings. An intricate starter might see flakes of salmon bundled up in Cromarty smoked trout, alongside salmon mousse in a mango dressing, while main courses impress for the quality of meats such as West Highland venison, perhaps the roast saddle served with caramelised red cabbage in a rosemary-scented sauce. Finish with a zesty lemon tartlet, its citric tang offset by whisky ice cream.

Chef Walter Walker **Owner** Terry & Irina Mackay **Times** 12-1.45/7-9 Closed 23-26 Dec **Prices** Fixed L 3 course £23.50, Fixed D 3 course £39.50, Service optional **Wines** 56 bottles over £20, 19 bottles under £20, 4 by glass **Notes** Sunday L, Vegetarian available, Civ Wed 92 **Seats** 32, Pr/dining room 14 **Children** Portions, Menu **Parking** 40

Contrast Brasserie

Modern, Traditional **NEW**

Riverside views and local produce

☎ 01463 223777
Glenmoriston Town House Hotel, 20 Ness Walk IV2 4SF
e-mail: reception@glenmoristontownhouse.com
dir: On riverside opposite theatre

If you're after a (dining) room with a view they don't come much better than at this smart riverside brasserie (sister to Abstract - see entry below) with its vista over the River Ness. The décor is chic – think simply laid tables and wooden venetian blinds in the conservatory – and the atmosphere relaxed. Alfresco dining is an option in warmer weather. Local produce is complemented by a global wine list, plus, of course, a good selection of malt whiskies. Start with hand-dived scallops roasted in the shell with lemon and chive butter and Thai salad, then move onto red deer fillet with Savoy cabbage, roasted mushroom and mashed potato. For coffee or afternoon tea, the terraces offer views of the Scottish Highlands.

Abstract Restaurant & Bar

INVERNESS **Map 23 NH64**

Modern French V

Intelligent, confident cooking with river views

☎ 01463 223777
Glenmoriston Town House Hotel, 20 Ness Bank IV2 4SF
e-mail: reception@glenmoristontownhouse.com
dir: 2 mins from city centre, on river opposite theatre

On the River Ness, part of the contemporary Glenmoriston Town House Hotel, Abstract diners would do well to bagsy a window seat. However, the French-accented food based on tip-top Scottish produce hits the spot wherever you sit. First though, take a pit stop at the stylish piano bar decked out in sumptuous leather chairs, for one of the 250 malt whiskies on offer or a cocktail or two. The restaurant doesn't let the side down in the design stakes – think highly polished wooden floors, colourful lightshades and linen-covered tables with sparkling glassware. The kitchen is big on flair, exhibiting original flavour combinations using the best of Scottish produce combined with modern French techniques. Expect the likes of hand-dived West Coast scallops roasted in sorrel butter, or a main of Scottish beef fillet with celeriac purée, braised oxtail, little gem and horseradish sauce. Strawberry soufflé makes a fittingly exalted finish. The chef's table by the pass serves a tasting menu to parties of up to six. Some classic French vintages make for an excellent wine list. The Contrast Brasserie (see entry) is a less formal alternative.

Chef Geoffrey Malmedy **Owner** Larsen & Ross South **Times** 6-10 Closed 26-28 Dec, Sun-Mon, L all week **Prices** Food prices not confirmed for 2011. Please telephone for details **Wines** 90% bottles over £20, 10% bottles under £20, 11 by glass **Notes** Vegetarian menu, Civ Wed 100 **Seats** 26, Pr/dining room 15 **Children** Portions, Menu **Parking** 50

Chef Geoffrey Malmedy **Owner** Barry Larsen **Times** 12-2.30/5-10 **Prices** Fixed L 2 course £9.95, Fixed D 2 course £11.95, Service optional **Wines** 40 bottles over £20, 5 bottles under £20, 8 by glass **Notes** Pre-theatre menu 2 course Mon-Sat 5-6.30pm £9.95, Sunday L, Vegetarian available, Civ Wed 90 **Seats** 70, Pr/dining room 20 **Children** Portions, Menu **Parking** 40

Culloden House Hotel

Modern Scottish

Serious Scottish cuisine in historic setting

☎ 01463 790461
Culloden IV2 7BZ
e-mail: info@cullodenhouse.co.uk
dir: From A96 left turn at junction of Balloch, Culloden, Smithton. 2m, hotel on right

A sweeping expanse of green lawns frames Culloden House, the magnificent Palladian mansion where Bonnie Prince Charlie spent the night before his army was defeated at the battle of Culloden in 1746. The sense of history inside is palpable: crystal chandeliers hang from lofty ceilings garlanded with ornate plasterwork in the entrance hall, but there's no airs and graces in the friendly welcome you receive. Settings don't come much more grand than the Adam dining room, where the kitchen showcases Scotland's finest produce in classic dishes with a modern spin. To start, pan-roasted scallops are teamed with crispy pork belly, squash purée and tomato salsa, before main-course roasted sea bass appears in the company of crushed crab potatoes, crayfish ravioli and saffron cream. Baked apple terrine with walnut brittle is a good way to finish.

Times 12.30-2/7-9 Closed 25-26 Dec

The New Drumossie Hotel

Modern Scottish

Art-deco Highland hotel with classy modern menu

☎ 01463 236451
Old Perth Rd IV2 5BE
e-mail: stay@drumossiehotel.co.uk
dir: From A9 follow signs for Culloden Battlefield, hotel on left after 1m

The Drumossie is a member of the Macdonald hotel group, and is another singularly enchanting place, full of unexpected charm. It's an art-deco building about 10 minutes' drive out of Inverness, with nine acres of beautifully kept grounds, and the seductive scenery of the Scottish Highlands all about. An appealing menu of fresh, lively dishes, soundly based on classic Scottish ingredients, achieves profound fullness of flavour in pairings such as Skye scallops and confit belly pork, a dish executed with well-nigh scientific precision and panache. What might be seen as the corporate signature main course, grilled rib-eye with field mushrooms, an improbably light green peppercorn sauce and big chips, is rendered with great attention to detail, or there may be wild venison loin with a mushroom ragoût and juniper jus.

Chef Kenny McMillan **Owner** Ness Valley Leisure **Times** 12.30-2/7-9.30 **Prices** Food prices not confirmed for 2011. Please telephone for details **Wines** 10 by glass **Notes** Vegetarian available, Civ Wed 400 **Seats** 90, Pr/dining room 500 **Children** Portions, Menu **Parking** 200

Riverhouse

British

Informal dining on banks of the River Ness

☎ 01463 222033
1 Greig St IV3 5PT
e-mail: riverhouse.restaurant@unicombox.co.uk
dir: On corner of Huntly St & Greig St

True to its name, this charming bistro-style restaurant sits on the north bank of the River Ness right by the Greig Street footbridge. Chef-proprietor Allan Little greets guests as they arrive in the intimate dining room, a clean-cut space decked out with chocolate-brown high-backed leather chairs, unclothed tables and fishy-themed wall art that reflects the penchant for piscine produce. An open kitchen lets diners watch as the chefs get stuck into preparing unpretentious, imaginative modern food using great Scottish materials – steamed Arisaig mussels in Thai red curry sauce with spring onion and coriander, for starters, followed by pan-roasted cod on Orkney crab risotto with roasted red pepper sauce. For carnivores, a rib-eye steak with béarnaise sauce and chunky chips should hit the spot.

Times 12-2.15/5.30-10 Closed Mon, L Sun

Rocpool

Modern European

Sleek design and eclectic, stylish cooking

☎ 01463 717274
1 Ness Walk IV3 5NE
e-mail: info@rocpoolrestaurant.com
web: www.rocpoolrestaurant.com
dir: On W bank of River Ness close to the university

Since it opened in 2002, this effervescent Inverness brasserie has built a loyal fan base. Its winning formula relies on a prime riverside spot, overlooking the River Ness through walls of glass, a cool contemporary décor with lots of bare wood and bold colours, and a buzzy vibe. The kitchen builds its repertoire of eclectic modern dishes on Scotland's matchless produce sprinkled with Mediterranean sunshine, plus a pinch of exotic spice here and there. King scallops might appear in the company of oriental duck ragú, oven-roasted pineapple, and sweet soy and lemongrass dressing with crispy shallots to start; there's lots going on too in a main-course fillet of John Dory with tomato and basil, shellfish butter, new potatoes and buttered vegetables. Hot lemon meringue pie cooked to order hits the spot for dessert.

Rocpool

Chef Steven Devlin **Owner** Mr Devlin **Times** 12-2.30/5.45-10 Closed 25-26 Dec, 1-2 Jan, Sun (Oct-Mar), L Sun (Apr-Sep) **Prices** Fixed L 2 course fr £10.95, Fixed D 2 course fr £12.95, Starter £3.95-£9.95, Main £11.95-£17.95, Dessert £5.45-£7.90, Service optional **Wines** 25 bottles over £20, 17 bottles under £20, 11 by glass **Notes** Early D 5.45-6.45pm 2 course £12.95, Vegetarian available **Seats** 55 **Children** Portions **Parking** On street

KINGUSSIE Map 23 NH70

The Cross at Kingussie

– *see page 514*

KYLE OF LOCHALSH Map 22 NG72

The Waterside Seafood Restaurant

Modern, Traditional Seafood

Quirky setting for fresh seafood and stunning views

☎ 01599 534813 & 577230
Railway Station Buildings, Station Rd IV40 8AE
e-mail: seafoodrestaurant@btinternet.com
dir: Off A87

Housed in the former railway ticket office and waiting room at the end of the pier, with stunning views across the platform towards Skye Bridge and up Loch Duich, this relaxed, friendly and simply furnished eaterie serves generous portions of fresh, locally-landed seafood. Try the seafood chowder or a plate of Skye oysters baked with herb butter, follow with smoked haddock with clapshot and white wine and parsley sauce, or a meat dish such as aromatic Moyle lamb slow-cooked in red wine with baked roots, butterbeans and crushed potatoes.

continued

KYLE OF LOCHALSH ***continued***

Chef Jann MacRae **Owner** Jann MacRae **Times** 11-3/5-9.30 Closed end Oct-beginning Mar, Sun (please phone to confirm opening hrs) **Prices** Food prices not confirmed for 2011. Please telephone for details **Wines** 2 bottles over £20, 15 bottles under £20, 2 by glass **Notes** Vegetarian available **Seats** 35 **Children** Portions **Parking** 5

LOCHINVER **Map 22 NC02**

Inver Lodge Hotel & Chez Roux

Traditional French V

Classic French cooking in stunning Highland location

☎ 01571 844496
IV27 4LU
e-mail: stay@inverlodge.com
dir: A835 to Lochinver, left at village hall, private road for 0.5m

Hidden away in an elevated hillside position overlooking the bay, this classy, comfortably and traditionally furnished hotel sits in its own attractive grounds surrounded by the unspoiled wilderness of this part of the Highlands. The Chez Roux restaurant has stunning views over the small fishing village of Lochinver and the ocean beyond, and, on a clear day, you can see the Western Isles through the picture windows. The Roux in the title is Albert, at least his company, so the smart, elegant restaurant with well-dressed, well-spaced tables and windows that frame the majestic views, is the setting for some confident French country cooking. Tip-top produce from the region, including freshly landed salmon and lobster, and Highland lamb, venison and beef, get a good showing. Start with the Roux signature, soufflé Suissesse, and move on to pan-fried duck breast in red wine and olives, finishing with a classic caramelised lemon tart served with a raspberry sorbet.

Chef Albert Roux, Lee Pattie **Owner** Robin Vestey **Times** 12-2/7-9.30 Closed Nov-Mar **Prices** Fixed D 3 course fr £40, Starter £8-£12, Main £16-£21, Dessert £7.50-£10.50, Service optional **Wines** 62 bottles over £20, 6 by glass **Notes** Fixed L 4 course from £15.50, Sunday L, Vegetarian menu, Civ Wed 50 **Seats** 50 **Children** Portions, Menu **Parking** 30

MUIR OF ORD **Map 23 NH55**

Ord House Hotel

Traditional British

Country-house comforts and fresh local produce

☎ 01463 870492
Ord Dr IV6 7UH
e-mail: admin@ord-house.co.uk
dir: off A9 at Tore rdbt onto A832. 5m, through Muir of Ord. Left towards Ullapool (A832). Hotel 0.5m on left

Converted into a country-house hotel over 40 years ago, this elegant 17th-century manor house still retains it original features and charm. It stands in 60 acres of glorious gardens and woodlands - plenty of room to supply the kitchen with fresh vegetables, herbs and fruit. Husband-and-wife-team John and Eliza Allen have taken the traditional route with their elegant hotel, and the kitchen stays in step, with simple country-house classics prepared from fresh, local, seasonal produce. West Coast oysters or smoked salmon pâté are typical starters, with Aberdeen Angus sirloin steak with Roquefort sauce to follow. Comforting desserts include plum crumble and treacle tart.

Chef Eliza Allen **Owner** Eliza & John Allen **Times** 7-9 Closed Nov-end Feb **Prices** Fixed D 3 course £28-£30, Starter £8-£14, Main £14-£25, Dessert £5-£7.50, Service included **Wines** 14 bottles over £20, 18 bottles under £20, 4 by glass **Notes** Vegetarian available **Seats** 26 **Children** Portions **Parking** 24

NAIRN **Map 23 NH85**

The Boath House

– ***see opposite page***

The Cross at Kingussie

KINGUSSIE **Map 23 NH70**

Modern Scottish

Top-notch restaurant with rooms in an idyllic setting

☎ 01540 661166
Tweed Mill Brae, Ardbroilach Rd PH21 1LB
e-mail: relax@thecross.co.uk

David and Katie Young's classy restaurant with rooms sits beside the babbling Gynack Burn in four acres of flowery gardens and woodland in the Cairngorm National Park. Red squirrels and colourful birds are frequently in attendance at aperitif time on the waterside terrace, before you move indoors for a leisurely-paced dinner. The Cross ticks all the right boxes: the mood is unbuttoned and unhurried thanks in no small part to the personable, clued-up staff, while the building's whitewashed rough-stone walls and heavy beams are a perfect foil to the food - everything that leaves the kitchen is built on the principle of treating fantastic produce with respect, and knowing when to stop before overworking sets in. Local sourcing is the kitchen's guiding principle, but quality comes first, so the finest materials are hauled in from around Scotland. Creative fixed price menus change daily, offering a couple of choices at each stage. What could be more simple than local wild mushroom soup with truffles and truffle oil to start the ball rolling? Next, the kitchen comes up with the more elaborate seared Kyle of Lochalsh scallops teamed with fennel, broad beans and pea shoots, orange, vanilla and cardamom dressing, ahead of roast coffee-marinated rump of Perthshire Blackface lamb with sweetcorn relish, wilted spinach and a rich maple syrup mash. A modern marriage of bitter chocolate torte with salted pistachio ice cream ends on a high note. Serious thought has gone into the wine list, which comes with witty tasting notes and nudges in the right direction to help with food matching; it's fairly priced too.

Chef Becca Henderson, David Young **Owner** David & Katie Young **Times** 7-8.30 Closed Xmas & Jan (excl New Year), Sun-Mon, L all week **Prices** Fixed D 4 course fr £50, Service included, Groups min 6 service 10% **Wines** 200 bottles over £20, 20 bottles under £20, 4 by glass **Notes** Vegetarian available **Seats** 20 **Parking** 12

The Boath House

NAIRN Map 23 NH85

Modern French, Traditional Scottish

Stunning food and effortless service in small country-house hotel

01667 454896
Auldearn IV12 5TE
e-mail: wendy@boath-house.com
dir: 2m E of Nairn on A96 (Inverness to Aberdeen road)

As you crunch along the long gravel drive leading to what has been called 'the most beautiful Regency house in Scotland', a sense of anticipation builds. Badgers and roe deer roam in the woods in its 20 acres of grounds, and swans, wild geese and ducks freckle the pretty lake stocked with brown and rainbow trout. Hard to believe, then, that this bucolic vision of Palladian elegance designed by celebrated architect Archibald Simpson was on the endangered list in the early '90s, when owners Don and Wendy Matheson fell in love with the place and carefully restored it to open as a splendid small hotel. They are a chatty, welcoming team whose hands-on enthusiasm has not dimmed. If Boath has the timeless, soft-focus familiarity of a glossy interior magazine spread, that's probably because it has been used for photo shoots by Bentley cars and numerous high-end fashion houses. And you can see why: the décor is a warmly-coloured, cosy, eclectic mix of antiques and colourful paintings, tasteful ceramics and sculpture in elegantly-proportioned lounges; Boath is designated an art gallery and exhibits many contemporary Highland artists. The beautiful gardens and lake, viewed through lovely French windows, are a backdrop to leisurely six-course dinners in the candlelit romance of the dining room. With a maximum of 26 guests to cater for, chef Charles Lockley can keep a tight rein on quality control as he brings a supreme level of skill to bear on his creations. Inspired by the idea of slow food, and driven by sourcing the finest organic and wild ingredients, his cooking is inspirational stuff that 'lets the ingredients do the talking'. Just about everything here is either home-grown in the walled garden, including honey from their own hives, or if it moos, oinks, baas or clucks it's sourced from local meat and dairy suppliers; if it swims, it's delivered fresh daily from the West Coast. Simple menu descriptions belie the combinations of deep flavours in each dish. An intense carrot soup with basil oil has the flavour of carrots plucked straight from the earth, while the sweetness of rabbit and lentils is pointed up by a tangy plum purée. Next up, salmon is teamed with beetroot jelly and quail's eggs, ahead of roe deer with crushed peas, chanterelles and truffle jus. Then comes the plate of exemplary artisanal cheeses before dessert - perhaps a vodka slammer berry sorbet combination with gingerbread and custard. Equally stunning are oyster fritters on celeriac, nut and summer truffle bonbon, lavender marshmallows and ginger chocolate pitched in as amuses and treats.

Chef Charles Lockley **Owner** Mr & Mrs D Matheson **Times** 12.30-1.45/7-7.30 **Prices** Fixed L 2 course fr £21, Service included **Wines** 153 bottles over £20, 5 bottles under £20, 7 by glass **Notes** Fixed D 6 course £65, Sunday L, Vegetarian available, Dress restrictions, Smart casual, no shorts/T-shirts/jeans, Civ Wed 30 **Seats** 28, Pr/dining room 8 **Children** Portions **Parking** 25

NAIRN *continued*

Golf View Hotel & Leisure Club

Traditional, Modern Scottish V

Sound modern Scottish cooking in hotel with sea views

01667 452301
Seabank Rd IV12 4HD
e-mail: golfview@crerarhotels.com
dir: Off A96 into Seabank Rd & continue to end

This fine coastal hotel has wonderful sea views and overlooks the Moray Firth and Black Isle. The championship golf course at Nairn is adjacent and guests have direct access to the long, sandy beaches. The hotel has plenty of period detail, as does the comfortable restaurant, which is the place to go for some serious fine dining. The contemporary Scottish cooking is schooled in traditional French techniques and local produce is the cornerstone of the kitchen; start with chicken and game terrine with beetroot purée and carrot crisp and follow with fillet of West Coast halibut served with an oxtail and barley cassoulet and wilted spinach. Baked chocolate tart with orange crème fraîche makes a fine end to proceedings.

Chef Lee Pattie **Owner** Crerar Hotels **Times** 6.45-9 Closed L Mon-Sat **Prices** Fixed D 4 course £27-£34, Service optional **Wines** 22 bottles over £20, 23 bottles under £20, 8 by glass **Notes** Sunday L, Vegetarian menu, Dress restrictions, Smart casual **Seats** 50 **Children** Portions, Menu **Parking** 30, and next to hotel on street

Newton Hotel

Scottish, European

Enjoyable food in baronial-style hotel

01667 453144
Inverness Rd IV12 4RX
e-mail: salesnewton@ohiml.com
dir: A96 from Inverness to Nairn. In Nairn hotel signed on left

Fantasy turrets and a crenellated tower jut from this Baronial pile overlooking Nairn golf course and the Moray Firth - a fine location that made it a winner for Harold Macmillan and Charlie Chaplin on their hols (not together, of course). The demands of modern life have seen it extended to cater for conferences and larger numbers of guests, who have a choice of eating in the traditional restaurant or the more modern bistro. Expect straightforward Scottish dishes with a modern spin, kicking off with something that waves the flag for local produce, such as haggis and black pudding croquettes, followed by pan-fried collops of venison and beef with dauphinoise potatoes and braised red cabbage. End with the homely comfort of apple crumble and vanilla crème anglaise.

Chef Eric Matthews, Marcin Pawlak **Owner** Oxford Hotels & Inns **Times** 12-2.30/6-9 Closed Xmas & New Year **Prices** Food prices not confirmed for 2011. Please telephone for details **Wines** 10 bottles over £20, 25 bottles under £20, 4 by glass **Notes** Sunday L, Vegetarian available **Seats** 65, Pr/dining room 65 **Children** Portions, Menu **Parking** 100

NETHY BRIDGE — Map 23 NJ02

The Restaurant at The Mountview Hotel

Modern British

Highland retreat with scenery as appetising as the cooking

01479 821248
Grantown Rd PH25 3EB
e-mail: info@mountviewhotel.co.uk
dir: From Aviemore follow signs for Nethy Bridge, through Boat of Garten. In Nethy Bridge over humpback bridge & follow hotel signs

Wild nature starts at the very doorstep of this grand Victorian country-house hotel. The snow-dusted peaks of the Cairngorm National Park rise above the Caledonian pines of the RSPB-owned Abernethy Forest, while for those with more spiritual pursuits in mind, the whisky mecca of Grantown-on-Spey lies a short drive away. The Mountview's restaurant basks in sweeping views of this dramatic landscape, which is a window onto the provenance of the superb local produce that finds its way into the kitchen's skilful modern British cooking. The basic material for a beetroot soup comes from Mountview's garden, pointed up with smoked bacon and sour cream, while main-course local estate venison is teamed with celeriac and potato cake, and a port and juniper sauce.

Chef Lee Beale **Owner** Kevin & Caryl Shaw **Times** 6-11 Closed 25-26 Dec, Mon, L all week **Prices** Starter £3.95-£7.50, Main £12.50-£24.95, Dessert £3.50-£7.25, Service optional **Wines** 6 bottles over £20, 15 bottles under £20, 5 by glass **Notes** Vegetarian available **Seats** 24 **Children** Portions, Menu **Parking** 20

ONICH — Map 22 NN06

The Restaurant at The Onich Hotel

Traditional Scottish

Fine Scottish food and stunning loch views

01855 821214
PH33 6RY
e-mail: enquiries@onich-fortwilliam.co.uk
dir: Beside A82, 2m N of Ballachulish Bridge lochside

With beautiful landscaped gardens in a heavenly location on the shores of Loch Linnhe, it's no wonder that this welcoming hotel does a brisk trade in wedding parties kitted out in full Highland regalia. Whether you're in the bar, sun lounge or restaurant, the hotel's focus is firmly on the sweeping panoramas of the loch and mountains beyond. The kitchen takes traditional country-house cuisine built on excellent Scottish produce - including herbs and salad from the hotel's own garden - and gives it a modern spin, delivering accurately cooked, uncomplicated dishes with beautifully balanced flavours. Expect the likes of local venison served as peppered loin, spiced kebab and a tart filled with casserole, followed by West Coast scallops and langoustines with mint pea purée, baby potatoes and chive hollandaise.

Chef Graeme Kennedy **Owner** James MacDonald, Maria Wilson **Times** 7-9 Closed 24 Dec, 26 Dec, L all week **Prices** Food prices not confirmed for 2011. Please telephone for details **Wines** 2 bottles over £20, 15 bottles under £20, 4 by glass **Notes** Sunday L, Vegetarian available, Civ Wed 150 **Seats** 50, Pr/dining room 120 **Children** Portions, Menu **Parking** 50

SHIEL BRIDGE — Map 22 NG91

Grants at Craigellachie

Modern Scottish

Stunning backdrop for bold modern Scottish cooking

01599 511331
Craigellachie, Ratagan IV40 8HP
e-mail: info@housebytheloch.co.uk
dir: A87 to Glenelg, 1st right to Ratagan opposite the Youth Hostel sign

This homely conservatory restaurant is at the back of the house, overlooking the tranquil shores of Loch Duich and the Five Sisters mountains beyond. They call themselves 'The Little Restaurant with Rooms', and although small, it is perfectly formed. Service from the owners is pleasingly unruffled and the diminutive kitchen team is headed up by chef-patron Tony Taylor. Expect plenty of top-notch Scottish produce among the modern Scottish repertoire, starting perhaps with a terrine of Glen Gloy rabbit and wild boar with a caramelised red onion and beetroot relish, following on with oven-baked cuts of Minch-caught hake with a fresh parmesan and spring onion crust with a watercress and cashew nut pesto. Vanilla and cumin blinis with loganberries, West Highland crowdie, warm heather honey and toasted sesame seeds is a fabulous finish. The well-constructed wine list includes a good range of dessert wines.

Chef Tony Taylor **Owner** Tony & Liz Taylor **Times** 7-11 Closed Dec-mid Feb, L all week, D Sun **Prices** Starter £5-£10, Main £14-£25, Dessert £5-£9, Service optional **Wines** 48 bottles over £20, 12 bottles under £20, 7 by glass **Notes** Restaurant open only by reservation, Vegetarian available **Seats** 14 **Children** Portions

SHIELDAIG — Map 22 NG85

Tigh an Eilean Hotel Restaurant

Modern Scottish

Innovative cooking in a lochside inn

01520 755251
IV54 8XN
e-mail: tighaneilean@keme.co.uk
dir: From A896 follow signs for Shieldaig. Hotel in village centre on water's edge

Chris and Cathryn Field's white-painted hotel dates from around 1800 and stands in tiny Shieldaig fishing village on the banks of Loch Torridon. Stunning views of islands and hills to the open sea beyond can be savoured from its light and airy dining room. Chris's modern Scottish cuisine with French and Spanish influences offers exciting, accurately prepared dishes where nothing is more important than flavour. Daily-changing dinner menus rely on local produce, including seafood (hand-dived scallops and clams) delivered directly from the village jetty to the kitchen door. Start with langoustine risotto with truffle-scented langoustine broth, following on, perhaps, with roast venison with red onion and quince marmalade and Ben Shieldaig chanterelles. Raspberry cranachan with champagne and raspberry sauce makes a fitting finale. Slightly more straightforward dishes are served in the refurbished bar, now renamed the Shieldaig Bar and Coastal Kitchen.

Times 7-9 Closed end Oct-mid Mar (except private booking), L all week

SPEAN BRIDGE **Map 22 NN28**

Russell's at Smiddy House

◎◎ Modern Scottish

Good cooking in friendly Highland hotel

☎ 01397 712335
Roy Bridge Rd PH34 4EU
e-mail: enquiry@smiddyhouse.co.uk
dir: In village centre, 9m N of Fort William, on A82 towards Inverness

Occupying a prominent position in the heart of Spean Bridge, Smiddy House makes the ideal base for exploring the Great Glen and scaling the slopes of Ben Nevis, which looms high above the town. Russell's, located on the ground floor in the 'Smiddyhouse', once the village blacksmith's, is an intimate, candelit restaurant sporting original features and crisp linen-clothed tables decked with sparkling glasses, quality china and fresh flowers. Well-presented and well-balanced modern Scottish cuisine makes good use of top-notch local seasonal produce via a fixed-price menu. Start with twice-baked cheese soufflé with ham hock tarlet, then move onto accurately-cooked herb-crusted rack of lamb with carrot and parsnip mash and hollandaise sauce, and baked vanilla cheesecake with rhubarb sorbet and compôte.

Chef Glen Russell **Owner** Glen Russell, Robert Bryson **Times** 6-9 Closed 2 days a week (Nov-Apr), L all week **Prices** Food prices not confirmed for 2011. Please telephone for details **Wines** 21 bottles over £20, 11 bottles under £20, 5 by glass **Notes** Vegetarian available, Dress restrictions, Smart casual **Seats** 38 **Children** Portions, Menu **Parking** 15

STRONTIAN **Map 22 NM86**

Kilcamb Lodge Hotel & Restaurant

◎◎ Modern European V

Contemporary Scottish cooking in a ravishing setting

☎ 01967 402257
PH36 4HY
e-mail: enquiries@kilcamblodge.co.uk
dir: Take Corran ferry off A82. Follow A861 to Strontian. 1st left over bridge after village

The Scottish Highlands may have the tranquility market cornered but, even so, it's hard to imagine anywhere more majestically peaceful than the shores of Loch Sunart, where Kilcamb Lodge is perched. It goes without saying that views over loch and mountains are ravishing, so grab a window table if you can. Crisp linen and sparkling glassware set the tone for the highly refined culinary achievements, which are naturally based on local fish and game, but presented with an eye for novelty. Daily-changing dinner menus offer three- or seven-courses, embracing the likes of tortellini of duck confit with seared foie gras in star anise jus, through to frozen bitter chocolate mousse with orange sorbet. In between come main dishes of great flair, perhaps monkfish with Orkney crab quenelles, or slow-poached pork loin with braised cheeks, celeriac and caramelised apples.

Chef Tammo Siemers **Owner** Sally & David Fox **Times** 12-1.30/7.30-9.30 Closed 1 Jan-1 Feb **Prices** Fixed L 2 course £14.50, Fixed D 4 course £48-£60, Service optional, Groups min 10 service 10% **Wines** 45 bottles over £20, 20 bottles under £20, 10 by glass **Notes** Chef's tasting menu available Mon-Fri, Sunday L, Vegetarian menu, Dress restrictions, Smart casual, no jeans, T-shirts or trainers, Civ Wed 60 **Seats** 26 **Parking** 28

TAIN **Map 23 NH78**

Glenmorangie Highland Home at Cadboll

◎◎ French, International

House party-style dining in Highland hideaway

☎ 01862 871671
Cadboll, Fearn IV20 1XP
e-mail: relax@glenmorangie.co.uk
dir: N on A9, at Nigg Rdbt turn right onto B9175 (before Tain) & follow signs for hotel

The Glenmorangie whisky company has come up with a formula to gladden the hearts of malt whisky and food fans: bring the two together in a remote, stylish bolthole with its own beach on the wild Dornoch Firth. It helps if you're the gregarious type, as the house party vibe brings guests together in the drawing room for drinks before seating everyone at a long table bedecked with candles, fresh flowers, silver and crystal. The kitchen's approach is focused on Highland produce with a strong line in fish from local boats, game from nearby estates, plus fresh materials from its own walled kitchen gardens and orchards. Four-course dinner might open with pan-fried halibut on wilted spinach with toasted pine kernels and sauce vierge, and progress via soup - perhaps seasonal mushrooms with sautéed girolles and truffle oil - to herb-crusted fillet of pork with braised belly, confit potato, and apple-scented jus. Valrhona chocolate torte with white chocolate sauce ends on a high note.

Chef David Graham **Owner** Glenmorangie Ltd **Times** 8pm Closed 23-31 Dec, 4-27 Jan, L except by prior arrangement **Prices** Food prices not confirmed for 2011. Please telephone for details **Wines** 38 bottles over £20, 5 bottles under £20, 15 by glass **Notes** Fixed D 5 course £50, Vegetarian available, Dress restrictions, Smart casual, no jeans or T-shirts, Civ Wed 60 **Seats** 30, Pr/dining room 12 **Parking** 60

THURSO Map 23 ND16

Forss House Hotel & Restaurant

Modern Scottish

Elegant dining in spectacular Highland surroundings

☎ 01847 861201
Forss KW14 7XY
e-mail: anne@forsshousehotel.co.uk
dir: On A836, 5m outside Thurso

This 200 year-old shooting lodge, tucked away in a sylvan glen beneath a waterfall, is a natural choice for fans of fishing, hunting, hiking and golfing. When you've had your fill of the great outdoors, a classy country-house interior awaits, complete with the River Forss meandering by the romantic dining room. First-class materials underpin a menu of unfussy modern Scottish dishes that does not lack imagination. Sinclair Bay crab is teamed with the tenderness of globe artichoke, pickled ginger, garden herbs and lemon dressing. Next up, loin of hake comes with salsify, mussel cream and potato purée, while desserts could involve raspberry tart and home-made ice cream.

Chef Kevin Dalgleish, Gary Leishman **Owner** Ian & Sabine Richards **Times** 7-9 Closed 23 Dec-4 Jan, L all week **Prices** Starter £5.95-£7.95, Main £18.50-£24, Dessert £4.95-£6.95, Service optional **Wines** 34 bottles over £20, 6 bottles under £20, 2 by glass **Notes** Vegetarian available **Seats** 26, Pr/dining room 14 **Children** Portions **Parking** 14

See advert below

TONGUE Map 23 NC55

Ben Loyal Hotel

Modern British

Fantastic local produce and hilly views

☎ 01847 611216
Main St IV27 4XE
e-mail: benloyalhotel@btinternet.com
dir: In village centre at junction of A836 & A838

With spectacular views over the rugged glens and mountains of the Sutherland landscape is the Ben Loyal Hotel. The An Garbh restaurant (Gaelic for hilly area) has picture windows so diners get great views of the said terrain. The kitchen is rightly proud of its local produce and uses it liberally to create simple but flavoursome food. If you can resist the Kyle of Tongue oysters - fresh every day - choose a traditional starter of Cullen skink or haggis en croûte with a whisky sauce before tucking into monkfish with tarragon cream, new potatoes and seasonal vegetables. Desserts are nursery favourites – crumbles and sticky toffee pudding reign supreme.

Chef Eddie McDermott **Owner** Caspian Steilfish **Times** 6-9 Closed Jan, L all week **Prices** Starter £4-£5.70, Main £8.25-£16.50, Dessert £3.30-£6.75, Service optional **Wines** All bottles under £20, 4 by glass **Notes** Sunday L, Vegetarian available **Seats** 50 **Children** Portions, Menu **Parking** 20, plus opposite hotel, and on main street

TORRIDON Map 22 NG95

The Torridon Restaurant

Modern British V NOTABLE WINE LIST

Stunning lochside setting for confident, locally-inspired cooking

☎ 01445 791242
IV22 2EY
e-mail: info@thetorridon.com
dir: From Inverness take A9 N, follow signs to Ullapool (A835). At Garve take A832 to Kinlochewe; take A896 to Torridon. Do not turn off to Torridon Village. Hotel on right after Annat

The whisky bar at The Torridon, a grandly turreted Victorian former shooting lodge, is worthy of attention. With 350 malts to choose from, it would require a prolonged stay to work through them. Whether or not you're a fan of the strong stuff, the view of Upper Loch Torridon will bring the same warm glow - it's as quintessentially 'Highland' as you could hope for, and with 58 acres of wooded grounds to explore, the fresh air will clear the head for sure. Inside, comforting luxury and a happy blend of original features and chic contemporary touches blend together harmoniously. The interconnecting dining rooms, with glorious panelled walls, benefit from the view, and the kitchen makes much of the excellent produce from loch, sea and land. Start with canapés in the elegant drawing room or whisky bar, before tucking into leek and potato espuma with Sleepy Hollow smoked salmon, followed by roast haunch of venison or pan-fried fillet of halibut with hand-rolled macaroni and langoustine essence. The ambitious modern British cooking style continues with dessert; perhaps a yoghurt and gingerbread terrine with a fig poached in red wine and ginger caramel.

Chef Jason Bruno Birkbeck **Owner** Daniel & Rohaise Rose-Bristow **Times** 7-9 Closed 2 Jan for 5 wks, L all week **Prices** Fixed D 4 course £45, Service optional **Wines** 156 bottles over £20, 27 bottles under £20, 8 by glass **Notes** Vegetarian menu, Dress restrictions, No jeans or trainers, Civ Wed 42 **Seats** 38, Pr/dining room 16 **Children** Portions, Menu **Parking** 20

INVERCLYDE

KILMACOLM Map 20 NS37

Windyhill Restaurant

Modern British V

Carefully sourced contemporary British cuisine

01505 872613 & 610512
4 St James Ter, Lochwinnoch Rd PA13 4HB
e-mail: matthewscobey@hotmail.co.uk
dir: From Glasgow Airport, A737 take Bridge of Weir exit. Onto A761 to Kilmacolm. Left into High Street

Inspired by the great architect Charles Rennie Mackintosh's house, Windyhill, the black shop-front façade of this contemporary restaurant opens into a classily casual setting with moody lighting, darkwood furniture and modern artwork to inject splashes of colour to pristine white walls. The cooking is founded on top-drawer, locally-sourced produce, put to good use in uncomplicated but effective dishes with some interesting flavour combinations. Monthly menus offer a half-dozen choices at each stage; salmon, herb and potato fishcakes with rocket salad, followed by chicken with mushroom and black pudding risotto and basil oil. Leave room for a pudding, perhaps baked banana and chocolate cheesecake with toffee sauce.

Chef Matthew Scobey **Owner** Matthew Scobey & Careen McLean **Times** 12-3/6-10 Closed Xmas-New Year, last wk Jul, 1st wk Aug, Sun-Mon, L Tue-Thu, Sat **Prices** Fixed L 2 course £15-£25, Fixed D 3 course £20-£30, Starter £3.95-£6.95, Main £9.95-£19.95, Dessert £4.95-£6.50 **Wines** 5 bottles over £20, 18 bottles under £20, 6 by glass **Notes** Vegetarian menu **Seats** 45 **Children** Portions, Menu **Parking** On street, car park opposite

LANARKSHIRE, SOUTH

EAST KILBRIDE Map 20 NS65

Macdonald Crutherland House

British

Accomplished cooking in surroundings of great elegance

01355 577000
Strathaven Rd G75 0QZ
e-mail: general.crutherland@macdonald-hotels.co.uk
dir: Follow A726 signed Strathaven, straight over Torrance rdbt, hotel on left after 250yds

A supremely elegant panelled dining room with restful lighting and comfortable high-backed leather chairs sets a formal tone at the heart of this one-time 18th-century dower house turned wedding-venue plus health-spa. The menu takes an upmarket crowd-pleasing bistro-style route, bolstered with special dishes appearing on designated days of the week (Thursday is beef and ale pie day), with sound-quality produce from the abundant Scottish larder evident throughout. Take a duo of outdoor-reared pork (fillet and belly) served with apple and sage gravy, or perhaps hake fillet in a cockle and saffron broth. Desserts keep things equally uncomplicated, perhaps a vanilla crème brûlée (with home-made shortbread) or sticky toffee pudding.

Chef Kevin Hay **Owner** Macdonald Hotels **Times** 6-9 Closed L all week **Prices** Starter £5.50-£7.50, Main £14.50-£23.50, Dessert £6-£8, Service optional **Wines** 53 bottles over £20, 11 bottles under £20, 15 by glass **Notes** Vegetarian available, Dress restrictions, Smart dress, Civ Wed 300 **Seats** 80, Pr/dining room 300 **Children** Portions, Menu **Parking** 200

STRATHAVEN Map 20 NS74

Rissons at Springvale

Modern Scottish

Relaxed restaurant with modern Scottish cuisine

01357 520234 & 521131
18 Lethame Rd ML10 6AD
e-mail: rissons@msn.com
dir: M74 junct 8, A71, through Stonehouse to Strathaven

Anne and Scott Baxter's small and friendly restaurant with rooms continues to go from strength to strength. Refurbished in a clean-cut contemporary style, the Victorian merchant's house overlooks the local park, making for a relaxed setting in the light and airy restaurant and adjoining conservatory. It's an easy-going place with clued-up service, and the kitchen likes to keep things simple with a modern-bistro repertoire to match the mood. Dishes are kept unfussy and put together with attention to detail and well-balanced flavours, such as in a starter of tender confit duck leg on Puy lentils with a sharp balsamic glaze. Follow on with curried salmon with fresh pasta and a well-cooked mussel sauce, and end indulgently with sticky toffee pudding with lashings of sweet butterscotch sauce.

Chef Scott Baxter, Leonard Allen **Owner** Scott & Anne Baxter **Times** 12-2.30/6-9.30 Closed New Year, 1 wk Jan, 1st wk July, Mon-Tue, L Sat, D Sun **Prices** Fixed L 2 course £10.50-£14.95, Fixed D 3 course £16.95, Starter £4-£7, Main £9-£16, Dessert £4.75-£6.50, Service optional **Wines** 13 bottles over £20, 23 bottles under £20, 6 by glass **Notes** Sunday L, Vegetarian available **Seats** 40 **Children** Portions, Menu **Parking** 10

LOTHIAN, EAST

GULLANE Map 21 NT48

La Potinière

Modern British

Excellent cooking in cottage-style restaurant

01620 843214
Main St EH31 2AA
dir: 20m SE of Edinburgh. 3m from North Berwick on A198

Keith Marley and Mary Runciman run their resolutely traditional restaurant as a double act, sharing the cooking, while Keith shuttles between stove and tables to keep front-of-house simmering nicely. The unassuming chintzy dining room is not a place where anyone stands on ceremony - it has a comfy old-school charm. The left-hand side of the menu lists all suppliers (local and Scottish, of course) for every ingredient, from meat and fish to eggs, potatoes, and fresh herbs - the latter coming from La Potinière's own garden. The menu keeps things uncomplicated, offering a couple of choices at each stage to allow the cooks to keep execution and timing spot on throughout. Dinner might kick off with poached and seared pigeon with cranberry and beetroot compôte, toasted brioche, foie gras and truffle butter, then progress via soup - perhaps Thai coconut with poached scallops - to roast rack and Bobotie of lamb with apricot, sage and onion mash and lamb jus.

Chef Mary Runciman, Keith Marley **Owner** Mary Runciman **Times** 12.30-1.30/7-8.30 Closed Xmas, Jan, Mon-Tue, D Sun (Oct-May) **Prices** Fixed L 2 course £18.50, Fixed D 4 course £40, Service optional **Wines** 39 bottles over £20, 8 bottles under £20, 5 by glass **Notes** Sunday L, Vegetarian available, Dress restrictions, Smart casual **Seats** 30 **Children** Portions **Parking** 10

NORTH BERWICK Map 21 NT58

Macdonald Marine Hotel & Spa

European

Grand setting for fine dining

0870 400 8129
Cromwell Rd EH39 4LZ
e-mail: sales.marine@macdonald-hotels.co.uk
dir: from A198 turn into Hamilton Rd at lights then 2nd right

This majestic Grade II listed Victorian property offers delightful views of the Firth of Forth and has a long golfing tradition. It overlooks the 16th green of East Lothian's famous championship golf course, a view best enjoyed from the Craigleith Restaurant, which sports rich red walls, deep red, gold and brown striped curtains and lighting that is a mix of spotlights and chandeliers. The menu features classic European cooking with some modern elements, made using top-notch local and seasonal ingredients. Expect simply presented starters such as seared bream with prawn brandade, samphire and citrus velouté, followed by braised shin of beef with truffled mash, baby vegetables and creamy wild mushrooms. Finish with cranachan mousse with whisky ice cream.

Chef John Paul McLachlan **Owner** Donald Macdonald **Times** 12.30-2.30/6.30-9.30 **Prices** Fixed D 3 course £35, Service optional **Wines** 80 bottles over £20, 40 bottles under £20, 12 by glass **Notes** Sunday L, Vegetarian available, Dress restrictions, Smart casual, Civ Wed 250 **Seats** 80, Pr/dining room 20 **Children** Portions, Menu **Parking** 50

LOTHIAN, WEST

LINLITHGOW Map 21 NS97

Champany Inn

@@ Traditional British NOTABLE WINE LIST

A homage to fine Aberdeenshire beef

☎ 01506 834532 & 834388
Champany Corner EH49 7LU
e-mail: reception@champany.com
dir: 2m NE of Linlithgow. From M9 (N) junct 3, at top of slip road turn right. Champany 500yds on right

A rambling collection of buildings, some dating back to the 16th century, the Champany is one couple's homage to one of Scotland's finest products - properly hung prime beef. The dining room makes a suitably grand arena for it, with its stone walls, brass fitments and the all important chilled display of beef in all its cuts. There are entrecotes, sirloins, rib-eyes, T-bones and Chateaubriands for two, carved at the table, with sauces to match in the way of peppercorn cream, Stilton and horseradish, or wild mushroom and mustard. And that about says it all, other than to add that the depth of flavour, tenderness and careful timing are everything you would hope for. A seafood counter provides oysters and other shellfish to whet the appetite and, if you've any spare capacity, you might finish with blood orange cheesecake with matching granité.

Chef C Davidson, D Gibson, R Miller **Owner** Mr & Mrs C Davidson **Times** 12.30-2/7-10 Closed 25-26 Dec, 1-2 Jan, Sun, L Sat **Prices** Fixed L 2 course £19.50, Fixed D 3 course £39.50, Starter £8.50-£16.50, Main £28-£48, Dessert £8.50, Service added 10% **Wines** 650 bottles over £20, 8 bottles under £20, 8 by glass **Notes** Vegetarian available, Dress restrictions, Smart casual, no jeans or T-shirts **Seats** 50, Pr/dining room 30 **Parking** 50

Livingston's Restaurant

@@ Modern Scottish V

Modern Scottish cooking in a charming family-run restaurant

☎ 01506 846565
52 High St EH49 7AE
e-mail: contact@livingstons-restaurant.co.uk
web: www.livingstons-restaurant.co.uk
dir: Opposite post office

At one time a stable for Linlithgow Palace, family-run Livingston's stands tucked away in peaceful landscaped gardens and is reached via an arch off the bustling main street. Although recently spruced up and extended, it remains a wonderfully intimate restaurant with exposed stone walls, interesting objets d'art, and flickering candles on wooden tables in both the main dining room and conservatory extension. Chef Chris McCall is cooking up a storm, preparing beautifully presented modern Scottish dishes, which showcase top-drawer local ingredients to great effect and offer interesting flavour combinations. Take perfectly executed slow-roasted duck and foie gras cannelloni with spinach and chanterelles, followed by well-cooked sea bass, squat lobster and calamari with herb risotto and lemon and caper dressing, and Valrhona dark chocolate mousse with thyme shortbread.

Chef Chris McCall **Owner** The Livingston Family **Times** 12-2.30/6-9.30 Closed 1 wk Jun, 1 wk Oct, 2 wks Jan, Sun (except Mothering Sun)-Mon **Prices** Fixed L 2 course £16.95, Fixed D 3 course £36.95, Service optional, Groups min 8 service 10% **Wines** 37 bottles over £20, 24 bottles under £20, 6 by glass **Notes** Vegetarian menu, Dress restrictions, Smart casual **Seats** 60, Pr/dining room 15 **Children** Portions **Parking** NCP Linlithgow Cross, on street

Ship 2 Shore 24

@ Modern Scottish

The best of Scottish seafood

☎ 01506 840123
57 High St EH49 7ED
dir: On the High St, across road from the Palace

The name leaves no doubt to this outfit's seafood orientation, and the menu comes awash with daily-landed fish from the east coast port at Eyemouth (the '24' signifying it's on your plate within 24 hours). Expect the like of halibut fillet, grilled and served with lemon and chervil braised vegetables and fresh horseradish cream, or perhaps more wallet-stretching whole lobster with sautéed new potatoes and sauce vièrge. The menu is not exclusively seafood, but everything is fuss-free and main-ingredient led. Service is appropriately informal, with daily specials revealed with enthusiasm, while the dining room comes decorated with vibrant Scottish artworks. And, as freshness and quality is the draw here, you can also take-out from their wet fish counter.

Chef Douglas Elliman **Owner** James Boyd **Times** 12-2/6-9 Closed 25 Dec, 1 Jan, Sun-Mon **Prices** Fixed D 3 course £30-£50, Starter fr £4, Main £6-£25, Dessert fr £4, Service optional **Wines** 42 bottles over £20, 18 bottles under £20, 9 by glass **Notes** Early D menu Tue-Fri 6-7.15pm 2/3 course £13.95/£16.95, Vegetarian available **Seats** 50

UPHALL Map 21 NT07

The Tower

@ Traditional British

Good Scottish fare in doomed Queen's old place

☎ 0844 879 9043
Macdonald Houstoun House EH52 6JS
e-mail: houstoun@macdonald-hotels.co.uk
dir: M8 junct 3 follow Broxburn signs, straight over rdbt then at mini-rdbt turn right towards Uphall, hotel 1m on right

The white 16th-century hotel in the country to the west of Edinburgh has plenty of history behind it, not least in that it was once home to the doomed Mary, Queen of Scots. Ascend the winding staircase in the tower to find not a horrid dungeon, but the ineffably stylish hotel dining room, with its panelled walls, shuttered windows and open fires. Here you will feast on good Scottish fare, in the shapes of Cullen skink, belly and fillet of outdoor-reared pork in apple and sage gravy, and dark chocolate tart with vanilla ice cream.

Chef David Murray **Owner** Macdonald Hotels **Times** 6.30-9.30 Closed L all week **Prices** Food prices not confirmed for 2011. Please telephone for details **Wines** 74 bottles over £20, 16 bottles under £20, 13 by glass **Notes** Vegetarian available, Dress restrictions, Smart casual, no jeans or trainers, Civ Wed 200 **Seats** 65, Pr/dining room 30 **Children** Portions, Menu **Parking** 200

MIDLOTHIAN

DALKEITH Map 21 NT36

The Sun Inn

@ Modern British NEW

Contemporary cooking in a revamped Scottish inn

☎ 0131 663 2456 & 663 1534
Lothian Bridge EH22 4TR
e-mail: thesuninn@live.co.uk
dir: Opposite Newbattle Viaduct on the A7 near Eskbank

Recently restyled as a gastro-pub and boutique hotel, the smartly refurbished Sun Inn is the perfect country bolt-hole close to Edinburgh. Expect a contemporary Scottish décor, with part-panelled walls, wooden floors, blazing log fires and upholstered furnishings mixing effortlessly with modern wall coverings featuring fish, game and flowers. Food is well cooked with great balance and accuracy of flavours achieved through the sourcing of top-drawer local ingredients, notably fish and seafood. Dishes range from pub classics like bangers and mash and posh fish pie to Thai fishcakes with coconut and lentil broth and rack of lamb with baby shepherd's pie, pea purée and red wine jus. Bread and puddings (chocolate and Cointreau mousse, perhaps) are made in-house.

Chef Ian & Craig Minto **Owner** Bernadette McCarron **Times** 12-2/5-9 Closed Mon **Prices** Fixed L 2 course £10, Starter £5-£8, Main £8-£22, Dessert £5-£7, Service optional **Wines** 27 bottles over £20, 24 bottles under £20, 13 by glass **Notes** Vegetarian available, Dress restrictions, Smart casual **Seats** 90 **Children** Portions, Menu **Parking** 125

MORAY

ARCHIESTOWN Map 23 NJ24

Archiestown Hotel

Modern British, International

International cuisine in small Victorian country-house hotel

01340 810218
AB38 7QL
e-mail: jah@archiestownhotel.co.uk
dir: Turn off A95 onto B9102 at Craigellachie

A sympathetically renovated Victorian country house set in an attractive Speyside village deep in whisky and salmon fishing country. Popular with the fishing fraternity, the intimate bistro-style restaurant also draws a loyal local dining clientele. It offers a seasonally-changing menu of dishes with an international influence. A typical meal may begin with twice-baked cheese soufflé with crab and cream, followed by pork fillet wrapped in ham and stuffed with mushrooms and olives, served with tomato, basil and parmesan risotto, with sticky toffee pudding to finish.

Times 12-2/7-9 Closed Xmas, 3 Jan-10 Feb

CRAIGELLACHIE Map 23 NJ24

Craigellachie Hotel

Traditional Scottish

Victorian hotel with good local ingredients and whisky galore

01340 881204
AB38 9SR
e-mail: reservations.craigellachie@ohiml.com
dir: 12m S of Elgin, in village centre

This impressive and popular hotel is located in the heart of Speyside so no prizes for guessing what you might be offered to drink in the Quaich Bar. That's right, a vodka and tonic. Only kidding – there are nearly 700 different types of whisky to choose from, reflecting the area's importance as Scotland's malt whisky distilling area. But Craigellachie not only satisfies the thirst, for the Ben Aigen restaurant has a nice line in confidently traditional Scottish cooking, where local meat and seafood are the star of the show. Start with Buckie potted crab served with crisp croûtons and pea shoots or perhaps a spicy parsnip soup, before a main course such as seared rump of Cabrach lamb accompanied by Arran mustard mash, wilted spinach and a red wine jus.

Chef Stuart Aitken **Owner** Oxford Hotels & Inns **Times** 12-2/6-9 **Prices** Fixed D 3 course £27.95, Service optional **Wines** 64 bottles over £20, 30 bottles under £20, 7 by glass **Notes** Sunday L, Vegetarian available, Dress restrictions, Smart casual, Civ Wed 60 **Seats** 30, Pr/dining room 60 **Children** Portions, Menu **Parking** 25

CULLEN Map 23 NJ56

Cullen Bay Hotel

Traditional Scottish

Glorious sea views and traditional Scottish fare

01542 840432
AB56 4XA
e-mail: stay@cullenbayhotel.com
dir: On A98, 0.25 m W of Cullen

Dolphins, porpoises and minke whales are frequently sighted in the Moray Firth, and this small family-run hotel perched above Cullen Bay's beach gets grandstand views of their playground. The views through the full-length picture windows in the restaurant are nothing short of stunning, while the food is traditional Scottish with a few modern European influences. Local boats provide seafood, while the verdant hills of the hinterland cater for meat, game and cheese. While you're in the homeland of Cullen skink, that seems the obvious way to start. Tartan chicken - breast of chicken stuffed with haggis and wrapped in smoked bacon in a whisky sauce - could be one way to proceed, with sticky toffee pudding with cream or ice cream to finish.

Times 12-2/6.30-9 Closed From 2 Jan for 10 days

PERTH & KINROSS

AUCHTERARDER Map 21 NN91

Andrew Fairlie @ Gleneagles

– see page 522

The Strathearn

British, French

Traditional fine dining in elegant ballroom

01764 694270
The Gleneagles Hotel PH3 1NF
e-mail: resort.sales@gleneagles.com
web: www.gleneagles.com
dir: Off A9 at exit for A823 follow signs for Gleneagles Hotel

The world-renowned Gleneagles golf resort offers plenty of r&r opportunities outside the game itself, not least its range of dining options. The 850-acre estate in the Scottish glens is as impressive as they come, and The Strathearn restaurant tries very hard to leave a lasting impression: the elegant ballroom-style dining room is vast, with high ceilings and pillars, and there's a pianist, too. Classical dishes are given a contemporary slant on the seasonal menu, while a whole brigade of staff provides formal but by no means stuffy service. Flambés and carving trolleys add an element of theatre and the notable wine list is worthy of serious examination. Expect a choice of hot or cold starters such as seared rose veal sweetbreads with petit pois and braised lettuce, or steak tartare. Main courses might include fillet of Scotch beef with liquorice-cooked cheek, neep fondant and bordelaise sauce.

The Strathearn

Chef Paul Devonshire **Owner** Diageo plc **Times** 12.30-2.30/7-10 Closed L Mon-Sat **Prices** Fixed L 3 course fr £40, Fixed D 3 course fr £56, Service optional **Wines** 100% bottles over £20, 15 by glass **Notes** Sunday L, Vegetarian available, Dress restrictions, Smart casual, no jeans or trainers, Civ Wed 250 **Seats** 322 **Children** Portions, Menu **Parking** 1000

COMRIE Map 21 NN72

Royal Hotel

Traditional British

Elegant hotel with confident cooking

01764 679200
Melville Square PH6 2DN
e-mail: reception@royalhotel.co.uk
dir: In main square, 7m from Crieff, on A85

This stylish former coaching house turned luxury small hotel occupies a charming position amongst the splendour of Strathearn and the Southern Scottish Highlands. Dating back to the 18th century (Queen Victoria bestowed its name), it was carefully renovated by the Milsom family in 1996. Now expect luxurious fabrics, polished wooden floors, antiques and roaring log fires. Chef-patron David Milsom's menu takes fresh local ingredients and presents them prettily whether you're eating in the main restaurant, clubby lounge bar or walled garden. Try coarse venison and pork terrine with griddled bread and beetroot chutney to start, followed by fillet of Scottish hake wrapped in Parma ham over braised cabbage and bacon, tomato butter sauce and new potatoes. Don't leave without sampling one of the 100-plus malt whiskies on offer.

Times 12-2/6.30-9 Closed Xmas

Andrew Fairlie @ Gleneagles

AUCHTERARDER Map 21 NN91

Modern French V  

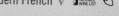

France meets Scotland in luxurious Perthshire hotel

☎ 01764 694267
The Gleneagles Hotel PH3 1NF
e-mail: andrew.fairlie@gleneagles.com
web: www.andrewfairlie.com
dir: From A9 take Gleneagles exit, hotel in 1m

Amid 850 spectacular acres of Perthshire countryside, the luxurious Gleneagles Hotel with its three top Scottish championship golf courses is home to local lad Andrew Fairlie's technically fabulous, refined cooking. Enter the independent restaurant on the ground floor and revel in the luxury – floor-to-ceiling silk drapes, dark-panelled walls and beautifully covered banquettes, plus original artwork by Archie Frost. Don't think the sumptuous surroundings mean you're in for a stuffy meal – on the contrary, it's slick but by no means overbearing, aided by polished and well-judged service with no unnecessary intrusions. Winner of the first Roux Scholarship at the tender age of 20, Andrew trained under legendary Michel Guérard in Gascony, picking up more experience in top Paris kitchens before Perthshire beckoned in 2001 and he returned to set up shop at Gleneagles. His cooking style takes all that he has learned from France and marries it with the unrivalled local and seasonal Scottish produce on his doorstep. Beautifully composed tasting and market menus are available for the whole table. Meanwhile, typical dishes from the seasonally-changing à la carte might include home-smoked Scottish lobster, warm lime and herb butter followed by roast loin of Perthshire lamb, confit neck and grilled kidney. Top-notch French artisanal cheeses are worth indulging in before a technically impressive dessert of hazelnut praline soufflé with chocolate ice cream and poire eau de vie sauce. All the little extra touches you'd expect to find at an establishment of such quality, like super amuse-bouche, are present and correct and the superb wine list and knowledgeable sommelier both add to the experience.

Chef Andrew Fairlie **Owner** Andrew Fairlie **Times** 6.30-10 Closed 24-25 Dec, 3 wks Jan, Sun, L all week **Prices** Starter £25-£35, Main £36, Dessert £14, Service optional **Wines** 300 bottles over £20, 12 by glass **Notes** Degustation 6 course £95, Du Marché 6 course £85, Vegetarian menu, Dress restrictions, Smart casual **Seats** 54 **Parking** 300

FORTINGALL **Map 20 NN74**

Fortingall Hotel

@@ Modern Scottish

Imaginative cooking in luxurious small hotel

☎ 01887 830367 & 830368
PH15 2NQ
e-mail: hotel@fortingallhotel.com
dir: B846 from Aberfeldy for 6m, left signed Fortingall for 3m. Hotel in village centre

An impressively refurbished hotel tucked away in a peaceful valley with views of wooded slopes and towering peaks, close to the Arts and Crafts village of Fortingall. The main dining room follows the Arts and Crafts theme with its furniture and tweed curtains, and a second slightly more informal room, the Yew dining room, has views over the garden. The daily-changing menu makes good use of regional produce, with seasonal vegetables, herb and fruits alongside venison and salmon sourced from the surrounding Glenlyon Estate. The confident modern Scottish cooking extends to venison carpaccio with pesto sauce, followed by line-caught sea bass with aubergine caviar, chorizo, braised baby gem and sauce vièrge, and almond pannacotta with chocolate foam for pudding. Friendly service comes from a young team.

Times 12-2/6.30-9

GLENFARG **Map 21 NO11**

The Famous Bein Inn

@ Modern Scottish

Traditional inn offering good Scottish food

☎ 01577 830216
PH2 9PY
e-mail: enquiries@beininn.com
web: www.beininn.com
dir: 2m N of Glenfarg, on the intersection of A912 & B996

Tucked away in a sylvan valley just south of Perth, the whitewashed Bein Inn is a grand old Georgian property offering a hearty Scottish welcome in its buzzy bar and restaurant. It's a cheerful sort of place with log fires, blue tartans on the floor and a kitchen that has garnered a strong local following for its fuss-free Scottish cuisine. Whether you choose to eat in the bistro or the Balvaird restaurant, top-class local and seasonal produce is the order of the day. Unpretentious dishes such as hot-smoked salmon rillettes with pickled cucumber and crème fraîche get the ball rolling, while mains deliver the likes of pan-fried Dunkeld fallow deer with potato mash and sultana jus. To finish, Scottish cheeses served with chutney and oatcakes offer a savoury alternative to dessert.

Chef Peter Carey **Owner** John & Alan MacGregor **Times** 12-9 Closed 25 Dec **Prices** Fixed D 3 course fr £22.95, Starter £3.50-£6.25, Main £9.95-£18.95, Dessert £4.25-£5.75, Service optional **Wines** 8 bottles over £20, 14 bottles under £20, 5 by glass **Notes** Sunday L, Vegetarian available **Seats** 65 **Children** Portions, Menu **Parking** 27

KENMORE **Map 21 NN74**

Taymouth Restaurant

@ Traditional Scottish

Historic inn with Tay views and quality Scottish cooking

☎ 01887 830205
Kenmore Hotel, The Square PH15 2NU
e-mail: reception@kenmorehotel.co.uk
web: www.kenmorehotel.co.uk
dir: off A9 at Ballinluig onto A827, through Aberfeldy to Kenmore, hotel in village centre

When you're a people's poet like Rabbie Burns you can get away with scribbling on the chimney breast of

continued

KENMORE ***continued***

Scotland's oldest inn: his verses to the area's beauty are preserved behind glass in the Poet's Bar. Since the historic Kenmore Hotel was built in 1572, the 'model' 18th-century village sprung up all around, but the inn still hogs the prime spot overlooking the River Tay - a glorious view seen at its best from the floor-to-ceiling picture windows in the conservatory-style restaurant. On the food front, unfussy Scottish cuisine with big, hearty flavours is the order of the day - you could start with venison and cranberry sausages in Puy lentil and vegetable broth, while main courses might involve oven-baked salmon filled with Aberfeldy whisky and haggis soufflé.

Chef Duncan Shearer **Owner** Kenmore Estates Ltd **Times** 12-6/6-9.30 **Prices** Starter £3.65-£5.95, Main £10.75-£17.65, Dessert £4.05-£5.65, Service optional **Wines** 17 bottles over £20, 30 bottles under £20, 13 by glass **Notes** Sunday L, Vegetarian available, Civ Wed 150 **Seats** 140, Pr/dining room 65 **Children** Portions, Menu **Parking** 40

See advert on page 523

KILLIECRANKIE **Map 23 NN96**

Killiecrankie House Hotel

@@ Modern British V

Country-house cooking in tranquil Perthshire

☎ 01796 473220
PH16 5LG
e-mail: enquiries@killiecrankiehotel.co.uk
dir: off A9 at Pitlochry, hotel 3m along B8079 on right

Built for a local church minister in 1840, the pristine white house is set in a tranquil part of the Perthshire countryside, not far from Pitlochry. Beautifully landscaped gardens and a riot of period features within pile on the charm, while the eating options are divided between an intimate dining room with tartan-upholstered seating, and a more informal conservatory bar. The food aims to reassure rather than challenge with some well-wrought country-house dishes, such as twice-baked Crottin soufflé with balsamic-dressed beetroot salad, pinkly roasted duck with curly kale and Parisienne carrots, or sea bream and scallops in orange butter sauce. To finish, a perfectly executed pannacotta is flavoured with coconut and lime, and comes with home-made shortbread and seasonal fresh raspberries.

Chef Mark Easton **Owner** Henrietta Fergusson **Times** 6.30-8.30 Closed Jan/Feb, L all week **Prices** Fixed D 3 course fr £31, Service optional, Groups min 10 service 10% **Wines** 62 bottles over £20, 12 bottles under £20, 7 by glass **Notes** Vegetarian menu, Dress restrictions, No shorts **Seats** 30, Pr/dining room 12 **Children** Portions, Menu **Parking** 20

KINCLAVEN **Map 21 NO13**

Ballathie House Hotel

@@ Modern Scottish

Country-house cooking in a Perthshire mansion

☎ 01250 883268
PH1 4QN
e-mail: email@ballathiehousehotel.com
dir: From A9, 2m N of Perth, take B9099 through Stanley & follow signs, or from A93 at Beech Hedge follow signs for Ballathie, 2.5m

Given a wholesale makeover in the Edwardian era, Ballathie is a pinnacled mansion in the Perthshire countryside, near a spot where the Glasgow to Aberdeen train used to halt. Its position by the river Tay makes it a favoured bolt-hole for anglers, and the atmosphere of fine living, with squashy sofas, open fires and a palatial dining room, exerts its own kind of pull. Tried-and-true country-house cooking using the best of the Scottish larder is the name of the game, including Skye smoked salmon with rocket, cucumber and caper salad and shallot purée, chargrilled sirloin with stuffed flatcap mushrooms and garlic butter, and date and toffee pudding in butterscotch sauce. Wine-tasting dinners are an alluring option at certain times of the year.

Times 12.30-2/7-9

KINLOCH RANNOCH **Map 23 NN65**

Dunalastair Hotel

@ Modern British

Traditional Highland hotel with confidently prepared food

☎ 01882 632323 & 632218
PH16 5PW
e-mail: info@dunalastair.co.uk
dir: From Pitlochry N, take B8019 to Tummel Bridge then B846 to Kinloch Rannoch

Modern boutique chic is all very well in the right circumstances, but sometimes you want a hotel to speak of its past and have a sense of place. At Dunalastair there's no doubting that you have left England behind and are north of the border: the dyed-in-the-wool Highland house dates from 1770, and has been used as barracks for Jacobite soldiers as well as a staging post in the days of horse-drawn transport. The restaurant is a classic venue in the oak panelling, antlers and tartan carpets vein - perfect for the kitchen's up-to-date reworkings of the country-house idiom, and superb Scottish ingredients hammer home the locality. Start with smooth chicken liver parfait, ahead of pan-seared sea bass with wilted pak choi, cherry tomatoes and black olive dressing, and close with a rich hot chocolate fondant.

Times 12-2.30/6.30-9

KINROSS **Map 21 NO10**

Basil's Restaurant

@ Modern International

Contemporary restaurant with classic-based modern cuisine

☎ 01577 863467
The Green Hotel, 2 The Muirs KY13 8AS
e-mail: reservations@green-hotel.com
dir: M90 junct 6 follow Kinross signs, onto A922 for hotel

The hotel started out as an 18th-century staging post for travellers heading north from Edinburgh - nowadays guests turn up for the lure of trout fishing on Loch Leven, or a spot of curling on the hotel's own rink, as well as - the clue is in the name - the two 18-hole golf courses. All that fresh air should produce a healthy appetite for dinner in Basil's Restaurant, a cheerful venue with colourful splashes of artwork and flower displays. The kitchen puts a modern spin on classic dishes, so you might begin with goats' cheese pannacotta with toasted brioche and cranberry compôte, before a classic marriage of pan-fried salmon with spring onion mash and herb beurre blanc. Puddings are well worth a dalliance - maybe iced mango parfait with marinated raspberries and passionfruit syrup.

Chef Gerard Lee **Owner** Sir David Montgomery **Times** 7-9.30 Closed L all week **Prices** Fixed D 3 course fr £29.50, Service optional **Wines** 8 bottles over £20, 14 bottles under £20, 6 by glass **Notes** Vegetarian available, Dress restrictions, Smart casual, Civ Wed 120 **Seats** 90, Pr/dining room 22 **Children** Portions, Menu **Parking** 80

MUTHILL **Map 21 NN81**

Barley Bree Restaurant with Rooms

@ Modern Scottish **NEW** V

Locally-sourced food in friendly contemporary restaurant

☎ 01764 681451
6 Willoughby St PH5 2AB
e-mail: info@barleybree.com
dir: A9 onto A822 in centre of Muthill

A charming contemporary restaurant with rooms in the centre of the village, with plain, scrubbed wooden tables, wooden floors and a double-sided wood burning stove, Barley Bree has a cosy, welcoming atmosphere. Artwork by a local artist adds interest along with the original oak beams and exposed stone walls, and the small residents' lounge is ideal for pre-dinner drinks. To start you could have clear-flavoured ham hock and pig's cheek terrine, with endive marmalade and pickled cucumber; follow that, perhaps, with tender, moist guinea fowl supreme, accompanied by lentils, pancetta and baby onion, finishing appealingly with pineapple and rhubarb cinnamon crumble. This is simple, rustic food with a twist.

Chef Fabrice Bouteloup **Owner** Fabrice & Alison Bouteloup **Times** 12-2/6-9 Closed mid Feb-early Mar, 2 wks Oct, Mon-Tue **Prices** Food prices not confirmed for 2011. Please telephone for details **Notes** Food served 12.30-7.30 Sun, Sunday L, Vegetarian menu **Children** Portions, Menu

PERTH Map 21 NO12

Acanthus Restaurant

Modern British

Creative, technically adept cooking in a smart setting

☎ 01738 622451
Parklands Hotel, St Leonards Bank PH2 8EB
e-mail: info@acanthusrestaurant.com
dir: Adjacent to Perth station, overlooking South Inch Park

The Parklands Hotel occupies the former residence of the Lord Provost in a handy location near to the station, with excellent views over South Inch Park to Kinnoull Hill. The smart Acanthus Restaurant is its fine-dining option, an uncluttered space with leather high-backed chairs at linen-clothed tables on herrringbone parquet floors – all very tasteful with nothing to distract from the food. The kitchen takes a creative modern approach to its output. Sound technical skills are evident in starters such as pan-fried wood pigeon with foie gras and truffle vinaigrette, while mains could deliver monkfish paired fashionably with braised oxtail, parsley risotto and smoked bacon jus. Poached pear with cinnamon mousse and cider sorbet makes an imaginative finale.

Chef Graeme Pallister, Steven McPhee **Owner** Scott & Penny Edwards **Times** 7-9 Closed 26 Dec-7 Jan, Sun-Tue, L all week **Prices** Fixed D 4 course £28.95-£32.95, Service optional, Groups min 8 service 10% **Wines** 33 bottles over £20, 55 bottles under £20, 6 by glass **Notes** Vegetarian available, Dress restrictions, Smart casual, no shorts or jeans, Civ Wed 30 **Seats** 36, Pr/dining room 22 **Children** Portions, Menu **Parking** 25

Best Western Huntingtower Hotel

Traditional British V

Traditional cooking in secluded country house

☎ 01738 583771
Crieff Rd PH1 3JT
e-mail: reservations@huntingtowerhotel.co.uk
dir: 3m W off A85

Once the home of a mill owner, this Edwardian country-house on the outskirts of Perth is set within six acres of secluded landscaped gardens and grounds. Inside, a mix of period features and modern facilities makes for a comfortable hotel with plenty of character. Lunch is served in the conservatory, while the charming oak-panelled dining room offers a more formal, intimate dining experience in the evening. The traditional menu features British cuisine with European influences, making good use of local produce, and might include starters such as breast of wood pigeon with red marmalade, pancetta, mushroom and truffle oil followed by breast of Gressingham duck with spring cabbage, fondant potato and pineapple chilli.

Chef Bill McNicoll **Owner** Portland Hotels **Times** 12-2.30/6-9.30 **Prices** Fixed L 2 course £12.95, Fixed D 3 course £19.95, Starter £3.50-£5, Main £3.50-£17, Dessert £3.50-£4, Service optional **Wines** 23 bottles over £20, 26 bottles under £20, 4 by glass **Notes** Sunday L, Vegetarian menu, Dress restrictions, Smart casual, Civ Wed 135 **Seats** 34, Pr/dining room 24 **Children** Portions, Menu **Parking** 200

Deans@Let's Eat

Modern Scottish

Skilled modern Scottish cooking in smart setting

☎ 01738 643377
77-79 Kinnoull St PH1 5EZ
e-mail: deans@letseatperth.co.uk
web: www.letseatperth.co.uk
dir: On corner of Kinnoull St & Atholl St, close to North Inch & cinema

Willie and Margo Deans have been wowing local foodies since they took over the helm at this friendly down-to-earth restaurant near the centre of Perth in October 2005. The eye-catching bottle-green frontage opens into a richly-hued interior of claret and terracotta, with tables swathed in crisp white linen, while service is personable and relaxed. Willie Deans stocks his kitchen with the pick of local produce for food with an emphatic seasonal accent. Vibrant modern Scottish dishes come together in creative combinations, occasionally taking an exotic tangent, as in a starter of West Coast fish curry with coconut, coriander and naan bread. Mains return to the robust mainstream with a slow-cooked daube of venison with glazed onions, creamed parsnips and shallot mash, while desserts end strongly - for example, marbled terrine of dark and white chocolate paired with winter fruit crumble and custard.

Chef Willie Deans, Fraser Allan **Owner** Mr & Mrs W Deans **Times** 12-2.30/6.30-10 Closed Sun-Mon **Prices** Fixed L 2 course £13.95, Fixed D 3 course £23.45, Starter £4.95-£9.50, Main £13.50-£19.75, Dessert £5.75-£7.50, Service optional **Wines** 40 bottles over £20, 23 bottles under £20, 8 by glass **Notes** Early eve supper Tue-Thu from 6pm, Vegetarian available, Dress restrictions, Smart casual **Seats** 70 **Children** Portions **Parking** Multi-storey car park (100 yds)

Murrayshall House Hotel

Modern British

Modern British cooking with ravishing Perthshire views

☎ 01738 551171
New Scone PH2 7PH
e-mail: info@murrayshall.co.uk
dir: From Perth A94 (Coupar Angus) turn right signed Murrayshall before New Scone

You'd expect a Perthshire hotel in 350 acres to be devoted principally to golf, and indeed Murrayshall is not about to disappoint you, but it has many other attractions too, not least the stunning views, which reach all the way to the nearby city of Perth. The tone in the Old Masters dining room leaves nothing to be desired, with panoramic vistas over the grounds from leaded windows, fine linen and glassware, high-backed chairs, and plenty of original artworks. Expect to eat highly polished modern British dishes such as Jerusalem artichoke pannacotta with salade Niçoise, breast of pigeon on red cabbage in blueberry jus, and champagne jelly with mixed fruit brunoise.

Chef Jonathan Greer **Owner** Old Scone Ltd **Times** 12-2.30/7-9.45 Closed 26 Dec, L Sat **Prices** Fixed L 2 course £12.50, Fixed D 3 course £28-£40, Service optional **Wines** 30 bottles over £20, 20 bottles under £20, 8 by glass **Notes** Sunday L, Vegetarian available, Civ Wed 130 **Seats** 55, Pr/dining room 40 **Children** Portions, Menu **Parking** 120

PERTH *continued*

Opus One

Modern British

Exciting culinary developments in city-centre boutique hotel

01738 623355
The New County Hotel, 22-30 County Place PH2 8EE
e-mail: enquiries@newcountyhotel.com
dir: A9 junct 11, Perth. Follow signs for town centre. Hotel on right after library

The white façade of the boutique New County Hotel looks spruce in the centre of Perth next to the Bell Library - a handy spot whether you're in town for theatre, concert and gallery visits or suited and booted for business. Clean-cut, minimal design gives a cool, cosmopolitan vibe throughout to please all comers. On the food front, there's nothing complicated on the menus in Café 22 or the cheerful, pubby bar-bistro. But move into the Opus One restaurant, and the cooking shifts into top gear, with Ryan Young's modern British cooking making bold statements. Take seared king scallops with white asparagus pannacotta and caviar oil to see the sort of ambition coming out of the kitchen; next up, pan-roasted venison loin is partnered with venison tartare, celeriac dauphinoise, and a red onion tarte Tatin with shallot jus. It all ends as you hope it will, with a lush sticky toffee pudding with vanilla ice cream and butterscotch sauce.

Chef Ryan Young, Lesley Young **Owner** Mr Owen Boyle, Mrs Sarah Boyle **Times** 12-2/6.30-9 Closed Sun-Mon **Prices** Fixed L 2 course £18.50-£22, Fixed D 3 course £32-£39.50, Service optional **Wines** 50 bottles over £20, 14 bottles under £20, 10 by glass **Notes** Vegetarian available **Seats** 48 **Children** Portions **Parking** 10, plus opposite on street

63 Tay Street

Modern Scottish V

Local, honest cooking by the River Tay

01738 441451
63 Tay St PH2 8NN
e-mail: info@63taystreet.com
dir: In town centre, on river

This large period building housing a stylish modern restaurant benefits from a location in the centre of Perth next to the River Tay. A popular light and airy lunch venue, come evening, the restaurant morphs into more of a formal, sophisticated dining affair. Local lad and 63 Tay Street chef-patron, Graeme Pallister, presents modern Scottish cooking with a great deal of flair and imagination and a liberal sprinkling of fresh local produce. Jerusalem artichoke soup with honey truffle and croûtons might lead to crumbed oxtail, Stornoway black pudding, duck egg and horseradish. Lemon posset comes with lemon curd ice cream and glass biscuits. The wide-ranging wine list is complemented by malt whiskies and a decent Cognac and liqueur selection.

Chef Graeme Pallister **Owner** Scott & Penny Edwards, Graeme Pallister **Times** 12-2/6.30-9 Closed Xmas, New Year, 1st wk Jul, Sun-Mon **Prices** Fixed L 2 course £17.95-£19.95, Fixed D 4 course £29.95-£39.95, Starter £5.25-£9.45, Main £17.50-£27.50, Dessert £5.45-£7.45, Service optional, Groups min 6 service 10% **Wines** 80 bottles over £20, 32 bottles under £20, 12 by glass **Notes** Vegetarian menu **Seats** 38 **Children** Portions

PITLOCHRY Map 23 NN95

Green Park Hotel

British

Fine cuisine in a lochside country-house hotel

01796 473248
Clunie Bridge Rd PH16 5JY
e-mail: bookings@thegreenpark.co.uk
dir: Turn off A9 at Pitlochry, follow signs for 0.25m through town

The Green Park Hotel has a loyal fan-base that returns again and again to switch off on the lushly-forested shores of Loch Faskally. What brings them to this glorious corner of Perthshire - apart, of course, from the glorious setting - is the genuinely welcoming family-run ambience, and reliable traditional comforts. Equally important is the classic Scottish country-house cuisine, served in the restful setting of the damson and honey-hued dining room. Perthshire's splendid produce lies at the heart of the kitchen's output on menus majoring on seafood and game, as well as seasonal herbs and salads from the kitchen garden. You could start with game and pistachio terrine with sweet onion compôte, then follow with deep-fried haddock in crispy chive and beer batter with coriander mayonnaise.

Chef Chris Tamblin **Owner** Green Park Ltd **Times** 12-2/6.30-8.30 **Prices** Fixed D 3 course £12-£18, Service optional **Wines** 10 bottles over £20, 65 bottles under £20, 8 by glass **Notes** Pre-theatre menu available from 5.45pm, Vegetarian available, Dress restrictions, Reasonably smart dress **Seats** 100 **Children** Portions, Menu **Parking** 52

ST FILLANS Map 20 NN62

Achray House Hotel, Restaurant & Lodges

Modern Scottish

Modern Scottish cooking in an idyllic location

01764 685231
PH6 2NF
e-mail: info@achrayhouse.com
dir: Follow A85 towards Crainlarich, from Stirling follow A9 then B822 at Braco, B827 to Comrie. Turn left onto A85 to St Fillans

Achray House was known in the 19th century as Victoria Cottage, as local legend has it that Queen Victoria commented favourably on its location as she made her way back to Balmoral. It's easy to see why she may have been taken with this charming, family-run hotel with its splendid views of Loch Earn and the mountains beyond. The restaurant, in a modern conservatory, makes the most of what nature offers and service is friendly and attentive. Modern Scottish cooking is the order of the day. Think scallops with a Talisker syrup and trio of root vegetable purées followed by, for the patriotic, haggis in filo pastry with an Irn-Bru chilli jam.

Chef Alan Bristow **Owner** Alan & Jane Gibson **Times** 12-2.30/6-8.30 Closed 3-31 Jan, L Mon-Wed in low season **Prices** Fixed L 2 course £9.99, Starter £4.95-£6.95, Main £10.95-£19.95, Dessert £4.95-£7.95, Service optional **Wines** 20 bottles over £20, 18 bottles under £20, 9 by glass **Notes** Sunday L, Vegetarian available **Seats** 44, Pr/dining room 12 **Children** Portions, Menu **Parking** 20

The Four Seasons Hotel

Modern British V

Breathtaking lochside scenery and bold cuisine

01764 685333
Lochside PH6 2NF
e-mail: info@thefourseasonshotel.co.uk
dir: From Perth take A85 W, through Crieff & Comrie. Hotel at west end of village

The view along Loch Earn from this 19th-century lochside lodge is hard to beat on a fine summer's evening. Dramatic wooded hills enfold the waters, and you're connected to the beauty of Perthshire's great outdoors as soon as you set foot out of this romantic small hotel. Country-house chintz has definitely been chucked out in this stylish bolt-hole - particularly in the waterside Meall Reamhar restaurant; cool white walls hung with original artwork and stunning views are the setting for a modern British menu built on spectacular Scottish ingredients brought together in inventive pairings. Pan-seared hand-dived Scrabster scallops with Aberdeenshire black pudding and asparagus cream is a signature starter, followed by a gâteau of Scotch Angus beef fillet with Comrie haggis, pistou crust, turnip purée and red wine jus.

Chef Mathew Martin **Owner** Andrew Low **Times** 12-2.30/6-9.30 Closed Jan-Feb & some wkdays Mar, Nov & Dec **Prices** Fixed D 2 course fr £25, Fixed D 4 course £35, Service optional **Wines** 71 bottles over £20, 29 bottles under £20, 8 by glass **Notes** Sunday L, Vegetarian menu, Dress restrictions, No jeans or trainers, Civ Wed 80 **Seats** 40, Pr/dining room 20 **Children** Portions, Menu **Parking** 30

SPITTAL OF GLENSHEE — Map 23 NO17

Dalmunzie Castle

Traditional British

Cooking fit for a laird

01250 885224
PH10 7QG
e-mail: reservations@dalmunzie.com
dir: On A93 at Spittal of Glenshee, follow signs to hotel

In case the 6,500-acre estate around the fairytale turrets of this fantastic Laird's mansion isn't enough for seekers of seclusion, Dalmunzie Castle has 600 square miles of elemental mountain wilderness on the doorstep. Inside, it is a home from home, as long as your home is a baronial hideaway where log fires crackle in comfy wood-panelled lounges that are tailor-made for retreating with a wee dram. The blue and cream dining room is a romantic, softly-lit affair, where excellent Scottish produce takes pride of place on a classical menu with flourishes of modern style. Expect the likes of seared crab cake with beetroot confit, chermoula-spiced prawn and truffle-scented velouté, followed by sea bass with cumin and parsnip purée, fennel gratin, pak choi, salsa verde and vanilla balsamic.

Chef Katie Cleary **Owner** Scott & Brianna Poole **Times** 12-2.30/7-9 Closed 1-28 Dec **Prices** Fixed D 4 course £45, Service included **Wines** 45 bottles over £20, 17 bottles under £20, 4 by glass **Notes** Vegetarian available, Dress restrictions, Smart casual, Jacket & tie preferred, Civ Wed 70 **Seats** 40, Pr/dining room 18 **Children** Portions **Parking** 40

RENFREWSHIRE

HOWWOOD — Map 20 NS36

Country Club Restaurant

Modern British

Converted mill offering modern bistro cooking

01505 705225
Bowfield Hotel & Country Club, Bowfield Rd PA9 1DZ
e-mail: enquiries@bowfieldhotel.co.uk
dir: From M8 take A737 (Irvine Rd), exit at Howwood, take 2nd right up country lane, turn right at top of hill

The hotel and country club enjoys a tranquil location within landscaped grounds, yet it's not that far from Glasgow airport. The restaurant is all quiet intimacy beneath its low ceiling, with original photographs on walls of whitewashed brick. Modern bistro dishes are the order of the day, with slow-roast wood pigeon and haggis croquette a memorable starter, and a main course of baked smoked haddock, Welsh rarebit and ratatouille offering lots of upstanding flavour. Finish with correctly gooey tarte Tatin on light, crisp pastry, and satisfaction is complete.

Chef Ronnie McAdam **Owner** Bowfield Hotel & Country Club Ltd **Times** 6.30-9 Closed L all week **Prices** Food prices not confirmed for 2011. Please telephone for details **Wines** 8 bottles over £20, 21 bottles under £20, 7 by glass **Notes** Sunday L, Vegetarian available, Dress restrictions, Smart casual, Civ Wed 120 **Seats** 40, Pr/dining room 20 **Children** Portions, Menu **Parking** 100

RENFREWSHIRE, EAST

UPLAWMOOR — Map 10 NS45

Uplawmoor Hotel

Modern Scottish

Good Scottish cuisine in former smugglers' haunt

01505 850565
66 Neilston Rd G78 4AF
e-mail: info@uplawmoor.co.uk
dir: M77 junct 2, A736 signed Barrhead & Irvine. Hotel 4m beyond Barrhead

Extensive renovation in the 1950s by architect James Gray added the Charles Rennie Mackintosh-inspired exterior to this charm-packed mid-1700s coaching inn hidden away in a sleepy village close to Glasgow and the airport. Fashioned from an old barn, the restaurant may be deeply traditional in style, with rich furnishings and a central copper canopied fireplace, but the food is bang up to date, the well-balanced menu featuring local fish, beef and game. Typically, tuck into chicken liver parfait with red onion marmalade, follow with baked cod with tomato compôte and saffron oil, leaving room for warm chocolate fondant with vanilla ice cream.

Chef Ewan McAllister **Owner** Stuart & Emma Peacock **Times** 12-3/6-9.30 Closed 26 Dec, 1 Jan, L Mon-Sat **Prices** Fixed L 2 course £15, Fixed D 3 course £18, Starter £4.25-£8.95, Main £7.95-£29.95, Dessert £4.95-£7.75, Service optional **Wines** 7 bottles over £20, 19 bottles under £20, 9 by glass **Notes** Early evening menu available 5.30-7pm Sun-Fri, Sunday L, Vegetarian available, Dress restrictions, Smart casual **Seats** 30 **Children** Portions, Menu **Parking** 40

SCOTTISH BORDERS

EDDLESTON — Map 21 NT24

The Horseshoe Inn

– *see page 528*

KELSO — Map 21 NT73

The Roxburghe Hotel & Golf Course

Modern, Traditional

Scottish country-house with confident fine-dining restaurant

01573 450331
TD5 8JZ
e-mail: hotel@roxburghe.net
dir: From A68, 1m N of Jedburgh, take A698 for 5m to Heiton

Owned by the Duke of Roxburghe, this grand Jacobean country-house hotel stands tucked away amongst woodland close to the River Teviot on the Duke's vast estate. The Scottish Borders are prime huntin' shootin' fishin' territory, renowned for top-notch fish, meat and game which the kitchen puts to good use, together with wild mushrooms from the estate and herbs from the garden, in menus of French-accented modern country-house cuisine. Served in the traditional country-house dining room at crisp linen-clothed tables, expect starters like seared scallops with Eyemouth crab and beetroot dressing to precede roast breast and stuffed leg of guinea fowl with wild mushroom ravioli and pancetta jus. The Duke's cellar is a treasure trove of bottles for all occasions.

Times 12-2/7.30-9.45

The Horseshoe Inn

EDDLESTON Map 21 NT24

French

Refined French cuisine on the Scottish borders

☎ 01721 730225
Edinburgh Rd EH45 8QP
e-mail:
reservations@horseshoeinn.co.uk
web: www.horseshoeinn.co.uk
dir: On A703, 5m N of Peebles

A smart golden sign and horseshoe-shaped windows are clues that this was once the village blacksmith's place. In a peaceful roadside spot near Peebles in magnificent Scottish border country, the Horseshoe Inn may sound like a country pub, but this is a classy set-up of an entirely different ilk. At its heart is Bardoulet's restaurant, a flamboyant pillared dining room with a touch of empire (French empire, that is) glamour in its ornate gilt-framed mirrors and trendy high-backed chairs; articulate staff are clued-up on the intricacies of the menu and help foster a real buzz as dishes arrive. Patrick Bardoulet brings a pedigree CV to the kitchen, and shows that the Auld Alliance is alive and kicking in his marriage of red-hot modern French techniques with top-drawer Scottish materials. Dishes fizz with creativity and amazing clarity of flavour, starting with carpaccio of smoked scallops - oak-smoked under a dome at the table - teamed with pineapple salsa and coconut sauce. An unusual rocket sorbet intervenes before pot-roast pork belly with langoustines, pumpkin purée, chestnuts and Madeira jus. An assiette of desserts climaxes with an explosion of foodie fireworks: pink praline crème brûlée with pistachio and olive oil cake and almond milkshake, as well as a Normandy omelette soufflé with roasted apple and apple brandy sauce, and a chocolate délice with meringue, dried banana and banana sorbet.

Chef Patrick Bardoulet **Owner** Border Steelwork Structures Ltd
Times 12-2.30/7-9 Closed 25 Dec, early Jan, mid Nov, Mon, D Sun **Prices** Fixed L 3 course £19.50, Starter £10.95-£14.95, Main £15.95-£26.50, Dessert £6.50-£15.95, Service optional, Groups min 8 service 10% **Wines** 71 bottles over £20, 31 bottles under £20 **Notes** Sunday L, Vegetarian available, Dress restrictions, Smart casual, Jackets for men preferred
Seats 40 **Parking** 20

MELROSE Map 21 NT53

Burt's Hotel

Modern Scottish

Friendly, family-run Borders hotel with modern Scottish menu

01896 822285
Market Square TD6 9PL
e-mail: enquiries@burtshotel.co.uk
web: www.burtshotel.co.uk
dir: A6091, 2m from A68, 3m S of Earlston. Hotel in market square

Dating from 1722, Burt's stands proudly on the market square of this quiet borders town. A well-maintained, family-run hotel, it serves the needs of the local community and visitors alike, whether it is for a three-course meal in the restaurant, North Sea haddock in beer batter in the bar-bistro, or simply a wee dram (the range of 90 single malts should sort you out). The décor in the restaurant suits the 18th-century heritage of the building, being both comfortable and traditional, and the tables are formally laid with white linen. Seasonally-driven menus are based around quality local produce, so roast butternut squash and smoked bacon soup might precede cod three ways or beef fillet with red onion compôte, root vegetables, fondant potato and roast garlic jus. Finish with a perfectly cooked chocolate fondant.

Chef Trevor Williams **Owner** The Henderson family **Times** 12-2/7-9 Closed 26 Dec, 4-9 Jan **Prices** Fixed L 2 course £20-£24, Fixed D 3 course £35-£39, Service optional **Wines** 40 bottles over £20, 20 bottles under £20, 8 by glass **Notes** Sunday L, Vegetarian available, Dress restrictions, Jacket & tie preferred **Seats** 50, Pr/dining room 25 **Children** Portions **Parking** 40

PEEBLES Map 21 NT24

Cringletie House

Modern British V

Locally-sourced, creative cooking within a beautiful baronial house

01721 725750
Edinburgh Rd EH45 8PL
e-mail: enquiries@cringletie.com
dir: 2.5m N of Peebles on A703

A towering Scottish baronial mansion and former hunting lodge, Cringletie is surrounded by 28 acres of achingly romantic gardens and woodlands. Whilst relaxing amid the formal, comforting grandeur of the house you can take in those views, although you're just as likely to be bowled over by the magnificent trompe l'oeil ceiling in the grand dining room. Smartly laid tables and rich, contemporary fabrics await. The menu is locally-sourced with passion and the overwhelming majority of fruits, herbs and vegetables come from the hotel's own 400-year-old walled garden. The cooking is in the modern vein, so contemporary ideas are based on sound classical foundations; start, perhaps, with a goats' cheese mousse served alongside garden beetroot, beetroot jelly and a pear compôte, following on with a duck breast, served up with roasted foie gras, pommes purée, Lyonnaise onions, toasted walnuts and natural juices. Indulgent desserts include a supremely decadent Cringletie banoffee pie with banana sorbet, caramel purée, vanilla cheesecake and glazed bananas.

Chef Craig Gibb **Owner** Jacob & Johanna van Houdt **Times** 6.30-9 Closed L Mon-Sat **Prices** Fixed L 2 course £15-£20, Fixed D 3 course £30-£43, Starter £7, Main £23, Dessert £6, Service optional **Wines** 68 bottles over £20, 9 by glass **Notes** Tasting menu £65, with wines £95, Sunday L, Vegetarian menu, Dress restrictions, Smart casual, No jeans or trainers, Civ Wed 55 **Seats** 55, Pr/dining room 12 **Children** Portions, Menu **Parking** 30

Renwicks

Modern British

Uncomplicated modern cooking with ravishing border-country views

0844 879 9024 & 01896 833600
Macdonald Cardrona Hotel, Golf & Country Club, Cardrona Mains EH45 8NE
e-mail: general.cardrona@macdonald-hotels.co.uk
dir: From Edinburgh on A701 signed Penicuik/Peebles. Then A703, at 1st rdbt beside garage turn left onto A72, hotel 3m on right

A golfing and spa resort owned by the Macdonald group, the Cardrona is surrounded by the gently rolling hills of the Scottish border country. Enjoy those ravishing views of hills and golfing from the second-floor Renwicks restaurant, where an alluring, uncomplicated style distinguishes the cooking. A meal might start out with seared peppered tuna with couscous in coriander and lime butter, proceed to braised shoulder of Highland lamb with roast roots and garlic mash, and conclude with hot pineapple tarte Tatin and passionfruit parfait. British cheeses come with grape and apple chutney.

Chef Ivor Clark **Owner** Macdonald Hotels **Times** 12-2.30/6.30-9.45 **Prices** Food prices not confirmed for 2011. Please telephone for details **Wines** 70 bottles over £20, 12 bottles under £20, 18 by glass **Notes** Vegetarian available, Dress restrictions, Smart casual, Civ Wed 150 **Seats** 70, Pr/dining room 200 **Children** Portions, Menu **Parking** 100

ST BOSWELLS Map 21 NT53

The Tweed Restaurant

Scottish

Modern Scottish cooking in a Victorian baronial house

01835 822261
Dryburgh Abbey Hotel TD6 0RQ
e-mail: enquiries@dryburgh.co.uk
dir: B6356 signed Scott's View & Earlston. Through Clintmains, 1.8m to hotel

Set amid an estate of 10 acres on the banks of the River Tweed, the magnificent early Victorian baronial house stands next to the abbey after which it is named. The views from The Tweed Restaurant, all soft-focus rural tranquility, are almost as nourishing as Mark Greenaway's locally-sourced, conscientious cooking, which offers a comprehensive guide to the modern Scottish idiom. Start with a confit duck leg, served with beetroot carpaccio, hot orange jelly, and a raspberry-dressed herb salad. Mains might take in seared salmon with pea purée, clam chowder and vanilla foam, or more mainstream roast rump of Aberdeen Angus in rosemary jus. Desserts include the rather fragile-sounding 'broken' lemon tart.

Times 7.30-9 Closed L all week

Roman Camp Country House Hotel

CALLANDER Map 20 NN60

Modern French V

Innovative French-influenced cooking in luxurious manor house

☎ 01877 330003
FK17 8BG
e-mail: mail@romancamphotel.co.uk
web: www.romancamphotel.co.uk
dir: N on A84 through Callander, Main St turn left at East End into drive

The nearby Roman earthworks are what gives this country-house hotel its name. Built in the 16th century as a shooting lodge for the Earls of Moray, the luxurious manor house played host to Prime Ministers, generals, painters, and famous actresses in its socialite Victorian and Edwardian heyday. Inside, it is a deeply traditional place that has no truck with the angular harshness of contemporary minimalism: linenfold oak panelling, ornate plasterwork ceilings, a silk-lined drawing room - every surface is plushly upholstered, swagged and tapestried and done out in opulent colour schemes. Two spacious dining rooms have a pastel-hued soft-focus look, with navy blue damask chairs and crisp white linen, all romantically candlelit for dinner. The larder is clearly well-stocked with diligently-sourced Scottish produce, brought together in intelligent modern Scottish combinations, with a distinctly French influence. Caramelised hand-dived scallops are teamed creatively with apple jelly, walnut purée and Calvados foam in a rather modern starter. Next up, an aged fillet of Scotch beef might be served with a slow-cooked cheek and bone marrow bonbon, while dessert concludes with an exotic flourish of iced coconut parfait with mango sorbet and passionfruit jelly.

Chef Ian McNaught **Owner** Eric Brown **Times** 12-2/7-9 **Prices** Fixed L 2 course £20-£23, Fixed D 4 course £47-£49, Starter £10.50-£16.50, Main £24.50-£38, Dessert £9.50-£14, Service optional **Wines** 185 bottles over £20, 15 bottles under £20, 16 by glass **Notes** Sunday L, Vegetarian menu, Dress restrictions, Smart casual, Civ Wed 120 **Seats** 120, Pr/dining room 36 **Children** Portions **Parking** 80

STIRLING

CALLANDER Map 20 NN60

Callander Meadows

Modern British

Classic cooking from a husband-and-wife-team

01877 330181
24 Main St FK17 8BB
e-mail: mail@callandermeadows.co.uk
dir: M9 junct 10, A8 for 15m, restaurant 1m in village on left past lights

Built around 1800, this charming restaurant with rooms in the heart of town is run, lovingly, by husband-and-wife-team Nick and Susannah Parkes. Both are trained chefs with past experience working in some of the country's top restaurants, so you can expect some skilful cooking, careful sourcing of produce and a keen eye for detail. The house is impeccably maintained, with plenty of original features, and the service is refreshingly relaxed and informal. Dinner might begin with steamed mussels in a spicy tomato sauce, with baked rump of lamb with potato cake, spring greens and a rosemary jus to follow.

Times 12-2.30/6-9 Closed 25-26 Dec, Tue-Wed

Roman Camp Country House Hotel

– *see opposite page*

CRIANLARICH Map 20 NN32

The Crianlarich Hotel

Traditional British NEW

Simple, accurate cooking in refurbished hotel

01838 300272
FK20 8RW
e-mail: info@crianlarich-hotel.co.uk
dir: At junct of A85 Oban & Fort William to Perth and A82 Glasgow road, in Crianlarich

The white-fronted hotel stands at a crossroads next to the railway line, but the views further afield over the Scottish Lowlands are stunning. Recent refurbishment has made the dining room a comfortable and stylish place to sit, and the locally-sourced cooking combines appealing simplicity with accurate timing and assured balancing of flavours. Good dishes include the flawlessly timed king scallops, served with Stornoway black pudding and a salad of crisp-fried bacon and apple, and a main course of tender, pink-cooked Perthshire venison with creamed Savoy cabbage in a reduction of red wine and rosemary. Finish with rhubarb and ginger brûlée and home-made shortbread.

Chef Calum Marr **Owner** Byrne Ventures Ltd **Times** 7-9.30 Closed L all week **Prices** Fixed D 3 course £37.50, Service optional **Wines** 7 bottles over £20, 19 bottles under £20, 4 by glass **Notes** Sunday L, Vegetarian available **Seats** 70, Pr/dining room 10 **Children** Portions, Menu **Parking** 50

STRATHYRE Map 20 NN51

Creagan House

French, Scottish NOTABLE WINE LIST

17th-century Trossachs farmhouse with warm hospitality and good food

01877 384638
FK18 8ND
e-mail: eatandstay@creaganhouse.co.uk
dir: 0.25m N of village, off A84

The setting for this welcoming country restaurant with rooms is rather special: glorious views of the Strathyre Valley will set you up for the day as soon as you're awake, and the place is run with good-natured enthusiasm by husband-and-wife-team Gordon and Cherry Gunn. The converted 17th-century farmhouse has a baronial dining room with a grand stone fireplace, vaulted ceiling and burnished refectory tables. Gordon works alone in the kitchen, delivering classical French dishes with clear Scottish overtones, and believes passionately in local provenance: vegetables and herbs come from their garden and local small-holdings, while meat is all reared on Perthshire farms. Seared hand-dived scallops on chicory and orange risotto with a port and sesame reduction gets things off to a flying start, followed by noisette of local venison with a croustade of chestnut and cranberry and a poivrade sauce. The 100-bin wine list and 50-odd malts are worthy of special mention.

Chef Gordon Gunn **Owner** Gordon & Cherry Gunn **Times** 7.30-8.30 Closed 9-24 Nov, Xmas, 19 Jan-10 Mar, Wed-Thu, L all week (ex parties) **Prices** Fixed D 3 course fr £31.50, Service optional **Wines** 48 bottles over £20, 19 bottles under £20, 8 by glass **Notes** Vegetarian available, Dress restrictions, Smart casual **Seats** 15, Pr/dining room 6 **Children** Portions **Parking** 25

SCOTTISH ISLANDS

ARRAN, ISLE OF

BRODICK Map 20 NS03

Kilmichael County House Hotel

Modern British

Refined cooking in stylish country-house hotel

01770 302219
Glen Cloy KA27 8BY
e-mail: enquiries@kilmichael.com
dir: Turn right on leaving ferry terminal, through Brodick & left at golf club. Follow brown sign. Continue past church & onto private drive

Reputed to be the oldest on the island, and less than five minutes' drive from the ferry terminal, this elegant, white-painted house has been lovingly restored to create a very stylish hotel. Surrounded by attractive gardens in a peaceful glen, the house is adorned with antiques, interesting artworks and fabulous china from around the world. In the light and airy restaurant overlooking the garden, the menu features first-class produce, including eggs from their own chickens and ducks, and fruit and vegetables and herbs from the garden or the estate. Expect canapés, followed by a starter such as lime, pea and mango soup. After a sorbet follow with a main course of lamb with rosemary and redcurrants, perhaps finishing with raspberry and champagne jelly.

Times 7-8.30 Closed Nov-Mar, Tue, L all week

MULL, ISLE OF

TOBERMORY Map 22 NM55

Highland Cottage

◎◎ Modern Scottish, International

Hospitable island hotel with locally-sourced cooking

☎ 01688 302030
24 Breadalbane St PA75 6PD
e-mail: davidandjo@highlandcottage.co.uk
web: www.highlandcottage.co.uk
dir: Opposite fire station. Main St up Back Brae, turn at top by White House. Follow road to right, left at next junct into Breadalbane St

In the heart of town, only a few minutes from the Mull waterfront, David and Jo Currie's hotel and restaurant is a little more extensive than the designation 'Cottage' might suggest. They have decluttered some of the old bric-à-brac, they say, but the tone of a restful island escape is maintained. The fixed-price dinner menus proceed from appetiser to coffee through a wide range of choice, with a sorbet intervening after the starter. Local seafood finds its way into Croig crab cakes with chilli caper sauce, or Inverlussa mussels under a gratin topping of breadcrumbs and garlic, while mains offer Ardnamurchan venison with red cabbage and juniper, or breast and confit leg of duck in orange and ginger sauce. Finish with Rusty Nail parfait, based on the classic cocktail combination of Scotch and Drambuie.

Chef Josephine Currie **Owner** David & Josephine Currie **Times** 7-9 Closed Nov-Mar, L all week **Prices** Fixed D 4 course £47.50, Service included **Wines** 33 bottles over £20, 21 bottles under £20, 11 by glass **Notes** Vegetarian available, Dress restrictions, Smart casual **Seats** 24 **Children** Portions **Parking** On street in front of establishment

Tobermory Hotel

◎ Modern Scottish

Modern Scottish cooking on the harbourside

☎ 01688 302091
53 Main St PA75 6NT
e-mail: tobhotel@tinyworld.co.uk
dir: On waterfront

Situated on what was recently shortlisted as Google Earth's most picturesque street, head to these 18th-century fishermen's cottages turned hotel if you're after unruffled service and the best of local produce. The aptly named Water's Edge restaurant and lounge are decorated in neutral tones so as not to distract from the harbour side views over Tobermory Bay, while local artworks hang on the walls. The modern Scottish dishes might include potato soup with horseradish cream, Tobermory smoked trout and crispy bacon. For main course, perhaps a roast rack and loin of Lagganulva lamb with walnut and mint crusted goats' cheese, redcurrant sauce and creamed potatoes.

Chef Helen Swinbanks **Owner** Mr & Mrs I Stevens **Times** 6-9 Closed Xmas, Jan, L all week **Prices** Fixed D 3 course £31.50, Service optional **Wines** 18 bottles over £20, 24 bottles under £20, 6 by glass **Notes** Vegetarian available **Seats** 30 **Children** Portions, Menu **Parking** On street

ORKNEY ISLANDS

ST MARGARET'S HOPE Map 24 ND49

The Creel Restaurant with Rooms

◎◎ British

Deserved reputation for first-class Orkney produce done right

☎ 01856 831311
The Creel, Front Rd KW17 2SL
e-mail: alan@thecreel.freeserve.co.uk

It takes a wee bit of effort to get to The Creel, unless you happen to live on far-flung South Ronaldsay, so its three rooms certainly come in handy for a stopover. Chef Alan Craigie has run The Creel for 25 years with a relaxed vibe that is apparent in the easygoing honesty of the place - local artwork on the walls, wooden seabird sculptures and elemental Orcadian sea views. Fish fans are in for a treat: not only is the piscine produce as good as it gets, but the menu features species that don't often find their way on to the plate, such as wolf-fish, torsk and sea-witch. The Creel's own smoked fishcakes come with freshly made tomato and tartare sauces, while main-course scallops are paired classically with cauliflower purée and Stornoway black pudding. It's not all about fish though: North Ronaldsay mutton fed on seaweed to impart a memorable flavour might turn up as a slow-braised shoulder served simply with barley broth and mash. Beers from the island's award-winning brewery, and malts from the Highland Park and Scapa distilleries, are worth exploring.

Chef Alan Craigie **Owner** Alan & Joyce Craigie **Times** 7-8.30 Closed mid Oct-April, Mon-Tue, L all wk **Prices** Food prices not confirmed for 2011. Please telephone for details. **Wines** 14 bottles over £20, 8 bottles under £20, 2 by glass **Notes** Vegetarian available **Seats** 20, Pr/dining room 12 **Children** Portions **Parking** 10

SKYE, ISLE OF

COLBOST Map 22 NG24

The Three Chimneys

◎◎◎ – *see opposite page*

continued

The Three Chimneys

COLBOST Map 22 NG24

Modern Scottish 

Peerless produce immaculately cooked in a wild remote location

☎ 01470 511258
IV55 8ZT
e-mail:
eatandstay@threechimneys.co.uk
dir: 5m W of Dunvegan take B884 signed Glendale. On left beside loch

This century-old crofter's cottage hunkered down on the wild shores of Loch Dunvegan is something of a place of pilgrimage for foodies. Three Chimneys is in its third decade now, a testament to the enduring virtues of remoteness and sympathy for the environment. The whole slow food, organic ethos was championed here long ago, and the very location uplifts the spirit: seals, otters and whales play in the waters; bolts of rain and shafts of sunlight take their turn to spear the elemental landscapes, while inside there're bare stone walls, head-skimming beams and squat fireplaces. The culinary magic wells from where all great food begins: matchless produce - much of it from the Isle of Skye itself - is celebrated on daily-changing fixed-price menus that are crafted to showcase the best of what the seasons bring and the day boats land. This is highly-polished modern Scottish food, brimming with creativity and razor-sharp technical skills that delineate flavours with precision. The sweetness of Colbost crab is pointed up by a tangy melon and mango salsa, land cress and a punchy shellfish essence. Next comes a fish soup that would make a memorable meal by itself, before a roast loin of Glenhinnisdale lamb with its own haggis, colcannon and bashed neeps and juniper gravy. Fish and seafood are strong suits too - the tang of the sea is in the air, and you can be sure that what's on your plate will have been swimming around not long ago; try steamed Gigha halibut and squid with crushed pink fir potatoes, courgettes and hazelnut and razor clam velouté. It would be rude not to try the signature finale, Shirley's legendary hot marmalade pudding with Drambuie custard, but home-made gingerbread with toffee pears, crème fraîche and pear Calvados syrup runs a close second.

Chef Michael Smith **Owner** Eddie & Shirley Spear **Times** 12.45-2.15/ 6.45-10.15 Closed 3 Jan-5 Feb, L Sun & Nov-Mar **Prices** Fixed L 2 course £27.50-£37.50, Fixed D 3 course £55, Tasting menu £80, Service optional, Groups min 8 service 10% **Notes** Tasting menu 7 course, Vegetarian tasting menu on request, Vegetarian available, Dress restrictions, Smart casual preferred **Seats** 40, Pr/ dining room 12 **Children** Portions

ISLEORNSAY Map 22 NG71

Hotel Eilean Iarmain

Modern Scottish

Stunning views and accomplished Scottish cooking

01471 833332
IV43 8QR
e-mail: hotel@eileaniarmain.co.uk
dir: Mallaig & cross by ferry to Armadale, 8m to hotel or via Kyle of Lochalsh

Once used as a hunting lodge on Lord McDonald's estate, the 19th-century hotel offers spectacular views and traditional Scottish cuisine. Overlooking the Sound of Sleat, be prepared for some dramatic scenery from the charming wood-panelled restaurant - right on the water's edge, diners look out across to Isle Ornsay lighthouse and the mainland hills. A pre-dinner drink in front of a log fire in the lounge should not be missed. The nearby old stone pier lands much of the seafood used by the kitchen in essentially modern Scottish dishes with some French influences; expect the likes of seared West Coast scallops with creamed Stornoway black pudding, Granny Smith apple and walnut velouté, followed by rump of Highland lamb with fondant potato, roast garlic, pea purée, tomato and saffron jus, and iced amaretto parfait with almond praline to finish.

Chef Billy Broderick **Owner** Sir Ian Andrew Noble **Times** 12-2.30/6.30-8.45 **Prices** Food prices not confirmed for 2011. Please telephone for details **Wines** 60 bottles over £20, 10 bottles under £20, 6 by glass **Notes** Sunday L, Vegetarian available, Dress restrictions, Smart casual, Civ Wed 80 **Seats** 40, Pr/dining room 22 **Children** Portions, Menu

Iona Restaurant

Modern Scottish V

Stylish haven of peace serving Skye's wonderful produce

01471 820200
Toravaig House Hotel, Knock Bay IV44 8RE
e-mail: info@skyehotel.co.uk
web: www.skyehotel.co.uk
dir: Cross Skye Bridge, turn left at Broadford onto A851, hotel 11m on left. Ferry to Armadale, take A851, hotel 4m on right

The Isle of Skye is a good starting point for time out from the modern world. But if you want to be sure this hit of escapism comes with the urbane comforts of a plush boutique hotel and seriously good food, head for Toravaig House. This heavenly bolt-hole delivers dollops of contemporary style in a heartbreakingly beautiful setting overlooking the Sound of Sleat and the Knoydart Hills marching away on the wild mainland. While you're at it, go sailing in the briny air on board the hotel's own yacht, and you'll come to dinner in the Iona restaurant ready to do full justice to menus that dazzle with intelligent, well-balanced simplicity. The island's finest produce is showcased in starters such as crab soufflé with smoked crab bisque, crab tuile and confit lemon zest, while main-course could play a riff on pork, teaming fillet, braised belly and cheek with walnut ravioli, braised endive and carrot purée.

Iona Restaurant

Chef Ritchie Gilfillan **Owner** Anne Gracie & Ken Gunn **Times** 12.30-2/6.30-9.30 **Prices** Fixed L 2 course £18.50, Service optional **Wines** 20 bottles over £20, 20 bottles under £20, 6 by glass **Notes** Fixed D 5 course £45, Vegetarian menu, Dress restrictions, Smart casual, Civ Wed 18 **Seats** 25 **Parking** 20

See advert below

Kinloch Lodge

– see opposite page

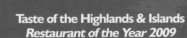

Kinloch Lodge

ISLEORNSAY Map 22 NG71

French, Scottish V NOTABLE WINE LIST

The best of the Skye larder in Baronial splendour

☎ 01471 833214 & 833333
Sleat IV43 8QY
e-mail: reservations@kinloch-lodge.co.uk
web: www.kinloch-lodge.co.uk
dir: 1m off main road, 6m S of Broadford on A851, 10m N of Armadale

Kinloch Lodge is the 16th-century seat of the High Chief of Clan Donald and what a location they chose: the lodge is bathed in jaw-dropping views over the elemental landscapes of Sleat and the wild waters of Na Dal sea loch, and steeped in clan history. Memorabilia is all around, including letters from Queen Victoria and a lock of Bonnie Prince Charlie's hair; centuries of Macdonalds are celebrated in oils on the walls of the formal dining room, surveying tables decorously clothed with starchy linen and laid with posh plates and vintage silver cutlery. As it happens, the love of good food is rooted deeply into the Macdonald household: this impressive pile is home to food and cookery writer Claire Macdonald (Lady Claire Macdonald), who is committed to making the best use of regional and seasonal produce. While chef Marcello Tully has his roots in the French classics, he happily raids the local larder for his intelligent and imaginative modern Scottish dishes. Dinner starts with a soup (a rustic French-style fish soup, perhaps), following on with a well-balanced dish of seared pigeon breast marinated in gin, with parsnip purée, sautéed wild mushrooms, citrus Puy lentils and game jus, then slow-roasted pork cheeks with West Coast scallops - seared and as a mousse - caramelised apples and rich port jus. A zingy lemon tart on crispy vanilla pastry with honey and Cointreau sauce finishes strongly.

Chef Marcello Tully **Owner** Lord & Lady Macdonald **Times** 12-2.30/6.30-9 Closed 1 wk Xmas **Prices** Fixed L 2 course fr £24.95, Fixed D 3 course fr £55, Service optional **Wines** 16 by glass **Notes** Sunday L, Vegetarian menu **Seats** 40, Pr/dining room 20 **Children** Portions **Parking** 20

ISLEORNSAY *continued*

Restaurant at the Duisdale

Modern Scottish

Pace-setting culinary style in remote Skye

01471 833202
Duisdale House Hotel & Restaurant, Sleat IV43 8QW
e-mail: info@duisdale.com
web: www.duisdale.com
dir: 7m N of Armadale ferry & 12m S of Skye Bridge on A851

The elegant restoration of a former hunting-lodge in a particularly remote part of Skye has seen a chic modern hotel arise from bare beginnings. On a summer evening, the only sound hereabouts is that of birdsong, and perhaps the faint plashing of the waves in the nearby Sound of Sleat. Gorgeous sunsets light up the mountain view from the conservatory dining room. A wealth of local produce, with seafood naturally to the fore, comes teeming on to the contemporary Scottish menus, which echo the surroundings for pace-setting style. Sconser scallops are creatively teamed with black olives, yoghurt and caramelised peanuts for an intriguing composition, while mains might offer saddle of the all-too-rarely-seen hare, the leg-meat preserved as confit and then made into a mini-lasagne, its richness offset with beetroot jelly and blueberries. Desserts mobilise interesting textural variants, perhaps with a light and fluffy apple 'cloud', served with punchy apple sorbet, mascarpone and a fine pistachio cake.

Chef Nick Fisher **Owner** K Gunn & A Gracie
Times 12-2.30/6.30-9 **Prices** Fixed L 2 course £18.50, Fixed D 4 course £44.50, Starter fr £5.95, Main fr £11.95, Dessert fr £5.95, Service optional **Wines** 39 bottles over £20, 11 bottles under £20, 9 by glass **Notes** Tasting menu available, Vegetarian available, Civ Wed 60
Seats 50 **Children** Portions **Parking** 30

See advert below

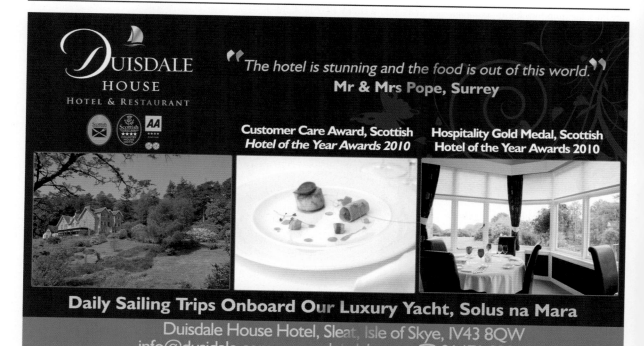

PORTREE Map 22 NG44

Bosville Hotel

Modern British

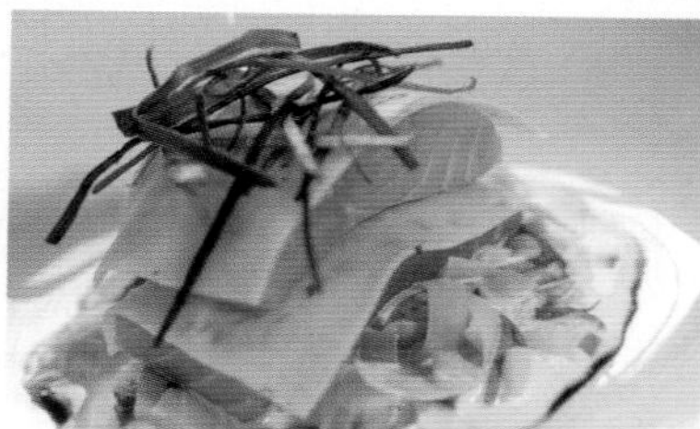

Superb cooking of local produce with great harbour views

01478 612846
9-11 Bosville Ter IV51 9DG
e-mail: bosville@macleodhotels.co.uk
web: www.bosvillehotel.co.uk
dir: A87 signed Portree, then A855 into town. Cross over pedestrian crossing, follow road to left

An extended and beautifully refurbished old fisherman's cottage overlooking the pretty fishing village of Portree is the stylish setting for the Chandlery Restaurant and the Bosville's popular bar and bistro. Themed around a ships' chandlery, the restaurant is smart and modern with innovative monthly menus built around the fantastic produce to be found on Skye. John Kelly's cooking is creative and focused on flavour and starters may include venison loin on barley risotto with thyme jus and herb salad. For main course, try Mallaig halibut with herb mash, Skye oyster, mussel and saffron broth and wilted spinach, then finish, perhaps, with apple and almond flan with pink grapefruit compôte and cardamom ice cream.

Bosville Hotel

Chef John Kelly **Owner** Donald W Macleod
Times 12-2.30/6.30-9.30 Closed L all week, D 25 Dec **Prices** Food prices not confirmed for 2011. Please telephone for details. **Wines** 20 bottles over £20, 20 bottles under £20, 12 by glass **Notes** Sunday L, Vegetarian available **Seats** 30 **Children** Portions, Menu **Parking** 10, On street

Cuillin Hills Hotel

Modern Scottish

Modern Scottish cooking in hotel with stunning views

☎ 01478 612003
IV51 9QU
e-mail: info@cuillinhills-hotel-skye.co.uk
dir: 0.25m N of Portree on A855

Set within 15 acres of mature private grounds overlooking Portree Bay, with magnificent views over the Sound of Raasay and the Cuillin Mountain range, this former hunting lodge was built for the Isle of Skye's Lord Macdonald. It is now a splendid country-house hotel with an elegant split-level restaurant, presided over by relaxed and friendly staff. West coast ingredients are allowed to shine in the Scottish-inspired cooking, but there are also plenty of European, particularly French, influences. Start, perhaps, with pan-fried hand-dived Sconser scallops with sautéed potato, pork belly, tomato and avocado salsa, move on to Isle of Skye lamb loin with shoulder croquette, pea crust and Provençal vegetables, and tarte Tatin with vanilla ice cream to finish.

Chef Chris Donaldson **Owner** Mr Kevin Wickman
Times 6.30-9 Closed L all week **Prices** Starter £5-£15, Main £17-£30, Dessert £5-£6, Service optional **Wines** 11 bottles under £20, 45 by glass **Notes** Vegetarian available, Civ Wed 45 **Seats** 40 **Parking** 58

See advert on page 538

Rosedale Hotel

Traditional Scottish

Welcoming waterfront hotel with seafood a speciality

☎ 01478 613131
Beaumont Crescent IV51 9DB
e-mail: rosedalehotelsky@aol.com
dir: On harbour front

Three former fisherman's houses have been joined together to create this charming family-run hotel right on the harbour in Portree. It's a quirky place, with a labyrinth of corridors and stairs connecting the lounges, bar and restaurant which are set on different levels. Try and grab a window seat in the delightful first-floor restaurant with fine views overlooking the bay, where sightings of golden eagles, sea eagles, otters, seals and dolphins are not out of the ordinary. An inspired Scottish menu is driven by local produce, including a good smattering of seafood, prepared with panache. Kick off with a bowl of Loch Eishort mussels in a creamy garlic and parsley sauce, before moving on to grilled Portree langoustines with garlic and herb butter and Orbost salad.

Times 7-8.30 Closed Nov-1 Mar, L all week

SKEABOST BRIDGE **Map 22 NG44**

Skeabost Country House

Traditional Scottish **NEW**

Classic cuisine beside the loch

☎ 01470 532202
IV51 9NP
e-mail: reservations.skeabost@ohiml.com

This enchanting white-painted house, sitting in lovely grounds on the edge of Loch Snizort, was originally built as a hunting lodge in 1850. These days it's a luxurious small hotel, with an attractive wood-panelled dining room overlooking the water. Here you can expect friendly and efficient service from a small, eager-to-please team, and some carefully executed classic cuisine based around prime, locally-sourced ingredients. Hebridean hot-smoked salmon served with crème fraîche, home-made chilli jam and Highland oatcakes makes a fine starter, while rack of Scottish lamb with roast garlic and olive oil mash, wilted greens and a redcurrant jus is a typically well-balanced main course. Vanilla pannacotta served with compôte of summer fruits and a sweet basil dressing is one way to finish.

Times 12-3/7-9.30

STAFFIN **Map 22 NG46**

Flodigarry Country House Hotel

Modern Scottish V

Glorious views and superb fish and seafood at intimate country house

☎ 01470 552203
IV51 9HZ
e-mail: info@flodigarry.co.uk
dir: Take A855 from Portree, through Staffin, N to Flodigarry, signed on right

A sensational setting beneath the sheer walls of Trotternish Ridge with elemental views across the sea to the mainland Torridon mountains is reason enough to come to this small-scale country hotel bolt-hole on the Isle of Skye. Add to that the romantic element that attaches to the former home of Scots heroine Flora MacDonald, and excellent food to boot, and you see the formula that keeps Flodigarry dear to visitors' hearts. As you ponder the enticing menu of modern Scottish cuisine, that view is the backdrop - you're looking at the provenance of the fish, shellfish and game that stars in dishes such as Skye seafood chowder packed with local salmon, langoustines, scallops and mussels in white wine, cream, shallots and garlic, and rack of Scottish lamb served with apple and potato cake, confit garlic and honey and mint sauce.

Chef Joseph Miko **Owner** Robin Collins
Times 12-2.30/7-9.30 Closed Nov & Jan **Prices** Starter £4.95-£16.75, Main £20-£32, Dessert £5.95-£8, Service included **Wines** 29 bottles over £20, 8 bottles under £20, 4 by glass **Notes** Sunday L, Vegetarian menu, Dress restrictions, Smart casual, Civ Wed 80 **Seats** 30, Pr/dining room 24 **Children** Portions, Menu **Parking** 40

The Glenview

British, French

Homely but creative cooking in north-eastern Skye

☎ 01470 562248
Culnacnoc IV51 9JH
e-mail: enquiries@glenviewskye.co.uk
dir: 12m N of Portree on A855, 4m S of Staffin

On the north-eastern corner of this hauntingly beautiful island, The Glenview is an example of croft architecture dating from the turn of the last century. It used to be the village shop, but is now a highly agreeable restaurant with rooms, in which to find some well-wrought, homely but creative, Hebridean cooking. Leek soup with Loch Eishort mussels and roast garlic oil, Highland free-range chicken with sautéed potatoes and champagne tarragon sauce, and Drambuie pannacotta with orange caramel add up to one particularly satisfying evening; save room at the end for a plate of fine Scottish cheeses.

Times 7-8.30 Closed Jan, Mon, L all week

STEIN **Map 22 NG25**

Loch Bay Seafood Restaurant

British Seafood

Simple fish cookery in a cottage setting by the loch

☎ 01470 592235
MacLeod Ter IV55 8GA
e-mail: david@lochbay-seafood-restaurant.co.uk
dir: 4m off A850 by B886

Stein was an unfinished project of the great engineer Thomas Telford, a dyed-in-the-wool model fishing village, and this charming, homely restaurant by the loch occupies what were once fishermen's cottages. The drill could hardly be simpler: daily-changing blackboard menus of the freshest fish, cooked with a minimum of contrivance or complication. Lightly cooked razor clams with herb butter, grilled king prawns in garlic butter, and poached organic salmon are among the attractions, as are more regal dishes such as shellfish platters and lightly dressed lobsters. Even the pannacotta turns out in full Scots figuration, judiciously flavoured with Drambuie.

Chef David Wilkinson **Owner** David & Alison Wilkinson **Times** 12-2/6-9 Closed Nov-Etr, Sat-Mon **Prices** Starter £3.75-£10, Main £12-£17.50, Dessert £5.20-£6.50, Service optional **Wines** 15 bottles over £20, 17 bottles under £20, 5 by glass **Notes** Extensive blackboard choices **Seats** 23 **Children** Portions **Parking** 6

STRUAN **Map 22 NG33**

Ullinish Country Lodge

– *see below*

Ullinish Country Lodge

STRUAN **Map 22 NG33**

Modern French V

Culinary paradise for foodies in an idyllic Skye setting

☎ 01470 572214
IV56 8FD
e-mail: ullinish@theisleofskye.co.uk
web: www.theisleofskye.co.uk
dir: 9m S of Dunvegan on A863

Owners Brian and Pam Howard relocated from the gently rolling hills of Devon to the wilderness of Skye in 2005. They couldn't have chosen a more elemental part of Scotland, guarded by lochs on three sides and watched over by the Black Cuillins and MacLeod's Tables. The Howards have transformed Ullinish into a remote hideaway complete with jaw-dropping views and food to evoke a similar reaction. Inside, it's comfortingly homely with wood-panelling and tartans in the dining room. Most of the kitchen's raw materials are sourced on Skye - a solid foundation for scintillating cooking that relies on excellent ingredients and flawless skills. Chef Craig Halliday's dishes are strikingly presented, often complex, but flavours are expertly fine-tuned so that they balance rather than fight with each other: for example in a starter of Loch Harport crab 'cannelloni' with soy marshmallows, cucumber velouté and edible organic flowers adding a wow factor. Contrasts are well handled in a pan-roasted fillet of hake with white onion purée, langoustine 'chorizo', crispy duck, sautéed radishes and chanterelle foam. Desserts are outstanding too, in colour, design and execution - take, for example, a 'taste of Skye berries', which throws every trick in the book at seasonal local fruit in the form of blueberry and apple jelly-milk foam, blackberry soufflé with crème brûlée ice cream, raspberry pannacotta with white chocolate tuile and a strawberry sorbet with strawberry and mint salad.

Chef Craig Halliday **Owner** Brian & Pam Howard **Times** 12-2.30/7.30-8.30 Closed Jan, 1 wk Nov **Prices** Fixed D 4 course £39.50, Starter £8.95-£9.25, Main £29-£32, Dessert £7.95-£9.25, Service optional **Wines** 55 bottles over £20, 10 bottles under £20, 22 by glass **Notes** Sunday L, Vegetarian menu, Dress restrictions, Smart casual, No T-shirts **Seats** 22 **Parking** 10

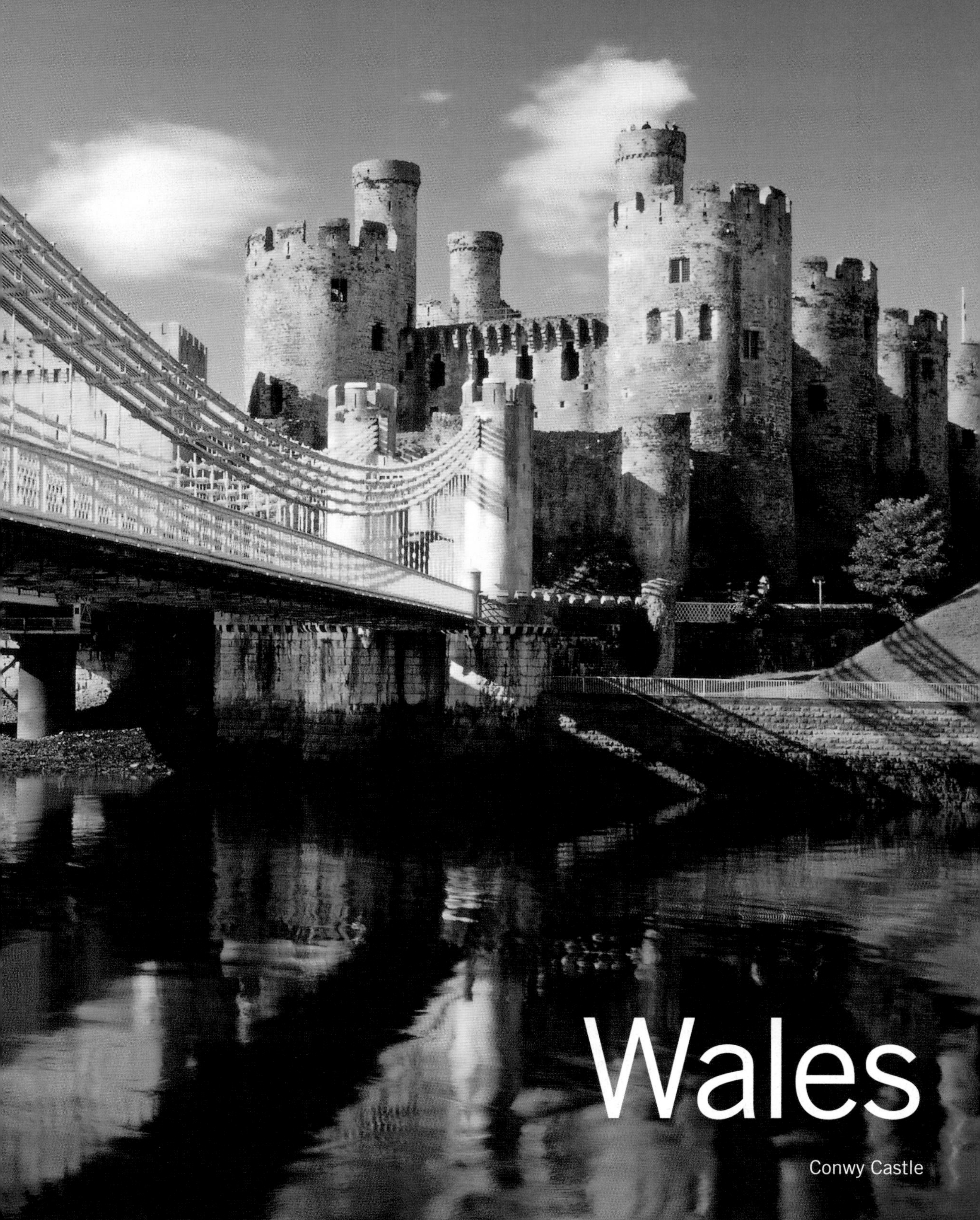

Wales

Conwy Castle

WALES

ANGLESEY, ISLE OF

BEAUMARIS Map 14 SH67

Bishopsgate House Hotel

Traditional Welsh

Unfussy dining overlooking the Menai Strait

☎ 01248 810302
54 Castle St LL58 8BB
e-mail: hazel@bishopsgatehotel.co.uk
dir: from Menai Bridge onto A545 to Beaumaris. Hotel on left in main street

The jaunty green façade of Bishopsgate House stands out from the neighbours along the Georgian terrace overlooking Beaumaris Green and the peaks of Snowdonia across the Menai waterfront. The intimate, low-ceilinged restaurant has a strong following with locals who know they can rely on good quality and value from the kitchen's straightforward crowd-pleasing menus, as well as a healthy showing of top-class local produce. Local sea bass with braised leeks and cherry tomato, tarragon and lime sauce sits alongside meaty mains such as loin of lamb teamed with crushed new potatoes with chives and port and redcurrant jus.

Times 12.30-2.30/7-9.30 Closed L Mon-Sat

Ye Olde Bulls Head Inn

Modern British

Historic inn serving top-notch Anglesey produce

☎ 01248 810329
Castle St LL58 8AP
e-mail: info@bullsheadinn.co.uk
dir: Town centre, main street

Built in 1472, this Bull's Head fully deserves its Ye Olde name tag. Tucked away by the walls of Beaumaris Castle, it featured on the travel itineraries of roving gourmets Charles Dickens and Dr Samuel Johnson, and still puts on a fine show for modern foodies. Two dining venues keep the kitchen hard at it: a buzzy, clean-cut contemporary brasserie done out with Welsh slate floors and oak tables serves unfussy crowd-pleasers - perhaps pan-fried sea bass with orange and basil butter sauce and black pasta. Fine dining takes place in the Loft Restaurant, a stylish and intimate modern space up in the eaves beneath ancient exposed beams. Top-class Anglesey produce - Welsh Black beef and salt marsh lamb, for example - stars in creative modern British dishes along the lines of Earl Grey-smoked duck with crispy confit duck fritter and burnt orange, ahead of cannon of Welsh lamb with leek porridge, shank ragoût, and coriander jus. Desserts are also works of skill and artistry - such as champagne rhubarb mousse with ginger crumbs and Armagnac anglaise.

Ye Olde Bulls Head Inn

Chef Hefin Roberts, Stuart Briggs **Owner** D Robertson, K Rothwell **Times** 7-9.30 Closed 25-26 Dec, 1 Jan, Sun-Mon, L all week **Prices** Fixed D 3 course £39.50-£40.50, Service optional **Wines** 93 bottles over £20, 28 bottles under £20, 6 by glass **Notes** Vegetarian available **Seats** 45 **Parking** 10

BRIDGEND

BRIDGEND Map 9 SS97

Bokhara Brasserie

Mediterranean, Indian NEW V

Mix of Indian and European cuisine in country manor

☎ 01656 720212
Court Colman Manor, Pen-y-Fai CF31 4NG
e-mail: experience@court-colman-manor.com
dir: M4 junct 34/A4063 in direction of Maesteg, after lights take 1st exit at rdbt to Bridgend, continue under motorway, take next right & follow hotel signs

As Indian restaurants go, the much-lauded Bokhara Brasserie stands out from the crowd. First, there's its classy location in an upmarket Georgian country-manor hotel set in six acres of landscaped gardens complete with a waterfall. Then, there's its one-off mix of Indian and Mediterranean-inspired dishes. The Brasserie itself has a metropolitan look in glowing shades of orange, terracotta and sun-bathed yellow - a reflection, perhaps, of the India-meets-Mediterranean cuisine it serves. On the sub-continental side, you'll find classic Indian dishes such as seekh kebabs to start, then murgh makhani - tandoori chicken cooked with tomatoes, cream, butter, cashews and ginger-garlic paste; if the curry muse doesn't appear, go continental instead and opt for monkfish in herb and butter sauce, or roast duck with honey, orange and Cointreau sauce.

Chef Sarvesh Jadon, Tulsi Kandel, Ganga Kandel **Owner** Sanjeen Bhagotra **Times** 12-3/7-10 Closed 25 Dec, L Mon-Sat, D Sun **Prices** Starter £2.10-£9.95, Main £3.95-£28.95, Dessert £2.95-£3.50, Service optional **Wines** 3 bottles over £20, 10 bottles under £20, 3 by glass **Notes** Sunday L, Vegetarian menu, Civ Wed 150 **Seats** 65, Pr/dining room 120 **Children** Portions, Menu **Parking** 100

The Great House & Restaurant

Modern British

Modern British in a delightful Grade II listed building

☎ 01656 657644
High St, Laleston CF32 0HP
e-mail: enquiries@great-house-laleston.co.uk
dir: On A473, 300yds from junct with A48

This French restaurant with rooms is housed in an interesting historic building; made of stone, it dates back to the 16th century and the finely decorated restaurant embraces its heritage with a feature inglenook fireplace. A chocolate-painted wall and wall lights lend a modern touch and well-spaced tables are dressed in high quality cream cloths. Modern British dishes are technically crafted from local produce and simply presented. Start with a retro Great House cheese fondue with confit egg and grilled baguette soldiers. Main courses include ox tongue, slowly cooked and served warm on potato salad with leeks, shallots and vinaigrette, and desserts such as a praline and fromage blanc tartlet and verbena sorbet.

Times 12-2/6-9.30 Closed Xmas, BH Mon, D Sun

CARDIFF

CARDIFF Map 9 ST17

Cardiff Marriott Hotel

British, French

Stylish city centre brasserie with judicious cooking

☎ 029 2078 5872 & 0870 4007290
Mill Ln CF10 1EZ
dir: M4 junct 29/A48M E follow signs city centre & Cardiff Bay. Continue on Newport Rd for 3m then turn right onto Mill Lane

This two-tiered contemporary city centre brasserie suits all comers, whether you're in town for business, shopping, or simply looking for some carefully prepared, well-judged French-inspired food. It's a pretty traditional set-up inside, with bare-wood tables and well rehearsed table settings all set off by clever lighting. Service is relaxed and well drilled and the traditional French dishes - with a British slant or two - deliver good, honest flavours. A delicious pile of wild mushrooms served up on toasted brioche hits the spot, following on, perhaps, with an entrée of breaded veal with mash, parsley and capers. For pudding, a good chocolate fondant with crème anglaise is a winner.

Chef Tino Pardon **Owner** Marriott International
Times 12-2.30/6-10 Closed D Sun **Prices** Fixed L 3 course fr £11.50, Starter £5-£7.25, Main £13-£22, Dessert fr £5, Service optional **Wines** 9 bottles over £20, 15 bottles under £20, 7 by glass **Notes** Sunday L, Vegetarian available, Civ Wed 350 **Seats** 120 **Children** Portions, Menu **Parking** 140

First Floor Restaurant

Traditional British

City views and appealing British menu

☎ 0870 122 0020
Mercure Holland House, 24-26 Newport Rd CF24 0DD
e-mail: H6622-am@accor.com
dir: Newport Rd 300mtrs from Queen St. Adjacent to Institute for the Blind & Cardiff University buildings

Elevated views of busy city life are the order of the day at this restaurant in the modern Mercure Holland House Hotel and Spa in the heart of Cardiff. The First Floor restaurant is a bistro style affair with a smart contemporary interior, open kitchen, unclothed tables and jazz in the background. The short daily-changing market menu of British cooking with broader European leanings features light dishes alongside more fine-dining options. There's smoked duck with celeriac, apple and walnut salad and carpaccio of beetroot to start, then a main-course cottage pie with roasted seasonal vegetables. Classic puds include knickerbocker glory, black forest sundae or an unusual liquorice and blackcurrant ice cream.

Chef Joseph Procak **Owner** Accor Hotels
Times 12-2/6-10 Closed L 1 Jan, D 25 Dec **Prices** Fixed L 2 course £10-£15, Fixed D 3 course £19.50-£35, Starter £5-£8, Main £10-£25, Dessert £5-£8 **Wines** 21 bottles over £20, 16 bottles under £20, 11 by glass **Notes** Vegetarian available, Civ Wed 700 **Seats** 120, Pr/dining room 500 **Children** Portions, Menu **Parking** 90, On street, NCP

Le Gallois-Y-Cymro

– *see below*

The Laguna Kitchen & Bar

Traditional European

Modern hotel restaurant with plenty of style

☎ 029 2011 1103 & 2011 1111
Park Plaza Cardiff, Greyfriars Rd CF10 3AL
e-mail: ppcres@parkplazahotels.co.uk
dir: City centre, next to New Theatre

This fashionable brasserie is part of the town centre's Park Plaza hotel but is a popular relaxed dining option in its own right. The contemporary design features low lighting, naked tables, dark wooden floor, plentiful glass and cream leather banquettes all brought together with an open-plan kitchen. It looks good. Meanwhile, the menu successfully combines local ingredients and international influences in, for example a dessert of locally-farmed Jersey cream crème brûlée with mini Welsh cakes. Working backwards, expect mains such as slow-cooked lamb shank, bubble-and-squeak and roasting jus, and chicken liver parfait to kick things off.

Chef Mark Freeman **Owner** Martin Morris
Times 12-2.30/5.30-10.30 **Prices** Fixed L 2 course £13.50, Fixed D 3 course £15.50, Starter £4-£8, Main £8-£18, Dessert £4-£6, Service added but optional 10% **Wines** 44 bottles over £20, 36 bottles under £20, 12 by glass **Notes** Sunday L, Vegetarian available, Civ Wed 140 **Seats** 110, Pr/dining room 150 **Children** Portions, Menu **Parking** NCP

Le Gallois-Y-Cymro

CARDIFF **Map 9 ST17**

British, French

Franco-Welsh inventiveness near the Millennium Stadium

☎ 029 2034 1264
6-10 Romilly Crescent CF11 9NR
e-mail: info@legallois.co.uk
dir: From town centre, follow Cowbridge Rd East. Turn right to Wyndham Crescent, then to Romilly Crescent. Restaurant on right

Rugby fans will be heartened to know that this stylish French restaurant is barely more than a touch-kick from the Millennium Stadium. There's a decidedly Parisian feel to the room, with its simple undressed tables and big picture windows - just the setting for some impeccably up-to-date Franco-Welsh cooking. An amuse-bouche of asparagus velouté gets things off to a flying start, the addition of fresh crab meat giving it a subtle sweetness. First course ris de veau is a well-crafted dish, the veal light and perfectly cooked, served with asparagus mousse, tête de porc and pecan butter. The quality of the produce shines out along with the sharp technical skills of chef Grady Atkins. For main course, belly and loin of Richard Vaughan's pork, moist and full of flavour, is partnered with organic Welsh shiitake mushrooms, a small quail's Scotch egg and smoked tea sauce. There are millefeuilles and croustillants to finish, perhaps an excursion over the Spanish border for churros with toasted marshmallow and hot chocolate, or flourless orange cake rich with sticky marmalade. The wine list follows the Francophile path, and there's now a deli and tea room next door.

Chef Grady Atkins **Owner** The Dupuy Family
Times 12-2.30/6.30-9.30 Closed Xmas, New Year, Sun-Mon **Prices** Fixed L 2 course £20-£25, Fixed D 3 course £30-£35, Service added but optional 10% **Wines** 60 bottles over £20, 5 bottles under £20, 11 by glass **Notes** Tasting menu available, Vegetarian available **Seats** 60 **Children** Portions **Parking** 20

CARDIFF *continued*

The Old Post Office Restaurant

@@ British, European

Assured modern cooking in a village near Cardiff

☎ 029 2056 5400
Greenwood Ln, St Fagans CF5 6EL
e-mail: info@theoldpostofficerestaurant.co.uk
dir: A48 E through Cardiff to St Fagans sign. Right at lights, 1.4m, in village turn right into Croft-y-Genau Rd, right into Greenwood Lane

In the picture-perfect village of St Fagans, four miles outside the Welsh capital, the name of this country restaurant is telling only half the story. It is cobbled together from the former post office and the old police station too, and is these days a white-fronted restaurant with rooms that entices Cardiff folk to make the journey. Eating goes on in a modern extension, and the style is modern British with a slight Italian accent. Begin with a big bowl of creamy, accurately judged crab risotto or a serving of home-cured local ham, before cod with bubble-and-squeak and mustard dressing, or a sensationally flavoured piece of Welsh lamb, served with pearl barley, onion cream and root veg on a platter of Welsh slate.

Times 12-3/7-9.30 Closed Xmas, 1st 2 wks Jan, Mon, D Sun

Raglans Restaurant

@@ Modern European

Confident cooking on the outskirts of Cardiff

☎ 029 2059 9100
Copthorne Hotel Cardiff, Copthorne Way, Culverhouse Cross CF5 6DH
e-mail: sales.cardiff@millenniumhotels.co.uk
dir: M4 junct 33 take A4232 (Culverhouse Cross), 4th exit at rdbt (A48), 1st left

Situated in the contemporary Copthorne Hotel, Raglans benefits from its position at the centre of a business and shopping park on Cardiff's outskirts. That's not to suggest that the restaurant is a room with an urban view though; full-length windows overlook the hotel's small lake replete with birdlife. Baby cacti on each green-clothed table, wooden panelling and romantic night-time lighting characterise the interior. Fresh home-made bread is a treat, but save room for modern European dishes confidently cooked using good produce; start, perhaps, with red split-pea and chorizo soup with paprika crème fraîche, followed by duo of Welsh new season lamb (neck and rack), smoked aubergine caviar and rosemary infused jus. Service is formal, yet friendly.

Chef Damien Pondevie **Owner** Millennium & Copthorne Hotels **Times** 12.30-2/6.30-9.45 **Prices** Food prices not confirmed for 2011. Please telephone for details **Wines** 25 bottles over £20, 10 bottles under £20, 12 by glass **Notes** Sunday L, Vegetarian available, Dress restrictions, Smart casual, Civ Wed 200 **Seats** 100, Pr/dining room 220 **Children** Portions, Menu **Parking** 225

The Thai House Restaurant

@ Thai V

First-rate Thai cooking in Cardiff

☎ 029 2038 7404
3-5 Guildford Crescent, Churchill Way CF10 2HJ
e-mail: info@thaihouse.biz
dir: At junct of Newport Rd & Queen St turn left past Queen St station, before lights turn left into Guildford Crescent

When Thai House brought the full-on flavours of its national cuisine to Wales in 1985, there were only a few places serving Thai food in the whole of the UK - all in London. Twenty-five years later, its ethos of total authenticity keeps it in the top rank of the country's Thai eateries. The local area is first port of call for ingredients, but obviously Wales doesn't produce much home-grown lemongrass or kaffir lime leaves, so exotica are flown in from Bangkok for a wide-ranging menu of health-conscious dishes that keep fat low and kick nasty E-numbers into touch. Start with soft-shelled crab with tangy green mango salad, and move on to spicy roast duck red curry with Thai fragrant rice, or Welsh lamb flash-fried with garlic, pepper, spring onions and Thai basil with a sloosh of Welsh whisky.

Chef Sujan Klingson **Owner** Noi & Arlene Ramasut **Times** 12-2.30/5.30-10.30 Closed Xmas, 1 Jan, Sun **Prices** Fixed L 2 course fr £10.50, Fixed D 3 course £25-£35.95, Starter £4.95-£11.95, Main £8.50-£17.95, Dessert £4.50-£6.25, Service optional, Groups min 8 service 10% **Wines** 34 bottles over £20, 23 bottles under £20, 16 by glass **Notes** Vegetarian menu, Dress restrictions, Smart casual **Seats** 130, Pr/dining room 20 **Children** Portions **Parking** On street & NCP opposite

Woods Brasserie

@ Modern European

Modern brasserie in fashionable Cardiff Bay

☎ 029 2049 2400
Pilotage Building, Stuart St, Cardiff Bay CF10 5BW
e-mail: serge@woods-brasserie.com
dir: In heart of Cardiff Bay. From M4 junct 33 towards Cardiff Bay, large stone building on right

Enormous glass windows make the best of the views over the water from the old grey-stone customs house building overlooking Cardiff Bay, with a table on the terrace perfect for watching the world go by in fair weather. The stylish conversion comes with an open-plan kitchen and bare-wood tables which confirm its modern take on the brasserie genre, as does a crowd-pleasing menu where Welsh produce is delivered with accomplished modern-European flair. Take pan-roasted grey mullet teamed with potato gratin and saffron and mussel cream, or perhaps roasted rump of lamb served with braised lentils and confit potato and a roasted vegetable salad. Finish with passionfruit tart or lemon and thyme posset.

Times 12-2/5.30-10 Closed 25-26 Dec & 1 Jan, D Sun (Sep-May)

CARMARTHENSHIRE

LAUGHARNE — **Map 8 SN31**

The Cors Restaurant

@@ Modern

Clear, confident flavours in the heart of Dylan Thomas country

☎ 01994 427219
Newbridge Rd SA33 4SH
e-mail: nickpriestland@hotmail.com
dir: A40 from Carmarthen, left at St Clears & 4m to Laugharne

Set back off the country road in Laugharne – Dylan Thomas country – this old rectory is now an idiosyncratic restaurant with a friendly and relaxing ambience. The name means 'bog', which it's hard to believe was in the place of a now-glorious garden complete with ponds and modern sculptures. The moody bohemian interior features plum and turquoise walls, wrought-iron seating for 24 in the dining areas, stone flooring, stained-glass windows and low lighting. Classical music on the sound system and well-paced service help maintain the laidback vibe. The kitchen produces accurately cooked seasonally-changing Welsh dishes to a high standard with no unnecessary frills or fussiness. Try the signature smoked haddock crème brûlée before moving on to roasted rack of Welsh salt marsh lamb with rosemary garlic crust and caramelised onion gravy.

Times 7-9.30 Closed 25 Dec, Sun-Wed

Dylan's at Seaview

@@ Modern Mediterranean **NEW**

Modern European cooking in the former home of Dylan Thomas

☎ 01994 427030
Market Ln SA33 4SB
e-mail: info@seaview-laugharne.co.uk
dir: From A40 take Laugharne/Pendine road through Laugharne village, left at Three Mariners pub then right at bakery

It seems remarkable that this place was allowed to fall into a state of near ruin: Seaview is a former home of Dylan Thomas and his young family, and he was visited here by T.S. Eliot and Arthur Miller amongst others. The handsome Georgian house has been restored to its former glory by its current owners and turned into a delightful restaurant with rooms, kitted out in uncluttered style with oak floors, wooden tables and chairs, crisp whitewashed stone walls and white-painted beamed ceilings. A wood-burning stove stacked all around with logs completes the picture of simple, rustic chic. The modern European menu is flannel-free and reads enticingly, delivering natural flavours extracted from quality, seasonal ingredients. Seared diver scallops with minted pea purée and crispy Carmarthen ham appears among starters, while main-course roast rump of Welsh lamb comes with black pudding, mixed bean salad and salsa verde.

Chef Gordon Jones **Owner** Gordon Jones
Times 12-2.30/6-9 Closed Mon, D Sun **Prices** Fixed L 2 course £9.95, Starter £4.50-£6.95, Main £9.95-£15.95, Dessert £4.95-£6.50, Service optional, Groups min 10 service % **Wines** 8 bottles over £20, 14 bottles under £20, 6 by glass **Notes** Sunday L, Vegetarian available **Seats** 34, Pr/dining room 16 **Children** Portions, Menu **Parking** 150 yds

LLANDEILO Map 8 SN62

The Angel Salem

Modern

Well-rendered locally-based cooking amid the Welsh mountains

☎ 01558 823394
Angel Salem SA19 7LY
e-mail: eat@angelsalem.co.uk
dir: From Llandeilo A483 cross River Towy, keep forward at rdbt, take 2nd exit onto A40 (signed Llandovery), turn left onto B4302 (signed Talley). Entering New Inn B4302 turn left on to unclassified into Salem

Wedged between the Cambrian and Black Mountains in rural Carmarthenshire, the Angel Inn stands on the main road through the village. A pair of beamed dining areas is adorned with pictures of local scenes against a green and cream colour scheme, and the service team is a model of friendly efficiency. The locally-based menus provide some homely but well-rendered cooking, along the lines of duck meat and potato hash cake with a fried egg in pea velouté, braised Welsh beef with tarragon dumpling and béarnaise, or salmon escalope crusted with tomato, rocket and parmesan. It's all distinguished by accurate cooking, good balance of flavours and eye-catching presentations. Finish with an apple crème brûlée served with vanilla ice cream.

Chef Rod Peterson **Owner** Rod Peterson & Liz Smith
Times 12-3/7-9 Closed 2 wks in Jan, Mon (ex BHs), L Tue, D Sun **Prices** Fixed D 3 course £24.95, Service optional **Wines** 18 bottles over £20, 21 bottles under £20, 5 by glass **Notes** Sunday L, Vegetarian available **Seats** 70 **Children** Portions **Parking** 25

The Plough Inn

Traditional International

Varied menu in friendly roadside hotel

☎ 01558 823431
Rhosmaen SA19 6NP
e-mail: info@ploughrhosmaen.com
dir: On A40 1m N of Llandeilo towards Llandovery. From M4 onto A483 at Pont Abraham

This smartly-updated small hotel and restaurant sits in the Towy Valley at the foot of the Brecon Beacons National Park. Whether you eat in the bar or the smart modern dining room, you can be sure that what's on the plate will be made from fresh ingredients judiciously sourced from local Welsh suppliers. Old favourites take in liver and onions with mash, crispy bacon and gravy, or battered fish of the day, or you could go for more ambitious modern Welsh cooking with occasional influences from further afield, as in a home-made spring roll of confit duck breast served with oriental salad and sweet chilli drizzle. Main course pan-fried sea bass comes with creamy pasta and a warm salsa of tomato, cucumber and prawns. Finish in the comfort zone with sticky toffee pudding.

Chef Andrew Roberts, Abi Kumar **Owner** Andrew Roberts
Times 11.30-3.30/5.30-9.30 Closed 1 Jan **Prices** Fixed L 2 course £11, Fixed D 3 course £16, Starter £3.95-£6.25, Main £7.95-£20.95, Dessert £4.50-£5.65, Service optional **Wines** 15 bottles over £20, 28 bottles under £20, 7 by glass **Notes** Sunday L, Vegetarian available, Civ Wed 100 **Seats** 190, Pr/dining room 35 **Children** Portions, Menu **Parking** 70

NANTGAREDIG Map 8 SN42

Y Polyn

Modern British

Skilled cooking in picturesque southwest Wales

☎ 01267 290000
SA32 7LH
e-mail: ypolyn@hotmail.com
dir: Follow brown tourist signs to National Botanic Gardens, Y Polyn signed from rdbt in front of gardens

In a rustic Carmarthenshire setting of great charm, Y Polyn has built up a reputation as a destination pub-restaurant. Locally-sourced ingredients inform the menus, and there is a heartening home-made ethos that overarches the kitchen output, from stunning breads to sumptuous ice creams. The Welsh note rings strong and clear through dishes like Carmarthen ham with celeriac remoulade and Brecknock lamb with onion and garlic purée, with French friends warmly welcomed; perhaps a textbook fish soup with gruyère and rouille, and an exquisite rendering of coq au vin packed with shallots, mushrooms and sheer flavour. Finish with pear and chocolate frangipane tart, served with Pembrokeshire clotted cream, or embark on a Welsh cheese odyssey with Golden Cenarth, Hafod and Luddesdown goats' cheese, served with fruit and nut bread, oat cakes, wheat wafers and walnut chutney.

Chef Susan Manson, Maryann Wright **Owner** Mark & Susan Manson, Simon & Maryann Wright **Times** 12-2/7-9 Closed Mon, D Sun **Prices** Fixed L 2 course £12.50, Fixed D 3 course £29.50, Starter £5-£8.50, Main £10.50-£16.50, Dessert £5.50, Service included **Wines** 20 bottles over £20, 31 bottles under £20, 9 by glass **Notes** ALC prices for L only, Sunday L, Vegetarian available **Seats** 40 **Children** Portions **Parking** 25

CEREDIGION

ABERAERON Map 8 SN46

Harbourmaster

Modern Welsh

Modern Welsh cooking overlooking the harbour

☎ 01545 570755
Pen Cei SA46 0BT
e-mail: info@harbour-master.com
dir: A487 (coast road). In town follow signs for Tourist Information Centre. Restaurant next door on harbourside

This Georgian Grade II listed building on Aberaeron's harbour may no longer be involved with managing the comings and goings from the harbour, but it benefits from the dramatic quayside location. It has been sympathetically restored, including the adjacent grain warehouse which is now a spacious bar with views over the bobbing boats. There are unpretentious pub classics in the bar or more ambitious cooking in the bright, airy brasserie with its ships' chandlery décor and striking spiral staircase. Relaxed service delivers modern Welsh dishes from bi-lingual menus that make good use of prime Welsh produce. Start with the Rhydlewis smoked salmon with honey and dill before a main course of pan-fried fillet of sea bream, Cardigan Bay crab risotto and sweet chilli sauce.

Chef Tom Holden **Owner** Glyn & Menna Hevlyn
Times 12-2.30/6-9 Closed 25 Dec **Prices** Fixed L 2 course £13, Starter £4.50-£9.50, Main £10.50-£22, Dessert £5.50, Service optional, Groups min 8 service 10% **Wines** 50 bottles over £20, 30 bottles under £20, 16 by glass **Notes** Sunday L, Vegetarian available **Seats** 50 **Children** Portions, Menu **Parking** 8, On street

Ty Mawr Mansion

Modern British, Welsh

Impressive cooking with local produce in a Georgian country house

☎ 01570 470033
Cilcennin SA48 8DB
e-mail: info@tymawrmansion.co.uk
dir: 4m from Aberaeron on A482 to Lampeter road

Chef Jeremy Jones' British cooking using the best of the local Welsh larder has people travelling from far and wide to dine at this Georgian mansion. In a commanding position above the Aeron Valley in 12 acres of grounds, the grey stone and slate exterior gives way to an interior where Georgian features and modern comforts are successfully combined. The unstuffy dining room is an intimate space in which to enjoy Jones' technically impressive modern cooking. Ty Mawr is blessed with fantastic produce on its doorstep and the kitchen makes good use of this, sourcing over 90% of ingredients from within 10 miles. Start, perhaps, with Cardigan Bay lobster bisque with shellfish beignet and brandy crème fraîche, and move on to sirloin of Welsh Black beef, steak-and-kidney pudding, buttered curly kale, red wine shallot and thyme jus, followed by Ty Mawr gooseberry and elderflower fool with lemon milk sorbet and shortbread biscuit.

Times 7-9 Closed 26 Dec-7 Jan, Sun, L all week

ABERPORTH — Map 8 SN25

The Penrallt

Modern British NEW

Fine cuisine in a country-house setting

01239 810227
SA43 2BS
e-mail: info@thepenrallt.co.uk
dir: Take B4333 signed Aberporth. Hotel 1m on right

There's room to relax and find your own space in the 42 acres of grounds surrounding this Edwardian mansion, with gorgeous views over Aberporth Bay as a bonus. A recent makeover has blended period features with a sleek, modern look, seen at its best in the fine-dining Bay Restaurant; fashionably unclothed darkwood tables are set against russet-hued half-panelled walls and an ornately beamed ceiling. The kitchen deals in a modern British repertoire with strong Welsh influences courtesy of the fine local produce brought in from the fields and seas all around. Start with sautéed lamb's kidneys teamed with wilted rocket, black-eyed bean purée and lamb jus, then follow with line-caught sea bass from New Quay with crab mash, local marsh samphire, and cockle and laverbread broth.

Owner Mr & Mrs P Miners **Times** 6.30-9.30 Closed Sun-Wed, L all week **Prices** Starter £4.45-£8.95, Main £14.95-£21.50, Dessert £5.45-£8.15, Service optional **Wines** 20 bottles over £20, 13 bottles under £20, 5 by glass **Notes** Sunday L, Vegetarian available, Dress restrictions, No shorts or flip-flops, Civ Wed 60 **Seats** 44, Pr/dining room 12 **Children** Menu **Parking** 60

EGLWYS FACH — Map 14 SN69

Ynyshir Hall

– *see below*

LAMPETER — Map 8 SN54

Valley Restaurant at the Falcondale Mansion

Modern British V

Grand house with confident cooking

01570 422910
Falcondale Dr SA48 7RX
e-mail: info@falcondalehotel.com
dir: 1m from Lampeter take A482 to Cardigan, turn right at petrol station, follow for 0.75m

Amidst breathtaking scenery and surrounded by valleys in the heart of Wales, this Victorian mansion is surrounded by 14 acres of manicured grounds, renowned for its spectacular springtime shows of rhododendrons and azaleas. Once the home to a wealthy banking family, the house retains an air of grandeur but the atmosphere is far from stuffy these days. Classic dishes are given a contemporary gloss, with the pick of Ceredigion and Carmarthenshire produce allowed to shine. A starter of laverbread and chicken roulade with tomato salsa and rocket dressing might precede a loin of Capeli lamb served with braised red cabbage, fondant potato, and a redcurrant and rosemary sauce. Leave room for the melting chocolate pudding with mint chocolate ice cream and the excellent selection of Welsh cheeses.

Chef Michael Green **Owner** Chris & Lisa Hutton **Times** 12-2/6.30-9 **Prices** Fixed L 2 course fr £13.50, Fixed D 4 course fr £40, Starter £6-£11, Main £13-£21, Dessert £6.50-£9.50, Service optional, Groups min 8 service 10% **Wines** 31 bottles over £20, 22 bottles under £20, 15 by glass **Notes** Tasting menu 8 course (pre-booked), Sunday L, Vegetarian menu, Dress restrictions, Smart casual, no shorts, Civ Wed 80 **Seats** 36, Pr/dining room 20 **Children** Portions **Parking** 60

Ynyshir Hall

EGLWYS FACH — Map 14 SN69

Modern British NOTABLE WINE LIST

Adventurous and sensational country-house cuisine

01654 781209
SY20 8TA
e-mail: ynyshir@relaischateaux.com
dir: On A487, 6m S of Machynlleth

The term 'destination hotel' is particularly apt for this tranquil country house: in 14 acres of splendid gardens within a 1,000-acre RSPB reserve on the Dovey Estuary, Ynyshir Hall is not the sort of place you simply stumble upon. The intimate scale of this retreat is a further bonus: there are just nine rooms. Long-time owner Joan Reen still manages Ynyshir several years after partnering with a top-end hotel group, thus leaving that special personal touch in place. For foodies, the restaurant needs no introduction: it's one of the finest tables in Wales, kept at the top of the culinary Premier League by chef Shane Hughes's intelligent, ambitious cooking. First-rate Welsh materials, including wild herbs and vegetables from the walled kitchen garden, are given modish treatment, but while the foams and jellies delight the eye, they are underpinned by skilled classical training. Razor-sharp flavours are a hallmark: you might start with cheese soufflé, apple, celery and hazelnut with parmesan cappuccino, or crayfish and crispy bacon risotto. Next up, Welsh Black beef is showcased with marrowbone, sweetbread, truffled linguine, salsa verde and Madeira emulsion, while a sea bass 'cassoulet' partners tip-top fish with foie gras, spiced lentils and saucisse de Morteau. Desserts hold form to the end - a deeply-satisfying treacle tart comes with walnuts, clotted cream and banana.

Chef Shane Hughes **Owner** von Essen Hotels, Rob & Joan Reen **Times** 12.30-1.30/7-8.45 **Prices** Fixed L 3 course fr £21.50, Fixed D 4 course £70-£85, Service optional **Wines** 250 bottles over £20, 5 bottles under £20, 25 by glass **Notes** Tasting menus available 6/8 course, Sunday L, Vegetarian available, Dress restrictions, No jeans, beachwear or shorts, Civ Wed 40 **Seats** 30, Pr/dining room 16 **Parking** 15

CONWY

ABERGELE Map 14 SH97

The Kinmel Arms

Modern Welsh

Sound cooking in local produce-driven gastro-pub

☎ 01745 832207
The Village, St George LL22 9BP
e-mail: info@thekinmelarms.co.uk

This converted 17th-century inn is close to the church in the village of St George in the beautiful Elwy Valley. Oak floors, a conservatory with marble tables and a central slate-topped bar with a stained glass header make for a stylish and atmospheric setting for the unfussy and well presented food. The restaurant specialises in local produce, offered alongside a good wine selection and some well-kept real ales. There are daily fish specials, and recommendations include king scallops served with broad bean and bacon purée, bacon crisp and chervil dressing, or tenderloin of St George lamb topped with tarragon and wild mushroom mousseline. Finish, perhaps, with warm rhubarb sponge pudding.

Times 12-2/6.30-9.30 Closed 25 Dec, 1-2 Jan, Sun-Mon

BETWS-Y-COED Map 14 SH75

Craig-y-Dderwen Riverside Hotel & Restaurant

Modern international

Creative modern cooking in idyllic country setting

☎ 01690 710293
LL24 0AS
e-mail: info@snowdoniahotel.com
dir: On A5 near Waterloo Bridge

On the banks of the River Conwy, up a private tree-lined driveway and within 16 acres of beautiful gardens, Craig-y-Dderwen is a late-Victorian country-house hotel of considerable charm. Contemporary British cuisine is the order of the day, with good use of seasonal Welsh produce and most of the fruit and vegetables sourced from the extensive kitchen garden. Other influences are present, however, so to start might be shredded duck and sweet chilli pancake served with pak choi salad. It's back to Europe for main-course confit of local belly pork with a pickled apple Tatin, and to finish a seasonal fruit and frangipane tart with warm vanilla pod custard.

Chef Paul Goosey **Owner** Martin Carpenter
Times 12.30-5/6.30-9 Closed 2 Jan-1 Feb **Prices** Fixed D 3 course £27.50, Service optional **Wines** 52 bottles over £20, 40 bottles under £20, 3 by glass **Notes** Sunday L, Vegetarian available, Dress restrictions, Smart casual, Civ Wed 125 **Seats** 82, Pr/dining room 40
Children Portions, Menu **Parking** 50

Llugwy Restaurant @ Royal Oak Hotel

Modern British, Welsh

Former coaching inn with confident Welsh cooking

☎ 01690 710219
Royal Oak Hotel, Holyhead Rd LL24 0AY
e-mail: royaloakmail@btopenworld.com
web: www.royaloakhotel.net
dir: on A5 in town centre, next to St Mary's Church

The Royal Oak Hotel sits in the chocolate-box honeypot of Betws-y-Coed, where the peaks of Snowdonia crowd all

continued

Tan-y-Foel Country House

BETWS-Y-COED Map 14 SH75

Modern British

Fine food and chic style in Snowdonia

☎ 01690 710507
Capel Garmon LL26 0RE
e-mail: enquiries@tyfhotel.co.uk
dir: A5 onto A470; 2m N towards Llanrwst, then turning for Capel Garmon. Country House on left 1m before village

Tan-y-Foel offers a classy contemporary take on the country-house idiom that is the very antithesis of chintz. The 17th-century Welsh stone house is an oasis of peace and good taste, perched above the madding crowds in the tourist honeypot village of Betws-y-Coed in six acres of woodland with uplifting views of Snowdonia and the Conwy Valley. The most picky style slave could find no fault with the chic, light and modern, minimalist interior, but what makes Tan-y-Foel stand out is the hands-on family-run ambience that delivers impeccable attention to detail to all aspects of the operation. Just a dozen diners fit into the intimate restaurant, allowing chef-proprietor Janet Pitman to bring razor-sharp technical precision to her imaginative modern ideas. Built on cracking Welsh produce, including herbs and veg from the hotel's 30-metre greenhouse, dinner menus change daily and are sensibly restricted to a choice of two dishes at each course, opening with grilled fillet of mackerel with orange chicory marmalade and a balsamic reduction dressing. Next up, pan-seared Welsh beef fillet is topped with devilled kidneys and puff pastry, and served with Anna potatoes, Nero kale and rich beef gravy. To finish, it's a tough call between excellent Welsh cheeses and a perfect raspberry Pavlova.

Chef Janet Pitman **Owner** Mr & Mrs P Pitman
Times 7-7.30 Closed Dec-Jan, Mon, L all week
Prices Fixed D 3 course £48, Service optional **Wines** 81 bottles over £20, 7 by glass **Notes** Dress restrictions, No jeans, trainers, tracksuits, walking boots **Seats** 10
Parking 14

BETWS-Y-COED ***continued***

around. Hungry hikers and ice cream-licking tourists keep the kitchen of the popular old coaching inn hard at it, serving up inventive modern Welsh dishes in the contemporary Grill Bar and the more traditional Llugwy Restaurant. Local produce is the mainstay: trout is home-smoked, and Pant-y-Gawen goats' cheese pannacotta with raisin and white wine jelly, or pan-fried Menai mussels with Dragon cider and double cream might appear among starters. Next up, sea bass might be matched with spaghetti vegetables, king prawns, chilli and lemon; to finish, bara brith (Welsh fruit cake to the uninitiated) and butter terrine with marmalade ice cream keeps the dragon flying.

Chef Dylan Edwards **Owner** Royal Oak Hotel Ltd **Times** 12-3/6.30-9 Closed 25-26 Dec, Mon-Tue, L Wed-Sat, D Sun **Prices** Fixed L 2 course £11.75-£12.95, Fixed D 4 course £25-£35, Starter £4.95-£8.50, Main £12.50-£21.95, Dessert £5.25-£7.50, Service optional **Wines** 16 bottles over £20, 40 bottles under £20, 11 by glass **Notes** Welsh tasting menu available 4-5 course, Sunday L, Vegetarian available, Dress restrictions, Smart casual, no jeans, shorts or T-shirts, Civ Wed 85 **Seats** 60, Pr/dining room 20 **Children** Portions, Menu **Parking** 100

Tan-y-Foel Country House

@@@ – *see page 547*

CONWY — **Map 14 SH77**

Dawsons @ The Castle Hotel Conwy

@@ Modern British

Fine Welsh produce in local landmark

☎ 01492 582800
High St LL32 8DB
e-mail: mail@castlewales.co.uk
dir: A55 junct 18, follow town centre signs, cross estuary (castle on left). Right then left at mini-rdbts onto one-way system. Right at Town Wall Gate, right onto Berry St then High St

Formerly an old coaching-inn, this family-run hotel built on the site of a Cistercian abbey showcases the best of Welsh seasonal produce in its restaurant. The well-maintained, impressive exterior is matched by plenty of original features on the inside, where a sympathetic and rather cool and classy renovation has brought the place well and truly up to date. Dawsons restaurant is named after John Dawson-Watson, the painter and illustrator responsible for the hotel's frontage. Quality Welsh produce is used to good effect in modern British dishes, so expect starters such as deep-fried blue cheese fritters with caramelised pear and cranberry dressing or locally-smoked haddock and chorizo risotto, topped with a soft-poached hen's egg and parmesan. Main course might bring roast rump of Welsh lamb with apple-scented sticky red cabbage, potato and onion cake and creamed spinach.

Dawsons @ The Castle Hotel Conwy

Chef Graham Tinsley **Owner** Lavin Family & Graham Tinsley **Times** 12-10 Closed D 25 Dec **Prices** Food prices not confirmed for 2011. Please telephone for details **Wines** 16 bottles over £20, 20 bottles under £20, 15 by glass **Notes** Sunday L, Vegetarian available **Seats** 70 **Children** Portions, Menu **Parking** 36

The Groes Inn

@ Traditional British

Honest, wholesome food in a characterful inn

☎ 01492 650545
Tyn-y-Groes LL32 8TN
e-mail: reception@groesinn.com
dir: On B5106, 3m from Conwy

This ancient inn in the Conwy Valley was the first house in Wales to be granted a licence back in 1573. It's an easygoing sort of place, all cosy nooks and crannies with beamed ceilings and well-worn settles. This is a genuine family-run affair, with owners who take pride in the warmth of their welcome and the quality of the cuisine that leaves the kitchen. The valleys and seas around Conwy and Anglesey provide top-drawer materials, among them salt marsh lamb, game, crab, wild salmon and oysters, all served in comforting traditional combinations - perhaps home-made salmon fishcakes with chunky tartare sauce and new potatoes, or local Conwy sausages with creamy mash and onion gravy.

Chef Lewis Williams **Owner** Dawn & Justin Humphreys **Times** 12-2.15/6.30-9 Closed 25 Dec **Prices** Starter £5-£8, Main £10-£24, Dessert £5-£7, Service added but optional, Groups min 8 service 10% **Wines** 12 bottles over £20, 27 bottles under £20, 16 by glass **Notes** Sunday L, Vegetarian available, Dress restrictions, Smart casual **Seats** 54, Pr/dining room 20 **Children** Portions, Menu **Parking** 100

Sychnant Pass House

@ Modern British

Modern British cuisine in Snowdonia National Park

☎ 01492 596868
Sychnant Pass Rd LL32 8BJ
e-mail: info@sychnant-pass-house.co.uk
dir: Pass Visitors Centre in Conwy, take 2nd left into Uppergate St. Up hill for 2m, restaurant on right

Tucked away in the foothills of the Snowdonia National Park above Conwy, the substantial white-painted country house stands in three acres of glorious grounds that include a stream, a pond and woods. Built in 1890, it is family-run and its modern facilities include a smart swimming pool, gym, hot tub and fire pits. The restaurant has a relaxed and informal feel with wooden tables and slate place mats. The fixed-price menu offers a good choice of modern British food. Expect the likes of creamy chorizo risotto with parmesan as a starter, followed by sorbet and then a main course of cannon of Welsh lamb with a light peppercorn sauce.

Times 12.30-2.30/7-9 Closed Xmas & Jan, L Mon-Sat

DEGANWY — **Map 14 SH77**

The Grill Bar & Restaurant

@@ Modern Welsh V

Panoramic views, contemporary surrounds and appealing food

☎ 01492 564100
Quay Hotel & Spa, Deganwy Quay LL31 9DJ
e-mail: info@quayhotel.com
dir: From S, M6 junct 20 signed North Wales/Chester. From N, M56 onto A5117 then A494. Continue on A55 to junct 18 (Conwy). Straight over 2 rdbts, at lights left over rail crossing, right at mini rdbt, hotel on right

The classy Quay Hotel sits on Deganwy Quay on the Conwy estuary, with glorious views of the ruined castle sweeping inland towards the peaks of Snowdonia. A waterside terrace makes the most of this spectacular setting, but if bad weather drives you indoors, the views are the same in the first-floor Grill Bar and Restaurant, a stylish, informal contemporary brasserie setting for the kitchen's modern Welsh repertoire. Top Welsh produce - particularly Welsh Black beef grazed on Anglesey - is proudly espoused on a menu of straightforward crowd-pleasing ideas. Take salmon from the Llandudno Smokery paired simply with horseradish cream, then follow with Great Orme lobster with chips and home-made ketchup, or for card-carrying devotees of red meat, there's grilled rib-eye of Welsh Black beef.

Chef Neil Wiggins **Owner** Exclusive Hotels **Times** 12-11 **Prices** Fixed D 3 course £32.50, Starter £3.95-£7.95, Main £12.95-£21.50, Dessert £5.95, Service optional **Wines** 76 bottles over £20, 18 bottles under £20, 19 by glass **Notes** Sunday L, Vegetarian menu, Civ Wed 240 **Seats** 120, Pr/dining room 240 **Children** Portions, Menu **Parking** 120

LLANDUDNO Map 14 SH78

Bodysgallen Hall and Spa

@@@ – *see below*

Empire Hotel

@ Traditional British

Traditional cooking in long-established family-run hotel

☎ 01492 860555
Church Walks LL30 2HE
e-mail: reservations@empirehotel.co.uk
web: www.empirehotel.co.uk
dir: Follow signs to Promenade, turn right at war memorial & left at rdbt. Hotel 100yds on right

Owned and run by the Maddocks family for over 50 years, this grand Victorian hotel in the heart of Llandudno is a short walk from the promenade, pier and shops. Situated at the base of the Great Orme mountain, it is the ideal location for exploring the magnificent Snowdonia National Park and medieval castles nearby. In the Watkins & Co restaurant, crowd-pleasing old favourites might include a starter of brandy-flavoured chicken liver pâté with home-made apricot and onion marmalade, while mains range from deep-fried cod fillet in batter with mushy peas and tartare sauce to baked chicken breast stuffed with mushrooms and shallots in a smoked bacon and leek sauce with seasonal vegetables.

Empire Hotel

Chef Michael Waddy, Larry Mutisyo **Owner** Len & Elizabeth Maddocks **Times** 12.30-2/6.30-9.30 Closed 19-30 Dec, L Mon-Sat **Prices** Fixed D 4 course £20.75-£27.75, Service optional **Wines** 39 bottles over £20, 47 bottles under £20, 7 by glass **Notes** Sunday L, Vegetarian available, Dress restrictions, Smart casual **Seats** 110, Pr/dining room 18 **Children** Portions, Menu **Parking** 44, On street

Imperial Hotel

@ Modern, Traditional British

Contemporary cooking on the seafront

☎ 01492 877466
The Promenade LL30 1AP
e-mail: reception@theimperial.co.uk
dir: On the Promenade

Llandudno's Victorian seafront is a magnificent sight, and this grand traditional hotel smack on the esplanade stands out with a splendidly ornate stucco façade like a

continued

Bodysgallen Hall and Spa

LLANDUDNO Map 14 SH78

Modern V

Sumptuous dining in classic country-house setting

☎ 01492 584466
LL30 1RS
e-mail: info@bodysgallen.com
web: www.bodysgallen.com
dir: From A55 junct 19 follow A470 towards Llandudno

Set in 200 acres of parkland, parterres and rose gardens, Bodysgallen feels rooted into the landscape, master of all it surveys. And that, by the way, is a view to die for, sweeping all the way from Conwy Castle to Snowdonia, then across to the Isle of Anglesey, and the Great Orme. Inside, step back into a bygone era of dark oak panelling, antiques, oil paintings, and open fires. Obliging, on-the-ball and courteous service, plus a kitchen that deals in sophisticated cooking with modern and classic influences, complete the picture. Skilled French technique is brought to bear on superb Welsh produce, with a trademark lightness of touch that is apparent in a starter of hand-dived scallops with lobster and mango salsa, and cucumber tagliatelle. A sorbet - perhaps lemon and thyme - intervenes before a main course of roe deer and trompette mushroom boudin, served with caramelised cauliflower and truffle jus. Inventive desserts, along the lines of caramelised pineapple tart, teamed with kaffir lime leaf, green tea jelly and peppercorn ice cream come beautifully presented.

Chef Gareth Jones **Owner** The National Trust **Times** 12.30-1.45/7-9.30 Closed Mon (winter), D Sun (winter) **Prices** Food prices not confirmed for 2011. Please telephone for details **Wines** 100 bottles over £20, 30 bottles under £20, 8 by glass **Notes** Pre-theatre D available, Sunday L, Vegetarian menu, Dress restrictions, Smart casual, no trainers/T-shirts/tracksuits, Civ Wed 55 **Seats** 60, Pr/dining room 40 **Children** Portions **Parking** 40

LLANDUDNO *continued*

piece of Wedgwood pottery. When the weather plays ball, the terrace is a great place to dine with views across the bay, but for a more elegant experience - with the same views - Chantrey's Restaurant is the place to head for. The kitchen puts a modern spin on traditional classics based on top-class Welsh supplies. The seasonally-changing menu has a broad appeal: a pressed terrine of ham hock, seasonal vegetables and chestnut mushrooms with Bramley apple and thyme chutney makes a well-constructed opener, before a main event starring roast loin of Welsh lamb wrapped in mint mousse, served with ratatouille, buttered leeks and fondant potato.

Times 12.30-3/6.30-9.30

The Lilly Restaurant with Rooms

Modern British **NEW**

Ambitious cooking in coastal restaurant with rooms

☎ 01492 876513
West Pde LL30 2BD
e-mail: thelilly@live.co.uk
dir: Just off A546 at Llandudno

On Llandudno's seafront with views over the Great Orme and Conwy Estuary, The Lilly is a restaurant with rooms that offers a choice to suit your mood: a brasserie and a fine dining restaurant. The latter, with its dramatic black and white styling (black leather chairs, curtains and pelmets contrasting with white tablecloths and white walls and ceiling) serves up some good modern dishes based on carefully-sourced produce and with an eye for precise presentations. Service is by a friendly young team. Duck liver and foie gras parfait with home-made chutney and toasted brioche might start things off, before wild sea bass with oyster tortellini, quinoa and sweetcorn emulsion. Hot chocolate fondant with white chocolate pannacotta and milk chocolate ice cream is a typical dessert. The food is matched by a well-priced wine list.

Chef Phillip Ashe, Jonathon Goodman **Owner** Roxanne & Phillip Ashe **Times** 12-3/6-9 Closed Mon, L Tue-Sat, D Sun **Prices** Fixed L 2 course £21.95-£24.95, Starter £5.25-£9.25, Main £10.45-£29.95, Dessert £4.95-£6.95, Service included **Notes** Sunday L, Vegetarian available, Dress restrictions, Smart **Seats** 35 **Children** Portions, Menu

Osborne House

Modern British

Grand setting for all-day dining

☎ 01492 860330
17 North Pde LL30 2LP
e-mail: sales@osbornehouse.com
web: www.osbornehouse.co.uk
dir: A55 at junct 19, follow signs for Llandudno then Promenade, at War Memorial turn right, Osborne House on left opposite entrance to pier

Right on the promenade, this grand townhouse hotel offers all-day dining from an extensive menu. The interior is theatrical and ornate in style - large glass chandeliers, Roman pillars, huge imposing portraits and a vast number of mirrors certainly make a bold statement. In this environment you might not expect a bistro-style menu, but here it is, and it works a treat. The small kitchen team turn out modern British dishes on the all-day menu that truly satisfy, plus there's a set lunch and early bird menu. Expect the likes of a well-balanced mushroom and sage soup, simply griddled sea bass on a bed of couscous with an olive, tomato and anchovy dressing and creamed cabbage and bacon, and to finish, dark chocolate and toffee sponge.

Chef Michael Waddy, Tim McAll **Owner** Len & Elizabeth Maddocks **Times** 12-3/5-10 Closed 19-30 Dec **Prices** Fixed L 2 course £10.25, Fixed D 3 course £18.50, Starter £3.95-£7.70, Main £11.55-£17.60, Dessert £3.60-£4.55, Service optional, Groups min 12 service 10% **Wines** 17 bottles over £20, 24 bottles under £20, 6 by glass **Notes** Pre-theatre menu 5pm, Sunday L, Vegetarian available, Dress restrictions, Smart casual **Seats** 70, Pr/dining room 20 **Children** Portions **Parking** 6, On street

St Tudno Hotel and Restaurant

Modern French

Accomplished cuisine in elegant surroundings on the seafront promenade

☎ 01492 874411
The Promenade LL30 2LP
e-mail: sttudnohotel@btinternet.com
dir: In town centre, on Promenade, opposite pier entrance (near Great Orme)

This classic Victorian seaside hotel has been in the Bland family for 35 years, bringing a sense of tradition, stability and well-honed service to the operation. It has Llandudno's prime position, smack on the seafront looking over the Victorian pier and gardens towards the Great Orme. Inside, a genteel period feel prevails, except in the dainty Terrace restaurant, where Italian chandeliers hang from a tented ceiling above a soft-focus mural of Lake Como. The kitchen turns top-class Welsh produce into dishes with modern and traditional influences, as shown in starters such as St Tudno bouillabaisse with Orme lobster boudin, or pan-seared chicken livers with café au lait sauce and herb gnocchi. These may be followed by loin of roe deer with game pudding and truffled Welsh honey glaze, with a tonka bean and pistachio pannacotta with Toblerone ice cream to finish.

Chef Ian Watson **Owner** Mr Bland **Times** 12.30-2/7-9.30 **Prices** Fixed L 2 course £15, Starter £5.75-£7.50, Main £15.50-£19.95, Dessert £5.50-£7.50, Service optional **Wines** 154 bottles over £20, 18 bottles under £20, 12 by glass **Notes** Pre-theatre menu available, Sunday L, Vegetarian available, Dress restrictions, Smart casual, no shorts, tracksuits or jeans, Civ Wed 70 **Seats** 60 **Children** Portions, Menu **Parking** 9, On street

Terrace Restaurant, St George's Hotel

Modern, Traditional

Patriotic Welsh cooking in a grand seafront hotel

☎ 01492 877544 & 862184
The Promenade LL30 2LG
e-mail: info@stgeorgeswales.co.uk
web: www.stgeorgeswales.co.uk
dir: A55, exit at Glan Conwy for Llandudno. A470 follow signs for seafront (distinctive tower identifies hotel)

Despite some contemporary design touches, the St George's retains the feel of a traditional seafront hotel, occupying pride of place among a grand sweep of buildings overlooking the bay. Drink in those views from the Terrace Restaurant, where traceability and ethical production are the watchwords of the menu. Leek and saffron cawl with Conwy mussels and flaked haddock makes for an impressive, regionally-based first course, or there might be a pannacotta of Anglesey goats' cheese with pear and walnut salad in hemp oil dressing. Welsh lamb and beef are hard to ignore, the former served with parsnip purée and thyme sauce, the latter with béarnaise. Finish with sticky toffee pudding and Penderyn ice cream, or Welsh cheeses.

Times 12-2.30/6.30-9.30

DENBIGHSHIRE

LLANDEGLA — Map 15 SJ15

Bodidris Hall

Modern British

Modern cooking in a historic country-hotel setting

☎ 01978 790434
LL11 3AL
e-mail: reception@bodidrishall.com
dir: A483/A525 (Wrexham-Ruthin). Turn right onto A5104. Hotel signed 1m on left

Built in 1465 AD, this elegant and impressive former stately home oozes history from every mullion window and oak beam. Watch out for the sheep and pheasants meandering across your path as you head up the mile-long drive. As you reach the top, the lake with ducks and swans comes into view, and you may well spot a peacock or two strutting across the lawns. Once inside the hotel, you'll find plenty of original features, along with quality art and furnishings. In the baronial-style restaurant the daily-changing fixed-price modern British repertoire is driven by fresh local produce. Expect accurate cooking and clear flavours, as in brown shrimps in clarified butter with toasted brioche, rump of Welsh lamb with roasted root vegetables and reduced pan juices, and coconut and mandarin cheesecake with raspberry coulis.

Chef Brian Eccles, Gary Turnbull **Owner** Stephanie & David Booth **Times** 12-2/7-9 **Prices** Fixed L 2 course £15, Fixed D 3 course £24.95, Service optional **Wines** 24 bottles over £20, 11 bottles under £20, 6 by glass **Notes** Sunday L, Dress restrictions, Smart casual, Civ Wed 90 **Seats** 40, Pr/dining room 25 **Children** Portions **Parking** 50

RHYL — Map 14 SJ08

Barratt's at Ty'n Rhyl

Traditional French

Confident cooking in an historic house

☎ 01745 344138
Ty'n Rhyl, 167 Vale Rd LL18 2PH
e-mail: ebarratt5@aol.com
dir: From A55 take Rhyl exit onto A525. Continue past Rhuddlan Castle, supermarket, petrol station, 0.25m on right

Standing somewhat majestically in an acre of elegant gardens, this 16th-century building, the oldest house in Rhyl, was once home to the Welsh bard, Angharad Llwyd. These days it is an extremely comfortable family-run hotel done out in some style - traditional and elegant. You can eat in the Georgian dining room with its antique furniture and a roaring open fire for those cold winter nights, or opt for the large conservatory with its views over the pretty lawns. The menu changes with the ebb and flow of the local produce that comes to the door and the cooking focuses on letting the top-notch ingredients shine. Cream of mushroom and truffle soup is one opener, or there might be breast of wood pigeon in a blackberry sauce. Main-course sees fillets of bream and bass lightly roasted and dressed in a creamy dill sauce, and to finish, perhaps strawberry pancakes with a hot toffee sauce.

Chef David Barratt **Owner** David Barratt **Times** 12-2.30/7.30-9 Closed 26 Dec, 1 wk holiday **Prices** Fixed L 3 course £15-£20, Starter £7, Main £24, Dessert £6.50, Service optional **Wines** 3 bottles over £20, 18 bottles under £20, 4 by glass **Notes** Sunday L, Vegetarian available, Dress restrictions, Smart casual **Seats** 24, Pr/dining room 16 **Children** Portions **Parking** 20

RUTHIN — Map 15 SJ15

Bertie's @ Ruthin Castle

Modern British

Historic Welsh castle serving imaginative food

☎ 01824 702664
Castle St LL15 2NU
e-mail: reservations@ruthincastle.co.uk
web: www.ruthincastle.co.uk
dir: From town square take road towards Corwen for 100yds

Popular with Edward VII when he was Prince of Wales, this romantic retreat is a perfect foil for flavoursome modern British cooking. It's Victorian in style, although the original ruthin (or red fort) was built in the 13th century before being redone in the 1820s. Bertie's is sumptuously furnished with deep comfortable seating, crisp napery and magnificent chandeliers. Views over the lawns make for a romantic setting. Seared breast of guinea fowl with a cassoulet sauce and Toulouse sausage is a fine start before fillet of sea bream with a Thai green broth and tempura baby veg. Finish with an intriguing Ruthin Castle five sorbet terrine. If medieval banquets are your thing, note they are held in the medieval banquet hall.

Times 12.30-2/7-9.30

ST ASAPH Map 15 SJ07

The Oriel

Modern British

Good food in tranquil surroundings

01745 582716
Upper Denbigh Rd LL17 0LW
e-mail: reservations@orielhousehotel.com
dir: A55 onto A525, left at cathedral, 1m on right

Just a gentle stroll from St Asaph, The Oriel is a charmingly done-out country-house hotel in peaceful, picturesque North Wales countryside. It's popular for weddings and can sort you out for all your pampering requirements, too. The Terrace Restaurant is also part of the appeal, with its unbuttoned, Mediterranean feel - tiled floors, neutral tones on the walls, high-backed wicker chairs and, of course, a large terrace for when the Welsh sun shines. Cooking is simple, effectively so, using regional ingredients to create accurate, flavoursome dishes that suit the Med leanings of the space. Start with tempura salmon with beetroot and goats' cheese salad before moving on to roast duck breast with confit leg and wilted bok choy, crispy sweet potato and cumin-scented caramel, with vanilla and raspberry pannacotta with walnut ice cream an appropriately sunny finale.

Chef Salvatore Tassiari **Owner** Gary Seddon **Times** 12-9.30 **Prices** Fixed L 2 course fr £19.95, Fixed D 3 course fr £27.95, Service included **Wines** 37 bottles over £20, 17 bottles under £20, 6 by glass **Notes** Sunday L, Vegetarian available, Dress restrictions, Smart casual, Civ Wed 220 **Seats** 30, Pr/dining room 240 **Children** Portions **Parking** 100

GWYNEDD

ABERSOCH Map 14 SH32

Neigwl Hotel

British, European

Unshowy cooking in a family hotel by Cardigan Bay

01758 712363
Lon Sarn Bach LL53 7DY
e-mail: relax@neigwl.com
dir: on A499, through Abersoch, hotel on left

With seductive views over Cardigan Bay and the islands of St Tudwalls, the Neigwl is a family-run hotel in picturesque North Wales. It's the kind of place that feels like a home from home, where the kids are welcome, and the cooking doesn't try to make an undue show of itself. The house speciality fish soup is worth a go, though, as a prelude perhaps to grilled fillet steak with peppercorn sauce, or duck breast with classic orange sauce. Give the kitchen 24 hours' notice, and you could just find yourself living it up with a whole lobster Thermidor.

Chef J David, J Smith **Owner** Mark Gauci & Susan Turner **Times** 7-9 Closed Jan, L all week **Prices** Food prices not confirmed for 2011. Please telephone for details **Wines** 7 bottles over £20, 16 bottles under £20, 5 by glass **Notes** Vegetarian available, Dress restrictions, Smart casual **Seats** 40 **Children** Portions, Menu **Parking** 30

Porth Tocyn Hotel

Modern, Traditional NOTABLE WINE LIST

Classic country-house hotel with excellent cooking

01758 713303
Bwlch Tocyn LL53 7BU
e-mail: bookings@porthtocyn.fsnet.co.uk
web: www.porthtocynhotel.co.uk
dir: 2m S of Abersoch, through Sarn Bach & Bwlch Tocyn. Follow brown signs

This archetypal country hotel has been in the same family for over 60 years and as the business has gently evolved over that time, one thing has never changed - the stunning views of the North Wales coastline. There's a refreshing lack of stuffiness here, with the staff genuine in their desire to make the place a home-from-home for their guests. Inside is a pleasing mix of traditional charm and contemporary comfort. The kitchen also reflects this lack of stuffiness, using local, seasonal produce to create British food which combines traditional values with some modern sensibilities. A first-course confit salmon and crab tian with pickled cucumber and sorrel oil might precede pan-fried pork fillet with champ potato, blue cheese fritter, baby vegetables and a Calvados jus. Warm croissant-and-butter pudding with marmalade glaze and mascarpone cream is an indulgent finale. The wine list is particularly well put together.

Chef L Fletcher-Brewer, J Bell, M Green **Owner** The Fletcher-Brewer Family **Times** 12.15-2/7.30-9 Closed mid Nov, 2 wks before Etr, L Mon-Sat **Prices** Fixed L 3 course £41, Fixed D 3 course £41, Service included **Wines** 63 bottles over £20, 37 bottles under £20, 4 by glass **Notes** Sunday L, Vegetarian available, Dress restrictions, Smart casual preferred **Seats** 50 **Children** Portions

BARMOUTH Map 14 SH61

Bae Abermaw

Modern British

Contemporary cooking in hotel with sea views

01341 280550
Panorama Rd LL42 1DQ
e-mail: enquiries@baeabermaw.com
web: www.baeabermaw.com
dir: From Barmouth centre towards Dolgellau on A496, 0.5m past garage turn left into Panorama Rd, restaurant 100yds

Occupying an enviable spot high above Cardigan Bay and right on the edge of the Snowdonia National Park, Bae Abermaw is an impressive Victorian house which has been completely restored to its original splendour. It may have a dark stone façade, but inside it's bright and contemporary, with wooden floors, fresh white walls, exposed brickwork, marble and slate fireplaces and modern art prints helping to create a vibrant and warm ambience. In the restaurant, French doors open on to the landscaped garden, and top-notch local produce is put to good use in a modern British repertoire which might include toasted peppered Pant-Ysgawn goats' cheese salad with roasted cherry tomatoes and fresh basil pesto, and roast rack of Meirionnydd mountain lamb with garlic scented potatoes and rosemary jus.

Chef Jackie Foster, Chris Wright **Owner** Suzi & David Reeve **Times** 7-9 Closed L all week (ex parties of 10+ pre booked) **Prices** Starter £5.25-£5.95, Main £12.50-£17.95, Dessert £5.25-£6.50, Service optional **Wines** 19 bottles over £20, 24 bottles under £20, 7 by glass **Notes** Sunday L, Vegetarian available, Dress restrictions, Smart casual, Civ Wed 100 **Seats** 28, Pr/dining room 80 **Children** Portions, Menu **Parking** 40

CAERNARFON Map 14 SH46

Rhiwafallen Restaurant with Rooms

Modern British

Sympathetically renovated farmhouse and local seasonal food

01286 830172
Rhiwafallen, Llandwrog LL54 5SW
e-mail: robandkate@rhiwafallen.co.uk
dir: A487 from Caernarfon, A499 restaurant 1m on left

This family-run converted Welsh farmhouse has been renovated in boutique style and serves up locally-sourced ingredients cooked with flair. Set in a particularly attractive part of north west Wales close to the Snowdonia National Park and the Coast of the Llyn Peninsula, Rhiwafallen provides a lovely base to explore the dramatic surroundings. Chef-Patron Rob and his wife Kate are effortlessly hospitable, having run the show for 20 years. The contemporary conservatory restaurant is intimate and features original modern art on the walls, pale wooden tables and richly upholstered chairs. Local fish, meat, fruit and vegetables take centre stage on the concise seasonally-changing dinner menu, offering the likes of carpaccio of local buffalo with pecorino, crushed black pepper, rocket and virgin olive oil, and grilled breast of guinea fowl with sautéed wild mushroom spätzle and tarragon cappuccino sauce. To finish, try the eggy bara brith with roasted nectarines and cinnamon ice cream.

Times 12.30-7 Closed 25-26 Dec, 1-2 Jan, Mon, L Tue-Sat, D Sun

Seiont Manor Hotel

Modern British V

Culinary hideaway in Snowdonia

☎ 01286 673366
Llanrug LL55 2AQ
e-mail: seiontmanor@handpicked.co.uk
dir: From Bangor follow signs for Caernarfon. Leave Caernarfon on A4086. Hotel 3m on left

Developed from the farmstead of a Georgian manor, this tranquil, sensitively refurbished hotel stands in 150 acres of parkland close to Snowdonia and the Isle of Anglesey. Public rooms, including a traditional oak-panelled bar, ooze period charm and character, with stone slab floors and exposed brickwork combining with modern fabrics and subtle decorative techniques to create an upmarket, contemporary feel throughout. High-backed leather chairs, modern artwork on crisp white walls, fresh flowers and gleaming tableware set the scene for sound classical cooking from a skilled kitchen with a good understanding of flavours. Food is fresh, honest and traditional with an emphasis on regional dishes and locally-sourced produce. Typically, tuck into seared scallops with pea purée, nutmeg foam and crispy pancetta for starters, move on to chargrilled chicken with cumin cabbage, butternut squash and red wine reduction, and finish with a delicious creamy rice pudding served with a chilled fruit broth.

Chef Martyn Williams **Owner** Hand Picked Hotels **Times** 12-2/7-9.30 **Prices** Fixed D 3 course £29.50, Starter £6.25-£8.95, Main £17.50-£25.95, Dessert £6.95-£8.95, Service optional **Wines** 104 bottles over £20, 2 bottles under £20, 18 by glass **Notes** Sunday L, Vegetarian menu, Dress restrictions, Smart casual, Civ Wed 100 **Seats** 55, Pr/dining room 30 **Children** Portions, Menu **Parking** 60

CRICCIETH Map 14 SH53

Bron Eifion Country House Hotel

Modern British

Elegant country-house hotel in stunning setting

☎ 01766 522385
LL52 0SA
e-mail: enquiries@broneifion.co.uk
dir: A497, between Porthmadog & Pwllheli

A fine example of the Victorian country house, Bron Eifion was built to benefit from beautiful views over the coastline, and it stands just outside the Snowdonia National Park. The modern day incarnation sees original features in abundance and an elegance in the furnishing which is entirely in keeping. The Great Hall impresses with its minstrels' gallery - a splendid setting for a pre-dinner drink - and the Orangery Restaurant delivers modern British cooking alongside panoramic views. Local produce gets a good showing on a menu that delivers a trio of smoked fish (salmon, mackerel and trout) dressed with anchovies, capers and lemon, followed by Welsh Black beef with Perl Las (a Welsh blue cheese), dauphinoise potatoes and a rich port and thyme reduction. The service is well organised.

Chef Matthew Philips **Owner** John & Mary Heenan **Times** 12-2/6.30-9 **Prices** Fixed L 3 course £18.95, Fixed D 3 course £30, Service included **Notes** Gourmand menu 8 course £55, Sunday L, Vegetarian available, Dress restrictions, No jeans, T-shirts, Civ Wed 50 **Seats** 50, Pr/dining room 16 **Children** Portions, Menu **Parking** 50

DOLGELLAU Map 14 SH71

Dolserau Hall Hotel

Traditional

Country-house cooking with a local flavour

☎ 01341 422522
LL40 2AG
e-mail: welcome@dolserau.co.uk
dir: 1.5m from Dolgellau on unclassified road between A470/A494 to Bala

A converted Victorian mansion set in five acres of attractive grounds deep in the Snowdonia National Park is the setting for the Winter Garden Restaurant. A conservatory-style dining room, it is attractively decorated in red and gold and enjoys stunning views of Snowdonia. The daily-changing menu focuses on local and seasonal meat, fruit and vegetables, and fish from a private fleet in Anglesey. Chicken liver parfait with sweetcorn relish might precede pheasant with a rich tomato and red wine sauce, or Dover sole with spring vegetables. Finish with Amaretto and dark chocolate mousse.

Times 7-9 Closed Nov-Feb, L all week

Penmaenuchaf Hall Hotel

Modern British

Conservatory dining against a Snowdonia backdrop

☎ 01341 422129
Penmaenpool LL40 1YB
e-mail: relax@penhall.co.uk
dir: From A470 take A493 (Tywyn/Fairbourne), entrance 1.5m on left by sign for Penmaenpool

The Hall is a solid greystone mansion built in the 1860s and set in 21 landscaped and wooded acres. It looks out over lush, undulating countryside, with the mountains of Snowdonia in the background. Dining takes place in a conservatory room with a Welsh slate floor and quality table settings, and there is a terrace area for summer days. Enthusiastic use is made of pedigree Welsh produce, from the Nant Hir pork belly with caramelised apple starter, to Bala spring lamb sauced in redcurrants and port that comes with root veg baked under parmesan. Fish might be Aberdovey grey mullet with creamed leeks in red wine, and meals end with the likes of variations on lemon (chiboust, tart and sorbet) or great Welsh farmhouse cheeses.

Chef J Pilkington, T Reeve **Owner** Mark Watson, Lorraine Fielding **Times** 12-2/7-9.30 **Prices** Fixed L 2 course fr £15.95, Fixed D 4 course fr £40, Starter £8.50-£9.50, Main £22-£26, Dessert £8.50-£9.50, Service optional **Wines** 123 bottles over £20, 33 bottles under £20, 6 by glass **Notes** Sunday L, Vegetarian available, Dress restrictions, Smart casual, no jeans or T-shirts, Civ Wed 50 **Seats** 36, Pr/dining room 16 **Children** Portions **Parking** 36

PORTHMADOG Map 14 SH53

Royal Sportsman Hotel

British NEW

Friendly hotel with interesting menu of modern Welsh dishes

☎ 01766 512015
131 High St LL49 9HB
e-mail: enquiries@royalsportsman.co.uk
dir: Near junct of A497 & A487

This Victorian coaching hotel in the bucket-and-spade resort of Porthmadog has had a full makeover in recent years and has won many fans - including a certain Bill Bryson - who appreciate the sincerely friendly staff and the great food in the smartly-restored restaurant overlooking the patio garden. A skilled kitchen team brings an arsenal of multinational influences to bear on top-grade Welsh produce, so expect an eclectic menu that ranges from good honest Sunday roasts to a modern British repertoire. Scallops are served with sorrel, black pudding, chilli tomato, coriander cress and saffron foam to start, followed by, perhaps, Asian influences in a dish of organic sea trout with basil crushed potatoes, wilted spinach, and lemongrass and coconut cream.

continued

PORTHMADOG *continued*

Chef Felix Prem, Dylan Williams, Ryan Agnew, Stefan Draghici **Owner** L Naudi **Times** 12-2.30/6-9 **Prices** Fixed L 2 course £10-£12, Fixed D 3 course £30, Starter £4.95-£8, Main £12.95-£21.95, Dessert £5.95-£6.25 **Wines** 5 bottles over £20, 20 bottles under £20, 8 by glass **Notes** Sunday L, Vegetarian available, Dress restrictions, Smart casual **Seats** 60 **Children** Portions, Menu **Parking** 17, On street

PORTMEIRION **Map 14 SH53**

Castell Deudraeth

Modern Welsh

Stylish dining in the North Wales fantasy village

☎ 01766 772400
LL48 6ER
e-mail: castell@portmeirion-village.com
dir: Off A487 at Minffordd. Between Porthmadog & Penryndeudraeth

This pocket-sized Gothic castle is a classic piece of Victorian folly sitting happily alongside the Italianate fantasy village of Portmeirion. While Castell Deudraeth could easily star in a '60s Hammer Horror film, the shock comes once you're inside; forget any notions involving suits of armour and medieval banqueting – the interior designers have pulled off a seriously stylish modern look involving textures of Welsh oak and slate, pine tables and blue leather high-backed chairs in the chic brasserie-style restaurant. The kitchen gardens supply much of the veg, while the local hillsides and the waters of the Lleyn Peninsula and the Menai Straits take care of meat and seafood for a relaunched gastro-pub-style menu. Scallops turn up on a bed of creamy mushroom risotto in an unfussy opener, ahead of a meaty main course of braised belly pork teamed with a ham hock croquette, Swiss chard, and bacon and onion sauce. Unlike Patrick McGoohan in *The Prisoner*, no-one feels like a number here these days, thanks to smiling, clued-up staff.

Times 12-2.30/6.30-9.30

Hotel Portmeirion

Modern Welsh

Stunning, unique setting for imaginative cooking

☎ 01766 770000 & 772440
LL48 6ET
e-mail: hotel@portmeirion-village.com
dir: Off A487 at Minffordd

Sir Clough Williams-Ellis's fairytale Italianate village on a secluded peninsula was created in the 1920s and the beautifully restored hotel, based on an early-Victorian villa, lies beneath its wooded slopes in a haven of tranquility. Close to the shore, looking out over the sandy estuary towards Snowdonia, it contains some stunning rooms, all filled with fine art, antiques and memorabilia. The splendid, light, spacious, curvilinear dining room enjoys fine vistas over the estuary and provides a romantic setting in which to savour some accomplished modern Welsh cooking based on wonderful local produce, in particular fresh fish. Handled with flair and care, full-flavoured dishes on the daily bi-lingual menu may take in juicy scallops with belly pork and a trio of cauliflower, served on eye-catching Welsh slate, followed by venison with blackcurrant and sloe gin jus, and white chocolate soufflé to round things off. The mainly Welsh-speaking staff are warm, hospitable and efficient.

Times 12-2.30/6.30-9 Closed 11-22 Jan

PWLLHELI **Map 14 SH33**

Plas Bodegroes

Modern British

Elegant restaurant with rooms with intelligent, confident cooking

☎ 01758 612363
Nefyn Rd LL53 5TH
e-mail: gunna@bodegroes.co.uk
dir: On A497, 1m W of Pwllheli

A Georgian manor house of distinction standing in its own secluded grounds in an Area of Outstanding Natural Beauty, Plas Bodegroes is on to a winner from the off. The wild and rugged Llyn Peninsula, a mile from the sandy beaches, is only part of the attraction, though – it is Chris Chown's cooking that put Plas Bodegroes on the map. The beautifully restored restaurant with rooms has a contemporary décor that suits the feel of the house and is enhanced with original art by local artists. Crisp linen-draped tables and a polished wooden floor add to the feeling that this is a restaurant where the finer points are important, down to the knowledgeable and personable service. The kitchen takes advantage of excellent local produce in well judged and intelligently balanced dishes. Start with pan-fried local quail breast with a confit of its leg, black pudding and a fried quail's egg, followed, perhaps, by a roast rump of Llyn lamb with devilled kidneys, potato gratin and rosemary jus, with plum and almond tart with cardamom ice cream to finish.

Chef Chris Chown, Aled Williams & Hugh Bracegirdle **Owner** Mrs G Chown & Chris Chown **Times** 12.30-2.30/7-9.30 Closed Dec-Feb, Mon, L Tue-Sat, D Sun **Prices** Fixed D 4 course fr £42.50, Service optional **Wines** 261 bottles over £20, 72 bottles under £20, 8 by glass **Notes** Sunday L, Vegetarian available **Seats** 40, Pr/dining room 24 **Parking** 20

MONMOUTHSHIRE

ABERGAVENNY **Map 9 SO21**

Angel Hotel

Modern British, European

Popular venue with confident brasserie-style menu

☎ 01873 857121
15 Cross St NP7 5EN
e-mail: mail@angelhotelabergavenny.com
dir: Follow town centre signs from rdbt, S of Abergavenny, past rail & bus stations. Turn left by hotel

The Angel is a handsome dove-grey Georgian coaching inn, refurbished to offer modern travellers a haven of chintz-free contemporary style. Inside, the vibe is convivial and relaxed in the bar, which is rather a social hub in Abergavenny. The region has become something of a gastronomic destination in recent years, thanks, in part, to its own annual food festival showcasing the endeavours of local producers. Plenty of top-class materials at hand, then, for the kitchen's modern European, brasserie-style cooking. The menu has broad appeal, taking in starters such as Black Mountain smoked salmon or smoked haddock, horseradish and potato cake with tartare sauce, and roast herb-crusted cod on tagliatelle with spinach and cream sauce from the fish and shellfish section. Welsh lamb comes simply with green beans and potato gratin. Afternoon tea is a bit of a speciality, too.

Chef Mark Turton **Owner** Caradog Hotels Ltd **Times** 12-2.30/7-10 Closed 25 Dec, D 24-26 Dec **Prices** Starter £5.40-£9.20, Main £9.80-£25, Dessert £4.80-£5.80, Service optional **Wines** 64 bottles over £20, 18 bottles under £20, 8 by glass **Notes** Sunday L, Vegetarian available, Civ Wed 200 **Seats** 80, Pr/dining room 120 **Children** Portions, Menu **Parking** 40

The Foxhunter

Modern British NOTABLE WINE LIST

Carefully-sourced ingredients cooked with flair

☎ 01873 881101
Nantyderry NP7 9DN
e-mail: info@thefoxhunter.com
dir: Just off A4042 between Usk & Abergavenny

Built as a stationmaster's house, and having served time as a pub, The Foxhunter, in a quiet little hamlet on the edge of the Brecon Beacons, is these days in the hands of Matt and Lisa Tebbutt. Matt's pedigree as a chef goes back to stints with Marco Pierre White and Alastair Little, and in recent years he's become a regular on TV. A touch of 21st-century style and comfort complements the charms of the Welsh flagged floors and wood-burning stoves, and amiable service brings a smile to the face. At the heart of things is a passion for local produce and a desire to keep things relatively simple, alongside keen technical skills. This modern British sensibility sees pan-fried ox tongue invigorated by pickled beetroot and a horseradish and thyme cream, and a haunch of Brecon venison paired with sweet braised red cabbage and sautéed wood blewits. The menu changes twice a day and the excellent wine list embraces both Old and New Worlds.

Chef Matt Tebbutt **Owner** Lisa & Matt Tebbutt **Times** 12-2.30/7-9.30 Closed Xmas, 1 Jan, Mon (exceptions apply), D Sun **Prices** Fixed L 2 course £18.95, Starter £6.95-£9.95, Main £12.95-£20.95, Dessert £6.95-£8.95, Service optional, Groups min 8 service 10% **Wines** 50 bottles over £20, 26 bottles under £20, 5 by glass **Notes** Sunday L, Vegetarian available **Seats** 50, Pr/dining room 30 **Children** Portions **Parking** 25

RESTAURANT OF THE YEAR

The Hardwick

Modern British

Top British food from a top British chef

☎ 01873 854220
Old Raglan Rd NP7 9AA
e-mail: info@thehardwick.co.uk

The setting, in an old country pub on a main road close to Abergavenny, is pleasant enough, but what lies within is a bit special, definitely worthy of a detour. This is down to chef-proprietor Stephen Terry. He's a man with over 20 years cooking experience under his belt and a CV that reads like a dream (from Marco Pierre White's Harveys and the Canteen in London to the nearby Walnut Tree in Abergavenny, with plenty of sexy foreign stages in-between), so you know you're in safe hands. There's nothing flashy about the interior - bare wooden tables and chairs confirm its country pub status. As we go to print the dining room and bar are being extended with eight bedrooms added. Making excellent use of high quality local produce, the daily-changing menu of rustic modern British grub shows some Italian influences and offers a remarkable choice given the high quality. To start, how about a generous portion of house-cured salt duck breast with Italian stem and globe artichokes, fontina and rocket? Main course might bring forth a hot raised venison pie with mashed potato, organic carrots and cavolo nero, or a superb piece of pan-fried organic Shetland salmon, served with a Black Mountain smoked salmon and fennel risotto cake. This is rustic, honest, compelling British cooking. 'Terry's orange chocolate Italian leafy orange fool and curd with Amedei chocolate and an orange polenta biscuit' makes an engaging finish. Customers feel well cared for here even if they forego Terry's food for a liquid lunch.

Chef Stephen Terry **Owner** Stephen Terry **Times** 12-3/6.30-10 Closed 3-16 Jan **Prices** Fixed L 2 course £18.50-£19.50, Starter £7-£14, Main £13-£25, Dessert £6-£8 **Notes** Sunday L, Vegetarian available **Seats** 100, Pr/dining room 30 **Children** Portions, Menu **Parking** 30

Llansantffraed Court Hotel

Modern British NOTABLE WINE LIST

Good views and accomplished cooking in elegant country-house hotel

☎ 01873 840678
Old Raglan Rd, Llanvihangel Gobion, Clytha NP7 9BA
e-mail: reception@llch.co.uk
dir: M4 junct 24/A449 to Raglan. At rdbt take last exit to Clytha. Hotel on right in 4.5m

Set against a breathtaking backdrop of the Brecon Beacons, this elegant neo-classical Georgian house stands in 20 acres of landscaped grounds between Abergavenny and Raglan on the fringe of the Usk Valley. An impressive foyer with arched ceilings leads to relaxing, sumptuous lounges and roaring log fires, which set the requisite country-house tone. The beamed Court Restaurant, located in the oldest part of this Grade II listed former mansion, has recently been refurbished in a light contemporary style. The modern British menu comprises classical dishes with unfussy, modern presentation, based on high-quality local produce. Daily menus may highlight tortellini of scallops and basil with warm tomato presse and scallop tartare, followed by Bwlch Farm venison with cranberry compôte, spiced gnocchi and venison faggot, and bitter chocolate tart with fudge ice cream and vanilla syrup. There's a very good wine list, too. The south-facing terrace is just the ticket for alfresco dining in summer.

Chef Steve Bennett **Owner** Mike Morgan **Times** 12-2/7-9 **Prices** Fixed L 2 course £14.50, Fixed D 4 course £29.50, Starter £5.50-£9.50, Main £16.50-£22, Dessert £6-£9, Service optional **Wines** 94 bottles over £20, 21 bottles under £20, 94 by glass **Notes** Tasting menu with matched wines, Sunday L, Vegetarian available, Civ Wed 150 **Seats** 50, Pr/dining room 35 **Children** Portions, Menu **Parking** 300

Restaurant 1861

Modern British

Country setting for relaxed modern fine dining

☎ 0845 388 1861
Cross Ash NP7 8PB
web: www.18-61.co.uk
dir: On B4521, 9m from Abergavenny, 15m from Ross-on-Wye, on outskirts of Cross Ash

In the small hamlet of Cross Ash, not far from Abergavenny, surrounded by a white-picket fence, is Simon and Kate King's restaurant, a serious addition to the regional dining scene. The Victorian building - 1861, of course - was a pub in a former life, but has been transformed into a comfortably rustic restaurant, with a small reception lounge containing comfortable sofas and a dining area with exposed beams and stonework. It's an unpretentious setting with bare-wood tables and a lack of fuss all round, and the food is similarly focused, revealing Simon's classical training and allowing the top quality local and regional produce to shine. That's not to say the food is unsophisticated, far from it, as revealed by a classy amuse-bouche of pork terrine with pickles, first-class bread presented as a mini loaf, and a pre-dessert chilled soup (apple and cinnamon, perhaps). First-course seared scallops are top quality, served up with celeriac purée and chicken juices, while main-course roast cod is partnered with a dazzling champagne and parsley sauce.

Chef Simon King **Owner** Simon & Kate King **Times** 12-2/7-9 Closed 1st 2 wks Jan, Mon, D Sun **Prices** Fixed L 2 course fr £18, Fixed D 3 course fr £32, Starter £7-£12.50, Main £16.50-£22, Dessert £6.50-£8, Service optional **Wines** 44 bottles over £20, 11 bottles under £20, 9 by glass **Notes** Tasting menu 7 course, Sunday L, Vegetarian available **Seats** 32 **Children** Portions **Parking** 20

Walnut Tree Inn

– see page 556

Walnut Tree Inn

ABERGAVENNY Map 9 SO21

Modern British NOTABLE WINE LIST

Shaun Hill working his magic near Abergavenny

☎ 01873 852797
Llandewi Skirrid NP7 8AW
e-mail: mail@thewalnuttreeinn.com
web: www.thewalnuttreeinn.com
dir: 3m NE of Abergavenny on B4521

This once again iconic restaurant in a lovely hamlet near food haven Abergavenny in Wales, is lucky enough to have Shaun Hill, the similarly revered chef, at its helm. While Hill was cooking his socks off solo at Ludlow's Merchant House from 1994 to 2005, the Walnut Tree was enjoying the end of a 30-year long golden period under founders Franco and Ann Taruschio, before hitting hard times and going into receivership under new owners. Hill and the Walnut Tree have proved to be a match made in heaven. Off a B road close to the Black Mountains, the simple décor with lots of white and wood is the perfect foil for Hill's confidently unpretentious food. Around 20 tables are serviced by a friendly bunch, with no hovering or constant wine topping up going on. Hill and his team of chefs focus on quality ingredients, seasonally sourced, on the daily-changing menu. Food geeks might spot a couple of signature dishes from Merchant House on the menu (samloi – Hungary's version of trifle with apricots, walnuts and rum, for instance) and the style of food is certainly based on the same principles of careful shopping and sound cooking skills. You might find a starter of monkfish with mustard and cucumber, a main of saddle of hare with roasted salsify and celeriac purée or iced nougat parfait with mango for pudding.

Chef Shaun Hill **Owner** Shaun Hill, William Griffiths **Times** 12-2.30/7-10 Closed Sun-Mon **Prices** Fixed L 2 course £17.50, Starter £7-£12, Main £14-£25 **Wines** 65 bottles over £20, 8 bottles under £20, 8 by glass **Notes** Vegetarian available **Seats** 70, Pr/dining room 26 **Children** Portions, Menu **Parking** 30

RAGLAN Map 9 SO40

The Beaufort Arms Coaching Inn & Brasserie

Modern British

Historic Welsh Marches inn with modern style and food to match

01291 690412
High St NP15 2DY
e-mail: enquiries@beaufortraglan.co.uk
dir: M4 junct 24 (Newport/Abergavenny), north on A449 to junct with A40, 1 min from turning to Abergavenny

The Beaufort Arms has been rooted in to Raglan village life for 400 years. Roundhead soldiers took time out from besieging medieval Raglan castle to drop into the Beaufort for a pint, and Prime Ministers have stayed while fishing the Wye and the Usk. Hands-on owners have given the venerable building a stylish modern facelift, but without sacrificing an ounce of the character in its slate floors, ancient beams and wood panelling; locals reckon that the grand stone fireplace in the lounge was 'recycled' from the castle. Modish shades of coffee and claret in the airy Brasserie restaurant set just the right tone to go with the kitchen's skilful modern British cooking. Crispy Thai fishcakes with fresh chilli jam and green leaves might start things off, followed by sea bass fillets with red mullet broth and sticky Thai rice.

Chef Colin Saunders, Paul Webber **Owner** Eliot & Jana Lewis **Times** 12-3/6-10 Closed 25 Dec **Prices** Starter £4.75-£7.50, Main £8.95-£16.50, Dessert £5-£5.95, Service optional **Wines** 10 bottles over £20, 25 bottles under £20, 12 by glass **Notes** Sunday L, Vegetarian available **Seats** 60, Pr/dining room 26 **Children** Menu **Parking** 30

ROCKFIELD Map 9 SO41

The Stonemill & Steppes Farm Cottages

British, French

Confident cooking in a converted 16th-century mill

01600 716273
NP25 5SW
e-mail: enquiries@thestonemill.co.uk
dir: A48 to Monmouth, B4233 to Rockfield. 2.6m from Monmouth town centre

A beautifully converted barn in a 16th-century mill complex with self-catering/bed and breakfast cottages, just a few miles west of Monmouth, provides the impressive setting for some good modern British cooking. Inside it's a riot of oak beams and vaulted ceilings, with chunky rustic tables around an ancient stone cider press. The kitchen's modern approach makes sound use of fresh regional and Welsh ingredients and wholesome dishes are accurately cooked and simply presented. Flavours shine through in dishes such as grilled sardines on home-made focaccia bread with roasted cherry tomatoes and salsa verde, and a moist and succulent breast of local pigeon served with braised red cabbage and sautéed potatoes. Round off with a classic white rum crème brûlée with crisp almond biscotti.

Chef Carl Hammett, Richard Bryan **Owner** Mrs M L Decloedt **Times** 12-2/6-9 Closed 25-26 Dec, 2 wks Jan, Mon, D Sun **Prices** Fixed L 2 course fr £12.95, Fixed D 3 course fr £18.95, Starter £4.95-£8.50, Main £14.95-£23.50, Dessert fr £5.95, Service optional **Wines** 15 bottles over £20, 28 bottles under £20, 8 by glass **Notes** Sunday L, Vegetarian available, Civ Wed 60 **Seats** 56, Pr/dining room 12 **Children** Portions **Parking** 40

SKENFRITH Map 9 SO42

The Bell at Skenfrith

Modern British NOTABLE WINE LIST

Restaurant with rooms and all-round appeal

01600 750235
NP7 8UH
e-mail: enquiries@skenfrith.co.uk
dir: N of Monmouth on A466 for 4m. Left on B4521 towards Abergavenny, 3m on left

Impressive on many counts, this lovingly refurbished 17th-century former coaching inn stands by the bridge spanning the River Monnow, just a stone's throw from the imposing ruins of Skenfrith Castle. It oozes sophisticated charm with Welsh slate floors, oak settles and original oak beams blending effortlessly with deep sumptuous sofas and beautiful fabrics in the stylish interior. Seasonally-changing menus are built around local ingredients (note the blackboard list of suppliers) and freshly harvested produce from the inn's organic kitchen garden. Accomplished cooking from an experienced team displays good technical skill. Well-presented dishes may include seared pigeon breast with caramelised figs, red wine and balsamic reduction, followed by Brecon beef fillet with steak-and-kidney pudding, horseradish bubble-and-squeak and beef jus, with toffee soufflé served with caramelised banana and brown bread ice cream making a grand finale. A large walk-in wine cellar and award-winning wine list completes the picture.

Chef Rupert Taylor **Owner** Mr & Mrs W Hutchings **Times** 12-2.30/7-9.30 Closed last wk Jan, 1st wk Feb, Tue (Nov-Mar) **Prices** Starter £5.50-£9.50, Main £14.50-£18.50, Dessert £6.50, Service optional **Wines** 254 bottles over £20, 34 bottles under £20, 14 by glass **Notes** Sunday L, Vegetarian available, Dress restrictions, Smart casual **Seats** 60, Pr/dining room 40 **Children** Portions, Menu **Parking** 35

USK Map 9 SO30

The Newbridge

Modern British

Good local produce in a riverside country inn

01633 451000
Tredunnock NP15 1LY
e-mail: thenewbridge@tinyonline.co.uk
dir: A449 to Usk exit through town & turn left after bridge through Llangiby. After approx 1m Cwrt Bleddyn Hotel is on the right, turn left opposite hotel. Drive through village of Tredunnock, down hill, inn on banks of River Usk

The Newbridge is a modern reinvention of a classic country inn set beside an ancient stone bridge on the banks of the River Usk. The place has gone all gastro with its country chic interior, and there are six stylish bedrooms to allow you to make the most of its easy-going vibe and put the kitchen through its paces. When the weather is fine you can eat alfresco on riverside tables and soak up views of the valley, since that is where a goodly proportion of the local game, fish and meat are sourced from. The kitchen cooks in a classic modern gastro-pub idiom, producing unfussy dishes such as parmesan risotto with braised pork belly and Madeira jus, followed by local lamb with polenta cake, white beans, braised spinach and red wine sauce.

Times 12-6/7-10

Raglan Arms

Modern British

Unpretentious atmosphere and good, honest food

01291 690800
Llandenny NP15 1DL
e-mail: raglanarms@aol.com
dir: M4 junct 26. Turn off A449 towards Usk, then immediately right towards Llandenny

Transformed from a traditional boozer to an upmarket dining pub in recent years, you'll find this flint-built local in a sleepy village deep in Monmouthshire farming country. If you prefer a pubby vibe, seat yourself in the bar, where well-kept ales are on tap, otherwise most activity centres on the conservatory extension. There's a clear Gallic flavour to the modern British dishes; the menu mixes old favourites with inventive options, and daily blackboard specials take advantage of the seasons. Expect unaffected presentation and sound, clean flavours. Start with red asparagus with morcilla salad and fried duck egg, followed by rump of Welsh lamb with baked aubergines and lamb kofta, then dark chocolate and raspberry delice with malt mousse.

Times 12-2.30/7-9.30 Closed 25-26 Dec & BHs, Mon, D Sun

USK *continued*

Three Salmons Hotel

Modern Welsh NEW

Unpretentious cooking with a clear Welsh accent

☎ 01291 672133
Bridge St NP15 1RY
e-mail: salmonshotel@aol.com
dir: M4 junct 24/A449, 1st exit signed Usk. On entering town hotel on main road

New owners took over this 17th-century coaching inn on the pretty town of Usk's central square at the start of 2010, bringing quite a buzz to the local dining scene. The Three Salmons offers traditional charm in spades, and after a day's walking in the Usk valley, the smartly-refurbished restaurant serves a nice line in unpretentious modern Welsh cooking based on plenty of local ingredients, with suppliers name-checked on the menu. Salmon tortellini with fennel purée and horseradish foam might precede a patriotic rump of Welsh lamb teamed with potato and onion cake, spinach, and carrot purée. Welsh artisan cheeses come with quince jelly, while warm chocolate fondant is served with ginger ice cream.

Chef James Bumpass **Times** 12-2.30/6.30-9.30 Closed D Sun **Prices** Food prices not confirmed for 2011. Please telephone for details **Notes** Civ Wed 100 **Seats** 34, Pr/dining room 22 **Children** Portions, Menu **Parking** 40

WHITEBROOK **Map 4 SO50**

Crown at Whitebrook

Modern British V Notable Wine List

Stylish restaurant with rooms with first-class cooking

☎ 01600 860254
NP25 4TX
e-mail: info@crownatwhitebrook.co.uk
web: www.crownatwhitebrook.co.uk
dir: From Monmouth take B4293 towards Trellech, in 2.7m left towards Whitebrook, continue for 2m

This tranquil restaurant with rooms in a 17th-century drover's inn in the densely-wooded Wye Valley near to Tintern Abbey has an inspiring Welsh setting, although there's something of the romantic French country auberge about the place. In the dining room, pastel shades make for a restful, minimal décor, while the switched-on service and contemporary cooking is the match of many a cosmopolitan restaurant. The kitchen here is firing on all cylinders under head chef James Sommerin, who pulls some unexpected combinations out of his toque. The modern cooking has sound classical French foundations as a basis for letting the creative juices flow through a menu of skilfully prepared, intelligent dishes. Take the bold partnership of poached and roast squab with duck liver, butterscotch and gingerbread for starters, while pan-fried halibut might be teamed with roasted scallop, spiced razor clam, tomato and cardamom. Technical skill is once again to the fore in desserts such as baked fig cream, with flapjack, caramel and cinnamon. An outstanding wine list completes the picture. The Crown has extended its reach to include a venue at swish golfing resort Celtic Manor (see entry).

Chef James Sommerin **Owner** The Crown Hotels & Restaurants Ltd **Times** 12-2/7-9.30 Closed 2 wks Xmas, New Year, D Sun **Prices** Fixed L 2 course fr £25, Tasting menu £55-£70, Main £48, Service optional, Groups min 8 service 12.5% **Wines** 200+ bottles over £20, 10 bottles under £20, 10 by glass **Notes** Fixed D 5 course £60.00, Tasting menu 6 or 9 course, Sunday L, Vegetarian menu, Dress restrictions, Smart casual, No T-shirts, shorts or sandals **Seats** 30, Pr/dining room 12 **Parking** 20

The Crown at the Celtic Manor Resort

NEWPORT **Map 9 ST38**

Modern British Notable Wine List

Fine restaurant in Welsh landmark hotel

☎ 01633 413000
Celtic Manor Resort, Coldra Woods NP18 1HQ
e-mail: thecrown@celtic-manor.com
web: www.crown.celtic-manor.com
dir: From M4 junct 24 take B4237 towards Newport, turn right after 300yds

The Celtic Manor Resort hosts the Ryder Cup as we publish this guide - did we win? The mammoth five-star development involves two separate hotels, a brace of spas and health clubs, three championship golf courses and five restaurants. Of these, the Crown gets top billing. The sister restaurant to the Crown at Whitebrook (see entry) is an oasis of understated taste with its chic high-backed leather chairs, polished darkwood floors and glamorous blue and gold lighting. Executive chef James Sommerin oversees proceedings at both Crowns, delivering polished precisely-cooked food with big, bold flavours in elegantly-presented packages. Welsh produce forms the backbone of the kitchen's output, which has a classic feel, reworked with flair and imagination. The tone is set by starters such as roasted pigeon breast teamed with confit duck liver and black treacle, while fillet of brill is presented with parsley fumet and frogs' legs. Main courses again handle flavours deftly - say local duck breast with pickled shiitake mushrooms, celeriac and spiced maple syrup, while desserts might take an exotic turn, as in coconut pannacotta with tropical fruit, mango and passionfruit sorbet, or stick to more classically-inclined ideas with a rhubarb soufflé, white chocolate ice cream and Sauternes. The stimulating wine list has some fine choices available by the glass.

Chef Tim McDougall **Times** 12-2/7-10 Closed 1-14 Jan, Sun-Mon **Prices** Fixed L 2 course £14.95-£29.95, Fixed D 3 course £47.50, Tasting menu £65, Service optional, Groups min 8 service 10% **Wines** 242 bottles over £20, 22 by glass **Notes** Tasting menu 6 course, Vegetarian available, Dress restrictions, Smart casual, Civ Wed 100 **Seats** 50, Pr/dining room 12 **Children** Portions **Parking** 100

NEWPORT

NEWPORT Map 9 ST38

The Crown at the Celtic Manor Resort

◎◎◎ – *see page 558*

The Manor House

◎ Modern, French NEW

Classic French cuisine in a relaxed setting

☎ 01633 413000
The Celtic Manor Resort, Coldra Woods NP18 1HQ
e-mail: bookings@celtic-manor.com
dir: M4 junct 24, B4237 towards Newport. Hotel 1st on right

The vast golf-centric Celtic Manor Resort offers a mind-spinning variety of eating options, including the exceptional fine-dining Crown restaurant (see entry). As its name might suggest, Le Patio Bistro in The Manor House itself is staunchly French in its approach, and has a quieter, more intimate ambience than the other eating venues spread around the huge complex. You enter through the original 19th-century building past the grand oak staircase into a tranquil restaurant with simple bare wooden tables and floor-to-ceiling windows looking over the immaculate grounds. The kitchen sources intelligently from Welsh farms and producers for its classic bistro-style dishes. Chicken liver parfait with plum and ginger chutney sets the tone, ahead of main-course roasted rump of rosemary and garlic-marinated Welsh lamb, served with silky carrot and parsnip purée, broad beans and fondant potato.

Chef James Sommerin **Times** 12-2/7-10 **Prices** Food prices not confirmed for 2011. Please telephone for details

Rafters

◎ Modern British

Good, contemporary cooking at the 19th hole

☎ 01633 413000
Celtic Manor Resort, Usk Valley NP18 1HQ
dir: M4 junct 24. At rdbt take the B4237 towards Newport, after 100mtrs turn right at Celtic Manor sign

With wonderful views over the Ryder Cup golf course, and a striking beamed interior, Rafters is a stylish and agreeable place for lunch or dinner. The service is full of enthusiasm, and what arrives on the plate is a notch or two above your typical clubhouse. The menu throws its culinary net wide over much of Europe, although there's a good amount of Welsh produce at the heart of things. Ballottine of chicken has some pickled turnip to cut through the richness in a well-judged first course; next up, belly of pork with excellent crackling, served with caramelised apple, sage mash and slices of black pudding. Finish with a rich milk chocolate mousse with fresh raspberries (in season) and a tuile.

Chef Simon Searle **Owner** Celtic Manor Resort **Times** 12-2.30/6-10 Closed D Mon-Wed (Oct-Mar) **Prices** Fixed L 2 course fr £14.95, Starter fr £5.50, Main fr £10.95, Dessert fr £5.50, Service optional **Wines** 34 bottles over £20, 1 bottle under £20, 6 by glass **Notes** Sunday L, Dress restrictions, Smart casual (no trainers/flip-flops) **Seats** 80, Pr/dining room 96 **Children** Portions **Parking** 115

PEMBROKESHIRE

HAVERFORDWEST Map 8 SM91

Wolfscastle Country Hotel

◎ British, International

Enjoyable food in peaceful country hotel

☎ 01437 741225 & 741688
Wolf's Castle SA62 5LZ
e-mail: info@wolfscastle.com
dir: From Haverfordwest take A40 towards Fishguard. Hotel in centre of Wolf's Castle

Very much a family affair, in ambience and character, this stone-built former vicarage turned hotel sits in the lush mid-Pembrokeshire countryside and is still known locally by its original name of Allt-yr-Afon ('Hill by the River'). It has a good reputation for its accurate, fuss-free cooking and use of quality local produce, with the same menu offered in both bar and restaurant. The choice divides into crowd-pleasing traditional options (grilled Welsh sausages with colcannon and caramelised onion gravy, for example) to more international-inspired dishes, such as roast fillet of salmon teriyaki to pan-fried duck confit served with mash, flageolet beans in tomato sauce and a red wine jus.

Chef Owen Hall **Owner** Mr A Stirling **Times** 12-2/6.30-9 Closed 24-26 Dec **Prices** Fixed L 2 course £11.95, Starter £4.95-£7.50, Main £9.95-£18.95, Dessert £4.95, Service optional **Wines** 33 bottles over £20, 15 bottles under £20, 9 by glass **Notes** Sunday L, Vegetarian available, Civ Wed 60 **Seats** 55, Pr/dining room 32 **Children** Portions, Menu **Parking** 75

NARBERTH Map 8 SN11

The Grove

◎ Modern British NEW

Modern British cuisine in a stylish country house

☎ 01834 860915
Molleston SA67 8BX
e-mail: info@thegrove-narberth.co.uk
dir: From A40, take A478 to Narberth. Continue past castle, turn right bottom of hill

This small restaurant with rooms hits a romantically relaxed balance, avoiding the coolness of many hip boutique hotels and stuffy chintz of some small country houses. The quirky cocktail of Georgian and Arts and Crafts interiors makes a good starting point, into which the owners have injected their own style - a mix of sumptuous fabrics, tasteful colours and ever-changing exhibitions of artworks. Served in either a gorgeous wood-panelled dining room, or the airy bistro-style Garden Room, food is at the heart of the house these days, cooked in a modern British vein with Welsh influences. Flavour combinations are kept simple and appealing, as in a starter of home-made Caerphilly and leek ravioli with truffle oil and main-course venison, matched with the less orthodox tang of poached nectarines and sweet potatoes.

Chef Emilio Fragacomo **Owner** Neil Kedward & Zoe Agar **Times** 12-2.30/5-9 Closed L Mon-Wed **Prices** Fixed L 2 course £15-£22, Starter £6-£10, Main £13-£26, Dessert £6-£9, Service optional **Wines** 50 bottles over £20, 10 bottles under £20, 4 by glass **Notes** Sunday L, Vegetarian available **Seats** 60, Pr/dining room 25 **Children** Portions, Menu **Parking** 25

NEWPORT Map 8 SN03

Llys Meddyg

◎◎ British

Welsh produce in a former coaching inn

☎ 01239 820008 & 820753
East St SA42 0SY
e-mail: contact@llysmeddyg.com
dir: A487 to Newport, located on the Main Street, through the centre of town

This restaurant with rooms in a Georgian townhouse on Newport's high street started off life as a coaching inn. Eclectically decorated with old and new furnishings, sea-green walls feature Welsh art and dark wooden tables come with comfortable leather-seated wooden chairs. The restaurant is small but on summer nights extra space is available in the conservatory, while in colder times the cosy cellar bar area accommodates any overflow. Welsh influences prevail on the modern British menu. Fresh seasonal ingredients sourced locally and accurately cooked are served by laid-back but efficient staff. Try Newport Bay crab spring rolls and tamarind ketchup followed by local hake fillet, Welsh bacon and gingered butternut squash. Coconut baked Alaska and passionfruit soup finishes things off nicely.

Chef Scott Davis **Owner** Ed & Louise Sykes **Times** 12-2/7-9 Closed Mon, L Tue, D Sun **Prices** Food prices not confirmed for 2011. Please telephone for details **Wines** 27 bottles over £20, 16 bottles under £20, 6 by glass **Notes** Sunday L, Vegetarian available, Civ Wed 50 **Seats** 30, Pr/dining room 14 **Children** Portions **Parking** 8

PORTHGAIN Map 8 SM83

The Shed

Traditional British, Mediterranean

Local seafood dining in sea-going surroundings

01348 831518
SA62 5BN
e-mail: caroline@theshedporthgain.co.uk
dir: 7m from St David's. Off A40

Seafood fans should beat a path to this simple beach hut-style bistro and wine bar right on the quayside in the adorable fishing village of Porthgain. Formerly a carpenter's workshop and fisherman's storehouse, you couldn't ask for a more authentic venue for tucking into fish and seafood landed on the doorstep - much of which is caught by the owners themselves. Slate floors, gingham tablecloths, and whitewashed walls all work to create a laid-back ambience for unpretentious dishes, starting with pan-fried sardine fillets with orange and basil dressing; a main-course sea bream is baked en papillotte with garlic, lemon, thyme and olive oil, or you could go for the fish stew served with croûtons and rouille.

Chef Viv Folan **Owner** Rob & Caroline Jones **Times** 10-4.30/6.30 Closed Nov-Apr open only wknds (except half term & Xmas hols), D Tue (off peak) **Prices** Food prices not confirmed for 2011. Please telephone for details **Wines** 26 bottles under £20, 6 by glass **Notes** Sunday L, Vegetarian available **Seats** 36 **Children** Portions **Parking** On village street

ST DAVID'S Map 8 SM72

Cwtch

Modern Welsh, British

Confident modern cooking using great local produce

01437 720491
22 High St SA62 6SD
e-mail: info@cwtchrestaurant.co.uk

Cutsh is the way to pronounce it by the way (it means 'hug'). This smart townhouse in a terrace of properties on the high street of Britain's smallest city has a rustic charm. Wooden and slate floors, whitewashed stone walls and a serious cross-beam add to the homely feel, but the mood is very much of relaxed contemporary dining. The small upstairs kitchen produces classy modern food, conjured from well-sourced local ingredients. Potted Abercastle crab with lemon dill mayonnaise and Bloody Mary is a fine opener, and might be followed by local Welsh Black rib-eye with garlic butter, onion confit and beef dripping chips, or fillet of Lechryd sea trout with cockles and sauce vièrge. Make sure there's room for Spring Meadow rhubarb crumble with Drim Farm clotted cream.

Chef Matt Cox **Owner** Rachael Knott **Times** 6-9.30 Closed L all week, D Sun-Tue (Nov-Mar) **Prices** Fixed D 3 course £29, Service optional **Wines** 8 by glass **Notes** Vegetarian available **Seats** 50 **Children** Portions, Menu **Parking** On street

Warpool Court Hotel

Modern British

Beautiful coastal views and ambitious, confident cooking

01437 720300
SA62 6BN
e-mail: info@warpoolcourthotel.com
dir: From Cross Sq in centre of St David's, left by HSBC bank into Goat St, at fork follow hotel signs

Bordering National Trust parkland and boasting outstanding views over St Brides Bay to the offshore islands, Warpool Court was built in the 1860s to house the cathedral choir. The glass-dominated restaurant makes the most of the vista and looks out to sea across the glorious gardens. Inside, it's the collection of 1,700 armorial and ornamental tiles that catch the eye. Expect a daily-changing set menu that concentrates on fresh local ingredients used in an innovative fashion that manages to remain true to the flavours of the produce. Accurately cooked and simply presented dishes may include roast quail on a bed of grapes, pine nuts and bacon, followed by cannon of lamb with dauphinoise potatoes and red pepper jus, and a silky, creamy vanilla pannacotta with blackberries and wild flower honey.

Chef Barry Phillips **Owner** Peter Trier **Times** 12-1.30/7-9.15 Closed Nov **Prices** Fixed L 2 course fr £33, Service included **Wines** 101 bottles over £20, 21 bottles under £20, 4 by glass **Notes** Sunday L, Vegetarian available, Civ Wed 120 **Seats** 50, Pr/dining room 22 **Children** Portions, Menu **Parking** 100

POWYS

BRECON Map 9 SO02

The Felin Fach Griffin

British NOTABLE WINE LIST

Splendid gastro-pub with great wine list and organic cooking

01874 620111
Felin Fach LD3 0UB
e-mail: enquiries@eatdrinksleep.ltd.uk
dir: 3.5m N of Brecon on A470. Large terracotta building on left, on edge of village

If you've been walking in the Brecon Beacons, or maybe just reading a book you bought in Hay on Wye, The Griffin is the kind of charmingly rustic bolt-hole you might have been dreaming of. This chintz-free gastro-pub with rooms retains a rustic allure with scuffed up leather sofas, wooden beams and warm colours. And with a serious approach to food, a genuine locals' bar and an outstanding wine list, what's not to like? Around 50 wines are available on the main list and there are 20 or so by the glass or carafe. With wine this good, the food has some talking to do, but it's up to the challenge. The pub's organic kitchen garden provides much of the produce for simple gastro-pub dishes and gaps are filled with an impressive network of local suppliers. Expect dressed Portland crab with ginger mayonnaise, tomato and avocado salsa, moving on to wild venison with butternut squash purée, fondant potato and elderberries, and finish up with a dark chocolate marquise with pistachio ice cream and cherry mousse.

Times 12.30-2.30/6.30-9.30 Closed 24-25 Dec, few days Jan

Peterstone Court

Modern British, European

Excellent local food on the edge of the Brecon Beacons

01874 665387
Llanhamlach LD3 7YB
e-mail: info@peterstone-court.com
dir: 1m from Brecon on A40 to Abergavenny

A handsome Georgian country house near to lovely Brecon, Peterstone Court has an inspirational backdrop of the brooding Brecon Beacons - a view to savour during a swim in the heated outdoor pool. This gourmet bolt-hole is a polished act: the interior blends funky contemporary touches with period elegance, and there's an intimate small-scale spa to chill out and soothe away the aches after hiking the hills. And the food is worth going out of your way for. The white minimal style of the restaurant suits the restful mood, and delivers seriously good modern cooking from a kitchen team with razor-sharp technical skills and an eye for beautiful presentation. Food miles are kept to a minimum by breeding most of the meat and poultry on the family farm seven miles away. You might start with a pressing of Glaisfer Farm pork with apple purée, while main courses could bring together herb-crusted pollock with grilled Hafod cheddar and a mussel, potato and bacon chowder, or a Welsh lamb plate, comprising best end, a mini shepherd's pie and rillettes with purple sprouting broccoli and redcurrant jus.

Chef Sean Gerrard, Ian Sampson **Owner** Jessica & Glyn Bridgeman, Sean Gerrard **Times** 12-2.30/7-9.30 **Prices** Fixed L 2 course fr £11.50, Starter £5-£8.95, Main £12.50-£18.95, Dessert £6.50-£7.95, Service optional **Wines** 30 bottles over £20, 31 bottles under £20, 12 by glass **Notes** Sunday L, Vegetarian available, Civ Wed 120 **Seats** 45, Pr/dining room 120 **Children** Portions, Menu **Parking** 40

CAERSWS Map 15 SO09

The Talkhouse

British, European

Friendly service and hearty portions in a cosy pub

☎ 01686 688919 & 07876 086183
Ty Siarad, Pontdolgoch SY17 5JE
e-mail: info@talkhouse.co.uk
dir: 1.5m W of Caersws on A470 (Machynlleth road)

British cooking with some European influences is on the menu at this 17th-century inn with many original features and bags of character. The cosy reception area-cum-library leads to a warming bar with a log burning fire. Eat in the bar or a second dining area looking out over well-tended gardens, or venture outside for summer dining. Bare wooden tables are laid with white linen napkins and high quality glassware. A daily-changing blackboard menu includes hearty portions of fresh fish and locally-sourced meat and poultry popular with the nearby farming fraternity. You might find a classic pan-fried skate wing with caper butter, then roasted local Welsh lamb rump with dauphinoise potatoes, carrots, Savoy cabbage, swede mash and new potatoes with a lamb gravy, and a textbook vanilla crème brûlée to finish.

Times 12-1.30/6.30-8.45 Closed 25-26 Dec, Mon (only open for group booking of 15 or more), L Sat, D Sun

CRICKHOWELL Map 9 SO21

The Bear Hotel

Modern British

Convivial dining in a late-medieval inn

☎ 01873 810408
High St NP8 1BW
e-mail: bearhotel@aol.com
dir: Town centre, off A40 (Brecon road). 6m from Abergavenny

Once visited, never forgotten: the Bear is one of those timeless coaching inns that has no need for an identikit 'gastro' makeover, as it has been thriving at the heart of its village community between Abergavenny and the Brecon Beacons since 1432. Its legacy is safe in the hands of the Hindmarsh family, who have run the Bear for over 30 years, going their own way without chasing the latest trends. After all, what's not to like about flagstoned floors, cosy log fires, venerable oak beams and stone walls? The kitchen keeps an eye open for good ideas from the modern British comfort food repertoire, relying on the quality of local produce for unfussy dishes such as home-made venison terrine with apple and plum chutney, followed by roast rack of Welsh lamb with celeriac dauphinoise, ratatouille and rosemary jus.

Times 12-2/7-9.30 Closed 25 Dec, Mon, L Tue-Sat, D Sun

Gliffaes Country House Hotel

Modern British

Serious commitment to local produce

☎ 01874 730371
Gliffaes Rd NP8 1RH
e-mail: calls@gliffaeshotel.com
dir: 1m off A40, 2.5m W of Crickhowell

Set in 33 acres of well-tended gardens and woods by the River Usk, this privately owned Italianate-styled Victorian country house has appeared in a movie or two and is in an area beloved of fly fishing enthusiasts. The formal restaurant looks great with its wooden panelling and artwork from Welsh artists on the walls, and there's a terrace for sunny days. Changing daily, the imaginative, modish dinner menu is likely to feature non-intensively reared beef or lamb or game in season from the Brecon Beacons National Park, plus plenty of other local ingredients – a member of the Slow Food Movement, the hotel endeavours to source 65% of the produce from within a 50-mile radius. Start with pan-fried Cornish sardines with confit fennel and smoked potato salad, before a main-course such as slow-cooked belly of pork with crab beignet, Puy lentils and a sharp apple sauce.

Chef Karl Cheetham **Owner** Mr & Mrs Brabner & Mr & Mrs Suter **Times** 12-2.30/7.30-9.15 Closed 2-31 Jan, L Mon-Sat **Prices** Fixed L 3 course £26, Fixed D 3 course £36.75, Service included **Wines** 45 bottles over £20, 33 bottles under £20, 8 by glass **Notes** Sunday L, Vegetarian available, Dress restrictions, Smart casual preferred, Civ Wed 40 **Seats** 60, Pr/dining room 18 **Children** Portions, Menu **Parking** 30

Manor Hotel

Traditional, International

Dramatic mountain backdrop with good, unfussy cooking

☎ 01873 810212
Brecon Rd NP8 1SE
e-mail: info@manorhotel.co.uk
web: www.manorhotel.co.uk
dir: 0.5m W of Crickhowell on A40 (Brecon road)

The views over the lush green valley and River Usk from this impressive manor-house hotel's bistro-style dining room are nothing short of stunning, while quality local produce (including meats from its own Glaisfer Farm) catches the eye on the menu. The kitchen keeps things simple and unfussy; think a duo of Glaisfer Farm lamb (confit leg and rack) served with roasted butternut squash and a rosemary and garlic jus. And, though meat and poultry may be a mainstay, fish isn't forgotten; pan-fried hake steak, perhaps, with a pesto and parmesan herb crust served with garlic potato mash. Desserts hit the comfort zone, from sticky toffee pudding to tarte au citron.

Chef Mr G Bridgeman **Owner** Mr G Bridgeman **Times** 12-2.30/6.30-9.30 **Prices** Fixed L 2 course fr £11.50, Fixed D 3 course fr £18.95, Starter £4.50-£8.95, Main £7.95-£20, Dessert £5.50-£6.50, Service optional **Wines** 31 bottles over £20, 35 bottles under £20, 15 by glass **Notes** Sunday L, Vegetarian available, Civ Wed 250 **Seats** 54, Pr/dining room 26 **Children** Portions, Menu **Parking** 200

HAY-ON-WYE Map 9 SO24

The Old Black Lion

British

Traditional cooking in historic inn

☎ 01497 820841
26 Lion St HR3 5AD
e-mail: info@oldblacklion.co.uk
dir: 1m off A438. From TIC car park turn right along Oxford Rd, pass NatWest Bank, next left (Lion St), hotel 20yds on right

Close to the Lions Gate, one of the original entrances to the old walled town, this historic whitewashed inn is packed with character and charm. It dates from the 17th-century, with parts going all the way back to the 1300s, and it is reputed that Oliver Cromwell stayed here when

continued

HAY-ON-WYE *continued*

the Roundheads besieged Hay Castle. With beams aplenty, there's a traditional bar, which is also used for dining, and a smart restaurant area that leads to a patio which provides alfresco opportunities in the warmer months. The traditional, carefully cooked food includes simple starters of cured goose breast with grapefruit and watercress, and main courses like loin of pork with black pudding, peppercorn sauce and gratin potatoes.

Chef Peter Bridges **Owner** Dolan Leighton **Times** 12-2/6.30-9 Closed 24-26 Dec, **Prices** Food prices not confirmed for 2011. Please telephone for details **Wines** 16 bottles over £20, 23 bottles under £20, 7 by glass **Notes** Sunday L, Vegetarian available **Seats** 60, Pr/dining room 20 **Parking** 20

KNIGHTON **Map 9 SO27**

Milebrook House

Modern, Traditional British V

Good food in a beautiful setting

01547 528632
Milebrook LD7 1LT
e-mail: hotel@milebrook.kc3ltd.co.uk
web: www.milebrookhouse.co.uk
dir: 2m E of Knighton on A4113 (Ludlow)

Travellers may be fascinated to learn that this rather grand 18th-century stone house in the Teme Valley is the former home of legendary explorer Sir Wilfred Thesiger. Originally built as a dower house to Stanage Castle, Milebrook sits in the embrace of the buxom Marches hills amid immaculately-tended formal gardens, including a handy kitchen garden which provides a good proportion of the vegetables that end up on your plate. It's a deeply traditional place, much-loved by shooting parties, and with a skilled hand in the kitchen to tailor the menus accordingly. The owners have tracked down the best local suppliers and deliver country-house classics cooked with flair and imagination. Chicken and tarragon rillettes come with red onion marmalade and toasted thyme brioche, ahead of rump of local lamb with roasted Mediterranean vegetables, roasted new potatoes and rosemary jus.

Chef Christopher Marsden **Owner** Mr & Mrs R T Marsden **Times** 12-2/7-9 Closed Mon (open for residents D), D Sun **Prices** Fixed L 2 course fr £12.95, Fixed D 3 course fr £32.95, Service optional **Wines** 40 bottles over £20, 25 bottles under £20, 5 by glass **Notes** Sunday L, Vegetarian menu **Seats** 40, Pr/dining room 16 **Children** Portions **Parking** 24

LLANDRINDOD WELLS **Map 9 SO06**

The Metropole

Modern British V

Stylish spa hotel with sound modern cooking

01597 823700
Temple St LD1 5DY
e-mail: info@metropole.co.uk
dir: In centre of town off A483

A family-owned hotel in a Welsh spa town, the Metropole exudes professionalism and a grandeur that radiates from the green façade, and continues as you head inwards towards the smartly appointed Radnor restaurant at the heart of the operation. Here, a variety of easy-to-understand modern cooking is offered, featuring dishes such as game terrine with beetroot jelly, fillet of bream in fennel cream sauce, and rack of Welsh lamb with a rarebit potato cake and thyme-infused jus. Valrhona chocolate rarely disappoints, and here it is fashioned into a tart with good light pastry and properly vibrant vanilla sauce.

Chef Nick Edwards **Owner** Justin Baird-Murray **Times** 12.30-1.45/7-9.30 **Prices** Starter £4.25-£7.95, Main £13.95-£18.75, Dessert £5.50-£7.50, Service included **Wines** 30 bottles over £20, 23 bottles under £20, 9 by glass **Notes** Sunday L, Vegetarian menu, Civ Wed 200 **Seats** 200, Pr/dining room 250 **Children** Portions, Menu **Parking** 150

LLANFYLLIN **Map 15 SJ11**

Seeds

Modern British

Accurate cooking in an intimate, relaxed setting

01691 648604
5-6 Penybryn Cottages, High St SY22 5AP
dir: In village centre. Take A490 N from Welshpool, follow signs to Llanfyllin

To say that the atmosphere in Seeds is laid-back is something of an understatement: with cool jazz in the background, a head-skimming beamed ceiling, slate floors, local art and personal travel mementoes dotted around, the atmosphere is that of a cosy dinner party with friends. Run by a husband-and-wife-team, amiable staff provide easygoing service, while Mark Seager works alone in a pocket-sized kitchen to produce some seriously flavoursome and unfussy modern British bistro cooking. Try a filo parcel of Camembert with sweet chilli sauce, followed by rack of Welsh lamb with Dijon mustard and herb crust or simple grilled sea bass with Mediterranean vegetables.

Chef Mark Seager **Owner** Felicity Seager, Mark Seager **Times** 11-2.30/7-8.30 Closed 25 Dec, 2 wks Mar, 1 wk Oct, Sun-Mon, L Tue **Prices** Fixed D 3 course £25.75-£29.50, Starter £3.50-£6.95, Main £8.95-£18.50, Dessert £4.95-£6.95, Service optional **Wines** 20 bottles over £20, 70 bottles under £20, 3 by glass **Notes** Vegetarian available **Seats** 20 **Children** Portions **Parking** Free car park in town, street parking

LLANGAMMARCH WELLS **Map 9 SN94**

Lake Country House Hotel & Spa

British, European

Intricate modern British cooking in magisterial country house

01591 620202 & 620474
LD4 4BS
e-mail: info@lakecountryhouse.co.uk
dir: 6m from Builth Wells on A483 from Garth, turn left for Llangammarch Wells & follow signs to hotel

Fifty acres of parkland, full of rhododendron-lined pathways and riverside walks, are only the half of it at this magisterial country-house spa hotel. Inside is a riot of soft colour, with peaches and blues lightening the mood, while the main dining room is all ruched drapes, oil portraits and garden views. It's a tonic for the soul, which might also be said of the intricately creative modern British cooking on offer. Dinner might be crab bavarois with spiced tomato coulis, avocado cream and pink grapefruit, followed by roast pheasant with caramelised chicory, parsnip purée, morcilla, apples and dates in blackcurrant dressing, finishing with green tea and lemon pannacotta with confit lemon, lime sorbet and chocolate croquant.

Times 12.30-2/7.30-9.15

LLANGATTOCK **Map 9 SO21**

The Old Rectory Hotel

Modern European NEW

Smart village hotel with skilled locally-inspired cooking

01873 810373
NP8 1PH
e-mail: oldrectoryhotel@live.com

The 16th-century building was once home to the not-much-remembered poet Henry Vaughan, and stands in a sleepy village near Crickhowell. A fine-dining restaurant in two shades of creamy brown aims to put the place on the gastronomic map. Golf is another big draw here, and the dining room looks out on to the 9-hole course. Locally-sourced ingredients such as Welsh beef and lamb and Brecon venison are pressed enthusiastically into service, and the fish and seafood show well too. Lobster and crab ravioli comes with an excellent shellfish sauce, while a selection of Cornish fish cooked with leeks, vermouth and cream is generous to a fault, encompassing John Dory, Dover sole, brill and scallops. That venison might be fashioned into burger and sausage accompaniments to a serving of the loin, sauced with berries and port.

LLANWDDYN Map 15 SJ01

Lake Vyrnwy Hotel & Spa

Modern British

Accomplished seasonal cooking with a stunning view

01691 870692
Lake Vyrnwy SY10 0LY
e-mail: info@lakevyrnwyhotel.co.uk
web: www.lakevyrnwyhotel.co.uk
dir: on A4393, 200yds past dam turn sharp right into drive

The view will leave a lasting impression. The elegantly restored Victorian sporting lodge overlooks the breathtaking Lake Vyrnwy and the vista is best enjoyed from the comfort of the conservatory restaurant. The food has a lot to compete with but can be diverting in its own right. The kitchen is adept at sourcing tip-top Welsh produce and putting them to good use on the menu. Grilled goats' cheese en croûte or quenelles of smoked trout mousse get things off to a good start, before shoulder and roast cutlet of Welsh lamb, served up with smoked bacon, pea and leek compôte and braised shallots. Chocolate fondant with Baileys butterscotch sauce and vanilla ice cream is an accomplished finale.

Lake Vyrnwy Hotel & Spa

Chef David Thompson **Owner** The Bisiker family **Times** 12-2/6.45-9.15 **Prices** Food prices not confirmed for 2011. Please telephone for details **Wines** 50 bottles over £20, 30 bottles under £20, 10 by glass **Notes** Sunday L, Vegetarian available, Dress restrictions, Smart casual preferred, Civ Wed 220 **Seats** 85, Pr/dining room 220 **Children** Portions **Parking** 80

LLANWRTYD WELLS Map 9 SN84

Carlton Riverside

– see below

Lasswade Country House Restaurant with Rooms

Modern British

Organically minded Edwardian country-house dining

01591 610515
Station Rd LD5 4RW
e-mail: info@lasswadehotel.co.uk
dir: On A483, follow signs for station, opposite Spar shop, adjacent to tourist info office, 400yds on right before station

Run with aplomb by a husband-and-wife-team who treat their diners as house guests, this unpretentious Edwardian house stands on the edge of the Victorian spa town and enjoys wonderful views from its elegant lounge. The Welsh Marches setting plays its part, too, in providing that much sought-after commodity - complete relaxation, which together with accomplished modern Welsh cuisine, adds up to a tempting package. There's a strong commitment to organic local produce here, like smoked organic salmon from the Welsh borders or fish fresh from Milford Haven. Cooking from the skilled chef-patron is confident, simple and down-to-earth, as in a starter of

continued

Carlton Riverside

LLANWRTYD WELLS Map 9 SN84

Modern British

Good honest cooking in delightful family-run riverside restaurant

01591 610248
Irfon Crescent LD5 4SP
e-mail: info@carltonriverside.com
web: www.carltonriverside.com
dir: In town centre beside bridge

Alan and Mary Ann Gilchrist's restaurant with rooms is set beside the bridge over the River Irfon smack in the centre of Llanwrtyd Wells. It's not hard to spot: the sky-blue paintwork stands out from the grey stone-built town. You're assured of a sincere welcome on arrival - maybe over an aperitif in the basement bar-bistro. The restaurant is smartly contemporary with high-backed chocolate leather chairs, Welsh slate place mats and an understated décor of coffee and cream. Alan looks after front-of-house with unobtrusive diligence, while Mary Ann's cooking hits top form, blending imagination with great natural skills and obvious passion. There's no flim-flammery of foams or gels on her à la carte menu, just perfectly cooked tip-top materials brought together in thoughtful combinations. You might start with an exemplary twice-baked cheese soufflé, ahead of roast rack and slow-braised breast of Irfon Valley lamb with new potatoes, buttered leeks and sherried lamb jus. Puddings could include warm almond Pithiviers with crème Chantilly or rice pudding with warm prunes in Earl Grey syrup.

Chef Mary Ann Gilchrist **Owner** Dr & Mrs Gilchrist **Times** 7-9 Closed L all week, D Sun (ex BH) **Prices** Fixed D 3 course £25-£39.50, Service optional **Wines** 60 bottles over £20, 15 bottles under £20, 4 by glass **Notes** Vegetarian available **Seats** 20 **Children** Portions, Menu **Parking** Car park opposite

LLANWRTYD WELLS *continued*

warm salad of black pudding and smoked bacon with poached free-range egg and basil oil, or a main course of cannon of Elan Valley organic lamb with leek soufflé and roast winter vegetables. Finish with a classic lemon tart with raspberry coulis.

Chef Roger Stevens **Owner** Roger & Emma Stevens **Times** 7.30-9.30 Closed 25 Dec, L all week **Prices** Fixed D 3 course £32, Service optional **Wines** 9 bottles over £20, 17 bottles under £20, 2 by glass **Notes** Vegetarian available, Dress restrictions, Smart casual **Seats** 20, Pr/dining room 20 **Parking** 6

LLYSWEN Map 9 SO13

Llangoed Hall

◎◎ Modern, Traditional British **NEW** V

Accomplished cooking in grand old house

☎ 01874 754525
LD3 0YP
e-mail: generalmanager@llangoedhall.com
dir: On A470, 2m from Llyswen towards Builth Wells

An impressive old building dating way back to 1632, Llangoed Hall, is surrounded by lush green fields in the Wye Valley. With the Black Mountains looming large, there are seven acres of beautiful landscaped gardens to explore. A memorable collection of fine artwork adorns the walls, complemented by antique furniture and richly luxurious fabrics. In the light and elegant restaurant, with its blue and white Wedgwood and outstanding paintings, service is just the ticket, and the appealing menu offers adventurous and accomplished dishes featuring plenty of local ingredients, including fruit and vegetables from the kitchen garden. Expect starters like seared scallops with truffle cauliflower purée and baked Carmarthenshire ham, followed by duo of Welsh lamb with dauphinoise potatoes, green beans and rosemary jus. First-class desserts may include Kirsch cherry crème brûlée with cinnamon doughnuts.

Chef Sean Ballington **Owner** The Ashley Llangoed Partnership **Times** 12.30-2/7-9 **Prices** Food prices not confirmed for 2011. Please telephone for details **Wines** 110 bottles over £20, 9 by glass **Notes** Sunday L, Vegetarian menu, Dress restrictions, Jacket at D, smart casual, no ripped denim, Civ Wed 80 **Seats** 50, Pr/dining room 80 **Children** Portions **Parking** 50

MONTGOMERY Map 15 SO29

Dragon Hotel

◎ Modern, Traditional

Historic inn serving simple food in restaurant and bar

☎ 01686 668359 & 668287
Market Square SY15 6PA
e-mail: reception@dragonhotel.com
dir: Behind town hall

Beams and timbers from the ruined nearby castle, destroyed by Cromwell, can be seen in the lounge and bar of this handsome, black-and-white timbered 17th-century former coaching inn, which stands in the heart of this Welsh Marches market town. Simple, generously served modern British dishes, prepared from locally-sourced produce, are served in the cosy, beamed and traditionally decorated dining room. Expect well-presented classic dishes like chicken liver pâté with plum and brandy chutney, lamb shank with redcurrant gravy, salmon supreme, and rib-eye steak with peppercorn sauce.

Dragon Hotel

Chef Thomas Fraenzel **Owner** M & S Michaels **Times** 12-2/7-9 **Prices** Fixed L 2 course £13.50, Fixed D 3 course £25, Starter £4.25-£5.95, Main £11.25-£21.95, Dessert £4.25-£5.50, Service optional **Wines** 7 bottles over £20, 43 bottles under £20, 12 by glass **Notes** Sunday L, Vegetarian available **Seats** 42, Pr/dining room 50 **Children** Portions **Parking** 20

WELSHPOOL Map 15 SJ20

Royal Oak Hotel

◎ Welsh

Enjoyable food in stylish former coaching inn

☎ 01938 552217
The Cross SY21 7DG
e-mail: relax@royaloakhotel.info

A traditional market town hotel in the heart of Welshpool, the Royal Oak dates back more than 350 years. The décor may be in the contemporary minimalist vein but it retains period features, including exposed beams, polished wood floors and open fires. There is a choice of two dining rooms - red or green - and service is friendly, attentive and well informed in both. The predominantly Welsh cuisine is based on a secure footing of local produce, and dishes achieve clarity of flavour. A starter of pheasant breast simmered in port with a walnut and grape sauce might be followed by pan-fried fillet of sea bass with seafood risotto and a shellfish bisque.

Chef Sam Regan **Owner** Malcolm & Emma Bebb **Times** 11-6.30/6.30-9.30 **Prices** Starter £4.75-£7.95, Main £9.95-£21.95, Dessert £5.75-£7.50 **Wines** 10+ bottles over £20, 10+ bottles under £20, 8 by glass **Notes** Sunday L, Vegetarian available, Civ Wed 30 **Seats** 80, Pr/dining room 32 **Children** Portions, Menu **Parking** 19, Car park

RHONDDA CYNON TAFF

MISKIN Map 9 ST08

Miskin Manor Country Hotel

◎◎ Modern British V

Inventive modern British cooking in tranquil South Wales

☎ 01443 224204
Pendoylan Rd CF72 8ND
e-mail: info@miskin-manor.co.uk
dir: M4 junct 34, exit onto A4119, signed Llantrisant, hotel 300yds on left

Not far from the M4, and yet managing to be an island of tranquility, Miskin is a majestic manor house in 22 acres of grounds. Wood panelling and swagged curtains create an appealingly antique feel in the Meisgyn dining room, but the cooking is fully up to date. Modern British combinations are much favoured, as in tuna carpaccio with balsamic-glazed belly pork, or spring pea soup with sesame-toasted cod and a quail's egg. Meats get all the fashionable treatments, lamb appearing in two cuts with a curry sabayon and trompette mushrooms, while seared red mullet is aptly teamed with razor clams, a raviolo of smoked eel and herb butter. Nor does the crème brûlée rest on its laurels, being sharpened up with Pendyryn whisky, roasted pineapple, and Earl Grey ice cream.

Chef Mark Beck **Owner** Mr & Mrs Rosenberg **Times** 12-2.30/6-10 **Prices** Fixed L 2 course £16.30-£18, Fixed D 3 course £20.38-£22.50, Starter £6.25-£8.90, Main £16.50-£24.50, Dessert £6.50-£8 **Wines** 34 bottles over £20, 6 bottles under £20, 12 by glass **Notes** Sunday L, Vegetarian menu, Dress restrictions, Smart casual, Civ Wed 120 **Seats** 50, Pr/dining room 30 **Children** Portions, Menu **Parking** 200

PONTYCLUN Map 9 ST08

Brookes Restaurant & Private Dining Room

◎ Modern International

Vibrant modern eatery with a global cocktail of cuisine

☎ 01443 239600
79-81 Talbot Rd, Talbot Green CF72 8AE
e-mail: staffbrookes@btconnect.com
dir: M4 junct 34, follow signs for Llantrisant, turn left at 2nd lights

Brookes is a vibrant eatery with a bright contemporary look - you can't miss the bold blue canopied façade on Talbot Road. Inside, it's a chic spot - all mirrored and whitewashed walls hung with vibrant modern art, and bare wooden tables. The kitchen goes for a modern international style, cooked and presented simply; the wide-ranging menu changes with the seasons, and delves freely into the cuisines of the Mediterranean and Asia. Daily-changing tapas-style specials offer casual grazing and sharing options. Tempura of spiced salmon with Caesar salad, and confit duck leg on bubble-and-squeak with lentil, red wine and thyme sauce shows the style.

Times 12-2.30/7-10.30 Closed 24 Dec, 1 Jan & BHs, Mon, L Sat, D Sun

PONTYPRIDD Map 9 ST08

Llechwen Hall Hotel

Modern Welsh

Valley views and a sense of history

☎ 01443 742050 & 743020
Llanfabon CF37 4HP
e-mail: reservations@llechwenhall.co.uk

A popular venue for functions and weddings, this privately owned country-house hotel is set in six acres of grounds at the top of a hill, overlooking the valleys. The property has housed a magistrates' court and private school in its 200-year history. The fine-dining restaurant in the 17th-century beamed Welsh longhouse boasts well-dressed tables and deep red furniture. There's a small, affordable New World wine list to complement the imaginative Welsh cookery which uses locally-sourced ingredients simply presented. Expect warm stilton tart with a compôte of sweet-and-sour shallots, then slow-cooked lamb shank with Puy lentils and a thyme jus, and a pudding of apricot and almond tart.

Times 12-2/7-9

SWANSEA

BISHOPSTON Map 8 SS58

Winston Hotel

Modern, Traditional

Gower hotel and restaurant with good, honest cooking

☎ 01792 232074
11 Church Ln SA3 3JT
e-mail: enquiries@winstonhotel.com
dir: A4067 from Swansea onto B4436 signed Bishopston. In 2.7m left to Bishopston & immediately right into Church Ln

The Winston Hotel is a family-run place, and as such the intimate Churchill's restaurant has a relaxed, informal feel, the tone set by the use of lots of natural darkwood. The kitchen places great emphasis on Welsh produce and everything - from the bread to the ice cream - is made in-house. Start, typically, with laverbread parcels - laverbread with bacon and onions cooked in crisp filo parcels with a light tomato sauce - and follow on in simple style with an exemplary steak and kidney pie. Dessert could be something a little less traditional, such as white chocolate cheesecake.

Times 12-2/7-9

LLANRHIDIAN Map 8 SS49

The Welcome to Town

British, French

Homely country bistro on the Gower peninsula

☎ 01792 390015
SA3 1EH
dir: 8m from Swansea on B4231. M4 junct 47 towards Gowerton. From Gowerton take B4295

Previously a magistrates' court with its own cells, the Bennetts' country bistro stands next to a green adorned with stone whipping-posts, so the name of the place represents a good attempt at overcoming a host of forbidding associations. The welcome is warm indeed these days, not least for the locally oriented, distinctly polished cooking. A lot of work goes into the dishes, and yet they manage to seem effortless. A twice-baked goats' cheese soufflé is offset with carpaccio-sliced beetroot and a celery and apple salad, while mains from the winter menu might take in noisette of Kirroughtree venison, grandly accompanied by braised Savoy cabbage, glazed chestnuts, fondant potato and a sauce of poached pear. You might be glad to finish by fortifying yourself against the peninsular winds outside with steamed ginger pudding and proper custard. Fine home-made breads shouldn't be missed.

Times 12-2/7-9.30 Closed 25-26 Dec, 1 Jan, last 2 wks Feb, 1 wk Oct, Mon, D Sun

PARKMILL Map 8 SS58

Maes-Yr-Haf Restaurant with Rooms

Modern British NEW

A taste of Wales in modish surroundings

☎ 01792 371000
SA3 2EH
e-mail: enquiries@maes-yr-haf.com

Set in the heart of the Gower, within easy reach of Swansea and just a short stroll from magnificent Three Cliffs Bay, this former private residence was transformed into a contemporary restaurant with rooms in 2007. In a stylish modern setting of cream and leather chairs, black and beige carpet, minimalist wall coverings and a feature carved glass screen, you can savour some accurate modern European cooking using quality local ingredients. Follow twice-baked crab soufflé with mango salsa, with moist, full-flavoured line-caught sea bass with a tartare of wild garlic, mussels, cockles and crayfish, and a saffron and tomato vièrge. To finish, try a deliciously creamy honey and cardamom pannacotta with rhubarb and blackberry compôte.

Chef Christos Georgakis **Owner** Colin Ford
Times 12-2.30/7-9.30 Closed 2 wks Jan, Mon, D Sun
Prices Fixed L 2 course fr £14.95, Fixed D 3 course fr £17.95, Starter £3.75-£6.75, Main £11.45-£24.95, Dessert £4.25-£6.50, Service optional **Wines** 8 bottles over £20, 23 bottles under £20 **Notes** Sunday L, Vegetarian available **Seats** 44 **Children** Menu **Parking** 17

REYNOLDSTON Map 8 SS48

WINE AWARD OF THE YEAR

Fairyhill

Modern British V NOTABLE WINE LIST

Elegant country-house hotel with real local flavour

☎ 01792 390139
SA3 1BS
e-mail: postbox@fairyhill.net
dir: M4 junct 47, take A483 then A484 to Llanelli, Gower, Gowerton. At Gowerton follow B4295 for approx 10m

Style, low-key luxury, top-notch food and a fantastic wine list are the attractions of this Gower favourite. And with just eight rooms, you won't have trouble finding a quiet corner - after all, with 24 acres of grounds to get lost in, peace and seclusion are virtually guaranteed. The elegant interior is kitted out in stylish modern country-house idiom, with well-spaced tables in the two dining rooms. The kitchen is keen on keeping food miles to a minimum, so most of the ingredients - Welsh Black beef, salt marsh lamb, Penclawdd cockles and fresh fish, for example - come from Gower and the surrounding area, and form the backbone of modern Welsh dishes. Starters might include cumin seared scallops with boudin noir, chorizo and pea purée, followed by loin and sausage of local venison with stwnch (that's mashed potato and swede to non-Welsh readers), apple mash and red wine and chocolate gravy. A clued-up and efficient front-of-house team is the icing on the cake.

Chef Paul Davies, James Hamilton
Owner Mr Hetherington, Mr Davies **Times** 12-2/7-9 Closed 26 Dec, 1-25 Jan **Prices** Fixed L 2 course fr £15.95, Fixed D 3 course fr £45, Starter £6.95-£12.50, Main £9.95-£24.50, Dessert £5.50-£6.25, Service optional **Wines** 400 bottles over £20, 50 bottles under £20, 10 by glass **Notes** Sunday L, Vegetarian menu, Civ Wed 40 **Seats** 60, Pr/dining room 40 **Children** Portions **Parking** 45

SWANSEA Map 9 SS69

The Dragon Hotel

Modern European

Modern European-style cuisine in the heart of Swansea

☎ 01792 657100 & 657159
The Kingsway Circle SA1 5LS
e-mail: enquiries@dragon-hotel.co.uk
web: www.dragon-hotel.co.uk
dir: M4 junct 42. At lights (after supermarket) turn right. Left into Kings Ln. Hotel straight ahead

Base yourself in the stylishly-renovated Dragon Hotel and you'll be in the thick of the action. The buzzy Dragon Brasserie is the place to watch the world go by through full-length windows onto the high street; its darkwood tables, wooden floors and shades of caramel and chocolate make for a smart modern setting, and the menu follows suit with straightforward, European-accented contemporary cooking. Start with a hearty leek and potato soup with chicken, and follow with breast of roast chicken stuffed with a herb farce, fondant potato and French garlic beans. Desserts might offer a mascarpone and raspberry crème brûlée with shortbread.

Chef Sam Thomas **Owner** Dragon Hotel Ltd **Times** 12-2.30/6-9.30 **Prices** Fixed L 2 course £9.95-£23.95, Fixed D 3 course £19.95-£23.95, Tasting menu fr £35, Starter £4.95-£8.95, Main £9.95-£22.95, Dessert £5.50-£6.95, Service optional **Wines** 9 bottles over £20, 24 bottles under £20, 12 by glass **Notes** Tasting menu by reservation only, Sunday L, Vegetarian available, Civ Wed 220 **Seats** 65, Pr/dining room 80 **Children** Menu **Parking** 50

Hanson at the Chelsea Restaurant

Modern British, French

Modern bistro eating in the city centre

☎ 01792 464068 & 07971 163 148
17 St Mary St SA1 3LH
e-mail: andrew_hanson@live.co.uk
dir: In small lane between St Mary Church & Wine St

An intimate venue down a side street in the city centre, this is a friendly, informal city bistro serving modern Anglo-French food. Tables may be a little cheek-by-jowl, but that's all part of the ambience; the seating is comfortable enough, there are two floors to choose from, and the red-shirted staff are highly proficient. Fortnightly-changing menus deliver some simple but effective dishes, with fish and seafood a speciality. Start with a deep-pile fishcake crammed with hake, salmon and cod, garnished with cockle and tomato relish, and then consider the pin-sharp timing of a piece of Cornish monkfish, well-supported by a spicy noodle stirfry incorporating prawns and pak choi. Three miniaturised desserts - apple pie, bread-and-butter pudding and silky crème brûlée - make a splendid finish. A separate vegetarian menu is offered.

Chef Andrew Hanson **Owner** Andrew & Michelle Hanson **Times** 12-2/7-10 Closed 25-26 Dec, BHs, Sun **Prices** Fixed L 2 course £12.50-£16.50, Fixed D 3 course £19.95, Starter £4.50-£7.50, Main £11.95-£19.95, Dessert £4.50 **Wines** 20 bottles over £20, 20 bottles under £20, 8 by glass **Notes** Vegetarian available, Dress restrictions, Smart casual **Seats** 50, Pr/dining room 20 **Children** Portions, Menu

VALE OF GLAMORGAN

HENSOL Map 9 ST07

Vale Grill

Modern British

Locally-sourced brasserie food at a luxurious resort hotel

☎ 01443 667800
Vale Hotel, Golf & Spa Resort, Hensol Park CF72 8JY
e-mail: sales@vale-hotel.com
dir: M4 junct 34, exit signed Pendoylan, turn 1st right twice, then 1st left before white house on bend. Hotel on right

A luxurious modern resort hotel not far from the majestic Glamorgan coast and Cardiff Bay, the Vale has all the modern amenities you could conjure a desire for. In the Grill, it also has a stylish venue for accomplished, locally-inspired brasserie cooking that keeps things light and reasonably simple. Start with beetroot risotto with Pant-Ysgawn goats' cheese, candied orange zest and watercress, and proceed to one of those grills, whether it be sea bass in tomato and olive dressing, or a steak of pedigree Welsh Black beef, served with a choice of dressings, from béarnaise to aïoli. A dramatic ending comes in the form of pumpkin pie with mascarpone sorbet and spiced chocolate sauce.

Chef Daniel James **Owner** Leekes Family **Times** 7-11 Closed L all week **Prices** Starter £2-£8, Main £13-£25, Dessert £6-£8 **Wines** 71 bottles over £20, 18 bottles under £20, 18 by glass **Notes** Sunday L, Vegetarian available, Dress restrictions, Smart casual, Civ Wed 700 **Seats** 80, Pr/dining room 350 **Children** Menu **Parking** 500

LLANTWIT MAJOR Map 9 SS96

Illtud's 216

Modern Welsh

Wales meets Austria in a 16th-century malt house

☎ 01446 793800
Church St CF61 1SB
e-mail: info@illtuds216.co.uk

This delightful restaurant in a 16th-century malt house showcases the cooking of Georg Fuchs, previously of the Savoy and, most recently, St David's Hotel in Cardiff. In the medieval hall style dining room there's a rustic feel. High ceilings with canopies and paintings of the eponymous Illtud – a monk rumoured to have brewed beer here. On the menu is modern Welsh cuisine, with the best from the sea and the valleys, imbued with Austrian flavours from Fuchs' heritage. Expect 'Llantwit Major particular' – ale and sage flavoured lamb cawl and crusty bread with Cadog mature cheddar, followed by sea bass fillet wrapped in smoked bacon and sage on creamed green lentils, fine vegetables and Illtud's potatoes. For desserts choose between the Austrian apple strudel or chocolate berry trifle.

Times 12-2.30/6-9.30 Closed Mon, D Sun

WREXHAM

LLANARMON DYFFRYN CEIRIOG Map 15 SJ13

The Hand at Llanarmon

Welsh

Local fresh produce in a hidden village inn

☎ 01691 600666
Ceiriog Valley LL20 7LD
e-mail: reception@thehandhotel.co.uk
dir: Leave A5 at Chirk onto B4500 signed Ceiriog Valley, continue for 11m

Lost among the quiet lanes of the Welsh Marches and guarded by the Berwyn mountains, the Hand has been at the heart of village life in Llanarmon Dyffryn Ceiriog for over four centuries. It is a real country pub with a beating heart, where visitors and locals mix in a chatty atmosphere beneath the venerable beams and glinting brasses in the rustic bar. The village's name is abbreviated to Llanarmon DC (perhaps to fit onto road signs), but the kitchen takes no short cuts with its down-to-earth food: everything is cooked from scratch from the area's superb produce, with local suppliers duly name-checked. The menu is a roll call of the sort of unfussy dishes you want to see - slow-braised shank of Welsh salt marsh lamb with redcurrant and red wine sauce, or grilled Ceiriog Valley trout with herbs, almonds and curry butter.

Times 12-2.20/6.30-8.45

West Arms Hotel

@@ British, French

Great local food in historic drovers' inn

☎ 01691 600665 & 600612
LL20 7LD
e-mail: gowestarms@aol.com
dir: Exit A483 (A5) at Chirk (mid-way between Oswestry & Llangollen). Follow signs for Ceiriog Valley (B4500), 11m

A remote location guarded by the Berwyn mountains has helped this authentic 16th-century inn retain its character intact: the bar is a classic assemblage of gnarled beams, flagstone floors, inglenooks and grand fireplaces popular with locals, and visitors that actually manage to find the place (it's worth the effort, so press on). The traditional menu doesn't set out to scare the horses: its bedrock is local Welsh Marches produce, cooked with an eye to the classics and with a contemporary touch here and there. Grilled sea bass with prawn risotto and tomato confit might precede a patriotic fillet of Welsh beef wrapped in watercress, with stilton, wild mushrooms and Burgundy sauce. Welsh cheeses with locally-made wine jellies are a savoury alternative to puddings such as glazed lemon tart with roasted plums and pineapple sorbet.

Chef Grant Williams **Owner** Mr & Mrs Finch & Mr G Williams **Times** 12-2/7-9 Closed L Mon-Sat **Prices** Fixed D 3 course £32.90, Service added but optional 10% **Wines** 16 bottles over £20, 21 bottles under £20, 9 by glass **Notes** Sunday L, Vegetarian available, Civ Wed 70 **Seats** 34, Pr/dining room 10 **Children** Portions, Menu **Parking** 20

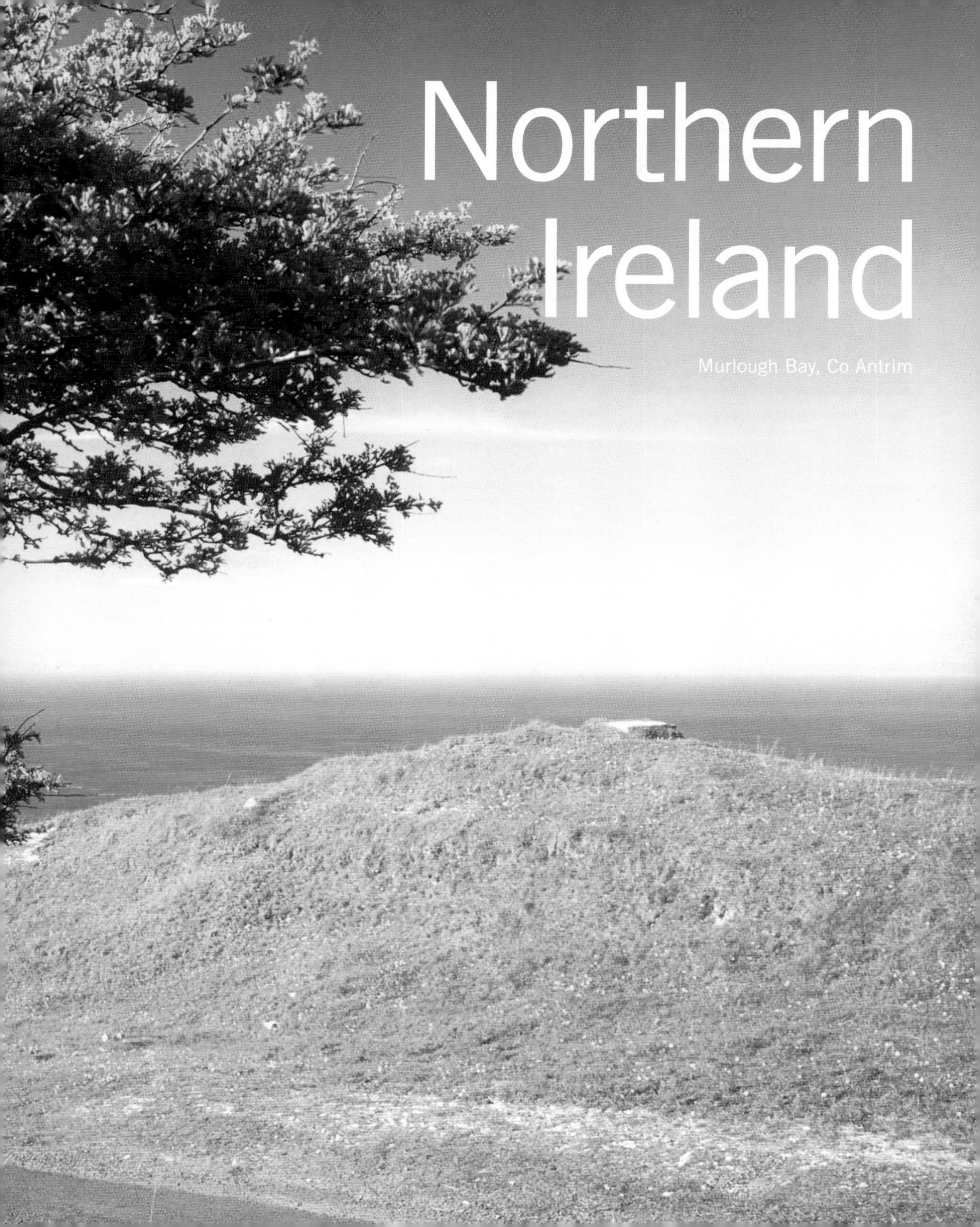

Northern Ireland

Murlough Bay, Co Antrim

CO ANTRIM

BALLYMENA Map 1 D5

Galgorm Resort & Spa

◎◎ International

Riverside dining on locally-sourced ingredients

☎ 028 2588 1001
BT42 1EA
e-mail: info@galgorm.com
web: www.galgorm.com

This luxury hotel and spa may be just 30 minutes from Belfast, but the setting amid 163 acres of parkland, through which the River Maine flows, is as rural as can be. Relaxation is obligatory here, though you won't be bored – walk, cycle or saddle up a horse and breathe in that country air. The River Room's selling point, if you hadn't guessed, is floor-to-ceiling windows looking out over the Maine - a glimpse of a heron is a distinct possibility. Fine glassware and crisp linen, together with immaculate flower displays, are a sophisticated backdrop to the creative modern cooking. Think fricassée of rabbit, red onions and leeks, then Glenarm salmon with rainbow chard and dry-cured ham.

Times 12-2.30/7-9.30 Closed Mon-Tue, L Wed-Sat

BUSHMILLS Map 1 C6

Bushmills Inn Hotel

◎ Traditional NEW V

Irish food in traditional surroundings

☎ 028 2073 3000 & 2073 2339
9 Dunluce Rd BT57 8QG
e-mail: mail@bushmillsinn.com
dir: 2m from Giant's Causeway on A2 in Bushmills after crossing river

Whether en route to the Giant's Causeway or on a pilgrimage to the home of Irish whiskey, the old inn is worth a dalliance. It's full of history, dating back to 1608, and has plenty of period charm to match the genuinely warm welcome. The restaurant is brimming with atmosphere with its wooden booth tables, intimate snugs and characterful original features. The kitchen aims to provide a true taste of Ulster and shows no little ambition, including in its diligent sourcing of the best seasonal Antrim produce. Begin, perhaps, with a seafood chowder full of local seafood and bacon, then move on to apple- and herb-stuffed pork fillet on buttered cabbage with praline-glazed pork medallion and spiced red wine jus. Home-made treacle tart with a scoop of Bushmills whiskey ice cream is the way to end a meal.

Chef Gordon McGladdery, Donna Thompson **Owner** Alan Dunlop **Times** 12-9.30 **Prices** Starter £5.25-£8.45, Main £16.15-£21, Dessert £4.85-£8, Service optional **Wines** 53 bottles over £20, 29 bottles under £20, 8 by glass **Notes** Sunday L, Vegetarian menu **Seats** 128 **Children** Menu **Parking** 70

CARNLOUGH Map 1 D6

Frances Anne Restaurant

◎ Modern

Unfussy modern Irish dishes in historic coastal hotel

☎ 028 2888 5255
Londonderry Arms Hotel, 20 Harbour Rd BT44 0EU
e-mail: ida@glensofantrim.com
dir: 14m N of Larne on Causeway coastal route

If you're up on the spectacular Antrim coast to see the Giant's Causeway, make sure to schedule in a foodie pitstop at the Londonderry Arms Hotel in the pretty fishing village of Carnlough. Sir Winston Churchill owned the place for a while, and the past is preserved in spades in its comfortingly chintzy décor, carved oak fireplaces, antiques and driftwood sculptures. The kitchen has moved with the times, taking an up-to-date tack with its unpretentious, full-flavoured cooking. Showcasing fine Ulster produce, dinner in the Frances Anne Restaurant might kick off with deep-fried Irish brie with fresh apple and thyme compôte, ahead of grilled medallions of pork fillet and pancetta with wholegrain mustard mash and Irish cider cream.

Times 12.30-2.45/7-8.15 Closed 24-25 Dec, L Mon-Sat

BELFAST

BELFAST Map 1 D5

Beatrice Kennedy

◎ Modern, Traditional V

Brasserie dining close to Queen's University

☎ 028 9020 2290
44 University Rd BT7 1NJ
e-mail: reservations@beatricekennedy.co.uk
web: www.beatricekennedy.co.uk
dir: Adjacent to Queen's University

With its rich, plum-coloured walls, wooden floors, leather chairs, chandeliers and candles, bookshelves aplenty and the sounds of big band jazz, this intimate restaurant in a former townhouse is reminiscent of a French bistro circa 1940. It's a short walk from Queen's University and takes its name from a former owner. Expect good value international cuisine along the lines of hot-smoked salmon with beetroot confit and horseradish ice cream or Barbary duck breast with polenta mash, asparagus, fig and apricot chutney. Smartly turned out staff are well informed and friendly.

Chef Jim McCarthy, Tim Quinn **Owner** Jim McCarthy **Times** 12.30-3/5-10.30 Closed 24-26 Dec, 1 Jan, Etr, Mon, L Mon-Sat **Prices** Fixed L 3 course £18.50, Fixed D 2 course fr £14.95, Starter £4-£9, Main £15-£19, Dessert £4.75, Groups min 6 service 10% **Wines** 20 bottles over £20, 15 bottles under £20, 4 by glass **Notes** Sunday L, Vegetarian menu **Seats** 75, Pr/dining room 25 **Children** Portions, Menu **Parking** On street

Cayenne

◎ Modern International

Trendy décor and eclectic food in Belfast

☎ 028 9033 1532
7 Ascot House, Shaftesbury Square BT2 7DB
e-mail: belinda@rankingroup.co.uk
dir: Top of Great Victoria St

There's something to appeal to all the senses at Cayenne – TV chef Paul Rankin and wife Jeanne's flagship restaurant. A vivid colour scheme and innovative, interactive artworks by local-born artist Peter Anderson are set to music and provide a bit of theatre to go with the confidently put together menu. Predominantly oriental influences exert their sway over well-sourced Irish ingredients, although Pacific, Indian and Mediterranean touches also vie for attention. The result is imaginative dishes without overly fussy presentation. Try, perhaps, crab and salmon tortellini in a ginger crab bisque, or a main of tea-smoked duck breast with seared scallops, Szechuan pickled cucumber and steamed jasmine rice.

Times 12-2.15/6-late Closed 25-26 Dec, Etr Mon, May Day BH, 12-13 Jul, L Sun-Wed

Deanes Restaurant

◎◎◎◎ *– see opposite page*

Deanes Restaurant

BELFAST Map 1 D5

Modern French, Irish  NOTABLE WINE LIST

Casual, modern dining from a Northern Irish culinary maestro

☎ 028 9033 1134
36-40 Howard St BT1 6PF
e-mail: info@michaeldeane.co.uk
dir: At rear of City Hall. Howard St on left opposite Spires building

Michael Deane's eponymous restaurant right at the hub of things in Belfast city centre has been through a fair amount of change lately. A burst pipe caused significant damage to the building in January 2010, and it was forced to close for nearly four months. Deane took the opportunity to fully refurbish the restaurant and - in his own words - to 'recreate a menu which contains more of the spirit of Deanes when I was first awarded three Rosettes in 1997'. The intention is to simplify the menu and make it more accessible. As ever, ingredients are sourced from the best local producers, but the whole experience is designed to be more relaxed and affordable. Certainly the new-look dining area has a modern, casual feel, with its pale wooden floor and darkwood and leather seating contrasting with bright pinkish red walls, while the service is friendly and knowledgeable. From the open kitchen come starters such as pan-fried Shetland scallops with Clonakilty black pudding, cauliflower purée and potato and scallion bread, and baked Ryefield goats' cheese, flaky pastry, carrot jam and salad of watercress. Main-course might be rump of Lough Erne new season lamb with spinach, sauce Niçoise and gratin dauphinoise, or fish of the day from the local market. Sticky toffee pudding with toffee sauce and yellowman ice cream could round things off, unless you prefer to go down the savoury route with a selection of farmhouse Irish and Continental cheeses from the trolley. The old bar area has been turned into a seafood bar with its own street entrance, serving the likes of local rock oysters, sardines on toast, moules frites and smoked haddock chowder. As we went to print we learned that the former Restaurant Michael Deane upstairs was to reopen as The Circle - a fine-dining restaurant (named after the turning circle in Helen's Bay) serving dinner on Thursday, Friday and Saturday only. The Circle (due to open in August 2010) will seat a maximum of 20 diners, plus a chef's table, and will offer a tasting menu changing weekly to reflect the best seasonal produce. Expect the likes of foie gras parfait with sourdough toast and quince chutney, roast breast and leg of local wood pigeon with pickled carrot and orange salad, and dark chocolate fondant served cold with white chocolate ice cream.

Chef Michael Deane, Simon Toye **Owner** Michael Deane, Derek Creagh **Times** 12-2.30/6-9.30 Closed 25 Dec, BHs, 11-18 Jul, Sun **Prices** Food prices not confirmed for 2011. Please telephone for details **Wines** 99 bottles over £20, 8 bottles under £20, 9 by glass **Notes** Vegetarian available **Seats** 70, Pr/dining room 40 **Children** Portions, Menu **Parking** On street (after 6pm), car park Clarence St

BELFAST ***continued***

Green Door Restaurant

Modern international

028 9038 8000
Malone Lodge Hotel, 60 Eglantine Av, Malone Rd BT9 6DY
e-mail: info@malonelodgehotel.com
dir: At hospital rdbt exit towards Bouchar Rd. At 1st rdbt, right at lights onto Lisburn Rd, 1st left into Eglantine Ave

The chic Malone Lodge Hotel occupies a row of Victorian townhouses in a leafy street just a few minutes from the centre of Belfast, and the Green Door is its suitably stylish restaurant. It's a split-level space, with tables smartly dressed in crisp white linen, high-backed chairs, aubergine hues on the walls and subdued lighting. The menu has an international feel but makes good use of local produce. Monkfish wrapped in prosciutto with tomato and chilli jam and a saffron couscous is a typically well-balanced main course, while butter cake with liqueur cherries and vanilla ice cream makes for a fine finish.

Times 12-3/6.30-10 Closed D Sun

James Street South Restaurant & Bar

Modern European

Intimate city-centre restaurant offering imaginative cooking

028 9043 4310
21 James Street South BT2 7GA
e-mail: info@jamesstreetsouth.co.uk
dir: Located between Brunswick St & Bedford St

Contemporary big-city style is stamped all over this well-frequented restaurant in Belfast centre. Inside the revamped former linen mill, the setting is stripped-out neutral chic: stark white walls are jazzed up with bright modern artwork, and smart leather seats stand on a bare wooden floor. The classical French-inspired cooking wells from chef-proprietor Niall McKenna's time spent in the kitchens of the sort of chefs who go by just one name - Nico and Marco. Exquisitely light dishes use top-grade Ulster produce, treated in a modern way to deliver precisely-executed food; scallop, smoked haddock brandade and chorizo all pull together in a marriage of pepper and smoke, for example. Sea bass, clams and pancetta presents the fish beneath a froth of clams and mussels, while espresso mousse is partnered successfully with chocolate cake, plum and Amaretto sorbet. Go for the fixed price lunch menus for top value.

Chef Niall McKenna **Owner** Niall & Joanne McKenna **Times** 12-2.45/5.45-10.45 Closed 25-26 Dec, 1 Jan, Etr Sun & Mon, 12 Jul, L Sun **Prices** Fixed L 2 course £14.50-£20.50, Fixed D 3 course £18.50-£37.50, Service optional, Groups min 5 service 10% **Wines** 90 bottles over £20, 6 bottles under £20, 8 by glass **Notes** Pre-theatre menu Mon-Fri 2 course £16.50, 3 course £18.50, Vegetarian available **Seats** 60 **Children** Portions **Parking** On street

Malmaison Belfast

Modern British, French

Contemporary-style converted seed mill offering satisfying brasserie dishes

028 9022 0200
34-38 Victoria St BT1 3GH
e-mail: mdavies@malmaison.com
dir: M1 along Westlink to Grosvenor Rd. Follow city centre signs. Pass City Hall on right, turn left onto Victoria St. Hotel on right

The Malmaison formula of taking characterful old buildings and kitting them out with decadent style-led contemporary interiors has worked its magic on a former seed mill for its Belfast outpost. The look is a plush modern take on cocktail bar glamour, all butch textures of wood and leather and boldly theatrical colours brought together in a funky style. Champagne and cocktails in the bar are de rigueur before settling into the brasserie for straightforward, well-cooked modern dishes delivered by cheerful staff. Presentation on slates and individual carving boards adds a touch of panache, and it's good to see that the 'home-grown and local' menu is still a crucial aspect of the Malmaison dining ethos. Mackerel rillettes with toasted soda bread is a good way to start, ahead of chargrilled entrecôte with pepper sauce, hand-cut chips and aïoli.

Times 12-2.30/6-12.30

The Merchant Hotel

Modern Irish, French

Modern Irish cooking in an opulent setting

028 9023 4888
35-39 Waring St BT1 2DY
e-mail: info@themerchanthotel.com
dir: In city centre, 2nd left at Albert clock onto Waring St. Hotel on left

Squillions have been lavished on restoring the derelict Victorian HQ of the Ulster Bank into a truly grand 21st-century hotel with an opulent restaurant to match. 'The Great Room' is exactly right: a high-domed ceiling with gold leaf and marble statuary propped up by Corinthian columns, and a sumptuous rich red and gold décor make an imposing setting for French-influenced modern Irish cooking. The kitchen draws on the local meat, fish and shellfish and treats them intelligently and without undue fuss. Off the tasting menu comes smoked venison carpaccio with shaved foie gras and pickled pear, followed by a silky cream of Jerusalem artichoke soup; next up roast quail with cassoulet garnish ahead of seared scallop with black pudding rösti and leek purée.

Times 12-2.30/6-10 Closed L Sat (afternoon tea only)

Shu

Modern Irish, European

Modern Irish cooking in a smart quarter

028 9038 1655
253-255 Lisburn Rd BT9 7EN
e-mail: eat@shu-restaurant.com
dir: From city centre take Lisburn Rd (lower end). Restaurant in 1m, on corner of Windsor Ave

A whitewashed terraced house in a stylish quarter of Belfast, Shu is named after the Egyptian god of the atmosphere. The open-plan, breezy ambience of the place echoes the theology, while the cooking tacks to a Euro-Irish wind, with French and Italian influences brought to bear on some high-gloss dishes. Expect well-made risottos, as well as duck confit, onion tarte Tatin, and organic Glenarm salmon with champ to be among the repertoire. A menu stalwart to write home about is the crisp-roasted pork belly with puréed cauliflower, potato gratin and cidery raisins. The raisins get to enjoy a bath in Sauternes when they turn up with steamed syrup sponge and custard, or you might finish on a more up-to-date note with a chocolate brownie and banana ice cream.

Chef Brian McCann **Owner** Alan Reid **Times** 12-2.30/6-10 Closed 25-26 Dec, 1 Jan, 12-13 Jul, Sun **Prices** Fixed L 2 course £12, Fixed D 3 course £20.50, Starter £4.25-£8.75, Main £12-£19.75, Dessert £5.50-£6.50, Service optional, Groups min 6 service 10% **Wines** 55 bottles over £20, 16 bottles under £20, 20 by glass **Notes** Supper menu Mon-Thu 5.30-6.30 1 course £8.50, 2 courses £12, Vegetarian available, Civ Wed 120 **Seats** 100, Pr/dining room 24 **Children** Portions, Menu **Parking** 4, On street

CO DOWN

BANGOR **Map 1 D5**

Clandeboye Lodge Hotel

Modern

Appealing cooking in a contemporary country setting

028 9185 2500
10 Estate Rd, Clandeboye BT19 1UR
e-mail: info@clandeboyelodge.co.uk
dir: M3 follow signs for A2 (Bangor). Before Bangor, turn right at junct signed Newtownards/Clandeboye Lodge Hotel & Blackwood Golf Course

There's no excuse for not working up a fine appetite for dinner at this contemporary country-house-style hotel near Belfast. Next door to 200 acres of woodland and gardens of the historic Clandeboye Estate, the Lodge has golf on the doorstep, and the seaside resort of Bangor is just a few minutes away. The Swiss chalet-style building sports a clubby décor, with wood panelling, leather chairs and unclothed wood- and marble-topped tables in the smart Clanbrasserie Restaurant. In tune with the setting, the kitchen takes a straightforward contemporary line with its output - expect dishes along the lines of lightly-smoked salmon fillet with lime and tarragon beurre blanc and chive mash, or rib-eye of beef from the grill, teamed with horseradish beignets and watercress mayonnaise.

Times 12-9.30 Closed 25-26 Dec

1614

@@ Modern, Traditional British

Atmospheric inn serving seasonal food

☎ 028 9185 3255
The Old Inn, 15 Main St, Crawfordsburn BT19 1JH
e-mail: info@theoldinn.com
web: www.theoldinn.com
dir: From Belfast along A2, past Belfast City Airport. Contine past Holywood & Belfast Folk & Transport museum. 2m after museum left at lights onto B20 for 1.2m

The Old Inn deserves its name - not far shy of 400 years old, it is steeped in history. The 1614 restaurant is housed in the oldest section of the building, which is Ireland's most ancient thatched hotel, with oak panels, brass chandeliers and local coats of arms to make for an atmospheric setting. After a reshuffle in 2009, the kitchen team has a clear focus on keeping things simple to emphasise flavour from top-class produce supplied by the ports of County Down as well as local beef, lamb, game and vegetables. Lough Neagh eel is teamed with smoked salmon and beetroot with horseradish dressing to great effect, ahead of roast pork fillet and crispy belly with Portavogie scallop, cauliflower purée and apple fondant.

Chef Neill Graham **Owner** Danny Rice
Times 12.30-2.30/7-9.30 Closed 25 Dec, L Mon-Sat, D Sun **Prices** Fixed D 4 course £30-£35, Service optional **Wines** 10 by glass **Notes** Sunday L, Vegetarian available, Dress restrictions, Smart casual, Civ Wed 85 **Seats** 64, Pr/dining room 25 **Children** Portions, Menu **Parking** 100

DUNDRUM Map 1 D5

Mourne Seafood Bar

@ Seafood

Vibrant fish restaurant 30 minutes from Belfast

☎ 028 4375 1377
10 Main St BT33 0LU
e-mail: bob@mourneseafood.com
dir: On main road from Belfast to The Mournes, on village main street

The Mourne Seafood Bar is a restaurant that 'does what it says on the tin'. As you would hope from a place that garners its materials from its own oyster and mussel beds, shellfish are the star of the show. The setting is easy on the eye too: a handsome Georgian building in a pretty fishing village, with the Mourne Mountains as a backdrop. Inside, it's an easygoing place with wooden floors and chunky wooden tables, and a buzzy vibe to go with straightforward fish and shellfish dishes that leave the freshness and purity of the ingredients to do the talking. Classics come in the form of roasted crab claws with chilli butter, seafood chowder, or grilled kippers with a fried egg, while mains might toss in a hint of Spain - hake fillet with chorizo and chick pea broth - or a modish mix of meat and fish, teaming sea bass with sauté potatoes and black pudding cream.

Chef Wayne Carville **Owner** Bob & Joanne McCoubrey
Times 12-9.30 Closed 25 Dec, Tue-Wed (winter)
Prices Fixed L 2 course £9.95, Fixed D 3 course £24.95, Starter £3.50-£6.50, Main £8.50-£17.50, Dessert £4.95, Service included **Wines** 18 bottles over £20, 22 bottles under £20, 5 by glass **Notes** Fixed D menu Sat only, Sunday L, Vegetarian available **Seats** 75, Pr/dining room 16 **Children** Portions, Menu **Parking** On street

STRANGFORD Map 1 D5

The Cuan Licensed Guest Inn

@ Traditional NEW V

Imaginative cooking in charming village inn

☎ 028 4488 1222
6-12 The Square BT30 7ND
e-mail: info@thecuan.com
dir: A7 to Downpatrick, follow A25 for Strangford ferry. Located in centre of village

In a conservation village on the shores of Strangford Lough, this family-owned and run hotel is an ideal base for exploring an area that includes the burial site of St Patrick in nearby Downpatrick. Dating back 200 years, the pub overlooks the village square and retains its original character with an open fire in the winter. The traditional cooking keeps things simple and lets the local produce speak for itself. A starter of steamed Dundrum Bay mussels might be followed by baked Glenarm salmon with spinach and a fresh parsley cream.

Chef Peter McErlean **Owner** Caroline & Peter McErlean
Times 9.30-10 **Prices** Food prices not confirmed for 2011. Please telephone for details **Notes** Sunday L, Vegetarian menu **Seats** 80, Pr/dining room 60 **Children** Portions, Menu **Parking** 5

CO FERMANAGH

ENNISKILLEN Map 1 C5

The Catalina Restaurant, Lough Erne Resort

@@ Modern, Traditional V

Modern golf and spa resort with contemporary and classic cuisine

☎ 028 6632 3230
Lough Erne Resort, Belleek Rd BT93 7ED
e-mail: info@loughernegolfresort.com
dir: A46 from Enniskillen towards Donegal, hotel in 3m

This luxurious purpose-built hotel sits on its own 600-acre peninsula jutting into the eponymous lough. Golfers are in heaven with a championship course designed by Nick Faldo, while others can seek nirvana in the luxurious Thai Spa. When the day's exertions and pampering are over, the Catalina Restaurant is the place to head for. Its name is taken from the curvaceous seaplanes that were based on the lough during the Second World War, immortalised in framed black-and-white photos on the walls; it's an expansive space with a classic look involving heavy drapes and linen-clothed tables beneath vaulted ceilings and arched windows opening over the lake. The home-grown chef's modern menus showcase prime local produce in imaginative dishes with ambitious flourishes. Saddle of rabbit is oak-smoked in-house and matched with caramelised peach, and roast hazelnut and rocket salad; French technique is brought to bear on main-course herb-crusted loin of Fermanagh lamb with dauphinoise potato, vegetable fricassée and tarragon jus.

Chef Noel McMeel **Owner** Jim & Eileen Treacy
Times 1-2.30/6.30 Closed L Mon-Sat **Prices** Food prices not confirmed for 2011. Please telephone for details **Wines** 120 bottles over £20, 8 bottles under £20, 3 by glass **Notes** Sunday L, Vegetarian menu, Civ Wed 315 **Seats** 75, Pr/dining room 30 **Children** Portions, Menu **Parking** 200

CO LONDONDERRY

LIMAVADY Map 1 C6

The Lime Tree

Traditional Mediterranean

Enjoyable food in popular neighbourhood restaurant

☎ 028 7776 4300
60 Catherine St BT49 9DB
e-mail: info@limetreerest.com
dir: Enter Limavady from Derry side. Restaurant on right on small slip road

The Lime Tree was named after the lime trees planted in the town to commemorate the inauguration of Limavady-born William Massey as prime minister of New Zealand. This relaxed restaurant's French- and Mediterranean-style classic cooking keeps loyal supporters coming back time and again, the frequently-changing menus showcasing excellent local fish and seafood. A starter of home-made crab cakes using Malin Head crabmeat, and served with a balsamic dressing, might precede a main course of roast saddle of rabbit with a leek and bacon stuffing and roasted garlic sauce. Round things off with steamed Seville orange marmalade sponge and vanilla custard.

Chef Stanley Matthews **Owner** Mr & Mrs S Matthews **Times** 6-9 Closed 25-26 Dec, 12 Jul, Sun-Mon, L all week (except by prior arrangement) **Prices** Starter £4.75-£9.50, Main £15.95-£24.50, Dessert £5.50-£6.95, Service optional **Wines** 17 bottles over £20, 24 bottles under £20, 5 by glass **Notes** Early bird menu Tue-Fri 6-7pm 2-3 course £13.95-£16.95, Vegetarian available **Seats** 30 **Children** Portions, Menu **Parking** 15, On street

Radisson Blu Roe Park Resort

Modern

Relaxed atmosphere in Irish country-house hotel

☎ 028 7772 2222
BT49 9LB
e-mail: reservations@radissonroepark.com
dir: On A6 (Londonderry-Limavady road), 0.5m from Limavady. 8m from Derry airport

Close to Derry and the Giant's Causeway, this Irish country house sits in over 150 acres of parkland on the River Roe and boasts an excellent golf course, spa and leisure facilities. The elegant Greens restaurant is the place to head to for fine dining and a modern European menu served by friendly staff. Expect crumbed crab and seafood cake with green lip mussels, rocket salad and a beurre blanc sauce, and seared scallops on a bed of saffron-infused and sun-blushed tomato orzo with spring onions and dried pancetta. The Coach House Brasserie serves sandwiches and pub-style grub.

Times 12-3/6.30-10 Closed Tue-Thu in Jan, Mon, L Tue-Sat, D Sun (Oct-May)

LONDONDERRY Map 1 C5

Beech Hill Country House Hotel

Modern Irish **NEW**

Elegant country house serving modish food

☎ 028 7134 9279
32 Ardmore Rd BT47 3QP
e-mail: info@beech-hill.com
dir: From A6 take Faughan Bridge turn, 1m to hotel opposite Ardmore Chapel

Beech Hill is an imposing 18th-century house standing in a 32-acre estate replete with woodland walks, lakes and sweeping lawns. The hotel is family-run and has a relaxed feel, which extends to the Ardmore Restaurant, an elegant room which opens out into a conservatory to make the most of the lovely garden views. Skilfully cooked dishes are prepared from carefully-sourced Irish ingredients, with a strong emphasis on sustainable and organic produce. Start with Clare Island organic smoked salmon with horseradish potato salad and a lemon and caper dressing, followed by roast crown of Fermanagh chicken marinated in garlic, lemon and thyme with jus gras.

Chef Trevor Hambley **Owner** Mr S Donnelly, Mrs P O'Kane **Times** 12-2.30/6-9.45 Closed 24-25 Dec **Prices** Fixed L 2 course £17.95, Fixed D 3 course £29.95, Starter £4.50-£11.95, Main £17-£24.95, Dessert £5.95, Service optional **Wines** 22 bottles over £20, 46 bottles under £20, 8 by glass **Notes** Early evening menu 3 course £19.95, Sunday L, Vegetarian available, Civ Wed 80 **Seats** 90, Pr/dining room 80 **Children** Portions **Parking** 50

MAGHERA Map 1 C5

Ardtara Country House

Modern International

Modern cuisine in a period country-house setting

☎ 028 7964 4490
8 Gorteade Rd BT46 5SA
e-mail: valerie_ferson@ardtara.com
dir: Take A29 to Maghera/Coleraine. Follow B75 (Kilrea) to Upperlands. Past sign for W Clark & Sons, next left

Forget modern boutique makeovers: Ardtara is a dyed-in-the-wool classic country hotel and proud to stay that way. That's not to say that this grand Victorian house has turned its back on the modern world – service is on the ball, and although the wood-panelled walls, glass skylight and unique hunting frieze in the dining room say traditional through-and-through, the kitchen deals in creative modern cooking with fine local materials featuring prominently. Fixed-price dinner menus could kick off with cider braised pork belly, well-partnered with apple purée and apple crisp, then pause for a sorbet before continuing with something like dry-aged beef fillet with gratin potatoes, celeriac purée, baby onions and a pepper cream reduction, and end with vanilla pannacotta with strawberry and balsamic soup.

Times 12.30-2.30/6.30-9

PORTSTEWART Map 1 C6

Preference Brasserie

European **NEW**

Imaginative cooking in a buzzy seaside brasserie

☎ 028 7083 3959 & 07933 489323
81 The Promenade BT55 7AF
e-mail: neilgibson@talktalk.net
dir: Enter Portstewart on Coleraine Rd, straight on at next 2 rdbts. Restaurant located on right next to church

In pole position for people watching on Portstewart's busy promenade, this stylish little brasserie has become a firm favourite with locals and holidaymakers since it set up shop in November 2008. The intimate dining room looks sharp in monochrome with its black leather chairs and lampshades and crisp white linen, and offers a suitably modern European menu to match. The kitchen keeps an eye out for the best of Ulster's seasonal produce and comes up with plenty of good, uncomplicated ideas, as in dry-spiced Wicklow wood pigeon with Madeira creamed lentils, bacon and red chard, followed by pan-fried sea bass with celeriac and vanilla mousseline, roast baby beets and beurre noisette.

Chef Neil Gibson **Owner** Neil & Louise Gibson **Times** 6-9.30 Closed 25-26 Dec, 1 Jan & BHs, Sun-Mon, L all week **Prices** Fixed D 2 course fr £14, Starter £4.50-£7.95, Main £13.95-£19.95, Dessert £5, Service optional, Groups min 6 service 10% **Wines** 4 bottles over £20, 8 bottles under £20, 2 by glass **Notes** Vegetarian available **Seats** 34 **Children** Portions **Parking** Car park

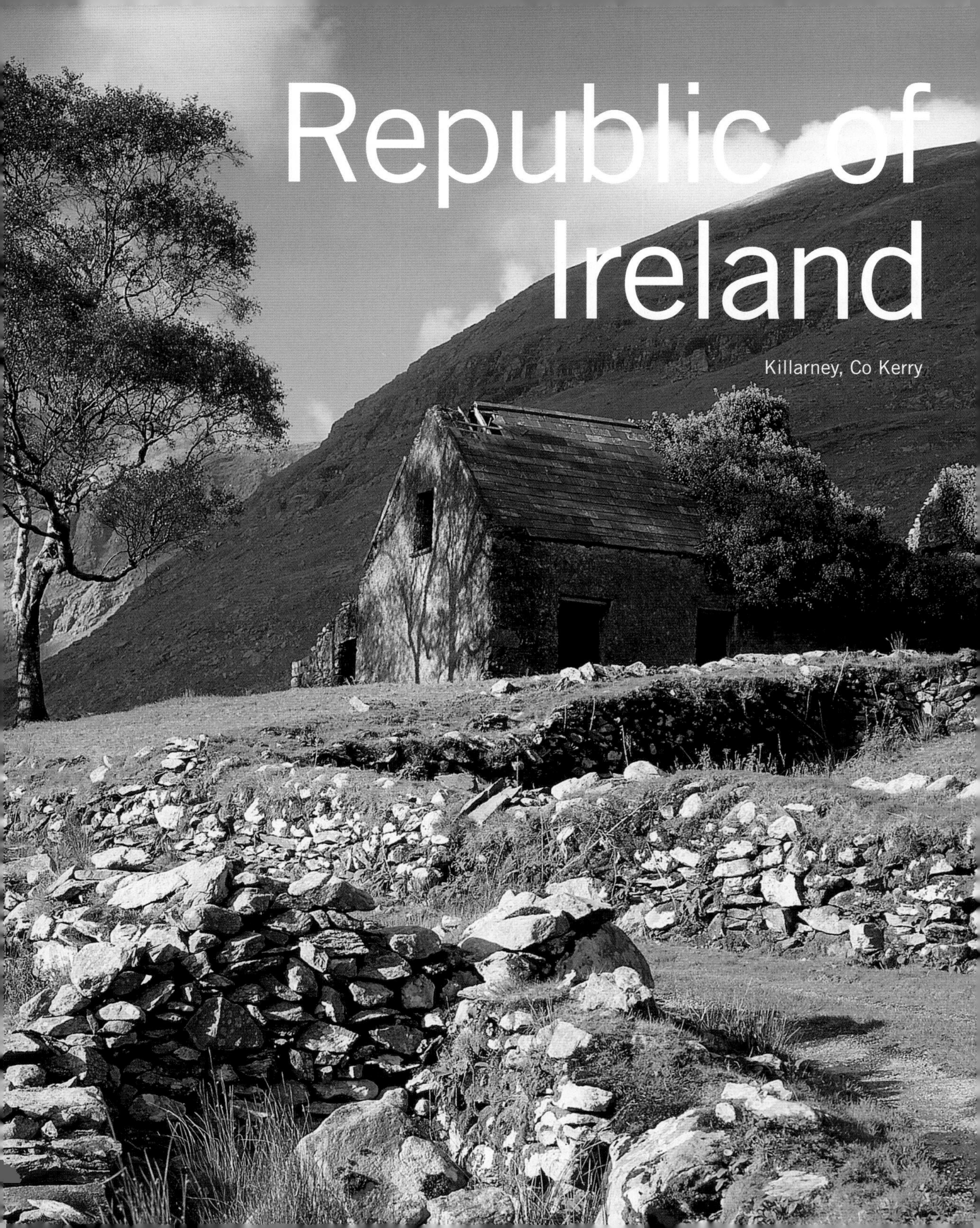

Republic of Ireland

Killarney, Co Kerry

CO CARLOW

TULLOW Map 1 C3

Mount Wolseley Hotel, Spa & Country Club

Modern European V

Confident modern cooking at a luxury golf resort

☎ 059 9180100
e-mail: sales@mountwolseley.ie
dir: Take N7 from Dublin. In Naas take N9 towards Carlow. In Castledermot turn left for Tullow

Occupying 200 acres on the estate once owned by Frederick Wolseley - the man behind the famous car marque - this luxurious resort is a must-visit course for golfers from all over the world. The hotel's light and airy main restaurant caters well to an international clientele with its modern European menu. Pan-seared scallops on endive salad with truffle croûtons and light pumpkin velouté gets things off to a good start, while main-course roast loin of venison is served with a glazed shallot Tatin, Jameson's-soaked raisins and chestnut crumb. Finish with iced lemon soufflé with pineapple and mango salsa.

Chef David Cuddihy, Ken Harker **Owner** Donal & I Morrissey **Times** 12.30-2.30/6-9.30 Closed 24-26 Dec, L Mon-Sat **Prices** Fixed L 2 course €100, Service optional **Wines** 6 by glass **Notes** Early bird menu available 6-7 €29.95 (not Sat), Vegetarian menu, Civ Wed 500 **Seats** 150, Pr/dining room 40 **Children** Portions, Menu **Parking** 500

CO CAVAN

CAVAN Map 1 C4

Cavan Crystal Hotel

Modern

Innovative cooking in contemporary hotel

☎ 049 4360600
Dublin Rd
e-mail: info@cavancrystalhotel.com
dir: Approach Cavan on N3, straight over rdbt, hotel immediately on left

As its name might suggest, the Cavan Crystal Hotel is operated by Ireland's second oldest crystal manufacturer on the same site as the factory. It is a striking contemporary operation, with the stylish Opus One restaurant acting as a showcase for the company's fine crystal products - chandeliers, glasses and dishes all twinkling away as a backdrop to the kitchen's beautifully-presented, creative reworkings of classic dishes. Top-class local produce is deployed in confident, well-balanced ideas, as in a tart of oak-smoked trout, teamed with pickled cucumber, beetroot, and savoury lemon and thyme ice cream. At main course, roast duck breast is partnered by onion mousseline, wild mushroom ragoût and cherry purée, while dessert delivers another demonstration of sound technique in a duo of Valrhona chocolate mousses with candied brioche and a shot glass of hot chocolate. A parade of peripheral amuses and pre-desserts all display the same level of inventiveness and attention to detail.

Times 12.30-3.30/6-10 Closed 24-25 Dec

VIRGINIA Map 1 C4

The Park Hotel

European, International

Estate-fresh produce served in a former hunting lodge

☎ 049 8546100
Virginia Park
e-mail: reservations@parkhotelvirginia.com
dir: exit N3 in Virginia onto R194. Hotel 500yds on left

This long, low-slung country hotel started life in the 18th century as the Marquis of Headfort's hunting lodge. With woodland walking trails, trout and bream fishing on Loch Ramor and a nine-hole golf course in its 100-acre estate, there's plenty to keep guests busy until dinner. In the Marquis dining room, period plasterwork, high ceilings, marble fireplaces and antiques add up to a sense of occasion for the kitchen's straightforward take on the classic country-house idiom. Expect plenty of home-grown organic ingredients courtesy of the estate's orchards, greenhouses and kitchen garden in dishes like chicken liver parfait with redcurrant jelly and olive oil croûtes, followed by slow-roast belly pork with red cabbage and cranberry, macerated apricots, toasted almonds and honey jus.

Times 12.30-3.30/6.30-9.30 Closed Jan, Xmas, Mon, L Tue-Sat, D Sun

Gregans Castle

BALLYVAUGHAN Map 1 B3

Modern European

Imaginative cooking in a haunting limestone landscape

☎ 065 7077005
e-mail: stay@gregans.ie
dir: On N67, 3.5m S of Ballyvaughan

The unassuming-looking house on the N67, just south of Ballyvaughan, stands opposite the original Gregans Castle, a towered house once the residence of successive Princes of the Burren – the Burren being the haunting limestone landscape all about you. Inside the hotel, an elegant dining room overlooks the gardens and those dramatic views, while the businesslike ingredient-listing of Mickael Viljanen's menu descriptions belies a level of intricacy and technical skill in the execution of the dishes. And what imaginative dishes they are. A fillet of fried mackerel comes with mackerel tartare set in cucumber and seawater jelly, with a shot glass of warm miso, and a creamy avocado mousse. Even greater complexity comes in a main dish that comprises boulangère potato, a ragoût of calf's sweetbreads and ceps, a wafer-thin onion tart and parsnip purée, not to mention a pair of sauces (sherry vinegar jus and an allspice emulsion), all supporting an impeccably timed fillet of local rose veal. At dessert, a selection of raspberry treatments includes an almond biscuit and violet sandwich and a smooth tart sorbet, as well as fennel pollen and a cube of hibiscus jelly. The list includes a wide selection of organic and biodynamic wines.

Chef Mickael Viljanen **Owner** Simon Haden **Times** 6-9 Closed seasonal, L all week (served in bar only) **Prices** Fixed L 2 course €21, Fixed D 3 course €50, Tasting menu €80, Service included **Wines** 95 bottles over €20, 14 by glass **Notes** Fixed menu D 6 course €65, Sunday L, Vegetarian available, Dress restrictions, No shorts, Civ Wed 45 **Seats** 50, Pr/dining room 36 **Children** Portions, Menu **Parking** 20

CO CLARE

BALLYVAUGHAN Map 1 B3

Gregans Castle

@@@ – *see opposite page*

ENNIS Map 1 B3

Temple Gate

@ Modern International

Modern dining in a Gothic-style building

☎ 065 6823300
The Square
e-mail: info@templegatehotel.com
dir: Exit N18 onto Tulla Rd for 0.25m, hotel on left

A short walk from the historic town centre of Ennis, the Temple Gate hotel is built on the site of the 19th-century Convent of Mercy. The sisters moved out in 1995 before a characterful conversion turned the place into a smart contemporary townhouse hotel with a touch of Victorian Gothic style, backed up by all the 21st-century mod cons you could reasonably ask for. The Legends restaurant is a clean-cut contemporary space kitted out with wooden floors, neutral tones and slatted window blinds - a setting that hits the right note for a wide-ranging menu of modern, European-accented dishes. Pan-fried organic chicken is layered with mozzarella and served with crispy speck ham and spiced plum chutney, followed by West Clare seafood - sea bass, crab claws, mussels and salmon - poached in basil-infused white wine broth and teamed with prawn crostini drizzled with white truffle oil.

Chef Paul Shortt **Owner** John Madden
Times 12.30-3/6-10 Closed 25-26 Dec, L ex by request only Mon-Sat **Prices** Fixed L 2 course €16.95, Fixed D 3 course €19, Service added 5% **Wines** 19 bottles over €20, 4 bottles under €20, 3 by glass **Notes** Sunday L, Vegetarian available, Civ Wed 200 **Seats** 90
Children Portions, Menu

LAHINCH Map 1 B3

Moy House

@ Modern, Traditional NEW

Modern Irish cooking and fabulous sea views

☎ 065 7082800
e-mail: moyhouse@eircom.net
dir: Located 1km from Lahinch on the Miltown Malbay road

Originally built in the mid 18th century as a private house, this attractive small hotel sits in 15 acres of grounds looking out over picturesque Lahinch Bay. Inside it's a happy blend of contemporary design and classical elegance, and that extends to the conservatory-style restaurant, which has fabulous sea views and flickering candles at night. The restaurant is small and intimate (booking is advised) and the menu changes daily and features plenty of local produce from both sea and land. Start, perhaps, with Liscannor Bay lobster, bisque risotto, coconut and lemongrass, before moving on to new season lamb chump with green peas, aubergine salsa and redcurrant jus. Save room for the warm chocolate truffle cake with a hot chocolate shot and hazelnut ice cream.

Times 7-8.30 Closed Jan

LISDOONVARNA Map 1 B3

Sheedy's Country House Hotel

@@ Modern Irish

Country-house cooking with classic and modern influences

☎ 065 7074026
e-mail: info@sheedys.com
dir: 20m from Ennis on N87

Sheedy's has been in the family's ownership since the 18th century and is the oldest house in the lovely village of Lisdoonvarna on the fringes of The Burren. It exudes the kind of family-run, unchanging tradition that keeps a loyal fan base returning year after year, particularly when the kitchen has chef-patron John Sheedy at the stoves turning out a strong line in classic cuisine revved up with a sprinkling of modern ideas. The hotel's kitchen garden does its bit to supplement excellent local materials, as typified by a rack of Burren lamb, roasted and served with pearl barley, baby onions and smoked bacon, or rabbit loin stuffed with black pudding and wrapped in smoked bacon and served with pear sauce.

Chef John Sheedy **Owner** John & Martina Sheedy
Times 6.45-8.30 Closed mid Oct-mid Mar, 1 day a week Mar-Apr **Prices** Fixed D 3 course fr €27.50, Starter €5.50-€13, Main €22-€29, Dessert €7.80-€9, Service optional **Wines** 11 bottles over €20, 2 by glass **Seats** 28
Children Portions **Parking** 25

NEWMARKET-ON-FERGUS Map 1 B3

Carrygerry Country House

@ Modern Irish NEW

Modern Irish cooking overlooking the Shannon

☎ 061 360500
Carrygerry
e-mail: info@carrygerryhouse.com

This Georgian house in the west of Ireland, set amid rolling country acres despite being a short drive from Shannon airport, feels like a home from home. Crackling fires and expansively friendly staff will warm your cockles in their different ways, and the conservatory dining room makes a welcoming setting for the modern Irish cuisine, which respects the seasons via the produce of some fine local growers and producers. Start with a well-made filo tartlet of creamy ricotta, spinach and pine nuts, served with organic saladings, before cruising onwards with cannon of Clare lamb marinated in red wine and mint, sauced in port and redcurrants, and served with a fried potato and spring onion cake.

Chef Niall Ennis **Owner** Niall & Gillian Ennis **Times** 6-10 Closed Xmas, Sun-Mon **Prices** Fixed D 3 course fr €30, Service optional **Wines** 25 bottles over €20, 8 bottles under €20, 8 by glass **Notes** Vegetarian available, Civ Wed 100 **Seats** 50 **Children** Portions, Menu **Parking** 25

Dromoland Castle

@@ Traditional Irish, European V

Classically-based cooking amid breathtaking opulence

☎ 061 368144
e-mail: sales@dromoland.ie
dir: From Ennis take N18, follow signs for Shannon/Limerick. 7m follow Quin. Newmarket-on-Fergus sign. Hotel 0.5m. From Shannon take N18 towards Ennis

The 16th-century castle with its round tower and battlements is now one of Ireland's most opulent hotels. Superbly decorated throughout, with layers of unapologetic chintz, rich reds and burnished golds, it feels like an enormous film set. Dine in baronial style among crystal chandeliers and vast mirrors, and the experience could barely be more ravishing. Executive chef David McCann offers a classically-based style of cuisine teased into the modern era with some inventive touches. Mussel and chorizo risotto with butternut squash and peas might be the prelude to mignon of milk-fed veal with Savoy cabbage, lentils and wild mushrooms in Madeira sauce. Depth of flavour is achieved throughout, even in the context of the featherlight texture required in a passionfruit soufflé, served with coconut sorbet.

Chef David McCann **Owner** Earl of Thomond **Times** 7-10 Closed 24-27 Dec, L all week **Prices** Fixed D 4 course €55 **Wines** 10 bottles under €20, 10 by glass
Notes Vegetarian menu, Dress restrictions, Smart dress **Seats** 80, Pr/dining room 40 **Children** Portions, Menu **Parking** 140

CO CORK

BALLYCOTTON Map 1 C2

Bayview Hotel

Modern Irish, French V

Accomplished cuisine in comfortable country house with dramatic views

☎ 021 4646746
e-mail: res@thebayviewhotel.com
web: www.thebayviewhotel.com
dir: At Castlemartyr on N25 (Cork-Waterford road) turn onto R632 to Garryvoe, then follow signs for Shanagarry & Ballycotton

True to its name, the Bayview has heavenly views along the coast from its clifftop perch above the fishing harbour of Ballycotton. When fish and seafood is landed fresh on your doorstep every day, it should quite rightly be the star of the show, but there's plenty of local meat and game action too. With views like this, the window tables in the restaurant are snapped up quickly, while the kitchen delivers imaginative modern Irish food that aims to satisfy all palates and preferences. A lengthy menu brims with ambitious ideas and clever touches – starters might find sautéed prawns with Reblochon cheese gnocchi, potato and wild garlic foam, alongside terrine of smoked ham hock with cabbage, potato and mustard dressing, while main courses cover all the bases from pan-fried turbot with Jerusalem artichoke purée, sautéed ceps, salsify and vanilla butter, to roast saddle of rabbit teamed with caramelised pork belly, squash purée and a sweet-and-sour Madeira reduction.

Chef Ciaran Scully **Owner** John & Carmel O'Brien **Times** 1-3/7-9 Closed Nov-Apr, L Mon-Sat **Prices** Starter €7.50-€15, Main €24-€32, Dessert €8.50, Service optional **Wines** 28 bottles over €20, 7 by glass **Notes** Sunday L, Vegetarian menu, Dress restrictions, Smart casual **Seats** 65, Pr/dining room 30 **Children** Portions, Menu **Parking** 40

BALLYLICKEY Map 1 B2

Sea View House

Traditional

Impressive Irish cooking in a delightful country house

☎ 027 50073 & 50462
e-mail: info@seaviewhousehotel.com
dir: 3m N of Bantry towards Glengarriff, 70yds off main road, N71

True to its name, this welcoming hotel in beautifully-kept gardens overlooks Bantry Bay and the mountains beyond. It is the sort of place where guests return again and again for its sincere friendliness and the promise of consistently excellent food, which is served in three interconnecting dining rooms done out in restful hues of green, and furnished with polished mahogany tables, antiques and fresh flowers; a new conservatory restaurant is flooded with light and looks over the gardens. The kitchen utilises superb local ingredients - sparklingly fresh, locally-landed fish is a real plus - and draws on classic country-house themes. A feather-light scallop mousse with vermouth sauce gets proceedings under way, followed by lemon sole, served as a paupiette filled with local Beara prawns, and as fillets poached in a Bonne Femme sauce.

Times 12.30-1.45/7-9.30 Closed Nov-Mar, L Mon-Sat

BLARNEY Map 1 B2

Blarney Golf Resort

Modern Irish, International

Luxurious golf resort with impressive modern cooking

☎ 021 4384477
Kerry Rd, Tower
e-mail: reservations@blarneygolfresort.com
dir: Exit N20 for Blarney, 4km to Tower, turn right onto Old Kerry Rd. Hotel 2km on right

Close to the historic town of Blarney, this luxury golf hotel is in a wonderful position set against a backdrop of 170 acres of beautiful woods in the Shournagh valley. After drinks in Cormac's Bar, move through to the spacious Inniscarra Restaurant which occupies a split-level room with contemporary décor. Seasonal local produce is the cornerstone of the kitchen, and the cooking is modern Irish with international influences. Start with home-made duck spring roll served with Asian salad and sweet chilli sauce and follow with braised shank of Irish lamb with honey and rosemary, roasted garlic mashed potato, confit of root vegetables and rosemary sauce. Milk chocolate and mint mousse rounds things off.

Chef Shane McClements **Times** 6-8.45 Closed 24-25 Dec, L all week **Prices** Fixed L 2 course fr €18, Fixed D 4 course fr €80, Starter €7.50-€10, Main €22.95-€29, Dessert €6.50, Service optional **Wines** 16 bottles over €20, 2 bottles under €20, 4 by glass **Notes** Sunday L, Vegetarian available, Dress restrictions, Smart casual, Civ Wed 150 **Seats** 130, Pr/dining room 40 **Children** Portions, Menu **Parking** 300

CLONAKILTY Map 1 B2

Inchydoney Island Lodge & Spa

Modern French

Fine West Cork ingredients in a glorious coastal setting

☎ 023 8833143 & 8821100
Inchydoney
e-mail: reservations@inchydoneyisland.com
dir: From Cork take N71 following West Cork signs. Through Innishannon, Bandon & Clonakilty, then follow signs for Inchydoney Island

Undisturbed views of the Atlantic Ocean and the Blue Flag beach at Inchydoney are just part of the appeal at this luxurious resort hotel, reached by a causeway from the mainland. The rest is down to the sumptuous, designer interior, the state-of-the-art spa and the fine-dining Gulfstream Restaurant. The hotel's main dining room (there's also a pub and bistro) has a chic, contemporary look, and glorious sea views as befits its name. French and Mediterranean influences underpin the menu, with plenty of fresh local seafood and organic produce to the fore, as in seared West Cork scallops with a cauliflower purée, sweet-and-sour cauliflower, asparagus and a sauce Antiboise. For main course, pan-fried fillet of hake comes with a red onion and basil polenta, spring cabbage, pancetta, honey-glazed carrots and a clam beurre blanc. Ginger flavoured crème brûlée with seasonal berries and pistachio biscotti makes a fitting finale.

Times 1-3/6.30-9.45 Closed 24-26 Dec, L Mon-Sat

CORK Map 1 B2

Maryborough Hotel & Spa

Modern International V

Modern cooking in popular hotel restaurant

☎ 021 4365555
Maryborough Hill
e-mail: info@maryborough.ie
dir: From Jack Lynch Tunnel take 2nd exit signed Douglas. Right at 1st rdbt, follow Rochestown road to fingerpost rdbt. Left, hotel on left 0.5m up hill

Just minutes from Cork city centre, this beautifully renovated 18th-century house stands in 14 acres of listed gardens and woodland. A modern extension houses a luxurious spa and leisure centre, while the smart, split-level restaurant offers an extensive contemporary menu with a broad appeal. Go for smoked haddock and cod fishcakes with braised leeks and parsley cream sauce to start, followed by slow-roasted belly of pork with soy and honey glaze, Chinese leaf, sesame carrots, spring onion and coriander. End with a sumptuous chocolate and Maltesers mousse cake with mocha syrup.

Chef Gerry Allen **Owner** Dan O'Sullivan **Times** 12.30-2.30/6.30-10 Closed 24-26 Dec, L Sat, D Sun-Mon **Prices** Fixed L 2 course €20-€25, Fixed D 3 course fr €40, Starter €5.50-€9, Main €18.50-€25, Dessert €6.95-€9, Service optional, Groups min 10 service 10% **Wines** 44 bottles over €20, 11 bottles under €20, 4 by glass **Notes** Sunday L, Vegetarian menu, Dress restrictions, Smart casual, Civ Wed 100 **Seats** 120, Pr/dining room 60 **Children** Portions, Menu **Parking** 300

DURRUS — Map 1 B2

Blairscove House & Restaurant

International NEW

Confident cooking in carefully-restored old house

☎ 027 61127
e-mail: antje_gersche@eircom.net
dir: R591 from Durrus to Crookhaven, in 1.5m restaurant on right through blue gate

Phillipe and Sabina de Mey's impressive restaurant is in the sympathetically restored outbuildings of an 18th-century manor house, set in landscaped gardens with glorious views over Dunmanus Bay. A lofty, church-like room with timbered ceiling, exposed stone walls hung with fine gilt-framed portraits, and a magnificent central chandelier, make the restaurant a most appealing setting in which to tuck into skilfully prepared and presented dishes from a seasonal menu that is brimful of local seafood and artisan produce. The simplicity of the menu belies the care and attention given to each dish and the subtle combination of ingredients ensures that no one flavour predominates. Take a selection of delicious marinated seafood for starters, perhaps céviche of salmon with hints of ginger, lime and chilli, and a main course of succulent, tender and gamey, slow-roasted pheasant with a port cream sauce. A stunning assiette of desserts, including a rum baba and coconut and rice pudding, shows a lightness of touch.

Chef Richard Milnes **Owner** Phillipe & Sabina de Mey **Times** 12.30-2.30/5.30-9.30 Closed 1-16 Jan. Nov, Mon, L Tue-Sat, D Sun **Prices** Fixed D 3 course €58, Service optional, Groups min 8 service 10% **Wines** 1 bottle under €20, 6 by glass **Notes** Early bird 5.30-6.45pm 2/3 course €30-€40, 4 course L €35, Vegetarian available, Dress restrictions, Smart casual **Seats** 75 **Children** Portions **Parking** 30

GARRYVOE — Map 1 C2

Garryvoe Hotel

Modern Irish

Seafood-rich menu with Bay views

☎ 021 4646718
Ballycotton Bay, Castlemartyr
e-mail: res@garryvoehotel.com
web: www.garryvoehotel.com
dir: From N25 at Castlemartyr (Cork-Rosslare road) take R632 to Garryvoe

The luxurious hotel on the beach at Garryvoe has come a long way since its humble Edwardian beach hut origins, but the glorious five-mile beach and views of Ballycotton and the island remain the same. You're greeted by the genuine warmth of a family-run operation, and an interior that has been brought smartly up to date. The sea-gazing views make a sublime backdrop to the kitchen's unfussy modern cooking – a simple but effective formula that takes great local produce (plenty of seafood, naturally) and doesn't faff about with it. Spiced crab cake is spiked with chilli and served with lemongrass dressing, while main course delivers sea bream with sautéed leeks in a cream sauce; at dessert, a tart berry coulis cuts through the richness of chocolate roulade and fresh cream.

Chef Kevin O'Sullivan **Owner** Carmel & John O'Brien **Times** 1-2.30/6.45-8.45 Closed 24-25 Dec, L Mon-Sat **Prices** Fixed L 3 course €28, Fixed D 4 course €44, Starter €6.50-€12, Main €24-€32, Dessert €7-€8.50, Service optional **Wines** 6 by glass **Notes** Sunday L, Vegetarian available, Civ Wed 100 **Seats** 80, Pr/dining room 40 **Children** Portions, Menu **Parking** 80

GOLEEN — Map 1 A1

The Heron's Cove

Traditional Irish NEW

Fresh fish and seafood on the harbourside

☎ 028 35225
The Harbour
e-mail: suehill@eircom.net
dir: In Goleen village, turn left to harbour

This delightful restaurant with rooms sits in an idyllic spot on Goleen harbour near to Mizen Head, where the lonely Fastnet Rock lighthouse beams out across the Atlantic at Ireland's most south-westerly point. The former cow shed is traditionally rustic, fitted out cosily with simple pine furniture and wooden floors. This is an exceptionally easygoing, friendly place, where the kitchen subscribes to the Slow Food ethos, taking time to source the best local, mostly organic, ingredients that are the backbone of its output. The menu is as straightforward and unfussy as its surroundings; typical of starters are crispy crabcakes spiked with ginger, garlic, red chilli and lemon, and served with wasabi mayonnaise. Super-fresh local seafood is showcased once more in a main course of seared Dunmanus Bay scallops with bacon cream sauce. Large windows look out from the airy restaurant to an alfresco terrace.

Chef Irene Coughlan **Owner** Sue Hill **Times** 7-9.30 Closed Nov-Apr (open for weekend, Xmas & New Year bookings) **Prices** Fixed D 3 course €30, Starter €5.50-€10.95, Main €19.50-€37.95, Service optional **Wines** 36 bottles over €20, 11 bottles under €20, 2 by glass **Notes** Vegetarian available **Seats** 30 **Children** Portions, Menu **Parking** 10

GOUGANE BARRA — Map 1 B2

Gougane Barra Hotel

Irish, French

Traditionally-based cooking in stunningly beautiful lakeside setting

☎ 026 47069
e-mail: gouganebarrahotel@eircom.net
dir: Off R584 between N22 at Macroom & N71 at Bantry. Take Keimaneigh junct for hotel

Sitting by the side of the eponymous lake in west Cork, in a stunningly beautiful glen, the hotel is the very model of a tranquil retreat. From the dining room, you can catch glimpses of fish jumping in the lake, and the wild flowers and crisp white napery on tables create an elegant tone. Presentations of dishes on triangular plates garnished with all manner of herbs, berries and wild flowers are almost as luscious as the views, and the cooking is based on tried-and-true traditional principles. A meal might take in St Tola goats' cheese, roast aubergine and red onion galette adorned with dill flowers, roast Kenmare hake with sugar snaps in a silky-smooth hollandaise, with soup or sorbet in between, and a finisher of bread-and-butter pudding with Murphy's stout ice cream.

Times 12.30-2.30/5.30-8.45 Closed 18 Oct-10 Apr, L Mon-Sat

KINSALE Map 1 B2

Pier One

Modern, Traditional

Waterfront hotel with modern cuisine and harbour views

☎ 021 4779300
Trident Hotel, Worlds End
e-mail: info@tridenthotel.com
dir: From Cork take R600 to Kinsale. Hotel at end of Pier Rd

The Trident Hotel has bagged the best spot on the waterfront of historic Kinsale for its Pier One restaurant. Inside it has a light-drenched, clean-cut contemporary feel, with works by well-known Irish artists on exposed stone walls vying for attention with the views over the bustle in the harbour below. The kitchen takes a wide-ranging modern European tack, using peerless local ingredients in straightforward dishes along the lines of seared scallops with lemon and black pepper, ahead of crusted rack of lamb with redcurrant jus. Given the location, seafood has to be a strong suit – perhaps baked fillet of cod with a herb and parmesan crust and butter sauce, or a platter of local sea bass, monkfish, salmon and mussels with garlic and chilli butter sauce.

Times 1-2.30/7-9.30 Closed 24-26 Dec, L Mon-Sat

The White House

Traditional, International

Buzzy bistro-style food in the centre of Kinsale

☎ 021 4772125
Pearse St, The Glen
e-mail: whitehse@indigo.ie

This atmospheric family-run bistro and bar is housed in one of the oldest buildings in the heart of Kinsale, dating back to the 1850s. Inside the Restaurant d'Antibes the design is smart and modern with red banquettes and covered chairs against white and black walls. Live music can often be found in the next-door bar. Good quality local ingredients (many of the vegetables and herbs come from the owners' garden) are used in traditional Irish dishes presented in a rustic manner. Make the most of the local seafood with chef's special of seafood chowder to start or seafood pancake for a main course. Or for the more carnivorous, try crispy half-roast duck with apple and walnut stuffing, star anise and redcurrant jelly sauce.

Chef Martin El Sahen **Owner** Michael Frawley **Times** 12-10 Closed 25 Dec **Prices** Food prices not confirmed for 2011. Please telephone for details **Wines** 24 bottles over €20, 2 bottles under €20, 9 by glass **Notes** Sunday L, Vegetarian available **Seats** 45 **Children** Portions, Menu **Parking** Car park at rear of building

SHANAGARRY Map 1 C2

Ballymaloe House

Traditional NEW

Simply superb cooking in a delightful country house

☎ 021 4652531
e-mail: res@ballymaloe.ie
dir: From R630 at Whitegate rdbt, left onto R631, left onto Cloyne. Located on Ballycotton Rd

The Allen family have run Ballymaloe, a historic country house in 400 acres of East Cork, for 40 years. The concept of local sourcing was going strong here long before it became a foodie buzzword - the restaurant has always gathered fresh produce from its own garden and glasshouses, reared meat on the estate and taken fish fresh from the boats in Ballycotton just a few minutes away. Country-house tradition reigns in each of four dining rooms - white linen, gleaming silver and crystal on the tables, backed by polite, professional service - and the kitchen takes a similarly simple approach, letting the peerless produce talk for itself. Roast cod paired simply with salsa verde opens a five-course dinner, while main course brings Ballymaloe Farm's home-reared roast loin of organic pork with perfect crackling, Bramley apple sauce, red cabbage with cinnamon, and pommes duchesse. Go for a selection of desserts: poached rhubarb with star anise and ginger, a coffee roulade with a sweet marshmallow centre, and a Bavarian apple tart.

Chef Jason Fahey **Owner** The Allen Family **Times** 1/7-9.30 **Prices** Food prices not confirmed for 2011. Please telephone for details **Notes** Sunday L, Vegetarian available **Children** Menu

YOUGHAL Map 1 C2

Ahernes

Irish, Seafood

Seafood restaurant beside the sea

☎ 024 02424
163 North Main St
e-mail: ahernes@eircom.net

This long-established family operated small luxury hotel and seafood restaurant makes the most of its location near Ballycotton Bay to source the best of local produce. Situated in the historic walled seaside resort of Yougal on the south coast, Ahernes attracts a strong local following. The simple, daily-changing menu always features the catch of the day but there's also good local meat and vegetables if that takes your fancy. Expect classical garnishing and sauces. Start with seafood chowder before tucking into grilled black sole on the bone or buttered lobster.

CO DONEGAL

DONEGAL Map 1 B5

Harvey's Point Country Hotel

Modern V

High-impact cooking in a soothing lakeside location

☎ 074 9722208
Lough Eske
e-mail: sales@harveyspoint.com
dir: From Donegal 2m towards Lifford, left at Harvey's Point sign, follow signs, take 3 right turns to hotel gates

The Swiss family Gysling stumbled upon a little piece of Switzerland in the Donegal Hills by the shores of Lough Eske, and founded this upmarket modern hotel. It grew quickly from its modest beginning as a four-room guesthouse - nowadays, guests are known to arrive by helicopter to recharge in such a tranquil setting, with the bonus of excellent food served with a lough view through a wall of full-length windows. The kitchen scours the local area for top-class local and organic ingredients for modern flavour-packed cooking. Roast saddle of rabbit wrapped in ham is delivered on wilted spinach and lentils, with diced spicy poached pear as an interesting counterpoint to its earthy punch. Next up, an exotic breast of Peking duck comes with a vanilla-perfumed swede purée, a clove-scented quenelle of braised red cabbage and a duck and black cherry jus.

Chef Paul Montgomery **Owner** Marc Gysling, Deirdre McGlone **Times** 12.30-2.30/6.30-9.30 Closed Mon-Tue (Nov-Etr) **Prices** Fixed L 2 course €20-€30, Fixed D 3 course €49-€55, Starter €12, Main €35, Dessert €12, Service included **Wines** 26 by glass **Notes** Sunday L, Vegetarian menu, Dress restrictions, Smart casual, Civ Wed 250 **Seats** 100, Pr/dining room 100 **Children** Menu **Parking** 300

DUNFANAGHY Map 1 C6

Seascapes Restaurant

Traditional NEW

Accomplished cooking in a glorious wild setting

☎ 074 9136208
Arnolds Hotel, Main St
e-mail: enquiries@arnoldshotel.com
dir: On N56 from Letterkenny, hotel on left entering the village

This traditional family-run hotel in Donegal's spectacular Sheephaven Bay sits in the perfect spot to take on the great outdoors. The dunes of Killahoey Strand start at the doorstep, the Atlantic breakers are surfers' heaven, and when you're done working up an appetite, there's the warmth of open turf fires and good old-fashioned hospitality back in the hotel. The aptly-named Seascapes Restaurant has knockout views of Killahoey Beach, and deals in straightforward Irish cuisine that makes good use of the finest local produce, especially fresh fish. A goats' cheese tart makes a fine starter, served with roasted red peppers and red onion marmalade, and with such a wealth of superb piscine produce to hand, follow on with the fresh seafood platter.

Chef Joseph Gallagher **Owner** Arnold Family **Times** 5-9.30 **Prices** Fixed L 3 course €19.95-€30, Fixed D 3 course €25-€35, Starter €5.50-€8.95, Main €15.95-€23.95, Dessert €5.50-€7.75 **Notes** Sunday L, Vegetarian available, Civ Wed 90 **Seats** 60 **Children** Portions, Menu **Parking** 40

DUNKINEELY **Map 1 B5**

Castle Murray House and Restaurant

Traditional & Modern French

Excellent local seafood and great coastal views

☎ 074 9737022
St Johns Point
e-mail: info@castlemurray.com
dir: From Donegal take N56 towards Killybegs. Left to Dunkineely

Overlooking the ruins of McSwyne's Castle, this clifftop hotel is in a fabulous location with stunning sea and coastal views. An ideal base for exploring beautiful Donegal, the building was once a farmhouse and the floors were fashioned from stones from Castle Murray. In the comfortable restaurant, enjoy fresh seafood landed that day on a French-influenced menu that changes with the seasons; pigeon and foie gras terrine with a jelly of carrots and honey might precede grilled lobster with garlic butter and brandy. Round things off with caramelised apple and bourbon vanilla crumble.

Chef Remy Dupuy **Owner** Marguerite Howley **Times** 1.30-3.30/6.30-9.30 Closed mid Jan-mid Feb, L Mon-Sat, D Mon-Tue (low season) **Prices** Fixed D 3 course €31 **Wines** 24 bottles over €20, 28 bottles under €20, 5 by glass **Notes** Fixed L 4 course €31, Sunday L, Vegetarian available, Civ Wed 40 **Seats** 80, Pr/dining room 40 **Children** Portions, Menu **Parking** 25

RATHMULLAN **Map 1 C6**

Fort Royal Hotel

Modern Irish, Seafood

Country-house dining in mature gardens sloping down to the sea

☎ 074 9158100
Fort Royal
e-mail: fortroyal@eircom.net
dir: R245 from Letterkenny, through Rathmullan, hotel signed

The Fletcher family have run Fort Royal for over half a century, so you can take it as read that this small-scale country house runs like clockwork. And who can blame them for wanting to stay put? This is the sort of country that makes you glad to be alive, with walks on sandy beaches and the shores of Lough Swilly, plus the hotel has 18 acres of lovely grounds with tennis and a 9-hole pitch and putt course. When it comes to dining, the light-flooded restaurant looks through vast floor-to-ceiling windows over the gardens to glimpses of the bay. The kitchen sticks to the classic country-house idiom, making maximum use of home-grown fruit, vegetables and herbs, backed by exemplary local fish and meat in its daily set dinner menus. Kick off with a toasted local goats' cheese tartlet, and proceed to fillet of turbot served simply with sherry vinaigrette, garden herbs, broad beans and new potatoes.

Times 7.30-8.30 Closed L all week

Rathmullan House

Modern Irish V

Modern Irish cooking in a romantic setting

☎ 074 9158188
e-mail: info@rathmullanhouse.com
dir: R245 Letterkenny to Ramelton, over bridge right onto R247 to Rathmullan. On entering village turn at Mace shop through village gates. Hotel on right

On the shores of Lough Swilly, this charming family-owned country-house hotel stands on the edge of pretty Rathmullan village and port. In the Weeping Elm restaurant the tent-like canopied ceiling of three hexagonal sunrooms are dotted with fairy lights, creating a romantic soft glow in which to enjoy dinner. Take in the views of the gardens and lawns as they sweep down to the shore. Genuinely friendly service adds to the relaxed vibe. New head chef Kelan McMichael, previously of Roscoffs and Deane's in Belfast, is big on home-grown, sustainable produce and makes the most of organic fruit, salad leaves and herbs from the hotel's walled garden, while also making use of several artisan producers for his modern Irish menu. You might find Rathmullan House Burtonport crab cocktail with seasonal leaves and Granny Smith apple, followed by slow-roast crispy Silverhill duck with pea, barley, chorizo and apricots, and Bob's home-made marmalade steamed pudding with whiskey custard, raisins and toasted almonds.

Chef Ian Orr, Kelan McMichael **Owner** Wheeler Family **Times** 7.30-8.45 Closed Jan-mid Feb **Prices** Fixed D 3 course €45, Starter €10-€15, Main €25-€35, Dessert €12-€15, Service added 10% **Wines** 3 bottles under €20, 10 by glass **Notes** Vegetarian menu, Dress restrictions, Smart casual, Civ Wed 70 **Seats** 70, Pr/dining room 30 **Children** Portions, Menu **Parking** 40

DUBLIN

DUBLIN **Map 1 D4**

Finnstown Country House

European, International

Traditional cuisine in grand country house

☎ 01 6010700
Newcastle Rd
e-mail: manager@finnstown-hotel.ie
dir: From M1 take 1st exit onto M50 southbound. 1st exit after toll bridge. At rdbt take 3rd left (N4 W). Left at lights. Over next 2 rbts, hotel on right

Peacocks are the leitmotif of this elegant Georgian country house on the fringes of Dublin: the feathered dandies strut around 45 acres of splendid grounds and lend their name to the Peacock Restaurant. This light-drenched Georgian-styled room with an octagonal sunroom extension is the setting for the kitchen's straightforward treatment of cracking local produce. The internationally-inspired menu kicks off, not with peacock in any form at all, but with a well-made chicken liver pâté with melba toast and a tangy red onion relish, before putting excellent seafood to use in a medley involving sea bass, salmon and mussels in a prawn bisque sauce.

Times 12.30-2.30/7.30-9.30 Closed 24-26 Dec, D Sun

The Park Restaurant

Traditional, International

Contemporary brasserie in country club setting

☎ 01 6406300
Castleknock Hotel & Country Club, Porterstown Rd, Castleknock
e-mail: info@chcc.ie
dir: M50 exit 3 to Castleknock village, left at Myos junct & follow signs

A base for the All Blacks rugby squad when they play in Europe, this contemporary country club hotel is also a mile from Luttrellstown Castle where David and Victoria Beckham tied the knot. Only 9km from Dublin city centre, the hotel feels surprisingly rural with an 18-hole golf course, leisure centre and beauty salon. Guests have a wide choice of dining options, including The Brasserie and The Park Restaurant, a modern bistro and steak house with panoramic views of the golf course. Classic dishes include pan-fried tiger prawns with sun-dried tomato cream and linguine, pan-fried calves' liver with bacon, horseradish creamed potatoes and red onion marmalade or a selection of aged Irish steaks with traditional accompaniments.

Chef Lewis Bannerman **Owner** FBD Group **Times** 12.30-3/5.30-10 Closed 24-26 Dec, L Sat **Prices** Food prices not confirmed for 2011. Please telephone for details **Wines** 57 bottles over €20, 12 by glass **Notes** Sunday L, Vegetarian available, Civ Wed 150 **Seats** 65, Pr/dining room 400 **Children** Portions, Menu **Parking** 200

Restaurant Patrick Guilbaud

DUBLIN Map 1 D4

Modern French V

Unadulterated class at Dublin's premier restaurant

☎ 01 6764192
Merrion Hotel, 21 Upper Merrion St
e-mail: restaurantpatrickguilbaud@eircom.net
dir: Opposite government buildings, next to Merrion Hotel

Whether you're looking to impress a client, or simply have a good reason for treating yourself, Patrick Guilbaud's restaurant at the Merrion Hotel is the outstanding address in the Irish capital. It's a more modern looking room than you may be expecting amid the surrounding Georgian splendour, with assertive contemporary artworks, but there is as much sparkling crystal and gleaming silverware as you can handle. Service is precise and measured, without losing the personal touch. The cooking is at the top end of culinary achievement, with great care and attention to detail evident in all dishes, which, while made up of many elements and requiring a deal of technical skill, are nonetheless deftly balanced. It's hardly any wonder that there's a waiting-list for getting in at weekends. A brace of seared scallops are served on a cake of shredded crubeens and capers, garnished with a strip of crisp smoked bacon, and accompanied by a serving of tiny mushrooms infused with anise. After a stunning starter like that, main courses have a lot to live up to, but manage a further gear. Lightly grilled John Dory is bedded on saffron-scented quinoa, with sautéed squid in bouillabaisse, or there may be medium-rare magret of duck on spinach, with parsnips cooked two ways (roasted strips and a smooth cream), a seared lobe of foie gras and a crystal-clear sauce of mead. Dessert may come in a martini glass, and consist of prettily layered mango, pineapple and pomegranate seeds in yoghurt, the whole garnished with pineapple sorbet finished with gold-leaf. All other details, from breads to petits fours, are present and correct in what will add up to an undeniably expensive but memorable dining occasion.

Chef Guillaume Lebrun **Owner** Patrick Guilbaud **Times** 12.30-2.15/7.30-10.15 Closed 25 Dec, 1st wk Jan, Sun-Mon **Prices** Fixed L 2 course €38, Starter €28-€44, Main €46-€80, Dessert €22-€25, Service optional **Wines** 1000 bottles over €20, 12 by glass **Notes** Tasting menu 7 course, Vegetarian menu, Dress restrictions, Smart casual **Seats** 80, Pr/dining room 25 **Children** Portions **Parking** In square

DUBLIN *continued*

Restaurant Patrick Guilbaud

@@@@ – *see opposite page*

The Shelbourne

@ European, Irish

Comforting classics in luxurious Dublin hotel

☎ 01 6634500
27 St Stephen's Green
e-mail: www.Lemeridien-hotels.com
dir: In City Centre

The Shelbourne is a Victorian Grand Hotel built on a scale designed to impress on St Stephen's Green in the heart of Dublin. Opulently restored to its full glory, it is the place to base yourself amid the city's cultural and historical heritage. A pint of the black stuff in the Horseshoe Bar makes a fittingly butch aperitif before taking on the steak and seafood-based fare in the Saddle Room Restaurant. An open kitchen provides culinary theatre while you dig into traditional dishes driven by the seasons – expect starters such as chicken liver parfait with spicy red onion marmalade and home-made toasted brioche, followed by prime slabs of Irish beef, or fish in the shape of sole, grilled simply on the bone and served with lemon, capers, green beans, parsley and croûtons.

Times 12.30-2.30/6-10.30

Stillorgan Park Hotel

@ Traditional International

Stylish hotel with contemporary international menus

☎ 01 2881621 & 2001800
Stillorgan Rd
e-mail: sales@stillorganpark.com
dir: On N11 follow signs for Wexford, pass RTE studios on left, through next 5 sets of lights. Hotel on left

The Irish equivalent of the BBC is next-door to this striking contemporary hotel, so the place is usually fertile territory for spotting famous faces - notably in the Turf Club Bar, a buzzy place where people meet up for a bit of banter before dining in the Purple Sage restaurant. This series of interconecting small rooms has an eye-catching modern look, done out with hand-painted frescoes, mosaic tiling, modern artwork and striking floral-patterned chairs at contemporary bare wooden tables. The kitchen takes a modern approach, using quality Irish produce in a repertoire that roams widely from classic French dishes to modern international ideas. Duck liver parfait with red onion jam, apple and vanilla purée and toasted brioche is a typical starter, while mains might deliver pan-fried cod with saffron and shrimp risotto and red pepper beurrre blanc.

Times 12.30-3/5.45-10.15 Closed 25 Dec, L Sat, D Sun

The Tea Room @ The Clarence

@@ Irish, French

Modern brasserie dishes overlooking the Liffey

☎ 01 4070800
The Clarence, 6-8 Wellington Quay
e-mail: tearoom@theclarence.ie
web: www.theclarence.ie
dir: from O'Connell Bridge, W along Quays, through 1st lights (at Ha'penny Bridge) hotel 500mtrs

Sitting on the south bank of the Liffey, in the Temple Bar quarter of the Irish capital, The Clarence has been coaxed into the 21st century through a mixture of contemporary styling, modern cookery and its ownership by two members of U2. The tone is more relaxed elegance than rock'n'roll, with bracing river views from the high-ceilinged restaurant known, with some irony, as the Tea Room. Modern brasserie dishes of distinct flair are produced here. The scallops come with mushroom and parmesan polenta, diced chorizo, pine nuts and capers for a piquant, savoury starter, while mains might enterprisingly bring on a seared and roasted breast of goose, alongside little filo baskets of the confit leg meat and a fruity accompaniment of caramelised apricots. Sauce bigarade provides a big hit of orange tang. Toffee soufflé with hazelnuts is nicely offset by a sharp banana and lime ice cream for a well-balanced dessert.

Times 7-10.30 Closed 25-26 Dec, L all week

CO DUBLIN

KILLINEY Map 1 D4

PJ's Restaurant

@ Traditional, International

Fine dining overlooking Dublin Bay

☎ 01 2305400
Fitzpatrick Castle Hotel
e-mail: reservations@fitzpatricks.com
dir: From Dun Laoghaire port turn left, on coast road right at lights, left at next lights. Follow to Dalkey, right at Ivory pub, immediate left, up hill, hotel at top

The dapper oxblood-red and white façade of Fitzpatrick Castle Hotel looks majestic up on Killiney Hill, just a 9-mile drive from Dublin. The sweeping views across Dublin Bay from this grand 18th-century pile are worth coming out here for in their own right, but it's worth planning the trip around a visit to PJ's, the classy fine-dining restaurant. Crystal chandeliers and well-spaced tables done out in crisp linen create a fine sense of occasion for tackling the wide-ranging menu of skilfully-cooked seasonal dishes built on super local produce. Seared West Cork scallops with anise and citrus velouté are a good way to start, followed by roasted tarragon pheasant breast with leek and pancetta risotto and curry oil.

Chef Sean Dempsey **Owner** Eithne Fitzpatrick
Times 12.30-2.30/6-10 Closed 25 Dec, Mon, Tue, L Wed-Sat, D Sun **Prices** Fixed D 3 course €45, Service added 10% **Wines** 25 bottles over €20, 14 bottles under €20, 2 by glass **Notes** Sunday L, Vegetarian available **Seats** 65, Pr/dining room 50 **Children** Portions **Parking** 200

PORTMARNOCK Map 1 D4

Osborne Brasserie

@@ Modern International

Creative cuisine in a superb seaside location

☎ 01 8460611
Portmarnock Hotel & Golf Links, Strand Rd
e-mail: sales@portmarnock.com
dir: N1 towards Drogheda. Take R601 to Malahide. In 2m left at T-junct, through Malahide, 2.2m hotel on left. Off M1 take Malahide junct, then onto Portmarnock

Set between the sea and an impressive Bernhard Langar-designed 18-hole golf course, this handsome Victorian mansion was once home to the Jameson family (of Irish whiskey fame). The sophisticated Osborne Brasserie is named for the artist who painted the very view of the gardens and hills that form a scenic backdrop to the culinary endeavours. The menu follows a modern international route using the area's best ingredients. Start with local fish, shellfish and smoked pork chowder, followed by baked salmon with scallion mash and warm winter bean salad, traditional Irish stew, or confit pork belly with bean and sausage cassoulet. End with apple crème brûlée with hazelnut ice cream.

Times 6-9.45 Closed Sun-Mon, L all week

CO GALWAY

CASHEL Map 1 A4

Cashel House

@@ Traditional V

A wealth of seafood in a heavenly location

☎ 095 31001
e-mail: res@cashel-house-hotel.com
dir: S of N59. 1m W of Recess

Standing at the head of Cashel Bay in 50 acres of delightful, award-winning gardens, Cashel House is a gracious 19th-century country house that has been in the hands of the McEvilly family since 1968. When you have worked up a serious appetite on the local golf courses and woodland walks, the restaurant offers a repertoire of French-accented classics, served in either an airy

continued

CASHEL *continued*

conservatory extension, or a polished traditional setting amid antiques and artworks. Connemara's lakes, rivers, hillsides and the fishermen out in the bay supply the kitchen with the finest produce it could wish for, which are handled simply and with the confidence to let the flavours do the talking. You might start with Cashel crayfish, simply-poached and served with wasabi mayonnaise and a classic Marie Rose sauce. Next, nothing could be more local than a main course of rabbit from the hill above the hotel, casseroled until tender and fragrant with tomatoes, onions and cider and served with dauphinoise potatoes.

Chef Arturo Amit, Arturo Tillo **Owner** Kay McEvilly & family **Times** 12.30-2.30/7-8.30 Closed 2 Jan-2 Feb **Prices** Fixed D 4 course €60, Service added 12.5% **Wines** 90 bottles over €20, 4 bottles under €20, 5 by glass **Notes** Sunday L, Vegetarian menu, Dress restrictions, Smart casual **Seats** 70, Pr/dining room 20 **Children** Portions, Menu **Parking** 30

GALWAY — Map 1 B3/4

Camilaun Restaurant

Modern International

Modern cooking in restaurant with garden views

☎ 091 521433
The Ardilaun Hotel, Taylor's Hill
e-mail: info@theardilaunhotel.ie
dir: 1m from city centre, towards Salthill on west side of city, near Galway Bay

On the outskirts of Galway city, the much-extended Ardilaun Hotel has at its heart a 19th-century building that was once home to a prominent Galway family. Since St Patrick's Day 1962 it has been run as a hotel by the Ryan family. The Camilaun Restaurant overlooks five acres of landscaped grounds, and has built a loyal local fan base for its consistent cooking. The kitchen deals in dishes that take their influence from around the globe, and their ingredients from rather closer to home. Fresh salmon from Cleggan is paired with local crab in crispy dill-scented cakes, with chilli-spiked avocado salsa and fennel salad, followed by a crispy roast leg of confit Barbary duck served with mustard mash and lentils and a pancetta and coriander jus.

Chef David O'Donnell **Owner** John Ryan
Times 1-2.15/6.30-9.15 Closed 23-27 Dec, L Mon-Sat **Prices** Food prices not confirmed for 2011. Please telephone for details **Wines** 62 bottles over €20, 2 bottles under €20, 11 by glass **Notes** Sunday L, Vegetarian available, Dress restrictions, Smart dress, Civ Wed 650 **Seats** 180, Pr/dining room 380 **Children** Portions, Menu **Parking** 300

Park House Hotel & Park Room Restaurant

International

Appealing menu in bustling city-centre hotel

☎ 091 564924
Forster St, Eyre Square
e-mail: parkhousehotel@eircom.net
dir: In city centre, off Eyre Sq

Park House is a stalwart of the Galway dining scene with a strong local fan base built up over 33 years of doing business in a former Victorian grain store with a splendid stone façade. It's a favourite all-day spot for everything from bustling lunchtime meet-ups to lingering evening meals in a more intimate low-lit ambience. The wide-ranging menu covers most bases with a modern style of cooking taking in local oysters served as nature intended or Mornay-style, through to salmon and prawn in filo pastry, ahead of main-course breast of orange and honey-glazed duckling served with pink peppercorn and gin sauce, pine nut and herb stuffing, and raspberry compôte.

Times 12-3/6-10 Closed 24-26 Dec

River Room

Modern Irish, International

Modern cuisine in an 18th-century country residence

☎ 091 526666
Glenlo Abbey Hotel, Bushypark
e-mail: info@glenloabbey.ie
dir: Approx 2.5m from centre of Galway on N59 to Clifden/ Connemara

Five-star luxury is the name of the game at this magnificent hotel in the 18th-century abbey that was once home to Galway's tribal elders. Inside are soaring ceilings necklaced with fancy plasterwork, lovely stained glass and antiques to foster an opulent ambience after a day on the fairways of the 138-acre lakeside golf estate. The River Room restaurant is done out in soft-focus hues of peaches and cream, and a split-level layout ensures that all tables gets the views over Lough Corrib through its semi-circular walls of lofty windows. The kitchen shows a healthy regard for top-drawer ingredients and puts a creative, modern fine-dining spin on them. Breast of quail is marinated in honey and soy, and served with green beans, rocket and a cranberry dressing, while main course delivers monkfish poached in white wine and partnered with chorizo-infused polenta cake, tempura vegetables and lemongrass vinaigrette.

Times 6.30-9.30 Closed 24-27 Dec, Mon-Tue, L all week

RECESS (SRAITH SALACH) — Map 1 A4

Ballynahinch Castle

Modern International V

Classical cooking in fishing hotel with stunning views

☎ 095 31006 & 31086
e-mail: bhinch@iol.ie
dir: Take N59 from Galway. Turn right after Recess towards Roundstone (R331) for 2m

A haven of peace and tranquility set in 450 acres of gardens, lakes and walks, this grand Victorian mansion occupies a stunning location in the heart of Connemara, overlooking the famous Ballynahinch River. A renowned fishing hotel, it offers high levels of comfort and friendliness in elegantly furnished lounges, drawing rooms, and the inviting restaurant with its crisp linen and relaxing river views. The accomplished cooking is based on excellent local produce, including seafood landed at nearby Cleggan and wild salmon and game from the estate. A typical meal may kick off with Cleggan white crab meat with ginger and coriander, lemongrass foam, fennel powder and toasted brioche, with roast rack of lamb, gratin potato, stuffed cabbage, garlic and rosemary jus to follow.

Chef Xin Sun **Owner** Ballynahinch Castle Hotel Inc **Times** 6.30-9 Closed 2 wks Xmas, Feb, L all week **Prices** Food prices not confirmed for 2011. Please telephone for details **Wines** 42 bottles over €20, 20 bottles under €20, 5 by glass **Notes** Vegetarian menu, Dress restrictions, Smart casual **Seats** 90 **Parking** 55

Lough Inagh Lodge

Irish, French

Fabulous setting for Irish country cooking

☎ 095 34706 & 34694
Inagh Valley
e-mail: inagh@iol.ie
dir: From Galway take N344. After 3.5m hotel on right

Sitting on the shore of Lough Inagh, one of Connemara's most spectacular lakes, and surrounded by mountains, this former 19th-century fishing lodge delivers modern comforts in a delightful old-world atmosphere. There are comfortable lounges with turf fires, a cosy oak-panelled bar and an intimate dining room. The simple country-house cooking focuses on flavour and makes good use of local produce; seafood and wild game are specialities of the house. Start with nutty breaded deep-fried Irish brie with redcurrant sauce, then baked Killary lobster with lemon butter, and finish with lemon meringue tart with cream anglaise.

Times 7-8.45 Closed mid Dec-mid Mar

CO KERRY

CAHERDANIEL (CATHAIR DÓNALL) Map 1 A2

Derrynane Hotel

Irish, European

Simple cooking with a fabulous coastal backdrop

☎ 066 9475136
e-mail: info@derrynane.com

Jaw-dropping views of Kenmare Bay and the ocean are guaranteed at this welcoming family-run hotel, perched on a clifftop on the spectacular Ring of Kerry. The surrounding countryside is stunning and well worth exploring, and there are many outdoor activities on the doorstep to help you work up a hearty appetite for dinner. The airy dining room has full-length picture windows on two sides, so you get those incredible views of the rugged Atlantic shoreline as a backdrop to the kitchen's repertoire of straightforward modern Irish dishes. Warm Derrynane smoked mackerel on potato salad with sweet mustard dressing might start things off, followed by steamed fillet of hake on roasted peppers and courgettes with an almond pesto dressing. Rhubarb from the garden is put to good use in a fool for dessert.

Times 7-9 Closed Oct-mid Apr

KENMARE Map 1 B2

La Cascade

European V

Imaginative cooking with a soundtrack of rushing water

☎ 06466 41600
Sheen Falls Lodge
e-mail: info@sheenfallslodge.ie
dir: From Kenmare take N71 to Glengarriff. Take 1st left after suspension bridge. 1m from Kenmare

Cascading falls, dramatically floodlit at night, tumble past vast picture windows and enhance the magical atmosphere in the elegantly designed restaurant at this former fishing lodge, set high on a promontory with expansive views of Kenmare Bay. It's an inviting setting in which to savour consistent modern Irish and European cooking, where the emphasis is firmly on fresh, local ingredients, including home-smoked salmon and home-cured lamb. Typically, start with smoked eel with beetroot and potato salad and horseradish foam, or duo of quail and foie gras with spiced pumpkin and fig mustard, and follow with monkfish saltimbocca with saffron risotto, or Skeaghanore duck breast with braised red cabbage, parsnip ragout and blackberry jus. Order the spiced Irish coffee mousse or the pineapple carpaccio with coconut ice cream for a satisfying finale.

Chef Heiko Riebandt **Owner** Sheen Falls Estate Ltd **Times** 7-9.30 Closed 2 Jan-1 Feb, L all week **Prices** Food prices not confirmed for 2011. Please telephone for details **Wines** 805 bottles over €20, 6 bottles under €20, 16 by glass **Notes** Tasting menu available, Vegetarian menu, Dress restrictions, Smart casual (jacket), No jeans or T-shirts **Seats** 120, Pr/dining room 20 **Children** Portions, Menu **Parking** 75

KILLARNEY Map 1 B2

Cahernane House Hotel

Modern European, International V

Artisanal produce in the former Earl of Pembroke's abode

☎ 06466 31895
Muckross Rd
e-mail: marketing@cahernane.com
dir: From Killarney follow signs for Kenmare, then from Muckross Rd over bridge. Hotel signed on right. Hotel 1m from town centre

Dating back to the 1600s, Cahernane sits in the tranquil surroundings of its own private estate within the Killarney National Park but just a 10-minute walk to the town centre. Meander down the long avenue to the three-storey house which features plenty of period details such as original fireplaces, woodwork on the ceilings and traditional portraits. The fine-dining Herbert Room Restaurant has views of the well-tended grounds and lake while the kitchen makes good use of seasonal, artisan and locally-sourced produce. The confident kitchen turns out modern dishes such as roast loin of rabbit with a Clonakilty black pudding mousse, black olive and pineapple dressing, moving onto lime and coriander marinated salmon, confit fennel, citrus beurre blanc with baby shrimp, and finishing with a rich chocolate tart with orange-scented sweet cream and chocolate sauce. A bistro menu is available in the Cellar Bar.

Chef Maurice Prendiville **Owner** Mr & Mrs J Browne **Times** 12-14.30/7-9.30 Closed Jan-Feb, L all week ex by arrangement **Prices** Fixed L 2 course €30, Fixed D 3 course €40, Starter €7-€12, Main €27-€32, Dessert €7-€9, Service optional **Wines** 98 bottles over €20, 22 bottles under €20, 20 by glass **Notes** Tasting menu available, Sunday L, Vegetarian menu, Dress restrictions, Smart casual, no shorts, Civ Wed 60 **Seats** 50, Pr/dining room 18 **Children** Portions, Menu **Parking** 50

Killeen House Hotel

Modern International

Accomplished cooking in charming country-house hotel

☎ 06466 31711 & 31773
Aghadoe, Lakes of Killarney
e-mail: charming@indigo.ie
dir: 4m from Killarney town centre, in Aghadoe, just off Dingle Road

Originally built as a rectory in 1838, this charming small hotel sits in mature gardens on the edge of town. It's a family-run place, with a welcoming atmosphere and traditional elegance in its relaxed sitting rooms and restaurant. The kitchen's country-house cooking suits the surroundings and is driven by prime seasonal, local ingredients. Dinner might begin with rosette of smoked salmon with a spicy gâteau of fresh flaked salmon and gravad lax with a cucumber and mango dressing, followed by roast rack of Kerry lamb with a rosemary and pine nut crust and garlic potato gratin, served with a Tuscan bean dressing. Finish off with tangy lemon tart with a praline mascarpone cream and citrus syrup.

Times 6.30-9.30 Closed 20 Oct-20 Apr

KILLORGLIN Map 1 A2

Carrig House Country House & Restaurant

Modern Irish, European

Fine dining in country house overlooking lake

☎ 066 9769100
Caragh Lake
e-mail: info@carrighouse.com

Located on the shores of Caragh Lake in acres of woodland gardens, which by all accounts contain 935 plant species, this restored Victorian country manor has stunning views across the lake to the Kerry Mountains. Furnished in period style, it has log fires in the public rooms, formal linen tablecloths and delightfully friendly service. The innovative cuisine makes excellent use of seasonal products, cooked with care and with judicious use of herbs and spices. Starters might include Dingle seafood chowder, and mains such as maple-glazed duck with celeriac purée, onion tarte Tatin and cinnamon jus, and roast cod with saffron sauce.

Times 7-9

TRALEE Map 1 A2

The Walnut Room

Modern, Traditional

Smart, modern hotel restaurant using fresh local produce

☎ 066 7194500 & 066 7194505
Manor West Hotel, Killarney Rd
e-mail: info@manorwesthotel.ie
dir: On main Killarney road adjacent to Manor West Retail Park

A large retail park close to the town centre is the unlikely setting for this smart modern hotel but it's the perfect venue to rest and refuel after a hard day's shopping. Relax over a drink in the cocktail lounge - complete with piano - before taking your place for dinner in the fine-dining Walnut Room, a comfortable contemporary restaurant with rich, warm décor. High quality ingredients, cooked with flair and due attention without the need for over-embellishment, feature on the seasonal menu, which includes the freshest of fish from nearby Dingle Bay and a carvery option at lunch. A starter of local crab cakes with saffron aïoli might be followed by beef fillet with basil mash and red onion marmalade.

Times 6-11 Closed 25 Dec, L all week

The Byerley Turk

STRAFFAN Map 1 C/D4

Modern, Traditional Irish

Fine dining in a country hotel with championship golf courses

☎ 01 6017200
The K Club
e-mail: hotel@kclub.ie
web: www.kclub.ie
dir: 30 minutes from Dublin. From Dublin Airport follow M4 to Maynooth, turn for Straffan, just after village on right

Named after a legendary Arab stallion who was one of the founders of the modern thoroughbred racing horse bloodstock, the Byerley Turk is a fitting image for the flagship restaurant of the high-flying golf and spa-oriented K Club hotel. The place is certainly built to impress with its French château-style façade, and an interior fully-laden with plush fabrics, gilt-framed mirrors, oil paintings and antiques. The Byerley Turk dining room also comes replete with plenty of old-school opulence – grandiose marble columns and walls upholstered in rich brocade, while a pianist tinkles away in the background at dinner, and clued-up staff ensure a silkily-orchestrated country-house experience. The formal mood demands that male diners wear jacket-and-tie. Dinner takes the format of seven- or nine-course tasting menus, involving a modern Irish take on classical themes. A roll call of luxury ingredients is imported to back up the country's finest produce in dishes that are realised with a serious level of technical ability. An arsenal of cheffy tricks is unleashed on Dordogne foie gras, served seared and as a marbled terrine, with celeriac foam and a five spice tuile, while seared scallops might be teamed with onion ice cream, fennel seed oil and 25-year-aged balsamic; the main event could be a signature creation of beef fillets with wild mushrooms and mead sauce. In fitting with the tasting ethos, an assiette of desserts delivers mango mousse 'cannelloni', a tangy lemon posset and a chocolate baba.

Chef Finbarr Higgins **Owner** Michael Smurfit **Times** 7-9 Closed Nov-mid Mar (except D Sat 6 Nov-18 Dec), Sun-Thu, L all week **Prices** Tasting menu €75-€95, Service optional **Wines** 600 bottles over €20, 8 by glass **Notes** Tasting menu 7/9 course, Vegetarian available, Dress restrictions, Jacket & tie **Seats** 36, Pr/dining room 16 **Children** Portions **Parking** 100

CO KILDARE

NAAS Map 1 D4

Killashee House Hotel & Villa Spa

Irish, Mediterranean

Elegant dining in magnificent surroundings

☎ 045 879277
e-mail: sales@killasheehouse.com
dir: 1m from Naas on old Kilcullen road. On left past Garda (police station)

There's a real sense of occasion as you wind along the driveway through 200 acres of immaculately-kept grounds to arrive at this dove-grey ivy-clad Victorian manor house. After a good leg-stretcher in the Wicklow Hills, or rather more indulgent de-stress in the spa, you'll probably feel like putting on the best bib and tucker to dine in the majestic Turner's restaurant, amid a palatial décor of painted panelling, chandeliers and fancy plasterwork; tall candelabra on the tables add a romantic edge, boosted further still on Saturday nights when a harpist plays a soulful accompaniment to the Mediterranean-accented dishes. Expect the likes of roulade of Irish salmon and prawns with wasabi mayonnaise, ahead of pan-fried sea bass with Provençal vegetables and tapenade oil.

Times 1-2.45/7-9.45 Closed 24-25 Dec, L Sat

Virginia Restaurant at Maudlins House Hotel

Modern French

Comfort and good cooking in Kildare

☎ 045 896999
Dublin Rd
e-mail: info@maudlinshousehotel.ie
dir: Exit N7 approaching large globe, at rdbt head towards Naas, restaurant 200mtrs on right

A sensitive restoration has brought this creeper-swathed Victorian country house on the outskirts of Naas gently up to date. The interior still has a full complement of period character to go with its new image, with plush swagged drapes and linen-clothed tables on a capacious polished wood floor in the Virginia Restaurant. The kitchen deals in modern French cooking, skilfully prepared and presented to impress: goats' cheese soufflé might turn up with pickled beetroot and tomato and tarragon cream, while main courses involve the likes of poached turbot with choucroute, Toulouse sausage, new potatoes and grain mustard velouté. For local meat fans there could be roast loin of West Wicklow lamb with Provençal stuffed aubergine, tomato confit, aubergine caviar and tarragon jus.

Times 12.30-9.30

NEWBRIDGE Map 1 C3

Keadeen Hotel

International NEW

Stylish dining in family-run hotel

☎ 045 431666
e-mail: info@keadeenhotel.ie
dir: N7 from Dublin to Newbridge. Hotel 1m from Curragh racecourse & 0.5m from Newbridge town centre

Established by the O'Loughlin family over 40 years ago, and still under the same ownership, Keadeen is a timelessly elegant hotel sitting in beautifully manicured gardens. The hotel's Derby restaurant is a stylish venue for sophisticated country-house dining. Service is formal but unobtrusive, befitting the elegant décor and fine table settings, while the menu makes use of the very best local produce. Timbale of fresh seafood with sauce Marie Rose, and crisp salad of smoked chicken, mango and Westphalian ham with balsamic dressing are typical starters. Main course could be roast prime sirloin of beef with sauce chasseur, or pan-fried fillets of sea bass with a fine ratatouille and fish cream essence.

Times 12.30-2.30/6-9.30

STRAFFAN Map 1 C/D4

Barberstown Castle

Irish, French

Classic cooking in a 13th-century castle with pretty grounds

☎ 01 6288157
e-mail: info@barberstowncastle.ie
dir: R406, follow signs for Barberstown

Built originally in the 13th century, this former castle is now a popular country-house hotel close to Dublin city centre and airport. The elegant Victorian and Elizabethan dining rooms occupy the extensions to its original battlements, which come decked out with period furniture and overlook the gardens. Lunch can be taken in the airy conservatory tearoom, but dinner is a more formal candlelit occasion with appropriately professional service. The Irish country-house cooking is firmly rooted in the French classics and makes the best of quality local produce. Take roast Cherry Valley duck breast with confit leg, sautéed Savoy cabbage and foie gras sauce, while dessert might feature an orange and cardamom crème brûlée with home-made shortbread.

Chef Bertrand Malabat **Owner** Kenneth Healy
Times 7.30-9.30 Closed 24-28 Dec, Jan, L all week
Prices Fixed D 3 course €55-€65, Tasting menu €75, Service optional **Wines** 105 bottles over €20, 15 bottles under €20, 2 by glass **Notes** Vegetarian available, Dress restrictions, Smart dress, Civ Wed 300 **Seats** 100, Pr/dining room 32 **Parking** 100

The Byerley Turk

– see opposite page

CO KILKENNY

KILKENNY Map 1 C3

Riverside Restaurant

Traditional, International

International cuisine next to Kilkenny Castle

☎ 056 7723388
Kilkenny River Court Hotel, The Bridge, John St
e-mail: reservations@rivercourthotel.com
dir: In town centre, opposite castle

Kilkenny Castle is an ever-present neighbour when you're in this upmarket contemporary hotel smack on the riverside in the heart of town. Floor-to-ceiling picture windows look out from the elegant Georgian-styled restaurant across the terrace - the place to be for dining alfresco on balmy days - to the imposing 12th-century fortress. Local produce is showcased with pride on a wide-ranging menu that takes a globetrotting canter around international influences. Home-made spring rolls of aromatic beef and wok-fried vegetables teamed with sweet chilli chutney might precede an entrecote of local beef, pan-fried and flamed with Cognac, and served with wild garlic and herb butter and spicy potatoes. Finish with sticky ginger pudding with honeycomb ice cream and butterscotch sauce.

Chef Gerrard Dunne **Owner** Xavier McAuliffe
Times 12.30-2.30/6-9.30 Closed 24-26 Dec, L Mon-Sat, D Sun (excl BHs) **Prices** Fixed L 3 course €29, Fixed D 3 course €37, Starter €6.50-€14.50, Main €18.25-€35, Dessert €8.50-€12.50 **Wines** 40 bottles over €20, 20 bottles under €20, 10 by glass **Notes** Pre-booking for Sun L essential, Sunday L, Vegetarian available, Dress restrictions, Smart casual preferred, Civ Wed 200
Seats 90, Pr/dining room 200 **Children** Portions, Menu
Parking 70, NCP

THOMASTOWN Map 1 C3

Kendals Restaurant

French

A taste of France beside the golf course

☎ 056 7773000
Mount Juliet Conrad Hotel
e-mail: info@mountjuliet.ie
dir: Just outside Thomastown, south on N9

French brasserie classics are the name of the game at Kendals Restaurant, the second dining option at the luxurious Mount Juliet. Kendals is set away from the main Georgian building, within the golf clubhouse, and it's a light and airy room with large windows looking out over the Jack Nicklaus-designed course. Bare wooden tables, wooden floors and an open fire create a casual, relaxed setting for dishes like salade Lyonnaise, tarte Provençal, bouillabaisse and faux-fillet de boeuf (dry-aged sirloin of Irish 'Aberdeen Angus' beef, served with crispy red onions, thick-cut fries and béarnaise sauce). Dessert could be les tarte maison (home-made lemon and lime tartlets), or you could go for les fromages du jour.

Times 6-9.30 Closed Sun & Tue

THOMASTOWN *continued*

The Lady Helen Restaurant

Modern Irish, French

Modern Irish cooking in impressive mansion hotel

☎ 056 7773000
Mount Juliet Conrad Hotel
e-mail: info@mountjuliet.ie
dir: Just outside Thomastown, south on N9

Overlooking the River Nore and surrounded by 1,500 acres of parkland, the Mount Juliet Hotel retains many original 18th century features, including in the formal and classically elegant Lady Helen Restaurant, which is decorated in grand country-house style and has lovely views across the estate and down to the river. The menu is probably best described as modern Irish with French influences, and showcases plenty of fine local produce, including fresh herbs from the garden and game from the estate in season. Duncannon crab ravioli with cauliflower purée, lobster reduction and vermouth foam, and Wicklow venison Wellington with braised red cabbage and shiraz jus are typical of the style.

Times 7-9.45 Closed L all week

CO LEITRIM

CARRICK-ON-SHANNON Map 1 C4

Boardwalk Café

Modern International

Modern dining in a waterfront setting

☎ 071 9622222
The Landmark Hotel
e-mail: reservations@thelandmarkhotel.com
dir: From Dublin on N4 approaching Carrick-on-Shannon, take 1st exit at rdbt, hotel on right

Carrick is the cruising capital of the Shannon, and the modern Landmark Hotel sits in pole position looking over boats moored in the marina. The Boardwalk Café offers a funky modern setting for all-day riverside dining, kitted out with vibrant damson leather seating and bare, darkwood tables. The food fits the setting - fun, light-hearted and appealing stuff, built on solid foundations of locally-sourced seasonal ingredients. The kitchen might typically send out roasted sea trout in the company of sweet potato, olive, tomato and corn salsa, and chive and lime sauce, or combine slow-cooked lamb shank with celeriac, redcurrant sauce and rosemary champ potato.

Owner Ciaran & John Kelly **Times** 12-4/5-9 Closed 24-25 Dec **Prices** Food prices not confirmed for 2011. Please telephone for details **Wines** 12 bottles over €20, 24 bottles under €20, 8 by glass **Notes** Sunday L, Vegetarian available, Civ Wed 300 **Seats** 180, Pr/dining room 125 **Children** Portions, Menu **Parking** 125

MOHILL Map 1 C4

The Sandstone Restaurant

Modern French V

Big flavours and a secluded setting

☎ 071 9632700 & 071 9632714
Lough Rynn Castle
e-mail: enquiries@loughrynn.ie
dir: N4 (Dublin to Sligo), hotel 8km off N4 & 2km from Mohill

The ancestral home of Lord Leitrim was built to impress: Lough Rynn Castle sits in 300 acres of idyllic Ireland beside the eponymous lough, complete with its own championship golf course. The Sandstone Restaurant is an intimate space in the converted stables that showcases its bare stone walls (hence the name), and comes plushly furnished with well-upholstered high-backed chairs and linen-clothed tables. The kitchen takes pride in sourcing the finest County Leitrim ingredients, put together with skill and imagination in French-accented dishes. A warm torte of rabbit opens in the company of wild mushrooms and potato gratin with Madeira jus, ahead of fillet of Fermanagh beef with pommes Maxime, sautéed salsify, celeriac purée, crispy bacon and red wine jus.

Chef Jean Michel Chevet **Owner** Hanly Group **Times** 12-2.30/6-9.45 Closed L Mon-Fri (Private bkgs only) **Prices** Food prices not confirmed for 2011. Please telephone for details **Wines** 90+ bottles over €20, 8 by glass **Notes** Sunday L, Vegetarian menu, Civ Wed 450 **Seats** 65, Pr/dining room 10 **Children** Portions, Menu **Parking** 100

CO LIMERICK

ADARE Map 1 B3

Dunraven Arms

Traditional, Modern European

Accomplished cooking in charming village hotel

☎ 061 605900
e-mail: reservations@dunravenhotel.com
dir: N18 from Limerick, change to N21

The Dunraven Arms may sound like a pub, but this thatched coaching inn in a postcard-pretty village feels more like an intimate country-house hotel. It is an atmospheric, traditional sort of place with dollops of true Irish cosiness thanks to its leather settles by open fires, warm colours and clubby country vibe. The dining room favours a smart look with heavy drapes, cherry-red walls and linen-clad tables as a setting for the kitchen's accomplished, largely modern European cuisine. Beef from the village butcher is a stalwart of the menu, carved from the trolley and served with red wine jus and horseradish sauce, while fish landed fresh each day by local boats could turn up as fillet of plaice with brown butter and capers, and tomato salsa balanced nicely with fennel purée. Plum and almond flan with home-made vanilla ice cream and blueberry coulis ends on a high note.

Chef David Hayes **Owner** Bryan & Louis Murphy **Times** 12.30-2.30/7-9.30 Closed L Mon-Sat **Prices** Food prices not confirmed for 2011. Please telephone for details **Wines** 25 bottles over €20, 25 bottles under €20, 6 by glass **Notes** Sunday L, Vegetarian available, Dress restrictions, Smart casual **Seats** 80, Pr/dining room 30 **Children** Portions **Parking** 60

LIMERICK Map 1 B3

No 1 Pery Square Hotel & Spa

Modern European NEW

Elegant brasserie dining in townhouse hotel

☎ 061 402402
Pery Square
e-mail: info@oneperysquare.com

Overlooking a leafy square in Limerick's Georgian quarter, this boutique townhouse hotel offers luxury and historic charm in spades. Looking out over the street on the first floor is the elegant Brasserie One, with its smartly set clothless tables, wooden floors, a mixture of antique and modern furnishings and open kitchen. The menu pays great heed to the seasons and features plenty of local produce in inventive dishes such as loin of rabbit stuffed with langoustines, peas à la Française and a carrot emulsion, and roasted red mullet with black olive gnocchi, red pepper purée, courgette and basil. Check out the on-site wine shop, where you can buy a bottle to enjoy with your meal rather than choosing from the list (although a small corkage charge applies).

Times 6-9

CO MAYO

BALLINA Map 1 B4

The Kitchen Restaurant

Modern V

A French interpretation of Ireland's natural bounty

☎ 096 74472
Mount Falcon Country House Hotel, Foxford Rd
e-mail: info@mountfalcon.com
dir: On N26, 6m from Foxford & 3m from Ballina. Hotel on left

A Victorian romantic decided that his bride should live in a castle and built this grand baronial house in 100 acres of woodland on the banks of the River Moy. As for dining, the clue is in the name: the luxury hotel's restaurant occupies the stylishly-converted old kitchens and pantries of the manor house. Shooting and fishing have always figured large on the agenda at Mount Falcon, so there's never a shortage of local game and freshly-caught wild Atlantic salmon, trout and eel for the chefs, who are big on sourcing artisan supplies, and using offal and humble ingredients in a 'snout to tail' approach. Head chef Phillipe Farineau's motto says it all: 'Irish product, French heart'. Scallops from nearby Clew Bay are seared and served with a purée of smoked onion, oxtail croquettes and wedges of Cox apple, ahead of lamb neck, slow-braised to melting tenderness and teamed simply with creamed root vegetables and potato gratin.

Chef Phillipe Farineau **Owner** Alan Maloney **Times** 12.30-2/6.30-9.30 Closed 25-26 Dec **Prices** Food prices not confirmed for 2011. Please telephone for details **Wines** 140 bottles over €20, 12 by glass **Notes** Sunday L, Vegetarian menu, Civ Wed 200 **Seats** 80, Pr/dining room 14 **Children** Portions, Menu

The Pier Restaurant

Modern NEW V

Creative cuisine in a strikingly modern riverside restaurant

☎ 096 23500
The Ice House Hotel, The Quay Rd, Ballina
e-mail: chill@theicehouse.ie

The 19th-century trade in salmon netted in the weirs of the River Moy grew to such a level that this Victorian ice house was built to handle the tonnage of fish. Now transformed into a chic hotel and spa for the 21st century, the building is still a haven of cool, in the slick designer sense of the word. The Pier Restaurant is a stylish space shared between the whitewashed brickwork of the original barrel vaulted ice store and a striking modernist glass extension supported by soaring wooden buttresses, and with glorious views along the river. Creative modern Irish cuisine is the order of the day, done in a simple but effective style, with well-balanced dishes built from quality local produce; spiced pork belly, for example, with pearl onions and apple relish, followed by Irish beef fillet teamed with ravioli of osso buco, buttered leeks and truffle oil.

Chef Gavin O'Rourke **Owner** Pearse Farrell **Times** 12/6.30-10.30 Closed 24-27 Dec **Prices** Food prices not confirmed for 2011. Please telephone for details **Wines** 2 bottles under €20, 6 by glass **Notes** Sunday L, Vegetarian menu, Civ Wed 150 **Seats** 100, Pr/dining room 16 **Children** Portions, Menu **Parking** 32

CONG Map 1 B4

The George V Restaurant

European

Lavish castle dining room serving classical cuisine

☎ 094 9546003
Ashford Castle
e-mail: ashford@ashford.ie

Let's face it – anywhere that was once the Guinness family seat is hardly going to be modest, but the romantic vision that is 13th-century Ashford Castle exceeds even the wildest expectations. When King George V came to stay, a room was designed to impress the royal guest with its opulent crystal chandeliers, oak panelling, and ornate plasterwork ceilings. That room is now the restaurant that bears his name, and nothing has changed since that would ruffle George's feathers, right down to the formal table service and jacket-and-tie dress code for gentlemen. The cooking, however, might cause a raised eyebrow: the kitchen's output may be guided by the French classics, but there's a wealth of creative ideas to keep modernists entertained. Perfectly seared foie gras comes partnered with figs and a Sauternes jelly, ahead of scallops and pork belly flavoured with star anise. Roasts are still carved from a trolley – perhaps baked fillet of pork in puff pastry teamed with a mousseline of wild mushrooms and foie gras.

Times 1-2/7-9.30 Closed L Mon-Sat

Lisloughrey Lodge Hotel

Modern International

Modern cooking with spectacular lake views

☎ 094 9545400
The Quay
e-mail: lodge@lisloughrey.ie
dir: Take N84 from Galway to Cross. Left at Cong sign. Left at sign for hotel

It's a beautiful setting - looking out at the many small sailing boats resting on the calm, clear waters of Lough Corrib, with tall trees all around. There are 10 acres of grounds to explore and the house itself retains all the charm you'd expect of a dwelling built in 1824, along with the modern facilities and style of a contemporary boutique hotel. The Salt Restaurant is spread across four intimate rooms spanning the whole of the first floor, all individual in style and with spectacular lake views through original sash windows. Here you can enjoy modern international cuisine prepared from top-notch local ingredients, such as roasted breast of wood pigeon with confit leg ravioli, sautéed girolles, baby chard, burnt butter and cabernet vinegar reduction, followed by butter basted monkfish tail with sautéed Irish lobster and watercress risotto. Save room for the baked filo parcel of bramley apple and goats' cheese with port wine ice cream.

Chef Wade Murphy **Owner** Lisloughrey Lodge Trading **Times** 6.30-10 Closed 24-26 Dec, D Sun-Mon **Prices** Food prices not confirmed for 2011. Please telephone for details, Service optional **Wines** 112 bottles over €20, 8 bottles under €20, 8 by glass **Notes** Fixed D 6 course €65, Vegetarian available, Civ Wed 180 **Seats** 56, Pr/dining room 14 **Children** Portions, Menu **Parking** 100

MULRANY Map 1 A4

Nephin Restaurant

Modern V

Atlantic views and contemporary cooking

☎ 098 36000
Mulranny Park Hotel
e-mail: info@mulrannyparkhotel.ie
web: www.mulrannyparkhotel.ie
dir: From Westport take N59 through Newport. R311 to Mulranny, hotel on right

The Nephin is idyllically located within The Mulrany Hotel, a beautiful old building overlooking the Atlantic Ocean. There are spectacular views of Clew Bay and the tumultuous waters from the bay windows of the elegant period dining room. Cooking is classically French-based, using the finest local Irish ingredients, especially the abundance of local seafood. Begin with fillet of lamb on petit ratatouille with Madeira jus, follow with pan-seared salmon in a nage of mussels with garden peas and a raviolo of scallop. For dessert, there might be Grand Marnier flavoured orange crème brûlée.

Chef Ollie O'Regan **Owner** Tom Bohan & Tom Duggan **Times** 6.30-9 Closed Jan, L Mon-Sat **Prices** Fixed L 2 course €19.50, Fixed D 3 course €39, Service optional **Wines** 38 bottles over €20, 7 bottles under €20, 4 by glass **Notes** Tasting menu available, Sunday L, Vegetarian menu, Civ Wed 320 **Seats** 100, Pr/dining room 50 **Children** Portions, Menu **Parking** 200

WESTPORT Map 1 B4

Bluewave Restaurant

Modern European

Fine local produce and spectacular views

098 29000
Carlton Atlantic Coast Hotel, The Quay
e-mail: info@atlanticcoasthotel.com
dir: From Westport take coast road towards Louisburgh for 1m. Hotel on harbour on left

The original stone-built façade of the 18th-century woollen mill lives on in this otherwise modern hotel sitting in the shadow of Croagh Patrick above Westport Harbour. The rooftop Bluewave Restaurant has glorious views to the islands of Clew Bay to go with its unfussy modern cooking. Superb local ingredients - fresh fish and seafood, naturally - get a European tweak in dishes such as roast fillet of cod with ratatouille, pineapple and coriander salsa, and tomato and rocket pesto, and oven-baked rump of lamb with turnip purée, black olive tapenade, fondant potato and shallot and thyme jus.

Chef Anthony Holland **Owner** Carlton Hotel Group **Times** 6.30-9.15 Closed 20-27 Dec, L all week **Prices** Fixed L 2 course €14.95-€19.95, Fixed D 3 course €21.95-€28.95, Starter €5.95-€8.95, Main €14.95-€24.95, Dessert €6.95-€9.95, Service optional **Wines** 12 bottles over €20, 14 bottles under €20, 1 by glass **Notes** Early bird menu available 6.30-7.30pm, Sunday L, Vegetarian available, Civ Wed 140 **Seats** 85, Pr/dining room 140 **Children** Portions, Menu **Parking** 80

Knockranny House Hotel

Modern, Classical

Ambitious cooking and fabulous views

098 28600
e-mail: info@khh.ie
dir: On N5 (Dublin to Castlebar road), hotel on left before entering Westport

Knockranny is a luxurious modern hotel with a glitzy spa set in enchanting scenery, with to-die-for views of Clew Bay and Croagh Patrick. The split-level La Fougère restaurant pulls out all the stops to create a sense of relaxed refinement: well-spaced tables wear their finest white linen and gleaming silverware, and huge windows take in those stunning views. Choose from table d'hôte, à la carte and tasting menus - whichever route you take, expect skilled, intelligent classical cooking with a serious dedication to the region's top seasonal produce, including fish and meat smoked in-house. A typically labour-intensive starter involves a raviolo of Killala Bay lobster in a light sole mousse served with mousseline of lovage and a mustard and brandy flavoured 'Thermidor' foam; next, wild mallard comes as roast breast, braised leg wrapped in cabbage, and its liver in a wild mushroom tart. Complex to the end, dessert brings an assiette of lemon and lime.

Chef Seamus Commons **Owner** Adrian & Geraldine Noonan **Times** 6.30-9.30 Closed Xmas, L Mon-Sat (open selected Sun) **Prices** Tasting menu €74, Service optional **Wines** 6 by glass **Notes** Fixed D 6 course €54, Sunday L, Vegetarian available, Dress restrictions, Smart casual, Civ Wed 300 **Seats** 90 **Children** Portions **Parking** 200

CO MEATH

KILMESSAN Map 1 D5

The Station House Hotel & Signal Restaurant

European, Mediterranean

Country-house dishes in a former railway station

046 9025239
e-mail: info@thestationhousehotel.com
dir: From Dublin N3 to Dunshaughlin, R125 to Kilmessan

The last passenger train may have puffed through Kilmessan as long ago as the 1940s, but the place is still recognisably a former railway station, albeit one with 12 acres of landscaped gardens and trimly kept lawns. In the Signal Restaurant, it has a tastefully designed dining room too. Menus furnish a bewildering variety of options, among them classic country-house dishes such as warm goats' cheese on toasted ciabatta with roasted peppers and caramelised onions, seared sea bass with root vegetable ratatouille, and rack of local lamb with spring onion mash and rosemary jus.

Chef David Mulvihill **Owner** Chris & Thelma Slattery **Times** 12.30-4.30/5-10.30 **Prices** Fixed L 2 course €30, Starter €4.50-€12.95, Main €12.95-€24.95, Dessert €6.95-€9.95, Service optional **Wines** 43 bottles over €20, 3 bottles under €20, 6 by glass **Notes** Fixed L 4 course €19.95-€24.95, D 5 course €24.95-€44.95, Sunday L, Vegetarian available, Civ Wed 120 **Seats** 90, Pr/dining room 180 **Children** Portions, Menu **Parking** 200

CO MONAGHAN

CARRICKMACROSS Map 1 C4

Restaurant at Nuremore

– see opposite page

CO SLIGO

CASTLEBALDWIN Map 1 B4

Moira's Restaurant

Modern Irish NEW V

Classic dishes with a modern twist in glorious location

071 9165155
Cromleach Lodge, Country House Hotel & Spa, Lough Arrow
e-mail: info@cromleach.com
dir: 6km off N4 Dublin-Sligo road at Castlebaldwin

Moira's Restaurant is the culinary heart of the upmarket Cromleach Lodge Country House Hotel, a soothing hideaway embraced by the hills above Lough Arrow. The hotel started life 30 years ago as a small B&B catering for anglers, but its restaurant proved so popular that it has been the driving force behind the hotel's ever-expanding business. What keeps the foodies beating a path to Moira's door is classic dishes done well; produce is well-sourced and cooked with care - that's all that's needed. Scallops served on pommes Anna with cherry tomatoes and herbes de Provence dressing is typical of the style, followed by pistachio and herb-crusted rack of lamb with turnip and prune gratin and a Madeira reduction.

Chef Lanka Fernando **Owner** Christy & Moira Tighe **Times** 1-6/6-9 Closed Nov, Xmas, Mon-Tue **Prices** Starter €12-€15, Main €27-€35, Dessert €10, Service optional **Wines** 84 bottles over €20, 4 by glass **Notes** Sunday L, Vegetarian menu, Civ Wed 160 **Seats** 80, Pr/dining room 25 **Children** Portions, Menu **Parking** 50

Restaurant at Nuremore

CARRICKMACROSS Map 1 C4

Modern French V

Intelligent, complex cooking at first-class country house

042 9661438
e-mail: info@nuremore.com
web: www.nuremore.com
dir: 11m from M1 junct 14 Ardee exit (N33)

This classic country-house hotel is set in the stunning rolling Monaghan countryside, but there's plenty on-site to keep visitors occupied. There's a spa and leisure centre, beautifully landscaped gardens, not to mention one of Ireland's most impressive championship golf courses, and that's before we've even got started on the restaurant. The split-level room overlooking the gardens and lake features well-spaced tables laid with high quality Irish linen and silverware. Head chef Ray McArdle earned his spurs under top Irish chefs Paul Rankin and Michael Deane and has been at Nuremore for 10 years now. His style is underscored with classical French cooking and utilises local ingredients combined with well-sourced international produce. Great technical skills are evident in some complex dishes, which are of a consistently high standard, due in part to the kitchen's use of techniques like sous vide. All butchery and bakery is done in-house. Try pressed foie gras mi-cuit with toasted brioche and fig salad followed by line-caught turbot braised with lemongrass, tomato tartar, buttered leeks and spinach and a light lemongrass velouté. Textures of rhubarb is a virtuoso finish.

Chef Raymond McArdle **Owner** Gilhooly Family **Times** 12.30-2.30/6.30-9.45 Closed L Mon-Sat **Prices** Fixed D 3 course fr €40, Starter €6.50-€12.50, Main €23-€29.50, Dessert €9.50, Service optional **Wines** 153 bottles over €20, 18 by glass **Notes** Prestige menu €80, Sunday L, Vegetarian menu, Civ Wed 200 **Seats** 120, Pr/dining room 50 **Children** Portions, Menu **Parking** 200

SLIGO Map 1 B5

The Glasshouse

Modern V

Contemporary cuisine overlooking the Garravogue River

☎ 071 9194300
The Glasshouse Hotel, Swan Point
e-mail: info@theglasshouse.ie
web: www.theglasshouse.ie
dir: N4 to Sligo town. Continue through rdbt, on entering relief road take 2nd turning on right, continue to Wine Street, Hotel on left on Hyde Bridge

Sligo's iconic Glasshouse Hotel stands out for its striking, ultra-modern design and its wonderful riverside location. Set along the river boardwalk, the bright Kitchen Restaurant is intimate and colourful with a Mediterranean vibe and fantastic views of the River Garravogue. Contemporary interpretations of classic dishes are on offer, with some unusual but effective combinations. Expect accurate cooking of well-sourced local ingredients, as seen in a starter of creamy smoked haddock risotto, a full-flavoured main course of roast rack of lamb with fondant potato, ratatouille and root vegetable mash, and a well-baked frangipane pear tart served with chilled anglaise and vanilla ice cream. There's also a swish ground-floor bar.

Chef Enda Delaney **Owner** Michael O'Heir, Ronnie Grenoey **Times** 12-5/6.30-9.30 Closed 25 Dec **Prices** Starter €5.50-€8.50, Main €19.50-€27.50, Dessert €6.50-€7, Service included **Wines** 34 bottles over €20, 8 bottles under €20 **Notes** Sunday L, Vegetarian menu, Dress restrictions, Smart casual, Civ Wed 60 **Seats** 108, Pr/dining room 140 **Children** Portions, Menu **Parking** 215

CO WATERFORD

ARDMORE Map 1 C2

The House Restaurant

Modern Irish NEW

Cutting-edge cooking using superb local produce

☎ 024 87800 & 87801
The Cliff House Hotel
e-mail: info@thecliffhousehotel.com
dir: N25 to Ardmore. Hotel at the end of village via The Middle Road

Cliff House has earned a reputation as a destination hotel for those in search of a sybaritic spa and dining experience. Its statement architecture is a dramatic exercise in slate and glass on the cliffs of Ardmore Bay, with a view that is straight out of a glossy magazine. The kitchen turns out some pretty cutting edge work and clearly likes to play with interesting flavours and textures. Take a star ingredient and play a riff on it - as in cod, which is presented filleted, poached and as brandade and croquettes, then things get seriously creative with the addition of leeks, sea vegetable vinegar and 62 degree egg yolk. Locally-reared lamb is carefully butchered and served in three ways: a cutlet is topped with chicken mousse, wrapped in caul and roasted; loin is roasted pink with a fragrant herb crust, and sweetbreads are tossed in a light crumb coating and briefly fried - all served with tangy lemon potato purée and steamed baby artichokes.

Times 7-10 Closed Xmas & Jan, Occasional Sun, Mon

WATERFORD Map 1 C2

Faithlegg House Hotel

Irish

Traditional country-house dining

☎ 051 382000
Faithlegg
e-mail: reservations@fhh.ie

Now boasting an 18-hole golf course and fully equipped leisure centre, this 18th-century mansion still offers a traditional country-house experience. The Roseville Rooms restaurant in the carefully restored original dining room has a high ceiling and views over the gardens. Traditional fare using Irish produce, but with European influences, is on offer. Start with Faithlegg spiced beef with home-made tomato and pear chutney and ciabatta croûtons before baked breast of chicken with goats' cheese stuffing and a wholegrain mustard cream, and finish with classic lemon tart with champagne sorbet and lemon martini syrup.

Times 6.30-9.30 Closed Xmas, L Mon-Sat

Waterford Castle - Munster Dining Room

French, European

Modern French cooking in a medieval castle on an island

☎ 051 878203
The Island
e-mail: info@waterfordcastle.com
dir: From city centre turn onto Dunmore East Rd, 1.5m, pass hospital, 0.5m left after lights, ferry at bottom of road

The ferry collects you to take you to the 15th-century castle at Waterford, which stands aloof on its own private island. Elizabethan oak panelling, mullioned windows and ornately moulded ceilings are as grand as it gets, and the place comes with its own golf course. Gentlemen won't be surprised to hear that a jacket is required. Modern French cooking based on impeccably sourced ingredients is on offer in the sumptuous Munster Dining Room. A trio of accurately seared scallops comes with locally made boudin noir, together with chive mash and a rich oxtail jus, for a high-octane starter. That might be followed by chargrilled beef fillet with celeriac purée and earthy cep cream sauce, or wild sea bass served with pearl barley 'risotto', soft polenta and warm leek vinaigrette. An individual frangipane-based fig tart with anglaise sauce makes a satisfying finale.

Chef Michael Quinn **Owner** Munster Dining Room **Times** 12.30-1.45/7-9 Closed Xmas, early Jan, L Mon-Sat **Prices** Fixed L 3 course €36, Fixed D 3 course fr €29, Service added but optional 10% **Wines** 50+ bottles over €20, 8 by glass **Notes** Early bird menu Sun-Thu, Vegetarian available, Dress restrictions, Jacket or shirt required for D, Civ Wed 100 **Seats** 50, Pr/dining room 80 **Children** Portions, Menu **Parking** 200

CO WESTMEATH

ATHLONE Map 1 C4

Wineport Lodge

Modern, Classical

Modern Irish cuisine in glorious lakeside setting

☎ 090 6439010
Glasson
e-mail: lodge@wineport.ie

Wineport has the natural, clean-cut contemporary lines of a country retreat among the wilderness lakes of Scandinavia. The low-slung cedar-clad structure dovetails unobtrusively with the watery landscapes of Lough Ree, and its vast windows and expansive balconies allow guests to feel a real sense of connection with the environment. You can even arrive by boat if that's your preferred mode of transport, and dine out on the decking terrace, or if the weather doesn't oblige, the light-drenched dining room offers the same inspirational views. While the kitchen takes a globetrotting approach to its modern Irish output, the ingredients are strictly local, whether you're ordering from the à la carte, bistro, or 'wild and organic' tasting menu. Seared foie gras with Clonakilty black pudding and sherry-marinated prunes is a typical opener, ahead of butter-basted John Dory with crab mayonnaise, sea asparagus and leeks.

Times 3-10/6-10 Closed 24-26 Dec, L Mon-Sat

MULLINGAR Map 1 C4

Mullinger Park Hotel

Modern Irish NEW

Modern Irish cooking in stylish hotel restaurant

☎ 044 9344446 & 9337500
Dublin Rd
e-mail: Info@mullingarparkhotel.com
dir: N4 junct 9, take exit for Mullingar

Close to the bustling town of Mullingar, this modern hotel has two dining areas: the popular Horseshoe bar offers a relaxed bistro menu all day, whilst the elegant and airy Terrace restaurant delivers modern Irish cooking using plenty of local produce. Fish comes from Galway and the beef from Westmeath. Flavours are bold and well defined in dishes such as Irish oak-smoked salmon with pickled red onion, capers, seasonal leaves and wheaten bread, and braised beef cheek with parsnip mash. Finish with pear millefeuille with vanilla ice cream and sago.

Chef Michael Roth **Owner** Josephine Hughes
Times 12.30-2.30/5.30-10 Closed 25-26 Dec **Prices** Fixed L 2 course €15.50, Fixed D 3 course €29.95, Starter €5.50-€7.95, Main €15.50-€28.95, Dessert €7.50-€8, Service included **Wines** 8 by glass **Notes** Sunday L, Vegetarian available, Dress restrictions, Smart Casual, Civ Wed 200 **Seats** , Pr/dining room 700
Children Portions, Menu **Parking** 800

CO WEXFORD

GOREY Map 1 D3

Marlfield House

Classic

Grand hotel dining in the heart of Wexford

☎ 053 9421124
Courtown Rd
e-mail: info@marlfieldhouse.ie
dir: N11 junct 23, follow signs to Courtown. Turn left for Gorey at Courtown Road Rdbt, hotel 1m on the left

Formerly the Wexford residence of the Earls of Courtown back in the 1830s, today Marlfield House is still all about entertaining in its latest guise as a luxurious country-house hotel with a delightful conservatory restaurant. Family-run and with family members always very much in evidence, the Regency-style house offers a sense of occasion from cocktails in the library to dinner with fittingly formal service in the restaurant overlooking the garden. Fresh herbs, fruit and vegetables are gathered daily and Wexford's bounteous larder provides much of the fish and meat on the modern French-European-accented menu. Expect the likes of crab brûlée with sesame seeds, pickled cucumber salad and melba toast, then seared fillet of salmon with courgette spaghetti, wild garlic mash and basil pesto. A mini dessert selection of Marlfield rhubarb crumble, chocolate marquise, warm chocolate brownie and cinnamon ice cream is a decadent finish.

Chef Paul O'Loughlin **Owner** The Bowe Family
Times 12.30-2/7-9 Closed Jan-Feb, L Mon-Sat
Prices Food prices not confirmed for 2011. Please telephone for details **Wines** 200 bottles over €20, 20 bottles under €20, 10 by glass **Notes** Sunday L, Vegetarian available, Dress restrictions, Smart dress, no jeans, Civ Wed 140 **Seats** 80, Pr/dining room 50
Parking 100

The Rowan Tree Restaurant

Modern International

Enjoyable dining in modern hotel spa

☎ 053 9480500
Ashdown Park Hotel, The Coach Rd
e-mail: info@ashdownparkhotel.com
dir: On approach to Gorey town take N11 from Dublin. Take left signed for Courtown. Hotel on left

On the edge of lovely Gorey town, the Ashdown Park Hotel is within easy striking distance of sandy beaches and grassy golf courses - although the classy modern spa and leisure facilities mean that there's plenty to keep you occupied without setting foot outside the modern complex. When it comes to dining, the smart Rowan Tree Restaurant looks over the rooftop garden, where you can eat outside in good weather. The kitchen deals in simple, straightforward ideas from the modern repertoire, showcasing fine Irish materials. Take chorizo and emmental tartlet for starters, and follow with rump of wild venison marinated in herbs and red wine, served with parsnip purée, creamed potato and a rich gamey thyme jus. Apple and berry crumble with crème anglaise makes a comforting finale.

Times 12.30-2.30/6-9.30 Closed 24-25 Dec, L Mon-Sat

ROSSLARE Map 1 D2

Beaches

European

Beachside resort hotel with modern cooking

☎ 053 9132114
Kelly's Resort Hotel & Spa
e-mail: kellyhot@iol.ie

Family-run since 1895, Kelly's Resort Hotel sits on five miles of glorious golden sands in Rosslare, a location that its Beaches restaurant makes the most of. It's a soothing spot, light-drenched and done out with pastel shades, potted plants and white linen, but while there's an unchanging air about the place, it has been all change in the kitchen. New broom Eugene Callaghan has taken over from the long-standing incumbent, and ushered in a new, more contemporary style of dining. Starters team organic local goats' cheese with roasted beetroot and toasted rustic bread, while mains deliver hake stuffed with shrimp and crab mousse; pecan pudding with rich butterscotch sauce and vanilla bean ice cream makes a happy ending for dessert-lovers.

Times 1-2/7.30-9 Closed mid Dec-mid Feb

La Marine Bistro

Modern

Bistro-style cooking at a smart seaside resort hotel

☎ 053 9132114
Kelly's Resort Hotel & Spa
e-mail: kellyhot@iol.ie

The stand-alone restaurant of this resort hotel has a maritime theme to its décor and views of the busy kitchen. The atmosphere is casual and relaxed, and the menu offers uncomplicated cooking of the freshest produce with an emphasis on allowing the natural flavours of the main ingredient to shine through. There's a good choice of seafood, including starters of creamy seafood and saffron chowder and Bannow Bay mussels with garlic and parsley butter. Follow with monkfish with warm saffron and garlic mayonnaise, or rib-eye steak with Burgundy snails and garlic and red wine jus, and pear, chocolate and almond pithivier to finish.

Times 12.30-2/6.30-9

WEXFORD Map 1 D3

Newbay Country House & Restaurant

Modern European

Popular country-house dining with excellent, simply-prepared dishes

☎ 053 9142779
Newbay, Carrick
e-mail: newbay@newbayhouse.com
dir: Take Cork road from Wexford, left after Citroen garage, at x-rds turn right, restaurant on right

Newbay is a striking coral-pink Georgian country house in 25 acres of well-tended gardens and parkland just a short drive from Wexford town. When it comes to dining there are two attractive options: the more casual venue is the Cellar Bistro, a bright and breezy place done out with pale wood floors and shades of sunny yellow; move upstairs, and you have the fine-dining restaurant, where the menu offers an eclectic array of modern dishes showcasing the best of the region's produce. As the hotel has its own trawler, fish and seafood ought to be a good bet - kick off with Kilmore crabmeat wontons served in a shrimp and tomato bisque, and follow with grilled turbot teamed with garlic and rosemary, courgettes and wild mushrooms.

Times 12-3/6-9.30 Closed Xmas, New Year, L Mon-Thu

WEXFORD *continued*

Seasons Restaurant

Irish, European

Enjoyable food in popular family-run hotel

☎ 053 9143444
Whitford House Hotel, New Line Rd
e-mail: info@whitford.ie
dir: From Rosslare ferry port take N25. At Duncannon Rd rdbt right onto R733, hotel immediately on left. 1.5m from Wexford

Located just outside the medieval town of Wexford, the family-run Whitford House Hotel is a well-established and popular base for breaks to the sandy beaches and golf courses of Ireland's sunny South East. The food in the Seasons Restaurant is modern Irish with European influences and the cooking is skilled and confident. A starter of chunky Atlantic seafood chowder might precede a main course of braised lamb shank on colcannon mash with roast garlic and rosemary jus. Apple, cinnamon and hazelnut crumble with vanilla anglaise is one of the comforting puddings.

Chef Siobhan Devereux **Owner** The Whitty Family
Times 12.30-3/7-9 Closed 24-27 Dec, Sun-Wed out of season, L Mon-Sat **Prices** Fixed L 2 course €15.50-€17.50, Fixed D 3 course €19.95-€31.95, Starter €5-€9, Main €14.95-€24.50, Dessert €4.95-€7.95, Service optional **Wines** 4 bottles over €20, 29 bottles under €20, 4 by glass **Notes** Sunday L, Vegetarian available, Civ Wed 100 **Seats** 100 **Children** Portions, Menu **Parking** 150

CO WICKLOW

DUNLAVIN Map 1 D3

Rathsallagh House

Traditional European NEW

Traditional country-house cookery with modern twists

☎ 045 403112
e-mail: info@rathsallagh.com
dir: M7 junct 3 towards Baltinglass, left at T-junct & take 2nd right, signposted Rathsallagh

Built in the former stables of a Queen Anne house which burned down in 1798, this rambling hotel stands in endless acres of rolling parkland, with its own walled garden and 18-hole golf course. The kitchen team delivers confident country-house cooking using top-drawer local ingredients, including lamb and beef from the family farm. Careful saucing allows natural flavours to shine through. Typical choices may include rabbit loin stuffed with foie gras, wild rice and wild mushrooms for starters, followed by loin of lamb served with vegetable and couscous terrine and a well-reduced and flavoured rosemary scented jus. Round off with an unctuous chocolate fondant.

Chef Eric Kavanagh **Owner** Joe O'Flynn
Times 12.30-4.30/7-9 **Prices** Fixed L 2 course €28-€30, Fixed D 3 course €45-€50, Starter €10-€15, Main €18-€35, Dessert €8-€14, Service optional, Groups min 8 service 10% **Wines** 80 bottles over €20, 5 by glass **Notes** Sunday L, Vegetarian available, Dress restrictions, Smart casual, no jeans, no trainers, Civ Wed 200 **Seats** 130, Pr/dining room 40 **Children** Portions **Parking** 60

MACREDDIN Map 1 D3

The Strawberry Tree Restaurant

Modern Irish

Dramatic dining venue specialising in organic and wild food

☎ 0402 36444
Brooklodge Hotel & Wells Spa
e-mail: info@brooklodge.com
dir: From Dublin take N11, turn off at Rathnew for Rathdrum, then through Aughrim to Macreddin (2m)

The top-drawer Brooklodge Hotel's Strawberry Tree Restaurant has led the way in serving only wild and organic food for 21 years. Ireland's first certified organic restaurant is the brainchild of the three Doyle brothers, who developed this foodie destination made up of a pub and micro-brewery, café, bakery, smokehouse, Italian restaurant, 18-hole golf course and spa on the site of a deserted village in the Wicklow Valley. The Strawberry Tree is an eye-catching space sprawling through a trio of glamorous rooms with mirrored ceilings, glitzy contemporary chandeliers and deep blue décor. The ingredients are the stars here, so the kitchen brings this peerless produce together in a creative way, balancing fine flavours in a starter of pan-fried pigeon breast with pancetta, celeriac purée, glazed beetroot and thyme jus. Main-course baked hake is given modern treatment with a lime crust, capers, Bulgur wheat and tomato foam.

Chef Tim Daly, Evan Doyle **Owner** The Doyle Family
Times 7-9.30 Closed L all week **Prices** Food prices not confirmed for 2011. Please telephone for details **Wines** 10 bottles under €20, 21 by glass **Notes** Vegetarian available, Dress restrictions, Smart casual, Civ Wed 200 **Seats** 90, Pr/dining room 50 **Children** Portions **Parking** 200

RATHNEW Map 1 D3

Hunter's Hotel

Traditional French

Beautiful views and 300 years of history

☎ 0404 40106
e-mail: reception@hunters.ie
dir: N11 exit at Wicklow/Rathnew junct. 1st left onto R761. Restaurant 0.25m before village

Five generations of the Gelletlie family have run Ireland's oldest coaching inn since 1820. Set in lovely gardens on the banks of the River Varty, this traditional hostelry has an inimitable charm that only comes from such stability and a healthy disinterest in the ephemeral vagaries of fashion, bolstered by excellent hospitality from friendly staff. The kitchen sticks resolutely to its repertoire of classic country-house cooking, letting first-class local and seasonal produce speak for itself in accurately-cooked dishes. Typical starters include céviche of prawns with lentil vinaigrette, followed by chargrilled beef fillet with scallion mash and mushroom velouté, and toffee, pecan and hazelnut roulade for dessert.

Times 12.45-3/7.30-9 Closed 3 days Xmas

KEY TO ATLAS

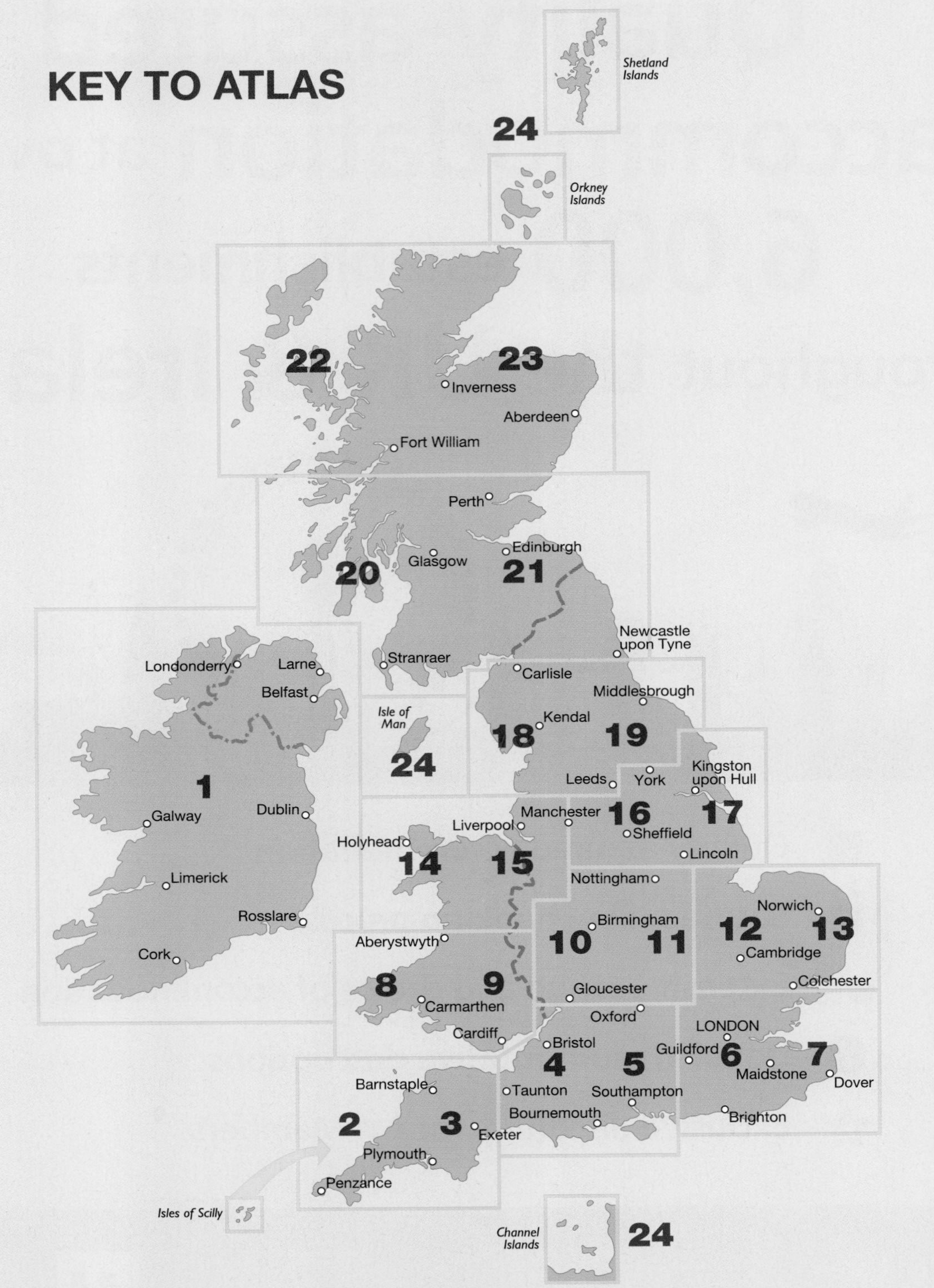

Shetland Islands
24
Orkney Islands
22
23
Inverness
Aberdeen
Fort William
Perth
Edinburgh
Glasgow
20
21
Newcastle upon Tyne
Stranraer
Carlisle
Londonderry
Larne
Belfast
Middlesbrough
Isle of Man
Kendal
18
19
24
1
Leeds
York
Kingston upon Hull
Galway
Dublin
Manchester
16
17
Liverpool
Sheffield
Holyhead
Lincoln
14
15
Limerick
Nottingham
Norwich
Rosslare
Birmingham
12
13
Aberystwyth
10
11
Cork
Cambridge
Colchester
8
9
Gloucester
Carmarthen
Oxford
LONDON
Cardiff
Bristol
Guildford
4
5
6
7
Barnstaple
Maidstone
Dover
Taunton
Southampton
Bournemouth
Brighton
2
3
Exeter
Plymouth
Penzance
Isles of Scilly
Channel Islands
24

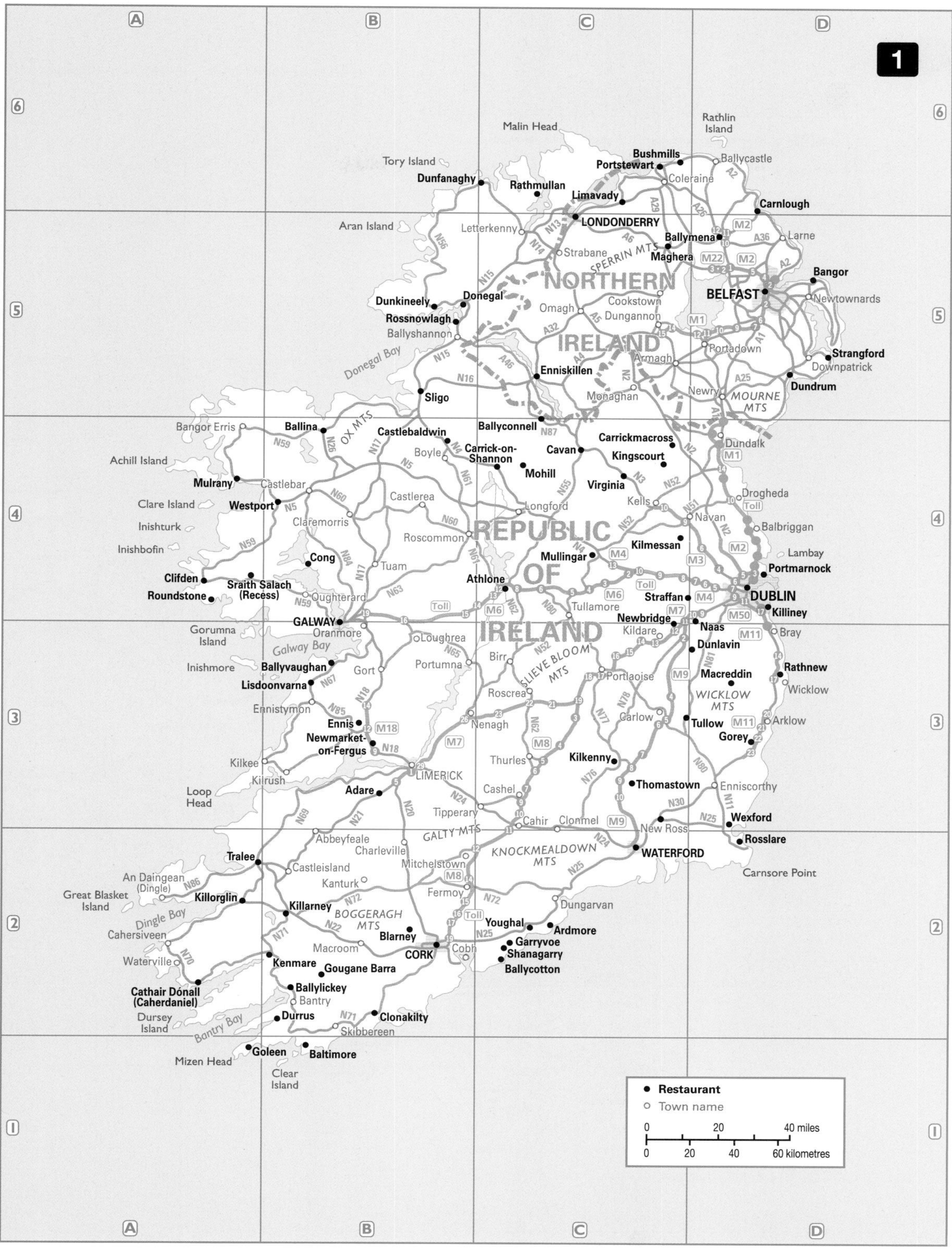
1
A
B
C
D
6
5
4
3
2
I
Malin Head
Rathlin Island
Tory Island
Bushmills
Portstewart
Ballycastle
Coleraine
Dunfanaghy
Rathmullan
Limavady
Carnlough
Aran Island
LONDONDERRY
Letterkenny
Ballymena
Larne
Strabane
SPERRIN MTS
Maghera
Bangor
NORTHERN
BELFAST
Dunkineely
Donegal
Cookstown
Newtownards
Omagh
Dungannon
Rossnowlagh
Ballyshannon
IRELAND
Portadown
Donegal Bay
Armagh
Strangford
Downpatrick
Enniskillen
Dundrum
Sligo
Monaghan
Newry
MOURNE MTS
Bangor Erris
Ballina
OX MTS
Castlebaldwin
Ballyconnell
Carrickmacross
Dundalk
Achill Island
Boyle
Carrick-on-Shannon
Cavan
Kingscourt
Mohill
Mulrany
Castlebar
Virginia
Drogheda
Clare Island
Westport
Castlerea
Kells
Longford
Navan
Inishturk
Claremorris
Balbriggan
REPUBLIC
Roscommon
Kilmessan
Inishbofin
Mullingar
Lambay
Cong
Tuam
OF
Portmarnock
Clifden
Sraith Salach (Recess)
Athlone
DUBLIN
Roundstone
Oughterard
Straffan
Tullamore
Killiney
Gorumna Island
GALWAY
Newbridge
Naas
Oranmore
IRELAND
Kildare
Bray
Galway Bay
Loughrea
Dunlavin
Birr
SLIEVE BLOOM MTS
Inishmore
Ballyvaughan
Portumna
Rathnew
Gort
Macreddin
Lisdoonvarna
Portlaoise
Wicklow
Roscrea
WICKLOW MTS
Ennistymon
Carlow
Ennis
Nenagh
Tullow
Arklow
Newmarket-on-Fergus
Gorey
Kilkee
Thurles
Kilkenny
Kilrush
LIMERICK
Loop Head
Thomastown
Enniscorthy
Cashel
Adare
Tipperary
Cahir
Clonmel
Wexford
New Ross
GALTY MTS
Abbeyfeale
Rosslare
KNOCKMEALDOWN MTS
Charleville
WATERFORD
Tralee
Mitchelstown
An Daingean (Dingle)
Castleisland
Carnsore Point
Kanturk
Great Blasket Island
Killorglin
Fermoy
Dungarvan
Killarney
BOGGERAGH MTS
Dingle Bay
Youghal
Ardmore
Cahersiveen
Blarney
Garryvoe
Macroom
Cobh
Shanagarry
Waterville
CORK
Kenmare
Ballycotton
Gougane Barra
Cathair Dónall (Caherdaniel)
Ballylickey
Bantry
Dursey Island
Durrus
Clonakilty
Bantry Bay
Skibbereen
Goleen
Baltimore
Mizen Head
Clear Island
Restaurant
Town name
0
20
40 miles
0
20
40
60 kilometres

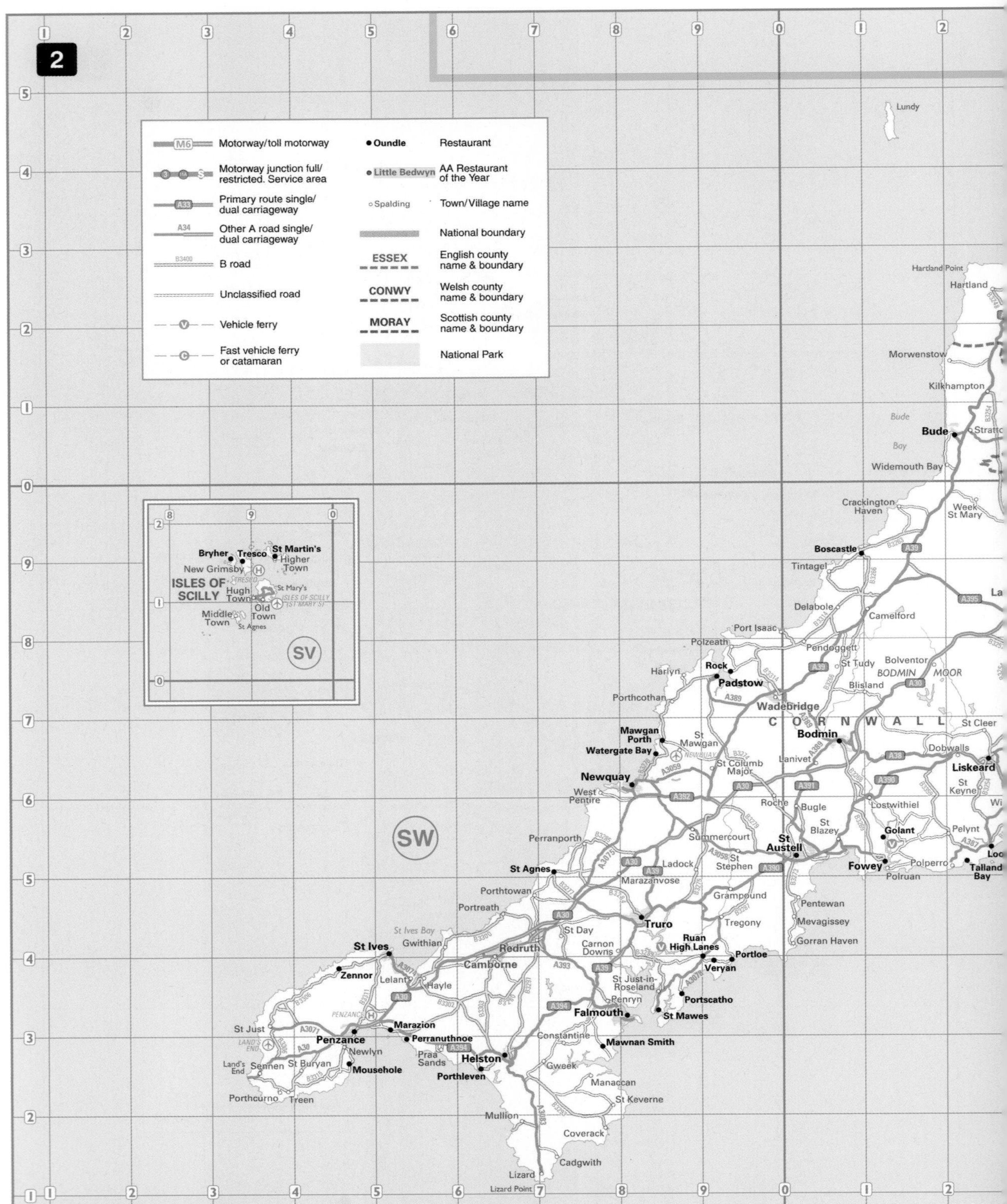
Motorway/toll motorway
Motorway junction full/ restricted. Service area
Primary route single/ dual carriageway
Other A road single/ dual carriageway
B road
Unclassified road
Vehicle ferry
Fast vehicle ferry or catamaran
Oundle
Restaurant
Little Bedwyn
AA Restaurant of the Year
Spalding
Town/Village name
National boundary
ESSEX
English county name & boundary
CONWY
Welsh county name & boundary
MORAY
Scottish county name & boundary
National Park
Lundy
Hartland Point
Hartland
Morwenstow
Kilkhampton
Bude Bay
Bude
Widemouth Bay
Crackington Haven
Week St Mary
Boscastle
Tintagel
Delabole
Camelford
Port Isaac
Polzeath
Pendoggett
St Tudy
Bolventor
BODMIN MOOR
Blisland
Harlyn
Rock
Padstow
Porthcothan
Wadebridge
CORNWALL
Mawgan Porth
Watergate Bay
St Mawgan
Bodmin
St Cleer
Dobwalls
Liskeard
Lanivet
St Columb Major
Newquay
West Pentire
St Keyne
Roche
Bugle
Lostwithiel
St Blazey
Golant
Pelynt
Perranporth
Summercourt
St Austell
Fowey
Polperro
Talland Bay
Polruan
St Agnes
Ladock
St Stephen
Marazanvose
Porthtowan
Grampound
Pentewan
Mevagissey
Gorran Haven
Portreath
Truro
Tregony
St Ives Bay
St Day
Carnon Downs
Ruan High Lanes
Portloe
Veryan
St Ives
Gwithian
Redruth
Camborne
Zennor
Lelant
Hayle
St Just-in-Roseland
Penryn
Portscatho
St Mawes
Falmouth
St Just
Penzance
Marazion
Perranuthnoe
Constantine
Mawnan Smith
Land's End
Sennen
St Buryan
Newlyn
Mousehole
Praa Sands
Helston
Porthleven
Gweek
Manaccan
St Keverne
Porthcurno
Treen
Mullion
Coverack
Cadgwith
Lizard
Lizard Point
ISLES OF SCILLY
Bryher
Tresco
St Martin's
Higher Town
New Grimsby
St Mary's
Hugh Town
Old Town
Middle Town
St Agnes
SV
SW

For continuation pages refer to numbered arrows

3
BRISTOL CHANNEL
9
SUPER-MARE
Bridgwater Bay
Ilfracombe
Lynton
Lynmouth
Combe Martin
Brendon
Porlock Weir
Porlock
Minehead
Mortehoe
Lee
Woolacombe
Parracombe
EXMOOR
Wootton Courtenay
Dunster
Blue Anchor
Watchet
Kilve
Stogursey
Georgeham
Challacombe
NATIONAL
Carhampton
Holford
Croyde
Muddiford
Bratton Fleming
Simonsbath
Exford
PARK
Wheddon Cross
Sampford Brett
Nether Stowey
Cannington
Bridgwater
Barnstaple Bay
Saunton
Braunton
Withypool
Crowcombe
QUANTOCK HILLS
Goathurst
Brayford
Winsford
Brompton Regis
Elworthy
Barnstaple
Bideford Bay
Appledore
Instow
Westward Ho!
Northam
North Molton
Dulverton
Wiveliscombe
Fitzhead
Bishops Lydeard
Clovelly
Horns Cross
Bideford
South Molton
SS
Exbridge
Petton
Milverton
Taunton
Knowstone
Umberleigh
Chittlehamholt
Bampton
Sampford Arundel
Wellington
Monkleigh
Great Torrington
Rackenford
Burrington
Little Torrington
Beaford
Stibb Cross
Merton
Dolton
Chulmleigh
Chawleigh
Witheridge
Tiverton
Halberton
Culmstock
Hemyock
Uffculme
Willand
Bradworthy
Milton Damerel
Shebbear
Black Torrington
Sheepwash
Meeth
Winkleigh
Eggesford
Lapford
Morchard Bishop
Cheriton Fitzpaine
Cullompton
Bickleigh
Upottery
Chilsworthy
Holsworthy
Highampton
Hatherleigh
Copplestone
Silverton
Halwill Junction
Clawton
Beaworthy
Crediton
Stoke Canon
Fenny Bridges
Honiton
Ashwater
Okehampton
DEVON
Newton St Cyres
Tedburn St Mary
Broadclyst
Whimple
Rockbeare
Ottery St Mary
Bratton Clovelly
South Zeal
Whiddon Down
Crockernwell
EXETER
Bridestowe
Sourton
Dunsford
Clyst St Mary
Newton Poppleford
Chagford
Topsham
Lewdown
DARTMOOR
Moretonhampstead
Kenford
Exminster
Woodbury
Sidmouth
Lifton
Lydford
Otterton
Kenton
Budleigh Salterton
Milton Abbot
Bovey Tracey
Chudleigh
Exmouth
Mary Tavy
Postbridge
Widecombe in the Moor
Haytor Vale
Lamerton
Two Bridges
NATIONAL
Ilsington
Chudleigh Knighton
Ideford
Dawlish
Tavistock
Princetown
Bishopsteignton
Gunnislake
Gulworthy
Kingsteignton
Teignmouth
Shaldon
Pensilva
Callington
Horrabridge
Hexworthy
Ashburton
Newton Abbot
Dousland
Holne
Kingskerswell
Bere Alston
Yelverton
PARK
Buckfastleigh
Maidencombe
Pillaton
Bere Ferrers
Ipplepen
Shaugh Prior
Dartington
TORQUAY
Landrake
South Brent
Cornwood
Totnes
Paignton
Saltash
Wrangaton
Stoke Gabriel
Tor Bay
Plympton
Ivybridge
Churston Ferrers
Polbathic
Harbertonford
Dittisham
Brixham
Torpoint
Ugborough
Portwrinkle
Crafthole
PLYMOUTH
Halwell
Millbrook
Heybrook Bay
Brixton
Yealmpton
Modbury
Kingswear
Cawsand
Dartmouth
Holbeton
Aveton Gifford
Wembury
Newton Ferrers
Stoke Fleming
Slapton
Strete
SX
Bigbury-on-Sea
Kingsbridge
Chillington
Bigbury Bay
Start Bay
Thurlestone
Torcross
Hope
Salcombe
Beesands
Malborough
Hallsands
Start Point
East Prawle
Bleadon
Winscombe
Blagdon
Biddisham
Berrow
Brent Knoll
Draycott
Burnham-on-Sea
Mark
Wedmore
Highbridge
West Huntspill
Bleadney
Meare
Glastonbury
Ashcott
Walton
Middlezoy
Othery
North Petherton
SOMERSET
Somerton
Lyng
Curry Rivel
Langport
ST
North Curry
Long Sutton
Hatch Beauchamp
Ilchester
Corfe
Martock
Staple Fitzpaine
South Petherton
Montacute
Horton
Ilminster
Chard
Crewkerne
Yarcombe
Winsham
Misterton
Mosterton
Tytherleigh
Broadwindsor
Beaminster
Wilmington
Shute
Axminster
North Chideock
Colyton
Charmouth
Colyford
Uplyme
Branscombe
Seaton
Axmouth
Lyme Regis
West Bay
Bridport
Beer
Burton Bradstock
Lyme Bay
SY
4
0 10 miles
0 10 20 kilometres

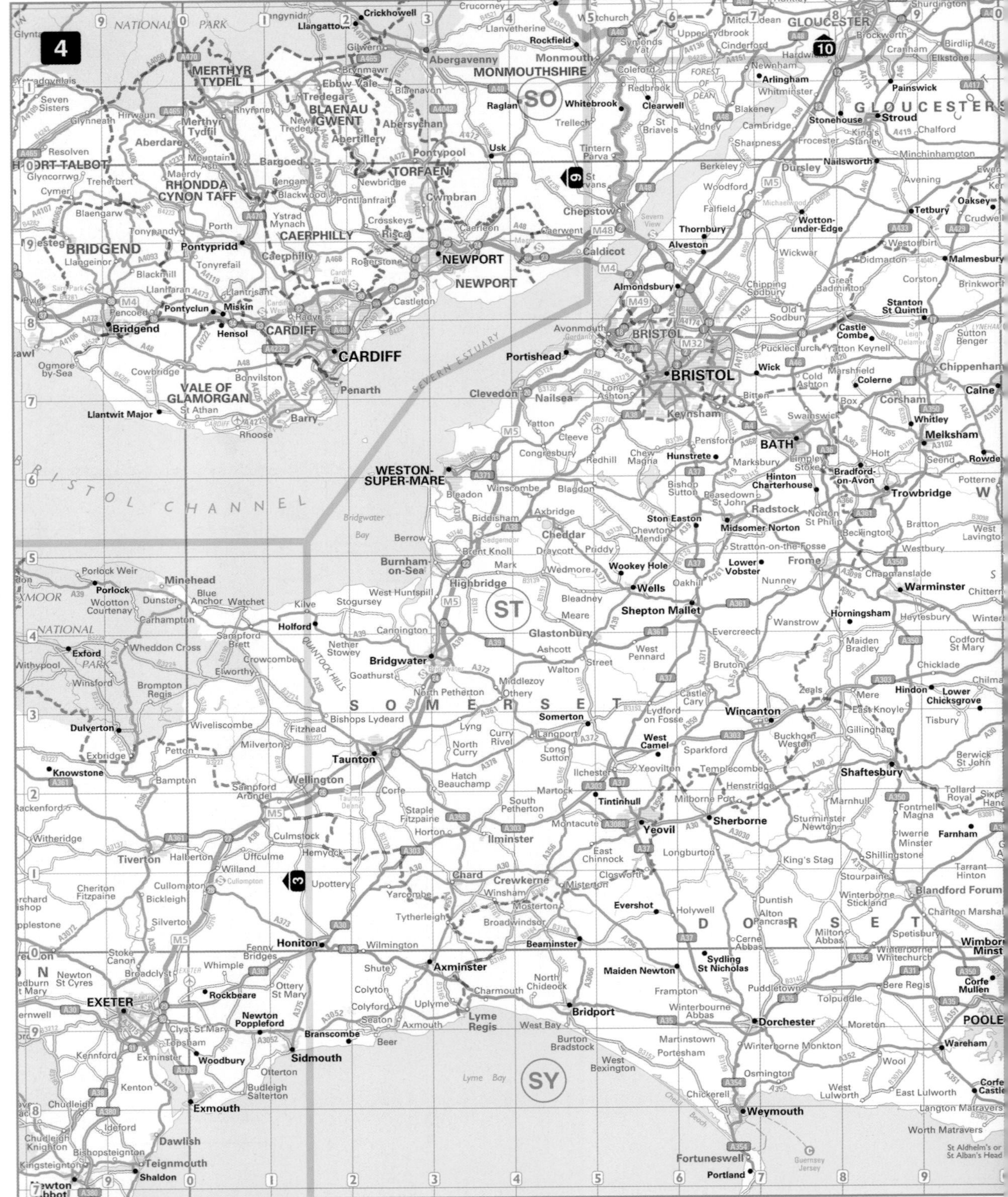

For continuation pages refer to numbered arrows

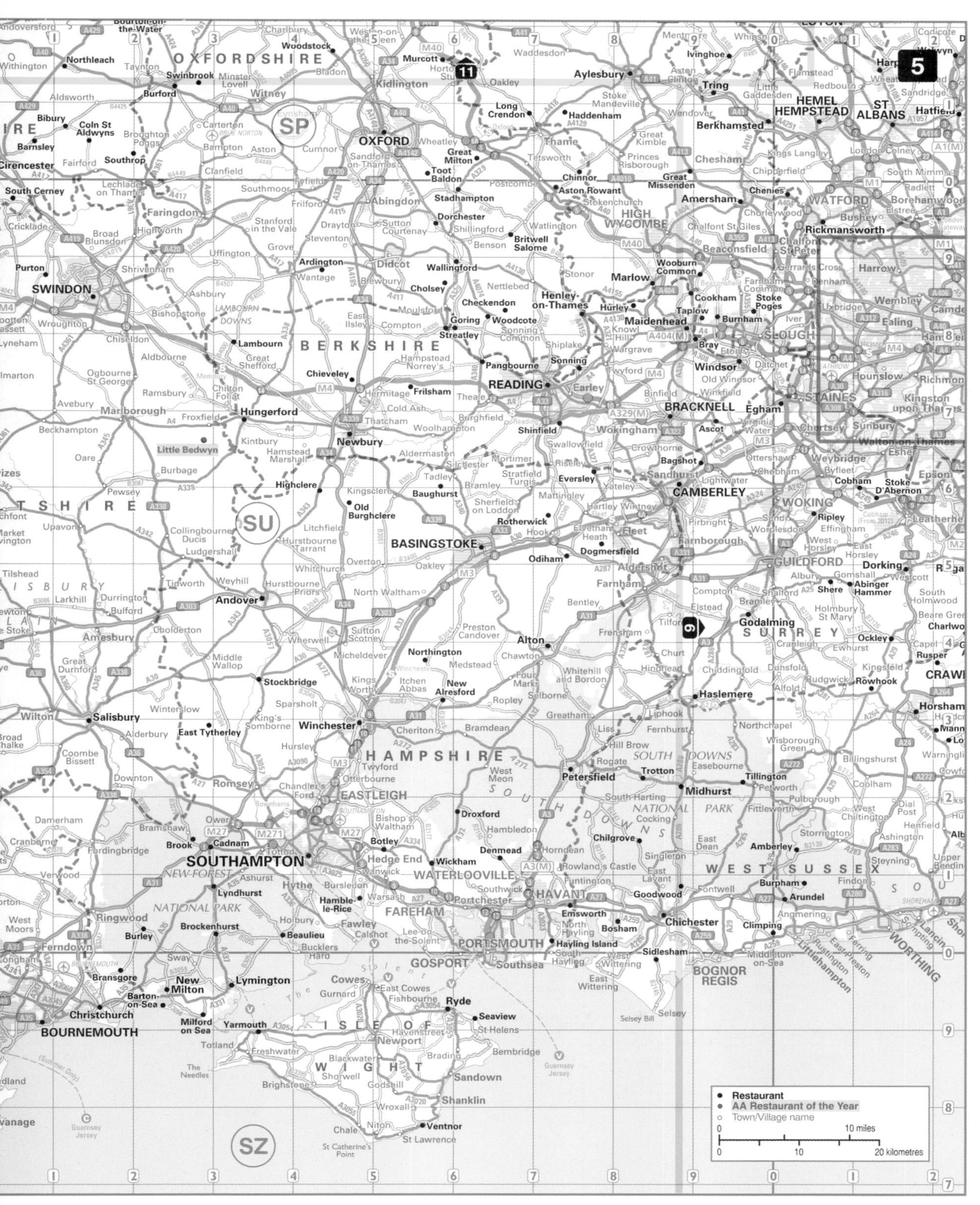
5
OXFORDSHIRE
BERKSHIRE
HAMPSHIRE
SURREY
WEST SUSSEX
ISLE OF WIGHT
SOUTH DOWNS NATIONAL PARK
NEW FOREST NATIONAL PARK
SP
SU
SZ
Woodstock
Northleach
Withington
Swinbrook
Burford
Taynton
Minster Lovell
Witney
Kidlington
Murcott
Oakley
Waddesdon
Aylesbury
Ivinghoe
Tring
Bibury
Coln St Aldwyns
Barnsley
Cirencester
Carterton
Bampton
Aston
Cumnor
OXFORD
Wheatley
Great Milton
Long Crendon
Haddenham
Thame
Tetsworth
Chinnor
Aston Rowant
Princes Risborough
Great Missenden
Amersham
Chesham
Berkhamsted
HEMEL HEMPSTEAD
ST ALBANS
Hatfield
Harpenden
WATFORD
Rickmansworth
Chenies
Bushey
Borehamwood
Toot Baldon
Stadhampton
Dorchester
Abingdon
Faringdon
South Cerney
Cricklade
Fairford
Southrop
Lechlade on Thames
HIGH WYCOMBE
Beaconsfield
Chalfont St Peter
Britwell Salome
Watlington
Benson
Wallingford
Cholsey
Didcot
Ardington
Wantage
Purton
SWINDON
Shrivenham
Marlow
Wooburn Common
Cookham
Stoke Poges
Taplow
Burnham
Maidenhead
SLOUGH
Bray
Windsor
Henley-on-Thames
Hurley
Checkendon
Goring
Woodcote
Streatley
Pangbourne
Sonning
READING
Earley
Lambourn
Chieveley
Frilsham
Hungerford
Little Bedwyn
Newbury
Shinfield
Wokingham
BRACKNELL
Ascot
Egham
Staines
Bagshot
Sandhurst
CAMBERLEY
Eversley
Highclere
Old Burghclere
Baughurst
Rotherwick
BASINGSTOKE
Odiham
Dogmersfield
Fleet
Farnborough
Aldershot
Farnham
WOKING
Ripley
Cobham
Stoke D'Abernon
GUILDFORD
Dorking
Shere
Abinger Hammer
Godalming
Ockley
Rusper
Horsham
Rowhook
Haslemere
Andover
Alton
Northington
New Alresford
Stockbridge
Salisbury
East Tytherley
Winchester
Petersfield
Trotton
Midhurst
Tillington
Droxford
Botley
Wickham
Denmead
Chilgrove
Amberley
Burpham
Arundel
SOUTHAMPTON
Brook
Cadnam
Lyndhurst
Hedge End
Hamble-le-Rice
Emsworth
Bosham
Chichester
Goodwood
Climping
Sidlesham
Brockenhurst
Beaulieu
Burley
Bransgore
New Milton
Lymington
Barton-on-Sea
Milford on Sea
Christchurch
BOURNEMOUTH
Yarmouth
Ryde
Seaview
Newport
Sandown
Shanklin
Ventnor
PORTSMOUTH
Hayling Island
GOSPORT
FAREHAM
HAVANT
WATERLOOVILLE
EASTLEIGH
BOGNOR REGIS
WORTHING
Littlehampton
Restaurant
AA Restaurant of the Year
Town/Village name
0
10 miles
0
10
20 kilometres

For continuation pages refer to numbered arrows

7
COLCHESTER
Coggeshall
Tendring
Witham
Tolleshunt Knights
Maldon
CLACTON-ON-SEA
Walton on the Naze
Brightlingsea
West Mersea
Bradwell-on-Sea
Burnham-on-Crouch
Southminster
Rayleigh
Rochford
SOUTHEND-ON-SEA
Canvey Island
Great Wakering
TM
TR
Sheerness
Minster
Eastchurch
Leysdown-on-Sea
Isle of Sheppey
GILLINGHAM
Sittingbourne
Faversham
Whitstable
Herne Bay
Reculver
MARGATE
Broadstairs
Ramsgate
Sandwich
Canterbury
Deal
Kingsdown
St Margaret's at Cliffe
DOVER
KENT
Ashford
Charing
Lenham
Bearsted
Boughton Monchelsea
Biddenden
Sissinghurst
Cranbrook
Tenterden
Rye
Winchelsea
Camber
Lydd
New Romney
Dymchurch
St Mary's Bay
Hythe
FOLKESTONE
CHANNEL TUNNEL TERMINAL
Channel Tunnel (Rail)
STRAIT OF DOVER
Dungeness
Westfield
HASTINGS
St Leonards
Restaurant
AA Restaurant of the Year
Town/Village name
10 miles
10
20 kilometres

For continuation pages refer to numbered arrows

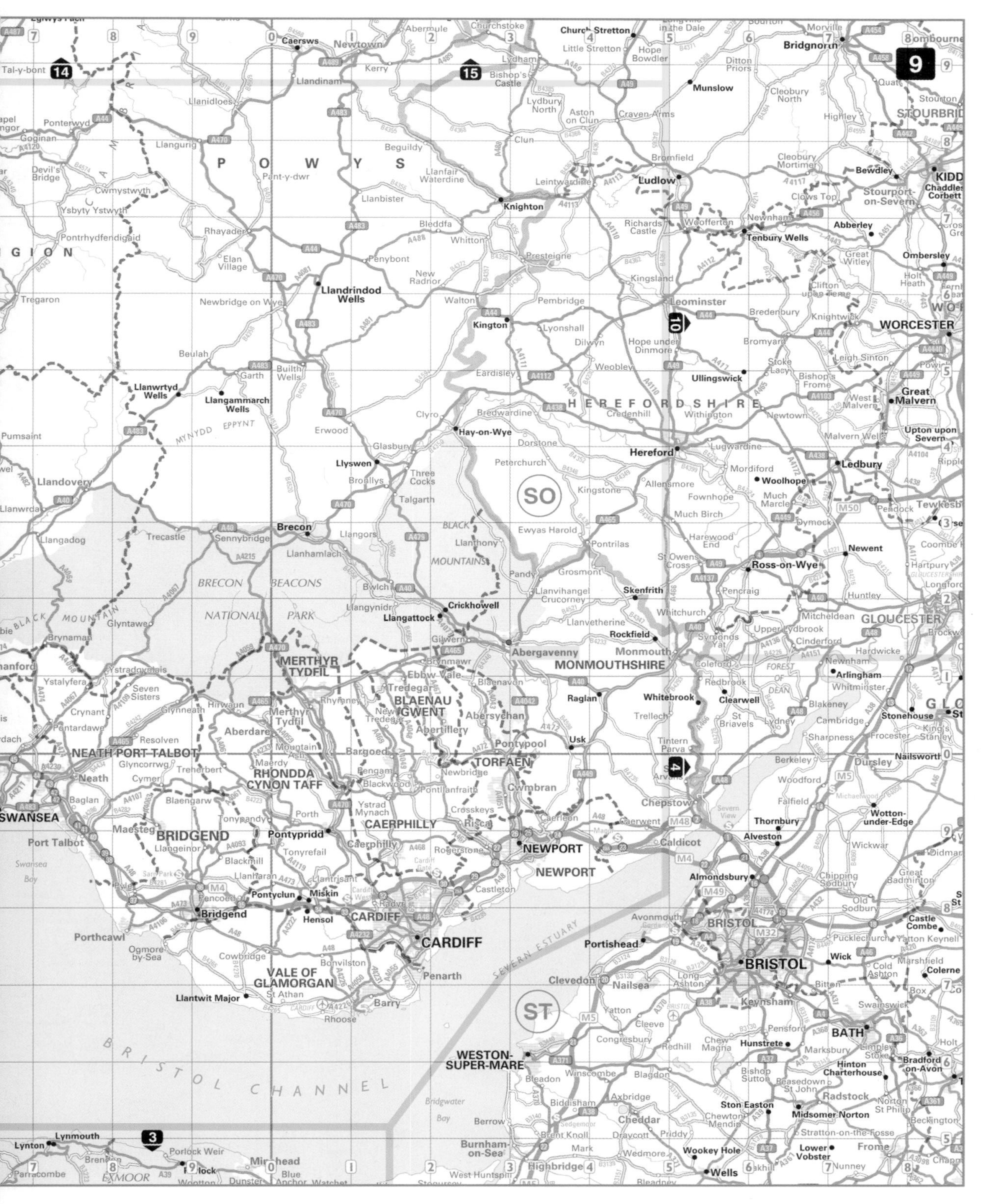
9
POWYS
HEREFORDSHIRE
MONMOUTHSHIRE
Aberystwyth
Newtown
Knighton
Ludlow
Leominster
Tenbury Wells
Llandrindod Wells
Builth Wells
Kington
Hay-on-Wye
Hereford
Ledbury
WORCESTER
Great Malvern
Brecon
Crickhowell
Abergavenny
Ross-on-Wye
GLOUCESTER
Monmouth
MERTHYR TYDFIL
BLAENAU GWENT
RHONDDA CYNON TAFF
CAERPHILLY
TORFAEN
NEATH PORT TALBOT
BRIDGEND
SWANSEA
NEWPORT
CARDIFF
VALE OF GLAMORGAN
Chepstow
BRISTOL
BATH
WESTON-SUPER-MARE
BRECON BEACONS NATIONAL PARK
BLACK MOUNTAINS
BRISTOL CHANNEL
SEVERN ESTUARY
SO
ST

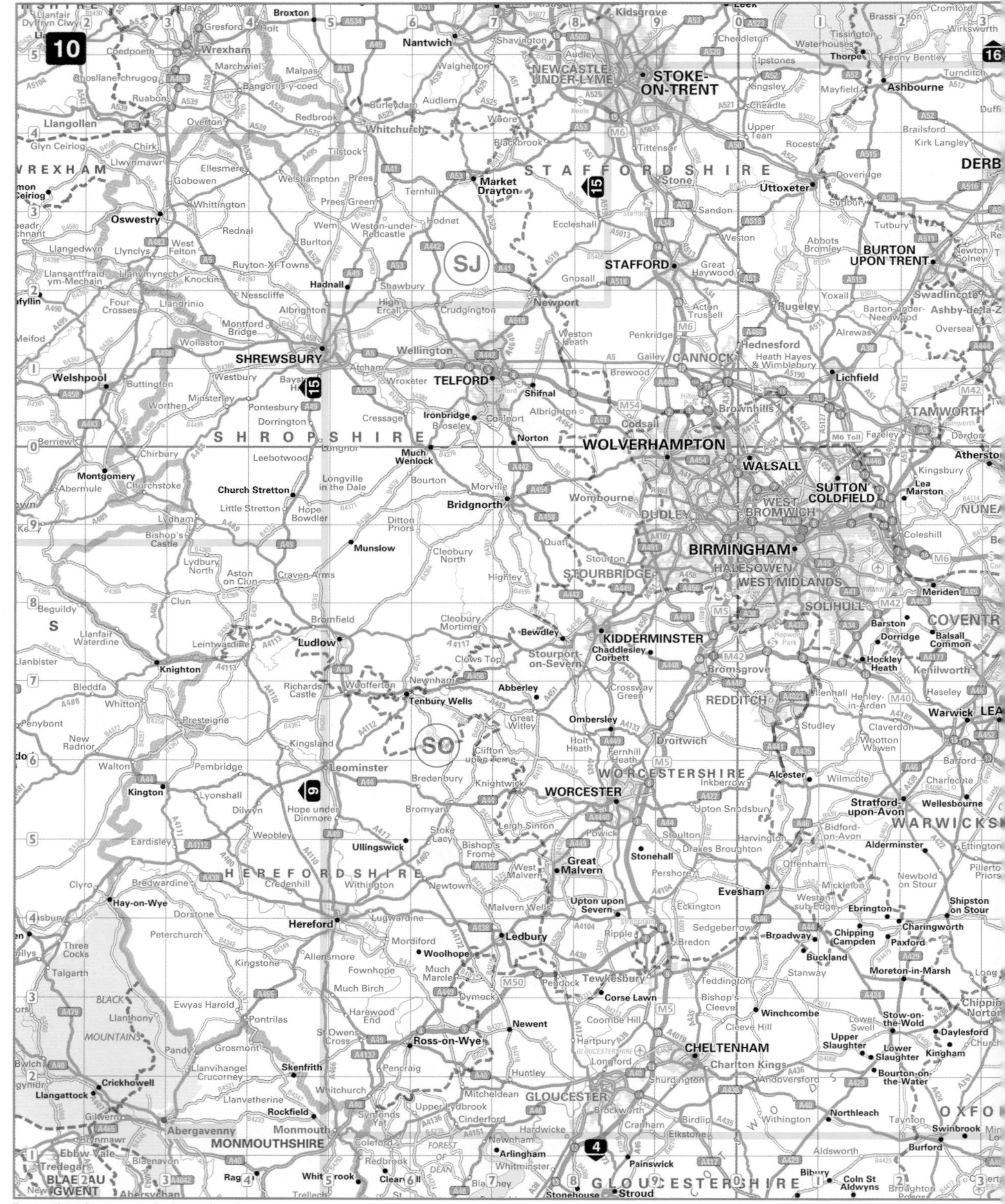

For continuation pages refer to numbered arrows

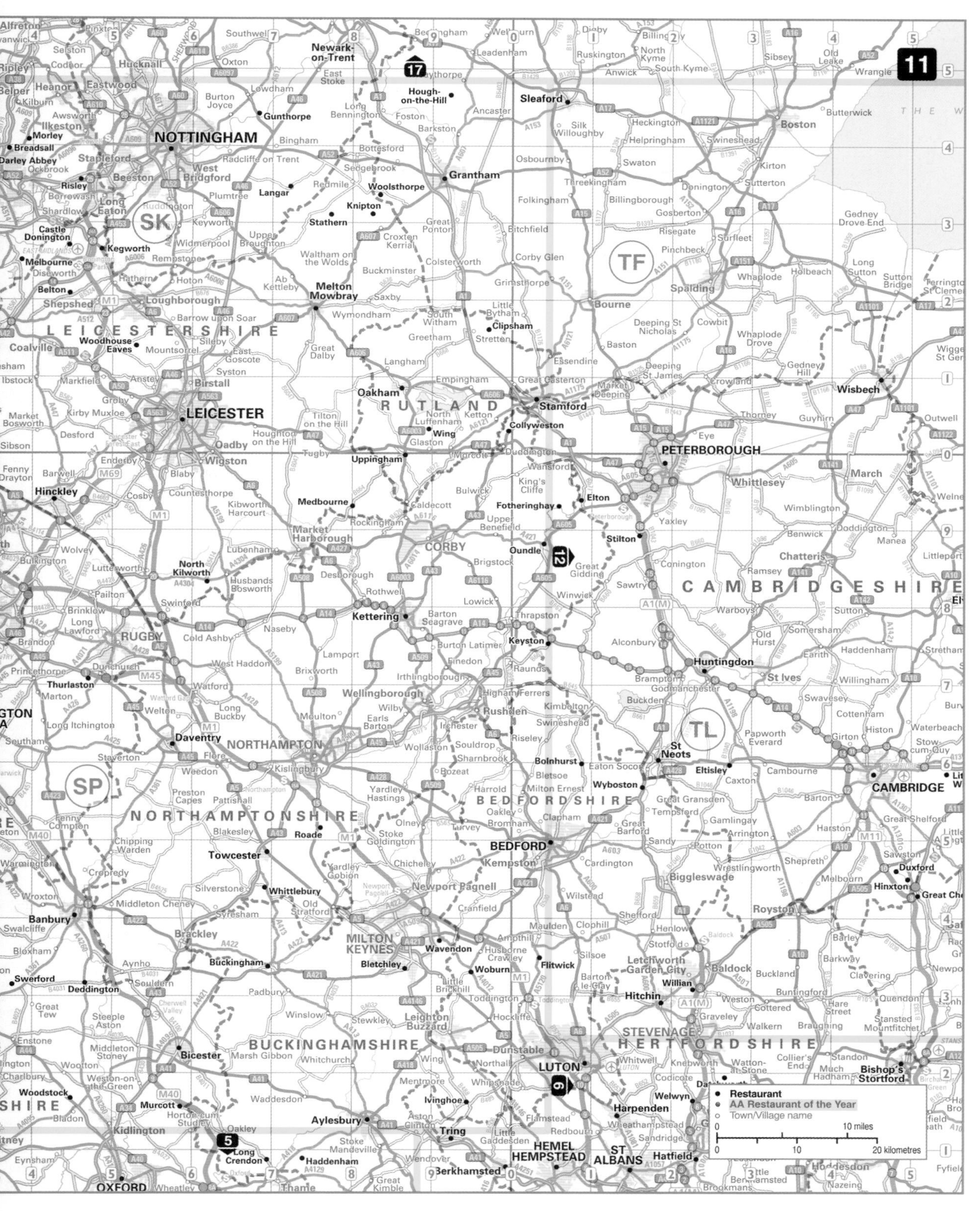

11
Restaurant
AA Restaurant of the Year
Town/Village name
10 miles
20 kilometres
SK
TF
SP
TL
LEICESTERSHIRE
RUTLAND
NORTHAMPTONSHIRE
BEDFORDSHIRE
CAMBRIDGESHIRE
BUCKINGHAMSHIRE
HERTFORDSHIRE
NOTTINGHAM
LEICESTER
PETERBOROUGH
CAMBRIDGE
NORTHAMPTON
BEDFORD
LUTON
MILTON KEYNES
OXFORD
CORBY
STEVENAGE
HEMEL HEMPSTEAD
ST ALBANS
Newark-on-Trent
Sleaford
Boston
Grantham
Melton Mowbray
Loughborough
Stamford
Oakham
Uppingham
Kettering
Wellingborough
Market Harborough
Huntingdon
St Neots
St Ives
Spalding
Bourne
Wisbech
March
Whittlesey
Chatteris
Oundle
Rugby
Daventry
Towcester
Banbury
Bicester
Brackley
Buckingham
Aylesbury
Tring
Berkhamsted
Dunstable
Hitchin
Baldock
Royston
Biggleswade
Harpenden
Hatfield
Welwyn
Bishop's Stortford
Hinckley
Coalville
Beeston
West Bridgford
Long Eaton
Stapleford
Hucknall
Eastwood
Heanor
Ripley
Belper
Alfreton
Ilkeston
Kegworth
Castle Donington
Hough-on-the-Hill
Gunthorpe
Langar
Woolsthorpe
Knipton
Stathern
Clipsham
Wing
Collyweston
Medbourne
Fotheringhay
Elton
Stilton
Keyston
Rushden
Roade
Whittlebury
Bolnhurst
Wyboston
Eltisley
Woburn
Flitwick
Bletchley
Wavendon
Ivinghoe
Haddenham
Long Crendon
Murcott
Deddington
Swerford
Woodstock
Thurlaston
North Kilworth
Woodhouse Eaves
Birstall
Belton
Breadsall
Morley
Darley Abbey
Risley
Duxford
Hinxton
Great Chesterford
William
Kidlington
Thame
Leighton Buzzard
Newport Pagnell
Kempston
Sandy
Potton
Letchworth Garden City

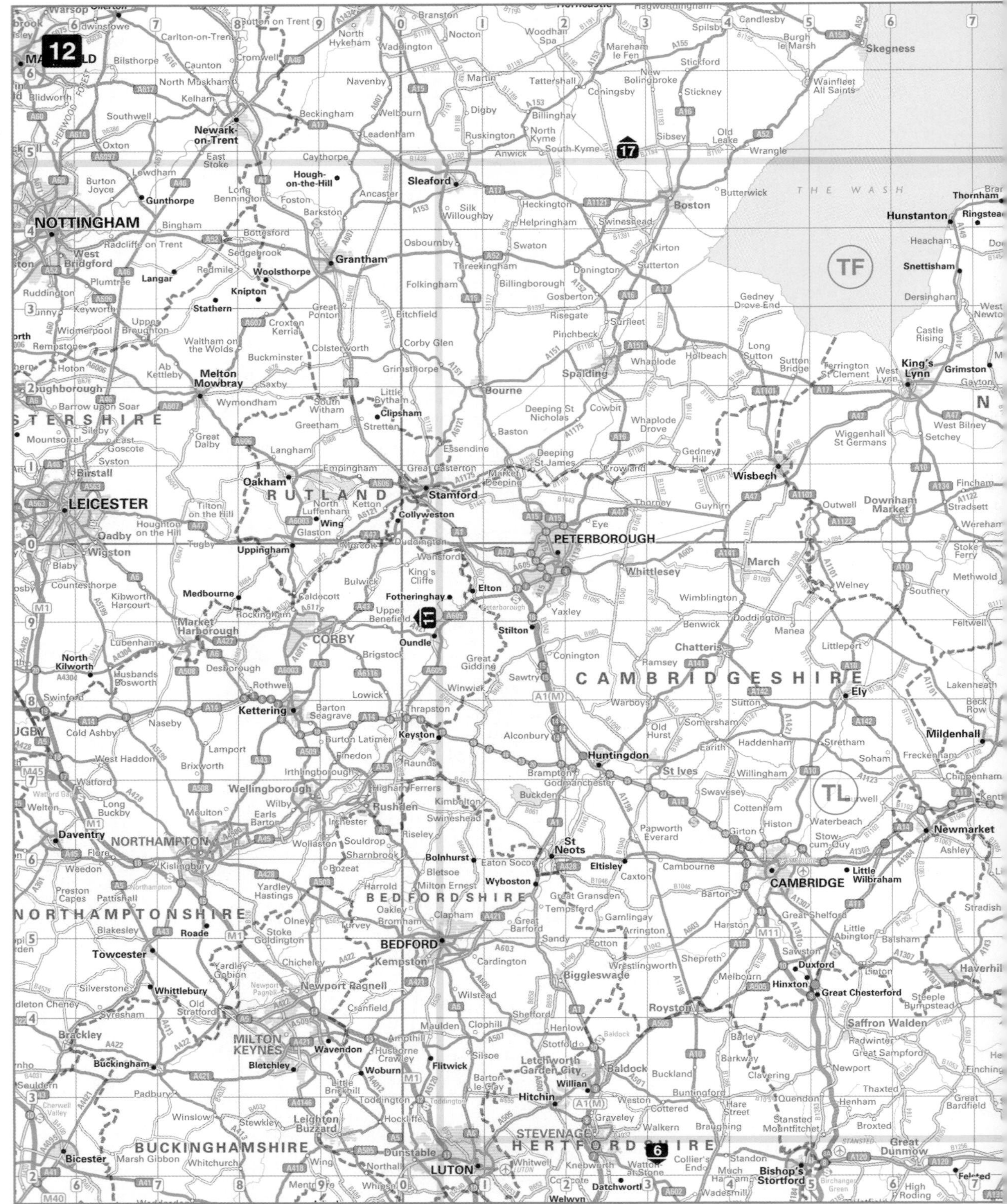

For continuation pages refer to numbered arrows

TG
TM
N O R F O L K
S U F F O L K
Brancaster Staithe
Burnham Overy Staithe
Wells-next-the-sea
Blakeney
Cley next the Sea
Sheringham
Cromer
Titchwell
Holkham
Burnham Market
Stiffkey
Morston
Wiveton
Weybourne
West Runton
Little Walsingham
Holt
Trimingham
North Creake
Roughton
Southrepps
Mundesley
Syderstone
Thursford
Bacton
Great Bircham
Melton Constable
Itteringham
North Walsham
Happisburgh
East Rudham
Fakenham
Saxthorpe
Blickling
Aylsham
Sea Palling
South Raynham
Guist
Stalham
Weasenham All Saints
North Elmham
Reepham
Catfield
Horsey
Bawdeswell
Coltishall
Ludham
Beetley
Attlebridge
Spixworth
Wroxham
Hemsby
Castle Acre
Litcham
Taverham
Rackheath
Rollesby
Ormesby St Margaret
Dereham
Drayton
Thorpe End
South Walsham
Filby
Honingham
Acle
Caister-on-Sea
Swaffham
Necton
Barnham Broom
NORWICH
Brundall
GREAT YARMOUTH
Shipdham
Cringleford
THE BROADS
Burgh Castle
Hethersett
Kimberley
Belton
Hingham
Stoke Holy Cross
Yelverton
Reedham
Watton
Wymondham
Scoulton
Brooke
Loddon
Fritton
Hopton on Sea
Hales
Corton
Haddiscoe
Attleborough
Bunwell
Long Stratton
Hempnall
Mundford
Great Hockham
Ellingham
LOWESTOFT
Gillingham
New Buckenham
Bungay
Beccles
Banham
Earsham
Alburgh
East Harling
Pulham St Mary
Brandon
Kenninghall
Homersfield
Henstead
Kessingland
Thetford
Harleston
Garboldisham
Diss
Metfield
Wrentham
Elveden
Scole
Brockdish
Redgrave
Hoxne
Botesdale
Brome
Fressingfield
Halesworth
Southwold
Honington
Yaxley
Stradbroke
Walberswick
Eye
Stanton
Laxfield
Bramfield
Ixworth
Dunwich
Yoxford
Westleton
Finningham
Brockford Street
Worlingworth
Dennington
Theberton
Thurston
Framlingham
Bury St Edmunds
Saxmundham
Debenham
Woolpit
Brandeston
Great Glemham
Leiston
Horringer
Stowmarket
Easton
Thorpeness
Stratford St Andrew
Whepstead
Helmingham
Snape
Aldeburgh
Needham Market
Wickham Market
Hawkedon
Tunstall
Hartest
Coddenham
Chillesford
Witnesham
Butley
Hitcham
Great Blakenham
Glemsford
Lavenham
Orford
Bildeston
Claydon
Woodbridge
Long Melford
Monks Eleigh
Kesgrave
Clare
IPSWICH
Shottisham
Martlesham Heath
Sudbury
Hadleigh
Hintlesham
Boxford
Copdock
Capel St Mary
Nacton
Bawdsey
Great Yeldham
Stoke-by-Nayland
Shotley
Holbrook
East Bergholt
Bures
Nayland
Felixstowe
Colne Engaine
Dedham
Manningtree
Harwich
Ardleigh
Earls Colne
Aldham
COLCHESTER
Wix
Marks Tey
Coggeshall
Copford Green
Elmstead Market
Thorpe-le-Soken
Walton on the Naze
Wivenhoe
Silver End
Kelvedon
Frinton-on-Sea
Brightlingsea
Restaurant
AA Restaurant of the Year
Town/Village name
10 miles
10
20 kilometres

For continuation pages refer to numbered arrows

15
PRESTON
BLACKBURN
Accrington
Great Harwood
Lytham St Anne's
18
Freckleton
Longton
Leyland
Bamber Bridge
Rawtenstall
Todmorden
Hebden Bridge
HALIFAX
Brighouse
Clifton
Sowerby Bridge
Elland
Ripponden
Bacup
Darwen
Tarleton
SOUTHPORT
SD
Rufford
Chorley
Littleborough
ROCHDALE
HUDDERSFIELD
Burscough Bridge
Wrightington
Horwich
BOLTON
BURY
Marsden
Meltham
Holmfirth
Formby
Ormskirk
Skelmersdale
Standish
WIGAN
Prestwich
Chadderton
OLDHAM
Delph
Maghull
Atherton
Leigh
Failsworth
Liverpool Bay
CROSBY
KIRKBY
Golborne
GT MAN
Ashton-under-Lyne
MANCHESTER
Stockport
BOOTLE
MERSEYSIDE
ST HELENS
Stretford
Denton
Hyde
Glossop
WALLASEY
LIVERPOOL
Risley
Hoylake
BIRKENHEAD
Sale
STOCKPORT
PEAK DISTRICT
Lymm
WARRINGTON
Cheadle
Hazel Grove
West Kirby
Altrincham
Bebington
WIDNES
Bucklow Hill
Manchester Airport
Poynton
Disley
Furness Vale
Chapel-en-le-Frith
Castleton
Hope
Prestatyn
Thurstaston
RUNCORN
16
Wilmslow
Whaley Bridge
NATIONAL
Meliden
Mostyn
Heswall
Thornton Hough
ELLESMERE PORT
Mobberley
Knutsford
Alderley Edge
Prestbury
Bollington
Fernilee
Rhuddlan
Greenfield
Bagillt
Neston
Childer Thornton
Frodsham
Tideswell
Grindleford
St Asaph
Holywell
Burton
Helsby
Northwich
Lower Peover
Chelford
Macclesfield
Buxton
Wardlow
Caerwys
Flint
Puddington
Weaverham
Davenham
Cuddington
Sandiway
Goostrey
Connah's Quay
Great Saughall
Bodfari
Northop
Queensferry
Holmes Chapel
PARK
Bakewell
Denbigh
FLINTSHIRE
CHESTER
Tarvin
Winsford
Cotebrook
Middlewich
Monyash
Mold
Hawarden
Tarporley
Brereton Green
Congleton
Longnor
Youlgreave
Gwernymynydd
Buckley
Arclid Green
Hartington
Llanbedr Dyffryn-Clwyd
Hope
Pulford
Aldford
CHESHIRE
Sandbach
Warslow
Beeston
Ruthin
DENBIGHSHIRE
Handley
Peckforton
CREWE
Alsager
Biddulph
Leek
Llanfair Dyffryn Clwyd
Rossett
Kidsgrove
Brassington
Broxton
Llandegla
Gresford
Holt
Nantwich
Shavington
Audley
Cheddleton
Tissington
Waterhouses
Thorpe
Coedpoeth
Wrexham
Marchwiel
NEWCASTLE-UNDER-LYME
STOKE-ON-TRENT
Ipstones
Malpas
Walgherton
SJ
Rhosllanerchrugog
Bangor-is-y-coed
Kingsley
Mayfield
Ashbourne
Ruabon
Audlem
Burleydam
Cheadle
Corwen
Llangollen
Overton
Redbrook
Whitchurch
Woore
Upper Tean
Glyn Ceiriog
Chirk
Blackbrook
Tittensor
Rocester
Llandrillo
WREXHAM
Llwynmawr
Tilstock
Ellesmere
Gobowen
Welshampton
Prees
Market Drayton
STAFFORDSHIRE
Stone
10
Uttoxeter
Doveridge
Llanarmon Dyffryn Ceiriog
Ternhill
Whittington
Prees Green
Sudbury
Oswestry
Sandon
Llanrhaeadr-ym-Mochnant
Rednal
Wem
Weston-under-Redcastle
Hodnet
Eccleshall
Weston
Tutbury
Abbots Bromley
Llangedwyn
West Felton
Burlton
BURTON UPON TRENT
Llynclys
STAFFORD
Great Haywood
Ruyton-XI-Towns
Llansantffraid-ym-Mechain
Llanymynech
Knockin
Hadnall
Shawbury
Gnosall
Llanwddyn
Llanfyllin
Nesscliffe
Four Crosses
Llandrinio
High Ercall
Crudgington
Newport
Acton Trussell
Rugeley
Yoxall
Barton-under-Needwood
Albrighton
Montford Bridge
Penkridge
Meifod
Weston Heath
Alrewas
Hednesford
Wollaston
Wellington
Gailey
CANNOCK
Heath Hayes & Wimblebury
SHREWSBURY
Atcham
Llanerfyl
Brewood
Lichfield
Welshpool
Buttington
Westbury
Bayston Hill
Wroxeter
TELFORD
Shifnal
Llanfair Caereinion
Minsterley
Pontesbury
Dorrington
Ironbridge
Coalport
Albrighton
Brownhills
Worthen
Cressage
Broseley
Codsall
SHROPSHIRE
Berriew
Longnor
Norton
WOLVERHAMPTON
Chirbury
Much Wenlock
Leebotwood
WALSALL
Montgomery
Churchstoke
Longville in the Dale
Bourton
Morville
SUTTON COLDFIELD
Abermule
Church Stretton
WEST BROMWICH
Caersws
Newtown
Little Stretton
Hope Bowdler
Bridgnorth
Wombourne
Lydham
SO
DUDLEY
Kerry
Bishop's Castle
Llandinam
9
Munslow
Cleobury North
Quatt
BIRMINGHAM
Lydbury North
Aston on Clun
Craven Arms
Highley
Stourton
STOURBRIDGE
HALESOWEN
WEST MIDLANDS
M6 Toll
Douglas (Mar-Nov)
Douglas (Nov-Mar)

16

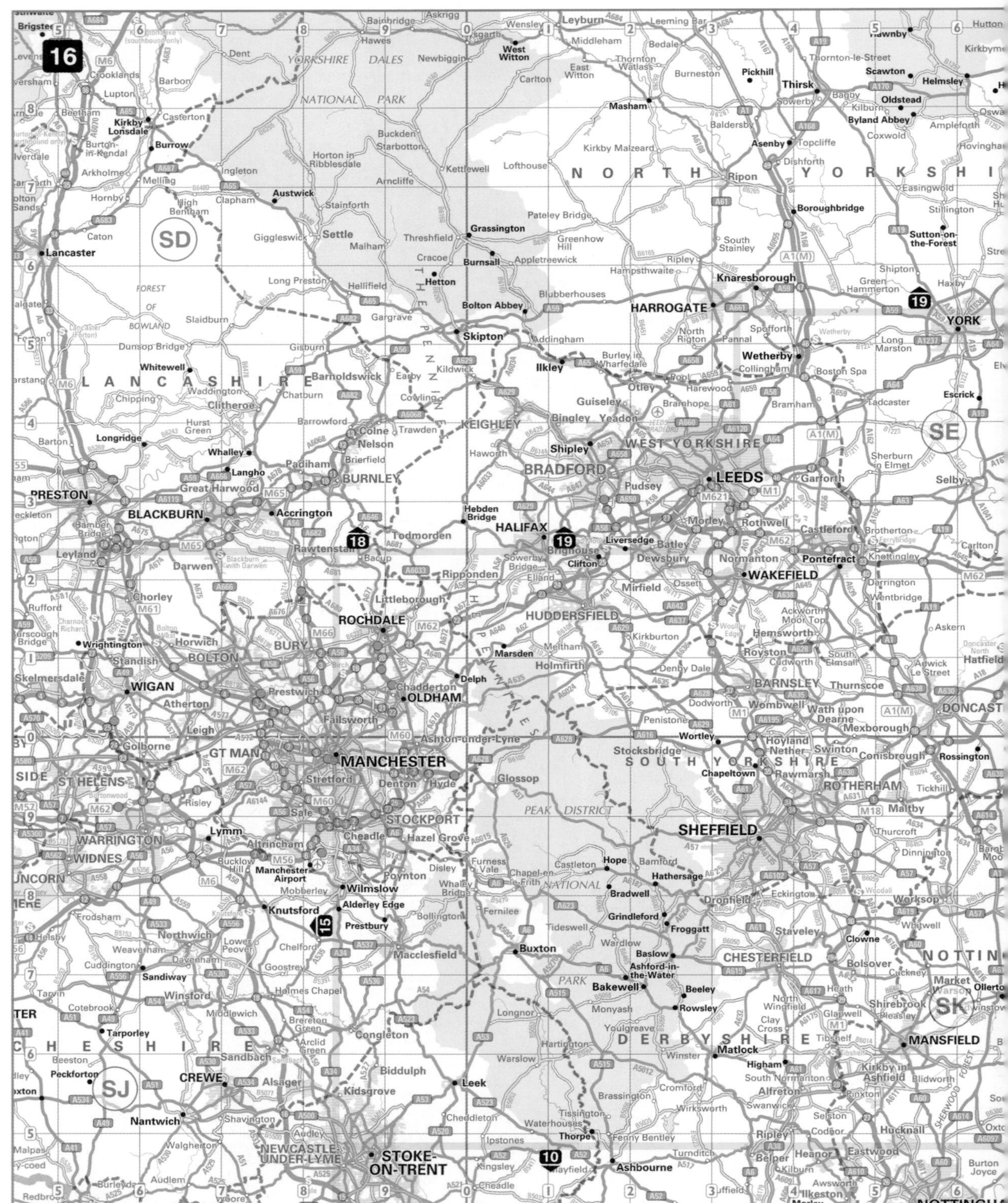

For continuation pages refer to numbered arrows

Restaurant
AA Restaurant of the Year
Town/Village name
0 10 miles
0 10 20 kilometres
TA
TF
EAST RIDING OF YORKSHIRE
LINCOLNSHIRE
Scarborough
Filey
Pickering
Malton
Bridlington
Flamborough
Flamborough Head
Driffield
Beverley
Willerby
KINGSTON UPON HULL
Hornsea
Withernsea
Patrington
Easington
Spurn Head
Howden
Goole
Winteringham
Thorne
SCUNTHORPE
Brigg
GRIMSBY
Cleethorpes
Immingham
Gainsborough
Retford
Market Rasen
Louth
Mablethorpe
Sutton on Sea
Alford
Chapel St Leonards
Ingoldmells
Skegness
Wainfleet All Saints
LINCOLN
Horncastle
Woodhall Spa
Coningsby
Tattershall
Newark-on-Trent
Hough-on-the-Hill
Sleaford
Boston
Hunstanton
Ringstead
Brancaster Staithe
Burnham
THE WASH
River Humber
Hessle
North Ferriby
Barton upon Humber
Pocklington
Market Weighton
Stamford Bridge
Hedon
Saltfleet
Spilsby
Wragby
Binbrook
Caistor
Humberston
Waltham
Laceby
Hecking
Swineshead
Wrangle
Old Leake
Sibsey
Stickney
Navenby
Waddington
North Hykeham
Saxilby
Torksey
Tuxford
Ancaster
Caythorpe

For continuation pages refer to numbered arrows

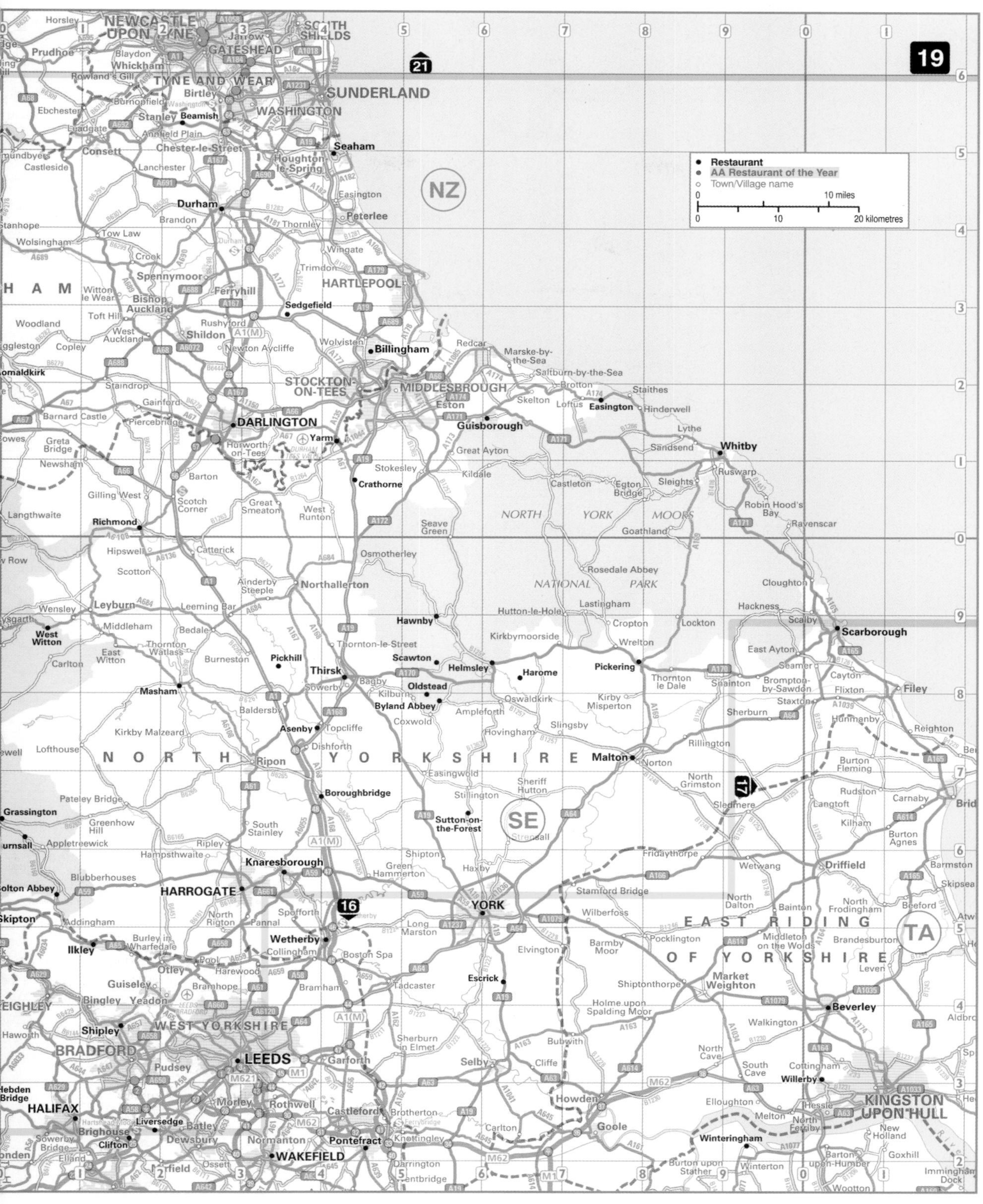
Restaurant
AA Restaurant of the Year
Town/Village name
0
10 miles
0
10
20 kilometres
NZ
SE
TA
NEWCASTLE UPON TYNE
GATESHEAD
SOUTH SHIELDS
TYNE AND WEAR
SUNDERLAND
WASHINGTON
Seaham
Durham
HARTLEPOOL
Sedgefield
Billingham
STOCKTON-ON-TEES
MIDDLESBROUGH
DARLINGTON
Yarm
Guisborough
Easington
Whitby
Crathorne
Richmond
Northallerton
NORTH YORK MOORS
NATIONAL PARK
Hawnby
Scarborough
Pickhill
Thirsk
Scawton
Helmsley
Harome
Pickering
Masham
Oldstead
Byland Abbey
Asenby
NORTH YORKSHIRE
Ripon
Malton
Boroughbridge
Sutton-on-the-Forest
Grassington
Knaresborough
HARROGATE
Driffield
YORK
EAST RIDING OF YORKSHIRE
Wetherby
Ilkley
Escrick
Beverley
Shipley
WEST YORKSHIRE
BRADFORD
LEEDS
Selby
Willerby
KINGSTON UPON HULL
HALIFAX
Liversedge
Brighouse
Clifton
WAKEFIELD
Pontefract
Goole
Winteringham
16
17
21

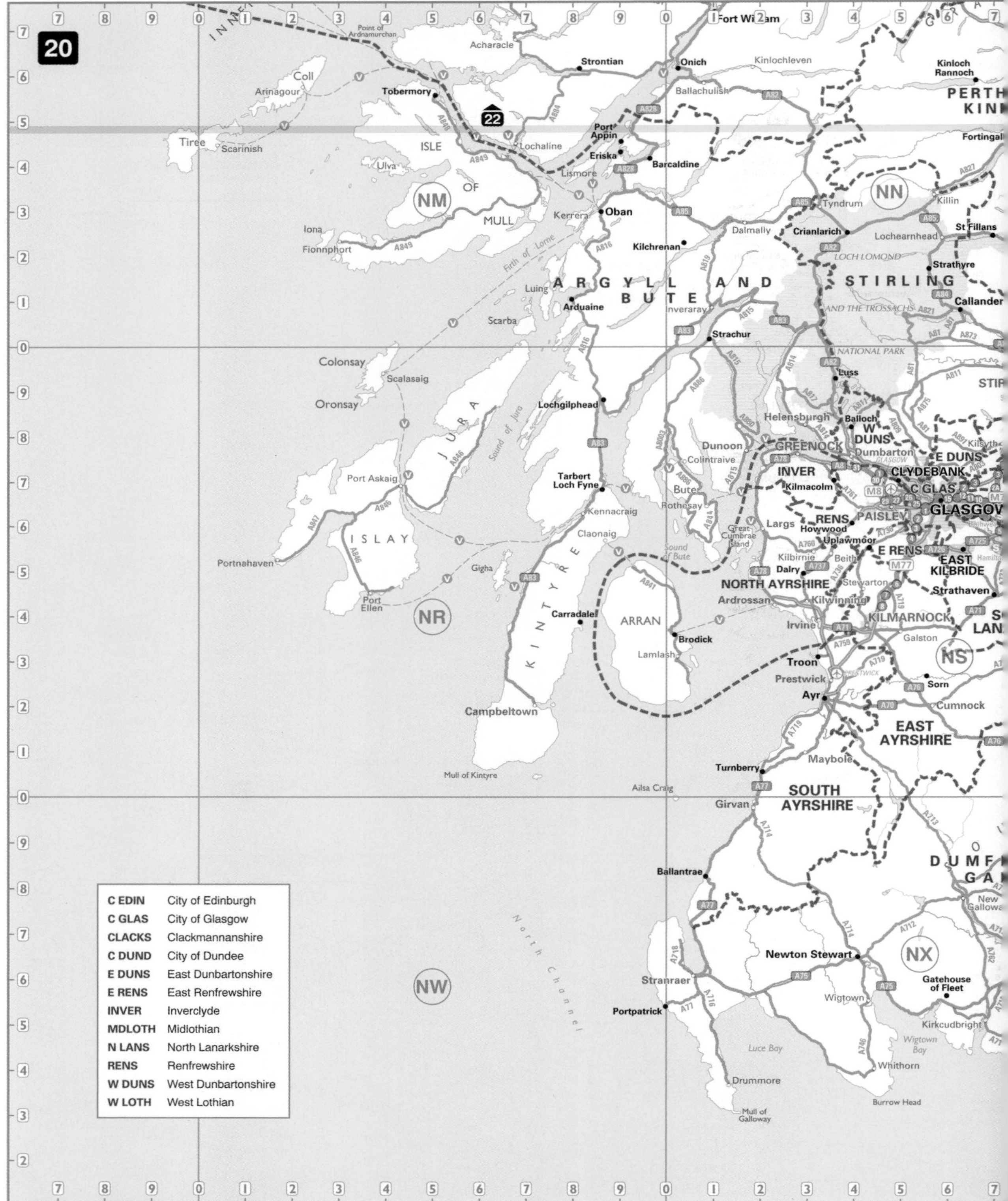

C EDIN	City of Edinburgh
C GLAS	City of Glasgow
CLACKS	Clackmannanshire
C DUND	City of Dundee
E DUNS	East Dunbartonshire
E RENS	East Renfrewshire
INVER	Inverclyde
MDLOTH	Midlothian
N LANS	North Lanarkshire
RENS	Renfrewshire
W DUNS	West Dunbartonshire
W LOTH	West Lothian

For continuation pages refer to numbered arrows

Restaurant
AA Restaurant of the Year
Town/Village name
20 miles
30 kilometres
ANGUS
FIFE
EDINBURGH
SCOTTISH BORDERS
NORTH SEA
NORTHUMBERLAND
NEWCASTLE UPON TYNE
GATESHEAD
SUNDERLAND
CARLISLE
CUMBRIA
DURHAM
DUNDEE
Perth
St Andrews
Berwick-upon-Tweed
Alnwick
Hexham
Dumfries
Moffat
Penrith
Keswick
MIDDLESBROUGH
HARTLEPOOL
STOCKTON-ON-TEES
DARLINGTON

For continuation pages refer to numbered arrows

Restaurant
AA Restaurant of the Year
Town/Village name
0 10 20 miles
0 10 20 30 kilometres
NC
ND
NH
NJ
NK
NN
NO
HIGHLAND
MORAY
ABERDEENSHIRE
ANGUS
PERTH AND KINROSS
CITY OF ABERDEEN
Thurso
Wick
Tongue
Brora
Dornoch
Tain
Invergordon
Nairn
INVERNESS
Contin
Muir of Ord
Abriachan
Brachla
Fort Augustus
Kingussie
Grantown-on-Spey
Nethy Bridge
Boat of Garten
Archiestown
Craigellachie
Cullen
Peterhead
Oldmeldrum
Balmedie
ABERDEEN
Banchory
Crathes
Ballater
Strathdon
Stonehaven
Spittal of Glenshee
Kinloch Rannoch
Killiecrankie
Pitlochry
Fortingall
Kenmore
Dunkeld
Kinclaven
Inverkeilor
Carnoustie
Perth
St Fillans
Cairngorms National Park
Grampian Mountains
Monadhliath Mountains
Moray Firth
Pentland Firth
Elgin
Forres
Keith
Huntly
Banff
Fraserburgh
Ellon
Inverurie
Montrose
Brechin
Forfar
Arbroath
Dundee
Blairgowrie
Aviemore
John o' Groats
Helmsdale
Golspie
Lairg
Dingwall
21

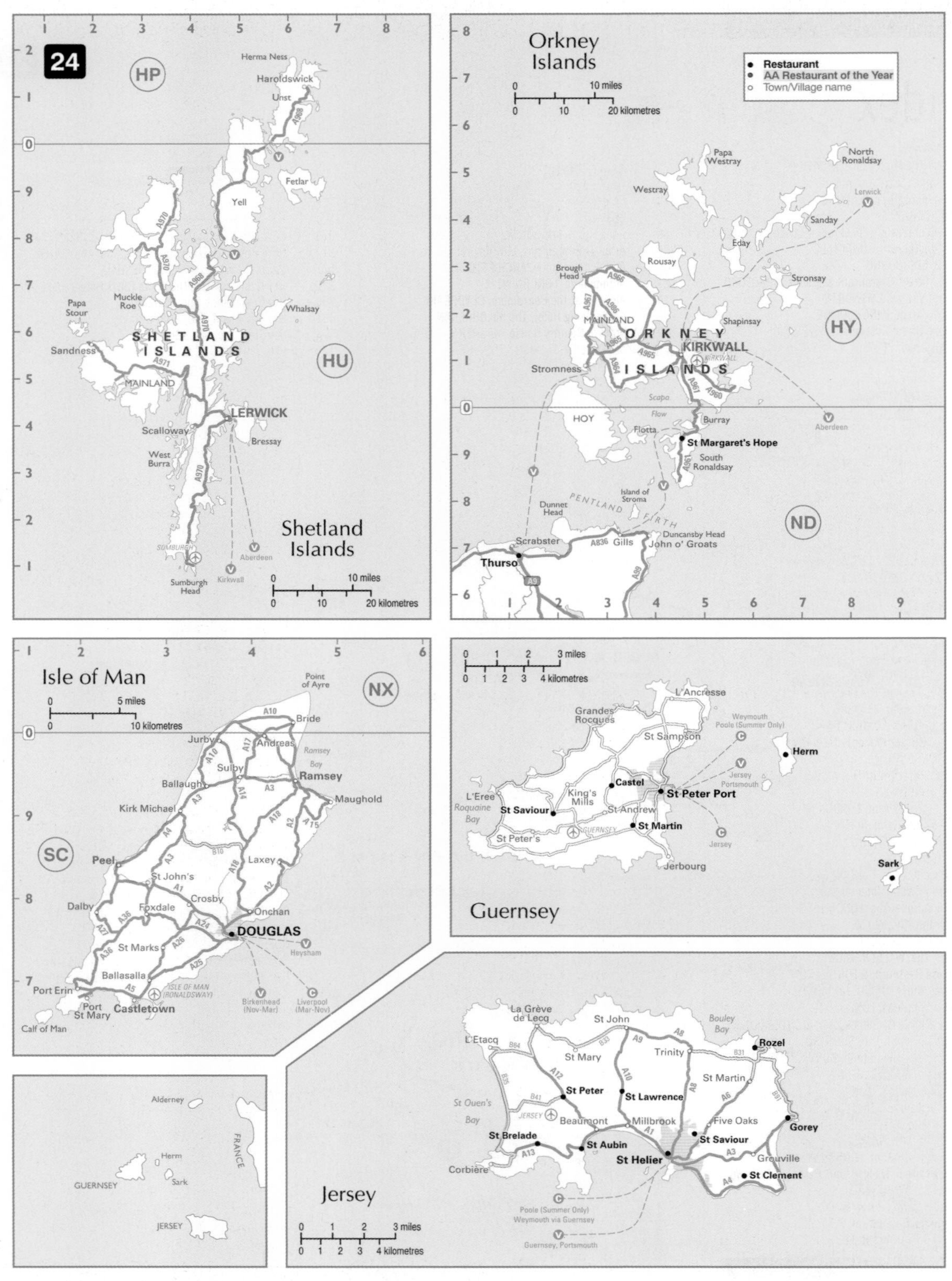
Shetland Islands
Herma Ness
Haroldswick
Unst
Fetlar
Yell
Whalsay
Papa Stour
Muckle Roe
SHETLAND ISLANDS
Sandness
MAINLAND
LERWICK
Scalloway
Bressay
West Burra
Sumburgh Head
Kirkwall
Aberdeen
HP
HU
10 miles
20 kilometres
Orkney Islands
Restaurant
AA Restaurant of the Year
Town/Village name
Papa Westray
North Ronaldsay
Westray
Lerwick
Sanday
Eday
Rousay
Brough Head
Stronsay
Shapinsay
MAINLAND
ORKNEY ISLANDS
KIRKWALL
Stromness
Scapa Flow
HOY
Flotta
Burray
St Margaret's Hope
South Ronaldsay
Aberdeen
Island of Stroma
Dunnet Head
PENTLAND FIRTH
Duncansby Head
John o' Groats
Scrabster
Gills
Thurso
HY
ND
Isle of Man
Point of Ayre
Bride
Jurby
Andreas
Ramsey Bay
Sulby
Ramsey
Ballaugh
Maughold
Kirk Michael
Laxey
Peel
St John's
Crosby
Dalby
Foxdale
Onchan
DOUGLAS
St Marks
Heysham
Ballasalla
Port Erin
Port St Mary
Castletown
ISLE OF MAN (RONALDSWAY)
Birkenhead (Nov-Mar)
Liverpool (Mar-Nov)
Calf of Man
NX
SC
5 miles
10 kilometres
Guernsey
3 miles
4 kilometres
L'Ancresse
Grandes Rocques
St Sampson
Weymouth Poole (Summer Only)
Herm
Castel
Jersey Portsmouth
L'Eree
Roquaine Bay
King's Mills
St Peter Port
St Saviour
St Andrew
St Martin
St Peter's
GUERNSEY
Jersey
Jerbourg
Sark
Alderney
Herm
Sark
GUERNSEY
JERSEY
FRANCE
Jersey
La Grève de Lecq
St John
Bouley Bay
L'Etacq
St Mary
Trinity
Rozel
St Martin
St Ouen's Bay
St Peter
St Lawrence
Five Oaks
JERSEY
Beaumont
Millbrook
Gorey
St Brelade
St Aubin
St Saviour
St Helier
Grouville
Corbière
St Clement
Poole (Summer Only)
Weymouth via Guernsey
Guernsey, Portsmouth
3 miles
4 kilometres

Index of Restaurants

0-9

A

B

M

AA Media Limited would like to thank the following photographers, companies and picture libraries for their assistance in the preparation of this book.
Abbreviations for the picture credits are as follows: (t) top; (b) bottom; (l) left; (r) right; (c) centre; (AA) AA World Travel Library

1 Graffiti at Hotel Felix, The Waterside Inn, photography by Richard Trussell; 3 Galvin Café a Vin; 4 AA; 5 Canteen, Royal Festival Hall; 6 The New Mill Riverside Restaurant; 9 Galvin Café a Vin 10 Restaurant Martin Wishart; 12 & 13 Goring Hotel; 14 (l) The Harrow Inn (r) Galvin La Chapelle; 15 (l) The Peat Inn (r) The Hardwick; 18 Photodisc; 19 (l) Hambleton Hall (c) The Kitchin (r) Fairyhill; 20 Chapters All Day Dining; 22 (l) Chapters All Day Dining (r) Galvin Café a Vin; 23 Sam's Brasserie; 24 (t) The Modern Pantry (b) The Print Room; 25 (l) The Print Room (r) The Left Bank; 26 Absolute Taste at Harvey Nichols; 27 British Cheese Board; 28 (t & b) British Cheese Board; 29 (t) AA/J A Tims (b) Denhay Cheese (r) British Cheese Board; 30 British Cheese Board; 31 Terre à Terre, Brighton; 32, 34 & 35 The Waterside Inn, photography by Richard Trussell; 37 Opus; 41 Terre à Terre, photography by Lisa Barber; 46/7 AA/D Hall; 212/3 AA/S Montgomery; 472/3 AA/D W Robertson; 540/1 AA/N Jenkins; 568/9 AA/I Dawson; 575 Stockbyte

Every effort has been made to trace the copyright holders, and we apologise in advance for any accidental errors. We would be happy to apply the corrections in the following edition of this publication.

Readers' Report Form

Please send this form to:–
Editor, The Restaurant Guide,
Lifestyle Guides,
AA Publishing,
13th Floor, Fanum House,
Basingstoke RG21 4EA

or fax: 01256 491647
or e-mail: lifestyleguides@theAA.com

Please use this form to tell us about any restaurant you have visited, whether it is in the guide or not currently listed. Feedback from readers helps us to keep our guide accurate and up to date. Please note, however, that if you have a complaint to make during a visit, we strongly recommend that you discuss the matter with the restaurant management there and then, so that they have a chance to put things right before your visit is spoilt. The AA does not undertake to arbitrate between you and the restaurant management, or to obtain compensation or engage in correspondence.

Date ....

Your name (BLOCK CAPITALS) ....

Your address (BLOCK CAPITALS) ....

....

....

Post code ....

E-mail address ....

Restaurant name and address: (If you are recommending a new restaurant please enclose a menu or note the dishes that you ate.)

....

....

....

Comments ....

....

....

....

....

(please attach a separate sheet if necessary)

We may use information we hold about you to write, e-mail or telephone you about other products and services offered by us and our carefully selected partners, but we can assure you that we will not disclose it to third parties.

Please tick here ☐ if you DO NOT wish to receive details of other products or services from the AA.

PTO

Readers' Report Form *continued*

Have you bought this guide before? ☐ YES ☐ NO

Please list any other similar guides that you use regularly

What do you find most useful about The AA Restaurant Guide?

Please answer these questions to help us make improvements to the guide
What are your main reasons for visiting restaurants (tick all that apply)
Business entertaining ☐ Business travel ☐ Trying famous restaurants ☐ Family celebrations ☐
Leisure travel ☐ Trying new food ☐ Enjoying not having to cook yourself ☐
To eat food you couldn't cook yourself ☐ Because I enjoy eating out regularly ☐
Other (please state)

How often do you visit a restaurant for lunch or dinner? (tick one choice)
Once a week ☐ Once a fortnight ☐ Once a month ☐ Less than once a month ☐
Do you use the location atlas ☐ YES ☐ NO?
Do you generally agree with the Rosette ratings at the restaurants you visit in the guide?
(If not please give examples)

Who is your favourite chef?

Which is your favourite restaurant?

Which type of cuisine is your first choice e.g. French

Which of these factors is most important when choosing a restaurant?
Price ☐ Service ☐ Location ☐ Type of food ☐ Awards/ratings ☐ Décor/surroundings ☐
Other (please state)

Which elements of the guide do you find most useful when choosing a restaurant?
Description ☐ Photo ☐ Rosette rating ☐ Price ☐
Other (please state)

Readers' Report Form

Please send this form to:–
Editor, The Restaurant Guide,
Lifestyle Guides,
AA Publishing,
13th Floor, Fanum House,
Basingstoke RG21 4EA

or fax: 01256 491647
or e-mail: lifestyleguides@theAA.com

Please use this form to tell us about any restaurant you have visited, whether it is in the guide or not currently listed. Feedback from readers helps us to keep our guide accurate and up to date. Please note, however, that if you have a complaint to make during a visit, we strongly recommend that you discuss the matter with the restaurant management there and then, so that they have a chance to put things right before your visit is spoilt. The AA does not undertake to arbitrate between you and the restaurant management, or to obtain compensation or engage in correspondence.

Date ....

Your name (BLOCK CAPITALS) ....

Your address (BLOCK CAPITALS) ....

....

....

.... Post code ....

E-mail address ....

Restaurant name and address: (If you are recommending a new restaurant please enclose a menu or note the dishes that you ate.)

....

....

....

Comments ....

....

....

....

....

(please attach a separate sheet if necessary)

We may use information we hold about you to write, e-mail or telephone you about other products and services offered by us and our carefully selected partners, but we can assure you that we will not disclose it to third parties.

Please tick here ☐ if you DO NOT wish to receive details of other products or services from the AA.

PTO

Readers' Report Form *continued*

Have you bought this guide before? ☐ YES ☐ NO

Please list any other similar guides that you use regularly

What do you find most useful about The AA Restaurant Guide?

Please answer these questions to help us make improvements to the guide
What are your main reasons for visiting restaurants (tick all that apply)
Business entertaining ☐ Business travel ☐ Trying famous restaurants ☐ Family celebrations ☐
Leisure travel ☐ Trying new food ☐ Enjoying not having to cook yourself ☐
To eat food you couldn't cook yourself ☐ Because I enjoy eating out regularly ☐
Other (please state)

How often do you visit a restaurant for lunch or dinner? (tick one choice)
Once a week ☐ Once a fortnight ☐ Once a month ☐ Less than once a month ☐
Do you use the location atlas ☐ YES ☐ NO?
Do you generally agree with the Rosette ratings at the restaurants you visit in the guide?
(If not please give examples)

Who is your favourite chef?

Which is your favourite restaurant?

Which type of cuisine is your first choice e.g. French

Which of these factors is most important when choosing a restaurant?
Price ☐ Service ☐ Location ☐ Type of food ☐ Awards/ratings ☐ Décor/surroundings ☐
Other (please state)

Which elements of the guide do you find most useful when choosing a restaurant?
Description ☐ Photo ☐ Rosette rating ☐ Price ☐
Other (please state)

Readers' Report Form

Please send this form to:–
Editor, The Restaurant Guide,
Lifestyle Guides,
AA Publishing,
13th Floor, Fanum House,
Basingstoke RG21 4EA

or fax: 01256 491647
or e-mail: lifestyleguides@theAA.com

Please use this form to tell us about any restaurant you have visited, whether it is in the guide or not currently listed. Feedback from readers helps us to keep our guide accurate and up to date. Please note, however, that if you have a complaint to make during a visit, we strongly recommend that you discuss the matter with the restaurant management there and then, so that they have a chance to put things right before your visit is spoilt. The AA does not undertake to arbitrate between you and the restaurant management, or to obtain compensation or engage in correspondence.

Date

Your name (BLOCK CAPITALS)

Your address (BLOCK CAPITALS)

Post code

E-mail address

Restaurant name and address: (If you are recommending a new restaurant please enclose a menu or note the dishes that you ate.)

Comments

(please attach a separate sheet if necessary)

We may use information we hold about you to write, e-mail or telephone you about other products and services offered by us and our carefully selected partners, but we can assure you that we will not disclose it to third parties.

Please tick here ☐ if you DO NOT wish to receive details of other products or services from the AA.

PTO

Readers' Report Form *continued*

Have you bought this guide before? ☐ YES ☐ NO

Please list any other similar guides that you use regularly

What do you find most useful about The AA Restaurant Guide?

Please answer these questions to help us make improvements to the guide
What are your main reasons for visiting restaurants (tick all that apply)
Business entertaining ☐ Business travel ☐ Trying famous restaurants ☐ Family celebrations ☐
Leisure travel ☐ Trying new food ☐ Enjoying not having to cook yourself ☐
To eat food you couldn't cook yourself ☐ Because I enjoy eating out regularly ☐
Other (please state)

How often do you visit a restaurant for lunch or dinner? (tick one choice)
Once a week ☐ Once a fortnight ☐ Once a month ☐ Less than once a month ☐
Do you use the location atlas ☐ YES ☐ NO?
Do you generally agree with the Rosette ratings at the restaurants you visit in the guide?
(If not please give examples)

Who is your favourite chef?

Which is your favourite restaurant?

Which type of cuisine is your first choice e.g. French

Which of these factors is most important when choosing a restaurant?
Price ☐ Service ☐ Location ☐ Type of food ☐ Awards/ratings ☐ Décor/surroundings ☐
Other (please state)

Which elements of the guide do you find most useful when choosing a restaurant?
Description ☐ Photo ☐ Rosette rating ☐ Price ☐
Other (please state)

AA Lifetime Achievement Award 2010-2011

Above: George Goring OBE

Opposite: Al fresco dining at the Goring Hotel

George GORING

The term 'family-run' can be applied to many establishments listed within the pages of this guidebook, but few can match the historic connections of the Goring Hotel and lifetime commitment of George Goring – born in room 114 of the hotel and having worked for 43 dedicated years behind its elegant Edwardian walls, Mr Goring embodies the very best of the hospitality industry.

The Goring Hotel opened its doors in 1910 and has remained in the family ever since. From day one the hotel made an impact – the eye-catching innovation being every bedroom having its own 'en-suite' bathroom, the first in the world to do so. It's fair to say the notion caught on rather well.

George Goring was born into the business and quite literally 'in' the business (room 114) in 1938. He received an education and training in the hospitality industry at the Swiss Hotel School and went on to work in Germany, returning to the UK to work for British Transport Hotels.

It was 1962 when George Goring took the helm of the family business from his father to become the third generation to do so. The development and improvement of the hotel never ceased; his fervent commitment to high quality in all departments never dinted, and his focus on people – both customers and staff – resulted in loyalty and affection being afforded to both him and the hotel.

Throughout his career, George Goring played an important role within the hospitality industry, becoming a much respected and admired figure, culminating in the award of an OBE by her Majesty for services to the hotel industry.

When, following his retirement, the mantle was passed to his son, Jeremy, a fourth generation of Goring took the helm. The Goring is the only family-run AA 5 Red Star hotel in London, a landmark London establishment with a great past, a bright future and a proud family name.

well be described as the beating heart of the Scottish restaurant scene, with Restaurant Martin Wishart a leading light.

Wishart has always shown a peerless attention to detail in his cooking; a refinement that is matched by a lightness of touch. There is nothing parochial about this Scottish chef, though, as witnessed in his travels abroad – including a stint with Charlie Trotter in the US – and with his on-going friendships and professional relationships with a number of top chefs around Europe.

It was not until 2008 that he looked to open up a second venue, and he chose a place where he had previously served time, the majestic Cameron House. At Martin Wishart at Loch Lomond, Wishart has created a restaurant that is another essential address on any culinary tour of Scotland, and in Stewart Boyles, Wishart has installed a head chef who is equally passionate about superb Scottish produce and skilled in the French-accented techniques that is the Wishart style.

The opening of Wishart's Cook School meant some of the craft and skills learned over his career could be passed onto willing enthusiasts – spreading the word and raising standards.

The award by his peers of the AA Chefs' Chef 2010-2011 is reward for Wishart's industry, skill and ambition. And we do not doubt there is much more to come from this precociously talented chef.

On The Menu

Roasted Kilbrannan scallops with bellota ham, black cherry juice and sweet-and-sour pepper

•

Loin, trotter and crispy ear of Drumlanrig pork with choucroute, apricot chicharrón and grain mustard sauce

•

Grapefruit with hazelnut caramel, fromage frais and yuzu sorbet

PREVIOUS WINNERS

Michael Caines
Gidleigh Park, Chagford, Devon
p122

Andrew Fairlie
Andrew Fairlie @ Gleneagles, Scotland
p522

Germain Schwab
Winteringham Fields (former chef), Lincolnshire

Raymond Blanc
Le Manoir aux Quat' Saisons, Great Milton, Oxfordshire
p354

Shaun Hill
Walnut Tree Inn, Abergavenny, Monmouthshire, Wales
p556

Heston Blumenthal
The Fat Duck, Bray, Berkshire
p51

Jean-Christophe Novelli

Gordon Ramsay
Restaurant Gordon Ramsay, London SW3
p266

Rick Stein
The Seafood Restaurant, Padstow, Cornwall
p88

Marco Pierre White
Marco Pierre White's Yew Tree Inn, Highclere, Hampshire,
p175

Kevin Viner

Philip Howard
The Square, London
p303

Marcus Wareing
Marcus Wareing at The Berkeley
p256

AA Chefs' Chef 2010-2011

This is the annual poll of all the chefs in The Restaurant Guide. Around 2,000 of the country's top chefs were asked to vote to recognise the achievements of one of their peers from a shortlist chosen by the AA's team of Inspectors.

Martin Wishart

This year's AA Chefs' Chef Award goes to Martin Wishart, chef-patron of Restaurant Martin Wishart in Edinburgh's thriving Leith dockside.

Scotland is a country which, it is probably fair to say, is not renowned for its culinary ambition and achievement. But a quick scan through the pages of this guide will reveal a growing confidence. In fact, compared with many other parts of the UK, Scotland is somewhere you'll find restaurant menus showing an ever-increasing sense of place. At the forefront of this new spirit and appreciation of Scottish produce, matched by acute ability and ambition, is Martin Wishart.

The winner of this year's Chefs' Chef is a Scotsman who takes exquisite Scottish produce from land, sea and loch and turns them into dishes of compelling technical virtuosity, whilst ensuring the flavour and freshness of the ingredients shine out.

The winner of this year's Chefs' Chef is a Scotsman who takes exquisite Scottish produce from land, sea and loch and turns them into dishes of compelling technical virtuosity, whilst ensuring the flavour and freshness of the ingredients shine out.

Martin Wishart received a grounding in classical French cooking from some of the very best names in the business - Albert Roux, Marco Pierre White and Michel Roux jnr to name but a few - and it was to his home country that he headed when he came to open his first restaurant in 1999, preferring the up-and-coming area of Leith than the centre of Edinburgh. It was a good call, as these days Leith could

How the AA Assesses for Rosette Awards

The AA's Rosette award scheme was the first nationwide scheme for assessing the quality of food served by restaurants and hotels. The Rosette scheme is an award, not a classification, and although there is necessarily an element of subjectivity when it comes to assessing taste, we aim for a consistent approach throughout the UK. Our awards are made solely on the basis of a meal visit or visits by one or more of our hotel and restaurant Inspectors, who have an unrivalled breadth and depth of experience in assessing quality. They award Rosettes annually on a rising scale of one to five.

So what makes a restaurant worthy of a Rosette Award?
For our Inspectors, the top and bottom line is the food. The taste of a dish is what counts, and whether it successfully delivers to the diner the promise of the menu. A restaurant is only as good as its worst meal. Although presentation and competent service should be appropriate to the style of the restaurant and the quality of the food, they cannot affect the Rosette assessment as such, either up or down. The summaries below indicate what our Inspectors look for, but are intended only as guidelines. The AA is constantly reviewing its award criteria, and competition usually results in an all-round improvement in standards, so it becomes increasingly difficult for restaurants to reach award level. For more detailed Rosette criteria, please visit theAA.com.

One Rosette

- Excellent restaurants that stand out in their local area
- Food prepared with care, understanding and skill
- Good quality ingredients

Around 50% of restaurants have one Rosette.

Two Rosettes

- The best local restaurants
- Higher standards
- Better consistency
- Greater precision apparent in the cooking
- Obvious attention to the quality and selection of ingredients

About 40% of restaurants have two Rosettes.

Three Rosettes

- Outstanding restaurants demanding recognition well beyond local area
- Selection and sympathetic treatment of highest quality ingredients
- Timing, seasoning and judgement of flavour combinations consistent
- Excellent intelligent service and a well-chosen wine list

Around 10% of restaurants have three Rosettes.

Four Rosettes

Dishes demonstrate:

- intense ambition
- a passion for excellence
- superb technical skills
- remarkable consistency
- appreciation of culinary traditions combined with desire for exploration and improvement
- Cooking demands national recognition

Twenty-six restaurants have four Rosettes.

Five Rosettes

- Cooking stands comparison with the best in the world
- Highly individual
- Breathtaking culinary skills
- Setting the standards to which others aspire
- Knowledgeable and distinctive wine list

Seven restaurants have five Rosettes.